Psychology

Fourth Edition

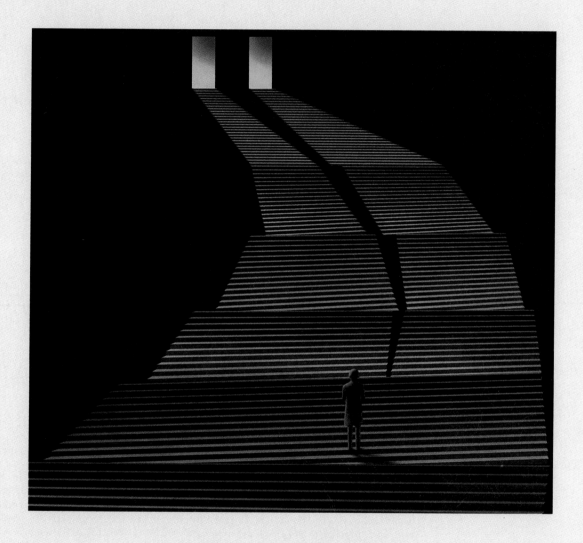

Carole Wade
Dominican College of San Rafael

Carol Tavris

HarperCollins*CollegePublishers*

Acquisitions Editor: Jill Lectka
Developmental Editor: Melissa Mashburn
Project Editor: Donna DeBenedictis
Design Manager/Text Design Adaptation: Jill Little
Cover Designer: Bass/Yager & Associates
Photo Researcher: Sandy Schneider
Electronic Production Manager: Alexandra Odulak
Electronic Pre-Press Manager: Heather A. Peres
Desktop Administrators/Electronic Page Makeup: LaToya Wigfall and Joanne Del Ben
Manufacturing Manager: Hilda Koparanian
Printer and Binder: R. R. Donnelley & Sons Company
Cover Printer: New England Book Components, Inc.

For permission to use copyrighted material, grateful acknowledgement is made to the copyright holders on pp. C-1–C-4, which are hereby made part of this copyright page.

Psychology, Fourth Edition

Library of Congress Cataloging-in-Publication Data

Wade, Carole.
    Psychology / Carole Wade, Carol Tavris.—4th ed.
       p. cm.
    Includes bibliographical references and indexes.
    ISBN 0-673-99647-6
      1. Psychology. I. Tavris, Carol. II. Title.
BF121.W27 1996
  150–dc20   95-23139
                                 CIP

95 96 97 98 9 8 7 6 5 4 3 2 1

Contents at a Glance

Contents

Part One

An Invitation to Psychology

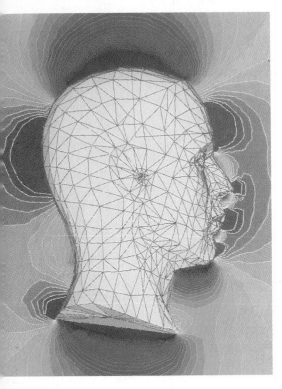

Part Two

Biology and Behavior

Part Three

Learning, Thinking, and Feeling

Part Four

Motivation, Personality, and Development

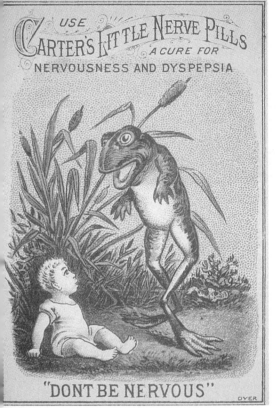

Part Six

Society and Behavior

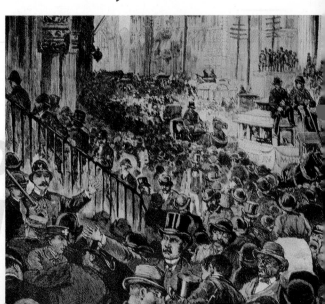

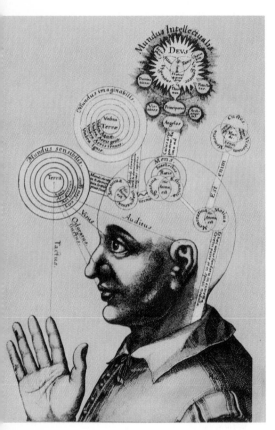

To the Instructor

When we began work on the first edition of this textbook over ten years ago, we had several goals in mind that were considered quite daring at the time: to make critical thinking integral to the introductory psychology course, to mainstream issues of culture and gender, to acknowledge controversies and debates in the field, and to reevaluate the way specific topics were treated. Preparing this introduction to our fourth edition has provided us with an opportunity to reflect on what has happened to these goals, and to the field of psychology, since we began this project.

■ GOALS OF THIS BOOK: PAST AND PRESENT

Thinking About Critical and Creative Thinking. Our first ambition was not only to convey the basic content of psychology, but also to get students to reflect on and use what they learn—to show them what it is like to think like a psychologist. Psychology, we have always believed, is not only a body of knowledge; it is also a way of approaching and analyzing the world. It is a way of asking questions about everything from the smallest curiosities to the largest matters of life and death. From the beginning, therefore, our approach has been based on **critical and creative thinking:** the understanding that knowledge is advanced when people resist leaping to conclusions on the basis of personal experience alone (so tempting in psychological matters!), when they apply rigorous standards of evidence, and when they listen to competing views.

One of our greatest satisfactions over the years has been observing the success of this effort to define and implement critical thinking, and make it an integral part of the study of psychology. We rarely get reactions anymore such as "Isn't critical thinking the same as debunking?" or "Isn't it just a gimmick?" At its best, critical thinking is neither negative thinking nor an added-on embellishment. Sometimes, of course, critical thought does require skepticism and doubt, but it also involves the ability to generate ideas, see implications, be creative with explanations, and ask imaginative questions. It means breaking out of preconceived categories. It means being open-minded—although not so open-minded, as philosopher Jacob Needleman observed, "that your brains fall out."

Given these meanings, it is clear that true critical thinking cannot be reduced to a set of rhetorical questions or to a formula for analyzing studies; it is a process of reporting and evaluating research and ideas that must be woven seamlessly into a book's narrative. In this book, we apply it to concepts that many students approach uncritically, such as astrology, "premenstrual syndrome," and the "instinctive" nature of sexuality. We also apply it to some assumptions that many psychologists have accepted unquestioningly, such as the decisive importance of childhood to later life, the hierarchical nature of motives, and the disease model of addiction. By probing beneath assumptions and presenting the most recent evidence available, we hope to convey the excitement and open-ended nature of psychological research and inquiry.

Mainstreaming Culture and Gender. Our second goal, from the start, was to make the study of psychology the study of all human beings. We felt the time had finally come for psychologists to acknowledge that universal principles of behavior cannot be deduced from a narrow sample of humanity—Americans, say, or white college sophomores, or middle-class men. At the time of our first edition, the idea of mainstreaming issues of gender, ethnicity, and culture in college textbooks was considered radical. Today, the issue is no longer whether to include these topics, but how best to do it. From the beginning, our own answer has been to raise relevant studies in the main body of the text, and we continue to do so. Are there sex differences in the brain? This controversial and fascinating issue belongs in the brain chapter (Chapter 4). Do women and men differ in the meanings and motives they attach to love and sex? That topic belongs in the discussion of motivation (Chapter 11). Similarly, when we talk about the supposedly universal milestones of infant development, that is the place to show how those milestones differ depending on an infant's cultural environment (Chapter 13).

Our approach to culture, however, continues to evolve and change. When we first wrote this book, some psychologists believed (and some still do) that "culture" is a frothy topic that somehow trivializes the serious business of scientific research. We respectfully disagree. Over the past decade, the exploding fields of cultural and cross-cultural psychology have demonstrated convincingly that culture is not merely a superficial gloss on human behavior, but a profound influence that affects virtually all aspects of life (Lonner & Malpass, 1994). The proper study of culture, therefore, makes our field more scientific, not less so.

Nevertheless, we have been disheartened to see a growing confusion between the scientific study of culture and the popular movement called multiculturalism. The study of culture, in our view, should increase students' understanding of what culture means, how and why ethnic and national groups differ, what our common human needs are, and why no culture is inherently superior to any other—in spite of the universal ethnocentric inclination to believe so. In some books and in many classrooms, however, multiculturalism is neither "multi" nor "cultural," but a pretext for celebrating one's own particular ethnic identity. There is a place for celebrating one's own ethnic identity! We fear, however, that the original reason for bringing the study of culture into psychology—to create a bigger tent that will encompass all the diversity of humankind—is in some quarters generating the construction of dozens of little separate tents.

In this edition we feel the time has come to address these issues squarely. Therefore, although we continue to mainstream research on culture and ethnicity where relevant throughout the book, we have also added an entirely new chapter on cultural psychology (Chapter 18). There we discuss the emotionally laden subject of "political correctness" in group names; why the study of culture so often deteriorates into stereotyping and value judgments; the touchy matter of moral evaluations of other cultures' practices (and how we feel when other cultures morally evaluate our practices); and, most of all, what the *scientific* study of culture means—problems of definition, method, and interpretation, along with some fascinating research.

Some instructors may want to assign the "Psychology and Popular Culture" feature from Chapter 18 at the beginning of the course, because this box concerns the psychology and politics of group names, an issue relevant to the classroom itself. Is it better to say Hispanic or Latino? Chicano or Mexican-American? Black, African-American, or, as social critic Henry Louis Gates prefers for himself, colored? Anglo, European-American, or white? Crippled, handicapped, disabled, or "differently abled"? Native American, the politically appropriate term, or American Indian, the term the American Indian Movement itself prefers? Each of these labels has different emotional connotations in different parts of North America. Rather than focus on which terms are "correct," we encourage teachers to raise the question of the *psychology* of labels and of ethnic identity. What do students prefer to call themselves and other groups? Their answers will reveal a great deal about their own identities and sense of place in society.

Facing the Controversies. As the study of culture shows, psychology has always been full of lively, sometimes angry, debates, and we feel that students should not be sheltered from these controversies. They are what make psychology so interesting! Sociobiologists and feminist psychologists differ strongly in their analyses of gender relations (Chapter 3). Psychodynamic clinicians and experimental psychologists differ strongly in their assumptions about memory, child development, and trauma; these differences have important repercussions for, among other things, "recovered memory" therapy and the questioning of children as eyewitnesses (Chapter 9). The "scientist–practitioner" gap between researchers and psychotherapists is continuing to widen (Chapter 16). In this book we candidly address these and other debates, try to show why they are occurring, and suggest the kinds of questions that might lead to useful answers in each case.

Reflecting New Directions in the Field. Psychology is an expanding, constantly evolving enterprise. New areas of interest emerge, and suddenly research on a topic previously overlooked explodes into prominence. Often, however, there is a time lag between such an explosion and its impact on psychology textbooks. When we first wrote this book, for example, emotion, if it was discussed at all in the introductory course, was typically combined with motivation, for reasons more historical than logical. Yet, by the mid-1980s emotion had become a major area of study and research, and exciting findings had emerged on its physiological, cognitive, and cultural components; thus, we broke with tradition and gave emotion its own proper chapter.

The discipline of psychology itself continues to shape the organization of the book. Accordingly, this edition features two new chapters that reflect two increasingly important and exciting topics within the field: *evolutionary psychology* (Chapter 3) and, as we just noted, *cultural psychology* (Chapter 18). We see these topics as the bookends of behavior, for biology and culture combine to create our human similarities and human differences. (In "What's New" on page xix we discuss our decisions to drop some topics and rearrange others to accommodate these new chapters without adding length to the book.)

■ IMPLEMENTING THE GOALS

Our goals of incorporating critical thinking, mainstreaming research on culture and gender, confronting controversies, and reflecting new research directions are carried out throughout the text. Here we want to draw your attention to some of the particular ways in which these goals are addressed.

Pedagogical Supports for Critical and Creative Thinking

As we noted, the primary way we try to "do" critical and creative thinking is by modeling it in our evaluations of research and popular ideas.

- We start right off, in the first chapter, with **an extended discussion of what critical thinking is and what it isn't.** This discussion covers eight specific guidelines to critical thinking and includes an explanation of why critical thought is particularly relevant to the study of psychology (see pages 28–35). A pictorial essay (on pages 38–39) further illustrates the guidelines discussed.

- A feature in each chapter titled **Think About It** raises psychological, social, or philosophical issues that have no easy answers. These essays pose provocative questions for the student to ponder. (Some instructors have students debate these questions in class, write short essays on them, or choose one or more for term papers.) Topics include the social implications of genetic testing (Chapter 3), whether praise and high grades raise self-esteem or diminish it (Chapter 7), which kinds of "love stories" are beneficial and which are not (Chapter 11), how far fetal protection policies should go (Chapter 13), and the delicate balance between understanding other cultures' practices and accepting them, as illustrated by the debate over female genital mutilation (Chapter 18).

- A new boxed feature, **Psychology and Popular Culture,** which appears in ten chapters, shows how psychological research might be brought to bear in critically assessing an issue that has captured the attention of the culture at large. North America is increasingly inundated with what R. D. Rosen (1977) once called "psychobabble"—quasi-psychological ideas covered in a thin veneer of psychological language. So pervasive are these ideas, and in some cases so relevant to people's personal lives and a nation's social policies, that we thought the time was right to acknowledge them head-on. Topics include the national furor over *The Bell Curve* and matters of race and intelligence in general (Chapter 3), "subliminal persuasion" (Chapter 6), the debate over the origins of homosexuality (Chapter 11), what social psychological research on crowd behavior means for the "deindividuation defense" in the law (Chapter 17), and, as mentioned earlier, the argument about political correctness in the use of group names (Chapter 18).

- *Critical thinking questions* are included in many of the self-tests (Quick Quizzes) found in each chapter, and give students plenty of opportunities to practice specific critical thinking skills. These items, which are identified by a "flash" symbol such as the one in the margin, invite the student to reflect on the implications of findings and consider how psychological principles might illuminate real-life issues. For example: What kinds of questions should a critical thinker ask about a new biological treatment for depression? How might a hypothetical study of testosterone and hostility be improved? How might findings on working conditions and job motivation help us think critically about the reasons for an employee's habitual tardiness? Although we offer some possible responses to such questions, most of them do not have a single correct answer, and students may have valid, well-reasoned answers that differ from our own.

- *Marginal signposts* throughout the book raise provocative questions that alert students to some (though by no means all) of the critical discussions in the text. These signposts, accompanied by the flash symbol for easy identification, are not, in themselves, illustrations of critical thinking. Rather, they serve as pointers to critical analyses in the text of a chapter and invite the reader into the discussion.

Applications: Taking Psychology With You

Few disciplines have as many real-world implications as does psychology. Psychological principles and findings can be applied to individuals, groups, institutions, and society as a whole. We cover such applications not only in the main body of the text but also in a feature at the end of each chapter called **Taking Psychology with You.** Drawing on research reported in the chapter, this feature tackles topics of practical concern, such as living with chronic pain (Chapter 6), becoming more creative (Chapter 8), managing anger (Chapter 10), assessing your work motivation (Chapter 11), choosing a therapist (Chapter 16), and evaluating the manipulations of advertisements (Chapter 17).

The final "Taking Psychology with You" feature is an **Epilogue,** which represents a unique effort to show students that the vast number of seemingly disparate studies and points of view they have just read about are related. The epilogue contains two real-life problems that most students can be expected to encounter, if they haven't already—the end of a love relationship and difficulties at work. We show how topics discussed in previous chapters can be applied to understanding and coping with these situations. Readers learn that solving a real problem requires more than finding the "right" study from the "right" school of psychology. Many instructors have told us that they find this epilogue a useful way to help students integrate some of the diverse approaches of contemporary psychology. Asking students to come up with research findings that might apply to other problems in living makes for a good term-paper assignment as well.

▓ INVOLVING THE STUDENT

One of the soundest findings about learning is that it requires the active encoding of material. In this textbook, two features in particular encourage students' active involvement and provide pedagogical support:

- **Quick Quizzes** are periodic self-tests that encourage students to check their progress and to go back and review if necessary. These quizzes do more than just test for memorization of definitions; they tell students whether they comprehend the issues. Mindful of the common tendency to skip quizzes or to peek at the answers, we have used various formats and have included entertaining examples in order to motivate students to test themselves. As we mentioned, many of the quizzes also include critical thinking items. We believe that the incorporation of these items makes this pedagogical feature, more than ever, a useful one for students of all abilities.

- A **running glossary** defines boldfaced technical terms on the pages where they occur for handy reference and study. Students are enthusiastic about this feature. All entries can also be found in a cumulative glossary at the back of the book.

Other pedagogical features include chapter outlines, lists of key terms, and chapter summaries in numbered paragraph form.

▓ CONTENT UPDATES: WHAT'S NEW?

In addition to the two new chapters on evolutionary and cultural psychology, and the new "Psychology and Popular Culture" box, this edition includes revised content and updated research throughout. We have purposely avoided making purely cosmetic changes, especially in the stories and examples that students enjoy. We did, however, add a great deal of recent, cutting-edge research in every chapter, and we reorganized some sections to make them clearer and easier to study and teach. Here are a few highlights:

- *Chapter 3* (evolution, genes, and behavior) combines research in behavioral genetics and evolutionary psychology to illustrate the origins of human commonalities and individual differences. This chapter includes topics particularly suited to the nature–nurture debate, including research on body shape and weight (formerly discussed in motivation), the capacity for language (formerly discussed in thinking), and the origins of intelligence (formerly discussed in a separate chapter on intelligence), as well as a discussion of the debate on the evolutionary origins of gender differences.

- *Chapter 4* (neurons, hormones, and the brain) contains an up-to-date discussion of research on sex differences in the brain, including remarkable new studies using MRIs. We continue to caution students, however, about exaggerating the implications of such research.

- *Chapter 6* (sensation and perception) includes new research on the physiology of sound localization, individual differences in the ability to taste bitter substances, the ability of infants to coordinate visual and auditory cues, and parapsychology.

- *Chapter 8* (thinking and intelligence) now includes psychometric and cognitive approaches to intelligence (formerly in a separate intelligence chapter); an expanded section on animal cognition; cognitive dissonance as a bias in rational thinking (formerly in the motivation chapter); and research on reflective judgment in adolescents and adults.

- *Chapter 9* (memory) has been extensively reorganized, and in addition now includes coverage of the controversial recovered-memory debate in psychotherapy and of studies of children's memory, so relevant to their testimony as eyewitnesses.

- *Chapter 11* (motivation) consists now of fewer topics in greater depth: love (including attachment theory), sexuality, and work.

- We have reorganized the material on child, adolescent, and adult development, which used to involve two chapters. At the request of many users of the book, we now cover child and adolescent development in one chapter (*Chapter 13*), and have moved the findings on adulthood to other chapters where appropriate. (There are those who say the entire rest of the textbook is about adults, after all!) For example, Erik Erikson's theory of adult stages is now discussed under psychodynamic theories of personality; ethical and psychological issues about death and dying are discussed in the context of health psychology (*Chapter 14*); and sexuality over the life cycle is discussed in the section on sexuality (*Chapter 11*).

- *Chapter 15* (psychological disorders) contains a revised and expanded discussion of the complex issues involved in defining and diagnosing mental disorder, an extended discussion of the controversy surrounding multiple personality disorder (now officially called dissociative identity disorder), and new research on the causes of antisocial personality disorder.

- The sociocultural unit now consists of two chapters: social psychology (*Chapter 17*) and cultural psychology (*Chapter 18*). This organization allowed us to move the topics of ethnocentrism, stereotyping, and prejudice into cultural psychology, and expand the social psychology chapter to include more on attitude change (friendly and coercive), group behavior, and altruism and dissent.

A detailed explanation of all deletions, additions, and changes in the fourth edition of *Psychology* is available to all adopters of the previous edition, so that they will not have to guess why we made particular changes. We hope this support will make the transition from one edition to the next as painless for instructors as possible. You can obtain this description from your HarperCollins representative or by writing to: Marketing Manager, Psychology, HarperCollins College Publishers, 10 E. 53rd Street, New York, NY 10022.

■ SUPPLEMENTS PACKAGE

Psychology, Fourth Edition, is supported by a complete teaching package.

For the Instructor:

Instructor's Resource Manual. This manual contains a wealth of teaching aids for each chapter: learning objectives, chapter outlines, lecture supplements, classroom demonstrations, and critical thinking exercises; mini-experiments, self-test exercises, and suggestions for additional readings; and an extensive guide to audiovisual materials. The IRM comes in a three-ring binder for easy reproduction of student handouts. The binder may also serve as a storage unit for collecting favorite lecture supplements and teaching materials.

Test Banks I & II. These two comprehensive test banks are the result of a unique collaboration. Grace Galliano of Kennesaw State University, Scott Johnson of John Wood Community College, and Carolyn Meyer of Lake Sumter Community College worked together to create a pool of class-tested, thoroughly revised test items. Of these, the best test items have been chosen to create the two test banks that accompany the fourth edition. The test banks feature an assortment of multiple-choice, short answer, true/false, and essay items that test applied, factual, and conceptual knowledge. Items are referenced by learning objectives, cognitive type, topic, and skill.

Testmaster Computerized Testing System. This flexible, easy-to-master computer test bank includes all the test items in the two test banks. The Test Master software allows you to edit existing questions and add your own items. Tests can be printed in several different formats and can include figures, such as graphs and tables. Testmaster is available in Macintosh- and IBM- compatible formats.

Lecture Shell. The chapter outlines of the entire text are available on disc for use in creating your own lecture outlines.

Transparencies. A new Introductory Psychology Transparency Package contains 200 full-color acetates designed to accompany the text. The package features many transparencies specifically designed for large lecture halls.

Other Media. Fully updated **CD-ROM, laserdiscs, electronic transparencies, presentation software,** and **videos** are also available to qualified adopters of *Psychology,* Fourth Edition. Please contact your HarperCollins sales representative for more information.

For the Student:

Study Guide. Written by Tina Stern of Dekalb College, this manual has been extensively updated to reflect the new coverage in the fourth edition. It includes learning objectives, chapter outlines, thinking questions illustrating concepts in the text, three sets of practice tests with suggested answers, key-term reviews, and a "How To Study" section.

ESL Study Guide. Written by Amy Tickle of Michigan State University, this manual is an adaptation of the fourth-edition study guide for ESL students. Like the original study guide, each chapter contains learning objectives, chapter outlines, and practice tests, in addition to a pronunciation guide, and activities designed to help meet the needs of ESL students.

Psychobabble and Biobunk. A new handbook to accompany the fourth edition of *Psychology,* this short paperback features a selection of opinion essays written for *The Los Angeles Times* by Carol Tavris. These essays, which apply psychological research and findings to current issues in the news, may be used to encourage debate in the classroom or as a basis for student papers. Students can be asked to write or present their own points of view on a topic, drawing on evidence from the textbook, lectures, or independent research to support their conclusions.

Practice Tests. Written by the test bank authors, these tests, consisting of 15 multiple-choice questions per chapter with annotated answers, are designed to help students prepare for exams.

Interactive Media for the Student:

Psychology CD-ROM. Prepared in consultation with James Hilton of the University of Michigan and Charles Perdue of West Virginia State College, the CD-

ROM is an interactive, digital presentation of *Psychology*, Fourth Edition. Video, audio, animated graphics, and other interactive activities are integrated within the book presentation. The CD is fully annotated with multimedia that extends, reinforces, and enlivens the text and still graphics. The CD also features an electronic study guide and self-tests.

SuperShell Computerized Tutorial. Created by Catherine Strathern and Gary Grey, both of the University of Cincinnati, this interactive program helps students learn important psychological facts and concepts through drill and practice exercises and diagnostic feedback. SuperShell provides immediate correct answers and the text page numbers on which the material is discussed. A running score of the student's performance is maintained on the screen throughout the session. SuperShell is available for both IBM and Macintosh Computers.

Journey II. Students are guided through a concept-building tour of the experimental method, the nervous system, learning, development, and psychological assessment with this program developed by Intentional Educations. Each module is self-contained and comes complete with step-by-step pedagogy. This program is available in Macintosh- and IBM-compatible formats.

■ ACKNOWLEDGMENTS

Like any other cooperative effort, writing a textbook requires a support team. The following reviewers and consultants made many valuable suggestions during the development of this and previous editions of *Psychology*, and we are indebted to them for their contributions.

Benton E. Allen
Mt. San Antonio College

Susan M. Andersen
University of California, Santa Barbara

Lynn R. Anderson
Wayne State University

Emir Andrews
Memorial University of Newfoundland

Alan Auerbach
Wilfrid Laurier University

Lynn Haller Augsbach
Morehead State University

Brian C. Babbitt
Missouri Southern State College

MaryAnn Baenninger
Trenton State College

Patricia Barker
Schenectady County Community College

Ronald K. Barrett
Loyola Marymount University

Allan Basbaum
University of California, San Francisco

Carol Batt
Sacred Heart University

William M. Baum
University of New Hampshire

Bill E. Beckwith
University of North Dakota

Helen Bee
Madison, WI

David F. Berger
SUNY at Cortland

Michael Bergmire
Jefferson College

Philip J. Bersh
Temple University

Randolph Blake
Vanderbilt University

Richard Bowen
Loyola University of Chicago

Laura L. Bowman
Kent State University

Edward N. Brady
Belleville Area College

John R. Braun
University of Bridgeport

Sharon S. Brehm
SUNY at Binghamton

Sylvester Briggs
Kent State University

Gwen Briscoe
College of Mt. St. Joseph

Barbara Brown
DeKalb College

Robert C. Brown, Jr.
Georgia State University

Linda L. Brunton
Columbia State Community College

Peter R. Burzynski
Vincennes University

Frank Calabrese
Community College of Philadelphia

Jean Caplan
Concordia University

Bernardo J. Carducci
Indiana University Southeast

Sally S. Carr
Lakeland Community College

Paul Chance
Laurel, DE

Herbert H. Clark
Stanford University

Samuel Clement
Marianopolis College

Eva Conrad
San Bernardino Valley College

Richard L. Cook
University of Colorado

Robert Cormack
New Mexico Institute of Mining and Technology

Wendi Cross
Ohio University

Gaylen Davidson-Podgorny
Santa Rosa Junior College

Robert M. Davis
Purdue University School of Science, IUPUI

Michael William Decker
University of California, Irvine

Geri Anne Dino
Frostburg State University

Susan H. Evans
University of Southern California

Fred Fahringer
Southwest Texas State University

Ronald Finke
SUNY at Stony Brook

John H. Flowers
University of Nebraska–Lincoln

William F. Ford
Bucks County Community College

Donald G. Forgays
University of Vermont

Sheila Francis
Creighton University

Grace Galliano
Kennesaw State College

Mary Gauvain
Oregon State University

Ron Gerrard
SUNY at Oswego

David Gersh
Houston Community College

Jessica B. Gillooly
Glendale Community College

Margaret Gittis
Youngstown State University

Carlos Goldberg
*Indiana University–Purdue University
at Indianapolis*

Carol Grams
Orange Coast College

Patricia Greenfield
University of California, Los Angeles

Richard A. Griggs
University of Florida

Sarmi Gulgoz
Auburn University

Jimmy G. Hail
McLennan Community College

Pryor Hale
Piedmont Virginia Community College

Len Hamilton
Rutgers University

George Hampton
University of Houston

Algea Harrison
Oakland University

Neil Helgeson
The University of Texas at San Antonio

John E. Hesson
Metropolitan State College

Robert Higgins
Oakland Community College

John P. Hostetler
Albion College

John Hunsley
University of Ottawa

James Johnson
*University of North Carolina at
Wilmington*

Robert D. Johnson
Arkansas State University

Timothy P. Johnston
*University of North Carolina at
Greensboro*

Chadwick Karr
Portland State University

Yoshito Kawahara
San Diego Mesa College

Geoffrey Keppel
University of California, Berkeley

Harold O. Kiess
Framingham State College

Gary King
Rose State College

Jack Kirschenbaum
Fullerton College

Donald Kline
University of Calgary

Stephen M. Kosslyn
Harvard University

Michael J. Lambert
Brigham Young University

George S. Larimer
West Liberty State College

S. David Leonard
University of Georgia

Herbert Leff
University of Vermont

Robert Levy
Indiana State University

Lewis Lieberman
Columbus College

R. Martin Lobdell
Pierce College

Nina Lott
National University

Bonnie Lustigman
Montclair State College

Debra Moehle McCallum
University of Alabama at Birmingham

D. F. McCoy
University of Kentucky

C. Sue McCullough
Texas Woman's University

Elizabeth McDonel
University of Alabama

Susanne Wicks McKenzie
Dawson College

Mark B. McKinley
Lorain County Community College

Ronald K. McLaughlin
Juniata College

Frances K. McSweeney
Washington State University

Marc Marschark
*University of North Carolina at
Greensboro*

Monique Martin
Champlain Regional College

Maty Jo Meadow
Mankato State University

Linda Mealey
College of St. Benedict

Dorothy Mercer
Eastern Kentucky University

Laura J. Metallo
Five Towns College

Maribel Montgomery
Linn-Benton Community College

Douglas G. Mook
University of Virginia

T. Mark Morey
SUNY at Oswego

James S. Nairne
University of Texas at Arlington

Douglas Navarick
California State University, Fullerton

Robert A. Neimever
Memphis State University

Nora Newcombe
Temple University

Linda Noble
Kennesaw State College

Keith Oatley
Ontario Institute for Studies in Education

Peter Oliver
University of Hartford

Patricia Owen-Smith
Oxford College

David Page
Nazareth College

M. Carr Payne, Jr.
Georgia Institute of Technology

Dan G. Perkins
Richland College

Gregory Pezzetti
Rancho Santiago Community College

Wayne Poniewaz
University of Arkansas, Monticello

Paula M. Popovich
Ohio University

Robert Prochnow
St. Cloud State University

Janet Proctor
Purdue University

Reginald L. Razzi
Upsala College

Jayne Rose
Augustana College

Gary Ross-Reynolds
Nicholls State University

Gerald Rubin
Central Virginia Community College

Joe Rubinstein
Purdue University

Nancy Sauerman
Kirkwood Community College

H. R. Schiffman
Rutgers University

Lael Schooler
Indiana University

David A. Schroeder
University of Arkansas

Marvin Schwartz
University of Cincinnati

Shelley Schwartz
Vanier College

Joyce Segreto
Youngstown State University

Kimron Shapiro
University of Calgary

Phillip Shaver
University of California, Davis

Susan A. Shodahl
San Bernardino Valley College

Dale Simmons
Oregon State University

Art Skibbe
Appalachian State University

William P. Smotherman
SUNY at Binghamton

Samuel Snyder
North Carolina State University

Barbara A. Spellman
University of Texas at Austin

Larry R. Squire
University of California, San Diego

Tina Stern
DeKalb College

A. Stirling
John Abbott College

Milton E. Strauss
Johns Hopkins University

Judith Sugar
Colorado State University

Shelley E. Taylor
University of California, Los Angeles

Barbara Turpin
Southwest Missouri State University

Ronald J. Venhorst
Kean College of New Jersey

Wayne A. Viney
Colorado State University

Benjamin Wallace
Cleveland State University

Phyllis Walrad
Macomb Community College

Charles R. Walsmith
Bellevue Community College

Phillip Wann
Missouri Western State College

Thomas J. Weatherly
DeKalb College–Central Campus

Mary Wellman
Rhode Island University

Gary L. Wells
University of Alberta

Warner Wilson
Wright State University

Loren Wingblade
Jackson Community College

Judith K. Winters
DeKalb College

Rita S. Wolpert
Caldwell College

Our editorial and production team at HarperCollins has been, as always, superb, and we are enormously grateful to these talented people for their hard work and commitment to quality. In particular, we thank developmental editor Melissa Mashburn, for her unwavering enthusiasm for this book, her day-to-day editorial suggestions, and her unruffled good nature in helping us meet every deadline; acquisitions editor Jill Lectka, for expertly shepherding this complicated project from start to finish; editorial director Marcus Boggs, whose insights and knowledge about psychology and about books were especially beneficial to this fourth edition; project editor Donna DeBenedictis, whose humor, calm manner, and brilliant organizational skills guided this project through its complicated production schedule; and marketing manager Mark Paluch, for superbly organizing and implementing the marketing plan. Under Jill Little's excellent art direction, the book has acquired a clean new design that weaves the many elements together with clarity and elegance. And we are eternally grateful to photo researcher Sandy Schneider for her wonderful selections of photos and illustrations that visually illustrate abstract concepts or raise thought-provoking questions.

We cannot begin to thank Saul Bass for once again giving us a unique and stunning cover design. Throughout the four editions of this text, Saul's covers have conveyed the mystery, the challenge, the risk, and the rewards in thinking critically and creatively. His work represents art and psychology at their best. Our appreciation also goes to Art Goodman, Nancy Von Lauderbach, and the rest of the fine staff at Saul Bass/Herb Yager and Associates.

Most of all, we thank Howard Williams and Ronan O'Casey, who from the beginning of this endeavor have bolstered us with their love, humor, and good cheer, not to mention an endless supply of freshly brewed coffee.

We have enjoyed writing this book, and we hope you will enjoy reading and using it. Your questions, comments, and reactions on the first three editions helped us make many improvements. Please let us hear from you.

CAROLE WADE
CAROL TAVRIS

To the Student

If you are reading this introduction, you are starting your introductory psychology course on the right foot. It is always a good idea to get a general picture of what you are about to read before charging forward, just as it is best to find out what Wyoming looks like before moving there from Maine.

Our goal in writing this book is to guide you to think critically and imaginatively about what you read, and to apply what you learn to your own life and the world around you. We ourselves have never gotten over our initial excitement about psychology, and we have done everything we can think of to make the field as absorbing for you as it is for us. However, what you bring to this book is as important as what we have written. This text will remain only a collection of pages with ink on them unless you choose to interact with its content. The more actively you are involved in your own learning, the more successful the book and your course will be, and the more enjoyable, too.

In our years of teaching, we have found that certain study strategies can vastly improve learning, and so we offer the following suggestions. (Reading Chapter 7, on learning, and Chapter 9, on memory, should also be helpful!) Do not read the text in the same way as you might a novel, taking in large chunks at a sitting. To get the most from your studying, we recommend that you read only a part of each chapter at a time. Instead of simply reading silently, try to restate what you have read in your own words at the end of each major section. Some people find it helpful to write down main points on a piece of paper or on index cards. Others prefer to recite main points aloud to someone else or to themselves (which may require some privacy). Do not count on getting by with just one reading of a chapter. Most people need to go through the material at least twice, and then review the main points several times before an exam.

Individuals often develop their own strategies for studying, and we don't want to discourage you from doing so. Whatever approach you use, though, it should involve an *active response* to the material. Here are some further hints for enhancing your learning:

- A good first step is to read the chapter title and outline to get an idea of what is in store. Browse through the chapter, looking at the pictures and reading the headings.

- Every chapter contains several **Quick Quizzes** that permit you to test your understanding and retention of what you have just read and your ability to apply the material to examples. Do not let the word "quiz" give you a sinking feeling. These quizzes are for your practical use and, we hope, for your enjoyment. When you can't answer a question, do not go on to the next section; pause right then and there, review what you've read, and then try again.

- Some of the Quick Quizzes contain a *critical-thinking item,* denoted by a flash symbol such as the one in the margin. The answers we give for these items are only suggestions; you may come up with different (and possibly better) ones. Quick Quizzes containing critical-thinking items are not really so quick, because they ask you to reflect on what you have read and to apply the guidelines to critical thinking that are introduced in Chapter 1. But if you take the time to respond thoughtfully to them, we think you will learn more and become a more sophisticated user of psychology.

- Every important new term in this textbook is printed in **boldface** and is defined in the margin of the page on which it appears or on the facing page. The **marginal glossary** permits you to find all key terms and concepts easily, and will help you when you study for exams. A *full glossary* also appears at the end of the book.

- **Critical thinking signposts**, found in the margins and accompanied again by the flash symbol, indicate where critical thinking analyses or issues appear.
- When you have finished a chapter, read the **summary.** Some students tell us they find it useful to write down their own summary first, then compare it with the book's.
- Use the **key terms** list at the end of each chapter as a checklist. Try to define and discuss each term in the list to see how well you understand and remember it. If you need to review a term, a page number is given to tell you where it is first mentioned in the chapter.

You should know about some other features of this book, too. In each chapter, a **Think About It** box poses a provocative question that has no easy answer. We hope you will have as much fun pondering these questions as we did writing about them. Another box, called **Psychology and Popular Culture,** examines pop-psych topics that appear in the news and on talk shows—and discusses what good psychological research might have to say about those topics. At the end of each chapter, a feature called **Taking Psychology with You** draws on research to suggest ways you can apply what you have learned to everyday problems and concerns, such as living with stress and getting a better night's sleep, as well as to more serious ones, such as knowing when and how to select a psychotherapist or how to help a friend who seems suicidal.

You will notice that discussions of studies and theories are followed by one or more *citations* in parentheses. A citation tells the reader where the original research report or theoretical work was published. It consists of the author's name and the date of publication—for example: (Smith, 1984). The full reference, with the name of the article or book and other information, can be found in a *bibliography* at the end of the book. Students often find citations useful, especially for locating material for term projects and reports.

At the back of the book you will also find an *author index* and a *subject index.* The author index lists the name of every author cited in the book and the pages where the person's work is discussed. If you want to review a study by someone named Snodgrass, but you can't recall where it was covered, look under "Snodgrass" in the author index. The subject index provides a listing of all the major topics mentioned in the book. If you want to review material on, say, depression—a topic discussed in several chapters—you can look up "depression" in the subject index and find each place it is mentioned.

Most psychology textbooks stop abruptly with the last chapter, leaving the reader with the impression that early lessons have little to do with later ones. At the end of this book, you will find an **Epilogue** that shows how you might integrate and use the findings and theories you have read about to understand events, make wise decisions, and cope with life's inevitable challenges and changes. We consider the Epilogue to be important because it suggests how you can carry psychology out of your classroom and into the rest of your life.

We also recommend the **Study Guide** that is available at your bookstore to help you study and expand upon the material in this book. The *Study Guide* contains review material, exercises, and practice tests to help you understand and apply the concepts in the book.

We have done our utmost to convey our own enthusiasm about psychology, but in the end, it is your efforts as much as ours that will determine whether you find psychology to be exciting or boring, and whether the field will matter in your own life. We welcome your ideas and reactions so that we will know what works for you and what doesn't. In the meantime, welcome to psychology!

CAROLE WADE
CAROL TAVRIS

About the Authors

CAROLE WADE earned her Ph.D. in cognitive psychology at Stanford University. She began her academic career at the University of New Mexico, where she initiated a new course on gender roles; was professor of psychology for ten years at San Diego Mesa College; then taught at College of Marin; and is now affiliated with Dominican College of San Rafael, where she teaches undergraduate courses in psychology. She is coauthor with Sarah Cirese of *Human Sexuality* and coauthor with Carol Tavris of *Psychology in Perspective* and *The Longest War: Sex Differences in Perspective*. A former associate editor of *Psychology Today* magazine, where she met Dr. Tavris, Dr. Wade has a long-standing interest in making psychology accessible to students and the general public through public lectures, workshops, general interest articles, and the electronic media. For many years she has focused her efforts on the teaching and promotion of critical thinking skills and the enhancement of undergraduate education in psychology. She has served as chair of the American Psychological Association's Public Information Committee; as a member of the APA's Committee on Undergraduate Education; as a member of the Steering Committee for the APA's National Conference on Enhancing the Quality of Undergraduate Education; and on the Panel on Precollege and Undergraduate Education of the APA's Board of Educational Affairs. Dr. Wade is a Fellow of Divisions 1 and 2 and a member of Divisions 8, 9, and 35 of the American Psychological Association, and is a charter member of the American Psychological Society.

CAROL TAVRIS earned her Ph.D. in the interdisciplinary program in social psychology at the University of Michigan, and ever since has sought to bring interdisciplinary research from the many fields of psychology to the public. She is author of *The Mismeasure of Woman*, which won the 1992 Distinguished Media Contribution Award from the American Association of Applied and Preventive Psychology, and the Heritage Publications Award from Division 35 of the APA. Dr. Tavris is also the author of *Anger: The Misunderstood Emotion* and coauthor with Carole Wade of *Psychology in Perspective* and *The Longest War: Sex Differences in Perspective*. She has written on psychological topics for a wide variety of magazines, journals, and edited books, and also contributes essays to *The Los Angeles Times,* which have been reprinted in many newspapers across the United States and Canada. A highly regarded lecturer, she has given keynote addresses and workshops on, among other topics, critical thinking, anger, gender, and psychology and the media. She has taught at the Human Relations Center of the New School for Social Research and in the psychology department at UCLA. Dr. Tavris is a Fellow of Divisions 1, 9, and 35 of the American Psychological Association and a member of Division 8; a charter Fellow of the American Psychological Society; and a Fellow of the Committee for the Scientific Investigation of Claims of the Paranormal.

PSYCHOLOGY

Fourth Edition

Carole Wade
Dominican College of San Rafael

Carol Tavris

ISBN 0--673-99647-6

The first text to seamlessly integrate critical thinking, gender, age, and culture into the study of psychology, *Psychology,* now in its fourth blockbuster edition, remains at the forefront of the discipline, by continuing to weave these topics into its narrative more thoroughly than any other text of its kind. This enables students not only to learn the content of psychology, but also to think critically about a variety of issues influencing human development and behavior: they learn to "think" like psychologists. In addition to retaining these hallmark features, celebrated pedagogy, and inviting conversational tone, the widely anticipated fourth edition has been updated to feature two new cutting-edge chapters on *evolutionary psychology* and *socio-cultural psychology,* which reflect state-of-the-art psychological research and theory. Building on the text's acclaimed critical-thinking emphasis, new "Psychology and Popular Culture" boxes discuss how educated psychology students might approach an issue that has captured the attention of the public.

PART ONE ■ AN INVITATION TO PSYCHOLOGY

■ THINKING CRITICALLY AND CREATIVELY ABOUT PSYCHOLOGY

We believe that one of the greatest benefits of studying psychology is that you learn not only how the brain works in general but also how to use yours in particular—by thinking critically. **Critical thinking** is the ability and willingness to assess claims and make objective judgments on the basis of well-supported reasons. It is the ability to look for flaws in arguments and to resist claims that have no supporting evidence. It is the ability to defend a conclusion as reasonable or plausible. Critical thinking, however, is not merely negative thinking. It also fosters the ability to be *creative and constructive:* to come up with various explanations for events, think of implications of research findings, and apply new knowledge to a broad range of social and personal problems. You can't separate critical thinking from creative thinking, for it is only when you question *what is* that you can begin to imagine *what can be.*

Here is an example of what we mean. Many people, when faced with a setback to their expectations, narrow their horizons instead of expanding them. We know a fellow named Victor whose entire dream in life was to be a veterinarian. Victor's love of animals was legendary: At age 3, he wouldn't let you kill a bug in his presence. However, Victor wasn't admitted to any of the veterinary schools he applied to, and his reaction was panic and despair: "My whole life is ruined!" Victor was not thinking critically; he had divided his possibilities into only two alternatives: become a veterinarian, or nothing. But by examining this assumption and by thinking creatively about all the possible occupations that would make use of his love of animals, Victor realized his choices were endless: pet-shop owner, Hollywood "pet therapist," animal trainer, designer of humane zoos, organizer for an endangered-species group, ecologist, wildlife photographer. . . .

These days, most people know that you have to exercise the body to keep it in shape, but they may assume that thinking doesn't take any effort at all, and certainly no practice. All around us we can see examples of flabby thinking, lazy thinking, emotional thinking, and nonthinking.

■ **critical thinking**
The ability and willingness to assess claims and to make objective judgments on the basis of well-supported reasons.

Ask Questions; Be Willing to Wonder. What is the one kind of question that most exasperates parents of young children? "Why is the sky blue, Mommy?" "Why doesn't the plane fall?" "Why don't pigs have wings?" Unfortunately, as children grow up, they tend to stop asking "why" questions. (Why do you think this is?)

It is not enough to say that something "could be" true; critical thinkers demand that claims be supported by convincing evidence.

CRITICAL AND CREATIVE-THINKING EMPHASIS

The text's acclaimed critical- and creative-thinking emphasis begins with an extended discussion in Chapter 1, which includes eight specific guidelines for critical and creative thinking and an explanation of why critical thought is particularly relevant to the study of psychology.

MARGINAL SIGNPOSTS

Found throughout the text, *marginal signposts* raise provocative questions that alert students to some of the critical discussions in the text. Flagged by a "flash" symbol for easy identification, these signposts serve as pointers to critical analyses inviting the reader into the discussion.

As you might imagine, it is often difficult for clinicians to determine when people in fugue states have a true disorder and when they are faking (Schacter, 1986). This problem is also apparent in the remarkable disorder of multiple personality.

Dissociative Identity Disorder ("Multiple Personality")

The DSM-IV has dropped the familiar term "multiple personality disorder" (MPD) in favor of **dissociative identity disorder** to describe the appearance, within one person, of two or more distinct identities. (In our discussion, however, we will retain the more commonly used term.) In this disorder, each identity appears to have its own memories, preferences, handwriting, and medical problems (Braun, 1988). In a case study of one person with four identities, for example, the researcher concluded that it was "as if four different people had been tested" (Larmore et al., 1977).

Cases of multiple personality are extremely dramatic: Those portrayed in the films *The Three Faces of Eve* and *Sybil* fascinated audiences for years, and so do the legal cases that make the news. A woman charges a man with rape, claiming that only one of her personalities consented to have sex with him while another objected; a man kills his wife and claims his "other personality" did it. Among mental health professionals, however, there are two competing and *totally incompatible* views of MPD. Some think it is a real disorder, all too common but often underdiagnosed. Others are skeptical: They think that most cases are concocted by psychiatrists and psychologists who believe in it, in unwitting collusion with vulnerable and suggestible patients, and that if it exists at all it is extremely rare.

A man charged with murder claims that one of his "other personalities" committed the crime. You are on the jury, and you know that psychologists disagree about the validity of his defense. What questions would you want to ask about this man's claim, and how would you reach a decision about it?

Quick QUIZ

A. Keeping in mind that both sides of the brain are involved in most activities, see whether you can identify which side is *most* closely associated with each of the following:
1. Enjoying a musical recording
2. Wiggling the left big toe
3. Giving a speech in class
4. Balancing a checkbook
5. Recognizing a long-lost friend

B. Over the past two decades, thousands of people have taken courses and bought tapes that promise to turn them into right-brained types. What characteristics of human thought might explain the eagerness of some people to glorify "right-brainedness" and disparage "left-brainedness" (or vice versa)?

Answers:

A. 1, 2, and 5 are most closely associated with the right side; 3 and 4 with the left. B. One possible answer: Human beings like to make sense of the world, and one easy way to do that is to divide humanity into opposing categories, such as right-brained versus left-brained types. This sort of dualistic, either-or thinking can lead to the conclusion that "fixing up" one of the categories (e.g., left-brained types) will make individuals happier and the world a better place. (If only it were that simple.)

QUICK QUIZZES

Helping students ascertain whether they truly comprehend the issues they have just covered, these periodic self-tests encourage readers to check their progress and to go back and review if necessary. Certain questions are marked with a "flash" symbol to call attention to their critical thinking nature.

Psychology and Popular Culture

What's in a Name? The Debate over "Political Correctness"

■ In 1994, the *Los Angeles Times* published its "Guidelines on Racial and Ethnic Identification," a list that bans some 150 words and phrases that are potentially insulting to various groups. *Times* writers may not say "welsh on a bet," an affront to the Welsh. They may not use the word "invalid" because it literally means "not valid" and is thus considered offensive to disabled persons, who are to be called "disabled" and not "crippled." Writers may not use the term "New World," as if there were no indigenous cultures in the Americas that preceded Columbus's voyage, or "Dutch treat," a term presumably offensive to the Dutch. And for some reason, the *Times* prohibits the word "deaf" in favor of "people who cannot hear," although most deaf people have no reluctance to say they are deaf, and the National Theater of the Deaf is not planning to change its name to the National Theater of People Who Cannot Hear.

In North America today, the question of what various groups should be called and what terms are "offensive"—and whether newspapers, universities, the government, and other institutions should try to establish language guidelines for correct usage—evokes much controversy. One side argues that because language shapes attitudes and prejudices, we must be ever vigilant about the mindless use of labels or phrases that offend or perpetuate untruths. Although most Americans do not realize the derivation of the term "to welsh" on a bet, it is as offensive to people from Wales as the expression "to Jew him down" is to Jews.

The opposing side argues that efforts to legislate "political correctness" in language produce tedious or comical gobbledegook, impede clear thinking, and don't change anyone's prejudices anyway. Moreover, in this view, when everyone is focused on the correct word and quick to take offense if someone uses the "wrong" one, it becomes easy to forget the bottom line: How people are actually being treated. Nancy Mairs (1986), a writer who suffers from multiple sclerosis, says:

> I am a cripple. I choose this word to name me. . . . "cripple" seems to me a clean word, straightforward and precise. . . . As a lover of words, I like the accuracy with which it describes my condition: I have lost the full use of limbs. "Disabled," by contrast, suggests any incapacity, physical or mental . . . Most remote

is the recently coined euphemism "differently abled," which partakes of the same semantic hopefulness that transformed countries from "undeveloped" to "underdeveloped," then to "less developed," and finally to "developing" nations. People have continued to starve in those countries during the shift. Some realities do not obey the dictates of language.

The one thing everyone can agree on is that labels have great symbolic and emotional significance. For example, the *Times* would be in trouble in some quarters for its use of the word "racial" in its guidelines. As we noted in Chapter 2, some social scientists want to abandon the term *race* on the grounds that racial classifications are arbitrary, and that they confuse cultural differences with biological ones (Betancourt & López, 1993; Yee et al., 1993).

Psychological research from arenas as different as social-identity theory and psycholinguistics offers some insights into this debate. As social-identity theory suggests, the name a group chooses for itself has an important symbolic function. Around the world, many ethnic groups are rejecting names that were imposed on them by the majority culture, insisting instead on a name that reflects their own cultural identity. This is why the Eskimos of Canada are now called the Inuit, their own name for themselves. In addition, a group's name reflects its history, status, and self-concept. In the early 1970s, William Cross (1971) analyzed "The Negro-to-Black conversion experience," arguing that this change was critical for "the psychology of Black liberation." In the 1980s, Halford Fairchild (1985) analyzed the significance of labels that are based on skin color ("black"), race ("Negro"), or national origin ("Afro-American"), for each term has different historical and emotional connotations. Only a few years after that article appeared, African-American became a popular term to identify people of African descent living in the Americas; those who like the term argue that it is analogous to Polish-American or Italian-American.

If Nancy Mairs considers herself a cripple, and Thurgood Marshall favored the word Negro, and Joseph Trimble calls himself an Indian, how rigid should we all be about names? If the goal is tolerance of all groups, is what people say ultimately as important as how they behave toward one another? ■

Think About It

What Is a Good Love Story?

■ As we have seen earlier in this book, the stories we tell to describe our lives have become a key metaphor in understanding human behavior (see Chapter 9). According to Robert Sternberg (1994), love too is a story: an implicit narrative about what love means, what a love relationship should be like, and how it should work. "Each relationship is a different story," he observes. "We choose the person who presents us with the love story we like best, even though that person might not be the most compatible partner for us." The reason people don't fall in love with someone who is otherwise their best friend, or who is objectively "right," says Sternberg, is that the friend fits their story of friendship, but not their story of love.

Relationships may come to an end, says Sternberg, if the two partners have different stories about what love is and should be. For example, Dan's love story is that a loving relationship should be calm and free of conflict. If two people love each other, in his view, they accept each other as they are and try to avoid confrontation. Susan's love story is that two people in love *do* confront their differences and together find a solution. So, because she loves him, Susan confronts Dan when she feels they have a problem—and he regards these confrontations as evidence that she does not love him! "The relationship is deteriorating," says Sternberg, but "not because the two people don't love each other. Rather, they have different stories about love, which lead them to interpret events in opposite ways. The relationship may fall apart simply because neither partner has understood the other partner's story about love."

Are some love stories better or healthier than others? Many philosophers and social critics believe that by defining love as a passionate emotion instead of as a relationship or an experience, people set themselves up for disappointment. For example, Robert Solomon (1994) argues that "We conceive of [love] falsely—as a feeling, as novelty, as bound up with youth and beauty. We fall into domestic habits and routine relationships and assume that love will take care of itself, which, of course, it will

not. We expect an explosion at the beginning powerful enough to fuel love through all of its ups and downs instead of viewing love as a process over which we have control, a process that tends to *increase* with time rather than wane."

As Solomon's remarks suggest, the way we define love, and the love stories we choose to guide our lives, deeply affect our feelings and satisfaction with relationships. If you believe that love "just happens," that you have no control over it, that love is defined by sexual passion and hot emotion, then you may decide you are "out of love" when the initial phase of attraction fades, as it eventually must. Worse yet, critics argue, maladaptive stories about romantic love can lead women and men to behave in irrational and self-defeating ways. Writer Bonnie Kreps (1990) worries especially about the many women, who, she feels, are too quick to sacrifice their self-interest, talents, and achievements when romantic love comes along. They become what she calls a reverse Sleeping Beauty: They kiss the prince and promptly fall asleep.

Critics of romantic love maintain that it is a relatively modern, Western invention. It is a love story that people in community-oriented cultures tend to distrust (Dion & Dion, 1993) and that people in postmodern cultures tend to regard with cynicism and skepticism (Gergen & Gergen, 1994). But evolutionary psychologists believe that passionate love is universal, even if it takes different forms, and that we could no more eliminate it than we could eliminate the need for food. In their view, romantic love sees to it that couples bond together, reproduce, look after each other, and stay together in spite of illness, mortgages, and housework (Buss, 1994).

Why do the popular love stories in Western culture almost exclusively celebrate romantic, passionate love rather than the kinds of love that abide for decades? How can people cultivate a more realistic view of what it takes to sustain love over the long haul? What are the ingredients essential to a loving relationship, and what is *your* ideal love story? Think about it. ■

"TAKING PSYCHOLOGY WITH YOU"

Found at the end of each chapter, *Taking Psychology with You* sections draw on real-world research reported in the chapter and tackle topics of practical concern, such as becoming more creative, choosing a therapist, and living with chronic pain.

Taking Psychology with You

"Let It Out" or "Bottle It Up"? The Dilemma of Anger

What do you do when you feel angry? Do you tend to brood and sulk, collecting your righteous complaints like acorns for the winter, or do you erupt, hurling your wrath upon anyone or anything at hand? Do you discuss your feelings when you have calmed down? Does "letting anger out" get rid of it for you, or does it only make it more intense? The answer is crucial for how we get along with our families, neighbors, employers, and strangers. Increasingly, it seems, people are freely venting their anger in the home and in public with rude gestures and insulting remarks, and the level of public debate about serious issues seems to have degenerated into name calling and the exchange of hostilities.

Although some schools of therapy once advised people to "get it out of your system," psychologists have found that this advice often backfires. Chronic feelings of anger and an inability to control anger can be as emotionally devastating and unhealthy as chronic problems with depression or anxiety (Deffenbacher, 1994; Williams, 1989). In contrast to much pop-psych advice, research shows that expressing anger does not always get rid of anger; often it prolongs it. When people talk about their anger or act on that feeling, they tend to rehearse their grievances, create a hostile disposition, and pump up their blood pressure (Averill, 1982; Tavris, 1989). Conversely, when people learn to control their tempers and express anger constructively, they usually feel better, not worse; calmer, not angrier. Charles Darwin (1872/1965) observed this fact more than a century ago. "The free expression by outward signs of an emotion intensifies it," he wrote. "On the other hand, the repression, as far as this is possible, of all outward signs softens our emotions. He who gives way to violent gestures will increase his rage."

Some people behave aggressively when they are angry, but others behave in a friendly, cooperative way to try to solve the problem that is causing their anger. When people are feeling angry, after all, they can do many things: write letters, play the piano, jog, bake bread, kick the sofa, abuse their friends or family, or yell. If a particular action soothes their feelings or gets the desired response from other people, they are likely to acquire a habit. Soon that habit feels "natural," as if it could never be changed; indeed, many people justify their violent tempers by saying "I just couldn't help myself." But they can. If you have learned an abusive or aggressive habit, the research in this chapter offers prac-

tical suggestions for relearning constructive ways of managing anger:

- *Don't sound off in the heat of anger; let bodily arousal cool down.* Whether your arousal comes from background stresses such as heat, crowds, or loud noise, or from conflict with another person, take time to relax (Gottman, 1994). Time allows you to decide if you are "really" angry or just tired and tense. This is the reason for that sage old advice to count to 10, count to 100, or sleep on it. Other "cooling-off" strategies include taking a time-out in the middle of an argument, meditating or relaxing, and calming yourself with a distracting activity.
- *Remember that anger depends on the perception of insult; check your perceptions for accuracy, and then see if you can rethink the problem.* People who are quick to feel anger tend to interpret other people's actions as intentional offenses. People who are slow to anger tend to give others the benefit of the doubt and they are not as focused on their own injured pride. Empathy ("Poor guy, he's feeling rotten") is usually incompatible with anger, so practice seeing the situation from the other person's perspective (Miller & Eisenberg, 1988; Tangney, 1992).
- *If you decide that expressing anger is appropriate, think carefully about how to do it so that you will get the results you want.* As we saw, different cultures have different display rules. Be sure the recipient of your anger understands what you are feeling and what complaint you are trying to convey—and this is true whether the recipient is your parent, friend, annoying neighbor, employer, or city hall.

Ultimately, the decision about whether to express anger depends not only on whether you will feel good if you do, but also on what you hope to accomplish. Do you want to restore your rights, change the other person, improve a bad situation, or achieve justice? If those are your goals, then learning how to express anger so the other person will listen and respond is essential. People who have been the targets of discrimination or other injustices have learned that outbursts of anger may draw society's attention to a problem—but real change requires sustained political effort, challenges to unfair laws, and the use of tactics that persuade rather than alienate the opposition.

The disease model, popular though it is, has an additional problem: It cannot adequately account for the often rapid rise and fall in addiction rates. Between 1942 and 1976 there was a 20-fold increase in the number of alcoholics in treatment (Peele, 1989), and more and more people are becoming addicted to other drugs as well. Further, people can become "addicted" to activities and to television as well as to drugs; what "disease" are they catching? A growing number of television addicts compulsively watch TV the way drug addicts compulsively use drugs—to relieve loneliness, sadness, or anger (Jacobvitz, 1990). "Exercise addicts" have a compulsion to exercise that far exceeds any health benefits (Chan & Grossman, 1988).

Opponents of the disease model of addiction marshal three lines of support for their argument:

1. *Addiction patterns vary according to culture and learning.* Study after study has found that alcoholism is much more likely to occur in cultures that forbid children to drink but condone drunkenness in adults (such as Ireland) than in cultures that teach children how to drink responsibly but condemn adult drunkenness (such as Italy, Greece, France, and colonial America). In cultures with low rates of alcoholism, adults demonstrate correct drinking habits to their children, gradually introducing them to alcohol in safe family settings. Alcohol is not used as a rite of passage into adulthood, nor is it associated with masculinity and power (Peele, 1989; Vaillant, 1983). Drinking is considered neither a virtue nor a sin. Abstainers are not sneered at and drunkenness is not considered charming, comical, or manly; it's considered stupid or obnoxious.

2. *Not all drug users go through withdrawal symptoms when they stop taking the drug.* During the Vietnam War, nearly 30 percent of American soldiers were taking heroin in doses far stronger than those available on the streets of U.S. cities. These men believed themselves to be addicted. Experts predicted a drug-withdrawal disaster among the returning veterans. It never materialized (see Figure 15.3). Over 90 percent of the men simply gave up the drug, without withdrawal pain, when they came home (Robins, Davis, & Goodwin, 1974). Studies find that the majority of people who are addicted to alcohol, cigarettes, tranquilizers, or painkillers are also able to stop taking these drugs, without outside help and without withdrawal symptoms (Lee & Hart, 1985).

Rates of alcoholism depend on when and where people drink. In cultures in which people drink moderately with meals, and children learn the social rules of drinking along with their families, alcoholism rates are much lower than in cultures in which drinking occurs in bars, in binges, or in privacy.

■ **Figure 15.3 Drugs and Vietnam Veterans: Failure of the Addiction Prediction**

U.S. soldiers who tested "drug positive" when they were in Vietnam showed a dramatic drop in drug use when they returned to civilian life—contrary to prediction and to the "disease model" of addiction (Robins, Davis, & Goodwin, 1974).

■ Total "drug positive" group
■ Those reporting addiction in Vietnam
■ Those reporting post-Vietnam drug use
■ Those showing narcotic dependency

INTEGRATED EMPHASIS ON CRITICAL AND CREATIVE THINKING

Encouraging students to become more active learners, Wade and Tavris seamlessly weave critical thinking throughout the text and apply it to concepts that many students approach uncritically, such as astrology, PMS, and the "instinctive" nature of sexuality. In the example depicted here, the disease model of addiction, often accepted unquestioningly by psychologists, is exposed to critical analysis.

3

Evolution, Genes, and Behavior

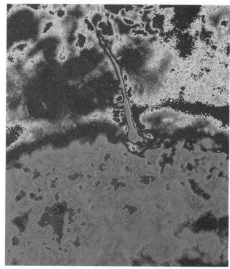

A human sperm enters an ovum at the moment of conception. The DNA in the two cells will combine to form a human being with a unique genetic pattern.

18

The Cultural Context

This 1457 map shows Spain as the head and crown of Europe, reflecting the mapmaker's belief that Spain was the most important country in Europe. Ethnocentrism—the belief that one's own culture or ethnic group is superior to all others—is probably universal.

The Older Infant

Babies grow as fast as weeds during their first two years. Most infants double their birth weight in five months. By 1 year of age, on the average, they have tripled their birth weight and grown 10 to 12 inches in length. (The custom of talking about a baby's "length" but a child's "height" is charming; the language changes as soon as the baby is upright!) By age 2, most toddlers are half the height they will be as adults. The baby not only grows in height and weight, but also changes proportion. An infant's head is nearly one-third of the whole body; a 2-year-old's head is about one-fourth; an adult's head is only one-eighth to one-tenth of total height.

A baby's motor skills develop accordingly. At about 1 month, infants can hold their chins up when lying on their stomachs. At about 2 months, they can raise the upper body. At 4 months, they can sit if someone supports them. At about 7 months, they can sit upright without support. From then on, parents have to look sharp. Babies soon crawl and stand with help (9 months), walk with help (10 months), and toddle off on their own (13 months). These milestones are only averages, however; some babies develop more quickly, others more slowly.

✳ *Most childrearing manuals advise parents to teach their 5-month-old infants to sleep through the night by not responding to the babies' cries for attention. What assumptions about babies and about the parent-child relationship are these books making? Are these assumptions the same everywhere?*

Although babies and infants everywhere develop according to the same maturational sequence, many aspects of their development depend on cultural customs. Parents in different cultures treat their babies differently right from the start, in how often they hold, touch, feed, or talk to them (Super & Harkness, 1994). For example, infant sleep patterns vary according to a culture's rules for sleeping arrangements. In the United States, babies are expected to sleep for eight uninterrupted hours by the age of 4 or 5 months. This milestone is considered a sign of neurological maturity, although many babies weep and wail when the parent puts them in the crib at night and leaves the room. Yet for people in many cultures, including Mayan Indians, rural Italians, African villagers, and urban Japanese, this nightly clash of wills never occurs because the infant sleeps with the mother for the first few years of life. Mothers have no incentive to get their babies to sleep through the night, and infants continue to wake and nurse about every four hours. Cultural differences in babies' sleep arrangements in turn reflect cultural values. Mayan mothers believe it is important to sleep with the baby in order to forge a close bond with the child; American parents believe it is important to foster the child's independence as soon as possible (Morelli et al., 1992).

▶ *A good example of the intersection between maturation and culture is the case of the cradleboard. Most Navaho babies (left) calmly accept the Navaho custom of being strapped to a cradleboard until they are about 6 months old; Caucasian babies (right) protest vigorously when strapped in one. Yet despite cultural differences in such practices, babies in every culture sit, crawl, and walk at the same average maturational age.*

MAINSTREAMING CULTURE

Wade and Tavris' integrated coverage of culture increases students' understanding of what culture means, how and why ethnic and national groups differ, what our common human needs are, and why no culture is inherently superior to any others.

Are There "His" and "Hers" Brains?

A second stubborn controversy concerns the existence of sex differences in the brain. Efforts to distinguish male from female brains have a long and not always glorious history. Findings on male–female brain differences have often flip-flopped in a most suspicious manner, a result of the biases of the observers rather than the biology of the brain (Shields, 1975). During the nineteenth century, scientists doing dissection studies reported that women's frontal lobes were smaller than men's, and that their parietal lobes were larger; this finding was said to explain women's intellectual shortcomings. Then, around the turn of the century, people began (mistakenly) to attribute intellect to the parietal lobes rather than the frontal lobes. Suddenly, there were reports that women had *smaller* parietal lobes and larger frontal lobes. You probably won't be surprised to learn that these researchers often knew the sex of the brains they were dissecting.

✳ *Perhaps no topic in brain research generates as much muddy thinking and jumping to conclusions as that of sex differences in the brain. Does the existing evidence warrant significant conclusions about real-life behavior?*

Since the 1960s, theories about male–female brain differences have come and gone just as quickly. Three decades ago, there was speculation that women were more "right-brained" and men were more "left-brained." Then, when the virtues of the right hemisphere were discovered, there was speculation that *men* were more right-brained. Whichever side is the valued one, it is now clear that the abilities popularly associated with the two sexes do not fall neatly into the two hemispheres of the brain. The left side is more verbal (presumably a "female" trait), but it is also more mathematical (presumably a "male" trait). The right side is more intuitive ("female"), but it is also more spatially talented ("male").

To evaluate the issue of sex differences in the brain, we need to ask two questions: Do male and female brains physically differ? And if so, what, if anything, does this have to do with behavior?

Let's consider the first question. A number of anatomical sex differences have been found in animal brains, especially in areas related to reproduction.

Popular magazines have been quick to run stories on purported differences in the brains of males and females. Often these articles (such as this one from Time) conclude—from interesting but still tentative findings—that gender differences in behavior must be biologically based. Is this conclusion justified? What kind of evidence is necessary to establish a link between an observed brain difference and an observed behavioral difference? And why do studies of gender differences make the covers of national magazines when studies that find gender similarities do not?

MAINSTREAMING GENDER

Because it is important to point out that universal principles of behavior can not be deduced from a narrow sample of humanity, Wade and Tavris continue to raise relevant studies pertaining to gender throughout the text.

UPDATED CONTENT

This fourth edition contains a great deal of revised content and updated research throughout to maintain its emphasis on renowned, cutting-edge studies in each chapter.

Some psychotherapists think that it is impossible to measure the effectiveness of therapy; researchers disagree. What assumptions does each side bring to this debate? How can it be resolved?

The Scientist–Practitioner Gap

Is it possible to measure the effectiveness of therapy, or is this human exchange too varied and complex to be captured by the researcher's empirical arsenal? Many psychotherapists believe that measuring psychotherapy is a futile task. Psychotherapy is an art, not a science, they say, and research is simply irrelevant to what they do. Most believe that clinical experience is more valuable and accurate than the methods of traditional research, and that laboratory and survey studies capture only a small and shadowy image of the real person. They wish that academic psychologists would pay more attention to *clinical* evidence and observations in the research they do (Edelson, 1994). A survey of 400 clinical psychologists found that the great majority paid little attention to empirical research at all, stating that they gained their most useful information from "clinical work with clients." The majority also believed that research on therapy's effectiveness fails to incorporate the complexities of psychotherapy, obscures essential differences among therapies, and ignores the importance of the relationship between therapist and client (Elliott & Morrow-Bradley, 1994).

The clients who are most likely to do well in therapy have a strong sense of self and also sufficient distress to motivate them to change. For example, one study of depressed elderly people found that cognitive, behavioral, and brief dynamic therapy were equally likely to be successful. What made the difference between good outcomes and poor ones were the clients' *commitment* to the therapy, *willingness* to work on their problems, and their *expectations* of success. In turn, the people who were committed and willing had support from their families and a personal style of dealing actively with problems instead of avoiding them (Gaston et al., 1988, 1989).

THE SEVEN DWARFS AFTER THERAPY

How much can therapy change a person, and how can we evaluate that change?

---

ing tasks that should have been easy. For example, a pig was supposed to drop large wooden coins in a box. Instead, the pig would drop the coin, push at it with its snout, throw it in the air, and push at it some more. This odd behavior actually delayed reinforcement, so it was hard to explain in terms of operant principles. Apparently the pig's rooting instinct—its tendency to use its snout to uncover edible roots—was keeping it from learning the task. The Brelands called such a reversion to instinctive behavior **instinctive drift.**

Positive and Negative Reinforcers and Punishers

Reinforcement and punishment may seem to be the proverbial carrot and stick, but they are not quite so simple as they seem. In our example of reinforcement, something pleasant (a doggie biscuit or a pat on the dog's head) followed the dog's response (heeling). This type of procedure is known as **positive reinforcement.** But there is another brand of reinforcement, negative reinforcement, that involves the *removal* of something *unpleasant*. If you politely ask your roommate to turn off some music you can't stand, and your roommate immediately complies, the likelihood of your being polite when making similar requests will probably increase. Your politeness has been strengthened (negatively reinforced) by the removal of the unpleasant music.

The distinction between positive and negative reinforcement has been a source of confusion and frustration for generations of students, and has been known to turn strong and confident people into quivering heaps. We can assure you that if *we* had been around when these terms were first coined, we would have complained loudly. One eminent behaviorist, Gregory Kimble (1993), argues that it's still not too late to change their meanings so that they conform better to ordinary usage. But we doubt that changing the definitions at this point would help much because students who went on in psychology would still have to read articles and books using the old definitions, and in introductory courses, some books would be teaching one set of definitions and others a different set. That is why as textbook authors, we've resigned ourselves to the traditional terms, irksome though they are.

■ **instinctive drift**
The tendency of an organism to revert to an instinctive behavior over time; can interfere with learning.

■ **positive reinforcement**
A reinforcement procedure in which a response is followed by the presentation of, or increase in intensity of, a reinforcing stimulus; as a result, the response becomes stronger or more likely to occur.

PEDAGOGICAL SUPPORT

Psychology, 4/e, contains a number of learning aids that support its critical thinking emphasis and involve students' active learning, including *Psychology and Popular Culture* and *Think About It* boxes, *Taking Psychology with You* sections, *Quick Quizzes,* marginal signposts, running marginal glossary, numbered summaries, chapter outlines, and key terms.

Psychology

1
What Is Psychology?

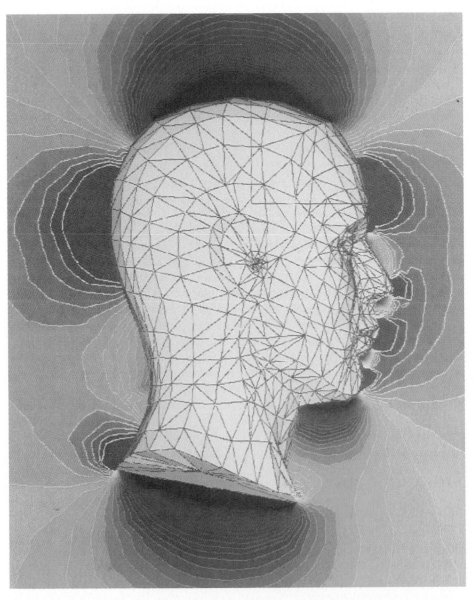

This image shows the human head's magnetic fields, with red-to-orange areas the strongest. Psychologists study the many "fields" of influence that affect human beings— biological, environmental, cognitive, psychodynamic, and sociocultural.

*The purpose of psychology
is to give us a completely different idea
of the things we know best.*

■ PAUL VALÉRY ■

In 1945, a 15-year-old Jewish girl named Anne Frank died of typhus at Bergen-Belsen, a notorious Nazi death camp. She had spent the previous two years with her parents, her sister, and four others in a cramped apartment in Amsterdam, hiding from German troops occupying Holland. Unable to go outside, the group depended entirely on Christian friends for food and other necessities. Anne, who was a gifted writer and astute observer, recorded in her diary the fears, frustrations, and inevitable clashes of people forced to live 24 hours a day in close proximity. Yet she never despaired or lost her sense of wonder at life's joys. With humor and grace, she described the pleasure of family celebrations, the thrill of first love, the excitement of growing up. Shortly before the Gestapo discovered the hideout, Anne wrote, "It's really a wonder that I haven't dropped all my ideals, because they seem so absurd and impossible to carry out. Yet I keep them, because in spite of everything I still believe that people are really good at heart. I simply can't build up my hopes on a foundation consisting of confusion, misery, and death."

Anne Frank (1929–1945)

Many years later, and thousands of miles away, Jeffrey Dahmer grew up in what seems to have been a fairly normal American household. As a small child, Jeffrey seemed happy and animated. Gradually, however, he drifted into a private fantasy world and showed obvious signs of abnormality. He collected animal bones and carcasses, which he stored in formaldehyde-filled jars in his childhood clubhouse; he sulked alone in the woods whenever his parents fought; his eyes developed a dull and vacant look. At age 18, Jeffrey began committing a series of unspeakable crimes. Over a 13-year period, he lured 17 young men to his home and then tortured, murdered, and mutilated them, keeping body parts as souvenirs and even cannibalizing one of the victims. In *A Father's Story* (1994), Jeffrey's father Lionel asked himself how his son could have become such a ghoulish monster. Perhaps it was the medication his wife took during pregnancy. Perhaps he himself had been too emotionally aloof. Perhaps the parents' frequent fights and ultimate divorce were to blame. Perhaps an apparent incident of sexual abuse by a neighborhood boy had played a role. Or perhaps, the father speculated, the "potential for great evil . . . resides deep in the blood that some of us . . . may pass on to our children at birth."

How did Anne Frank, living in a world gone mad, manage to retain her love of humanity? Why did Jeffrey Dahmer, whose early life was not all that unusual, develop bizarre urges that led him to commit gruesome acts of violence? More generally, how can we explain why some people are overwhelmed by their problems, whereas others, despite enormous difficulties, remain strong and mentally healthy? Why do some human beings pursue their dreams and others succumb to nightmares? What principles can help us understand why some of us are confident players in the game of life, while others angrily reject its basic rules?

If you have ever asked yourself such questions, welcome to the world of psychology. You are about to explore a discipline that studies the many complexities and contradictions of human behavior. Psychologists do not confine their attention to personal problems or the extremes of behavior. They take as their subject the entire spectrum of brave and cowardly, wise and silly, intelligent and foolish, beautiful and brutish things that human beings do. Their aim is to understand how human beings—and animals, too—learn, remember, solve problems, perceive, feel, and get along with others. They are therefore as likely to study commonplace experiences as exceptional ones—experiences as universal and ordinary as rearing children, gossiping, remembering a shopping list, daydreaming, making love, and making a living. Most of us, after all, are neither saints nor sinners but a curious combination of positive and negative qualities. In short, psychology is not only about martyrs and murderers; it is also about you.

■ A MATTER OF DEFINITION

Over the years, psychology has been defined in various ways, but most psychologists today would agree that **psychology** is the scientific study of behavior and mental processes and how they are affected by an organism's physical state, mental state, and external environment. We realize, however, that this brief definition of psychology is a little like defining a car as "a vehicle for transporting people from one place to another." Such a definition is accurate as far as it goes, but it doesn't tell you what a car looks like, how a car differs from a train or a bus, how a Ford differs from a Ferrari, or how a catalytic converter works. Similarly, to get a good, clear picture of what psychology is, you need to have more information—about its methods, its findings, and its ways of interpreting information. Your psychology course and the rest of this textbook will give you this information.

Psychology and Common Sense

Let's begin by considering what psychology is *not.* First, the psychology that you are about to study bears little relation to the popular psychology ("pop psych") found in many self-help books or to the popular but nonscientific ideas that get media attention on TV shows such as "Geraldo" and "Oprah." Serious psychology is more complex, more informative, and, we think, far more helpful. As we will see in the next chapter, psychology is based on rigorously conducted research and evidence that can be verified by others. In recent decades, the public's appetite for psychological information has created a huge market for what R. D. Rosen (1977) called "psychobabble"—pseudoscience and quackery covered by a veneer of psychological language. Today, more than ever, when so many simplistic pop psych ideas have filtered into public consciousness, education, and even the law, people need to know the difference between psychobabble and serious psychology, between unsupported *popular opinion* and documented *research evidence.*

Second, psychology is not just a fancy name for common sense, as some of its critics have charged. It is true that psychological research sometimes confirms what many people already believe to be so. When that happens, it is easy to conclude that a little intelligence and the accumulated wisdom of the ages are all you need to understand why people act as they do, and that scientific studies are a waste of time and money. Often, however, the obviousness of a psychological finding is only an illusion. Armed with the wisdom of hindsight, people may maintain that they "knew it all along" when in fact they did not (Locke & Latham, 1991).

Consider this demonstration: An instructor tells an introductory psychology class that "according to research, couples whose careers require them to live apart are more likely to divorce than other couples." Most students, on hearing

Do hypnotized people remember past events with special clarity, or do they make things up that never happened and only appear to "remember" them? Whichever answer we gave you, you might say, "I knew that all along." (You'll find out the actual answer in Chapter 5.)

■ **psychology**

The scientific study of behavior and mental processes and how they are affected by an organism's physical state, mental state, and external environment; the term is often represented by Ψ, the Greek letter psi (usually pronounced "sy").

this finding, will claim they are not surprised. After all, as everyone knows, "out of sight, out of mind." But then, in another class, the instructor changes the report, this time saying that couples whose careers require them to live apart are *less* likely to divorce than other couples. This purported finding is exactly the reverse of the first one, yet, again, most students will claim they could have predicted it. After all, as everyone knows, "Absence makes the heart grow fonder." Both results, once they are stated, seem intuitively obvious, whether true or not, because common sense is full of contradictions (Myers, 1980; Wood, 1984). Psychologists interested in close relationships will go beyond popular folk sayings to investigate the *conditions* under which absence may or may not make the heart grow fonder. One factor, for example, is the degree of emotional attachment felt by the couple before they part; absence often intensifies a bright flame but extinguishes a weak one (Brehm, 1992).

Further, psychological research often does produce surprises, findings that are not commonsensical at all. For example, according to popular belief, "the child is father to the man" (or mother to the woman, as the case may be); that is, early experiences are said to determine how a person turns out, for better or for worse. The evidence, however, shows that although experiences during childhood greatly influence adult personality, intelligence, and behavior, a human being is never a finished product. As we will see in later chapters, many abilities, behaviors, and attributes can change throughout life in response to new situations. Even children traumatized by abuse, neglect, or war can become happy, secure adults if their circumstances improve (Garmezy, 1991; Werner, 1989).

The finding that we may ultimately triumph over tragedies reassures us. Unfortunately, however, some findings in psychology are troubling. For example, studies show that most people are willing to inflict physical harm on another person if they are told to do so by an authority figure. Those inflicting the harm are likely to suffer terrible emotional distress because of their actions, but they obey anyway (Milgram, 1963, 1974). This is a disturbing finding, with important political and moral implications. To take another example: Despite all the warnings against judging a book by its cover, most people do exactly that. Research shows that good-looking individuals are more likely than others to attract dates and to get jobs. Attractive people even receive shorter jail sentences (Berscheid, 1985). This information is sobering for a society that considers itself to be democratic and egalitarian.

People sometimes think that psychology is "only common sense." But common sense does not tell us why people dress up in funny outfits, do self-destructive things such as starving themselves to death, or jump from a hot-air balloon suspended only by a bungee cord.

Psychology, then, may or may not confirm what you already believe about human nature. We want to emphasize, however, that findings do not have to be surprising to be scientifically important. Psychologists may enjoy announcing results that startle people, but they also seek to extend and deepen our understanding of generally accepted facts. After all, long before the laws of gravity were discovered, people knew that an apple would fall to the ground if it dropped from a tree. But it took Isaac Newton to discover the principles that explain why the apple falls and why it travels at a particular speed while falling. Psychologists, too, strive to deepen our understanding of an already familiar world.

Psychology's Relatives

Psychology belongs to a family of disciplines known as the social (or sometimes the behavioral) sciences. All of these sciences encourage us to analyze human problems objectively and to search for reliable patterns in behavior. Each of these disciplines teaches us to appreciate both the similarities and the differences among individuals and groups. But there are some important differences in emphasis, as we can see by comparing psychology with two other social sciences—sociology and anthropology.

Sociology is the study of groups and institutions within society, such as the family, religious institutions, the workplace, and social cliques. A sociologist might study, for example, how family roles change when women enter the paid workforce, or how and why urban gangs come into being. In general, sociologists pay less attention than psychologists do to personality traits and individual differences. However, one specialty, *social psychology*, falls on the border between psychology and sociology; it deals with the ways in which social groups and situations affect an individual's behavior, and vice versa.

Anthropology is concerned with the physical and cultural origins and development of the human species. Anthropologists typically focus on a large social unit—a tribe, a community, or even an entire society. They explore human diversity by comparing customs and beliefs across different cultures, often participating in the daily lives and activities of the social group they are observing. In contrast, most psychologists study behavior only in their own society, and they study the specific behaviors or mental processes of individuals rather than the customs of entire groups. Again, however, the boundary between disciplines is not rigid: Some anthropologists study psychological issues, and researchers in the growing field of *cross-cultural psychology* investigate differences and similarities among cultures.

Of all the social sciences, psychology relies most heavily on laboratory experiments and observations. At the same time, it is the most personal of the disciplines, focusing more than the others on the individual and his or her well-being. Psychology also makes more use of biological information than the other fields do (except for physical anthropology, which is concerned with the physical evolution of the human species). In fact, some psychologists classify psychology with the biological and life sciences rather than the social sciences. However, whereas biologists are chiefly concerned with understanding the structure and functioning of all living things, from trees to turtles, psychologists are mainly interested in doing biological research as a way to deepen their insight into human behavior and mental activities. A psychologist might study the communication of nerve cells in the brain, for example, in order to better understand the processes of learning and memory.

Psychology also has links with several other fields, including linguistics, computer science, medicine, neuroscience, and management science. Most of the findings in this book come from research done by psychologists, but we will occasionally refer to results from related disciplines as well. When scholars and scientists cultivate only their own gardens, they may miss ways to improve their intellectual harvest. Now and then it's a good idea to glance over to see what is happening in someone else's yard.

Quick QUIZ

Pause now to test your understanding of the previous section. Do you have the distinctions among the various fields straight? Can you match each topic on the left with a discipline on the right?

1. How the structure of a bureaucracy affects job satisfaction.
2. Sexual customs in a Polynesian society.
3. The molecular structure of bodily cells.
4. The effects of anxiety on IQ scores.

a. biology
b. anthropology
c. psychology
d. sociology

Answers:

1.d 2.b 3.a 4.c

(*Note:* This self-test does not ask you to parrot back a memorized list of definitions but rather to recognize an example of each discipline we have discussed. If you can do this, you have not merely memorized; you have understood. If you had any difficulty, we recommend that you reread the preceding section before going on.)

■ PSYCHOLOGY'S PAST: FROM THE ARMCHAIR TO THE LABORATORY

Most of the great thinkers of history, from Aristotle to Zoroaster, raised questions that today would be considered psychological. They wanted to know how people take in information through their senses, use information to solve problems, and become motivated to act in brave or villainous ways. They wondered about the elusive nature of emotion, and whether it controls us or is something we can control. Like modern psychologists, they wanted to describe, understand, predict, and modify behavior and mental processes in order to add to human knowledge and increase human happiness. But unlike modern psychologists, scholars of the past did not rely heavily on **empirical** evidence—evidence gathered by careful observation, experimentation, and measurement. Often, their observations were based simply on anecdotes or descriptions of individual cases.

This does not mean that the forerunners of modern psychology were always wrong. Hippocrates (c. 460 B.C.–c. 377 B.C.), the ancient Greek known as the father of modern medicine, observed patients with head injuries and inferred that the brain must be the ultimate source of "our pleasures, joys, laughter, and jests as well as our sorrows, pains, griefs, and tears." And so it is. In the first century A.D., the Stoic philosophers observed that people do not become angry or sad or anxious because of actual events but because of their explanations of those events. And so they do.

But without empirical methods, the forerunners of psychology also committed some terrible blunders. Even the great philosopher Aristotle, one of the first to advocate the use of empirical methods, did not always use them correctly himself. He thought that the brain could not possibly be responsible for sensation because the brain itself feels no pain, and he concluded that the brain must be a radiator for cooling the blood. Aristotle was absolutely right

■ **empirical**
Relying on or derived from observation, experimentation, or measurement.

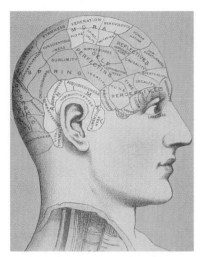

Prescientific theories of human behavior were often wrong, but many contained a grain of truth. For example, nineteenth-century phrenologists, inspired by the writings of Austrian physician Joseph Gall (1758–1828), thought that different brain areas accounted for specific character traits, such as "stinginess" and "religiosity," and that such traits could be "read" from bumps on the skull. Phrenology, though wildly popular, was sheer nonsense, but its underlying assumption of specialized brain parts has since been confirmed by many studies, as we will see in Chapter 4.

about the brain being insensitive, but he was wrong about the brain being a radiator, and about many other things. (For instance, he believed that small people have poor memories!)

A good example of how prescientific psychology could lead down a blind alley comes from the seventeenth century. At that time, when physics and physiology were still young sciences, scholars were puzzled about how living things could move about. The French mathematician and philosopher René Descartes [Day-CART] (1596–1650) suggested that animals operated much like machines. Descartes concocted a complicated theory of motion that compared muscles and tendons to engines and springs. But he could not quite bring himself to call his own species a mere mechanical contraption. Human beings, he decided, possessed a mind, which he equated with an immortal soul. According to Descartes, this mind/soul squeezed the *pineal* [pie-NEE-ul] *gland,* a small blob of tissue in the center of the brain, this way and that. The pineal gland, the bridge between the soul and the body, in turn caused "animal spirits" (brain fluids) to flow down nerves, which Descartes believed were hollow tubes leading to muscles. When the brain fluid entered a muscle, the fluid made the muscle billow out like a balloon, resulting in the movement of a limb. Most of these ideas, which seem so outlandish today, were based on pure speculation.

It would be wrong, however, to ridicule the outmoded ideas of the past—as the psychologists of the future may be tempted to do someday when they look back at us. Even without scientific methods, the great thinkers of history often had insights and made observations that led to later advances. Descartes, for example, argued that stimulating a sense organ caused a signal of some sort to travel to the brain, which then *reflected* the signal back to the muscles. Thus was born the concept of a *reflex.* Although Descartes' description of reflexes was not anatomically correct, his work led to the idea that the actions of living things are determined by *stimuli,* physical changes in the environment. The concept of the reflex and the view of behavior as a response to stimuli greatly influenced psychology some three centuries later. More generally, Descartes helped promote scientific thinking by rejecting the then-common belief that human behavior is governed by unknowable forces, by openly doubting conventional wisdom, and by searching for physical explanations of behavior.

Still, until the nineteenth century, psychology was pretty much a hit-or-miss sort of business. It was not recognized as a separate field of study, and few formal rules guided how it was conducted.

The Birth of Modern Psychology

Psychologists usually regard 1879 as the year in which psychology as a formal science was officially born. In that year the first psychological laboratory was established in Leipzig, Germany, by Wilhelm Wundt (VIL-helm Voont], who is generally acknowledged as the founder of psychology as a separate discipline. Wundt (1832–1920), who was trained in medicine and philosophy, was a prolific writer; over a period of six decades, he turned out volume after volume on psychology, physiology, natural history, ethics, and logic. What most people remember about him, however, is that he was the first person to announce (in 1873) that he intended to make psychology a science.

Actually, psychology had many forefathers (and several foremothers too, although their accomplishments were often unacknowledged or even credited to others [Scarborough & Furumoto, 1987]). For two centuries, philosophers, such as John Locke in England, had paved the way by arguing that all knowledge must be based on sensory experience and not on speculation or pure reasoning. By the time Wundt set up his laboratory, a number of individuals in

Wilhelm Wundt (1832–1920), third from left, with co-workers.

Europe and in North America were already doing some psychological research and teaching some psychological topics. The Leipzig laboratory, however, was the first to be formally established and to have its results published in a scholarly journal. Although it started out as just a few rooms in an old building, it soon became the place to go for anyone who wanted to become a psychologist. Many of America's first psychologists got their training there.

Researchers in Wundt's laboratory did not study the entire gamut of topics that today's psychologists do. Most concentrated on sensation, perception, reaction times, imagery, and attention, and avoided learning, personality, and abnormal behavior. Wundt himself doubted that higher mental processes, such as abstract thinking, could be studied experimentally. He thought such topics were better understood by studying culture and natural history.

One of Wundt's favorite research methods was **trained introspection,** in which specially trained people carefully observed and analyzed their own mental experiences under controlled conditions. Looking inward wasn't as easy as it sounds. Wundt's introspectors had to make 10,000 practice observations before they were allowed to participate in an actual study. Once trained, they might take as long as 20 minutes to report their inner experiences during a 1.5-second experiment (Lieberman, 1979). Wundt hoped trained introspection would yield reliable, verifiable results. Ironically, although Wundt made his mark on history by declaring psychology to be an objective science, introspection was soon to be abandoned by other psychologists because it wasn't considered objective enough.

Two Early Psychologies

Wundt's ideas were popularized in America in somewhat modified form by one of his students, E. B. Titchener (1867–1927), whose brand of psychology became known as **structuralism.** Structuralists hoped to analyze sensations, images, and feelings into basic elements, much as a chemist might analyze water into hydrogen and oxygen atoms. For example, a person might be asked

■ **trained introspection**
A form of self-observation in which individuals examine and report the contents of their own consciousness.

■ **structuralism**
An early psychological approach that stressed analysis of immediate experience into basic elements.

to listen to a metronome clicking and report exactly what he or she heard. Most people said they perceived a pattern (such as, CLICK click click CLICK click click), even though the clicks of a metronome are actually all the same. Or a person might be asked to break down all the different components of taste when biting into an orange (sweet, tart, wet, etc.).

Despite an intensive program of research, structuralism soon went the way of the dinosaur. After you have discovered the building blocks of a particular sensation or image and how they link up, then what? Years after structuralism's demise, Wolfgang Köhler (1959) recalled how he and his colleagues had responded to it as students: "What had disturbed us was . . . the implication that human life, apparently so colorful and so intensely dynamic, is actually a frightful bore."

The structuralists' reliance on introspection also got them into hot water. To see why, imagine that you are a structuralist who wants to know what goes on in people's heads when they hear the word *triangle*. You round up some trained introspectors, say the word *triangle*, and ask them about their mental experience. Most of your respondents report a visual image of a form with three sides and three corners. Elbert, however, reports a flashing red form with equal angles, whereas Endora insists that she saw a revolving colorless form with one angle larger than the other two. Which attributes of *triangle* would you conclude were basic? This sort of conflict is exactly what occurred in structuralist studies; people disagreed. Some even claimed they could think about a triangle without forming any visual image at all (Boring, 1953).

Another early school of psychology was **functionalism,** which emphasized the function, or purpose, of behavior. One of its leaders was William James (1842–1910), an American philosopher, physician, and psychologist who argued that searching for building blocks of experience was a waste of time because the brain and the mind are constantly changing. Permanent ideas—of triangles or anything else—do not appear periodically before the "footlights of consciousness." Attempting to grasp the nature of the mind through introspection, wrote James (1890/1950), is "like seizing a spinning top to catch its motion, or trying to turn up the gas quickly enough to see how the darkness looks." (James was a wonderful writer who is still a joy to read, both for his ideas and his eloquence in expressing them.)

Where the structuralists asked *what* happens when an organism does something, the functionalists asked *how* and *why*. They were inspired in part by the evolutionary theories of British naturalist Charles Darwin (1809–1882). Darwin had argued that a biologist's job is not merely to describe, say, the brilliant plumage of a peacock or the drab markings of a lizard but also to figure out how these attributes enhance survival. Do they help the animal attract a mate or hide from its enemies? Similarly, the functionalists wanted to know how various behaviors help a person or animal adapt to the environment, so they looked for underlying causes and practical consequences of specific behaviors and mental strategies. Unlike the structuralists, they felt free to pick and choose among many methods, and they broadened the field of psychology to include the study of children, animals, religious experiences, and what James called the "stream of consciousness"—a term still used because it so beautifully describes the way thoughts flow like a river, tumbling over each other in waves, sometimes placid, sometimes turbulent.

As a distinct school of psychology, functionalism had a rather short life. It seems to have lacked the sort of precise theory or program of research that inspires passion or wins recruits. Also, it endorsed the study of consciousness just as that concept was about to fall out of favor. However, the functionalists' emphasis on the causes and consequences of behavior was to set the course of modern psychology.

William James (1842–1910)

■ **functionalism**

An early psychological approach that stressed the function or purpose of behavior and consciousness.

Quick QUIZ

Check your memory for the preceding section by choosing the correct response from the pair in parentheses.

1. Psychology has been a science for about (2,000/100) years.
2. The forerunners of modern psychology depended heavily on (casual observation/empirical methods).
3. Credit for founding modern psychology is generally given to (William James/Wilhelm Wundt).
4. Early psychologists who emphasized how behavior helps an organism adapt to its environment were known as (structuralists/functionalists).
5. Introspection was rejected as a research method because it was too (subjective/time-consuming).

Answers:

1. 100 2. casual observation 3. Wilhelm Wundt 4. functionalists 5. subjective

▪ PSYCHOLOGY'S PRESENT: BEHAVIOR, BODY, MIND, AND CULTURE

Today, five major theoretical perspectives predominate in psychology: the *learning, psychodynamic, biological, cognitive,* and *sociocultural* perspectives. These approaches reflect different questions that psychologists ask about human behavior; different assumptions about how the mind works; and, most important, different kinds of explanations of why people do what they do.

We know that at this early point in your study of psychology, attempting to remember a bunch of abstract theories can be like trying to hold water in a sieve. For that reason, we are going to try to make these five approaches more memorable for you by discussing how they might apply to a concrete issue, the issue of violence. Violence, of course, takes many forms: spouse and child abuse, street crime, political terrorism, mass murder, war. Armchair speculation has done little to curb violence or to prevent the suffering it causes, but we believe that psychological theories and research can help people understand why different kinds of aggression occur and can even suggest possible solutions. As we describe the major perspectives in psychology, see whether you can predict how each one might go about explaining why human beings are so often willing to mistreat, maim, and even murder one another.

The Learning Perspective

In 1913, a psychologist named John B. Watson (1878–1958) published a paper that rocked the still-young science of psychology. In "Psychology as the Behaviorist Views It," Watson argued that if psychology were ever to be as objective as physics, chemistry, and biology, it would have to give up its preoccupation with the mind and consciousness. Psychologists, he said, should throw out introspection as a method of research and should reject such terms as *mental state, mind,* or *emotion* in explanations of behavior. They should stick to what they can observe and measure directly: acts and events actually taking place in the environment. In short, they should give up mentalism for **behaviorism.**

Watson wrote approvingly of studies by the Russian physiologist Ivan Pavlov (1849–1936). Pavlov had shown that many kinds of automatic or involuntary

John B. Watson (1878–1958)

▪ **behaviorism**
A psychological approach that emphasizes the study of observable behavior and the role of the environment as a determinant of behavior.

The astonishing diversity of human behavior is vividly captured in Pieter Brueghel's depiction of Dutch proverbs, rhymes, and folk sayings. Psychologists approach the study of this diversity from five major perspectives.

behavior, such as salivating at the sight of food, were learned responses to specific changes, or stimuli, in the environment. Like Pavlov, Watson believed that basic laws of learning could explain the behavior of both human beings and animals. Later, another psychologist, B. F. Skinner (1904–1990), extended the behavioral approach, with important modifications, to voluntary acts such as turning on a light switch, riding a bike, or getting dressed. Skinner showed that the consequences of an act powerfully affect the probability of its occurring again: Acts that are followed by pleasant consequences are more likely to be repeated, whereas acts that are followed by unpleasant consequences are likely to cease.

The behavioral approach excited not only psychologists but also sociologists and political scientists. Here, at last, was a way for the social sciences to be hard-headed and earn the respect of a skeptical world. In many ways, stimulus–response or "S–R" psychology, as it was informally called, narrowed the scope of psychology. But in other ways it broadened it, for (like functionalism) it fostered the study of groups that could not be studied at all through introspection, including animals, infants, and mentally disturbed persons. Behaviorism soon became the predominant American school of experimental psychology and remained so until the early 1960s.

Critics of behaviorism have often accused its proponents of denying the existence of ideas and thoughts—of believing "that human beings do not think or

For behavioral psychologists, human behavior, even such an ordinary event as an intimate conversation between friends, is explainable largely in terms of its environmental consequences. One such consequence is the rewarding attention we get from others.

ponder or worry, but instead only *think* that they do" (Sherif, 1979). This criticism, however, is unfair. In everyday conversation, behaviorists are as likely as anyone else to say that they think or feel this or that. They realize that they themselves are conscious! It's true that Watson wanted to eliminate thoughts, emotions, and visual images as topics of psychological study. Skinner, however, held that private events could be studied, so long as they were treated as types of behavior. Verbal reports, he said, could provide imperfect clues to these events. Where Skinner and other behaviorists parted company with nonbehaviorists was in their insistence that mental events could not *explain* behavior. For behaviorists, thoughts and feelings were simply behaviors to be explained. The prediction and modification of behavior depended on specifying the environmental conditions that maintained the behavior, not in describing people's thoughts or feelings. That is why behaviorists viewed discussions of the mind with suspicion.

Eventually, however, it became apparent to most psychologists that behavioral principles were not the only principles of learning. People also learn by observation, imitation, and insight; and they learn by thinking about what they see around them. One outgrowth of behaviorism, **social-learning theory** (often called today *cognitive social-learning theory*), which began to take hold in the 1960s, combines elements of classic behaviorism with research on thinking and consciousness. It emphasizes, for example, how people's plans, perceptions, and expectations influence their behavior. As Albert Bandura (1986), one leading proponent of this approach, has observed, "If actions were determined solely by external rewards and punishments, people would behave like weather vanes, constantly shifting direction to conform to whatever momentary influence happened to impinge on them." According to Bandura, the fact that people don't (always) act like weather vanes means that much of human learning is *self-regulated*—shaped by a person's thoughts, values, self-reflections, and intentions. Today, many psychologists feel comfortable combining elements of behaviorism with approaches that incorporate the study of thinking and consciousness.

What can learning approaches tell us about violence and aggression? Behaviorists do not probe the inner lives or motives of violent people. Instead, they seek

■ **social-learning theory (or cognitive social-learning theory)**
The theory that behavior is learned and maintained through observation and imitation of others, positive consequences, and cognitive processes such as plans and expectations.

to identify the sorts of situations that promote violence and the payoffs it earns for its perpetrators. They argue that violent behavior can be reduced or eliminated by withdrawing the rewards that maintain it and by rewarding cooperative, friendly behavior instead. Social-learning research also suggests that many children learn to be aggressive by imitating the aggressive behavior of others, including behavior depicted on television and in movies (Bandura, 1973; Eron, 1980). It follows that a society that wishes to reduce violence should not present aggressive bullies or lawless vigilantes as role models to be admired, and that parents should not model violence in the home by using it against their children or each other.

Because of its many practical applications, the learning perspective has touched many lives. It has helped people eliminate unreasonable fears, quit smoking, lose weight, toilet-train infants, become better parents, and acquire better study habits. Historically, behaviorism's insistence on precision and objectivity did much to advance psychology as a field, and learning research in general has given psychology some of its most reliable findings.

The Psychodynamic Perspective

In 1900, a few years before John Watson published his behaviorist manifesto, an obscure Viennese physician published a book titled *The Interpretation of Dreams.* The book was not exactly an overnight sensation. In fact, during the next eight years the publisher managed to sell only 600 copies. Who could possibly have known that the author's ideas would have a profound influence on the psychology, literature, and art of the twentieth century?

That author was Sigmund Freud (1856–1939), whose name today is as much a household word as Einstein's. A neurologist by training, Freud originally hoped for a career as a medical researcher, but research did not pay well, and family responsibilities forced him to go into private practice as a physician. As Freud listened to his patients' reports of depression, nervousness, and obsessive habits, he became convinced that many of their symptoms had mental, not bodily, causes. Psychological distress was due, he concluded, to conflicts, memories, and emotional traumas that often went back to early childhood. Freud's ideas eventually evolved into a broad theory of personality, and both his theory and his methods of treating people became known as **psychoanalysis.**

Freud argued that conscious awareness is merely the tip of a mental iceberg. Beneath the visible tip, he said, lies the unconscious part of the mind, containing unrevealed wishes, ambitions, passions, guilty secrets, unspeakable yearnings, and conflicts between desire and duty. We are not aware of our unconscious urges and thoughts as we go blithely about our daily business, yet they do make themselves known—in dreams, slips of the tongue, apparent accidents, and even jokes. Freud (1905a) wrote, "No mortal can keep a secret. If the lips are silent, he chatters with his fingertips; betrayal oozes out of him at every pore." In the Freudian view, unconscious forces have more power over behavior than consciousness does. Whereas a behaviorist is concerned with observable acts, a psychoanalyst tries to dig below the surface of a person's behavior to uncover the roots of personality. And whereas a behaviorist emphasizes the external environment, the psychoanalyst emphasizes processes that go on within the individual. Psychoanalysts think of themselves as archeologists of the mind.

Unlike the behaviorists, Freud viewed aggression not as a learned behavior but as a biological instinct. The duty of society, he said, is to get people to channel their aggressive energy into productive, socially useful activities. Aggressive energy that is not channeled in this way will inevitably be released in violent actions such as murder and war. It follows that if society wishes to minimize aggression, it must establish clear rules about the expression of aggression, reinforce those rules, and provide people with ways to rechannel their aggres-

Sigmund Freud (1856–1939), with his daughter Anna, who also became an influential psychoanalyst.

▪ **psychoanalysis**

A theory of personality and a method of psychotherapy, originally formulated by Sigmund Freud, that emphasizes unconscious motives and conflicts.

sive impulses. A Freudian might say that a butcher, a boxer, and a surgeon are all channeling their aggressive energy in healthy directions.

Psychoanalysis continues today as a school of therapy and an approach to explaining human nature. Its major role has been as an influence on modern **psychodynamic theories** of personality, which emphasize unconscious dynamics within the individual, such as inner forces, conflicts, or instinctual energy (see Chapter 12). *Dynamics* is a term from physics that refers to the motion and balance of systems under the action of external or internal forces. (For example, the science of thermodynamics studies the relationship between heat and mechanical energy.) Freud borrowed the idea of the conservation of energy from nineteenth-century physics: Within any system, he thought, energy can be shifted or transformed, but the total amount of energy remains the same. Psychological energy—the energy it takes to carry out mental and emotional processes—was, to Freud, a form of physical energy. Although modern psychodynamic theories differ in various ways from classical psychoanalysis, they share Freud's **intrapsychic** view of the individual, emphasizing the internal, hidden mechanisms of the psyche or mind.

Psychodynamic psychology is the thumb on the hand of psychology: It is connected to the other fingers but also set apart from them because it differs radically from the others in its language, methods, and standards of acceptable evidence. Many research psychologists working from the biological, learning, cognitive, and sociocultural perspectives don't think that psychodynamic psychology belongs in academic psychology at all (Gardner, 1992). Whereas the other perspectives originated in scientific research, they argue, the psychodynamic perspective originated in psychoanalysis and therefore belongs with philosophy, literature, or therapy rather than social science.

Nevertheless, the psychodynamic perspective has influenced mainstream psychology in many important ways. Some research psychologists study the processes of rationalization, denial, and self-delusion—concepts that stemmed from Freud's theory that the conscious mind strives to protect itself from threatening information. Others are investigating the nature and mechanisms of the unconscious—for example, how people can perceive something without being aware of it. Most researchers today agree that thoughts and rational behavior can be distorted by guilt, anxiety, and shame. Moreover, the psychodynamic perspective is the only one that tries to deal with the great existential human dilemmas, such as alienation in a lonely world and the fear of death.

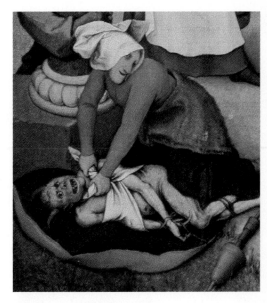

In the psychodynamic perspective, behavior is explained primarily by unconscious needs and motives. Psychoanalysts argue that everyone must struggle to control the instinctive "demons" of aggression and sexuality that threaten to disrupt civilization. Other psychodynamic theorists emphasize different unconscious drives.

The Biological Perspective

Many people, when they first study psychology, are surprised to find that psychologists are interested not only in actions and thoughts, but also in genes, hormones, and nerve cells. Yet the biological approach to psychology has been important from the beginning. Wilhelm Wundt's best-known work was titled *Principles of Physiological Psychology,* and for good reason: He and most other early researchers expected their science to rest on a firm foundation of anatomy and biology.

During the 1920s and 1930s, interest in mental processes and the brain flourished within *Gestalt psychology,* a movement that had begun in Germany in 1912. In German, *gestalt* means "pattern" or "configuration." The Gestalt psychologists studied how people interpret sensory information as patterns in order to acquire knowledge (see Chapter 6). In America, however, biological research in psychology languished until the 1960s, when new drugs were developed to treat mental disorders, and new technologies permitted increasingly sophisticated ways of measuring brain activity. These new methods have made it possible to explore areas of an organism's "inner space" where no one has ventured before.

The premise behind the **biological perspective** in psychology is that all actions, feelings, and thoughts are associated with bodily events. Electrical

■ **psychodynamic theories**
Psychological approaches that emphasize unconscious dynamics within the individual, such as inner forces, conflicts, or the movement of instinctual energy.

■ **intrapsychic**
Within the mind (psyche) or self.

■ **biological perspective**
A psychological approach that emphasizes bodily events and changes associated with actions, feelings, and thoughts.

Some people literally bang their heads against a wall. Biological psychologists look for the causes of such abnormal behavior, and of normal actions as well, in genes, brain circuits, and bodily processes, and in the evolutionary development of our species.

impulses shoot along the intricate pathways of the nervous system. Hormones course through the bloodstream, signaling internal organs to slow down or speed up. Chemical substances flow across the tiny gaps that separate one microscopic brain cell from another. *Biological psychologists* (sometimes called *behavioral neuroscientists, biopsychologists,* or *psychobiologists*) want to know how these bodily events interact with events in the external environment to produce perceptions, memories, and behavior. They study how biology affects the rhythms of life, perceptions of reality, the ability to learn, the experience of emotion, temperaments, and vulnerability to emotional disorder. And in a popular new specialty, *evolutionary psychology,* researchers have been studying how our species' evolutionary past may help explain some of our present behaviors and psychological traits; we will focus on their contributions in Chapter 3.

One result of the biological perspective has been a better understanding of how mind and body interact in illness and in health. Researchers are learning that although bodily processes can affect one's moods and emotions, the converse is also true: Emotions, attitudes, and perceptions can influence the functioning of the immune system and thus a person's susceptibility to certain diseases, as we will see in Chapter 14. Psychobiological research has also renewed interest in the age-old debate over the relative contributions made by "nature" (genetic dispositions) and "nurture" (upbringing and environment) to the development of abilities and personality traits, as we will see in Chapter 3.

Many biological psychologists hope that their discoveries, along with those of biochemists and other biological scientists, will help solve some of the mysteries of mental and emotional problems. Some of that research might help us understand some kinds of impulsive, unprovoked violence, which may be traceable to brain tumors, brain injuries, diseases, or subtle neurological disorders. Dutch researchers have reported evidence, from one large family, that a genetic abnormality may help explain some very unusual cases of lifelong aggression in males (Brunner, Nelen, & van Zandvoort, 1993).

People often mistakenly think that the explanation for some puzzle of behavior must be *either* physical *or* psychological, and they fail to appreciate how complex the interactions between body and mind really are. But the biological approach has a useful message for us all: We cannot know ourselves if we do not know our bodies. That is why biological discoveries will be discussed in many sections of this book.

The Cognitive Perspective

For the first half of this century, behaviorism and psychoanalysis ruled in psychology, with the former governing most research and the latter guiding most psychotherapy. Then, during the 1950s and 1960s, an emerging movement to study the workings of the human mind gathered momentum from an expected source: the development of the computer. The computer gave scientists a method and a metaphor for studying problem solving, informational feedback, and other mental processes. The result was the rise of the **cognitive perspective** in psychology. (The word *cognitive* comes from the Latin for "to know.")

Cognitive psychologists argued that in order to understand how people use language, acquire moral codes, experience emotions, or behave in groups, psychologists must know what is going on in people's heads. Therefore they must study how people perceive, think, remember, solve problems, explain experiences, and form beliefs—and the consequences that follow from these mental events. However, cognitive researchers did not wish to return to the structuralists' dependence on introspection. Instead, they developed new ways to infer mental processes from observable behavior. For example, by examining the kinds of errors people make when they try to recall words from a list, cognitive psychologists could draw conclusions about whether words are stored in mem-

■ **cognitive perspective**

A psychological approach that emphasizes mental processes in perception, memory, language, problem solving, and other areas of behavior.

Cognitive psychologists emphasize people's perceptions, thought processes, and explanations of events. When a problem arises, a person's behavior will depend in part on whether he or she interprets it as a challenge or "cries over spilt milk."

ory in terms of either sounds or meanings. With the development of such techniques, the mind again became a respectable topic of scientific study.

One of the most important contributions of this perspective has been to show that people's explanations and perceptions affect what they do and feel. All of us are constantly seeking to make sense of the world around us and of our own physical and mental states. Our ideas may not always be realistic or sensible, but they continually influence our actions and choices. For example, people who are quick to behave violently often assume that others are insulting them, even in the absence of much evidence. If someone does something they dislike, they attribute the action to meanness and malice. They see provocation everywhere. They accept negative stereotypes about those who are different from themselves, and they divide the world up into "us" versus "them." In contrast, nonviolent people are able to take another person's perspective. If someone does something they dislike, they are apt to say, "He had a bad day" instead of "He's a rotten person." They avoid blowing disputes out of proportion. They can generate alternative ways of solving disagreements. Thus, in the cognitive view, the solution to violence (and to other human problems as well) is to change destructive and distorted thinking patterns.

Hardly a topic in psychology has remained unaffected by what is now called the "cognitive revolution" (Gardner, 1985). Cognitive researchers have studied how people explain their own behavior, understand a sentence, solve intellectual problems, reason, form opinions, and remember events. They have busily rushed into areas of study where behaviorists feared to tread, such as sleeping, dreaming, hypnosis, and drug-induced states of consciousness. They are designing computer programs that perform complex cognitive tasks and that predict how humans will perform, too (Simon, 1992).

Like every other approach to psychology, the cognitive perspective has its critics. They point out that although perceptions and interpretations are important, we must not overlook the impact of external events—job conditions, family situations, experiences and losses—on our behavior. Critics also complain that often there is no way to choose among competing cognitive explanations. However, the cognitive approach is one of the strongest forces in psychology today, and it has inspired an explosion of research on the complex workings of the mind.

The Sociocultural Perspective

For the most part, the study of psychology has been the study of the individual—that is, the behavioral, psychodynamic, cognitive, or biological forces that affect an individual's behavior. After World War II, some psychologists began to question this focus. They wanted to know how dictators such as Adolf Hitler could persuade people to commit the atrocities that led to the deaths of Anne Frank and millions of others. They wondered why apparently nice people often hold hateful prejudices and whether such attitudes could be changed. They asked how cultural values and political systems affect everyday experience. The view that emerged from these questions is one that we call the **sociocultural perspective.**

Researchers working from this perspective have demonstrated that social contexts shape every aspect of human behavior, from how (and whether!) we kiss to what and where we eat. Yet most of us underestimate the influence of the particular historical and social context in which we happen to find ourselves. We are like fish that are unaware they live in water, so obvious is water in their lives. Sociocultural psychologists study the water and ask how it affects everything that swims in it.

Psychologists who emphasize the "socio-" side of the sociocultural perspective might study how standards of masculinity and femininity influence the expression of emotion (Chapter 10); how job opportunities affect a person's goals and ambitions (Chapter 11); or how being in a group affects attitudes and the desire to conform (Chapter 17). They study how we are affected by other people—spouses, lovers, friends, bosses, parents, and strangers. They study how we emulate our heroes, conform to peer groups, obey authorities, and blossom or wilt in relationships.

Psychologists who emphasize the "cultural" side of the perspective study how cultures affect behavior (Lonner & Malpass, 1994). In general, *culture* refers to a program of shared rules that govern the behavior of members of a community or society, and a set of values, beliefs, and attitudes shared by most members of that community. Sometimes the rules are explicit: "Every adult woman must cover her face and hair in public." Sometimes the rules are implicit: "The correct nose-to-nose distance for talking to a friend is about twenty inches." (Try it, and see if that is your culture's rule for conversational

■ **sociocultural perspective**

A psychological approach that emphasizes social and cultural influences on behavior.

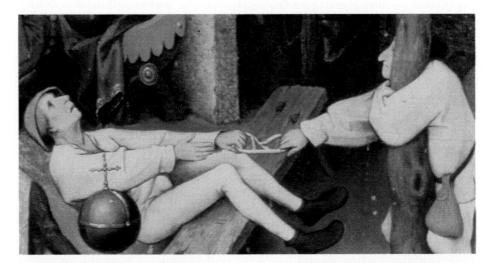

For psychologists who take a sociocultural perspective, human behavior depends on many outside influences, ranging from the immediate situation to the larger culture. They might ask why relationships in some societies are a tug-of-war, whereas those in other societies are more cooperative.

distance!) Cultural psychologists might look at how a society's emphasis on individualism or loyalty to family affects people's motives and goals, how cultural expectations about children's family responsibilities affect moral development, or how cultural attitudes toward personal control affect the experience of stress.

In the sociocultural view, the reasons for violence do not reside in instincts, brain circuits, or personal dispositions, but in economic and political arrangements and in social and cultural rules about when to aggress and against whom. When societies are small and close-knit, and when individuals must cooperate to survive, people tend to fear and avoid aggression. The Inuit (Eskimos), for example, often regard the mildest protest, the slightest raised tone, the merest hint of a frown as serious threats. The Inuit consider anger to be dangerous and intolerable, appropriate only for babies, the insane, the sick—and *kaplunas,* white people (Briggs, 1970). In contrast, societies that value competition or power often foster anger and aggression, both within the society and against outsiders. To reduce violence, then, there must be social and cultural change, not merely personal change.

We will be examining the influence of society and culture in our discussions of perception, emotion, child development, and many other topics throughout this book, and Chapter 18 will specifically explore findings from the fields of cultural and cross-cultural psychology. The sociocultural perspective can lead to glib generalizations and stereotypes about ethnic groups, nations, and cultures. But because we are social animals, this perspective has made psychology a more representative and scientific discipline.

Two Influential Movements in Psychology

Not all schools of psychology fall neatly into one of the five perspectives we have discussed. In the 1960s, for example, Abraham Maslow, Rollo May, and Carl Rogers rejected the psychoanalytic emphasis on unconscious hostility and conflict as being too pessimistic a view of human nature, and they rejected the behavioral approach as being too mechanistic and "mindless" a view of human nature. Human behavior, they said, is not completely determined by either unconscious dynamics or by the environment. People are capable of free will and therefore have the ability to make more of themselves than psychoanalysis or behaviorism would predict. As Maslow (1971) wrote, "When you select out for careful study very fine and healthy people, strong people, creative people, saintly people, sagacious people . . . then you get a very different view of mankind. You are asking how tall can people grow, what can a human being become?" It was time, therefore, for a "third force" in psychology, which they called **humanistic psychology** (or *humanism*). Its goal would be to help people express themselves creatively and achieve their full potential.

Although humanism is no longer a dominant school in psychology, it has had considerable influence both inside and outside the field. Many psychologists across all perspectives consider themselves humanists, although they regard humanism as a philosophy of life rather than a systematic approach to psychology. Further, many of the topics the humanists raised, such as altruism (unselfish helpfulness to others) and creativity, have been studied by scientific psychologists in other perspectives. Humanism has probably had its greatest influence in psychotherapy and in spiritual and self-help movements. Many of the descendants of the early humanists abandoned mainstream psychology in order to form popular human-potential movements; humanism is their philosophical parent.

Another movement that emerged in the 1970s, one that continues to wield great influence today, is **feminist psychology.** The women and men who call

■ **humanistic psychology**
A psychological approach that emphasizes personal growth and the achievement of human potential more than the scientific understanding, prediction, and control of behavior.

■ **feminist psychology**
A psychological approach that analyzes the influence of social inequities on gender relations and on the behavior of the two sexes.

themselves feminist psychologists draw on research from all five psychological perspectives in order to analyze how social, economic, and political inequities affect gender relations and the behavior of the sexes. As women began to enter psychology in greater numbers during the 1970s, they documented evidence of a pervasive bias in the research methods of psychology and in the very questions that researchers had been asking (Bem, 1993; Crawford & Marecek, 1989; Hare-Mustin & Marecek, 1990). They observed the large number of studies that used only men as subjects—and usually only young, white, middle-class men, at that—and showed why it was inappropriate to generalize to everyone else from such a narrow research base. They found that when researchers did include women in their studies, gender differences were typically described as deficiencies in women (Denmark et al., 1988). For instance, women were said to be "more gullible" than men, not "more open-minded."

Feminist psychologists have also spurred research on topics that have traditionally been of little or no interest to most men in the field, such as menstruation, motherhood, the dynamics of power in close relationships, women's life-span issues, and reasons for the changing definitions of masculinity and femininity. They have critically examined the male bias in psychotherapy, starting with Freud's own case studies (Hare-Mustin, 1991). They have also analyzed the social consequences of psychological findings, showing how research has often been used to justify the lower status of women and other disadvantaged groups.

Although feminist psychologists are committed to redressing gender bias in psychology, they differ in their views of how best to achieve that goal, the best research methods to use, and the conclusions that can be drawn from various studies. Some are concerned about a tendency among some of their colleagues to replace a male bias in research with a female bias (Yoder & Kahn, 1993)—for example, by doing studies of women only and then drawing conclusions about gender differences. Others worry that the overriding goal of feminist psychologists—the promotion of gender equality—has led some theorists to embrace conclusions that are intuitively appealing but that lack empirical support (Mednick, 1989; Peplau & Conrad, 1989).

Feminist psychologists, however, remind us that research and psychotherapy are social processes, affected by all the influences that people bring to any enterprise. To improve psychology and the uses to which it is put, they say, we must become aware of our biases and attempt to correct them. This argument has inspired other movements in psychology that are striving to eliminate bias in studies of ethnic and cultural groups, gay men and lesbians, old people, disabled people, and the poor.

A Note on Psychology's Multiple Personalities

The differences among the perspectives of psychology are very real; they have produced passionate arguments and sometimes stony silences among their defenders. But not all psychologists feel they must swear allegiance to one approach or another. Many, if not most, are *eclectic*, using what they believe to be the best features of diverse theories and schools of thought. Further, most psychologists agree on certain broad guidelines about what is and what is not acceptable in their discipline. Most believe in gathering empirical evidence instead of arriving at conclusions through reasoning alone. Nearly all reject supernatural explanations of events—evil spirits, psychic forces, miracles, and so forth. This insistence on rigorous standards of proof sets psychology apart from other, nonscientific explanations of human experience (see "Think About It").

Think About It

Sense and Nonsense About Human Experience

■ You have probably heard that human beings are different from other animals because we have language, use tools, or can think. But to communications psychologist George Gerbner (1988), we are unique because we tell stories—and live by the stories we tell. All of us have a need to explain ourselves and the workings of the world around us. We are constantly constructing stories that will make sense of confusing, surprising, or unfair events. Which stories are right? Marriages have broken up and wars have been waged over that question.

Psychology and other sciences offer certain kinds of stories about human behavior; they are called "theories." But psychology has plenty of nonscientific competitors. Are you having romantic problems? An astrologer may advise you to choose an Aries instead of an Aquarius as your next love. Are you unable to make decisions? A "channeler" will put you in touch with a 5,000-year-old equivalent of Dear Abby. Are you fighting the battle of the bulge? An expert in "past lives regression" will explain that the problem is not in your unhappy childhood but in your unhappy previous life; perhaps in the fourteenth century, you were a starving serf. By analyzing personality and dispensing advice, many of these self-defined healers operate in effect as unlicensed psychological counselors. You hear about their famous clients all the time—movie stars, rock singers, Wall Street brokers, even politicians. During former President Ronald Reagan's term of office, Nancy Reagan sought the advice of an astrologer before permitting White House staffers to set her husband's schedule.

When deciding which stories about human behavior to believe, it helps to distinguish two questions that are often confused: *Does it work?* and *Is it true?* Many stories work for people; that is, they help people feel better, provide entertainment, reassure people that they are normal, or simplify a complicated world. But for a story, theory, or system to be *true,* or valid, it must explain or predict behavior or events more reliably and accurately than could be done by mere guessing.

Throughout history, people have turned to religion for answers to ultimate questions of life and death, spirituality, and meaning. Religious explanations are for the most part impossible to test for accuracy; they are a matter of faith. But other nonscientific systems of belief are testable in principle, although their followers often ignore the rules of evidence. One such rule is that you have to make predictions in advance of, not after, the fact. For instance, you don't get to experience an earthquake and then argue that the planets predicted it.

When you look closely, you find that nonscientific predictions are rarely correct *in advance.* For example, in a review of many studies, Geoffrey Dean (1986/1987, 1987) found that predictions made by trained astrologers have only chance-level accuracy. The astrologers' occasional on-target predictions are the result of shrewd guesses ("Mideast tensions will continue"), vagueness ("A tragedy will strike the country this spring"), or inside information ("Movie star A will marry director B"). (It is interesting that not a single astrologer in these studies predicted the 1993 Israel–PLO peace agreement!) Astrologers are no better at describing individuals' personalities based on their birth charts. Dean concludes that astrology is "psychological chewing gum, satisfying but ultimately without real substance."

Even when people know about a system's inadequacies, they may ignore those flaws, out of a need to believe. The task of the scientist is to separate belief from evidence and to consider all of the available information, including any counterevidence. James Randi, a magician who devotes his time to debunking pseudoscientific claims, once sent a birth chart to a noted astrologer for analysis. The astrologer, thinking the chart was Randi's own, sent back a glowing description of a virtuous, steadfast fellow. In fact, the chart was based on the birthdate, birth hour, and birthplace of a convicted rapist.

In this book, you will learn that psychology tells more than one story. A psychoanalyst's explanation of your personality will not be the same as a cognitive psychologist's, and neither account will be the same as a behaviorist's. In later chapters, we will be offering you ways to think critically about various psychological approaches, as well as about those of psychology's nonscientific competitors.

In the meantime, ask yourself what else you need to know to evaluate a theory besides the fact that it is coherent and appealing, and you want it to be true. What is the harm in accepting an explanation of behavior that has no evidence to support it? Does it matter whether we attribute our fates to the alignment of heavenly bodies, past lives, spirit guides, psychic energy, or our own decisions and actions? Think about it. ■

Some psychologists hope that in time they will be able to resolve their differences and settle on a limited set of fundamental principles that apply to all forms of behavior (Kimble, 1990). Some even hope for a single, unifying *paradigm*—a guiding model or theory—that will define what psychologists should study and how they should study it. They hope that such a paradigm will do for psychology what the laws of motion did for physics and evolutionary theory did for biology. Given the complexity of their subject matter, however, a unifying paradigm may be as elusive as the Holy Grail (Gardner, 1992; Hilgard, 1991; Koch, 1992).

Even as psychologists yearn for unity, individual researchers are heading off in different directions. While some seek the answers to psychological problems in biology, others are studying the effects of social pathology—poverty, unemployment, racism, sexism, ageism, and urban crowding. While some want to bring psychology back to its philosophical roots, others are investing their energy in computer simulations and space-age technology. Grand theories have been replaced by more specific ones that address particular questions. Human behavior does not seem to lend itself to simple, all-encompassing theories. It is like a giant mosaic made up of many fragments, so complicated that no single approach can take in the whole picture. Put all the approaches together, though, and the result is a rich, multicolored, absorbing psychological portrait.

Quick QUIZ

A. Anxiety is a common problem. To find out if you fully understand the five major perspectives in psychology, try to match each possible explanation of anxiety on the left with a perspective on the right.

1. Anxious people often think about the future in distorted ways.
2. Anxiety is due to forbidden, unconscious desires.
3. Anxiety symptoms often bring hidden rewards, such as being excused from exams.
4. Excessive anxiety can be caused by a chemical imbalance.
5. A national emphasis on competition and success promotes worry and anxiety about failure.

   a. behavioral
   b. psychodynamic
   c. sociocultural
   d. biological
   e. cognitive

 B. Different assumptions about human behavior can lead to different conclusions. What assumption distinguishes cognitive psychology from behaviorism? What assumption distinguishes the psychodynamic perspective from the sociocultural perspective?

Answers:

A. 1. e 2. b 3. a 4. d 5. c **B.** Cognitive psychologists assume that thoughts and feelings can explain behavior; behaviorists assume that thoughts and feelings are behaviors to be explained. Psychodynamic psychologists assume that behavior is driven largely by internal (intrapsychic) factors, such as unconscious urges and personality traits; the sociocultural perspective assumes that behavior is determined largely by social and cultural contexts.

■ WHAT PSYCHOLOGISTS DO

Now you know the main viewpoints that guide psychologists in their work. But what do psychologists actually do with their time between breakfast and dinner?

When people hear the word *psychologist,* they often imagine a therapist listening intently while a client, perhaps stretched out comfortably on a couch, pours forth his or her troubles. Many psychologists do in fact fit this image, though chairs are more common than couches these days. However, many others do not (see Table 1.1). The professional activities of psychologists generally fall into three categories: (1) teaching and doing research in colleges and universities; (2) providing health or mental health services, often referred to as *psychological practice*; and (3) conducting research or applying its findings in nonacademic settings such as business, sports, government, law, and the military. Many psychologists wear more than one professional hat, moving flexibly among teaching, research, and practice. A teacher at a university might spend half the day doing laboratory research and the other half teaching psychology courses, besides occasionally serving as a professional consultant in legal cases or for government policy makers. A scientist–practitioner might see patients in a mental health clinic three days a week and do research in a hospital on the causes of depression the other two.

Psychological Research

Psychological researchers work for universities and colleges, the government, the military, schools, and business. Some, seeking knowledge for its own sake, work in **basic psychology,** doing "pure" research. Others, concerned with the practical uses of knowledge, work in **applied psychology.** A psychologist doing basic research might ask, "How do children, adolescents, and adults differ in their approach to moral issues such as honesty?" An applied psychologist might ask, instead, "How can knowledge about moral development be used to

■ **basic psychology**
The study of psychological issues in order to seek knowledge for its own sake rather than for its practical application.

■ **applied psychology**
The study of psychological issues that have direct practical significance and the application of psychological findings.

Table 1.1　　*What Is a Psychologist?*

A psychologist has an advanced degree; some psychologists are psychotherapists (clinicians), but many do research, teach, work in business, or consult.

Academic/Research Psychologists	Clinical Psychologists	Psychologists in Industry, Law, or Other Settings
Specialize in areas of pure or applied research, such as:	May work in any of these settings, or some combination:	Do research or consult to institutions in the community on, e.g.:
Developmental	Private practice	Sports
Psychometric	Mental health clinics/services	Consumer issues
Health	Hospitals	Advertising
Educational	Research	Environmental issues
Social	Teaching	Public policy analysis
Industrial/organizational		Survey research/opinion polls
Consumer		
Physiolgical		
Perception and sensation		

prevent teenage violence?" A psychologist in basic science might ask, "Can a chimpanzee or a gorilla learn to use sign language?" An applied psychologist might ask, "Can techniques used to teach language to a chimpanzee be used to help mentally impaired or disturbed children who do not speak?"

Applied psychologists have made important contributions in areas as diverse as health, education, marketing, management, consumer behavior, industrial design, worker productivity, and urban planning. For many years, however, the basic approach had far more prestige among psychologists than did the applied approach (Sherif, 1979). This began to change during World War II, when the U.S. government encouraged psychological scientists to apply their findings to the training, education, and health-care problems facing the country. Many well-known psychologists answered the call. Today, most psychologists recognize that basic and applied psychology are both necessary. Although basic psychology can sometimes lead to useful discoveries by accident, such accidents cannot be depended on. On the other hand, insisting that psychological research always be relevant is like trying to grow flowers by concentrating only on the blossoms and ignoring the roots (Walker, 1970). Basic research is root research. Without it there would be little scientific knowledge to apply.

Psychologists' findings, both basic and applied, fill this book, so you can get a good idea of *what* psychologists study and teach by scanning the Table of Contents on pages vi to xiv. Here are a few of the major nonclinical specialties in psychology:

- *Experimental psychologists* conduct laboratory studies of learning, motivation, emotion, sensation and perception, physiology, human performance, and cognition. Don't be misled by the term *experimental,* though; other researchers also run experiments.

- *Educational psychologists* study psychological principles that explain learning and search for ways to improve learning in educational systems. Their interests range from the application of findings on memory and thinking to the use of rewards to encourage achievement.

- *Developmental psychologists* study how people change and grow over time, physically, mentally, and socially. In the past, their focus was mainly on childhood, but many now study adolescence, young adulthood, the middle years, or old age.

- *Industrial/organizational psychologists* study behavior in the workplace. They are concerned with group decision making, employee morale, work motivation, productivity, job stress, personnel selection, marketing strategies, equipment design, and many other issues.

- *Psychometric psychologists* design and evaluate tests of mental abilities, aptitudes, interests, and personality. Nearly all of us have had firsthand experience with one or more of these tests in school, at work, or in the military.

- *Social psychologists* study how groups, institutions, and the social context influence individuals and vice versa. Among their interests are conformity, obedience, competition, cooperation, leadership styles, group decision making, and prejudice.

The Practice of Psychology

Psychological practitioners, whose goal is to understand and improve physical and mental health, work in mental hospitals, general hospitals, clinics, schools, counseling centers, and private practice. Over the past two decades, the proportion of psychologists who are practitioners has greatly increased;

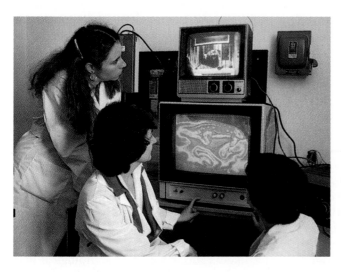 

Some psychologists are researchers, others are practitioners, and some are both. In the photograph on the left, Patricia Goldman-Rakic (center) and her colleagues use technology to study the brain mechanisms underlying mental processes. In the photograph on the right, a clinical psychologist helps a client cope with an emotional problem.

today, practitioners account for well over two-thirds of new psychology doctorates, and a similar proportion of the members of the American Psychology Association (APA) identify themselves as health-care providers (Kohout & Wicherski, 1991; Shapiro & Wiggins, 1994). Some practitioners are *counseling psychologists,* who generally help people deal with problems of everyday life, such as test anxiety, family and marital problems, or low job motivation. Others are *school psychologists,* who work with parents, teachers, and students to enhance students' performance and emotional development. The majority, however, are *clinical psychologists,* who diagnose, treat, and study mental or emotional problems and disabilities. Clinicians are trained to do psychotherapy with highly disturbed people as well as those who are mildly troubled or unhappy or who want to learn to handle their problems better. (As we will see in Chapter 16, there are many different kinds of psychotherapy.)

In almost all states, a license to practice clinical psychology requires a doctorate. Most clinical psychologists have a Ph.D., some have an Ed.D. (doctorate in education), and a smaller but growing number have a relatively new degree called a Psy.D. (doctorate in psychology, pronounced "sy-dee"). Clinical psychologists typically do four or five years of graduate work in psychology, plus at least a year's internship under the direction of a practicing psychologist. Clinical programs leading to a Ph.D. or Ed.D. are designed to prepare a person both as a scientist and a clinical practitioner; they require completion of a dissertation, a major scholarly work (usually involving research) that contributes to knowledge in the field. Programs leading to a Psy.D. focus on professional practice and do not usually require a dissertation. However, they do require the student to complete a research study, theoretical paper, literature review, or other scholarly project.

People often confuse the terms *psychotherapist, psychoanalyst, clinical psychologist,* and *psychiatrist,* but these terms do not mean the same thing. Anyone who does any kind of psychotherapy is a psychotherapist. In fact, in most states anyone can say that he or she is a "therapist" of one sort or another without having any training at all. A psychoanalyst is a person who practices one particular form of therapy, psychoanalysis. To call yourself a psychoanalyst, you must get specialized training at a recognized psychoanalytic institute, and you must usually undergo extensive psychoanalysis yourself. **Psychiatry** is the medical specialty concerned with mental disorders, maladjustment, and abnormal behavior. Psychiatrists are medical doctors (M.D.s) who have had three or four years

■ **psychiatry**
The medical specialty concerned with mental disorders, maladjustment, and abnormal behavior.

of general medical training, a yearlong internship in general medicine, and a three-year residency in psychiatry. During the residency period, a psychiatrist learns to diagnose and treat psychiatric patients under the supervision of more experienced physicians. Some psychiatrists go on to do research on mental problems rather than to work with patients.

Although there are many similarities in what psychiatrists and clinical psychologists do, there are also important differences. Psychiatrists are more likely than psychologists to treat severe mental disorders. They tend to be more medically oriented because they have been trained to diagnose physical problems that can cause mental ones. In addition, psychiatrists can write prescriptions, and clinical psychologists cannot (at least not yet; many psychologists are pressing for prescription-writing privileges). Psychiatrists, however, often are not thoroughly trained in the theories and methods of modern psychology. These differences can affect approaches to treatment (see Chapter 16). For example, if a patient is depressed, a psychiatrist will often prescribe an antidepressant drug. A clinical psychologist is more likely to look for the psychological and social origins of depression and to offer nonmedical solutions.

Marriage, family, and child counselors, school counselors, and social workers also do mental health work. These professionals ordinarily treat general problems in adjustment and not serious mental disturbance. Licensing requirements vary somewhat from state to state but usually include a master's degree in psychology or social work and one or two years of supervised experience. (For a summary of the various types of psychotherapists and the training they receive, see Table 1.2.)

Many research psychologists are worried about a flood tide of poorly trained psychotherapists across America (Dawes, 1994; Ofshe & Watters, 1994). Some of these people have no credentials at all, many are entirely unschooled in research methods and the empirical findings of psychology, and many use therapy techniques that have not been validated. Some practitioners, too, are concerned about the lack of a uniform, national standard of professional education (Fox, 1994). A few years ago, such concerns contributed to the formation of the American Psychological Society, an organization devoted to the needs and interests of psychology as a science. Many practitioners, on the other hand, accuse psychological scientists of living in an ivory tower and of showing too little concern for helping people to solve problems in the real world. (As for those psychologists whose professional commitment is mainly to teaching, they sometimes feel that their concerns are ignored by both researchers *and* practitioners!)

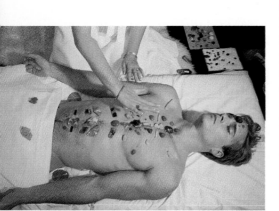

Many psychologists are concerned about the popularity of such pseudoscientific therapies as "crystal healing," which lack empirical support.

Table 1.2 Types of Psychotherapists

Psychotherapist	A person who does psychotherapy: may have anything from no degree to an advanced professional degree; the term is unregulated.
Clinical psychologist	Has a Ph.D., Ed.D., or Psy.D.
Psychoanalyst	Has specific training in psychoanalysis after an advanced degree (M.D. or Ph.D.).
Psychiatrist	A medical doctor (M.D.) with a specialty in psychiatry.
Other mental health professionals: counselors; school psychologists; licensed social workers (LSWs); marriage, family, and child counselors (MFCCs)	Licensing requirements vary; generally has at least an M.A. in psychology or in social work.

Partly because of these tensions, and partly because the media and the public persist in equating "psychologist" with "psychotherapist," some psychological scientists think it is time to come up with new labels to describe what they do and yield the word *psychologist* to its popular meaning. Research psychologists, they say, should call themselves "cognitive scientists," "behavioral scientists," "neuroscientists," and so forth, depending on their area of study (Gardner, 1992). This change in language is already underway and gathering steam. At present, however, the word *psychologist* still embraces all the cousins in psychology's sprawling family.

Psychology in the Community

In the past few decades, psychology has probably expanded more quickly than any other field, in terms of scholars, publications, and specialties. The American Psychological Association (APA), psychology's largest professional organization, now has 49 divisions. Some of these divisions represent the major fields described in this chapter, such as developmental psychology and physiological psychology; others represent special research or professional interests, such as the psychology of women, ethnic minority issues, sports, the arts, environmental concerns, gay and lesbian issues, consumer behavior, peace, psychology and the law, and health.

Look around your community, and you are apt to find psychologists. Besides teaching, doing research, and treating patients, they consult with companies to improve worker satisfaction and productivity. They establish programs to improve race relations and reduce tensions among different ethnic communities. They advise commissions on how pollution and noise affect mental health. They do research for the military. They do rehabilitation training for people who are physically or mentally disabled. They educate judges and juries about the reliability of eyewitness testimony. They assist the police in emergencies involving hostage takers and other violent persons. They conduct public opinion surveys. They run suicide-prevention hot lines. They advise zoos on the care and training of animals. They help coaches improve the athletic performance of their teams. And on and on.

Psychologists work in many settings, from classrooms to courtrooms. On the left, prison psychologist Patricia Frish counsels an inmate at San Quentin. On the right, researcher Louis Herman studies the ability of dolphins to learn and understand an artificial language comprised of hand signals. In response to Herman's gestural sequence for "person" and "over," Ake will leap over the person in the pool.

Is it any wonder that people are a little fuzzy about what a psychologist is? Cognitive psychologist George Miller has related what happens when he tells people his profession:

> Some people say: "So you're a psychologist. I think my wife's calling," and off they go. Then there's the opposite reaction: "So you're a psychologist. Well I'm something of a psychologist myself," and they describe how they trained their dog to bring in the newspaper. Other people ask about their children's test scores, and still others want me to interpret their dreams. All I can say is: "I'm not that kind of psychologist!" (in J. Miller, 1983)

*Q*uick QUIZ

Let's try a quick game of "What's My Line?" Which kinds of psychologists are most likely to have the following job descriptions?

1. Studies emotional development during childhood.
2. Does laboratory studies of visual perception in animals.
3. Treats eating disorders of patients in a mental health clinic.
4. Consults with industry on marketing strategies.

Answers:

1. developmental 2. experimental 3. clinical 4. industrial/organizational

■ THINKING CRITICALLY AND CREATIVELY ABOUT PSYCHOLOGY

We believe that one of the greatest benefits of studying psychology is that you learn not only how the brain works in general but also how to use yours in particular—by thinking critically. **Critical thinking** is the ability and willingness to assess claims and make objective judgments on the basis of well-supported reasons. It is the ability to look for flaws in arguments and to resist claims that have no supporting evidence. It is the ability to defend a conclusion as reasonable or plausible. Critical thinking, however, is not merely negative thinking. It also fosters the ability to be *creative and constructive:* to come up with various explanations for events, think of implications of research findings, and apply new knowledge to a broad range of social and personal problems. You can't separate critical thinking from creative thinking, for it is only when you question *what is* that you can begin to imagine *what can be.*

Here is an example of what we mean. Many people, when faced with a setback to their expectations, narrow their horizons instead of expanding them. We know a fellow named Victor whose entire dream in life was to be a veterinarian. Victor's love of animals was legendary: At age 3, he wouldn't let you kill a bug in his presence. However, Victor wasn't admitted to any of the veterinary schools he applied to, and his reaction was panic and despair: "My whole life is ruined!" Victor was not thinking critically; he had divided his possibilities into only two alternatives: become a veterinarian, or nothing. But by examining this assumption and by thinking creatively about all the possible occupations that would make use of his love of animals, Victor realized his choices were endless: pet-shop owner, Hollywood "pet therapist," animal trainer, designer of humane zoos, organizer for an endangered-species group, ecologist, wildlife photographer. . . .

■ **critical thinking**

The ability and willingness to assess claims and to make objective judgments on the basis of well-supported reasons.

These days, most people know that you have to exercise the body to keep it in shape, but they may assume that thinking doesn't take any effort at all, and certainly no practice. You just do it, like breathing. Yet thinking does need practice. All around us we can see examples of flabby thinking, lazy thinking, emotional thinking, and nonthinking. Sometimes people justify their mental laziness by proudly telling you they are open-minded. Critical thinkers reply that it's good to be open-minded, but not so open that your brains fall out.

One increasingly prevalent misreading of what it means to be open-minded is the idea that all opinions are created equal and that everybody's beliefs are as good as everybody else's. On matters of religious faith or personal preferences, that's true; if you prefer the look of a Camaro to the look of a Honda, no one can argue with you. But if you say, "The Camaro is a better car than a Honda," you have uttered a statement that is more than mere opinion. Now you have to support your belief with evidence of the car's reliability, track record, safety, and the like (Ruggiero, 1988). And if you say, "Camaros are the best in the world, and Hondas do not exist; they are a conspiracy of the Japanese government," you forfeit the right to have your opinion taken seriously. Your opinion, if it ignores reality, is *not* equal to any other.

In the United States, the idea that there are two sides to every issue has added to the confusion between beliefs based on matters of taste, preference, and wishful thinking and beliefs based on good reasoning and solid evidence. The "two sides" idea has been used by some college newspaper editors to explain why they accept advertisements for revisionist books claiming that the Holocaust never took place. But as Deborah Lipstadt, author of *Denying the Holocaust* (1993), observes, there are *not* two sides to the question of whether the Holocaust occurred; debating such a question is like debating whether the Roman Empire existed or whether there really was a French Revolution. The First Amendment states that Congress shall make no law abridging freedom of speech, but, notes Lipstadt (1994), "It says nothing about a paper's obligation to publish every absurd claim that comes its way," nor does it require that every opinion, no matter how half-baked, be given the same standing.

Critical thinking involves a set of skills that will help you distinguish arguments based on solidly grounded evidence from those that float along on delusion or wishful dreams. Patricia King and Karen Kitchener, who have studied what they call *reflective judgment* and we call critical thinking, find that people don't usually use such skills until their mid-20s or until they have had many years of higher education—if then (Kitchener & King, 1990; King & Kitchener, 1994). (We will be discussing this research further in Chapter 8.) That does not mean, however, that people *can't* think critically. Even young children often do so, though they may not get much credit for it. We know one fourth-grader, who when told that ancient Greece was the "cradle of democracy," replied, "But what about women and slaves, who couldn't vote and had no rights? Was Greece a democracy for them?" That's critical thinking. And it is also creative thinking, for once you question the assumption that Greece was a democracy for everyone, you can begin to imagine other interpretations of ancient Greek civilization.

Many educators, philosophers, and psychologists believe that the American educational system shortchanges students by not encouraging them to think critically and creatively. Too often, say these critics, both teachers and students view the mind as a bin for storing the right answers or a sponge for soaking up knowledge. The mind is neither a bin nor a sponge. Remembering, thinking, and understanding are all active processes. They require judgment, choice, and the weighing of evidence. Unfortunately, children who challenge prevailing opinion at home or in school are often called "rebellious" rather than "involved." As a result, say the critics, many high school and college graduates cannot formulate a rational argument or see through misleading advertisements and propaganda that play on emotions. They do not know how to go about deciding whether to have children, make an investment, or support a political proposal. They do not know how to come up with imaginative solutions to their problems.

You can apply critical thinking to any subject you study or problem you encounter, but it is particularly relevant to psychology, for three reasons. First, the field itself includes the study of thinking, problem solving, creativity, and curiosity, and so by its very nature fosters critical and creative thinking. In one study, graduate students in psychology substantially improved their ability to reason about the events of everyday life, whereas graduate students in chemistry showed no improvement (Lehman, Lempert, & Nisbett, 1988). Second, psychology also includes the study of *barriers* to clear thinking, such as the human propensity for rationalization, self-deception, and biases in perception. Third, the field of psychology generates many competing findings on topics of personal and social relevance, and people need to be able to evaluate these findings and their implications. Critical thinking can help you separate psychology from the psychobabble that clutters the airwaves and bookstores.

In part, learning to think critically means following the rules of logic. But there are also more general guidelines involved (Ennis, 1985; Halpern, 1995; Paul, 1984; Ruggiero, 1988). Here are eight of the essential ones, which we emphasize throughout this book.

Ask Questions; Be Willing to Wonder. What is the one kind of question that most exasperates parents of young children? "Why is the sky blue, Mommy?" "Why doesn't the plane fall?" "Why don't pigs have wings?" Unfortunately, as children grow up, they tend to stop asking "why" questions. (Why do you think this is?)

Psychologist Bob Perloff (1992) has reflected on a few questions he would like to have answered:

> Why are moths attracted to wool but indifferent to cotton? How is it that there exist minuscule organisms so small that they cannot be seen by the naked eye? And speaking about naked, why is it that there are so few nude beaches when many of us, truth to tell, like to look at naked bodies (except our own)? . . . Why is dust? Why is a rainbow arched? I used to feel foolish, even dumb, because I didn't know why or how the sun shines until I learned very recently that the astrophysicists themselves are in a quandary about this.

"The trigger mechanism for creative thinking is the disposition to be curious, to wonder, to inquire," writes Vincent Ruggiero (1988). "Asking 'What's wrong here?' and/or 'Why is this the way it is, and how did it come to be that way?' leads to the identification of problems and challenges." Some occupations actually teach their trainees to think this way. Industrial engineers are taught to walk through a company and question everything, even procedures that have been used for years. But other occupations teach trainees to accept the existing system as "received wisdom" and they discourage criticism.

We hope that you will not approach psychology as received wisdom but will ask many questions about the theories and findings we present in this book. Be on the lookout, too, for questions about human behavior that are *not* answered in the chapters that follow. If you do that, you will not only be learning psychology, you will also be learning to think the way psychologists do.

Define the Problem. Once you've raised a question, the next step is to identify the issues in clear and concrete terms. "What makes people happy?" is a fine question for midnight reveries, but it will not lead to answers unless you have specified what you mean by "happy." Does happiness require being in a constant state of euphoria all the time? Does it mean feeling a pleasant contentment with life? Does it mean the absence of serious problems or pain?

It is not enough to say that something "could be" true; critical thinkers demand that claims be supported by convincing evidence.

The inadequate formulation of a question can produce misleading or incomplete answers. For example, asking, "Can animals learn language?" assumes that language is an all-or-none ability, and the question allows for only two possible answers, yes or no. But putting the question another way—"Which aspects of language might certain animals be able to acquire?"—takes into account the fact that language requires many different abilities. It also acknowledges that there are differences among species and opens up a range of possible answers, as we will see in Chapter 8.

Examine the Evidence.   Have you ever heard someone in the heat of argument exclaim, "I just know it's true, no matter what you say" or "That's my opinion; nothing's going to change it" or "If you don't understand my position, I can't explain it"? Have you ever made such statements yourself? Accepting a conclusion without evidence, or expecting others to do so, is a sure sign of uncritical thinking. A critical thinker asks, *What evidence supports or refutes this argument and its opposition? How reliable is the evidence?* If it is not possible to check the reliability of the evidence, the critical thinker considers whether its source has been reliable in the past.

Some pop-psych claims have been widely accepted on the basis of poor evidence or even no evidence at all. For example, many people believe that it is psychologically and physically healthy to ventilate their anger at the first person, pet, or piece of furniture that gets in their way. Actually, studies across many different fields suggest that sometimes expressing anger is beneficial, but more often it is not. Often it makes the angry person angrier, makes the target of the anger angry back, lowers everybody's self-esteem, and fosters hostility and aggression (see Chapter 10). Yet the belief that expressing anger is always healthy persists, despite the lack of evidence to support it. Can you think of some reasons why this might be so?

Analyze Assumptions and Biases.   Critical thinkers evaluate the assumptions and biases that lie behind arguments, asking how they influence claims and conclusions in the books they read, the political speeches they hear, the news programs they watch, and the ads that bombard them every day. Here is an example: The manufacturer of a popular pain reliever advertises that hospitals prefer its product over all others. The natural assumption—the one the advertiser wants you to make—is that this product is better than all others. Actually, hospitals prefer the product because they get a bigger discount on it than on its competitors.

Critical thinkers also are aware of their own assumptions and are willing to question them. For example, many people automatically adopt their parents' ways of doing things. When faced with difficult problems, they will reach for familiar solutions, saying, "If my dad voted Republican (or Democratic), then I should," or "I was brought up to believe that the best way to discipline children is to spank them." But critical thinking requires us to examine our biases when the evidence contradicts them. All of us, of course, carry around a headful of assumptions about how the world works: Do people have free will or are they constrained by biology and upbringing? Are government programs the solution to poverty, or would private programs do better? If we don't make our assumptions explicit, our ability to interpret evidence objectively can be seriously impaired.

Avoid Emotional Reasoning: "If I Feel This Way, It Must Be True." Emotion has a place in critical thinking. Passionate commitment to a view can motivate a person to think boldly without fear of what others will say, to defend an unpopular idea, and to seek evidence for creative new theories. Moreover, in the absence of the emotions of compassion and pity, logic and reason can lead to misguided or even destructive decisions and actions; some of the most sadistic killers and military strategists in history have been bright, even brilliant, thinkers. But when gut feelings replace clear thinking, the results are equally dangerous. "Persecutions and wars and lynchings," observes Edward de Bono (1985), "are all a result of gut feeling."

Because our feelings seem so right, it is hard to understand that people with opposing viewpoints feel just as strongly. But they usually do, which means that feelings alone are not a reliable guide to the truth. As you begin this book, you may hold strong, passionate beliefs about child rearing, drugs, astrology, the causes of crime, racism, the origins of intelligence, gender differences, and many other issues. As you read about research on these topics, you may find yourself quarreling with certain findings that you dislike. Disagreement with what you read is fine; it means you are reading actively. All we ask is that you ask yourself *why* you are disagreeing: Is it because the results cause you to question an assumption that you hold to be true, or because the evidence is unpersuasive? Keep in mind the words of the English poet and essayist Alexander Pope: "What reason weaves, by passion is undone."

Don't Oversimplify. A critical thinker looks beyond the obvious, resists easy generalizations, and rejects either/or thinking. For example, when life serves up a miserable situation, should you deny your problems ("Everything's fine; let's go to the movies") or face them head-on? Either answer oversimplifies. As we will see in Chapter 14, sometimes denial can keep people from solving their problems, but at other times, it helps them get through painful situations that can't be changed (Taylor, 1991).

Often, in a disagreement, you will hear someone arguing by anecdote—generalizing from a personal experience or one tiny bit of evidence to the whole world. One crime committed by a paroled ex-convict means parole should be abolished; one friend of yours who hates his or her school means that everybody who goes there hates it. Anecdotal generalizations are the source of stereotyping as well: One dishonest welfare mother means they are all dishonest; one encounter with an unconventional Californian means that they are all flaky. Many people make themselves miserable by generalizing from a single unfortunate event to a whole pattern of defeat: "I did poorly on this test, and now I'll never get through college or have a job or kids or anything." Critical thinkers want more evidence than one or two stories before making generalizations about the world or about their own lives.

Is this a UFO? Some people, reasoning emotionally, believe passionately in the existence of "flying saucers" from outer space. They jump from "I want them to exist" to "They do exist." (To find out more about this particular "UFO," see page 34.)

Consider Other Interpretations.   A critical thinker creatively formulates hypotheses that offer reasonable explanations of characteristics, behavior, and events. The ultimate goal is to find an explanation that accounts for the most evidence with the fewest assumptions. (This is called the *principle of Occam's razor*, after the fourteenth-century philosopher William of Occam, who proposed it.) On the other hand, critical thinkers are also careful not to shut out alternative explanations too soon. They generate as many interpretations of the evidence as possible before settling on the most likely one.

Consider, for example, a study of Swedish couples in which those who lived together before marriage were 80 percent more likely to separate or divorce than those who had lived apart (Bennett, Blanc, & Bloom, 1988). *Time* magazine promptly concluded that "premarital cohabitation may be hazardous to your marriage," and Dear Abby advised a reader that if she wanted her forthcoming marriage to last, she shouldn't cohabit beforehand. Neither *Time* nor Dear Abby considered another plausible conclusion: that people who cohabit before marriage are less committed to the institution of marriage and therefore more inclined to leave an unhappy marriage. This was the interpretation the researchers themselves favored.

Tolerate Uncertainty.   Ultimately, learning to think critically teaches us one of the hardest lessons of life: how to live with uncertainty. It is important to examine the evidence before drawing conclusions, but sometimes there is little or no evidence available. Sometimes the evidence merely allows us to draw some tentative conclusions. And sometimes, the evidence seems good enough to permit strong conclusions . . . until, exasperatingly, new evidence throws our beliefs into disarray. Critical thinkers are willing to accept this state of uncertainty. They are not afraid to say, "I don't know" or "I'm not sure." This admission is not an evasion but a spur to further creative inquiry.

The desire for certainty often makes people uncomfortable when they go to experts for a single correct answer, and the experts cannot give it to them. Patients may demand of their doctors, "What do you mean you don't know what's wrong with me? Find out, and fix it!" Students may demand of their professors, "What do you mean it's a controversial issue? Just tell me the answer!" Critical thinkers, however, know that the more important the question, the less likely it is to have a single simple answer.

The need to accept a certain amount of uncertainty does not mean that we must live without beliefs and convictions. "The fact that today's knowledge may be overturned or at least revised tomorrow," says Ruggiero (1988), "could lead us to the kind of skepticism that refuses to embrace any idea. That would be foolish because, in the practical sense, it is impossible to build a life on that view. Besides, it is not the embracing of an idea that causes problems—it is the refusal to relax that embrace when good sense dictates doing so. It is enough to form convictions with care and carry them lightly, being willing to reconsider them whenever new evidence calls them into question."

Like the man who was delighted to learn he had been speaking prose all his life, many people are pleased to find that they already know some of these guidelines of critical and creative thinking. They do it, we might say, without thinking about it. Still, all of us could benefit from shaping up our mental muscles. In the remaining chapters, you will have many opportunities to apply critical thinking to psychological theories and to everyday life. From time to time, questions in the margin, accompanied by a small flash symbol like the one next to this paragraph, will draw your attention to discussions in which critical and creative thinking is particularly important. (Feel free to find others!) The photographs on pages 38 and 39 give a preview of some of the issues to be dis-

These odd objects may look like spaceships, but they are really lenticular (lens-shaped) clouds over Santos, Brazil. When people reason emotionally about UFOs, or anything else, they may overlook relevant evidence and ignore alternative interpretations.

cussed. The flash symbol will also appear from time to time in Quick Quizzes, to signal a question that gives you practice in critical thinking skills. In addition, a feature called "Psychology and Popular Culture," which appears in many chapters, will discuss some things to consider when you evaluate pop-psych claims that make the headlines and the talk shows.

Keep in mind, though, that critical thinking is as much an attitude as it is a set of skills. And it is a process, not a once-and-for-all accomplishment. No one ever becomes a perfect critical thinker, unaffected by emotional reasoning and wishful thinking in every area of life. We are all less open-minded than we think. We take comfort from believing that only *other* people are biased or need to think more clearly. But critical thinking requires a willingness to submit even your most cherished beliefs to honest analysis. That is why intelligent people are not always critical thinkers. Clever debaters can learn to poke holes in the arguments of others, while twisting facts or conveniently ignoring arguments that might contradict their own position. True critical thinking, in the words of philosopher Richard W. Paul (1984), is "fair-mindedness brought into the heart of everyday life."

Critical thinking is not for people who want psychology to give them final answers and simple solutions. Psychological facts do not pile up like a collection of postage stamps or trading cards. As new facts are added to our store of knowledge, others are discarded. Existing facts are continually being reorganized, reinterpreted, and assigned new meanings.

Some philosophers of science argue that, in a sense, all scientific theories *must* eventually fail. As knowledge grows, so does ignorance, for the more we know, the more questions we think to ask (Kuhn, 1981). As findings accumulate, existing theories become strained. Eventually, they cannot explain all the evidence, no matter how they are stretched. It is like trying to fit a queen-sized sheet onto a king-sized bed. When you tuck the sheet in at the head of the bed, it is too short at the bottom; when you tuck it in at the bottom, it is too short at the top. Eventually you have to get a new sheet or a new bed. Similarly, the scientist eventually is forced either to show that the new findings are wrong or to get a new theory.

Does all this mean that there is no such thing as intellectual progress? Not at all. After each failure, a new and better theory arises from the ashes of the previous one, explaining more facts, solving more puzzles. This can be frustrating for those who want psychology and other sciences to hand them some absolute truths. But it is exciting for those who love the pursuit of understanding as much as the collection of facts. As neuroscientist John C. Eccles (1981) once

recalled, his training taught him to "rejoice in the refutation of a cherished hypothesis, because that, too, is a scientific achievement and because much has been learned by the refutation."

If you are ready to share in the excitement of studying psychology—if you, like Eccles, love a mystery—then you are ready to read on.

*T*aking Psychology with You

What Psychology Can Do for You—and What It Can't

*I*f you intend to become a psychologist or a mental health professional, you have an obvious reason for taking a course in psychology. But psychology can contribute to your life in many ways, whether you plan to work in the field or not. Here are a few things psychology can do for you:

- *Make you a more informed person.* One purpose of education is to acquaint people with their cultural heritage and with humankind's achievements in literature, the humanities, and science. In contemporary society, being a well-informed person requires knowing something about psychology. One psychologist has written, "What geology was to the early nineteenth century, biology to the late nineteenth century, and physics to the first half of the twentieth century, so psychology is [to] the latter half of the twentieth century, its central major science" (Jaynes, 1973). Geologists, biologists, and physicists might not agree, but certainly psychology plays a large role in our culture.

- *Satisfy your curiosity about human nature.* When the Greek philosopher Socrates admonished his fellow human beings to "know thyself," he was only telling them to do what they wanted to do anyway. The topic that seems to fascinate human beings most is human beings. Psychology, along with the other social sciences, literature, history, and philosophy, can contribute to a better understanding of yourself and others.

- *Help you increase control over your life.* Throughout this book we will be suggesting ways in which you can apply the findings of psychology to your own life. Psychology cannot solve all your problems, but it does offer techniques that may help you handle your emotions, improve your memory, and eliminate unwanted habits. It can also foster an attitude of objectivity that is useful for analyzing your behavior and your relationships with others.

- *Help you on the job.* A bachelor's degree in psychology is useful for getting a job in a helping profession, for example, as a welfare caseworker or a rehabilitation counselor. But the study of psychology is helpful in all jobs in which psychological insights are useful. Anyone who works as a nurse, doctor, social worker, member of the clergy, police officer, or teacher can put psychology to work on the job. So can people whose jobs involve dealing with customers, such as waiters, flight attendants, bank tellers, salespeople, and receptionists. Finally, psychology can be useful to those whose jobs require them to predict people's attitudes and behavior—for example, labor negotiators, politicians, advertising copywriters, merchandise buyers, personnel managers, product designers, market researchers, magicians. . . .

- *Give you insights into political and social issues.* Crime, drug abuse, discrimination, and war are not only social issues but also psychological ones. Psychological knowledge alone cannot solve the complex political, social, and ethical problems that plague every society, but it can help you make informed judgments about them. For example, if you know that involuntary crowding often leads to stress and abnormal behavior, this knowledge may affect your views on conditions in schools and prisons. Knowing that being sexually harassed lowers a person's self-esteem and sense of control may influence your views on antiharassment legislation.

We are optimistic about psychology's role in the world, but we want to caution you that sometimes people expect things from psychology that it cannot deliver. For example,

- *It can't tell you the meaning of life.* Some people follow individual psychologists the way others follow religious leaders and gurus, hoping for enlightenment (Albee, 1977). There is no such thing, however, as instant wisdom. A philosophy about the purpose of life requires not only the acquisition of knowledge but also reflection and a willingness to learn from life's experiences.

- *It won't relieve you of responsibility for your actions.* It is one thing to understand the origins of offensive or antisocial behavior and another thing to *excuse* it. Knowing that your short temper is partly a result of your unhappy childhood doesn't give you a green light to behave abusively toward your loved ones. Nor does scientific neutrality mean that *society* must be legally or morally neutral. A better understanding of the origins of child beating may help us to reduce child abuse and to treat offenders, but we can still hold child beaters accountable.

- *It doesn't provide simple answers to complex questions.* You have already learned that psychologists, like other scientists, often disagree among themselves. This disagreement is a normal result of their differing perspectives and methods, and it reflects the fact that most human phenomena—from violence to love—do not lend themselves to one-note explanations. Rather than becoming attached to any one approach, therefore ("Medication will one day cure all mental illnesses"; "With the right environment, any child can become a Mozart"), the critical thinker will try to integrate the best contributions of each. In the epilogue to this book, we suggest how such an integration might apply to love and work.

Almost three decades ago, in a presidential address to the APA, George Miller (1969) called on his colleagues to "give psychology away." It was time, he said, for them to emerge from their laboratories and to make an impact on the world. "Psychological facts," he said, "should be passed out freely to all who need and can use them."

Ever since, critics have complained that psychologists don't know enough to "give it away." We don't agree. Behavioral scientists know that the questions they raise are difficult, harder than those tackled by such "hard" sciences as physics and chemistry (Diamond, 1987). You can't put an attitude, emotion, or thought in a test tube or measure it with calipers. But that doesn't mean human behavior is beyond understanding. Even love is yielding its secrets. At the end of each chapter, starting with the next one, you will have the opportunity to decide whether psychology does, in fact, have something to give away. The "Taking Psychology with You" section will suggest ways to apply psychological findings to your own life—at school, on the job, or in your relationships.

Summary

1. *Psychology* is the study of behavior and mental processes and how they are affected by an organism's external and internal environment. In its methods and its reliance on evidence, it differs from pseudoscience and "psychobabble."

2. Psychological findings sometimes confirm, but often contradict, common sense. When psychological results do seem obvious, it is often because people overestimate the ability they might have had to predict the outcome of a study in advance. In any case, a result does not have to be surprising to be scientifically important.

3. Until the late 1800s, psychology was not a science. A lack of *empirical evidence* often led to serious errors in the description and explanation of behavior. But psychology's forerunners, such as Descartes, also made valid observations and had useful insights.

4. The official founder of scientific psychology was Wilhelm Wundt, whose work led to *structuralism*, the first of many approaches to the field. Structuralism emphasized the analysis of immediate experience into basic elements. It was soon abandoned because of its reliance on introspection. Another early approach, *functionalism*, emphasized the purpose of behavior. It, too, did not last long as a distinct school of psychology, but it greatly affected the course of psychological science.

5. Five points of view predominate today in psychology. The *learning (or behavioral) perspective* emphasizes the study of observable behavior and rejects mentalistic explanations. The *psychodynamic perspective*, which originated with Freud's theory of psychoanalysis, emphasizes unconscious motives, conflicts, and desires. The *biological perspective* emphasizes bodily events associated with actions, thoughts, and feelings. The *cognitive perspective* emphasizes mental processes in perception, problem solving, belief formation, and other human activities. The *sociocultural perspective* emphasizes how social and cultural rules, values, and expectations affect individual beliefs and behavior. Each of these approaches has made an important contribution to psychology, and each also has its critics.

6. Not all approaches to psychology fit neatly into one of the five major perspectives. Two important social movements, *humanistic psychology* and *feminist*

psychology, have influenced the questions researchers ask, the methods they use, and their awareness of biases in the field.

7. Many, if not most, psychologists are *eclectic,* drawing on more than one school of psychology. However, they disagree about whether it will ever be possible to unite psychology under a single unifying *paradigm* or whether the discipline will continue to be a mosaic of smaller theories and findings.

8. Psychologists teach, do research, and provide mental-health services (psychological practice). *Applied* psychologists are concerned with the practical uses of psychological knowledge. *Basic* psychologists are concerned with knowledge for its own sake. Psychological specialties include, among many others, experimental, educational, developmental, industrial/organizational, psychometric, social, counseling, school, and clinical psychology.

9. *Psychotherapist* is an unregulated word for anyone who does therapy, including even persons who have no credentials or training at all. Licensed therapists differ according to their training and approach: Clinical psychologists have a Ph.D. or Psy.D.; psychiatrists have an M.D.; psychoanalysts must be trained in special psychoanalytic institutes; and social workers, counseling and school psychologists, and marriage and family counselors may have a variety of postgraduate degrees. Psychologists of all kinds also do research outside of academia, working in a wide variety of occupations and settings.

10. One of the greatest benefits of studying psychology is the development of *critical thinking* skills and attitudes. The critical thinker asks questions, defines problems clearly and accurately, examines the evidence, analyzes assumptions and biases, avoids emotional reasoning, avoids oversimplification, considers alternative interpretations, and tolerates uncertainty. Critical thinking is not for those who want psychology to give final answers and simple solutions, but it can open up many exciting paths in the pursuit of understanding.

Key Terms

Use this list to check your understanding of terms in this chapter. If you have trouble with a term, you can find it on the page listed.

psychology   *4*
sociology   *6*
anthropology   *6*
cross-cultural psychology   *6*
empirical   *7*
Wilhelm Wundt   *8*
trained introspection   *9*
structuralism   *9*
functionalism   *10*
William James   *10*
Charles Darwin   *10*
John B. Watson   *11*
behaviorism   *11*
Ivan Pavlov   *11*
B. F. Skinner   *12*
social-learning theory   *13*
Sigmund Freud   *14*
psychoanalysis   *14*
psychodynamic theories   *15*
intrapsychic   *15*
Gestalt psychology   *15*
biological perspective   *15*
evolutionary psychology   *16*

cognitive perspective   *16*
sociocultural perspective   *18*
culture   *18*
humanistic psychology   *19*
feminist psychology   *19*
paradigm   *22*
psychological practice   *23*
basic psychology   *23*
applied psychology   *23*
experimental psychologist   *24*
educational psychologist   *24*
developmental psychologist   *24*
industrial/organizational
   psychologist   *24*
psychometric psychologist   *24*
social psychologist   *24*
counseling psychologist   *25*
school psychologist   *25*
clinical psychologist   *25*
psychiatry   *25*
psychotherapist   *25*
critical thinking   *28*

What's Ahead

Thinking Critically and Creatively About Psychology

In the pages ahead, we will apply the eight guidelines to critical and creative thinking discussed in Chapter 1 to a variety of psychological topics.

1. Ask questions; be willing to wonder. *The sight of this Chinese man standing alone against awesome military might inspired millions of people around the world during the May 1989 rebellion in Tiananmen Square. What gives some people the courage to risk their lives for their beliefs? Why, in contrast, do so many people "go along with the crowd" and mindlessly obey authority? Social psychologists have probed these questions in depth, as we will see in Chapter 17.*

2. Define the problem. *People talk about "intelligence" all the time, but what is it exactly? Does the musical genius of a world-class violinist like Anne-Sophie Mutter count as a kind of intelligence? Is intelligence confined to what IQ tests measure, or does it also include other kinds of wisdom, knowledge, and "smarts." Is intelligence, however we might define it, an inborn trait, is it acquired through experience—or both? We will be taking up these issues in Chapters 3 and 8.*

3. Examine the evidence. *Illusionists such as Siegfried and Roy, when demonstrating levitation, take advantage of the fact that people are willing to trust the evidence of their own eyes even when such evidence is misleading, as discussed in Chapter 6.*

4. Analyze assumptions and biases. *Cultural and personal biases lead many people to believe that men are "naturally" less expressive emotionally than women. But which men, which emotions, and in which cultures? This Palestinian man, grieving over his dead son, does not fit Western stereotypes. As we will see in Chapters 10 and 18, cultural display rules have a powerful influence on when, how, and to whom we express our feelings.*

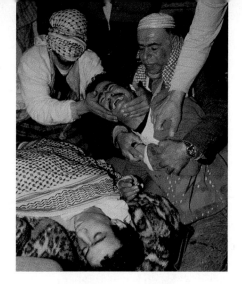

5. Avoid emotional reasoning. *Chances are that this photograph inspires an emotional reaction in you. Passionate feelings about controversial issues such as abortion can keep us from considering other viewpoints. The resolution of differences requires that we move beyond emotional reasoning ("I feel this way strongly, so I must be right") and think dialectically, weighing point and counterpoint, as discussed in Chapter 8.*

The snack for your left brain. Nutritious!
- High in fiber
- Cholesterol free
- Low in sodium and calories
- No artificial anything

© 1989 Natural Nectar Corporation

The snack for your right brain. Great taste!

Save 30¢. See reverse for coupon.

6. Don't oversimplify. *Is the left side of the brain entirely analytic, rational, and sensible? Is the right side always intuitive, emotional, and spontaneous? As we will see in Chapter 4, the two hemispheres of the brain do have some specialized talents, but it's easy to exaggerate the differences.*

7. Consider other interpretations. *These young Jamaican children, members of the Rastafarian church, are smoking ganja (marijuana), which their religion regards as a "wisdom weed." Will they react in the same way as a North American who buys the drug on the streets and smokes it alone or at a party? Many people attribute the effects of psychoactive drugs solely to the properties of the drugs themselves. An alternative explanation, however, supported by much evidence, emphasizes the importance of setting, motives, and cultural expectations, as we will see in Chapters 5 and 15.*

8. Tolerate uncertainty. *Some questions have no easy answers and may even be unanswerable in principle. For example: What are the origins of sexual orientation? Many theories have been offered, but no single explanation can account for the many variations of homosexuality or of heterosexuality, as we will see in Chapter 11.*

How Psychologists Know What They Know

In seventeenth-century France, people sought answers to their problems by throwing dice and matching the numbers to the Roman numerals and adjoining planets on this astrological "map." A separate chart matched the combinations with the answers "yes" and "no." Psychological science offers more useful and reliable methods.

The negative cautions of science
are never popular.

■ MARGARET MEAD ■

Imagine that you are the parent of a 9-year-old boy who has been diagnosed as autistic. Your child seems to live in a silent world of his own, cut off from normal social interaction with others. He rarely looks you in the eyes. He rocks back and forth for hours, staring aimlessly at the light streaming through the window. Sometimes he does such alarmingly self-destructive things as biting through the skin on his fingers or poking pencils in his ears. He does not speak, and he cannot function in a public classroom. You are determined to do something to help him.

Imagine your excitement, then, when you hear glowing reports on TV about a new technique, devised by an Australian teacher, that seems to offer your child a way out of his mental prison. According to the proponents of this technique (called "facilitated communication"), when children who are autistic or mentally impaired are placed in front of a keyboard and an adult gently places a hand over the child's hand or forearm, children who have never used words before are able to peck out complete, sensible sentences. One child reportedly typed, "I amn not a utistivc on thje typ" (I am not autistic on the typewriter). You do some investigating and find a clinic that will try facilitated communication with your son. The fee is steep, but what desperate parent wouldn't be willing to pay the price?

"Facilitated communication" is thought by some to be a breakthrough for autistic people. What does controlled research show?

The situation we have described is not hypothetical. In the past few years, thousands of hopeful parents have been drawn to the promise of facilitated communication, and many have been amazed at the results. After years of profound impairment, their children are suddenly able to answer questions, convey their needs, and divulge their inner thoughts. Some children have even requested high school level math and reading, and done well on them. Facilitated communication, say its boosters, is a miracle.

Or is it?

Psychological scientists would not be content with clinical claims alone, nor would they be persuaded by the poignant stories of parents who believe in the value of facilitated communication. They would want to test those claims and to check out those stories in a controlled, unbiased manner—and that is just what they have done, in research involving hundreds of autistic children and adults (Jacobson et al., 1994; Mulick, 1994; Ogletree et al., 1993; Szempruch & Jacobson, 1993). In one experiment, researchers arranged things so that the child's facilitator could not see a series of pictures presented to the child or hear the questions the child was being asked about the pictures. Under these conditions, autistic children showed no unexpected linguistic or communicative abilities, even after 20 hours of training (Eberlin et al., 1993). In another study, 12 facilitators chosen because of their reputed talents were asked to work with 12 young and middle-aged autistic adults. The autistic individual and the facilitator each saw a series of pictures, which the autistic person was supposed to describe by typing some words on the keyboard. On some trials they saw the same picture and on other trials they saw different ones. Whenever the pictures

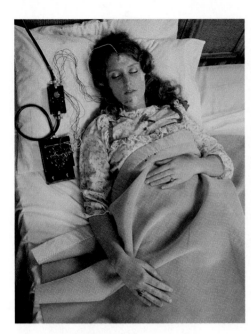

Innovative research methods have enabled psychologists to study many questions that once seemed unanswerable. Here, a volunteer in a sleep experiment slumbers while researchers measure her brain and muscle activity. If awakened during periods of rapid eye movement, she is likely to report that she has been dreaming.

differed, the only correct descriptions typed out by the autistic subjects were for the pictures that had been shown to the *facilitator* but not the autistic person (Wheeler et al., 1993).

What happens in facilitated communication, it seems, is exactly what happens when a medium or spiritualist guides a person's hand over a Ouija board to help the person receive "messages" about the future: The person doing the facilitating is unconsciously nudging the other person's hand in the desired direction (Dillon, 1993). Facilitated communication, on closer inspection, turns out to be *facilitator* communication (Cummins & Prior, 1992; Green, 1994). This finding is important, because if parents waste their time and money on a treatment that doesn't work, they may never get the kind of help for their children that is actually helpful—and they may suffer terribly when their false hopes are finally demolished by reality.

You can see, then, why research methods are so important to psychologists. These methods are the tools of the psychologist's trade. They allow researchers to separate the kernel of truth from the chaff of unfounded belief. They offer a way to sort out conflicting views and to correct false ideas that may otherwise cause people enormous harm. They encourage the replacement of simplistic questions by more sophisticated and valuable ones. As we will see in this book, an innovative or clever research method can even reveal answers to questions about behavior that once seemed impossible to study.

■ SCIENCE VERSUS PSEUDOSCIENCE

Perhaps you are saying to yourself, "Okay, psychologists need to know about research methods. But why do *I* have to? Why not get right to the findings?" In this section, we will give you two answers. Then we will look at the assumptions and procedures that you will need to understand if you are to distinguish good science from bad.

Why Study Methodology?

One reason to study methodology is that it can help you identify fallacies in your own or other people's thinking. For instance, we are all vulnerable to the *confirmation bias*, the tendency to look for evidence that supports our ideas and to ignore evidence that does not. Sometimes this bias can have profound personal consequences. Some adults who were physically or sexually abused early in life are afraid to have children of their own because they think their experience has ruined them as potential parents. Social workers, judges, and other professionals sometimes make the same assumption: One judge denied a woman custody of her children solely because the woman had been abused as a child, even though she had never harmed her own children. Judgments such as these rely on the notion that abuse inevitably breeds abuse—an inference based mainly on the confirming cases of abused children who later became abusive adults. What about children who suffer abuse but do not grow up to mistreat their children? A person knowledgeable about scientific methodology would consider both groups, as well as people who were not abused as children and then grew up to be—or not to be—abusive parents (see Table 2.1). When you take all the existing data into account, you find that although being abused is definitely a risk factor for becoming an abusive parent, and for other destructive behaviors as well, most abused children do *not* grow up to mistreat their own offspring (Kaufman & Zigler, 1987; Widom, 1989). (Many other mental stumbling blocks also interfere with the ability to make sound decisions and to predict behavior accurately; you will find some further examples in "Taking Psychology with You" at the end of this chapter and later in Chapter 8.)

A second reason for studying methodology is to become a more critical and sophisticated consumer of psychological findings. Psychology can be useful to you in many ways, but you should not accept every reported finding uncritically. You are constantly being barraged with conflicting claims about matters that can affect your life—claims about how you should break bad habits, manage your emotions, dress for success, settle disputes, overcome shyness, improve your love life, or reduce stress. Not all studies on such matters are good ones, and some advice from self-styled experts is based on no evidence at all.

Psychologists have shown that when college students lack an adequate understanding of research methods, they tend to base their responses to research on how well the results happen to confirm their own expectations. If

✸ A psychologist has published a paper in which she states that nearly all the abusive parents in a sample from large midwestern city were mistreated as children. Does this mean that most children who are abused will grow up to become abusive parents?

Table 2.1   Examining the Evidence

Is an abused child likely to become an abusive parent? People often base their answers solely on confirming cases, represented by the upper left-hand cell of this table. Psychological researchers consider all four types of evidence in the table.

		Abused as a child?	
		Yes	**No**
Abusive parent?	**Yes**	Abused children who become abusive parents	Nonabused children who become abusive parents
	No	Abused children who do not become abusive parents	Nonabused children who do not become abusive parents

the findings match their expectations, students usually feel confident about accepting them, even when the study's methods do not justify such confidence. But after students learn how to evaluate specific aspects of a study's design (for example, the way in which the participants were selected), they stop to consider the procedures used before drawing any conclusions (Forsyth, Arpey, & Stratton-Hess, 1992). We hope that when you hear and read about psychological issues, you, too, will consider how the information was obtained and how the results were interpreted, using guidelines presented in this chapter.

What Makes Research Scientific?

When we refer to psychologists as scientists, we do not mean that they work with complicated gadgets and machines or wear white lab coats (although some do). The scientific enterprise has more to do with attitudes and procedures than with apparatus. Philosophers and scientists have written many fat books on the features that distinguish science from other ways of knowing. Here are a few key characteristics of the ideal scientist:

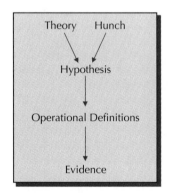

1. *Precision.* Scientists usually start out with a **hypothesis,** a statement that attempts to describe or explain behavior. Initially, the hypothesis may be stated in general terms, as in "Misery loves company." But before any research can be done, the hypothesis must be put into specific terms; for example, "People who are anxious about a threatening situation tend to seek out others who face the same threat."

Some hypotheses are suggested by previous findings or casual observations. Others are derived from a general **theory,** an organized system of assumptions and principles that purports to explain certain phenomena and how they are related. A scientific theory is not just a bunch of hunches or opinions (as in "It's only a theory"). Theories that come to be accepted by a large part of the scientific community are consistent with many different observations and inconsistent with only a few (Stanovich, 1992).

A hypothesis leads to explicit predictions about what will happen in a particular situation. In a prediction, vague terms such as *anxiety* or *threatening situation* are given **operational definitions** that specify how they are to be observed and measured. For example, *anxiety* might be defined as a score on an anxiety questionnaire and *threatening situation* as the threat of an electric shock. The prediction might be, "If you raise people's anxiety scores by telling them they are going to receive electric shocks, and then you give them the choice of waiting alone or with others in the same situation, they will be more likely to choose to wait with others than they would be if they were not anxious." The prediction is then tested, using scientific procedures.

In contrast, *pseudoscientists*—people who pretend to be scientific but aren't—often hide behind vague and empty terms and make predictions that are nearly meaningless. If your astrological forecast tells you that "today will be a good time to take care of unfinished tasks," what have you learned? Isn't every day a good one for tackling chores?

2. *Skepticism.* Scientists do not accept ideas on faith or authority; their motto is "Show me!" Some of the greatest scientific advances have been made by those who dared to doubt what everyone else assumed to be true: that the sun revolves around the earth, that illness can be cured by applying leeches to the skin, that madness is a sign of demonic possession. In the world of the researcher, skepticism means accepting conclusions, both new and old, with caution. Caution, however, must be balanced by an openness to new ideas and evidence. Otherwise, the scientist may wind up as shortsighted as the famous

■ **hypothesis**

A statement that attempts to predict or to account for a set of phenomena. Scientific hypotheses specify relationships among events or variables and are supported or disconfirmed by empirical investigation.

■ **theory**

An organized system of assumptions and principles that purports to explain a specified set of phenomena and their interrelationships.

■ **operational definition**

A precise definition of a term in a hypothesis, which specifies the operations for observing and measuring the process or phenomenon being defined.

physicist Lord Kelvin, who at the end of the nineteenth century reputedly declared with great confidence that radio had no future, X rays were a hoax, and "heavier-than-air flying machines" were impossible.

3. *Reliance on empirical evidence.* Unlike plays and poems, scientific theories and hypotheses are not judged by how artistically pleasing or entertaining they are. An idea may initially generate excitement because it is plausible, imaginative, or appealing; but no matter how true or right it may seem, eventually it must be backed by evidence if it is to be taken seriously. As Nobel Prize–winning scientist Peter Medawar (1979) wrote, "The intensity of the conviction that a hypothesis is true has no bearing on whether it is true or not." Further, as we noted in Chapter 1, the evidence for a scientific idea must be *empirical,* that is, based on systematic observation. A collection of personal accounts or anecdotes, or an appeal to authority, will not do.

Consider, again, the problem of childhood autism. At one time, many clinicians thought that this disorder was caused by a rejecting, cold "refrigerator mother." They were influenced in this belief by the writings of the eminent psychoanalyst Bruno Bettelheim. Bettelheim's evidence was meager, to say the least. In his book *The Empty Fortress* (1967), he presented case studies of three autistic children whose mothers had a history of psychological problems. He also alluded to 37 other cases but published no facts about any of them. Yet Bettelheim's authority was so great that many people accepted his claims unquestioningly, despite the flimsiness of his argument.

Then some researchers began to have doubts about Bettelheim's notion that bad mothers cause autistic children. They decided to compare the parents of autistic children with parents who did not have an autistic child. Instead of relying on subjective impressions, as Bettelheim had done, these researchers used standardized tests of psychological adjustment and analyzed their data statistically. The results were clear: On personality traits, marital adjustment, or family life, parents of autistic children were no different, on the average, than parents of normal children (DeMyer, 1975; Koegel et al., 1983). Bruno Bettelheim had been wrong. Yet because of his advice, thousands of parents had been led to believe that they were responsible for their children's disorder, suffering needless guilt and remorse. Today there is general agreement that autism stems from a neurological problem rather than any psychological problems of the parents.

4. *Willingness to make "risky predictions."* A scientist must state an idea in such a way that it can be *refuted,* or disproved by counterevidence. This principle, known as the **principle of falsifiability,** does not mean that the idea *will* be refuted, only that it *could* be if contrary evidence were to be discovered. Another way of saying this is that a scientist must predict not only what will happen, but also what will *not* happen. A willingness to make such risky predictions forces scientists to take negative evidence seriously. Any researcher who refuses to go out on a limb and risk disconfirmation is not a true scientist.

This characteristic is a little tricky, so let's take an example. Some people believe that they can find subterranean water by holding a "dowsing rod" out in front of them and walking around until the rod bends down toward water hidden belowground. Some dowsers use special steel rods; others prefer such mundane objects as a straightened coat hanger or a forked branch. Dowsers believe that they are psychically tuned in to the presence of water and that this accounts for the rod's behavior; actually it is due to involuntary movements of their own hands. (Unconscious hand movements again!)

James Randi (1982), who has been using his professional training as a magician to debunk the fraudulent claims of psychics and others who claim to have paranormal abilities, has been challenging the claims of dowsers for years by conducting controlled tests using scientific procedures to which the dowsers themselves agree. Randi offers a prize of thousands of dollars to any dowser who proves

■ **principle of falsifiability**
The principle that a scientific theory must make predictions that are specific enough to expose the theory to the possibility of disconfirmation— that is, the theory must predict not only what will happen, but also what will not happen.

Can this "dowser" find water by pointing a stick at the ground? Believers in parapsychology often ignore the negative evidence.

him wrong. He has never lost a cent; invariably the dowsers perform at levels no better than chance. Yet despite these failures, the dowsers rarely lose faith in their abilities. Instead, they blame the alignment of the planets, or sunspots, or bad vibes from spectators. Thus it really doesn't matter at all how the dowsing demonstration turns out, because the dowser already has all the bases covered in advance. *Any theory that purports to explain everything that could conceivably happen is unscientific.*

If you keep your eyes open, you will find many violations of the principle of falsifiability around you every day. For example, psychiatric workers and FBI and police investigators have been unable to substantiate the supposedly murderous activities of satanic cults, but that doesn't keep some police officers from believing in the reality of such cults' misdeeds (Hicks, 1991). The officers, and others who believe that such cults are widespread, say they are not surprised by the lack of evidence because satanic cults cover up their murders by eating bodies or burying them. The lack of evidence, they say, is actually a sign of the cults' success. But think about that claim. If a lack of evidence can count as evidence, what could possibly count as *counter*evidence?

5. *Openness.* Scientists must be willing to tell others where they got their ideas, how they tested them, and what the results were. They must do this clearly and in detail so that other scientists can repeat, or *replicate*, their studies and verify the findings.

Replication is an important part of the scientific process, because sometimes what seems to be a fabulous finding turns out to have been only a fluke. Many decades ago, a team of researchers trained flatworms to cringe in response to a flashing light. Then they killed the worms, ground them into a mash, and fed the mash to a second set of worms. This cannibalistic diet, the researchers reported, sped up acquisition of the cringe response in the second group of worms (McConnell, 1962). As you can imagine, this report generated tremendous excitement. If worms could learn faster by ingesting the memory molecules of their fellow worms, could memory pills be far behind? Students joked about grinding up professors; professors joked about doing brain transplants in students. But alas, the results proved difficult to replicate, and talk of memory pills eventually faded away.

Do psychologists and other scientists always live up to the lofty standards expected of them? Of course not. Being human, they may put too much trust in their personal experiences. They may deceive themselves. They may permit ambition to interfere with openness. They may fail to put their theories fully to the test: It is always easier to be skeptical about someone else's ideas than about your own pet theory. Even Albert Einstein sometimes resisted data that might have disconfirmed his own ideas.

Commitment to one's theories is not in itself a bad thing. Passion is the fuel of progress. It motivates researchers to think boldly, defend unpopular ideas, and do the exhaustive testing that is often required to support an idea. But passion can also cloud perceptions and in some sad cases has even led to deception and fraud. That is why science must be a *communal activity*. Scientists are expected to share their evidence and procedures with others. They are expected to present their results in professional journals, which submit the findings to critical review by other experts in the field before publishing them. Through this process of "peer review," scientists demonstrate to the satisfaction of others that their position is well supported. The scientific community—in our case, the psychological community—acts as a jury, scrutinizing and sifting the evidence, approving some viewpoints and relegating others to the scientific scrap heap. This public process is not perfect, but it does give science a built-in system of checks and balances. Individuals are not necessarily objective or even rational, but science forces them to justify their claims.

Quick QUIZ

Test your understanding of science by identifying which of its rules was violated in each of the following cases.

1. For years, writer Norman Cousins told how he had cured himself of a rare and life-threatening disease through a combination of humor and vitamins. His book about his experience, *Anatomy of an Illness,* became a huge best-seller.
2. Alfred Russel Wallace hit upon the theory of evolution at about the same time that Charles Darwin did. Later, he became fascinated by attempts to communicate with the dead. To prove that such communication was possible, he had mediums conduct séances. He trusted these mediums and was persuaded by their demonstrations.
3. Benjamin Rush, a physician and signer of the Declaration of Independence, believed that illnesses accompanied by fever should be treated by bloodletting. During an outbreak of yellow fever, many patients whom he treated in this manner died. Yet Rush did not lose faith in his approach; he attributed each case of improvement to his treatment and each death to the severity of the disease (Stanovich, 1992).

Answers:

1. Cousins offered only a personal account and ignored disconfirming evidence. 2. Wallace was gullible rather than skeptical. 3. Rush violated the principle of falsifiability: He interpreted a patient's survival as support for his treatment and explained a death by saying that the person had been too ill for the treatment to work. Thus there was no possible counterevidence that could refute the theory (which, by the way, was dead wrong—the "treatment" was actually as dangerous as the disease).

■ FERRETING OUT THE FACTS: DESCRIPTIVE STUDIES

Psychologists use several different methods in their research, depending on the kinds of questions they want to answer. These methods are not mutually exclusive. Just as a police detective may use a magnifying glass *and* a fingerprint duster *and* interviews of suspects to figure out "who done it," psychological sleuths often draw on different techniques at different stages of an ongoing investigation.

Many psychological methods are descriptive in nature. **Descriptive methods** allow a researcher to describe and predict behavior, but they usually do not allow the researcher to choose one explanation over other, competing ones. Some of these methods are used primarily by clinicians to describe individual traits and problems. Others are used primarily by researchers to compare groups of people and to arrive at generalizations about behavior. And some methods can be used in either way. In this section, we will discuss the most common descriptive methods. As you read, you might want to list each method's advantages and disadvantages on a piece of paper. When you finish this and the next two sections, check your list against the one in Table 2.2 on p. 63.

Case Studies

A **case study** (or *case history*) is a detailed description of a particular individual. It may be based on careful observation or on formal psychological testing.

■ **descriptive methods**
Methods that yield descriptions of behavior but not necessarily causal explanations.

■ **case study**
A detailed description of a particular individual under study or treatment.

It may include information about the person's childhood, dreams, fantasies, experiences, relationships, and hopes—anything that will increase insight into the person's behavior. Case studies are most commonly used by clinicians, but they are occasionally used by academic researchers as well. They are especially valuable in the investigation of a new topic. Many early language researchers started out by keeping detailed diaries on the language development of their own children. A case study can be a rich source of hypotheses for future research.

Case studies illustrate psychological principles in a way that abstract generalizations and cold statistics never can. They also produce a more detailed picture of an individual than other methods do. Often, however, case studies depend on people's memories of the past, and such memories may be both selective and inaccurate. Moreover, it can be hard to choose one interpretation of a case over another. Most important, the case method has limited usefulness for psychologists who want to generalize about human behavior, because a person who is the subject of a case study may be unlike most other people about whom the researcher would like to draw conclusions. One of Bettelheim's errors, you will recall, was to assume that the three mothers he studied were representative of all parents of autistic children.

Still, case studies can be enlightening when practical or ethical considerations prevent information from being gathered in other ways, or when unusual circumstances shed light on a general issue. Let's take an example. Many psychologists believe that a critical period for normal language development occurs between age 1 and age 5 or 6, with the likelihood of mastering a first language declining steadily after that and falling off drastically at puberty (Curtiss, 1977; Pinker, 1994b; Tartter, 1986). During these years, children need to hear speech (or if they are deaf, to see signs) and to enjoy close relationships with people who give them an opportunity to practice the arts and skills of conversation. If children lack these early experiences, they will be unable to catch up completely later on, no matter how much tutoring they are given. How can psychologists test this hypothesis? Obviously, they cannot put children in solitary confinement until adolescence! However, they can study the tragic cases of children who were abandoned, abused, and isolated by their parents and were therefore prevented from acquiring language until they were rescued, sometimes after many years of solitude. Such cases often leave important questions unanswered: How long was the child alone? At what age was the child isolated or abandoned? Was the child born mentally impaired? Did the child have a chance to learn any language before the ordeal began? Nonetheless, these cases can still provide valuable information.

One such case involved a 13-year-old girl whose parents had locked her up in one small room since age 1½. During the day they usually strapped her in a child's potty seat. At night, they confined her to a straitjacket-like sleeping bag. The mother, a battered wife who lived in terror of her severely disturbed husband, barely cared for her daughter. Although the child may have been able to hear some speech through the walls of her room, there was no television or radio in the home, and no one spoke a word to her. If she made the slightest sound, her father beat her with a large block of wood.

Genie, as researchers later called her, hardly seemed human when she was finally set free. She did not know how to chew or to stand erect, and she was not toilet trained. She slobbered uncontrollably, masturbated in public, and spit on anything that was handy, including herself and other people. When she was first observed by psychologists, her only sounds were high-pitched whimpers. She understood only a few words, probably learned shortly after her release.

This picture was drawn by Genie, the adolescent girl described in the text who endured years of isolation and mistreatment. It shows one of Genie's favorite pastimes: listening to researcher Susan Curtiss play classical music on the piano. Genie's drawings were used along with other case material to study her mental and social development.

Yet Genie was alert and curious. Placed in a hospital rehabilitation center and then a foster home, she made rapid progress. She developed physically, learned some basic rules of social conduct, and established relationships. Gradually she began to use words and understand short sentences, and to use language to convey her needs, describe her moods, and even tell lies. However, her grammar and pronunciation of words remained abnormal. She could not use pronouns correctly, ask questions, produce proper negative sentences, or use the little word endings that communicate tense, conjunction, number, and possession (Curtiss, 1977, 1982; Rymer, 1993). Susan Curtiss, who studied Genie's language development as part of her doctoral work, concluded that Genie's case supported the critical-period hypothesis.

Ironically, then, unusual cases can sometimes shed light on a general question about human functioning. Most case studies, however, are *sources* rather than *tests* of hypotheses. You should be extremely cautious about pop-psych books and TV programs that present only testimonials and vivid case histories as evidence.

Observational Studies

In **observational studies,** the researcher systematically observes and records behavior without interfering in any way with the people being observed. Unlike case studies, observational studies usually involve many different subjects. Often an observational study is the first step in a program of research; it's helpful to have a good description of behavior before you try to explain it.

The primary purpose of *naturalistic observation* is to describe behavior as it occurs in the natural environment. Ethologists such as Jane Goodall and the late Dian Fossey used this method to study apes and other animals in the wild. Psychologists use naturalistic observation wherever people happen to be—at home, on playgrounds, and in schoolrooms and offices. In one study using naturalistic observation, a social psychologist and his students ventured into a common human habitat: bars. They wanted to know whether people in bars drink more when they are in groups than when they are alone. They visited all 32 pubs in a midsized city, ordered beers, and recorded on napkins and pieces of newspaper how much the other patrons imbibed. They found that drinkers in groups consumed more than individuals who were alone. Those

▪ **observational study**
A study in which the researcher carefully and systematically observes and records behavior without interfering with the behavior; includes naturalistic and laboratory observations.

Psychologists often venture into the field to do observational studies. The man asking for a handout is actually a psychologist studying how people react to panhandlers. A tape recorder hidden under his shirt records their responses. (Copyright © 1990, Los Angeles Times.)

in groups didn't drink any faster; they just lingered in the bar longer (Sommer, 1977).

Note that the student researchers in this study did not rely on their impressions or memories of how much people drank. In observational studies, it is important to *count*, *rate*, or *measure* behavior in a systematic way. This procedure helps to minimize the tendency of most observers to notice only what they expect or want to see. Careful record keeping ensures accuracy and allows different observers to cross-check their observations. Cross-checking is necessary to make sure the observations are reliable, or consistent, from person to person. Note, too, that the researchers who studied drinking habits took pains to avoid being obvious about what they were doing. If they had marched in with video cameras and announced that they were psychology students, people might not have behaved naturally. In other studies, researchers have often concealed themselves entirely. When such precautions are taken, naturalistic observation gives us a glimpse of subjects as they really are, in their normal social contexts. However, it does *not* tell us what caused their behavior. For example, the barroom results do not necessarily mean that being in a group makes people drink a lot. People may join a group because they are already interested in drinking and find it more comfortable to hang around the bar if they are with others.

Sometimes it is preferable or necessary to make observations in the laboratory rather than in real-world settings. In *laboratory observation*, the psychologist has more control. He or she can use sophisticated equipment, determine how many people will be observed at once, maintain a clear line of vision while observing, and so forth. Suppose, for example, that you want to know how infants of different ages respond when left with a stranger. You could observe children at a nursery school, but most would probably already be toddlers and would know the nursery school teachers. You could visit private homes, but that might be slow and inconvenient. A solution would be to have parents and their infants come to your laboratory, observe them together for a while through a one-way window, then have a stranger enter the room and, a few minutes later, have the parent leave. You could record signs of distress, interactions with the stranger, and other behavior. If you used this procedure, you would find that

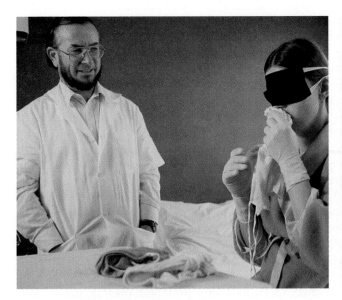

In the laboratory, researchers have better control over the factors they are investigating than they do in ordinary settings. For example, in the natural environment, it might be hard to know if mothers and infants can recognize one another's odors because of other distractions and scents (such as the aroma of dinner cooking). But by using laboratory methods, French ethologist Hubert Montagner (1985), shown on the left, has found that mothers can distinguish their own baby's shirt from the shirts of other newborns on the basis of smell alone. Similarly, parent–child interactions can sometimes be observed more efficiently in the laboratory, where there are no interruptions and researchers can take advantage of technical equipment, as in the photo on the right.

very young infants carry on cheerfully with whatever they are doing when the parent leaves. However, by the age of about 8 months they often burst into tears or show other signs of what child psychologists call "separation anxiety" (Ainsworth, 1979).

One shortcoming of laboratory observation, however, is that the presence of researchers and special equipment may cause subjects to behave differently than they would in their normal surroundings. Another is that laboratory observations, like naturalistic observations, are more useful for describing behavior than for explaining it. When we observe infants wailing whenever a parent leaves the room, we cannot be sure *why* they are protesting. Is it because they have become attached to their parents and want them nearby, or have they learned from experience that crying brings attention and affection? It is hard to answer such questions on the basis of observational studies alone.

Tests

Psychological tests are procedures used for measuring and evaluating personality traits, emotional states, aptitudes, interests, abilities, and values. Typically, such tests require people to answer a series of written or oral questions. The answers may then be totaled to yield a single numerical score (or a set of scores) that reveals something about the person. *Objective tests,* also called "inventories," measure beliefs, feelings, or behaviors of which an individual is aware. In contrast, *projective tests* are designed to tap unconscious feelings or motives (see Chapter 12).

At one time or another, most people have probably taken a psychological test, such as an intelligence test, achievement test, or vocational aptitude test.

■ **psychological tests**
Procedures used to measure and evaluate personality traits, emotional states, aptitudes, interests, abilities, and values.

Computerized psychological tests are in wide use.

You may have taken other kinds of tests when applying for a job, joining the military, or starting psychotherapy. Hundreds of psychological tests are used in industry, education, research, and the helping professions. Some are given to individuals, others to large groups. These measures help clarify differences among individuals, as well as differences in the reactions of the same individual on different occasions or at different stages of life. They may be used to promote self-understanding, to evaluate treatments and programs, or, in scientific research, to draw generalizations about human behavior.

One test of a good test is whether it is **standardized**—that is, whether there are uniform procedures for giving and scoring it. It would hardly be fair to give some people detailed instructions and plenty of time and others only vague instructions and limited time. Those who administer the test must know exactly how to explain the tasks involved, how much time to allow, and what materials to use. Scoring is usually done by referring to **norms,** which are established standards of performance. The usual procedure for developing norms is to give the test to a large group of people who resemble those for whom the test is intended. Norms tell users of the test which scores can be considered high, low, or average.

Test construction, administration, and interpretation present many challenges. For one thing, the test must be **reliable**—that is, it must produce the same results from one time and place to the next. A vocational interest test is not reliable if it tells Tom that he would make a wonderful engineer but a poor journalist, and then gives different results when Tom retakes the test a week later. Psychologists evaluate a test's reliability in several ways. For example, they may measure *test–retest reliability* by giving the test twice to the same group of people, then comparing the two sets of scores statistically. If the test is reliable, individuals' scores will be similar from one session to another. This method has a drawback, however. People tend to do better the second time they take a test, after they have become familiar with the strategies required and the actual test items used. Another approach is to compute *alternate-forms reliability,* by giving different versions of the same test to the same group on two separate occasions. The items on the two forms are similar in format but are not identical in content. With this method, performance cannot improve because of familiarity with the items, although people may still do somewhat better the second time around because they have learned the general strategies and procedures expected of them.

In order to be useful, a test must also be **valid;** that is, it must measure what it sets out to measure. A creativity test is not valid if what it actually measures is verbal sophistication. If the items are broadly representative of the trait in question, the test is said to have *content validity.* Suppose you constructed a test to measure employees' job satisfaction. If your test tapped a broad sampling of relevant beliefs and behaviors (e.g., "Do you feel you have reached a dead end at work?" "Are you bored with your assignments?"), it would have content validity. If the test asked only how workers felt about their salary level, it would lack content validity and would be of little use; highly paid people are not always satisfied with their jobs, nor are poorly paid people always dissatisfied.

Most tests are also judged on *criterion validity,* the ability to predict other, independent measures, or criteria, of the trait in question. A test can have criterion validity and thus be useful even when some individual items don't *look* valid or sensible to the test-taker. The criterion for a scholastic aptitude test might be college grades; the criterion for a test of shyness might be behavior in social situations. To find out if your job-satisfaction test had criterion validity, you might return a year later to see whether it correctly predicted absenteeism, resignations, or requests for job transfers.

Unfortunately, teachers, parents, and employers do not always stop to question a test's validity, especially when results are summarized in a single number such as an IQ score or a job applicant's ranking. Enthralled by the test score, they may simply assume that the test measures what it claims to measure.

■ **standardize**

In test construction, to develop uniform procedures for giving and scoring a test.

■ **norms**

In test construction, established standards of performance.

■ **reliability**

In test construction, the consistency, from one time and place to another, of scores derived from a test.

■ **validity**

The ability of a test to measure what it was designed to measure.

Robert Sternberg (1988) has noted that this assumption is especially common with mental tests, even though, he argues, such tests tap only a limited set of abilities important for intelligent behavior. "There is allure to exact-sounding numbers," says Sternberg. "An IQ of 119, a SAT score of 580, a mental abilities score in the 74th percentile—all sound very precise. . . . But the appearance of precision is no substitute for the fact of validity."

Among psychologists and educators, the validity of even some widely used tests is controversial. For example, "integrity tests," which probe for such personality traits as hostility to authority, conscientiousness, and "wayward impulses," are given to millions of job applicants each year in an effort to predict dishonesty and drug use in the workplace. Such tests may be more reliable and valid than interviews and other methods, but they generally fail to meet the standards of experts in assessment. Experts disagree about what these tests are actually measuring, and some are extremely worried that many people who fail such tests are misclassified and are not actually dishonest (Camera & Schneider, 1994; Sackett, 1994; Saxe, 1994).

How would you feel if you had to take a test on entering college that would supposedly reveal whether you are likely to cheat? Would you take it? Why or why not?

The Scholastic Assessment Test—formerly called the Scholastic Aptitude Test—has also come under fire. Stuart Katz and his colleagues studied the Reading Comprehension section of this test, which requires students to read a passage and then answer multiple-choice questions about it (Katz, Blackburn, & Lautenschlager, 1991; Katz & Lautenschlager, 1994). Undergraduates, they found, can do well on most questions *even without reading the passages,* although not as well as when they do read them. Consider this item, from the 1983 version of the SAT:

According to the author, it is the duty of children's literature to:

   a. protect children from learning anything unpleasant or distressing
   b. simplify moral issues so that children can understand them
   c. force children to deal with the facts of pain and suffering
   d. reassure children that every problem has a solution
   e. present truth in a way that children can accept and understand

Did you get the answer? It's *e.* Many people can figure out the right response by drawing on their knowledge of cultural values concerning children. Katz and his colleagues concluded that SAT reading-comprehension items do not measure pure reading comprehension as they are purported to do; these items also tap general knowledge and test-taking skills. That conclusion might be important for test-takers to know because guidelines for taking the SAT advise them to *ignore* background knowledge when answering the items.

Criticisms and reevaluations of psychological tests are what keep psychological assessment honest and scientifically rigorous. In contrast, the pseudoscientific psychological tests frequently found in magazines and newspapers usually have not been evaluated for validity or reliability. These questionnaires often have inviting headlines such as "How's Your Power Motivation?" or "Are You Self-destructive?" or "The Seven Types of Lover." But these tests are really only lists of questions that someone thought up without any concern for reliability or validity.

Surveys

Psychological tests generate information about people indirectly. Questionnaires and interviews that gather information about people by asking them *directly* about their experiences, attitudes, or opinions are called **surveys.** Most people are familiar with surveys in the form of national opinion polls, such as the Gallup and Roper polls. Surveys have been done on many topics, from consumer preferences to sexual preferences—and sometimes they not only reflect people's attitudes and behavior but also influence them (see "Think About It").

■ **surveys**
Questionnaires and interviews that ask people directly about their experiences, attitudes, or opinions.

Surveys provide a lot of information quickly, but the information may or may not be useful, depending on the procedures used to construct the questions and select the participants.

■ *Your favorite magazine has just published a sensational survey of its female readers, called "The Sex Life of the American Wife." The survey reports that "Eighty-seven percent of all wives like to make love in rubber boots." Is this claim justified? What would be a more accurate title for the survey?*

■ **sample**

A group of subjects selected from a population for study, in order to estimate characteristics of the population.

■ **representative sample**

A sample that matches the population in question on important characteristics such as age and sex.

■ **volunteer bias**

A shortcoming of findings derived from a sample of volunteers instead of a representative sample.

Surveys produce bushels of data, but they are not easy to do well. The biggest hurdle is getting a **sample,** a group of subjects, that is **representative** of the larger population that the researcher wishes to describe. Suppose you want to know about drug use among college sophomores. You can't question every college sophomore in the country; instead, you must choose a sample. Special procedures can be used to ensure that this sample will be representative—that is, that it will contain the same proportion of women, men, blacks, whites, poor people, rich people, Catholics, Jews, and so on, as the general population of college sophomores.

A sample's size is less critical than its representativeness; a small but representative sample may yield extremely accurate results, whereas a survey or poll that fails to use proper sampling methods may yield questionable results no matter how large the sample. A radio station that asks its listeners to vote yes or no by telephone on a controversial question is not conducting a scientific poll. Only those who feel quite strongly about the issue *and* who happen to be listening to that particular station are likely to call in, and those who feel strongly may be likely to take a particular side. A psychologist or statistician would say that the poll suffers from a **volunteer bias:** Those who volunteer probably differ from those who stay silent.

Many magazines—*Redbook, Cosmopolitan, Playboy, The Ladies' Home Journal*—have done highly publicized surveys on the sexual habits of their readers, but these surveys, too, are vulnerable to the volunteer bias. Readers motivated to respond to these surveys may be more (or possibly less) sexually active, on the average, than those who do not respond. In addition, people who read magazines regularly tend to be younger, more educated, and more affluent than the population as a whole, and these characteristics may affect the results. When you read about a survey (or any other kind of study), always ask what sorts of people participated. A biased, nonrepresentative sample does not necessarily mean that a survey is worthless or uninteresting, but it does mean that the results may not hold for other groups.

A final problem with surveys is that people sometimes lie. This is especially likely when the survey is about a touchy topic ("What? Me do that? Never!"). The likelihood of lying is reduced when respondents are guaranteed anonymity. Also, there are some ways to check for lying—for example, by asking a question several times in different ways. But not all surveys use these techniques, and even when people do not intentionally lie, they may misinterpret the survey questions or misremember their own past behavior (Tanur, 1992). For example, in studies of stress and coping strategies, men sometimes recall using "instrumental" (problem-focused) strategies more than women do, and women recall using "expressive" (emotion-focused) strategies more than men do. But when Sandra Hamilton and Beverly Fagot (1988) interviewed college students three times a week over an eight-week period about stressful events of the preceding 24 hours, using a checklist of common stressful events, the gender difference evaporated.

When you read the results of any survey, you need to ask how the questions were phrased. Political pollsters often design questions intended to produce the results they want: The item "Do you think we should cut the crime rate by locking felons up for life after they commit three violent crimes?" will get a different response than "Are you prepared to pay higher taxes to enforce a three-

*T*hink About It

*S*urveys, Public Opinion, and You

- According to a nationwide survey, 87 percent of all students have had sexual intercourse by age 16.
- According to a nationwide survey, 37 percent of all students have had sexual intercourse by age 16.

Do you find yourself wanting to believe one of these results rather than the other because it matches your own sexual history? Would one figure make you feel normal and the other make you feel odd? Might either finding influence you to change your own behavior? If so, you are not alone. Opinion polls and surveys not only reflect but can also *affect* people's feelings and behavior.

Many people form their views by studying a sample of one: themselves. Or perhaps they expand the sample a bit to include their sister, their best friend, and the neighborhood grocer. They assume that their own beliefs and actions, or those of people they know, are typical of "most people." Gary Marks and Norman Miller (1987) call this tendency the *false-consensus effect.* By overestimating the degree of agreement between themselves and others, say Marks and Miller, people maintain their self-esteem and reduce the discomfort of feeling different or weird. But the false-consensus effect can also keep people from recognizing other points of view and can make them discount information that challenges their own ways.

In addition to thinking that everyone is like them, people tend to think that they themselves ought to be like everyone else. As a consequence, when they find themselves in the minority, they may become apathetic, feeling that "there's no point trying to do anything." Or they may do things they consider wrong, or even alter their beliefs, because it appears

that everybody (according to the surveys) is doing something or holds some opinion, and they don't want to be different. Sociologist Elisabeth Noelle-Neumann (1984) has argued that this tendency to unconsciously tailor opinions to fit prevailing trends makes public opinion a potent form of social control. She describes a German election in which two parties were neck and neck until polls gave one party a slight edge. "And then, right at the end, people jumped on the bandwagon," she writes. "As if caught in a current, 3–4 percent of the votes were swept in the direction of the general expectation of who was going to win."

How can people resist the false-consensus effect? What can be done to limit the influence of political polls during elections? How will you be influenced by studies in this book showing that your own opinions or habits are not shared by everybody? Think about it. ▪

Every time I think I'm part of a normal relationship...

Someone publishes a new survey.

strikes law that may or may not be effective?" Moreover, ambiguous phrases may mean different things to different people. In 1992, a national survey asked people this question: "As you know, the term Holocaust usually refers to the killing of millions of Jews in Nazi death camps during World War II. Does it seem possible or does it seem impossible to you that the Nazi extermination of the Jews never happened?" Not only does the question contain a double negative, which is confusing, but some people might take "extermination" to mean *total* annihilation, in which case the answer "no" is appropriate. In response to this question, 22 percent of Americans expressed doubts about the Holocaust. But when a follow-up survey asked a much clearer question—"Do you doubt that the Holocaust actually happened, or not?"—the number of doubters fell to 9 percent (*Skeptic* magazine, 1994). As you can see, although surveys can be extremely informative, they must be conducted and interpreted carefully.

Quick QUIZ

A. Which descriptive method would be most appropriate for studying each of the following topics? (All these topics, by the way, have been the focus of study.)

1. Ways in which the games of boys differ from those of girls
2. Changes in attitudes toward nuclear disarmament after a television movie about nuclear holocaust
3. The math skills of U.S. versus Japanese children
4. Physiological changes that occur when people watch violent movies
5. The development of a male infant who was reared as a female after his penis was accidentally burned off during a supposedly routine circumcision involving electro-cauterization

   a. case study
   b. naturalistic observation
   c. laboratory observation
   d. survey
   e. test

B. Professor Flummox gives his new test of aptitude for studying psychology to his psychology students at the start of the year. At the end of the year, he finds that those who did well on the test averaged only a C in the course. The test lacks _____.

C. Over a period of 55 years, an 80-year-old British woman sniffed large amounts of cocaine, which she obtained legally under British regulations for the treatment of addicts. Yet the woman appeared to show no negative effects, other than drug dependence (Brown & Middlefell, 1989). What does this case tell us about the dangers or safety of cocaine?

Answers:

A. 1. b 2. d 3. e 4. c 5. a B. validity (more specifically, criterion validity) C. Not much. "Snorting" cocaine may be relatively harmless for some people, such as this woman, but extremely harmful for others. Also, the cocaine she received may have been less potent than cocaine purchased on the street. Critical thinking requires that we resist generalizing from a single case.

■ LOOKING FOR RELATIONSHIPS: CORRELATIONAL STUDIES

In descriptive research, psychologists often want to know whether two or more phenomena are related, and if so, how strongly. To obtain this information, they do **correlational studies.** If a researcher simply surveys college students to find out how many hours a week they spend watching television, the study is not a correlational one. However, if the researcher looks for a relationship between hours in front of the television set and grade point average, then it is.

The word **correlation** is often used as a synonym for relationship. Technically, however, a correlation is a numerical measure of the *strength* of the relationship between two or more things. The "things" may be events, scores, or anything else that can be recorded and tallied. In psychological studies, such things are called **variables** because they can vary in quantifiable ways. Height, weight, age, income, IQ scores, number of items recalled on a memory test, number of smiles in a given time period—anything that can be measured, rated, or scored can serve as a variable.

Correlations always occur between *sets* of observations. Sometimes the sets come from one individual. Suppose you measured a person's temperature and the person's alertness several times during the day. To check for a relationship between temperature and alertness, you would need several measurements, or numerical values, for each variable. Of course, your results would hold only for that individual. In psychological research, sets of correlated observations usually come from many individuals or are used to compare groups of people. For example, in research on the origins of intelligence, psychologists look for a relationship between the IQ scores of parents and children. To do this, the researchers must gather scores from a *set* of parents and from the children of these parents. You cannot compute a correlation if you only know the IQs of one particular parent–child pair. To say that a relationship exists, you need more than one pair of values to compare.

A **positive correlation** means that high values of one variable are associated with high values of the other, and that low values of one variable are associated with low values of the other. Height and weight are positively correlated, for example; so are IQ scores and school grades. Rarely is a correlation perfect, however. Some tall people weigh less than some short ones; some people with average IQs are superstars in the classroom and some with high IQs get poor grades. Figure 2.1(a) on page 58 shows a positive but imperfect relationship between educational level and annual income.

A **negative correlation** means that high values of one variable are associated with *low* values of the other (see Figure 2.1[b]). The older the car, the lower the price, except for antiques and models favored by collectors. As for human beings, in general the older adults are, the fewer miles they can run and the fewer hairs they have on their heads. See whether you can think of some other variables that are negatively correlated. Remember, though, a negative correlation still indicates that a relationship exists. If there is *no* relationship between two variables, we say they are *uncorrelated.* Shoe size and IQ scores are uncorrelated.

The statistic used for expressing a correlation is called the **coefficient of correlation.** This number conveys both the size of the correlation and its direction. A perfect positive correlation has a coefficient of +1.00. Suppose you weighed ten people and listed them in order, from lightest to heaviest. Then suppose you measured their heights and listed them in order, from shortest to tallest. If the names on the two lists were in exactly the same order, the correlation between weight and height would be +1.00. A perfect negative correlation has a coefficient of −1.00. If you hear that the correlation between two variables is +.80, it means that they are very strongly related. If you hear that the correla-

■ **correlational study**

A descriptive study that looks for a consistent relationship between two phenomena.

■ **correlation**

A measure of how strongly two variables are related to one another.

■ **variables**

Characteristics of behavior or experience that can be measured or described by a numeric scale; variables are manipulated and assessed in scientific studies.

■ **positive correlation**

An association between increases in one variable and increases in another.

■ **negative correlation**

An association between increases in one variable and decreases in another.

■ **coefficient of correlation**

A measure of correlation that ranges in value from −1.00 to +1.00.

■ Figure 2.1   Correlations

Graph (a) shows a positive correlation between education and income in a group of men. Each dot represents a man. You can find each man's educational level by drawing a horizontal line from his dot to the vertical axis, and his income by drawing a vertical line from his dot to the horizontal axis. Graph (b) shows a negative correlation between average income and the incidence of dental disease for groups of 100 families. In general, the higher the income, the fewer the dental problems. (From Wright, 1976.)

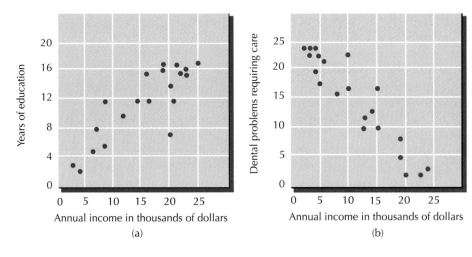

(a)

(b)

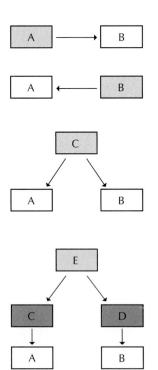

■ Figure 2.2   Correlation and Causation

If two variables, A and B, are correlated, there are many possible patterns of causation, including the four shown here. The arrows show the direction of causation, and C, D, and E represent other variables.

tion is −.80, the relationship is just as strong, but it is negative. When there is no association between two variables, the coefficient is zero or close to zero.

Correlations allow researchers, using statistical techniques, to make general predictions about a variable if they know how it is related to another one. But because correlations are rarely perfect, predictions about a particular *individual* may be inaccurate. If you know that a person is well educated, you might predict, in the absence of any other information, that the person is fairly well-off, because education and income are positively correlated. You would not be able to say exactly how much the person earned, but you would probably guess that the person's income was relatively high. You could be wrong, though. Some people with doctorates earn low salaries, and some people with only a grade-school education make fortunes.

Correlational studies in the social sciences are common and are often reported in the news. But beware; they can be extremely misleading. The important thing to remember is that *a correlation does not show causation*. It is easy to assume that if A predicts B, A must be causing B—that is, making B happen—but that is not necessarily so (see Figure 2.2). The number of storks nesting in some European villages is reportedly correlated positively with the number of human births in those villages. But clearly that doesn't mean that storks bring babies or that babies attract storks! Human births seem to be somewhat more frequent at certain times of the year (you might want to speculate on the reasons), and the peaks just happen to coincide with the storks' nesting periods.

The coincidental nature of the correlation between nesting storks and human births may be obvious, but in other cases, unwarranted conclusions about causation are more tempting. For example, knowing there is a modest correlation between self-esteem and grades in school, many people conclude that high self-esteem boosts grades. But it is also possible that getting high grades boosts self-esteem, or that causation runs in both directions. A correlation alone doesn't tell. Here's another example: Television watching is positively correlated with children's aggressiveness. Many people therefore assume that watching television causes aggressiveness. On the other hand, perhaps it is the case that being highly aggressive causes children to watch more television with violent shows. Or a third factor, growing up in a violent household, could cause children both to be aggressive *and* to watch television. Psychologists are still debating which of these causal relationships is the strongest; actually, there is evidence for all three (APA Commission on Violence and Youth, 1993; Eron, 1982; Eron & Huesmann, 1987; Oskamp, 1988).

The moral of the story: When two variables are associated, one variable may or may not be causing the other.

Quick QUIZ

1. Are you clear about correlations? Find out by identifying each of the following findings as indicative of either a positive correlation or a negative correlation.

   a. The higher a child's score on an intelligence test, the less physical force her mother is likely to use in disciplining her.

   b. The higher a male monkey's level of the hormone testosterone, the more aggressive he is likely to be.

   c. The older people are, the less frequently they tend to have sexual intercourse.

   d. The hotter the weather, the more crimes against persons (such as muggings) tend to occur.

2. Now see if you can generate two or three alternative explanations for each of the above findings.

Answers:

1. a. Negative correlation b. Positive correlation c. Negative correlation d. Positive correlation 2. a. Physical force may impair a child's intellectual growth; brighter children may elicit less physical discipline from their parents; brighter mothers may have brighter children and may also tend to use less physical force. b. The hormone might cause aggressiveness, or acting aggressively might stimulate hormone production. c. Older people may have less interest in sex than younger people, may have less energy, or may think they are supposed to have less interest in sex and behave accordingly; older people may also have trouble finding sexual partners. d. Hot temperatures may make people edgy and cause them to commit crimes; victims may be more plentiful in warm weather because more people stroll outside and go out at night; criminals may find it more comfortable to be out committing their crimes in warm weather than in cold. (Our explanations for these correlations are not the only ones possible.)

▪ HUNTING FOR CAUSES: THE EXPERIMENT

Researchers often propose explanations of behavior on the basis of descriptive studies, but for actually tracking down the causes of behavior, they rely heavily on the experimental method. An **experiment** allows the researcher to *control* the situation being studied. Instead of being a passive recorder of what is going on, the researcher actively does something that he or she thinks will affect the subjects' behavior, then observes what happens.

Experimental Variables

Suppose you are a psychologist and you come across reports that cigarette smoking improves performance on simple reaction time tasks. You do not question these findings, but you have a hunch that nicotine may have the opposite effect on more complex or demanding kinds of behavior, such as driving. You know that on the average, smokers have more car accidents than nonsmokers, even when differences in alcohol consumption, age, and other factors are taken into account (DiFranza et al., 1986). But this relationship doesn't prove that smoking *causes* accidents. Smokers may be greater risk takers than nonsmokers, whether the risk is lung cancer or trying to beat a red light. Or perhaps the distraction of falling ashes or fumbling for matches explains the relationship, rather than smoking itself. So you decide to do an experiment. In a laboratory, you ask smokers to "drive" using a computerized driving simulator equipped with a stick

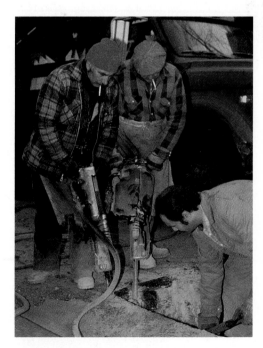

Everyone knows that alcohol and the operation of heavy machinery don't mix—but what about the effects of nicotine on such work? What sort of experiment might answer the question?

▪ **Figure 2.3 Do Smoking and Driving Mix?**

The text suggests an experiment to test the hypothesis that the nicotine in cigarettes impairs driving skills. The independent variable is use or nonuse of nicotine. The dependent variable is the number of rear-end collisions while operating a driving simulator. A similar study, using more complex procedures, was reported by Spilich, June, and Renner (1992).

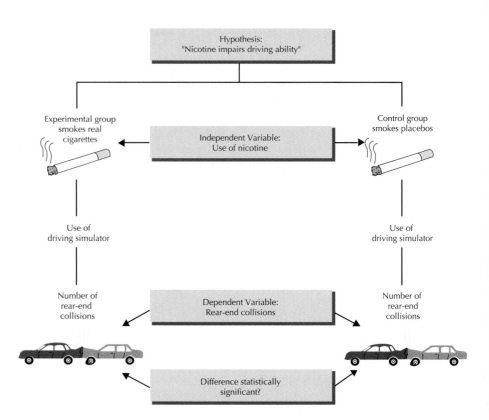

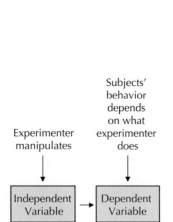

▪ **experiment**

A controlled test of a hypothesis in which the researcher manipulates one variable to discover its effect on another.

▪ **independent variable**

A variable that an experimenter manipulates.

▪ **dependent variable**

A variable that an experimenter predicts will be affected by manipulations of the independent variable.

shift and a gas pedal. The object, you tell them, is to maximize distance by driving as fast as possible on a winding road while avoiding rear-end collisions. At your request, some of the subjects smoke a cigarette immediately before climbing into the driver's seat. Others do not. You are interested in comparing how many collisions the two groups have. (The basic design of this experiment is illustrated in Figure 2.3. You may want to refer to the figure from time to time as you read the next few pages.)

The aspect of an experimental situation manipulated or varied by the researcher is known as the **independent variable.** The reaction of the subjects—the behavior that the researcher tries to predict—is called the **dependent variable.** Every experiment has at least one independent and one dependent variable. In our example, the independent variable is nicotine use: one cigarette versus none. The dependent variable is the number of rear-end collisions.

Ideally, everything about the experimental situation *except* the independent variable is held constant—that is, kept the same for all subjects. You would not have some people use a stick shift and others an automatic, unless shift type were an independent variable. Similarly, you would not have some people go through the experiment alone and others perform in front of an audience. Holding everything but the independent variable constant ensures that whatever happens is due to the researcher's manipulation and nothing else. It allows you to rule out other interpretations.

Understandably, students often have trouble keeping independent and dependent variables straight. You might think of it this way: The dependent variable—the outcome of the study—*depends* on the independent variable. When psychologist Smith sets up an experiment, she thinks, "If I do (such and such), the subjects in my study will do (such and such)." The first "such and such" represents the independent variable; the second represents the dependent variable. Most variables may be either independent or dependent, depending on what the experimenter is manipulating and trying to predict. If you want to know whether eating chocolate makes people nervous, then the amount of chocolate eaten is the independent variable. If you want to know whether feeling nervous makes people eat chocolate, then the amount of chocolate eaten is the dependent variable.

Quick QUIZ

Name the independent and dependent variables in studies designed to answer the following questions:

1. Whether sleeping after learning a poem improves memory for the poem
2. Whether the presence of other people affects a person's willingness to help someone in distress
3. Whether people get agitated from listening to heavy-metal music
4. Whether drinking caffeinated coffee makes people more talkative

Answers:

1. Opportunity to sleep after learning is the independent variable; memory for the poem is the dependent variable. 2. The presence of other people is the independent variable; willingness to help others is the dependent variable. 3. Exposure to heavy-metal music is the independent variable; agitation is the dependent variable. 4. Coffee drinking (caffeinated versus decaffeinated) is the independent variable; talkativeness is the dependent variable. (Now, can you think up some ways to do experiments that might answer these questions?)

Experimental and Control Conditions

Experiments usually require both an experimental condition and a comparison or **control condition.** In the control condition, subjects are treated exactly like those in the experimental condition, except that they are not exposed to the same treatment, the manipulation of the independent variable. Without a control condition, you can't be sure that the behavior in which you are interested would not have occurred anyway, even without your manipulation. In some studies, the same subjects can be used in both the control and the experimental conditions; they are said to serve as their own controls. In other studies, subjects are assigned to either an *experimental group* or a *control group.*

In the nicotine experiment, the people who smoke before driving make up the experimental group, and those who refrain from smoking make up the control group. We want these two groups to be roughly the same in terms of average driving skill. It wouldn't do to start out with a bunch of reckless roadrunners in the experimental group and a bunch of tired tortoises in the control group. We probably also want the two groups to be similar in average intelligence, education, smoking history, and other characteristics, so that none of these variables will affect our results. To ensure comparability of the two groups, we can use **random assignment** to place people in the groups. We might randomly give each person a number, then put all those with even numbers in the experimental group and all those with odd numbers in the control group. At the beginning of the study, each subject will have the same probability as any other subject of being assigned to a given group. If we have enough subjects in our study, individual differences among them are likely to be roughly balanced in the two groups. However, for some characteristics, such as sex, we may decide not to depend on random assignment. Instead, we may deliberately assign an equal number of people from each category (e.g., male and female) to each group.

Sometimes, researchers use several different experimental or control groups. For example, in our nicotine study, we might want to examine the effects of different levels of nicotine by having people smoke one, two, or three cigarettes before starting the simulated driving, and comparing each of these experimental groups to each other and to a control group of nonsmokers as well. For now, however, let's focus just on experimental subjects who smoked one cigarette.

We now have two groups. We also have a problem. In order to smoke, the experimental subjects must light up and inhale. These acts might set off expecta-

You've developed a new form of therapy that you believe cures anxiety: Sixty-three percent of the people who go through your program improve. Why shouldn't you rush out to open an anxiety clinic?

■ **control condition**
In an experiment, a comparison condition in which subjects are not exposed to the same treatment as in the experimental condition.

■ **random assignment**
A procedure for assigning people to experimental and control groups in which each individual has the same probability as any other of being assigned to a given group.

tions of feeling relaxed, getting nervous, feeling confident, or whatever. These expectations, in turn, might affect driving performance. It would be better to have the control group do everything the experimental group does *except* use nicotine. Therefore, let's change the experimental design a bit. Instead of having the control subjects refrain from smoking, we will give them a **placebo,** a fake treatment. Placebos, which are used frequently in drug research, often take the form of pills or injections containing no active ingredients. Assume that it's possible in the nicotine study to use phony cigarettes that taste and smell like the real thing but that contain no active ingredients. Our control subjects will not know their cigarettes are fake and will have no way of distinguishing them from real ones. Now if they have substantially fewer collisions than the experimental group, we will feel safe in concluding that nicotine increases the probability of an auto accident. (Placebos, by the way, sometimes produce effects that are as strong or nearly as strong as those of a real treatment. Thus, phony injections are often surprisingly effective in eliminating pain. Such placebo effects are a puzzle awaiting scientific solution.)

Experimenter Effects

Because expectations can influence the results of a study, subjects should not know whether they are in an experimental or a control group. When this is so, as it usually is, the experiment is said to be a **single-blind study.** But subjects are not the only ones who bring expectations to the laboratory; so do researchers. Their expectations and hopes for a particular result may cause them inadvertently to influence the participants' responses through facial expressions, posture, tone of voice, or some other cue.

Several years ago, Robert Rosenthal demonstrated how powerful such **experimenter effects** can be. He had students teach rats to run a maze. Half the students were told their rats had been bred to be "maze bright," half that their rats had been bred to be "maze dull." In reality, there were no genetic differences between the two groups of rats, but the supposedly brainy rats actually did learn the maze more quickly! If an experimenter's expectations can affect a rodent's behavior, reasoned Rosenthal, surely they can affect a human being's. He went on to demonstrate this in many other studies (Rosenthal, 1966, 1994).

Unfortunately, the cues an experimenter may give to subjects can be as subtle as the smile on the Mona Lisa. In fact, the cue may *be* a smile. In one of his studies, Rosenthal found that male researchers were far more likely to smile at female subjects than at males. Since one smile tends to invite another, such behavior on the part of the experimenter could easily ruin a study on friendliness or cooperation. "It may be a heartening finding to know that chivalry is not dead," noted Rosenthal, "but as far as methodology is concerned it is a disconcerting finding."

One solution to the problem of experimenter effects is to do a **double-blind study.** In such a study, the person running the experiment, the one having actual contact with the subjects, does not know which subjects are in which groups until the data have been gathered. Double-blind procedures are common in drug research. Different doses of a drug are coded in some way, and the person administering the drug is kept in the dark about the code's meaning until after the experiment. To run the nicotine study in a double-blind fashion, we would keep the person dispensing the cigarettes from knowing which ones were real and which were placebos. In psychological research, double-blind studies are often more difficult to design than those that are single-blind.

Because experiments allow conclusions about cause and effect, they have long been the method of choice in psychology. However, like all methods, the laboratory experiment has its limitations. As we noted earlier, the laboratory creates an artificial setting that may call forth behavior rarely seen elsewhere. Moreover, the laboratory encourages a special relationship between researchers and their subjects, in which the researcher determines what the questions are and which behaviors will be recorded. In their desire to cooperate, subjects may act in ways

A smile is nice, but not if it produces an experimenter effect.

▪ **placebo**

An inactive substance or fake treatment used as a control in an experiment or given by a medical practitioner to a patient.

▪ **single-blind study**

An experiment in which subjects do not know whether they are in an experimental or a control group.

▪ **experimenter effects**

Unintended changes in subjects' behavior due to cues inadvertently given by the experimenter.

▪ **double-blind study**

An experiment in which neither the subjects nor the researchers know which subjects are in the control group(s) and which in the experimental group(s) until the results are tallied.

Table 2.2 *Research Methods in Psychology: Their Advantages and Disadvantages*

Method	Advantages	Disadvantages
Case history	Good source of hypotheses Provides in-depth information on individuals Unusual cases can shed light on situations/ problems that are unethical or impractical to study in other ways	Individual may not be representative or typical Difficult to know which subjective interpretation is best
Naturalistic observation	Allows description of behavior as it occurs in the natural environment Often useful in first stages of research program	Allows researcher little or no control of the situation Observations may be biased Does not allow firm conclusions on cause and effect
Laboratory observation	Allows more control than naturalistic observation Allows use of sophisticated equipment	Allows researcher only limited control of the situation Observations may be biased Does not allow firm conclusions on cause and effect Behavior in the laboratory may differ from behavior in the natural environment
Test	Yields information on personality traits, emotional states, aptitudes, abilities	Difficult to construct tests that are valid and reliable
Survey	Provides large amount of information on large numbers of people	If sample is nonrepresentative or biased, it may be impossible to generalize from the results Responses may be inaccurate or untrue
Correlational study	Shows whether two or more variables are related Allows general predictions	Does not permit identification of cause and effect
Experiment	Allows researcher to control the situation Permits researcher to identify cause and effect	Situation is artificial and results may not generalize well to the real world Sometimes difficult to avoid experimenter effects

that they ordinarily would not. Thus the psychologist confronts a dilemma: The more control he or she exercises over the situation, the more unlike real life it may be. For this reason, many psychologists are calling for more field research, involving the careful study of behavior in natural contexts. (For a comparison of the advantages and disadvantages of various research methods, see Table 2.2.)

Quick QUIZ

1. What's wrong with these two studies?
   a. A kidney specialist and a psychiatrist treated mentally disordered patients by filtering their blood through a dialysis machine (normally used with kidney patients). They reported several cases of dramatic improvement, which they attributed to the removal of an unknown toxin (Wagemaker & Cade, 1978).
   b. A sex researcher surveyed women on their feelings about men and love. She sent out 100,000 lengthy questionnaires to women's groups and got back 4,500 replies (a 4.5 percent return). On the basis of these replies, she reported that 84 percent of women are dissatisfied with their relationships, 98 percent want more communication, and 70 percent of those married five years or more have had extramarital affairs (Hite, 1987).

 2. Suppose you hear that a researcher reported a dramatic improvement in the functioning of patients with Alzheimer's disease who took an experimental drug. As a critical thinker, what questions would you want to ask about this study? Try to come up with as many questions as you can.

Answers:

1. a. The dialysis study had no control group and was not double-blind. Patients' expectations that the "blood-cleansing" equipment would wash their madness out of them might have influenced the results, and so might the researchers' expectations. In later studies, using double-blind procedures, control subjects had their blood circulated through the machine but the blood was not actually filtered. Little improvement occurred in either the experimental or the control condition, and the real treatment was no better than the fake treatment (Carpenter et al., 1983). **b.** Because of the way the sample was recruited and the low return rate, the findings may be flawed by a volunteer bias. Although the study produced information on the feelings of many women, figures and percentages from the study are not necessarily valid for the general population. **2.** Some possible questions: How many people were studied? Was there a control group? If so, did the control subjects receive placebos? How were patients assigned to the experimental and control groups? Were double-blind procedures used? How was improved functioning measured? How long did the effects last? Did the effects make any difference in the everyday lives of the patients or their families? Were there any negative effects? Has the experiment been replicated by other researchers?

■ EVALUATING THE FINDINGS: WHY PSYCHOLOGISTS USE STATISTICS

If you are a psychologist who has just done an observational study, a survey, or an experiment, your work has only just begun. Once you have some results in hand, you must do three things with them: (1) describe them, (2) assess how reliable and meaningful they are, and (3) figure out how to explain them.

Descriptive Statistics: Finding Out What's So

Let's say that 30 people in the nicotine experiment smoked real cigarettes, and 30 smoked placebos. We have recorded the number of collisions for each person on the driving simulator. Now we have 60 numbers. What can we do with them?

The first step is to summarize the data. The world does not want to hear how many collisions each person had. It wants to know what happened in the nicotine group as a whole, compared to what happened in the control group. To provide this information, we need numbers that sum up our data. Such numbers, known as **descriptive statistics,** are often depicted in graphs and charts.

A good way to summarize the data is to compute group averages. The most commonly used type of average is the **arithmetic mean.** (For two other types, see the Appendix.) It is calculated by adding up all the individual scores and dividing the result by the number of scores. We can compute a mean for the

■ **descriptive statistics**

Statistics that organize and summarize research data.

■ **arithmetic mean**

An average that is calculated by adding up a set of quantities and dividing the sum by the total number of quantities in the set.

Averages can be misleading if you don't know how much events deviated from the statistical mean and how they were distributed.

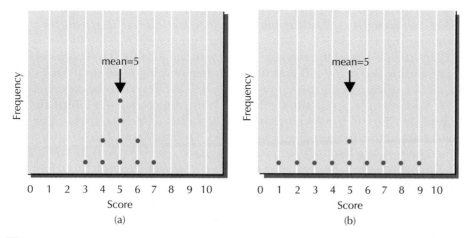

■ **Figure 2.4   Same Mean, Different Variances**

In both distributions of scores the mean is 5, but in (a) the scores are clustered around the mean, whereas in (b) they are widely dispersed.

nicotine group by adding up the 30 collision scores and dividing by 30. Then we can do the same for the control group. Now our 60 numbers have been boiled down to 2. For the sake of our example, let's assume that the nicotine group had an average of 10 collisions, while the control group's average was only 7.

We must be careful, however, about how we interpret these averages. An arithmetic mean does *not* necessarily tell us what is typical; it merely summarizes a mass of data. It is possible that *no one* in our nicotine group actually had 10 collisions. Perhaps half the people in the nicotine group were motoring maniacs and had 15 collisions, while the others were more cautious and had only 5. Perhaps almost all the subjects had 10 or 11 collisions. Perhaps accidents were evenly distributed between zero and 15.

The mean does not tell you about the variation in subjects' responses. For that, there are other statistics. One, the **range,** gives the difference between the lowest and highest scores in a distribution of scores. If the lowest number of collisions in the nicotine group was 5 and the highest was 15, the range would be 10. Another, the **variance,** is more informative; it tells you how clustered or spread out the individual scores are around the mean (see Figure 2.4). The more spread out they are, the less "typical" the mean is. Knowing about variance can help you to understand certain passionate debates in psychology. The concept of variance has been important, for example, in arguments over the meaning of group differences in IQ (see Chapter 3). But when research is reported in the media, you usually hear only about the mean. There are other kinds of descriptive statistics as well, including the coefficient of correlation, which we covered earlier. Descriptive statistics are discussed in greater detail in the Appendix.

Inferential Statistics: Asking "So What?"

At this point in our nicotine study, we have one group with an average of 10 collisions and another with an average of 7. Should we break out the champagne? Try to get on TV? Call our mothers?

Better hold off. Descriptive statistics do not tell us whether the outcome is anything to write home about. Perhaps if one group had an average of 15 and the

■ **range**

A measure of the spread of scores, calculated by subtracting the lowest score from the highest score.

■ **variance**

A measure of the dispersion of scores around the mean.

other an average of 1 we could get excited. But rarely does a psychological study hit you between the eyes with a sensationally clear result. In most cases, there is a possibility that the difference between the two groups was due simply to chance. Perhaps the people in the nicotine group just happened to be more accident-prone during the study, and their behavior had nothing to do with smoking. It would be surprising if the two groups had *exactly* the same number of collisions.

To find out how significant the data are, the psychologist uses **inferential statistics.** They permit a researcher to draw *inferences* (conclusions based on evidence) about the findings. There are many inferential statistics to choose from, depending on the kind of study and what the researcher wants to know. Like descriptive statistics, inferential statistics involve the application of mathematical formulas to the data (see Appendix).

Inferential statistics do not merely describe or summarize the data. *They tell the researcher how likely it is that the result of the study occurred by chance.* More precisely, they reveal the probability of obtaining an effect as large as (or larger than) the one observed, if manipulating the independent variable actually has no reliable effect on the behavior in question. It is impossible to rule out chance entirely. However, if the likelihood of the result occurring by chance is extremely low, we say the result is **statistically significant.** This means that the probability that the difference is "real" is overwhelming—not certain, mind you, but overwhelming. By convention, psychologists consider a result significant if it would be expected by chance 5 or fewer times in 100 repetitions of the study. Another way of saying this is that the result is significant at the .05—"point oh five"—level.

Inferential statistics are necessary because a result that seems unlikely may not be unlikely at all. For example, how probable is it that in a room of 25 people, at least 2 will have the same birthday? The odds seem remote, but in fact they are better than even. Even if there are only 10 people in the room, the chances are 1 in 9. Among U.S. presidents, two had the same birthday (Warren Harding and James Polk), and three died on the fourth of July (John Adams, the second president; Thomas Jefferson, the third; and James Monroe, the fifth). Surprising? No. Such coincidences are not statistically striking at all.

With inferential statistics, we can find out whether an experimental result would be truly a rare event if only chance were operating. In our nicotine study (which was summarized in Figure 2.3 on page 60), these statistics would tell us how likely it is that the difference between the nicotine group and the placebo group occurred by chance. If the difference could be expected to occur by chance in 6 out of 100 studies, we would have to say that the results failed to support the hypothesis—that the difference we obtained might well have occurred merely by chance. You can see that psychologists refuse to be impressed by just any old result.

Statistically significant results allow psychologists to make many general predictions about human behavior. These predictions are usually stated as probabilities ("On average, we can expect 60 percent of all students to do X, Y, or Z"). However, they do not usually tell us with certainty what a particular individual will do in a given situation. Probabilistic results are typical of all the sciences. Medical research, for example, can tell us that the odds are high that someone who smokes will get lung cancer, but because many different variables interact to produce any particular case of cancer, research can't tell us for sure whether Aunt Bessie, a two-pack-a-day smoker, will come down with the disease.

By the way, a nicotine study similar to our hypothetical example has actually been done (Spilich, June, & Renner, 1992). Smokers who lit up before driving got a little farther on the simulated road, but they also had significantly more rear-end collisions on average (10.7) than temporarily abstaining smokers (5.2)

■ **inferential statistics**
Statistical tests that allow researchers to assess how likely it is that their results occurred merely by chance.

■ **statistically significant**
A term used to refer to a result that is extremely unlikely to have occurred by chance.

or nonsmokers (3.1). After hearing of this research, the head of Federal Express banned smoking on the job among all of the company's 12,000 drivers (George Spilich, personal communication).

Quick QUIZ

Check your understanding of the descriptive/inferential distinction by placing a check in the appropriate column for each phrase:

	Descriptive statistics	Inferential statistics
1. Summarize the data	_____	_____
2. Give likelihood of data occurring by chance	_____	_____
3. Include the mean	_____	_____
4. Give measure of statistical significance	_____	_____
5. Tell you whether to call your mother	_____	_____

Answers:

1. descriptive 2. inferential 3. descriptive 4. inferential 5. inferential

---

From the Laboratory to the Real World: Interpreting the Findings

The last step in any study is to figure out what the findings mean. Trying to understand behavior from uninterpreted findings is like trying to become fluent in Portuguese by reading a Portuguese-English dictionary. Just as you need the grammar of Portuguese to tell you how the words fit together, the psychologist needs hypotheses and theories to explain how the facts that emerge from research fit together.

Sometimes it is hard to choose between competing explanations. Does nicotine disrupt driving because it impairs coordination, increases a driver's vulnerability to distraction, interferes with the processing of information, clouds judgment, or distorts the perception of danger? In general, the best explanation is the one that accounts for the greatest number of findings and makes the most accurate predictions about new findings.

Often the explanation for a finding will need to take into account many different factors. We saw earlier, for example, that being abused as a child does not inevitably turn a person into an abusive parent. Many influences, including life stresses, exposure to violence on television, and the nature of the abuse, interact in complicated ways to determine the kind of parent a person becomes (Widom, 1989). Fortunately, with special statistical procedures, psychologists can analyze how much each variable contributes to a result and how factors interact.

In interpreting any particular study, we must also not go too far beyond the facts. There may be several explanations that fit those facts equally well, which means that more research will be needed to determine the best explanation. Rarely does one study prove anything, in psychology or any other field. That is why you should be suspicious of headlines that announce a major scientific breakthrough. Scientific progress usually occurs gradually, not in one fell swoop.

Sometimes the best interpretation of a finding does not emerge until a hypothesis has been tested in different ways. Although the methods we have described tend to be appropriate for different questions (see Table 2.3), differ-

Table 2.3   Psychological Research Methods Contrasted

Psychologists may use different methods to answer different questions about a topic. To illustrate, this table shows some ways in which the methods described in this chapter can be used to study different questions about aggression. The methods listed are not necessarily mutually exclusive. That is, sometimes two or more methods can be used to investigate the same question. As discussed in the text, findings based on one method may extend, support, or disconfirm findings based on another.

Method	Purpose	Example
Case study	To understand the development of aggressive behavior in a particular individual; to formulate research hypotheses about the origins of aggressiveness	Developmental history of a serial killer
Naturalistic observation	To describe the nature of aggressive acts in early childhood	Observation, tally, and description of hitting, kicking, etc., during free-play periods in a preschool
Laboratory observation	To find out if aggressiveness in pairs of same-sex and opposite-sex children differs in frequency or intensity	Observation through a one-way window of same-sex and opposite-sex pairs of preschoolers; pairs must negotiate who gets to play with an attractive toy that has been promised to each child
Test	To compare the personality traits of aggressive and nonaggressive persons	Administration of personality tests to violent and nonviolent prisoners
Survey	To find out how common domestic violence is in the United States	Questionnaire asking anonymous respondents (in a sample representative of the U.S. population) about the occurrence of slapping, hitting, etc., in their homes
Correlational study	To examine the relationship between aggressiveness and television viewing	Administration to college students of a paper-and-pencil test of aggressiveness and a questionnaire on number of hours spent watching TV weekly; computation of correlation coefficient
Experiment	To find out whether high air temperatures elicit aggressive behavior	Arrangement for individuals to "shock" a "learner" (actually a confederate of the experimenter) while seated in a room heated to either 72°F or 85°F

■ **cross-sectional study**
A study in which subjects of different ages are compared at a given time.
■ **longitudinal study**
A study in which subjects are followed and periodically reassessed over a period of time.

ent methods can also complement each other. That is, one method can be used to confirm, disconfirm, or extend the results obtained with another. If the findings of studies using various methods converge, there is greater reason to be confident about them. On the other hand, if they conflict, researchers will know they must modify their hypotheses or do more research.

As an example, when psychologists compare the mental test scores of young people and old people, they usually find that young people outscore older ones. This type of research, in which groups are compared at a given time, is called **cross-sectional.** Other researchers have used **longitudinal studies** to investigate mental abilities across the life span. In a longitudinal study, people are followed over a period of time and reassessed at regular intervals. In contrast to cross-sectional studies, longitudinal studies find that as people age, they often continue to perform as well as they ever did on many types of mental tests. A general decline in ability does not usually occur until the seventh or eighth decade of life, if at all (Baltes, Dittman-Kohli, & Dixon, 1984; Schaie, 1993). Why do results from the two types of studies conflict? Apparently, cross-sectional studies measure generational differences; younger generations tend to outperform older ones on many tests, perhaps because they are better educated or more familiar with the types of items used on the tests. Without longitudinal studies, we might falsely conclude that mental ability inevitably declines with age.

Sometimes psychologists agree on the reliability and meaning of a finding, but not on its importance for theory or practice. Statistical significance alone does not provide the answer, because *statistical significance does not always imply real-world importance.* A result may be statistically significant at the "point oh-five level," but at the same time be small and of little consequence in everyday life (Rosnow & Rosenthal, 1989). Psychologists are now using other kinds of statistics to estimate how much of the variance among the scores in a study was accounted for by the independent variable. Often this *effect size* turns out to be quite small (see Figure 2.5).

One useful new technique, called **meta-analysis,** statistically combines and analyzes data from many studies, instead of assessing each study's results separately. Meta-analysis reveals how much of the variation in scores across *all* the studies examined can be explained by a particular variable, such as gender. For example, one recent meta-analysis of nearly fifty years of research found that gender differences on some spatial-visual tasks are substantial, with males doing better on the average (Voyer, Voyer, & Bryden, 1995). In contrast, other meta-analyses show that differences in verbal ability, aggressiveness, and suggestibility, although reliable, are surprisingly small, with gender accounting for only 1 to 5 percent of the variance in scores (Eagly & Carli, 1981; Feingold, 1988; Hyde, 1981, 1984; Hyde & Linn, 1988).

Critics of meta-analysis argue that this method is like combining apples and oranges; the blend is interesting, but it is bland—and obliterates the distinctive flavors of the original ingredients. For example, research on verbal abilities has often relied on studies of high school students. But students who don't read well are more likely to drop out of high school, and these drop-outs are more likely to be male than female. Thus a meta-analysis may fail to identify an overall female advantage on verbal tests (Halpern, 1989). Similarly, a meta-analysis that combines studies of all math skills will miss a male advantage on problems of spatial visualization (McGuinness, 1993). Meta-analyses that turn up no overall sex differences in cognitive abilities are appealing to many people but ultimately unhelpful, critics believe, because such analyses gloss over differences that educators should know about if they want *all* children to do well. Nevertheless, on topics that have generated dozens and even hundreds of studies, meta-analysis has been the most promising way of finding patterns of results, as long as its limitations are taken into account.

⭐ *A study reports that women are "significantly" better than men at tongue twisters. On closer examination, you find that women are "better" by an average of three seconds. Does this finding make any difference in real life?*

■ **meta-analysis**
A procedure for combining and analyzing data from many studies; it determines how much of the variance in scores across all studies can be explained by a particular variable.

■ **Figure 2.5 Is This a Meaningful Difference?**

Group differences that are statistically significant are not always useful for predicting behavior. Seventh-grade boys do better, on the average, than seventh-grade girls on the mathematics section of the SAT. But as this graph shows, the difference is small, and the scores greatly overlap. Thus, it is impossible to predict reliably whether a particular boy will outperform a particular girl (from Sapolsky, 1987, based on data from Benbow & Stanley, 1983).

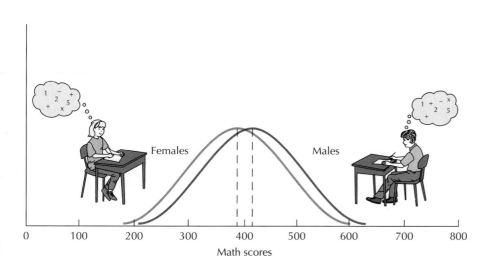

Females   Males

0   100   200   300   400   500   600   700   800
Math scores

Laboratory and field studies are both important in psychological research. An industrial/organizational psychologist might be interested in doing a field study to investigate group processes such as teamwork and group cohesion; the consequences of being the only minority member; or how groups are affected by the ratio of women to men.

▪ EVALUATING RESEARCH METHODS: SCIENCE UNDER SCRUTINY

Rigorous research methods are the very heart of science, so it is not surprising that psychologists spend much time discussing and debating their procedures for collecting, evaluating, and presenting data. In recent years, such debates have gone far beyond such matters as when to use questionnaires versus interviews or how best to analyze the data.

Keeping the Enterprise Ethical

One set of issues has to do with the ethics of research. The APA (American Psychological Association) recognizes the need for ethical guidelines and has a formal code that all members must follow, both in clinical practice and in psychological research. The APA code calls on psychological scientists to respect the dignity and welfare of their subjects. It states that human subjects must voluntarily consent to participate in a study and must know enough about it to make an intelligent decision, a doctrine known as *informed consent.* Once a study begins, a subject must be free to withdraw from it at any time. Federal regulations also govern scientific research, and in most colleges and universities, an ethics committee must approve all proposed studies.

Most ethical issues are not controversial, but two have provoked continuing debate. One has to do with the practice of deception. Many studies require that researchers mislead their subjects about the purpose of the research until the study is completed. If participants in a study knew in advance why it was being done, the results might not be valid. If they knew the study concerned the willingness to help others, they might try to outdo Mother Teresa; or if they knew the study was measuring verbal ability, they might become as talkative as a sportscaster at the Super Bowl. The obvious solution is for researchers to disguise the purpose of their studies, or, to put it more bluntly, to lie.

But what if the deception causes the subjects to suffer anxiety or embarrassment during the study? What if the participants are misled into thinking they will have to deliver electric shock to another person? What if they are going to be insulted or humiliated by a confederate of the researcher so that the researcher can study their reactions? Because of growing concern about the morality of deceptive procedures, the APA's ethical guidelines now require that a researcher who plans to use deception show that it is necessary and that it is justified by the study's potential scientific, educational, or applied value. The investigator must also protect participants from physical and mental discomfort or harm, and if any risk of harm or discomfort exists, must tell them.

An even more controversial issue concerns the use of animals in research. Animals are used in about 7 or 8 percent of psychological studies, and 95 percent of the animals used are rodents (American Psychological Association, 1984). Psychologists are especially partial to the Norwegian white rat, which is bred specifically for research purposes and is relatively cheap and healthy. But they also occasionally use pigeons, cats, monkeys, apes, and other species. Most studies involve no harm or discomfort to the animals (such as research on mating in hamsters), but some do (such as studies in which infant monkeys are reared apart from their mothers and as a consequence develop abnormal behaviors). Some even require the animal's death, as when rats brought up in deprived or enriched environments are sacrificed so that their brains can be examined for specific effects.

Animals are used in psychological research to study learning, memory, emotion, motivation, and other topics. Here a rat learns to find food in a radial maze.

Psychologists who study animals are sometimes interested in comparing different species, or they hope to learn more about a particular species. Their work generally falls into the area of basic science, but it often produces practical benefits. For example, using behavioral principles, farmers have been able to reduce crop destruction by birds and deer without resorting to their traditional method—shooting the animals. Other psychologists are primarily interested in principles that apply to both animals and people. Because many animals have biological systems or behavioral patterns similar to those of human beings, using animals often allows more control over variables than would otherwise be possible. In some cases, practical or ethical considerations prevent the use of human beings as subjects. And studying animals can clarify important theoretical issues. For example, we might not attribute the greater life expectancy of women solely to "lifestyle" factors and health practices if we find that a male–female difference exists in other mammals as well.

Animal studies have led to many improvements in human health and well-being. They have helped researchers develop methods for treating bed-wetting; teach retarded children to communicate; devise behavioral therapies for treating emotional problems and substance abuse; combat life-threatening malnutrition caused by chronic vomiting in infants; rehabilitate patients with neurological disorders and sensory impairment; teach people to control high blood pressure and headaches; treat suicidal depression; develop better ways to reduce chronic pain; train animal companions for the disabled; and understand the mechanisms underlying memory loss and senility—to name only a few benefits (Feeney, 1987; Greenough, 1991; N. Miller, 1985).

In recent years, however, animal research has provoked angry disputes over the welfare of animals and even over whether to do any animal research at all. Much of the criticism has centered on the medical and commercial use of animals, but psychologists have also come under fire. In one survey, 85 percent of committed animal rights activists, versus 17 percent of a comparison group, endorsed the statement, "If it were up to me, I would eliminate all research using animals" (Plous, 1991). For their part, some psychologists have refused to acknowledge that confinement in laboratories can be psychologically and physically harmful for some species. The controversy has often degenerated into vicious name-calling by extremists on both sides. Some animal rights activists have vandalized laboratories and threatened and harassed researchers and their families; some scientists have unfairly branded all animal-welfare activists as terrorists (Blum, 1994).

On the positive side, this conflict has motivated many psychologists to find ways to improve the treatment of animals that are needed in research. The APA's ethical code has always contained provisions covering the humane treatment of animals, and in the past few years, more comprehensive guidelines have been formulated. New federal laws have strengthened regulations on the housing and care of research animals. Every experiment involving vertebrates must now be reviewed by a committee that includes representatives from the research institution and the community.

Most scientists, however, oppose proposals to ban or greatly reduce animal research. The APA and other organizations feel that protective legislation for animals is desirable but must not jeopardize research that increases scientific understanding and improves human welfare. The difficult task—one that promises to be with us for many years—is to balance the many benefits of animal research with an acknowledgment of past abuses and a compassionate attitude toward species other than our own.

The Meanings of Knowledge

The continuing arguments over ethical issues show that research methods in psychology can provoke as much disagreement as research findings do. Conflict exists not only about how to do research, but also about what research in general can and cannot reveal. Indeed, heated exchanges are raging in all the sciences and humanities about the very meaning of knowledge itself.

For the past three centuries, the answer seemed clear enough. Knowledge was the discovery of an absolute, knowable reality existing outside the human mind, and the way to uncover that reality was to be objective, value-free, and detached. The purpose of a theory was to map or reflect this reality. A clear line was assumed to exist between the knower, on one side, and the phenomenon under study, on the other—and the knower wasn't supposed to cross that line.

Today, many scholars are questioning these assumptions. Adherents of *postmodernism* argue that detached objectivity, long considered the cornerstone of Western science, is a myth. In the postmodern view, the observer's values, judgments, and status in society inevitably affect how events are studied, how they are explained, and even how they take place. Scholars and researchers, in this view, are not exempt from human subjectivity. Because they do their work at a particular time and in a particular culture, they bring with them shared assumptions and worldviews that influence what they count as an important fact, what parts of reality they notice, and how they determine standards of excellence. If you have encountered arguments about which books should be counted as classics—the familiar greats of Western literature or modern works by African-Americans, women, and non-European writers—you have already observed a postmodern conflict.

In the social sciences, one postmodern theory, **social constructionism,** holds that knowledge isn't so much discovered as it is *created* or invented (Gergen, 1985; Guba, 1990; Hare-Mustin & Marecek, 1990; Rosaldo, 1989). Our understanding of things does not merely mirror what's "out there"; it organizes and orders it.

Consider the concept of race. Many people speak of "blacks" or "Asians" or "whites" as if the boundaries between these groups were self-evident based on physical differences. But there are many ways to define *race*. Some societies base their definitions on ancestry, not on any obvious physical attribute such

■ **social constructionism**

The view that there are no universal truths about human nature, because people construct reality differently, depending on their culture, the historical moment, and power arrangements within their society.

as skin color; a person can look white but be considered black if he or she has a single black ancestor. Indeed, as recently as 1970, Louisiana laws held that anyone with as little as ½₂ "Negro blood" was black (Jones, 1991). South Africa has used ancestry to differentiate blacks from "coloreds" (people of mixed ancestry) for political and legal purposes; but in South America, where people come in all shades and Many combinations of European, Indian, and African ancestry, this kind of classification does not exist. And why should skin color or hair type be the primary basis for distinguishing races? As physiologist Jared Diamond (1994) observes, "There are many different, equally valid procedures for defining races, and those different procedures yield very different classifications." You could, for example, make distinctions based on gene frequencies for sickle-cell anemia, on types of fingerprints, on amount of body hair or shape of buttocks, or on body shape. One classification would group Italians, Greeks, and most African blacks into one race and the Xhosas of South Africa and Swedes into another. "Still another procedure," says Diamond, "would keep Swedes and Italians separate from all African blacks but would throw [them] into the same race as New Guineans and American Indians."

Racial labels obscure the fact that few if any of us are pure anything, a fact that is causing all sorts of problems for the U.S. Census Bureau, which valiantly keeps trying to construct new terms. Racial labels also vastly exaggerate the differences between groups; there is far more genetic and physical variation *within* groups than between them (Betancourt & López, 1993; Jones, 1991; Zuckerman, 1990a). Of course, behavior can be profoundly affected by the way people label and identify themselves and others, as we will see in Chapter 18. And *racism*—hatred or intolerance toward others because of their race, however it is defined—is a lamentably real human problem. But both in society at large and within the discipline of psychology, there are no agreed-on definitions of race itself (Yee et al., 1993). Because the concept of race falsely implies the existence of physically unique groups and is problematic from a scientific point of view, in this book we will be avoiding the term *race* whenever possible. Instead we will use the term *ethnic group* to refer to people who share a common culture, religion, or language.

In psychology, social-constructionist debates about science are especially challenging. Psychologists have always sought to understand the behavior and mental processes of human beings. Now they are being asked to analyze their own behavior as psychologists and to examine how their own values, gender, place in society, and cultural experiences affect their conclusions. In this task, they have a rich variety of research methods to aid them, and research findings as well. For example, cognitive psychologists have shown that people's emotions and behavior often depend more on how they interpret events than on some actual state of affairs. And sociocultural psychologists have shown that social and cultural roles profoundly influence how people view the world and the conclusions they draw about reality.

Nevertheless, many people, including many psychologists, react to postmodern views with alarm. They fear that these criticisms mean we can never know the truth about anything and so we might as well give up on science, uniform standards of criticism, and the effort to apply objective methods. They fear that a legitimate critique of the limitations of research is turning into an attack on *all* methods of research and on science itself, which in effect is throwing the baby (useful findings) out with the bath water (bias and narrow-mindedness) (Peplau & Conrad, 1989; Smith, 1994).

This is a serious and interesting debate that is not going to be resolved soon, which is why we have raised it here. Our own position, which guides our approach in this book, falls somewhere between extreme traditionalism and extreme postmodernism. We think that understanding how knowledge is constructed by scholars and researchers is essential to the study of psychology. And we believe that new ways of looking at knowledge and of doing research have the potential to expand and enrich our understanding of behavior (see Gergen, 1994). But for us, as for all scientific psychologists, some things will remain the same: an insistence on standards of evidence, a reliance on verifiable results, and an emphasis on critical thinking. That is why we hope that as you read the following chapters, you will resist the temptation to skip descriptions of how studies were done. If the assumptions and methods of a study are faulty, so are the results and the conclusions based on them. Ultimately, what we know about human behavior is inseparable from how we came to know it.

Taking Psychology with You

"Intuitive Statistics": Avoiding the Pitfalls

Everyone uses intuition and hunches to generate hypotheses about human behavior. Scientists are required to confirm their hypotheses through careful research and rigorous statistical analysis. In daily life, though, people usually test their ideas through casual observation and the use of "intuitive statistics," notions about probabilities that may or may not be correct. These unscientific methods often work well but can sometimes lead to errors. You can take Chapter 2 with you by watching out for common statistical mistakes in your own thinking.

For example, you have learned how misleading it can be to "accentuate the positive and eliminate the negative" by ignoring nonoccurrences of a phenomenon (see p. 43). Sherlock Holmes, the legendary detective, was aware of the value of nonoccurrences. In one adventure he invited a police inspector to consider "the curious incident of the dog in the nighttime." The inspector protested that the dog did nothing in the nighttime. Holmes replied that *that* was the curious incident: The dog's silence proved that the intruder in the mystery was someone well known to the dog (Ross, 1977). Like Sherlock Holmes, we all need to be aware of what nonoccurrences can tell us.

Other intuitive statistics can trap us in false conclusions. For example, how would you answer the following questions?

1. If black has come up three times in a row on the roulette wheel, would you be inclined to bet next on red or on black?

2. Where are you more worried about safety, in a car or in an airplane?

3. If your psychology instructor has a friend who is a professor, and if that person is socially rather shy, is slight of stature, and likes to write poetry, is the friend's field more likely to be Chinese studies or psychology?

When presented with the first question, many people say that it is red's "turn" to win. Yet black and red are equally likely to win on the fourth play, just as they were on the first three (assuming that the wheel is fair). How could the probabilities change from one play to the other? A roulette wheel has no memory! The same is true for tossing coins. If you get three heads, the chance of a head on the fourth toss is still .50. The probability of a head or a tail does not change from toss to toss, and it is perfectly normal to get a run of either heads or tails, though over the long run (if the coin is fair), there will be a balance of heads and tails. Because many people don't understand these facts of probability, they often succumb to the gambler's fallacy, the belief that a "run" of one event alters the chances of that event occurring again. The gambler's fallacy is common outside the casino as well. Many people think that parents with three girls are due for a boy, but the odds are the same as they always were: 50 percent for most people; more or less than 50 percent when the man produces an above-average supply of male-producing or female-producing sperm.

What about the second question? You may already know that airplanes are far safer than cars, even controlling for number of passenger miles traveled. Yet most of us still feel safer in cars, because we overestimate the probability of an event when examples are readily available in memory (Tversky & Kahneman, 1973). We can all recall specific airplane disasters; they make headlines because so many people die at once. A single vivid plane crash lingers longer in memory than the many auto accidents regularly reported in the local newspaper. Thus airplane fatalities *seem* more likely. On the other hand, we don't want to simplify; driving may not be riskier for everyone. Your age, driving habits, and seat-belt use, as well as the type of car you drive, all affect your risk of dying in a traffic accident.

Finally, on the third question, many people predict that the instructor's friend is a professor of Chinese studies (Ross, 1977). But this is unlikely, since there are very few professors of Chinese studies in the United States, and there are thousands of professors of psychology. Also, a psychology instructor is likely to have more friends in psychology than in Chinese studies. People go astray on this question because they are influenced by their stereotypes about people, and they ignore statistical probabilities.

This little exercise shows you how intuitions can be clouded by biases and fallacies despite people's best efforts to be rational. The scientific approach is the psychologist's way of avoiding such pitfalls.

Summary

1. Research methods provide a way for psychologists to separate well-supported conclusions from unfounded belief. An understanding of these methods can also help people think critically about psychological issues and become astute consumers of psychological and other scientific findings.

2. The ideal scientist states hypotheses and predictions precisely; is skeptical of claims that rest solely on faith or authority; relies on empirical evidence; is willing to comply with the principle of falsifiability and make "risky predictions"; and is open about methods and results so that findings can be replicated. The public nature of science gives it a built-in system of checks and balances.

3. *Descriptive methods* allow a researcher to describe and predict behavior but not necessarily to choose one explanation over others. Such methods include case studies, observational studies, psychological tests, surveys, and correlational methods. Some descriptive methods are used both by clinicians and by researchers.

4. *Case studies* are detailed descriptions of individuals. They are often used by clinicians, and in research, they can be valuable in exploring new topics and addressing questions that would otherwise be difficult or impossible to study. But because the person under study may not be representative of people in general, case studies are typically sources rather than tests of hypotheses.

5. In *observational studies*, the researcher systematically observes and records behavior without interfering in any way with the behavior. *Naturalistic observation* is used to obtain descriptions of how subjects behave in their natural environments. *Laboratory observation* allows more control and the use of special equipment; behavior in the laboratory, however, may differ in certain ways from behavior in natural contexts.

6. *Psychological tests* are used to measure and evaluate personality traits, emotional states, aptitudes, interests, abilities, and values. A good test has been standardized and is both valid and reliable. Teachers, parents, and employers do not always stop to question a test's validity, especially when results are summarized in a single number. The validity of some widely used tests is controversial.

7. *Surveys* are questionnaires or interviews that ask people directly about their experiences, attitudes, and opinions. Precautions must be taken to obtain a sample that is *representative* of the larger population that the researcher wishes to describe and that yields results that are not skewed by a *volunteer bias*. Findings can be affected by the fact that respondents sometimes lie, misremember, or misinterpret the questions.

8. In descriptive research, studies that look for relationships between phenomena are known as *correlational*. A *correlation* is a measure of the strength of the relationship between two variables; it may be positive or negative. A correlation does *not* show a causal relationship between the variables.

9. *Experiments* allow researchers to manipulate an *independent variable* and to assess the effects of the manipulation on a *dependent variable.* An experiment usually requires both an experimental condition and a control condition. *Single-blind* and *double-blind* procedures can be used to prevent the expectations of the subjects or of the experimenter from affecting the results. Although experiments create a special kind of situation that may call forth behavior not typical in other environments, they have been the method of choice for drawing conclusions about cause and effect relationships.

10. Psychologists use *descriptive statistics,* such as the mean, range, and variance, to summarize their data. They use *inferential statistics* to find out how likely it is that the results of a study occurred merely by chance. The results are said to be *statistically significant* if this likelihood is very low. Statistically significant results allow predictions about human behavior, but, as in all sciences, probabilistic results do not tell us with certainty what a particular individual will do in a situation.

11. It can be hard to choose between competing interpretations of a specific finding. Care must be taken to avoid going beyond the facts or exaggerating the real-world significance of the findings. Sometimes the best interpretation does not emerge until a hypothesis has been tested in more than one way—for example, by using both *cross-sectional* and *longitudinal* studies. A technique called *meta-analysis* reveals how much of the variation in scores across many different studies can be explained by a particular variable. It is useful for finding patterns of results, so long as some limitations of this method are kept in mind.

12. Two controversial ethical issues in psychological research are the use of deception in studies of human subjects and the use of animals in research. Debate on these issues has led to the revision and expansion of ethical guidelines.

13. Some fundamental assumptions about the meaning of knowledge are currently under scrutiny. Adherents of *postmodernism* argue than an observer's values, judgments, and status in society inevitably affect which events are studied, how they are studied, and how they are explained. One postmodern theory, *social constructionism,* holds that knowledge is not so much discovered as it is created or invented. Some scholars are alarmed by postmodernism, fearing that a legitimate critique of the limitations of research is turning into an attack on all traditional methods. However, these new ideas, if combined with a traditional insistence on critical thinking and standards of evidence, have the potential for expanding and enriching our understanding of human behavior.

Key Terms

confirmation bias   *43*
hypothesis   *44*
theory   *44*
operational definition   *44*
principle of falsifiability   *45*
replicate   *46*
descriptive methods   *47*
case study   *47*
observational studies   *49*
naturalistic observation   *49*
laboratory observation   *50*
psychological tests   *51*
standardization   *52*
norms (in testing)   *52*
reliability   *52*
test–retest reliability   *52*

alternate-forms reliability   *52*
validity   *52*
content validity   *52*
criterion validity   *52*
surveys   *53*
sample   *54*
representative sample   *54*
volunteer bias   *54*
correlational study   *57*
correlation   *57*
variable   *57*
positive correlation   *57*
negative correlation   *57*
coefficient of correlation   *57*
experiment   *59*
independent variable   *60*

3

Evolution, Genes, and Behavior

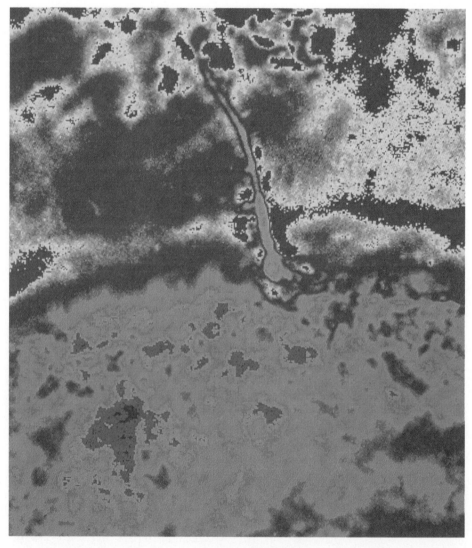

A human sperm enters an ovum at the moment of conception. The DNA in the two cells will combine to form a human being with a unique genetic pattern.

The tough-minded . . . respect difference.
Their goal is a world made safe for differences.

■ RUTH BENEDICT ■

Think of all the ways that human beings are alike. Everywhere, no matter what their backgrounds or where they live, people love, work, argue, dance, sing, complain, and gossip. They rear families, celebrate marriages, and mourn losses. They reminisce about the past and plan for the future. They help their friends and fight with their enemies. They tell jokes and laugh, and they frown with displeasure. Where do all these commonalities come from?

Think of all the ways that human beings differ. Some are extroverts, always ready to throw a party, make a new friend, or speak up in a crowd; others are shy and introverted, preferring the safe and familiar. Some are trailblazers, ambitious and enterprising; others are placid, content with the way things are. Some take to book learning like a cat to catnip; others don't do so well in school but have lots of street smarts and practical know-how. Some are overwhelmed by even the most petty of problems; others, faced with severe difficulties, remain calm and resilient. Where do all these differences come from?

For many years, psychologists trying to answer these questions tended to fall into two camps. On one side were the *nativists,* who emphasized genes and inborn characteristics, or nature; on the other side were the *empiricists,* who focused on learning and experience, or nurture. Edward L. Thorndike (1903), one of the leading psychologists of the early 1900s, staked out the nativist position when he claimed that "in the actual race of life . . . the chief determining factor is heredity." But his contemporary, behaviorist John B. Watson (1925), insisted that experience could write virtually any message on the blank slate of human nature: "Give me a dozen healthy infants, well-formed, and my own specified world to bring them up in and I'll guarantee to take any one at random and train him to become any type of specialist I might select—doctor, lawyer, artist, merchant-chief and yes, even beggar-man and thief, regardless of his talents, penchants, tendencies, abilities, vocations, and race of his ancestors."

In this chapter, we focus mostly on the nature side of the debate and the findings of two related fields in psychology. Researchers in **behavioral genetics** study the contribution of heredity to individual differences in personality, mental ability, and other human characteristics. Researchers in **evolutionary psychology** (sometimes called *Darwinian psychology*) emphasize the evolutionary mechanisms that might help explain commonalities in language learning, attention, perception, memory, sexual behavior, reasoning, decision making, emotion, and many other aspects of human psychology (Barkow, Cosmides, & Tooby, 1992; Buss, 1995; Mealey, in press). Evolutionary psychology, which has emerged in the past few years as a dominant force in psychology, overlaps with **sociobiology,** an interdisciplinary field that looks for evolutionary explanations of social behavior in animals, including human beings.

In the past, exchanges between the two sides of the nature–nurture issue sometimes sounded like a boxing match: "In this corner, we have Heredity and in this corner, we have Environment. Okay, you guys, come out fighting." Today,

The long and short of it: Human beings are similar and different.

■ **behavioral genetics**
An interdisciplinary field of study concerned with the genetic bases of behavior and personality.

■ **evolutionary psychology**
A field of psychology emphasizing evolutionary mechanisms that may help explain human commonalities in cognition, development, emotion, social practices, and other areas of behavior.

■ **sociobiology**
An interdisciplinary field of study that emphasizes evolutionary explanations of social behavior in animals, including human beings.

no one argues in terms of nature *or* nurture; all scientists understand that heredity and environment interact to produce not only our psychological traits but even most of our physical ones. There is evidence, for instance, that children can inherit a tendency to be nearsighted, but whether nearsightedness actually develops may depend on whether a child reads a lot or sits for hours at a TV set or video monitor (Curtin, 1985; Gwiazda et al., 1993). In societies that lack a written language—societies in which nobody reads—nearsightedness is extremely rare.

▪ WHAT'S IN A GENE?

Let's begin by looking more closely at what genes are and how they operate. **Genes,** the basic units of heredity, are located on **chromosomes,** rod-shaped structures found in every cell of the body. Each sperm cell and each egg cell (ovum) possesses 23 chromosomes, so when a sperm and egg unite at conception, the fertilized egg, and all the body cells that eventually develop from it (except for sperm cells and ova), contain 46 chromosomes—23 pairs.

One of these chromosome pairs usually determines a person's anatomical sex; it consists of an X chromosome from the mother's egg and either an X or a Y chromosome from the father's sperm. Because all eggs carry only an X, whereas sperm can carry either an X or a Y, it is the father's sperm that determines the offspring's sex. If the father contributes an X, the offspring is female (XX); if the father contributes a Y, the offspring is male (XY). (When Henry VIII blamed Anne Boleyn for bearing a daughter instead of a son, he was following a long tradition—still alive in some societies—of assuming that the mother determines a child's sex. Had he known then what we know now about genetics, his unfortunate queen might have kept her crown and her head!) The only exceptions to the genetic rules governing anatomical sex are children born with hormonal or chromosomal anomalies that cause their anatomy to conflict with their genetic sex (that is, their sex chromosomes).

Chromosomes consist of threadlike strands of **DNA (deoxyribonucleic acid)** molecules, and genes consist of small segments of this DNA. Each human chromosome contains thousands of different genes, each with a fixed location; collectively the 100,000 or so human genes are referred to as the human **genome.** Within each gene, four basic elements of DNA (called *bases*)—identified by the letters A, T, C, and G, and numbering in the thousands or even tens of thousands—are arranged in a particular order: for example, ACGTCTCTATA. . . . This sequence forms a chemical code that helps determine the synthesis of a particular protein by specifying the sequence of amino acids that are the protein's building blocks. In turn, proteins directly or indirectly affect virtually all of the structural and biochemical characteristics of the organism.

In the simplest type of inheritance, first described in the late nineteenth century by the Austrian monk Gregor Mendel, a single pair of genes is responsible for the expression of a particular trait. In many cases, one member of the pair is said to be *dominant* and the other *recessive*, which means that if an individual has one gene of each type, he or she will show the trait corresponding to the dominant gene. The ability to curl one's tongue lengthwise, for example, follows this pattern. If both of your parents contribute a gene for this ability (call it *A*), you will have it too, and if both parents contribute the other form of the gene, the one associated with lack of the ability (call it *a*), you too will lack the ability. However, if one parent contributes an *A* and the other contributes an *a*, you will be able to curl your tongue, because the gene for the ability is dominant. You can still pass your "inability gene" on to your offspring, but it will not affect your own ability to curl your tongue.

Most human traits, even such seemingly straightforward ones as height and eye color, depend on more than one gene pair; this complicates matters enormously and makes tracking down the genetic contributions to a trait extremely difficult. Identifying even a single gene is daunting; biologist Joseph Levine and

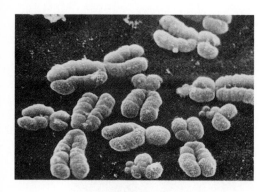

Human chromosomes, magnified almost 55,000 times.

▪ **genes**
The functional units of heredity; they are composed of DNA and specify the structure of proteins.

▪ **chromosomes**
Rod-shaped structures within every body cell that carry the genes.

▪ **DNA (deoxyribonucleic acid)**
The chromosomal molecule that transfers genetic characteristics by way of coded instructions for the structure of proteins.

▪ **genome**
The full set of genes in each cell of an organism.

geneticist David Suzuki (1993) compare the task to searching for a particular person when all you know is that the person lives somewhere on earth. There are about 3 *billion* units of DNA (all those As, Ts, Cs, and Gs) in the complete set of human chromosomes. So to locate a gene, you cannot just peer through a microscope. Instead, researchers must clone (produce copies of) several different stretches of DNA on a chromosome, then use indirect methods to locate particular genes.

One such method, which has been used to search for the genes associated with physical and mental conditions, involves doing **linkage studies.** These studies take advantage of the tendency of some genes lying close together on a chromosome to be inherited together across generations. The researchers start out by looking for *markers,* DNA segments that vary considerably among individuals and whose locations on the chromosomes are already known. Then they look for patterns of inheritance of these markers in large families in which a particular condition is common. If a certain marker tends to exist in individuals who have the condition and not in those who don't, then the variant of the gene involved in the condition is apt to be located nearby on the chromosome, and the researchers have some idea where to search for it. The linkage method was recently used to locate the gene that causes Huntington's disease, a fatal condition that usually strikes people in middle age, causing involuntary spasms and twisting movements of the body, facial grimacing, memory lapses, impulsive behavior, and sometimes paranoia, depression, and other psychological symptoms (Gusella et al., 1993; Huntington's Disease Collaborative Research Group, 1993). Only one gene was involved, yet the search took a decade of painstaking work.

An international collaboration of researchers is now rushing to map the entire human genome—all 3 billion units of DNA—and some optimistic scientists expect success within only a few years. They are working not only with linkage studies but also with high-tech methods that have been devised only recently. But finding any particular gene is still a long, laborious process, and even when you find it, you don't automatically know its role in physical or psychological functioning. That is one reason why the human genome project has been controversial; no one is quite sure what the ultimate payoffs will be. (One possibility is increased genetic testing, which we discuss in "Think About It.")

Although scientists commonly refer to *the* human genome, each of us, with the exception of identical twins, is a unique genetic mosaic, one that never existed before and never will again. Our uniqueness is due to the way inheritance operates. When the body cells that produce sperm cells and egg cells divide, one member of each original chromosome pair goes to one new cell and the other member goes to the other new cell. That is why sperm cells and egg cells contain only 23 *unpaired* chromosomes.

Chance alone decides which member of each chromosome pair goes to a particular sperm or egg. When you work out the mathematics, you find that each sperm- or egg-producing cell has the potential to produce over 8 million different chromosome combinations in each new sperm or egg. But the actual diversity is far greater, because genes can change spontaneously, or *mutate,* during formation of a sperm or an egg, due to an error in the copying of the original DNA sequence, and because small segments of genetic material are apt to *cross over* (exchange places) between members of a chromosome pair before the final division.

The upshot is that each of us is the potential parent (given the time and energy) of billions of genetically different offspring. And because it takes two to make a baby, and each parent contributes one of billions of possible combinations to each child, the potential number of genetic combinations from any given set of parents is staggering. Thus siblings, who share, on the average, half their genes, can be unlike each other in many ways. And children, who share, on the average, half their genes with each parent, can be unlike their parents in purely *genetic* terms.

■ **linkage studies**
Genetic studies that look for patterns of inheritance of genetic markers in large families in which a particular condition is common; the markers consist of DNA segments that vary considerably among individuals and that have known locations on the chromosomes.

That's not all. Some fascinating research with mice suggests that two individuals would turn out to be different even if they had identical genes *and* identical environments! Robert Collins (1985, 1991), who is both a geneticist and a psychologist, has studied mice that were inbred for more than 100 generations and were reared in similar cages. Just as humans have a preference for which hand they use, it turns out that mice have a preference for which paw they use. Collins finds, and other researchers have confirmed, that although the *degree* of handedness (pawedness?) in mice is affected by heredity, half of these genetically similar mice become left-pawed and half right-pawed. This result suggests that a given gene or set of genes does not always have the same outcome, even in the same environment. No one knows exactly why this is so. Perhaps slight differences in chemical reactions involved in the synthesis of proteins affect the expression of a gene. In any case, there appears to be an element of chance in the making of any individual. As Collins told us, "Nature can build a slot machine, but it can't specify the outcome of every gamble."

Other research with animals suggests that environmental factors, such as stress and nutrition, can cause specific genes to turn "on" and "off" over the course of a lifetime (McClearn, 1993). To say, then, that some trait is genetic does not mean that a child is destined to be a chip off the old block.

*T*hink About It

*G*enetic Testing: Promise or Threat?

■ Suppose you read in the paper that scientists have located a gene that increases the risk of developing Alzheimer's disease at ages 50–60. There happen to be many cases of this condition in your family tree. Would you want to be tested to find out if you have the gene?

This question is no longer hypothetical. In the past few years, scientists have located genes known or thought to be involved in a number of disorders, including heart disease, some kinds of colon cancer, cystic fibrosis, Huntington's disease, certain types of early-onset Alzheimer's disease, and one kind of inherited breast cancer. Supporters of genetic research are exhilarated by these findings. Such discoveries, they hope, will lead to new ways of testing for genetic mutations involved in diseases and to new treatments, including the insertion of normal genes directly into patients' tissues. Indeed, the media recently reported the case of a little girl who benefited from an experimental genetic treatment of cystic fibrosis. It is impossible not to feel thrilled at the possibility that science will prolong her life and allow her to play like other children. You can see why scientists are excited.

But genetic breakthroughs also raise many disturbing questions about how the new information will be used. One possibility, for example, is that insurance companies will refuse coverage to adults and children who are currently healthy but who, because of their DNA, have some genetic predisposition for developing a disease or disorder later in life. Employers who pay insurance premiums for their workers may refuse to hire people whose DNA is not up to company standards. And even if the information can be kept private, people might become needlessly depressed and anxious if they know that *someday* they may die of a specific disease that currently has no cure.

Of course, it is natural, if you are going to be a parent, to want to avoid having a child who will suffer the agonies of a fatal or painful disease. But what if prenatal genetic testing reveals that there is some chance your child will have a mild or treatable disease, or a disease that will not strike until old age? As one writer asks, "Many parents now abort fetuses with genes for Huntington's and cystic fibrosis, but what do you do with the knowledge that your unborn child has a sixty-five-per-cent chance of contracting breast cancer in her forties, or a ninety-per-cent chance of developing Alzheimer's in his fifties? Or that your child carries a gene for manic depression? Or a gene for obesity?" (Seabrook, 1994). What if the condition is dyslexia, which makes it hard but not impossible to learn to read; or homosexuality, which is not a disorder at all but which some people fear; or being very short, which in some quarters is a social disadvantage but is hardly a disability? What if the condition is femaleness? In many cultures, parents prefer sons to daughters; indeed, in China and India, the use of prenatal sonograms to determine the sex of the fetus has resulted in the abortion of millions of females. As a result, the sex ratio in these societies has become seriously skewed.

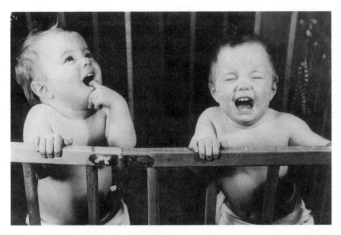 

Even identical twins don't always resemble each other psychologically, as you can see in these pictures of the same pair of identical twins at different ages. In both infancy and childhood the twin on the left was cheerful and easygoing whereas the one on the right was negative and difficult. Basic research with animals suggests that even when environments are similar the same genes can have different outcomes.

The ability to reject fetuses that are deemed not good enough could lead, in turn, to a tendency to view children as products. Will anyone want to be stuck with an imperfect model? Daniel Koshland (1988–1989), a molecular biologist and former editor in chief of *Science,* the foremost scientific journal in the United States, has asked, "If a child destined to have a permanently low IQ could be cured by replacing a gene, would anyone really argue against that?" Well, yes, some people might. For one thing, as this chapter will emphasize again and again, genes don't destine someone to have a particular IQ or any other trait. For another, variations in human abilities and traits—even those that cause individual hardship—are necessary for the adaptive functioning of complex societies, and eliminating them might have unexpected but disastrous social consequences. Further, what would the effects be on a child whose parents expected him or her to be perfect and were disappointed when, inevitably, the child was not?

Critics also worry about the social implications of genetic research. Once people learn that a gene is associated with some condition, they often ignore the economic and environmental factors that contribute to it. It is easy to make this mistake because of the language that researchers themselves sometimes use. As biologist Ruth Hubbard and writer Elijah Wald (1993) have observed, when scientists say that genes "control," "program," or "determine" behavior, or when they refer to genes "for" this or that trait, their words imply an inevitability that

does not actually exist. (We have made a concerted effort to avoid this kind of deterministic language.)

For example, interest in genetic factors in intelligence may deflect attention from social and environmental influences, such as poorly equipped classrooms and toxins that cause subtle brain damage and learning problems. Likewise, the recent discovery of an "obesity gene" could divert attention from the fact that high-fat foods and inactivity are the primary causes of overweight in our society. In an opinion essay in *The New York Times* (December 15, 1994), Kelly Brownell, a scientist who has studied weight and eating for many years, notes that when laboratory rats are given cheese curls, chocolate bars, marshmallows, and cookies, they ignore nutritious food and become obese. "Yet we do not fault these animals for a lack of discipline, nor need we change their biology," writes Brownell. "Remove bad foods and the rats stay thin."

In the coming years, many of us will have to face decisions about genetic testing. Would you be tested if some of your relatives had a disease that was influenced by heredity? How would you cope if the results were unfavorable? How serious and how likely would an inherited condition have to be before you would consider aborting a fetus? Would you want your employer to have information about your DNA? Would you want to know, while you are still young, that you carry genes associated with Alzheimer's disease, Huntington's disease, or other disorders that usually don't strike until old age? How might this information change your life? Think about it. ▪

Quick QUIZ

1. The basic units of heredity are called (a) chromosomes, (b) Xs and Ys, (c) genes, (d) DNA molecules.
2. True or false: Typically, a human trait can be traced to a single gene or pair of genes.
3. Each of us is a unique genetic mosaic. What three processes during formation of sperm and eggs explain this uniqueness?

Answers:

1. c 2. false 3. The random nature of chromosome-pair division, spontaneous genetic mutations, and crossover of genetic material between members of a chromosome pair before the final division.

▓ OUR HUMAN HERITAGE: THE GENETICS OF SIMILARITY

Just as diversity is inherent in the way genes function, so are many fundamental human similarities. These similarities can be traced to our evolutionary history. British geneticist Steve Jones (1994) writes, "Genetics is the key to the past. Every human gene must have an ancestor. . . . Each gene is a message from our forebears and together they contain the whole story of human evolution."

Evolution is basically a change in the gene frequencies within a population over many generations. As genes become more or less common in the population, so do genetically influenced characteristics. Why do these frequencies change? For one thing, although parents pass on their genes to their offspring, new genetic variations keep arising as genes spontaneously mutate and recombine. According to the principle of **natural selection,** first formulated in general terms by the British naturalist Charles Darwin in *On the Origin of Species* (1859/1964), the fate of these genetic variations depends on the environment. (Darwin didn't actually know about genes, which hadn't yet been discovered. But he did know that characteristics must somehow be transmitted from one generation to the next.) If, in a particular environment, individuals with a genetically influenced trait tend to be more successful in finding food, surviving the elements, fending off enemies, and staying alive until they can reproduce, their genes will become more and more common in the population; over many generations, these genes may spread throughout the species. In contrast, individuals whose traits are not as adaptive in the struggle for survival will not be as reproductively fit: They will tend to die before reproducing, so their genes (and traits) will become less and less common and may eventually become extinct. There is debate about how gradually or abruptly such changes occur and whether competition for survival is always the primary mechanism of change (Gould & Eldredge, 1977), but scientists agree on the basic processes of evolution, and evolutionary principles guide all of the biological sciences.

Often, scientists who study evolution start with some observed phenomenon (such as why the male peacock has such fabulous feathers) and then try to explain it in evolutionary terms after the fact (his preening display got the attention of the female). But some evolutionary psychologists are taking a different tack. They begin by asking what sorts of challenges human beings might have faced in their prehistoric past—having to decide which foods were safe to eat, for example, or needing to size up a stranger's intentions quickly. They

When Darwin first proposed his theory of evolution, many people were outraged. Cartoonists ridiculed the notion that humans and nonhuman primates are descended from a common ancestor. In this nineteenth-century cartoon, a monkeylike Darwin holds a mirror to show an ape how closely he resembles human beings. Today, evolutionary principles, which have long guided the biological sciences, are having a growing influence on psychological science as well.

Although evolutionary changes tend to be slow and gradual, sometimes they occur rapidly in response to sudden changes in the environment. In England, the peppered moth has both a light form and a dark form. At one time, dark moths were rare; because they stood out against the light green lichen on trees and could be spotted easily by predators, they often did not survive long enough to reproduce and pass on their genes. Light moths, however, were camouflaged against the trees and were able to reproduce in great numbers. In the nineteenth century, pollution from coal-burning factories blackened the lichen (left), dark wings became adaptive and white wings maladaptive, and the species changed; by the late 1940s, 98 percent of all peppered moths were dark. Then pollution-control devices were installed and the trees became lighter once again (right). In the years since then, white moths have made a comeback.

then draw inferences about the behavioral tendencies and psychological mechanisms that might have evolved to solve these survival problems and enhance reproductive fitness: Taste preferences might have evolved so that people would not eat poisonous or rancid food, and universal facial expressions might have evolved so that people would recognize the difference between a friendly stranger and an angry one. Evolutionary psychologists then design empirical studies, including experiments, to see whether their inferences are correct. Their guiding assumption is that the human mind is not a general-purpose computer but instead evolved as a collection of specialized and independent "modules" to handle specific survival problems (Buss, 1995; Cosmides, Tooby, & Barkow, 1992; Mealey, in press).

Critics of evolutionary psychology worry about the tendency of its advocates to assume that *every* behavior has biological, adaptive origins. They argue that the idea of mental modules is no improvement over instinct theory, the once popular notion in psychology that virtually every human activity and capacity, from cleanliness to cruelty, is innate. Evolutionary psychologists, however, think that by drawing on different kinds of evidence they can distinguish behavior that has a biological origin from behavior that does not. As Steven Pinker (1994b) explains,

> Using biological anthropology, we can look for evidence that the problem is one that our ancestors had to solve in the environments in which they evolved—so language and face recognition are at least candidates for innate modules, but reading and driving are not. Using data from psychology and ethnography, we can test the following prediction: when children solve problems for which they have mental modules, they should look like geniuses, knowing things they have not been taught; when they solve problems that their minds are not equipped for, it should be a long hard slog. Finally, if a module for some problem is real, neuroscience should

■ **evolution**
A change in gene frequencies within a population over many generations; a mechanism by which genetically influenced characteristics of a population change.

■ **natural selection**
The evolutionary process in which individuals with genetically influenced traits that are adaptive in a particular environment tend to survive and to reproduce in greater numbers than other individuals; as a result, their traits become more common in the population over time.

discover that the brain tissue computing the problem has some kind of physiological cohesiveness, such as constituting a circuit or subsystem.

Innate Human Characteristics

Because of our common evolutionary history, many abilities, traits, and characteristics are universal in human beings and are either present at birth or develop as the child matures, given certain experiences. For example, babies are born with a number of reflexes, such as sucking and grasping (see Chapter 13). In addition, an attraction to novelty seems to be part of our evolutionary heritage, and that of many other species, as well. If a rat has had its dinner, it will prefer exploring an unfamiliar wing of a maze rather than the familiar wing where food is. Human babies, too, reveal a surprising interest in looking at and listening to unfamiliar things—which, of course, includes most of the world. A baby will even stop nursing if someone new enters his or her range of vision. A third innate characteristic in birds and mammals is a motive to explore and manipulate objects. Primates especially like to "monkey around" with things, taking them apart and scrutinizing the pieces, apparently for the sheer pleasure of it (Harlow, Harlow, & Meyer, 1950).

Many species, including our own, seem to have an innate motive to play, to fool around, and to imitate others (Huizinga, 1950). Think of kittens and lion cubs, puppies and pandas, and all young primates, who will play with and pounce on each other all day until hunger or naptime calls. Some researchers argue that play and exploration are biologically adaptive because they help members of a species find food and other necessities of life and learn to cope with their environments. Indeed, the young of many species enjoy *practice play*, behavior that will later be used for serious purposes when they are adults (Vandenberg, 1985). A kitten, for example, will stalk and attack a ball of yarn. In human beings, play is part of a child's socialization, teaching children how to get along with others and giving them a chance to practice their motor and linguistic skills (Harlow & Harlow, 1966; Pelligrini & Galda, 1993).

Evolutionary psychologists have speculated on other kinds of behavior that might be influenced by tendencies inherited because they were useful during the history of our species (see Table 3.1). In later chapters, we will consider the adaptive aspects of sensory and perceptual abilities (Chapter 6), learning (Chapter 7), emotion (Chapter 10), attachment (Chapter 11), and stress reac-

All primates, including human beings, are innately disposed to explore the environment, manipulate objects, play, and "monkey around."

Table 3.1	*Some Candidates for Evolved Abilities and Behaviors*

The following list, proposed by Steven Pinker (1994b), includes human emotional and cognitive capacities that might have developed as evolutionary adaptations to the environment. Pinker's list is speculative; there is evidence of specialized neurological mechanisms underlying some of these capacities, but not all. Other writers have proposed evolutionary origins for humor, deceit, tool making, and crying. Which capacities do you think warrant being on this list?

Intuitive mechanics: basic knowledge of the motions, forces, and deformations that objects undergo

Intuitive biology: basic understanding of how plants and animals work

Number

Mental maps for large territories

Habitat selection: seeking of safe, information-rich, productive environments

Danger, including the emotions of fear and caution; phobias for stimuli such as heights, confinement, risky social encounters, and venomous and predatory animals; and a motive to learn the circumstances in which each is harmless

Food: what is good to eat

Contamination, including the emotion of disgust and intuitions about contagion and disease

Monitoring of current well-being, including the emotions of happiness and sadness, and moods of contentment and restlessness

Intuitive psychology: predicting other people's behavior from their beliefs and desires

A mental Rolodex: a database of individuals, with blanks for kinship, status or rank, history of exchange of favors, and inherent skills and strengths

Self-concept: gathering and organizing information about one's value to other people, and packaging it for others

Justice: sense of rights, obligations, and deserts, including the emotions of anger and revenge

Kinship, including nepotism and allocations of parenting effort

Mating, including feelings of sexual attraction, love, and intentions of fidelity and desertion

Source: Adapted from Pinker, 1994b, p. 420.

tions (Chapter 14). For now, let us look more closely at two areas that have been of great interest to evolutionary psychologists: the development of language and mating practices around the world.

The Capacity for Language

Try to read this sentence aloud:

Kamaunawezakusomamanenohayawewenimtuwamaanasana.

Can you tell where one word begins and another ends? Unless you happen to know Swahili, the syllables of this sentence probably sound like gibberish.*

Well, to a baby learning its native tongue, *every* sentence must, at first, be gibberish. How, then, does an infant pick out discrete syllables and words from the jumble of sounds in its environment, much less figure out what those words mean? Is there something about a baby's brain that is special, something that allows the baby to tune in to language and discover how it works?

*Kama unaweza kusoma maneno haya, wewe ni mtu wa maana sana, in Swahili means, "If you can read these words, you are a remarkable person."

Human beings seem to have an inborn facility for acquiring language, even when they can't hear speech. In North America, deaf people use American Sign Language (ASL) to express not only everyday meanings but also poetic and musical ones, and deaf infants acquire ASL as easily as hearing infants acquire spoken language. These teenagers at a summer camp in New York State are animatedly conversing in sign.

To understand this issue, we must first appreciate that a **language** is not just any old communication system; it is a system for combining elements that are in themselves meaningless into utterances that convey meaning. The elements are usually sounds, but not always. In the United States and Canada, many hearing-impaired people use as their primary language American Sign Language (ASL), which is based on gesture rather than sound, and in other countries, deaf people have developed other gestural languages.

Whether spoken or signed, language allows us to express and comprehend an infinite number of novel utterances, created on the spot. We seem to be the only species that does this naturally. Other primates use a variety of grunts and screeches to warn each other of danger, attract attention, and express emotions, but the sounds are not combined to produce original sentences (at least, as far as we can tell). Bongo may make a certain sound when he encounters food, but he cannot say, "The bananas in the next grove are a lot riper than the ones we ate last week and sure beat our usual diet of termites."

Except for a few fixed phrases ("How are you?" "Get a life"), most of the utterances we produce or hear over a lifetime are new. Thus you will find few, if any, sentences in this book that you have read, heard, or spoken before in exactly the same form. Yet you can understand what you are reading, and you can produce new sentences of your own. According to most *psycholinguists* (researchers who study the psychology of language), you do this by applying a large but finite set of rules that make up the grammar of your language. Rules of *syntax* tell you which strings of sounds or gestural signs form acceptable utterances and which ones do not. Most people cannot actually state the syntactic rules of their grammar ("Adjectives precede the noun they describe"), yet they are able to apply them, without even thinking about it. No native speaker of English would say, "He threw the ball big."

For adults, mastering the rules of a new language can be an intimidating task. But children acquire new words at an amazingly rapid rate—about 9 a day, for a total of more than 14,000 new words during the preschool years. They absorb these words as they encounter them in conversation, typically after hearing only one or two uses of a word in context (Rice, 1989). In a few short years, a child is able to string all those new words together in sentences that make sense, and, most impressive of all, produce and understand an infinite number of new word combinations. A 5-year-old we know was walking home with his

■ **language**

A system that combines meaningless elements such as sounds or gestures to form structured utterances that convey meaning.

Last night, Maurice ate food that disagreed with him.

To "get" this cartoon, you must realize that the caption could have two different meanings and that one of these meanings violates an expectation about the way words can be used in context. The human ability to master language and its sophisticated uses in a relatively short time has persuaded many psycholinguists that the capacity for language is innate.

mother, who was carrying a large shopping bag that kept bumping into him. The boy protested, "It's hitting me in the armpit of my leg!" (Well, how would you describe the back of the knee?)

Where do these dazzling abilities come from? Until the middle of this century, many psychologists assumed that children learned to speak simply by imitating adults and paying attention when adults corrected their mistakes. Then along came linguist Noam Chomsky (1957, 1980), who argued that language was far too complex to be learned bit by bit, as one might learn a list of U.S. presidents or the rules of algebra. Chomsky observed that children not only can figure out which sounds form words but also can take the *surface structure* of a sentence—the way the sentence is actually spoken—and apply rules of syntax to infer an underlying *deep structure* that contains meaning. For example, although "Mary kissed John" and "John was kissed by Mary" have different surface structures, a 5-year-old knows that the two sentences have essentially the same deep structure, in which Mary is the actor and John the recipient of the action. The human brain, said Chomsky, must therefore contain a *language acquisition device*, a mental module that allows young children to develop language if they are exposed to an adequate sampling of speech. Just as a bird is designed to fly, human beings are designed to use language.

Chomsky and others have presented several arguments to support this position (Crain, 1991; Pinker, 1994b):

1. *Children everywhere seem to go through similar stages of linguistic development,* whether they are learning Polish, English, or Chinese (Bloom, 1970; Brown & Fraser, 1964; Brown & Hanlon, 1970; Slobin, 1970). For example, children first form negatives simply by adding *no* or *not* at the beginning or end of a sentence ("No get dirty"); and at a later stage, they will often use double negatives ("He don't want no milk" "Nobody don't like me"), even when their language does not allow such constructions (Klima & Bellugi, 1966; McNeill, 1966). Such facts fit the theory that children are born with a sort of "universal grammar," which is another way of saying that the brain is disposed to notice the features common to all languages (nouns, verbs, phrase structures, and so forth) as well as the variations that can occur. In this view, it is the universal grammar that enables a child to hear the sentence "John likes fish," infer its deep structure, and come up with the similar sentence "Mary eats apples." And it is the same universal grammar that allows the child to know that "John likes fish" is *different* from "John might fish," because otherwise the child would say "John might apples" (Pinker, 1994b). (We will discuss the stages of language development further in Chapter 13.)

2. *Children combine words in ways that adults never would, so children could not simply be imitating.* They reduce a parent's sentences ("Let's go to the store!") to their own two-word version ("Go store!") and make errors an adult would not ("The alligator goed kerplunk," "Daddy taked me," "Hey, Horton heared a Who") (Ervin-Tripp, 1964; Marcus et al., 1992). Such errors are not random, however; they show that the child has grasped a grammatical rule (add the *t* or *d* sound to make a verb past tense, as in *walked* and *hugged*) and is overgeneralizing it (*taked, goed*). Helen Bee (1995) reported this charming conversation between a 6-year-old and a 3-year old, who were arguing about the relative dangers of forgetting to feed pet goldfish or feeding them too much:

> **6-year-old:** It's worse to forget to feed them.
> **3-year-old:** No, it's badder to feed them too much.
> **6-year-old:** You don't say badder, you say worser.
> **3-year-old:** But it's baddest to give them too much food.
> **6-year-old:** No it's not. It's worsest to forget to feed them.

These children had learned a rule for comparisons (*-er* and *-est* endings) but had not yet learned all the exceptions. Such errors, which are called *overregularizations*, are really quite smart, because they show that children are actively seeking regular, predictable rules of language.

3. *Adults do not consistently correct their children's syntax.* Learning explanations of language acquisition assume that children are rewarded for saying the right words and are punished for making errors. But parents don't stop to correct every error in their children's speech, so long as they can understand what the child is trying to say (Brown, Cazden, & Bellugi, 1969). Indeed, parents often *reward* children for incorrect statements! The 2-year-old who says "Want milk!" is likely to get it; most parents would not wait for a more grammatical (or polite) request. Yet, by the tender age of 3, as Steven Pinker (1994b) writes, the child has become "a grammatical genius—master of most constructions, obeying rules far more often than flouting them, respecting language universals, erring in sensible, adultlike ways, and avoiding many kinds of errors altogether."

4. *Even children who are profoundly retarded acquire language.* Indeed, they typically show a facility for language that exceeds by far their abilities in other areas (Bellugi et al., 1992).

Chomsky's ideas so revolutionized thinking about language and human nature that some linguists now refer to the initial publication of his ideas as The Event (Rymer, 1993). Chomsky completely changed the way researchers ask questions about language development, and even the terms they use (language "acquisition" replaced language "learning"). Since then, there have been some efforts to revive the learning approach, based on computer models that mimic aspects of language acquisition without assuming any prior mental rules of grammar (Rumelhart & McClelland, 1987). And research now shows that in addition to the many similarities in the speech of children learning different languages, there are also many dissimilarities (Slobin, 1985, 1991). However, many if not most psycholinguists accept Chomsky's argument that the human faculty for language is biologically based. Although Chomsky himself has avoided the evolutionary implications, others argue that language evolved in our species because it permitted our forebears to convey precise information about time, space, objects, and events, and to negotiate alliances that were necessary for survival (Pinker, 1994b).

The next logical step might be to identify the specific brain mechanisms and genes that contribute to our ability to acquire language. One clue comes from the study of a large three-generation British family with a rare genetic disorder that prevents normal language acquisition. Tests show that people affected with this disorder, although they have normal overall intelligence, cannot infer general grammatical features of words. For example, they can learn the distinction between *mice* and *mouse* but cannot learn the general rule about adding an *s, z,* or *ez* sound to make a noun plural; instead, they must learn each plural as a separate item, and they make many errors. The pattern followed by the disorder suggests that it may be due to a single dominant gene (Gopnik, 1990, 1991).

Findings that support an innate mechanism in language acquisition have inspired evolutionary psychologists to look for similar mechanisms in perception, reasoning, and other aspects of mental life. But remember: In matters as complex as human behavior, nature and nurture nearly always interact. For example, in recent years, studies of middle-class parents have shown that even though parents may not go around correcting their children's speech all day, neither do they ignore their children's errors. They are more likely to repeat verbatim a child's well-formed sentence than a sentence with errors ("That's a horse, mommy!" "Yes, that's a horse"). And when the child does make a mistake or produce a clumsy sentence, parents almost invariably respond by recasting it ("That are monkey!" "Yes, that *is* a monkey") or expanding its basic elements ("Monkey climbing!" "Yes, the monkey is climbing the tree") (Bohannon & Stanowicz, 1988). In turn, children are more likely to imitate adult recasts and expansions, suggesting that they are learning from them (Bohannon & Symons, 1988). They also imitate their parents' accents, inflections, and tone of voice, and they will repeat some words that the parent tries to teach ("This is a ball, Erwin." "Baw"). Children may have a basic capacity to acquire language from mere exposure to it, but many parents help things along.

Language therefore depends on both biological readiness and social experience. Children who are abandoned and abused, and who are not exposed to language for years (such as Genie, whom we discussed in Chapter 2), rarely speak normally. Such sad evidence suggests that there may be a *critical period* in language development, possibly the years between ages 1 and 5, possibly the entire first decade of life (Curtiss, 1977; Lenneberg, 1967). During these years, children do not need to hear speech—deaf children's acquisition of sign language parallels the development of spoken language—but they do need close relationships and practice in conversation.

Quick QUIZ

How evolved is your understanding of evolutionary psychology?

1. Which is the *best* statement of the principle of natural selection? (a) During evolution, the environment naturally selects some traits over others. (b) Genetic variations become more common over time if they are adaptive in a particular environment. (c) A species constantly improves as parents pass along their best traits to their offspring.
2. The guiding principle of evolutionary psychology is that the human mind evolved as (a) a general-purpose computer that adapts to any situation; (b) a blank slate on which experience can write any message; (c) a collection of specific instincts for every human activity or capacity; (d) a collection of specialized modules to handle specific survival problems.
3. According to evolutionary psychologists, which of the following is *not* part of our biological heritage? (a) a sucking reflex at birth; (b) a motive to explore and manipulate objects; (c) an avoidance of novel, unfamiliar objects; (d) a tendency to play and imitate others.
4. Name four arguments for the existence of an innate "universal grammar."

Answers:

1. b 2. d 3. c 4. Children everywhere seem to go through similar stages of linguistic development; children combine words in ways that adults never would; adults do not consistently correct their children's syntax; and even profoundly retarded children acquire language.

Courtship and Mating

Most psychologists would agree that the evolutionary history of our species has made certain kinds of learning either difficult or easy for human beings. Most would agree that human beings inherit some of their perceptual, emotional, and linguistic capacities. There is great disagreement, however, about the biological and evolutionary origins of complex *social* customs, such as those surrounding mating and marriage.

In psychology, and in other social sciences as well, the evolutionary viewpoint on mating practices has been strongly influenced by the writings of sociobiologists. In sociobiology, the focus is not on the species, as it was for Darwin, but on the individual. Sociobiologists contend that evolution has bred into each of us a tendency to act in ways that maximize our chances of passing on our genes, and to help our close biological relatives, with whom we share many genes, do the same. This impulse to act in ways that ensure the survival of our personal genetic code, the sociobiologists argue, is the primary motivation behind much of our social behavior, from altruism (concern for others) to xenophobia (fear of strangers) (Wilson, 1975, 1978). In the sociobiological view, just as nature has selected physical characteristics that have proved adaptive, so it has selected psychological traits and social customs that aid individuals in propagating their genes. Social customs that enhance the odds of reproductive success survive in the form of kinship bonds, courtship rituals, dominance arrangements, taboos against female adultery, and many other aspects of social life.

Sociobiologists argue that because the males and females of most species have faced different kinds of survival and mating problems, they have evolved to differ profoundly in aggressiveness, social dominance, and sexual strategies (Symons, 1979; Trivers, 1972). In this view, it pays for males to compete with other males for access to young and fertile females, and to try to win and then inseminate as many females as possible. The more females a male mates with, the more genes he can pass along. (The world's record in this regard was achieved by a man who fathered 899 children [Daly & Wilson, 1983].) But females need to shop for the best genetic deal, as it were, because they can conceive and bear only a limited number of offspring. Having a large biological investment in each pregnancy, they can't afford to make mistakes. Besides, mating with a lot of different men would produce no more offspring than staying with just one. So, according to sociobiologists, females try to attach themselves to dominant males, who have resources and status and are likely to have "superior" genes. The result of these two opposite sexual strategies is that, in general, males want sex more often than females do; males are often fickle and promiscuous, whereas females are usually devoted and faithful; males are drawn to sexual novelty and even rape, whereas females want stability and security; males are relatively undiscriminating in their choice of partners, whereas females are cautious and choosy; and males are competitive and concerned about dominance, whereas females are less so.

Evolutionary psychologists agree with much of this argument (Buss, 1994). However, unlike the sociobiologists, most evolutionary psychologists do not consider human beings to be "reproductive-fitness maximizers" whose main

This Kenyan man has 40 wives and 349 children. Although he is unusual, in cultures around the world it is far more common for men to have many wives than for women to have many husbands. Sociobiologists and evolutionary psychologists argue that this difference reflects the evolutionary adaptiveness of different sexual and marital strategies.

motive is to perpetuate their genes. As evolutionary psychologist David Buss (1995) points out, if men had a conscious or unconscious motive to maximize their reproductive fitness, they would be lining up to make donations to sperm banks! Instead, say evolutionary psychologists, evolved behavioral tendencies are simply the *end products* of a process of natural selection that took place in the past.

According to evolutionary psychologists, among these end products are mating preferences and strategies similar to those described by the sociobiologists. Supporting evidence comes from many cross-cultural studies, such as one massive project in which 50 scientists studied 10,000 people in 37 cultures located on six continents and five islands (Buss, 1994). Such studies have found that around the world, men are more violent than women, more socially dominant, more interested in the youth and beauty of their sexual partners (presumably because youth is associated with fertility), less discriminating in their choice of partners, quicker to have sex with partners they don't know well, and more inclined toward polygamy and promiscuity. Women, on the other hand, tend to emphasize the financial resources or prospects of a potential mate, his status, and his willingness to commit to a relationship (Buss, 1989, 1994; Daly & Wilson, 1983; Kenrick & Trost, 1993; Sprecher, Sullivan, & Hatfield, 1994). A recent study found that many of these sex differences are shared by gay men and lesbians (Bailey et al., 1994).

It is no accident, say evolutionary psychologists, that these are the very sex differences found among other mammals. Douglas Kenrick and Melanie Trost (1993) observe that hamadryas baboons and Ugandan kob antelopes are unlikely to have been influenced by American television and social customs, so some other explanation of the similarities between people and other species is necessary. That explanation, they believe, starts with our genes.

Critics of the evolutionary approach acknowledge that sex differences exist; but they differ in their explanations for them. It is a mistake, they say, to argue by analogy. Two species may behave in a similar fashion, but this does not necessarily mean that the *origins* of the behavior are the same in both species. For example, a male scorpion fly that coerces a female into copulation can hardly have the same motives as a human rapist, but some sociobiologists use the word *rape* to apply to the behavior of both the fly and the man (Thornhill, 1980). In this way, says geneticist Richard Lewontin (1993), "Human categories are laid

A basic sociobiological assumption is that females across species have a greater investment in child rearing than males do. But there are many exceptions. Female emperor penguins, for example, take off every winter, leaving males like this one behind to take care of the kids.

on animals by analogy, partly as a matter of convenience of language, and then these traits are 'discovered' in animals and laid back on humans as if they had a common origin."

In fact, not all animal behavior or human behavior conforms to the stereotypes of the sexually promiscuous male and the coy and choosy female (Hrdy, 1988; Hubbard, 1990). In many species—including birds, fish, mammals, and primates—females are sexually ardent and often have many male partners. In these species the female's sexual behavior does not seem to depend simply on the goal of being fertilized by the male, because females actively solicit males when the females are not ovulating and even when they are already pregnant! And in many primate species, males do not just mate and run; they stick around, feeding the infants, carrying them on their backs, and protecting them against predators (Hrdy, 1988; Taub, 1984).

These findings have sent primatologists and evolutionary theorists scurrying to figure out the evolutionary benefits of female promiscuity and male nurturance. Perhaps, in some species, females need sperm from several males in order to ensure conception by the healthiest sperm. Perhaps, in some species, females mate with numerous males precisely to make paternity uncertain (Hrdy, 1988). That way, male partners will be more invested in, and tolerant of, the female's infants, and more involved with their infants' survival.

But critics of evolutionary theories take exception to this entire line of reasoning. The evidence of female promiscuity in other species, they say, has no more relevance to human behavior than does evidence of female fidelity. Among human beings, sexual behavior is extremely varied and changeable. Human cultures range from those in which women have many children to those in which they have very few; from those in which men are intimately involved in child rearing to those in which they do nothing at all; from those in which women may have many lovers to those in which women may be killed if they have sex outside of marriage. Even within a given culture, there are startling variations. For example, a recent nationally representative sex survey found that the number of partners a person has over a lifetime varies by education and religion, with educated people and Jewish or nonreligious people of both sexes having the most partners (Laumann et al., 1994). Such variations, say the critics, argue against a single, genetically determined sexual strategy. In rebuttal, evolutionary theorists reply that cultural variation does not negate the importance of biology. "Evolutionary theorists do not deny that there is a great variation in the range of human social behavior," observe Kenrick and Trost (1993), but "they believe that, underneath all the variation, it is possible to discern some regularities in human behavior."

This may seem like a moderate conclusion, but debate over these matters can get quite heated, mostly because evolutionary arguments have troublesome political implications. Critics worry that these arguments will be used to justify existing social and political arrangements and behavior patterns. Do men rape women? The evolutionary perspective could be used to argue that rape is a biological imperative—modifiable, perhaps, but impossible to eliminate. Do men dominate women and control business and politics everywhere? Well, given the history of our species, one could argue that that's just the way it has turned out; after all, who are we to question thousands of years of evolution? Indeed, Edward Wilson (1975), one of the leading proponents of sociobiology, once wrote that because of genetics, "Even with identical education and equal access to all professions [for both sexes], men are likely to continue to play a disproportionate role in political life, business, and science." This is not a message that people who hope for gender equality welcome! In 1978, demonstrators at a meeting of the American Association for the Advancement of Science dumped water on Wilson's head, chanting "Wilson, you're all wet!" The American Anthropological Association even considered censuring him until Margaret Mead, an ardent environmentalist if there ever was one, defended him by reminding the association that censure would be equivalent to book burning (Wilson, 1994).

Ultimately, the central issue in this debate has to do with the relative power of biology and culture. In *On Human Nature* (1978), Wilson argued that genes hold culture on a leash. The big question, replied paleontologist Stephen Jay Gould (1987), is: How long and tight is that leash? Is it only 1 foot long, in which case a society doesn't have much room to maneuver and change, or is it 10 feet long, in which case biology merely establishes a broad range of possibilities? To most sociobiologists, the near universality of certain human customs is evidence that the leash is short and tight. To most psychologists working from other perspectives, the enormous variation among individuals and societies is evidence that the leash is a long and loose one. The majority of evolutionary psychologists seem to fall somewhere in the middle. They emphasize the adaptive nature of mating and courtship customs in the environments in which our species evolved, but they also acknowledge that some of these customs may no longer be adaptive or intelligent in our current environments (Buss, 1995; Mealey, in press). They note that human beings have evolved to be flexible enough to change when environmental demands change.

In a simple study that illustrates this point, social psychologist Linda Carli and her associates (1993) asked students to rate the desirability of various characteristics in a mate or a marriage partner. Half the students were asked to imagine that they were independently wealthy; the other half, the control subjects, were given no special instructions. In the control group, women were more likely than men to say they desired a wealthy and successful partner, and men were more likely than women to want youth and physical attractiveness—just as the sociobiologists would predict. But in the group that imagined themselves to be wealthy, there were *no* gender differences! Perhaps as women's status and resources rise, their mating preferences and actual choices may change accordingly. Time—and more research—will tell.

Certain sex differences in courtship and mating are common in cultures around the world—and among other mammals as well. But there are also many variations in human sexual behavior. Do genes hold culture on a tight leash, a long and flexible one, or none at all? How might we go about answering this question?

Quick QUIZ

1. According to sociobiologists, human social customs reflect a tendency of individuals to act in ways that ensure the survival of (a) the species, (b) their particular ethnic or national group, (c) their personal genetic code.
2. Which of the following, if any, would a sociobiologist or evolutionary psychologist expect to be more typical of males than of females? (a) promiscuity, (b) choosiness about sexual partners, (c) concern with dominance, (d) interest in young partners, (e) emphasis on physical attractiveness of partners.
3. A friend of yours, who has read some sociobiology, tells you that men will *always* be more sexually promiscuous than women because during evolution, the best reproductive strategy for male primates has been to inseminate lots of females. What kind of evidence would you need to examine to evaluate this claim?

Answers:

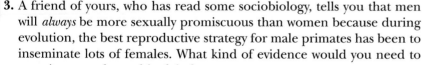

1. c   2. all but b   3. You would not want to look just for confirming evidence (recall the principle of falsifiability). You would want to look also for evidence of female promiscuity and male monogamy among humans and other species and changes in sexual customs in response to changing social conditions.

■ OUR HUMAN DIVERSITY: THE GENETICS OF DIFFERENCE

We turn now to the second great issue in the nature–nurture debate: the origins of the differences among us. We begin with a critical discussion of what heritability means and how it can be estimated. Then, to illustrate how behavioral geneticists study differences that might be partly heritable, we will examine two (unrelated!) topics: weight and intelligence. In Chapter 12, we will discuss behavioral-genetic explanations of personality, and in Chapter 15, we will consider behavioral-genetic explanations of mental disorders.

The Heritability Hunt

✦ *What does it mean to say that some trait is "highly heritable"? If you want to improve your flute playing and someone tells you that musical ability is heritable, should you stop practicing?*

Suppose you want to measure flute-playing ability in a large group of music students. You have some independent raters assign each student a score, from 1 to 20, and when you plot the scores you see that they vary considerably. Some people are what you might call melodically disadvantaged and should forget about a career in music; others are flute geniuses, practically ready for Carnegie Hall; and the rest fall somewhere in between. What causes the variation in this group of students? Why are some so musically talented and others so inept? Are these differences primarily genetic, or are they the result of experience and motivation?

The methods used by behavioral geneticists to study such questions typically yield a statistical estimate of the *proportion of the total variance* in a trait that is attributable to *genetic variation within a group*. This estimate is known as the trait's **heritability.** Because the heritability of a trait is expressed as a proportion, the maximum value it can have is 1.0. Height is highly heritable; that is, within a group of equally well-nourished individuals, most of the variation among them will be accounted for by their genetic differences. In contrast, table manners have low heritability because most variation among individuals is accounted for by differences in upbringing. Our guess is that flute-playing ability falls somewhere in the middle.

Many people hold completely mistaken ideas about heritability. You can't understand the nature–nurture issue without understanding this concept, and in particular, the following five important facts:

1. *"Heritable" does not mean the same thing as "genetic."* The reason is that estimates of heritability apply only to traits that vary in a population. Many genetic traits, such as breathing, are crucial for life and therefore do not vary; if you are alive, you breathe. Such traits are 100 percent genetic, but their calculated heritability would be zero because there is no variation to explain. Of course, a tendency to develop a breathing disorder, such as asthma, can be partly heritable.

2. *An estimate of heritability applies only to a particular group living in a particular environment, and estimates may differ for different groups.* Suppose that all the children in Oz County are affluent, eat plenty of high-quality food, have kind and attentive parents, and go to the same top-notch schools. The intellectual differences among them will probably be due largely to their genetic differences, because their environments are similar and are optimal for intellectual development. In contrast, the children who live in Normal County are rich, poor, and in between. Some of them have healthy diets; others live on fatty foods and cupcakes. Some attend good schools; others go to miserably inadequate ones. Some have doting parents, and some have unloving and neglectful ones. Because these children's intellectual differences might be due to their environmental differences, estimates of the heritability of intelligence may be lower in this group.

■ **heritability**
A statistical estimate of the proportion of the total variance in some trait within a group that is attributable to genetic differences among individuals within the group.

3. *Heritability estimates do not apply to individuals, only to variations within a group.* No one can determine the impact of heredity on any *particular* individual's intellectual or emotional makeup. Journalistic accounts of behavioral-genetics research often overlook this fact. In a *Time* article on the heritability of intelligence (January 12, 1987), we found this passage: "How much of any individual's personality is due to heredity? The . . . answer: about half." That statement is extremely misleading. As we saw, each individual is a unique genetic mosaic. Each individual also has a unique history in terms of family relationships, intellectual training, and motivation. For these reasons, no one can say whether your particular genius at, say, flute playing is a result of inherited musical talent, living all your life in a family of devoted flute players, a private obsession that you acquired at age 6 when you saw the opera *The Magic Flute*—or a combination of all three. For one person, genes may make a tremendous difference in some aptitude or disposition; for another, the environment may be far more important.

4. *Even highly heritable traits can be modified by the environment.* Although height is highly heritable, malnourished children may not grow to be as tall as they would with sufficient food. Conversely, if children eat a supernutritious diet, they may grow to be taller than anyone thought they could. The same principle applies to psychological traits, although some writers have failed to realize this. Some biological determinists, for example, have argued that because IQ is highly heritable, IQ and school achievement cannot be boosted much. But even if the first part of the statement is true, the second part does not necessarily follow.

5. *Heritable behavioral traits are usually influenced by many genes working in combination.* It is unlikely that any single gene confers musical talent, mathematical ability, or a sunny disposition. Nor do genes produce behavior directly; remember, what genes do is encode instructions for the structure of proteins, which in turn affect the structure and functioning of the body and brain, with potential implications for behavior.

There is no way for scientists to estimate the heritability of a particular trait or behavior directly, so they must *infer* it by studying people whose degree of genetic similarity is known. The simplest approach might seem to be a comparison of blood relatives within families. Everyone knows of families that are famous for some talent or trait. But anecdotes and isolated examples can always be answered with counterexamples. There were seven generations of musical Bachs, but Mendelssohn's father was a banker, Chopin's a bookkeeper, and Schubert's a schoolmaster, and their mothers were not known to have musical talent (Lewontin, 1982). Results from controlled studies of families are also inconclusive, for close relatives usually share environments as well as genes. If Carlo's parents and siblings all love lasagna, that doesn't mean a taste for lasagna is heritable. The same applies if everyone in Carlo's family has a high IQ, is mentally ill, or is moody.

There are two ways out of this bind. One is to study adopted children (e.g., Loehlin, Horn, & Willerman, in press; Plomin & DeFries, 1985). Such children share half their genes but not their environment with each birth parent. On the other hand, they share an environment but not their genes with their adoptive parents and adoptive siblings. Researchers can compare correlations between the children's traits and those of their biological and adoptive relatives and use the results to estimate heritability.

The other approach is to compare **identical (monozygotic) twins** with **fraternal (dizygotic) twins.** Identical twins are created when a fertilized egg divides into two parts that then develop into two separate embryos. Because the twins come from the same fertilized egg, they share all their genes, barring genetic mutations or other accidents. (They may be slightly different at birth,

▪ **identical (monozygotic) twins**
Twins born when a fertilized egg divides into two parts that develop into separate embryos.

▪ **fraternal (dizygotic) twins**
Twins that develop from two separate eggs fertilized by different sperm; they are no more alike genetically than any other pair of siblings.

Some identical twins love to accentuate their similarities. To psychologists, the similarities—and differences—between twins are important for what they tell us about heritability.

however, because of birth complications, differences in the blood supply to the two fetuses, or the chance factors mentioned earlier in this chapter.) In contrast, fraternal twins develop when a woman's ovaries release two eggs instead of one, and each egg is fertilized by a different sperm. Fraternal twins are wombmates but are no more alike genetically than any other two siblings and may be of different sexes. By comparing groups of same-sex fraternal twins to groups of identical twins, psychologists can try to estimate heritability. The assumption is that if identical twins are more alike than fraternal twins, the increased similarity must be genetic.

Perhaps, however, environments shared by identical twins differ from those shared by fraternal twins. People may treat identical twins, well, identically, or go to the other extreme by emphasizing their differences. To avoid this problem, investigators have studied identical twins who were separated early in life and reared apart. (Until recently, adoption policies and attitudes toward illegitimacy permitted such separations to occur.) In theory, separated identical twins share all their genes but not their environments. Any similarities between them should be primarily genetic and should thus permit a direct estimate of heritability.

Past studies of twins reared apart had some serious flaws. Most twins supposedly reared apart had not been so far apart after all. Many had visited one another during childhood or were reared by relatives in the same town or went to the same school. Of 121 sets studied between 1922 and 1973, only 3 were strangers at the time of study. Also, ratings of similarity were typically based on only a few tests, self-reports, or casual observations (Farber, 1981).

Research on twins today has addressed many of these problems. In one project, begun in 1979, an interdisciplinary team at the University of Minnesota has been testing and interviewing identical and fraternal twins reared apart (Bouchard, 1984, 1995, in press; Bouchard et al., 1990, 1991; Tellegen et al., 1988). Subjects undergo six days of psychological and medical monitoring and answer some 15,000 written questions. Information has been reported on many sets of reunited twins and also on many twins reared together. This kind of research is transforming our understanding of behavior that was once explained solely in psychological terms, and nowhere is this more true than in the study of body weight and shape.

Drawing by Chas. Addams; ©1981 The New Yorker Magazine, Inc.

Separated at birth, the Mallifert twins meet accidentally.

Quick QUIZ

1. Diane hears that basket-weaving ability is highly heritable and concludes that her own low performance must be due mostly to genes. What's wrong with her reasoning?
2. Bertram reads that an ability is highly heritable in adults and concludes that schools should stop trying to instill the ability in those who seem low in it. What's wrong with his reasoning?
3. Carpentry skills seem to run in Andy's family. Why shouldn't Andy conclude that his talent is genetic?

Answers:

1. Heritability applies only to differences among individuals within a group, not to particular individuals. 2. A trait can be highly heritable *and* susceptible to modification. 3. Family members share environments as well as genes.

Body Weight and Shape

At one time, most psychologists thought that being fat was a sign of emotional disturbance. If you were overweight, it was because you hated your mother, or feared intimacy, or were trying to fill an emotional hole in your psyche by loading up on rich desserts. The evidence for this belief, however, came mainly from self-reports, and many studies were seriously flawed: They lacked control groups, and they overlooked the possibility that people were saying what they thought researchers wanted to hear (Allison & Heshka, 1993). When researchers put this popular idea to the test, they found no support for it. On average, fat people are no more and no less emotionally disturbed than average-weight people (Stunkard, 1980).

Even more surprising, studies show that *heaviness is not always caused by overeating* (C. Bouchard et al., 1990). Many heavy people do eat enormous quantities of food, but so do some very thin people. Some thin people eat very little, but so do some obese people. In one study that carefully monitored every-

Obesity is caused mainly by psychological problems that drive people to overeat, isn't it? This idea is logical, obvious, . . . and wrong. What other theories might explain why some slender people eat a lot and some overweight people eat very little?

Is this man heavy because of his genes, his diet, or both? Does your answer affect how you feel about him—sympathetic, neutral, or contemptuous?

thing that subjects were eating, two 260-pound women maintained their weights while consuming only 1,000 calories a day (Wooley, Wooley, & Dyrenforth, 1979). In another study, in which volunteers were required to gorge themselves for months, it was as hard for slender people to gain weight as it is for most heavy people to lose weight. The minute the study was over, the slender people lost weight as fast as dieters gained it back (Sims, 1974).

One theory that integrates these findings argues that a biological mechanism keeps a person's body weight at a genetically influenced **set point**—the weight the person stays at when not thinking about it (Lissner et al., 1991). According to this theory, everyone has a genetically programmed *basal metabolism rate,* the rate at which the body burns calories for energy, and a fixed number of *fat cells,* cells in the body that store fat for energy. The fat cells can change in size but not in number. An interaction of metabolism, fat cells, and hormones keeps people at the weight their bodies are designed to be. Set-point theory explains why the majority of people who go on restricted diets eventually gain their weight back; they are returning to their set-point weight (Lissner et al., 1991).

In twin and adoption studies, estimates of the heritability of body weight and shape vary considerably, ranging from 25 percent to 80 percent (Allison et al., 1994; C. Bouchard et al., 1990; Stunkard et al., 1990). But it seems clear that size and weight differences among people can be explained to some extent by their genetic differences. When a heavy person diets, the body's metabolism may slow down to conserve energy and fat reserves. When a thin person overeats, metabolism may speed up, burning energy. Set-point theory has been supported by dozens of studies of animals and human beings (Keesey, 1980; Leibel, Rosenbaum, & Hirsch, 1995; Levitan & Ronan, 1988). For example:

- In a study of 171 Pima Indians in Arizona, researchers found that two-thirds of the women and half of the men became obese over time, and the slower their metabolisms, the greater the weight gain. After adding anywhere from 20 to 45 pounds, however, the Pimas stopped gaining weight. Now their metabolism rates rose, and their weights stabilized at the new, higher level (Ravussin et al., 1988). Many Pimas apparently have a set point for plumpness.

- In a study of 18 infants at 3 months of age, the babies of overweight mothers generated 21 percent less energy than the babies of normal-weight mothers, although all the babies were eating the same amount. By age 1, these lower-metabolism babies had become overweight (Roberts et al., 1988).

- Genes also affect whether the body will convert excess calories into fat or muscle, and what the basic body *shape* will be (pear, apple, hourglass, tree trunk, and so on). In a study of 12 pairs of adult male identical twins, Claude Bouchard and his colleagues (1990) confined the men to a dormitory for 100 days, where they were forbidden to exercise and were given a diet that contained 1,000 extra calories a day. Each *pair* of twins gained almost exactly the same amount of weight, but the differences *between* different twin pairs was astonishing. One pair of twins gained 9½ pounds, but another pair gained almost 30—all of them on only 1,000 extra calories a day. Some twins gained weight on their hips and thighs, but others gained weight around the waist. And in another study, pairs of adult identical twins who had been raised in different families were just as similar in body weight and shape as twins raised together. The early family environment had almost no effect at all on body shape, weight gain, or percentage of fat in the body (Stunkard et al., 1990).

■ **set point**
According to one theory, the genetically influenced weight range for an individual, thought to be maintained by a biological mechanism that regulates food intake, fat reserves, and metabolism.

Recently, researchers have identified a genetic variation in mice that could help explain some types of obesity in humans (Zhang et al., 1994). The usual

Body shape and weight are strongly influenced by genetic factors. Set-point theory helps explain why the Pima tribe of the American Southwest (left) gain weight easily but lose it slowly, whereas the Bororo nomads of Niger (right) can eat a lot of food yet remain slender.

form of the gene causes fat cells to secrete a hormonelike substance that travels through the blood to a brain area called the hypothalamus, which is involved in the regulation of appetite. Varying levels of this substance signal how large or small the fat cells are, and the brain can then regulate appetite to maintain the animal's set point. When the variant form of the gene, called "obese" or *ob* for short, is present, fat cells make less of the substance or perhaps none at all, and the animal becomes obese. If the ob variant is present in human beings, as it appears to be, it may cause the person to feel hungry and keep eating even when the body has enough stored fat to meet current energy demands. According to evolutionary psychologists, obesity genes probably exist in our species because in our prehistoric past, starvation was all too often a real possibility. Thus, a tendency to store calories in the form of fat provided a definite survival advantage.

Most people in our culture still mistakenly blame obesity on slothfulness, gluttony, and weakness of will (Crandall, 1994). Therefore, the discovery of genetic influences on body weight and shape may help to combat society's rampant prejudice toward obese individuals. Yet to many researchers, obesity is a legitimate matter of medical concern because it is associated with a higher risk of heart dis-

Research with mice finds that some forms of obesity can be traced to genes. One of these mice has been bred to be thin, whereas the other has been bred to be chubby.

Although heredity contributes to weight and body size, genes alone do not explain overweight. Sedentary lifestyles and a fondness for high-fat fast foods are the main reasons that average weights in North America have been increasing for many years.

ease, hypertension, diabetes, some cancers, and other diseases. Should seriously overweight people try to fight their set points or society's prejudices?

The behavioral-genetics research on obesity shows again the danger of thinking that *either* heredity *or* environment is the whole story. Genes set limits for body weight and shape, but other factors affect weight within that range. One such factor is eating habits—what a person eats and how much of it. If you consume the high-fat junk food diet that so many Americans love (indeed, that human beings might be evolutionarily primed to love), and if you eat such food in the large quantities that most Europeans and Asians find excessive and alarming, you are likely to be heavier than if you eat a low-fat diet in moderate portions. As one physician wrote to *The New York Times,* "Perhaps the flaw lies not so much in our mutations as in McDonald's."

A second factor is exercise, which boosts the body's metabolic rate and may lower the set point. In one study of 18 obese women who were on severely restricted diets, metabolism rates dropped sharply, as set-point theory would predict. But the women who combined the diet with modest physical activity—daily walking—lost weight, and their metabolic rates rose almost to previous levels (Wadden et al., 1990). This study suggests why changes in weight often accompany major changes in habits and activity levels. People start walking to work (or stop). They become lethargic after losing a job (and gain weight), or excited when they fall in love (and lose weight).

In turn, culture has an enormous influence on how and what people eat and how much exercise they get. During the 1950s and 1960s, surveys found that about 7 percent of American men and 14 percent of women were trying to lose weight. Over the years, the numbers rose steadily, until today about a quarter of all men and two-fifths of all women say they are dieting (Horm & Anderson, 1993; Serdula et al., 1993). Yet all this dieting has not produced a thinner population. In fact, the prevalence of obesity has doubled since 1900 and has continued to rise dramatically in recent years (Kuczmarski et al., 1994). The reasons are less likely to have to do with obesity genes than with the increased abundance of high-fat foods, the habit of eating high-calorie food on the run rather than leisurely meals, the rise in energy-saving (fat-conserving!) devices, the popularity of television over active hobbies, and increasingly sedentary lifestyles (Brownell & Rodin, 1994).

The research on weight contains a lesson that applies to many other areas of behavior: Within a given environment, genes and other biological factors place some limits on how much a person can change. Even if you make daily trips to the gym and eat a healthy diet, you may never look like the current cultural ideal, which is biologically impossible for many people. But there is much you can do to maintain your healthiest personal weight, as we discuss in "Taking Psychology with You."

Quick QUIZ

1. According to set-point theory, when a thin person overeats, metabolism tends to _____, whereas when a heavy person diets, metabolism tends to _____.
2. Research on twins indicates that genes contribute not only to differences in weight but also to differences in body _____.
3. Animal research on the ob gene suggests that obese people may lack a hormonelike substance that helps the brain regulate _____.

 4. Bill, who is thin, reads in the paper that genes set the range of body weight and shape. "Oh, good," he exclaims, "now I can eat all the junk food I want; I was born to be skinny." What's wrong with Bill's conclusion?

Answers:

do with overweight.
don't exercise; also rich junk food is unhealthy for reasons that have nothing to
leanness will gain some weight on fatty foods and excess calories, especially if they
simplifying and jumping to conclusions. Even people who have a set point for
that there may be limits to how heavy he can become. But he may also be over-
1. increase; slow down **2.** shape **3.** appetite or hunger **4.** Bill is right to recognize

Origins of Intelligence

Most people think that differences in body weight are due entirely to psychological factors, but as we have seen, heredity is also involved. In contrast, many people think that individual differences in intelligence are due entirely to hereditary factors, but as we will see, psychology is also very much involved. Likewise, many people think that weight is easier to change than it is—and that IQ is harder to change than it is. In this section, we consider how biology and learning affect intelligence just as they affect weight.

In heritability studies, the usual measure of intellectual functioning is an **intelligence quotient,** or **IQ** score. The term "IQ" is a holdover from the early days of psychological testing, when intelligence tests were given only to children. A child's *mental age* (MA)—the child's level of intellectual development relative to other children's—was divided by the child's chronological age (CA) and multiplied by 100 to yield an *intelligence quotient* (IQ). Thus a child of 8 who performed like the average 6-year-old would have a mental age of 6 and an IQ of 75 (6/8 times 100); and a child of 8 who scored like an average 10-year-old would have a mental age of 10 and an IQ of 125 (10/8 times 100). All average children, regardless of age, would have an IQ of 100 because MA and CA would be the same. In actual calculations, months were used, not years, to yield a more precise figure.

This method of figuring IQ had a serious flaw. At one age, scores might cluster tightly around the average, whereas at another age, they might be somewhat more dispersed. As a result, the IQ score necessary to be in the top 10 or 20 or 30 percent of one's age group varied, depending on one's age. Because of this problem, and because the IQ formula did not make much sense for adults, today's intelligence tests are scored differently. Usually, the average is arbitrarily set at 100, and test scores—still informally referred to as "IQs"—are computed from tables. A score still reflects how a person compares with other people, either children of a particular age or adults in general. At all ages, the distribution of scores approximates a bell-shaped curve, with scores near the average (mean) most common and very high or very low scores rare (see Figure 3.1).

■ **intelligence quotient (IQ)**
A measure of intelligence originally computed by dividing a person's mental age by his or her chronological age and multiplying the result by 100; it is now derived from norms provided for standardized intelligence tests.

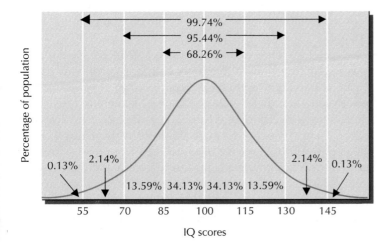

■ **Figure 3.1 Expected Distribution of IQ Scores**

In a large population, IQ scores will tend to be distributed on a normal (bell-shaped) curve. On most tests, about 68 percent of all people are expected to score between 85 and 115; about 95 percent will score between 70 and 130; and about 99.7 percent will score between 55 and 145. In any actual sample, however, the distribution will depart somewhat from the theoretical ideal. In particular, very low scores will usually outnumber very high ones because of mental retardation caused by neurological disorders.

IQ tests have many critics, and, in fact, the entire concept of intelligence is controversial. Contrary to the assumption that intelligence is a single quality that can be summed up by a single number, intelligence comes in many varieties; moreover, the ability to perform well on standard intelligence tests is deeply affected by culture. (We will discuss kinds of intelligence and their cultural origins in Chapter 8.) Keep in mind, then, that heritability studies are estimating only the heritability of those mental skills that contribute to IQ test scores, not necessarily all aspects of mental performance, and that the tests are likely to be more valid for some groups than for others.

Variations Within Groups. With these important qualifications, we can say, on the basis of behavioral-genetics studies, that variations in IQ test scores are partly heritable. On the average, studies of children and adolescents estimate heritability to be about .50; that is, about half of the variance in IQ scores is explainable by genetic differences (Chipuer, Rovine, & Plomin, 1990; Plomin, 1989). And studies of adults tend to get higher estimates—in the .70 to .80 range (McGue et al., 1993). Although heritability estimates range widely across different studies and different tests, from as low as .10 to almost .90, the scores of identical twins are always more highly correlated than those of fraternal twins. In fact, the scores of identical twins reared apart are more highly correlated than those of fraternal twins reared together. In adoption studies, the scores of adopted children are more highly correlated with those of their birth parents than with those of their adoptive parents, and by adolescence, the scores of adopted children correlate only weakly with those of their biologically unrelated adoptive siblings (Plomin, 1988).

Of course, if heredity accounts for only part of why people differ in their scores on mental tests, the environment (and random errors in measurement) must account for the rest. As Robert Plomin (1989), a leading behavioral geneticist, has observed, "The wave of acceptance of genetic influence on behavior is growing into a tidal wave that threatens to engulf the second message of this research: These same data provide the best available evidence for the importance of environmental influences."

The following environmental influences can have a large impact on mental ability, even when heritability is fairly high, and some have been implicated in the lower IQ scores of children from poor and working-class families, as compared with those from middle-class families:

- *Prenatal care.* If a pregnant woman is malnourished, contracts infections, takes certain drugs, smokes or drinks excessively, or is exposed to environmental pollutants, the fetus is at risk of having a reduced IQ and learning disabilities.

- *Nutrition.* Early malnutrition slows brain growth and mental development (Stoch & Smythe, 1963; Winick, Meyer, & Harris, 1975). The average IQ gap between severely malnourished and well-nourished children can be as high as 20 points.

- *Exposure to toxins.* Children exposed to toxins such as lead, which can damage the nervous system, have lower IQ scores and more problems paying attention than do other children. These children also continue to perform more poorly on mental tests and school-achievement tests when they reach adolescence (Needleman, Leviton, & Bellinger, 1982; Needleman et al., 1990). Nearly 9 percent of all children in the United States ages 1 to 5 are exposed to dangerous levels of lead from lead paint and old lead pipes, and for black children ages 1 and 2 the percentage rises to 21.6 (Brody et al., 1994).

- *Mental stimulation.* Dozens of animal studies show that a stimulating environment actually alters the structure of the brain. Rats that learn complicated tasks or grow up in cages equipped with lots of rat toys develop thicker and heavier cortexes and richer networks of connections in some brain areas than do rats in unchallenging environments (Greenough & Anderson, 1991; Greenough & Black, 1992; Rosenzweig, 1984). Stimulation is important in human mental development, as well. A study examined nearly a thousand premature infants who, because of their prematurity, were at risk for delayed development. A combination of intensive educational efforts, home visits by specialists, and training of parents about how to stimulate cognitive and social development through games and other activities resulted in an average IQ score at age 3 that was significantly higher than that of a control group (Infant Health and Development Program, 1990). These results are especially impressive because the children were assigned randomly to the two groups, the testers were unaware of which group the children were in, and the children came from a variety of income levels and ethnic origins.

One of the most important things parents can do is to stimulate their children intellectually by reading to them, asking them questions, and providing books and games.

- *Family size.* The average IQ in a family tends to decline as the number of children rises (Belmont & Marolla, 1973). Birth order also makes a difference: IQ tends to decline slightly in each successive child (Zajonc & Markus, 1975). Most researchers attribute these facts to the reduced time parents with many children can spend with each child.

- *Individual experiences.* General environmental factors, such as parents' education or social class, do not explain why siblings who grow up together in the same household often have different interests and talents. Increasingly, psychologists are finding that individual experiences that are not shared with other family members, such as having an inspiring teacher, being favored or not favored by a parent, or winning a prize in a science fair, can affect a child's aptitudes and achievements (Dunn & Plomin, 1990).

- *Stressful family circumstances.* In a project known as the Rochester Longitudinal Study, researchers have been tracking several hundred children from birth through early adolescence, correlating family risk factors with the children's intellectual competence and general adjustment (Sameroff et al., 1987; Sameroff & Seifer, 1989). These risk factors include a father who does not live with the family, a mother with a history of mental illness, low parental work skills, and a history of stressful events during the child's early life. On average, each risk factor reduces a child's IQ score by 4 points. Children with no risk factors score more than *30 points higher* than those with seven or eight risk factors (see Figure 3.2).

- *Parent–child interactions.* In general, children who score well on IQ tests have parents who spend time with them, encourage them to think things through, read to them, provide appropriate toys and field trips, and

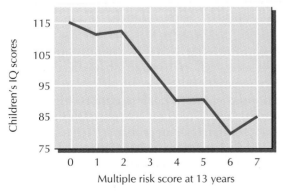

Children's IQ scores

Multiple risk score at 13 years

■ **Figure 3.2 Family Risk Factors and Children's IQ Scores**

The greater the number of stressful family circumstances, the lower a child's IQ score is likely to be (Sameroff & Seifer, 1989). An enormous gap exists between the average IQ score of children with no family risk factors and the scores of those with many, as you can see from this graph.

The children of migrant workers (left) often spend long hours in backbreaking field work, and may miss out on the educational opportunities and intellectual advantages available to middle-class children (right).

expect them to do well (Bee et al., 1982; Bradley & Caldwell, 1984). Such parents talk to their children about many topics and describe things accurately and fully (Clarke-Stewart, VanderStoep, & Killian, 1979; Dickson et al., 1979). Most important, their reactions to their children are tied directly to what the children do (Beckwith & Cohen, 1984). By answering their children's questions and responding to their actions, these parents give their children a sense of competence and teach them that their efforts matter.

These parenting skills can be taught. In one study of 30 middle-class parents and their toddlers, parents learned during two brief training sessions to ask open-ended questions when reading to their offspring ("What is the cat doing?") instead of merely asking the children to point out objects or answer yes–no types of questions ("Is the cat asleep?"). The parents also learned to expand on the child's answers, provide alternative responses, correct inaccurate responses, and give plenty of praise. Parents in a control group read just as often to their children but did not get the special instruction. After only a month, the children in the experimental group were 8½ months ahead of those in the control group in their expressive-language skills and 6 months ahead of them in vocabulary skills (Whitehurst et al., 1988). A similar study, in which parents and child-care teachers read interactively with low-income children, also produced highly significant vocabulary enhancement (Whitehurst et al., 1994). The implications are enormous when you consider that by one estimate, the average low-income child enters first grade with only 25 hours of one-on-one picture-book reading, compared to 1,000 to 1,700 hours for middle-class children (Adams, 1990).

We see, then, that heredity may provide the range of a child's intellectual potential, but many other factors affect where in that range the child will fall. The same heritability studies illustrate both conclusions. For example, as we noted, the IQ scores of adopted children correlate more highly with their birth parents' scores than with those of their adoptive parents. This fact supports the heritability of intelligence as measured by IQ tests. However, in *absolute* terms, Johnny's IQ may differ considerably from the scores of his birth parents: Indeed, on the average, adopted children have IQs that are 10 to 20 points *higher* than those of their birth parents (Scarr & Weinberg, 1977). Most psychologists believe that this difference exists because adoptive families are generally smaller, wealthier, and better educated than other families—and these family characteristics are associated with higher IQs in children.

Variations Between Groups.

So far, we have considered intellectual differences only *within* a group of individuals. For many years, researchers have also wondered about the origins of differences *between* groups. Unfortunately, the history of this issue has been marred by ethnic, class, and gender prejudice (see "Psychology and Popular Culture" on pages 108–109). Too often, in the words of Stephen Jay Gould (1981), interpretations of research have been bent to support the belief that some groups are destined by "the harsh dictates of nature" to be subordinate to others.

In recent years, most of the interest in group differences has focused on black–white differences in IQ. African-American children score, on average, some 10 to 15 points lower on IQ tests than do white children. Keep in mind that we are talking about *averages;* the distributions of scores for black and white children overlap considerably.

A few psychologists have proposed a genetic explanation of this difference (Jensen, 1969, 1981; Rushton, 1988). As you can imagine, these theories have provoked an emotional response. Genetic explanations, however innocent of racism their academic advocates may be, are music to the ears of people who consider whites to be inherently superior to blacks and who consider racial inequality to be inevitable (but who usually ignore the fact that Asians, on the average, score higher on IQ tests than whites do). Racists often cite such theories to justify their own hatreds and discrimination. It is vital, therefore, that we all know how to evaluate genetic theories of group differences. What are the facts?

One fatal flaw in genetic theories of black–white differences is their use of heritability estimates based mainly on white samples to estimate the role heredity plays in *group* differences. This problem sounds pretty technical, but it is not really difficult to understand, so stay with us.

Consider, first, not people but tomatoes. (This "thought experiment," illustrated in Figure 3.3, is based on Lewontin, 1970.) Suppose you have a bag of tomato seeds that vary genetically; all things being equal, some will produce tomatoes that are puny and tasteless, and some will produce tomatoes that are plump and delicious. Now you take a bunch of seeds in your left hand and a bunch in your right. Though one seed differs genetically from another, there is no *average* difference between the seeds in your left hand and those in your right. You plant the left hand's seeds in pot A with some soil that you have doctored with nitrogen and other nutrients, and you plant the right hand's seeds in pot B with soil from which you have extracted nutrients. When the tomatoes grow, they will vary in size *within* each pot, purely because of genetic differences. But there will also be an average difference between pot A and pot B. This difference *between* pots is due entirely to the different soils—even though the *within*-pot heritability is 100 percent.

The principle is the same for people as it is for tomatoes. Most psychologists believe that differences *within* groups are at least partly genetic. But that does not mean that differences *between* groups are genetic. Blacks and whites do not grow up, on the average, in the same kinds of environments. Because of a long legacy of racial discrimination and de facto segregation, black children (as well as Latino and other minority children) often receive far fewer nutrients—literally, in terms of food, and figuratively, in terms of education, encouragement by society, and intellectual opportunities. Moreover, groups differ in countless cultural ways that affect their performance on IQ tests (as we will discuss in detail in Chapter 8).

✴ *Behavioral-genetics studies, on the average, show the heritability of intelligence to be high. A popular book argues that heredity must play a similarly large role in average IQ differences between ethnic groups. What's wrong with that reasoning?*

Poor Soil   Rich Soil

■ Figure 3.3   The Tomato Plant Experiment

Even if the differences among plants within each pot were due entirely to genetic differences, the average difference between pots could be entirely environmental. The same principle applies to individual and group differences among human beings.

Psychology and Popular Culture

Genes, Intolerance, and IQ

■ A hammer is a tool that can be used to build a house or to bash a head. Mental tests are tools, too, and the way they are used depends on the temper of the times, political trends in society, and scientists' own intentions and prejudices. History amply documents that scientific research about intelligence is not a neutral matter, like the study of musical talent or perception.

Consider the origins of the IQ test itself. In 1904, the French Ministry of Education asked psychologist Alfred Binet (1857–1911) to design a test that would identify slow learners. School attendance had just been made mandatory, but some children did not learn well in an ordinary classroom and needed special help. The ministry was reluctant to let teachers identify such children because the teachers might have prejudices about poor children or might assume that shy or disruptive children were retarded. What was needed was an objective test that would reveal who would benefit from remedial work, and that test is what Binet developed. But something happened to Binet's test and the French intentions to help *individual* children when the test crossed the ocean to America. In America, a revised version of the test was used to assign children to school tracks, according to their alleged natural ability—not to bring slow learners up to average. IQ scores also became a political tool, used to argue that some ethnic groups were inherently smarter than others.

For example, as soon as he got his hands on the IQ test, Henry Goddard (1917), a leading American educator, gave it to a group of immigrants at Ellis Island. Many of the immigrants knew little or no English and could neither read nor write their own language. Yet no sooner did they get off the boat after a long and tiring journey than they found themselves taking an IQ test. The results: 83 percent of the Jews, 80 percent of the Hungarians, 79 percent of the Italians, and 87 percent of the Russians scored as "feeble-minded," with a mental age lower than 12. Goddard concluded that low intelligence and poor character were inherited and that "undesirables" should be prevented from having children. He acknowledged that deprivation might explain these results, but he did not recognize that the results themselves had no validity, given the conditions under which they were obtained.

Henry Goddard, giving an early IQ test.

A more ambitious study of IQ was done during World War I, when 1.5 million soldiers took the first mass-produced intelligence tests in America. The purpose was to eliminate "feeble-minded" recruits and to determine who should become an officer. To everyone's astonishment, the average mental age of white men was only 13, just a notch above the "moron" level; blacks and eastern and southern Europeans scored even lower, on average. Once again many citizens (of northern European extraction, anyway) concluded that the nation's intelligence was declining because of the influx of immigrants and their "breeding habits," ignoring the abominable conditions under which the tests were given, the confusing instructions used, and the lack of education of many of the men.

The 1920s saw a growth in eugenics movements in North America and Europe. Eugenicists argued that government should help improve humanity by discouraging births among the lower classes and others presumed to have genetically inferior traits. Some called for the forced sterilization of low-IQ people and strict limits on immigration. They were inspired by *Social Darwinism,* the theory that the prevailing social order reflects the "survival of the fittest" (the phrase was coined by the English political philosopher Herbert Spencer in the 1840s).

These ideas were taken to their extreme during World War II by the Nazis, who used them as a rationale for exterminating 12 million people in the Holocaust.

When the extent of the Nazi atrocities became known, most scholars turned away in disgust from all biological explanations of mental abilities. For three decades, the prevailing doctrine was that culture and environment were the primary if not the sole determinants of intelligence. But now behavioral-genetics research, as we report in this chapter, has called that belief into question; few can dispute that differences among individuals are due in part to heredity—that a Forrest Gump can never become an Einstein.

What does this research mean for individuals or social policies? In 1994, the interaction of science and culture exploded in a heated debate about *The Bell Curve: Intelligence and Class Structure in American Life* (1994), written by the late psychologist Richard Herrnstein and conservative political theorist Charles Murray. If the book were about the bell curve of intelligence *within* groups, it would not have generated much controversy. But, in the old American tradition, it is really about differences *between* groups, and some of its arguments would be familiar to any Social Darwinist.

Herrnstein and Murray argue that (a) IQ tests are a valid indicator of a single quality called intelligence; (b) intelligence is largely heritable; (c) because low-IQ people are having more children than high-IQ people, the nation's intelligence level is declining; (d) the United States may soon be divided into a huge low-IQ underclass and a "cognitive meritocracy" of wealthy, well-educated high-IQ people; and (e) educational programs can do little to raise IQs. For many people, Herrnstein and Murray write, there is nothing they can learn that will repay the cost of teaching, and resources spent on such people would be better spent on the gifted. Although most of *The Bell Curve* is not about race or ethnicity, the implication is that the gap between the average white and the average black IQ can never be closed, and that it is foolish to waste money trying to do so.

Critical reviewers of the book have attacked its scholarship, methods, assumptions, and conclusions (Gould, 1994; Holt, 1994; Lane, 1994; Steele,

1994). They point out, as noted in this chapter, that heritability estimates based on differences within a group cannot be used to compare differences between groups. They reject the notion that intelligence can be captured by a single number. They acknowledge that programs such as Head Start fail to permanently alter preschoolers' IQs, but they don't think that this failure is a reason to abandon or curtail such remedial efforts. A program that children attend for only two or three hours a week, for only a year or two, cannot be expected to reverse permanently the effects of a childhood of poverty and intellectual deprivation. If anything, say the critics, remedial efforts must therefore be expanded.

Supporters of hereditarian arguments reply that their opponents have their own political ax to grind. They complain that their position has brought them a great deal of scorn and abuse, and that they have a right to do research into matters that they regard as interesting intellectual questions, without being branded, ipso facto, as racists or elitists (Rushton, 1993). Flaws in the studies of environmentalists, they argue, are overlooked or rationalized, whereas the methods of hereditarians are scrutinized and attacked. The critics, in turn, note that the political implications of "interesting intellectual questions" can't be ignored. Stephen Jay Gould (1994) observes that *The Bell Curve* appeared at a moment in American history when taxpayers are in the mood to slash social programs. At such times, people are more likely to accept uncritically the message that the beneficiaries of these programs cannot be helped anyway.

The political nature of the IQ controversy raises some hard questions about the relationship between society and science. Why have Americans been so concerned about group differences in IQ for so many decades? Can the study of such differences truly be beneficial, or, given today's climate and the persistence of prejudice, does it promote class and racial bias? Should scientists consider the political ramifications of their research, or should they leave that problem to others? Finally, once we have research on an issue as explosive as group differences in some ability, what lesson should be drawn—to accept those differences, or try to eliminate them? ■

One sure way to settle the question of inherent racial differences would be to gather IQ information on blacks and whites reared in exactly the same circumstances. This task is nearly impossible at present in the United States, where racism affects the lives of even affluent, successful African-Americans (Cose, 1994; Staples, 1994). However, we know that as economic, social, political, and educational opportunities have opened up to black Americans, the performance of black children on achievement and aptitude tests has climbed considerably, and black–white differences have shrunk (L. Jones, 1984). Further, the studies that have overcome past methodological problems have failed to reveal any genetic differences between blacks and whites in whatever it is that IQ tests measure (Lewontin, 1982; Mackenzie, 1984). Consider:

- Children fathered by black and white American soldiers in Germany after World War II, and reared in similar German communities by similar families, did not differ significantly in IQ (Eyferth, 1961).

- Black and interracial children adopted during their first year by white families with above-average incomes and education score 10 to 20 points higher on IQ tests than black children being reared by black families. Their performance on vocabulary and reading-achievement tests is somewhat higher than the national average and is generally comparable to that of other adopted children reared in an environment that fosters the particular skills emphasized in schools and on IQ tests (Scarr & Weinberg, 1976; Weinberg, Scarr, & Waldman, 1992).

- Degree of African ancestry (which can be roughly estimated from skin color, blood analysis, and genealogy) is not related to measured intelligence, as a genetic theory of black–white differences would predict (Scarr et al., 1977).

An intelligent reading of the research on intelligence, therefore, would not direct us to conclude that differences among cultural, ethnic, or national groups are permanent, genetically determined, or signs of any group's superiority. On the contrary, the research suggests that we should try to make sure that all children grow up in the best possible soil, with room for the smartest and the slowest to find a place in the sun.

Quick QUIZ

1. Estimates of the heritability of intelligence based on twin and adoption studies (a) put heritability at about .90, (b) show heritability to be low at all ages, (c) average about .50 for children and adolescents.
2. Name at least four environmental factors that affect mental abilities.
3. True or false: If a trait is highly heritable within a group, then between-group differences in the trait must also be due mainly to heredity.
4. The available evidence does/does not show that ethnic differences in average IQ scores are due to genetic differences.

Answers:

1. c 2. prenatal factors, nutrition, exposure to toxins, mental stimulation, family size, individual experiences, family circumstances, parent–child interactions 3. false 4. does not

■ IN PRAISE OF HUMAN VARIATION

This chapter opened with two simple questions: What makes us alike as human beings, and why do we differ? Here is the pop-psych answer to these questions:

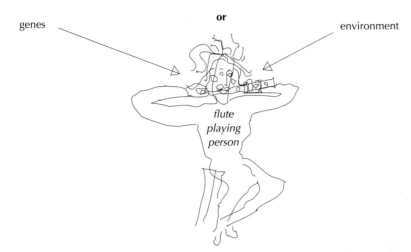

And here is the more complicated view that emerges from the study of human development:

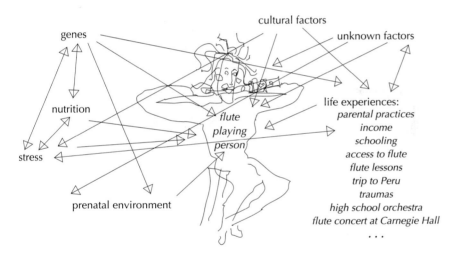

As we have seen, heredity and environment always interact to produce the unique mixture of qualities that make up a human being. Yet even this answer is too simple, because each of us is, in a sense, *more* than the sum of the individual influences on us. Once these influences become a part of us, they blend and become indistinguishable. A geneticist, a neurobiologist, and a psychologist offer this analogy. Think, they say, of the baking of a cake: "The taste of the product is the result of a complex interaction of components—such as butter, sugar, and flour—exposed for various periods to elevated temperatures; it is not dissociable into such-or-such a percent of flour, such-or-such of butter, etc., although each and every component . . . has its contribution to make to the final product" (Lewontin, Rose, & Kamin, 1984). The "cake" that is a person is never done. Each moment, a slightly different self interacts with a slightly different environment. We can no more speak of genes or of the environment *causing* personality or intelligence than we can speak of butter, sugar, or flour individually *causing* the taste of a cake. Yet we do speak that way. Why? Perhaps out of a desire to make things clearer than they actually are, or sometimes, to justify prejudices about culture, ethnicity, gender, or class.

It's easy to oversimplify the nature–nurture issue. How can we think about this issue while avoiding either–or reasoning? Should we think of a human being as a jigsaw puzzle, made up of separate components, or as more like a cake, with blended ingredients?

Nature, however, loves diversity. Biologists agree that the fitness of any species depends on this diversity. If all members of a species were alike, with exactly the same strengths and weaknesses, the species could not survive changes in the physical or social environment. With diversity, at least some members have a good chance of survival. When we see the world as behavioral geneticists and evolutionary psychologists do, we realize that each of us has something valuable to contribute, whether it is artistic talent, academic ability, creativity, social skill, athletic prowess, a sense of humor, mechanical aptitude, practical wisdom, a social conscience, or the energy to get things done. The challenge, for any society, is to promote the potential of each of its members.

Taking Psychology with You

How to Lose Weight—and Whether You Should

Over the years, "ideal weight" charts have become more flexible, giving a range of healthy weights for various heights and allowing for normal weight gain as people age. Fashion, however, has not followed suit; the cultural ideal in North America and Europe has been getting decidedly thinner. Brett Silverstein and his colleagues documented the changing female ideal in this century by computing a bust-to-waist ratio of the measurements of models in popular women's magazines (Silverstein, Peterson, & Perdue, 1986). The ideal body type became thin, as opposed to voluptuously curvy, twice during this century, in the mid-1920s and from the mid-1960s to the present.

Why did these changes occur? Silverstein found that men and women associate the curvy, big-breasted female body with femininity; and they associate femininity with domesticity, nurturance, and, alas, incompetence. (For men, too, overweight is now considered a sign of softness and lack of masculinity.) Thus, in every era in which women have been admitted to colleges and have had professional careers in greater numbers, women have tried to look boyishly thin to avoid the risk of appearing feminine and dumb. Lately, a new female ideal, another biological impossibility for most women, has appeared, possibly reflecting national ambivalence about whether women's proper role is domestic or professional: the big-breasted but narrow-hipped body shape.

Many women, therefore, face a dilemma. Evolution has programmed them for a reserve of fat necessary for the onset of menstruation, healthy childbearing, nursing, and, after menopause, production and storage of the hormone estrogen. The result of the battle between biological design and social standards is that many women today—as in the 1920s—are obsessed with weight, continually dieting, or suffering from eating disorders such as anorexia nervosa (self-starvation) or bulimia (bingeing and vomiting).

The obsession about achieving the ideal female body shape, Silverstein hypothesized, should be most likely to occur in women who value achievement, higher education, and careers, especially male-dominated careers. Being thin allows them to identify with male competence and to actively distance themselves from femininity. And that is just what research finds. College women who develop eating disorders are also more likely than other women to say that their parents believe a woman's place is in the home, their mothers are unhappy with their lives, their fathers think their mothers are unintelligent, and their fathers treat sons as being more intelligent than daughters (Silverstein et al., 1988).

While many normal-weight women struggle to fit the cultural ideal, many overweight men and women struggle to fit the medical ideal. Almost a third of American men and about a quarter of women are overweight—that is, their body mass exceeds the healthy standard by 25 to 30 percent—and 12 percent of both sexes are severely overweight (National Academy of Sciences, 1989). Among the experts, there is disagreement about the best solution for overweight people. Many researchers believe that dieting is unhealthy and may even contribute to medical problems and eating disorders (Garner & Wooley, 1991). But others conclude that dieting and weight loss can help reduce the health risks associated with overweight. They point to research showing that even modest weight losses have medical benefits, such as lowered blood pressure. And they note that findings on the risks of dieting are inconsistent (Brownell & Rodin, 1994). So what's an overweight person to do? Research offers some suggestions:

- Be realistic about your need to diet. As Kelly Brownell and Judith Rodin (1994) observe, dieting and a 10 percent reduction in weight may be of benefit to an obese older man with high blood pressure but unhealthy for a teenage girl who is not overweight.

- Avoid fad diets that restrict you to only a few foods or put you on starvation rations. People on these diets often become obsessed with food, get depressed and anxious when they slip off the diet, and ultimately binge, which restores the lost weight—plus some. It is far better to permanently alter your eating habits by reducing fat intake and eating more fruits and vegetables.

- Get more exercise, which may raise the metabolic rate and which, when combined with a low-fat diet, is associated with more weight loss than dieting alone (Foreyt et al., 1993). You do not have to become a marathon runner, but you can increase your activity level—for example, by walking instead of driving to work or school.
- Avoid yo-yo dieting, in which you repeatedly lose and gain weight. Many studies show a link between yo-yo dieting and a higher-than-normal risk of cardiovascular disease, hypertension, and other chronic diseases (Brownell & Rodin, 1994; Ernsberger & Nelson, 1988; Lissner et al., 1991). Some researchers believe that weight fluctuations are a greater risk to health than high weight is (Garner & Wooley, 1991), though other research suggests the opposite. In any case, yo-yo dieting is psychologically debilitating and may cause an obese person to give up.

- Find ways to nurture and reward yourself other than eating. People who develop eating disorders are more self-critical than healthy eaters, and they are more likely to use food to assuage hurt feelings and low self-esteem (Lehman & Rodin, 1989).
- Avoid amphetamines and other diet pills, which can be far more dangerous to your health than a few pounds and can become addictive. Diet pills raise the metabolic rate only as long as you take them. When you stop taking them, the pounds return.
- If you are mistakenly trying to control weight by frequent vomiting and abuse of laxatives, you can break this harmful pattern by joining an eating-disorders program; school counselors and health clinics can direct you to suitable programs.
- Remember that the biological disposition to gain weight varies from person to person, and that even with exercise, there are genetic factors that limit how much you can change.

Most of all, think carefully and critically about the reasons that you are dieting. Are you really overweight? Whose standards are you following, and why?

Summary

1. From the perspective of *behavioral geneticists* and *evolutionary psychologists,* a key to understanding the qualities that unite human beings as a species and the qualities that differentiate them as individuals can be found in genes. Yet all scientists also understand that heredity and environment interact to produce not only psychological traits but even most physical ones.

2. *Genes,* the basic units of heredity, are located on *chromosomes,* which consist of strands of *DNA.* Within each gene, the sequence of four basic elements constitutes a chemical code that helps determine the synthesis of a particular protein by specifying the sequence of amino acids that are the protein's building blocks. In turn, proteins directly or indirectly affect virtually all of the structural and biochemical characteristics of the organism.

3. In the simplest type of inheritance, a single pair of genes is responsible for the expression of a trait; in many cases, one member of the pair is *dominant* and the other *recessive.* Most human traits, however, depend on more than one gene pair, which makes tracking down the genetic contributions to a trait extremely difficult.

4. The way in which heredity operates ensures that each individual (with the exception of identical twins) will be a unique genetic mosaic. Each sperm- or egg-producing cell has the potential to produce millions of different chromosome combinations in each new sperm or egg, and mutations and the crossover of segments of genetic material produce even greater genetic diversity.

5. The guiding assumption in evolutionary psychology is that the mind is not a general-purpose computer, but instead evolved as a collection of specialized and independent mental modules to handle specific survival problems. Many fundamental human similarities can be traced to the evolutionary workings of *natural selection*—for example, inborn reflexes, an attraction to novelty, a

motive to explore and manipulate objects, and a motive to play and to imitate others.

6. Human beings are the only species that uses language naturally, to express and comprehend an infinite number of novel utterances. Noam Chomsky argued that the ability to take the *surface structure* of an utterance and apply rules of *syntax* to infer its underlying *deep structure* must depend on an innate faculty for language, a universal grammar; many others have supported this view and explored its evolutionary implications. However, certain parental practices, such as speaking more slowly and repeating correct sentences verbatim, appear to aid in language acquisition. Case studies of children deprived of exposure to language suggest that a *critical period* exists for acquiring language.

7. There is controversy about the biological and evolutionary origins of mating and marriage practices. *Sociobiologists* maintain that people's tendency to act in ways that ensure the survival of their personal genetic code is the primary motivation behind most social customs, including those surrounding courtship and sexual behavior. In this view, males and females have developed different reproductive strategies, so that, for example, males are on the average more promiscuous than females. Most evolutionary psychologists reject the assumption of a reproductive-fitness motive, but they agree that psychological mechanisms adaptive in the evolutionary past often continue to affect human behavior, including mating preferences. Cross-cultural studies support many evolutionary predictions, but critics argue that human sexual behavior is extremely varied and changeable, and many take exception to the entire line of evolutionary reasoning. The debate can get quite heated because of the political implications of the sociobiological argument.

8. Behavioral geneticists study differences among individuals by trying to estimate the heritability of traits and abilities. These estimates are most often based on studies of twins and adopted children. *Heritability* refers to the extent to which differences in a trait within a group of individuals are accounted for by genetic differences. Heritability estimates do not apply to specific individuals. They apply only to differences within a particular group living in a particular environment and not to differences between groups. Even a highly heritable trait may be susceptible to environmental modification. Heritable behavior traits are usually influenced by many genes working in combination.

9. Biological and behavioral-genetics research is altering our understanding of body weight and shape. Overweight is usually not caused by emotional problems, and it does not always involve overeating. According to *set-point theory*, hunger, weight, and eating are regulated by a complex set of bodily mechanisms that keep people within a certain genetically influenced weight range. Genes influence body shape, distribution of fat, and whether the body will convert excess calories into fat, and may help account for certain types of obesity. However, weight is also influenced by eating habits and by exercise, which may raise metabolism and lower a person's set point. Culture, in turn, influences how much and what people eat and how much exercise they get.

10. Heritability estimates for intelligence (as measured by IQ tests, which have come under fire by critics) vary widely, but these estimates average about .50 for children and adolescents and .70 to .80 for adults. Individual differences in mental performance are also influenced by a variety of environmental factors, including prenatal care, nutrition, exposure to toxins, mental stimulation, family size, individual experiences, family circumstances, and parent–child interactions.

11. Research on group differences in IQ has focused on average black–white differences. The history of debate on this issue has often been marred by ethnic, class, and gender prejudice, as we discussed in "Psychology and Popular Culture." Genetic explanations have often mistakenly used heritability estimates derived from one group to estimate the genetic contribution to group differences—an invalid procedure. The available evidence fails to support genetic explanations of these differences.

12. There are some limitations in behavioral-genetics studies and some common errors in interpreting their results. Measures of environmental influences on behavior are still crude, so the impact of these influences may be underestimated; people often overlook interactions between genetic factors and the environment; and many people also confuse heritability with invulnerability to environmental influence.

13. Neither nature nor nurture can completely explain people's similarities or differences. Genetic and environmental influences blend and become indistinguishable in the development of any individual.

Key Terms

nativists versus empiricists   *79*
behavioral genetics   *79*
evolutionary psychology   *79*
sociobiology   *79*
genes   *80*
chromosomes   *80*
DNA (deoxyribonucleic acid)   *80*
genome   *80*
bases   *80*
dominant/recessive genes   *80*
linkage studies   *81*
mutate   *81*
evolution   *84*
natural selection   *84*
Charles Darwin   *84*
language   *88*

syntax   *88*
surface structure/deep structure   *89*
language acquisition device   *89*
universal grammar   *89*
overregularizations   *90*
critical period (for language acquisition)   *91*
heritability   *96*
identical (monozygotic) twins   *97*
fraternal (dizygotic) twins   *97*
set point   *100*
intelligence quotient (IQ)   *103*
mental age   *103*
Social Darwinism   *108*

4

Neurons, Hormones, and the Brain

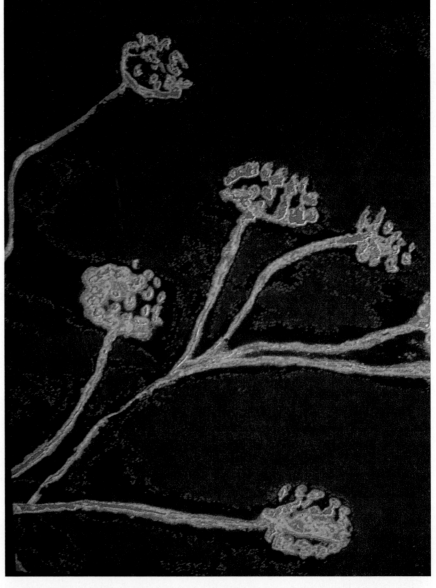

This photograph, taken with the aid of a powerful microscope, captures the beauty and delicacy of specialized neurons that function as sensory receptors in the skin.

It's amazing to think that the body feeds the brain sugar and amino acids, and what comes out is poetry and pirouettes.

■ NEUROLOGIST ROBERT COLLINS ■

Emily D., a former English teacher and poet, had a tumor in an area on the right side of the brain that processes the expressive qualities of speech, such as rhythm, inflection, and intonation. Although Emily D. could understand words and sentences perfectly well, she could not tell whether a speaker was indignant, cheerful, or dejected unless she carefully analyzed the person's facial expressions and gestures, and unfortunately, fading vision limited her ability to do so. Emily D.'s brain damage had left her entirely deaf to the emotional nuances of speech, the variations of tone and cadence that can move a listener to laughter, tears, or outrage. But she had one skill that many people lack. Because she could not be swayed by histrionics or tone of voice, she could easily spot a liar.

Dr. P., a cultured and charming musician of great repute, had suffered damage in a part of the brain that handles visualization. Although his vision was sharp, he could no longer recognize people or objects, or even dream in visual images. He would pat the heads of water hydrants and parking meters, thinking them to be children, or chat with pieces of furniture and wonder why they did not reply. He could spot a pin on the floor but did not know his own face in the mirror. Lost in a world of abstractions, he could not comprehend the simplest concrete image. Once, when looking around for his hat, he thought his wife's head was the hat and tried to lift it off. Neurologist Oliver Sacks, who studied Dr. P., came to call him "the man who mistook his wife for a hat" (Sacks, 1985).

These two fascinating cases, reported along with others by Sacks, show us that the brain is the bedrock of behavior. **Neuropsychologists,** along with other neuroscientists from a variety of disciplines, explore that bedrock, searching for the basis of behavior in the structure, biochemistry, and circuitry of the brain and the rest of the nervous system. Among neuropsychologists' many interests are the biological foundations of consciousness (Chapter 5), perception (Chapter 6), memory (Chapter 9), emotion (Chapter 10), stress (Chapter 14), and mental disorders (Chapter 15). In this chapter, we describe the structure of the brain and the rest of the nervous system as background for our later discussions.

At this very moment, your own brain, assisted by other parts of your nervous system, is busily taking in these words. Whether you are excited, curious, or bored, your brain is registering some sort of emotional reaction to the material. As you continue reading, your brain will (we hope) store away much of the information in this chapter for future use. Later on, your brain may enable you to smell a flower, climb the stairs, greet a friend, solve a personal problem, or chuckle at a joke. But the brain's most startling accomplishment, by far, is its knowledge that it is doing all these things. This self-awareness makes brain research different from the study of anything else in the universe. Scientists must use the cells, chemicals, and circuitry of their own brains to understand the cells, chemicals, and circuitry of brains in general.

■ **neuropsychology**
The field of psychology concerned with the neural and biochemical bases of behavior and mental processes.

Because the brain is the site of consciousness, people disagree vehemently about what language to use in describing it. One reviewer who read this chapter before publication took issue with the way we wrote the preceding paragraph. How, he wanted to know, could we talk about "your" brain doing this or that; after all, if the brain is where consciousness happens, where is the "you" that is "using" that brain? Another reviewer had just the opposite complaint; she objected when we wrote that the brain interprets, stores information, or registers emotions, because she felt we were depersonalizing human beings and implying that brain mechanisms completely explain behavior. "I think people do these things," she wrote, "not brains. Brains are not actors." You can see our problem. After much discussion, we finally decided to stick with everyday constructions such as "We use our brains," but we want you to know that we are simply resorting to a convenient linguistic shorthand, without assuming the existence of an independent brain "operator" that is doing the using. On the other hand, we also do not want to imply that brain mechanisms are all you need to understand about behavior.

William Shakespeare had an opinion on this matter; he once called the brain "the soul's frail dwelling house." Actually, the brain is more like the main room in a house filled with many alcoves and passageways—the "house" being the nervous system as a whole. Before we can understand the windows, walls, and furniture of this house, we need to become acquainted with the overall floor plan. It's a pretty technical floor plan, which means that you will be learning many new terms, but you will need to know these terms in order to understand how psychologists with a biological perspective go about explaining psychological topics.

■ THE NERVOUS SYSTEM: A BASIC BLUEPRINT

The function of a nervous system is to gather and process information, produce responses to stimuli, and coordinate the workings of different cells. Even the lowly jellyfish and the humble worm have the beginnings of such a system. In very simple organisms that do little more than move, eat, and eliminate wastes, the "system" may be no more than one or two nerve cells. In human beings, who do such complex things as dance, cook, and take psychology courses, the nervous system contains billions of cells. For purposes of description, scientists divide this intricate network into two main parts, the central nervous system and the peripheral (meaning "outlying") nervous system (see Figure 4.1).

The Central Nervous System

The **central nervous system (CNS)** receives, processes, interprets, and stores incoming sensory information—information about tastes, sounds, smells, color, pressure on the skin, the state of internal organs, and so forth. It also sends out messages destined for muscles, glands, and internal organs. It is usually conceptualized as having two components: the brain, which we will consider in detail later, and the **spinal cord.** The spinal cord is actually an extension of the brain. It runs from the base of the brain down the center of the back, protected by a column of bones (the *spinal column*), and acts as a sort of bridge between the brain and the parts of the body below the neck.

The spinal cord produces some behaviors on its own, without any help from the brain. These spinal **reflexes** are automatic, requiring no conscious effort. For example, if you accidentally touch a hot iron, you will immediately pull your hand away, even before the brain has had a chance to register what has happened. Nerve impulses bring a message to the spinal cord (hot!), and the spinal cord immediately sends out a command via other nerve impulses, telling muscles in your arm to contract and to pull your hand away from the iron.

■ **central nervous system (CNS)**

The portion of the nervous system consisting of the brain and spinal cord.

■ **spinal cord**

A collection of neurons and supportive tissue running from the base of the brain down the center of the back, protected by a column of bones (the spinal column).

■ **reflex**

An automatic response to a stimulus.

◾ Figure 4.1 The Central and Peripheral Nervous Systems

The central nervous system, shown here in yellow, consists of the brain and spinal cord. The peripheral nervous system, shown in purple, consists of 43 pairs of nerves that transmit information to and from the central nervous system. Twelve pairs of cranial nerves in the head enter the brain directly. Thirty-one pairs of spinal nerves enter the spinal cord at the spaces between the vertebrae of the spine.

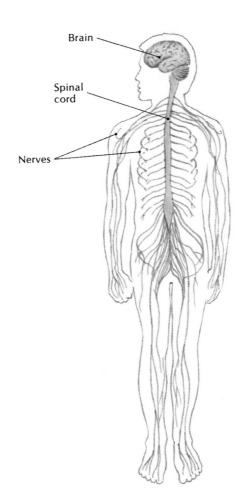

Brain

Spinal cord

Nerves

(Reflexes above the neck, such as sneezing and blinking, involve the lower part of the brain rather than the spinal cord.)

The neural circuits underlying many spinal reflexes are linked to other neural pathways that run up and down the spinal cord, to and from the brain. Because of these connections, reflexes can sometimes be influenced by thoughts and emotions. An example is erection in men, a spinal reflex that can be inhibited by anxiety or distracting thoughts, and initiated by erotic thoughts. Some reflexes can be brought under conscious control. If you concentrate, you may be able to keep your knee from jerking when it is tapped, as it normally would. Similarly, most men can learn to delay ejaculation voluntarily, also a spinal reflex.

The Peripheral Nervous System

The **peripheral nervous system (PNS)** handles the central nervous system's input and output. It contains all portions of the nervous system outside the brain and spinal cord, right down to nerves in the tips of the fingers and toes. If your brain could not get information about the world by means of a peripheral nervous system, it would be like a radio without a receiver. In the peripheral nervous system, **sensory nerves** carry messages from special receptors in the skin, muscles, and other internal and external sense organs to the spinal cord, which sends them along to the brain. These nerves put us in touch with both the outside world and the activities of our own bodies. **Motor nerves,** in contrast, carry orders from the central nervous system to muscles, glands, and internal organs. They enable us to move our bodies, and they cause glands to contract and to secrete substances, including chemical messengers called *hormones.*

◾ **peripheral nervous system (PNS)**

All portions of the nervous system outside the brain and spinal cord; it includes sensory and motor nerves.

◾ **sensory nerves**

Nerves in the peripheral system that carry sensory messages toward the central nervous system.

◾ **motor nerves**

Nerves in the peripheral system that carry messages from the central nervous system to muscles, glands, and internal organs.

Some patients with spinal cord injuries lose consciousness when they sit upright because their blood pressure plunges. Here, Neal Miller, a pioneer in biofeedback research, trains a patient to control her blood pressure at will, using biofeedback techniques.

■ **somatic nervous system**
The subdivision of the peripheral nervous system that connects to sensory receptors and skeletal muscles; sometimes called the skeletal nervous system.

■ **autonomic nervous system**
The subdivision of the peripheral nervous system that regulates the internal organs and glands.

Scientists further divide the peripheral nervous system into two parts: the somatic (bodily) nervous system and the autonomic (self-governing) nervous system. The **somatic nervous system,** sometimes called the *skeletal nervous system,* consists of nerves that are connected to sensory receptors and to the skeletal muscles that permit voluntary action. When you sense the world around you, or when you turn off a light or write your name, your somatic system is active. The **autonomic nervous system** regulates blood vessels, glands, and internal (visceral) organs such as the bladder, stomach, and heart. When you happen upon the secret object of your desire and your heart starts to pound and your hands get sweaty, you can blame your autonomic nervous system.

The autonomic nervous system works more or less automatically, without a person's conscious control. We say more or less because some people can learn to heighten or suppress their autonomic responses. In India, some yogis can slow their heartbeats and metabolisms so dramatically that they can survive in a sealed booth long after most of us would have suffocated. And in the 1960s and 1970s, Neal Miller and his colleagues showed that you don't have to be a yogi to control visceral responses; many other people can do so, using a technique called *biofeedback* (Miller, 1978). In biofeedback, monitoring devices track the bodily process in question and deliver a signal, such as a light or a tone, whenever a person makes the desired response. Instructions may include specific methods for producing the response, or the person may simply be told to try to increase the frequency of the signal.

There is little question that biofeedback can help people control *voluntary* responses. For example, it has helped teenagers with scoliosis (curvature of the spine) alter their posture and overcome the disorder (Dworkin & Dworkin, 1988). Some clinicians are using biofeedback training to help patients learn to control *involuntary* autonomic responses in order to treat high blood pressure, asthma, and migraine headaches (although there is great controversy about success rates). It is not clear, however, whether the control that occurs over autonomic responses is direct or indirect. When people learn to raise or lower their heart rates, for example, are they doing so directly, or are they producing the response indirectly by using skeletal muscles in the chest to speed up or slow down their breathing, which in turn affects their heart rates? Research has been inconclusive, and we still do not have an explanation for the autonomic effects of biofeedback.

■ **Figure 4.2 The Autonomic Nervous System**

The two divisions of the autonomic nervous system have different functions. In general, the sympathetic division prepares the body for an expenditure of energy, and the parasympathetic division restores and conserves energy. Sympathetic nerve fibers exit from areas of the spinal cord shown in yellow in this illustration. Parasympathetic nerve fibers exit from the base of the brain and from areas of the spinal cord shown here in purple.

Sympathetic division
Dilates pupils
Weakly stimulates salivation
Stimulates sweat glands
Accelerates heartbeat
Dilates bronchial tubes in lungs
Inhibits digestion
Increases epinephrine,
   norepinephrine secretion
   by adrenal glands
Relaxes bladder wall
Decreases urine volume
Stimulates glucose release by liver
Stimulates ejaculation in males

Parasympathetic division
Constricts pupils
Stimulates tear glands
Strongly stimulates salivation
Slows heartbeat
Constricts bronchial tubes in lungs
Activates digestion
Inhibits glucose release by liver

Contracts bladder wall
Stimulates genital erection (both
   sexes) and vaginal lubrication
   (females)

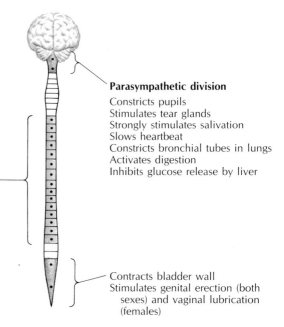

The autonomic nervous system is itself divided into two parts: the **sympathetic nervous system** and the **parasympathetic nervous system.** These two parts work together, but in opposing ways, to adjust the body to changing circumstances (see Figure 4.2). To simplify, the sympathetic system acts like the accelerator of a car, mobilizing the body for action and an output of energy. It makes you blush, sweat, and breathe more deeply, and it pushes up your heart rate and blood pressure. When you are in a situation that requires you to fight, to flee, or to cope, the sympathetic nervous system whirls into action.

The parasympathetic system, on the other hand, is more like a brake: It does not stop the body, but it does tend to slow things down and keep them running smoothly. It helps the body to conserve and store energy. If you have to jump out of the way of a speeding motorcyclist, sympathetic nerves increase your heart rate. Afterward, parasympathetic nerves slow it down again and keep your heart rhythm regular. Both systems are involved in emotion and stress.

■ **sympathetic nervous system**
The subdivision of the autonomic nervous system that mobilizes bodily resources and increases the output of energy during emotion and stress.

■ **parasympathetic nervous system**
The subdivision of the autonomic nervous system that operates during relaxed states and that conserves energy.

Quick QUIZ

Speaking of stress, you may be feeling a bit overwhelmed by the many terms introduced in the preceding paragraphs. Pause now to test your memory by mentally filling in the missing parts of the nervous system "house." Then see if you can briefly describe what each part of the system does.

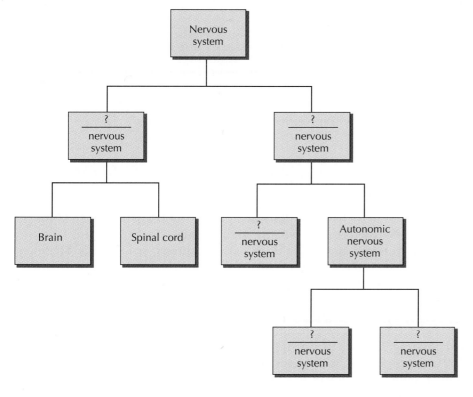

Answers:

Check your answers against Figure 4.3 on the next page. If you had any difficulty, or if you could label the parts but could not remember what they do, review the preceding section and try again.

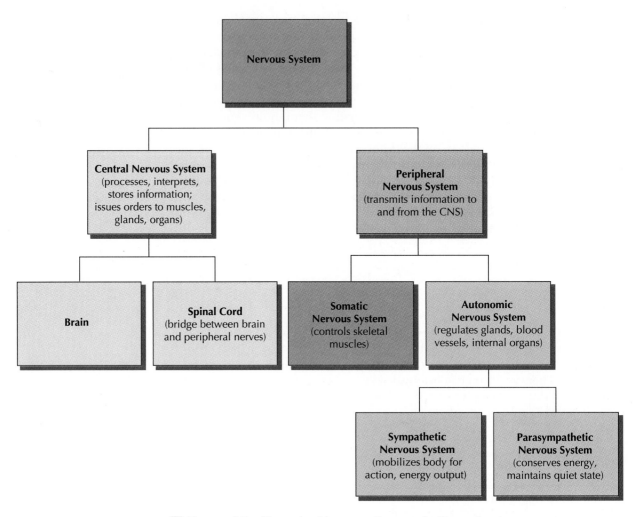

■ **Figure 4.3   How the Nervous System Is Organized**

■ COMMUNICATION IN THE NERVOUS SYSTEM: THE NUTS AND BOLTS

The blueprint we have just described provides only a general idea of the nervous system's structure. Now we turn to the details.

The nervous system is made up in part of **neurons,** or *nerve cells.* These neurons are held in place by **glial cells** (from the Greek for "glue"). Glial cells, which greatly outnumber neurons, also provide the neurons with nutrients, insulate them, and remove cellular debris when the neurons die. Many neuroscientists suspect that glial cells carry electrical or chemical signals between parts of the nervous system, and that they somehow influence the activity of neighboring neurons (Cornell-Bell et al., 1990; Murphy, 1993; Nedergaard, 1994). It is the neurons, however, that are the communication specialists, transmitting signals to, from, or within the central nervous system.

Although neurons are often called the building blocks of the nervous system, they look nothing like blocks; they are more like snowflakes, exquisitely delicate, differing from one another greatly in size and shape (see Figure 4.4). In the giraffe, a neuron that runs from the spinal cord down the animal's hind leg may be nine feet long! In the human brain, neurons are microscopic. No one is sure how many neurons the brain contains, but a typical estimate is 100 billion, about the same number as there are stars in our galaxy—and some estimates go much higher.

■ **neuron**
A cell that conducts electrochemical signals; the basic unit of the nervous system; also called a nerve cell.

■ **glial cells**
Cells that hold neurons in place, insulate neurons, and provide them with nutrients.

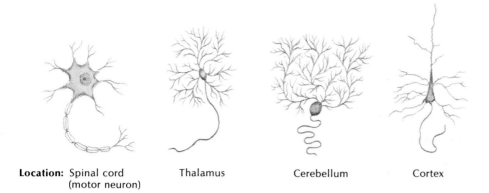

Location: Spinal cord   Thalamus   Cerebellum   Cortex
(motor neuron)

■ **Figure 4.4 Different Kinds of Neurons**

Neurons vary in size and shape, depending on their location and function. More than 200 types of neurons have been identified in mammals.

The Structure of the Neuron

As you can see in Figure 4.5, a neuron has three main parts: *dendrites*, a *cell body*, and an *axon*. The **dendrites** look like the branches of a tree; indeed, the word *dendrite* means "little tree" in Greek. Dendrites act like antennas, receiving messages from as many as 10,000 other nerve cells and transmitting these messages toward the cell body. The **cell body,** which is shaped roughly like a sphere or a pyramid, contains the biochemical machinery for keeping the neuron alive. It also determines whether the neuron should "fire"—that is, transmit a message to other neurons—based on the number of inputs from other neurons. The **axon** (from the Greek for "axle") is like the tree's trunk, though more slender. It transmits messages away from the cell body to other neurons or to muscle or gland cells. Axons commonly divide at the end into branches, called *axon terminals.* In adult human beings, axons vary from only four one-thousandths of an inch to a few feet in length. Dendrites and axons give each neuron a double role: As one researcher puts it, a neuron is first a catcher, then a batter (Gazzaniga, 1988).

■ **dendrites**

Branches on a neuron that receive information from other neurons and transmit it toward the cell body.

■ **cell body**

The part of the neuron that keeps it alive and determines whether it will fire.

■ **axon**

Extending fiber of a neuron that conducts impulses away from the cell body and transmits them to other neurons.

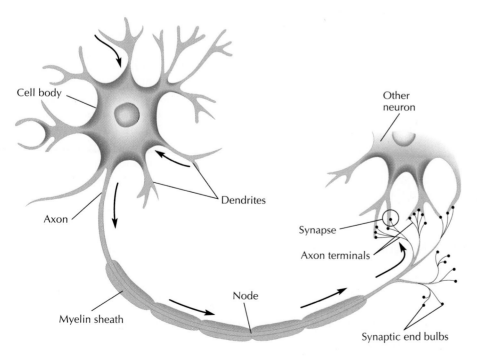

Cell body

Axon

Myelin sheath

Dendrites

Node

Other
neuron

Synapse

Axon terminals

Synaptic end bulbs

■ **Figure 4.5 The Structure of a Neuron**

Incoming neural impulses are received by the dendrites of a neuron and are transmitted to the cell body. Outgoing signals pass along the axon to terminal branches. The arrows show the direction in which impulses travel.

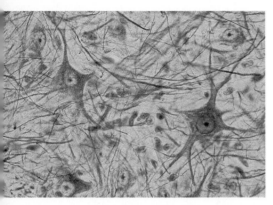

This photograph, taken through a microscope, reveals the delicate fibers of a human motor neuron.

In the peripheral nervous system, the fibers of individual neurons (axons and sometimes dendrites) are collected together in bundles called **nerves,** rather like the lines in a telephone cable. (In the central nervous system, similar bundles of neuron fibers are called *tracts*.) The human body has 43 pairs of peripheral nerves, one nerve from each pair on the left side of the body and the other on the right. Most of these nerves enter or leave the spinal cord, but the 12 pairs that are in the head, the *cranial nerves,* connect directly to the brain. In Chapter 6, we will describe three cranial nerves involved in sensory processing: the olfactory nerve, involved in smell; the auditory nerve, involved in hearing; and the optic nerve, involved in vision.

Many axons, especially the larger ones, are insulated by a layer of fatty material called the **myelin sheath,** which is derived from glial cells. One purpose of this covering is to prevent signals from adjacent cells from interfering with each other. Another is to speed up the conduction of neural impulses. The myelin sheath is divided into segments that make the axon look a little like a string of link sausages. Beneath the myelin sheath, conduction of a neural impulse is impossible, in part because conduction involves the passage of certain ions (charged particles) across the cell's membrane (enclosing cover) and into the cell, and in myelinated parts of the axon, there is no way for these ions to enter. Instead, when a neural impulse travels down the axon, it "hops" from one break between two "sausages" to the next break. This arrangement allows the impulse to travel faster than it could if it moved along the entire axon. Nerve impulses travel more slowly in babies than in older children and adults because when babies are born their myelin sheaths are not yet fully developed.

Until a few years ago, neuroscientists thought that except for some specialized cells in the nose, neurons in the central nervous system could not reproduce or regenerate to any significant degree. They assumed that if these cells were injured or damaged, there was nothing anyone could do about it. But animal studies have challenged these assumptions. In one study, researchers got severed axons in the spinal cords of rats to regrow by blocking the effects of nerve-growth inhibiting substances found in the myelin sheath (Schnell & Schwab, 1990). In another study, researchers induced severed optic nerves in hamsters to regenerate by laying down a trail of transplanted nervous tissue from the animals' legs (Keirstead et al., 1989). What's more, Canadian neuroscientists have discovered that certain undifferentiated cells from the brains of mice, when immersed in a growth-promoting protein in the laboratory, will produce new neurons, which then continue to divide and multiply (Reynolds & Weiss, 1992). One of the researchers, Samuel Weiss, said that this result was hard to believe at first: "It challenged everything I had read; everything I had learned when I was a student" (quoted in Barinaga, 1992).

Each year brings ever more astonishing findings on neurons. Many of these results will not only alter our understanding of the nervous system but may also lead to new treatments for neurological damage and brain diseases (Barinaga, 1994). As we saw in Chapter 2, the willingness to question conventional wisdom is a characteristic of the ideal scientist. Critical thinking about commonly accepted assumptions ("Neurons in the central nervous system can't regenerate, period"), when combined with empirical evidence, makes possible new discoveries.

How Neurons Communicate

Individual neurons do not form a continuous chain, with each neuron directly touching another, end to end. If they did, the number of connections would be inadequate for the vast amount of information the nervous system must handle. Instead, individual neurons are separated by a minuscule space

▪ **nerve**
A bundle of nerve fibers (axons and sometimes dendrites) in the peripheral nervous system.

▪ **myelin sheath**
A fatty insulating sheath surrounding many axons.

called the *synaptic cleft*, where the axon terminal of one neuron nearly touches a dendrite or the cell body of another. The entire site—the axon terminal, the cleft, and the membrane of the receiving dendrite or cell body—is called a **synapse.** Because a neuron's axon may have hundreds or even thousands of terminals, a single neuron may have synaptic connections with a great many others. As a result, the number of communication links in the nervous system runs into the trillions or perhaps even the quadrillions.

Although we seem to be born with nearly all the neurons we will ever have, many synapses have not yet formed at birth (see Figure 4.6). Research with animals shows that axons and dendrites continue to grow as a result of both physical maturation and experience with the world, and tiny projections on dendrites called *spines* increase both in size and in number. Throughout life, new learning results in the establishment of new synaptic connections in the brain, with stimulating environments producing the greatest changes (Greenough & Anderson, 1991; Greenough & Black, 1992). Conversely, some unused synaptic connections are lost as cells or their branches die and are not replaced (Camel, Withers, & Greenough, 1986). The brain's circuits are not fixed and immutable; they are continually developing and being pruned in response to information and to challenges and changes in the environment.

Neurons speak to one another, or in some cases to muscles or glands, in an electrical and chemical language. A neural impulse—a wave of electrical voltage—travels down a transmitting axon somewhat as fire travels along the fuse of a firecracker. The physics of this process involves the sudden inflow of positively charged sodium ions followed by the outflow of positively charged potassium ions, a change called an *action potential.* When the impulse reaches the axon terminal's buttonlike tip (*synaptic end bulb*), it must get its message across the synaptic cleft to another cell. At this point, *synaptic vesicles*, tiny sacs in the end bulb, open and release a few thousand molecules of a chemical substance called a **neurotransmitter,** or *transmitter* for short. Like sailors carrying a message from one island to another, these molecules then diffuse across the synaptic cleft (see Figure 4.7 on the next page).

When they reach the other side, the transmitter molecules bind briefly with special molecules called *receptor sites* in the membrane of the receiving neuron, fitting these sites much as a key fits into a lock. This produces changes in the membrane of the receiving cell. The result is a brief change in electrical potential caused largely by the momentary inflow of positively charged sodium ions across the membrane. The ultimate effect of this change is either *excitatory* (a voltage shift in a positive direction) or *inhibitory* (a voltage shift in a negative direction), depending on which receptor sites have been activated. If the effect is excitatory, the probability increases that the receiving neuron will fire; if it is inhibitory, the opposite is true. Inhibition in the nervous system is extremely important. Without it, we could not sleep or coordinate our movements. Excitation of the nervous system would be overwhelming, producing convulsions.

What any given neuron actually does at any given moment depends on the net effect of all the neurons that are sending messages to it. Only when the cell's voltage reaches a certain threshold will it fire. Thousands of messages, both excitatory and inhibitory, may be coming into the cell. Essentially, the neuron must average them. But how it does this, and how it "decides" whether to fire, is still a puzzle. The message that reaches a final destination depends on the rate at which individual neurons are firing, how many are firing, what types of neurons are firing, and where the neurons are located. It does *not* depend on how strongly the neurons are firing, however, because a neuron always either fires or it doesn't. In other words, the firing of a neuron, like the turning on of a light switch, is an *all-or-none* event.

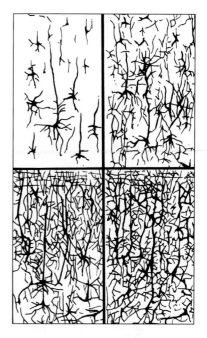

■ **Figure 4.6 Getting Connected**

At birth, neurons in the infant's brain are widely spaced (upper left), but they begin to form connections immediately. These drawings show the marked increase in the size and number of neurons in the baby's first 15 months of life.

■ **synapse**

The site where transmission of a nerve impulse from one nerve cell to another occurs; it includes the synaptic end bulb, synaptic cleft, and receptor sites in the membrane of the receiving cell.

■ **neurotransmitter**

A chemical substance that is released by a transmitting neuron at the synapse and that alters the activity of a receiving neuron.

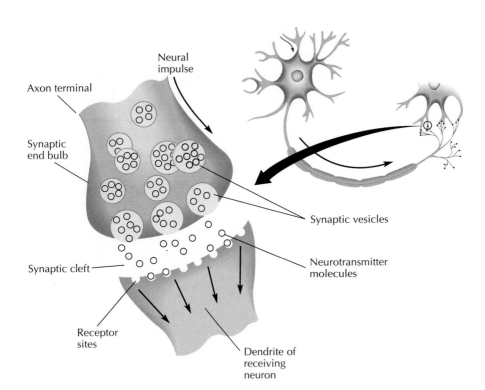

Neural impulse

Axon terminal

Synaptic end bulb

Synaptic cleft

Receptor sites

Synaptic vesicles

Neurotransmitter molecules

Dendrite of receiving neuron

▪ **Figure 4.7**
Neurotransmitter Crossing a Synapse

Neurotransmitter molecules are released into the synaptic gap between two neurons from vesicles (chambers) in the transmitting neuron's axon terminal. After crossing the gap, the molecules bind to receptor sites on the receiving neuron. As a result, the electrical state of the receiving neuron changes, and it becomes either more or less likely to fire an impulse, depending on the type of transmitter substance. A neuron may have synaptic connections with hundreds or even thousands of other neurons.

Chemical Messengers in the Nervous System

It takes a lot of nerve to make up the nervous system "house," but that house would remain forever dark and lifeless without chemical couriers such as the neurotransmitters. We now look more closely at neurotransmitters, and at two other types of chemical messengers: endorphins and hormones.

Neurotransmitters: Versatile Couriers.   As we have seen, neurotransmitters make it possible for one neuron to excite or inhibit another. Dozens of different substances are known or suspected to be transmitters, and the number keeps growing. Each neurotransmitter binds only to specific types of receptor sites. This means that if some of those "sailors" we mentioned (the transmitter molecules) get off course and reach the wrong "islands" (receiving neurons), their messages will not be heard (no binding will occur). The existence of different neurotransmitters and receptor sites ensures that messages go where they are supposed to go.

Neurotransmitters exist not only in the brain, but also in the spinal cord, the peripheral nerves, and certain glands. Through their effects on specific nerve circuits, these substances can affect your mood, memory, and well-being. The nature of the effect depends on the level of the neurotransmitter and its location. Here are a few of the better understood neurotransmitters and some of their known or suspected effects:

- *Serotonin* affects neurons involved in sleep, appetite, sensory perception, temperature regulation, pain suppression, and mood.

- *Dopamine* affects neurons involved in voluntary movement, learning, memory, and emotion.

- *Acetylcholine* affects neurons involved in muscle action, cognitive functioning, memory, and emotion.

- *Norepinephrine* affects neurons involved in increased heart rate and the slowing of intestinal activity during stress, and neurons involved in learning, memory, dreaming, waking from sleep, and emotion.

- *GABA* (gamma-aminobutyric acid) functions as the major inhibitory neurotransmitter in the brain.

- *Glutamate* functions as an important excitatory neurotransmitter in the brain.

Harmful effects can occur when these neurotransmitters are in either too great or too short supply. Low levels of serotonin and norepinephrine have been associated with severe depression. Abnormal GABA levels have been implicated in sleep and eating disorders and in convulsive disorders, including epilepsy (Bekenstein & Lothman, 1993). Elevated levels of serotonin, along with other biochemical and brain abnormalities, have been implicated in childhood autism, the disorder described at the beginning of Chapter 2 (du Verglas, Banks, & Guyer, 1988).

Deficiencies in a number of neurotransmitters have also been implicated in *Alzheimer's disease,* a devastating condition, most common in the elderly, which leads to memory loss, personality changes, and eventual disintegration of all physical and mental abilities. In Alzheimer's patients, many of the brain cells responsible for producing acetylcholine have been destroyed, which may account for memory loss. Also, in the early stages of the disease, serotonin receptors normally present in certain layers of brain cells nearly disappear (Cross, 1990). This deficit could be related to the increased aggressiveness and moodiness often observed in Alzheimer's patients, although such reactions could also be understandable responses to having the disease.

The degeneration of brain cells that produce and use another neurotransmitter, dopamine, appears to cause the symptoms of Parkinson's disease, a condition characterized by tremors, muscular spasms, and increasing muscular rigidity. Patients with advanced Parkinson's may "freeze" for minutes or even hours. Injections of dopamine do not help, because dopamine molecules cannot cross the *blood–brain barrier,* a system of densely packed capillary and glial cells whose function is to prevent potentially harmful substances from entering the brain. Symptoms can be lessened by the administration of levodopa (L-dopa), which is a precursor (building block) of dopamine, but patients must take larger and larger doses; after a while, adverse effects, including depression, confusion, and even episodes of psychosis, may be worse than the disease itself.

During the past few years, surgeons have pioneered a dramatic new approach to treating Parkinson's disease and potentially other diseases as well. They have grafted dopamine-producing brain tissue from aborted fetuses into the brains of Parkinson's patients and also the brains of patients who developed symptoms similar to those of Parkinson's after having used a botched designer drug that killed their dopamine-producing cells (e.g., Freed et al., 1992, 1993). Not all patients have improved, but some who were virtually helpless before the operation can now move freely and even dress and feed themselves. Animal research suggests that transplants might also be able to help people with Huntington's disease, which involves the degeneration of neurons that make acetylcholine and GABA (Giordano et al., 1990; Sanberg et al., 1992, 1993). Although the long-term risks and benefits of brain tissue transplants are not yet known, and although at present the technique is not feasible on any large scale, this work is generating a lot of excitement.

We want to warn you, however, that establishing a cause-and-effect relationship between neurotransmitter abnormalities and behavioral abnormalities is extremely difficult, and many conclusions remain tentative. Each neurotransmitter plays multiple roles; its effect depends on the location of the neurons it serves and whether it excites or inhibits those neurons. Further, the functions of different substances often overlap. In addition, it is always possible that something about a disorder leads to abnormal neurotransmitter levels, instead of the other way around. Although drugs that boost or decrease levels of particular neurotransmitters are sometimes effective in treating disorders, that does not necessarily mean that abnormal neurotransmitter levels are *causing* the disorders. After all, aspirin can relieve a headache, but headaches are not caused by a lack of aspirin!

While scientists try to unravel the relationships between neurotransmitters and medical and psychological disorders, many of us are already doing things that affect our own neurotransmitters, usually without knowing it. For example, many recreational and therapeutic drugs produce their effects by either blocking or enhancing the actions of individual neurotransmitters (see Chapter 5). Even ordinary foods can influence the availability of neurotransmitters in the brain, as we discuss in "Taking Psychology with You" at the end of this chapter.

Endorphins: The Brain's Natural Opiates.   Another intriguing group of chemical messengers is known collectively as *endogenous opioid peptides,* or more popularly as **endorphins.** Endorphins have effects similar to those of natural opiates; that is, they reduce pain and promote pleasure. They are also thought to play a role in appetite, sexual activity, blood pressure, mood, learning, and memory. Some endorphins function as neurotransmitters, but most act primarily as **neuromodulators,** which increase or decrease the actions of specific neurotransmitters.

Endorphins were identified two and a half decades ago. Candace Pert and Solomon Snyder (1973) were doing research on *morphine,* a pain-relieving and mood-elevating opiate derived from heroin, which is made from poppies. They found that morphine works by binding to receptor sites in the brain. This seemed odd. As Snyder later recalled, "We doubted that animals had evolved opiate receptors just to deal with certain properties of the poppy plant" (quoted in Radetsky, 1991). Pert and Snyder reasoned that if opiate receptors exist, then the body must produce its own internal, or *endogenous,* morphinelike substances, which they named "endorphins." Soon, they and other researchers confirmed this hypothesis.

Endorphin levels seem to shoot up when an animal or a person is afraid or under stress. This is no accident; by making pain controllable in such situations, endorphins give a species an evolutionary advantage (Levinthal, 1988). When an organism is threatened, it needs to do something fast. Pain, however, can interfere with action: A mouse that pauses to lick a wounded paw may become a cat's dinner; a soldier who is overcome by an injury may never get off the battlefield. Of course, the body's built-in system of counteracting pain is only partly successful, especially when painful stimulation is prolonged. Researchers are now searching for ways to stimulate endorphin production or to administer endorphins directly to alleviate pain. One method is to apply mild electrical shock via a device inserted beneath the skin (transcutaneous electrical nerve stimulation, or TENS), a technique that alleviates chronic pain in many people, possibly by causing endorphins to be released (Pomeranz, 1989).

Other research, using animals, has demonstrated a link between endorphins and the pleasures of social contact. In one series of studies, Jack Panksepp and his colleagues (1980) gave low doses of morphine or endorphins to young puppies, guinea pigs, and chicks. After the injections, the animals showed much less distress than usual when separated from their mothers. (In all other respects, they behaved normally.) The injections seemed to provide a biochemical replacement for the mother, or, more specifically, for the endorphin surge presumed to occur during contact with her. Conversely, when young guinea pigs and chicks received a chemical that *blocks* the effects

■ **endorphins [en-DOR-fins]**
Neuromodulators that are similar in structure and action to opiates. They are involved in pain reduction, pleasure, and memory, and are known technically as endogenous opioid peptides.

■ **neuromodulators**
Chemical messengers in the nervous system that increase or decrease the action of specific neurotransmitters.

of opiates, their crying increased. These findings suggest that endorphin-stimulated euphoria may be a child's initial motive for seeking affection and cuddling—that in effect, a child attached to a parent is a child addicted to love.

Hormones: Long-Distance Messengers.   The third class of chemical messengers is the **hormones,** substances that are produced in one part of the body but that affect another. Hormones originate primarily in **endocrine glands,** which release them directly into the bloodstream. The bloodstream then carries the hormones to organs and cells that may be far from their point of origin. Some endocrine glands are activated by nervous-system impulses. Conversely, hormones affect the way the nervous system functions. The parts of the nervous and endocrine systems that interact are often referred to as the *neuroendocrine system.* Hormones have dozens of jobs, from promoting bodily growth to aiding digestion to regulating metabolism. The following hormones are of particular interest to psychologists:

1.   *Insulin,* which is produced by the *pancreas,* plays a role in the body's use of *glucose* (a sugar) and affects appetite.

2.   *Melatonin,* which is secreted by the *pineal body,* a small gland deep within the brain, appears to regulate biological rhythms (see Chapter 5).

3.   *Adrenal hormones,* which are produced by the adrenal glands (organs that are perched right above the kidneys), are involved in emotion and in responses to stress (see Chapter 10). Each adrenal gland is composed of an outer layer, or *cortex,* and an inner core, or *medulla.* The outer part produces *cortisol,* which increases blood-sugar levels and boosts energy. The inner part produces *epinephrine* and *norepinephrine.* (Most scientists prefer these last two terms to their older names, adrenaline and noradrenaline, although the older terms are still in common use.) When epinephrine and norepinephrine are released in your body, they activate the sympathetic nervous system, which in turn increases your arousal level and prepares you for action.

4.   *Sex hormones* are secreted by tissue located within the gonads—testes in men, ovaries in women. There are three main types of **sex hormones,** all occurring in both sexes, though in differing amounts and proportions after puberty. *Androgens* (the most important of which is *testosterone*) are masculinizing hormones produced mainly in the testes but also in the ovaries and adrenal cortex. Androgens set in motion the physical changes males experience at puberty—for example, a deepened voice and facial and chest hair—and cause pubic and underarm hair to develop in females. They also appear to influence sexual arousal in both sexes. *Estrogens* are feminizing hormones produced primarily in the ovaries but also in the testes and adrenal cortex. In women, they bring on the physical changes of puberty, such as breast development and the onset of menstruation, and influence the course of the menstrual cycle. *Progesterone* is a hormone that contributes to the growth and maintenance of the uterine lining in preparation for a fertilized egg. It is produced mainly in the ovaries, but small amounts are also produced in the testes and adrenal cortex. In the next chapter, we will examine the popular belief that fluctuating sex hormones make women (but not men) "emotional."

Although we have discussed hormones and neurotransmitters as separate substances, they are not always chemically distinct. The two classifications are like clubs that admit some of the same members. A chemical, such as norepinephrine, may belong to more than one classification, depending on where it is located and what function it is performing. Nature has been efficient, giving many of these substances more than one task to perform.

■ **hormones**
Chemical substances, secreted by organs called glands, that affect the functioning of other organs.

■ **endocrine glands**
Internal organs that produce hormones and release them into the bloodstream.

■ **sex hormones**
Hormones that regulate the development and functioning of reproductive and sex organs and that stimulate the development of male and female sexual characteristics; they include estrogens, progesterone, and testosterone.

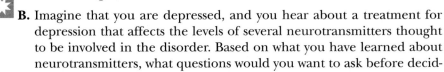

Quick QUIZ

A. Each definition below is followed by a pair of words. Which word best fits the definition?

1. Basic building blocks of the nervous system (*nerves/neurons*)
2. Cell parts that receive nerve impulses (*axons/dendrites*)
3. Site where communication between neurons takes place (*synapse/ myelin sheath*)
4. Opiatelike substance in the brain (*dopamine/endorphin*)
5. Chemicals that make it possible for neurons to communicate (*neurotransmitters/hormones*)
6. Hormone closely associated with emotional excitement (*epinephrine/estrogen*)

B. Imagine that you are depressed, and you hear about a treatment for depression that affects the levels of several neurotransmitters thought to be involved in the disorder. Based on what you have learned about neurotransmitters, what questions would you want to ask before deciding whether to try the treatment?

Answers:

A. 1. neurons **2.** dendrites **3.** synapse **4.** endorphin **5.** neurotransmitters **6.** epinephrine **B.** You might want to ask, among other things, about side effects (each neurotransmitter has several functions, all of which might be affected by the treatment); about evidence that the treatment works; and about whether there is any reason to believe that your own neurotransmitter levels are abnormal or whether there may be other reasons for your depression.

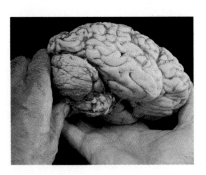

The human brain: Its modest appearance gives no hint of its powers.

▪ EAVESDROPPING ON THE BRAIN

We come now to the main room of the nervous system "house," the brain. A disembodied brain is not much to look at. Stored in a formaldehyde-filled container, it is a putty-colored, wrinkled glob of tissue that looks a little like a walnut whose growth has gotten out of hand. It takes an act of imagination to envision this modest-looking organ writing *Hamlet*, discovering radium, or inventing the paper clip.

In a living person, of course, the brain is encased in a thick protective vault of bone. How, then, can scientists study it? One approach is to study patients who have had a part of the brain damaged or removed because of disease or injury. Another, called the *lesion method*, involves damaging or removing sections of brain in animals, then observing the effects.

The brain can also be probed by using devices called *electrodes*. Some electrodes are coin-shaped and are simply pasted or taped onto the scalp. They detect the electrical activity of millions of neurons in every brain region and are widely used in research and medical diagnosis. The electrodes are connected by wires to a machine that translates the electrical energy from the brain into wavy lines on a moving piece of paper or visual patterns on a screen. That is why electrical patterns in the brain are known as "brain waves." Different wave patterns are associated with sleep, relaxation, and mental concentration, as we will see in Chapter 5.

▪ **electroencephalogram (EEG)**

A recording of neural activity detected by electrodes.

A brain-wave recording is called an **electroencephalogram (EEG).** An EEG is useful, but not very precise, because it reflects the firing of many cells at once. "Listening" to the brain with an EEG machine is like standing outside a sports

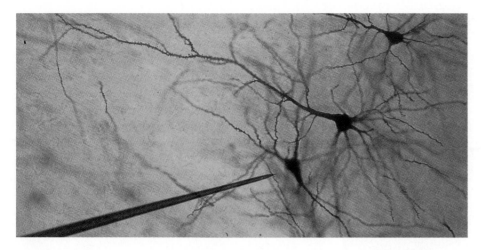

A microelectrode is used to record the electrical impulses generated by a single cell in the brain of a monkey.

stadium: You know when something is happening, but you can't be sure what it is or who is doing it. Fortunately, computer technology can be combined with EEG technology to get a clearer picture of brain activity patterns associated with specific events and mental processes. To analyze such patterns, or **evoked potentials,** researchers use a computer to suppress all the background "noise" being produced by the brain, leaving only the pattern of electrical response to the event.

For even more specific information, researchers use *needle electrodes,* very thin wires or hollow glass tubes that can be inserted into the brain, either directly in an exposed brain or through tiny holes in the skull. Only the skull and the membranes covering the brain need to be anesthetized during insertion; the brain itself, which processes all sensation and feeling, paradoxically feels nothing when touched. Therefore, a human patient or an animal can be awake and not feel pain during the procedure. Needle electrodes can be used both to record electrical activity from the brain and to stimulate the brain with weak electrical currents. *Microelectrodes* are so fine that they can be inserted into single cells.

During the past decade or two, even more amazing doors to the brain have opened. The most widely used method, the **PET scan (positron-emission tomography),** goes beyond anatomy to record biochemical changes in the brain as they are happening. One type of PET scan takes advantage of the fact that nerve cells convert glucose, the body's main fuel, into energy. A researcher can inject a patient with a glucoselike substance that contains a harmless radioactive element. This substance accumulates in brain areas that are particularly active and are therefore consuming glucose rapidly. The substance emits radiation, which is a telltale sign of activity, like cookie crumbs on a child's face. The radiation is detected by a scanning device, and the result is a computer-processed picture of biochemical activity on a display screen, with different colors indicating different activity levels.

PET scans were originally designed to diagnose abnormalities, and in the past few years, they have produced evidence that certain brain areas in people with emotional disorders are either unusually quiet or unusually active. But PET technology can also be used to find out which parts of the brain are normally active during specific activities and emotions (see Figure 4.8a on page 132). It lets researchers see which areas are busiest when a person hears a song, feels elated, or shifts attention from one task to another.

PET scans are also being used to study the physiological correlates of intelligence. Most neuropsychologists doubt that intelligence has anything to do with the gross anatomy of the brain—no one, for instance, has been able to find any-

■ **evoked potentials**
Patterns of brain activity produced in response to specific events.

■ **PET scan (positron-emission tomography)**
A method for analyzing biochemical activity in the brain, using injections of a glucoselike substance containing a radioactive element.

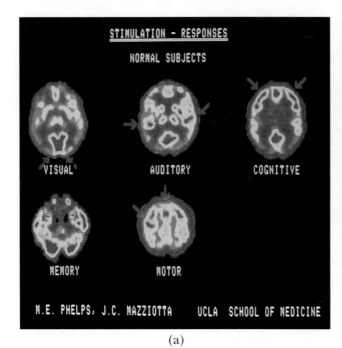

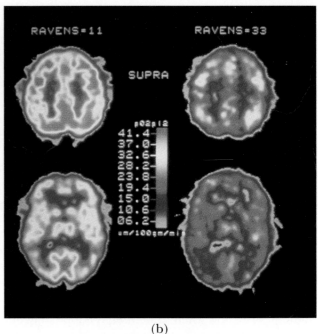

(a)   (b)

■ **Figure 4.8   PET Scans of Metabolic Activity in the Brain**

In the PET scans in photo (a), red indicates areas of highest activity, and violet areas of lowest activity. The arrows point to regions that are most active when a person looks at a complicated visual scene (top left), listens to a sound (top center), performs a mental task (top right), recalls information from stories heard previously (bottom left), or moves the right hand (bottom center). The PET scan in photo (b) suggests a link between intellect and brain activity. During an abstract-reasoning task, the brains of high scorers (right) metabolized less glucose per minute than the brains of low scorers (left), suggesting that the brains of those who did well were working more efficiently (Haier et al., 1988).

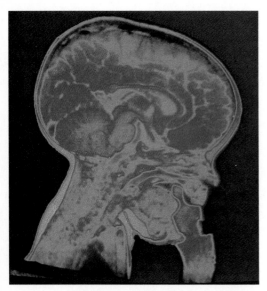

■ **Figure 4.9 MRI at Work**

This MRI shows a child's brain—and the bottle given to him to quiet him during the seven minutes it took to obtain the image.

thing remarkable about Einstein's brain. What more probably matters is the wiring of neural circuits, the amount or efficiency of neurotransmitters, or metabolism rates (Gazzaniga, 1988). PET-scan studies find, for example, that when people are working on intellectual tasks, the brains of those who score high are *less active* than those of people who do poorly (Haier et al., 1988; Parks et al., 1988) (see Figure 4.8b). A plausible explanation is that in high scorers, fewer circuits are required for the task, or perhaps fewer neurons per circuit; neurologically, in other words, their brains are operating more efficiently. Such biological differences could be genetic, but they could also develop as the result of experience. When participants in one study were given the opportunity to practice a computer game over a period of several weeks, their glucose metabolism rates during the sessions gradually fell (Haier et al., 1992).

Another technique, **MRI (magnetic resonance imaging),** allows the exploration of "inner space" without injecting chemicals. Powerful magnetic fields and radio frequencies produce vibrations in the nuclei of atoms making up body organs, and these vibrations are picked up as signals by special receivers. A computer then analyzes the signals, taking into account their strength and duration, and converts them into a high-contrast picture (see Figure 4.9). Like the PET scan, MRI is used both for diagnosing disease and for studying normal brains. Conventional MRI is too slow to map activity over time, but recent breakthroughs in computer hardware and software have led to faster techniques that can capture brain changes during specific mental activities, such as thinking of a word or looking at a scene (Rosen et al., 1993). Fast or "func-

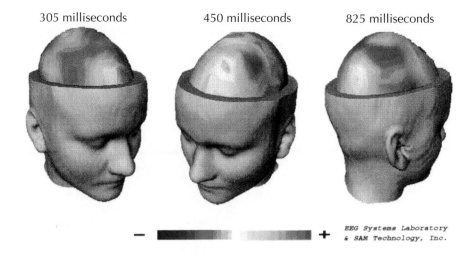

305 milliseconds   450 milliseconds   825 milliseconds

EEG Systems Laboratory & SAM Technology, Inc.

■ **Figure 4.10   Brain Activity in 3-D**

By combining a new technology, MRI, with an old technology, EEG, researchers can now monitor electrical changes in brain cells from moment to moment as a person works on a specific task. The models in this figure show changes on the brain's surface during a one-second interval as a person compares the location of a new stimulus with the location of one seen moments before. Different regions on the front and sides of the cerebral cortex are activated as the person performs the task.

tional," MRI works indirectly; it detects blood flow by picking up magnetic signals from blood that has given up its oxygen to active brain cells.

Still other techniques, although not yet widely used for psychological research, are becoming available with each passing year. One of the newest techniques combines EEG and MRI technology. The researcher or clinician first uses electrodes to record electrical signals from 128 points on the scalp. A new reading is taken every few milliseconds. A computer is then used to map ongoing, changing neuronal activity at the surface of a three-dimensional MR image of the brain (Gevins et al., 1994). The result is something like a movie of ongoing changes in brain-cell activity (see Figure 4.10).

As you can see, the brain can no longer hide from researchers behind the fortress of the skull. It is now possible to get a clear visual image of our most enigmatic organ without so much as lifting a scalpel.

■ A TOUR THROUGH THE BRAIN

Neurosurgeon Joseph Bogen (1978) once suggested that a 30-story replica of the brain be built so that people could learn about brain anatomy the way they learn about a neighborhood—by strolling through it. No one has followed up on that suggestion, so we must make do with an imaginary tour. Pretend, now, that you have shrunk to a microscopic size and that you are wending your way through the "soul's frail dwelling house" starting at the lower part, just above the spine. For ease of description, we can think of that house as having three main sections: the *hindbrain,* the *midbrain,* and the *forebrain.* (These terms have fallen somewhat out of favor, but they do provide a useful way of organizing the areas of the brain.) In general, the more reflexive or automatic a behavior is, the more likely it is to be controlled by areas in the hindbrain and midbrain, and the more complex a behavior, the more likely it is to involve the forebrain. Major structures of the brain are shown in Figure 4.11 on the next page; you may want to refer to it as we take our tour.

■ **MRI (magnetic resonance imaging)**
A method for studying body and brain tissue, using magnetic fields and special radio receivers.

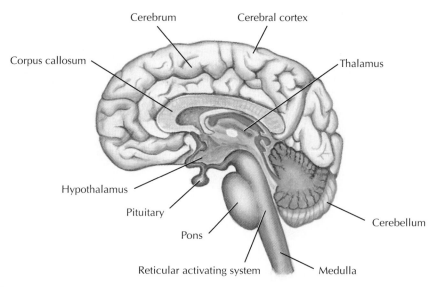

■ Figure 4.11   The Human Brain

This cross-sectional drawing shows the brain as though it were split in half. The view is of the inside surface of the right half. The pons, medulla, cerebellum, and lower part of the reticular activating system (RAS) make up what has traditionally been called the hindbrain. The reticular activating system extends into an area called the midbrain. The other structures labeled in the figure belong to the forebrain.

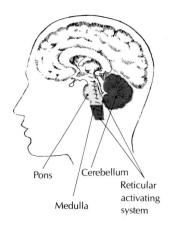

The Hindbrain: Vital Functions

We begin at the base of the skull with the **brain stem,** which began to evolve some 500 million years ago in segmented worms. The brain stem looks like a stalk rising out of the spinal cord. Pathways to and from upper areas of the brain pass through its two main structures, the **medulla** and the **pons.** The pons is involved in (among other things) sleeping, waking, and dreaming. The medulla is responsible for bodily functions that do not have to be consciously willed, such as breathing and heart rate. Hanging has long been used as a method of execution because when it breaks the neck, nervous pathways from the medulla are severed, stopping respiration.

Extending upward from the core of the brain stem is the **reticular activating system (RAS).** This dense network of neurons, which has connections with many higher areas of the brain, screens incoming information and arouses the higher centers when something happens that demands their attention. Without the RAS, we could not be alert or perhaps even conscious.

Standing atop the brain stem and looking toward the back part of the brain, we see a structure about the size of a small fist. It is the **cerebellum,** or "lesser brain," which contributes to a sense of balance and coordinates the muscles so that movement is smooth and precise. If your cerebellum were damaged, you would probably become exceedingly clumsy and uncoordinated. You might have trouble using a pencil, threading a needle, riding a bicycle, or, as we will see in Chapter 9, remembering some kinds of skills.

The Midbrain: Important Way Stations

Above the brain stem is the *midbrain,* which contains neural tracts that run to and from the upper and lower portions of the brain. One area of the midbrain receives information from the visual system and is involved in eye movements. Some researchers consider the midbrain to be part of the brain stem. In this book we will not be concerned with details about the midbrain's structure.

The Forebrain: Emotions, Memory, and Thought

Above the brain stem, in the brain's interior, we can see the **thalamus,** the busy traffic officer of the brain. As sensory messages come into the brain, the thalamus directs them to higher centers. For example, the sight of a sunset sends signals that the thalamus directs to a vision area, and the sound of an oboe sends signals that the thalamus sends on to an auditory area. The only sense that completely bypasses the thalamus is the sense of smell, which has its own private switching station, the *olfactory bulb.* The olfactory bulb lies near areas that control emotion. Perhaps that is why particular odors—the smell of fresh laundry, gardenias, a steak sizzling on the grill—often rekindle memories of important personal experiences.

Beneath the thalamus sits a structure called the **hypothalamus** (*hypo* means "under"). It is involved in drives associated with the survival of both the individual and the species—hunger, thirst, emotion, sex, and reproduction. It also regulates body temperature by triggering sweating or shivering, and it controls the complex operations of the autonomic nervous system. And, as we will see in the next chapter, it contains a neurological clock that regulates the body's biological rhythms.

Hanging down from the hypothalamus, connected to it by a short stalk, is a cherry-sized endocrine gland called the **pituitary gland.** The pituitary is often called the body's "master gland" because the hormones it secretes affect many other endocrine glands. The master, however, is really only a supervisor. The true boss is the hypothalamus, which sends chemicals to the pituitary that tell it when to "talk" to the endocrine glands. The pituitary, in turn, sends hormonal messages out to the glands.

The hypothalamus has many connections to a set of loosely interconnected structures that form a sort of border on the underside of the brain's "cauliflower." Together, these structures make up the **limbic system** of the brain (see Figure 4.12 on page 136). (*Limbic* comes from the Latin word for "border.") Some brain specialists include the hypothalamus and parts of the thalamus in the limbic system. The limbic system is heavily involved in emotions, such as rage and fear, that we share with other animals.

Many years ago, James Olds and Peter Milner reported the existence of "pleasure centers" in the limbic system (Olds, 1975; Olds & Milner, 1954). They found that rats could be trained to press a lever in order to get a buzz of electricity delivered through tiny electrodes to their limbic systems. Some rats would press the bar thousands of times an hour, for 15 or 20 hours at a time, until they collapsed from exhaustion. When they revived, they went right back to the bar. When forced to make a choice, the little hedonists opted for electrical stimulation over such temptations as water, food, and even an attractive rat of the other sex that was making provocative gestures. (You may be either relieved or disappointed to know that human beings do not act like rats in this regard. Patients who volunteered to have their pleasure areas stimulated as an experimental treatment for depression said that the experience was merely "pleasant" [Sem-Jacobsen, 1959].) Today, researchers believe that brain stimulation activates various neural pathways rather than discrete centers, and that such stimulation causes changes in neurotransmitter or neuromodulator levels. Several lines of research have focused on the possible role of endorphins, since the limbic system contains some of the highest concentrations of endorphins and endorphin receptors in the brain.

Two parts of the limbic system of special concern to psychologists are the amygdala and the hippocampus. The **amygdala** appears to be responsible for

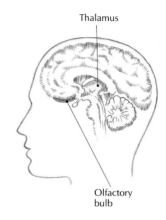

Thalamus

Olfactory bulb

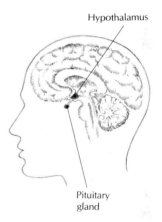

Hypothalamus

Pituitary gland

■ **brain stem**
The part of the brain at the top of the spinal cord; responsible for automatic functions such as heartbeat and respiration.

■ **medulla**
A structure in the brain stem responsible for certain automatic functions, such as breathing and heart rate.

■ **pons**
A structure in the brain stem involved in, among other things, sleeping, waking, and dreaming.

■ **reticular activating system (RAS)**
A dense network of neurons found in the core of the brain stem; arouses the cortex and screens incoming information.

■ **cerebellum**
A brain structure that regulates movement and balance.

■ **thalamus**
The brain structure that relays sensory messages to the cerebral cortex.

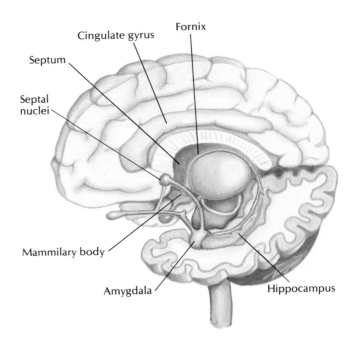

■ Figure 4.12 The Limbic System

Structures of the limbic system play an important role in memory and emotion.

■ hypothalamus

A brain structure involved in emotions and drives vital to survival, such as fear, hunger, thirst, and reproduction; it regulates the autonomic nervous system.

■ pituitary gland

A small endocrine gland at the base of the brain, which releases many hormones, and which regulates other endocrine glands.

■ limbic system

A group of brain areas involved in emotional reactions and motivated behavior.

■ amygdala

A brain structure involved in the arousal and regulation of emotion; it may also play a role in the association of memories formed in different senses.

■ hippocampus

A brain structure thought to be involved in the storage of new information in memory.

evaluating sensory information and quickly determining its emotional importance, and also for the initial decision to either approach or withdraw from a person or situation. The other important limbic structure, the **hippocampus,** has a shape that must have reminded someone of a sea horse, for that is what its name means. This structure is larger in human beings than in any other species. One of its tasks seems to be to compare sensory messages with what the brain has learned to expect about the world. When expectations are met, the hippocampus tells the reticular activating system, the brain's arousal center, to "cool it." It wouldn't do to be highly aroused in response to *everything*. What if neural alarm bells went off every time a car went by, a bird chirped, or you felt your saliva trickling down the back of your throat?

The hippocampus has been called the "gateway to memory," because (along with other brain areas) it seems to enable us to store new information for future use. We know about this role of the hippocampus in part from research on brain-damaged patients with severe memory problems. One man, known to researchers as H. M., was studied for many years by Brenda Milner and later by Suzanne Corkin and is still being studied today (Corkin, 1984; Milner, 1970; Ogden & Corkin, 1991). In 1953, when H. M. was 27, surgeons removed most of his hippocampus, along with part of the amygdala. The operation was a last-ditch effort to relieve H. M.'s severe and life-threatening epilepsy. People who have epilepsy, a neurological disorder that has many causes and that takes many forms, often have seizures. Usually, the seizures are brief, mild, and controllable by drugs, but in H. M.'s case, they were unrelenting and uncontrollable.

The operation did, in fact, achieve its goal: Afterward, the young man's seizures were milder and could be managed with medication. His memory, however, had been affected dramatically. Although H. M. continued to recall most events before the operation, he could no longer remember new experiences for much longer than 15 minutes. They vanished like water down the drain. Milner and H. M.'s physicians had to reintroduce themselves every time they saw him. He would read the same magazine over and over without realizing it. He could not recall the day of the week, the year, or even his last meal. Today, many years later, he will occasionally recall an unusually emotional event, such as the assassination of someone named Kennedy. He has managed to learn some new manual, perceptual, and problem-solving skills, which may draw on a different part of the brain than do facts and events. However, he forgets the training sessions. For the most part, history stopped for H. M. on the day of his operation. H. M. says that living his life is like constantly waking from a dream. Today, this gentle, good-natured man can no longer recognize a photograph of his own face; he is stuck in a time warp from the past. We will meet H. M. again when we discuss memory in Chapter 9.

At this point in our tour, the largest part of the brain still looms above us. It is the cauliflowerlike **cerebrum,** where the higher forms of thinking take place. The complexity of the human brain's circuitry far exceeds that of any computer in existence, and much of its most complicated wiring is packed into this structure. Compared to many other creatures, we humans may be ungainly, feeble, and thin-skinned, but our well-developed cerebrum enables us to overcome these limitations and to control our environment creatively (and, some would say, to mess it up).

The cerebrum is divided into two separate halves, or **cerebral hemispheres,** connected by a large band of fibers called the **corpus callosum.** In general, the right hemisphere is in charge of the left side of the body, and the left hemisphere is in charge of the right side of the body. The two hemispheres also have somewhat different tasks and talents, a phenomenon known as **lateralization.**

Working our way right up through the top of the brain, we find that the cerebrum is covered by several thin layers of densely packed cells known collectively as the **cerebral cortex.** Cell bodies in the cortex, as in many other parts of the brain, produce a grayish tissue—hence the term *gray matter.* In other parts of the brain and nervous system, long, myelin-covered axons prevail, producing *white matter.* Although the cortex is only about 3 millimeters thick, it contains almost three-fourths of all the cells in the human brain (Schneider & Tarshis, 1986). In only 1 square *inch* of the cortex there are around 10,000 miles of synaptically connected nerve cells. In the entire cortex there are enough connections to stretch from the earth to the moon and back again, and then back to the moon (Davis, 1984).

Standing atop the cortex, we note that it has many deep crevasses and wrinkles. These folds and fissures in the brain's surface enable it to contain its billions of neurons without requiring us to have the heads of giants—heads that would be too big to permit us to be born. In other mammals, which have fewer neurons, the cortex is less crumpled; in the rat, it is quite smooth. From our vantage point we can see that on each cerebral hemisphere, certain especially deep fissures divide the cortex into four distinct regions, or lobes (see Figure 4.13):

- The *occipital lobes* (from the Latin for "in back of the head") are at the lower back part of the brain. Among other things, they contain the *visual cortex,* where visual signals are processed. Damage to the visual cortex can cause impaired visual recognition or blindness.

- The *parietal lobes* (from the Latin for "pertaining to walls") are at the top of the brain. They contain the *somatosensory cortex,* which receives information about pressure, pain, touch, and temperature from all over the body. This sensory information tells you what the movable parts of your body are doing at every moment. The areas of the somatosensory cortex that receive signals from the hands and the face are disproportionately large because these body parts are particularly sensitive.

- The *temporal lobes* (from the Latin for "pertaining to the temples") are at the sides of the brain, just above the ears, behind the temples. They are involved in memory, perception, emotion, and language comprehension, and they contain the *auditory cortex,* which processes sounds.

- The *frontal lobes,* as their name indicates, are located toward the front of the brain, just under the skull in the area of the forehead. They contain

■ **cerebrum [suh-REE-brum]**
The largest brain structure, consisting of the upper part of the forebrain; it is in charge of most sensory, motor, and cognitive processes; from the Latin for "brain."

■ **cerebral hemispheres**
The two halves of the cerebrum.

■ **corpus callosum**
The bundle of nerve fibers connecting the two cerebral hemispheres.

■ **lateralization**
Specialization of the two cerebral hemispheres for particular psychological operations.

■ **cerebral cortex**
A collection of several thin layers of cells covering the cerebrum; it is largely responsible for higher mental functions; cortex is Latin for "bark" or "rind."

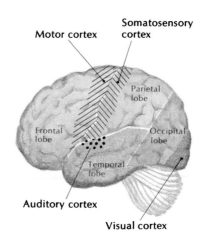

■ **Figure 4.13 Lobes of the Cerebrum**

Crosshatched areas show regions specialized for movement and bodily sensation; dotted areas show regions specialized for vision and hearing.

"Well, time for our weekly brain-stem storming session."

the *motor cortex,* which issues orders to the 600 muscles of the body that produce voluntary movement. They also seem to be responsible for the ability to make plans, think creatively, and take initiative.

When a surgeon probes these four pairs of lobes with an electrode, different things tend to happen. If current is applied to the somatosensory cortex in the parietal lobes, the patient may feel tingling in the skin or a sense of being gently touched. If the visual cortex in the occipital lobes is stimulated, the person may report a flash of light or swirls of color. However, there is considerable overlap in what the lobes do. And in most areas of the cortex, nothing happens as a result of electrical stimulation. These "silent" areas, sometimes called the *association cortex,* appear to be responsible for higher mental processes.

The silent areas of the cortex are just beginning to reveal their secrets. Psychologists are especially interested in new information about the forwardmost part of the frontal lobes, the *prefrontal cortex.* This area barely exists in mice and rats and takes up only 3.5 percent of the cerebral cortex in cats, about 7 percent in dogs, and 17 percent in chimpanzees. In human beings, it accounts for fully 29 percent of the cortex (Pines, 1983).

Scientists have long known that the frontal lobes, and the prefrontal cortex in particular, must have something to do with personality. The first clue appeared in 1848, when a bizarre accident drove an inch-thick iron rod, over three and a half feet long, clear through the head of a young railroad worker named Phineas Gage. The rod (which is still on display at Harvard University, along with Gage's skull) entered beneath the left eye and exited through the top of the head, destroying much of the front of the brain (see Figure 4.14). Miraculously, Gage survived this extraordinary trauma. What's more, he retained

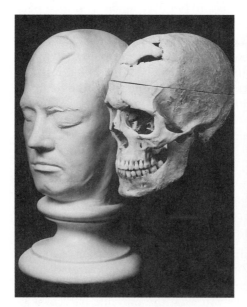 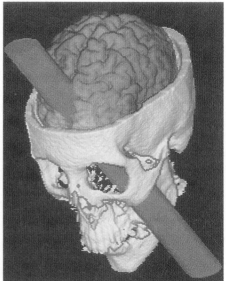

■ **Figure 4.14   A Famous Skull**

At the left is Phineas Gage's skull and a cast of his head, on display at Harvard Medical School. You can see where the tamping iron penetrated, so dramatically altering his behavior and personality that his friends said he was "no longer Gage." The exact location of the brain damage remained controversial until recently, when Hanna Damasio and her colleagues (1994) used photographs and measurements of Gage's skull and MRIs of normal brains to plot possible trajectories of the tamping iron. On the right is a reconstruction showing the trajectory that best fits the evidence: The damage occurred in an area in the right and left prefrontal cortex thought to be involved in rational decision making and the processing of emotion.

the ability to speak, think, and remember. But his friends complained that he was "no longer Gage": He had changed from a friendly, efficient, well-respected worker into a foul-mouthed, ill-tempered, undependable lout who could not hold a steady job or stick to a plan. His employers had to let him go, and he was reduced to exhibiting himself as a circus attraction.

This sad case and other cases of frontal-lobe damage suggest that parts of the frontal lobes are involved in social judgment and the ability to set goals and make and carry through plans—or what is commonly called "will." As neurologist Antonio Damasio (1994) writes, "Gage's unintentional message was that observing social convention, behaving ethically, and, in general, making decisions advantageous to one's survival and progress, require both knowledge of rules and strategies *and* the integrity of specific brain systems." Interestingly, the mental deficits that characterize damage to these areas are accompanied by a flattening out of emotion and feeling, which suggests that normal emotions are necessary for everyday reasoning and decision making.

The frontal lobes also govern the ability to do a series of tasks in the proper order and to stop doing them at the proper time. The pioneering Soviet psychologist Alexander Luria (1980) studied many patients in whom damage to the frontal lobes had disrupted these abilities. One man who was observed by Luria kept trying to light a match after it was already lit. Another planed a piece of wood in the hospital carpentry shop until it was gone, and then went on to plane the workbench!

Scientists are now trying to map the circuitry of the frontal lobes by studying brain-injured patients and monkeys. Their tools are the sophisticated techniques discussed earlier—microelectrodes and brain scans. These researchers hope to link specific areas of the frontal lobes with specific mental abilities. Some believe that damage to the prefrontal cortex, caused by birth complications or child abuse, might help account for many cases of criminally violent behavior (Raine, Brennan, & Mednick, 1994). A recent PET-scan study found that accused murderers had less brain activity in this area than did control subjects who were matched for age and sex (Raine et al., 1994). These results, if verified by other researchers, will raise troubling legal questions: Should violent individuals who have damage in the frontal cortex be held responsible for their acts? And what treatment or punishment should they receive?

Quick QUIZ

Match each of the descriptions on the left with one of the terms on the right.

1. Filters out irrelevant information
2. Known as the "gateway to memory"
3. Controls the autonomic nervous system; involved in drives associated with survival
4. Consists of two hemispheres
5. Wrinkled outer covering of the brain
6. Site of the motor cortex; associated with planning, thinking creatively, and taking initiative.

   a. reticular activating system
   b. cerebrum
   c. hippocampus
   d. cerebral cortex
   e. frontal lobes
   f. hypothalamus

Answers:

1.a 2.c 3.f 4.b 5.d 6.e

■ THE TWO HEMISPHERES OF THE BRAIN

We have seen that the cerebrum is divided into two hemispheres that control opposite sides of the body. Although similar in structure, these hemispheres have somewhat separate talents, or areas of specialization.

Split Brains: A House Divided

In a normal brain, the two hemispheres communicate with one another across the corpus callosum, the bundle of fibers that connects them. Whatever happens in one side of the brain is instantly flashed to the other side.

What would happen, though, if the communication lines were cut? An early clue occurred in a case study published in 1908. A mentally disturbed woman repeatedly tried to choke herself with her left hand. She would try with her right hand to pull the left hand away from her throat, but she claimed that the left hand was beyond her control. She also did other destructive things, like throwing pillows around and tearing her sheets—but only with her left hand. A neurologist suspected that the woman's corpus callosum had been damaged, and that as a result the two sides of the brain could no longer communicate. When the woman died, an autopsy showed that he was right (Geschwind, in J. Miller, 1983).

This case suggests that the two sides of the brain can feel different emotions. What would happen if they were completely out of touch? Would they think different thoughts and store different memories? In 1953, Ronald E. Myers and Roger W. Sperry took the first step toward answering this question by severing the corpus callosum in cats. They also cut parts of the nerves leading from the eyes to the brain. Normally, each eye transmits messages to both sides of the brain. After this procedure, a cat's left eye sent information only to the left hemisphere; its right eye sent information only to the right hemisphere.

At first, the cats did not seem to be affected much by this drastic operation. But Myers and Sperry showed that something profound had happened. They trained the cats to perform tasks with one eye blindfolded. For example, a cat might have to push a panel with a square on it to get food but to ignore a panel with a circle. Then the researchers switched the blindfold to the cat's other eye and tested the animal again. Now the cats behaved as if they had never learned the trick. Apparently, one side of the brain didn't know what the other side was doing. It was as if the animals had two minds in one body. Later studies confirmed this result with other species, including monkeys (Sperry, 1964).

In all the animal studies, ordinary behavior, such as eating and walking, remained normal. Encouraged by this finding, a team of surgeons led by Joseph Bogen decided in the early 1960s to try cutting the corpus callosum in patients with debilitating, uncontrollable epilepsy. In some forms of epilepsy, disorganized electrical activity spreads from an injured area to other parts of the brain. The surgeons reasoned that cutting the connection between the two halves of the brain might stop the spread of electrical activity from one side to the other. As in H. M.'s case, the operation was a last resort.

The results of this *split-brain surgery* generally proved successful. Seizures were reduced and sometimes disappeared completely. As an added bonus, these patients gave scientists a chance to find out what each half of the brain can do when it is quite literally cut off from the other. It was already known that the two hemispheres are not mirror images of one another. In most people, language is largely handled by the left hemisphere: speech production in an area of the left frontal lobe known as *Broca's area*, meaning and language comprehension in an area of the left temporal lobe known as *Wernicke's area*. (The two areas are named after the scientists who first described them.) Thus, a person who suffers brain damage because of a stroke (a blockage in or rupture of a blood vessel in the brain) is much more likely to have language problems if the damage is in the left hemisphere than if it is in the right. How would splitting the brain affect language and other abilities?

In their daily lives, split-brain patients did not seem much affected by the fact that the two sides of their brains were incommunicado. Their personalities and general intelligence remained intact; they could walk, talk, and in general lead normal lives. Apparently, connections in the undivided brain stem kept body movements normal. But in a series of ingenious studies, Sperry and his colleagues (and later other researchers) showed that perception and memory had been profoundly affected, just as they had been in earlier animal research. In 1981, Sperry won a Nobel Prize for this work.

To understand this research, you must know how nerves connect the eyes to the brain. (The human patients, unlike Myers and Sperry's cats, did not have these nerves cut.) If you look straight ahead, everything in the left side of the scene before you—the "visual field"—goes to the right half of your brain, and vice versa. This is true for *both* eyes (see Figure 4.15).

The basic procedure was to present information only to one or the other side of the subjects' brains. In one early study (Levy, Trevarthen, & Sperry, 1972), the researchers took photographs of different faces, cut them in two, and pasted different halves together (see Figure 4.16). The reconstructed photographs were then presented on slides. The person was told to stare at a dot on

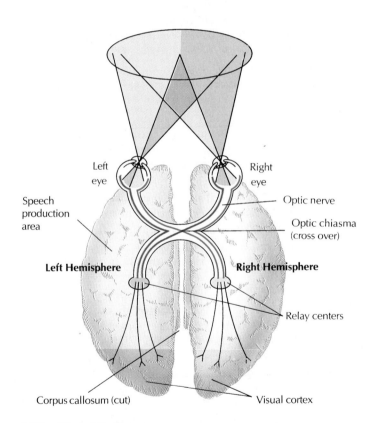

▪ Figure 4.15   Visual Pathways

Each hemisphere of the brain receives information about the opposite side of the visual field. For example, if you stare directly at the corner of a room, everything to the left of the juncture is represented in your right cerebral hemisphere and everything to the right is represented in your left cerebral hemisphere. This is so because half the axons in each optic nerve cross over (at the optic chiasma) to the opposite side of the brain. Normally, each hemisphere immediately shares its information with the other one. However, in split-brain patients, severing of the corpus callosum prevents such communication from occurring.

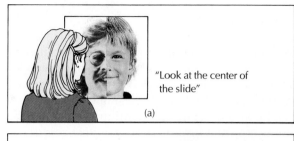

"Look at the center of the slide"

(a)

"Point to the person you saw"

(b)

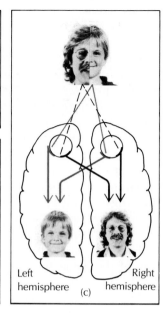

Left hemisphere   Right hemisphere

(c)

■ Figure 4.16   Divided Brain, Divided View

Split-brain patients were shown composite photographs, then asked to pick out the face they had seen from a series of intact photographs. These patients said they had seen the face on the right side of the composite, yet they pointed with their left hands to the face that had been on the left. Because the two hemispheres of the brain could not communicate, the verbal left hemisphere was aware of only the right half of the picture and the relatively mute right hemisphere was aware of only the left half.

the middle of the screen, so that half the image fell to the left of this point and half to the right. Each image was flashed so quickly that there was no time for the person to move his or her eyes. When the subjects were asked to say what they had seen, they named the person in the right part of the image. But when they were asked to *point* with their left hands to the face they had seen, they chose the person in the left side of the image. Further, they claimed they had noticed nothing unusual about the original photographs! Each side of the brain saw a different half-image and automatically filled in the missing part. Neither side knew what the other side had seen.

Why did the patients name one side of the picture but point to the other? Speech centers are in the left hemisphere. When the person responded with speech, it was the left side of the brain doing the talking. When the person pointed with the left hand, which is controlled by the right side of the brain, the right brain was giving *its* version of what the person had seen.

In another study, the researchers presented slides of ordinary objects, and then suddenly flashed a slide of a nude woman. Both sides of the brain were amused, but because only the left side has speech, the two sides responded differently. When the picture was flashed to her left hemisphere, one woman laughed and identified it as a nude. When it was flashed to her right hemisphere, she said nothing but began to chuckle. Asked what she was laughing at, she said, "I don't know . . . nothing . . . oh—that funny machine." The right hemisphere could not describe what it had seen, but it reacted emotionally, just the same (Gazzaniga, 1967).

A Question of Dominance

Since the initial split-brain studies, many others have been carried out. (Several dozen people have undergone the split-brain operation during the past

"It's finally happening, Helen. The hemispheres of my brain are drifting apart."

few decades.) Research on left–right hemispheric differences has also been done with people whose brains are intact. Electrodes and PET scans have been used to gauge activity in the left and right sides of the brain while people perform different tasks. The results confirm that nearly all right-handed people and a majority of left-handers process language mainly in the left hemisphere. The left side is also more active than the right during some logical, symbolic, and sequential tasks, such as solving math problems and understanding technical material. Because of its cognitive "talents," many researchers refer to the left hemisphere as *dominant.* They believe that the left hemisphere usually exerts control over the right hemisphere. One well-known split-brain researcher, Michael Gazzaniga (1983), has argued that without help from the left side, the right side's mental skills would probably be "vastly inferior to the cognitive skills of a chimpanzee." He also believes that the left hemisphere is constantly trying to explain actions and emotions generated by brain parts whose workings are nonverbal and outside of awareness.

You can see in split-brain patients how the left brain concocts such explanations. In one classic example, a picture of a chicken claw was flashed to a patient's left hemisphere, a picture of a snow scene to his right. The task was to point to a related image for each picture from an array, with a chicken the correct choice for the claw and a shovel for the snow scene. The patient chose the shovel with his left hand and the chicken with his right. When asked to explain why, he responded (with his left hemisphere) that the chicken claw went with the chicken, and the shovel was for cleaning out the chicken shed. The left brain had seen the left hand's response but did not know about the snow scene, so it interpreted the response by using the information it did have (Gazzaniga, 1988). In people with intact brains, says Gazzaniga, the left brain's interpretations account for the sense of a unified, coherent identity. (For more on the brain and self-awareness, see "Think About It.")

Other researchers, including Sperry (1982), have rushed to the right hemisphere's defense. The right side, they point out, is no dummy. It is superior in problems requiring spatial–visual ability, the ability you use to read a map or to follow a dress pattern, and it excels in facial recognition. (Dr. P., at the beginning of this chapter, had damage in the right hemisphere.) It is active during the creation and appreciation of art and music. It recognizes nonverbal sounds, such as a dog's barking. The right brain also has some language ability. Typically,

✳ *Some popular self-improvement programs promise to sharpen up your logical "left brain" and liberate your artistic "right brain." Why do so many people get carried away with the right brain/left brain dichotomy? Does the evidence support their enthusiasm—and the claims of self-improvement programs?*

it can read a word briefly flashed to it and can understand an experimenter's instructions. In a few split-brain patients, language ability has been quite well developed. Research with other brain-damaged people finds that the right brain actually outperforms the left at understanding familiar idioms and metaphors (such as "turning over a new leaf") (Van Lancker & Kempler, 1987). Some researchers have also credited the right hemisphere with having a cognitive style that is holistic (sees things as wholes) and intuitive, in contrast to the left hemisphere's more rational and analytic mode.

However, many researchers are concerned about popular interpretations of such conclusions. Books and programs that promise to "beef up your brain,"

*T*hink About It

*W*here Is Your "Self"?

■ When you say, "I am feeling unhappy," all sorts of brain parts and processes are active, but who, exactly, is the "I" doing the feeling? When you say, "I've decided to have a hot dog instead of a hamburger," who is the "I" doing the choosing? When you say, "My mind is playing tricks on me," who is the "me" watching your mind play those tricks, and who is it that's being tricked? How can the self observe itself? Isn't that a little like a finger pointing at its own tip?

The ancient Egyptians reportedly believed that the "self" controlling actions and thoughts was a little person, a *homunculus,* residing in the head. Descartes, as we saw in Chapter 1, thought the soul made contact with the body in the brain's pineal gland. Western religions have resolved the problem by teaching that there is an immortal self or soul that exists entirely apart from the mortal brain—a position known in philosophy as *dualism.* But most modern brain scientists (with some notable exceptions) consider mind to be a matter of matter—a position known as *materialism.* Although they may have personal religious convictions about a soul, most assume that "mind" or "self-awareness" can be explained in physical terms as a product of the cerebral cortex; in the words of British philosopher Gilbert Ryle (1949), there is no "ghost in the machine." If that is so, then it makes no sense, really, to say "I have a brain" or "We think with our brains" or "Boy, she's really using her brain"—although we all use such everday constructions—because we *are* our brains! There's no one else in there.

Some scientists suggest that the sense of self is merely a kind of by-product of some sort of overall control mechanism in the brain. But neurologist Richard Restak (1983, 1994) has noted that many of our actions and choices seem to occur without direction by a conscious self. He concludes (1983)

that "there is not a center in the brain involved in the exercise of will any more than there is a center in the brain of the swan responsible for the beauty and complexity of its flight. Rather, the brains of all creatures are probably organized along the lines of multiple centers and various levels." Likewise, brain researcher Michael Gazzaniga (1985) has proposed that the brain is organized as a loose confederation of independent *modules,* or mental systems, all working in parallel. The sense of a unified self or consciousness is an illusion, he says; it occurs because the one verbal module, an "interpreter" (usually in the left side of the brain), is constantly constructing a theory to explain the actions, moods, and thoughts of the others. In a similar vein, cognitive scientist Daniel Dennett (1991) suggests that instead of one homunculus overseeing consciousness, the brain/mind consists of a "pandemonium of homunculi" that deal with different aspects of thought and perception, constantly conferring and collaborating with each other and revising their "drafts" of reality.

Curiously, such views come close to those of Eastern spiritual traditions. Buddhism, for example, teaches that the self is not a unified "thing" but rather a collection of thoughts, perceptions, concepts, and feelings that change from moment to moment. In this view, the unity and the permanence of the self are a mirage. Such notions are contrary, of course, to what most people in the West, including psychologists, have always assumed about their "selves."

We are not about to settle here a question that has plagued philosophers for thousands of years. Inevitably, though, as we think about the brain, we must think about how the brain can think about itself. What do you think about the existence and location of your "self," . . . and who, by the way, is doing the thinking? ■

It's easy to exaggerate differences between the left and right brain hemispheres.

they observe, tend to oversimplify and exaggerate hemispheric differences. Most studies find these differences to be relative, not absolute—a matter of degree. Most important, in most real-life activities, the two hemispheres seem to cooperate naturally, with each making a valuable contribution (Kinsbourne, 1982; J. Levy, 1985). As Sperry (1982) himself once noted, "The left–right dichotomy . . . is an idea with which it is very easy to run wild."

Quick QUIZ

A. Keeping in mind that both sides of the brain are involved in most activities, see whether you can identify which side is *most* closely associated with each of the following:

1. Enjoying a musical recording
2. Wiggling the left big toe
3. Giving a speech in class
4. Balancing a checkbook
5. Recognizing a long-lost friend

 B. Over the past two decades, thousands of people have taken courses and bought tapes that promise to turn them into right-brained types. What characteristics of human thought might explain the eagerness of some people to glorify "right-brainedness" and disparage "left-brainedness" (or vice versa)?

Answers:

A. 1, 2, and 5 are most closely associated with the right side; 3 and 4 with the left. **B.** One possible answer: Human beings like to make sense of the world, and one easy way to do that is to divide humanity into opposing categories, such as right-brained versus left-brained types. This sort of dualistic, either–or thinking can lead to the conclusion that "fixing up" one of the categories (e.g., making left-brained types more right-brained) will make individuals happier and the world a better place. (If only it were that simple!)

■ TWO STUBBORN ISSUES IN BRAIN RESEARCH

If you have mastered the definitions and descriptions in this chapter, you are prepared to read popular accounts of advances in neuropsychology intelligently. But many mysteries remain about how the brain works, and we will end this chapter with two of them.

How Specialized Are Separate Brain Parts?

Is a piece of information stored in one specific spot or distributed throughout the brain? Researchers have generally assumed that only one answer can be true. Could both be true?

One of the most persistent questions in brain research has been this: Where are specific memories, habits, perceptions, and abilities stored? Most theories assume that different brain parts perform different jobs and store different sorts of information. This concept, known as **localization of function,** goes back at least to Joseph Gall (1758–1828), an Austrian anatomist who thought that personality traits were reflected in the development of different areas of the brain. Objective research eventually showed that Gall's theory of *phrenology*, which enjoyed enormous popularity throughout Europe and America, was completely wrong-headed (so to speak). His basic notion of specialization, however, had merit. Over the next 150 years, researchers showed that numerous functions, such as visual processing, language production, and the generation of mental images, could be traced to specific brain areas; they discovered the location of the motor cortex and the somatosensory areas; and split-brain studies revealed that the two cerebral hemispheres have somewhat different talents.

Modern research finds that brain damage can have extremely specific effects on perception and memory, depending on exactly where the damage is. In one study, two female stroke patients both had problems with verbs! One woman could read or speak verbs but had trouble writing them; the other could do only the reverse. The first woman had no trouble writing down the word *crack* after hearing the sentence "There's a crack in the mirror" (in which *crack* is a noun), but she could not write the word after hearing "Don't crack the nuts in here" (in which *crack* is a verb). The other woman could write *crack* as both a noun and a verb, but she couldn't speak it as a verb (Caramazza & Hillis, 1991). In another study (Cubelli, 1991), two brain-damaged patients were unable to correctly write down the vowels in words, but had no trouble writing the consonants! Researchers have also studied patients who can recognize manufactured items, such as photographs, tools, or books, but not natural objects, or who can recognize most natural objects but cannot distinguish among different animals, or fruits, or vegetables (Damasio, 1990).

Because of such findings, localization remains the guiding principle of modern brain theories. However, a minority view holds that perceived, learned, or remembered information is *distributed* across large areas of the brain, perhaps even the entire cortex. One of the first to make this argument was Karl Lashley, who many years ago set out to find where specific memories were stored in the rat's brain. His search turned out to be as frustrating as looking for a grain of sugar in a pile of sand. Lashley trained rats to run a complicated maze in order to find food, then destroyed a part of each rat's cortex (without killing the rat). Destroying any section of the cortex led to some impairment in the rat's ability to find the food, though the size of the area damaged was more important than where the damage was located. Yet even when Lashley removed over 90 percent of a rat's visual cortex, the animal could still make its way through the maze. After a quarter of a century, Lashley (1950) finally gave up searching for specific memory traces. He jokingly remarked that perhaps "learning just is not possible." More seriously, he concluded that every part of the cortex must somehow influence every other part.

■ **localization of function**
Specialization of particular brain areas for particular functions.

How might the brain function as an integrated whole? According to E. Roy John (1976; John et al., 1986), when we learn that Columbus discovered America or remember that 6 times 8 equals 48, it is not because particular cells fire or because a connection among cells is formed. What matters is the *average pattern* of cell activity throughout the brain, a pattern that has a unique rhythm. The billions of cells in the brain are like the members of a gigantic orchestra. Each instrument is making noise in a more or less random way, as when an orchestra is tuning up. When a thought or memory occurs, most of the instruments in one section start to play a tune that has a definite rhythm. However, some instruments in other sections do so as well.

Another holistic approach compares brain processes to holography (Pribram, 1971, 1982). Holography is a system of photography in which a three-dimensional image is reproduced by means of light-wave patterns that are recorded on a photographic plate or film (the hologram). Information about any point in the image is distributed throughout the hologram. Thus any given area of the hologram contains the information necessary for producing the entire image. Similarly, some forms of knowledge may be dispersed throughout the brain, just as Karl Lashley thought.

Holistic theories have the virtue of being able to explain the remarkable *plasticity,* or flexibility, of the brain. Sometimes people who cannot recall simple words after a stroke regain normal speech within a matter of months, and some people who cannot move an arm after a head injury may regain full use of it after therapy. A few individuals have even survived and functioned well in their lives after a drastic surgical procedure—the removal of an entire cerebral hemisphere! Perhaps patients who have recovered from brain damage have learned to use new strategies to accomplish their mental and physical tasks. Another possibility, however, is that the brain is indeed like a giant orchestra, and the

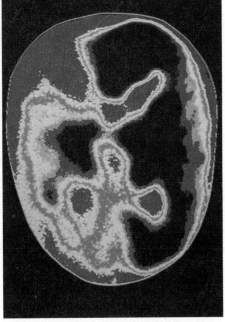

The child on the left, Ryan, suffered from continual, life-threatening seizures that could not be controlled by medication. When he was 15 months old, a PET scan (right) showed that much of his left hemisphere was diseased and not functioning properly, and surgeons removed the affected areas. The seizures diminished and Ryan's development improved dramatically. Cases like these demonstrate the remarkable plasticity of the human brain.

players know one another's music. If one violinist can't make it to the performance, another violinist or perhaps a cellist may fill in.

Well, is information in the brain localized or distributed? The best way out of this dilemma may be to recognize that both answers are probably true. Neuropsychologist Larry Squire (1986, 1987) observes that any perception, habit, or memory includes many bits and pieces of information, often gathered from more than one sense: sounds, images, locations, facts. Specific collections of neurons in the brain may handle specific pieces of information, and many such collections, distributed across wide areas of the brain, may participate in representing an entire event. This view reconciles apparently opposite positions: The parts of the event are localized but the whole is distributed. Although there are no single centers for vision, language, or anything else, there are *systems* composed of several interconnected areas, and these systems are dedicated to particular operations (Damasio, 1994). But we still are a long way from knowing how the many aspects of a memory or ability or perception finally link together to form a whole. Nor do we understand yet why some people recover from damage to the brain while others, with similar damage, are permanently disabled.

Are There "His" and "Hers" Brains?

Perhaps no topic in brain research generates as much muddy thinking and jumping to conclusions as that of sex differences in the brain. Does the existing evidence warrant significant conclusions about real-life behavior?

A second stubborn controversy concerns the existence of sex differences in the brain. Efforts to distinguish male from female brains have a long and not always glorious history. Findings on male–female brain differences have often flip-flopped in a most suspicious manner, a result of the biases of the observers rather than the biology of the brain (Shields, 1975). During the nineteenth century, scientists doing dissection studies reported that women's frontal lobes were smaller than men's, and that their parietal lobes were larger; this finding was said to explain women's intellectual shortcomings. Then, around the turn of the century, people began (mistakenly) to attribute intellect to the parietal lobes rather than the frontal lobes. Suddenly, there were reports that women had *smaller* parietal lobes and larger frontal lobes. You probably won't be surprised to learn that these researchers often knew the sex of the brains they were dissecting.

Since the 1960s, theories about male–female brain differences have come and gone just as quickly. Three decades ago, there was speculation that women were more "right-brained" and men were more "left-brained." Then, when the virtues of the right hemisphere were discovered, there was speculation that *men* were more right-brained. Whichever side is the valued one, it is now clear that the abilities popularly associated with the two sexes do not fall neatly into the two hemispheres of the brain. The left side is more verbal (presumably a "female" trait), but it is also more mathematical (presumably a "male" trait). The right side is more intuitive ("female"), but it is also more spatially talented ("male").

To evaluate the issue of sex differences in the brain, we need to ask two questions: Do male and female brains differ physically ? And if so, what, if anything, does this have to do with behavior?

Let's consider the first question. A number of anatomical sex differences have been found in animal brains, especially in areas related to reproduction. In rats, hormone differences before birth result in nerve-cell clusters in the hypothalamus that differ in size in males and females. There are also sex differences in the levels of neurotransmitters in rats' brains (McEwen, 1983). And in male rats, the right half of the cerebral cortex is thicker than the left in most areas, whereas in females, the opposite tends to be true, though most of the left–right differences are not statistically significant (Diamond et al., 1983). Human sex differences, however, have been more elusive. Of course, we would

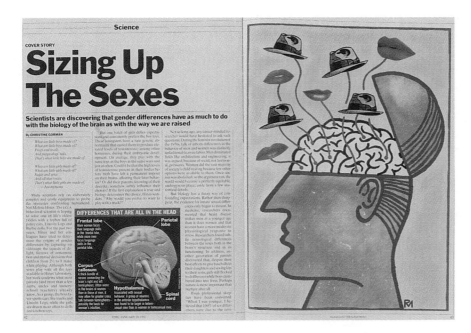

Popular magazines have been quick to run stories on purported differences in the brains of males and females. Often these articles (such as this one from Time*) conclude—from interesting but still tentative findings—that gender differences in behavior must be biologically based. Is this conclusion justified? What kind of evidence is necessary to establish a link between an observed brain difference and an observed behavioral difference? And why do studies of gender differences make the covers of national magazines when studies that find gender similarities do not?*

expect to find male–female brain differences that are related to the regulation of sex hormones and other aspects of reproduction. But many researchers want to know whether there are differences that affect how men and women think or behave—and here, the picture is murkier.

For example, in 1982, two anthropologists autopsied 14 human brains and reported an average sex difference in the size and shape of the splenium, a small section at the end of the corpus callosum, which connects the two cerebral hemispheres (de Lacoste-Utamsing & Holloway, 1982). The researchers concluded that women's brains are less *lateralized* for certain tasks than men's are—that is, that men rely more heavily on one or the other side of the brain, whereas women tend to use both sides. This conclusion quickly made its way into newspapers, magazines, and even textbooks as a verified sex difference. Now that more than a decade of research has passed, however, the picture is different. Neuroscientist William Byne (1993), in a review of the available studies, found that only the 1982 study reported the splenium to be larger in women. Two very early studies (in 1906 and 1909) found that it was larger in men, and 21 studies in the past decade have found no sex difference at all. Findings on the shape of the splenium are also mixed: Four studies find the splenium to be more bulb-shaped in women; one study finds it to be more bulbous in men; and six studies find no difference. These studies did not make the cover of *Newsweek*.

Researchers are now looking for specific sex differences in the density of neurons in different areas of the brain. For example, Sandra Witelson and her colleagues, who studied 9 brains from autopsied bodies, recently reported that the women had an average of 11 percent more cells in certain areas of the cortex associated with the processing of auditory information; all of the women had more of these cells than any of the men (Witelsen, Glaser, & Kigar, 1994).

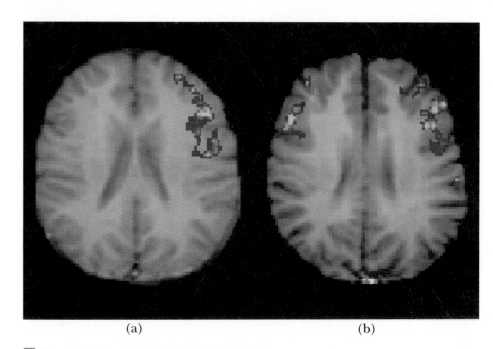

(a)   (b)

■ **Figure 4.17   Gender and the Brain**

In a study of 19 men and 19 women, researchers recently reported the first direct evidence that male and female brains tend to function differently during a specific task (Shaywitz et al., 1995). In these MRIs, the orientation is as if from below the brain, so the left hemisphere is on the right and vice versa. During the first step in the process of sounding out words, Broca's area, the small left-hemisphere area associated with speech, was active in the men's brains (a). Eight women also had this pattern, but the brains of the other 11 showed activity on both sides (b). The two sexes performed equally well on the task, leading the researchers to conclude that nature has efficiently provided the brain with different routes to the same ability. However, the results might help explain why women seem to compensate better than men do for reading disabilities.

Other researchers are using high-tech methods to search for average sex differences in the brain areas that are active when men and women work on the same task. One such difference has been reported by neurologist Bennett Shaywitz, behavioral scientist Sally Shaywitz, and their colleagues (1995). In their study, 19 men and 19 women (all right-handed) had to say whether pairs of nonsense words rhymed, a task that required them to process and compare sounds. In men and women alike, an area at the front of the left hemisphere was activated. But in 11 of the women (and none of the men), the corresponding area in the right hemisphere was *also* active (see Figure 4.17). These findings are further evidence for a sex difference in lateralization, at least for this one type of language function. Less lateralization in women could help explain why left-hemisphere damage is less likely to cause language problems in women than in men after a stroke (Inglis & Lawson, 1981; McGlone, 1978).

Over the next few years, research may reveal additional anatomical and information-processing differences in the brains of males and females. But even if such differences exist, we must then ask the second question raised at the beginning of this section: *What do the differences mean for the behavior of men and women in real life?* In the Shaywitz study, for example, there was no difference in how well the two sexes actually performed on the rhyme–judgment task, in spite of the average sex difference on their MRIs. When it comes to explaining how brain differences are related to more general abilities, speculations are as plentiful as ants at a picnic, but the fact is that no one knows

(Hoptman & Davidson, 1994). To arrive at an answer, we would need to have a clear picture of how brain organization and chemistry affect human abilities and traits in general, and as yet we don't. Even in animals whose brains have been studied for many years, the functions of many brain areas are unknown.

Nevertheless, some popular writers jump to the conclusion that brain differences explain, among other things, women's allegedly superior intuition, women's love of talking about feelings and men's love of talking about sports, women's greater verbal ability, men's edge in math ability, and why men won't ask for directions when they're lost. But these supposed gender differences are stereotypes; on any of these abilities or activities, the overlap between the sexes is greater than the difference between them. As neuroanatomist Roger Gorski told *The New York Times* (February 28, 1995), "There is so much overlap that if you take any individual man and women, they might show differences in the opposite direction" from the statistical findings. Moreover, as we saw in Chapter 2, verbal differences are shrinking (Feingold, 1988; Hyde & Linn, 1988); and mathematical and some spatial-visual differences have been exaggerated (Hyde, Fennema, & Lamon, 1990). The actual behavior of women and men has changed a lot faster than their brains could, which means that social and cultural influences must play an important role in shaping such behavior. While it is important, therefore, to keep an open mind about new findings on sex differences in the brain, it is also important to keep a cautious attitude about how such findings might be exaggerated and misused.

When thinking about sex differences in the brain, or about any of the findings discussed in this chapter, we need to keep two important points in mind. First, brain organization—the proportion of brain cells found in any part of the brain—varies considerably from person to person. As Roger Sperry (1982) noted, "The more we learn . . . the stronger the conclusion becomes that the individuality inherent in our brain networks makes that of fingerprints or facial features gross and simple by comparison." Therefore, any sweeping generalizations about the brain, whether they are about the left and right hemispheres, localization of function, or sex differences, are bound to be oversimplifications.

Second, experience is constantly sculpting the circuitry of the brain, and it can affect the way brains are organized. A cross-cultural example may make this point clear. The brains of the Japanese may not be lateralized in the same way as the brains of Westerners (including Americans of Japanese descent). There is some evidence that the Japanese process nonverbal human and animal sounds and Japanese instrumental music in the left hemisphere rather than the right, where we would expect them to be processed on the basis of split-brain studies. One speculation (not yet proven) is that because the Japanese language is rich in vowel sounds and therefore has a musical quality, the left hemisphere learns to process nonverbal tonal sounds (Sibatani, 1980; Tsunoda, 1985).

As we have seen in this chapter, the more we know about our physical selves, the better we understand our psychological selves. The challenge is to learn from biology without oversimplifying it. As science writer Ron Cowen (1989) has noted, "Nothing is black-and-white when it comes to the gray matter of the brain." And even if we could monitor every cell and circuit of the brain, we would still want to understand the circumstances, thoughts, and social rules that affect whether we are gripped by hatred, consumed by grief, lifted by love, or transported by joy. The human brain is a miraculous organ, but analyzing human behavior in terms of physiology alone is like analyzing the Taj Mahal solely in terms of the materials that were used to build it.

Taking Psychology with You

Food for Thought: Diet and Neurotransmitters

"Vitamin improves sex!"
"Mineral boosts brainpower!"
"Chocolate chases the blues!"

Claims such as these have long given nutritional theories of behavior a bad reputation. In the late 1960s, when Nobel Laureate Linus Pauling proposed that some mental illnesses might result from an unusual need for massive doses of vitamins, few serious researchers listened. Mainstream medical authorities classified Pauling's vitamin therapy with such infamous cure-alls as snake oil and leeches.

Today, most mental-health professionals remain skeptical of nutritional treatments for mental illness. But they may have to eat at least some of their words, as respect grows for the role that nutrients might play in mood and performance. The underlying premise of these treatments, that diet affects the brain and therefore behavior, is getting a second look. Claims that sugar or common food additives lead to undesirable behavior in otherwise normal people remain controversial. However, in some cases of disturbance, diet may make a difference. In one double-blind study, researchers asked depressed patients to abstain from refined sugar and caffeine. Over a three-month period, these patients showed significantly more improvement in their symptoms than did control patients who refrained from red meat and artificial sweeteners (Christensen & Burrows, 1990).

Some of the most exciting work on diet and behavior has looked at the role that nutrients play in the synthesis of neurotransmitters, the brain's chemical messengers. *Tryptophan,* an amino acid found in protein-rich foods (dairy products, meat, fish, and poultry), is a precursor (or building block) of the neurotransmitter serotonin. *Tyrosine,* another amino acid found in proteins, is a precursor of norepinephrine, epinephrine, and dopamine. *Choline,* a component of the lecithin found in egg yolks, soy products, and liver, is a precursor of acetylcholine.

In the case of tryptophan, the path between the dinner plate and the brain is indirect. Tryptophan leads to the production of serotonin, which appears to reduce alertness, promote relaxation, and hasten sleep. Since tryptophan is found in protein, you might think that a high-protein meal would make you drowsy and that carbohydrates (sweets, bread, pasta, potatoes) would leave you relatively alert. Actually, the opposite is true. High-protein foods contain several amino acids, not just tryptophan, and they all compete for a ride on carrier molecules headed for brain cells. Because tryptophan occurs in foods in small quantities, it doesn't stand much of a chance *if* all you eat is protein. It is in the position of a tiny child trying to push aside a crowd of adults for a seat on the subway. Carbohydrates, however, stimulate the production of insulin, and insulin causes all the other amino acids to be drawn out of the bloodstream while having little effect on tryptophan. So carbohydrates increase the odds that tryptophan will make it to the brain (Wurtman, 1982). Paradoxically, then, a high-carbohydrate, no-protein meal should make you relatively calm or lethargic and a high-protein one should promote alertness. Studies with human beings support this conclusion (Spring, Chiodo, & Bowen, 1987; Wurtman & Lieberman, 1982–1983).

How else might nutrition affect mental and physical performance? In a report commissioned by the U.S. Army, the National Academy of Sciences recently reviewed existing animal and human studies on this question (Marriott, 1994). These studies suggest that (1) tyrosine can reduce symptoms that occur in extreme cold and at high altitudes, such as fuzzy thinking, headache, and nausea; (2) carbohydrates can prolong endurance under stressful conditions, increase fine-motor coordination, improve mood, and help people sleep; (3) choline can enhance memory, improve muscle strength, and strengthen the immune system; and (4) caffeine improves alertness and mental performance. The army is now considering fortifying its food rations with these food components.

Keep in mind, though, that research in this area is just beginning. Individuals differ in how they respond to different nutrients. The effects of nutrients are subtle (many other factors also influence mood and behavior), and some of these effects depend on a person's age, the circumstances, and the time of day when a meal is eaten. Nutrients can and do affect the brain and behavior, but these nutrients interact with each other in complex ways. If you don't eat protein, you won't get enough tryptophan, but if you go without carbohydrates, the tryptophan found in protein will be useless. And trying to rev yourself up with too many nutritional supplements can actually be dangerous. The moral of the story: If you're looking for brain food, you are most likely to find it in a well-balanced diet.

Summary

1. The brain is the origin of consciousness, perception, memory, emotion, and reasoning. People debate what language to use in describing the brain, and where the "you" is that is "using" your brain.

2. The nervous system is the bedrock of behavior; its function is to gather and process information, produce responses to stimuli, and coordinate the workings of different cells. Scientists divide it into the *central nervous system* (CNS) and the *peripheral nervous system* (PNS). The CNS, which includes the brain and spinal cord, processes, interprets, and stores information, and it sends messages destined for muscles, glands, and organs. The PNS transmits information to and from the CNS by way of sensory and motor nerves.

3. The peripheral nervous system is made up of the *somatic nervous system,* which controls voluntary actions, and the *autonomic nervous system,* which regulates blood vessels, internal organs, and various glands. The autonomic system usually functions without conscious control. Some people can learn to heighten or suppress certain autonomic responses, using *biofeedback* techniques, but it is unclear whether this control is direct or indirect.

4. The autonomic nervous system is divided into the *sympathetic nervous system,* which mobilizes the body for action, and the *parasympathetic nervous system,* which conserves energy.

5. *Neurons,* supported by *glial cells,* are the basic units of the nervous system. Each neuron consists of *dendrites,* a *cell body,* and an *axon.* In the peripheral nervous system, axons (and sometimes dendrites) collect in bundles called *nerves.* Many axons are insulated by a *myelin sheath* that speeds up the conduction of neural impulses. Recent research has challenged the old assumption that neurons in the human central nervous system cannot be induced to regenerate or multiply.

6. Communication between two neurons occurs at the *synapse.* When a wave of electrical voltage (action potential) reaches the end of a transmitting axon, *neurotransmitter* molecules are released into the *synaptic cleft.* When these molecules bind to receptor sites on the receiving neuron, the receiving neuron becomes either more or less likely to fire. The message that reaches a final destination depends on how frequently particular neurons are firing, how many are firing, what types are firing, and where they are located.

7. Neurotransmitters play a critical role in mood, memory, and psychological well-being. Abnormal levels of particular neurotransmitters have been implicated in depression, Parkinson's disease, Alzheimer's disease, childhood autism, and other disorders. However, it is difficult to establish a cause-and-effect relationship between a particular neurotransmitter problem and a particular behavioral disorder.

8. *Endorphins,* which act primarily as *neuromodulators* that affect the action of neurotransmitters, reduce pain and promote pleasure. Endorphin levels seem to shoot up when an animal or person is afraid or is under stress. Endorphins also seem linked to the pleasures of social contact.

9. *Hormone* levels affect, and are affected by, the nervous system. Psychologists are especially interested in the effects of insulin, melatonin, the *adrenal hormones* (involved in emotions and stress), and the *sex hormones* (involved in the physical changes of puberty, the menstrual cycle, and sexual arousal).

10. Researchers study the brain by observing brain-damaged patients; by using the *lesion method* with animals; by using *electrodes* to detect electrical activity; and by using such techniques as electroencephalograms (*EEGs*), position emission tomography *(PET scans),* and magnetic resonance imaging (*MRI*).

11. In the hindbrain, the *brain stem* controls automatic functions such as heartbeat and breathing. The *reticular activating system* screens incoming information and is responsible for alertness. The *cerebellum* contributes to balance and muscle coordination.

12. In the forebrain, the *thalamus* directs sensory messages to appropriate centers. The *hypothalamus* is involved in emotion and in drives associated with survival, controls the operations of the autonomic nervous system, and sends to the *pituitary gland* chemicals that tell it when to "talk" to other endocrine glands.

13. The *limbic system* is involved in emotions that we share with other animals, and it contains pathways involved in pleasure. Within this system, the *amygdala* evaluates sensory information and quickly determines its emotional importance, and it is also responsible for the initial decision to approach or withdraw from a person or situation. The *hippocampus* has been called the "gateway to memory" because it plays a critical role in storage of long-term memories.

14. The *cerebrum,* the upper part of the forebrain, is divided into two hemispheres and is covered by thin layers of cells known as the *cerebral cortex.* The cortex is convoluted so that it can contain billions of neurons without requiring the brain to be too big for the skull. The *occipital, parietal, temporal,* and *frontal* lobes of the cortex have specialized (but partially overlapping) functions. The *association cortex* appears to be responsible for higher mental processes.

15. Studies of split-brain patients who have had the *corpus callosum* cut show that the two cerebral hemispheres have somewhat different talents. In most people, language is processed mainly in the left hemisphere, which generally appears to be specialized for logical, symbolic, and sequential tasks. The right hemisphere is associated with spatial–visual tasks, facial recognition, and the creation and appreciation of art and music. However, in most mental activities, the two hemispheres cooperate as partners, with each making a valuable contribution.

16. Most scientists believe that the brain stores different items of information in different areas, a phenomenon known as *localization of function.* Others argue that perceived, learned, or remembered information is *distributed* across large areas of the brain and that the brain functions as an integrated whole; this view accounts for the *plasticity* of the brain in recovering from some injuries. Both views may have merit: Specific locations in the brain may handle specific pieces of information, but many such collections, distributed across wide areas of the brain, may collaborate in representing an entire event, perception, or skill.

17. Sex differences have been observed in anatomical studies of animal brains. Sex differences in human brains, however, have been more elusive and contradictory, and there is controversy about their existence and their meaning. It is unclear how reported brain differences are related to actual behavior or talents, especially since traditional male–female differences in many abilities have been decreasing or even disappearing.

18. In evaluating research on the brain and behavior, it is important to remember that individual brains vary considerably in their organization, and also that experiences and environments affect brain development. Findings about the brain are most illuminating when they are integrated with psychological and cultural ones.

Key Terms

neuropsychology *117*	peripheral nervous system *119*
central nervous system *118*	sensory nerves *119*
spinal cord *118*	motor nerves *119*
reflex *118*	somatic nervous system *120*

5

Body Rhythms and Mental States

This drawing by a nineteenth-century British artist shows novelist Charles Dickens dreaming up his characters—literally, while napping. Psychologists have invented ingenious methods to study dreaming and other states of consciousness.

Like a bird's life, [consciousness] seems to be made of an alternation of flights and perchings.

■ WILLIAM JAMES ■

In Lewis Carroll's immortal story *Alice's Adventure in Wonderland,* the ordinary assumptions of everyday life keep dissolving in a sea of logical contradictions. First Alice shrinks to within only a few inches of the ground, then she shoots up taller than the treetops. The crazy antics of Wonderland's inhabitants make her smile one moment and shed a pool of tears the next. "Dear dear!" muses the harried heroine. "How queer everything is today! And yesterday things went on just as usual. I wonder if I've been changed in the night? Let me think: *was* I the same when I got up this morning? I almost think I can remember feeling a little different. But if I'm not the same, the *next* question is, 'Who in the world am I?' Ah, *that's* the great puzzle!"

In a way, we all live in a sort of Wonderland. For a third of our lives, we reside in a realm where the ordinary rules of logic and experience are suspended: the dream world of sleep. Throughout the day, mood, alertness, efficiency, and **consciousness** itself—the awareness of oneself and the environment—are in perpetual flux, sometimes shifting as dramatically as Alice's height.

Starting from the assumption that mental and physical states are as intertwined as sunshine and shadow, psychologists, along with other scientists, are exploring these fluctuations by relating subjective experience to predictable changes in brain activity, hormone levels, and the actions of neurotransmitters. They have come to view changing **states of consciousness** as part of an ebb and flow of experience over time, associated with predictable bodily events. For example, dreaming, traditionally classified as a state of consciousness, is also part of a 90-minute cycle of brain activity. Alternating periods of dreaming and nondreaming during the night occur in a regular pattern, or **biological rhythm.**

Examining subjective experience in terms of ongoing rhythms is a little like watching a motion picture of consciousness. Studying subjective experience in terms of distinct states is more like looking at separate snapshots of consciousness. In this chapter, we will first run the motion picture, to see how functioning and consciousness vary predictably over time. Then we will zoom in on one specific "snapshot" of the world of dreams, and examine it in some detail. Finally, we will turn to some ways in which people try to "retouch the film" by deliberately altering consciousness.

■ BIOLOGICAL RHYTHMS: THE TIDES OF EXPERIENCE

Wouldn't you like to know beforehand when you were about to have a bad day or be in top form? People who sell "biorhythm charts" claim you can. They cite an old theory that 28-day mood cycles, 33-day intellectual cycles, and 23-day physical cycles begin at birth and continue like clockwork throughout life. Half of each cycle is said to be positive and half negative, and the point at which a cycle changes from positive to negative is said to be "critical"—ripe for errors, accidents, and illness. Proponents of this theory will tell you that Clark Gable,

■ **consciousness**
The awareness of the environment and of one's own existence, sensations, and thoughts.

■ **states of consciousness**
Distinctive and discrete patterns in the functioning of consciousness, characterized by particular modes of perception, thought, memory, or feeling.

■ **biological rhythm**
A periodic, more or less regular fluctuation in a biological system; may or may not have psychological implications.

✳ *Purveyors of "biorhythm" charts would have us believe that famous people died when they did because their biorhythms were in a trough. What facts does this explanation leave out?*

Harry Truman, and other famous people had heart attacks or died on critical days. They may also cite "scientific studies" showing that accidents declined after bus drivers or pilots were given warnings to be particularly careful on critical days.

Can you spot the weaknesses in this evidence? One problem is that the anecdotal accounts ignore *negative* data, all the cases of people who have remained perfectly healthy on critical days or died on noncritical ones. As for the studies, as you might have guessed, they failed to include safety warnings to workers who were *not* entering a so-called critical period. Without control groups, biorhythm studies merely show that warning people to be careful makes them more careful! Even on the face of it, the biorhythm theory is implausible. Why should such rhythms start at birth, rather than at conception or during fetal development? Besides, we know that the human body is not rigidly regular; illness, fatigue, stress, excitement, exercise, and drugs can all affect how we function. So it's not surprising that when researchers have taken the trouble to test the biorhythm theory scientifically, by examining occupational accidents or the performance of sports stars, they have consistently failed to find any support whatsoever for it (Englund & Naitoh, 1980; Louis, 1978; Wheeler, 1990). Yet biorhythm charts continue to be marketed. Apparently, one human characteristic that does not fluctuate much is gullibility!

On the other hand, it *is* true that human beings, unlike robots and computers, do not operate in an unvarying way 24 hours a day, 7 days a week, 52 weeks a year. We've got rhythm; in fact, we experience dozens of periodic, more or less regular ups and downs in physiological functioning. Biological clocks in our brains govern the waxing and waning of hormone levels, urine volume, blood pressure, and even the responsiveness of brain cells to stimulation. Such physiological fluctuations are what scientists mean by biological rhythms.

The body's rhythms are typically synchronized with external events, such as changes in clock time and daylight. But many rhythms will continue to occur even in the absence of all external time cues; they are *endogenous*, or generated from within. These rhythms fall into three categories:

1. **Circadian rhythms** occur approximately every 24 hours. The best-known circadian rhythm is the sleep–wake cycle, but there are hundreds of others that affect physiology and performance. For example, body temperature fluctuates about 1 degree Fahrenheit each day, peaking, on average, in the late afternoon and hitting a low point, or trough, in the wee hours of the morning.

2. **Infradian rhythms** occur less often than once a day. In the animal world, infradian rhythms are common: Birds migrate south in the fall, bears hibernate in the winter, and marine animals become active or inactive, depending on bimonthly changes in the tides. In human beings, the female menstrual cycle, which occurs every 28 days on the average, is an example of an infradian rhythm.

3. **Ultradian rhythms** occur more often than once a day, frequently on roughly a 90-minute schedule. The most well-studied ultradian rhythm, as we will see, occurs during sleep, but an extraordinary array of other physiological changes and behaviors also follow an ultradian pattern when social customs do not intervene. They include stomach contractions, certain hormone levels, appetite for food, oral behavior (smoking, pencil chewing, snacking), susceptibility to visual illusions, performance on verbal and spatial tasks, brain-wave responses during specific cognitive or perceptual tasks, and alertness (Escera, Cilveti, & Grau, 1992; Klein & Armitage, 1979; Kripke, 1974; Lavie, 1976). Even daydreaming follows an ultradian rhythm: At the peak of each cycle, thoughts and images are likely to be emotional or even bizarre; at the trough, thoughts are more realistic, and they concern current problems or future plans (Kripke & Sonnenschein, 1978).

▪ **circadian [sur-CAY-dee-un] rhythm**
A biological rhythm with a period (from peak to peak or trough to trough) of about 24 hours; from the Latin circa, "about," and dias, "a day."

▪ **infradian [in-FRAY-dee-un] rhythm**
A biological rhythm that occurs less frequently than once a day; from the Latin for "below a day."

▪ **ultradian [ul-TRAY-dee-un] rhythm**
A biological rhythm that occurs more frequently than once a day; from the Latin for "beyond a day."

Psychologists and other researchers are just beginning to recognize the potential impact of biological rhythms on their studies. A review of research done with rats, mice, and hamsters found that most studies have been conducted during the day, with the lights on, even though these rodents are normally active at night and sleep during the day. The authors note that "The field of psychology has been frequently criticized for being extensively based on studies of white male rats. . . . Perhaps that indictment should be revised to read '*sleepy* white male rats'!" (Brodie-Scott & Hobbs, 1992). Results from human beings, too, can be influenced by the time of day when the research was conducted. In one study, most young adults said they preferred the evening for doing mental work, whereas most elderly adults expressed a preference for the morning. On a memory test given in the late afternoon, the younger subjects in this study performed much better than the older ones, but when the test took place in the early morning, the younger people's scores fell, the older people's scores rose, and there was no longer any significant difference between the two groups. These findings suggest that existing studies of aging and mental function, which are usually done in the afternoon, may give a false picture of age differences in memory (May, Hasher, & Stoltzfus, 1993).

Findings on biological rhythms have many implications for everyday functioning. With better understanding of these internal tempos, we may be able to design our days to take the best advantage of our bodies' natural cycles. Let's look more closely at these cycles.

Circadian Rhythms

Circadian rhythms exist in plants, animals, insects, and human beings. They reflect the adaptation of organisms to the many changes associated with the rotation of the earth on its axis, such as changes in light, air pressure, temperature, and wind.

During ordinary living, time cues abound and our bodies adapt to a strict 24-hour schedule. To explore endogenous circadian rhythms, therefore, scientists must isolate volunteers from sunlight, clocks, environmental sounds, and all

A morning glory is only "glorious" in the morning. Animals and human beings also have daily physical and behavioral rhythms.

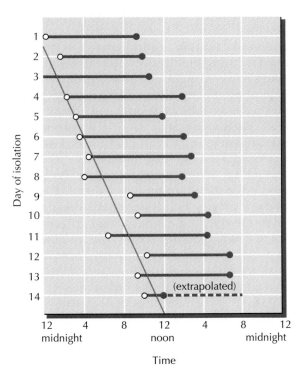

■ Figure 5.1   The Days Grow Longer

This is a chart of sleep periods for a volunteer living in isolation from all time cues. Open circles show when the person went to bed; solid circles show when the person rose. Like most volunteers living in isolation, this individual tended to retire and awaken later and later as the study wore on—in this case, an average of 49 minutes later each day. The pattern is represented by the diagonal red line. (From Webb & Agnew, 1974.)

other cues to time. Artificial light is kept constant, varied by the researcher, or turned on and off by the volunteers when they retire or awaken. Some hardy souls have spent weeks or even months alone in caves and salt mines, linked to the outside world only by a one-way phone line and a cable transmitting physiological measurements to the surface. More often, volunteers live in specially designed bunkers or rooms equipped with stereo systems, comfortable furniture, and temperature controls.

In a typical study, a person sleeps, eats, and works whenever he or she wishes, free of the tyranny of the timepiece. Living on a self-imposed schedule in this way is called *free-running.* In the absence of time cues, some people live a "day" that is far shorter or longer than 24 hours, but most people soon settle into a "day" that averages about 25 hours in length. During each successive cycle, the person tends to go to sleep a little later and get up a little later (see Figure 5.1). Temperature, blood pressure, and hormone cycles usually follow suit (Aschoff & Wever, 1981; Moore-Ede, Sulzman, & Fuller, 1984).

Several self-sustaining but interrelated biological clocks or pacemakers seem to be ticking away in various parts of the brain, controlling the dozens of different circadian rhythms. The evidence indicates that these clocks are linked to each other and also to a "super clock," or overall coordinator, located in a tiny teardrop-shaped area in the hypothalamus called the *suprachiasmatic nucleus (SCN).* Normally, the various rhythms governed by these clocks are synchronized, just as wristwatches can be synchronized. Their peaks may occur at different times, but they occur in phase with one another; if you know when one rhythm peaks, you can predict when another will. This synchrony is choreographed by rising and falling levels of various hormones and neurotransmitters.

One hormone, **melatonin,** which is secreted by the pineal gland deep within the brain, is responsive to changes in light and dark and appears to keep the superclock in phase with the light–dark cycle (Lewy et al., 1992; Reppert et al., 1988). Animal studies suggest that information about light and dark reaches the pineal gland via a neural pathway that leads from the back of the eyes

■ melatonin

A hormone secreted by the pineal gland; it is involved in the regulation of circadian rhythms.

through the hypothalamus and on to the pineal gland. In at least two cases, melatonin treatments have been used to synchronize the disturbed sleep–wake cycle of blind men whose sleep problems apparently stemmed from their inability to sense light and dark (Arendt, Aldhous, & Wright, 1988; Tzischinsky et al., 1992). Carefully monitored melatonin supplements may also be useful in treating people who suffer from severe chronic insomnia associated with abnormally low levels of melatonin.

When a person's normal routine changes, circadian rhythms may be thrown out of phase with one another. Such *internal desynchronization* often occurs when people take airplane flights across several time zones. Sleep and wake patterns usually adjust quickly, but temperature and hormone cycles can take several days to return to normal. The resulting "jet lag" affects mental and physical performance. A miniversion of jet lag seems to occur in some people when they have to "spring forward" into daylight savings time, losing an hour from the 24-hour day. They may sleep less well than usual and feel a little out of sorts during the week following the time change. In contrast, "falling back" into standard time, which produces a 25-hour day and time for extra sleep, does not seem to be a strain (Monk & Aplin, 1980).

Internal desynchronization also occurs when workers must adjust to a new shift. Efficiency drops, the person feels tired and irritable, accidents become more likely, and sleep disturbances and digestive disorders may occur. For people such as police officers, emergency-room personnel, airline pilots, truck drivers, and nuclear power plant operators, the consequences can be very serious. In 1991, a National Commission on Sleep Disorders noted that lack of alertness in night-shift equipment operators may have contributed to the 1989 *Exxon Valdez* oil spill off the coast of Alaska and the accidents at the Three Mile Island and Chernobyl nuclear power plants. And in 1995 the National Transportation Safety Board reported that truck drivers who fall asleep at the wheel are responsible for up to 1,500 road deaths a year; driver fatigue is more of a safety problem than alcohol or other drugs.

Night work itself is not necessarily the problem: With a schedule that always stays the same (even on weekends), people can often adapt. However, many swing and night-shift assignments are made on a rotating basis, so circadian rhythms never have a chance to resynchronize. Moreover, many shift workers fail to sleep enough during the day. Ideally, a rotating work schedule should follow circadian principles by switching workers as infrequently as possible and by always moving them forward to a later schedule rather than backward to an ear-

Travel is often exhausting, and jet lag can make it worse. Because most people when freed from the clock have a natural day that is somewhat longer than 24 hours, jet lag tends to be more noticeable and long-lasting after eastbound travel (which shortens the day) than after westbound (which lengthens it).

lier one. (For example, if you've been working from midnight to 8:00 A.M., your next shift should be 8:00 A.M. to 4:00 P.M.)

Researchers are now working on ways to hasten recovery from jet lag and ease people's adjustment to new work shifts. One approach is to use bright lights to "reset" the superclock in the SCN, just as you would reset a real clock forward or backward (Dawson, Lack, & Morris, 1993). Another is to give small amounts of melatonin on a controlled schedule, or to combine light treatments with melatonin (Lewy et al., 1992; Samel et al., 1991). However, procedures that seem promising in the laboratory may not work out so well in the real world, where people are exposed to many natural and artificial time cues. In one study, adults went to bed two hours later on each of five nights and were also exposed to bright lights, which in the laboratory can shift the rhythm of the body's temperature. Under the more natural conditions of this study, the subjects' temperature rhythms stubbornly refused to conform to their new sleep schedule (Gallo & Eastman, 1993).

We want to emphasize that under normal circumstances, circadian rhythms are not perfectly regular and are affected by ordinary daily experiences. Hormones rise and fall in a characteristic pattern, but stress can alter the pattern. Animal research suggests that even the timing of exercise can influence circadian rhythms, and may help determine, along with genetic influences, whether one is a "night owl" or an "early bird" (Mistlberger, 1991). Further, circadian rhythms differ greatly from individual to individual: Some people are feeling their oats by 7 in the morning; others aren't ready for action until noon. You may be able to learn about your own personal pulses through careful self-observation, and you may want to trying putting that information to use when planning your daily schedule.

The Menstrual Cycle and Other Long-term Rhythms

According to Ecclesiastes, "To every thing there is a season, and a time for every purpose under heaven." Modern science agrees: Long-term (infradian) cycles have been observed in everything from the threshold for tooth pain to mortality and conception rates.

Some psychologists believe that in some people, mood follows an infradian cycle. Clinicians report that such people usually become depressed in the winter, when periods of daylight are short, and improve every spring, as daylight increases—a pattern that has come to be known as "seasonal affective disorder" (SAD). One theory holds that the winter doldrums are related to abnormal fluctuations in melatonin, which usually peaks during the night and falls with the approach of day (Lewy et al., 1987). So some physicians and therapists have been treating "SAD" patients by having them sit in front of fluorescent lights at specific times of the day (Dahl et al., 1993; Rosenthal et al., 1985).

But the link between "SAD" and melatonin is *not* an established fact. A British study found no differences at all in the melatonin rhythms of "SAD" patients and controls (Checkley et al., 1993), and even the researchers who originally proposed the theory no longer argue that melatonin abnormalities play a direct role. Further, clinicians doing light-therapy studies have often failed to include a control group, making it impossible to rule out placebo effects when patients improve. Most important, it has not been proven that long-term cycles in depression are actually endogenous. The winter blues could be caused by the mental association of short days with cold weather, inactivity, or even the holidays, which some people find depressing. Similarly, some people report *summer* depression (Wehr, Sack, & Rosenthal, 1987), but this does not necessarily mean their depression reflects an internal biological rhythm. Perhaps summer depressives are simply people who can't take the heat.

One infradian rhythm that clearly *is* endogenous, however, is the menstrual cycle. Several hormones in human females ebb and flow over a period of roughly 28 days. During the first half of the cycle, an increase in estrogen causes the lining of the uterus to thicken in preparation for a possible pregnancy. At midcycle, the ovaries release a mature egg, or ovum. After ovulation, the ovarian sac that contained the egg begins to produce progesterone, which helps prepare the uterine lining to receive the egg. Then, if conception does not occur, estrogen and progesterone levels fall, the uterine lining sloughs off as the menstrual flow, and the cycle begins again.

For psychologists, the interesting question is whether emotional or intellectual changes are correlated with the physical ones. Starting in the early 1970s, a cluster of symptoms associated with the days preceding menstruation—including fatigue, headache, irritability, and depression—has come to be thought of as an illness and has been given a label: "premenstrual syndrome (PMS)." Some books refer to "millions" of sufferers or assert that "most" women have "PMS," although there are no statistics to back up such claims. Proposed explanations of the syndrome include progesterone deficiency, estrogen/progesterone imbalance, water retention, high sodium, and a fall in the level of endorphins, the brain's natural opiates. Yet biomedical research reveals no consistent support for *any* of these theories, and evidence against many of them. For example, in one study, researchers gave "PMS" patients a drug that blocks the hormonal changes characteristic of the premenstrual period; the women still reported symptoms, indicating that hormone changes could not be responsible (Schmidt et al., 1991). Further, despite many anecdotes and testimonials, no treatment—including progesterone, the most commonly prescribed remedy—works any better than a placebo (Freeman et al., 1990).

Discussions of "PMS" often fail to distinguish between physical and emotional symptoms, and this distinction is crucial. No one disputes that there are physical symptoms associated with menstruation, which typically include cramps, breast tenderness, and water retention, although women vary tremendously in the symptoms they have, with some having none and others many. But there is reason to question claims that *emotional* symptoms are reliably and universally tied to the menstrual cycle. Many women do report having "PMS," but remember, self-reports can be a poor guide to reality, no matter how valid they feel to the person doing the reporting (see Chapter 2). A woman might easily attribute a blue mood to her impending period, although at other times of the month she would blame a stressful day or a poor grade on an English paper. She might notice that she feels depressed or irritable when these moods happen to occur premenstrually but overlook times when such moods are *absent* premenstrually.

A woman's perceptions of her own emotional ups and downs can also be influenced by her expectations and attitudes toward menstruation and by beliefs about menstruation that are prevalent in popular culture. Even the form of the questionnaire used in a study can bias a woman's perceptions. When studies ask women to complete a widely used measure called the Menstrual Distress Questionnaire (MDQ)—which, as its names implies, asks primarily about negative symptoms—women tend to report many such symptoms. But if they are first given a "Menstrual Joy Questionnaire" that asks about "high spirits," "vibrant activity," and other potentially *positive* aspects of menstruation, they later report positive as well as negative changes on the MDQ (Chrisler et al., 1994). (Some respondents said that the very title of the Menstrual Joy Questionnaire made them think critically about their own attitudes toward menstruation!)

To get around these methodological problems, some researchers have polled women about their psychological and physical well-being *without revealing the true purpose of the study* (for example, Alagna & Hamilton, 1986; Burke,

✴ *Many women say they become more irritable or depressed premenstrually. Then why do their own daily reports fail to bear them out? And why do men report as many mood changes as women do over the span of a month?*

Burnett, & Levenstein, 1978; Englander-Golden, Whitmore, & Dienstbier, 1978; Parlee, 1982; Slade, 1984; Vila & Beech, 1980). Using a double-blind procedure, these psychologists have had women report symptoms for a single day and have then gone back to see what phase of the menstrual cycle the women were in; or they have had women keep daily records over an extended period of time. And some studies have included a control group that is usually excluded from research on hormones and moods: men! Here are some of the major findings that emerge from this research:

- Overall, women and men *do not differ* significantly in the emotional symptoms they report or the number of mood swings they experience in the course of a month, as you can see in Figure 5.2 (McFarlane, Martin, & Williams, 1988).

- A few women do become irritable or depressed before menstruation; others become happier or more energetic. But for most women, the relationship between cycle stage and symptoms is weak or nonexistent. They may recall their moods as having been more unpleasant before or during menstruation, but, as you can also see in Figure 5.2, their own daily reports fail to bear them out.

- Even when women know that menstruation is being studied, most do not consistently report negative (or positive) psychological changes from one cycle to the next. Their moods and emotional symptoms vary far more in degree and direction from one month to another than we would expect if predictable hormone fluctuations were the main reason for these changes (Walker, 1994).

- There is *no* reliable relationship between cycle stage and work efficiency, problem solving, motor performance, exam scores, or any other behavior that matters in real life (Golub, 1988).

Do these findings surprise you? Results like these, reported many times over the past 15 years, are unknown to most people and are often ignored by doctors, therapists, and the media, for reasons we discuss in "Psychology and Popular Culture." The same chasm between reality and belief may be found in women's experience of *menopause,* the midlife cessation of menstruation, which is brought on when the ovaries stop producing estrogen and progesterone. Many people think that the typical menopausal woman suffers from a "syndrome" or "deficiency disease" that makes her depressed, irritable, and irrational. Menopause does produce physical symptoms in many women, notably "hot flashes," as the vascular system adjusts to the decrease in estrogen. But in a large survey of thousands of randomly chosen women, most viewed menopause positively (with relief that they no longer had to worry about pregnancy or periods) or with no particular feelings at all. Only 3 percent reported regret at having reached menopause. The vast majority had no serious physical symptoms and did not suffer from depression, unless they had a history of depressive episodes in their lives. Apart from having some "temporarily bothersome symptoms," most women said that menopause is no big deal (McKinlay, McKinlay, & Brambilla, 1987). Over and over, large-scale studies of normal populations find that menopause has no effect on most women's mental health (Matthews et al., 1990). The people who have the most positive attitudes toward menopause are the women who have been through it (Gannon & Ekstrom, 1993).

The focus in the research community and in the general culture on women's moods and symptoms obscures the fact that men also have emotional ups and downs. Could these changes be linked to hormones? Testosterone, an important androgen (masculinizing hormone), fluctuates daily in all men, usually reaching a peak in the morning. It also seems to follow a longer, infradian cycle in some men, the length of the cycle varying from one individual to another (Doering et al., 1974). So far, the evidence on the relationship of testosterone

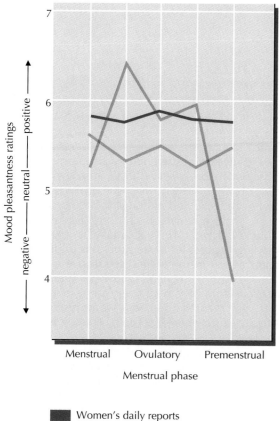

■ **Figure 5.2 Mood Changes in Women and Men: Are They Cyclical?**

In a study that challenged popular stereotypes about "PMS," college students of both sexes recorded their moods daily for 70 days without knowing the purpose of the study. This graph shows three of the study's findings. First, at no time of the month were the women grumpier or feeling less pleasant than the men. Second, when women were asked to recall their moods, they said their moods had been more negative premenstrually. Third, the women's daily reports showed that in fact their moods did not show wild swings over the menstrual cycle: their moods varied only moderately, just as the men's did (McFarlane, Martin, & Williams, 1988).

levels to psychological state has been sparse, conflicting, and hard to interpret. In one study, which measured daily mood and hormone changes in young men for a month, high testosterone levels predicted high hostility for some men, but low hostility for others (Doering et al., 1975). In another study, testosterone rose in men who were feeling elated after winning a $100 prize in a tennis match (Mazur & Lamb, 1980), but in a third study, teenagers with characteristically high testosterone levels had a tendency to feel sad, not elated (Susman et al., 1987).

A few years ago, in a survey of 4,462 men, James Dabbs and Robin Morris (1990) found that unusually high testosterone levels were associated with delinquency, drug use, having many sex partners, abusiveness, and violence—and were not associated with any positive behaviors. However, these results do not mean that men are victims of their hormones or that high testosterone levels constitute a syndrome. The causes of antisocial behavior are far more complicated than simple shifts in hormones, and besides, the findings were only correlational.

In actuality, the evidence shows that few people of either sex are likely to undergo personality shifts because of their hormones. It is true that hormonal abnormalities may produce psychological symptoms, just as a brain tumor might. A person's circumstances also affect physical or emotional symptoms: In one study, full-time homemakers with young children reported the most severe "PMS" (Sanders et al., 1983). Chronic pain or discomfort can affect mood in both women and men. But for most people, the relationships between body rhythms and mental states are subtle and varied. An increased state of arousal

Thinking Calmly About Raging Hormones

■ Imagine this cartoon: Joan of Arc, in a full coat of armor, with sword resting in her hand, sits forlornly on a grassy hill, weeping her heart out and vowing to "raise such a battle-cry that you will remember it forever!" The cartoon's caption reads, "PMS Attacks in History."

Cartoons like this one have been making the rounds in recent years. In fact, entire books of cartoons and gags about PMS have appeared. Popular magazines, too, have promoted the view that women's hormones drive them a bit bonkers, with article titles such as "Dr. Jekyll and Ms. Hyde" and "The Taming of the Shrew Inside of You" (Chrisler et al., 1994). And down at the local bookstore, best-sellers such as Gail Sheehy's *The Silent Passage: Menopause* warn women that just when they thought the menstrual blues were behind them, it's time to prepare for all the dire problems supposedly associated with menopause, from depression to dwindling sexual desire.

As we discuss in the text of this chapter, medical and psychological research shows that serious distress due to menstruation or menopause is rare. So what is going on here? Why do people so readily accept the notion that women are emotionally unstable because of their hormones? And why, we might wonder, is the hormonal excuse for the goose ("Of course she's angry, she's having her period") not the same for the gander ("Of course he's angry, he has all those male hormones")? Why has so much attention and funding been devoted to "PMS" and not to, say, "HTS"—HyperTestosterone Syndrome?

To answer these questions, we must consider cultural attitudes toward women's bodies and normal reproductive processes, and also how social, economic, and political forces shape research and the public's reaction to research findings.

As Emily Martin (1987) has shown, a negative attitude toward female reproductive processes pervades many cultures. This bias turns up subtly in supposedly objective anatomy textbooks, which describe the process of menstruation only in terms of deprivation, deficiency, loss, and shedding of the lining of the uterus. The lining of the stomach is shed and replaced regularly too, Martin observes, but textbooks do not describe this process as one of degenerating or shedding of the stomach lining. They emphasize the "production" of mucus, Martin

found, and "in a phrase that gives the story away—the periodic *renewal* of the lining of the stomach." Stomachs, which both sexes have, are described positively; uteruses, which only women have, are described negatively. And although a large proportion of the male ejaculate is composed of waste material, adds Martin, "The texts make no mention of a shedding process let alone processes of deterioration and repair in the male reproductive tract." Only 1 out of every 100 billion sperm ever manages to fertilize an egg. "From the very same point of view that sees menstruation as a waste product," notes Martin, "surely here is something really worth crying about!"

Psychologists, physicians, and other researchers are just as much a part of their culture as anyone else, and they are just as likely to be influenced by prevailing attitudes toward the female body. For many years, little work was done on menstruation, menopause, and other biological events that can affect women's reproductive health. When the PMS label came along in the early 1970s, many women welcomed it as a validation of the normal physical changes of the menstrual cycle and a sign that women's health issues were finally being taking seriously. Throughout the 1980s, however, a significant shift occurred: Premenstrual symptoms shifted from being seen as a normal process to a *medical and psychiatric disorder* (Parlee, 1989; Tavris, 1992). Insurance companies began to compensate psychiatrists and gynecologists for treating it, although, as we have seen, no treatment has been successful and there is no general agreement about what "PMS" even is.

"PMS" became a part of the popular culture because of several interwoven trends: women's welcoming it as a validation of their own physical changes; the medical and psychiatric establishments' welcoming it as another disorder suitable for treatment and insurance compensation; and the abiding attitude that women, but not men, are at the mercy of their fluctuating hormones. In such a cultural context, there is a danger that PMS will be used to justify the stigmatization of women and the trivialization of their genuine complaints, as research is already finding (Koeske, 1987). The critical thinker, in reflecting on popular culture's fondness for PMS jokes, might do well to ask who is having the last laugh. ■

or sensitivity may contribute either to nervousness and restlessness or to creative energy and vitality.

Symptoms are not "all in your head"; physical changes and mood changes are real. The body provides the clay for our symptoms; it's real clay—but it's only clay. Learning and culture mold that clay, by teaching us which physical changes are important or worrisome and which are not. The impact of any bodily change—whether it is circadian, ultradian, or infradian—depends on how we interpret it and how we choose to respond to it.

Quick QUIZ

Has your concentration peaked, or is it in an ultradian trough? Take this quiz to find out.

1. In the absence of time cues, most people would live a day that is about _____ hours long.
2. Jet lag occurs because of internal _____.
3. Which term describes the menstrual cycle? (a) circadian, (b) infradian, (c) ultradian.
4. For most women, the days before menstruation are reliably associated with (a) depression, (b) irritability, (c) elation, (d) creativity, (e) none of these, (f) all of these.
5. You are a psychologist studying testosterone in men. You tell your subjects that testosterone peaks in the morning and that you believe this hormone causes hostility. You then ask them to fill out a "HyperTestosterone Syndrome (HTS) Survey" in the morning and again at night. Based on menstrual-cycle findings, what result might you get? How could you improve your study?

Answers:

1. 25 2. desynchronization 3. b 4. e 5. Because of the expectations that the men now have about testosterone, they may be biased to report more hostility in the morning. It would be better to keep them in the dark about your hypothesis, give them a questionnaire with a neutral title (such as "Health and Mood Checklist"), and measure their actual hormone levels early and late in the day (since individuals vary in the timing of their peaks). Also, you might add a control group of women, to see whether their hostility levels vary in the same way as men's do.

The Rhythms of Sleep

Perhaps the most perplexing of all our biological rhythms is the one governing sleeping and wakefulness. Human beings and most animals curl up and go to sleep once every 24 hours, but the reason remains something of a puzzle. After all, sleeping puts an organism at risk: Muscles that are usually ready to respond to danger relax, and senses grow dull. As the late British psychologist Christopher Evans (1984) noted, "The behavior patterns involved in sleep are glaringly, almost insanely, at odds with common sense." Then why is sleep such a profound necessity?

Why We Sleep.   One likely function of sleep is to provide a time-out period, so that the body can restore depleted reserves of energy, eliminate waste products from muscles, repair cells, strengthen the immune system, or recover physical abilities lost during the day. The idea that sleep is for recuperation

During the Great Depression of the 1930s, marathon dancers competed for prize money by trying to dance longer than other contestants, and inadvertently demonstrated some of the effects of sleep deprivation.

accords with the undeniable fact that at the end of the day we feel tired and crave sleep. Though most people can function fairly normally after a day or two of sleeplessness, especially when doing interesting, nonrepetitive tasks, sleep deprivation that lasts for four days or longer is quite uncomfortable. In animals, forced sleeplessness leads to infections and eventually death (Rechtschaffen et al., 1983), and the same may be true for people. There is a case on record of a man who abruptly began to lose sleep at age 52. After sinking deeper and deeper into an exhausted stupor, he developed a lung infection and died. An autopsy showed he had lost almost all of the large neurons in two areas of the thalamus that have been linked to sleep and hormonal circadian rhythms (Lugaresi et al., 1986).

Nonetheless, when people go many days without sleep, they do not then require an equal period of time to catch up; one night's rest usually eliminates all symptoms of fatigue (Dement, 1978). Moreover, the amount of time we sleep does not necessarily correspond to how active we have been; even after a relaxing day on the beach, we usually go to sleep at night as quickly as usual. For these reasons, simple rest or energy restoration cannot be the sole purpose of sleep.

Many researchers now believe that sleep must have as much to do with brain function as with bodily restoration. Despite the fact that most people still function pretty well after losing a single night's sleep, mental flexibility, originality, and other aspects of creative thinking may suffer (Horne, 1988). Chronic sleepiness can impair performance on tasks requiring vigilance or divided attention, and it can lead to automotive and industrial accidents (Dement, 1992; Roehrs et al., 1990). Laboratory studies and observations of people participating in "wake-athons" have shown that after several days of sleep loss, people become irritable and begin to have hallucinations and delusions (Dement, 1978; Luce & Segal, 1966). The brain, then, needs periodic sleep. Researchers are now trying to find out how sleep may contribute to the regulation of brain metabolism, the maintenance of normal nerve-cell activity, and the replenishment of neurotransmitters. It is clear, however, that during sleep, the brain is not just resting. On the contrary, most of the brain remains quite active, as we are about to see.

The Realms of Sleep.   Until the early 1950s, little was known about sleep. Then a breakthrough occurred in the laboratory of physiologist Nathaniel Kleitman, who at the time was the only person in the world who had spent an

Whatever your age, sometimes the urge to sleep is irresistible. However, the physical and psychological functions of sleep are still not fully understood.

entire career studying sleep. Kleitman had assigned one of his graduate students, Eugene Aserinsky, the tedious task of finding out if the slow, rolling eye movements that characterize the onset of sleep continue throughout the night. To both men's surprise, Aserinsky discovered that eye movements did indeed occur, but they were rapid, not slow (Aserinsky, & Kleitman, 1955). Using the electroencephalograph to measure the brain's electrical activity (see Chapter 4), these researchers, along with another of Kleitman's students, William Dement, were able to correlate the rapid eye movements of sleepers with changes in their brain-wave patterns (Dement, 1992). Adult volunteers were soon spending their nights sleeping in laboratories while scientists observed them and measured changes in their brain activity, muscle tension, breathing, and other physiological responses.

As a result of this research, today we know that sleep is not an unbroken state of rest. In adults, periods of **rapid eye movement (REM)** alternate with periods of fewer eye movements, or *non-REM* (NREM), in an ultradian cycle that recurs, on the average, every 90 minutes. The REM periods last from a few minutes to as long as an hour, averaging about 20 minutes in length. Whenever they begin, the pattern of electrical activity from the sleeper's brain changes to resemble that of alert wakefulness. Non-REM periods are themselves divided into shorter, distinct stages, each associated with a particular brain-wave pattern (see Figure 5.3).

When you first climb into bed, close your eyes, and relax, your brain emits bursts of **alpha waves.** On an EEG recording, alpha waves have a regular rhythm, high amplitude (height), and a low frequency of 8–12 cycles per second. Alpha activity is associated with relaxing or not concentrating on anything in particular. Gradually, these waves slow down even further, and you drift into the Land of Nod, passing through four stages, each deeper than the previous one.

■ **rapid eye movement (REM) sleep**
Sleep periods characterized by eye movement, loss of muscle tone, and dreaming.

■ **alpha waves**
Relatively large, slow brain waves characteristic of relaxed wakefulness.

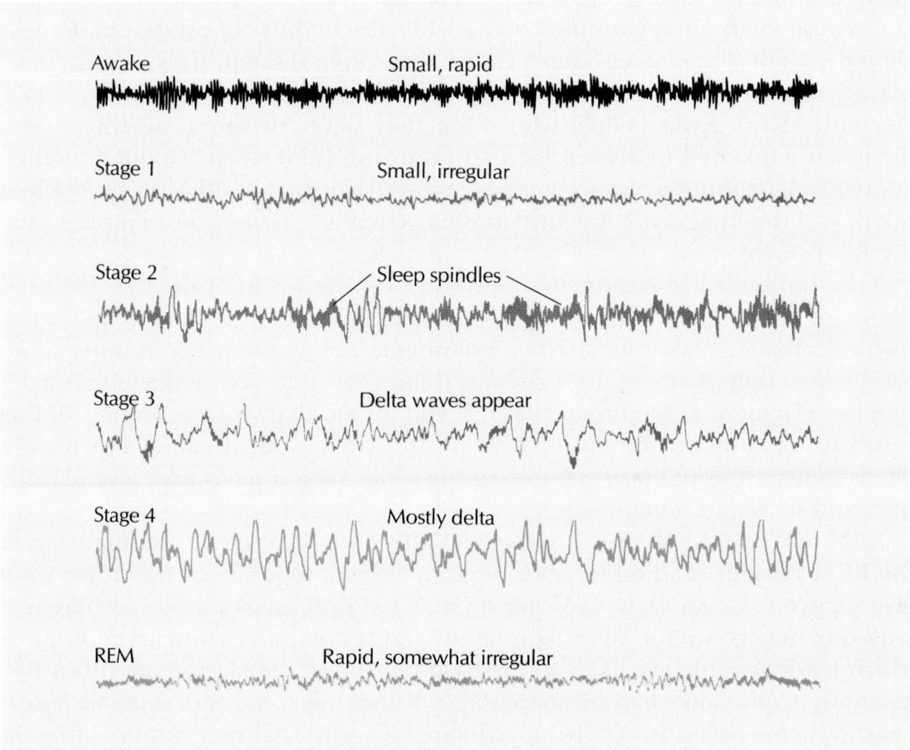

Figure 5.3 Brain-Wave Patterns During Sleep

Most types of brain waves are present throughout sleep, but different ones predominate at different stages.

1. *Stage 1.* Your brain waves become small and irregular, indicating activity with low voltage and mixed frequencies. You feel yourself drifting on the edge of consciousness, in a state of light sleep. If awakened, you may recall fantasies or a few visual images.

2. *Stage 2.* Your brain emits occasional short bursts of rapid, high-peaking waves called *sleep spindles.* Minor noises probably won't disturb you.

3. *Stage 3.* In addition to the waves characteristic of stage 2, your brain occasionally emits very slow waves of about 1–3 cycles per second, with very high peaks. These **delta waves** are a sure sign that you will be hard to arouse. Your breathing and pulse have slowed down, your temperature has dropped, and your muscles are relaxed.

4. *Stage 4.* Delta waves have now largely taken over, and you are in deep sleep. It will take vigorous shaking or a loud noise to awaken you, and you won't be very happy about it. Oddly enough, though, if you talk or walk in your sleep, this is when you are likely to do so.

Because cats sleep so much—up to 80 percent of the time!—it's easy to catch them in the various stages of slumber. A cat in NREM sleep (top) remains upright, but during REM sleep (bottom) its muscles go limp and it flops onto its side.

This sequence takes about 30–45 minutes. Then it reverses, and you move back up the ladder from stage 4 to 3 to 2 to 1. At that point, about 70–90 minutes after the onset of sleep, something peculiar happens. Stage 1 does not turn into drowsy wakefulness, as one might expect. Instead, your brain begins to emit long bursts of very rapid, somewhat irregular waves, similar to those produced during stage 1. Your heart rate increases, your blood pressure rises, and your breathing becomes faster and more irregular. There may be small, convulsive twitches in the face and fingers. In men, the penis becomes somewhat erect as vascular tissue relaxes and blood fills the genital area faster than it exits. In women, the clitoris enlarges, the vaginal walls become engorged, and vaginal lubrication increases. At the same time, most of your skeletal muscles go as limp as a rag doll, preventing your aroused brain from producing physical movement. Though you are supposedly in a "light" stage of sleep, you are hard to awaken. You have entered the realm of REM.

Because the brain is extremely active while the body is almost devoid of muscle tone, REM sleep has also been called "paradoxical sleep." It is during these periods that you are most likely to dream (Aserinsky & Kleitman, 1955; Dement, 1955). Even people who claim they never dream at all will report dreams if awakened in a sleep laboratory during REM sleep (Goodenough et al., 1959). Dreaming is also sometimes reported during non-REM sleep, but less often, and the images are less vivid and more realistic than those reported during REM sleep.

The study of REM has opened a window on the world of dreams. We now know, for example, that dreams do not take place in an instant, as people used to think, but in "real time." When volunteers are awakened 5 minutes after REM starts, they report shorter dreams than when they are awakened after 15 minutes (Dement & Kleitman, 1957). If you dream that you are singing all the verses to "A Hundred Bottles of Beer on the Wall," your dream will probably last as long as it would take you to sing the song. Most dreams take several minutes, and some last much longer.

REM and non-REM sleep continue to alternate throughout the night, with the REM periods tending to get longer and closer together as the hours pass (see Figure 5.4). An early REM period may last only a few minutes, whereas a later one may go on for 20 or 30 minutes and sometimes as long as an hour—which is why people are likely to be dreaming when the alarm goes off in the morning. In the later part of sleep, stages 3 and 4 become very short or disappear. But the cycles are far from regular. An individual may bounce directly from stage 4 back to stage 2, or go from REM to stage 2 and then back to REM. Also, the time between REM and non-REM is highly variable, differing from person to person and also within a particular individual.

■ **delta waves**
Slow, regular brain waves characteristic of stage 3 and stage 4 sleep.

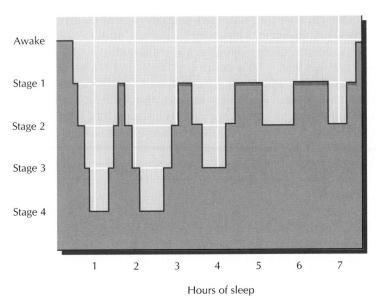

■ **Figure 5.4   The Changing Rhythms of Sleep**

This graph shows the pattern of a typical night's sleep for a young adult. Time spent in REM sleep is represented by the colored bars. REM periods tend to lengthen as the night goes on; but stages 3 and 4, which dominate non-REM sleep early in the night, may disappear as morning approaches. (From Kelly, 1981a.)

The purpose of REM sleep is still a matter of debate, but clearly it does have a purpose. If you wake people every time they lapse into REM sleep, nothing dramatic will happen. When finally allowed to sleep normally, however, they will spend a much longer time than usual in the REM phase. Electrical brain activity associated with REM may burst through into quiet sleep and even into wakefulness. The subjects seem to be making up for something they were deprived of. Many people think that in adults, at least, this "something" has to do with dreaming, to which we now turn.

Quick QUIZ

Match each term with the appropriate phrase.

1. REM periods
2. alpha
3. stage 4 sleep
4. stage 1 sleep

   a. delta waves and talking in one's sleep
   b. irregular brain waves and light sleep
   c. relaxed but awake
   d. active brain but inactive muscles

Answers:

1. d 2. c 3. a 4. b

■ EXPLORING THE DREAM WORLD

Every culture has its theories about dreams. In some cultures, dreams are thought to occur when the spirit leaves the body to wander the world or speak to the gods. In others, dreams are thought to reveal the future; in the Bible, it was while dreaming that Joseph learned there was to be a famine in Egypt. A Chinese Taoist of the third century B.C. pondered the possible reality of the dream world. He told of dreaming that he was a butterfly flitting about. "Suddenly I woke up and I was indeed Chuang Tzu. Did Chuang Tzu dream he was a butterfly, or did the butterfly dream he was Chuang Tzu?"

In dreaming, the focus of attention is inward, though sometimes an external event such as the sound of a siren can influence the dream. While a dream is in progress, it may be vivid or vague, terrifying or peaceful, colorful or bland. It may also seem to make perfect sense—until you wake up. Then it is often recalled as illogical and bizarre. The flow of a dream is usually not as smooth as the flow of waking consciousness; events occur without transitions. REM dreams, which as we noted are usually more vivid than non-REM dreams, are often reported as adventures or stories. Non-REM dreams tend to be described as vague, fragmentary, unemotional, and commonplace.

Ordinarily, during dreaming, you have no background awareness of where you are or of your own body. Some people, however, report dreams in which they know they are dreaming and they feel as though they are conscious. These **lucid dreams,** which occur at times of high cortical arousal, seem to involve a split in consciousness known as **dissociation.** During the dream, consciousness seems to divide into a dreaming part and an observing part. Some people have learned, with training, to produce lucid dreams at will and to control the action in them, much as a scriptwriter decides what will happen in a movie (Garfield, 1974; LaBerge, 1986, 1990). In the sleep laboratory, they may even be able to signal that they are having a lucid dream by moving their eyes in a prearranged way.

Studies of lucid dreamers have stirred up an issue that has been bothering sleep researchers for years: Do the eye movements of REM sleep correspond to events in a dream? Some researchers think that eye movements are no more related to dream content than are inner-ear muscle contractions, which also occur during REM sleep (Kelly, 1981b). Every mammal studied except the spiny anteater goes through REM sleep, as do human fetuses, but we might not want to credit mice, opossums, or human fetuses with what we ordinarily call dreams. Further, although children's eyes move during REM sleep, the imagery in children's dreams tends to be static until age 6 or so, and their cognitive limitations keep them from creating true narratives in dreams until age 7 or 8 (Foulkes, 1990; Foulkes et al., 1990). On the other hand, in adult dreamers, eye movements resemble those of waking life, when the eyes and head move in synchrony as the person moves about and changes the direction of his or her gaze—even though during dreaming the head and body stay still (J. H. Herman, 1992). Moreover, studies of skilled lucid dreamers find that their eye movements correspond to preplanned actions in their dreams (Schatzman, Worsley, & Fenwick, 1988). These findings suggest that in adults, at least, the eyes may indeed track dream images, actions, and events.

Why do these dream images arise at all? Why doesn't the brain just *rest,* switching off all thoughts and images and launching us into a coma? Why, instead, do we spend our nights flying through the air, battling monsters, or flirting with an old flame in the fantasy world of our dreams?

Dreams as Unconscious Wishes

The Iroquois of North America believed that dreams express hidden wishes and desires, and, like many cultures around the world, they developed rituals for the purpose of analyzing the underlying meanings of dreams (Krippner & Hillman, 1990). In psychology, one of the first theorists to take dreams seriously was Sigmund Freud, the founder of psychoanalysis; he too emphasized hidden messages from the mind. After analyzing many of his patients' dreams and some of his own, Freud concluded that our nighttime fantasies provide a "royal road to the unconscious." In dreams, said Freud, we are able to gratify forbidden or unrealistic wishes and desires, often sexual, that have been forced into the unconscious part of the mind. If we did not dream, energy invested in these wishes and desires would build up to intolerable levels, threatening our very sanity.

■ **lucid dream**
A dream in which the dreamer is aware of dreaming.

■ **dissociation**
Separation of consciousness into distinct parts.

According to Freud, every dream has meaning, no matter how absurd it might seem. But if a dream's message arouses anxiety, the rational part of the mind must disguise and distort it. Otherwise, the dream would waken the dreamer, intruding into consciousness. In dreams, therefore, one person may be represented by another—for example, a father by a brother—or even by several different characters. Similarly, thoughts and objects are translated into symbolic images. A penis may be disguised as a snake, umbrella, or dagger; a vagina, as a tunnel or cave; and the human body, as a house.

To understand a dream, Freud said, we must distinguish its *manifest content,* the aspects of it that we consciously experience during sleep and may remember upon wakening, from its *latent* (hidden) *content,* the unconscious wishes and thoughts being expressed symbolically. Freud warned against the simple-minded translation of symbols, however. Each dream had to be analyzed in the context of the dreamer's waking life, as well as the person's associations to the dream's contents. Not everything in a dream is symbolic. Sometimes, Freud cautioned, "A cigar is only a cigar."

Most psychologists today accept Freud's notion that dreams are more than incoherent ramblings of the mind, but many quarrel with his interpretations, which they find far-fetched. Critics of psychoanalysis point out that there are no clear rules for interpreting the latent content of dreams, and there is no objective way to know whether a particular interpretation is correct.

Dreams as Problem Solving

Another explanation holds that dreams reflect not deep-seated or infantile wishes but rather the ongoing emotional preoccupations of waking life—relationships, work, sex, or health (Webb & Cartwright, 1978). In this view, the symbols and metaphors in dreams convey the dream's true meaning, rather than disguising it. One psychologist, Gayle Delaney, tells of a woman who dreamed she was swimming underwater. Her 8-year-old son was on her back, his head above the water. Her husband was supposed to take a picture of them, but for some reason he wasn't doing it, and she was starting to feel as if she was going to drown. To Delaney, the message was obvious: The woman was "drowning" under the responsibilities of child care and her husband wasn't "getting the picture" (in Dolnick, 1990). Another psychologist, Alan Siegel (1991), tells of a father-to-be who dreamed of swimming downhill, with instructions from his wife's labor coach, and emerging in the locker room wrapped in a towel. When asked for his interpretation, the man said the dream meant he should swim more at the gym! To Siegel, however, the dream was about the man's anxiety over the impending childbirth and parenthood.

According to Rosalind Cartwright, dreams give us an opportunity to deal with emotional issues, even if we forget the dreams later. When we are relatively

These drawings, from dream journals kept by two sleep research subjects, show that dream images can be either abstract or literal. The two fanciful paintings on the left represent the dreams of a person who worked all day long with brain tissue, which the drawings rather resemble. The desk on the right was sketched in 1939 by a scientist to illustrate his dream about a mechanical device for instantly retrieving quotations—a sort of early desktop computer.

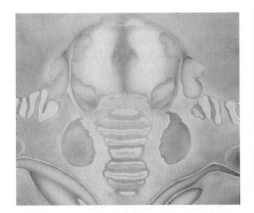

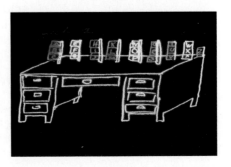

free of problems, we may use dreams simply to exercise our creativity. But during a crisis, our dream machinery goes into high gear, and emotional concerns activate images in memory. Cartwright (1989, 1991) finds that in depressed people going through a divorce, the first dream of the night often comes sooner than it does for others, the dream lasts longer, and it is more emotional and storylike—and this pattern, Cartright reports, relates to recovery. The content of these people's dreams suggests that they are working on issues of loss and new responsibilities. Cartwright (1990) concludes that getting through a divorce (and by implication, other crises) takes "time, good friends, good genes, good luck, and a good dream system."

Dreams as Information Processing

A third approach views dreams as opportunities for mental housekeeping. Christopher Evans (1984) argued that the brain must periodically shut out sensory input so that it can process and assimilate new data and update what has already been stored. It divides new information into "wanted" and "unwanted" categories, makes new associations, and revises old "programs" (to use a computer analogy) in light of the day's experiences. The data on which the brain works include not only recent events, but also ideas, obsessions, worries, wishes, and thoughts about the past. What we recall as dreams are really only brief snippets from an ongoing process of sorting, scanning, and sifting that occurs during REM sleep and possibly throughout the night. Because these snippets give us only a glimpse of the night's mental activity, they naturally seem odd and nonsensical when recalled.

Recent research in several different countries supports the idea that REM sleep helps us assimilate new information and integrate new experiences with old ones during "off-line processing." In rats and in human beings, REM sleep deprivation impairs memory for tasks that were recently learned (Li et al., 1991; Valatx, 1989). One study found that in rats, there appears to be a critical "window" of time when REM sleep is necessary for memory retention (Smith & MacNeill, 1993). On the basis of these and other findings, some researchers believe that REM is associated with *consolidation,* a process by which the synaptic changes associated with a recently stored memory become durable and stable (see Chapter 9). During consolidation, a memory will often continue to improve somewhat after initial learning has taken place. In a recent Israeli study, people learned a visual skill in the evening and then went to bed. On some nights, they were repeatedly awakened during stages 3 and 4 (slow-wave) sleep; on other nights, they were awakened the same number of times during REM sleep. When they were awakened during slow-wave sleep, their memories improved, despite the loss of sleep. But when they were deprived of REM sleep, their memories showed no improvement at all (Karni et al., 1994).

Information-processing approaches to dreaming might explain why REM sleep occurs in fetuses, babies, and other mammals as well as in adult human beings. They, too, need to "sort things out." Newborns, in fact, spend about 50 percent of their sleeping hours in REM sleep, versus only 20 percent for adults. Since everything that is happening to them is new, perhaps they have to do more writing, revising, and consolidating of "programs." As we noted, however, children's cognitive immaturity prevents them from creating the kinds of narratives and images that adult human beings experience during dreaming.

Dreams as Interpreted Brain Activity

A fourth approach to dreaming, the **activation–synthesis theory,** draws heavily on physiological research. According to this explanation, which was first proposed by Allan Hobson and Robert McCarley (1977) and later elaborated by

■ **activation–synthesis theory**
The theory that dreaming results from the cortical synthesis and interpretation of neural signals triggered by activity in the lower part of the brain.

Hobson (1988, 1990), dreams are not, in Shakespeare's words, "children of an idle brain." Rather, they are the result of neurons firing spontaneously in the lower part of the brain, specifically in the pons. These neurons control eye movement, gaze, balance, and posture, and they send messages to areas of the cortex responsible during wakefulness for visual processing and voluntary action. Such sleeptime signals have no psychological meaning in themselves, but the cortex tries to make sense of them by *synthesizing*, or combining, them with existing knowledge and memories to produce some sort of coherent interpretation—just as it would if the signals had come from sense organs during ordinary wakefulness.

Thus, according to the activation–synthesis theory, when neurons fire in the part of the brain that handles balance, the cortex may generate a dream about falling. When signals occur that would ordinarily produce running, the cortex may manufacture a dream about being chased. Because the signals themselves lack coherence, the interpretation—the dream—is also likely to be incoherent and confusing. And because cortical neurons that control storage of new memories are turned off during sleep (because certain neurotransmitter levels are low), we typically forget our dreams upon waking unless we write them down or immediately recount them to someone else.

Hobson (1988) explains why REM sleep and dreaming do not occur continuously through the night. Giant cells found in the reticular activating system of the pons, cells that are sensitive to the neurotransmitter acetylcholine, appear to initiate REM sleep. They then proceed to fire in unrestrained bursts, like a machine gun. Eventually, the gun's magazine is emptied, and other neurons, which inhibit REM sleep, take over. "If synapses are like cartridges," writes Hobson, "it may be that is why REM sleep ends; no more synaptic ammunition." Only when the neurons "reload" can firing, and REM sleep, resume. In support of this hypothesis, Hobson notes that when sleeping volunteers are injected with drugs that enhance the action of acetylcholine, REM sleep and dreaming increase. Conversely, when volunteers are injected with a drug that blocks the effects of acetylcholine, REM sleep and dreaming decrease (Gillin et al., 1985).

Wishes, according to Hobson, do not cause dreams; brain-stem mechanisms do. But that doesn't mean that dreams are meaningless. According to Hobson (1988), the brain "is so inexorably bent upon the quest for meaning that it attributes and even creates meaning when there is little or none to be found in the data it is asked to process." By studying these attributed meanings, you can learn about your unique perceptions, conflicts, and concerns—not by trying to dig below the surface of the dream, as Freud would, but by examining the surface itself. Or you can relax and enjoy the nightly entertainment that dreams provide.

The activation–synthesis model, like all dream theories, has its critics. Some argue that the cortex does not passively submit to "incoming volleys" from the pons, but instead takes an active role in controlling REM sleep and dreaming (J. H. Herman, 1992). In a review of findings about dreams and sleep, John Antrobus (1991) concludes that contrary to most theories, including Hobson's, dreaming is really just a modification of what goes on when we are awake. The difference is that when we are asleep we are cut off from sensory input from the external world and feedback from our own movements. It is this restricted input, argues Antrobus, that accounts for the bizarre imagery in dreams. Antrobus cites research in his laboratory suggesting that mental activity during wakefulness would be much like that during dreaming—with the same hallucinatory quality—if the person could be cut off from all external stimulation. As we will see in the next chapter, older studies have found the same thing.

How are we to evaluate these theories of dreaming? Each approach seems to explain certain kinds of evidence: the "aha" reactions of patients undergoing psychotherapy (psychoanalytic explanations); the dream experiences of people going through a crisis (problem-solving explanations); the existence of REM sleep in animals and infants (information-processing explanations); and the physiological evidence (the activation–synthesis theory). At present, no one theory seems to explain all dreams, and all the theories are proving difficult to test. Perhaps it will turn out that different kinds of dreams have different purposes and origins. Much remains to be learned about the purpose of dreaming and even of sleep itself.

Quick QUIZ

A dreamer imagines himself as an infant crawling through a dark tunnel looking for something he has lost. Which theory of dreams would be most receptive to each of the following explanations?

1. The dreamer has recently misplaced a valuable watch and is worried about possible memory problems.
2. While the dreamer was sleeping, neurons in his pons that would ordinarily stimulate leg-muscle movement were active.
3. The dreamer has repressed an early sexual attraction to his mother; the tunnel symbolizes her vagina.
4. The dreamer has broken up with his lover and is working through the emotional loss.

Answers:

1. the information-processing approach (the dreamer is processing information about a recent experience) 2. the activation–synthesis theory 3. psychoanalytic theory 4. the problem-solving approach

■ CONSCIOUSNESS-ALTERING DRUGS

- In Jerusalem, hundreds of male Hasidic Jews celebrate the completion of the annual reading of the holy Torah by dancing in the streets. Although it is warm and the men are dressed in long black coats, they go on for hours, never tiring. For them, dancing is not a diversion; it is a path to religious ecstasy.

- In South Dakota, several Sioux adults sit naked in the darkness of the sweat lodge, a circular hut covered with hides and blankets. A spiritual leader offers prayers and leads chants. Then he throws water on a pit of red-hot rocks, and a crushing wave of heat envelops the participants. They must concentrate all their thoughts on coping with it. Their reward will be euphoria, the transcendence of pain, and, according to Sioux belief, possible connection with the Great Spirit of the Universe.

- Deep in the Amazon jungle, a young man is training to be a shaman, a religious leader. For weeks, he has starved himself. Now he enters a trance, aided by a whiff of hallucinogenic snuff made from the bark of the virola tree. As a full shaman, he will be expected to enter trances regularly and to communicate with animals, spirits, and supernatural forces.

These three rituals, seemingly quite different, are all aimed at release from the confines of ordinary consciousness. Cultures around the world have devised such practices, often as part of their religions. Because attempts to alter

All cultures seem to find ways to alter ordinary consciousness. The Maulavis of Turkey (left), the famous whirling dervishes, spin in an energetic but controlled manner in order to achieve religious rapture and unite their souls with Allah. In many cultures, people learn to meditate (center) as a way to quiet the mind, experience immediate reality, and achieve spiritual enlightenment. And in some cultures, such as the Huichol Indian of western Mexico, psychoactive drugs are used for religious or artistic inspiration; the Huichol painting on the right, made of yarn and beeswax on wood, represents a peyote-induced hallucination of a tree.

consciousness appear to be universal, some writers believe they reflect a basic human need. Psychopharmacologist Ronald Siegel (1989) calls the motive to alter mood or consciousness a "fourth drive" (after sex, thirst, and hunger). William James (1902/1936), who was fascinated by alterations in consciousness, would have agreed. After inhaling nitrous oxide ("laughing gas"), he wrote, "Our normal waking consciousness, rational consciousness as we call it, is but one special type of consciousness, whilst all about it, parted from it by the filmiest of screens, there lie potential forms of consciousness entirely different."

James believed that psychologists should study these other forms of consciousness, but for half a century, few took his words seriously. Then, during the 1960s, attitudes changed. During that decade of social upheaval, millions of people began to explore techniques for deliberately producing **altered states of consciousness,** especially through the use of psychoactive drugs. Researchers became interested in the psychology, as well as physiology, of such drugs. The "filmy screen" described by James finally began to lift.

Classifying Drugs

A **psychoactive drug** is a substance that affects perception, mood, thinking, memory, or behavior by changing the body's biochemistry. Historically, the most widely used drugs have been tobacco, alcohol, marijuana, opium, cocaine, mescaline (peyote)—and, of course, coffee. Nearly every society has discovered at least one such substance and has used it either in rituals or recreationally. Many animals, too, like to get chemically "high" on occasion: Baboons ingest tobacco, elephants love the alcohol in fermented fruit, and reindeer and rabbits seek out intoxicating mushrooms (Siegel, 1989).

Most drugs can be classified as *stimulants, depressants, opiates,* or *psychedelics,* depending on their effects on the central nervous system and their impact on behavior and mood (see Table 5.1). (The following descriptions do not include

■ **altered state of consciousness**
A state of consciousness that differs from ordinary wakefulness or sleep.

■ **psychoactive drug**
A drug capable of influencing perception, mood, cognition, or behavior.

Table 5.1   Some Psychoactive Drugs and Their Effects

	Type of Drug	Common Effects	Results of Abuse/Addiction
Amphetamines	Stimulant	Wakefulness, alertness, raised metabolism, elevated mood	Nervousness, headaches, loss of appetite, high blood pressure, delusions, psychosis, heart damage, convulsions, death
Cocaine	Stimulant	Euphoria, excitation, boost of energy, suppressed appetite	Excitability, sleeplessness, sweating, paranoia, anxiety, panic, depression, heart damage, heart failure, injury to nose if sniffed
Tobacco (nicotine)	Stimulant	Varies, from alertness to calmness, depending on mental set, setting, and prior arousal; decreases appetite for carbohydrates	Nicotine: heart disease, high blood pressure, impaired circulation Tar: lung cancer, emphysema, mouth and throat cancer, many other health risks
Caffeine	Stimulant	Wakefulness, alertness, shortened reaction time	Restlessness, insomnia, muscle tension, heartbeat irregularities, high blood pressure
Alcohol (1–2 drinks)	Depressant	Depends on setting, mental set; tends to act like a stimulant because it reduces inhibitions, anxiety	
Alcohol (several/ many drinks)	Depressant	Slowed reaction time, tension, depression, reduced ability to store new memories or to retrieve old ones, poor coordination	Blackouts, cirrhosis, organic damage, mental and neurological impairment, psychosis, possibly death
Tranquilizers (e.g., Valium); Barbiturates (e.g., phenobarbital)	Depressant	Reduced anxiety and tension, sedation	Increased dosage needed for effects; impaired motor and sensory functions, impaired permanent storage of new information, withdrawal symptoms; possibly convulsions, coma, death (especially when taken with other drugs)
Opium, heroin, morphine	Opiate	Euphoria, relief of pain	Loss of appetite, nausea, constipation, withdrawal symptoms, convulsions, coma, possibly death
LSD, psilocybin, mescaline	Psychedelic	Exhilaration, visions and hallucinations, insightful experiences	Psychosis, paranoia, panic reactions
Marijuana	Mild psychedelic (classification controversial)	Relaxation, euphoria, increased appetite, reduced ability to store new memories, other effects depending on mental set and setting	Throat and lung irritation, lung damage (if smoked), impaired immunity; long-term effects not well established

▪ **stimulants**
Drugs that speed up activity in the central nervous system.

drugs used in the treatment of mental and emotional disorders; they are covered in Chapter 16.)

1. **Stimulants,** such as cocaine, amphetamines ("uppers"), nicotine, and caffeine, speed up activity in the central nervous system. In moderate amounts, they tend to produce feelings of excitement, confidence, and well-being or euphoria. In large amounts, they make a person anxious, jittery, and hyperalert. In very large doses, they may cause convulsions, heart failure, and death.

Amphetamines are synthetic drugs usually taken in pill form. Cocaine ("coke") is a natural drug, derived from the leaves of the coca plant. Rural workers in Bolivia and Peru chew coca leaf every day, without apparent ill effects. In the United States, the drug is usually inhaled ("snorted") or injected, or smoked in the highly refined form known as "crack." These methods give the drug a more immediate, powerful, and dangerous effect. Amphetamines and cocaine make users feel peppy but do not actually increase energy reserves. Fatigue, irritability, and depression may occur when the effects of these drugs wear off.

2. Depressants, such as alcohol, tranquilizers, and barbiturates, slow down activity in the central nervous system. Also known as *sedatives,* they usually make a person feel calm or drowsy, and they may reduce anxiety, guilt, tension, and inhibitions. In large amounts, they may produce insensitivity to pain and other sensations. Like stimulants, in very large doses, they can cause convulsions and death.

People are often surprised to learn that alcohol is a central nervous system depressant. In small amounts, alcohol has some of the effects of a stimulant, because it suppresses activity in parts of the brain that normally inhibit such behaviors as loud laughter and clowning around. Like barbiturates and opiates, alcohol can be used as an anesthetic; if you drink enough, you will eventually pass out. Extremely large amounts of alcohol can kill, by inhibiting the nerve cells in the brain areas that control breathing and heartbeat. But some studies find that *moderate* social drinking—a drink or two of wine or liquor a day—is associated with a variety of health benefits, including a reduction in the risk of heart attacks (Casswell, 1993; Peele, 1993).

3. Opiates include opium, derived from the opium poppy; morphine, a derivative of opium; heroin, a derivative of morphine; and synthetic drugs, such as methadone. All of these drugs relieve pain, mimicking the action of endorphins, and most have a powerful effect on the emotions. When injected, they may produce a sudden feeling of euphoria, called a "rush." There may be a decrease in anxiety and a decrease in motivation, although the effects vary.

4. Psychedelic drugs alter consciousness by disrupting the normal perception of time and space, as well as normal thought processes. Sometimes, psychedelics produce hallucinations, especially visual ones. Some psychedelics, such as lysergic acid diethylamide (LSD), are made in the laboratory. Others, such as mescaline (from the peyote cactus) and psilocybin (from mushrooms), are natural substances. Emotional reactions to psychedelics vary from person to person, and from one time to another for any individual. A "trip" may be mildly pleasant or unpleasant, a mystical revelation or a nightmare.

Two commonly used drugs—anabolic steroids and marijuana—fall outside these four classifications. *Anabolic steroids,* which have legitimate medical uses, are synthetic derivatives of testosterone that are taken in pill form or by injection. Because they are thought to increase muscle mass and strength when combined with weight-bearing exercise, they are often used illegally by athletes and bodybuilders. As reports of use by high school and even junior high school athletes have surfaced, concern about these drugs has grown. Numerous negative physical effects have been reported, including heart and liver disease, decreased testicular size, and erection problems (Pope & Katz, 1992). Whether anabolic steroids are psychoactive, however, is still an open question. There have been anecdotal and clinical reports both of positive psychological effects (increased sex drive, increased confidence, reduced fatigue during training) and of negative ones (increased aggression, irritability, anxiety, and even psychosis) (Lombardo & Sickles, 1992; Moss, Panzak, & Tarter, 1993; Pope & Katz, 1992; Yates, Perry, & Murray, 1992). However, to date only a few studies on the effects of anabolic steroids have been done, and many of these studies have used questionable sampling strategies or have relied on unverified self-reports (Bahrke, Yesalis, & Wright, 1990; Thompson, Zmuda, & Catlin, 1993). Because

■ **depressants**
Drugs that slow down activity in the central nervous system.

■ **opiates**
Drugs, derived from the opium poppy, that relieve pain and commonly produce euphoria.

■ **psychedelic drugs**
Consciousness-altering drugs that produce hallucinations, change thought processes, or disrupt the normal perception of time and space.

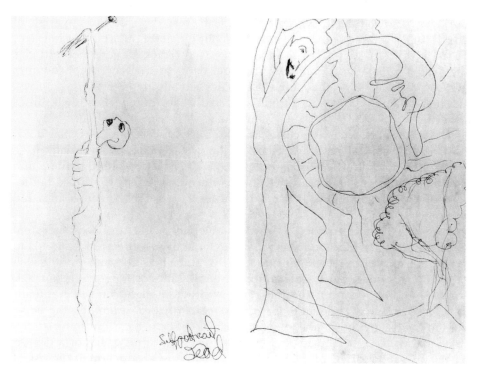

An LSD "trip" may be a ticket to agony or ecstasy. Both of these drawings were done while under the influence of the drug.

of such methodological problems, no firm conclusions can yet be drawn about the physical or psychological effects of these drugs.

Marijuana ("pot," "skunk," "weed"), which is smoked or, less commonly, eaten in foods such as brownies, is probably the most widely used illicit drug in the United States. Some researchers classify it as a mild psychedelic, but others feel that its chemical makeup and its psychological effects place it outside the major classifications. The active ingredient in marijuana is tetrahydrocannabinol (THC), derived from the hemp plant, *Cannabis sativa*. In some respects, THC appears to be a mild stimulant, increasing heart rate and making tastes, sounds, and colors seem more intense. But users report reactions ranging from mild euphoria to relaxation, or even sleepiness. Time often seems to go by slowly. In moderate doses, marijuana can interfere with the transfer of information to long-term memory, a characteristic it shares with alcohol. In large doses, it can cause hallucinations and a sense of unreality. Some studies also find that the drug impairs coordination, concentration, visual perception, and reaction times, though it is not clear how long these effects last.

The Physiology of Drug Effects

Psychoactive drugs produce their effects primarily by acting on brain neurotransmitters, the substances that carry messages from one nerve cell to another. Some psychoactive drugs cause more or fewer neurotransmitter molecules to be released at a synapse. Others prevent the reabsorption ("reuptake") of a neurotransmitter after its release. Still others block the effects of a neurotransmitter on a receiving nerve cell or bind to receptors that would ordinarily be triggered by a neurotransmitter or a neuromodulator. Figure 5.5 shows how one drug, cocaine, increases the amount of norepinephrine and dopamine in the brain by blocking the reabsorption of these substances.

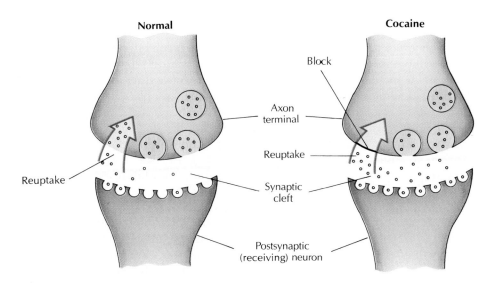

Figure 5.5 Cocaine's Effect on the Brain

Cocaine blocks the ability of brain cells to reabsorb the neurotransmitters dopamine and norepinephrine, so levels of these substances rise. The result is overstimulation of certain brain circuits and a brief euphoric "high." Then, when the drug wears off, a depletion of dopamine may cause the user to "crash," and become sleepy and depressed.

Such biochemical changes in the brain can have cognitive and emotional effects. For example, because of alcohol's effect on parts of the brain involved in judgment, drinkers often are unable to gauge their own competence. Even moderate amounts of alcohol can affect perception, response time, coordination, and balance, despite the drinker's own impression of unchanged or even improved performance (Poley, Lea, & Vibe, 1979). Liquor also affects memory, possibly by interfering with the work of the neurotransmitter serotonin. Information stored before a drinking session remains intact during the session but is retrieved more slowly (Stempel, Beckwith, & Petros, 1986). The ability to store new memories for later use also suffers, even after two or three drinks (Parker, Birnbaum, & Noble, 1976). Consuming small amounts does not seem to affect *sober* mental performance, but even occasional heavy drinking impairs later abstract thought. In other words, a Saturday night binge is more dangerous than a daily drink.

Animal studies suggest that repeated use of certain drugs, including *designer drugs* (potent synthetic chemicals that are easy to concoct and modify), are capable of causing permanent brain damage. For example, the drug "Ecstasy" (MDMA) may permanently damage cells that produce serotonin (Ricaurte et al., 1988). The dosages in animal studies, however, have been enormous, and the generalizability of such findings to human beings remains highly controversial. Some researchers have concluded that there is no evidence that *light or moderate* use of recreational drugs can cause enough brain damage in humans to affect cognitive functioning, although all agree that heavy or frequent use of any drug is another matter (see Chapter 15).

The use of some psychoactive drugs, such as heroin and tranquilizers, leads to **tolerance:** As time goes by, more and more of the drug is needed to get the same effect. When habitual heavy users stop taking a drug (whether it causes tolerance or not), they may suffer severe **withdrawal symptoms,** such as nausea, abdominal cramps, muscle spasms, depression, and sleep problems, depending on the drug. Tolerance and withdrawal are often assumed to be purely physiological matters, but in Chapter 7, we will see that learning also plays a role.

▪ **tolerance**
Increased resistance to a drug's effects accompanying continued use; as tolerance develops, larger doses are required to produce effects once brought about by smaller ones.

▪ **withdrawal symptoms**
Physical and psychological symptoms that occur when someone addicted to a drug stops taking it.

The Psychology of Drug Effects

✳   *One person takes a drink and flies into a rage. Another has a drink and "mellows out." What qualities of the user rather than the drug might account for this difference?*

People often talk about the effects of a drug as if such effects were automatic, the inevitable result of the drug's chemistry ("I couldn't help what I said; the booze made me do it"). But reactions to a psychoactive drug involve more than the drug's chemical properties. When people take an opiate such as heroin or morphine recreationally, for example, they usually get high. Yet when people take opiates to relieve chronic and incapacitating pain, the narcotics do *not* make them high or addicted; they just remove the pain (Portenoy, 1994). So if we want to understand drugs, we must know more than their biochemistry. Drug responses also depend on a person's physical condition, experience with the drug, environmental setting, and mental set:

1. *Physical condition* includes body weight, individual tolerance for the drug, and initial state of arousal. A drug may have a different effect after a tiring day than after a rousing quarrel. It may also affect a person differently at one time of the day than at another because of the body's circadian rhythms.

2. *Experience with the drug* refers to the number of times the drug has been used and the levels of past usage. Trying a drug—a cigarette, an alcoholic drink, a stimulant—for the first time is often a neutral or unpleasant experience. But reactions may change once a person has become familiar with the drug's effects.

3. *Environmental setting* greatly affects an individual's response to a drug. Setting is the reason that a person can have one glass of wine at home alone and feel sleepy but have three glasses of wine at a party and feel full of pep. It is the reason that a person might feel happy and high drinking with good friends but fearful and nervous drinking with strangers.

4. *Mental set* refers to expectations about the drug's effects, the reasons for taking the drug, and whether a person wants to justify some behavior by being "under the influence." Some people drink to become more sociable, friendly, or seductive; others drink in order to have an excuse for verbal abusiveness or physical violence.

People are often unaware of the effects of mental set when they try to explain behavior that occurs "under the influence." For example, because so many crimes of violence are committed when the participants have been drinking and because so many marital quarrels accompany drinking, alcohol is often assumed to "release" anger and aggression. Indeed, about half of all men arrested for assaulting their wives claim to have been drinking at the time. Yet

The motives for using a drug, expectations about its effects, and the setting in which it is used all contribute to a person's reactions to the drug.

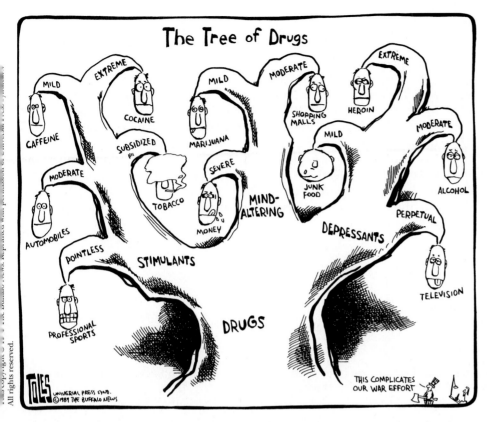

This cartoon, which pokes fun at the things people do to alter consciousness and make themselves feel better, reminds us that many stimulants and depressants are neither chemical nor illegal.

research finds that most of these men do not have enough alcohol in their bloodstreams to qualify as legally intoxicated, and most have not been drinking immediately prior to being violent (Gelles & Straus, 1988). This finding suggests that alcohol does not "make" these men violent, but rather that *their use of alcohol provided an excuse to behave violently.* Similarly, a recent meta-analysis of experimental studies found that alcohol increases the likelihood of aggressive behavior, but *not on its own:* People must be aware that they are consuming liquor (Bushman, 1993). The link between alcohol and aggression fades when people believe they will be held responsible for their actions while drunk (Critchlow, 1983).

Such research suggests that the real source of aggression is not in the alcohol but in the mind of the drinker. During the 1980s, several studies identified a "think–drink" effect by comparing people who were *actually* drinking liquor (vodka and tonic) with those who *thought* they were drinking liquor but were actually getting only tonic and lime juice. (Vodka has a subtle taste, and most people cannot tell the real and phony drinks apart.) Men behaved more belligerently when they thought they were drinking vodka than when they thought they were drinking plain tonic water, regardless of the actual content of the drinks. Both sexes reported feeling sexually aroused when they thought they were drinking vodka, whether they actually got vodka or not (Abrams & Wilson, 1983; Marlatt & Rohsenow, 1980).

None of this means that alcohol and other drugs are merely placebos; drugs do have physiological effects, many of them quite powerful. However, people must learn from their culture how to interpret these effects and how to behave when they occur. Most Americans start their day with a cup of coffee because it increases alertness. But when coffee was first introduced in Europe, there were protests against it. Women said it suppressed their husbands' sexual performance and made men inconsiderate, and maybe it did! In the nineteenth century, Americans regarded marijuana as a mild sedative with no "mind-altering" properties. They didn't expect it to give them a high, and it didn't; it merely put them to sleep (Weil, 1972/1986). Today's marijuana is more potent, but motives for using it have also changed, and these changes have no doubt affected how people respond to the drug's physiological effects.

Because the consequences of drug *abuse* are so devastating to individuals and to society, it is often difficult for people to think critically about drug *use*. (Drug abuse and addiction are discussed further in Chapter 15.) In "Think About It," we discuss the implications of research on drugs for social policy and personal choice.

*T*hink About It

*W*hat Should We Do About Drugs—and Which Drugs?

■ Debates about drug policy are typically framed by two extreme positions. At one extreme, some people cannot accept evidence that their favorite drug—such as coffee, tobacco, alcohol, or marijuana—might have harmful effects. At the other extreme, some people cannot accept the evidence that their most hated drug—such as alcohol, morphine, or the coca leaf—might not be dangerous in all forms or amounts, and might even have some beneficial effects. People often confuse extremely potent drugs with others that have only subtle effects or are safe in moderate amounts. They fail to distinguish light or moderate use of a drug from heavy or excessive use.

All societies draw a line between legal drugs that are considered "good" and illegal drugs that are considered "bad," but this distinction is usually made without any medical or biological basis (Gould, 1990; Weil, 1972/1986). As a result, some odd situations have occurred. For example, in the United States, methadone is a legal controlled substitute for heroin, yet both drugs are opiates. As Stephen Jay Gould (1990) observes, to say that methadone blocks the craving for heroin is like saying that a Coke blocks the craving for a Pepsi. Nicotine, which of course is legal, is as addictive as heroin and cocaine, which are illegal; and tobacco use contributes to more than 400,000 deaths in the United States every year, about 20 times the number of deaths from all other forms of drug use combined (McGinnis & Foege, 1993). Narcotics, which can devastate the lives of addicts, permit people with chronic pain to live productive, pain-free lives (Portenoy, 1994); but because narcotics are illegal, the people who most need them are often deprived

of them or are treated as "addicts" if they do use them.

The line between legal and illegal drugs is therefore an arbitrary one, drawn for social, economic, and cultural reasons. But once drawn, the line comes to be regarded as inevitable. When former Surgeon General Jocelyn Elders suggested, in 1993, that perhaps it would be worth studying the possibility of legalizing the drugs that many addicts commit theft or murder to get, her suggestion was met with waves of outrage. Once a drug is declared illegal, it seems, many people assume it is deadly even though some legal drugs are more dangerous than illegal ones.

Consider, for example, research on marijuana. In the 1970s, a research team studied a group of working-class Costa Rican men who had smoked an average of almost 10 marijuana cigarettes ("joints") daily for 17 years. They found no significant physical or psychological differences between these men and a matched group of nonusers. Years later, another team restudied some of the same men. On tests that had been used earlier, the marijuana users showed no evidence of deterioration, although the men had now been smoking for 30 years. On three *new* tests of sustained attention, organizing skills, and short-term memory, the users did do worse than the control subjects, but the differences were subtle (Page, Fletcher, & True, 1988).

Are you more impressed by these men's normal performance on the old tests or by their somewhat inferior performance on the new tests? Those who are worried about marijuana's effects emphasize the latter. In the United States and Canada, they point out, even slight impairment of performance might

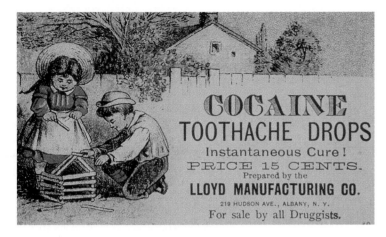

Before its sale was banned in the 1920s, cocaine was widely touted as a cure for everything from toothaches to timidity. The drug found its way into teas, tonics, throat lozenges, and even soft drinks (including, briefly, Coca-Cola, which derived its name from the coca plant). Ingesting it had a less powerful effect than sniffing, injecting, or smoking it, as is done today. However, as cocaine use became associated in the popular mind with criminality and as concerns about abuse grew, public opinion turned against it.

be troublesome because many people hold jobs requiring mental exertion and alertness. Others, however, note that very few Americans or Canadians smoke 10 joints a day for 30 years. Moreover, the slight deficits that were observed in Costa Rica could have been due to the temporary effects of recent smoking and not to any permanent effects of long-term use. The subjects were asked to abstain from smoking for two days before being tested, but it can take days or even weeks for the body to rid itself of THC.

Heavy, prolonged use of marijuana does pose some physical dangers, including lung damage when the drug is smoked (Wu et al., 1988). However, when used occasionally and in moderation, marijuana is less harmful than cigarettes or alcohol—unless, of course, it is mixed with other, hazardous drugs. It's true that much of the marijuana now available on the street has far greater concentrations of THC than it did a generation ago. But advocates point out that users have adjusted to this change by smoking less of the drug—just as a person might choose to drink one potent martini instead of two less potent vodka tonics (Danish, 1994).

In their book *Marihuana, the Forbidden Medicine,* psychiatrist Lester Grinspoon and James Bakalar (1993) review the evidence of marijuana's medical benefits: It reduces the nausea and vomiting that often accompany chemotherapy treatment for cancer and AIDS (acquired immune deficiency syndrome); it reduces the physical tremors, loss of appetite, and other symptoms caused by multiple sclerosis; it helps reduce the frequency of seizures in some epileptic patients; and it alleviates the retinal swelling caused by glaucoma. Critics reply that most of these claims have not been validated with controlled studies, but apparently the medical benefits of marijuana are known to many physicians. In a survey of 1,035 cancer specialists, half said they would prescribe marijuana if it were legal, and 44 percent had already recommended its illegal use to their patients (Doblin & Kleiman, 1991).

Some people are committed to the eradication of all illegal drugs, and some think that all drugs should be decriminalized. Others are more selective: They would legalize narcotics for people who are in chronic pain; they would legalize marijuana for recreational and medicinal use; but they would ban tobacco. Still others think that people who use drugs should not be punished, but that social policies should regulate the location of drug use (never at work, for example); that addicts should be treated in clinics rather than imprisoned; and that educational policy should encourage people to avoid drugs for their health—in short, the current approach to cigarette smoking. Andrew Weil, a physician who has been an outspoken critic of the war on drugs, nevertheless strongly advises people "to satisfy their [psychological] needs without using drugs at all" (Goldstein, 1980).

Where, given the research findings, do you stand on the drug debate? Given the near universality of drug use, is total prohibition of all drugs the answer? Which drugs, if any, should be prohibited? How might we create mental sets and environmental settings that promote safe recreational use of some drugs, minimize the likelihood of drug abuse, and permit the medicinal use of beneficial drugs? What do you think? ■

Quick QUIZ

A. See whether you can name the following:

1. An illegal stimulant
2. Two drugs that interfere with the formation of new long-term memories
3. Three types of depressant drugs
4. A legal "recreational" drug that acts as a depressant on the central nervous system
5. Four factors that influence a person's psychological reactions to a drug

 B. A bodybuilder who has been illegally taking anabolic steroids says the drugs make him more aggressive. What are some other possible interpretations?

Answers:

A. 1. cocaine; also some amphetamines **2.** marijuana and alcohol **3.** barbiturates, tranquilizers, and alcohol **4.** alcohol **5.** the person's physical condition, prior experience with the drug, mental set, and the environmental setting **B.** The bodybuilder's increased aggressiveness may be due to his expectations (a placebo effect); bodybuilding itself may increase aggressiveness; the culture of the body-building gym may encourage aggressiveness; other influences in the person's life (or other drugs he is taking) may be making him more aggressive; or he may only *think* he is more aggressive, and his behavior may contradict his self-perceptions.

■ THE RIDDLE OF HYPNOSIS

Hypnosis is usually defined as a heightened state of suggestibility or responsiveness. It is *not* sleep; brain waves during hypnosis are similar to those of ordinary wakefulness. The person almost always remains fully aware of what is going on and remembers the experience later, unless explicitly instructed to forget it. Even then, the memory can be restored by a prearranged signal. To induce hypnosis, the hypnotist typically suggests that the person being hypnotized feels relaxed, is getting sleepy, and feels the eyelids getting heavier and heavier. In a singsong or monotonous voice, the hypnotist assures the subject that he or she is sinking "deeper and deeper" but not actually falling asleep. Sometimes the hypnotist has the person concentrate on a color or a small object, or on certain bodily sensations. Some people can be hypnotized while they are doing something active, such as riding a bicycle (Bányai & Hilgard, 1976).

People who have been hypnotized report that the focus of attention turns outward, toward the hypnotist's voice. The experience is sometimes likened to total absorption in a good book, a play, or a favorite piece of music. People who can easily become absorbed in such activities, who can suspend ordinary reality and become involved in the world of imagination, make good hypnotic subjects (J. R. Hilgard, 1979; Nadon et al., 1991). Children are generally easier to hypnotize than adults, who often have learned to be wary of fantasy and are unwilling to suspend ordinary perceptions of reality. However, most people have at least some ability to respond to hypnotic suggestions, and even those who do not can be trained to be more hypnotizable (Gorassini & Spanos, 1986; Spanos, DuBreuil, & Gabora, 1991).

It is impossible to force hypnotized people to do things they do not want to do. An individual must *choose* to turn initiative over to the hypnotist and to cooperate with the hypnotist's suggestions (Lynn, Rhue, & Weekes, 1990). However, like psychoactive drugs, hypnosis can be used to justify letting go of

■ **hypnosis**
A condition in which attention is focused and a person is extremely responsive to suggestion.

inhibitions ("I know this looks silly, but after all, I'm hypnotized"). Hypnotized people may also do socially unacceptable things if they accept a suggestion that they are in an appropriate situation for doing so. They may take off their clothes if they are convinced they are in the shower or attack someone they are led to believe has killed one of their friends. In some cases, they have been willing to do something dangerous, like dipping their hand in what seems to be fuming acid (Orne & Evans, 1965).

Because hypnotic suggestions can affect perception, memory, and motivation, hypnosis has found many applications in medicine and psychology. It has been used effectively to treat headaches; anesthetize people undergoing dental work, surgery, or childbirth; eliminate unwanted habits such as smoking or nail biting; improve study skills; reduce nausea in cancer patients undergoing chemotherapy; and even pump up the confidence of athletes. Many studies have verified that it can reduce severe pain. In a typical experiment, a hypnotized volunteer places an arm in ice water for several seconds, then rates the pain. Normally, this is an excruciating experience. But when subjects are told that they will feel no pain, they report little or none, and they do not show any obvious signs of distress, such as groaning or grimacing. After the hypnotic session ends, they continue to deny that they felt pain (Hilgard & Hilgard, 1975).

Hypnosis as an Altered State

The traditional explanation of these findings is that hypnosis is a true altered state, different subjectively and objectively from normal wakefulness. Although hypnosis has not been consistently linked with predictable changes in brain waves, eye movements, skin resistance, or other physiological responses, Ernest Hilgard, who studied hypnosis for many years, has argued that such responses are not critical for concluding that hypnosis is different from ordinary waking consciousness. After all, he notes, scientists readily accepted the reality of dreams and the existence of sleep as a separate state before anyone knew about REM stages or EEG patterns.

Hilgard's own belief is that hypnosis is an altered state that involves *dissociation,* the split in consciousness that we mentioned when discussing lucid dreams (Hilgard, 1977, 1986). In dissociation, one part of the mind operates independently from another. In many hypnotized persons, says Hilgard, only one of the parts goes along with the hypnotic suggestion. The other part is like a *hidden observer,* watching but not participating. Unless given special instructions, the hypnotized person remains unaware of the observer.

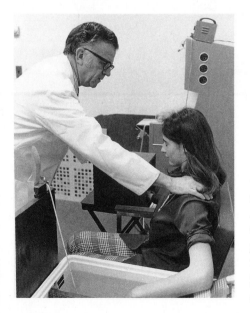

Ordinarily, a person whose arm is immersed in ice water feels intense pain. But Ernest Hilgard, a pioneer in hypnosis research, found that when hypnotized people are told the pain will be minimal they report little or no discomfort, and, like the young woman shown here in one of Hilgard's studies, they seem unperturbed.

In studies by Hilgard and his colleagues, the researchers attempted to question the hidden observer directly. For example, using the ice-water procedure, they told hypnotized subjects that although they would feel no pain, the nonsubmerged hand would be able to signal the level of any hidden pain by pressing a key. In this situation, many people said they felt little or no pain while at the same time their free hand was busily pressing one of the keys. After coming "out" of hypnosis, these people continued to insist that they were pain free—unless the hypnotist suggested that the hidden observer would be able to issue a separate report.

One appealing aspect of the altered-state explanation is that it fits in well with recent research on nonconscious mental processing (see Chapters 6 and 8). It is also consistent with recent brain theories, which propose that one part of the brain operates as an interpreter and reporter of activities carried out unconsciously by other brain parts (see Chapter 4). Nevertheless, many psychologists believe that there is less to the hypnotic trance than meets the eye. Theodore Barber has noted that there is no truly objective way to verify that the hypnotized person is in such a state (Barber, 1979; Barber & Wilson, 1977). In fact, the very notion of a hypnotic state is circular: How do we know that a person is hypnotized? Because he or she obeys the hypnotist's suggestions. And why does the person obey those suggestions? Because the person is hypnotized!

It's true, say the critics, that hypnosis *looks* like an altered state: There are the drooping eyelids, the fixed gaze, the slumped posture. However, hypnosis does not always involve these bodily reactions, and besides, most hypnotized subjects know from films or nightclub acts how a hypnotized person is *supposed* to behave. Moreover, claims about the powers of hypnosis are often overblown or poorly supported. For example, studies on how hypnotic suggestions might bolster the immune system have lacked good controls, and when proper procedures are used, the effects tend to disappear (Stam, 1989).

Most important, all the apparently astounding things that people do while hypnotized can also be done in the waking state, *if* people are sufficiently motivated and *if* they believe they can succeed (Spanos, 1986). For example, when a stage hypnotist has a hypnotized person stretch out rigid as a plank between two chairs, with the head on the back of one chair and ankles on the back of another, nothing special is actually occurring. Most unhypnotized people can do the same thing; they only think they can't. Although hypnotic suggestions sometimes lead to feats of great strength, pain reduction, hallucinations, and

Amazing, right? Or maybe not. Although the chair trick is a staple of the stage hypnotist's repertoire, most unhypnotized people can do it, too. The only way to find out if hypnosis produces unique results is to do research with control groups.

even the disappearance of warts, there is impressive evidence that suggestion alone, without the special procedures of hypnosis, can produce exactly the same results, so long as people are encouraged to relax, concentrate, and do their best (e.g., Chaves, 1989; Spanos, Stenstrom, & Johnson, 1988). Then what, exactly, is going on during hypnosis?

Hypnosis as a Social-Cognitive Process

A second leading view holds that hypnosis is explainable in terms of normal social and cognitive processes. For many years, Theodore Sarbin and his colleagues have argued that the hypnotized person is basically *playing the part* of a hypnotized person, a part that has analogies in ordinary life, where we willingly submit to the suggestions of parents, teachers, doctors, therapists, and television commercials (Coe & Sarbin, 1977; Sarbin, 1991). The person is not merely faking or playacting, however; the role of hypnotized person, like many other social roles, is so engrossing and involving that actions required by the role may occur without conscious intent. Thus a person who has been instructed to fake hypnosis to fool an observer will tend to overplay the role and will stop playing it as soon as the observer leaves the room, whereas hypnotized subjects will continue to follow the hypnotic suggestions even when they think they are not being watched (Kirsch et al., 1989; Spanos et al., 1993).

Sometimes, objective tests can penetrate the hypnotic role. Imagine that a person has been given a hypnotic suggestion to become deaf until she receives a tap on the shoulder. The suggestion seems to work; even the crash of cymbals behind her back fails to get her attention or startle her. But then the researcher has the subject participate in a procedure called *delayed auditory feedback*. As she reads a paragraph aloud, her words are recorded and played back to her through earphones with half a second delay. People with normal hearing respond to delayed auditory feedback with stuttering, slurring, and hesitation. They speak more loudly than usual and mispronounce words. (The same thing can happen when a bad long-distance telephone connection produces an echo of your own voice.) Studies have shown that hypnotized subjects, though apparently deaf to their own voices, will respond in exactly the same way as would a hearing person (Barber, 1979). Therefore, they must be able to hear.

But why don't they realize that they can hear? Research on a related phenomenon, "hypnotic blindness," suggests that hypnotized people use *active cognitive strategies* to experience what the hypnotist tells them to experience. They do not merely focus on the hypnotist's words; they try their best to meet the demands of the hypnotic setting. For example, when shown a page with a word on it, a person told to be "blind" may think of a white curtain coming down over the page and then believe that he or she is not seeing the word (Bryant & McConkey, 1990). Such findings have led many researchers to think of hypnosis as a social-cognitive process in which the person uses imagination in an attempt to comply with the hypnotist's suggestions.

What about the frequent claim that under hypnosis, people can actually relive a childhood event or recall a long forgotten experience? Stage hypnotists, "past-lives channelers," and some psychotherapists have reported dramatic performances by people who have been "age-regressed" to earlier years or even earlier centuries. A few therapists claim that hypnosis has helped their patients recall alleged abductions by extraterrestrials (Fiore, 1989). They make the assumption that any memory recovered by hypnosis must be accurate. But is that true?

Michael Nash (1987), who reviewed six decades of scientific studies on hypnotic age regression, found that when people are regressed to an earlier age, their mental and moral performance remains "essentially adult in nature."

Under hypnosis, Jim cheerfully describes the chocolate cake at his fourth birthday and Joan remembers a former life as a twelfth-century French peasant. As it turns out, lemon cake was served at Jim's birthday, and Joan can't speak twelfth-century French. What are some possible explanations of these vivid "memories"?

Their brain-wave patterns and reflexes do not become childish; they do not show any signs of outgrown emotional disorders; they do not reason as children do or show child-sized IQs. Nor does hypnosis reliably improve memory for specific early experiences, even though hypnotized people often swear that it does. In one of Nash's own studies, hypnotized subjects tried to recall what their favorite comforting object was at age 3 (teddy bears, blankets, and the like). Only 23 percent were accurate, compared to 70 percent of a nonhypnotized control group! (Mothers independently verified the accuracy of these memories.)

It is true, Nash says, that people undergo dramatic changes in behavior and subjective experience when they are hypnotically regressed; they may use baby talk or report that they feel 4 years old again. But the reason is not that they *are* 4; they are just willing to play the role. They will do the same when they are hypnotically *progressed* ahead—say, to age 70 or 80—or regressed to "past lives." Their belief that they are 7 or 70 or 7,000 years old may be sincere and convincing, but it is based on an elaborate fantasy and role playing. Unfortunately, some psychotherapists who use hypnosis are unaware of this finding. When Michael Yapko (1993, 1994), a clinical psychologist who uses hypnosis in his own practice, surveyed 869 members of the American Association of Marriage and Family Therapists, he discovered that more than half believed, despite all the evidence to the contrary, that "hypnosis can be used to recover memories from as far back as birth."

In a fascinating series of studies that dramatically demonstrated how false memories can be constructed under hypnosis, Nicholas Spanos and his colleagues (1991) directed hypnotized Canadian university students to regress past their own birth to a previous life. About a third of the students reported they could do so. But when they were asked, while supposedly "reliving" a past life, to name the leader of their country, say whether the country was at peace or at war, or describe the money used in their community, the students could not do it. One young man, who thought he was Julius Caesar, said the year was 50 A.D. and he was emperor of Rome—but Caesar died in 44 B.C. and was never crowned emperor (and besides, dating years as A.D. or B.C. did not begin until several centuries later).

This cartoon is funny because it reminds us that people who report "past lives" never seem to recall an average, ordinary existence. Why do so many think they were emperors, courtesans, crusaders, or priestesses?

In these studies, all of the students who believed they were reliving a past life were actually weaving events, places, and persons from their present lives into their accounts. Their descriptions and their acceptance of their regression experiences as "real" were also influenced by what the hypnotist told them. The researchers concluded that the act of "remembering" another "self" involves the construction of a fantasy that accords not only with one's own beliefs but also the beliefs of others.

A similar process occurs when people under hypnosis report spirit possession or "memories" of alien abductions (Baker, 1992; Dawes, 1994). Such persons may have a need to "escape the self" by turning control over to someone else (Newman & Baumeister, 1994). Often, the hypnotist readily assumes such control, shaping the person's story by giving subtle and not-so-subtle hints about what the person should say. Here is an exchange between one therapist who believes in UFO abductions and a supposed abductee who has been hypnotized (from Fiore, 1989, quoted, in Newman & Baumeister, 1994):

> **Dr. Fiore:** Now I'm going to ask you a few questions at this point. You will remember everything because you want to remember. When you were being poked everywhere, did they do any kind of vaginal examination?
>
> **Sandi:** I don't think they did.
>
> **Dr. Fiore:** Now you're going to let yourself know if they put a needle in any part of your body, other than the rectum.
>
> **Sandi:** No. They were carrying needles around, big ones, and I was scared for a while they were going to put one in me, but they didn't. [*Body tenses.*]
>
> **Dr. Fiore:** Now just let yourself relax. At the count of three you're going to remember whether they did put one of those big needles in you. If they did, know that you're safe, and it's all over, isn't it. And if they didn't, you're going to remember that too, at the count of three. One . . . two . . . three.
>
> **Sandi:** They did.

Even under the best of circumstances, when the focus is an event from real life, people often find it hard to distinguish an authentic memory from their inferences about what might have happened (see Chapter 9). Under hypnosis, this natural tendency to confuse fact and speculation is increased by a desire to please the hypnotist and by the fact that hypnosis encourages fantasy and detailed images. When hypnosis is used to jog the memories of crime victims and trial witnesses, occasionally there is a happy ending. After the 1976 kidnapping of a busload of schoolchildren in Chowchilla, California, the bus driver was able under hypnosis to recall all but one of the license plate numbers on the kidnappers' car. That clue provided a breakthrough in the investigation. But in other cases, hypnotized witnesses, despite feeling confident about their memories, have been dead wrong. Although hypnosis does sometimes boost the amount of information recalled, it also increases *errors*, perhaps because hypnotized people are more willing than nonhypnotized people to guess, or because they mistake vividly imagined possibilities for actual memories (Dinges et al., 1992; Dywan & Bowers, 1983; Whitehouse et al., 1988). Because pseudomemories and errors are so common in hypnotically induced recall, the American Psychological Association and the American Medical Association oppose the use of "hypnotically refreshed" testimony in courts of law.

In sum, the preponderance of evidence casts doubt on the idea that hypnosis creates a unique, altered state of consciousness in which people can do extraordinary things, memories become sharper, or early experiences can be replayed with accuracy. But whatever hypnosis is, by studying it, psychologists can learn much about human suggestibility, the power of imagination, and the way we perceive the present and remember the past.

Quick QUIZ

A. True or false:

1. Most people are at least somewhat susceptible to hypnotic suggestions.
2. According to Hilgard, hypnosis is a state of dissociation involving a "hidden observer."
3. Hypnosis gives us special powers we do not ordinarily have.
4. Hypnosis reduces errors in memory.
5. Hypnotized people are entirely passive and play no active part in their behavior and thoughts.

B. Some people believe that hypnotic suggestions can bolster the immune system and even help cure cancer. However, findings on this issue, mostly case reports, are contradictory, and positive results have been hard to replicate (Stam, 1989). One therapist dismissed this problem by saying that a negative result just means that the hypnotist is untalented or lacks the right kind of personality. As a critical thinker, can you spot what's wrong with his reasoning? (Think back to the qualities of the ideal scientist discussed in Chapter 2.)

Answers:

A. 1. true 2. true 3. false 4. false 5. false B. The therapist's argument violates the principle of falsifiability. If a result is positive, he counts it as evidence. But if a result is negative, he refuses to count it as counterevidence ("Maybe the hypnotist just wasn't good enough"). With this kind of reasoning, there is no way to tell whether the hypothesis is right or wrong.

As we have seen in this chapter, changes in consciousness, however they are initiated, allow us to explore how our expectations and explanations of behavior affect what we do and how we feel. States of consciousness are interesting in and of themselves. And under scientific scrutiny, hypnosis, drug-induced states, dreams, and biological rhythms—phenomena once thought beyond the pale of science—can also deepen our understanding of the intimate relationship between body and mind.

---

*T*aking Psychology with You

How to Get a Good Night's Sleep

You hop into bed, turn out the lights, close your eyes, and wait for slumber. An hour later, you're still waiting. Finally you drop off, but at 3:00 A.M., to your chagrin, you're awake again. By the time the rooster crows, you have put in a hard day's night.

Insomnia affects most people at one time or another—and many people most of the time. In search of relief, Americans spend hundreds of millions of dollars each year on sleeping aids. Usually, their money is not well spent. Over-the-counter pills are almost worthless for inducing sleep, and some prescription drugs can actually make matters worse. Barbiturates greatly suppress REM sleep, a result that eventually causes wakefulness, and they also suppress stages 3 and 4, the deeper stages of sleep. Other medications, known as benzodiazepines, lead to tolerance more slowly, but they produce a breakdown product that stays in the body during the day and causes diminished alertness and hand–eye coordination problems (Kelly, 1981a). Most physicians prescribe sleeping remedies for only very short periods of time. Said one well-known sleep researcher, "Let me put a person on sleeping pills for a month, and I'll guarantee broken sleep" (Webb, quoted in Goleman, 1982). Studies of sleep suggest better alternatives:

- *Be sure you actually have a sleep problem.* Many people only *think* they don't sleep well. People complaining of insomnia often greatly overestimate how long it takes them to nod off and underestimate how much sleep they actually get (Bonnet, 1990). In one study, 55 people reporting for help at a sleep clinic were observed for several nights in the laboratory. Most took less than 30 minutes to fall asleep. Only 30 got less than 6½ hours of sleep per night, and only 26 were awake more than 30 minutes total during the night (Carskadon, Mitler, & Dement, 1974).

  The amount of time spent sleeping is not a good criterion of insomnia in any case. Many people need more than the standard eight hours of sleep, and some research suggests that most of us would be more alert during the day if we could sleep longer at night (Dement, 1992; Roehrs et al., 1989). On the other hand, some people get by on as little as three or four hours. As people age, they typically sleep more lightly, and they often break up sleep into nighttime slumber and an afternoon nap. Young people, too, can benefit from napping, which many researchers feel is biologically beneficial. The real test for diagnosing a sleep deficit is how you feel during the day. Do you doze off without intending to? Do you feel drowsy at meetings or in class? If you function well with less sleep than most people get, you probably shouldn't worry about it, since worrying itself can cause insomnia (Lichstein & Fanning, 1990).

- *Get a correct diagnosis of the sleep problem.* Once you know you have a problem, you need to identify the cause. Disruption of sleep can result from psychological disturbances, such as depression, and from physical disorders. In *sleep apnea,* breathing periodically stops for a few moments, causing the person to choke and gasp. Breathing may stop hundreds of times a night, often without the person knowing it, and chronic apnea may lead to high blood pressure or irregular heartbeat. There are several causes of sleep apnea, from blockage of air passages to failure of the brain to control respiration correctly. In *narcolepsy,* another serious disorder, an individual is subject to irresistible and unpredictable daytime attacks of sleepiness lasting from 5 to 30 minutes. For reasons not yet clear, narcoleptics often lapse immediately into REM sleep, even during the briefest naps. Some researchers think that as many as a quarter of a million Americans may suffer from this condition, many without knowing it.

- *Avoid excessive use of alcohol or other drugs.* Many drugs interfere with sleep. Coffee, tea, cola, and chocolate all contain caffeine, which is a stimulant; alcohol suppresses REM sleep; and tranquilizers such as Valium and Librium reduce stage 4 sleep.

- *Don't associate the bedroom with wakefulness.* When environmental cues are repeatedly associated with some behavior, they can come to trigger the behavior (Bootzin, Epstein, & Wood, 1991). If you don't want your bedroom to trigger wakefulness, avoid reading, studying, and watching TV there. Also avoid lying awake for hours waiting for sleep, since your frustration will cause arousal that can be associated with the bedroom. If you can't sleep, get up and do something else, preferably something dull, in another room. When you feel drowsy, try sleeping again.

- *Take care of your health.* As your grandmother probably told you, good health habits are important for good sleep. Nutrition is one area to watch. The amino acid tryptophan promotes the onset of sleep, and there may be other dietary influences on alertness and relaxation. Exercise during the day also seems to enhance sleep, but it should be avoided right before bedtime because in the short term it heightens alertness.

Finally, because much if not most insomnia is related to anxiety and stress, it makes sense to get to the source of your problems. You can't expect to sleep well with adrenaline pouring through your bloodstream and worries crowding your mind. In an evolutionary sense, sleeplessness is an adaptive response to danger and threat. As Woody Allen once said, "The lamb and the lion shall lie down together, but the lamb will not be very sleepy." When your anxieties decrease, so may your sleepless nights.

Summary

1. *Consciousness* is the awareness of oneself and the environment. *States of consciousness* are distinct patterns of consciousness, and changes in these states are often associated with *biological rhythms*—periodic fluctuations in physiological functioning. *Circadian* fluctuations occur about once a day; *infradian*

fluctuations occur less often; and *ultradian* fluctuations occur more frequently than once a day, often on about a 90-minute cycle.

2. Circadian rhythms appear to be governed by biological clocks in the brain that seem to be linked to each other and to an overall coordinator in the hypothalamus. These rhythms are studied by allowing people to "free run." When volunteers live in isolation from all time cues, they typically live a "day" of about 25 hours. The hormone *melatonin* is responsive to changes in light and dark and appears to keep the body in phase with the light–dark cycle of the earth. In normal life, when a person's usual routine changes, the person may experience *internal desynchronization,* in which the usual circadian rhythms are thrown out of phase with one another.

3. Infradian rhythms of many types have been observed, including seasonal fluctuations in vulnerability to depression. However, it is hard to prove that they are endogenous—that is, that they originate within the body and are not due to social or cultural conventions or other external factors.

4. One infradian rhythm that is endogenous is the menstrual cycle, during which various hormones rise and fall predictably. Physical symptoms associated with the cycle usually have a biological cause. However, well-controlled (blind) studies on "PMS" do not support claims that emotional symptoms are reliably and universally tied to the menstrual cycle (or to the cessation of menstruation, *menopause*). Overall, women and men do not differ in the emotional symptoms they report or in the number of mood swings they experience over the course of a month. Expectations and learning affect how we interpret bodily and emotional changes. Few people of either sex are likely to undergo dramatic monthly mood swings or personality changes because of hormones.

5. Sleep, which recurs on a circadian rhythm, seems necessary not only for bodily restoration but also for normal brain function. During sleep, periods of *rapid eye movement,* or *REM,* alternate with non-REM sleep in an ultradian rhythm. Non-REM sleep is divided into four stages associated with certain brain-wave patterns. During REM sleep, the brain is active, and there are other signs of arousal, yet most of the skeletal muscles are limp; dreams are reported most often during REM sleep.

6. The *psychoanalytic explanation* of dreams is that they allow us to gratify forbidden or unrealistic wishes and desires that have been forced into the unconscious part of the mind. Thoughts and objects may be disguised as symbolic images that provide clues to the dream's meaning. Most psychologists today accept the notion that dreams are more than incoherent ramblings of the mind, but many psychologists quarrel with specific psychoanalytic interpretations.

7. The *problem-solving explanation* of dreams emphasizes the opportunity that dreams provide for working through emotional issues, especially during times of crisis. Findings on the dreams of divorced people provide support for this explanation.

8. The *information-processing explanation* of dreams views them as opportunities for mental housekeeping. According to this approach, sleep gives the brain an opportunity to scan and sort through new data; dreams are merely random snippets from an ongoing process that is otherwise inaccessible to consciousness. This explanation could explain why REM sleep occurs in human infants and in animals, who also need to "sort things out."

9. The *activation–synthesis theory* of dreaming holds that dreams occur when the cortex tries to make sense of spontaneous neural firing initiated in the pons. The resulting interpretation is a dream. In this view, dreams do not disguise unconscious wishes, but they can reveal a person's perceptions, conflicts, and concerns. The activation–synthesis theory is well developed, but not everyone agrees that the physiological evidence supports it, and alternative explanations of the evidence have been proposed.

10. In all cultures, people have found ways to produce *altered states of consciousness*. For example, *psychoactive drugs* alter the body's biochemistry, primarily by acting on neurotransmitters in the brain. Most psychoactive drugs are classified as *stimulants, depressants, opiates,* or *psychedelics,* depending on their central nervous system effects and their impact on behavior and mood. However, two common drugs, anabolic steroids and marijuana, fall outside these categories. The use of some psychoactive drugs leads to *tolerance,* in which increasing dosages are needed for the same effect, and *withdrawal symptoms* if an addict tries to quit.

11. The effects of a psychoactive drug cannot be explained solely in terms of its chemical properties. Reactions to a drug are also influenced by the user's physical condition, prior experience with the drug, environmental setting, and *mental set*—the person's expectations and motives for taking the drug. Public attitudes affect drug reactions and patterns of drug use.

12. *Hypnosis* is usually defined as a heightened state of suggestibility or responsiveness. Some researchers consider it to be an altered state that involves *dissociation,* a split in consciousness. Others regard it as a result of normal social and cognitive processes, a form of role-playing in which the role is so engrossing that the person interprets it as "real." These two interpretations can account for apparent age and past-life "regressions" and hypnotically induced "blindness" and "deafness." Hypnosis can sometimes improve memory, but the person's tendency to confuse fact with speculation is increased by a desire to please the hypnotist and by the fact that hypnosis encourages fantasy and detailed images; thus "hypnotically refreshed" memories are often full of errors. Like drug-induced states, dreams, and biological rhythms, hypnosis can shed light on the intricate relationship between body and mind.

Key Terms

consciousness *157*
states of consciousness *157*
biological rhythm *157*
endogenous *158*
circadian rhythm *158*
infradian rhythm *158*
ultradian rhythm *158*
free-running *160*
melatonin *160*
internal desynchronization *161*
menstrual cycle *162*
"premenstrual syndrome (PMS)" *163*
menopause *164*
rapid eye movement (REM) sleep *169*
non-REM sleep *169*
alpha waves *169*
delta waves *170*
lucid dreams *172*
dissociation *172*
psychoanalytic theory of dreams *172*

manifest/latent content of dreams *173*
problem-solving approach to dreams *173*
information-processing approach to dreams *174*
activation–synthesis theory of dreams *174*
altered states of consciousness *177*
psychoactive drug *177*
stimulants *178*
depressants *179*
opiates *179*
psychedelic drugs *179*
anabolic steroids *179*
marijuana *180*
tolerance *181*
withdrawal symptoms *181*
hypnosis *186*
hidden observer *187*
social-cognitive theory of hypnosis *189*

6

Sensation and Perception

Belgian artist René Magritte's The Human Condition *(1933) depicts the eerie and ambiguous boundary between illusion and reality and the fallible nature of perception.*

Minds that have nothing to confer
Find little to perceive.

■ WILLIAM WORDSWORTH ■

When he was only 10 months old, S. B. went blind. An infection damaged his corneas, the transparent membranes on the front surfaces of the eyes, leaving him sightless. As he grew into adulthood, S. B. adjusted well to his disability; a cheerful and independent man, he married, supported himself, and led an active life. But through the years, he continued to dream of regaining his sight.

At last, when S. B. was 52, a doctor successfully performed corneal transplant surgery. Almost as soon as the bandages were removed, S. B. was able to identify common objects and letters of the alphabet. Within days, he could make his way down corridors without touching the walls and could even tell time from a large wall clock. But there were also some strange gaps in his visual world. Although his eyes now functioned well, he seemed blind to objects or parts of objects that he had not previously touched. He could not read facial expressions well or recognize pictures of scenery. Gradually, his visual abilities improved, yet months after surgery his perception of the world remained limited and distorted by his previous sensory experiences. When asked to draw a bus, he produced the sketch in the margin—leaving out the front end, which he had never felt with his hands. In many ways, S. B. continued to lead the life of a blind man until his death three years after the operation (Gregory & Wallace, 1963).

S. B.'s story is an unusual one, but it contains some lessons for us all. Like S. B., we all depend on our senses for our everyday understanding of physical reality. Also like S. B., we have only a partial perception of that reality. Even with normal eyesight and hearing, we are blind to most of the electromagnetic energy waves around us and deaf to most of the pressure waves that fill the air. And because of expectations shaped by our previous experiences, even with normal sensory abilities, we may look but not see, listen but not hear.

Yet despite these limitations, our sensory and perceptual capacities are astonishingly complex and sensitive. In this chapter, you will learn both how your sense organs take in information from the environment and how your brain interprets and organizes that information to construct a reliable model of the world. The boundary between these two processes is not always easy to draw because they occur so quickly and because some organization occurs even before incoming signals reach the brain. However, as a way of conceptualizing what is going on, psychologists have traditionally called the first process *sensation* and the second *perception*.

Sensation is the detection and encoding of changes in physical energy caused by environmental or internal events. The cells that detect such changes are **sense receptors,** located in the *sense organs*—the eyes, ears, tongue, nose, skin, and internal body tissues. The receptors for smell, pressure, pain, and temperature are structural extensions (dendrites) of sensory neurons. The receptors for vision, hearing, and taste are distinct cells separated from sensory

■ **sensation**
The detection or direct experience of physical energy in the external or internal environment due to stimulation of receptors in the sense organs.

■ **sense receptors**
Specialized cells that convert physical energy in the environment to electrical energy that can be transmitted as nerve impulses to the brain.

neurons by synapses. The sensory processes made possible by these sense receptors produce an immediate awareness of sound, color, form, and other basic building blocks of consciousness. They tell us what is happening, both inside our bodies and in the world beyond our own skins.

Without sensation, we would lose touch—literally—with reality. Yet sensation alone is not sufficient for making sense of the world impinging on our senses; for that, we also need **perception,** the set of processes that organize and interpret sensory impulses. Perception tells us where one object begins and another ends, and assembles the building blocks of sensory experience into meaningful patterns. The sense of vision produces a two-dimensional image on the back of the eye, but we *perceive* the world in three dimensions. The sense of hearing brings us the sound of a C, an E, and a G played simultaneously on the piano, but we *perceive* a C-major chord.

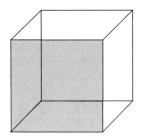

Look at the drawing of the cube in the margin. If you stare at the cube, it will flip-flop in front of your eyes. The surface on the outside and front will suddenly be on the inside and back, or vice versa. Sensory receptors at the back of your eyes detect black lines on a field of white, but because your brain can interpret the sensory image in alternative ways, you *perceive* two different cubes. The ambiguity is not in the picture but in the eye (actually, the brain) of the beholder. Something similar happens when you repeat certain speech sounds. Say the word "say" over and over again. "Say" will soon become "ace," and then "ace" will shift back to "say." The sound signal does not change, only your perception of it.

Psychologists study sensation and perception because together these processes are the foundation of learning, thinking, and acting. Much of the research in this area is of the "pure," or basic, sort. But knowledge about sensation and perception is often put to practical use—for example, in the design of color television sets, hearing aids, and robots that "see," "hear," and "feel," and in the training of flight controllers, astronauts, and others who must make important decisions based on what they sense and perceive.

■ OUR SENSATIONAL SENSES

At some point you probably learned that there are five senses corresponding to five sense organs: vision (eyes), hearing (ears), taste (tongue), touch (skin), and smell (nose). The senses have been categorized in this way at least since Aristotle's time. Actually, however, there are more than five senses, though scientists disagree about the exact number. The skin, which is the organ of touch or pressure, also senses heat, cold, and pain, not to mention itching and tickling. The ear, which is the organ of hearing, also contains receptors that account for a sense of balance. The internal muscles contain receptors responsible for a sense of bodily movement.

All of our senses evolved to help us survive. Even pain, which causes so much human misery, is an indispensable part of our evolutionary heritage, for it alerts us to illness and injury. In rare cases, people have been born without a sense of pain. Although free of the hurts and aches that plague the rest of us, they lead difficult lives. Because they feel none of pain's warnings, they burn, bruise, and cut themselves more than other people do. One young woman developed inflamed joints because she failed to turn over in her sleep or shift her weight while standing, acts that people with normal pain sensation perform automatically. At the age of only 29, she died from massive infections, due in part to skin and bone injuries (Melzack, 1973).

Sensory experiences contribute immeasurably to the quality of life, even when they are not directly helping us survive. They entertain us, amuse us, inspire us. If we really pay attention to our senses, said poet William Wordsworth, we can "see into the life of things" and hear "the still, sad music of humanity."

■ **perception**
The process by which the brain organizes and interprets sensory information.

The Riddle of Separate Sensations

Sensation begins with the sense receptors. When these receptors detect an appropriate stimulus—light, mechanical pressure, or chemical molecules—they convert the energy of the stimulus into electrical impulses that travel along nerves to the brain. This conversion of one form of energy into another is known as **transduction.** Sense receptors are biological transducers. Radio receivers, which convert radio waves into sound waves, are mechanical transducers, as are Geiger counters, television sets, and electronic eyes.

Sense receptors are like military scouts who scan the terrain for signs of activity and relay a message when they detect something. These scouts cannot make many decisions on their own. They must transmit what they learn to field officers—sensory neurons in the peripheral nervous system. The field officers in turn must report to generals at a command center—the cells of the brain. The generals are responsible for analyzing the reports, combining information brought in by different scouts, and deciding what it all means.

The "field officers" in the sensory system all use exactly the same form of communication, a neural impulse. It is as if they must all send their messages on a bongo drum and can only go "boom." How, then, are we able to experience so many different kinds of sensations? The answer is that the nervous system *encodes* the messages, using two basic kinds of code (Schneider & Tarshis, 1986). One kind, which is *anatomical,* was first described as far back as 150 A.D. by the Greek physician Galen, and was elaborated on in 1826 by the German physiologist Johannes Müller in his *doctrine of specific nerve energies.* According to this doctrine, different sensory modalities exist because signals received by the sense organs stimulate different nerve pathways, which terminate in different areas of the brain. Signals from the eye cause impulses to travel along the optic nerve to the visual cortex. Signals from the ear cause impulses to travel along the auditory nerve to the auditory cortex. Light and sound waves produce different sensations because of these anatomical differences.

Although some of the physiological details proposed by Müller have since been shown to be wrong, his fundamental concept is generally correct. The doctrine of specific nerve energies implies that what we know about the world ultimately reduces to what we know about the state of our own nervous system. Therefore, if sound waves could stimulate nerves that end in the visual part of the brain, we would "see" sound. In fact, a similar sort of crossover does occur when you close an eye, press lightly on the side of the lid, and "see" a flash of light. The pressure apparently produces an impulse that travels up the optic nerve to the visual area of the brain.

Anatomical encoding, however, does not completely solve the riddle of separate sensations. It accounts well for our ability to distinguish visual from auditory signals, but linking the different skin senses to distinct nerve pathways has proven difficult. The doctrine of specific nerve energies also fails to explain variations of experience within a particular sense—the sight of pink versus red, the sound of a piccolo versus the sound of a tuba, or the feel of a pinprick versus the feel of a kiss. An additional kind of code is therefore necessary.

This second kind of code has been called *functional* (Schneider & Tarshis, 1986). Functional codes rely on the fact that particular receptors and neurons fire, or are inhibited from firing, only in the presence of certain sorts of stimuli. At any particular time, then, some cells in the nervous system are firing, and some are not. Information about *which* cells are firing, *how many* cells are firing, the *rate* at which cells are firing, and the *patterning* of each cell's firing constitutes a functional code. You might think of such a code as the neurological equivalent of the Morse code. Functional encoding may occur all along a sensory route, starting in the sense organs and ending in the brain. As we will see, there is still a lot to learn about how functional encoding allows us to form an overall perception of an object.

■ **transduction**
The conversion of one form of energy to another; sensory receptors are biological transducers.

Measuring the Senses

Just how sensitive are our senses? The answer comes from the field of **psychophysics,** which is concerned with how the physical properties of stimuli are related to our psychological experience of them. Drawing on principles from both physics and psychology, psychophysicists have studied how the strength or intensity of a stimulus affects the strength of sensation in an observer.

Absolute Thresholds. One way to find out how sensitive the senses are is to present people with a series of weak signals, and ask them to say which ones they can detect. The smallest amount of energy that a person can detect reliably is known as the **absolute threshold.** The word *absolute* is a bit misleading, because people detect borderline signals on some occasions and miss them on others. "Reliable" detection is said to occur when a person can detect a signal 50 percent of the time.

If you were having your absolute threshold for brightness measured, you might be asked to sit in a dark room and look at a wall or screen. You would then be shown flashes of light varying in brightness. Your task would be to say whether you noticed a flash. Sometimes you would miss seeing a flash, even though you had noticed one of equal brightness on other trials. At other times, you would have a "false alarm," thinking that you saw a flash when there was none. Such errors seem to occur in part because of random firing of cells in the nervous system, which produces something like the background noise in a stereo system.

By studying absolute thresholds, psychologists have found that our senses are very sharp indeed. If you have normal sensory abilities, you can see a candle flame on a clear, dark night from 30 miles away. You can hear a ticking watch in a perfectly quiet room from 20 feet away. You can taste a teaspoon of sugar diluted in two gallons of water, smell a drop of perfume diffused through a

■ **psychophysics**
The area of psychology concerned with the relationship between physical properties of stimuli and sensory experience.

■ **absolute threshold**
The smallest quantity of physical energy that can be reliably detected by an observer.

*T*hink About It

*I*n Search of the Real World

■ Three baseball umpires were arguing about how to tell balls from strikes. The first said, "I calls 'em as I sees 'em." The second said, "I calls 'em as they is." The third said, "They ain't nothin' until I calls 'em!"

This old story raises an issue pondered by philosophers through the ages: Is reality "out there" in the environment or "in here" in a person's mind? Suppose a tree falls in the forest and there is no one around to hear the crash. Is there a noise? *Objectivists* say yes. They believe in the objective reality of a material world that exists completely apart from the perceiver. *Solipsists* (from the Latin words for "alone" and "self") say no. They argue that reality exists solely in the mind of the perceiver. For a solipsist, even the tree has no independent reality. Psychologists usually take the middle ground in this debate. They accept that there is a physical reality, that a falling tree disturbs air mole-

cules and produces pressure waves. But they also note that hearing, like all sensations, is a subjective experience, and so *noise* cannot be said to occur unless someone experiences it.

Because sensation is a subjective experience, our ideas about reality must be affected by our sensory abilities and limitations. That is, things appear to us as they do not only because of *their* nature but also because of *ours*. If the entire human race were totally deaf, we might still talk about pressure waves, but we would have no concept of sound. Similarly, if we were all completely color-blind, we might still talk about the wavelengths of light, but we would have no concept of color. The human way of sensing and perceiving the world is certainly not the only way. Because different species have different needs, their bodies are attuned to different aspects of physical reality. Bees are blind to red, but

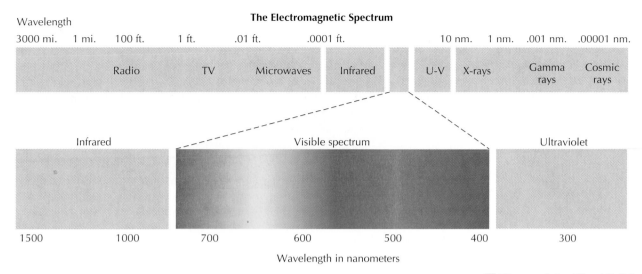

The Electromagnetic Spectrum

Wavelength

3000 mi.   1 mi.   100 ft.   1 ft.   .01 ft.   .0001 ft.   10 nm.   1 nm.   .001 nm.   .00001 nm.

| Radio | TV | Microwaves | Infrared | U-V | X-rays | Gamma rays | Cosmic rays |

Infrared   Visible spectrum   Ultraviolet

1500   1000   700   600   500   400   300

Wavelength in nanometers

■ **Figure 6.1 The Visible Spectrum of Electromagnetic Energy**

Our visual system detects only a small fraction of the electromagnetic energy around us.

three-room apartment, and feel the wing of a bee falling on your cheek from a height of 1 centimeter (Galanter, 1962).

Yet, despite these impressive sensory skills, our senses are tuned in to only a narrow band of physical energies. For example, as mentioned earlier, we are sensitive visually to only a tiny fraction of all electromagnetic energy (see Figure 6.1). Other species can pick up signals that we cannot. Dogs can detect high-frequency sound waves that are beyond our range, as you know if you have ever called your pooch with a "silent" doggie whistle. Bats and porpoises can hear sounds two octaves beyond our range. As we discuss in "Think About It," sensory differences among species raise some intriguing questions about the nature of reality.

they can see ultraviolet light, which merely gives human beings a sunburn. Because different parts of flowers reflect ultraviolet light at different rates, flowers that appear to us to be a single color must look patterned to a bee. Neither our perception nor the bee's is more "correct."

Some animal sensory systems seem to have no equivalent at all in human beings. Some snakes have an organ in a pit on the head that detects infrared rays. This organ permits them to sense heat given off by the bodies of their prey. The slightest change in temperature sends a message racing to the snake's brain. There the message is combined with information from the eyes, so that the snake actually sees an infrared pattern—and locates its prey with deadly accuracy even in the dark (Newman & Hartline, 1982). The sensory abilities of other animals, too, seem like something out of a science fiction story. For example, some fish apparently sense distortions of electrical fields through special receptors on the surface of their bodies (Kalmijn, 1982).

Our sensory windows on the world, then, are partly shuttered. But we can use reason, ingenuity, and technology to pry open those shutters. Ordinary perception tells us that the sun circles the earth, but the great astronomer Copernicus was able to figure out nearly five centuries ago that the opposite is true. Ordinary perception will never let us see ultraviolet and infrared rays directly (unless evolution or genetic engineering drastically changes the kind of organism we are), but we know they are there, and we can measure them.

If science can enable us to overturn the everyday evidence of our senses, who knows what surprises about "reality" are still in store for us? Think about it. ■

The sunflower on the left was photographed in normal light. The one on the right, photographed under ultraviolet light, is what a butterfly (equipped with ultraviolet receptors) might see. The bright spots are nectar sources, invisible to the naked eye of a human being.

Difference Thresholds.   Psychologists also study sensory sensitivity by having people compare two stimuli and judge whether they are the same or different. A subject might be asked to compare the weight of two blocks, the brightness of two lights, or the saltiness of two liquids. The smallest difference in stimulation that a person can detect reliably (again, half of the time) is called the **difference threshold,** or *just noticeable difference (jnd).* When you compare two stimuli, A and B, the difference threshold will depend on the intensity or size of A. The larger or more intense A is, the greater the change must be before you can detect a difference. If you are comparing the weights of two pebbles, you might be able to detect a difference of only a fraction of an ounce, but you would not be able to detect such a subtle difference if you were comparing two massive boulders.

According to **Weber's law** (named for Ernst Weber, who proposed it in the early 1800s), when a person compares two stimuli, the size of the change necessary to produce a jnd is a *constant proportion* of the original stimulus. Consider those pebbles and boulders again. Assume, for the sake of argument, that one pebble weighs 5 ounces, and you can just detect the difference between the two pebbles when the second one weighs one-tenth of an ounce more (one-fiftieth of 5 ounces). Assume, too, that the first massive boulder weighs 100 pounds. How much must the second boulder weigh in order for you to tell the difference? The answer is 102 pounds—an addition of one-fiftieth of 100 pounds, or 2 pounds. In both cases, the *proportion* of change necessary to produce the just noticeable difference is the same. Weber's law applies to stimuli in the midrange of many dimensions, from weight to smell. The value of the proportion depends on which dimension is being measured. For example, for you to perceive a change in loudness, the change must equal one-tenth of the original stimulus. In contrast, you can detect a change in the brightness of light when the change is equivalent to only one-sixtieth of the original stimulus.

In everyday life, we may sometimes think we can detect a difference between stimuli when we can't. For example, many people say they prefer one of the two leading colas to the other, and ads often capitalize on that claim. Years ago, as a class project, undergraduate students at Williams College put cola preference claims to the test. They presented tasters with three glasses of cola, two of one leading brand and one of the other (or vice versa), and asked them which drink they liked most and least. Each taster was given three trials. Most of the tasters were inconsistent in their preferences, indicating that they had trouble telling the two brands apart (Solomon, 1979). Apparently, the difference between the two tastes exceeded the students' difference thresholds.

Signal-Detection Theory.   Despite their usefulness, the procedures we have described for measuring sensory thresholds have a serious limitation. Measurements for any given individual may be affected by the person's general tendency, when uncertain, to respond, "Yes, I noticed a signal (or a difference)" or

■ **difference threshold**
The smallest difference in stimulation that can be reliably detected by an observer when two stimuli are compared; also called just noticeable difference (jnd).

■ **Weber's law**
A law of psychophysics stating that the change necessary to produce a just noticeable difference is a constant proportion of the original stimulus.

"No, I didn't notice anything." Some people are habitual yea-sayers, willing to gamble that the signal was really there. Others are habitual naysayers, cautious and conservative. In addition, motives and expectations can influence how a person responds on any given occasion. If you are in the shower and you're expecting an important call, you may think you heard the telephone ring when it didn't. In laboratory studies, when observers want to impress the experimenter, they may lean toward a positive response.

Fortunately, these problems of *response bias* are not insurmountable. According to **signal-detection theory,** an observer's response in a detection task can be divided into a *sensory process,* which depends on the intensity of the stimulus, and a *decision process,* which is influenced by the observer's response bias. There are methods for separating these two components. For example, the measurement of an absolute threshold includes some trials ("catch trials") in which no stimulus is presented and others in which a weak stimulus is presented. Yea-sayers will have more "hits" than naysayers when a weak stimulus is presented, but they will also have more "false alarms" when no stimulus is presented. As the number of catch trials increases, people in general will become more likely to say "nay." All this information can be fed into a mathematical formula that yields separate estimates of a person's response bias and sensory capacity. The individual's true sensitivity to a signal of any particular intensity can then be predicted.

The old method of measuring thresholds assumed that a person's threshold was determined entirely by the stimulus. Signal-detection theory assumes that the "threshold" depends on a decision actively made by the observer. Signal-detection methods have many real-world applications, from screening applicants for jobs requiring keen hearing to training air-traffic controllers, whose decisions about the presence or absence of a blip on a radar screen may mean the difference between life and death.

Sensory Adaptation

Variety, they say, is the spice of life. It is also the essence of sensation, for our senses are designed to respond to change and contrast in the environment (see Figure 6.2). When a stimulus is unchanging or repetitious, sensation fades or disappears. Receptors get "tired" and temporarily stop responding, or nerve cells higher up in the sensory system temporarily switch off. The resulting decline in

■ **signal-detection theory**
A psychophysical theory that divides the detection of a sensory signal into a sensory process and a decision process.

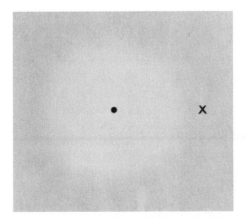 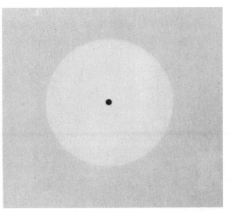

■ Figure 6.2   Now You See It, Now You Don't

Sensation depends on change and contrast in the environment. Hold your hand over one eye and stare steadily at the dot in the middle of the circle on the right. You should have no trouble maintaining an image of the circle. However, if you do the same with the circle on the left, the image will fade. The gradual change from light to dark does not provide enough contrast to keep the visual receptors in your eye firing at a steady rate. The circle only reappears if you close and reopen your eye or if you shift your gaze to the X.

sensory responsiveness is called **sensory adaptation.** You know that adaptation has occurred when you can no longer feel your watch on your wrist, or you no longer smell a gas leak that you noticed when you first entered the kitchen.

We never completely adapt to extremely intense stimuli—a terrible toothache, the odor of ammonia, the heat of the desert sun. And we rarely adapt completely to visual stimuli, whether they are weak or intense. Eye movements, voluntary and involuntary, cause the location of an object's image on the back of the eye to keep changing, so that visual receptors don't have a chance to "fatigue." But in the laboratory, researchers can stabilize the image of a simple pattern, such as a line, at a particular point on the back of a person's eye. They use an ingenious device consisting of a tiny projector mounted on a contact lens. Although the eyeball moves, the image of the object stays focused on the same receptors. In minutes, the image begins to disappear.

What would happen if our senses adapted to *most* incoming stimuli? Would we sense nothing, or would the brain substitute its own images for the sensory experiences no longer available by way of the sense organs? In early studies of **sensory deprivation,** researchers studied this question by isolating male volunteers from all patterned sight and sound. Vision was restricted by a translucent visor; hearing by a U-shaped pillow and noise from an air conditioner and fan; and touch by cotton gloves and cardboard cuffs. The volunteers took brief breaks to eat and use the bathroom, but otherwise, they lay in bed, doing nothing. The results were dramatic. Within a few hours, many of the men felt edgy. Some were so disoriented that they quit the study the first day. Those who stayed longer became confused, restless, and grouchy. Many reported hallucinations—at first simple images, then more bizarre visions, such as a squadron of marching squirrels, or a procession of marching eyeglasses. Few men were willing to remain in the study for more than two or three days (Heron, 1957).

These findings made headlines, of course. But the notion that sensory deprivation is unpleasant or even dangerous turned out to be an oversimplification (Suedfeld, 1975). In many of the studies, the experimental procedures themselves probably aroused anxiety. Participants were told about "panic buttons," asked to sign "release from legal liability" forms, and given inadequate orientation sessions. Later research, using better methods, showed that hallucinations are less dramatic and less disorienting than at first thought. In fact, many people enjoy time-limited periods of deprivation, and some perceptual and intellectual

You're in a dark room, isolated from sight, sound, smell, and taste. Will you hallucinate and beg to be released, or will you find the experience restful and soothing? What might affect your reaction?

■ **sensory adaptation**
The reduction or disappearance of sensory responsiveness that occurs when stimulation is unchanging or repetitious.

■ **sensory deprivation**
The absence of normal levels of sensory stimulation.

The effects of sensory deprivation depend on the circumstances. Choosing to relax for an hour in a solitary flotation tank is one thing; being imprisoned in a dark cell, alone and against your will, is another.

abilities actually improve. The response to sensory deprivation is affected by a person's expectations and interpretations of what is happening. Reduced sensation can be scary if you are locked in a room for an indefinite period, but relaxing if you have retreated to that room voluntarily for a little time out—or if you are paying cash money for a session in a "relaxation chamber."

Still, it is clear that the human brain requires a minimum amount of sensory stimulation during daily life to function normally. The absence of sensory input during sleep may help explain the sometimes bizarre imagery of dreams. And the need for sensory stimulation during waking life may help explain why people who live alone often keep the radio or television set running continuously and why prolonged solitary confinement is a form of torture.

Sensory Overload

If too little stimulation can be bad for you, so can too much. Excessive stimulation can lead to fatigue and mental confusion. If you have ever felt exhausted, nervous, and headachy after a day crammed with hectic activities—feeling you have too much to do with too little time to do it—you know first-hand about sensory overload.

When people find themselves in a state of overload, they often cope by blocking out unimportant sights and sounds and focusing only on those they find interesting or useful. Psychologists have dubbed this the "cocktail party phenomenon," because at a cocktail party, a person typically focuses on just one conversation, ignoring other voices, the clink of ice cubes, music, and bursts of laughter across the room. The competing sounds all enter the nervous system, enabling the person to pick up anything important—even the person's own name, spoken by someone several yards away. Unimportant sounds, though, are not fully processed by the brain.

The capacity for **selective attention** protects us in daily life from being overwhelmed by all the sensory signals impinging on our receptors. The brain is not forced to respond to everything the sense receptors send its way. The "generals" in the brain can choose which "field officers" get past the command center's gates. Those that don't seem to have anything important to say are turned back.

What would stock and commodity traders, who operate amid constant pandemonium, do without selective attention?

▪ **selective attention**
The focusing of attention on selected aspects of the environment and the blocking out of others.

Quick QUIZ

If you're not overloaded, try answering these questions.

1. Even on the clearest night, some stars cannot be seen by the naked eye because they are below the viewer's _____ threshold.
2. Mark is asked to judge whether two bars differ in length. When one bar is 10 millimeters long, the just noticeable difference (jnd) is 1 millimeter; that is, the second bar must be 11 millimeters before a difference is detected. Suppose the first bar is 20 millimeters long; what will the jnd be then?
3. If you jump into a cold lake, but moments later the water no longer seems so cold, sensory _____ has occurred.
4. If you are immobilized in a hospital bed, with no roommate and no TV or radio, and you feel edgy and disoriented, you may be suffering the effects of _____.
5. During a break from your job as a waiter, you decide to read. For 20 minutes, you are so engrossed that you fail to notice the clattering of dishes or orders being called out to the cook. This is an example of _____.

 6. In real-life detection tasks, is it better to be a "naysayer" or a "yea-sayer"?

Answers:

1. absolute 2. 2 millimeters (The jnd is a constant proportion of the first stimulus, in this case one-tenth.) 3. adaptation 4. sensory deprivation 5. selective attention 6. Neither; it depends on the consequences of a "miss" or "false alarm" and the probability of an event occurring. You might want to be a "yea-sayer" if you're just out the door, you think you hear the phone ringing, and you're expecting a call about a job interview. You might want to be a "naysayer" if you're just out the door, you think you hear the phone, and you're on your way to a job interview and don't want to be late.

▪ VISION

Vision is the most frequently studied of all the senses, and with good reason. More information about the external world comes to us through our eyes than through any other sense organ. Because we are most active in the daytime, we are "wired" to take advantage of the sun's illumination. Animals that are active at night tend to rely more heavily on hearing.

What We See

The stimulus for vision is light; even cats, raccoons, and other creatures famous for their ability to get around in the dark need *some* light to see. Visible light comes from the sun and other stars and from light bulbs, and is also reflected off objects. Light travels in the form of waves, and the way we see the world—our sensory experience—is affected by the characteristics of these waves:

1. **Hue,** the dimension of visual experience specified by color names, is related to the wavelength of light—that is, to the distance between the crests of a light wave. Shorter waves tend to be seen as violet and blue, and longer ones as orange and red. (We say "tend to" because other factors also affect color perception, as we will see later.) The sun produces white light, a mixture of all the visible wavelengths. Sometimes, drops of moisture in the air act like a prism: They separate the sun's white light into the colors of the visible spectrum, and we are treated to a rainbow.

2. **Brightness** is the dimension of visual experience related to the amount, or intensity, of the light that an object emits or reflects. Intensity corresponds to the amplitude (maximum height) of the wave. Generally speaking, the more light an object reflects, the brighter it appears. However, brightness is also affected by wavelength: Yellows appear brighter than reds and blues when physical intensities are actually equal. (For this reason, some fire departments have switched from red engines to yellow ones.)

3. **Saturation** (colorfulness) is the dimension of visual experience related to the **complexity of light**—that is, to how wide or narrow the range of wavelengths is. When light contains only a single wavelength, it is said to be "pure," and the resulting color is said to be completely saturated. At the other extreme is white light, which lacks any color and is completely unsaturated. In nature, pure light is extremely rare. Usually we sense a mixture of wavelengths, and we see colors that are duller and paler than completely saturated ones.

Note that hue, brightness, and saturation are all *psychological* dimensions of visual experience, whereas wavelength, intensity, and complexity are all *physical* properties of the visual stimulus, light.

An Eye on the World

Light enters the visual system through the eye, a wonderfully complex and delicate structure that is often compared, rather loosely, to a camera. As you

▪ **hue**
The dimension of visual experience specified by color names and related to the wavelength of light.

▪ **brightness**
Lightness or luminance; the dimension of visual experience related to the amount of light emitted from or reflected by an object.

▪ **saturation**
Vividness or purity of color; the dimension of visual experience related to the complexity of light waves.

▪ **complexity of light**
Refers to the number of different wavelengths contained in light from a particular source.

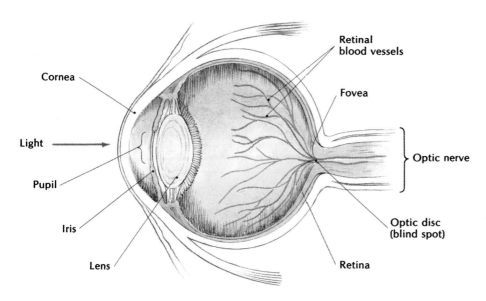

Cornea

Light →

Pupil

Iris

Lens

Retinal blood vessels

Fovea

Optic nerve

Optic disc (blind spot)

Retina

▪ **Figure 6.3   Major Structures of the Eye**

Light passes through the pupil and lens and is focused on the retina at the back of the eye. The point of sharpest vision is at the fovea.

read this section, examine Figure 6.3. Notice that the front part of the eye is covered by the transparent *cornea.* The cornea protects the eye and bends incoming light rays toward a *lens* located behind it. A camera lens works by moving closer to or farther from the opening. However, the lens of the eye works by subtly changing its shape, becoming more or less curved to focus light from objects that are close by or far away. The amount of light that gets into the eye is controlled by muscles in the *iris,* the part of the eye that gives it color. The iris surrounds the round opening, or *pupil,* of the eye. When you enter a dim room, the pupil widens, or dilates, to let more light in. When you emerge into bright sunlight, the pupil gets smaller, contracting to allow in less light. You can see these changes by watching your eyes in a mirror as you change the lighting.

The visual receptors are located in the back of the eye, or **retina.** In a developing embryo, the retina forms from tissue that projects out from the brain, not from tissue destined to form other parts of the eye; thus the retina is actually an extension of the brain. As Figure 6.4 shows, when the lens of the eye focuses light on the retina, the result is an upside-down image (which can actually be seen with an instrument used by eye specialists). Light from the top of the visual field stimulates light-sensitive receptor cells in the bottom part of the retina, and vice versa. The brain interprets this upside-down pattern of stimulation as something that is right side up.

About 120 to 125 million receptors in the retina are long and narrow and are called **rods.** Another 7 or 8 million receptors are cone-shaped and are called,

▪ **retina**
Neural tissue lining the back of the eyeball's interior, which contains the receptors for vision.

▪ **rods**
Visual receptors that respond to dim light but are not involved in color vision.

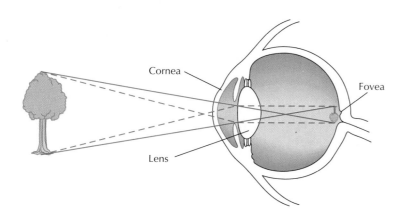

Cornea

Fovea

Lens

▪ **Figure 6.4   The Retinal Image**

When we look at an object, the light pattern focused on the retina is upside down. René Descartes was probably the first person to demonstrate this fact. He took an ox's eye, cut a piece from the back of it, and replaced the piece with paper. When he held the eye up to the light, he saw an upside-down image of the room on the paper!

appropriately enough, **cones.** The center of the retina, or *fovea,* where vision is sharpest, contains only cones, clustered densely together. From the center to the periphery, the ratio of rods to cones increases, and at the outer edges, there are virtually no cones.

Rods are more sensitive to light than cones are. They enable us to see in dim light and at night. Since they occupy the outer edges of the retina, they also handle side vision. That is why you can sometimes see a star from the corner of your eye although it is invisible when you gaze straight at it. But rods cannot distinguish different wavelengths of light and therefore are not sensitive to color. That is why it is often hard to distinguish colors clearly in dim light. The cones, on the other hand, are differentially sensitive to specific wavelengths of light and allow us to see colors. However, the cones need much more light than rods do to respond. Therefore they don't help us much when we are trying to find a seat in a darkened movie theater.

We have all noticed that it takes some time for our eyes to adjust fully to dim illumination. This process of **dark adaptation,** which involves chemical changes in the rods and cones, actually occurs in two phases. The cones adapt quickly, within 10 minutes or so, but never become very sensitive to the dim illumination. The rods adapt more slowly, taking 20 minutes or longer, but are ultimately much more sensitive. After the first phase of adaptation, you can see better but not well; after the second phase, your vision is as good as it will get.

Rods and cones are connected by synapses to *bipolar neurons,* which in turn communicate with neurons called **ganglion cells** (see Figure 6.5). Usually a single cone communicates (via a bipolar neuron) with a single ganglion cell; it has a "private line." Rods, in contrast, must communicate via a "party line." That is, whole groups of rods, covering a particular area of the retina, send their messages to a single ganglion cell.

The axons of the ganglion cells converge to form the *optic nerve,* which carries information out through the back of the eye and on to the brain. Where the optic nerve leaves the eye, at the *optic disc,* there are no rods or

■ **cones**
Visual receptors involved in color vision.

■ **dark adaptation**
A process by which visual receptors become maximally sensitive to dim light.

■ **ganglion cells**
Neurons in the retina of the eye that gather information from receptor cells (by way of intermediate bipolar cells); their axons make up the optic nerve.

■ **Figure 6.5   The Structures of the Retina**

For clarity, all cells in this drawing are greatly exaggerated in size. Notice that in order to reach the receptors for vision (the rods and cones), light must pass through the ganglion and bipolar cells as well as the blood vessels that nourish them. Normally we do not see the shadow cast by this network of cells and blood vessels. It always falls on the same place on the retina, and such stabilized images are not sensed (see text). But when an eye doctor shines a moving light into your eye, the treelike shadow of the blood vessels falls on different regions of the retina and you may see it—a rather eerie experience.

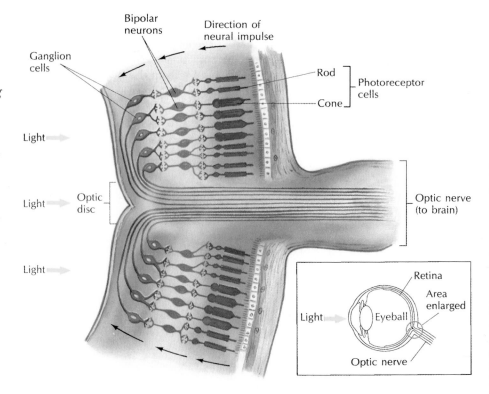

■ **Figure 6.6 Find Your Blind Spot**

To find the blind spot in your left eye, close your right eye and look at the magician. Then slowly move the book toward and away from yourself. The rabbit should disappear when the book is between 9 and 12 inches from your eye.

cones. The absence of receptors produces a blind spot in the field of vision. Normally we are unaware of the blind spot because (1) the image projected on the spot is hitting a different, "nonblind" spot in the other eye; (2) our eyes move so fast that we can pick up the complete image; and (3) the brain tends to fill in the gap. You can find your blind spot by following the instructions in Figure 6.6.

Why the Visual System Is Not a Camera

Because the eye is often compared with a camera, it is easy to assume that the visual world is made up of a mosaic of dots, as in a photograph. But unlike a camera, the visual system is not a passive recorder of the external world. Instead of simply registering spots of light and dark, neurons in the system build up a picture of the world by detecting its meaningful features.

Simple features of the environment, such as spots of light and dark, are coded in the ganglion cells and in an area in the thalamus of the brain. In mammals, more complex features are coded in special **feature-detector** cells in the visual cortex. This fact was first demonstrated by David Hubel and Torsten Wiesel (1962, 1968), who painstakingly recorded impulses from individual cells in the brains of cats and monkeys. (In 1981, they received a Nobel Prize for their work.) Hubel and Wiesel found that different neurons were sensitive to different patterns projected on a screen in front of the animal's eyes. Most cells responded maximally to moving or stationary lines that were oriented in a particular direction and located in a particular part of the visual field. One type of cell might fire most rapidly in response to a horizontal line in the lower right part of the visual field, another to a diagonal line at an angle in the upper left part of the visual field. In the real world, such features make up the boundaries and edges of objects.

Since this pioneering work was done, scientists have found that other cells in the visual system have more complex kinds of specialties (Tanaka et al., 1991). For example, certain cells in the visual cortex respond maximally to bull's-eyes, spirals patterns, or concentric circles (Gallant, Braun, & Van Essen, 1993), and certain visual cells in the temporal lobe "prefer" a starlike shape (Sáry, Vogels, & Orban, 1993). Even more intriguing, some cells in the temporal lobe respond maximally to *faces* (Desimone, 1991; Young & Yamane, 1992)! But no one is sure whether cells that respond to such complex forms are responding to the overall form or to some specific component of it. And to complicate matters further, studies suggest that it is not only the frequency of a cell's firing that contains information but also the *pattern* or *rhythm* with which it fires (Richmond & Optican, 1990).

The brain's job is to take all this fragmentary information about lines, angles, shapes, motion, brightness, texture, and other features of what we see,

■ **feature detectors**
Cells in the visual cortex that are sensitive to specific features of the environment.

and come up with a unified view of the world. How on earth does it do this? We saw in Chapter 4 that as neurons converge at a synapse, their overall pattern of firing determines whether the neuron on the other side of the synapse is excited or inhibited. The firing (or inhibition) of that neuron, then, actually conveys information to the *next* neuron along the sensory route about what was happening in many other cells. Eventually a single "hypercomplex" cell in the cortex of the brain may receive information that was originally contained in the firing of thousands of different visual receptors. But most researchers believe that the perception of a visual stimulus ultimately depends not just on the firing of a single hypercomplex cell but on the simultaneous activation of many different cells in different parts of the brain, and the overall pattern of firing of these groups of cells. Researchers are now using computer models to try to figure out how this intricate process might take place, but at present, it remains mostly a mystery.

How We See Colors

For 200 years, scientists have been trying to figure out why we see the world in living color. One approach, the **trichromatic theory** (also known as the *Young–Helmholtz theory*), assumed that there were three mechanisms in the visual system, each especially sensitive to a range of wavelengths, and that these mechanisms interacted in some way to produce all the different color sensations. Another approach, the **opponent-process theory,** assumed that the visual system treated pairs of colors as opposing or antagonistic, which would explain why we can describe a color as bluish green but not as reddish green. Modern research suggests that both views are valid, and that each explains a different level of processing.

The trichromatic theory applies to the first level of processing, which occurs in the retina. The retina contains three different types of cones. One type responds maximally to blue (or more precisely, to a range of wavelengths near the short end of the spectrum, which give rise to the experience of blue), another to green, and a third to red. The hundreds of colors we see result from the combined activity of these three types of cones.

Total color blindness is usually due to a genetic variation that causes cones of the retina to be absent or malfunctional. The visual world then consists of black, white, and shades of gray. Many animal species are totally color-blind, but the condition is extremely rare in human beings. Most "color-blind" people are actually *color deficient.* Usually, the person is unable to distinguish red and green; the world is painted in shades of blue, yellow, brown, and gray. In rarer instances, a person may be blind to blue and yellow and may see only reds, greens, and grays. Color deficiency is found in about 8 percent of white men, 5 percent of Asian men, and 3 percent of black men and Native American men (Sekuler & Blake, 1985). Because of the way the condition is inherited, it is very rare in women. One story has it that John Dalton, a respectable eighteenth-century Quaker physician who published the first study of color deficiency and was color deficient himself, once startled his colleagues by wearing red hose—which he saw as brown. But fortunately for people who are color deficient, this condition does not usually interfere with daily living. A person who is blind to red and green can respond correctly to traffic lights, for instance, because the lights differ in position and brightness as well as in hue.

The opponent-process theory applies to the second stage of color processing, which occurs in bipolar and ganglion cells in the retina and in neurons in the thalamus of the brain. These cells, known as *opponent-process cells,* either respond to short wavelengths but are inhibited from firing by long wavelengths, or vice versa (DeValois, 1960; DeValois & DeValois, 1975; Hurvich & Jameson, 1974). Some opponent-process cells respond in opposite fashion to red and

▪ **trichromatic theory**
A theory of color perception that proposes three mechanisms in the visual system, each sensitive to a certain range of wavelengths; their interaction is assumed to produce all the different experiences of hue.

▪ **opponent-process theory**
A theory of color perception that assumes that the visual system treats pairs of colors as opposing or antagonistic.

▪ **Figure 6.7   Change of Heart**
To produce a negative afterimage, stare at the black dot in the middle of the heart for at least 20 seconds. Then shift your gaze to a white piece of paper or white wall. You should see an image of a red heart with a blue border.

green; they fire in response to one and turn off in response to the other. Others respond in opposite fashion to blue and yellow. (A third system responds in opposite fashion to white and black and thus yields information about brightness.) The net result is a color *code* that is passed along to the higher visual centers. Opposing colors cannot be coded at the same time, which is why we never see a reddish green or a bluish yellow.

Opponent-process cells that are *inhibited* by a particular color seem to produce a burst of firing when the color is removed, just as they would if the opposing color were present. Similarly, cells that *fire* in response to a color stop firing when the color is removed, just as they would if the opposing color were present. These facts seem to explain why we are susceptible to *negative afterimages* when we stare at a particular hue—why we see, for instance, red after staring at green (see Figure 6.7). A sort of neural rebound effect occurs: The cells that switch on or off to signal the presence of "red" send the opposite signal ("green") when the red is removed. If you stare intently at a green screen, such as on a computer monitor, you may see the world through rose-colored glasses when you look away—a demonstration of the opponent process in action.

Unfortunately, two-stage theories do not yet provide a complete explanation of color vision. The wavelengths reflected by an object do not by themselves account for whether we see the object as mauve or magenta, purple or puce. Edwin Land (1959), inventor of the Polaroid camera, showed that the perceived color of an object depends on the wavelengths reflected by *everything around it.* Thus you never see a good, strong red unless there are other objects around that reflect the green and blue part of the spectrum. Land worked out precise rules that predict exactly how an object will appear, given the wavelengths reflected by all the objects in a scene. So far, however, researchers have not been able to explain fully how the brain follows these rules.

Constructing the Visual World

We do not see a retinal image; that image is merely grist for the mill of the mind, which actively interprets the image and constructs the world from the often fragmentary data of the senses (see Figure 6.8). In the brain, sensory signals that give rise to vision, hearing, taste, smell, and touch are combined from moment to moment to produce a unified model of the world. This is the process of perception.

Form Perception.   To make sense of the world, we must know where one thing ends and another begins, and we must do this in all our sensory modali-

■ **Figure 6.8   Perception Is Meaningful**

Perceptual processes actively organize and interpret data from our senses. For example, chances are that you see more than a random collection of light and dark splotches in this picture. If not, try holding the picture a little farther away from you.

ties. In vision, we must separate the teacher from the podium; in hearing, we must separate the piano solo from the orchestral accompaniment; and in taste, we must separate the marshmallow from the hot chocolate. This process of dividing up the world occurs so rapidly and effortlessly that we take it completely for granted—until we must make out objects in a heavy fog or words in the rapid-fire conversation of someone speaking a foreign language.

The Gestalt psychologists, whom we introduced in Chapter 1, were among the first to study how people organize the world visually into meaningful units and patterns. In German, *gestalt* means "pattern" or "configuration." The Gestalt psychologists' motto was "The whole is more than the sum of its parts." They observed that when we perceive something, properties emerge from the whole configuration that are not found in any particular component. When you watch a movie, for example, the motion you "see" is nowhere in the film, which consists of separate static frames projected at 24 frames per second.

Although the Gestalt psychologists had ideas about the physiology of visual perception that are no longer accepted, many of their observations remain useful. For instance, they noted that we always organize the visual field into *figure* and *ground*. The figure stands out from the rest of the environment, which provides a formless background (see Figure 6.9). Some things stand out as figure by virtue of their intensity or size; it is hard to ignore the blinding flash of a camera or a tidal wave approaching your piece of beach. Unique objects also stand out, such as a banana in a bowl of oranges. Moving objects in an otherwise still environment, such as a shooting star, will usually be seen as figure. Indeed, it is hard to ignore a sudden change of any kind in the environment because our brains are geared to respond to change and contrast. However, selective attention, the ability to concentrate on some stimuli and to filter out others, gives us some control over what we perceive as figure and ground.

Here are some other Gestalt strategies that the visual system uses to group sensory building blocks into perceptual units:

1. *Proximity.* Things that are near each other tend to be grouped together. Thus you perceive the dots on the left as three groups of dots, not as 12 separate, unrelated ones. Similarly, you perceive the pattern on the right as vertical columns of dots, not as horizontal rows:

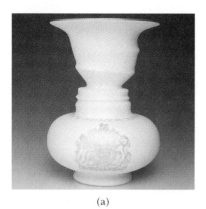

(a)

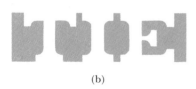

(b)

■ **Figure 6.9   Figure and Ground**

Both the photograph (a) and the drawing (b) have two possible interpretations, which keep alternating depending on which part is seen as figure and which as ground. Do you see the silhouettes and the goblet in the photograph and the word in the drawing?

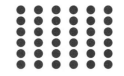

2. *Closure.* The brain tends to fill in gaps in order to perceive complete forms. This is fortunate because we often need to decipher less than perfect images. The following figures are easily perceived as a triangle, a face, and the letter *e*, even though none of the figures is complete:

3. *Similarity.* Things that are alike in some way (for example, in color, shape, or size) tend to be perceived as belonging together. In the figure on the left, you see the circles as forming an *x*. In the one on the right, you see horizontal bars rather than vertical columns because the horizontally aligned stars share the same color:

4. *Continuity.* Lines and patterns tend to be perceived as continuing in time or space. You perceive the figure on the left as a single line partially covered by a circle rather than as two separate lines touching a circle. In the figure on the right, you see two lines, one curved and one straight, instead of two curved and two straight lines, touching at one focal point:

One psychologist has estimated that adults must readily discriminate among 30,000 different familiar objects (Biederman, 1987). Gestalt and other perceptual principles help explain why we have trouble discriminating some of these visual forms. Objects manufactured by human beings may be designed with little thought for how the mind works, which is why it can be a major challenge to figure out how to use a new microwave, camera, or VCR (Norman, 1988). Good design requires, among other things, that crucial distinctions be visually obvious. For instance, knobs and switches with different functions should differ in color, texture, or shape, and should stand out as "figure." But on many VCRs, it is hard to tell the rewind button from the fast-forward button.

With a little ingenuity and a knowledge of perceptual principles, people can often correct such flaws in the design of machines and products. Control-room operators in one nuclear power plant cleverly solved the problem of similar knobs on adjacent switches: They placed distinctively shaped beer-keg handles over them, one labeled Heineken's, the other Michelob (Norman, 1988). Can you think of some ways to overcome problems of poor design in your own environment?

Depth and Distance Perception. Ordinarily we need to know not only what something is, but also where it is. Touch gives us this information directly, but vision does not, so we must use certain cues to *infer* an object's location by estimating its distance or depth.

To perform this remarkable feat, we rely in part on **binocular cues**—cues that require the use of two eyes. The eyes are about 2½ inches apart on the face. As

▪ **binocular cues**
Visual cues to depth or distance requiring two eyes.

they converge on objects close by or far away, the angle of convergence changes, providing information about distance. The two eyes also receive slightly different retinal images of the same object. You can easily prove this by holding a finger about 12 inches in front of your face and looking at it with only one eye at a time. Its position will appear to shift when you change eyes. Now hold up two fingers, one closer to your nose than the other. Notice that the amount of space between the two fingers appears to change when you switch eyes. The slight difference in lateral (sideways) separation between two objects as seen by the left eye and the right eye is called **retinal disparity.** Since retinal disparity increases as the distance between two objects increases, the brain can use this disparity to infer depth and calculate distance. Retinal disparity is mimicked by 3-D movies and slide viewers (stereoscopes), which project two images, one as seen by the left eye and one as seen by the right, to create the illusion of depth.

Binocular cues only help us locate objects up to about 50 feet away. For objects farther away, we rely on **monocular cues,** cues that do not depend on using both eyes. One such cue is *interposition:* When an object is interposed between the viewer and a second object, partly blocking the view of the second object, the first object is perceived as being closer. Another monocular cue is *linear perspective:* When two lines known to be parallel appear to be coming together or converging, they imply the existence of depth. For example, if you are standing between railroad tracks, they appear to converge in the distance. A third monocular cue is *relative size:* The smaller the retinal image of an object, the farther away the object appears to be. These and other monocular cues are illustrated in Figure 6.10.

Visual Constancies: When Seeing Is Believing.   You might be able to see what things are and where they are, but your perceptual world would be a confusing place without another important perceptual skill. Lighting conditions, viewing angles, and the distances of stationary objects are all continually changing as we move about, yet we rarely confuse these changes with changes in the objects themselves. This ability to perceive objects as stable or unchanging even though the sensory patterns they produce are constantly shifting is called **perceptual constancy.** The best-studied constancies are visual. They include the following:

1. *Shape constancy.* We continue to perceive objects as having a constant shape even though the shape of the retinal image changes when our point of view changes. If you hold a Frisbee directly in front of your face, its image on the retina will be round. When you set the Frisbee on a table, its image becomes elliptical, yet you continue to identify the Frisbee as round.

2. *Location constancy.* We perceive stationary objects as remaining in the same place even though the retinal image moves about as we move our eyes, heads, and bodies. As you drive along the highway, telephone poles and trees fly by—on your retina. But you know that objects like telephone poles and trees move by themselves only in cartoons, and you also know that your body is moving, so you perceive the poles and trees as staying put.

3. *Brightness constancy.* We continue to see objects as having a relatively constant brightness even though the amount of light they reflect changes as the overall level of illumination changes. Snow remains white even on a cloudy day. In fact, it is possible for a black object in strong sunlight to reflect more light than a white object in the shade. We are not fooled, though, because the brain registers the total illumination in the scene, and we automatically take this information into account in the perception of any particular object's brightness.

4. *Color constancy.* We see an object as maintaining its hue despite the fact that the wavelength of light reaching our eyes may change somewhat. For example, outdoor light is "bluer" than indoor light, and objects outdoors therefore reflect more "blue" light than those indoors. Conversely, indoor light from a lamp is rich in long wavelengths, and is therefore "yellower." Yet objects usually look the same color in both places. The explanation involves sensory adapta-

■ **retinal disparity**
The slight difference in lateral separation between two objects as seen by the left eye and the right eye.

■ **monocular cues**
Visual cues to depth or distance that can be used by one eye alone.

■ **perceptual constancy**
The accurate perception of objects as stable or unchanged despite changes in the sensory patterns they produce.

(a)

(b)

(c)

(d)

(e)

(f)

■ Figure 6.10   Monocular Cues to Depth

*Most cues to depth do not depend on having two eyes. Some monocular (one-eyed) cues are: (a) **Interposition** (partial overlap). An object that partly blocks or obscures another one must be in front of the other one and is therefore seen as closer. (b) **Motion parallax.** When an observer is moving, objects seem to move at different speeds and in different directions. The closer an object, the faster it seems to move. Close objects also appear to move backward, while distant ones seem to move forward. (c) **Light and shadow.** Both attributes give objects the appearance of three dimensions. (d) **Relative size.** The smaller the image of an object on the retina, the farther away it appears. (e) **Relative clarity.** Because of particles in the air (from fog, smog, or dust), distant objects tend to look hazier, duller, or less detailed. (f) **Texture gradients.** In a uniform surface, distant parts of the surface appear denser; that is, the elements that make it up seem spaced more closely together. (g) **Linear perspective.** Parallel lines will appear to be converging in the distance—the greater the apparent convergence, the greater the perceived distance. This cue is often exaggerated by artists to convey an impression of depth.*

(g)

BIZARRO　By DAN PIRARO

When size constancy fails.

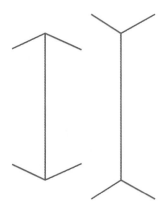

■ **perceptual illusion**
An erroneous or misleading perception of reality.

tion, which we discussed earlier. Outdoors, we quickly adapt to short-wavelength (bluish) light, and indoors, we adapt to long-wavelength light. As a result, our visual responses are similar in the two situations. Also, as we saw earlier, the brain takes into account all the wavelengths in the visual field when computing the color of a particular object. If a lemon is bathed in bluish light, so, usually, is everything else around it. The increase in blue light reflected by the lemon is "canceled" in the visual cortex by the increase in blue light reflected by the lemon's surroundings, and so the lemon continues to look yellow.

5. *Size constancy.* We continue to see an object as having a constant size even when its retinal image becomes smaller or larger. A friend approaching on the street does not seem to be growing; a car pulling away from the curb does not seem to be shrinking. Size constancy depends in part on familiarity with objects. You *know* people and cars don't change size just like that. It also depends on the apparent distance of an object. When you move your hand toward your face, your brain registers the fact that the hand is getting closer, and you correctly perceive its unchanging size. There is, then, an intimate relationship between perceived size and perceived distance.

Visual Illusions: When Seeing Is Misleading.　Perceptual constancies allow us to make sense of the world. Occasionally, however, we can be fooled, and the result is a **perceptual illusion.** For psychologists, illusions are valuable because they are *systematic* errors that provide us with hints about the perceptual strategies of the mind.

Although illusions can occur in any sensory modality, visual illusions have been studied most frequently. Visual illusions sometimes occur when the strategies that normally lead to accurate perception are overextended to situations where they don't apply. Compare the two lines in the margin. If you are like most people, you perceive the line on the right as slightly longer than the one on the left. Yet if you measure the lines, you will find that they are exactly the same length. This is the Müller-Lyer illusion, named after the man who first described it in 1889.

One explanation for the Müller-Lyer illusion is that the figures contain perspective cues that normally suggest depth (Gregory, 1963). The line on the left is like the near edge of a building; the one on the right is like the far corner of a room. The two lines produce the same-sized retinal image, but the one with the outward-facing branches suggests greater distance. We are fooled into perceiving it as longer because we automatically apply a rule about the relationship between size and distance that is normally very useful. The rule is that when two objects produce the same-sized retinal image and one is farther away, the farther one is larger. The problem, in this case, is that there is no actual difference in the distance of the two lines, so the rule is inappropriate.

Just as there are size, shape, location, brightness, and color constancies, so there are size, shape, location, brightness, and color illusions. Some illusions are simply a matter of physics. Thus a chopstick in a half-filled glass of water looks bent because water and air refract light differently. Other illusions are due to misleading messages from the sense organs, as in sensory adaptation. Still others, like the Müller-Lyer illusion, seem to occur because the brain misinterprets sensory information. Figure 6.11 shows some startling visual illusions.

In everyday life, most illusions are harmless, or even useful or entertaining. For example, electric signs often take advantage of the fact that when lights flash on and off in patterns, images occur successively across the retina, much as they do when actual objects move, and so we perceive the images in the sign as moving. The result of this apparent motion may be dancers kicking up their heels on a Las Vegas billboard or news headlines scrolling across a building in New York's Times Square.

But occasionally an illusion interferes with normal performance of some skill. In baseball, two types of pitches that drive batters batty are the rising fastball, in which the ball seems to jump a few inches when it reaches home plate, and the breaking curveball, in which the ball seems to loop toward the batter and then plummet at the last moment. Both of these pitches are physical impossibilities; according to one explanation, they are illusions that occur when batters misestimate a ball's speed and momentarily shift their gaze to where they think it will cross home plate (Bahill & Karnavas, 1993). Illusions may also lead on occasion to industrial and automobile accidents. For example, if a driver thinks that a pedestrian in the road is an adult when it is really a child, the driver may overestimate the pedestrian's size (a lapse in size constancy), and therefore miscalculate the person's distance from the car. As a result, the driver may not step on the brakes quickly enough to avoid striking the child (Stewart, Cudworth, & Lishman, 1993).

(b)

(a)

(c)   (d)   (e)

■ **Figure 6.11   Some Visual Illusions**

Although perception is usually accurate, we can be fooled. In (a) the cats as drawn are all the same size; in (b) the two figures are the same size; in (c) the diagonal lines are all parallel; and in (d) the sides of the square are all straight. To see the illusion depicted in (e), hold your index fingers 5 to 10 inches in front of your eyes, as shown, then focus straight ahead. Do you see a floating "fingertip frankfurter"? Can you make this apparition shrink or expand? Why do you think this illusion occurs?

*Q*uick QUIZ

Can you accurately perceive these questions?

1. How can two Gestalt principles help explain why you can make out the Big Dipper on a starry night?
2. True or false: Binocular cues help us locate objects that are very far away.
3. Hold one hand about 12 inches from your face and the other one about 6 inches away. (a) Which hand will cast the smaller retinal image? (b) Why don't you perceive that hand as smaller?

Answers:

1. *Proximity* of certain stars encourages you to see them as clustered together to form a pattern; *closure* allows you to "fill in the gaps" and see the contours of a "dipper." **2.** false **3.** a. The hand that is 12 inches away will cast a smaller retinal image. b. Your brain takes the differences in distance into account in estimating size; also, you know how large your hands are.

■ HEARING

Like vision, the sense of hearing, or *audition,* provides a vital link with the world around us. When damage to the auditory system causes hearing loss, the consequences go beyond the obvious loss of auditory information. Because we use hearing to monitor our own speech, when deafness is present at birth or occurs early in life, speech development is hindered. When people lose their hearing, they sometimes come to feel socially isolated because social relationships rely so heavily on hearing others. That is why many deaf people feel strongly about teaching deaf children American Sign Language (ASL), which allows them to communicate normally with and forge close relationships with other signers.

What We Hear

The stimulus for sound is a wave of pressure created when an object vibrates (or, sometimes, when compressed air is released, as in a pipe organ). The vibration (or release of air) causes molecules in a transmitting substance to move together and apart. This movement produces variations in pressure that radiate in all directions. The transmitting substance is usually air, but sound waves can also travel through water and solids. That is why, in old Westerns, Indian scouts would sometimes put an ear to the ground to find out whether anyone was approaching.

As with vision, psychological aspects of our auditory experience are related in a predictable way to physical characteristics of the stimulus—in this case, a sound wave:

1. Loudness is the dimension of auditory experience related to the intensity of a wave's pressure. Intensity corresponds to the amplitude, or maximum height, of the wave. The more energy contained in the wave, the higher it is at its peak. Perceived loudness is also affected by pitch—how high or low a sound is. If low and high sounds produce waves with equal amplitudes, the low sound may seem quieter.

Sound intensity is measured in units called *decibels* (dB). A decibel is one-tenth of a *bel,* a unit named for Alexander Graham Bell, the inventor of the tele-

■ **loudness**
The dimension of auditory experience related to the intensity of a pressure wave.

phone. The average absolute threshold of hearing in human beings is zero decibels. Decibels are not equally distant, as inches on a ruler are. A sound of 60 decibels (such as that of a sewing machine) is not one-fifth louder than one at 50 decibels (such as that of a refrigerator), but rather is ten times louder. Table 6.1 shows the intensity in decibels of some common sounds.

2. Pitch is the dimension of auditory experience related to the frequency of the sound wave and, to some extent, its intensity. **Frequency** refers to how rapidly the air (or other medium) vibrates—that is, the number of times per second the wave cycles through a peak and a low point. One cycle per second is known as 1 *hertz* (Hz). The healthy ear of a young person normally detects frequencies in the range of 16 Hz (the lowest note on a pipe organ) to 20,000 Hz (the scraping of a grasshopper's legs).

A remarkable line of research, however, is finding that under special conditions, people can detect *ultrasonic* frequencies previously thought to be beyond the range of human hearing. Martin Lenhardt and his colleagues (1991) have used a special laboratory device, placed directly against the skull, to deliver signals as high as 90,000 Hz through bone conduction. They find that even profoundly deaf people can clearly perceive words presented at 28,000 to 40,000 Hz in this manner. These results suggest that bone-conducted ultrasonic frequencies are processed by different auditory structures (yet to be identified) than audible frequencies are. If that is true, the findings may one day lead to a new type of hearing aid for the hearing impaired.

■ **pitch**
The dimension of auditory experience related to the frequency of a pressure wave; height or depth of a tone.

■ **frequency (of a sound wave)**
The number of times per second that a sound wave cycles through a peak and low point.

Table 6.1   Sound Intensity Levels in the Environment

The following decibel levels apply at typical working distances. Each 10-point increase on the decibel scale represents a tenfold increase in sound intensity over the previous level. Even some everyday noises can be hazardous to hearing if exposure goes on for too long a time.

Typical Level (Decibels)	Example	Dangerous Time Exposure
0	Lowest sound audible to human ear	
30	Quiet library, soft whisper	
40	Quiet office, living room, bedroom away from traffic	
50	Light traffic at a distance, refrigerator, gentle breeze	
60	Air conditioner at 20 feet, conversation, sewing machine	
70	Busy traffic, noisy restaurant (constant exposure)	Critical level begins
80	Subway, heavy city traffic, alarm clock at 2 feet, factory noise	More than 8 hours
90	Truck traffic, noisy home appliances, shop tools, lawn mower	Less than 8 hours
100	Chain saw, boiler shop, pneumatic drill	Less than 2 hours
120	Rock concert in front of speakers, sandblasting, thunderclap	Immediate danger
140	Gunshot blast, jet plane at 50 feet	Any length of exposure time is dangerous
180	Rocket launching pad	Hearing loss inevitable

Source: Reprinted with permission from the American Academy of Otolaryngology—Head and Neck Surgery, Washington, D.C.

3. Timbre is the distinguishing quality of a sound. It is the dimension of auditory experience related to the complexity of the sound wave—to the relative breadth of the range of frequencies that make up the wave. A pure tone consists of only one frequency, but in nature, pure tones are extremely rare. Usually what we hear is a complex wave consisting of several subwaves with different frequencies. A particular combination of frequencies results in a particular timbre. Timbre is what makes a note played on a flute, which produces relatively pure tones, sound different from the same note played on an oboe, which produces very complex sounds.

When many frequencies are present but are not in harmony, we hear noise. When all the frequencies of the sound spectrum occur, they produce a hissing sound called *white noise*. White noise is named by analogy to white light. Just as white light includes all wavelengths of the visible light spectrum, so white noise includes all frequencies of the sound spectrum.

An Ear on the World

As Figure 6.12 shows, the ear has an outer, a middle, and an inner section. The soft, funnel-shaped outer ear is well designed to collect sound waves, but hearing would still be quite good without it. The essential parts of the ear are hidden from view, inside the head.

A sound wave passes into the outer ear and through an inch-long canal to strike an oval-shaped membrane called the *eardrum*. The eardrum is so sensitive that it can respond to the movement of a *single molecule!* A sound wave causes it to vibrate with the same frequency and amplitude as the wave itself. This vibration is passed along to three tiny bones in the middle ear, the smallest bones in the human body. The bones move, one after the other, which has the effect of

■ **timbre**
The distinguishing quality of a sound; the dimension of auditory experience related to the complexity of the pressure wave.

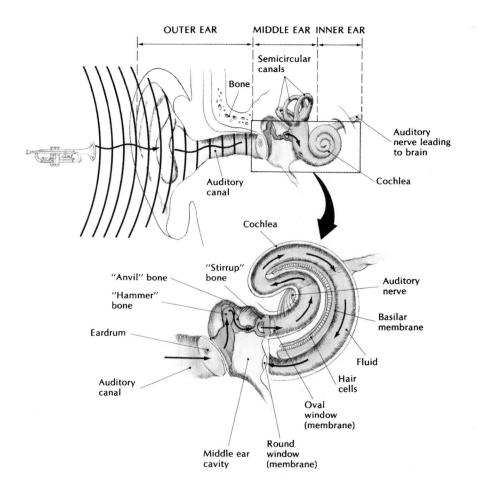

■ **Figure 6.12 Major Structures of the Ear**

Sound waves are collected by the outer ear and channeled down the auditory canal, causing the eardrum to vibrate. These vibrations are then passed along to the tiny bones of the middle ear. Movement of these bones intensifies the force of the vibrations and funnels them to a small membrane separating the middle and inner ear. The receptor cells for hearing (hair cells) are located in a small organ within the snail-shaped cochlea. The receptors initiate nerve impulses that travel along the auditory nerve to the brain.

intensifying the force of the vibration. The third bone pushes on a membrane that opens into the inner ear.

The actual organ of hearing, the *organ of Corti,* is a chamber inside the **cochlea,** a snail-shaped structure within the inner ear. The organ of Corti plays the same role in hearing that the retina plays in vision. It contains the all-important receptor cells, which in this case look like bristles and are called hair cells, or *cilia.* Exposure to extremely loud noise for a brief period, or more moderate levels of noise for a sustained period, can damage these fragile cells. They flop over, like broken blades of grass, and if the damage reaches a critical point, hearing loss occurs.

In our society, with its ubiquitous office machines, automobiles, power saws, leaf blowers, jackhammers, and stereos (often played at full blast and listened to through headphones), such impairment is common. According to one estimate, three of every five entering college students already have impaired hearing, most of them because of damage to the cilia (Lipscomb, 1972). Our noisy environment also helps explain why so many older people cannot hear as well as they once did (especially the higher frequencies), although some receptor cells in the ear are also lost normally with age. Recent research suggests that hair cells might be able to regenerate after damage if they are stimulated by a substance that promotes nerve growth (Defebvre et al., 1993). Someday this research may lead to techniques that restore hearing, but you shouldn't count on it; try to avoid the loud noises that damage these fragile cells.

The hair cells of the cochlea are embedded in the rubbery *basilar membrane,* which stretches across the interior of the cochlea. When pressure reaches the cochlea, it causes wavelike motions in fluid within the cochlea's interior. These motions push on the basilar membrane, causing it to move in a wavelike motion. Just above the hair cells is yet another membrane. As the hair cells rise and fall, their tips brush against it, and they bend. This causes the hair cells to initiate a signal that is passed along to the *auditory nerve,* which then carries the message to the brain. The particular pattern of hair cell movement is affected by the manner in which the basilar membrane moves. The pattern determines which neurons fire and how rapidly they fire, and the resulting code determines the sort of sound we hear.

Could anyone ever imagine such a complex and odd arrangement of bristles, fluids, and snail shells if it didn't already exist?

Constructing the Auditory World

Just as we do not see a retinal image, so we do not hear a chorus of brushlike tufts bending and swaying in the dark recesses of the cochlea. Just as we do not see a jumbled collection of lines and colors, so we do not hear a disconnected cacophony of pitches and timbres. Instead, we use our perceptual powers to organize patterns of sound and to construct a meaningful auditory world.

For example, in class, your psychology instructor hopes you will perceive his or her voice as *figure* and the hum of a passing airplane, cheers from the athletic field, or distant sounds of a construction crew as *ground*. Whether these hopes are realized will depend, of course, on where you choose to direct your attention. Other Gestalt principles also seem to apply to hearing. The *proximity* of notes in a melody tells you which notes go together to form phrases; *continuity* helps you follow a melody on one violin when another violin is playing a different melody; *similarity* in timbre and pitch helps you pick out the soprano voices in a chorus and hear them as a unit; *closure* helps you understand a radio announcer's words even when static makes some of the individual sounds unintelligible.

Besides organizing sounds, we also need to know where they are coming from. We can estimate the *distance* of a sound's source by using loudness as a cue. For example, we know that a train sounds louder when it is 20 yards away

The spiraled interior of a guinea pig's cochlea, shown here, is almost identical to that of a human cochlea.

■ **cochlea (KOCK-lee-uh)**
A snail-shaped, fluid-filled organ in the inner ear, containing the receptors for hearing.

than when it is a mile off. To locate the *direction* a sound is coming from, we depend in part on the fact that we have two ears. A sound arriving from the right reaches the right ear a fraction of a second sooner than it reaches the left. It may also provide a bit more energy to the right ear (depending on its frequency) because it has to get around the head to reach the left ear. It is hard to localize sounds that are coming from directly in back of you or from directly above your head because they reach both ears at the same time. When you turn or cock your head, you are actively trying to overcome this problem. Many animals don't have to do this; they can move their ears independently of the head.

Research with cats is clarifying the physiology of sound location. As we've seen, in the visual system, many cells are "tuned" to a specific part of the visual field. But in the auditory cortex of the brain, the number of times a cell fires does not depend on the location of a sound. Instead, any given cell can respond to any location, and sounds at different locations produce different *patterns* of firing over time (Middlebrook et al., 1994). One pattern might mean "in back of me" and another "off to the right side." The combined activity of many such neurons conveys the precise location of the sound. However, even people with normal hearing find it difficult to locate objects through sound alone, as you know if you have ever played blindfold games such as Marco Polo. Our eyes provide fuller information on distance than our ears do because they provide direct perception of a three-dimensional world.

*Q*uick **QUIZ**

How well can you detect the answers to these questions on hearing?

1. Which psychological dimensions of hearing correspond to the intensity, frequency, and complexity of the sound wave?
2. Willie Nelson has a nasal voice, and Ray Charles has a gravelly voice. Which psychological dimension of hearing describes the difference?
3. An extremely loud or sustained noise can permanently damage the _____ of the ear.
4. During a lecture, a classmate draws your attention to a buzzing fluorescent light that you had not previously noticed. What will happen to your perception of figure and ground?

Answers:

1. loudness, pitch, timbre 2. timbre 3. hair cells (cilia) 4. The buzzing sound will become figure and the lecturer's voice will become ground, at least momentarily.

■ OTHER SENSES

Psychologists have been particularly interested in vision and audition because of the importance of these senses to human survival. However, research on the other senses is growing dramatically, as awareness of how they contribute to our lives increases and new ways are found to study them.

Taste: Savory Sensations

Taste, or *gustation,* occurs because chemicals stimulate thousands of receptors in the mouth. These receptors are located primarily on the tongue, but

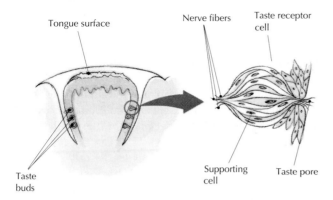

Tongue surface

Nerve fibers

Taste receptor cell

Taste buds

Supporting cell

Taste pore

■ **Figure 6.13   Taste Receptors**

The illustration on the left shows the tongue's surface; the one on the right shows an enlarged view of a single taste bud.

there are also some in the throat and on the roof of the mouth. If you look at your tongue in a mirror, you will notice many tiny bumps; they are called **papillae,** and they come in several forms. Each papilla contains many **taste buds** along its sides (see Figure 6.13). The buds, which up close look a little like a segmented orange, are commonly referred to, mistakenly, as the receptors for taste. The actual receptor cells, however, are inside the buds, 15 to 50 to a bud. These cells send tiny fibers out through an opening in the bud; the receptor sites are on these fibers. The receptor cells are replaced by new cells every 10 days or so. However, over time, the total number of taste buds (and therefore receptors) declines, which is why older people can often enjoy strong tastes that children may detest.

There appear to be four basic tastes: *salty, sour, bitter,* and *sweet,* each produced by a different type of chemical. Until recently, most textbooks (including, we confess, previous editions of this one) included a "tongue map," showing areas supposedly most sensitive to these tastes. But physiological psychologist Linda Bartoshuk (1993) has found that the map was based on a misleading graph published in 1942—and it is simply wrong. The four basic tastes can be perceived at any spot on the tongue where there are receptors, and differences among the areas are small.

When you bite into an egg or a piece of bread or an orange, its unique flavor is composed of some combination of the four basic taste types. The physiological details, however, are still not well understood. For example, it is not clear whether the four tastes are really points on a continuum, as colors are, or are distinct and are associated with different types of nerve fibers.

Human beings are born with a sweet tooth (Bartoshuk & Beauchamp, 1994). Just a few drops of sugar water will calm a crying newborn infant and raise an infant's pain threshold, perhaps because the sugar somehow activates endorphins, the body's natural opiates (Smith, Fillion, & Blass, 1990). Our species also seems to have a natural dislike for bitter substances, probably because many poisonous substances are bitter. But taste is also a matter of culture. For example, many North Americans who enjoy raw oysters, raw smoked salmon, and raw herring are nevertheless put off by other forms of raw seafood that are popular in Japan (such as sea urchin and octopus).

Individual tastes also vary. The French have a saying, *Chacun à son goût* ("each to his own taste"). Why do some people within a culture gobble up a dish that makes others turn green? Experience undoubtedly plays a role. As we will see in Chapter 7, one can acquire a taste or a distaste for a particular food. Recent evidence indicates that individual differences in taste sensitivity are also related to the density of taste buds; human tongues may have as few as 500 or as

■ **papillae (pa-PILL-ee)**
Knoblike elevations on the tongue, containing the taste buds. (Singular: papilla.)

■ **taste buds**
Nests of taste-receptor cells.

Nontaster   *Supertaster*

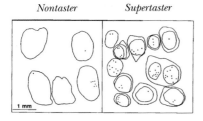

1 mm

■ Figure 6.14   On the Tip of the Tongue

"Supertasters" for certain bitter compounds have more taste buds and more fungiform (mushroom-shaped) papillae on the tip and sides of the tongue than "non-tasters," and their papillae are surrounded by rings of tissue not seen on a nontaster's papillae. Here you see tracings taken from videotapes of fungiform papillae in a non-taster (left) and a supertaster (right). The dots indicate openings to taste buds. These differences help explain why one person's bitter pill isn't always so bitter to another. (From Reedy et al., 1993.)

many as 10,000 taste buds (Miller & Reedy, 1990). Genetic differences probably make people more or less sensitive to the chemicals in particular foods (Bartoshuk, 1993). For example, some people experience a bitter taste from saccharin, caffeine, and other substances, but others do not. People who are "supertasters" for bitter substances have more taste buds on their tongues than do those who are less sensitive to such substances. Further, as Figure 6.14 shows, in supertasters, papillae of a certain type are smaller, are more densely packed, and look different than those in other people (Anliker et al., 1991; Reedy et al., 1993).

The attractiveness of a particular food can be affected by its temperature and texture. As Goldilocks found out, a bowl of cold porridge isn't nearly as delicious as one that is properly heated. And any peanut butter fan will tell you that chunky and smooth peanut butters just don't taste the same. Even more important for taste is a food's odor. Subtle flavors such as chocolate and vanilla would have little taste if we could not smell them (see Figure 6.15). The dependence of taste on smell explains why you have trouble tasting your food when you have a stuffy nose. Most people who chronically have trouble tasting things probably have a problem with smell, not taste per se. The total loss of taste is extremely rare; Linda Bartoshuk (1990) says that in a decade of evaluating disorders of smell and taste, she met only two people who could not taste a thing.

Smell: The Sense of Scents

The great author and educator Helen Keller, who was blind and deaf from infancy, once called smell "the fallen angel of the senses." Yet our sense of smell, or *olfaction*, although seemingly crude when compared to a bloodhound's, is actually quite good—and more useful than most people realize. People can detect thousands of different odors. And they can smell some substances before they can be detected by odor-sensitive machines, which is why

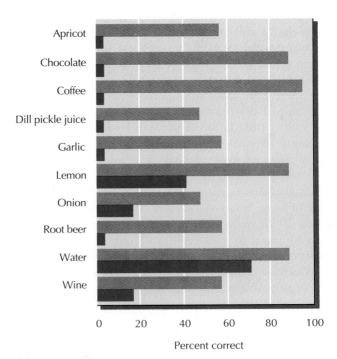

■ Figure 6.15   Taste Test

The red bars show the percentages of people who could identify a substance dropped on their tongues when they were able to smell it. The blue bars show the percentages who could identify a substance when they were prevented from smelling it. (From Mozell et al., 1969.)

human beings are often hired to detect odors in chemical plants and laboratories and to detect the freshness of fish at fish markets.

The receptors for smell are specialized neurons embedded in a tiny patch of mucous membrane in the upper part of the nasal passage, just beneath the eyes (see Figure 6.16). These receptors, about 5 million of them in each nasal cavity, respond to chemical molecules in the air. Certain molecules seem to fit certain receptors the way a key fits a lock. Somehow their effects combine to yield the yeasty smell of freshly baked bread or the spicy fragrance of a eucalyptus tree. But the neural code for smell, like that for taste, is still poorly understood.

One complicating factor is that there are many words to describe smells (rotten, burned, musky, fruity, spicy, flowery, resinous, putrid, . . .), but researchers do not agree on which smells are basic. Research suggests that there may be as many as a thousand different receptor types, with each possibly responding to only a few kinds of odor molecules (Buck & Axel, 1991). This kind of system is quite unlike the one involved in vision, where only three basic receptor cell types are involved, or the one involved in taste, where there are four basic types.

Signals from the receptors travel to the olfactory bulb in the brain. However, the discovery of so many different receptor types means that a great deal of the processing necessary for odor discrimination may occur within the nose itself. Such a system may have originally evolved because most animals were heavily dependent on smell for finding food or detecting predators. With their small brains, they needed a lot of specialized receptor cells to do the actual work of olfaction. Although smell is less vital for human survival than for the survival of other animals, it is still important. We sniff out danger by smelling smoke, food spoilage, or poison gases. Thus a deficit in the sense of smell is nothing to turn up your nose at. Such a loss can come about because of infection or disease, or because of cigarette or pipe smoking. In one study in which people took a whiff of 40 common odors, such as pizza, motor oil, and banana, smokers were nearly twice as likely as nonsmokers to show impaired ability. The researchers also found that a person who has smoked two packs a day for 10 years must abstain from cigarettes for 10 more years before odor detection will return to normal (Frye, Schwartz, & Doty, 1990).

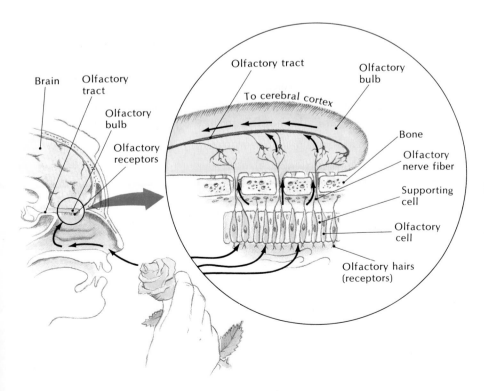

■ Figure 6.16   Receptors for Smell

Airborne chemical molecules (vapors) enter the nose and circulate through the nasal cavity, where the smell receptors are located. Sniffing draws more vapors into the nose and speeds their circulation. Vapors can also reach the nasal cavity through the mouth by way of a passageway from the throat.

Smell has not only evolutionary but also cultural significance. These pilgrims in Matsuyama, Japan, are purifying themselves with holy incense for good luck and health. Incense has always been an important commodity; the gifts of the Magi, after all, included frankincense and myrrh.

Folklore tells us that smells not only aid survival but also contribute to the sexual "chemistry" that seems to exist between some people. Interest has centered on *pheromones*, odorous chemical substances released by one member of a species that affect the physiology or behavior of other members. In many species, pheromones play a role in sexual behavior. A female cat in heat will attract, through scent, all the unneutered tomcats in the neighborhood. A female moth emits pheromones to entice male suitors who are miles away. There is some evidence that human beings, too, produce pheromones, a fact that has inspired one American perfume company to bring out a pheromone-based scent that it promises will "trigger an intense magnetic reaction" in persons of the other sex. But before you head for the perfume counter, we should tell you that there is no evidence that eau de pheromone can influence, let alone *compel*, human sexual behavior, or increase sexual allure. Natural or learned reactions to smells may well play a role in sexual attraction, but in sexual matters, human beings are generally more affected by what the brain learns and the eyes see than what the nose knows (Wade & Cirese, 1991).

Human odor preferences, like taste preferences, vary. In some societies, people use rancid fat as a hair pomade, but anyone in our culture who did so would quickly have a social problem. Within a particular culture, context and experience are all-important. The very same chemicals that contribute to unpleasant body odors and bad breath also contribute to the pleasant bouquet and flavor of cheese.

Senses of the Skin

The skin's usefulness is more than just skin deep. Besides protecting our innards, our 2 square yards of skin help us identify objects and establish intimacy with others. By providing a boundary between ourselves and everything else, the skin also gives us a sense of ourselves as distinct from the environment.

The skin senses include *touch* (or pressure), *warmth, cold,* and *pain.* At one time, it was thought that these four senses were associated with four distinct kinds of receptors, or "end organs," but this view is now in doubt. Although there are spots on the skin that are particularly sensitive to cold, warmth, pressure, and pain, no simple correspondence between the four sensations and the various types of receptors has been found. Recent research has concentrated more on the neural codes involved in the skin senses than on the receptors themselves.

Pain, which is both a skin sense and an internal sense, has come under special scrutiny. Pain differs from other senses in an important way: When the stimulus producing pain is removed, the sensation may continue—sometimes for years. Chronic pain disrupts lives, puts stress on the body, keeps people from their jobs, and causes depression and despair. (For ways of coping with pain, see "Taking Psychology with You.")

According to the **gate-control theory** of pain, the experience of pain depends partly on whether pain impulses get past a "gate" in the spinal cord and thus reach the brain (Melzack & Wall, 1965). The gate is made up of neurons that can either transmit or block pain messages from the skin, muscles, and internal organs. Pain fibers (like other kinds of fibers in the nervous system) are always active. When injury to tissue occurs, certain fibers open the gate. Normally, though, the gate is closed, either by impulses coming into the spinal cord from larger fibers that respond to pressure or by signals coming down from the brain itself. According to the gate-control theory, chronic pain occurs when disease, infection, or injury damages the fibers that ordinarily close the gate, and pain messages are able to reach the brain unchecked.

The gate-control theory may help explain the strange phenomenon of *phantom pain,* in which a person continues to feel pain that seemingly comes from an amputated limb or from a breast or internal organ that has been surgically removed. Although sense receptors that were in the body part no longer exist, the pain can nonetheless be excruciating. An amputee may feel the same aching, burning, or sharp pain from gangrenous ulcers, calf cramps, throbbing toes, surgical wounds, or even ingrown toenails that he or she endured before the surgery (Katz & Melzack, 1990).

One explanation of phantom pain is that impulses normally responsible for closing the pain "gate" are reduced or eliminated by the amputation or operation. Without these inhibitory impulses, pain fibers near the spinal cord are able to get their messages through, and pain pathways are permanently activated. Another possible explanation is that pain-producing activity in the brain, once it begins, somehow continues on its own without any further impulses from the spinal cord. This would explain why amputees who undergo complete transection (horizontal cutting) of the spinal cord may still report phantom pain (Melzack, 1990).

During the past three decades, researchers have learned that the occurrence of pain involves the release of several chemicals at the site of tissue damage and in the spinal cord and brain, including an important neurotransmitter called *substance P.* These chemicals promote inflammation and cause pain nerves to fire. The reason that chile peppers burn your tongue is that they contain capsaicin [cap-SY-a-sin], a chemical that causes nerve endings to release substance P. (But if you are exposed to enough capsaicin, substance P is eventually depleted and pain actually lessens; indeed, capsaicin is used in some arthritis remedies.) Conversely, the suppression of pain involves the release of endorphins in the brain (see Chapter 4). One effect of the endorphins is to prevent pain fibers from releasing substance P (Jessel & Iversen, 1979; Ruda, 1982).

Thus pain is far more complex than scientists thought when the gate-control theory was first proposed. However, although aspects of the gate-control theory have turned out to be incomplete or wrong, in its general outlines, the theory remains useful. It correctly predicts that mild pressure, as well as other types of stimulation, can interfere with severe or protracted pain by closing the spinal gate, either directly or by means of signals sent from the brain. When we vigorously rub a banged elbow, or apply ice packs, heat, or mustard plasters to injuries, we are acting on this principle. The idea of fighting fire with fire in order to close the pain gate has led to the development of a pain-relief device that delivers small amounts of electric current into spinal cord nerves. This

■ **gate-control theory**
The theory that the experience of pain depends in part on whether pain impulses get past a neurological "gate" in the spinal cord and thus reach the brain.

device can be installed under the skin, and patients can control the amount of stimulation themselves, with a resulting decrease in the pain they feel.

Much remains to be learned, not only about the four basic skin sensations, but also about itch, tickle, sensitivity to vibration, the sensation of wetness, and different types of pain. Researchers are trying to break the neural codes that explain why gently pricking pain spots with a needle produces itch; why lightly touching adjacent pressure spots in rapid succession produces tickle; and why the simultaneous stimulation of warm and cold spots produces not a lukewarm sensation but the sensation of heat. Decoding the messages of the skin senses will eventually tell us how we are able to distinguish sandpaper from velvet and glue from grease.

The Environment Within

We usually think of our senses as pipelines to the "outside" world, but two senses keep us informed about the movements of our own bodies. **Kinesthesis** tells us where our body parts are located and lets us know when they move. It uses pain and pressure receptors located in the muscles, joints, and tendons (tissues that connect muscles to bones). Without kinesthesis, you could not touch your finger to your nose with your eyes shut. In fact, you would have trouble with any voluntary movement. Think of how hard walking is when your leg has "fallen asleep" or how clumsy chewing is when a dentist has numbed your jaw with novocaine.

Equilibrium, or the sense of balance, gives us information about our bodies as a whole. Along with vision and touch, it lets us know whether we are standing upright or on our heads and tells us when we are falling or rotating. Equilibrium relies primarily on three **semicircular canals** in the inner ear (see Figure 6.12 on page 220). These thin tubes are filled with fluid that moves and presses on hairlike receptors whenever the head rotates. The receptors initiate messages that travel through a part of the auditory nerve that is not involved in hearing.

Normally, kinesthesis and equilibrium work together to give us a sense of our own physical reality, something we take utterly for granted but shouldn't. Oliver

▪ **kinesthesis (KIN-es-THEE-sis)**
The sense of body position and movement of body parts; also called kinesthesia.

▪ **equilibrium**
The sense of balance.

▪ **semicircular canals**
Sense organs in the inner ear that contribute to equilibrium by responding to rotation of the head.

Martha Graham photograph courtesy Barbara Morgan. Martha Graham, *Letter to the World* (Kick). 1940.

On the right, Olympic gold medalist Greg Louganis executes a winning dive that requires precise positioning of each part of his body. "I have a good kinesthetic awareness," said Louganis, with some understatement. "I am aware of where I am in space." Above is famed dancer and choreographer Martha Graham, who turned kinesthesis and balance into artistry.

Sacks (1985) tells the heartbreaking story of a young British woman named Christina, who suffered irreversible damage to her kinesthetic nerve fibers because of a mysterious inflammation. At first, Christina was as floppy as a rag doll; she could not sit up, walk, or stand. Then, slowly, she learned to do these things, relying on visual cues and sheer willpower. But her movements remained unnatural; she had to grasp a fork with painful force or she would drop it. More important, despite her remaining sensitivity to light touch on the skin, she could no longer experience herself as physically embodied: "It's like something's been scooped right out of me, right at the centre. . . ."

With equilibrium, we come, as it were, to the end of our senses. We have seen that the gathering of sensory data about the external and internal world is far from straightforward. Every second, millions of sensory signals reach the brain, which combines and integrates them to produce a model of reality from moment to moment. How does it know how to do this? Are our perceptual abilities inborn, or must we learn them? We turn next to this issue.

Quick QUIZ

Can you make some sense out of the following sensory problems?

1. April always has trouble tasting foods, especially those with subtle flavors. What's the most likely explanation of her difficulty?
2. May has chronic shoulder pain. How might the gate-control theory explain it?
3. June, a rock musician, discovers she can't hear as well as she used to. What's a likely explanation?

Answers:

1. An impaired sense of smell, possibly due to disease, illness, or cigarette smoking. 2. Nerve fibers that normally close the pain "gate" may have been damaged. Or it may be that pain-producing activity in the brain is, for some reason, continuing even without pain impulses from the spinal cord. 3. Hearing impairment has many causes, but in June's case, we might suspect that prolonged exposure to loud music has damaged the hair cells of her cochlea.

■ PERCEPTUAL POWERS: ORIGINS AND INFLUENCES

What happens when babies first open their eyes? Do they see the world the way adults do? Do they hear the same sounds that adults do, smell the same smells, taste the same tastes? Are their strategies for organizing the world innate, wired into their brains from the beginning? Or is an infant's world, as William James once suggested, only a "blooming, buzzing confusion," waiting to be organized by experience and learning? Modern research suggests that the truth lies somewhere between these two extremes.

Inborn Abilities and Perceptual Lessons

One way to study the origins of perceptual abilities is to see what happens when the usual perceptual experiences of early life fail to occur. To do so, researchers study animals whose sensory and perceptual systems are similar to our own, such as cats. What they find is that without certain experiences during critical periods of development, perception develops abnormally.

Researchers studying vision, for example, have found that when newborn animals are reared in total darkness for a period of weeks or months, or fitted with translucent goggles that permit only diffuse light to get through, or allowed to see only one visual pattern and no others, visual development is impaired. In one famous study, kittens were exposed to either vertical or horizontal black and white stripes. Special collars kept them from seeing anything else, even their own bodies. After several months, the kittens exposed only to vertical stripes seemed blind to all horizontal contours; they bumped into horizontal obstacles placed in their way and ran to play with a bar that an experimenter held vertically but not a to bar held horizontally. In contrast, those exposed only to horizontal stripes bumped into vertical obstacles and ran to play with horizontal bars but not vertical ones (Blakemore & Cooper, 1970).

How would you interpret these results? It would seem that cats need to learn to see horizontal and vertical lines in order to develop normal vision, but there is another possibility: Normal experience may merely ensure the survival of skills *already present* at birth in rudimentary form. Physiological studies suggest that this second interpretation is the correct one, at least in the case of line perception. The brains of newborn kittens are equipped with the same kinds of feature-detector cells that adult cats have. When kittens are kept from seeing lines of a particular orientation, such as horizontal or vertical ones, cells sensitive to those orientations deteriorate or change, and perception suffers (Hirsch & Spinelli, 1970; Mitchell, 1980). Moreover, there seems to be a critical period in cats, during the first 3 months after birth, when exposure to verticality and horizontality is crucial. If a kitten doesn't get this exposure, its vision will continue to be abnormal even after many years of living in a normal environment.

From findings such as these, psychologists have concluded that human infants are probably born with an ability to detect and discriminate the edges and angles of objects. Direct observations of infants and their reactions to different sensory stimuli show that they have other visual talents, as well. They can discriminate different sizes and colors very early, possibly at birth. They can distinguish contrasts, shadows, and complex patterns after only a few weeks. Even depth perception occurs early and may be present from the beginning.

Testing an infant's perception of depth requires considerable ingenuity. One clever procedure that was used for decades was to to place infants on a device called a *visual cliff* (Gibson & Walk, 1960). The "cliff" is a pane of glass covering both a shallow surface and a deep one (see Figure 6.17). The infant is placed on a board in the middle, and the child's mother tries to lure the baby across either the shallow or the deep side. Babies as young as 6 months of age will crawl to their mothers across the shallow side but will refuse to crawl out over the "cliff." Their hesitation shows that they have depth perception.

Of course, by age 6 months, a baby has had quite a bit of experience with the world. But infants younger than 6 months, even though they are unable to crawl, can also be tested on the visual cliff. At only 2 months of age, babies show a drop in heart rate when placed on the deep side of the cliff, but no change when they are placed on the shallow side. A slowed heart rate is usually a sign of increased attention. Thus, although these infants may not be frightened the way an older infant would be, it seems they can notice the difference in depth (Banks & Salapatek, 1984). By age 5 months, infants can even coordinate visual information with auditory cues to judge distance. Thus they are more likely to look at a video of an advancing or retreating train when increasing or decreasing engine noises "match" what they are seeing than when there is a conflict (Pickens, 1994).

Another line of evidence also supports the notion that some visual abilities are prewired: case histories of people who have gained sight after a lifetime of blindness. Like S. B., whose case we described at the start of this chapter, these individuals may have many visual limitations. On the other hand, even though they have never seen before, when their bandages are removed, they can dis-

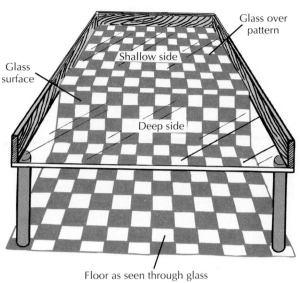

Glass over pattern

Shallow side

Glass surface

Deep side

Floor as seen through glass

▪ **Figure 6.17 A Cliff-hanger**

Infants as young as 6 months usually hesitate to crawl past the apparent edge of a visual cliff, which suggests that they are able to perceive depth.

tinguish figure from ground, scan objects, and follow moving objects with their eyes. Thus these abilities, at least, seem to be inborn.

We have been talking only about vision, but clearly other sensory abilities are also inborn or develop very early. For example, we saw earlier that infants show a distinct preference for sweet tastes but wrinkle up their noses at bitter ones. They also react strongly to particular smells, such as garlic and vinegar, but less strongly to others, such as licorice and alcohol, showing that they can discriminate among odors. And they will startle to a loud noise and turn their heads toward its source, showing that they perceive sound as being localized in space.

An infant's world, then, is far from the blooming, buzzing confusion that William James took it to be. A young child's perceptual world is not identical to an adult's; neurological connections are not completely formed, so an infant's senses are less acute. But if learning to perceive is compared to going to school, nature has allowed us to skip kindergarten and possibly even the first grade.

Psychological and Cultural Influences on Perception

The fact that some perceptual processes appear to be innate does not mean that all people perceive the world in the same way. A camera doesn't care what it "sees." A tape recorder doesn't ponder what it "hears." A robot arm on a factory assembly line holds no opinion about what it "touches." But because human beings care about what they see, hear, taste, smell, and feel, psychological factors can influence what we perceive and how we perceive it:

1. *Needs.* When we need something, have an interest in it, or want it, we are especially likely to perceive it. For example, hungry individuals are faster than others at seeing words related to hunger when the words are flashed briefly on a screen (Wispé & Drambarean, 1953).

Several decades ago, two researchers discovered that the desire of sports fans to have their team win can affect what they see during a game. Sports fans, of course, tend to regard their own team as the good guys and the opposing team as the dirty rats. In the study, Princeton and Dartmouth students were shown a

People often see what they want to see. This apartment building in a small French town drew huge crowds when some people thought they saw the face of Jesus on it. Actually, the pattern on the wall was the result of damage caused by water leaking from faulty plumbing in one of the apartments.

▪ **perceptual set**
A habitual way of perceiving, based on expectations.

movie of a football game between their two teams. The game, which Princeton won, was a rough one. Several players were injured, including Princeton's star quarterback. Princeton students viewing the film saw Dartmouth players commit an average of 9.8 rule infractions. They considered the game "rough and dirty." Dartmouth students, on the other hand, noticed only half as many infractions by their team. They considered the game rough but fair (Hastorf & Cantril, 1954).

2. *Beliefs.* What a person holds to be true about the world can affect the interpretation of ambiguous sensory signals. Suppose you spot a round object hovering high in the sky. If you believe that extraterrestrials occasionally visit the earth, you may "see" the object as a spaceship. But if you think such beliefs are hogwash, you are more likely to see a weather balloon. An image of a crucified Jesus on a garage door in Santa Fe Springs, California, caused great excitement among people who were ready to believe that divine messages may be found on everyday objects. The image was actually caused by two streetlights that merged the shadows of a bush and a "For Sale" sign in the yard.

3. *Emotions.* Emotions can also influence our interpretation of sensory information. A small child afraid of the dark may see a ghost instead of a robe hanging on the door, or a monster instead of a beloved doll. Pain, in particular, seems affected by emotion (Melzack & Dennis, 1978). Soldiers who are seriously wounded often deny being in much pain, even though they are alert and are not in shock. Their relief at being alive may offset the anxiety and fear that contribute so much to pain (although other explanations are also possible). Conversely, negative emotions such as anger, fear, sadness, or depression can prolong and intensify a person's pain (Fernandez & Turk, 1992; Fields, 1991).

4. *Expectations.* Previous experiences often affect how we perceive the world (see Figure 6.18). The tendency to perceive what you expect is called a **perceptual set.** Perceptual sets can come in handy. For example, at a noisy party, you may not catch every sound the person talking to you makes. But if she says, "How do you . . . " and then extends her hand, you may "hear" the word *do.* But perceptaul sets can also keep us from perceiving things. In Center Harbor, Maine, local legend has it that veteran newscaster Walter Cronkite was sailing into port one day when he heard a small crowd on shore shouting "Hello, Walter . . . Hello, Walter." Pleased, he waved and took a bow. Only when he ran aground did he realize what they had really been shouting: "Low water . . . low water." (By the way, there is a misspelled word right before this story. Did you

▪ **Figure 6.18   Overcoming Perceptual Expectations**

Can you draw a chair this well? If not, perhaps your perceptual expectations about chairs are getting in the way. Renowned art educator Betty Edwards (1986) uses several techniques to help people see (and then draw) what is really "out there." One of her assignments is to draw the empty spaces between the lines or shapes of an object, instead of the object itself. That technique produced this student's drawing. Why not try it yourself with some simple object, such as a chair, a cup, or your own hand with your index finger touching your thumb? You may find yourself perceiving the world around you in a fresh new way.

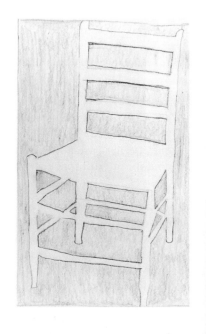

notice it? If not, probably it was because you expected all the words in this book to be spelled correctly.)

In turn, our needs, beliefs, emotions, and expectations are all affected by the culture we live in. Different cultures give people practice with different environments (see Figure 6.19). In a classic study done in the 1960s, researchers found that members of some African tribes were much less likely to be fooled by the Müller-Lyer illusion and other geometric illusions than were Westerners. Westerners, the researchers observed, live in a "carpentered" world, full of rectangular structures built with the aid of saws, planes, straight edges, and carpenter's squares. Westerners are also used to interpreting two-dimensional photographs and perspective drawings as representations of a three-dimensional world. As a result, they learn to interpret acute and obtuse angles as right angles extended in space—just the sort of habit that would increase susceptibility to the Müller-Lyer illusion. The rural Africans in the study, living in a less carpentered environment and in round huts, seemed more likely to take the lines in the figures literally, as two-dimensional, which could explain why they were less susceptible to the illusion (Segall, Campbell, & Herskovits, 1966).

This research was followed by a flurry of replications in the 1970s, showing that it was indeed culture that produced the differences between groups (Segall, 1994; Segall et al., 1990). Since then, there has been little further work on the fascinating intersection of culture and visual illusions. However, as we will be seeing throughout this book, culture affects perception in many other ways: by shaping our stereotypes, directing our attention, and telling us what is important to notice and what is not.

■ PUZZLES OF PERCEPTION

We come, finally, to two intriguing questions about perception that have captured the public's imagination for years. First, can we perceive, through our usual sensory channels, what is happening in the world without conscious awareness? Second, is it possible to pick up signals from the world or from other people without using our usual sensory channels at all?

Conscious and Nonconscious Perception

Certainly many aspects of perception occur outside of awareness. As we have seen, before something can be recognized or identified, its basic features must be analyzed. In the case of vision, we must make out edges, colors, textures, and differences in the reflectance of light. We must separate figure from ground, calculate distance or depth, and adjust for changing patterns of stimulation on the retina. All this we do without any conscious intention or awareness.

Persons who are blind to half of the visual field because of damage in the visual cortex provide striking evidence for the nonconscious nature of basic perceptual processes. When these people are presented with a brief flash of light in the part of the visual field affected, they deny seeing it. But when they are asked to *guess* where the light is by pointing to it or by directing their eyes toward it, some do much better than chance, although they continue to deny seeing anything—a phenomenon known as "blindsight." A patient may even be able to distinguish a vertical line from a horizontal one, or an *X* from an *O*, with better than chance accuracy. One research team argues that blindsight occurs because of "islands of functional brain tissue" in the brain area that have been damaged (Fendrich, Wessinger, & Gazzaniga, 1992). However, most researchers who study blindsight believe it occurs because messages from the eyes reach parts of the brain other than the visual cortex, areas that handle elementary kinds of visual information without a person's conscious awareness (Braddock et al., 1992; Ptito et al., 1991; Stoerig, 1993; Weiskrantz, 1992). They point out that blindsight has been observed in monkeys that have had both halves of the visual cortex removed and in children who have had an entire hemisphere removed.

What about more complicated perceptual tasks, such as registering and deciphering speech? Research on selective attention and the "cocktail party phenomenon," discussed earlier, shows that even when we are oblivious to unattended speech sounds, we are processing and recognizing them at some level. Other tantalizing evidence of nonconscious perception comes from studies of people anesthetized and apparently unconscious during surgery, who have later shown signs of having heard remarks made by doctors (or researchers) during the operation (Bennett, 1988; Kihlstrom et al., 1990; Millar & Watkinson, 1983; Sebel, Bonke, & Winograd, 1993). However, it is not always clear in this research just how deeply anesthetized the patients really were.

The sorts of nonconscious processes we have been discussing all involve stimuli that would be *above* the absolute threshold if a person were consciously attending to them. Is it also possible to perceive and respond to messages that are *below* the threshold—too quiet to be consciously heard (in the case of hearing) or too brief or dim to be consciously seen (in the case of vision), even when you are trying your best to hear or see them? Perhaps you have seen ads for products that will allow you to take advantage of such "subliminal perception." Or perhaps you have heard that subliminal perception doesn't really exist. What are the facts?

First, there is considerable evidence that a simple visual stimulus *can* affect a person's responses to a task even when the person has no awareness of seeing the stimulus. For example, in one study, people subliminally exposed to a face tended to prefer the face over one they did not "see" in this way (Bornstein, Leone, & Galley, 1987). In another study, words were briefly flashed on a screen and were then immediately masked by a pattern of *X*'s and *O*'s. Subjects said they could not read the words or even tell whether a word had appeared at all. But when an "invisible" word (e.g., *bread*) was followed by a second, visible word that was either related in meaning (e.g., *butter*) or unrelated (e.g., *bubble*), the subjects were able to read the related word more quickly (Dagenbach, Carr, & Wilhelmsen, 1989).

Findings such as these are remarkable and are potentially important for theories of how the mind works. They have convinced many psychologists that people often know more than they know they know (Greenwald, 1992; Moore, 1992). In fact, nonconscious processing appears to occur not only in perception, but also in memory, thinking, and decision making, as we will see in Chap-

For only $29.95, a "subliminal-perception tape" promises to tune up your sluggish motivation. It's true that many perceptual processes occur outside of awareness, but does that mean that "subliminal" tapes can change your behavior or improve your life?

ters 8 and 9. However, the real-world implications of subliminal perception are not as dramatic as you might think. Even in the laboratory, where researchers have considerable control, the phenomenon is hard to demonstrate, and subtle changes in procedure can affect the results. The strongest evidence comes from studies using simple stimuli (faces or single words, such as *bread*), rather than complex stimuli such as sentences ("Eat whole-wheat bread, not white bread"). Some psychoanalytic researchers have reported that the sentence "Mommy and I are one," presented subliminally, can make anxious, depressed, or disturbed patients feel better (Silverman & Weinberger, 1985). However, serious questions exist about the methods used by these researchers in their studies, and it is not clear how "subliminal" the "Mommy" sentence really was, so most psychologists remain skeptical about these claims (Greenwald, 1992; Moore, 1989). Timothy Moore, one such skeptic, told us he will be convinced when the "Mommy" stimulus gets positive results in comparison to a control stimulus that merely changes two letters: "Tommy and I ate one."

Moreover, while visual subliminal perception may occur under certain conditions, subliminal *persuasion,* the subject of many popular books and magazine articles, is quite another matter. Empirical research has uncovered no basis whatsoever for believing that Madison Avenue can seduce us into buying soft drinks or voting for political candidates by flashing subliminal slogans on television, or by slipping subliminal images into magazine ads or supermarket music—as we discuss further in "Psychology and Popular Culture," on page 236.

Quick QUIZ

Suppose you hear about a study that appeared to find evidence of "sleep learning"—the ability to perceive and retain material played on an audiotape while a person sleeps. What would you want to know about this research before deciding to tape this chapter and play it by your bedside all night instead of studying it in the usual way?

Answer:

You might ask about the kinds of stimuli used (in studies of nonconscious perception, positive results have been obtained with very simple stimuli, not running text); whether the results were large enough to have practical consequences; and most important, how it was determined that the subjects were really asleep while the tape was playing. (When EEG measurements are used to verify that subjects are actually sleeping, no "sleep learning" takes place. So if you want to learn the material in this chapter, you'll have to stay awake!)

Extrasensory Perception: Reality or Illusion?

Eyes, ears, mouth, nose, skin—we rely on these organs for our experience of the external world. Some people, however, claim they can send and receive messages about the world without relying on the usual sensory channels, by using *extrasensory perception,* or *ESP.*

Reported ESP experiences (also known as *Psi,* a shortening of "psychic phenomena") fall into four general categories: (1) *Telepathy* is direct communication from one mind to another without the usual visual, auditory, and other sensory signals. If you try to guess what number someone is thinking of or what card a person is holding out of sight, you are attempting telepathy. (2) *Clairvoyance* is the perception of an event or fact without normal sensory input. If a man

For the most part, the meeting was quite successful. Only a slight tension filled the air, stemming from the unforeseen faux pas of everyone wearing the same dress.

suddenly "knows" that his wife has just died, yet no one has informed him of the death, he might be called clairvoyant. (3) *Precognition* is the perception of an event that has not yet happened. Fortune-tellers make their livings by claiming to read the future in tea leaves or in a person's palm. (4) *Out-of-body experiences* involve the perception of one's own body from "outside," as an observer might see it. The person feels that he or she has left the physical body entirely. Such experiences are often reported by persons who have been near death, but some people say they can bring them on at will.

Some types of ESP are more plausible than others, given what we know about the physical world. Normal perception depends on the ability to detect changes in energy. Conceivably, telepathy could involve something similar: the sending and receiving of changes in energy through channels that have not yet

*P*sychology and *P*opular Culture

*S*ubliminal Persuasion

■ In 1957, a public-relations executive issued a press release that described a brave new tactic in advertising. Movie audiences in New Jersey, the executive said, had been unwittingly persuaded to "drink Coca-Cola" and "eat popcorn" when these messages were superimposed on the movie they were watching. The messages were flashed on the screen so quickly that no one could tell they were there, yet people had supposedly flocked to the refreshment counter with cravings for a Coke and a bad case of the munchies. Although the marketing firm reponsible for this gimmick offered no proof of these results, the report caused considerable public panic. If consumers could be induced by subliminal messages to buy snacks, what was to prevent unscrupulous politicians from using the same techniques for more sinister purposes? What was to prevent the media from using them for their own sneaky goals, as a Seattle radio station tried to do when it broadcast the "subaudible" message, "TV's a bore" (Moore, 1982)?

Later, it turned out that the whole thing had been a hoax; no study had ever been done (Rogers, 1992–1993). Hysteria over the threat of subliminal advertising and political manipulation soon faded, but claims about subliminal techniques refused to die. In the 1970s, a best-selling book called *Subliminal Seduction* warned that pictures cleverly hidden in magazine advertisements were inducing consumers to buy products they didn't really want. Finding these supposed pictures became a sort of parlor game—the 1970s version of "Where's Waldo?"

In the mid-1980s, subliminal persuasion was reborn in still another form: Parents worried that "subliminal" messages recorded on music albums were influencing young people to commit immoral

or dangerous acts. In 1990, the parents of two young men who had tried to commit suicide (one succeeded, one survived but was seriously injured) brought suit against the rock group Judas Priest. A subliminal message ("DO IT") on one of the band's albums, claimed the parents, had provoked the boys' suicidal impulses. Psychologists brought in to testify for the defense demonstrated that there is no evidence that such messages can affect behavior: Carefully controlled research shows that they aren't processed as meaningful speech and can't possibly affect either actions or attitudes (Begg, Needham, & Bookbinder, 1993; Vokey & Read, 1985). The defense also pointed out that millions of other people listened to the album without killing themselves, and, most important, that other factors were more likely to have led to the suicides. These young men, for example, had had a history of emotional disturbance, delinquency, drug abuse, and family violence (Moore, 1994; Pratkanis & Aronson, 1992). The parents lost their suit.

Today, the belief that subliminal persuasion exists lives on, except that now these techniques are said to be beneficial rather than harmful. Countless numbers of subliminal tapes promise, among other things, to help you slim down, stop smoking, relieve stress, read faster, lower your cholesterol, stop biting your nails, overcome jet lag, stop taking drugs, stop swearing, and enlarge your bust. One company even markets a tape "just for newborns." (Our favorite title is "Housekeeping with Love.") These tapes earn $50 million a year, and most laypeople assume they work. What can psychological research tell us about their effectiveness?

The answer is clear as a bell: A substantial body of research shows that the manufacturers' claims

been identified. Other forms of ESP, however, challenge everything we suppose to be true about the way the world and the universe operate. Precognition, for instance, contradicts our usual assumptions about time and space. If it exists, then tomorrow is as real as today, and future events can be known, even though they cannot have caused physical changes in the environment.

Evidence—or Coincidence?   Much of the "evidence" for extrasensory perception comes from anecdotal accounts. Unfortunately, people are not always reliable reporters. They often embellish and exaggerate, or recall only parts of an experience. They also tend to "forget" incidents that don't fit their beliefs, such as "premonitions" of events that fail to occur. Many ESP experiences could merely be unusual coincidences that are memorable because they are dramatic

It might be fun to have ESP, especially before a tough exam or a blind date. However, it's one thing to wish ESP existed and another to conclude that it does. What kind of evidence would convince you that ESP is real, and what kind is only wishful thinking?

have no support; people cannot discriminate a tape with a supposedly subliminal message from a placebo (Eich & Hyman, 1992; Merikle & Skanes, 1992; Moore, 1995). In one typical study, some 200 college students and other adults listened every day to commercially available tapes that claimed to improve memory or boost self-esteem. Some people thought they were using memory tapes but were actually using self-esteem tapes, or vice versa. Others listened to correctly labeled tapes. These people had all volunteered, and they wanted the tapes to work. At the end of a month, about half thought they had improved in the area corresponding to the label they had received, *whether the label was correct or not.* But in reality, there were *no* actual improvements beyond a general placebo effect (Greenwald et al., 1991).

In another study, Philip Merikle and Heather Skanes (1992) had female students and staff members at the University of Waterloo listen to weight-loss tapes. All of the women were overweight, and all believed the tapes could help them shed extra pounds. One group of women listened to tapes purchased from the manufacturer, another group listened to a "placebo" tape with no message on it, and a third group didn't listen to any tape at all. Each woman was weighed once a week for five weeks. By the end of the study, all of the women had lost weight, and the amount lost was about the same for all three groups. The researchers suggested that regular use of subliminal weight-loss tapes may simply make people more aware of weight and dieting.

A third study demonstrated how expectations can account for any "effects" that a subliminal tape may appear to have. College students listened to a

jazz tape that supposedly contained a subliminal message; actually, there was no message. Students who believed in subliminal persuasion were more likely than nonbelievers to think they heard a message, and they also reported greater mood changes while listening to the tape (Benoit & Thomas, 1992).

As we discuss in the text, subliminal *perception*—detection of a signal at better than chance levels even when you think you didn't see or hear it—appears to be a real phenomenon. But the conditions in which it occurs in the laboratory, where all extraneous stimulation is controlled and each participant's personal threshold is usually measured to determine what "below threshold" really means, rarely occur out in the real world. Timothy Moore (1995), who has studied subliminal perception for years, says that although future research could reveal some as-yet-undiscovered therapeutic use of sublimation stimulation, "given our current understanding of unconscious cognition the possibility seems very remote." As for subliminal tapes, Moore (1992) concludes that they are sheer quackery, part of a long tradition of selling useless products to vulnerable customers who want quick cures. (The tape companies are not pleased; one manufacturer called Moore an "intellectual terrorist," and other scientists who have criticized the tapes have also been subjected to personal attacks by some industry defenders.)

If advertisers want you to buy something, therefore, they would do better to spend their money on *above*-threshold messages that you can consciously evaluate. And if you want to improve yourself or your life, we encourage you to do so—but you'll probably have to do it the old-fashioned way: by working at it. ■

(see Chapter 2). What passes for telepathy, clairvoyance, or precognition could also be based on what a person knows or deduces through ordinary means. If Joanne's father has had two heart attacks, her "premonition" that her father will die shortly (followed, in fact, by her father's death) may not really be so impressive.

The scientific way to establish that a phenomenon exists is to produce it under controlled conditions. Extrasensory perception has been studied extensively by researchers in the field of **parapsychology.** In a typical study, a person might be asked to guess which of five symbols will appear on a card presented at random. A "sender" who can see the card before it is presented tries to transmit a mental image of the symbol to the person. Although most people do no better than chance at guessing the symbols, in some studies, a few people have consistently done somewhat better than chance. But ESP studies have often been sloppily designed, with inadequate precautions against fraud and improper statistical analysis. When skeptical researchers try to repeat the studies, they get negative results. After an exhaustive review, the National Research Council concluded that there was "no scientific justification . . . for the existence of parapsychological phenomena" (Druckman & Swets, 1988).

The issue has not gone away, however. Recently, a well-known social psychologist, Daryl Bem, made waves in the psychological community when he reported a series of ESP studies carried out with the late Charles Honorton, a British parapsychologist. Bem and Honorton (1994) studied telepathy (what they call the "anomalous process of information transfer") by using a variation of a method known as the *ganzfeld* ("total field") procedure. A sender sits in a soundproof room and concentrates on a picture or video clip selected at random by a computer. A receiver sits in another soundproof room; at the end of the transmission period, the receiver is shown four pictures or video clips and is asked to pick out the one that most closely matched his or her mental imagery during the transmission period. If the receiver selects the stimulus that was "sent," that trial is counted as a "hit." Bem and Honorton reported an overall hit rate of about 33 percent, whereas chance would predict only 25 percent.

The methods used by Bem and Honorton were far superior to those of previous researchers, but of course, their methods and findings have been subjected to much critical interpretation. Ray Hyman (1994), a leading critic of parapsychology, has pointed out possible flaws in the way the target stimuli were randomized and selected. Everyone agrees that the findings need to be replicated in other laboratories, and as we write this chapter, several researchers are gearing up to do the necessary studies. It will be interesting to see what happens, although we think it is safe to say that caution is warranted. The history of research on psychic phenomena has been one of initial enthusiasm followed by disappointment when results cannot be replicated, and the thousands of studies done over the past 50 years have failed to make a convincing case for ESP.

Lessons from a Magician.   Despite the lack of evidence for ESP, about half of all Americans say they believe in it. Perhaps you yourself have had an experience that seemed to involve ESP or have seen a convincing demonstration by someone else. Surely you can trust the evidence of your own eyes—or can you? We will answer with a true story that contains an important lesson, not only about ESP but about ordinary perception as well.

Several years ago, physician Andrew Weil (whose writings on drug use we discussed in Chapter 5) set out to investigate the claims of a self-proclaimed psychic named Uri Geller (Weil, 1974a, 1974b). Geller seemed able to bend keys without touching them, start broken watches, and guess the nature of simple drawings hidden in sealed envelopes. Although he had performed as a stage

■ **parapsychology**
The study of purported psychic phenomena such as ESP and mental telepathy.

magician in Israel, his native country, he denied using trickery. His powers, he said, came from energy from another universe.

Weil, who believed in telepathy, felt that ESP might be explained by principles of modern physics and was receptive to Geller's claims. When he met Geller at a private gathering, he was not disappointed. Geller correctly identified a cross and a Star of David sealed inside separate envelopes. He made a stopped watch start running and a ring sag into an oval shape, apparently without touching them. He made keys change shape in front of Weil's very eyes. Weil came away a convert. What he had seen with his own eyes seemed impossible to deny . . . until he met The Amazing Randi.

James Randi is a well-known magician who is dedicated to educating the public about psychic deception. To Weil's astonishment, Randi was able to duplicate much of what Geller had done. He, too, could bend keys and guess the contents of sealed envelopes. But Randi's feats were only tricks, and he was willing to show Weil exactly how they were done. Weil suddenly experienced "a sense of how strongly the mind can impose its own interpretations on perceptions; how it can see what it expects to see, but not see the unexpected."

Weil was dis-illusioned—literally. He was forced to admit that the evidence of one's own eyes is *not* always reliable. Even when he knew what to look for in a trick, he could not catch The Amazing Randi doing it. Weil learned that our sense impressions of reality are not the same as reality. Our eyes, our ears, and especially our brains can play tricks on us.

The great Greek philosopher Plato once said that "knowledge is nothing but perception," but in fact, simple perception is *not* always the best path to knowledge. The truth about human behavior is most likely to emerge if we are aware of how our beliefs and assumptions shape and alter our perceptions. As we have seen throughout this chapter, we do not passively register the world "out there." We mentally construct it.

"Seeing is believing," goes the old saying, but is it? The engraving on the left shows "a living half woman." The one on the right reveals how the illusion is produced: A diagonal mirror reflects the floor or carpet pattern, so onlookers think they see an unbroken expanse of floor. The moral: Be skeptical when someone claims to possess "supranormal" powers, even if you "saw it with your own eyes."

Taking Psychology with You

Living with Pain

*T*emporary pain is an unpleasant but necessary part of life, a warning of disease or injury. Chronic pain, which is ongoing or recurring, is another matter, a serious problem in itself. Back injuries, arthritis, migraine headaches, serious illnesses such as cancer—all can cause unrelieved misery to pain sufferers and their families. Chronic pain can also impair the immune system (Page et al., 1993), and such impairment can put patients at risk of further complications from their illnesses.

At one time, the only way to combat pain was with drugs or surgery, which were not always effective. Today, we know that the experience of pain is affected by attitudes, actions, emotions, and circumstances, and that treatment must take into account psychology as well as biology. Even social roles can influence a person's response to pain. For example, in pain experiments done in the laboratory, men tend to "tough it out" longer than women do. But a real-world study of people in constant pain for more than six months found that men suffered more severe psychological distress than women, possibly because the male role made it hard for them to admit their pain (Snow et al., 1986).

Many pain-treatment programs encourage patients to manage their pain themselves instead of relying entirely on health-care professionals. Usually, these programs combine several strategies:

- *Painkilling medication.* Doctors often worry that patients will become addicted to painkillers or will develop a tolerance to the drugs. The physicians will therefore give a minimal dose, then wait until the effects wear off and the patient is once again in agony before giving more. This approach is *ineffective* and ignores the fact that addiction depends in part on the motives for which a drug is taken and the circumstances under which it is used (see Chapters 5 and 15). The method now recommended by experts (although doctors and hospitals do not always follow the advice) is to give pain sufferers a continuous dose of painkiller in whatever amount is necessary to keep them pain-free, and to allow them to do this for themselves when they leave the hospital. This strategy leads to *reduced* dosages rather than increasing ones and does not lead to drug dependence (Hill et al., 1990; Portenoy, 1994).

- *Spouse or family involvement.* When a person is in pain, friends and relatives understandably tend to sympathize and excuse the sufferer from regular responsibilities. The sufferer takes to bed, avoids physical activity, and focuses on the pain. As we will see in Chapter 7, attention from others is a powerful reinforcer of whatever behavior produces the attention. Also, focusing on pain tends to increase it, and inactivity can lead to shortened muscles, muscle spasms, and fatigue. So sympathy and attention can sometimes backfire and may actually prolong the agony (Flor, Kerns, & Turk, 1987). For this reason, many pain experts now encourage family members to resist rewarding or reinforcing the pain and to reward activity, exercise, and wellness instead. This approach, however, must be used carefully, preferably under the direction of a professional, since a patient's complaints about pain are an important diagnostic tool for the physician (Rodgers, 1988).

- *Self-management.* When patients learn to identify how, when, and where their pain occurs, this knowledge helps them determine whether the pain is being maintained by external events. Just having a sense of control over one's pain can have a powerful pain-reducing effect. In a recent study, students who monitored their pain while their hand was submerged in freezing water showed more rapid recovery from the pain than did students who had tried to suppress their awareness of pain sensations or distract themselves, apparently because the monitoring students had a sense of control (Cioffi & Holloway, 1993). Patients also need muscle "reeducation"; instead of tensing muscles in response to pain, which only makes the pain worse, patients can learn to relax them (Keefe & Gil, 1986).

- *Biofeedback, hypnosis,* and *progressive relaxation.* These techniques have all been successful with some patients. (We discussed biofeedback in Chapter 4, hypnosis in Chapter 5.) It is unclear, however, whether biofeedback and progressive relaxation are applicable to all types of chronic pain.

- *Cognitive-behavioral therapy.* Cognitive-behavioral strategies teach people to recognize the connections among thoughts, feelings, and pain; substitute adaptive thoughts for negative ones; and use coping strategies such as distraction, relabeling of sensations, and imagery to alleviate suffering (see Chapter 16). All of these techniques increase feelings of control and reduce feelings of inadequacy.

For further information about help for pain, you can contact pain clinics or services in teaching hospitals and medical schools. There are many reputable clinics around the country, some specializing in specific disorders. But take care: There are also many untested therapies and quack practitioners who only prey on people's pain.

Summary

1. *Sensation* is the detection or encoding of changes in physical energy caused by environmental or internal events. *Perception* is the process by which sensory impulses are organized and interpreted.

2. Sensation begins with the sense receptors, which convert the energy of a stimulus into electrical impulses that travel along nerves to the brain, a conversion of energy called *transduction*. Separate sensations can be accounted for by *anatomical* codes (the *doctrine of specific nerve energies*) and *functional* codes in the nervous system. There is still controversy about how functional encoding yields an overall perception of a stimulus.

3. Psychologists in the area of *psychophysics* study sensory sensitivity by measuring *absolute and difference thresholds*. *Signal-detection theory* assumes that an observer's response in a detection task consists of both a sensory process and a decision process; the theory has led to improved methods for estimating individual thresholds.

4. Our senses respond to change and contrast in the environment. When stimulation is unchanging, *sensory adaptation* occurs. Too little stimulation can cause *sensory deprivation,* and too much stimulation can cause *sensory overload,* which is why we exercise *selective attention.*

5. Vision is affected by the wavelength, frequency, and complexity of light, which produce the psychological dimensions of visual experience—hue, brightness, and saturation. The visual receptors, *rods* and *cones,* are located in the *retina* of the eye. Rods are responsible for vision in dim light; cones are responsible for color vision. The visual world is not a mosaic of light and dark spots but a collection of lines and angles detected and integrated by special *feature-detector cells* in the visual areas of the brain. The eye is not a camera; the brain takes in fragmentary information about lines, angles, shapes, motion, brightness, texture, and other features of what we see, and comes up with a unified view of the world.

6. The *trichromatic* and *opponent-process* theories of color vision apply to different stages of processing. In the first stage, three types of cones respond selectively to different wavelengths of light. In the second, cells in the visual system known as *opponent-process cells* respond in opposite fashion to short and long wavelengths of light.

7. Perception involves the active construction of a model of the world from moment to moment. The *Gestalt principles* (such as *figure and ground, proximity, closure, similarity,* and *continuity*) describe visual strategies used in form perception. Gestalt and other perceptual principles can be used to improve the design of everyday objects.

8. We localize objects in visual space by using both *binocular* and *monocular* cues. Monocular cues to depth include interposition, linear perspective, and relative size. *Perceptual constancies* of shape, location, brightness, color, and size allow us to perceive objects as stable despite changes in the sensory patterns they produce. *Perceptual illusions* occur when sensory cues are misleading or when we misinterpret cues; illusions provide useful hints about perceptual processing.

9. Hearing, or *audition,* is affected by the intensity, frequency, and complexity of pressure waves in the air or other transmitting substance, corresponding to the experience of loudness, pitch, and timbre of the sound. The receptors for hearing are hair cells (cilia) embedded in the *basilar membrane,* in the interior of the *cochlea.* The sounds we hear are determined by patterns of hair-cell movement. Gestalt principles apply to auditory as well as visual perception. When we localize sounds, we use as cues subtle differences in how pressure waves reach the two ears.

10. Taste, or *gustation,* is a chemical sense. Elevations on the tongue, called *papillae,* contain many *taste buds.* There are four basic tastes—salty, sour, bitter,

and sweet. Responses to a particular taste depend on culture, genetic differences among individuals ("supertasters" can taste a bitter compound that nontasters cannot), the texture and temperature of the food, and above all, the food's smell.

11. Smell, or *olfaction,* is also a chemical sense. No basic odors have been identified, and the neural code for smell remains to be worked out. Research suggests that there may be as many as a thousand different receptor types for smell, and that much of the processing for smell occurs within the nose itself. Cultural and individual differences affect people's responses to particular odors. *Pheromones* have not yet been shown to play a role in human sexual response.

12. The skin senses include touch (pressure), warmth, cold, and pain. There does not seem to be a simple connection between these four senses and different types of receptors. Pain is both a skin sense and an internal sense. According to the *gate-control theory,* the experience of pain depends on whether neural impulses get past a "gate" in the spinal cord and reach the brain. This theory, although not correct in all its details, has led to important advances in pain treatment. Pain also depends on the release of certain chemicals at the site of tissue damage, and pain suppression involves the release of endorphins in the brain.

13. *Kinesthesis* tells us where our body parts are located, and *equilibrium* tells us the orientation of the body as a whole. Together, these two senses provide us with a feeling of physical embodiment.

14. Studies of animals, human infants, and blind people who have recovered their sight suggest that many fundamental perceptual skills are inborn or acquired shortly after birth. By using the *visual cliff,* for example, psychologists have learned that babies have depth perception by the age of 6 months and possibly even earlier. However, without certain experiences early in life, cells in the nervous system deteriorate, change, or fail to form appropriate neural pathways, and perception is impaired.

15. Psychological influences on perception include needs, beliefs, emotions, and expectations. All of these influences are affected by culture, which gives people practice with certain kinds of experiences. Because psychological factors affect the way we construct the perceptual world, the evidence of our senses is not always reliable.

16. Many perceptual processes occur outside of awareness and without conscious intention, and in the laboratory, simple visual subliminal messages can influence behavior. However, there is no evidence that complex behaviors (such as losing weight or raising self-esteem) can be manipulated by "subliminal-perception" tapes, as discussed in "Psychology and Popular Culture."

17. *Extrasensory perception* (ESP) refers to paranormal abilities such as telepathy, clairvoyance, precognition, and out-of-body experiences. Although many people believe that ESP exists, they tend to overlook disconfirming evidence—for example, times when they "knew" something bad was going to happen and it didn't. There is to date no replicated and convincing evidence for ESP. Many so-called psychics take advantage of people's desire to believe in ESP, but what they do is no different from the tricks of any good magician. The story of ESP supports the most important fact about human perception: that it does not merely capture objective reality, but also reflects our needs, biases, and beliefs.

Key Terms

sensation *197*
sense receptors *197*
perception *198*
transduction *199*
anatomical codes *199*

doctrine of specific nerve energies *199*
functional codes *199*
psychophysics *200*
absolute threshold *200*

7
Learning

In this drawing by a nineteenth-century French satirist, fish use jewels, wine, awards, and money as bait to catch people. As this chapter shows, people will indeed respond to such "lures," but they aren't everything.

[R]eward and punishment . . . these are the spur and reins whereby all mankind are set on work, and guided.

■ JOHN LOCKE ■

It's January 1, a brand-new year. The sins and lapses of the old year are behind you; you're ready for a fresh start. Optimistically, you sit down to record your New Year's resolutions:

1. Eat healthfully; no more extra-rich ice cream.
2. Raise grades; spend more time studying.
3. Be easier to get along with; control temper.
4. Get more exercise; take up jogging.
5. Control spending; pay off credit card.
6. (You fill in the blank.)

How likely are you to achieve these goals? Some people do fulfill most of their resolutions. For others, the road to frustration is paved with good intentions. Within weeks, days, or even hours, they find themselves backsliding ("Well, maybe just one *small* dish of ice cream"). They may end up feeling like the proverbial old dog, unable to learn new tricks. In fact, however, all of us can learn new tricks. By studying the laws of learning, we can improve our ability to change behavior in desirable ways—as we will see in this chapter.

In ordinary speech, the word *learning* often refers to classroom activities, such as memorizing the facts of geography, or the acquisition of practical skills, such as carpentry or sewing. But to psychologists, **learning** is *any* relatively permanent change in behavior that occurs because of experience (excluding changes due to fatigue, injury, or disease). Experience is the great teacher, altering an organism's nervous system and, through the nervous system, its behavior. Learning provides the essential link between the past and the future, enabling an organism to adapt to changing circumstances in order to survive and thrive. Our species is more dependent on learning than is any other; over a lifetime, each of us acquires not only those characteristics typical of our species but also thousands of attributes that make us unique as individuals. But learning is a fundamental process in all animals, from the lowliest backyard bug to the most eminent human scholar.

Research on learning has been heavily influenced by **behaviorism,** the view that psychologists should explain behavior in terms of observable events rather than hypothetical mental processes. Behavioral research has led to the discovery of many powerful principles of animal and human behavior, although not all psychologists believe that these principles are sufficient. Social-learning theorists and cognitive psychologists, in particular, argue that omitting mental processes from explanations of human learning is like omitting passion from descriptions of sex: You may explain the form, but you miss the substance. To them, learning is not so much a change in behavior as a change in *knowledge* that has the *potential* for affecting behavior.

■ **learning**
A relatively permanent change in behavior (or behavioral potential) due to experience.

■ **behaviorism**
An approach to psychology that emphasizes the study of observable behavior and the role of the environment as a determinant of behavior.

Ivan Pavlov is in the center, flanked by his students and a canine subject.

■ CLASSICAL CONDITIONING: NEW REFLEXES FROM OLD

At the turn of the century, the great Russian physiologist Ivan Pavlov (1849–1936) was studying salivation in dogs, as part of a research program on digestion. His work would shortly win him the Nobel Prize in physiology and medicine. One of Pavlov's procedures was to make a surgical opening in a dog's cheek, then insert a tube that conducted saliva away from the animal's salivary gland so it could be measured. To stimulate the reflexive flow of saliva, Pavlov placed meat powder or other food in the dog's mouth. This procedure was later refined by others (see Figure 7.1).

Pavlov was a truly dedicated scientific observer. Many years later, as he lay dying, he even dictated his sensations for posterity! During his salivation studies, Pavlov noticed something that most people would have overlooked or dismissed as trivial. After a dog had been brought to the laboratory a number of times, it would start to salivate *before* the food was placed in its mouth. The sight or smell of the food, the dish in which the food was kept, even the sight of the person who delivered the food or the sound of the person's footsteps were

■ **Figure 7.1   A Modification of Pavlov's Method**

Pavlov's work inspired others to refine his techniques. In this apparatus, saliva collected from a dog's cheek flowed down a tube and was measured by the movement of a needle on a revolving drum.

enough to start the dog's mouth watering. This new salivary response clearly was not inborn but was acquired through experience.

At first, Pavlov treated the dog's excessive drooling as an annoying "psychic secretion." But after reviewing the literature on reflexes, he realized that he had stumbled onto an important phenomenon, one that he came to believe was the basis of all learning in human beings and other animals. He called that phenomenon a "conditional" reflex—conditional because it depended on environmental conditions. Later, an error in the translation of his writings resulted in "conditional" becoming "conditioned," the word most commonly used today.

Pavlov soon dropped what he had been doing and turned to the study of conditioned reflexes, to which he would devote the last three decades of his life. Why were his dogs salivating to aspects of the environment other than food? Pavlov decided that it was pointless to speculate about his dogs' thoughts, wishes, or memories. Instead, he analyzed the environment in which the conditioned reflex arose. The original salivary reflex, according to Pavlov, consisted of an **unconditioned stimulus (US),** food, and an **unconditioned response (UR),** salivation. By an *unconditioned stimulus,* Pavlov meant an event or stimulus that elicits a response automatically or reflexively. By an *unconditioned response,* he meant the response that is automatically produced:

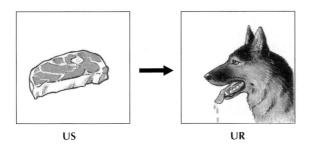

US   UR

Learning occurs, Pavlov said, when some neutral stimulus is regularly paired with an unconditioned stimulus. The neutral stimulus then becomes a **conditioned stimulus (CS),** which elicits a learned or **conditioned response (CR)** that is similar to the original, unlearned one. (We now know, however, that the CR need not be similar to the UR.) In Pavlov's laboratory, the sight of the food dish, which had not previously elicited salivation, became a CS for salivation:

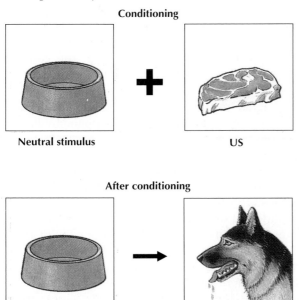

Conditioning

Neutral stimulus   US

After conditioning

CS   CR

■ **unconditioned stimulus (US)**
The classical-conditioning term for a stimulus that elicits a reflexive response in the absence of learning.

■ **unconditioned response (UR)**
The classical-conditioning term for a reflexive response elicited by a stimulus in the absence of learning.

■ **conditioned stimulus (CS)**
The classical-conditioning term for an initially neutral stimulus that comes to elicit a conditioned response after being associated with an unconditioned stimulus.

■ **conditioned response (CR)**
The classical-conditioning term for a response that is elicited by a conditioned stimulus; occurs after the conditioned stimulus is associated with an unconditioned stimulus.

In a series of experiments, Pavlov showed that a wide variety of stimuli can become a conditioned stimulus for salivation—the ticking of a metronome, the musical tone of a tuning fork, the vibrating sound of a buzzer, a triangle drawn on a large card, even a pinprick or an electric shock. None of these stimuli naturally elicits salivation, but if paired with food, all of them will. The optimal interval between the presentation of the CS and the presentation of the US depends on the kind of response being conditioned; in the laboratory, it is often less than a second.

The process by which a neutral stimulus becomes a conditioned stimulus became known as **classical conditioning** and is also sometimes called *Pavlovian* or *respondent conditioning*. Because the terminology of classical conditioning can be hard to learn, let's pause for a Quick Quiz before going on.

Quick QUIZ

See whether you can name the four components of classical conditioning in these two situations.

1. Five-year-old Samantha is watching a storm from her window. A huge bolt of lightning is followed by a tremendous thunderclap, and Samantha jumps at the noise. This happens several more times. There is a brief lull and then another lightning bolt. Samantha jumps in response to the bolt.
2. Gregory's mouth waters whenever he eats anything with lemon in it. One day, while reading an ad that shows a big glass of lemonade, Gregory notices his mouth watering.

Answers:

1. US = the thunderclap; UR = jumping elicited by the noise; CS = the sight of the lightning; CR = jumping elicited by the lightning. 2. US = the taste of lemon; UR = salivation elicited by the taste of lemon; CS = the picture of a glass of lemonade; CR = salivation elicited by the picture.

Since Pavlov's time, researchers have established that nearly any automatic, involuntary response can become a conditioned response—for example, heartbeat, stomach secretions, blood pressure, reflexive movements, blinking, or muscular contractions. For optimal conditioning, the conditioned stimulus should precede the unconditioned stimulus, not follow it or occur simultaneously. This makes sense, for in classical conditioning, the conditioned stimulus becomes a kind of signal for the unconditioned stimulus. It enables the organism to *prepare* for an event that is about to happen. In Pavlov's studies, for instance, a bell or buzzer was a signal that meat was coming, and the dog's salivation was preparation for digesting food.

Indeed, today, many psychologists contend that what an organism actually learns in classical conditioning is *information* conveyed by one stimulus about another. In studies supporting this view, Robert Rescorla showed that merely pairing an unconditioned stimulus and a neutral one is not enough to produce learning; the neutral stimulus must reliably *signal*, or *predict*, the unconditioned one (Rescorla, 1968, 1988; Rescorla & Wagner, 1972).

Suppose you are a budding behaviorist and you want to teach a rat to fear a tone. Following the usual procedure, you repeatedly sound the tone before an unconditioned stimulus for fear, such as electric shock; tone, shock, tone, shock, tone, shock. . . . After 20 such pairings, the rat shows signs of fear upon

■ **classical conditioning**
The process by which a previously neutral stimulus acquires the capacity to elicit a response through association with a stimulus that already elicits a similar or related response; also called Pavlovian and respondent conditioning.

hearing the tone. Now suppose you do this experiment again—on 20 trials the tone precedes the shock—but this time you randomly intersperse an additional 20 trials in which the shock occurs *without* the tone. With this method, the tone is paired with the shock just as often as in the standard procedure, but it signals shock only half of the time. In other words, the shock is equally likely to occur when the tone is absent as when it is present. Under these conditions, the tone does not provide any information about the shock, and hardly any conditioning occurs.

From this and similar findings, Rescorla (1988) concludes that "Pavlovian conditioning is not a stupid process by which the organism willy-nilly forms associations between any two stimuli that happen to co-occur. Rather, the organism is better seen as an information seeker using logical and perceptual relations among events, along with its own preconceptions, to form a sophisticated representation of its world." Not all learning theorists agree with this conclusion or with the findings on which it is based (Papini & Bitterman, 1990). An orthodox behaviorist would say that it's silly to talk about the preconceptions of a rat. The important point, however, is that for some researchers, concepts such as "information seeking," "preconceptions," and "representations of the world" have opened the door to a more cognitive view of classical conditioning.

Principles of Classical Conditioning

The basic principles that govern the learning of classically conditioned responses are common to all species, from worms to *Homo sapiens*. Some of the most important are extinction, higher-order conditioning, and stimulus generalization and discrimination.

Extinction. Conditioned responses do not necessarily last forever. If, after conditioning, the conditioned stimulus is repeatedly presented without the unconditioned stimulus, the conditioned response eventually disappears, and **extinction** is said to have occurred (see Figure 7.2). Suppose you train a dog to salivate to the sound of a bell, but then you ring the bell every five minutes and do *not* follow it with food. The dog will salivate less and less to the bell and will

■ **extinction**
The weakening and eventual disappearance of a learned response; in classical conditioning, it occurs when the conditioned stimulus is no longer paired with the unconditioned stimulus.

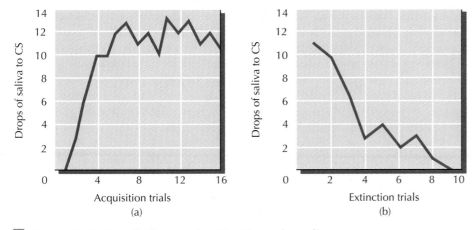

■ Figure 7.2 Acquisition and extinction of a salivary response
Graph (a) shows what happens when a neutral stimulus is consistently followed by an unconditioned stimulus for salivation. The neutral stimulus also comes to elicit salivation; that is, it becomes a conditioned stimulus. Graph (b) shows what happens when the conditioned stimulus is repeatedly presented without the unconditioned stimulus. The conditioned salivary response weakens and eventually disappears; it is extinguished.

soon stop salivating altogether; salivation has been extinguished. However, if you come back the next day and ring the bell, the dog may salivate again for a few trials. The reappearance of the response is called **spontaneous recovery,** and it explains why completely eliminating a conditioned response usually requires more than one extinction session.

Higher-Order Conditioning. Sometimes a neutral stimulus can become a conditioned stimulus by being paired with an already established CS, a procedure known as **higher-order conditioning.** Say a dog has learned to salivate to the ringing of a bell. Now you present a flash of light before ringing the bell. With repeated pairings of the light and the bell, the dog may learn to salivate to the light, although the light will probably elicit less salivation than the bell does. The procedure looks like this:

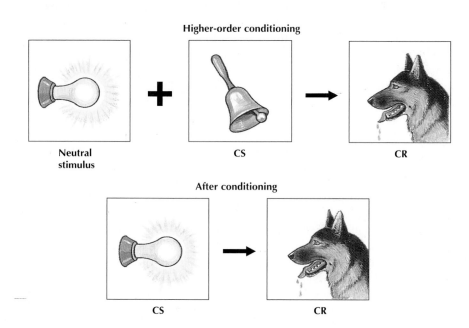

It may be that words acquire their emotional meanings through a process of higher-order conditioning. When they are paired with objects or other words that already elicit some emotional response, they, too, may come to elicit that response (Chance, 1994; Staats & Staats, 1957). For example, a child may learn a positive response to the word *birthday* because of its association with gifts and attention. Conversely, the child may learn a negative response to ethnic or national labels, such as *Swede, Turk,* or *Jew,* if those words are paired with already disagreeable words, such as *dumb* or *dirty.* Higher-order conditioning, in other words, may contribute to the formation of prejudices.

Stimulus Generalization and Discrimination. After a stimulus becomes a conditioned stimulus for some response, other, similar stimuli may produce a similar reaction—a phenomenon known as **stimulus generalization.** For example, a dog conditioned to salivate to middle C on the piano may also salivate to D, which is one tone above C, even though D was not paired with food. Stimulus generalization is described nicely by an old English proverb: "He who hath been bitten by a snake fears a rope."

The mirror image of stimulus generalization is **stimulus discrimination,** in which *different* responses are made to stimuli that resemble the conditioned stimulus in some way. Suppose you condition your poodle to salivate to middle C on the piano by repeatedly pairing the sound with food. At the same time, you play middle C on a guitar, *without* following it by food. Eventually, the dog

■ **spontaneous recovery**
The reappearance of a learned response after its apparent extinction.

■ **higher-order conditioning**
In classical conditioning, a procedure in which a neutral stimulus becomes a conditioned stimulus through association with an already established conditioned stimulus.

■ **stimulus generalization**
After conditioning, the tendency to respond to a stimulus that resembles one involved in the original conditioning; in classical conditioning, it occurs when a stimulus that resembles the conditioned stimulus elicits the conditioned response.

■ **stimulus discrimination**
The tendency to respond differently to two or more similar stimuli; in classical conditioning, it occurs when a stimulus similar to the CS fails to evoke the CR.

will learn to salivate to a C on the piano and not to salivate to the same note on the guitar; that is, the animal will discriminate between the two sounds.

Classical Conditioning in Real Life

If a dog can learn to salivate to the ringing of a bell, so can you. In fact, you probably have learned to salivate to the sound of a lunch bell, not to mention the sight of the refrigerator, the phrase *hot fudge sundae,* "mouth-watering" pictures of food in magazines, the sight of a waiter in a restaurant, and a voice calling out "Dinner's ready!" But the role of classical conditioning goes far beyond the learning of simple observable reflexes; conditioning affects us every day in many ways.

Accounting for Taste. We probably learn to like and dislike many things, including particular foods, through a process of classical conditioning. In the laboratory, researchers have taught animals to dislike various foods or odors by pairing them with drugs that cause nausea or other unpleasant symptoms. One researcher trained slugs to associate the smell of carrots, which slugs normally like, with a bitter-tasting chemical that they detest. Soon the slugs were avoiding the smell of carrots. The researcher then demonstrated higher-order conditioning by pairing the smell of carrots with the smell of potato. Sure enough, the slugs began to avoid the smell of potato as well (Sahley, Rudy, & Gelperin, 1981).

Whether we say "yum" or "yuck" to certain foods may depend on a past experience involving classical conditioning.

Martin Seligman, who has studied learned behavior in the laboratory for many years, tells how he himself was conditioned to hate béarnaise sauce. One night, shortly after he and his wife ate a delicious meal of filet mignon with béarnaise sauce, he came down with the flu. Naturally, he felt wretched. His misery had nothing to do with the béarnaise sauce, of course, yet the next time he tried it, he found he disliked the taste (Seligman & Hager, 1972). Similar conditioned food aversions may occur in cancer patients when a meal is followed by nausea-inducing chemotherapy (Bernstein, 1985).

Sometimes we like a food but our bodies refuse to tolerate it. This happens with allergies: You adore chocolate, say, but your skin breaks out in hives whenever you eat it. Some allergic reactions may be classically conditioned. In a study with guinea pigs, researchers paired the smell of either fish or sulphur with injection of a substance to which the animals were already allergic. After only ten pairings, the animals became allergic to the odor alone. Their blood histamine levels rose, just as they would have done after exposure to a true allergen (Russell et al., 1984). People, too, may learn to be allergic to substances that have been associated with substances to which they are already sensitive. A century ago, a physician reported that he used an artificial rose to provoke asthmatic symptoms in an allergic patient, and since then, several studies have confirmed that nonallergenic objects previously associated with allergens can induce asthmatic symptoms in some people (Ader & Cohen, 1993).

Learning to Love. Classical conditioning involves involuntary bodily responses, and many such responses are part and parcel of human emotions. It follows that this type of learning may explain how we acquire emotional responses to particular objects and events.

One of the first psychologists to recognize this implication of Pavlovian theory was John B. Watson, who founded American behaviorism and was an enthusiastic promoter of Pavlov's ideas. Watson believed that emotions were simply collections of gut-level muscular and glandular responses, a view later detractors derided as "muscle-twitch psychology" (Hunt, 1993). A few such responses, said Watson, are inborn. For the sake of convenience, he called these responses fear, rage, and love, but he was really referring to patterns of movement and changes in breathing, circulation, and digestion, and not to subjective feelings. In Watson's analysis, "love" included the smiling and burbling that babies are apt to do when they are stroked and cuddled. The stroking and cuddling are unconditioned stimuli; the smiling and burbling are unconditioned responses. According to Watson, an infant learns to "love" other things when they are paired with stroking and cuddling. The thing most likely to be paired with stroking and cuddling is, of course, a parent. Learning to love a parent (or anyone else, for that matter) is really no different from learning to salivate to the sound of a bell—at least in Watson's view.

A similar process may help explain unusual desires and preferences, such as *masochism*, the enjoyment of pain. We mentioned earlier that Pavlov could condition dogs to salivate to a pinprick or an electric shock. The animals showed none of the bodily upset usually associated with these painful stimuli. In fact, they seemed to enjoy being pricked or shocked. Similarly, masochism in human beings may result when painful stimuli are associated with an unconditioned stimulus for pleasure or satisfaction, such as sexual arousal and orgasm.

Conditioned Fears.

Dislikes and negative emotions such as fear, as we saw in our discussion of higher-order conditioning, can also be classically conditioned. According to behaviorists, many fears are conditioned responses to stimuli that were originally neutral. The original conditioning incident does not have to be remembered in order for the fear to persist.

When a fear of a specific object or situation is irrational and interferes with normal activities, it qualifies as a *phobia*. To demonstrate how a phobia might be acquired, John Watson and Rosalie Rayner (1920) deliberately established a rat phobia in an 11-month-old boy named Albert. The ethics, procedures, and findings of their study have since been questioned (Harris, 1979), and no researcher today would perform such a demonstration. Nevertheless, the study remains a classic, and its main conclusion, that fears can be conditioned, is still well accepted.

"Little Albert" was a rather placid tyke who rarely cried. When Watson and Rayner gave him a furry white rat to play with (a live one, not a toy), Albert showed no fear; in fact, he was delighted. However, like most children, Albert was afraid of loud noises. Whenever a steel bar behind his head was struck with a hammer, he would jump and fall sideways onto the mattress he was sitting on. The noise was an unconditioned stimulus for the unconditioned response of fear.

Having established that Albert liked rats, Watson and Rayner set about teaching him to fear them. Again they offered him a rat, but this time, as Albert reached for it, one of the researchers struck the steel bar. Startled, Albert fell onto the mattress. The researchers repeated this procedure several times. Albert began to whimper and tremble. Finally, the rat was offered alone, without the noise. Albert fell over, cried, and crawled away as fast as he could; the rat had become a conditioned stimulus for fear. Further tests showed that Albert's fear had generalized to other hairy or furry objects, including white rabbits, cotton wool, a Santa Claus mask, and even John Watson's hair.

Unfortunately, Watson and Rayner did not have an opportunity to reverse the conditioning, for reasons that are unclear. Later, however, Watson and Mary Cover Jones did accomplish a reversal in a 3-year-old named Peter (Jones, 1924). Peter was deathly afraid of rabbits. His fear was, as Watson put it, "homegrown" rather than psychologist induced. Watson and Jones eliminated it with a method called **counterconditioning**, which involved pairing the rabbit with another stimulus—a snack of milk and crackers—that produced pleasant feelings incompatible with the conditioned response of fear. At first, the researchers kept the rabbit some distance from Peter, so that his fear would remain at a low level. Otherwise, Peter might have learned to fear milk and crackers! But gradually, over several days, they brought the rabbit closer and closer. Eventually

■ **counterconditioning**
In classical conditioning, the process of pairing a conditioned stimulus with a stimulus that elicits a response that is incompatible with an unwanted conditioned response.

This photograph, made from a 1919 film, shows John Watson, in a mask, testing Little Albert for stimulus generalization. (Photo courtesy of Prof. Benjamin Harris.)

Peter was able to sit with the rabbit in his lap, playing with it with one hand while he ate with the other. A variation of this procedure, called *systematic desensitization,* was later devised for treating phobias in adults (see Chapter 16).

The Power of Drugs. Many researchers believe that classical conditioning has important implications for understanding aspects of drug addiction (Poulos & Cappell, 1991; Siegel, 1990; Siegel & Sdao-Jarvie, 1986). In this view, a drug's effect is the unconditioned stimulus for a *compensatory* bodily response, a response aimed at restoring a normal biological state. For example, when morphine causes numbness to pain, the body attempts to compensate by becoming increasingly sensitive to pain. Environmental cues that are paired with the drug's effects, such as needles or a particular location, may then become conditioned stimuli for this compensatory response:

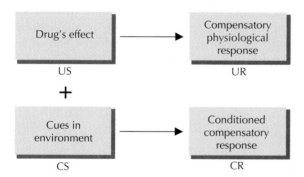

This analysis can help explain why *tolerance* to drugs often develops (see Chapter 5). In the presence of environmental cues associated with drug taking, a compensatory response occurs, so more of the drug is needed to produce the usual effects. On the other hand, a drug dose that would ordinarily be safe, given an addict's tolerance level, may be lethal when the drug is used in novel circumstances, because the usual conditioned compensatory response does not occur. The result may be sudden and seemingly inexplicable death.

Experiments with both animals and human beings, using a wide variety of drugs, support this theory. In one study, male college students drank large amounts of beer at the same place on each of four consecutive days. On the fifth day, some of the students downed their beers at a new place. Students who remained at the original location scored higher on tests of intellectual and perceptual-motor skills, apparently because their bodies had learned to moderate the effects of alcohol in the presence of familiar cues (Lightfoot, 1980). In another study, researchers gave rats a strong dose of heroin. Some of the rats were already "experienced" with the drug. In inexperienced rats, the injection was almost always fatal, but in experienced ones, the outcome depended on the setting: Two-thirds of the rats injected while in a strange environment died, versus only one-third of those who remained in a familiar place (Siegel et al., 1982).

The importance of environmental cues may help explain why in-hospital drug treatment programs so often fail: When people return to the neighborhoods where they used to take drugs, conditioned stimuli elicit the usual compensatory responses. In the absence of the drug, such responses are now experienced as a return of unpleasant withdrawal symptoms, and a craving for the drug again develops (Siegel, 1990). The implication is that people who want to overcome drug dependence either must move to a new environment or get treatment that systematically exposes them to familiar features of their usual environment until their conditioned physiological responses to these cues are extinguished.

We see, then, that many seemingly "natural" or biological responses—food preferences, fears, addictions—may have their origins in classical conditioning. Conversely, in recent decades, behavioral researchers have acknowledged the importance of innate tendencies and have integrated these factors into their theories.

Biological factors, for example, can help us understand the story of the psychologist who learned to hate béarnaise sauce. Unlike conditioning in the laboratory, this learning occurred after only one pairing of the sauce with illness and with a considerable delay between the conditioned and unconditioned stimuli. In addition, neither the psychologist's wife nor the plate from which he ate became conditioned stimuli for nausea, though they, too, were paired with illness. Controlled research suggests that certain animals (including, apparently, psychologists) are biologically prepared to associate sickness with taste rather than, say, with light and sound (Garcia & Koelling, 1966; Seligman & Hager, 1972). This tendency enhances the species' survival: Eating bad food is more likely to be followed by illness than are sights or sounds. Likewise, in human beings, it is easier to establish a conditioned fear of spiders, snakes, or heights than of butterflies, flowers, or toasters, probably because during the evolution of our species, the former objects presented a danger, whereas the latter did not.

Quick QUIZ

Supply the correct term to describe the outcome in each situation:

1. After a child learns to fear spiders, he also responds with fear to ants, beetles, and other crawling bugs.
2. A toddler is afraid of the bath, so her father puts just a little water in the tub and gives the child a lollipop to suck on while she is being washed. Soon, the little girl loses her fear of the bath.
3. A factory worker notices that his mouth waters whenever a noontime bell signals the beginning of his lunch break. One day, the bell goes haywire and rings every half hour. By the end of the day, the worker has stopped salivating to the bell.

Answers:

1. stimulus generalization 2. counterconditioning 3. extinction

▪ OPERANT CONDITIONING: THE CARROT AND THE STICK

At the end of the nineteenth century, in the first known scientific effort to study anger, G. Stanley Hall (1899) asked people to describe angry episodes they had experienced or observed. One informant told of a 3-year-old girl who broke out in furious, seemingly uncontrollable sobs when she was punished by being kept home from a ride. In the middle of her tantrum, the child suddenly stopped crying and asked in a perfectly calm voice if her father was in. Told no, she immediately resumed her sobbing.

Children, of course, cry for many valid reasons—pain, discomfort, fear, illness, fatigue—and these cries deserve an adult's sympathy and attention. However, studies show that even infants only a few weeks old will also learn to cry when they are *not* in physical distress if adults respond to such cries (Gewirtz, 1991). The child in Hall's study had learned, from prior experience, that an outburst of sobbing would bring her attention and possibly the ride she wanted—that it stood a reasonable chance of working. Her behavior, which some might label "naughty," was perfectly understandable, because it followed one of the most basic laws of learning: *Behavior becomes more or less likely, depending on its consequences.*

An emphasis on consequences is at the heart of the second major type of conditioning, **operant conditioning** (also called *instrumental conditioning*). In classical conditioning, the animal's or person's behavior does not have any environmental consequences; in Pavlov's procedure, the dog got food, whether it salivated or not. But in operant conditioning, the organism's response (the little girl's sobbing, for example) *operates* or produces effects on the environment. These effects, in turn, influence whether or not the response will occur again. Classical and operant conditioning also tend to differ in the types of responses they involve. In classical conditioning, the response is reflexive, an automatic reaction to something happening in the environment, such as the sight of food or the sound of a bell. Generally, responses in operant conditioning are complex and not reflexive, involving the entire organism—for instance, riding a bicycle, writing a letter, climbing a mountain, . . . or throwing a tantrum.

Operant conditioning has been studied since the turn of the century, although it wasn't called "operant" until later. Edward Thorndike (1898), then a young doctoral candidate, set the stage by observing cats as they tried to escape from a "puzzle box" to reach a scrap of fish that was just outside the box. At first, the cat would engage in trial and error, scratching, biting, or swatting at parts of the cage in an unorganized way. Then, after a few minutes, the cat would chance on the successful response (loosening a bolt, pulling a string, or hitting a button) and rush out to get the reward. Placed in the box again, the cat now took a little less time to escape, and after several trials, the animal immediately made the correct response. According to Thorndike's *law of effect,* the correct response had been "stamped in" by its satisfying effects (getting the food). In contrast, annoying or unsatisfying effects "stamped out" behavior. Behavior, said Thorndike, is controlled by its consequences.

This general principle was elaborated and extended to more complex forms of behavior by B. F. (Burrhus Frederic) Skinner (1904–1990). Calling his approach "radical behaviorism" to distinguish it from the behaviorism of John Watson, Skinner argued that what we need to know to understand behavior are the external causes of an action and the action's consequences. Skinner was careful to avoid such terms as "satisfying" and "annoying," which reflect assumptions about what an organism feels and wants. For Skinner, the explanation of behavior was to be found by looking outside the individual rather than within, a position he continued to defend until his death in 1990.

An instantaneous learning experience.

Reprinted with special permission of King Features Syndicate, Inc.

In operant conditioning, behavior is controlled by its consequences.

▪ **operant conditioning**
The process by which a response becomes more or less likely to occur, depending on its consequences.

Skinner has often been called the greatest of American psychologists, and certainly he is one of the best known. Yet despite his fame, or perhaps because of it, his position is often distorted by the general public, psychology students, and even some psychologists. For example, many people think Skinner denied the existence of human consciousness and the value of studying it. It is true that Skinner's predecessor John Watson thought that psychologists should study only public (external) events, not private (internal) ones. But Skinner maintained that we *can* study private events by observing our own sensory responses and the verbal reports of others, and the conditions under which such events occur. For Skinner, the private events we "see" when we examine our own "consciousness" are just the early stages of behavior, before the behavior begins to act on the environment. These private events are as real or physical as public ones, Skinner said, although they are less accessible and harder to describe (Skinner, 1972, 1990).

Because Skinner thought the environment could and should be manipulated to alter behavior, some critics have portrayed him as cold-blooded or even sinister. But Skinner, who was a quiet and mild-mannered man, felt that it would be unethical *not* to try to improve human behavior by applying behavioral principles. In recognition of his efforts, the American Humanist Association honored him with its Humanist of the Year Award.

One famous controversy regarding Skinner occurred when he invented the Air-Crib, an enclosure for his daughter Deborah. This "baby box," as it came to be known, was set up to eliminate the usual discomforts suffered by babies, including heat, cold, wetness, and confinement by bedding. It had temperature and humidity controls, so Deborah could go without any clothes. People mistakenly imagined that the Skinners were leaving the baby in the Air-Crib all the time and never cuddling or playing with her, and for years, rumors circulated that Deborah had grown up to be psychotic. Actually, both of Skinner's daughters turned out to be perfectly normal. One became a successful artist, the other a professor of educational psychology, who raised her own two daughters in an Air-Crib.

Whereas some other psychologists, notably the humanists, have argued for the existence of free will, Skinner steadfastly supported the view of *determinism.* Free will, he believed, is an illusion. Environmental consequences may not automatically "stamp in" operant behavior, but they do determine the probability that an action will occur. Skinner refused to credit personal traits, such as

B. F. Skinner, at work on a scale model of a Skinner box, described on pages 260–261.

curiosity, or mental events, such as goals, thoughts, or motives, for his own or anyone else's accomplishments. Indeed, he regarded himself not as a "self" but as a "repertoire of behaviors" resulting from an environment that encouraged looking, searching, and investigating (Bjork, 1993). "So far as I know," he wrote in the third volume of his autobiography (Skinner, 1983), "my behavior at any given moment has been nothing more than the product of my genetic endowment, my personal history, and the current setting."

Reinforcers and Punishers: A Matter of Consequence

In Skinner's analysis, which has inspired an immense body of research, a response ("operant") can lead to one of three types of consequences. The first type is neutral as far as future behavior is concerned: It neither increases nor decreases the probability that the behavior will recur. If a door handle squeaks each time you turn it, and the sound does not affect whether you turn the door handle in the future, the squeak is a neutral consequence.

A second type of consequence involves **reinforcement.** In reinforcement, a reinforcing stimulus, or *reinforcer,* strengthens or increases the probability of the response that it follows. When you are training your dog to heel, and you offer it a doggie biscuit or a pat on the head when it does something right, you are using reinforcement (see Figure 7.3). Reinforcers are roughly equivalent to rewards, and many psychologists have no objection to the use of the words *reward* and *reinforcer* as approximate synonyms. However, strict behaviorists avoid *reward* because it is the organism, not the response, that is rewarded; the response is *strengthened.* Also, in common usage, a reward is something earned that results in happiness or satisfaction. But technically, any stimulus is a reinforcer if it strengthens the preceding behavior, whether or not the organism experiences pleasure or any other positive state. And conversely, no matter how pleasurable a stimulus is, it is not a reinforcer if it does not increase the likelihood of a response. It's pleasurable to get a paycheck, but if you get paid regardless of the effort you put into your work, the money will not reinforce "hard-work behavior."

The third type of consequence involves **punishment.** Punishment occurs when the stimulus or event that follows a response weakens it or makes it less likely to recur. Any aversive (unpleasant) stimulus or event may be a *punisher.* A dog that runs into the street and is nearly hit by a passing car will be less likely to run into the street in the future when cars are around. Later, we will see that deliberate punishment as a way of controlling behavior has many drawbacks.

In a way, operant conditioning is a kind of natural selection applied to the constantly changing behavior of individuals. As we saw in Chapter 3, because the principle of natural selection operates during evolution, some genetically

▪ **reinforcement**
The process by which a stimulus or event strengthens or increases the probability of the response that it follows.

▪ **punishment**
The process by which a stimulus or event weakens or reduces the probability of the response that it follows.

(a) (b) (c)

▪ **Figure 7.3 Reinforcement in Action**
The dog's response, heeling (a), is followed immediately by a reinforcer, in this case praise and a pat (b). As a result, the response is strengthened (c).

Operant conditioning procedures work best when they capitalize on an animal's natural responses. For example, it's easy to train pigs to hunt for truffles, a fungus that grows underground, because pigs have a natural rooting instinct.

▪ **instinctive drift**

The tendency of an organism to revert to an instinctive behavior over time; can interfere with learning.

▪ **positive reinforcement**

A reinforcement procedure in which a response is followed by the presentation of, or increase in intensity of, a reinforcing stimulus; as a result, the response becomes stronger or more likely to occur.

▪ **negative reinforcement**

A reinforcement procedure in which a response is followed by the removal, delay, or decrease in intensity of an unpleasant stimulus; as a result, the response becomes stronger or more likely to occur.

influenced characteristics are selected by the environment and become more common in a population over time. Similarly, in operant conditioning, actions of an individual are "selected" by their environmental consequences, and these responses become more frequent in the behavior of the individual.

As in classical conditioning, what an animal can learn through operant conditioning depends first and foremost on its physical characteristics; a fish cannot be trained to climb a ladder. And operant conditioning procedures, like classical ones, work best when they capitalize on inborn tendencies. Keller and Marian Breland (1961), psychologists who became animal trainers, described what happens when biological constraints are ignored. The Brelands found that animals often had trouble learning tasks that should have been easy. For example, a pig was supposed to drop large wooden coins in a box. Instead, the pig would drop the coin, push at it with its snout, throw it in the air, and push at it some more. This odd behavior actually delayed reinforcement, so it was hard to explain in terms of operant principles. Apparently the pig's rooting instinct—its tendency to use its snout to uncover edible roots—was keeping it from learning the task. The Brelands called such a reversion to instinctive behavior **instinctive drift.**

Positive and Negative Reinforcers and Punishers

Reinforcement and punishment may seem to be the proverbial carrot and stick, but they are not quite so simple as they seem. In our example of reinforcement, something pleasant (a doggie biscuit or a pat on the dog's head) followed the dog's response (heeling). This type of procedure is known as **positive reinforcement.** But there is another brand of reinforcement, **negative reinforcement,** that involves the *removal* of something *unpleasant.* If you politely ask your roommate to turn off some music you can't stand, and your roommate immediately complies, the likelihood of your being polite when making similar requests will probably increase. Your politeness has been strengthened (negatively reinforced) by the removal of the unpleasant music.

As Table 7.1 shows, the positive–negative distinction can also be applied to punishment: Something unpleasant may occur (positive punishment) or something pleasant may be removed (negative punishment). However, the terms "positive" and "negative" are more often applied to reinforcement.

The distinction between positive and negative reinforcement has been a source of confusion and frustration for generations of students, and has been known to turn strong and confident people into quivering heaps. We can assure you that if *we* had been around when these terms were first coined, we would have complained loudly. One eminent behaviorist, Gregory Kimble (1993), argues that it's still not too late to change their meanings so that they conform better to ordinary usage. But we doubt that changing the definitions at this point would help much because students who went on in psychology would still have to read articles and books using the old definitions, and in introductory courses, some books would be teaching one set of definitions and others a different set. That is why as textbook authors, we've resigned ourselves to the traditional terms, irksome though they are.

You will master these terms more quickly if you understand that in reinforcement, "positive" and "negative" have nothing to do with "good" or "bad." They refer to *procedures*—giving something or taking something away. *In either case, a response becomes more likely.* If someone praises Ludwig for doing his homework, that is positive reinforcement (of studying). If Ludwig's headache goes away after he takes an aspirin, that is negative reinforcement (of aspirin taking). Think of a positive reinforcer as something that is added or obtained, and a negative reinforcer as avoidance of or escape from something unpleasant.

Recall again what happened with Little Albert. Albert learned to fear rats through a process of classical conditioning. Then, after he acquired this fear,

Table 7.1 Types of Reinforcement and Punishment

In operant conditioning, a response increases or decreases in likelihood depending on its consequences. The occurrence of a pleasant stimulus or the removal of an unpleasant one reinforces the response. The occurrence of an unpleasant stimulus or the removal of a pleasant one constitutes punishment, which weakens the response.

What event follows the response?

		Stimulus presented	Stimulus removed
What happens to the response?	**Response increases**	**Positive reinforcement** For example: Completion of homework assignments increases when followed by praise.	**Negative reinforcement** For example: Use of aspirin increases when followed by reduction of headache pain.
	Response decreases	**Positive punishment** For example: Nail biting decreases when followed by the taste of a bitter substance painted on the nails.	**Negative punishment** For example: Parking in a "no parking" zone decreases when followed by loss of money (a fine).

crawling away (an operant behavior) was negatively reinforced by escape from the now-fearsome rodent. The negative reinforcement that results from escaping or avoiding something unpleasant explains why so many fears are long-lasting. When you evade a feared object or situation, you also cut off all opportunities for extinguishing your fear.

Understandably, people often confuse negative reinforcement with positive punishment, since both involve an unpleasant stimulus. To keep the two straight, remember that punishment *decreases* the likelihood of a response. Reinforcement—either positive or negative—*increases* it. In real life, punishment and negative reinforcement often go hand in hand. If you use a choke collar on your dog to teach it to heel, a yank on the collar *punishes* the act of walking. But release of the collar *negatively reinforces* the act of standing still by your side.

Primary and Secondary Reinforcers and Punishers

Food, water, light stroking of the skin, and a comfortable air temperature are naturally reinforcing because they satisfy biological needs. They are therefore known as **primary reinforcers.** Similarly, pain and extreme heat or cold are inherently punishing and are therefore known as **primary punishers.** Primary reinforcers and punishers are powerful controllers of behavior, but they also have their drawbacks. For one thing, the organism may have to be in a deprived state for a stimulus to act as a primary reinforcer; a glass of water isn't much of a reward to someone who just drank three glasses. Also, there are ethical problems with using primary punishers or taking away primary reinforcers.

Fortunately, behavior can be controlled just as effectively by **secondary reinforcers** and **secondary punishers,** which are learned. Money, praise, applause, good grades, awards, and gold stars are common secondary reinforcers. Criticism, demerits, catcalls, scoldings, fines, and bad grades are common secondary punishers. Most behaviorists believe that secondary reinforcers and punishers acquire their ability to influence behavior by being paired with pri-

■ **primary reinforcer**
A stimulus that is inherently reinforcing, typically satisfying a physiological need; an example is food.

■ **primary punisher**
A stimulus that is inherently punishing; an example is electric shock.

■ **secondary reinforcer**
A stimulus that has acquired reinforcing properties through association with other reinforcers.

■ **secondary punisher**
A stimulus that has acquired punishing properties through association with other punishers.

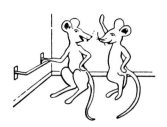

"Boy, do we have this guy conditioned. Every time I press the bar down he drops a pellet in."

mary reinforcers and punishers. If that reminds you of classical conditioning, reinforce yourself with a pat on the back! Indeed, secondary reinforcers and punishers are often called *conditioned* reinforcers and punishers.

Just because a reinforcer (or punisher) is secondary doesn't mean it is any less potent than a primary reinforcer (or punisher). Money has a great deal of power over most people's behavior; not only can it be exchanged for primary reinforcers such as food and shelter, but it also brings with it other secondary reinforcers, such as praise and respect. Still, like any conditioned stimulus, a secondary reinforcer such as money will eventually lose its ability to affect behavior if it cannot be paired at least occasionally with one of the stimuli originally associated with it. In 1930, a child who found a penny would be thrilled at the goodies it could buy. Today, U.S. pennies are so worthless that billions of them go out of circulation each year because people throw them away or leave them on the ground when they drop.

Quick QUIZ

Which kind of consequence is illustrated by each of the following? (You may want to refer to Table 7.1 if you have difficulty with the first three items.)

1. A child nags her father for a cookie; he keeps refusing, but she keeps pleading. Finally, unable to stand the "aversive stimulation" any longer, he hands over the cookie. For him, the ending of the child's pleas is a _____. For the child, the cookie is a _____.

2. A woman wants her husband to take more responsibility for household chores. One night, he clears the dishes. She touches him affectionately on the arm. The next night, he again clears the dishes. Her touch was probably a _____.

3. A hungry toddler gleefully eats his oatmeal with his hands after being told not to. His mother promptly removes the cereal and takes the messy offender out of the high chair. The removal of the cereal is a _____.

4. Which of the following are secondary (conditioned) reinforcers: quarters spilling from a slot machine, a winner's blue ribbon, a piece of candy, an A on an exam, "frequent-flyer" points.

5. During "happy hours" in bars and restaurants, typically held in the late afternoon, drinks are sold at a reduced price, and appetizers are often free. What undesirable behavior may be rewarded by this practice?

Answers:

1. negative reinforcer; positive reinforcer 2. positive reinforcer 3. punisher (or more precisely, a negative punisher) 4. All but the candy are secondary reinforcers. 5. One possible answer: The reduced prices, free appetizers, and convivial atmosphere all reinforce heavy alcohol consumption just before the commuter rush hour, and thus may contribute to drunk driving (see Geller & Lehman, 1988).

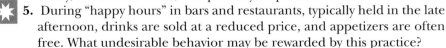

Principles of Operant Conditioning

Thousands of studies have been done on operant conditioning, many using animals. A favorite experimental tool is the *Skinner box,* a cage equipped with a device (called a "magazine") that delivers food into a dish when an animal makes a desired response (see Figure 7.4). A *cumulative recorder* connected to

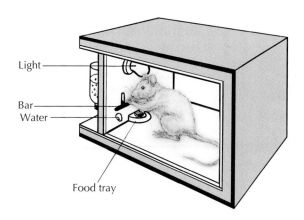

Light
Bar
Water
Food tray

▪ Figure 7.4 The Skinner Box

Rats have been popular research subjects in studies using this device. When a rat presses a bar, a food pellet or drop of water is automatically released. Skinner's own favorite subjects were pigeons, which are typically trained to peck at a disk or key.

the cage automatically records each response and produces a graph showing the cumulative number of responses across time.

Early in his career, Skinner (1938) used the Skinner box for a classic demonstration of operant conditioning. A rat that had previously learned to eat from the magazine was placed in the box. Because no food was present, the animal proceeded to do typically ratlike things, scurrying about the box, sniffing here and there, and randomly touching parts of the floor and walls. Quite by accident it pressed a lever mounted on one wall, and immediately a pellet of tasty rat food fell into the food dish. The rat continued its movements and again happened to press the bar, causing another pellet to fall into the tray. With additional repetitions of bar pressing followed by food, the animal began to behave less randomly and to press the bar more consistently. Eventually, Skinner had the rat pressing the bar as fast as it could shuttle back from the magazine.

Skinner's favorite experimental animals were pigeons, which usually are trained to peck at a disk or a key, but most behaviorists have worked with rats. By using the Skinner box and similar devices, behavioral researchers have discovered many techniques and applications of operant conditioning.

Extinction. In operant conditioning, as in classical, **extinction** is a procedure that causes a previously learned response to stop occurring. In operant conditioning, extinction takes place when the reinforcer that maintained the response is removed or is no longer available. At first, there may be a spurt of responding, but then the responses gradually taper off and eventually cease. Suppose you put a coin in a vending machine and get nothing back. You may throw in another coin, or perhaps even two, but then you will probably stop trying. The next day, you may put in yet another coin, an example of *spontaneous recovery*. Eventually, however, you will give up on that machine. Your response has been extinguished.

Immediate Versus Delayed Consequences. In general, the sooner a reinforcer or punisher follows a response, the greater its effect. This principle applies especially to animals and children, but human adults also respond more reliably when they don't have to wait too long for a paycheck, a smile, or a grade. When there is delay, other responses occur in the interval, and the connection between the desired or undesired response and the consequence may not be made.

Stimulus Generalization and Stimulus Discrimination. In operant conditioning, as in classical, **stimulus generalization** may occur. That is, responses may generalize to stimuli not present during the original learning situation that resemble the original stimuli. For example, a pigeon that has been trained to peck at a picture of a circle may also peck at a slightly oval figure. But if you

▪ **extinction**
The weakening and eventual disappearance of a learned response; in operant conditioning, it occurs when a response is no longer followed by a reinforcer.

▪ **stimulus generalization**
In operant conditioning, the tendency for a response that has been reinforced (or punished) in the presence of one stimulus to occur (or be suppressed) in the presence of other, similar stimuli.

wanted to train the bird to discriminate between the two shapes, you would present both the circle and the oval, giving reinforcers whenever the bird pecked at the circle and withholding reinforcers when it pecked at the oval. Eventually, **stimulus discrimination** would occur.

A somewhat different kind of discrimination occurs when an animal or human being learns to respond to a stimulus only when some other stimulus, called a **discriminative stimulus,** is present. The discriminative stimulus signals whether a response, if made, will "pay off." In a Skinner box, for example, a light may serve as a discriminative stimulus for pecking at a circle. When the light is on, pecking brings a reward; when it is off, pecking is futile. The light is said to exert **stimulus control** over the pecking by setting the occasion for reinforcement to occur if the response is made. However, the response is not *compelled,* as salivation was compelled by the ringing of the bell in Pavlov's studies. It merely becomes more probable (or occurs at a greater rate) in the presence of the discriminative stimulus.

Human behavior is controlled by many discriminative stimuli, both verbal ("Store hours are 9 to 5") and nonverbal (traffic lights, doorbells, the ring of a telephone, the facial expressions of others). Learning to respond correctly when these stimuli are present is an essential part of operant learning. In a public place, if you have to go to the bathroom, you don't just walk through any door that leads to a toilet. The words *Women* and *Men* are discriminative stimuli for entering. One word tells you the response will be rewarded by the opportunity to empty a full bladder, the other that it will be punished by the jeers or protests of others.

The failure to make appropriate discriminations can lead to accidents and errors. A behaviorist would say that when we go into the next room to do something and then can't remember why we're there, it is because the discriminative stimuli for the response are no longer present (Salzinger, 1990). But insufficient generalization also causes problems. For example, "personal-growth" workshops provide participants with lots of reinforcement for emotional expressiveness and self-disclosure. Participants often feel that their way of interacting with others has been dramatically transformed. But when they return home and to work, where the environment is full of the same old reinforcers, punishers, and discriminative stimuli, they may be disappointed to find that their new responses have failed to generalize. A grumpy boss or a cranky spouse may still be able to "push their buttons"—a relapse that is predictable from behavioral principles.

Learning on Schedule. Reinforcers can be delivered according to different schedules, or patterns over time. When a response is first acquired, learning is usually most rapid if the response is reinforced each time it occurs; this procedure is called **continuous reinforcement.** However, once a response has become reliable, it will be more resistant to extinction if it is rewarded on a **partial** or **intermittent schedule of reinforcement,** which involves reinforcing only some, but not all, responses. Skinner (1956) reported that he first happened on this property of partial reinforcement when he ran short of food pellets for his rats and was forced to deliver reinforcers less often. (Not all scientific discoveries are planned!) Years later, when he was asked how he could tolerate being misunderstood so often, he replied that he only needed to be understood three or four times a year—his own intermittent schedule of reinforcement.

Many kinds of intermittent schedules have been studied. *Ratio schedules* deliver a reinforcer after a certain number of responses have occurred. *Interval schedules* deliver a reinforcer if a response is made after the passage of a certain amount of time since the last reinforcer. The number of responses that must occur or the amount of time that must pass before the payoff may be

After a weekend of "getting in touch with your feelings," you are full of patience and goodwill toward others. Then why do you lose your temper just as easily on Monday morning as you did on Friday afternoon?

■ **stimulus discrimination**

In operant conditioning, the tendency of a response to occur in the presence of one stimulus but not in the presence of other, similar stimuli that differ from it on some dimension.

■ **discriminative stimulus**

A stimulus that signals when a particular response is likely to be followed by a certain type of consequence.

■ **stimulus control**

Control over the occurrence of a response by a discriminative stimulus.

fixed (constant) or *variable*. Combining the ratio/interval patterns and fixed/variable patterns yields four basic types of intermittent schedules (see Figure 7.5). These variations in how the reinforcers are delivered have powerful effects on the rate, form, and timing of behavior—effects that most people are not aware of.

1. *On a* **fixed-ratio (FR) schedule,** *reinforcement occurs after a fixed number of responses.* An FR-2 schedule delivers a reinforcer after every other response, an FR-3 schedule after every third response, and so forth. Fixed-ratio schedules produce very high rates of responding. In the laboratory, a rat may rapidly press a bar several hundred times to get a single reward. Outside the laboratory, fixed-ratio schedules are often used by employers to increase productivity. A salesperson who must sell a specific number of items before getting a commission or a factory worker who must produce a specific number of products before earning a given amount of pay (a system known as "piecework") are on fixed-ratio schedules. An interesting feature of high fixed-ratio schedules is that performance drops off just after reinforcement. If a writer must complete four chapters before getting a check, interest and motivation will sag right after the check is received.

2. *On a* **variable-ratio (VR) schedule,** *reinforcement occurs after some average number of responses, but the number varies from reinforcement to reinforcement.* A VR-5 schedule would deliver a reinforcer *on the average* after every fifth response but sometimes after one, two, six, or seven responses, or any other number, as long as the average was five. Variable-ratio schedules produce extremely high, steady rates of responding. The responses are more resistant to extinction than when a fixed-ratio schedule is used. The prime example of a variable-ratio schedule is delivery of payoffs by a slot machine. A player at a slot machine knows that the average number of responses necessary to win is set at a level that makes money for the house. Hope springs eternal, though. The gambler takes a chance on being in front of the machine during one of those lucky moments when fewer responses bring a payoff.

3. *On a* **fixed-interval (FI) schedule,** *reinforcement of a response occurs only if a fixed amount of time has passed since the previous reinforcer.* A rat on a FI-10-second schedule gets a food pellet the first time it presses the bar after the passage of a 10-second interval. Pressing the bar earlier does not hasten the reward. Animals on fixed-interval schedules seem to develop a sharp sense of time. After a rein-

■ **continuous reinforcement**
A reinforcement schedule in which a particular response is always reinforced.

■ **intermittent (partial) schedule of reinforcement**
A reinforcement schedule in which a particular response is sometimes but not always reinforced.

■ **fixed-ratio (FR) schedule**
An intermittent schedule of reinforcement in which reinforcement occurs only after a fixed number of responses.

■ **variable-ratio (VR) schedule**
An intermittent schedule of reinforcement in which reinforcement occurs after a variable number of responses.

■ **fixed-interval (FI) schedule**
An intermittent schedule of reinforcement in which a reinforcer is delivered for the first response made after a fixed period of time has elapsed since the last reinforcer.

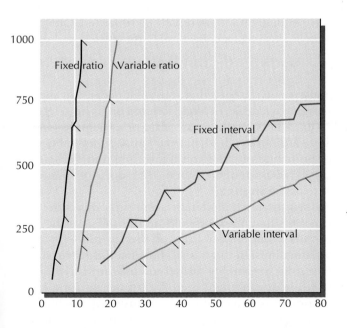

■ **Figure 7.5 Reinforcement Schedules and Behavior**

Different schedules of reinforcement produce different learning curves, or patterns of responding over time. In research using the Skinner box, these curves can be recorded by a device called a cumulative recorder. *Each time a response occurs, a pen moves up a notch on a moving strip of paper. The faster the rate of responding, the steeper the curve. In this figure, each crosshatch indicates the delivery of a reinforcer. Notice that when a fixed-interval schedule is used, responses drop off immediately after reinforcement, resulting in a scalloped curve. (Adapted from B. F. Skinner, "Teaching machines," November 1961, p. 96. Copyright 1961 by Scientific American, Inc. All rights reserved.)*

forcer is delivered, they often stop responding altogether. Then as the end of the interval approaches, responding again picks up, reaching a maximum rate right before reinforcement. Outside the laboratory, fixed-interval schedules are not common, but some behavior patterns do resemble those seen on such schedules. Suppose your sweetheart, who is away for a month, writes you a love letter every day. If the letter usually arrives at about noon, you probably won't check the mailbox at 8:00 A.M., but you will start checking as noon approaches. Once the delivery is received, you will not check again until the next day (Houston, 1981).

4. *On a* **variable-interval (VI) schedule,** *reinforcement of a response occurs only if a variable amount of time has passed since the previous reinforcer.* A VI-10-second schedule means that the interval will average 10 seconds but will vary from reinforcement to reinforcement. Since the animal or person cannot predict when a reward will come, responding is relatively low but steady. When you go fishing, you do not know whether a fish will bite in 5 seconds or 30 minutes or not at all. Under these conditions (assuming you really want that fish), you may steadily check your line every few minutes (Houston, 1981).

A basic principle of operant conditioning is that if you want a response to persist after it has been learned, you should reinforce it intermittently, not continuously. If an animal has been receiving continuous reinforcement for some response and then reinforcement suddenly stops, the animal will soon stop responding. Because the change in reinforcement is large (from continuous to none at all), the animal will easily distinguish the change. But if reinforcement has been intermittent, the change is not so dramatic, and the animal will keep responding for some period of time. Pigeons, rats, and people on intermittent schedules of reinforcement have responded in the laboratory thousands of times without reinforcement before throwing in the towel, especially on variable schedules. Animals will sometimes work so hard for an unpredictable, infrequent bit of food that the energy they expend is greater than that from the reward; theoretically, the animal could actually work itself to death.

It follows that if you want to get rid of a response, you should be careful *not* to reinforce it intermittently. If you are going to extinguish undesirable behavior by ignoring it—a child's tantrums, a friend's midnight phone calls, a parent's unasked-for advice—you must be *absolutely consistent* in withholding reinforcement (your attention). Otherwise, you will probably only make matters worse. The other person will learn that if he or she keeps up the screaming, calling, or advice giving long enough, it will eventually be rewarded. One of the most common errors people make, from a behavioral point of view, is to reward intermittently the responses they would like to eliminate.

Shaping. For a response to be reinforced, it must first occur. But suppose you want to train a rat to pick up a marble, or a dog to stand on its hind legs and turn around, or a child to use a knife and fork properly, or a friend to play terrific tennis. Such behaviors, and most others in everyday life, have almost no probability of appearing spontaneously. You could grow old and gray waiting for them to occur so that you could reinforce them. The operant solution to this dilemma is a procedure called **shaping.**

In shaping, you start by reinforcing a tendency in the right direction, then you gradually require responses that are more and more similar to the final, desired response. The responses that you reinforce on the way to the final one are called **successive approximations.** In the case of the rat and the marble, you might deliver a food pellet if the rat merely turned toward the marble. Once this response was well established, you might then reward the rat for taking a step toward the marble. After that, you could reward it for approaching the marble, then touching the marble, then putting both paws on the marble, and

■ **variable-interval (VI) schedule**
An intermittent schedule of reinforcement in which a reinforcer is delivered for a response made after a variable period of time has elapsed since the last reinforcer.

■ **shaping**
An operant-conditioning procedure in which successive approximations of a desired response are reinforced; used when the desired response has a low probability of occurring spontaneously.

■ **successive approximations**
In the operant-conditioning procedure of shaping, behaviors that are ordered in terms of increasing similarity or closeness to the desired response.

Animals can learn to do some surprising things, with a little help from their human friends and the application of operant conditioning techniques. Water skiing, anyone?

finally holding it. With the achievement of each approximation, the next one would become more likely, making it available for reinforcement.

Using shaping and other techniques, Skinner was able to train pigeons to play Ping-Pong with their beaks and to "bowl" in a miniature alley complete with a wooden ball and tiny bowling pins. Rats have learned equally impressive behaviors (see Figure 7.6). Animal trainers routinely use shaping to teach dogs to act as the "eyes" of the blind. And shaping can be equally effective with human beings. According to one story (probably apocryphal), some university students once used the secondary reinforcement of eye contact to shape the behavior of a famous professor who was an expert on operant conditioning. They decided to get him to deliver his lecture from one particular corner of the room. Each time he moved in the appropriate direction, they looked at him. Otherwise, they averted their gaze. Eventually, the professor was backed into the corner, never suspecting that his behavior had been shaped.

Superstition.   So far, we have been talking about responses that directly bring about some consequence. But a consequence can be effective even when it is entirely coincidental. Skinner (1948) demonstrated this fact by putting eight pigeons in boxes and rigging the boxes so that food was delivered every

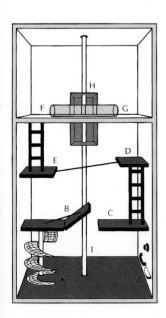

▪ Figure 7.6   A Rat's Route

To demonstrate the effectiveness of shaping and other operant procedures, a researcher trained a rat to perform a long sequence of activities in an apparatus resembling this one. Starting at point A, the rat climbs a ramp to B, crosses a drawbridge to C, climbs a ladder to D, crosses a tightrope to E, climbs another ladder to F, crawls through a tunnel to G, runs to H and enters an elevator, descends in the elevator to I, and runs out of the elevator to J, where it presses a lever and finally receives its well-deserved food. (After Cheney, in Chance, 1994.)

❋ *Farmers sometimes put hex signs like this one on the sides of their barns to ward off evil spirits. Such "good luck" objects and rituals don't "work" most of the time. Why do people superstitiously continue to believe in them?*

15 seconds, even if the bird didn't lift a feather. But pigeons, like rats, are often in motion, so when the food came, each animal was doing *something*. That something was then reinforced by delivery of the food. The behavior, of course, was reinforced entirely by chance, but it still became more likely to occur, and thus to be reinforced again. Within a short time, six of the pigeons were practicing some sort of consistent ritual—turning in counterclockwise circles, bobbing the head up and down, swinging the head to and fro, or making brushing movements toward the floor. None of these activities had the least effect on the delivery of the reinforcer; the birds were being "superstitious." It was as if they thought their movements were responsible for bringing the food.

You can see how coincidental reinforcement might account for some human superstitions. A baseball pitcher happens to scratch his left ear, then strikes out a star batter on the other team; ever after, he scratches his left ear before pitching. A student uses a purple pen on the first exam of the semester, gets an A, and from then on uses only purple pens for taking tests. Why, though, don't such superstitions extinguish? After all, the pitcher isn't going to strike out every batter, nor is the student always going to be brilliant. One answer: Intermittent reinforcement may make the response particularly resistant to extinction. If coincidental reinforcement occurs occasionally, the superstitious behavior may continue indefinitely (Schwartz & Reilly, 1985). Ironically, the fact that our little rituals only "work" some of the time ensures that we will keep using them.

Of course, there are other reasons that superstitions persist. Many superstitions (such as the belief that spilling salt will bring bad luck) are part of one's culture, and they are reinforced by the agreement, approval, or attention of others. Some superstitions are reinforced by the feeling of control over events that they provide. With good-luck charms and the like, as long as nothing awful happens when a person is carrying the charm, the person is likely to credit it with protective powers, but if something bad does occur, the person can always say that the charm has lost its powers. Yet even when we know the reasons for our superstitions, they can be hard to shake. As educator and psychologist Paul Chance (1988) writes, "A black cat means nothing to me now, nor does a broken mirror. There are no little plastic icons on the dashboard of my car, and I carry no rabbit's foot. I am free of all such nonsense, and I am happy to report no ill effects—knock wood."

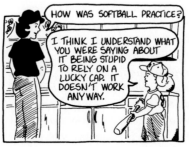

Quick QUIZ

Are you ready to apply the principles of operant conditioning? In each of the following situations, choose the best alternative, and give your reason for choosing it:

1. You want your 2-year-old to ask for water with a word instead of a grunt. Should you give him water when he says "wa-wa" or wait until his pronunciation improves?
2. Your roommate keeps interrupting you while you are studying even though you have asked her to stop. Should you ignore her completely or occasionally respond for the sake of good manners?
3. Your father, who rarely writes, has finally sent a letter. Should you reply quickly or wait a while so he will know how it feels to be ignored?

Answers:

forcement is more effective than delayed reinforcement.
reply quickly if you want to encourage letter writing, because immediate rein-
mittent reinforcement could cause her interruptions to persist. **3.** You should
behaviors need to be shaped. **2.** You should ignore her completely because inter-
1. You should reinforce "wa-wa," an approximation of *water,* because complex

Just Deserts? The Problem with Punishment

In his novel *Walden Two* (1948/1976), Skinner imagined a utopia in which reinforcers were used so wisely that undesirable behavior was rare. His book gives a revealing glimpse of how a behaviorist might go about designing an entire community, using "behavioral engineering." But in the real world, bloopers, bad habits, and antisocial acts abound. Then we are faced with how to get rid of those bad habits and behaviors.

An obvious approach might seem to be punishment. In the United States, the physical punishment of children has roots in the religious belief that you must beat children, or their innate wickedness will land them in hell (Greven, 1991). Most Western democracies and socialist countries have banned corporal (physical) punishment of schoolchildren by principals and teachers, but in the United States, 24 states still permit it (Hyman, 1994). Boys, minority children, and poor white children are the most likely to be hit. Our penal system, too, is based on punishment as a deterrent; the current rallying cry is "three strikes, and you're out." When Michael Faye, an 18-year-old American student, was caned on the buttocks for vandalizing cars in Singapore, many in the United States, including several politicians, called for importing this intensely painful method of punishing juvenile misbehavior. But does punishment work?

Sometimes punishment is unquestionably effective. Some highly disturbed children have been known to chew their own fingers to the bone, stick objects in their eyes, or tear out their hair. You can't ignore such behavior because the children are seriously injuring themselves. You can't respond with concern and affection because you may unwittingly reward the behavior. In these cases, punishment works: Clinical studies find that immediately punishing the self-destructive behavior eliminates it (Lovaas, 1977; Lovaas, Schreibman, & Koegel, 1974). Mild punishers, such as a spray of water in the face, are often just as effective as strong ones, such as electric shock; sometimes they are even more effective. A firm "No!" can also be established as a conditioned punisher.

The effects of punishment, however, are far less predictable than many people realize, as we can see in responses to domestic violence. In a widely publicized real-life experimental intervention, men who were arrested for assaulting their wives or girlfriends were less likely to repeat the offense within six months than men who were merely talked to by the police or ordered to stay away from the victim for a few hours (Sherman & Berk, 1984). On the basis of these results, police departments across the United States adopted mandatory arrest policies in cases of domestic assault. Then more research came along showing that the conclusions were premature: Although arrests do temporarily prevent a repeat attack, they do not usually deter domestic violence *in the long run* (Dunford, Huizinga, & Elliott, 1990; Hirschel et al., 1990; Sherman, 1992). A moral dilemma exists, then, between the immediate need to protect the victim and the long-term need to eliminate the violence entirely.

Further, Lawrence Sherman and his colleagues (Sherman, 1992; Sherman et al., 1991) have noted that if arrest is the aspirin of criminal justice, the pill has different effects on different people at different doses. They found that brief arrests of two or three hours were generally most effective in initially reducing the chances of renewed domestic violence (when compared with a warning), although this effect disappeared within a few weeks. However, for unemployed men in the inner city, being arrested actually *increased* the long-term chances of a repeat attack. The researchers speculated that for these men, the initial fear of being arrested again wore off quickly and was replaced by anger at the woman who "caused" the arrest or at women in general.

Because of such complexities, simplistic efforts to "crack down" on wrongdoers often fail to work. Laboratory and field studies show that punishment also has the following other disadvantages as a method of behavior control:

Is this scene familiar? Harried parents often resort to physical punishment without being aware of the many negative consequences for themselves and their children. Based on your reading of this chapter, what alternatives does this mother have?

1. *People often administer punishment inappropriately or when they are so enraged that they are unable to think through what they are doing and how they are doing it.* They swing blindly or yell wildly, applying punishment so broadly that it covers all sorts of irrelevant behaviors. Indeed, even when people are not carried away by anger, they often misunderstand the proper application of punishment. One student told us his parents used to punish their children before leaving them alone for the evening because of all the naughty things they were *going* to do. Naturally, the children didn't bother to behave like angels.

2. *The recipient of punishment often responds with anxiety, fear, or rage.* Through a process of classical conditioning, these emotional side effects may then generalize to the entire situation in which the punishment occurs—the place, the person delivering the punishment, and the circumstances. Negative emotional reactions tend to create more problems than the punishment solves. For example, instead of becoming obedient or respectful, a teenager who has been severely punished may strike back or run away. As in the case of domestic violence, emotional reactions to punishment may even produce an increase in the undesirable behavior that the punishment was intended to eliminate. That may be why the physical punishment of children is correlated with high rates of violence in children; violence breeds violence (Hyman, 1994; McCord, 1991; Straus, 1991; Weiss et al., 1992).

3. *The effects of punishment are sometimes temporary, depending heavily on the presence of the punishing person or circumstances.* We can probably all remember some transgressions of childhood that we never dared commit when our parents were around but which we promptly resumed as soon as they were gone. All we learned was not to get caught.

4. *Most misbehavior is hard to punish immediately.* Recall that punishment, like reward, works best if it quickly follows a response, especially with animals and children. Outside the laboratory, quick punishment is often hard to achieve.

5. *Punishment conveys little information.* If it immediately follows the misbehavior, it may tell the recipient what *not* to do. But it doesn't communicate what the person (or animal) *should* do. For example, spanking a toddler for messing in his pants will not teach him to use the potty chair. As Skinner (1968) wrote, "We do not teach [a student] to learn quickly by punishing him when he learns slowly, or to recall what he has learned by punishing him when he forgets, or to think logically by punishing him when he is illogical."

6. *An action intended to punish may instead be reinforcing because it brings attention.* Indeed, angry attention may be just what the offender is after. If a mother yells at a child who is throwing a tantrum, the very act of yelling may give him what he wants—a reaction from her. In the schoolroom, teachers who scold children in front of other students, thus putting them in the limelight, often unwittingly reward the very misbehavior they are trying to eliminate.

Because of these drawbacks, most psychologists believe that punishment, especially severe punishment, is a poor way to eliminate unwanted behavior and should be regarded only as a last resort. When punishment is used, it should not involve physical abuse, it should be accompanied by information about what kind of behavior would be appropriate, and it should be followed, whenever possible, by the reinforcement of desirable behavior.

Fortunately, in most situations there is a good alternative to punishment: extinction of the responses you want to discourage. Of course, extinction is sometimes difficult to achieve. It is hard to ignore the child nagging for a cookie before dinner, the roommate interrupting your concentration, or the dog barking its lungs out. Moreover, the simplest form of extinction—ignoring the behavior—is not always appropriate. A teacher cannot ignore a child who is hitting a playmate. The dog owner who ignores Fido's backyard barking may soon hear "barking" of another sort—from the neighbors. A parent whose child is a TV addict can't ignore the behavior, because television is rewarding to the child. One solution is to combine extinction of undesirable acts with reinforcement of alternative ones. If a child is addicted to TV, the parent might ignore the child's pleas for "just one more program" and at the same time encourage behavior that is incompatible with television watching, such as playing outdoors.

It is also important to understand the reasons for a person's misbehavior before deciding how to respond to it. Edward Carr and V. Mark Durand (1985) found, for example, that when autistic and other disturbed children throw tantrums, attack their teachers, or do self-destructive things such as punching or poking themselves, it is often because difficult demands are being placed on them or because they are bored and frustrated. Their bizarre behavior is actually a way of saying, "Hey, let me out of here!" And because the behavior often works, or is reinforced by attention from adults, it tends to persist. When these children are taught to use words to ask for praise or help ("Am I doing good work?" "I don't understand"), their problem behavior decreases and often even disappears. Similarly, a child screaming in a supermarket may be saying, "I'm going out of my head with boredom. Help!" A lover who sulks may be saying, "I'm not sure you really care about me; I'm frightened." Once we understand the purpose or meaning of behavior we dislike, we may be more effective in dealing with it.

Putting Operant Principles to Work

Over the years, behaviorists have carried operant principles out of the narrow world of the Skinner box and into the wider world of the classroom, athletic field, prison, mental hospital, nursing home, rehabilitation ward, child-care center, factory, and office. The use of operant techniques (and also classical ones) in such real-world settings is called **behavior modification.**

Many behavior-modification programs rely on a technique called the **token economy.** Tokens are secondary reinforcers that have no real value in themselves (for example, points or scrip money) but that are exchangeable for primary reinforcers or other secondary reinforcers. They provide an easy way to reinforce behavior on a continuous schedule. Once a particular behavior is

Warnings and threats of punishment often don't work.

■ **behavior modification**
The application of conditioning techniques to teach new responses or to reduce or eliminate maladaptive or problematic behavior.

■ **token economy**
A behavior-modification technique in which secondary reinforcers called tokens, which can be collected and exchanged for primary or other secondary reinforcers, are used for shaping behavior.

established, tokens can be phased out and replaced by more "natural" intermittent reinforcers, such as praise.

Behavior modification has its critics. They fear that its widespread use will crush creativity and turn people into sheep. To these critics, operant conditioning seems mechanistic, harsh, and unethical, especially when it involves the use of punishment or the withholding of reinforcers. But behaviorists contend that society needs *more*, not less, behavior modification. They point out that unethical manipulation existed long before behavioral principles were known. Reinforcement, punishment, and extinction are always occurring, whether in a planned or an unplanned way. The important question is whether society is willing to use behavioral procedures wisely to achieve humane goals.

Behavior modification has had some enormous successes. Behaviorists have taught parents how to toilet train their children in only a few sessions (Azrin & Foxx, 1974) and have taught teachers how to be "behavioral change agents" (Besalel-Azrin, Azrin, & Armstrong, 1977). They have taught autistic children who have never before spoken to use a vocabulary of several hundred words (Lovaas, 1977). They have trained disturbed and mentally retarded adults to communicate, dress themselves, mingle socially with others, and earn a living in the community (Lent, 1968; McLeod, 1985). They have taught brain-damaged patients to control inappropriate behavior, focus attention, and improve their language abilities (McGlynn, 1990). And they have helped ordinary folk to eliminate unwanted habits, such as smoking and nail biting, or to acquire wanted ones, such as practicing the piano or studying.

We do not mean to make behavioral modification sound easy. Sometimes it fails or even backfires. Unlike a rat or a pigeon, human beings may feel manipulated and may refuse to cooperate. Situations are often so complex and uncontrolled that well-planned programs can go awry, especially if those who must implement the programs have not been adequately trained. In one study, a token economy system that had worked well with juvenile offenders in a pilot project fell apart when it was tried in a different institution. The people in charge neglected to smile as they handed out the tokens, and apparently the young men took their stern expressions as an insult (related by Pryor, 1984). Operant techniques may also fail when the underlying cause of the behavior is

Behavioral principles have many practical applications. This capuchin monkey has been trained to assist her paralyzed owner by picking up objects, opening doors, helping with feeding, and performing a variety of other everyday tasks.

not altered. For example, rewarding your partner's cheerfulness may not do much good if his or her gloominess is caused by a boring job. The real solution may be for the person to change jobs.

Another complication is that human beings (and probably many animals, too) work not only for **extrinsic reinforcers,** such as money and gold stars, but also for **intrinsic reinforcers,** such as enjoyment of the task and the satisfaction of accomplishment. As psychologists have applied operant conditioning in real-world settings, they have sometimes found that extrinsic reinforcement can become too much of a good thing; in some circumstances, it can kill the intrinsic pleasure of an activity.

Consider what happened when psychologists gave nursery-school children the chance to draw with felt-tipped pens (Lepper, Greene, & Nisbett, 1973). The children already liked this activity and readily took it up during free play. First, the researchers recorded how long each child spontaneously played with the pens. Then they told some of the children that if they would draw with felt-tipped pens for a man who had come "to see what kinds of pictures boys and girls like to draw with Magic Markers," there would be a prize, a "Good Player Award," complete with gold seal and red ribbon. After drawing for six minutes, each child got the award, as promised. Other children did not expect a reward and were not given one. A week later, the researchers again observed the children's free play. Those children who had expected and received a reward were spending much less time with the pens than they had before the start of the experiment. In contrast, children who were not given an award continued to show as much interest in the activity as they had shown initially (see Figure 7.7). Similar results occurred among older children working on academic tasks.

Why should extrinsic rewards undermine intrinsic motivation? The researchers in these studies suggested that when we are paid for an activity, we interpret it as work. It is as if we say to ourselves, "I'm doing this because I'm being paid for it. Since I'm being paid, it must be something I wouldn't do if I didn't have to." When the reward is withdrawn, we refuse to "work" any longer. Others argue that extrinsic rewards are often seen as controlling, and therefore they reduce a person's sense of autonomy and choice ("I guess I should just do what I'm told to do") (Deci & Ryan, 1987). A third, more behavioral explanation is

People often work hard for money and good grades. Unhappily, these rewards can also kill the intrinsic pleasure of the activity. Could that be why so many college students stop reading after they graduate? What are the conditions under which rewards might not reduce intrinsic satisfactions?

■ **extrinsic reinforcers**
Reinforcers that are not inherently related to the activity being reinforced, such as money, prizes, and praise.

■ **intrinsic reinforcers**
Reinforcers that are inherently related to the activity being reinforced, such as enjoyment of the task and the satisfaction of accomplishment.

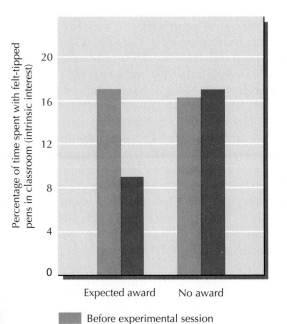

■ **Figure 7.7 Turning Play into Work**

Preschool children were promised a prize for drawing with felt-tipped pens, an activity they already liked. The time they voluntarily spent with the pens temporarily increased. But after the prize was awarded, the children spent less time with the pens than they had before the study. In contrast, children who were not promised or given an award continued to show interest in drawing with the pens. Such results suggest that extrinsic rewards can sometimes reduce intrinsic motivation.

*T*hink About It

*D*o High Grades and Praise Raise Self-esteem?

■ It is popular today to blame every problem of youth, from poor academic test scores to juvenile crime, on low self-esteem. Raise self-esteem, the argument goes, and the problems will disappear. In California, a Task Force on the Social Importance of Self-esteem was convened to confirm the allegedly beneficial effects of raising self-esteem (Smelser, Vasconcellos, & Mecca, 1989). Teachers everywhere are taking this goal to heart, handing out lavish praise and high grades in hopes that students' feelings of self-worth and academic performance will improve.

One obvious result is grade inflation. In one middle school, when teachers tried to use a cutoff of a 3.5 grade point average for membership in a new academic honor society, they found that *two-thirds* of the school's 600 students were eligible, although clearly not all were doing "A" work (Celis, 1993). The teachers apparently felt obligated to give out high grades whether students deserved them or not. Grade inflation has infiltrated higher education, as well. In some colleges and universities, C's, which once meant "average" or "satisfactory," are nearly extinct. (We heard about one student, who was complaining about strict course requirements and said, oblivious to the irony, "Gosh, it's impossi-

ble for an average student to get an A in this class.") Pressured by parents and administrators, and worried about how students will evaluate them, many teachers go along with the trend despite their misgivings.

The problem, from a learning theory point of view, is that to be effective, rewards must be tied to the behavior you are trying to increase. When rewards are dispensed indiscriminately, they become meaningless (they are no longer reinforcing), and when teachers praise mediocre work, that is what they are likely to get. Moreover, if a teacher gushes over work on a task that was actually easy, the hidden message may be that the child isn't very smart ("Gee, Minnie, you did a *fantastic* job . . . of adding two and two"). Even when the task is a challenging one, praise, if delivered too dramatically, may carry an unintended message—that the student's good work was a surprise ("Gee, Robert, you *really* did *well* on that paper [and who would have ever thought you could do it]"). The result is likely to be lower, not higher, self-esteem, and reduced expectations of doing well (Kohn, 1993).

Although many people assume that self-esteem is the main ingredient of success and achievement—and its absence a major reason that children

"That is the correct answer, Billy, but I'm afraid you don't win anything for it."

that extrinsic reinforcement raises the rate of responding above some optimal, enjoyable level, so the activity really does become work.

There is a trade-off, then, between the short-term effectiveness of extrinsic rewards and the long-term effectiveness of intrinsic ones. Extrinsic rewards work: How many people would trudge off to work every morning if they never got paid? In the classroom, a teacher who offers incentives to an unmotivated student may be taking the only course of action open. Further, you have to have the skill to do something before the activity can become intrinsically pleasurable (Chance, 1992). Reading a good novel may be intrinsically rewarding, but the painstaking process of learning, as a first-grader, to sound out words is less so. If a behavior is to last when the teacher isn't around, however, extrinsic reinforcers eventually must be phased out. As one mother wrote in a *Newsweek* essay, "The winners [of prizes for school work] will . . . suffer if they don't discover for themselves that they can gain the pleasure of health and strength from exercise, the joy of music from songs, the power of mathematics from counting and all of human wisdom from reading" (Skreslet, 1987). The fact that our school system relies heavily on grades and other extrinsic incentives may help explain why the average college graduate reads few books. Like all extrinsic rewards, grades induce temporary compli-

fail—there is actually no evidence to support this assumption, in spite of concerted efforts to find some. The California task force, after reviewing virtually every study done on the relationship of self-esteem to anything (and there are thousands of them), found *no support* for any of its "intuitively correct" ideas about self-esteem (Smelser, Vasconcellos, & Mecca, 1989). Lilian Katz (1993), a professor of early childhood education who heads the National Association for the Education of Young People, argues that "feel good about yourself" programs in schools, although well-intentioned, tend to confuse self-esteem with narcissism. Children are taught to turn their attention inward and to focus on personal gratification and self-celebration. Program after program asks children to write about such superficial things as physical attributes and consumer preferences ("What I like to watch on TV" or "What I like to eat"). In one typical curriculum she examined, Katz says, "Not once was the child asked to assume the role of producer, investigator, initiator, explorer, experimenter, wonderer, or problem-solver." The booklets never had pages with titles such as "What I want to know more about," or "What I am curious about" or want to explore, find out, solve, figure out, or make. Real self-esteem,

Katz argues, does not come from "cheap success in a succession of trivial tasks," from phony flattery by a teacher, or from gold stars and happy faces. It emerges from effort, persistence, and the gradual acquisition of skills, and is nurtured by a teacher's genuine appreciation of the *content* of the child's work.

In recent years, studies have revealed an appalling level of illiteracy in the United States. Some high school graduates cannot read well enough to decipher a bus schedule or a warning on a nonprescription medication. Millions of people have such poor arithmetic skills that they cannot balance a checkbook or verify the change they get at the supermarket. Many students are unaware that their writing and math skills are deficient; how could they know, since they have always received high grades? The time seems right to rethink the way children are taught and schools are organized. After reading this chapter, how would you design a school system that fostered achievement, competence, and an intrinsic love of learning? What role, if any, would grades and other extrinsic reinforcers play? How would you let students know about poor performance without making them feel like failures? Think about it. ▪

ance but not necessarily a lifelong disposition to learn. There is evidence that as children get older, they become more and more dependent on grades and the teacher's approval and less and less concerned with satisfying their own curiosity (Harter & Jackson, 1992). (In "Think About It," we discuss how grades and praise affect students' self-esteem.)

We do not want to leave the impression, however, that extrinsic reinforcers always decrease intrinsic motivation. Many businesses now recognize that workers' productivity depends both on pay incentives *and* on having interesting, challenging, and varied kinds of work to do (see Chapter 11). Money and praise do not necessarily interfere with intrinsic motivation when extrinsic rewards are clearly tied to competence rather than mere performance and when the activity is already well learned (Deci, 1975). Also, people who are extremely interested in an activity or task to begin with are likely to keep doing it even when extrinsic reinforcers are withdrawn (Mawhinney, 1990). Extrinsic rewards can even increase creativity, as long as they are given only for high-quality performance and are not so salient that they distract a person from the task at hand (Eisenberger & Selbst, 1994).

Effective behavior modification, as you can see, is not only a science but an art. In "Taking Psychology with You," we offer some guidelines for mastering that art.

Quick QUIZ

A. According to behavioral principles, what is happening here?

1. An adolescent whose parents have hit him for minor transgressions since he was small runs away from home.
2. A young woman whose parents paid her to clean her room while she was growing up is a slob when she moves to her own apartment.
3. Two parents scold their young daughter every time they catch her sucking her thumb. The thumb sucking continues anyway.

 B. Several states are trying to reduce truancy and school failures by experimenting with forms of punishment. For example, families on welfare may lose part of their payments if their children regularly skip school, students who earn poor grades may lose after-school activities or driving privileges, and students who quit high school may have to forfeit their driver's licenses. What assumptions underlie such programs?

Answers:

A. 1. The physical punishment was painful, and through a process of classical conditioning, the situation in which it occurred also became unpleasant. Because escape from an unpleasant stimulus is negatively reinforcing, the boy ran away. *2.* Extrinsic reinforcers are no longer available, and room-cleaning behavior has been extinguished. Also, extrinsic rewards may have displaced the intrinsic satisfaction of having a tidy room. *3.* Punishment has failed, possibly because it rewards thumb sucking with attention or because thumb sucking still brings the child pleasure whenever the parents aren't around. *B.* We do not know yet the effectiveness of such programs, but in any case, they rest on the following assumptions (among others): (a) The threat of punishment will motivate students to do better instead of alienating or discouraging them; (b) the problem is in the students, not the schools or the community; (c) if a student isn't doing well, the student must not be working hard; (d) enforcement will be adequate, and the punishers used will be effective; (e) extrinsic and intrinsic reinforcers can't do the job without punishment. (Based on your reading of this chapter, can you think of some reasons why some or all of these assumptions may be valid or invalid for certain students?)

▪ SOCIAL-LEARNING THEORIES

For half a century, most American learning theories held that learning could be explained by specifying the behavioral "ABCs"—*antecedents* (events preceding behavior), *behaviors,* and *consequences.* Early behaviorists, such as John Watson, assumed that what was learned was a stimulus–response connection. Skinner (1974) and later behaviorists rejected this approach and discussed complex cues for responding, classes of behavior, and the way that rules, in the form of language, can control behavior. In the 1960s, other theorists expounded a view known as "expectancy theory," emphasizing that when an organism behaves in a certain way, it acts *as if* it has expectations (Bolles, 1972; Bolles et al., 1980). Pavlov's dogs acted *as if* they expected the ringing of the bell (the CS) to be followed by food (the US). Skinner's rats acted *as if* they expected bar pressing to be followed by food. But expectancy theorists did not speculate about what an animal (or person) might consciously experience during learning. Like most other behaviorists, they believed that nothing was to be gained by theorizing about mental operations.

Yet even during the early glory years of behaviorism, a few behaviorists were rebelling against explanations of behavior that relied solely on conditioning principles. In the 1940s, two social scientists proposed a modification they called *social-learning theory* (Dollard & Miller, 1950). In human beings, they argued, most learning is acquired by observing other people in a social context, not through standard conditioning procedures. By the 1960s and 1970s, social-learning theory was in full bloom, and a new element had been added: the human capacity for higher-level cognitive processes. Its proponents agreed with behaviorists that human beings, along with the rat and the rabbit, are subject to the laws of operant and classical conditioning. They recognized the importance of situational reinforcers and the influence of the immediate environment on a person's actions. But they added that human beings, unlike the rat and the rabbit, are full of attitudes, beliefs, and expectations that affect the way they acquire information, make decisions, reason, and solve problems. All of these mental processes affect what individuals will do at any given moment and also, more generally, the kinds of people they become.

Today social-learning approaches also differ from behaviorism in their emphasis on the *interaction* between individuals and their environments. Radical behaviorists regard the relationship of environment to behavior primarily as a straight line, like this:

But social-learning theorists regard the environment, a person's qualities, and his or her behavior as forming a circle in which all elements mutually affect each other. This interaction of the person and the environment, called *reciprocal determinism* (Bandura, 1986), looks like this:

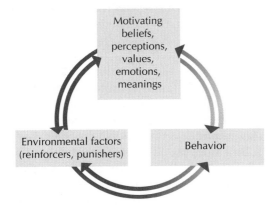

We speak of **social-learning theories** in the plural because they do not represent a single unified approach to behavior in the way that traditional behaviorism does. Researchers in this field differ, for example, in how much emphasis they place on cognitive processes and in how much they distance themselves from behaviorism. Some researchers continue to call themselves "social-learning theorists," but the two leading advocates of this approach, Walter Mischel and Albert Bandura, call their theories *cognitive social learning* (Mischel, 1973) and *social cognitive theory* (Bandura, 1986, 1994). In general, however, social-learning theories all emphasize observational learning and the role of models, as well as cognitive processes such as perceptions and interpretations of events.

Observational Learning: The Copycat Syndrome

Late one night, a friend who lives in a rural area was awakened by a loud clattering and banging. Her whole family raced outside to find the source of the

■ **social-learning theories**
Theories of learning that typically emphasize a person's reciprocal interaction with the environment and that involve observational learning, cognitive processes, and motivating beliefs.

Like father, like daughter. Parents can be powerful role models.

commotion. A raccoon had knocked over a "raccoon-proof" garbage can and seemed to be demonstrating to an assembly of other raccoons how to open it: If you jump up and down on the can's side, the lid will pop off.

According to our friend, the observing raccoons learned from this episode how to open stubborn garbage cans, and the observing humans learned how smart raccoons can be. In short, they all benefited from **observational learning** (which behaviorists call *vicarious conditioning*): learning by watching what others do and what happens to them for doing it. Social-learning theorists emphasize that operant conditioning can and often does occur vicariously, when an animal or person observes a *model* (another animal or person) behaving in certain ways and experiencing the consequences (Bandura, 1977). Sometimes the learner imitates the responses shortly after observing them. At other times the learning remains latent until circumstances allow or require it to be expressed in performance. A little boy may observe a parent setting the table, threading a needle, or tightening a screw, but he may not act on this learning for years. Then the child finds he knows how to do these things, even though he has never before done them. He did not learn by doing, but by watching.

None of us would last long without observational learning. We would have to learn to avoid oncoming cars by walking into traffic and suffering the consequences or to swim by jumping into a deep pool and flailing around. Learning would be not only dangerous but also inefficient. Parents and teachers would be busy 24 hours a day shaping children's behavior. Bosses would have to stand over their employees' desks, rewarding every little link in the complex behavioral chains we call typing, report writing, and accounting. Observational learning also explains why parents who hit their children for hitting other kids tend to rear children who are hitters, and why yellers ("Be quiet!") tend to rear yellers. The children do as their parents do, not as they say (Grusec, Saas-Kortsaak, & Simutis, 1978).

Many years ago, Albert Bandura and his colleagues (1963) showed just how important observational learning is, especially for children who are learning the rules of social behavior. In their study (Bandura, Ross, & Ross, 1963), nursery school children watched a short film of two men, Rocky and Johnny, playing

■ **observational learning**
A learning process in which an individual learns new responses by observing the behavior of another (a model) rather than through direct experience; sometimes called vicarious conditioning.

with toys. (Apparently the children did not think this behavior was odd.) In the film, Johnny refuses to share his toys, and Rocky responds by clobbering him. Rocky's actions are rewarded because he winds up with all the toys. Poor Johnny sits dejectedly in the corner, while Rocky marches off with a sack full of his loot and a hobby horse under his arm. After watching the film, each child was left alone for 20 minutes in a playroom full of toys, including some of the items shown in the film. The researchers found that the children were much more aggressive in their play than a control group that had not viewed the film. Sometimes the children's behavior was almost a direct imitation of Rocky's. At the end of the session, one little girl even asked the experimenter for a sack!

Commenting on the powerful effects of his "Rocky and Johnny show" and other instances of observational learning, Bandura (1973) noted that "Children have been apprehended for writing bad checks to obtain money for candy, for sniping at strangers with BB guns, for sending threatening letters to teachers and for injurious switchblade fights after witnessing similar performances on television." Today, alas, children (and adults) are being apprehended for far more violent acts of imitation.

Behaviorists have always acknowledged the importance of observational learning; they just think it can be explained in stimulus–response terms. But social-learning theorists believe that in human beings, observational learning cannot be fully understood without taking into account the thought processes of the learner (Meltzoff & Gopnik, 1993).

Cognitive Processes: Peering into the "Black Box"

Early behaviorists liked to compare the mind to an engineer's hypothetical "black box," a device whose workings must be inferred because they can't be observed directly. To most behaviorists, the box contained irrelevant wiring; it was enough to know that pushing a button on the box would produce a predictable response.

But even as early as the 1930s, a few behaviorists could not resist peeking into that black box. Edward Tolman (1938) committed virtual heresy at the time by noting that his rats, when pausing at turning points in a maze, seemed to be *remembering* and *deciding* which way to go. In his studies, Tolman found that sometimes the animals didn't behave as conditioning principles would predict. Sometimes the animals were clearly learning without any obvious behavioral change. What, he wondered, was going on in their little rat brains that might account for this puzzle?

In a classic experiment, Tolman and C. H. Honzik (1930) placed three groups of rats in mazes and observed their behavior each day for more than two weeks. The rats in Group 1 always found food at the end of the maze. Group 2 never found food. Group 3 found no food for ten days but then received food on the eleventh. The Group 1 rats, which had been reinforced with food, quickly learned to head straight for the end of the maze without going down blind alleys, whereas Group 2 rats did not learn to go to the end. But the Group 3 rats were different. For ten days they appeared to follow no particular route. Then, when food was introduced, they quickly learned to run to the end of the maze. As Figure 7.8 on page 279 shows, by the next day, they were doing as well as Group 1.

Group 3 had demonstrated **latent learning,** learning that is not immediately expressed. A great deal of human learning also remains latent until circumstances allow or require it to be expressed, as we saw in our discussion of observational learning. Latent learning poses problems for behavioral theories. Not only does it occur in the absence of any obvious reinforcer, but it also raises questions about what, exactly, is learned during learning. The rats that were not given food until the eleventh day had no reason to run toward the end during their first ten days in the maze. Yet clearly they had learned *something.*

■ **latent learning**
A form of learning that is not immediately expressed in an overt response; occurs without obvious reinforcement.

Tolman (1948) argued that this "something" was a **cognitive map,** a mental representation of the spatial layout of the environment. You have a cognitive map of your neighborhood, which is what allows you to find your way to 4th and Kumquat Streets even if you have never done so; and you have a cognitive map of the city you live in, which enables you to take three different unfamiliar routes across town to the movies and still get there. More generally, according to social-learning theories, what the learner learns in observational and latent learning is not a response but *knowledge* about responses and their consequences. We learn how the world is organized, which paths lead to which places, and which actions can produce which payoffs. This knowledge permits us to be creative and flexible in reaching our goals.

Social-learning theories also emphasize the importance of people's *perceptions* in what they learn: perceptions of the models they observe and also per-

■ **cognitive map**

A mental representation of the environment.

Psychology and Popular Culture

Media Violence: Getting Away with Murder

■ Many people are worried about what seems to be an epidemic among young people of violence and obliviousness to the pain caused by violence. One inner-city teacher decided to take some gang members to a hospital so they could see up close the results of violence on their streets. While they were there, they spotted a fellow gang member on a hospital gurney, bloodied and moaning in pain from a gunshot wound. The victim looked up and said, in a tone of astonishment, "I had no idea it hurt." In a Connecticut town, a group of teenage boys looking for excitement telephoned an order for Chinese food so that they could rob the delivery man. When he refused to hand over the cartons of food, one of the teenagers impulsively shot him to death. Later, the boys calmly ate the food.

Many psychologists and social critics blame such callous attitudes in part on television and movies. Social-learning theory predicts that children will imitate violent acts, or at least become more aggressive, if they are exposed to portrayals of violence in which the perpetrator is rewarded. A great deal of media violence fills the bill: Children in the United States and many other countries view endless killings and maimings that leave out all negative consequences. Victims are merely "blown away." Death doesn't mean grief, mourning, or pain; it means disappearing from the screen.

In this chapter, we discussed a classic study showing that some children become more aggressive from watching aggression on television. Other research has found the same thing (Comstock et al., 1978; Eron, 1980; Geen, 1978; Singer & Singer, 1988). A task force convened by the American Psy-

chological Association to study this issue concluded that "There is absolutely no doubt that higher levels of viewing violence on television are correlated with increased acceptance of aggressive attitudes and increased aggressive behavior" (APA Commission on Violence and Youth, 1993).

Children, however, watch many kinds of programs and movies and have many models to observe besides those they see in the media. There are many influences on a child's aggression, one of the most important of which is growing up in a violent family. That may be why, in most studies, the relationship between media violence and real violence is not strong (Freedman, 1988; Milavsky, 1988). Certainly not everyone who watches *The Terminator,* or even four "Freddy" films in a row, runs out to commit mayhem. Nor does everyone draw the same lessons from media violence. One person who watches Arnold Schwarzenegger destroy the bad guys might regard Arnold as the greatest hero of all times, while another sees him as an overpaid weightlifter who should take acting lessons. One person may learn from seeing people being "blown away" that violence is cool and masculine; another may conclude that violence is ugly, stupid, and self-defeating.

Still, movies and television programs are powerful shapers of values, attitudes, and reactions to events, including violent events. Critics of media violence point out that most research on the issue was done during the 1970s. Since then, depictions have become far more graphic, especially in action and slasher films, which are routinely shown on non-network TV stations and which feature, with

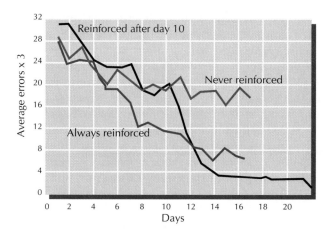

Figure 7.8   Latent Learning

In a classic experiment, rats were placed in a complicated maze. Rats that always found a food reward in the goal box made fewer errors over time, as shown by the gray curve on the graph. In contrast, rats that never found food showed little improvement, as shown by the red curve. A third group of rats found no food for the first ten days and then were given food on the eleventh day. As the black curve shows, these animals showed rapid improvement from then on, quickly equaling the performance of the rats that received food from the start. This result suggests that learning involves cognitive changes that can occur even in the absence of reinforcement, although such changes may not be acted on until a reinforcer becomes available (Tolman & Honzik, 1930).

monotonous regularity, people being sawed in half by chain saws, impaled, or blown to bits. To many young people, these films are a joke and fun; the rush of epinephrine the movies produce is enjoyable. To many psychologists, graphic violence is no joke. They believe that with repeated exposure to mindless murder, viewers' responses of horror or disgust tend to extinguish, people become numb to the consequences of brutality, and increasingly gruesome depictions are needed to produce an emotional effect. Support comes from studies of slasher films, which often link erotic scenes with grisly violence. In the laboratory, viewers of such films tend to become more callous in their attitudes toward women and toward real-life rape victims (Linz, Donnerstein, & Penrod, 1988).

Violence has always been a part of storytelling, in fairy tales, myths, novels, and plays. Modern media violence, however, whether bloodless or gory, is often notable not only for what it shows but also for what it leaves out: the human face and personality of the victim, the sorrow of those they leave behind (even bad guys usually have friends and families), and perhaps most important, alternative ways of resolving conflicts. People can identify with victims and survivors when violence has meaning; they will cry even for Bambi, a cartoon deer. But it is hard to feel empathy when killing is just a matter of awesome special effects.

In contrast to the glamorizing of fictional violence, news reports of actual violence are often sanitized. Since World War II, government censors have been concerned about media efforts to portray the realities of war: rape, disease, and bodies torn apart

in battle (Fussell, 1989). Since the Vietnam conflict, the first "TV war," battlefields and body bags have been off limits to cameras, presumably because seeing the real carnage of war might affect public support for it. During the 1991 Persian Gulf war, television viewers saw only sleek aircraft taking off and videos of "smart bombs" "surgically" destroying buildings. They did not get to witness the chaos and fear of battle; enemy fatalities were called "collateral damage." What are the effects of this censorship on viewers?

Some people hope to solve the problem of violence in popular culture by censoring other media images. This goal raises complex issues, not only because the American Constitution protects free speech, but also because of the problem of defining which violent images should be censored and who would do the censoring. Other social critics argue that media images only reflect the popular culture's existing fondness for violent entertainment and violent solutions to problems.

In the midst of this debate, understanding the basic principles of learning can be helpful. Learning theory suggests that violent films continue to be made because they make barrels of money for their producers—a powerful reinforcer! It follows that viewers can extinguish violent-film-making behavior by refusing to buy tickets to slasher and other violent action films or by turning to another station when such films are shown on television. The question is whether they would be willing to do so, or whether their own viewing behavior is being controlled by reinforcers that they have never stopped to analyze. ■

ceptions of themselves. Two people may observe the same event and come away with entirely different interpretations of it; they have learned, we might say, two different lessons from it. Individuals also bring different knowledge and assumptions to an event, and they notice and pay attention to different aspects of a situation. People make thousands of observations every day and theoretically could learn something from all of them; but if they don't *want* to learn what is being modeled, they could watch a hundred models and not get anywhere at all (Bandura, 1986, 1994). Individual differences in perceptions and interpretations help explain why observational learning does not produce the same results in all observers. (In "Psychology and Popular Culture," we discuss the implications of this fact in debates about the effects of media violence on children and adults.)

Behaviorists would say that the thing we call "personality" is a set of habits and beliefs that have been rewarded over a person's life. Social-learning theorists, however, maintain that these learned habits and beliefs eventually come to exert their own motivating effects on behavior. For example, to understand why some people work hard and persist even after failing many times, such theorists argue, we need to understand cognitive factors, such as the sense of control people have about their lives and whether they are confident in their own abilities. We will be discussing the influence of motivating beliefs and internalized goals further in Chapters 11 and 12.

■ COGNITIONS VERSUS CONNECTIONS: WHY DOES LEARNING OCCUR?

Today, most psychologists allow for cognitions in their theories and explanations of behavior. However, to the true behaviorist, mental explanations are misleading fictions, and nothing is to be gained by using them. As behaviorist William Baum (1994) writes, "I no more have a mind than I have a fairy godmother. I can talk to you about my mind or about my fairy godmother; that cannot make either of them less fictional. No one has ever seen either one . . . such talk is no help in a science."

The basic tension between behaviorism and cognitive approaches to psychology can be seen in how the two approaches treat the interesting problem of insight. **Insight** is learning that appears to occur in a flash: You suddenly "see" how to solve an equation, fix your carburetor, or finish a puzzle. The human species is not the only one capable of insight. In the 1920s, Wolfgang Köhler (1925) put chimpanzees in situations in which some tempting bananas were just out of reach, and then he watched to see what the apes would do. The apes turned out to be very clever. If the bananas were outside the cage, the animal might pull them in with a stick. If the bananas were hung overhead, and there were boxes in the cage, the chimpanzee might pile up the boxes and climb on top of them to reach the fruit. Often, the solution came after the animal had been sitting quietly for a while without actively trying to reach the bananas. It appeared as though the animal had been thinking about the problem and suddenly saw the answer.

To most people, insight seems to be an entirely cognitive phenomenon—a new way of perceiving logical and cause-and-effect relationships, in which a person or animal does not simply respond to a stimulus but instead solves a problem. But behaviorists argue that insight can be explained in terms of an organism's prior reinforcement history (Windholz & Lamal, 1985). Insight, they say, is just a label for a sudden change in behavior; it does not *explain* the behavior.

Behaviorists point out that even animals not credited with higher mental processes seem capable of what looks suspiciously like "insight," under some

When a chimpanzee suddenly finds a way to reach some bananas, we say it has "insight." But what if a pigeon does the same thing? Can a birdbrain have insight?

■ **insight**

A form of learning that occurs in problem solving and appears to involve the (often sudden) understanding of how elements of a situation are related or can be reorganized to achieve a solution.

(a)

(b)   (c)

▪ Figure 7.9   Smart Bird

"Now, let's see . . . ." In Robert Epstein's laboratory, a pigeon looks at a cluster of toy bananas strung overhead (a), pushes a small box beneath the bananas (b), then climbs on the box to peck at them (c). The bird previously learned separate components of this sequence through a process of operant conditioning. Behaviorists view this accomplishment, which resembles that of chimpanzees, as evidence against the cognitive view of insight. Cognitive psychologists disagree. What do you think?

conditions. In one ingenious study, Robert Epstein and his colleagues (1984) trained four pigeons to push boxes in a particular direction and also to climb onto a box to peck a toy banana overhead in order to obtain grain. The birds were also taught not to fly or to jump at the banana; these behaviors were extinguished. Then the pigeons were left alone with the banana suspended overhead, just out of reach, and the box at the edge of the cage. They quickly solved their feeding problem by pushing the box beneath the banana and climbing onto it, just as Köhler's chimps had done (see Figure 7.9). The pigeons had solved the problem, yet few people would want to credit pigeons with complex thought processes. Epstein (1990) has since devised a computer model that is amazingly accurate in predicting the pigeons' behavior in the banana-and-box situation, using only behavioral concepts. Cognitive researchers, however, are not convinced; cognitive studies, they maintain, show that in human beings (and possibly chimpanzees), insight requires *mentally* combining previously learned responses in new ways.

The debates between behaviorists and their critics over insight and many other kinds of learning promise to continue. In practice, behavioral and cognitive approaches are sometimes treated as different levels of analysis, rather than as conflicting approaches; many therapists, for example, combine behavioral principles with cognitive ones to treat people in psychotherapy (see Chapter 16). Nonetheless, as we will see in the next two chapters, cognitive psychologists have staked out many areas that behaviorists have traditionally regarded as foreign territory—areas in the vast country of the mind.

Taking Psychology with You

Shape Up!

Operant conditioning can seem deceptively simple. In the early 1980s, a tiny but expensive book titled *The One Minute Manager* became an enormous bestseller merely by advising managers to use praise and constructive criticism. In practice, though, behavior modification can be full of unwanted surprises, even in the hands of experts. Here are a few things to keep in mind if you want to modify someone's behavior.

- *Accentuate the positive.* Most people notice bad behavior more than good and therefore miss opportunities to use reinforcers. Parents, for example, often scold a child for bed-wetting but fail to give praise for dry sheets in the morning; or they punish a child for poor grades but fail to reward studying.

- *Reinforce small improvements.* A common error is to withhold reinforcement until behavior is perfect. Has your child's grade in math improved from a D to a C? Has your favorite date, who is usually an awful cook, managed to serve up a half-decent omelette? Has your messy roommate left some dirty dishes in the sink but vacuumed the rug? It's probably time for a reinforcer. On the other hand, you don't want to overdo praise or give it insincerely. Gushing about every tiny step in the right direction will cause your praise to lose its value, and soon nothing less than a standing ovation will do.

- *Find the right reinforcers.* You may have to experiment a bit to find which reinforcers a person (or animal) actually wants. In general, it is good to use a variety of reinforcers because the same one used again and again can get boring. Reinforcers, by the way, do not have to be *things*. You can also use valued activities, such as going out to dinner, to reinforce other behavior.

- *Always examine what you are reinforcing.* It is easy to reinforce undesirable behavior by responding to it. Suppose someone is always yelling at you at the slightest provocation, and you want it to stop. If you respond to it at all, whether by crying, apologizing, or yelling back, you are likely to reinforce it. An alternative might be to explain in a calm voice that you will henceforth not respond to complaints unless they are communicated without yelling—and then, if the yelling continues, leave. When the person does speak civilly, you can reward this behavior with your attention and goodwill.

Because you are with yourself more than with anyone else, it may be easier to modify your own behavior than someone else's. You may wish to reduce your nibbling, eliminate a smoking habit, or become more outgoing in public. Let's assume for the sake of discussion that you aren't studying enough. How can you increase the time you spend with your books? Some hints:

- *Analyze the situation.* Are there circumstances that keep you from studying, such as a friend who is always pressuring you to go out or a rock band that practices next door? If so, you need to change the discriminative stimuli in your environment during study periods. Try to find a comfortable, cheerful, quiet, well-lit place. Not only will you concentrate better, but you may also have positive emotional responses to the environment that may generalize to the activity of studying.

- *Set realistic goals.* People can achieve more by learning to set behavioral goals that are demanding but that they can realistically achieve. If a goal is too vague, as in "I'm going to work harder," you don't know what action to take to reach it or how to know when you get there (what does "harder" mean?). If your goal is focused, as in "I am going to study two hours every evening instead of one, and read 25 pages instead of 15," you have specified both a course of action and a goal you can achieve.

- *Reinforce getting started.* The hardest part of studying can be getting started. (This is true of many other activities, too, as writers, joggers, and people who prepare their own income-tax returns can tell you.) You might give yourself a small bit of candy or some other reward just for sitting down at your desk or, if you study at the library, getting there early.

- *Keep records.* Chart your progress in some way, perhaps by making a graph. This will keep you honest, and the progress you see on the graph will serve as a secondary reinforcer.

- *Don't punish yourself.* If you didn't study enough last week, don't brood about it or berate yourself with self-defeating thoughts, such as "I'll never be a good student" or "I'm a failure." Think about the coming week instead.

Above all, be patient. Shaping behavior is a creative skill that takes time to learn. Like Rome, new habits cannot be built in a day.

Summary

1. For almost half a century, until the 1960s, *behaviorism* was the dominant approach to the study of learning. Behaviorists have shown that two types of conditioning can explain much of human behavior: classical conditioning and operant conditioning.

2. *Classical conditioning* was first studied by Russian physiologist Ivan Pavlov. In this type of learning, when a neutral stimulus is paired with an *unconditioned stimulus (US)* that elicits some reflexive *unconditioned response (UR)*, the neutral stimulus comes to elicit a similar or related response. The neutral stimulus is then called a *conditioned stimulus (CS)*, and the response it elicits, a *conditioned response (CR)*.

3. In *extinction*, the conditioned stimulus is repeatedly presented without the unconditioned stimulus, and the conditioned response eventually disappears. In *higher-order conditioning*, a neutral stimulus becomes a conditioned stimulus by being paired with an already established conditioned stimulus. In *stimulus generalization*, after a stimulus becomes a conditioned stimulus for some response, other, similar stimuli may produce the same reaction. And in *stimulus discrimination*, different responses are made to stimuli that resemble the conditioned stimulus in some way.

4. The traditional behaviorist view was that an association is formed between the unconditioned and conditioned stimuli simply because the two stimuli occur close together in time. A more recent view holds that what an animal or a person learns is information conveyed by one stimulus about another.

5. Classical conditioning may account for the acquisition of likes and dislikes, emotional responses to particular objects and events, unusual desires, and fears and phobias. John Watson showed how fears may be learned and then unlearned through a process of *counterconditioning*. Classical conditioning may also be involved in such aspects of drug addiction as tolerance and withdrawal.

6. The basic principle of *operant conditioning* is that behavior becomes more or less likely to occur, depending on its consequences. Responses in operant conditioning are generally not reflexive and are more complex than in classical conditioning. Research in this area is closely associated with B. F. Skinner, who called his approach "radical behaviorism."

7. In the Skinnerian analysis, a response ("operant") can lead to one of three consequences: neutral, reinforcing, or punishing. *Reinforcement* strengthens or increases the probability of a response. *Punishment* weakens or decreases the probability of a response. Reinforcement (and punishment) may be positive or negative. *Positive reinforcement* occurs when something pleasant follows a response. *Negative reinforcement* occurs when something *un*pleasant is removed. Reinforcement is called *primary* when the reinforcer is naturally reinforcing (for instance, satisfying a biological need) and *secondary* when the reinforcer has acquired its ability to strengthen a response through association with other reinforcers. A similar distinction is made for punishers.

8. By using the Skinner box and similar devices, behaviorists have shown that extinction, stimulus generalization, and stimulus discrimination occur in operant as well as in classical conditioning. They also find that immediate consequences usually have a greater effect on a response than do delayed consequences.

9. The pattern of responding in operant conditioning depends in part on the *schedule of reinforcement*. *Continuous reinforcement* leads to the most rapid learning, but *intermittent*, or *partial*, reinforcement makes a response resistant to extinction. Intermittent schedules deliver a reinforcer after a given amount of time has passed since the last reinforcer (*interval schedules*) or after a given number of responses are made (*ratio schedules*). Such schedules may be *fixed* or *vari-*

able. One of the most common errors people make, from a behavioral point of view, is to reward intermittently the responses they would like to eliminate.

10. *Shaping* is used to train behaviors with a low probability of occurring spontaneously. Reinforcers are given for *successive approximations* to the desired response, until the desired response is achieved. Accidental or coincidental reinforcement can effectively strengthen behavior and probably helps account for the learning and the persistence of superstitions, although other factors are also involved.

11. Punishment can sometimes be effective in eliminating undesirable behavior, but it has many drawbacks and may have unintended consequences. It is often administered inappropriately, when a person is angry; it may produce rage and fear; its effects are often temporary; it is hard to administer immediately; it conveys little information about what kind of behavior is desired; and an action intended to punish may instead be reinforcing because it brings attention. Extinction of undesirable behavior, combined with reinforcement of desired behavior, is generally preferable to the use of punishment. It is also important to understand the reasons for a person's misbehavior instead of simply trying to get rid of it.

12. *Behavior modification,* the application of conditioning principles, has been used successfully in many settings, often by applying a *token economy.* However, problems in behavior modification also occur. For example, dependence on *extrinsic reinforcers* may undermine *intrinsic* motivation. But money and praise do not usually interfere with intrinsic pleasure when a person is rewarded for succeeding or making progress rather than for merely participating in an activity, or when a person is already extremely interested in the activity.

13. In the 1960s and 1970s, expectancy theory and new theories of classical conditioning opened the door to more cognitive interpretations of learning. One result was the rise of *social-learning theories,* whose proponents study not only environmental influences but also higher-level cognitive processes and the interaction between individuals and their environments (*reciprocal determinism*). Social-learning theorists emphasize *observational learning,* in which the learner imitates the behavior of a model; performance may be either immediate or delayed (*latent learning*). They also emphasize the role of people's perceptions and motivating beliefs in explaining behavior.

14. The tension between behaviorism and cognitive approaches to psychology can be seen in how the two approaches treat *insight,* learning that seems to occur suddenly and that involves the solving of a problem. Behaviorists believe insight can be understood in terms of the conditioning history of the organism. Cognitive psychologists believe that what is learned is knowledge rather than behavior. The behavioral and cognitive approaches are quite different, but many psychologists treat them as different levels of analysis and use concepts and techniques from both.

Key Terms

learning *245*

behaviorism *245*

unconditioned stimulus (US) *247*

unconditioned response (UR) *247*

conditioned stimulus (CS) *247*

conditioned response (CR) *247*

classical conditioning *248*

extinction (in classical conditioning) *249*

spontaneous recovery *250*

higher-order conditioning *250*

stimulus generalization (in classical conditioning) *250*

stimulus discrimination (in classical conditioning) *250*

phobia *252*

counterconditioning *252*

operant conditioning *255*

law of effect *255*

8

Thinking and Intelligence

Think About It
    Has Television Killed Off
    Reading—and If So, So What?

Taking Psychology with You
    Becoming More Creative

*Here's a mental challenge: Each room has two sides that are mirrors and two open sides.
Find the mirrored walls. Then place a clear sheet over the puzzle and starting in the middle draw a
line through all eight rooms consecutively without going through a room twice.
(The solution is on page 325.)*

What a piece of work is man! How noble in reason! How infinite in faculties! . . . in apprehension how like a god!

■ WILLIAM SHAKESPEARE ■

A great many people think they are thinking when they are merely rearranging their prejudices.

■ WILLIAM JAMES ■

Every day, in the course of ordinary living, we make plans, draw inferences, concoct explanations, analyze relationships, and organize and reorganize the flotsam and jetsam of our mental world. Descartes' famous declaration, "I think, therefore I am," could just as well have been reversed: "I am, therefore I think." Our powers of thought and intelligence inspired our forebears to give our species the immodest name *Homo sapiens,* Latin for "wise or rational man." But just how "sapiens" are we, really? Consider:

- As children, we all learn how clocks arbitrarily divide time into hours, minutes, and seconds. Yet every spring, when daylight savings time begins, there are people who fret about tampering with "God's time." One letter writer in Colorado even complained to a local newspaper that the "extra hour" of sunlight was burning up her front lawn!

- A national survey of ethnic attitudes (T. Smith, 1991) asked people to rank the social standing of 58 groups, including one called the Wisians. Although three-fifths of the respondents said they knew too little about the Wisians to rank them, the others had no such reservations, assigning the group a relatively low average score of 4.12 on a 9-point scale. In reality, there were no "Wisians"; they had been made up by the researchers.

- A few years ago, the pilots of an Air Florida flight were going over a pre-takeoff checklist. When the de-icer was mentioned, a crew member automatically responded "off," without giving it much thought. After all, it's always warm in Florida, isn't it? Unfortunately, on this occasion the weather was icy, and the plane crashed, killing 74 people.

He's thinking—but how well is he thinking?

The human mind, which has managed to come up with poetry, penicillin, and pantyhose, is a miraculous thing. But the human mind has also managed to come up with traffic jams, junk mail, and war. To better understand why the same species that figured out how to get to the moon is also capable of breathtaking bumbling here on earth, in this chapter we will examine how we reason, solve problems, and grow in intelligence, as well as some sources of our mental shortcomings.

■ THOUGHT: USING WHAT WE KNOW

Many cognitive psychologists who study thinking and other mental processes liken the human mind to an information processor, analogous to a computer but far more complex. Though the "mind" of a machine differs in many ways from the mind of a human being, information-processing approaches have proven useful because they capture the fact that the brain does not passively record information but actively alters and organizes it. (We will look at some departures from the information-processing approach in the next chapter.)

In information-processing models, **thinking** is defined as the mental manipulation of information. The ability to think frees us from the confines of the immediate present: We can think about a trip taken three years ago, a party planned for next Saturday, the War of 1812. It carries us beyond the boundaries of physical reality: We can imagine unicorns and utopias, Martians and magic. Because we think, we do not need to grope our way blindly through our problems but, with some effort and knowledge, can solve them intelligently and creatively.

The Elements of Cognition

When we take action, we physically manipulate the environment. When we think, we *mentally* manipulate internal representations of objects, activities, and situations. However, we do not manipulate all the information potentially available to us; if we did, making the simplest decision or solving the most trivial problem would be a time-consuming, and perhaps impossible, task. Imagine trying to decide whether to go out for a hamburger if that meant thinking about every hamburger you ever ate, saw a commercial for, or watched someone consume. Thinking is possible because our internal representations simplify and summarize information that reaches us from the environment.

Concepts. One type of representation, or unit of thought, is the **concept.** Essentially, a concept is a mental category that groups objects, relations, activities, abstractions, or qualities having common properties. The instances of a concept are seen as roughly similar. For example, *golden retriever, cocker spaniel,* and *Weimaraner* are instances of the concept *dog,* and *anger, joy,* and *sadness* are instances of the concept *emotion.* Because concepts simplify the world, we do not have to learn a new name for each thing, relation, activity, abstract state, or quality we encounter, nor do we need to treat each instance as though it were unique. You may never have seen a *Basenji* or eaten *escargots,* but if you know that the first is an instance of *dog* and the second an instance of *food,* you will know, roughly, how to respond.

We form concepts not only through direct contact with objects and situations, but also by contact with *symbols,* things that represent or stand for something else. Symbolic representations include words, mathematical formulas, maps, graphs, pictures, and even gestures. Symbols stand not only for objects but also for operations (for example, the symbols + and −), relationships (for example, = and <), and qualities (for example, the dot in musical notation that symbolizes an abrupt or staccato quality).

Certain concepts, called **basic concepts,** have a moderate number of instances and are easier to acquire than those that have either few or many instances (Rosch, 1973). What is the object pictured in the margin? You will probably call it an apple. The concept *apple* is more basic than *fruit,* which includes many more instances and is more abstract. It is also more basic than *McIntosh apple,* which is quite specific. Similarly, *book* is more basic than either *printed matter* or *novel.* Children seem to learn basic-level concepts earlier than others, and adults use them more often than others, because basic concepts convey an optimal amount of information in most situations.

All the qualities associated with a concept do not necessarily apply to every instance: Some apples are not red; some dogs do not bark; some birds do not fly or perch on trees. But all the instances of a concept do share a "family resemblance." Moreover, everyone within a culture can easily tell you which instances are most representative, or *prototypical,* of the concept (Rosch, 1973).

■ **thinking**
The mental manipulation of information stored in the form of concepts, images, or propositions.

■ **concept**
A mental category that groups objects, relations, activities, abstractions, or qualities having common properties.

■ **basic concepts**
Concepts that have a moderate number of instances and that are easier to acquire than those having few or many instances.

*According to the dictionary, a bachelor is an unmarried man—period. In real life, how-
ever, some instances of a concept are more representative, or prototypical, than others. For
example, consumer advocate Ralph Nader and politician Jerry Brown both clearly qualify as bachelors. But is the pope a bachelor? What about Robert Redford, who is divorced,
or Clint Eastwood, who is unmarried but has had the same "significant other" for several years and has a child with her? And what about a gay man in a committed relationship: Is he a bachelor?*

Which dog is doggier, a golden retriever or a chihuahua? Which fruit is more
fruitlike, an apple or a pineapple? Which activity is more representative of
sports, football or weight lifting? When we need to decide whether something
belongs to a concept, we are likely to compare it to a prototype.

Propositions, Schemas, and Images.   Concepts are the building blocks of
thought, but they would be of limited use if we simply stacked them up mentally. We must also represent their relationships to one another. One way we
accomplish this may be by storing and using **propositions,** units of meaning
that are made up of concepts and that express a unitary idea. A proposition can
express nearly any sort of knowledge (*Hortense raises Basenjis*) or belief (*Basenjis
are beautiful*). Propositions, in turn, are linked together in complicated networks of knowledge, associations, beliefs, and expectations. These networks,
which psychologists call **cognitive schemas,** serve as mental models of aspects of
the world. For example, gender schemas represent a person's beliefs and
expectations about what it means to be male or female. People also have
schemas about cultures, occupations, animals, geographical locations, and
many other features of the social and natural environment.

Most cognitive psychologists believe that **mental images** are also important in
thinking (Kosslyn, 1983; Paivio, 1983). Most people report experiencing visual
images, pictures in the mind's eye. Although no one can directly "see" another
person's visual images, psychologists are able to study them indirectly. One
method is to measure how long it takes people to rotate an image, scan from
one point to another, or "read off" some detail from the image. The results suggest that visual images are like images on a television screen: We can manipulate them, they occur in a mental "space" of a fixed size, and small ones contain
less detail than larger ones (Kosslyn, 1980; Shepard & Metzler, 1971).

Most people also report auditory images (for instance, when thinking about
a song or a conversation), and many report images in other sensory modalities—touch, taste, smell, or pain. Some even report kinesthetic images, feelings
in the muscles and joints. Although mental images often have no obvious purpose, people do sometimes use them to visualize the possible outcomes of a
decision, understand or formulate verbal descriptions, boost motivation, or
improve mood (Kosslyn et al., 1990). Imagining yourself performing an athletic skill, such as diving or sprinting, may even improve your actual perfor-

■ **proposition**
*A unit of meaning that is made up
of concepts and expresses a unitary
idea.*

■ **cognitive schema**
*An integrated mental network of
knowledge, beliefs, and expectations
concerning a particular topic or
aspect of the world.*

■ **mental image**
*A mental representation that mirrors
or resembles the thing it represents.
Mental images can occur in many
and perhaps all sensory modalities.*

mance (Druckman & Swets, 1988). A recent brain-scan study suggests that this mental practice activates most of the brain circuits involved in the activity itself (Stephan et al., 1995). (Of course, you have to know how to *do* the activity first!) Albert Einstein relied heavily on visual and kinesthetic imagery for formulating ideas. The happiest thought of his life, he once recalled, occurred in 1907, when he suddenly imagined a man falling freely from the roof of a house and realized that the man would not experience a gravitational field in his immediate vicinity. This insight led eventually to Einstein's formulation of the principle of general relativity, and physics was never again the same.

Quick QUIZ

1. Stuffing your mouth with cotton candy, licking a lollipop, and chewing on a piece of beef jerky are all instances of the _____ *eating.*
2. Which concept is most basic: *furniture, chair,* or *high chair?*
3. In addition to concepts and images, _____ have been proposed as a basic form of mental representation.

Answers:

1. concept 2. chair 3. propositions

Fortunately for this father, some well-learned tasks, such as typing, do not require much conscious thought, so we can do other things at the same time.

▪ **subconscious processes**
Mental processes occurring outside of conscious awareness but accessible to consciousness when necessary.

▪ **nonconscious processes**
Mental processes occurring outside of and not available to conscious awareness.

How Conscious Is Thought?

When we think about thinking, most of us have in mind those mental activities, such as solving problems or making decisions, that are carried out in a deliberate way with a conscious goal in mind. However, not all mental processing is conscious.

Subconscious processes lie outside of awareness but can be brought into consciousness when necessary. These processes allow us to handle more information and to perform more complex tasks than if we depended entirely on conscious thought, and they also enable us to perform more than one task simultaneously (Kahneman & Treisman, 1984). Consider all the automatic routines performed "without thinking," though they might once have required careful, conscious attention: knitting, typing, driving a car, decoding the letters in a word in order to read it. Because of the capacity for automatic processing, with proper training, people can even learn to perform simultaneously such complex tasks as reading and taking dictation (Hirst, Neisser, & Spelke, 1978).

Nonconscious processes remain outside of awareness but nonetheless affect behavior. For example, most of us have had the odd experience of having a solution to a problem "pop into mind" after we have given up trying to find one. Similarly, people will often say they rely on intuition rather than conscious reasoning to solve a problem. Research suggests that intuition is actually an orderly process that seems to involve two stages (Bowers et al., 1990). In the first stage, clues in the problem automatically activate memories or knowledge, and you begin to see a pattern or structure in the problem, although you can't yet say what it is. This nonconscious process guides you toward a hunch or a hypothesis. Then, in the second stage, your thinking becomes conscious, and you become aware of a possible solution. This stage may feel like a sudden revelation ("Aha, I've got it!"), but considerable mental work has already occurred, even though you are not aware of it.

Some decisions to act also seem to be made without awareness. In a fascinating study, physiologist Benjamin Libet (1985) told volunteers to flex a wrist or a finger whenever they felt like it. As soon as the urge to flex occurred, the person noted the position of a dot revolving on a clocklike screen. Electrodes monitored changes in brain activity occurring immediately before the volunteers' muscular movements, changes known as "readiness potentials." Libet found that readiness potentials occurred about half a second before muscle movement, but conscious awareness of an intention to move the muscle (as inferred from reports of dot position) occurred about three-tenths of a second *after* that. In other words, one part of the brain seemed to be initiating action before another part—the aware part—knew it.

Libet drew an analogy between these results and what happens when a sprinter hears a starter's pistol go off. The sprinter will take off in less than a tenth of a second after the gun fires, yet that is too short a time to perceive the sound consciously. According to Libet, the runner must be responding unconsciously. Then, after the sound enters awareness, the mind "corrects" the sequence, so the person thinks he or she heard the sound before actually moving.

Usually, of course, much of our thinking is conscious—but we may not be thinking very *hard*. Like the pilots who left the de-icer off, we may act, speak, and make decisions out of habit, without stopping to analyze what we are doing or why we are doing it. Ellen Langer (1989) has called this mental inertia *mindlessness*. She notes that mindless processing keeps people from recognizing when a change in context requires a change in behavior. In one study by Langer and her associates, a researcher approached people as they were about to use a photocopier and made one of three requests: "Excuse me, may I use the Xerox machine?" "Excuse me, may I use the Xerox machine, because I have to make copies," or "Excuse me, may I use the Xerox machine, because I'm in a rush." Normally, people will let someone go before them only if the person has a legitimate reason, as in the third request. In this study, however, people also complied when the reason sounded like an authentic explanation but was actually meaningless ("because I have to make copies"). They heard the form of the request, but not its content, and mindlessly stepped aside (Langer, Blank, & Chanowitz, 1978).

The mindless processing of information has benefits: If we stopped to think twice about everything we did, we would get nothing done ("Okay, now I'm reaching for my toothbrush; now I'm putting a quarter inch of toothpaste on it; now I'm brushing my upper right molars"). But it can also lead to errors and

Drawing by Weber; ©1989 The New Yorker Magazine, Inc.

"This CD player costs less than players selling for twice as much."

Mindlessness is a common source of irrationality.

Which cereal to buy? Without a certain degree of mindlessness, the decisions of everyday life would be overwhelming. But mindlessness also leads to miscalculations and poor choices. This consumer could be blindly loyal to the brand he has bought for years, or he could devote time and effort to making a thoughtful decision.

mishaps, ranging from the trivial (putting the butter in the dishwasher or locking yourself out of the car) to the serious (driving carelessly while on "automatic pilot").

Jerome Kagan (1989) argues that fully conscious awareness is needed only when we must make a deliberate choice, when events happen that can't be handled automatically, and when unexpected moods and feelings arise. "Consciousness," he says, "can be likened to the staff of a fire department. Most of the time, it is quietly playing pinochle in the back room; it performs [only] when the alarm sounds." That may be so, but most of us would probably benefit if our mental firefighters paid a little more attention to their jobs. Cognitive psychologists have, therefore, devoted a great deal of study to mindful, conscious, intentional thought and the capacity to reason.

▪ REASONING RATIONALLY

Reasoning is purposeful mental activity that involves operating on information to reach conclusions. Unlike impulsive or "intuitive" responding, reasoning requires us to draw inferences from observations, facts, or assumptions.

Deductive and Inductive Reasoning

Two of the most basic types of reasoning are deductive reasoning and inductive reasoning, both of which involve drawing conclusions from a series of observations or propositions (*premises*).

In **deductive reasoning,** if the premises are true, then the conclusion *must* be true. Often, deductive reasoning takes the form of a *syllogism,* a simple argument consisting of two premises and a conclusion:

premise	All human beings are mortal.
premise	I am a human being.
conclusion	Therefore I am mortal.

We all think in syllogisms, although many of our premises are implicit rather than explicitly spelled out: "I never have to work on Saturday. Today is Saturday. Therefore, I don't have to work today." However, applying deductive reasoning to abstract problems that are divorced from everyday life does not seem to come so naturally; it depends on experience and schooling. Years ago, in a study of the Kpelle tribe in Africa (Scribner, 1977), researchers gave an unschooled farmer this problem, a standard example of a Western syllogism: "All Kpelle men are rice farmers. Mr. Smith is not a rice farmer. Is he a Kpelle man?" The farmer insisted that the information did not allow a conclusion:

Kpelle man: I don't know the man in person. I have not laid eyes on the man himself.
Researcher: Just think about the statement.
Kpelle man: If I know him in person, I can answer that question, but since I do not know him in person, I cannot answer that question.

The interviewer concluded that because the Kpelle farmer was accustomed to drawing on personal knowledge alone to reach conclusions, he could not approach the task analytically. Yet in the exchange with the researcher, the man showed that he *could* reason deductively:

premise	If I do not know a person, I cannot draw any conclusions about that person.
premise	I do not know Mr. Smith.
conclusion	Therefore I cannot draw any conclusions about Mr. Smith.

▪ **reasoning**
The drawing of conclusions or inferences from observations, facts, or assumptions.

▪ **deductive reasoning**
A form of reasoning in which a conclusion follows necessarily from certain premises; if the premises are true, the conclusion must be true.

The answer that the Kpelle farmer gave was perfectly smart in *his* culture's terms; it just was not what his interviewer expected. Cross-cultural research has found that most people everywhere are able to learn to reason deductively, but the areas in which they apply deductive reasoning will depend on their experiences and needs (Serpell, 1994).

In **inductive reasoning,** the premises provide support for the conclusion, but the conclusion *could* still be false. The conclusion does not follow necessarily from the premises, as it does in deductive reasoning. Often, people think of inductive reasoning as the drawing of general conclusions from specific observations, as when you generalize from past experience: "I had three good meals at that restaurant; they sure have great food." But an inductive argument can also have general premises. Two logicians (Copi & Burgess-Jackson, 1992) give this example:

> All cows are mammals and have lungs.
>
> All whales are mammals and have lungs.
>
> All humans are mammals and have lungs.
>
> Therefore probably all mammals have lungs.

Conversely, inductive arguments can have specific conclusions:

> Most people with season tickets to the concert love music.
>
> Jeannine has season tickets to the concert.
>
> Therefore Jeannine probably loves music.

Science depends heavily on inductive reasoning. In their studies, researchers make many careful observations, then draw some conclusions that they think are probably true. But in inductive reasoning, no matter how much supporting evidence you gather, it is always possible that new information will turn up to show you are wrong. For example, you might discover that the three good meals you ate at that restaurant were not at all typical—that, in fact, all the other dishes on the menu are awful. Or you might learn that Jeannine bought season tickets to the concert only to impress a friend. Similarly, new scientific information may show that previous conclusions were faulty and must therefore be revised.

Almost everyone has trouble thinking logically in some situations. For example, they may say that the following syllogism is valid, when in fact it is not:

> All rich people live in big fancy houses.
>
> That person lives in a big fancy house.
>
> Therefore that person is rich.

"That person" may well be rich, but the conclusion does not follow from the premises, because some people may live in big fancy houses for other reasons—perhaps they inherited one or bought it when it was inexpensive. Errors of this type occur because people reverse a premise. In this case, they convert "All rich people live in big fancy houses" to "All people who live in big fancy houses are rich." The reversed premise is plausible, but it is not the one that was given.

Dialectical Reasoning and Reflective Judgment

Logic is a crucial weapon to have in your cognitive arsenal, but logic alone, whether inductive or deductive, is often inadequate for solving psychological difficulties and social problems. One reason is that people may reach different conclusions even when their logic is impeccable, if they start out with different premises. Logic only tells us that *if* the premises are true, a certain conclusion

▪ **inductive reasoning**
A form of reasoning in which the premises provide support for a certain conclusion, but it is still possible for the conclusion to be false.

"If people would only be logical, they could get along." But logic is not enough when people start with different assumptions and values. How can people who are operating from different premises reach agreement?

must follow (in deductive reasoning) or is probably true (in inductive reasoning). Logic does not tell us whether the premises *are,* in fact, true. Controversial issues tend to be those in which premises cannot be proven true or false to everyone's satisfaction. For example, your position on abortion rights will depend on your premises about when meaningful human life begins, what rights an embryo has, and what rights a woman has. People on opposing sides even disagree on how the premises should be phrased, because they have different emotional reactions to terms such as "rights," "meaningful life," and "control over one's body."

Even when we feel fairly confident about our premises, there may be no clearly correct solution to a problem (Galotti, 1989). In formal reasoning problems—the kind you might find, say, on an intelligence test or a college entrance exam—the information you need for drawing a conclusion is specified clearly, and there is a single right answer. Deductive and inductive reasoning are useful for these kinds of problems. But in *informal* reasoning problems, information may be incomplete; many approaches and viewpoints may compete, and you have to decide which one is most reasonable, based on what you know, even though there is no clear-cut solution (see Table 8.1). Philosophers call such problems "ill-structured." For example, should the government raise taxes or lower them? What is the best way to improve public education? Is this a good time to buy a car?

To think rationally about such issues, you need more than inductive and deductive logic. You also need to think *dialectically.* **Dialectical reasoning** is the ability to evaluate opposing points of view. Philosopher Richard Paul (1984) describes it as a process of moving "up and back between contradictory lines of reasoning, using each to critically cross-examine the other." This is what juries are supposed to do to arrive at a verdict. A jury decision is not reached by applying some formula or set of procedures but (ideally) by open-minded consideration of arguments for and against, point and counterpoint.

Many people have trouble with dialectical reasoning because their self-esteem depends on being right and having their beliefs accepted by others. We

▪ **dialectical reasoning**
A process in which opposing facts or ideas are weighed and compared, with a view to determining the best solution or to resolving differences.

Table 8.1   Two Kinds of Reasoning

In formal reasoning, we apply rules of logic to solve well-specified problems. In informal, everyday reasoning, we must solve problems that are less clearly defined. Below are some differences between the two modes of thought.

Formal	Informal
All premises are supplied.	Some premises are implicit and some are not supplied at all.
There is typically one correct answer.	There are typically several possible answers that vary in quality.
There are often established methods of inference that apply to the problem.	There are rarely established procedures for solving the problem.
You usually know when the problem is solved.	It is often unclear whether the current "best" solution is good enough.
The problem is often of limited real-world interest.	The problem typically has personal relevance.
Problems are solved for their own sake.	Problems are often solved as a means of achieving other goals.

Source: Adapted from Galotti, 1989.

Deductive and inductive reasoning alone will not enable the members of this jury to reach a conclusion. They will also need to reason dialectically, weighing the evidence for and against guilt or innocence and the reasonableness of the arguments made by the attorneys.

all have our convictions, of course, but the inability to listen with an open mind to competing views is a major obstacle to critical thinking. Some social commentators believe that the replacement of reading by television watching is partly to blame for the growing inability of young people to think dialectically. Television news often gives us "sound bites" instead of fully developed arguments, encouraging us to form quick, impulsive opinions instead of carefully considered ones (see Figure 8.1). The medium through which we get our information may affect our ability to evaluate the message, as we discuss further in "Think About It."

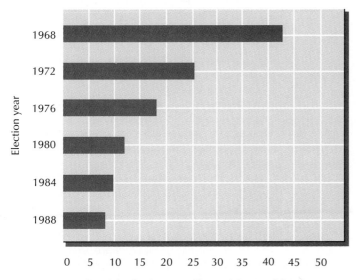

■ Figure 8.1 The Shrinking Sound Bite

Since 1968, the average number of seconds of uninterrupted speech by political figures during network news coverage of U.S. presidential campaigns has declined steadily (Hallin, 1991). At this rate, candidates will soon have barely enough time to say, "Vote for me." Length is no guarantee of substance, of course; and brevity, as Shakespeare said, is the soul of wit. But critics worry that chopping political discourse into fleeting "sound bites" discourages people from critically analyzing the issues.

In any case, it is clear that many adults have trouble thinking dialectically. Evidence comes from the research of Karen Kitchener and Patricia King, who for many years have been asking adolescents and adults of all ages and occupations where they stand on such issues as nuclear power, the safety of food additives, and the objectivity of the news media. Kitchener and King are not interested in how much people know about these issues, or even how they feel about them, but rather in how they think, and how their thinking changes over time. More specifically, these researchers want to know whether people use *reflective judgment* in thinking about everyday problems (King & Kitchener, 1994; Kitchener & King, 1981, 1990). Reflective judgment is basically what we have called "critical thinking": the ability to evaluate and integrate evidence, relate that evidence to a theory or opinion, and reach a conclusion that can be defended as reasonable or plausible. To think reflectively, you must question assumptions, consider alternative interpretations, and stand ready to reassess your conclusions in the face of new information.

To date, King and Kitchener and their colleagues have interviewed more than 1,700 adolescents and adults, ranging in age from 14 to 65. (Some of this research has followed the same individuals for up to a decade.) First, the researchers provide the interviewee with statements that describe opposing viewpoints on topics such as those we mentioned. Then the interviewer asks some questions: What do you think about these statements? On what do you base your point of view? Can you ever know for sure that your position is correct? Why do you suppose disagreement exists about this issue?

Think About It

Has Television Killed Off Reading—and If So, So What?

TELEVISION IS VERY USEFUL IN OCCUPYING TIME THAT MIGHT OTHERWISE BE USED FOR THINKING!

■ You find yourself with a free evening, and you decide to spend a quiet, cozy evening at home. A novel beckons from the bookshelf. The TV listings tempt you with a new sitcom. Which do you pick, the book or the tube?

A growing number of academics, writers, and social commentators think you'll make the wrong choice. We bet you can guess what it is. Reading, the critics say, appears to be going out of fashion. More books are being published than ever before, but many are sold as gifts and are not necessarily read or even skimmed. Writer Mitchell Stephens (1991) notes that more and more people are reading no books at all, and fewer and fewer people say they read a newspaper. Poet and writer Katha Pollitt (1991) notes that debates on college campuses

about which books students should be required to read miss the point that if students don't read *on their own*, they won't like reading and will forget the books on the required reading list the minute they finish them, no matter what the books are. "While we have been arguing so fiercely about which books make the best medicine," Pollitt writes, "the patient has been slipping deeper and deeper into a coma."

One reason people are reading less these days is that they are doing something else instead: watching TV, typically for 20 to 30 hours a week. The problem, say critics, is not just television's content, which is often mindless, but the medium itself, which creates mindlessness. We watch TV primarily to amuse ourselves, but in fact television has a negative impact on both mood and alertness. In a series of studies involving 1,200 subjects, Robert Kubey and Mihali Csikszentmihalyi (1990) found that although television relaxes people while they are watching, afterward viewers are likely to feel more tense, bored, irritable, and lonely than they did before, and less able to concentrate. In contrast, reading tends to leave people more relaxed, in a better mood, and with improved concentration.

A recent review of studies found that because television supplies the viewer with ready-made visual images, it may also discourage the development of imagination and novel ideas (Valkenburg & van der Voort, 1994). In one experiment, Patricia

King and Kitchener have identified seven cognitive stages on the road to reflective thought, some occurring in childhood and others unfolding throughout adolescence and adulthood. At each stage, a person makes different assumptions about how things are known and uses certain ways of justifying or defending beliefs. Each stage builds on the skills of the prior one and lays a foundation for successive ones. We will not be concerned here with the details of these stages, but only in their broad outlines.

In general, according to Kitchener and King, people in the early, *prereflective* stages assume that a correct answer always exists and that it can be obtained directly through the senses ("I know what I've seen") or from authorities ("They said so on the news"; "That's what I was brought up to believe"). If authorities don't yet have the truth, prereflective thinkers tend to reach conclusions on the basis of what "feels right" at the moment. They do not distinguish between knowledge and belief, or between belief and evidence, and they don't see any reason for justifying a belief (King & Kitchener, 1994):

> **Interviewer:** Can you ever know for sure that your position [on evolution] is correct?
> **Respondent:** Well, some people believe that we evolved from apes and that's the way they want to believe. But I would never believe that way and nobody could talk me out of the way I believe because I believe the way that it's told in the Bible.

Greenfield and Jessica Beagles-Roos (1988) found that children *remembered* more of a story when they saw it on TV than when they heard it on radio (because visual images are memorable), but their thinking became more *imaginative* when they heard the story on the radio (because they had to imagine what the characters looked like and what they were doing). The researchers fear that children who are raised on a mental diet limited to television "may have more information but be less imaginative, less verbally precise, and less mentally active" than earlier generations who grew up listening to the radio.

The replacement of reading by television watching may be contributing to a growing inability of young people to use dialectical reasoning and reflective judgment, and an unwillingness to spend time searching for answers to intellectual problems (Suedfeld et al., 1986). Because television lumps serious issues with silly ones, sells politicians the way it sells cereal, and relies on a format of quick cuts and hot music, its critics fear that it discourages sustained, serious thought (Postman, 1985). In contrast, reading requires us to sit still and follow extended arguments. It encourages us to think in terms of abstract principles and not just personal experience. It gives us the opportunity to examine connections among statements and to spot contradictions. As Mitchell Stephens (1991) notes, "All television demands is our gaze."

Defenders of television feel the criticisms are unfair. There are many possible causes of reading's decline: the pressures of modern life, the popularity of outdoor sports, the demands of juggling work and family obligations. Television not only entertains, but it also supplies information and intellectual enrichment (especially through public television programming). It gives families something to do together. It provides a diverse population with a common culture. *Mindful* television viewing, in which you analyze and discuss what you're seeing, can be mentally stimulating (Langer & Piper, 1988). And perhaps television will eventually be put to use in ways that haven't yet been thought of; after all, it took a century and a half after the printing press was invented for someone to think of producing novels and newspapers (Stephens, 1991). Interactive television and CD-Rom are already changing the way people use the tube.

What do you think of these arguments? Are there books you can't wait to read, or has reading become a chore (and if so, why)? Would you read more books if you watched less television? Do you know as much about world events after watching the nightly news as you do after reading a newspaper? Is disapproval of television just a reactionary, backward-looking response to a successful new technology? If not, what can be done to see that people control the TV knob instead of allowing it to control them? Think about it. ▪

Interviewer: In this case, then, is one view right and one point of view wrong?
Respondent: Well I think the evolved one is wrong.

During the middle, *quasi-reflective* stages, people recognize that some things cannot be known with absolute certainty, but they are not sure how to deal with these situations. They realize that judgments should be supported by reasons, but they pay attention only to evidence that fits what they already believe. They know that there are alternative viewpoints, but they seem to think that because knowledge is uncertain, any judgment about the evidence is purely subjective. Quasi-reflective thinkers will defend a position by saying that "Everyone has a right to their own opinion," as if all opinions are created equal. Here is the response of a college student who uses quasi-reflective reasoning:

Interviewer: Can you say you will ever know for sure that chemicals [in foods] are safe?
Student: No, I don't think so.
Interviewer: Can you tell me why you'll never know for sure?
Student: Because they test them in little animals, and they haven't really tested them in humans, as far as I know. And I don't think anything is for sure.
Interviewer: When people differ about matters such as this, is it the case that one opinion is right and one is wrong?
Student: No. I think it just depends on how you feel personally because people make their decisions based upon how they feel and what research they've seen. So what one person thinks is right, another person might think is wrong. . . . If I feel that chemicals cause cancer and you feel that food is unsafe without it, your opinion might be right to you and my opinion is right to me.

In the last stages, a person becomes capable of *reflective* judgment. He or she understands that knowing is an active, continual process of inquiry, and that although not everything can be known for sure, some judgments are more valid than others, depending on their coherence, their fit with the evidence, their usefulness, and so on. People at these stages are willing to consider evidence from a variety of sources and to reason dialectically. At the very highest stage, they are able to defend their conclusions as representing the most complte, plausible, or compelling understanding of an issue, based on currently available evidence. This interview with a graduate student illustrates reflective thinking:

Interviewer: Can you ever say you know for sure that your point of view on chemical additives is correct?
Student: No, I don't think so. I think . . . [that] even if the internal argument in your system is completely consistent, it might be that the assumptions are wrong. . . .
Interviewer: Is there anything else that contributes to not being able to be sure?
Student: Yes. Aside from assumptions, it might be that the research wasn't conducted rigorously enough. In other words, we might have flaws in our data or sample, things like that.
Interviewer: How then would you identify the "better" opinion?
Student: One that takes as many factors as possible into consideration. I mean one that uses the higher percentage of the data that we have, and perhaps that uses the methodology that has been most reliable.
Interviewer: And how do you come to a conclusion about what the evidence suggests?
Student: I think you have to take a look at the different opinions and studies that are offered by different groups. Maybe some studies

offered by the chemical industry, some studies by the government, some private studies. . . . You wouldn't trust, for instance, a study funded by the tobacco industry that proved that cigarette smoking is not harmful. You wouldn't base your point of view entirely upon that study. . . . you have to try to interpret people's motives and that makes it a more complex soup to try to strain out.

In King and Kitchener's studies, most people do not show evidence of reflective judgment until their middle or late twenties—if at all. That doesn't mean they're incapable of it; most studies have measured people's typical performance, not their *optimal* performance. When students get support for thinking reflectively and opportunities for practice, their thinking tends to become more complex, sophisticated, and well-grounded (Kitchener et al., 1993). This may be one reason that higher education seems to move people gradually closer to reflective judgment. Most undergraduates, whatever their age, tend to score at stage 3 during their first year of college, and at stage 4 as seniors; most graduate students score at stage 4 or 5; and many advanced doctoral students perform consistently at stage 6 (King & Kitchener, 1994). Longitudinal studies suggest that these differences do not occur only because lower-level thinkers are more likely to drop out along the way.

The gradual development of thinking skills among undergraduates, says Barry Kroll (1992), represents an abandonment of "ignorant certainty" in favor of "intelligent confusion." It may not seem so, but this is a big step forward! You can see why, in this book, we emphasize thinking about and evaluating psychological findings, and not just memorizing them.

Quick QUIZ

Put on your thinking cap to answer these questions.

1. Zelda discovers that she has dialed her boyfriend's number instead of her mother's number, as she intended. Her error can be attributed to
_____.

2. Most of the items Mervin bought as Christmas gifts this year cost more than they did last year, so he concludes that inflation is increasing. Is he using inductive, deductive, or dialectical reasoning?

3. Yvonne is arguing with Henrietta about whether real estate is a better investment than stocks. "You can't convince me," says Yvonne. "I just know I'm right." Yvonne needs training in _____ reasoning.

4. Seymour thinks the media have a liberal bias, and Sophie thinks they're too conservative. "Well," says Seymour, "I have my truth and you have yours. It's purely subjective." Which of King and Kitchener's levels of thinking is Seymour at?

5. What kind of evidence might resolve the issue that Seymour and Sophie are arguing about?

Answers:

1. mindlessness 2. inductive 3. dialectical 4. quasi-reflective 5. Researchers might have raters watch a random sample of TV news shows and measure the amount of time devoted to conservative and liberal politicians or viewpoints. Or they could have raters read a random sample of newspaper editorials from all over the country and evaluate the editorials as liberal or conservative in outlook. You can probably think of other strategies as well. However, having people judge whether *entire* TV programs or newspapers were slanted in one direction or the other, based solely on their own subjective impressions, might not be informative, because people often perceive only what they want or expect to perceive.

▪ CONFRONTING OUR COGNITIVE BIASES

In daily life, as we have seen, we must make many judgments and decisions under conditions of uncertainty. To solve a problem in long division, you need only apply an **algorithm**—a method guaranteed to produce a solution even if you don't know how it works. To make a cake, you need only apply an algorithm called a recipe. But to solve most common problems you need, in addition to a capacity for reflective judgment and dialectical reasoning, a knowledge of **heuristics**—rules of thumb that suggest a course of action without guaranteeing an optimal solution. An investor trying to predict the stock market, a renter trying to decide whether to lease an apartment, a doctor trying to determine the best treatment for a cancer patient, a marriage counselor advising a troubled couple, a factory owner trying to boost production: All are faced with incomplete information on which to base a judgment or decision and must therefore rely on heuristics.

Usually our heuristics are helpful and appropriate, but some are subject to predictable cognitive biases. Psychologists have shown that these biases frequently affect personal, economic, and political decision making (Simon, 1973; Tversky & Kahneman, 1986). There are literally dozens of such biases in the way people think and make decisions; here we report a few of them.

Exaggerating the Improbable

One bias is the inclination to exaggerate the probability of very rare events. Because of this bias, people will sometimes accept risk even though a gain is improbable and will sometimes avoid risk even though a loss is unlikely. The first tendency helps explain the popularity of lotteries. The second explains why people buy airline disaster insurance.

As we saw in Chapter 2, people are especially likely to exaggerate the likelihood of a rare event if its consequences are catastrophic. One reason is the **availability heuristic,** the tendency to judge the probability of an event by how easy it is to think of examples or instances. Catastrophes stand out in our minds and are therefore more "available" than other kinds of negative events. For example, in one study, people overestimated the frequency of deaths from tornadoes and underestimated the frequency of deaths from asthma, which occur 20 times as often but do not make headlines. And these same people estimated deaths from accidents and disease to be equally frequent, even though 16 times as many people die each year from disease as from accidents (Lichtenstein et al., 1978).

People will sometimes work themselves up into a froth about unlikely events, such as dying in an airplane crash, yet irrationally ignore real dangers to human life that are harder to visualize, such as a growth in cancer rates due to depletion of the ozone layer in the earth's atmosphere. Similarly, parents are often more frightened about real but unlikely threats to their children, such as being kidnapped by a stranger or having an adverse reaction to an immunization (both extremely unlikely), than they are about problems more common in children, such as depression, delinquency, or poor grades (Stickler et al., 1991).

Loss Aversion

In general, people making decisions try to avoid or minimize risks and losses. For example, suppose you had to choose between two health programs to combat a disease expected to kill 600 people. Which would you prefer, a program that would definitely save 200 people, or one with a one-third probability of saving all 600 people and a two-thirds probability of saving none? When subjects (including physicians) were asked this question, most said they preferred the first program. In other words, they rejected the riskier though potentially

▪ **algorithm**
A problem-solving strategy guaranteed to produce a solution even if the user does not know how it works.

▪ **heuristic**
A rule of thumb that suggests a course of action or guides problem solving but does not guarantee an optimal solution.

▪ **availability heuristic**
The tendency to judge the probability of a type of event by how easy it is to think of examples or instances.

more rewarding solution in favor of a sure gain. The same study, however, found that people *will* take a risk if they see it as a way to *avoid loss*. Subjects were asked to choose between a program in which 400 people would definitely die and a program in which there was a one-third probability of nobody dying and a two-thirds probability that all 600 would die. If you think about it for a while, you will see that the alternatives are exactly the same as in the first problem; they are merely worded differently. Yet this time, most people chose the second solution. They rejected risk when they thought of the outcome in terms of lives saved, but they accepted risk when they thought of the outcome in terms of lives lost (Tversky & Kahneman, 1981).

Few of us will have to face a decision involving hundreds of lives, but we may have to choose between different medical treatments for ourselves or a relative. Our decision may be affected by whether the doctor frames the choice in terms of mortality or survival.

The Confirmation Bias

When our primary objective is to make an accurate judgment, we will usually try to encode relevant information thoroughly and think about it carefully. But when our main motive is to reach a conclusion about ourselves, other people, or circumstances, we tend to give in to the **confirmation bias:** We pay attention to evidence that confirms what we want to believe while ignoring or finding fault with evidence that points in a different direction (Kunda, 1990). We may think we are being rational and impartial, but we are only fooling ourselves.

You can see the confirmation bias at work in yourself, friends, politicians, editorial writers—whenever people are defending their beliefs and seeking to confirm them. Politicians, for example, are likely to accept economic news that supports their philosophies and dismiss counterevidence as biased or unimportant. Police officers who are convinced of a suspect's guilt are likely to take anything the suspect says or does as evidence that confirms it. Unfortunately, the confirmation bias also affects many jury members. Deanna Kuhn and her colleagues had people listen to an audiotaped reenactment of an actual murder trial, then say how they would have voted and why. Instead of considering and weighing various possibilities against the evidence, many people quickly constructed a story about what had happened and then considered only the evidence that supported their version of events. These same people were the most confident in their decision and were most likely to vote for an extreme verdict (Kuhn, Weinstock, & Flaton, 1994).

The confirmation bias can also affect how students react to what they learn. When students read about scientific findings that dispute one of their own cherished beliefs or that challenge the wisdom of their own actions, they tend to acknowledge but minimize the strengths of the research. In contrast, when a study supports their view, they will acknowledge any flaws (such as a small sample or a reliance on self-reports) but will give these flaws less weight than they would otherwise (Sherman & Kunda, 1989). It seems that in thinking critically, people apply a double standard: They think most critically about results they don't like.

Biases Due to Expectations

In Chapter 6 we saw that expectations affect how we perceive the world. They also affect what we do with the information once we have perceived it. On July 3, 1988, a U.S. warship shot down an Iranian passenger jet taking off over the Persian Gulf, killing several hundred people aboard. The warship's computer system had at first misread the plane's altitude and identified it as an F-14 fighter jet but then corrected itself. Unfortunately, by that time, the initial information had created an expectation of an attack. The skipper thus paid

■ **confirmation bias**
The tendency to look for or pay attention only to information that confirms one's belief.

more attention to his crew's reports of an emergency than to new information being generated by the computer. The earlier information was never reevaluated, and the crew assumed that the airliner was descending rather than ascending—with tragic results (Nisbett, 1988).

One expectation that human beings cannot live without is that events will have meaning. We do not like to think that they are due to chance or to causes that are too complicated to understand. We want an *explanation*. This quest for meaning is adaptive because it helps us understand and exert some control over life's events. Sometimes, however, we see a meaningful pattern or explanation when it doesn't exist. For example, nearly every day, the news media analyze yesterday's rise or drop in stock prices. The change must have been due to international developments, or fear about rising interest rates, or what the president did or didn't do. In actual fact, however, much of the fluctuation in the stock market is completely random (Shiller, 1987).

The Hindsight Bias

Would you have been able to predict, beforehand, that in 1994 the Republicans would gain control of Congress for the first time in 40 years; that the World Series, having survived two world wars, would be cancelled; and that Michael Jackson would get married—and to Lisa Marie Presley, at that? If you think so, don't be so sure. People who are told the actual outcome of an event (or the answer to a question) tend to be overly sure that they "knew it all along." Armed with the wisdom of hindsight, they see the outcome that actually occurred as inevitable, and they overestimate the probability that they could have predicted in advance what happened. Compared to judgments made *before* an event takes place, their judgments about their own ability to predict the event are inflated (Fischhoff, 1975; Hawkins & Hastie, 1990).

This **hindsight bias** shows up in all kinds of opinions, including political judgments ("I always knew my candidate would win"), medical judgments ("I could have told you that mole was cancerous"), and evaluations of other people's job performance ("The officers in charge of Pearl Harbor in 1941 should have known it would be attacked"). In 1991, when a blinding dust storm along a stretch of highway in California caused the worst multicar crash in U.S. history, many people angrily concluded that the highway patrol should have recognized the danger and closed the road. But from the highway patrol's standpoint, the situation was ambiguous: There were plenty of dust storms that people had gotten through perfectly well by slowing down or pulling off the road. Hindsight no doubt made the situation seem more straightforward in retrospect than it was at the time.

Hindsight biases may be a side effect of adaptive learning. When we try to predict the future, we consider many possible scenarios. But when we try to make sense of the past, we focus on explaining just one outcome—the one that actually occurred. This is efficient: Explaining outcomes that didn't occur can be a waste of time. "In a sense," write Scott Hawkins and Reid Hastie (1990), "hindsight biases represent the dark side of successful learning and judgment." They are the dark side because when we are sure we knew something all along, we are less willing to find out what we need to know to make accurate predictions in the future. In medical conferences, for example, when doctors are told what the postmortem findings were for a patient who died, they tend to think the case was "easier" than it actually was ("I would have known it was a brain tumor"), so they learn less from the case than they should (Dawson et al., 1988).

Cognitive Dissonance

In 1994, Americans were stunned when football legend O. J. Simpson was charged with murdering his former wife and her friend. Glued to their televi-

■ **hindsight bias**

The tendency to overestimate one's ability to have predicted an event once the outcome is known; the "I knew it all along" phenomenon.

sion sets, viewers watched in shock as Simpson, who had always seemed the quintessential nice guy, was pursued by a caravan of police on a Los Angeles freeway, then arrested at his home and led away in handcuffs. Some reacted by quickly revising their opinion of their fallen hero. Others, however, groped to make sense of the unimaginable. Perhaps Simpson had run from the police not because he was guilty but because he was suicidal with grief over his ex-wife's death. Perhaps one of the police investigators had planted incriminating evidence. Perhaps the media were exploiting the case by exaggerating the evidence against him. Perhaps Simpson did kill his ex-wife, but only after she provoked the attack by taunting him and trying to extort money from him.

To psychologists, such strategies for coming to terms with information that conflicts with one's existing ideas are predictable. They can be explained, said Leon Festinger (1957), by the theory of **cognitive dissonance.** "Dissonance," the opposite of consistency ("consonance"), is a state of tension that occurs when a person simultaneously holds two cognitions (beliefs, thoughts, attitudes) that are psychologically inconsistent, or holds a belief that is incongruent with the person's behavior. This tension is uncomfortable, and someone in a state of dissonance will therefore be motivated to reduce it—by rejecting or changing a belief, by changing a behavior, by adding new beliefs, or by rationalizing.

For example, cigarette smoking is dissonant with the awareness that smoking causes illness. The smoker might change the behavior and try to quit; reject the cognition "smoking is bad"; persuade herself that she will quit later on ("after these exams"); emphasize the benefits of smoking ("A cigarette helps me relax"); or decide she doesn't want a long life, anyhow ("It will be shorter, but sweeter"). In an actual study of people who went to a clinic to quit smoking, those who later relapsed had to reduce the dissonance between "I tried to quit smoking because it's bad for me" and "I couldn't do it." Can you predict what they did? In contrast to the successful quitters, most of them lowered their perceptions of the health risks of smoking ("It's not really so dangerous") (Gibbons, McGovern, & Lando, 1991).

You can see cognitive-dissonance reduction at work among the growing number of true believers who are predicting that doomsday is at hand. Such predictions are especially popular at the end of every century, so we predict that you will be hearing some lulus as the year 2000 dawns. Do you ever wonder what happens to true believers when a doomsday prophecy fails? Do they ever say, "Boy, what a jerk I was"? What would dissonance theory predict?

Many years ago, Festinger and two associates were able to explore people's reactions to failed prophecies by taking advantage of an opportunity to observe a group of people who thought the world would end on December 21 (Festinger, Riecken, & Schachter, 1956). The group's leader, whom the researchers called Marian Keech, promised that the faithful would be picked up by a flying saucer and whisked to safety at midnight on December 20. Many of her followers quit their jobs and spent all their savings, waiting for the end. What would they do or say, Festinger and his colleagues wondered, to reduce the dissonance between "The world is still muddling along on the 21st" and "I predicted the end of the world and sold all my worldly possessions"? The researchers predicted that believers who had made no public commitment to the prophecy, who awaited the end of the world by themselves at home, would lose their faith. But those who acted on their conviction, waiting with Keech for the spaceship, would be in a state of dissonance. They would, said the researchers, have to *increase* their religious belief to avoid the intolerable realization that they had behaved foolishly. That is just what happened. At 4:45 A.M., long past the appointed hour of the saucer's arrival, the leader had a new vision. The world had been spared, she said, because of the impressive faith of her little band.

What were your feelings when you saw O. J. Simpson's face in this police photo? Did you feel shocked, angry, or upset? Did you tell yourself, "My hero could not possibly have committed murder" or "It's a tragedy, but even highly admired people sometimes commit awful crimes"?

✷ *Time and again, doomsday predictions fail. Have you ever wondered why people who wrongly predict a devastating earthquake or the end of the world don't feel embarrassed when their forecasts flop?*

■ **cognitive dissonance**
A state of tension that occurs when a person simultaneously holds two cognitions that are psychologically inconsistent, or when a person's belief is incongruent with his or her behavior.

Subsequent research has specified the conditions under which people are particularly likely to be motivated to reduce dissonance (Taylor, Peplau, & Sears, 1994):

1. *When people feel that they have freely made a decision.* If you do not think you freely chose to join a group, sell your possessions, or smoke a cigarette, you will not feel dissonance if these actions prove to be seriously misguided. There is no dissonance between "The Army drafted me; I had no choice about being here" and "I hate basic training."

2. *When people feel that the decision is important and irrevocable.* If you know that you can always change your mind about a decision, or if you aren't strongly committed to it, you will not feel dissonance if the decision proves foolhardy. There is no dissonance between "I just spent a fortune on ski equipment" and "I hate skiing" if you know you can return or sell your ski gear and get your money back.

3. *When people feel personally responsible for the negative consequences of their decisions.* If you choose a course of action that leads to disastrous but unforeseen results, you will not feel dissonance unless you feel responsible for the consequences. There is no dissonance between "I took my vacation in Hawaii" and "It rained the whole week I was there" if you don't feel personally responsible for causing the rain.

4. *When people have put a lot of effort into a decision, only to find the results are less than they hoped for.* The harder you work to achieve a goal, the more you will value the goal, even if the goal itself isn't so great after all (Aronson & Mills, 1959). This explains why hazing, whether in social clubs or the military, turns new recruits into loyal members. The cognition "I went through a lot of awful stuff to join this group" is dissonant with the cognition ". . . only to find I hate the group." Therefore, people must decide either that the hazing wasn't so bad or that they really like the group. This mental reevaluation is called the *justification of effort,* and it is one of the most popular methods of reducing dissonance.

There are limitations to dissonance theory. It can be hard to know when two cognitions are inconsistent: What is dissonant to you may be neutral or pleasingly paradoxical to another. Moreover, some people reduce dissonance by admitting their mistakes instead of rationalizing them. Still, there is vast evidence of a motive for cognitive consistency under certain conditions, and this motive can lead to irrational decisions as well as rational ones.

As you can see, the decisions people make are not always logical. This fact has enormous implications for decision makers in business, medicine, government, the marketplace—in fact, in all areas of life. But before you despair

Cognitive dissonance theory predicts the "justification of effort": The harder you work for a goal, the more you will like or value it. These men in basic training should become extremely devoted soldiers!

about the human ability to think clearly and rationally, we should tell you that the situation is not hopeless. People are not equally irrational in all situations. When they are doing things they have some expertise in, or making decisions that have real-life consequences, cognitive biases often diminish. Accountants who audit companies' books, for example, are less subject to the confirmation bias than are undergraduate students in psychology experiments, perhaps because auditors can be sued if they overestimate a firm's profitability or economic health (Smith & Kida, 1991).

Further, once we understand a bias, we may be able to reduce or eliminate it. For example, we saw that doctors are vulnerable to the hindsight bias if they already know what caused a patient's death. But Hal Arkes and his colleagues (1988) were able to reduce a similar bias in neuropsychologists. The psychologists were given a case study and asked to state one reason why each of three possible diagnoses—alcohol withdrawal, Alzheimer's disease, and brain damage—might have been applicable. This procedure forced the psychologists to consider all the evidence, not just evidence that supported the "correct" diagnosis. The hindsight bias evaporated, presumably because the psychologists realized that the correct diagnosis had not been so obvious at the time the patient was being treated.

Some people, of course, seem to think more clearly than others habitually; we call them "intelligent." But just what is intelligence, and how can we measure and refine it? We take up that question next.

Quick QUIZ

Think rationally about irrationality to answer these questions:

1. Stu takes a break from studying to grab a bite at the student cafeteria, where he meets a young woman. They hit it off, start to see each other regularly, and eventually get married. Says Stu, "I knew that day, when I headed for the cafeteria, that something special was about to happen. It was fate." What cognitive bias is affecting Stu's thinking?

2. In a classic study of cognitive dissonance (Festinger & Carlsmith, 1959), students did some boring, repetitive tasks and then had to tell another student, who was waiting to participate in the study, that the work was interesting and fun. Half the students were offered $20 for telling this lie and the others only $1. Which students decided that the tasks were fun after all?

3. We are all vulnerable to the confirmation bias. Which findings in previous chapters are you likely to think most or least critically about, because of your own pet opinions? Which facts or theories did you resist, and which did you accept readily? Be honest!

Answers:

1. The hindsight bias 2. The students who got only $1. They were in a state of dissonance, because "the task was as dull as dishwater" is dissonant with "I said I enjoyed it—and for a mere dollar, at that." Those who got $20 could rationalize that the large sum (which was *really* large in 1956) justified the lie. 3. We can't answer this one for you, but people often have biases about the strength and importance of gender differences, the psychological consequences of drug use, the use of animals in psychological research, and many other topics we haven't gotten into yet, such as drug abuse, child-rearing strategies, the accuracy of memory, recovering from trauma, and prejudice.

A school psychologist gives an elementary school student an intelligence test.

▪ INTELLIGENCE

The educator and writer Sylvia Ashton-Warner once called intelligence "the tool to find the truth"—a tool that must be kept sharpened. Yet much as we all desire this trait, it is hard to agree on what it is. Some psychologists equate it with the ability to reason abstractly, others with the ability to learn and profit from experience in daily life. Some emphasize the ability to think rationally, others the ability to act purposefully. These qualities are all probably part of what most people mean by **intelligence,** but theorists weigh them differently.

One of the longest-running debates in psychology is whether a global quality called "intelligence" even exists. A typical intelligence test asks you to do several things: provide a specific bit of information, notice similarities between objects, solve arithmetic problems, define words, fill in the missing parts of incomplete pictures, arrange pictures in a logical order, arrange blocks to resemble a design, assemble puzzles, use a coding scheme, or judge what behavior would be appropriate in a particular situation. Researchers often use a statistical method called **factor analysis** to try to identify which sorts of abilities underlie performance on the various items. This procedure identifies clusters of correlated items that seem to be measuring some common ability, or factor. Some psychologists believe that a general ability, or **g factor,** underlies specific abilities and talents (Herrnstein & Murray, 1994; Spearman, 1927; Wechsler, 1955). Other psychologists dispute the existence of a g factor, arguing that a person can excel in some tasks yet do poorly in others (Gould, 1994; Guilford, 1988). Disagreements over how to define intelligence have led some writers to suggest, only half-jokingly, that intelligence is "whatever intelligence tests measure."

Measuring Intelligence: The Psychometric Approach

The traditional approach to intelligence, the **psychometric** approach, focuses on how well people perform on standardized mental tests. The tests you take in your courses are called *achievement tests,* because they are designed to measure skills and knowledge that have been explicitly taught. *Aptitude tests,* in contrast, are designed to measure the ability to acquire skills or knowledge in the future. For example, vocational aptitude tests can help you decide whether you will do better as a mechanic or a musician, and IQ tests do a pretty good job of predicting school performance. But all mental tests are in some sense achievement tests because they assume past learning or experience with particular objects, words, or situations. The difference between achievement and aptitude tests is one of degree and intended use.

Binet's Brainstorm. As we saw in Chapter 3, the first intelligence test was devised at the beginning of the twentieth century by Alfred Binet (1857–1911), when the French Ministry of Education asked Binet to design an objective test that would identify slow learners in need of remedial help. Wrestling with the problem, Binet had a great insight: In the classroom, the responses of "dull" children resembled those of ordinary children of younger ages. Bright children, on the other hand, responded like ordinary children of older ages. The thing to measure, then, was a child's **mental age (MA),** or level of intellectual development relative to other children's. Then instruction could be tailored to the child's capabilities.

The test devised by Binet and his colleague, Theophile Simon, measured memory, vocabulary, and perceptual discrimination. Items ranged from those that most young children could do easily to those that only older children

▪ **intelligence**
An inferred characteristic of an individual, usually defined as the ability to profit from experience, acquire knowledge, think abstractly, act purposefully, or adapt to changes in the environment.

▪ **factor analysis**
A statistical method for analyzing the intercorrelations among various measures or test scores. Clusters of measures or scores that are highly correlated are assumed to measure the same underlying trait, ability, or aptitude (factor).

▪ **g factor**
A general intellectual ability assumed by some theorists to underlie specific mental abilities and talents.

▪ **psychometrics**
The measurement of mental abilities, traits, and processes.

▪ **mental age (MA)**
A measure of mental development expressed in terms of the average mental ability at a given age. A child with a mental age of 8 performs on a test of mental ability at the level of the average 8-year-old.

Table 8.2 Sample Items from the Stanford-Binet Intelligence Test, Form L-M

The older the test taker is, the more the test requires in the way of verbal comprehension and fluency.

Age   **Task**

4   Fills in the missing word when asked, "Brother is a boy; sister is a _____."
Answers correctly when asked, "Why do we have houses?"

9   Answers correctly when examiner says, "In an old graveyard in Spain they have discovered a small skull which they believe to be that of Christopher Columbus when he was about 10 years old. What is foolish about that?"
Examiner notices folded paper; child draws how it will look unfolded.

12   Completes "The streams are dry . . . there has been little rain."
Tells what is foolish about statements such as "Bill Jones's feet are so big that he has to put his trousers on over his head."

Adult   Can describe the difference between *misery* and *poverty*, *character* and *reputation*, *laziness* and *idleness*.
Explains how to measure 3 pints of water with a 5-pint and a 2-pint can.

Source: From Lewis M. Terman & Maud A. Merrill, *Stanford-Binet Intelligence Scale* (1972 norms ed.). Boston: Houghton-Mifflin, 1973. (Currently published by The Riverside Publishing Company.) Items are copyright 1916 by Lewis M. Terman, 1937 by Lewis M. Terman and Maud A. Merrill, © 1960, 1973 by The Riverside Publishing Company. Reproduced or adapted by permission of the publisher.

could handle, as determined by the testing of large numbers of children. A scoring system developed later by others used a formula in which the child's mental age (MA) was divided by the child's chronological age (CA) to yield an **intelligence quotient, or IQ.** Still later, the modern system of scoring was devised: The average is set arbitrarily at 100, and tests are constructed so that the *standard deviation*—a measure of how spread out the scores are around the mean—is always 15 or 16, depending on the test; individual test scores are then computed from tables (see Chapter 3).

Binet recognized that all children taking his test in France had similar cultural backgrounds, but that this might not be true elsewhere. He also emphasized that the test merely *sampled* intelligence and did not measure everything covered by that term. A test score, he said, could be useful, along with other information, for predicting school performance under ordinary conditions, but it should *not* be confused with intelligence itself. The purpose of testing was to identify children with learning problems, not to rank normal children.

In America, Stanford psychologist Lewis Terman revised Binet's test and established norms for American children. His version, the *Stanford-Binet Intelligence Scale*, was first published in 1916 and has been updated several times since. (For some sample items, see Table 8.2.) Two decades later, David Wechsler, chief psychologist at Bellevue Hospital in New York City, designed another test, expressly for adults, which became the *Wechsler Adult Intelligence Scale (WAIS)*. It was followed by the *Wechsler Intelligence Scale for Children (WISC)*. Although the Wechsler tests produce a general IQ score, they also provide specific scores for different kinds of ability, both verbal and nonverbal ("performance"). These tests, too, have since been revised. (For some sample items, see Figure 8.2 and Table 8.3 on the next page.)

■ **intelligence quotient (IQ)**
A measure of intelligence originally computed by dividing a person's mental age by his or her chronological age and multiplying by 100; now derived from norms provided for standardized intelligence tests.

■ **Figure 8.2   Performance Tasks on the Wechsler Tests**

Performance (nonverbal) items are particularly useful in measuring the abilities of those who have poor hearing, are not fluent in the tester's language, have limited education, or resist doing classroom-type tasks. A large gap between a person's verbal score and performance score on a Wechsler test sometimes indicates a specific learning problem. (Object assembly, digit symbol, and picture completion adapted from Cronbach, 1990).

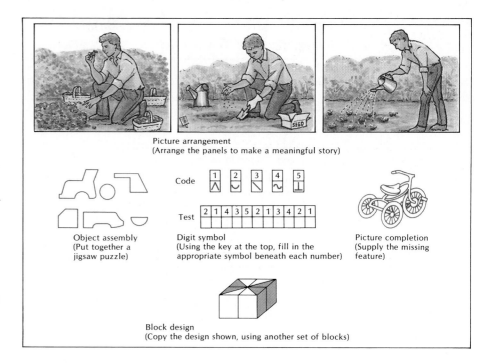

Picture arrangement
(Arrange the panels to make a meaningful story)

Object assembly
(Put together a jigsaw puzzle)

Code

Test

Digit symbol
(Using the key at the top, fill in the appropriate symbol beneath each number)

Picture completion
(Supply the missing feature)

Block design
(Copy the design shown, using another set of blocks)

Table 8.3   *Verbal Items Similar to Those on the WISC-R and the WAIS-R*

For each subtest, the first example illustrates the level of difficulty of the Wechsler Intelligence Scale for Children–Revised. The second example illustrates the level of difficulty of the Wechsler Adult Intelligence Scale–Revised. Digit-span items are similar on the two tests.

Subtest	Examples
Information	Who was Thomas Jefferson? Who wrote *Huckleberry Finn*?
Comprehension	Why is it important to use zip codes when you mail letters? Why do married people who want a divorce have to go to court?
Similarities	In what way are corn and macaroni alike? In what way are a book and a movie alike?
Vocabulary	What do we mean by *protect*? What does *formulate* mean?
Arithmetic	Dick had 13 pieces of candy and gave away 8. How many did he have left? How many hours will it take to drive 140 miles at the rate of 30 miles an hour?
Digit Span	I am going to say some numbers. Listen carefully, and when I am through, say them right after me: 3-6-1-7-5-8. Now I am going to say some more numbers, but this time when I stop, I want you to say them backward: 1-9-3-2-7.

Source: Adapted from Cronbach, 1990, and based on items from the Wechsler scales, published by The Psychological Corporation, 1958.

However, the purpose and use of intelligence testing were vastly different in America than in France. In France, Binet's test had been given to each child individually, so the test-giver could see whether a child was ill or nervous, had poor vision, or was not trying. In America, the revised Binet and the Wechsler tests were also given to individuals, but other, similar tests were given to huge

An intelligence test is useful only if it is used intelligently. Army intelligence testing during World War I often occurred under noisy, crowded, and confusing conditions. Many test items were culturally loaded, and some men refused to answer at all. Nevertheless, many people concluded that a high proportion of army recruits were "morons."

groups of people, usually students or soldiers, and the advantages of individualized testing were lost. Americans used the test not to bring slow learners up to the average, but to "track" people in school and in the armed services according to their presumed "natural" ability. The testers overlooked the fact that in America, with its many ethnic groups, people did not all share the same background and experience (Gould, 1981).

Intelligence tests developed or revised between World War I and the 1960s for use in schools favored city children over rural ones, middle-class children over poor ones, and white children over minority children. One item, for example, asked whether the Emperor Concerto was written by Beethoven, Mozart, Bach, Brahms, or Mahler. (The answer is Beethoven.) Critics complained that the tests did not measure the kinds of knowledge and skills that are intelligent in a minority neighborhood or in the hills of Appalachia (Scarr, 1984a). And they pointed out that because teachers thought IQ scores revealed the limits of a child's potential, low-scoring children would not get the educational attention or encouragement they needed; high-scoring children would. When teachers expect a child to do well, they respond more warmly, give more feedback, teach more material, and give the child more chances to ask and answer questions (Rosenthal, 1994; Rosenthal & Jacobson, 1992).

Culture-Free and Culture-Fair Tests. In the 1970s, group intelligence testing became a public issue. School boards and employers were sued for restricting the opportunities of low scorers. Some states prohibited the use of group tests for classifying children. Several test-makers responded by trying to construct tests that were *culture-free*. Such tests were usually nonverbal; in some, instructions were even pantomimed. Test constructors soon found, however, that culture can affect performance in unexpected ways. In one case, children who had emigrated from Arab countries to Israel were asked to show which detail was missing from a picture of a face with no mouth (Ortar, 1963). The children, who were not used to thinking of a drawing of a head as a complete picture, said that the *body* was missing!

Test constructors then tried to design tests that were *culture-fair*. Their aim was not to eliminate the influence of culture, but to find items that incorporate knowledge and skills common to many different cultures. So far the results have been less successful than originally hoped, because cultural values affect a person's attitude toward taking tests, comfort in the settings required for test-

"You can't build a hut, you don't know how to find edible roots and you know nothing about predicting the weather. In other words, you do terribly on our IQ test."

ing, motivation, rapport with the test-giver, competitiveness, and experience in solving problems independently (Anastasi, 1988). Moreover, cultures differ in which problem-solving strategies and skills they foster (Serpell, 1994). For example, children from white, middle-class families are typically trained to categorize things—to say that an apple and a peach are similar because they are both fruits. But children from other ethnic groups may have different expectations about what's being called for and answer that an apple and a peach are similar because they taste good—a response that test-givers interpret as less intelligent (Miller-Jones, 1989). That is why culture-fair items do not always eliminate differences in group performance.

In theory, it should be possible to establish norms that are not based on white urban children, by throwing out items on which such children score better than others. A similar strategy was used years ago to eliminate sex differences in IQ. On early tests, girls scored higher than boys at every age (Samelson, 1979). No one was willing to conclude that males were intellectually inferior, so in the 1937 revision of the Stanford-Binet test, Lewis Terman simply deleted items that showed sex differences.

But few people seem willing to do for cultural differences what Terman did for sex differences. The reason reveals a dilemma at the heart of intelligence testing. Intelligence tests put some groups of children at a disadvantage, yet they also measure skills and knowledge useful in the classroom. How can educators recognize and accept cultural differences and, at the same time, require students to demonstrate mastery of the skills, knowledge, and attitudes that will help them succeed in school and in the larger society? How can they eliminate bias from tests, while preserving the purpose for which the tests were designed? Anne Anastasi, an eminent expert in testing, contends that concealing the effects of cultural disadvantage by rejecting conventional tests is "equivalent to breaking a thermometer because it registers a body temperature of 101." Instead, she argues, special help should be given to any child who needs it (Anastasi, 1988). Others believe that IQ and other mental tests do more harm than good. Sociologist Jane Mercer (1988) has been trying for years to get testers to understand that children can be *ignorant* of information required by IQ tests without being *stupid,* but she has finally given up. Now, she says, "I'm out to kill the IQ test."

Beyond the IQ Test. The resolution of this debate may depend on whether test users can learn to use intelligence tests more intelligently. Most educators feel that the tests have value, as long as a person's background is kept in mind and the results are interpreted cautiously. IQ tests are well standardized, and they predict school performance fairly well. Correlations between IQ scores and current or future school grades, though far from perfect, are high, ranging between .40 and .60. IQ tests often identify not only the mentally retarded, but also gifted students who have not previously considered higher education.

In some schools, a child's placement in a special education program now depends not only on an IQ score, but also on other tests of specific abilities, medical data, and the child's demonstrated inability to get along in the family and community. And some schools are returning to Binet's original concept. Instead of using group tests to label and categorize children, they give individual tests to identify a child's strengths and weaknesses so that teachers can design individualized programs that will boost the child's performance.

This change in emphasis reflects an increasing awareness that the intellect—and IQ scores—can be improved, even in the mentally retarded (Butterfield & Belmont, 1977; Feuerstein, 1980; Sternberg, 1986). Psychologists and educators now realize, too, that a person may have a **learning disability**—a problem with a specific mental skill, such as reading or arithmetic—without having a

Suppose that a test finds IQ differences between two groups of children. Should we change the children in the group that does less well, or change the classroom or the test?

■ **learning disability**
A difficulty in the performance of a specific mental skill, such as reading or arithmetic; sometimes linked to perceptual or memory problems.

general intellectual impairment. Many children with learning disabilities have normal or even superior intelligence and can overcome or compensate for their handicaps.

Critics of traditional approaches to measuring intelligence, however, argue that when a child's abilities don't match those expected by teachers and testers, the best solution may be to "fix" not just the child, but also the classroom or the test. Anthropologist Shirley Brice Heath (1983) has shown how this approach can work. In a study of a small African-American community in a southern city, Heath found that black parents were less likely than white parents to ask their children "what," "where," "when," and "who" questions—the sorts of questions found on standardized tests and in schoolbooks ("What's this story about?" "Who is this?"). Black parents preferred to ask analogy questions ("What's that like?") and story-starter questions ("Did you hear about . . . "). Teachers in the community used this information to modify their teaching strategies. They encouraged their black pupils to ask "school-type" questions, but they also incorporated analogy and story-starter questions into their lessons. Soon the black children, who had previously been uncomfortable and quiet, became eager, confident participants.

Critics also point out that standardized tests don't reveal *how* a person goes about answering questions and solving problems. Nor do they explain why people with low scores on IQ tests often behave intelligently in real life. Psychologist Seymour Sarason tells of reporting for his first job, which was giving IQ tests at a school for the mentally retarded. Upon arriving, he learned that all of the students had escaped! When they were eventually rounded up and Sarason began to test them, he found that most could not do even the first problem. Yet these same students had outsmarted the school authorities by escaping, at least temporarily (in Sternberg, 1988). They might have had low IQs, but they had a sort of *practical intelligence*. Practical intelligence also reveals itself in the ordinary behavior of average citizens. For example, a study at a racetrack found that successful handicappers used an exceedingly complicated statistical method to predict winners. This ability was *not* related to the handicappers' IQs (Ceci & Liker, 1986). Another study found that shoppers in a supermarket can select the best buy even when they cannot do the formal mathematical computations that would allow them to compare prices of two brands (Lave, Murtaugh, & de la Roche, 1984).

Because of such findings, some researchers are taking a more cognitive approach to the measurement and study of intelligence.

Children with Down syndrome, who score low on standard IQ tests, are accomplishing more academically than anyone once thought they could. They show that intellectual performance is not as fixed and immutable as many people assume.

Dissecting Intelligence: The Cognitive Approach

In contrast to the psychometric approach to intelligence, which is concerned with how many answers a person gets right on a test, the cognitive approach emphasizes the *strategies* people use when thinking about problems and arriving at a solution. Intelligent behavior involves, among other things, encoding problems, noticing similarities and differences, spotting fallacies, and "reading" the environment, including other people.

The Triarchic Theory. One promising cognitive theory, Robert Sternberg's *triarchic theory of intelligence* (1988), distinguishes three aspects of intelligence. The first, *componential intelligence,* includes information-processing strategies that go on inside a person's head when the person is thinking intelligently about a problem: recognizing the problem, selecting a strategy for solving it, mastering and carrying out the strategy, and evaluating the result. People who are strong in componential intelligence tend to do well on conventional mental tests.

The second aspect of intelligence in Sternberg's theory, *experiential intelligence,* refers to how well you transfer skills to new situations. People with experiential intelligence cope well with novelty and learn quickly to make new tasks automatic; those who are lacking in this area perform well only under a narrow set of circumstances. For example, a student may do well in school, where assignments have specific due dates and feedback is immediate, but be less successful after graduation if her job requires her to set her own deadlines and her employer doesn't tell her how she is doing.

The third type of intelligence, *contextual intelligence,* refers to the practical application of intelligence, which requires taking into account different contexts in which you find yourself. If you are strong in contextual intelligence, you know when to adapt to the environment (you are in a dangerous neighborhood, so you become more vigilant); when to change environments (you had planned to be a teacher but you find you don't enjoy working with kids, so you switch to accounting); and when to fix the environment (your marriage is rocky, so you and your spouse go for counseling).

Most intelligence tests do not measure the experiential and contextual aspects of intelligence, yet these aspects help determine a person's personal and occupational success. For example, without contextual intelligence, you won't have the kind of practical savvy that allows you to pick up *tacit knowledge*—strategies for success that usually are not formally taught. In studies of college professors, business managers, and salespeople, scores on tests of tacit knowledge do not correlate strongly with conventional ability-test scores, but they do predict effectiveness on the job (Sternberg, Wagner, & Okagaki, 1993). Tacit knowledge about how to be a student—how to take notes during lectures, prepare for tests, do course papers—predicts college success as well as academic tests do (Sternberg & Wagner, 1989).

Cognitive psychologists are also recognizing the importance of **metacognition,** which is involved in componential intelligence. Metacognition is the knowledge or awareness of one's own cognitive processes and the ability to monitor and control them. Before you can solve a problem, you have to recognize that a problem exists—a metacognitive skill. For example, some students fail to notice when a textbook contains incomplete or inconsistent information, or when a passage is especially difficult. As a result, they spend no more time on difficult passages than on easy ones. They don't study the difficult material enough, and they spend more time than necessary on material they know (Nelson & Leonesio, 1988). Good students are better at assessing what they do and don't know (Maki & Berry, 1984). They check their comprehension by restating what they have read, backtracking when necessary, and questioning what they

■ **metacognition**
The knowledge or awareness of one's own cognitive processes.

Engineers drawing up plans for a new project must be strong in componential intelligence in order to analyze the problem, select a strategy, and evaluate potential solutions.

are reading (Bereiter & Bird, 1985). (If they are reading this textbook, they also take the Quick Quizzes!)

Domains of Intelligence. In other ways, too, cognitive approaches are expanding our understanding of what it means to be intelligent. As we have seen, traditional definitions have focused almost entirely on the kinds of behavior required or useful in the classroom. But Howard Gardner (1983), in his *theory of multiple intelligences*, suggests that there are actually seven "intelligences" or domains of talent: *linguistic, logical-mathematical, spatial, musical, bodily-kinesthetic* (which actors, athletes, and dancers have), *intrapersonal* (insight into yourself), and *interpersonal* (understanding of others). These talents are relatively independent, and each may have its own neural structures. People with brain damage often lose one of the seven without losing their competence in the others. And some autistic and retarded individuals, known by the unfortunate label "idiot savants" (*savant* means "learned" in French), have exceptional talents in one area, such as music, art, or rapid mathematical computation, despite poor functioning in all others.

Some schools are trying to incorporate Gardner's ideas to allow children to capitalize on their particular intelligences (or, as some prefer to call them, talents) (Krechevsky & Gardner, 1990; Scarnati, Kent, & MacKenzie, 1993). One little boy in Modesto, California, had trouble reading but was good in music; his teacher used folk songs such as "Fifteen Miles on the Erie Canal" to help him recall facts about the Erie Canal and the westward movement (Woo, 1995). So far, however, there is not enough research to assess the effectiveness of the new approaches, and no way to be sure that teachers won't misuse the theory to justify "fun" activities at the expense of teaching important content.

Intelligence is more than what IQ tests measure. A rock star has musical intelligence, a surveyor has spatial intelligence, and a compassionate friend has interpersonal intelligence.

People with emotional intelligence are skilled at reading nonverbal emotional cues. Which of these boys do you think feels the cockiest and which is most fearful? What cues are you using to answer?

Gardner's last two "intelligences" correspond to what some theorists call *emotional intelligence:* the undervalued ability to know how to identify your own and other people's emotions, express your emotions clearly, and regulate emotions in yourself and others (Mayer & Salovey, 1993). People who are low in emotional intelligence are often confused about their own emotions; they may insist that they're not angry, for example, while shouting and slamming doors. They express emotions inappropriately, such as by acting violently when they are suffering from grief or anxiety. And they misread nonverbal signals from others—for example, they will give a long-winded account of all their problems even when the listener is obviously bored.

People with high emotional intelligence use their emotions in adaptive ways, to motivate themselves and others or to spur creative thinking. Emotional intelligence even contributes to school achievement. One study with over a thousand children found that although difficulty in interpreting nonverbal emotional signals from others was not related to IQ, it was related to low academic achievement, especially in boys (Nowicki & Duke, 1989). Another study compared children whose parents had taught them to analyze and manage feelings of anger with children who had comparable IQs and socioeconomic backgrounds but whose parents were not good "emotional coaches." Those who had learned to understand their own emotions as preschoolers tended at age 8 to score higher on math and reading tests and to have longer attention spans (Gottman, Katz, & Hooven, in press). It may be that children who can't read emotional cues from their teachers and classmates, or who can't control their own emotions, have trouble learning because they feel anxious, confused, or angry.

Studies of brain-damaged adults, too, show that using your head also involves your heart. Neuroscientist Antonio Damasio (1994) tells of many patients with prefrontal damage who, as a result of the damage, became incapable of strong feelings. Although they scored in the normal range on mental tests, these patients persistently made "dumb," irrational decisions in their lives because they couldn't assign values to different options or read emotional cues from others. As Damasio explains, "We are faced by uncertainty when we have to make a moral judgment, decide on the course of a personal relationship, choose some means to prevent our being penniless in old age, or plan for the life that lies ahead. Emotion and feeling . . . assist us with the daunting task of predicting an uncertain future and planning our actions accordingly."

Quick QUIZ

How intelligent are you about intelligence?

1. In a sense, all mental tests are (aptitude/achievement) tests.
2. True or false: Culture-fair tests have eliminated group differences that show up on traditional IQ tests.
3. Some schools are returning to Binet's goal of using IQ tests as a tool for (a) labeling and categorizing children, (b) identifying children who could benefit from individualized programs, (c) studying intellectual differences among ethnic groups.
4. In your statistics class, you understand the material, but on tests, you plan your time poorly; you spend the entire period on the most difficult problems, never even getting to the problems you can solve easily. According to Sternberg, which aspect of intelligence do you need to work on?

 5. What's wrong with defining intelligence as "whatever intelligence tests measure"?

Answers:

traits other than intelligence.
intelligent in ways that the test fails to measure, and the test may be measuring
must be entirely the scorer's fault rather than the test's. But the test-taker may be
of the tests and efforts to improve them. People are led to assume that a low score
high? Because the person is intelligent! The definition also discourages criticisms
Because he or she scored high on an intelligence test. Why did the person score
tion) **5.** The definition is circular. How do we know someone is intelligent?
1. achievement **2.** false **3.** b **4.** componential (or, more specifically, metacogni-

■ ATTITUDES, MOTIVES, AND INTELLECT

You could have a high IQ, think logically, have emotional intelligence, be talented, and "know your way around," but without a few other qualities, you might still fall short of your own and other people's expectations. One of these qualities is motivation.

Consider a finding from one of the longest-running psychological studies ever conducted. Since 1921, researchers at Stanford University have been following 1,528 people with childhood IQ scores in the top 1 percent of the distribution. As boys and girls, these subjects were nicknamed "Termites," after Lewis Terman, who originally directed the research. The Termites started out bright, physically healthy, sociable, and well adjusted, and as they entered adulthood, most became successful in the traditional ways of the times: men in careers and women as homemakers (Sears & Barbee, 1977; Terman & Oden, 1959). However, some gifted men failed to live up to their early promise, dropping out of school or drifting into low-level work. When the researchers compared the 100 most successful men in the Stanford study with the 100 least successful, they found that motivation made the difference. The successful men were ambitious, were socially active, had many interests, and were encouraged by their parents. The least successful drifted casually through life. There was *no* average difference in IQ between the two groups.

In another study, researchers interviewed 120 of America's top artists, athletes, and scholars, along with their families and teachers, to find out what had made them so successful (Bloom, 1985). The research team expected to hear tales of extraordinary natural talent. Instead, they heard tales of extraordinary dedication. Musicians had practiced several hours a day for years. Swimmers told of rising early every morning to swim for two hours before school started. Talent, unlike cream, does not inevitably rise to the top; success depends on drive and determination. These high achievers were perfect illustrations of the old joke: A young man walking down a New York street asks an old woman, "How do I get to Carnegie Hall?" Her reply: "Practice, young man. Practice."

Yes, you say, but where do you get the discipline to practice? One factor has to do with your beliefs about the origins of intelligence and the reasons for achievement. For more than a decade, Harold Stevenson and his colleagues (1990a, 1990b) have been studying attitudes toward achievement in Japan, China, and the United States. The researchers began by comparing large samples of first- and fifth-grade children, their parents, and their teachers in Minneapolis, Sendai (Japan), and Taipei (Taiwan). In another project, they compared children from 20 schools in Chicago and 11 schools in Beijing. In 1990, Stevenson, along with Chuansheng Chen and Shin-Ying Lee (1993), revisited the original schools to collect new data on fifth-graders, and also retested many of the children who had been in the 1980 study. Their results have much to teach us about the cultivation of intellect.

In 1980, the Asian children far outperformed the American children on a broad battery of mathematical tests. On computations and word problems, there was virtually no overlap between schools, with the lowest-scoring Beijing schools doing better than the highest-scoring Chicago schools. By 1990, the gap between the Asian and American children had grown even greater. Only 4 percent of the Chinese children and 10 percent of the Japanese children had scores as low as those of the *average* American child. These differences could not be accounted for by educational resources: The Chinese had worse facilities and larger classes than the Americans. On the average, the American children's parents were far better off financially than the parents of the Chinese children, and they were better educated as well. Nor could the test differences be accounted for by differences in the children's fondness for math: 85 percent of the Chinese kids said they liked math, but so did almost 75 percent of the American children. Nor did it have anything to do with intellectual ability in general, because the American children did just as well as the Asian children on tests of general information—items not based on a school curriculum.

But the Asians and the Americans were worlds apart, so to speak, in their attitudes, expectations, and efforts:

- American parents, teachers, and children were far and away more likely than Asians to believe that mathematical ability is innate. They thought that if you "have it," you don't have to work hard, and if you don't have it, there's no point in trying. When Japanese teachers were asked to choose the most important factor in mathematical performance, 93 percent of them chose "studying hard"—compared to only 26 percent of the American teachers. Students picked up these attitudes: 72 percent of the Japanese but only 27 percent of the American eleventh-graders thought studying hard was the key to success in math.

- American parents had far lower standards for their children's performance. They said they would be satisfied with scores barely above average on a 100-point test; most felt that their children were doing fine in math and that the schools were doing a good or excellent job. In contrast, the Chinese and Japanese parents said they would be happy only with very high scores, and most were not highly satisfied with their children's schools or even with their children's excellent performance.

- American students had more stressful, conflicting demands on their time than their Asian counterparts did. Chinese and Japanese students were expected to devote themselves to their studies, but American students were expected to be "well-rounded"—to have after-school jobs (74 percent of them did, compared to only 21 percent of the Asians), to have dates and an active social life (85 percent to 37 percent), and to have time for sports and other activities. Contrary to the stereotype of the stressed and overworked Japanese student, it was the American students who were most likely to report that school was a source of stress and academic anxiety (Crystal et al., 1994). The Japanese eleventh-graders actually had the lowest incidence of stress, depression, insomnia, aggression, and physical symptoms.

- American students did not value education as much as Asian students did. When asked what they would wish for if a wizard could give them anything they wanted, more than 60 percent of the Chinese fifth-graders named something related to their education. Can you guess what the American children wanted? A majority said money or possessions.

The moral is: It's not just what you've got, but what you do with it. As Robert Sternberg (1986) writes, "We must never lose sight of the fact that what really matters in the world is not the level of our intelligence but what we achieve with this intelligence."

■ ANIMAL MINDS

A green heron swipes some bread from a picnicker's table and scatters the crumbs on a nearby stream. When a minnow rises to the bait, the heron strikes, swallowing its prey before you can say "hook, line, and sinker." A sea otter, floating calmly on its back, bangs a mussel shell against a stone that is resting on its stomach. When the shell cracks apart, the otter devours the tasty morsel inside, tucks the stone under its flipper, and dives for another shell, which it will open in the same way. A lioness appears behind a herd of wildebeests and chases them toward a ditch. Another lioness, lying in wait at the ditch, leaps up and kills one of the passing wildebeests. The first lioness then joins her companion for the feast.

Incidents such as these, summarized nicely in Donald Griffin's *Animal Minds* (1992), have convinced some biologists, psychologists, and ethologists that we are not the only animals with cognitive abilities—that "dumb beasts" are far smarter than we have realized. For many years, any scientist who claimed that animals could think was likely to get laughed at, or worse; today, the interdisciplinary field of **cognitive ethology,** the study of cognitive processes in nonhuman animals, is gaining increased attention (Griffin, 1992; Ristau, 1991). Cognitive ethologists argue that some animals can remember past events, anticipate future ones, make plans and choices, and coordinate their activities with those of their comrades (Cheney & Seyfarth, 1990; Crook, 1987; Griffin, 1984, 1992). In short, they can think.

Other scientists are skeptical, noting that even complex behavior can be genetically prewired. The assassin bug of South America catches termites by gluing nest material on its back as camouflage, but it is hard to imagine how the bug's tiny dab of brain tissue could enable it to plan this strategy consciously. Even trees and plants, which few people credit with consciousness, do things that *appear* intelligent. When willow trees are attacked by insects, they release a chemical into the air that causes leaves on nearby healthy willow trees to change chemically and become less palatable to the insects (Rhoades, 1985). Their "communication" does not imply thought; it is a genetically controlled adaptation to the environment. Even many cognitive ethologists are cautious about how *much* cognition they are willing to read into an animal's behavior. An animal could be "conscious," they argue, in the sense of being aware of its environment and "knowing" some things, without knowing that it knows and without being able to think about its own thoughts in the way that human beings do (Cheney & Seyfarth, 1990; Crook, 1987).

But explanations of animal behavior that leave out any sort of consciousness at all and attribute actions in all species entirely to instinct leave many questions unanswered. Like the otter who uses a stone to crack mussel shells, many animals are capable of using objects in the natural environment as rudimentary tools. One researcher has found that mother chimpanzees occasionally show their young how to use stone tools to open hard nuts (Boesch, 1991). In the laboratory, too, nonhuman primates have accomplished some truly surprising things. In one study, chimpanzees compared two pairs of food wells containing chocolate chips. One pair might contain, say, five chips and three chips, the other four chips and three chips. Allowed to choose which pair they wanted, the chimps almost always chose the one with the higher total, showing some sort of summing ability (Rumbaugh, Savage-Rumbaugh, & Pate, 1988). Other chimps have learned to use numerals to label quantities of items and simple sums (Boysen & Berntson, 1989; Washburn & Rumbaugh, 1991).

The primary ingredient in human cognition, of course, is language—our ability to shape thoughts into words. Language is often regarded as the last bastion of human uniqueness, a result of evolutionary forces (see Chapter 3). Do animals have anything comparable? To qualify as a language, a communication system must meet three criteria (Hockett, 1960):

How smart is this otter?

■ **cognitive ethology**
The study of cognitive processes in nonhuman animals.

1. *Meaningfulness.* In any language, reference to things, ideas, and feelings is achieved by the arbitrary but consistent combination of sounds or gestures into meaningful units such as words or signs. There must be enough words (or signs) to express all the concepts that a community might want or need to express.

2. *Displacement.* Languages permit communication about objects and events that are not present here and now—that are displaced in time or space. Merely pointing to things is not language.

3. *Productivity.* Language has a set of grammatical rules that allow the expression and comprehension of an infinite number of novel utterances.

By these criteria, no nonhuman species has its own language. Of course, animals do communicate, using gestures, body postures, facial expressions, vocalizations, and odors. And some of these signals have more specific meanings than previously thought. For example, vervet monkeys seem to have separate calls to warn about leopards, eagles, and snakes (Cheney & Seyfarth, 1985). But the sounds do not seem to be combined to produce entirely novel utterances.

Perhaps, however, some animals could acquire language if they got a little help from their human friends, beginning early in life. Dozens of researchers have tried to provide chimpanzees with just such help. Because the vocal tract of a chimpanzee does not permit speech, early efforts to teach chimpanzees spoken language were failures, although some comprehension did occur. During the 1960s and 1970s, researchers tried different approaches. In one project, chimpanzees learned to use as words geometric plastic shapes arranged on a magnetic board (Premack & Premack, 1983). In another, they learned to punch symbols on a computer-monitored keyboard (Rumbaugh, 1977). In yet another, they learned hundreds of signs from American Sign Language (ASL) (Fouts & Rigby, 1977; Gardner & Gardner, 1969). The animals in these and other studies learned to follow instructions, answer questions, and make requests. More important, they combined individual signs or symbols into longer utterances that they had never seen before. In general, their linguistic abilities resembled those of a 2-year-old child.

As you can imagine, accounts of the apes' abilities caused quite a stir. The animals were apparently using their newfound skills to apologize for being disobedient, scold their trainers, and even talk to themselves. Koko, a lowland gorilla, reportedly used signs to say that she felt happy or sad, to refer to past and future events, to mourn for her dead pet kitten named All-Ball, and to convey her yearning for a baby. She even lied on occasion, when she did something naughty (Patterson & Linden, 1981).

The animals in these studies were lovable, the findings appealing. But soon skeptics and some of the researchers themselves began to point out serious problems in interpreting these results (Seidenberg & Petitto, 1979; Terrace, 1985). In their desire to talk to the animals and their affection for them, researchers had not always been objective. They had overinterpreted the animal's utterances, reading all sorts of meanings and intentions into a single sign. In videotapes, they could be seen unwittingly giving nonverbal cues that might enable the apes to respond correctly. Further, the animals appeared to be stringing signs and symbols together in no particular order to earn a reward, instead of using grammatical rules to produce novel utterances; "Me eat banana" seemed to be no different for them than "Banana eat me." Longer utterances did not bring greater complexity in syntax, but mere repetition: "Give orange me give eat orange me eat orange give me eat orange give me you" (R. Brown, 1986).

Recent studies have benefited from such criticisms and are a marked improvement on past research. Carefully controlled experiments, in which the researchers are hidden from the animals and can't give them cues, have established that chimps can acquire the ability to use symbols to refer to objects (Sav-

It's hard not to be impressed by the smart accomplishments of so-called dumb beasts who use rudimentary tools and even seem able to add sums. And it's impossible not to love apes who use sign language or special symbols to request food, apologize, or lie when they are naughty. But are these animals really thinking and using language?

Researchers have used a number of innovative methods in their efforts to teach apes language. Here Kanzi, a pygmy chimp with the most advanced linguistic skill yet acquired by a nonhuman primate, answers questions and makes requests by punching symbols on a specially designed computer keyboard.

age-Rumbaugh, 1986). In some projects, chimpanzees have spontaneously used signs to converse with each other, suggesting that they are not merely imitating or trying to get a reward (Van Cantfort & Rimpau, 1982). A young chimp named Loulis has learned dozens of signs from Washoe, the original signing chimp (Fouts, Fouts, & Van Cantfort, 1989). Bonobo (pygmy) chimps are even more adept at language than are common chimpanzees. One bonobo named Kanzi has learned to understand English words and short sentences, and to understand keyboard symbols, *without formal training* (Savage-Rumbaugh & Lewin, 1994; Savage-Rumbaugh et al., 1990). He responds correctly to commands such as "Put the key in the refrigerator" and "Go get the ball that is outdoors" (as opposed to indoors). Kanzi picked up language as children do—by observing others using it, and through social interaction. He has also learned, with training, to manipulate keyboard symbols to request foods or activities (games, TV, visits to friends) or to announce his intentions, and he seems to use some simple grammatical ordering rules to convey meaning.

Other research suggests that even certain nonprimates can acquire some aspects of language. In Hawaii, Louis Herman and his colleagues have taught dolphins to respond to sentencelike requests made in two artificial languages, one consisting of computer-generated whistles and another of hand and arm gestures (Herman, 1987; Herman, Kuczaj, & Holder, 1993). To interpret a request correctly, the dolphins must take into account both the meaning of the individual symbols in a string of whistles or gestures and the order of the symbols (syntax). For example, they must understand the difference between "To left Frisbee, right surfboard take" and "To right surfboard, left Frisbee take." Remarkably, they can interpret sequences of gestures from a televised image of the trainer as well as they can from a live trainer (Herman, Morrel-Samuels, & Pack, 1990).

In another fascinating project, Irene Pepperberg (1988, 1990, 1994) has taught an African gray parrot named Alex to count, classify, and compare objects by vocalizing English words. When the bird is shown up to six items and is asked how many there are, he responds with spoken (squawked?) English phrases, such as "two cork(s)" or "four key(s)." He can even respond correctly to questions about items specified on two dimensions, as in "How many

Alex is one smart bird—but how smart? Alex's abilities raise intriguing questions about the intelligence of animals and their capacity for certain aspects of language.

blue key(s)?" Alex can also make requests ("Want pasta") and can answer questions about objects ("What color? Which is bigger?"). When presented with a blue cork and a blue key and asked "What's the same?" he will correctly respond "Color." He actually scores slightly better with new objects than with familiar ones, suggesting that he is not merely memorizing a set of stock phrases.

These recent results on animal language and cognition are impressive, but scientists are still divided over just what the animals in these studies are doing. Do they have language? Are they "thinking," in human terms? On one side are those who worry about *anthropomorphism,* the tendency to falsely attribute human qualities to nonhuman beings. They tell the story of Clever Hans, a "wonder horse" at the turn of the century, who was said to possess mathematical abilities (Fernald, 1984). Clever Hans would answer simple arithmetic problems by stamping his hoof the appropriate number of times. But a little careful experimentation by a psychologist, Oskar Pfungst (1911/1965), revealed that when Hans was prevented from seeing the questioner, his "powers" left him. It seems that questioners were staring at the horse's feet and leaning forward expectantly after stating the problem, then lifting their eyes and relaxing as soon as he completed the right number of taps. Clever Hans was indeed clever, but not at math. He was responding to nonverbal signals that people were inadvertently providing.

On the other side are those who warn against *anthropocentrism,* the tendency to think, falsely, that human beings have nothing in common with other animals. The need to see our own species as unique, they say, may keep us from recognizing that other species, too, have cognitive abilities, even if not as intricate as our own. Those who take this position point out that most modern researchers have gone to great lengths to avoid the Clever Hans problem.

The outcome of this debate is bound to have an effect on how we view ourselves and our place among other species on the planet. As Donald Griffin (1992) writes, "Cognitive ethology presents us with one of the supreme scientific challenges of our times, and it calls for our best efforts of critical and imaginative investigation."

Quick QUIZ

1. You've trained your pet cockatiel to say "Play it again, Sam" for a food reward when it is hungry. But it does not respond to the individual words or to the sentence as a whole in any consistent way. The animal does not have language, since its "speech" lacks _____.
2. A honeybee performs a little dance that communicates to other bees the direction and distance of food. Because the bee can "talk" about something that is located elsewhere, its communication system shows _____. But because the bee can create no utterances other than the ones that are genetically wired into its repertoire, its communication system lacks _____.
3. In thinking about animal cognition, it is important to avoid both _____ and _____.

Answers:

1. meaningfulness 2. displacement, productivity 3. anthropomorphism and anthropocentrism

In this chapter, we have seen that although we may be the smartest species in terms of our ability to adapt to changing environments and come up with novel solutions to problems, we are neither unique nor as savvy as we might suppose. Still, there is one crowning accomplishment we can boast of: *We are the only species that tries to understand its own misunderstandings.* This capacity for self-examination is perhaps our greatest accomplishment and the best reason to remain optimistic about our cognitive capacities.

In the next chapter, we invite you to exercise your own powers of understanding as we turn to an aspect of human cognition that is widely misunderstood—the mystery of memory.

*T*aking Psychology with You

Becoming More Creative

T ake a few moments to answer these items from the Remote Associates Test. Your task is to find a fourth, associated word that "goes with" each item in a set of three words (Mednick, 1962). For example, an appropriate answer for the set *news-clip-wall* is *paper.* Got the idea? Now try these (the answers are given on page 324):

1. piggy-green-lash
2. surprise-line-birthday
3. mark-shelf-telephone
4. stick-maker-tennis
5. blue-cottage-cloth

Associating elements in new ways by finding a common connection among them is an important component of creativity. People who are uncreative rely on *convergent thinking,* following a particular set of steps that they think will converge on one correct solution. Once they have solved a problem, they tend to develop a *mental set,* a tendency to solve new problems using the same heuristics, strategies, and rules that worked in the past.

Creative people, in contrast, exercise *divergent thinking;* instead of stubbornly sticking to one tried and true path, they explore some side alleys and generate several possible solutions. They come up with new hypotheses, break out of old mental sets, imagine alternative interpretations, and look for connections that may not be immediately obvious. As a result, they are able to use familiar concepts in unexpected ways. Creative thinking can be found in the auto mechanic who invents a new tool, the mother who designs and makes her children's clothes, or the office manager who devises a clever way to streamline work flow (Richards, 1991).

Interestingly, a high IQ does not guarantee creativity (Barron & Harrington, 1981). Personality characteristics seem more important and include these three essential ones (MacKinnon, 1962, 1968; McCrae, 1987; Schank, 1988):

- *Nonconformity and self-confidence.* Creative individuals are not overly concerned about what others think of them. They are willing to risk ridicule by proposing ideas that may initially appear foolish or off the mark. Geneticist Barbara McClintock's research was ignored or belittled by many for nearly 30 years. But she was sure she could show how genes move around and produce sudden changes in heredity. In 1983, McClintock was vindicated; she won the Nobel Prize. The judges called her work the second great genetic discovery of our time, after the discovery of the structure of DNA.

- *Curiosity.* Creative people are open to new experiences; they notice when reality contradicts expectations, and they are curious about the reason. For example, Wilhelm Roentgen, a German physicist, was studying cathode rays when he noticed a strange glow on one of his screens. Other people had seen the glow, but they ignored it because it didn't jibe with current understanding of cathode rays. Roentgen studied the glow, found it to be a new kind of radiation, and thus discovered X rays (Briggs, 1984).

- *Persistence.* This is perhaps the most important attribute of the creative person. After that imaginary lightbulb goes on over your head, you still have to work hard to make the illumination last. Or, as Thomas Edison, who invented the real lightbulb, reportedly put it, "Genius is one-tenth inspiration and nine-tenths perspiration." No invention or work of art springs forth full-blown from a person's head. There are many false starts and painful revisions along the way.

In addition to traits that foster creativity, there are *circumstances* that do. For example, the performance of students on creativity tests improved significantly after they watched a funny film or received a gift of candy, which put them in a good mood. In contrast, watching an upsetting film on concentration camps or a "neutral" film on math, or exercising to boost energy, had no effect on creativity (Isen, Daubman, & Nowicki, 1987). Cheerful situations, it seems, may loosen up creative associations.

Another situational factor is the encouragement of *intrinsic* rather than *extrinsic* motivation. Intrinsic motives include a sense of accomplishment, intellectual fulfillment, the satisfaction of curiosity, and the sheer love of the activity. Extrinsic motives include a desire for money, fame, and attention, or the wish to avoid punishment. Teresa Amabile and her colleagues found that artists' commissioned works were less creative than their non-commissioned works, both in their own eyes and in the estimation of "blind" judges. This was true even when the person commissioning the work allowed the artist complete freedom (Amabile, Phillips, & Collins, 1993).

In another study, Amabile (1985) asked 72 young poets and writers to create two poems. Before writing their second poem, half the writers evaluated a list of extrinsic motives for writing (such as "The market for freelance writing is constantly expanding" and "You enjoy public recognition of your work"). The other half evaluated a list of intrinsic motives ("You like to play with words"; "You achieve new insights"). Then a panel of 12 experienced poets judged all the poems for originality and creativity, without knowing which writers had read which motives. The writers who were exposed to extrinsic reasons for writing showed a significant drop in the creativity of their second poem. Those who paid attention to intrinsic motives wrote two poems of equal quality.

Other research shows that creativity flourishes when people (1) have control over how to perform a task or solve a problem; (2) are evaluated unobtrusively, instead of being constantly observed and judged; and (3) work independently (Amabile, 1983). In addition, organizations encourage creativity when they let people take risks, give them plenty of time to think about problems, and welcome innovation.

In sum, if you hope to become more creative, there are two things you can do. One is to cultivate the personal qualities that lead to creativity. The other is to seek out the kinds of situations that permit you to express them.

Summary

1. *Thinking* is the mental manipulation of information. Our mental representations simplify and summarize information from the environment.

2. A *concept* is a mental category that groups objects, relations, activities, abstractions, or qualities that share certain properties. *Basic concepts* have a moderate number of instances and are easier to acquire than concepts with few or many instances. Some instances of a concept are more *prototypical* than others. *Propositions* are made up of concepts and express a unitary idea; they may be linked together to form *cognitive schemas*, which serve as mental models of aspects of the world. Visual *images* and other sensory images also play a role in thinking.

3. Not all mental processing is conscious. *Subconscious* processes lie outside of awareness but can be brought into consciousness when necessary. *Nonconscious* processes remain outside of awareness but nonetheless affect behavior and may be involved in what we call "intuition." Conscious processing may be carried out in a mindless fashion if we overlook changes in context that call for a change in behavior.

4. *Reasoning* involves drawing inferences and conclusions from observations, facts, or assumptions (premises). In *deductive reasoning*, which often takes the form of a syllogism, if the premises are true then the conclusion must be true. The application of deductive reasoning is affected by experience and schooling. In *inductive reasoning*, the premises provide support for a conclusion, but the conclusion could still be false. Science depends heavily on inductive reasoning.

5. Logic alone is often inadequate for solving human problems. People make logical errors or disagree with others about basic premises. In informal reasoning problems, information may be incomplete, and there may be no clear-cut solution; in such cases, one needs to be able to reason *dialectically* about opposing points of view. Some critics believe that television watching is partly responsible for a decline in the ability to weigh and evaluate opposing arguments, as discussed in "Think About It."

6. Studies by King and Kitchener on *reflective judgment* show that many people have trouble thinking dialectically. People in the *prereflective* stages assume that a correct answer always exists; they do not distinguish between knowledge and belief, or between belief and evidence. Those in the *quasi-reflective* stages think that because knowledge is sometimes uncertain, any judgment about the evidence is purely subjective. Those who think *reflectively* understand that although some things cannot be known with certainty, certain judgments are more valid than others, depending on their coherence, usefulness, fit with the evidence, and so on. Higher education seems to move people gradually closer to reflective judgment.

7. *Heuristics*, rules of thumb used when making decisions and judgments, can be influenced by cognitive biases. People tend to exaggerate the likelihood of improbable events; avoid risks and losses; attend to evidence that confirms what they want to believe (the *confirmation bias*); perceive what they expect; and overestimate their ability to have made accurate predictions (the *hindsight bias*). The theory of *cognitive dissonance* holds that people are also motivated to reduce the tension that exists when two cognitions are in conflict—by rejecting or changing a belief, changing their behavior, or rationalizing. People are not always rational, but once we understand a bias, we may be able to reduce or eliminate it.

8. Although we all wish to think intelligently, intelligence is hard to define. Some theorists believe that a general ability (a *g factor*) underlies the many specific abilities tapped by intelligence tests, whereas other theorists do not.

9. The traditional approach to intelligence, the *psychometric* approach, focuses on how well people perform on standardized mental tests. The *intelligence quotient,* or *IQ,* represents how a person has done on an intelligence test, compared to other people. Alfred Binet designed the first widely used intelligence test for the purpose of identifying children who could benefit from remedial work. But in the United States, people assumed that intelligence tests revealed "natural" ability, and used the tests to "track" people in school and in the armed services.

10. IQ tests have been criticized for being biased in favor of white, middle-class people. However, efforts to construct culture-free and culture-fair tests have been disappointing. Some critics would like to dispense with IQ tests because they are so often interpreted unintelligently. Critics also argue that when a child's abilities don't match those expected by teachers and testers, the best solution may be to "fix" not just the child, but also the classroom or the test. Others believe the tests are useful for predicting school performance and diagnosing learning difficulties, as long as they are combined with other information.

11. In contrast to the psychometric approach, cognitive approaches to intelligence emphasize the strategies people use to solve problems and not just whether they get the right answers. Sternberg's *triarchic theory of intelligence* proposes three aspects of intelligence: componential, experiential, and contextual. Most intelligence tests do not measure experiential and contextual intelligence, yet these help determine a person's personal and occupational success. *Metacognition,* which is part of componential intelligence, also plays an important role in intelligent behavior.

12. Gardner, in his *theory of multiple intelligences,* argues that there are actually seven "intelligences": linguistic, logical-mathematical, spatial, musical, bodily-kinesthetic, intrapersonal, and interpersonal. The last two correspond roughly to *emotional intelligence,* which is related to personal and academic success.

13. Achievement also depends on motivation and attitudes. Cross-cultural work shows that beliefs about the origins of mental abilities, parental standards, and attitudes toward education can help account for differences in academic performance.

14. Some researchers argue that nonhuman animals have greater cognitive abilities than is usually thought. Many animals can use objects as rudimentary tools. Chimpanzees have learned to use numerals to label quantities of items and symbols to refer to objects. Several researchers have used visual symbol systems, American Sign Language, and other linguistic systems to teach primates language skills, and some animals (even some nonprimates) seem able to use simple grammatical ordering rules to convey meaning. However, scientists are still divided as to how to interpret these findings.

Key Terms

thinking *288*
concept *288*
basic concept *288*
prototypical instance *288*
proposition *289*
cognitive schema *289*
mental image *289*
subconscious processes *290*
nonconscious processes *290*
mindlessness *291*
reasoning *292*
premise *292*
deductive reasoning *292*
syllogism *292*
inductive reasoning *293*
informal vs. formal reasoning *294*
dialectical reasoning *294*
reflective judgment *296*
    prereflective stages *297*
    quasi-reflective stages *298*
    reflective stages *298*
algorithm *300*
heuristic *300*
availability heuristic *300*
loss aversion *300*
confirmation bias *301*
hindsight bias *302*
cognitive dissonance *303*
justification of effort *304*
intelligence *306*
factor analysis *306*
g factor *306*

psychometric approach to intelligence *306*
achievement vs. aptitude tests *306*
mental age (MA) *306*
intelligence quotient (IQ) *307*
Stanford-Binet Intelligence Scale *307*
Wechsler Adult Intelligence Scale (WAIS) *307*
Wechsler Intelligence Scale for Children (WISC) *307*
culture-free tests *309*
culture-fair tests *309*
learning disability *310*
practical intelligence *311*
cognitive approach to intelligence *312*
triarchic theory of intelligence *312*
    componential intelligence *312*
    experiential intelligence *312*
    contextual intelligence *312*
tacit knowledge *312*
metacognition *312*
theory of multiple intelligences *313*
emotional intelligence *314*
cognitive ethology *317*
anthropomorphism *320*
anthropocentrism *320*
convergent/divergent thinking *321*
mental set *321*

Answers to creativity test on page 321:

back, party, book, match, cheese

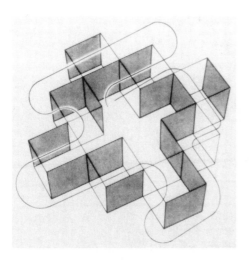

Solution to the puzzle on page 286:

The mirrored images of the figures provide clues as to which sides of the rooms are mirrored walls (shown as shaded here).

9

Memory

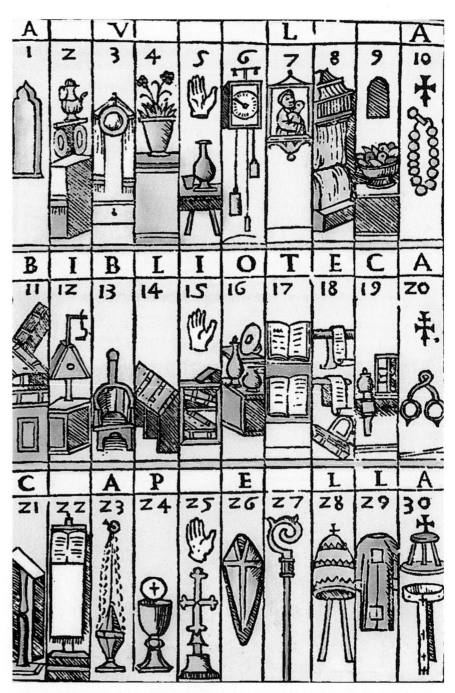

People are always searching for ways to improve memory. Sixteenth-century Dominican friars used the method of loci (places) to memorize speeches. Each idea in the speech was associated with an object on this chart, which was in turn mentally placed along a route through the abbey. The speaker then retraced the route, retrieving each object and idea in the correct order.

Better by far that you should forget and smile
Than that you should remember and be sad.

■ CHRISTINA ROSSETTI ■

In 1983, a writer we know took a trip to Italy with her husband and spent a few days exploring the beautiful city of Florence. Not long afterward, she read and saw the film of E. M. Forster's novel *Room with a View,* which is also set in Florence. Years went by, and a decade after her Italian vacation, she sat down on a winter's eve to rewatch the film of *Room with a View.* During the movie, a long camera shot of the Piazza Signoria suddenly brought back a flood of memories, one of them violent. Our friend remembered that during her trip, while she and her husband were in that piazza, a wild fight had broken out and a young man had been seriously injured. In her mind's eye, she once again saw the crowd, the commotion, the blood on the man's shirt. "At that moment," she says, "I would have sworn in a court of law that we had seen a fight in the Piazza Signoria."

Then, suddenly, she found herself watching, right up there on her television screen, the very same fight that she recalled witnessing a decade earlier. The fight she was so sure she had actually observed was a scene from the novel! Perhaps, she thought, some other violent event had occurred during her visit. Checking her journal of the trip, she found that on the day she and her husband were in the Piazza Signoria, they had spent some time admiring the sculptures, had sipped lemonade at a sidewalk cafe, and had watched a prostitute idly solicit business. There had been no fight, no disturbance—only a typical, peaceful Florentine morning in the Piazza Signoria.

Our friend's story illustrates an all-too-common glitch in the process of remembering: She imported subsequent information into an actual experience and assumed that the result was her own personal memory. How could our friend, who is known for her keen intelligence and devotion to accuracy, have been so wrong? Are such memory malfunctions the exception to the rule, or might they be the norm? If memory can be so unreliable, how can any of us be sure we know the story of our own life? How can we hope to understand the past?

In this chapter, we will see how psychologists investigate these uncomfortable questions. Psychological researchers want to know how a person can "remember" things that never happened. They also want to know why, despite our best efforts, we all forget many (perhaps most) events that did take place. They want to know why even very recent memories can evaporate like the morning dew: why we watch the evening news and half an hour later can't recall the main story; why we enjoy a meal and quickly forget what we ate; why, as students, we may study our heads off for an exam, only to find that some of the information isn't there when we most need it.

But psychologists also study the many astonishing feats of memory that all human beings are capable of—for, despite its lapses, memory is a true marvel of the human mind. Who fought whom in World War II? When are presidential elections held? What is the tune of your national anthem? How do you use an

How often and in what month do national elections take place? Why do you remember these facts? When did you learn them?

automated teller machine? What's the most embarrassing thing that ever happened to you? You can probably answer most of these questions—and hundreds of thousands of others—without hesitation. A mathematician once calculated that over the course of a lifetime, we store 500 times as much information as there is in the entire *Encyclopaedia Britannica* (Griffith, in Horn & Hinde, 1970). And a good thing, too. **Memory,** the capacity to retain and retrieve information, confers competence; without it we would be as helpless as newborns, unable to negotiate even the most trivial of our daily tasks. It also confers a sense of personal identity; we are each the sum total of our personal recollections, which is why we feel so threatened when people say our memories are wrong. Individuals and cultures alike rely on a remembered history for a sense of coherence and meaning; memory preserves the past and guides the future.

■ RECONSTRUCTING THE PAST

In ancient times, philosophers compared memory to a tablet of hot wax that would preserve anything that chanced to make an imprint on it. Then, with the advent of the printing press, they began to think of a memory as a sheet of paper, with all our memories filed away in a sort of giant mental filing cabinet, awaiting retrieval. Today, in the audiovisual age, many people think of memory as a mental tape recorder or videocamera, automatically recording each and every moment of their lives. One psychotherapist, who apparently never studied introductory psychology, expressed the modern pop-psych vision of memory this way:

> The subconscious mind has a memory bank of everything we ever experienced, exactly as we perceived it. Every thought, emotion, sound of music, word, taste and sight. Everything is faithfully recorded somehow in your mind. Your sub-conscious mind's memory is perfect, infallible. (Fiore, 1989)

Popular and appealing though this belief about memory is, however, it is utterly, absolutely wrong. As Robyn Dawes (1994) points out, this therapist has managed to ignore "every study that has ever been conducted on the nature of human memory." What those studies show is that *not* everything that happens to us or impinges on our senses is tucked away for later use. If it were, our minds would be cluttered with all sorts of mental junk—the temperature at noon Thursday, the price of turnips two years ago, a phone number needed only once. Memory must be selective. And recovering a memory, as we are about to see, is not at all like replaying a film of an event; it is more like watching a few unconnected frames and then figuring out what the rest of the scene must have been like.

The Manufacture of Memory

In 1932, the British psychologist Sir Frederic Bartlett asked people to read lengthy, unfamiliar stories from other cultures and then tell the stories back to him. Bartlett found that as the volunteers tried to retrieve the stories from memory, they made interesting errors: They often eliminated or changed elements, and they added details to make the story coherent. Memory, Bartlett concluded, must therefore be a *reconstructive* process. (Psychologists today sometimes call this process *confabulation*.) When we remember information, said Bartlett, we typically alter it in ways that help us make sense of the material, based on what we already know, or think we know. Since Bartlett's time, hundreds of memory studies have found this to be true for everything from stories to conversations. Often, like the writer who "remembered" the fight in Florence, people can't separate what they originally experienced from what they have added after the fact. It all feels like one integrated memory.

■ **memory**
The capacity to retain and retrieve information; also, the mental structure or structures that account for this capacity, and the material that is retained.

Research with patients who cannot form new memories for events is helping psychologists and neuroscientists understand how memory normally works. K. P. (left) became amnesiac a decade ago when her brain was robbed of oxygen for several minutes, possibly because of an accidental overdose of barbiturates. Although K. P. is fluent in three languages, she has trouble remembering events for more than 10 minutes. Working with researcher and clinician Bonnie Olsen, she has been able to acquire new skills and habits; mnemonic techniques, ranging from cue cards to an electronic voice reminder, are helping her to become more self-sufficient (Olsen et al., in preparation).

You can see the process of reconstruction at work in the tragic case of H. M., which we described briefly in Chapter 4 (page 136). Ever since 1953, when much of H. M.'s hippocampus and the adjacent cortex were surgically removed, he has suffered from **anterograde amnesia,** the inability to form lasting memories for new events and facts (Ogden & Corkin, 1991). Therefore, he cannot learn new words, songs, stories, or faces. Although he is now in his 60s, he does not know how old he is and usually guesses his age as much younger than it is. He can read the same magazine again and again without realizing that he has read it before. According to Suzanne Corkin, who has studied H. M. extensively, H. M. does have some "islands of remembering." For example, he sometimes recalls that both his parents are dead, and he knows that he has memory problems and that the operation done on him has never been done since. But these islands are the exceptions in a vast sea of forgetfulness.

To cope with his devastating condition, H. M. will sometimes try to reconstruct events. On one occasion, after eating a large chocolate Valentine's Day heart, H. M. stuck the shiny red wrapping in his shirt pocket. Two hours later, while searching for his handkerchief, he pulled out the paper and looked at it in puzzlement. When researcher Jenni Ogden asked why he had the paper in his pocket, he replied, "Well, it could have been wrapped around a big chocolate heart. It must be Valentine's Day!" Ogden could hardly contain her excitement about H. M.'s apparent recall of a recent episode. But a short time later, when she asked him to take out the paper again and say why he had it in his pocket, he replied, "Well, it might have been wrapped around a big chocolate rabbit. It must be Easter!" (Put H. M. in your long-term memory, as we will be seeing him again in this chapter.)

Of course, H. M. *had* to reconstruct the past; his damaged brain could not recall it in any other way. But those of us with normal memory abilities also reconstruct, far more than we realize. Suppose someone asks you to describe one of your early birthday parties. You may have some direct recollection of the event, especially if it was emotionally significant. But you have also stored information gleaned from family stories, photographs, or home videos. You may take all these bits and pieces and build one integrated account from them, and

▪ **anterograde amnesia**
The inability to form lasting memories for new events and facts.

later you may not be able to identify which information came from which source.

Despite the wealth of evidence for the reconstructive nature of memory, some people still believe that memories are permanently stored somewhere in the brain with perfect accuracy. As evidence, they will sometimes cite studies of recall under hypnosis. But as we saw in Chapter 5, hypnotically induced memories are as vulnerable to reconstruction as are any other memories, if not more so; and the information the person unwittingly adds may or may not be an accurate reflection of what really happened.

Another line of evidence often cited comes from neurosurgeon Wilder Penfield's studies of electrical brain stimulation. During the 1960s, Penfield reported that stimulating parts of a patient's brain during surgery would sometimes evoke reports of what seemed to be sharp memories from the distant past, thought by the patient to be long forgotten (Penfield & Perot, 1963). In one case, a woman told of rehearing a concert she had attended years before; she even hummed along with the music. Another woman said, "I hear voices. It is late at night, around the carnival somewhere—some sort of traveling circus."

For years, many psychologists unquestioningly accepted Penfield's brain-stimulation research as persuasive support for the permanent storage of memories. Then Elizabeth Loftus (1980) looked at his work more critically. First, she observed that although Penfield had electrically stimulated the brains of about 1,100 patients, only 40 of them—3.5 percent—reported having a "memory." Of those 40, most claimed to hear nothing more than some music or a person singing; hardly a memory of anything. As for the few that seemed to have more elaborate memories, closer examination suggested that they were not actually "reliving" a long-forgotten experience at all. Instead, they were re-creating one, drawing in part on actual memories and in part on their current interpretations of such memories—much as they might do while dreaming. One woman reported that she heard a female voice calling a child in her old neighborhood; but when the same brain area was stimulated 18 minutes later, the woman said the voice was coming from a lumberyard—and added that she had never in her life been in a lumberyard. Another woman's "memories" turned out to consist of whatever thoughts or bits of conversation had taken place just before and during the time of stimulation.

Loftus also pointed out what in retrospect should have been obvious: The recovery of *some* information stored long ago does not mean that *all* memories remain available and reflect what actually happened. According to Loftus, there is no solid evidence that all memories last forever. On the contrary, she argues, information in memory can be completely wiped out by new, misleading information, or can become permanently inaccessible. Although we can all produce some familiar facts without much reconstruction, literal recall is probably the exception, not the rule.

But, you may say, what about surprising, shocking, or emotional events that hold a special place in memory? Such experiences seem like moments frozen in time, with all the details seemingly intact. Years ago, Roger Brown and James Kulik (1977) labeled these memories **flashbulb memories** because that term captures the surprise, illumination, and seemingly photographic detail that characterize them. Brown and Kulik speculated that the capacity for flashbulb memories may have evolved because such memories had survival value. Remembering the details of a surprising or dangerous experience would have helped our ancestors avoid similar situations in the future.

Yet despite their intensity, even flashbulb memories are not always complete or accurate records of the past. Many people who were alive when John F. Kennedy was assassinated swear that they saw the assassination on television, as he was riding in his motorcade. In reality, no television cameras were present during the assassination, and the only film of the event, made by a bystander, was not shown until much later. Similarly, many people say they know exactly

✳ When their brains are electrically stimulated, some people seem to "relive" long-forgotten experiences. Should we conclude that all our memories are permanently on file, waiting to be retrieved?

■ **flashbulb memory**
A vivid, detailed recollection of a significant or startling event, or of the circumstances in which a person learned of such an event.

Do you recall where you were and what you were doing when you learned about the tragic explosion of the space shuttle Challenger *on January 28, 1986? If so, you may have a flashbulb memory of that moment.*

where they were and what they were doing when they learned of the 1986 explosion of the space shuttle *Challenger,* as well as who told them the news and what their own reactions were. Yet several studies done since the tragedy show that these memories, too, often grow dim with time.

In one such study, researchers interviewed people a few days after the explosion; most of them could provide many details about the experience. But nine months later, they gave much more general answers, and fully a quarter of them gave some responses that were inconsistent with their original reports (McCloskey, Wible, & Cohen, 1988). In another study, college students, on the morning after the event, reported how they had heard the news. Three years later, when they again recalled how they learned about the incident, not one student was entirely accurate and a third of them were *dead wrong,* although they *felt* they were remembering accurately (Neisser & Harsch, 1992). A third study found that after eight months, only those people who had been upset at the news of the disaster *and* who had often recounted their reactions could relate many details of the incident with a high degree of confidence (Bohannon, 1988).

Some shocking or surprising events do remain extremely memorable, especially when the person doing the remembering was personally involved in the event. Research finds, for example, that if you were living in the San Francisco Bay Area in 1989, you probably remember accurately where you were and what you were doing when the Loma Prieta earthquake hit on October 17 and what you did right afterward (Neisser, Winograd, & Weldon, 1991; Palmer, Schreiber, & Fox, 1991). Even with flashbulb memories, however, facts tend to get mixed with a little fiction. These findings remind us, once again, that remembering is an *active* process; it involves not only dredging up stored information but also putting two and two together to reconstruct the past.

The reconstructive nature of memory helps the mind work efficiently. We can store just the essentials of an experience, then use our knowledge of the world to figure out the specifics when we need them. But sometimes the same process gets us into hot water, which raises problems in legal cases that involve eyewitness testimony.

The Eyewitness on Trial

Imagine that as you leave an office building, you see a man running in the direction of a blue Dodge. You glance away for a moment, and when you look

THE FAR SIDE By GARY LARSON

More facts of nature: All forest animals, to this very day, remember exactly where they were and what they were doing when they heard that Bambi's mother had been shot.

The justice system depends on eye-witnesses to state "the facts and just the facts," but are the facts always reconstructed accurately?

back, you see that someone in the Dodge is pulling away from the curb. You are not paying much attention to this chain of events; why should you? But just then, a woman emerges from the building, points wildly at the receding car, and shouts, "Stop that man, he stole my purse!" Soon the police arrive and ask you to tell what you saw.

If we again compare memory to a film, you have actually seen only some of the frames: a man running toward a car, the car pulling away. Asked now for a description of what happened, you are likely to fill in the frames that are missing, the ones that would presumably show the man climbing into the car. In other words, you *infer* (deduce) what must have happened: "I saw a brown-haired man, about 5 feet 10 inches tall, with a mustache, and wearing a blue shirt, run over to the blue Dodge, get in, and drive away." To make matters worse, some aspects of this episode were undoubtedly hazy or incomplete, so you have probably gone back and "retouched" them, adding a little color here, a little detail there. What has happened is something like the perceptual closure we discussed in Chapter 6, except that in this case the closure has occurred in memory.

Will any harm result from your reconstruction? That depends. Perhaps the man you saw really did drive off in the car. Then again, perhaps another person was the purse snatcher, and the man you saw was someone else. Because mem-

Police often use lineups to jog eyewitnesses' memories, but lineups have a serious drawback. Sometimes witnesses compare the suspects and pick the one most like the criminal, even though all the suspects are actually innocent (Wells, 1993). Having witnesses observe suspects one at a time, instead of in a group, and respond to each one individually reduces such false identifications without reducing correct identifications (Cutler & Penrod, 1988).

ory is reconstructive, eyewitness testimony is not always reliable, even when the witness feels confident about the accuracy of his or her report. There is no easy solution to this problem. It does little good to give a polygraph ("lie-detector") test to a witness who is unwittingly reconstructing an event. Not only is the reliability of polygraph results questionable (see Chapter 10), but also, someone who is trying to reconstruct the past is not deliberately lying and should therefore pass the test. Nor, as we saw, will hypnosis necessarily help.

Of course, the accounts of eyewitnesses play a vital role in our justice system; without them, many guilty people would go free. But convictions based on such testimony occasionally turn out to be tragic mistakes. Errors are especially likely to occur when the suspect's race differs from that of the witness, perhaps because prejudices or lack of familiarity prevent people from attending to the distinctive features of members of other races (Brigham & Malpass, 1985; Chance & Goldstein, 1995; Luce, 1974).

To complicate matters further, our reconstructions of past events are heavily influenced by the way in which questions about those events are put to us. In a classic study of leading questions, Elizabeth Loftus and John Palmer (1974) showed people short films depicting car collisions. Afterward, they asked some of the viewers, "About how fast were the cars going when they *hit* each other?" Other viewers were asked the same question, but with the verb changed to *smashed, collided, bumped,* or *contacted.* These words imply different speeds, with *smashed* implying the greatest speed and *contacted* the least. Sure enough, the estimates of how fast the cars were going varied, depending on which word was used. *Smashed* produced the highest average speed estimates (40.8 mph), followed by *collided* (39.3 mph), *bumped* (38.1 mph), *hit* (34.0 mph), and *contacted* (31.8 mph).

In a similar study, the researchers asked some participants, "Did you see a broken headlight?" but asked of others "Did you see the broken headlight?" (Loftus & Zanni, 1975). Two other pairs of questions also differed only in the

Leading questions and misleading information can alter what we remember. When people who were shown the car with the yield sign (below) were asked if they had seen "the stop sign," many reported that they had; similarly, when those shown a stop sign were later asked if they had seen "the yield sign," many said yes (Loftus, 1980). In another study (right), subjects saw the face of a young man who had straight hair, then heard a description of the face supposedly written by another witness—a description that wrongly described the man as having light curly hair. When these subjects reconstructed the face using an Identi-kit of different features, 33 percent of their reconstructions contained the misleading detail, whereas only 5 percent contained it when curly hair was not mentioned. The top face shows one person's reconstruction in the absence of the misleading information; the bottom face shows another person's reconstruction of the same face after exposure to the misleading information (Loftus & Greene, 1980).

Some people claim that children never lie about or misremember sexual abuse; other people claim that children can't distinguish fantasy from reality and shouldn't be trusted. How can we avoid either–or thinking on this emotional issue? Is "do children lie" even the right question to be asking?

use of *a* or *the*. Note that the question with *the* presupposes a broken headlight, and merely asks whether the witness saw it, whereas the question with *a* makes no such presupposition. The researchers found that people who received questions with *the* were far more likely to report having seen something that had not really appeared in the film than were those who received questions with *a*. If a tiny word like *the* can lead people to remember what they never saw, you can imagine how the leading questions of police detectives and courtroom lawyers might influence a witness's recall.

Many people are especially concerned about the impact of leading questions on children's reports of sexual abuse. Some people argue that no child would ever lie about or misremember such a traumatic experience. Others say that you can't trust a child's testimony because children don't distinguish reality from fantasy and because they tend to say whatever adults expect. Who is right? Fortunately, we don't have to depend on opinion on this matter: Since 1979, there have been more than 100 studies on children's ability to give accurate testimony. In a lengthy review of this research, Stephen Ceci and Maggie Bruck (1993) conclude that extremists on both sides of the debate are wrong.

Ceci and Bruck found that in most of the studies that have been done, "Young children were able to accurately recollect the majority of the information they observed." For example, in studies of potentially embarrassing physical examinations, most children do not report that their genitals were touched if they were not touched—even when the children are asked leading questions. This is important, because without a few leading questions, some young children who have been abused will not volunteer information they feel is embarrassing or shameful. That is why most states now permit authorities to ask a child leading questions in sexual-abuse cases. On the other hand, some children *will* say that something happened when it did not. Like adults, they can be influenced to report an event in a certain way, depending on the frequency of the suggestions and the insistence of the person making them.

Ceci and Bruck suggest that instead of asking "Are children suggestible?" or "Do children lie?" and then staking out extreme positions, we need to recognize that *all people* can be suggestible under certain circumstances. A more useful question is: "Under what conditions are children apt to be suggestible?" Here are a few of those conditions:

- *When the child is very young.* Ceci and Bruck found that in 83 percent of all studies that looked at age differences, preschoolers were more vulnerable to suggestion than were school-aged children and adults.

- *When the child is influenced by other children's stories.* In one study, schoolchildren were asked for their recollections of an actual sniper who had terrorized their schoolyard. Many of the children who were not at the school during the shooting, including some who were on vacation at the time, reported "memories" of hearing shots, seeing someone lying on the ground, and other details they could not possibly have seen. Apparently, they were influenced by the accounts of the children who had been there (Pynoos & Nader, 1989). This finding has troubling implications for cases that appear to involve the abuse of many children, because in these cases, children often hear the stories of other youngsters and may come to doubt their own perceptions of what did or did not happen.

- *When the child has a desire to please an interviewer.* When an adult repeatedly asks the same question during an interview, children (especially preschoolers) will often change their answers, apparently because they interpret the repetition to mean that their answer is wrong or unacceptable (Cassel & Bjorklund, 1992; Poole & White, 1991). In some cases, the result may be a drop in accuracy from the first question to the second, especially among younger children (Moston, 1987). This finding, too, has important implications for sexual-abuse prosecutions, because interviewers have sometimes asked the same questions again and again. In one highly publicized case in Jordan, Minnesota, in which scores of parents were accused of horrific acts of abuse and murder, one child eventually admitted that he had made up detailed stories of abuse because "I could tell what they wanted me to say by the way they asked the questions" (Benedek & Schetky, 1987).

- *When the child is pressured by adults.* If the interviewer's manner is urgent or perceived as coercive, children may feel pressured to say what the adult wants them to say. In court cases, interrogators and social workers have sometimes used extremely questionable interview techniques, threatening the child, offering bribes, or repeatedly accusing children of lying if they don't give the "right" answers. Here, for example, is an excerpt from a long, intimidating interview conducted by a social worker and a detective (from Ceci & Bruck, 1993):

> **Social worker:** Did I tell you that this [the detective] is the guy that arrested her? . . . Well, we can get out of here quick if you just tell me what you told me the last time, when we met.
>
> **Child:** I forgot.
>
> **Social worker:** No, you didn't. I know you didn't.
>
> **Child:** I did! I did!
>
> .   .   .
>
> **Social worker:** Oh, come on. We talked to a few more of your buddies. And everyone told me about the nap room, and the bathroom stuff, and the music room stuff, and the choir stuff, and the peanut butter stuff, and everything. . . . All your buddies [talked]. . . . Come on, do you want to help us out? Do you want to keep her in jail? I'll let you hear your voice and play with the tape recorder. . . . Real quick, will you just tell me what happened with the wooden spoon? Let's go.
>
> **Child:** I forgot.
>
> **Detective:** Now listen, you have to behave.
>
> **Social worker:** Do you want me to tell him to behave? Are you going to be a good boy, huh? While you were here, did [the detective] show you his badge and his handcuffs? . . . Back to what happened to you with the spoon. If you don't remember words, maybe you can show me [with some anatomically correct dolls].
>
> **Child:** I forgot what happened, too.
>
> **Social worker:** You remember. You told your mommy about everything about the music room and the nap room, and all that stuff. You want to help her stay in jail, don't you? So she doesn't bother you anymore and so she doesn't tell you any more scary stories.

The accused teacher in this case, Margaret Kelly Michaels, was eventually convicted of 115 counts of sexual abuse against 20 preschoolers, some of the purported acts bizarre (for example, licking peanut butter off children's genitals). She was sentenced to 47 years in prison. After serving 5 years, she was released when an appeals court ruled that she had not received a fair trial because of the way the children were interrogated; the prosecution declined to retry her.

Investigators who must interview children in cases of suspected sexual abuse, therefore, face a difficult dilemma: They must somehow persuade a child who might be shy, embarrassed, or verbally unsophisticated to tell the truth about what happened, while avoiding questions that are coercive or that lead the child into making a false report. Investigators must also overcome their own confirmation bias, the tendency to seek only confirming evidence for their

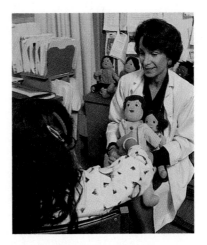

Designing reliable techniques for interviewing children about suspected sexual abuse is difficult. Many therapists say that anatomically correct dolls help children remember, and that preoccupation with a doll's genitals are signs of abuse. But even nonabused children will play with the dolls in a sexual manner, and independent raters often cannot distinguish abused and nonabused children on the basis of how they play with the dolls (Ceci & Bruck, 1993).

belief that abuse did (or did not) occur (see Chapter 8). Several researchers are now testing approaches for interviewing children that take into account the findings we have discussed. They hope to find better ways to help children be as accurate and truthful as possible. For the moment, it seems that the wisest course to take about children's testimony is to be open-minded but cautious, and to avoid extreme positions. Children, like adults, can be accurate in what they report and, also like adults, they can distort, forget, fantasize, and be misled. As research on memory shows, their memory processes are only human.

Quick QUIZ

See whether you can reconstruct what you have read to answer these questions.

1. Memory can be compared to (a) a wax tablet, (b) a giant file cabinet, (c) a videorecorder, (d) none of these.
2. In the old children's game "telephone," one person tells another person a story, the second person relates the story to a third, and so on. By the end of the game, the story will have changed considerably, which illustrates the principle that memory is _____.
3. Research suggests that the best way to encourage truthful testimony by children is to (a) tell them what other children said about an incident; (b) repeatedly ask them the same questions; (c) gently question them without pressuring; (d) refuse to accept answers you believe are wrong.
4. In psychotherapy, hundreds of people have claimed to recall long-buried memories of having taken part in bizarre satanic rituals involving animal and human torture and sacrifice. Yet law-enforcement investigators and research psychologists have been unable to confirm *any* of these reports (Goodman et al., 1995). Based on what you know about long-term memory, how might you explain such "memories"?

Answers:

1. d 2. reconstructive 3. c 4. Memories of satanic ritual abuse have so far been shown to be confabulations that confuse fantasy with fact. Therapists who uncritically accept the claim that satanic abuse cults are widespread may ask leading questions and make leading comments to their patients (Ganaway, 1991; Ofshe & Watters, 1994). Patients, who are susceptible to their therapists' interpretations, may then "remember" experiences that did not happen, "borrowing" ideas and descriptions from fictionalized accounts or other traumatic experiences in their lives. Networks of patients and therapists who believe in satanic ritual abuse may provide reinforcement and support for such false memories.

■ TAKING MEMORY'S MEASURE

Now that we have seen how memory *doesn't* work—namely, like a tape recorder, an infallible filing system, or a journal written in indelible ink—we turn to studies of how it *does* work. To understand how memory operates, however, you must know a little about how psychologists measure it. The ability to remember is not an absolute talent; it depends on the type of performance being called for. Students who express a preference for multiple-choice, essay, or true–false exams already know this.

Conscious recollection of an event or an item of information is called **explicit memory.** It is usually measured using one of two methods. The first method tests for **recall,** the ability to retrieve and reproduce information

■ **explicit memory**
Conscious, intentional recollection of an event or of an item of information.

■ **recall**
The ability to retrieve and reproduce from memory previously encountered material.

Rudolph the Red-Nosed Reindeer had eight reindeer friends. Name as many of them as you can.

■ Figure 9.1 Who Were Rudolph's Friends?

This is a test of recall. After you have done your best to remember all eight names, turn to page 338 for a recognition test on the same information.

encountered earlier. Essay and fill-in-the-blank exams and memory games such as Trivial Pursuit or Jeopardy require recall. The second tests for **recognition,** the ability to identify information you have previously observed, read, or heard about. The information is given to you, and all you have to do is say whether it is old or new, or perhaps correct or incorrect, or pick it out of a set of alternatives. The task, in other words, is to compare the information you are given with the information stored in your memory. True–false and multiple-choice tests call for recognition.

As all students know, recognition tests can be difficult (some might say "tricky"), especially when false items closely resemble correct ones. Under most circumstances, however, recall is the greater challenge (see Figure 9.1). This difference was once demonstrated in a study of people's memories of their high school classmates (Bahrick, Bahrick, & Wittlinger, 1975). The subjects, ages 17 to 74, first wrote down the names of as many classmates as they could remember. Recall was poor; most recent graduates could write only a few dozen names, and those out of school for 40 years or more recalled an average of only 19. Even when prompted with yearbook pictures, the youngest participants failed to name almost 30 percent of their classmates and the oldest ones failed to name over 80 percent. Recognition, however, was far better. The task was to look at ten cards, each containing five photographs, and say which picture on each card was that of a former classmate. Recent graduates were right 90 percent of the time, but so were people who had graduated 35 years earlier! Even those out of high school for *more than 40 years* could identify three-fourths of their classmates, and the ability to recognize names was nearly as impressive.

Sometimes, information is retained and affects our thoughts and actions even when there is no conscious or intentional remembering, a phenomenon known as **implicit memory** (Graf & Schacter, 1985; Schacter, 1987). To get at this subtle sort of knowledge, researchers must rely on indirect methods. One common method, **priming,** asks you to read or listen to some information and then tests you later to see whether the information is "activated" on another type of task. For example, you might read a list of words, then later try to complete word stems (such as DEF-) with the first word that comes to mind (such as *define* or *defend*). Even when recognition or recall for the original list is poor, people who see the original list are more likely than control subjects to complete the word fragments with words from the list. The fact that the original words "prime" (make more available) certain responses on the word-completion task shows that people can retain more implicit knowledge about the past than they realize. They know more than they know they know (Richardson-Klavehn & Bjork, 1988; Roediger, 1990).

How many of your high school classmates can you recall by name? Would you do better at recognizing their pictures or names?

■ **recognition**
The ability to identify previously encountered material.

■ **implicit memory**
Unconscious retention in memory, as evidenced by the effect of a previous experience or previously encountered information on current thoughts or actions.

■ **priming**
A method for measuring implicit memory in which a person reads or listens to information and is later tested to see whether the information is "activated" on another type of task.

Rudolph the Red-Nosed Reindeer had eight reindeer friends. From the following list, see whether you can identify their correct names:

Blitzen
Cupid
Kumquat
Bouncer
Dander
Dasher
Donder
Blintzes
Dancer
Prancer
Flasher
Trixie
Masher
Comet
Pixie
Vixen

If you took the recall test in Figure 9.1 (page 337), now try this recognition item. Which test was easier?

▪ **relearning method**
A method for measuring retention that compares the time required to relearn material with the time used in the initial learning of the material.

▪ **encoding**
The conversion of information into a form that can be stored in and retrieved from memory.

▪ **cognitive schema**
An integrated network of knowledge, beliefs, and expectations concerning a particular topic.

For example, to demonstrate the elusive effects of priming, researchers played a taped list of word pairs (such as *ocean–water*) while surgical patients were apparently unconscious. After their operations, the patients could not recall the word pairs, but when they were given the first word from each pair and asked to say any word that popped into mind, they were somewhat more likely than they would otherwise have been to respond with the associated words they had "heard" during surgery (Kihlstrom et al., 1990). Equally fascinating research has been done with patients who, because of damage to the brain, cannot identify familiar faces. In one study, two patients shown photographs of familiar and unfamiliar people could not consciously identify the faces of people they knew. Yet electrical conductance of the skin (a measure of autonomic nervous system arousal) changed while they were looking at the familiar faces, indicating that some sort of implicit, nonconscious recognition must have been taking place (Tranel & Damasio, 1985).

Yet another method of measuring memory, the **relearning method** (also called the *savings method*) seems to straddle the boundary between implicit and explicit memory tests. Devised by Hermann Ebbinghaus (1885/1913) over a century ago, the relearning method requires you to relearn information or a task that you learned earlier. If you fail to recall or recognize some or all of the material yet master it more quickly the second time around, you must be remembering something from the first experience. One eminent memory researcher whom we consulted said that he considers the relearning method to be a test of explicit memory. Another, however, maintained that it can sometimes function as a test of implicit memory, if the learner is unaware that the material being relearned was ever learned earlier.

▪ MODELS OF MEMORY

Although people usually refer to memory as if it were a single faculty, as in "I must be losing my memory" or "He has a memory like an elephant's," the term *memory* actually covers a complex collection of abilities, processes, and mental systems. If tape recorders or videocameras aren't accurate metaphors for capturing these diverse components of memory, then what metaphor would be better?

As we saw in Chapter 8, many cognitive psychologists liken the mind to an information processor, along the lines of a computer. Psychologists in this tradition have constructed *information-processing models* of memory, often borrowing liberally from the language of computer programming: Instead of stimuli, there are "inputs"; instead of responses, there are "outputs"; and between the inputs and outputs, information is actively processed in a series of "subroutines."

According to information-processing theories, remembering begins with **encoding,** the conversion of information to a form that the brain can process and store. Our memories are not an exact replica of experience. Sensory information is changed in form almost as soon as it is detected, and the form retained for the long run is different from that of the original stimulus. One reason is that whenever we are exposed to new information, we integrate it with what we already know or believe, by incorporating it into an existing web of knowledge called a **cognitive schema** (see Chapter 8). Often such schemas are useful because they help us make sense of separate pieces of information and thus remember them better. Many educators say that one reason American students frequently find history difficult is that they are asked to memorize dates, facts, and events that seem to have no connection with one another. Having an overall schema of the story of American history, and of the major issues involved, makes it easier to remember any specific bit of information. However, cognitive schemas can also lead to misremembering, because people often dis-

tort new information in order to make it "fit" their existing schemas. And if the new information doesn't fit, they may ignore it or forget it—a popular way of reducing cognitive dissonance.

Even when we don't distort, we simplify. For example, when you hear a lecture, you may hang on every word, but you do not store those words verbatim. Instead, you convert sentences to units of meaning, possibly in the form of *propositions* (Anderson & Bower, 1973). Propositions, as we saw in Chapter 8, are similar to sentences, but they express unitary ideas and are made up of abstract concepts rather than words. Thus the sentence, "The clever psychologist made an amazing discovery" contains three propositions that can be expressed by the words *the psychologist was clever, the psychologist made a discovery,* and *the discovery was amazing.* A man who emigrated from Germany at a young age and forgot all his German would still remember facts learned in the first grade because such information is stored as propositions, not as strings of German (or English) words.

As we saw in the previous chapter, most psychologists believe that information is also stored in the form of auditory or visual images—melodies, sounds, and "mental pictures." Visual images are often particularly memorable. In one study, Roger Shepard (1967) had students look at 612 colored slides. Then he paired those pictures with new ones, and the students had to select the ones they had previously seen. Immediately after seeing the original slides, the students identified 96.7 percent of them, and four months later, they still recognized more than 50 percent. Subsequent research showed that even if the original set of slides contained 2,560 different photographs, recognition remained high (Haber, 1970).

Other forms of encoding are also possible. For example, memories for specific motor skills, such as those involved in swimming or riding a bicycle, may be encoded and stored as sets of kinesthetic (muscular) instructions. Memories for motor skills are extremely long-lasting. If you learned to swim as a child, you will still know how to swim at age 30, even if you haven't been in a pool or lake for years.

With some kinds of information, encoding takes place automatically; you don't have to make a deliberate effort. Think about where you usually sit in your psychology class. When were you last there? You can probably provide this information easily, even though you never made a deliberate effort to encode it. In general, people automatically encode their location in space and time and the frequency with which they experience various situations (Hasher & Zacks, 1984). But other kinds of information require *effortful* encoding. To retain such information, you might have to label it, associate it with other material, or rehearse it until it is familiar. A friend of ours tells us that in her ballet class, she knows exactly what to do when asked to perform a *pas de bourrée,* yet she often has trouble recalling the term itself. Because she rarely uses it, she probably has not bothered to encode it well.

The photo fragments on the left suggest the fragmented way in which most students learn history: as a series of disconnected, meaningless facts. Little wonder that students find history boring and tend to forget most of what they learn. According to one recent report, two-thirds of American 17-year-olds cannot identify the century in which the Civil War was fought (Loewen, 1995). Psychological research suggests a solution: helping students build cognitive schemas by teaching them the major themes of history—the passionate issues, conflicts, and dramas—so that the facts cohere and make sense, as suggested by the photo on the right.

The motor skills we learn in our early years often last a lifetime.

Unfortunately, people sometimes count on automatic encoding when effortful encoding is needed. For example, when students study, they may wrongly assume that they can encode the material in a textbook as effortlessly as they encode where they usually sit in the classroom. Or they may assume that the ability to remember and perform well on tests is innate and that effort won't make any difference (Devolder & Pressley, 1989). As a result, they wind up in trouble at test time. Experienced students know that most of the information in a college course requires effortful encoding.

After encoding takes place, the next steps are *storage,* the maintenance of the material over time, and *retrieval,* the recovery of stored material (or what a computer programmer might call the "accessing" of information). In most information-processing theories, these processes involve three separate, interacting systems: *sensory memory,* which retains incoming sensory information for a second or two, until it can be processed further; *short-term memory* (STM), which holds a limited amount of information for a brief period of time, perhaps up to 30 seconds or so, unless a conscious effort is made to keep it there longer; and *long-term memory* (LTM), which accounts for longer storage—from a few minutes to decades. This model, which is sometimes informally called the "three-box model," has dominated research on memory for three decades. According to two of its leading proponents, Richard Atkinson and Richard Shiffrin (1968, 1971), information can pass from sensory memory to short-term memory and in either direction between short-term and long-term memory (see Figure 9.2).

The three-box model, however, does not explain all the findings on memory, and competing information-processing models also exist. Advocates of these models disagree regarding how information passes from one kind of memory system to another and how information gets encoded and stored in each system. Some question the very notion of distinct memory systems. They argue that there is just one system, with different mental processes called on for different tasks.

Further, although many psychologists agree with Philip Johnson-Laird (1988) that "the computer is the last metaphor for the mind," others are doubting the usefulness of the computer metaphor. They argue that the human brain does not operate like your average computer. Most computers process instructions sequentially and work on a single stream of data, so information-processing models of memory have also represented mental processing as sequential.

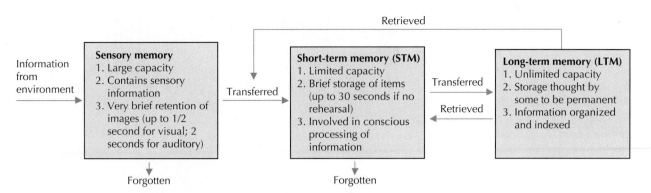

Retrieved

Sensory memory	Short-term memory (STM)	Long-term memory (LTM)

Information from environment

Sensory memory
1. Large capacity
2. Contains sensory information
3. Very brief retention of images (up to 1/2 second for visual; 2 seconds for auditory)

Transferred

Short-term memory (STM)
1. Limited capacity
2. Brief storage of items (up to 30 seconds if no rehearsal)
3. Involved in conscious processing of information

Transferred

Retrieved

Long-term memory (LTM)
1. Unlimited capacity
2. Storage thought by some to be permanent
3. Information organized and indexed

Forgotten

Forgotten

■ **Figure 9.2 Three Memory Systems**

Most memory models distinguish three separate but interacting memory systems, as shown in this diagram (although some models would draw the arrows a bit differently). When information does not transfer from sensory memory to short-term memory, or from short-term memory to long-term memory, it is assumed to be forgotten. Once in long-term memory, information can be retrieved for use in analyzing incoming sensory information or for temporary mental operations performed in short-term memory.

The human brain, however, performs many operations simultaneously—that is, in parallel. It recognizes patterns all at once rather than as a sequence of information bits. It monitors bodily functions, perceives the environment, produces speech, and searches memory all at the same time. It can do this because millions of neurons are active at once, and each neuron communicates with thousands of others, which in turn communicate with millions more. Although no single neuron is terribly smart or terribly fast, millions of them working simultaneously produce the complexities of cognition.

Some cognitive scientists, therefore, have rejected the traditional information-processing approach in favor of a **parallel distributed processing (PDP)** or *connectionist* model (Bechtel & Abrahamsen, 1990; Rumelhart, McClelland, & the PDP Research Group, 1986). In PDP models, knowledge is represented not as propositions or images but as connections among thousands and thousands of interacting processing units, distributed in a vast network and all operating in parallel—just like the neurons of the brain. As new information enters the system, the ability of these units to excite or inhibit each other is constantly adjusted to reflect new knowledge.

Although the details of PDP theory are beyond the scope of this book, we want to point out that it reverses the notion that the human brain can be modeled after a computer. PDP theorists say that for computers to be truly intelligent, they must be modeled after the human brain. Indeed, computer scientists are now designing machines called *neural networks* that attempt to imitate the brain's vast grid of densely connected neurons (Anderson & Rosenfeld, 1988; Levine, 1990). In these machines, thousands of simple processing units are linked up to one another in a weblike system, interacting with each other and operating in parallel. On the software side, researchers in the interdisciplinary field of *artificial intelligence* have been writing programs that simulate the way PDP theorists believe the human mind works. Like human beings, these programs do not always find the best solution to a problem, but they do tend to find a good solution quickly. They also have the potential to learn from experience by adjusting the strengths of their "neural" connections in response to new information.

It is too soon to say whether the connectionist approach will be an improvement on the more traditional information-processing models. Both approaches

■ **parallel distributed processing (PDP)**
An alternative to the information-processing model of memory, in which knowledge is represented not as propositions or images but as connections among thousands of interacting processing units, distributed in a vast network and all operating in parallel.

This cheerful piece of machinery informed visitors to the Boston Museum of Science, "Humans, you are witnessing the beginning of a great new era." Yet robots, and the computers that serve as their "brains," cannot contemplate the meaning of death, paint a great work of art, or know that it's time to prune the roses simply by looking at them. Unlike the human brain, most computers operate sequentially on information stored in memory, whereas human brains make multiple connections all at once.

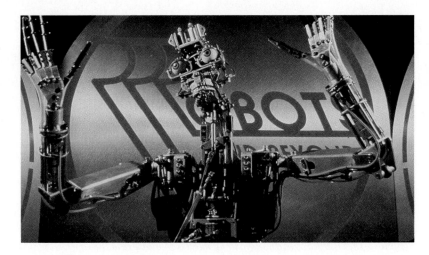

can explain many findings about memory, but neither one can explain all the findings. PDP models have the virtue of resembling the brain's actual wiring, and they are applicable not just to memory but also to perception, language, and decision making. But traditional information-processing models do a better job, at least for now, at explaining memory for a single event (Schacter, 1990). They are also better at explaining why well-learned information is sometimes forgotten when new information is learned (McCloskey & Cohen, 1989; Ratcliff, 1990).

In this chapter, we have decided to retain the three-box model with its three separate memory systems—sensory, short-term, and long-term—because it offers a convenient way to organize the major findings on memory and because it fits certain biological facts about memory (to be described later). But keep in mind that the model is only a metaphor, one that might someday find itself as outdated as the metaphor of memory as a camera.

Quick QUIZ

How well have you encoded what you just learned?

1. When making up multiple-choice tests, Joyce's physics teacher tends to make "c" the correct answer more often than other choices. Joyce does not consciously realize this is true, yet after taking several exams, she tends to choose "c" most often when she has to guess. Joyce's behavior may be influenced by an _____ memory of "c" having been most often correct on past tests.
2. The three basic memory processes are _____, storage, and _____.
3. Do the preceding two questions ask for recall, recognition, or relearning? (And what about *this* question?)
4. One objection to traditional information-processing theories of memory is that unlike most computers, which process information _____, the brain performs many independent operations _____.

Answers:

1. implicit 2. encoding, retrieval 3. The first two questions both measure recall; the third question measures recognition. 4. sequentially; simultaneously or in parallel

■ THE THREE-BOX MODEL

The fact that most information-processing theories refer to three interacting systems of memory does not mean that there are actually three separate places in the brain corresponding to the three memory storehouses. Talking about memory systems as places is merely a convenience. The three systems are actually clusters of mental processes that occur at different stages.

Fleeting Impressions: Sensory Memory

In the three-box model, all incoming sensory information must make a brief stop in **sensory memory,** the entryway of memory. Sensory memory includes a number of separate memory subsystems, or **sensory registers**—as many as there are senses. Information in sensory memory is short-lived. Visual images, or *icons,* remain for a maximum of half a second in a visual register. Auditory images, or *echoes,* remain for a slightly longer time, by most estimates up to two seconds or so, in an auditory register.

Sensory memory acts as a holding bin, retaining information just until we can select items for attention from the stream of stimuli bombarding our senses. *Pattern recognition,* the preliminary identification of a stimulus on the basis of information already contained in long-term memory, occurs during the transfer of information from sensory memory to short-term memory. Information that does not go on to short-term memory vanishes forever, like a message written in disappearing ink.

Images in sensory memory are fairly complete. How do we know that? In a clever experiment, George Sperling (1960) briefly showed people visual arrays of letters that looked like this:

X   K   C   Q

N   D   X   G

T   F   R   J

In previous studies, subjects had been able to recall only four or five letters, no matter how many they initially saw. Yet many people insisted that they had actually seen more items. Some of the letters, they said, seemed to slip away before they could be reported. To overcome this problem, Sperling devised a method of "partial report." He had people report the first row of letters when they heard a high tone, the middle row when they heard a medium tone, and the third row when they heard a low tone:

X K C Q	←———	High tone
N D X G	←———	Medium tone
T F R J	←———	Low tone

If the tone occurred right after they saw the array, people could recall about three letters from a row. Because they did not know beforehand which row they would have to report, they therefore must have had most of the letters in sensory memory right after viewing them. However, if the tone occurred after a delay of even one second, people remembered very little of what they had seen. The letters had slipped away.

In normal processing, too, sensory memory needs to clear quickly to prevent sensory "double exposures." It also acts as a filter, keeping out extraneous and unimportant information. Our brains process billions of bits of information during our lifetimes. Storing everything detected by our senses, including irrelevancies, would lead to inefficiency and confusion.

If you swing a flashlight rapidly in a circle, you see an unbroken circle of light instead of a series of separate points because the successive images remain briefly in sensory memory.

■ **sensory memory**
A memory system that momentarily preserves extremely accurate images of sensory information.

■ **sensory registers**
Subsystems of sensory memory; most memory models assume a separate register for each sensory modality.

If the sensory register did not clear quickly, multiple images might interfere with the accurate perception and encoding of information.

Memory's Work Area: Short-term Memory

Like sensory memory, **short-term memory (STM)** retains information only temporarily—for up to about 30 seconds by most estimates, although some researchers think the maximum interval may extend to a few minutes. In short-term memory, the material is no longer an exact sensory image but is an encoding of one, such as a word or a number. This material either transfers into long-term memory or decays and is lost forever. There are, however, ways to keep material in short-term memory beyond the usual limits, as we will see.

Certain cases of brain injury demonstrate the importance of transferring new information from short-term memory into long-term memory. H. M.'s case is again instructive. H. M., you will recall, can store information on a short-term basis; he can hold a conversation and appears normal when you first meet him. He also retains implicit memories. However, for the most part, H. M. cannot retain information about new facts and events for longer than a few minutes. Although he can learn some motor and perceptual skills, he cannot recall having learned them. H. M.'s problem is not in retaining information in long-term memory after it gets there; he, and other patients like him, can learn new visual information if they have extra time to study it, and then forgetting follows a normal course (McKee & Squire, 1992). Therefore, H. M.'s terrible memory deficits seem to involve a problem in transferring explicit memories from short-term storage into long-term storage in the first place.

Besides retaining new information for brief periods, short-term memory also holds information that has been retrieved from long-term memory for temporary use. For this reason, short-term memory is often called *working memory*. When you do an arithmetic problem, working memory contains the numbers and the instructions for doing the necessary operations ("Add the right-hand column, carry the 2"), plus the intermediate results from each step. The ability to bring information from long-term memory into working memory is not disrupted in patients such as H. M. They can do arithmetic, converse, relate events that occurred before their injury, and do anything else that requires retrieval of information from long-term into short-term memory.

People such as H. M. fall at the extreme end on a continuum of forgetfulness, but even those of us with normal memories know from personal experience how frustratingly brief short-term retention can be. We look up a tele-

■ **short-term memory (STM)**
In the three-box model of memory, a limited capacity memory system involved in the retention of information for brief periods; it is also used to hold information retrieved from long-term memory for temporary use.

phone number, dial it, get a busy signal, and then find after only a moment that the number has vanished from our minds. We meet someone at a party, and two minutes later, we find ourselves groping unsuccessfully for her name. Is it any wonder that short-term memory has been called a "leaky bucket"?

According to most memory models, if the bucket did not leak, it would quickly overflow, because at any given moment, short-term memory can hold only so many items. Years ago, George Miller (1956) estimated its capacity to be "the magical number 7 plus or minus 2." Five-number zip codes and seven-number telephone numbers fall conveniently in this range; 15-number credit card numbers do not. More recently, some researchers have questioned whether Miller's magical number is so magical after all. Estimates of STM's capacity have ranged from 2 items to 20, with most of the estimates at the lower end. Some psychologists believe it is not STM per se that is limited, but the processing capacity available to the entire memory system at any one time. Everyone agrees, however, that the number of items that short-term memory can handle at any one time is quite small.

If this is so, then how do we remember the beginning of a spoken sentence until the speaker reaches the end? After all, most sentences are longer than just a few words. According to most memory models, we overcome this problem by grouping small bits of information into larger units, or **chunks.** The real capacity of STM, it turns out, is not a few bits of information but a few chunks. A chunk may be a word, a phrase, a sentence, or even a visual image, and it depends on previous experience. For most of us, the acronym *FBI* is one chunk, not three, and the date *1492* is one chunk, not four. In contrast, the number *9214* is four chunks and *IBF* is three—unless your address is 9214 or your initials are IBF. To take another, more visual example: If you are not familiar with football and look at a field full of players, you probably won't be able to remember their positions when you look away. But if you are a fan of the game, you may see a single chunk of information—say, a wishbone formation—and be able to retain it.

Even chunking, however, cannot keep short-term memory from eventually filling up. Fortunately, much of the information we encounter during the day is needed for only a few moments. If you are multiplying two numbers, you need to remember them only until you have the answer. If you are talking to someone, you need to keep their words in mind only until you have understood them. But some information is needed for longer periods and must be transferred to long-term memory. Items that are particularly meaningful, have an emotional impact, or link up to something already in long-term memory may enter long-term storage easily, with only a brief stay in STM. The destiny of

■ **chunk**
A meaningful unit of information; it may be composed of smaller units.

Chunking increases the amount of information that can be held in short-term memory. If you don't play chess, the pieces on a chess board will look randomly placed and you won't be able to recall their positions when you look away. But experienced chess players, in the middle of a game, can remember the position of every piece after glancing only briefly at the board. They chunk the pieces into a few standard configurations, instead of trying to memorize where each piece is located.

other items depends on how soon new information displaces them in short-term memory. Material in short-term memory is easily displaced, unless we do something to keep it there—as we will discuss shortly.

Final Destination: Long-term Memory

The third box in the information-processing model of memory is the largest: **long-term memory (LTM).** The capacity of long-term memory seems to have no practical limits. The vast amount of information stored there enables us to learn, get around in the environment, and build a sense of identity and a personal history.

Organization in Long-term Memory.

Because long-term memory contains so much information, we cannot search through it exhaustively, as we can through short-term memory. According to most models of memory, the information must be organized and indexed, just as items in a library are, so we can find it. One way to index words (or the concepts they represent) is by the *semantic categories* to which they belong. *Chair,* for example, belongs to the category *furniture.* In a classic study, people had to memorize 60 words that came from four semantic categories: animals, vegetables, names, and professions. The words were presented in random order, but when people were allowed to recall the items in any order they wished, they tended to recall them in clusters corresponding to the four categories (Bousfield, 1953). This finding has since been replicated many times.

Evidence on the storage of information by semantic category also comes from case studies of people with brain damage. In one study, a patient called M. D. appeared to have made a complete recovery two years after suffering several strokes, with one odd exception: He had trouble remembering the names of fruits and vegetables (Hart, Berndt, & Caramazza, 1985). M. D. could easily name a picture of an abacus or a sphinx but not a picture of an orange or a peach. He could sort pictures of animals, vehicles, and other objects into their appropriate categories, but did poorly with pictures of fruits and vegetables. On the other hand, when M. D. was *given* the names of fruits and vegetables, he immediately pointed to the corresponding pictures. Apparently, he still had information about fruits and vegetables, but his brain lesion prevented him from using their names to get to the information when he needed it, unless the names were provided by someone else. This evidence supports the idea that information about a particular concept (such as *peach*) is linked in some way to information about the concept's semantic category (such as *fruit*).

Many models of long-term memory represent its contents as a vast network or grid of interrelated concepts (Collins & Loftus, 1975) and propositions (Anderson, 1983, 1990). A small part of a conceptual grid for *animals* might look something like the one in Figure 9.3. Network models assume that semantic networks are a universal way of organizing information. The way people use these networks, however, depends on experience and education. For example, cross-cultural studies of rural children in Liberia and Guatemala have shown that the more schooling children have, the more likely they are to use semantic categories in recalling lists of objects (Cole & Cole, 1993). This makes sense, because in school, children must memorize a lot of information in a short time, and semantic grouping can help. Unschooled children, having less need to memorize lists, do not cluster items and do not remember them as well. But this does not mean that unschooled children have poor memories. When the task is meaningful to them—say, recalling objects that were in a story or a village scene—they remember extremely well (Mistry & Rogoff, 1994; Rogoff & Mistry, 1985).

■ **long-term memory (LTM)**
In the three-box model of memory, the memory system involved in the long-term storage of information; theoretically, it has an unlimited capacity.

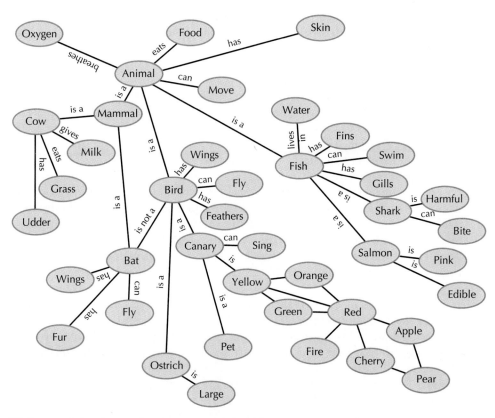

■ Figure 9.3   Part of a Conceptual Grid in Long-term Memory

In many models of memory, the contents of long-term semantic memory are represented as an immense network or grid of concepts and the relationships among them. This illustration shows a part of a hypothetical grid for animals.

We organize information in long-term memory not only by semantic groupings but also in terms of the way words sound or look. Have you ever tried to recall some word that was on the "tip of your tongue"? Nearly everyone experiences such *tip-of-the-tongue states,* especially when trying to recall the names of acquaintances or famous persons, the names of objects and places, or the titles of movies or books (Burke et al., 1991). One way to study this frustrating experience is to have people record tip-of-the-tongue episodes in daily diaries. Another is to give people the definitions of uncommon words and ask them to

Although there are certain basic ways of organizing long-term memories, culture affects how we encode, store, and retrieve information. Navaho healers, who use stylized, symbolic sand paintings in their rituals, must be able to commit to memory dozens of intricate visual designs. No permanent, exact copies are made, and after each ceremony the painting is destroyed.

supply the words themselves. When a word is on the tip of the tongue, people tend to come up with words that are similar in meaning to the right word before they finally recall it. For example, for "patronage bestowed on a relative, in business or politics" a person might say "favoritism" rather than the correct response, "nepotism." But verbal information in long-term memory also seems to be indexed by sound and form, and it is retrievable on that basis. Thus, incorrect guesses often have the correct number of syllables, the correct stress pattern, the correct first letter, or the correct prefix or suffix (A. Brown, 1991; R. Brown & McNeill, 1966). For the target word *sampan,* for example, a person might say "Siam" or "sarong."

Researchers are currently studying other ways in which we organize information in long-term memory, such as by its personal relevance, familiarity, or association with other information. The method a person uses in any given instance probably depends on the nature of the memory; you would probably store information about the major cities of Europe differently from information about your first date. To understand the organization of long-term memory, then, we must know what kinds of information can be stored there.

The Contents of Long-term Memory.   Most theories of LTM distinguish skills or habits ("knowing how") from abstract or representational knowledge ("knowing that"). **Procedural memories** are memories of knowing how—for example, knowing how to comb your hair, use a pencil, or swim. **Declarative memories** are memories of "knowing that," and they are usually assumed to be explicit. Declarative memories, in turn, come in two varieties, semantic memories and episodic memories (Tulving, 1985). **Semantic memories** are internal representations of the world, independent of any particular context. They include facts, rules, and concepts—items of general knowledge. On the basis of

■ **procedural memories**
Memories for the performance of actions or skills ("knowing how").

■ **declarative memories**
Memories of facts, rules, concepts, and events ("knowing that"); they include semantic and episodic memories.

■ **semantic memories**
Memories of general knowledge, including facts, rules, concepts, and propositions.

■ **Figure 9.4   Memories Are Made of This**

According to a widely accepted way of classifying memories, long-term memory contains procedural memories ("knowing how") and declarative memories ("knowing that"). Declarative memories, in turn, consist of semantic memories (general knowledge), and episodic memories (personal recollections). You might draw on procedural memories to ride a bike, semantic memories to identify a bird, and episodic memories to recall your graduation or wedding. Can you come up with some other examples for each type of memory?

your semantic memory of the concept *cat*, you can describe a cat as a small, furry mammal that typically spends its time eating, sleeping, prowling, and staring into space, even though a cat may not be present when you give this description and you probably won't know how or when you first learned it. **Episodic memories,** on the other hand, are internal representations of personally experienced events. When you remember how your cat once surprised you in the middle of the night by pouncing on your face as you slept, you are retrieving an episodic memory. Figure 9.4 summarizes these distinctions.

From Short-term to Long-term Memory: A Riddle.

The three-box model of memory has often been invoked to explain an interesting phenomenon called the **serial-position effect.** If you are shown a list of items and then immediately asked to recall them, your retention of any particular item will depend on its position in the list (Glanzer & Cunitz, 1966). Recall will be best for items at the beginning of the list (the **primacy effect**) and at the end of the list (the **recency effect**). When retention of all the items is plotted, the result will be a U-shaped curve, as shown in Figure 9.5. A similar serial position effect occurs when you are introduced to a roomful of people and find you can recall the names of the first few people and the last, but almost no one in the middle.

According to the three-box model, the first few items on a list are remembered well because they have the best chance of getting into long-term memory. Because short-term memory was relatively "empty" when they entered, there was little competition among these items to make it into long-term memory. They were verbally processed, so they remain memorable. The last few items are remembered for a different reason: At the time of recall, they are still sitting in short-term memory and can simply be "dumped." The items in the middle of a list, however, are not so well retained because by the time they get into short-term memory it is already crowded. As a result, many of these items drop out of short-term memory before they can be verbally processed and stored in long-term memory.

This explanation makes sense except for two things. First, under certain conditions, the last items on a list are well remembered even when the test is delayed past the time when short-term memory has presumably been "emptied" and filled with other information (Greene, 1986). In other words, the recency effect occurs even when, according to the three-box model, it should not. Second, serial-position curves occur in rats that have to remember a series of places in a maze (Kesner et al., 1984), so the primacy and recency effects can't be due to human verbal-processing strategies alone. Whatever is producing these effects, researchers are not yet sure what it is—another puzzle of memory.

■ **episodic memories**
Memories for personally experienced events and the contexts in which they occurred.

■ **serial-position effect**
The tendency for recall of the first and last items on a list to surpass recall of items in the middle of the list.

■ **primacy effect**
The tendency for items at the beginning of a list to be well recalled.

■ **recency effect**
The tendency for items at the end of a list to be well recalled.

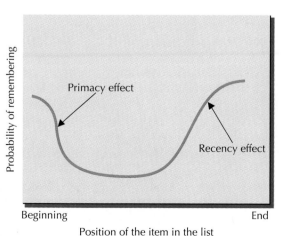

■ **Figure 9.5 The Serial-Position Effect**

When people try to recall a list of similar items immediately after learning it, they tend to remember the first and last items on the list best and the ones in the middle worst.

Quick QUIZ

Find out whether the findings discussed so far have transferred from your short-term memory to your long-term memory.

1. _____ memory holds images for a fraction of a second.
2. For most people, the abbreviation *U.S.A.* consists of _____ informational "chunk(s)."
3. Suppose you must memorize a long list of words that includes the following: *desk, pig, gold, dog, chair, silver, table, rooster, bed, copper,* and *horse.* You can recall the words in any order you wish. How are you likely to group these words in recall? Why?
4. When you roller-skate, are you relying on procedural, semantic, or episodic memory? How about when you recall the months of the year, or when you remember falling off your roller skates on an icy January day?
5. If a child is trying to memorize the alphabet, which sequence should present the greatest difficulty: *abcdefg, klmnopq,* or *tuvwxyz*? Why?

Answers:

1. sensory 2. one 3. *Desk, chair, table,* and *bed* would probably form one cluster; *pig, dog, rooster,* and *horse* a second; and *gold, silver,* and *copper* a third. Concepts tend to be organized in long-term memory in terms of semantic categories, such as *furniture, animals,* and *metals.* 4. procedural; semantic; episodic 5. *klmnopq,* because of the serial-position effect

■ HOW TO REMEMBER

Once we understand how memory works, we can use that understanding to remember better. One important technique for keeping information in short-term memory and increasing the chances of long-term retention is *rehearsal,* the review or practice of material. When people are prevented from rehearsing, the

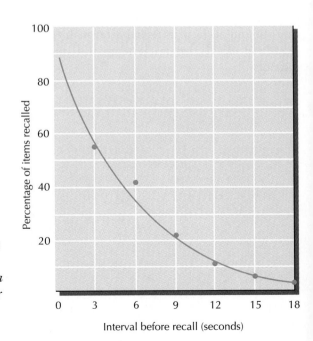

■ Figure 9.6   Retention in Short-term Memory: Going, Going, Gone

In a study that showed the importance of rehearsal, people heard a set of items consisting of three consonants, read aloud. After various intervals of time, they tried to recall the items. During each interval, a distracting task kept the subjects from rehearsing the items. The longer the interval, the poorer the recall; after only 18 seconds, recall fell to almost zero (Peterson & Peterson, 1959).

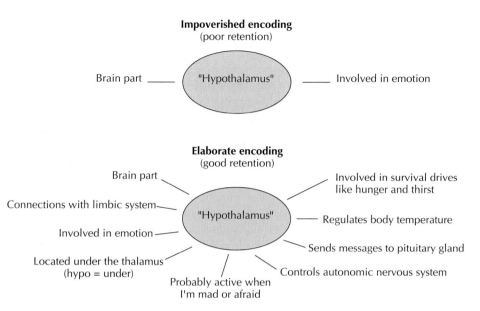

Figure 9.7 Elaboration of Encoding

In elaborated encoding, one encodes the features of an item and its associations with other items. When you studied the hypothalamus in Chapter 4, was your encoding elaborated or impoverished?

contents of their short-term memories quickly fade. In an early study of this phenomenon, people had to memorize meaningless groups of letters. Immediately afterward, they had to start counting backward by threes from an arbitrary number; this counting prevented them from rehearsing the letter groups. Within only 18 seconds, the subjects forgot most of the items (see Figure 9.6). But when they did not have to count backward, their performance was much better, probably because they were rehearsing the items to themselves (Peterson & Peterson, 1959). Similarly, if you repeat a telephone number over and over, you will be able to retain it in short-term memory for as long as you like; but if you look up a number and then get into a conversation with someone, you are apt to forget the number almost immediately.

A dramatic and poignant demonstration of the power of rehearsal once occurred during a research session with H. M. (Ogden & Corkin, 1991). The experimenter gave H. M. five digits to repeat and remember, but then she was unexpectedly called away. When she returned after more than an hour, H. M. was able to repeat the five digits correctly. He had been rehearsing them the entire time!

Short-term memory holds many kinds of information, including visual information and abstract meanings. In fact, some theorists believe that there are several STMs, each specializing in a particular type of information. But most people, or at least most hearing people, seem to favor speech for rehearsing the contents of short-term memory. The speech may be spoken aloud or spoken to oneself. When people make errors on short-term memory tests that use letters or words, they often confuse items that sound alike, such as *b* and *t*, or *bear* and *bare*. These errors suggest that they have been rehearsing verbally.

Some strategies for rehearsing are more effective than others. **Maintenance rehearsal** merely involves the rote repetition of the material. This kind of rehearsal is fine for maintaining information in STM, but it will not always lead to long-term retention. A better strategy if you want to remember for the long haul is **elaborative rehearsal,** also called *elaboration of encoding* (Cermak & Craik, 1979; Craik & Tulving, 1975). Elaboration involves associating new items of information with items that have already been stored or with other new items. It can also involve analyzing the physical, sensory, or semantic features of an item (see Figure 9.7).

Suppose that you are studying the concept of reinforcement in Chapter 7. Simply rehearsing the definition in a rote manner is unlikely to transfer the information you need from short-term to long-term memory. Instead, when

■ **maintenance rehearsal**
Rote repetition of material in order to maintain its availability in memory.

■ **elaborative rehearsal**
Association of new information with already stored knowledge and analysis of the new information to make it memorable.

going over (rehearsing) the concept, you could encode the information that a reinforcer follows a response, strengthens the response, and is similar to a reward. You might also note that the word *reinforcer* starts with the same letter as *reward*. And you might think up some examples of reinforcement and of how you have used it in your own life and could use it in the future. The more you elaborate the concept of reinforcement, the better you will remember it.

A related strategy for prolonging retention is **deep processing,** or the processing of meaning. If you merely process the physical or sensory features of a stimulus, such as how the word *reinforcement* is spelled and how it sounds, your processing will be shallow even if it is elaborated. If you recognize patterns and assign labels to objects or events ("Reinforcement is an operant procedure"), your processing will be somewhat deeper. If you fully analyze the meaning of what you are trying to remember, your processing will be deeper yet. Sometimes, shallow processing is useful; when you memorize a poem, for instance, you will want to pay attention to (and elaborately encode) the sounds of the words and the patterns of rhythm in the poem, and not just the poem's meaning. Usually, however, deep processing is more effective than shallow processing for remembering information. Unfortunately, students (and other people) often try to remember information that has little or no meaning for them, which explains why the information doesn't stick.

In addition to using elaborate rehearsal and deep processing, people who want to give their powers of memory a boost sometimes rely on **mnemonics** [neh-MON-iks], formal strategies and tricks for encoding, storing, and retaining information. (Mnemosyne—neh-MOZ-eh-nee—was the ancient Greek goddess of memory. Can you remember her?) Some mnemonics take the form of easily memorized rhymes ("Thirty days hath September / April, June, and

▪ **deep processing**
In the encoding of information, the processing of meaning rather than simply the physical or sensory features of a stimulus.

▪ **mnemonics**
Strategies and tricks for improving memory, such as the use of a verse or a formula.

Arthur Benjamin, a "lightning calculator," can compute the square of 85,211 in his head in only 90 seconds (the answer is 7,260,914,521). And it takes him only a second or so to square a three-digit number. In this photo, taken some years ago, he is racing a calculator and a desktop computer. Although Benjamin is clearly exceptional, the psychologists who studied him found that he relied on some simple memory tricks available to anyone. For example, he performed his calculations from left to right, saying the first three digits of the answer aloud in order to clear his working memory; and he organized intermediate results in such a way that the most recently memorized numbers were the first ones he needed. If ordinary people practice enough and learn to use mnemonics that make memory retrieval more efficient, they can often equal the performance of those with exceptional memories (Ericsson & Chase, 1982).

November ... "). Others use formulas (for example, "Every **g**ood **b**oy **d**oes **f**ine" for remembering which notes are on the lines of the treble clef in musical notation). Still others use visual images or word associations, which increase retention.

The best mnemonics force you to encode material actively and thoroughly. They may also reduce the amount of information by "chunking" it (as in the phone number 466-3293, which corresponds to the letters in GOOD-BYE—appropriate, perhaps, for a travel agency). Or they may make the material meaningful and thus easier to store and retrieve; facts and words to be memorized are often more memorable, for example, if they are woven into a coherent story (Bower & Clark, 1969). If you needed to remember the parts of the digestive system for a physiology course, you could construct a narrative about what happens to a piece of food after it enters a person's mouth, then repeat the narrative out loud to yourself or to a study partner.

Some stage performers with apparently amazing memories rely on more complicated mnemonics. We are not going to spend time on them here because for ordinary memory tasks such tricks are often no more effective than rote rehearsal, and they are sometimes actually worse (Wang & Thomas, 1992; Wang, Thomas, & Ouellette, 1992). In one survey of memory researchers, most said they did not use such mnemonics themselves (Park, Smith, & Cavanaugh, 1990). After all, why bother to memorize a grocery list using a fancy mnemonic when you can write down what you need to buy? The fastest route to a good memory is to follow the principles suggested by the findings in this section and by other research on memory (see "Taking Psychology with You").

"YOU SIMPLY ASSOCIATE EACH NUMBER WITH A WORD, SUCH AS 'TABLE' AND 3,476,029."

Very Quick Quiz

Camille is furious with her history professor. "I read the chapter three times, but I still failed the quiz," she fumes. "The quiz must have been unfair." What's wrong with Camille's reasoning, and what are some other possible explanations for her poor performance, based on what you have learned so far in this chapter?

Answers:

Camille is reasoning emotionally and is not examining the assumptions underlying her explanations. Perhaps she relied on automatic rather than effortful encoding, used maintenance instead of elaborative rehearsal, and used shallow instead of deep processing when she studied. She may also have tried to encode everything, instead of encoding selectively.

■ THE BIOLOGY OF MEMORY

So far, we have been discussing memory solely in terms of information processing. Psychologists would also like to know what happens in the brain while all that processing is going on. More specifically, they would like the answers to three questions: (1) What changes occur in neurons and synapses (the small gaps between neurons) when we store information about an event or a task? (2) Where in the brain do these changes occur? (3) How might hormones and other substances regulate or improve memory? In work on these issues, researchers draw on many of the concepts already covered in this chapter and in Chapter 4. (It might help you to encode the following information if you review Chapter 4 first.)

Changes in Neurons and Synapses

Nearly all scientists agree that memory involves chemical and structural changes at the level of neurons. But why do some memories last only a few seconds or minutes, whereas others persist for years or even a lifetime? Why, when a blow on the head or an electroconvulsive shock disrupts brain activity, do people often lose information stored during the past few minutes but not information stored weeks or years ago?

One answer is that *short-term memory and long-term memory involve different kinds of brain changes.* Short-term retention does not seem to involve permanent structural changes. Instead, temporary changes occur within neurons that alter their ability to release neurotransmitters, the chemicals that carry messages from one cell to another. Evidence comes from studies with the lowly sea snail, *Aplysia* (Kandel & Schwartz, 1982), and other organisms that have small numbers of easily identifiable neurons. These primitive animals can be taught simple conditioned responses, such as withdrawing or not withdrawing a part of their bodies in response to a light touch. When retention is only for the short term, a neuron's readiness to release neurotransmitter molecules temporarily increases or decreases, depending on the kind of response being learned.

In contrast, long-term memory seems to involve permanent structural changes in the brain. Thus, when rats learn new motor skills and retain them over time, they show more dendritic growth and more synaptic connections in the cerebellum, the roundish structure at the back of the brain, than do rats who have merely exercised, or rats that have been inactive "couch potatoes" (Black et al., 1990).

To mimic what they think may happen during the formation of a long-term memory, researchers apply brief, high-frequency electrical stimulation to groups of neurons in the brains of animals. In various brain areas, especially the hippocampus, this stimulation leads to a long-lasting increase in the strength of synaptic responsiveness known as **long-term potentiation** (McNaughton & Morris, 1987; Teyler & DiScenna, 1987). That is, certain synaptic pathways become more excitable. Long-term potentiation seems to occur as a result of two events: (1) an increase in the release of the neurotransmitter glutamate from transmitting neurons, and (2) a complex sequence of chemical reactions in receiving neurons that increases or alters ion channels in glutamate receptors, making the neurons more receptive to stimulation (Bliss & Collingridge, 1993). One result is that the tiny spines (projections) that cover the dendrites of the receiving neuron change shape, becoming rounder. This change in turn causes decreased electrical resistance and an increase in the responsiveness of the receiving neuron to the next signal that comes along. It is a little like what would happen if you increased the diameter of a funnel's neck to permit more flow through the funnel.

Other related changes also occur in long-term potentiation and, presumably, the formation of long-term memories. For example, dendrites branch out, and certain types of synapses increase in number (Greenough, 1984). At the same time, in a less well understood process called *long-term depression,* some cells become *less* responsive (Bolshakov & Siegelbaum, 1994). These changes all take time, which may explain why long-term memories remain vulnerable to disruption for a while after they are stored. Just as concrete takes time to set, memories require a period of **consolidation,** or stabilization, before they solidify. This process appears to be a gradual rather than an all-or-nothing process. If an animal gets electroconvulsive shock within the first hour after learning a task, it will forget what it has learned, which indicates that little if any consolidation has occurred. If the shock is delivered several hours or a few days after learning, the memory will be unaffected, which implies that consolidation has taken place by then. But *repeated* sessions of shock will again disrupt the memory, showing that the process is not yet complete (Squire, 1987). Consolidation can continue in animals for weeks and in human beings for several years.

■ **long-term potentiation**
A long-lasting increase in the strength of synaptic responsiveness, thought to be a biological mechanism of long-term memory.

■ **consolidation**
The process by which a long-term memory becomes durable and stable.

Keep in mind that the brain changes we have described are correlational. That is, they accompany the retention of learning, but no one can be absolutely certain that they actually reflect the storage of information. One way to find out might be to look at what happens in the brain after an animal's memory for some task (say, running a maze) begins to dim (Squire, 1987). Do the physical changes disappear, too? Future research will tell.

Locating Memories

We have been describing changes in neurons, but which neurons are they? Most scientists believe that the neural changes associated with specific memories are *localized,* confined to specific areas. However, some theorists argue that any given memory is *distributed* across large areas of the brain. As we saw in Chapter 4, these two views can be reconciled by recognizing that the typical "memory" is actually a complex cluster of information. When you recall meeting a man yesterday, you remember his greeting, his tone of voice, how he looked, and where he was. These different pieces of information may be processed separately and stored at different sites distributed across wide areas of the brain, with all these sites participating in the representation of the event as a whole. If this is so, then memories are both "localized" and "distributed" (Squire, 1986).

Researchers have discovered that particular brain structures seem to be responsible for the formation of certain *types* of memories (see Figure 9.8). In general, the formation of declarative memories (memory for facts and events, or "knowing that") involves different structures and pathways than does the formation of procedural memories (memory for skills and habits, or "knowing how"). Declarative memories, you will recall, are those you draw on when identifying a flower or recalling a vacation trip. Procedural memories are the kind you draw on to ride a bike, solve a jigsaw puzzle, or slam your foot on the brake.

The formation of long-term declarative memories involves the hippocampus and adjacent parts of the temporal lobe cortex (Squire & Zola-Morgan, 1991). The hippocampus is especially important: Damage that is limited to this structure results in amnesia for facts and events (Press, Amaral, & Squire, 1989). Procedural memories, however, seem to involve other brain areas. For example, the amygdala appears to be involved in the formation of conditioned fears and may also help link up memories formed in different senses. And in work

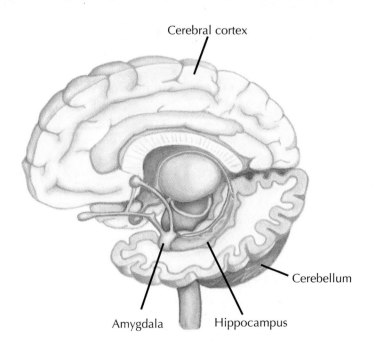

Cerebral cortex

Cerebellum

Amygdala   Hippocampus

■ **Figure 9.8   Brain Areas Critical for Memory**

The regions shown are particularly important in the formation or storage of memories.

with rabbits, Richard Thompson (1983, 1986) has shown that one kind of procedural memory, a simple, classically conditioned response to an unpleasant stimulus, is associated with specific changes in the cerebellum. After Thompson conditioned rabbits to blink in response to a tone, he discovered predictable changes in electrical activity in certain parts of the cerebellum. If he removed or destroyed the affected brain tissue, the animals immediately forgot the response and could not relearn it. In another study, Thompson and his colleagues used a drug to temporarily deaden either a specific part of the cerebellum or a specific part of the midbrain. In both cases, the rabbits failed to blink during training. When the drug wore off, the rabbits in the second group blinked away when the tone sounded, but the rabbits whose cerebellums had been drugged showed no sign of having learned the response (Krupa, Thompson, & Thompson, 1993).

But be careful: In the case of declarative memories, at least, we are talking about brain circuits involved in the *formation* and perhaps the temporary storage of memories, and *not* necessarily areas where the permanent changes required for long-term retention occur. Research with animals suggests that the role of the hippocampus is temporary, and that the ultimate destinations of declarative memories are in parts of the cerebral cortex. More specifically, long-term storage may take place in the same cortical areas that were involved in the original perception of the information (Mishkin & Appenzeller, 1987). The role of the hippocampus may be to somehow "bind together" the diverse aspects of a memory at the time it is formed, so that even though those aspects are stored in distinct cortical sites, the memory can be retrieved as one coherent entity (Squire & Zola-Morgan, 1991).

The formation of declarative and procedural memories in different brain areas could explain a curious finding about H. M. Despite his inability to form

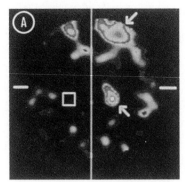 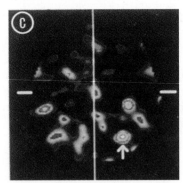

Explicit Memory   Implicit Memory

▪ **Figure 9.9   Brain Activity in Explicit and Implicit Memory**

These PET scans show average changes in blood flow for several subjects as they performed different kinds of memory tasks (Squire et al., 1992). In scan A, yellow and red represent increased blood flow, but the same colors represent decreased blood flow in scan C. Scan A shows that when people recalled words from a list—a test of explicit memory—neural activity increased in the right part of the hippocampus (lower arrow) and the right prefrontal cortex (upper arrow). (The right hemisphere may have been more active than the left because the task emphasized the visual form of the words rather than their sound or meaning.) In contrast, scan C shows that when people read the list and later just said the first words that came to mind in response to word stems—a test of implicit memory—there was a far smaller increase in activity in the hippocampus. In addition, activity in the right part of the visual cortex decreased (see arrow), presumably because seeing the initial list reduced the visual processing necessary for the word stems. Taken together, these findings support the view that different areas of the brain are involved in explicit and implicit memory tasks.

new declarative memories, H. M. can, with sufficient practice, acquire new procedural memories—cognitive, perceptual, and motor skills, such as solving a puzzle, reading mirror-reversed words, or playing tennis. Other patients with similar brain damage have shown the same pattern of memory loss, as have monkeys with lesions in the hippocampus (Mishkin & Appenzeller, 1987). Apparently, the parts of the brain involved in procedural memory have remained intact.

Patients such as H. M. not only retain procedural memories, but they also retain some implicit memory for verbal material. For example, if H. M. sees the word *define* on a list and later has to complete the stem "DEF" with the first word that comes to mind, he is more likely to say *define* than some other word, just as people with normal memories are (Keane, Gabrieli, & Corkin, 1987). Some psychologists conclude that there must be separate systems in the brain for implicit and explicit tasks (Sherry & Schacter, 1987; Tulving & Schacter, 1990). As Figure 9.9 shows, this view has been bolstered by PET scans, which reveal differences in the location of brain activity when normal subjects perform explicit versus implicit memory tasks (Squire et al., 1992).

Hormones and Memory

Have you ever smelled fresh cookies and recalled a tender scene from your childhood? Do you have a vivid memory of the first time you fell in love? In his classic novel *Remembrance of Things Past,* Marcel Proust evoked powerful emotional memories of tastes, sensations, and feelings. For the rest of us, too, emotional memories are often especially vivid and intense. The explanation may reside in our hormones.

Hormones appear to affect memory by regulating, or modulating, the storage of information. For example, hormones released by the adrenal glands during stress, including epinephrine (adrenaline) and certain steroids, appear to enhance memory (McGaugh, 1990). They do so, however, only at low or moderate levels. If you administer epinephrine to animals right after learning, their memory improves, but if the dosages are too high, memory suffers. Assuming that these findings apply also to human beings, they suggest that a moderate level of arousal is best when you are learning, just as it is best when you need to concentrate. If you want to remember information well, you should probably aim for an arousal level somewhere between "hyper" and "laid back."

How can hormones affect the remembrance of things past? One idea is that epinephrine affects the release of norepinephrine in the amygdala, which in turn sends out messages to other brain areas involved in memory storage (McGaugh, 1990). Another possibility involves, of all things, sugar. Paul Gold (1987) notes that epinephrine causes the level of glucose (a sugar) to rise in the bloodstream. Although epinephrine does not seem to enter the brain from the bloodstream readily, glucose does. Once in the brain, glucose may enhance memory either directly or by altering the effects of neurotransmitters. This "sweet memories" effect occurs both in aged rats and mice and in elderly human beings. In one fascinating study, healthy older people fasted overnight, drank a glass of lemonade sweetened with either glucose or saccharin, and then took two memory tests. The saccharine-laced drink had no effect on their performance, but drinking lemonade with glucose greatly boosted their ability to recall a taped passage 5 or 40 minutes after hearing it and their long- term ability to recall words from a list (Manning, Hall, & Gold, 1990). A similar study found that glucose enhanced the ability of Alzheimer's patients to recognize words, prose passages, and faces (Manning, Ragozzino, & Gold, 1993).

The apparent ability of hormones to regulate memory fits well with the view of many scientists that moderate emotional arousal is an essential ingredient in learning and memory. Arousal may signal the brain that an event or piece of information is important enough to store and may ensure that a person or ani-

Which of these students will remember best? Keep in mind that a moderate degree of emotional arousal enhances memory. One explanation may be biological: Retention seems to be best when hormones associated with arousal reach an optimal level.

mal will pay attention to what is happening. But the exact mechanisms remain unclear and controversial.

In this area, as in others in the biology of memory, we still have much to learn. Each new finding nudges the neuroscientist's dream of describing behavior in physical terms a bit closer to reality, but biological findings can be as slippery as any others. Technical obstacles often make it hard to get reliable results, and a finding with one animal or procedure may not apply to others. New discoveries are being made at a tremendous rate, but many of these findings are provisional, and as yet, there is no comprehensive biological model of memory. We do not yet know how the brain actually stores information, how distributed circuits link up with one another, or how a student is able to locate and retrieve information at the drop of a multiple-choice item. And, as we will see next, there is as much to be learned about why we forget as about why we remember.

Quick QUIZ

Find out whether your brain has recorded what you just read.

1. Is long-term potentiation associated with (a) increased responsiveness of a receiving neuron to a transmitting neuron, (b) a decrease in receptors on a receiving neuron, or (c) reaching your true potential?
2. The cerebellum has been associated with _____ memories; the hippocampus has been associated with _____ memories.
3. True or false: Hormone research suggests that if you want to remember well, you should be as relaxed as possible while learning.
4. After reading the findings on glucose and memory, should you immediately start gulping down lemonade? Why or why not?

Answers:

outweigh the benefits.
frequent glucose consumption may have adverse health consequences that would
elderly, there is an optimal dose (Parsons & Gold, 1992). Also, in some people,
do generalize, you would need to know how much glucose is effective; in the
younger people with normal memories (although they might). Even if the results
which older people tend to show deficits, will not necessarily generalize to
sugar yet. Results from elderly people, using certain measures of memory on
1. a **2.** procedural, declarative **3.** false **4.** You probably shouldn't pig out on

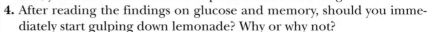

NEVER FORGETS   SOMETIMES FORGETS   ALWAYS FORGETS

■ WHY WE FORGET

Have you ever, in the heat of some deliriously happy moment, said to your-self, "I'll never forget this, never, *never*, NEVER"? Do you find you can more clearly remember saying those words than the deliriously happy moment itself? Sometimes you encode an event, you rehearse it, you analyze its meaning, you tuck it away in long-term storage—and still, you forget it. As we suggest in "Think About It," not all forgetting is bad. Most of us, however, would like to remember better than we do.

Over a century ago, in an effort to measure pure memory loss independent of personal experience, Hermann Ebbinghaus (1885/1913) memorized long lists of nonsense syllables, such as *bok, waf,* or *ged,* and then tested his retention over a period of several weeks. He reported that most forgetting occurred soon after the initial learning and then tapered off (see Figure 9.10). Ebbinghaus's method of studying memory was adopted by generations of psychologists, even though it didn't tell them much about the kinds of memories that people care about most.

A hundred years later, Marigold Linton decided to find out how people for-get real-life personal events, not nonsense syllables. Like Ebbinghaus, she used herself as a subject, but she charted the curve of forgetting over years rather than days. Every day for 12 years, she recorded on a 4- × 6-inch card two or more things that had happened to her that day. Eventually, she accumulated a catalogue of thousands of discrete events, both trivial ("I have dinner at the Canton Kitchen: delicious lobster dish") and significant ("I land at Orly Airport in Paris"). Once a month, she took a random sampling of all the cards accumu-lated to that point, noted whether she could remember the events on them,

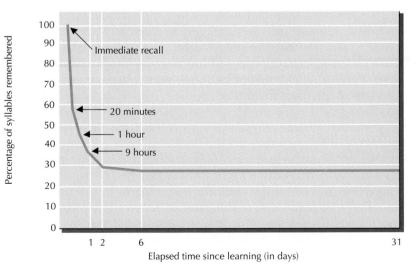

■ Figure 9.10 Ebbinghaus's Forgetting Curve

When Hermann Ebbinghaus tested his own retention of a list of nonsense syllables, memory loss was rapid soon after initial learning and then tapered off.

The Benefits of Forgetting

▪ Who has not wished, at some time or other, for a "photographic memory"? It's bad enough that we forget so much that we have worked diligently to learn in school. How can we formulate a realistic assessment of ourselves if our recollection of the past is inaccurate and incomplete?

Yet a perfect memory is not the blessing that one might suppose. The Russian psychologist Alexander Luria (1968) once told of a journalist, S., who could remember giant grids of numbers and long lists of words, and could reproduce them both forward and backward, even after the passage of 15 years. S. also remembered the exact circumstances under which he had originally learned the material. He used memory tricks to accomplish his astonishing feats, many involving the formation of visual images. But you shouldn't envy him, for he had a serious problem: He could not forget even when he wanted to. Images he had formed in order to remember kept creeping into consciousness, distracting him and interfering with his ability to concentrate. At times, he even had trouble holding a conversation because the other person's words would set off a jumble of associations. In fact, Luria called him "rather dull-witted." Eventually, unable to work at his profession, S. took to supporting himself by traveling from place to place as a per-

former, demonstrating his mnemonic abilities for audiences.

Perhaps you still think a perfect memory would be a terrific thing to have. Imagine, then, for a moment, what it would be like to remember *everything*. Each time you recalled the past, along with the diamonds of experience you would dredge up the pebbles. Remembering might take hours instead of seconds. The clutter in your mind might grow beyond your ability to organize it efficiently. With a perfect memory, you might also remember things better off forgotten. Would you really want to recall every angry argument, every embarrassing episode, every painful moment of your life? How would total recall affect your relationships with relatives and friends? Could it be that the success of a close relationship depends on a certain amount of forgiving forgetfulness? Could it be that self-confidence and optimism are possible only if we lock some grievances in a back drawer of memory, and stop ruminating on them?

Like remembering, a certain degree of forgetting contributes to our survival and our sanity. Where is the line between adaptive forgetting and disruptive forgetting? If you had the choice, what would you recollect with greater clarity, and what would you allow to fade? Think about it. ▪

and tried to date the events. Reporting on the results from the first 6 years of her study, Linton (1978) told how she had expected the kind of rapid forgetting reported by Ebbinghaus. Instead, as you can see in Figure 9.11, she found that long-term forgetting was slower and proceeded at a much more constant pace, as details gradually dropped out of her memories.

Of course, some personal memories never lose their distinctiveness. Events that mark important transitions (marriage, getting a first job) are more memorable than others. But why did Marigold Linton, like the rest of us, forget so many details? Psychologists have proposed five mechanisms to account for forgetting: decay; "erasure" of old memories by new ones; interference; motivated forgetting; and cue-dependent forgetting.

The Decay Theory. One commonsense view, the **decay theory,** holds that memory traces fade with time if they are not "called up" now and then. We have already seen that decay occurs in sensory memory and that it seems to occur in short-term memory as well, if we don't rehearse the material. However, the mere passage of time does not account so well for forgetting in long-term memory. People commonly forget something that happened only yesterday while remembering events from many years ago. Indeed, some knowledge is still accessible decades after learning. One study found that people could remember their

▪ **decay theory** *(of forgetting)*
The theory that information in memory eventually disappears if it is not reactivated; it appears to apply more to short-term than to long-term memory.

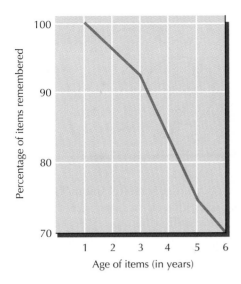

■ Figure 9.11 A Forgetting Curve for Personal Events

When Marigold Linton tested her own memory for personal events over a period of several years, she obtained a forgetting curve quite different from that of Ebbinghaus (see Figure 9.10). Her memory loss was minimal at first, but then retention fell off at a gradual but steady rate.

high-school Spanish up to 50 years later, although most had hardly used Spanish at all in the intervening years (Bahrick, 1984). Why didn't it decay?

New Memories for Old. Another explanation holds that new information can completely wipe out old information, just as rerecording on an audiotape or videotape will obliterate the original material. In one study supporting this view, described earlier on page 333, Elizabeth Loftus and her colleagues (1978) used a leading question to mislead people into thinking they had seen either a stop sign or a yield sign while viewing slides of a traffic accident. Other people were not misled in this way and identified accurately the sign they had actually seen. Later, all the subjects were told the purpose of the study and were asked to guess whether they had been misled. Almost all of those who were misled continued to insist that they had *really, truly* seen the sign whose existence had been "planted" in their minds by the leading question (Loftus, Miller, & Burns, 1978). Their original perception appears to have been "erased" by the misleading information.

Interference. A third explanation holds that forgetting occurs because similar items of information interfere with each other in either storage or retrieval; the information is in memory, but it becomes confused with other information (see Figure 9.12 on the next page). This type of forgetting, which occurs in both short- and long-term memory, is especially common when you have to recall isolated facts.

Suppose you are at a party and you meet someone named Julie. A half-hour later, you meet someone named Judy. You go on to talk to other people, and after an hour, you again bump into Julie, but by mistake, you call her Judy. The second name has interfered with the first. This type of interference, in which new information interferes with the ability to remember old information, is called **retroactive.** Retroactive interference is often illustrated by a story about an absent-minded professor of ichthyology (the study of fish) who complained that whenever he learned the name of a new student, he forgot the name of a fish.

Because new information is constantly entering memory, we are all vulnerable to the effects of retroactive interference. At least most of us are. H. M.'s memories of childhood and adolescence are unusually detailed and clear, and they rarely change. H. M. can remember actors and singers famous in his childhood, the films they were in, and who their costars were. He knows the names

■ retroactive interference
Forgetting that occurs when recently learned material interferes with the ability to remember similar material stored previously.

■ **Figure 9.12 Interference in Memory**

Retroactive interference occurs when new information interferes with memory for previously stored material. Proactive interference occurs when previously stored material interferes with memory for new information.

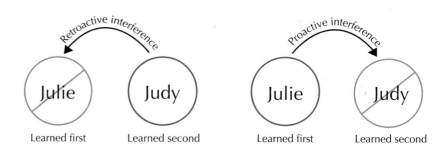

Learned first   Learned second   Learned first   Learned second

of friends from the second grade. Presumably, these declarative memories from early in life have not been subject to interference from memories acquired since the operation—because there have been no new memories!

Interference also works in the opposite direction. Old information (such as the Spanish you learned in high school) may interfere with the ability to remember new information (such as the French you're trying to learn now). This type of interference is called **proactive.** Over a period of weeks, months, and years, proactive interference may cause more forgetting than retroactive interference does, because we have stored up so much information that can potentially interfere with anything new. Fortunately, we can also use our old information to elaboratively encode new information and thus improve our ability to remember.

Motivated Forgetting. Sigmund Freud believed that people forget because they block from consciousness those memories that are too threatening or painful to live with, and he called this self-protective process *repression* (see Chapter 12). Today, many psychologists prefer a more general term, **motivated forgetting,** and they argue that there are many reasons why a person might be motivated to forget certain events, including embarrassment, guilt, shock, and a desire to protect one's pride. Motivated forgetting could explain some cases of **retrograde amnesia,** in which people can remember historical incidents and form new memories, but forget friends, relatives, or painful experiences from the past.

The concepts of repression and motivated forgetting are based mostly on clinical reports of people in psychotherapy who appear to recall long-buried

■ **proactive interference**
Forgetting that occurs when previously stored material interferes with the ability to remember similar, more recently learned material.

■ **motivated forgetting**
Forgetting because of a desire to eliminate awareness of painful, embarrassing, or otherwise unpleasant experiences.

■ **retrograde amnesia**
Loss of the ability to remember events or experiences that occurred before some particular point in time.

How common is it to repress traumatic memories and then recover them later? Memory researchers point out that people like this prisoner of war, who have been humiliated, mistreated, and tortured, might be expected to repress their memories of these horrible events; yet typically their problem is not forgetting what happened but remembering all too well. Some clinical researchers, in response, argue that adults may have different ways of coping with trauma than children do.

memories, typically of traumatic events in childhood. These people's stories, although compelling, are often difficult to verify, and they have rarely been corroborated by objective evidence. Because of what psychologists have learned about memory, claims of "repressed" memories of early trauma raise unsettling issues. How are we to know when a "memory" is being accurately retrieved or reconstructed? Should the validity of memories that are recovered in therapy be accepted in a court of law? To what extent are memories of events contaminated by what a person has heard from others since the event occurred, or by other traumatic experiences? In "Psychology and Popular Culture," we discuss the bitter debate over repressed memories of childhood sexual abuse.

Cue-dependent Forgetting. Often, when we need to remember, we rely on *retrieval cues,* items of information that can help us find the specific information we're looking for. When we lack such cues, we may feel as if we have lost the call number for an entry in the mind's library. This type of memory failure, which psychologists call **cue-dependent forgetting,** may be the most common type of all. Willem Wagenaar (1986), who, like Marigold Linton, recorded daily events in his life, found that within a year, he had forgotten 20 percent of the critical details, and after five years, he had forgotten 60 percent. However, when he gathered cues from witnesses about ten events that he thought he had forgotten, he was able to recall something about all ten, which suggests that some of his forgetting was cue dependent.

Cognitive psychologists think that retrieval cues may work by getting us into the general area of memory where an item is stored, or by making a match with information that is linked in memory with the item in question. Thus, if you are trying to remember the last name of an actor, knowing the person's first name or the name of a recent movie the actor starred in might help. Cues that were present at the time you learned a new fact or had a certain experience are apt to be especially useful as retrieval aids. That may explain why remembering is often easier when you are in the same physical environment as you were when an event occurred: Cues in the present context match those from the past. Many people have suggested that the overlap between present and past cues may also lead to a *false* sense of having been in exactly the same situation before; this is the eerie phenomenon of *déjà vu* (which means "already seen" in French). Ordinarily, however, contextual cues help us remember the past more accurately.

Even imagining the features of a past situation may aid in the recall of an experience that occurred in that situation. Because of this finding, many police departments have altered the way they interview witnesses to a crime. The old way was to question the witness in an effort to get a step-by-step account: "Then what did he do? And then what happened after that?" The new way is to encourage witnesses to reconstruct the circumstances of the crime and to recall *without interruption* everything they can about what they saw, even details that seem unimportant. Such "cognitive interview" strategies increase the number of available retrieval cues and produce better recall than standard "and-then-what-did-he-do" techniques (Geiselman, 1988).

Your mental or physical state may also act as a retrieval cue, evoking a **state-dependent memory.** For example, if you are drunk when something happens, you may remember it better when you are once again drunk than when you are sober. (This is not an endorsement of drunkenness! Your memory will be best if you are sober during both encoding and recall.) Likewise, if your emotional arousal is especially high or low at the time of an event, you may remember that event best when you are once again in the same emotional state. When victims of violent crimes have trouble recalling details of the experience, it may be in

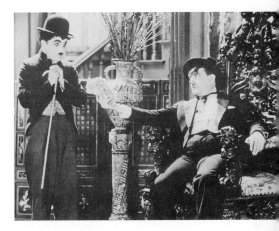

Charlie Chaplin's great film City Lights provides a classic illustration of state-dependent memory. After Charlie saves the life of a drunken millionaire, the two spend the rest of the evening in boisterous merrymaking. The next day, however, after sobering up, the millionaire fails to recognize Charlie and gives him the cold shoulder. Then, once again, the millionaire gets drunk—and once again he greets Charlie as a pal.

■ **cue-dependent forgetting**
The inability to retrieve information stored in memory due to a lack of sufficient cues for recall.

■ **state-dependent memory**
The tendency to remember something when one is in the same physical or mental state as during the original learning or experience.

Psychology and Popular Culture

The Debate over Repressed Memories of Sexual Abuse

■ For more than a decade, the emotionally charged subject of incest has captured public attention. During the late 1970s and 1980s, incest victims and social scientists began writing about the disturbing prevalence of the sexual abuse of children, which had previously been thought to be extremely rare (Armstrong, 1978/1987; Rush, 1980). Psychotherapists, educators, and members of the legal system began to take this issue seriously.

By the late 1980s, however, a new phenomenon emerged. Many therapists and pop-psych writers, in best-sellers such as *The Courage to Heal* and *Secret Survivors,* contended that incest is not just more common than once thought, it is epidemic. One therapist said that incest is "so common that I'll tell you that within 10 minutes, I can spot it as a person walks in the door, often before they even realize it" (quoted in Dawes, 1994). To support such claims, these therapists argued that traumatic events are almost always repressed, and that if a person cannot actually remember the abuse, that's all the more evidence that it happened. Whereas previous books on incest had been about experiences the victim could *not* forget, now survivors asserted that they had pushed their memories from consciousness, sometimes for decades, until they entered psychotherapy. In one typical case, a woman sued her father for hundreds of thousands of dollars, claiming that he had sexually abused her from the age of 6 months until she was 18 years old, but that she had completely repressed the memories until therapy helped her recover them (Loftus, 1993a, 1993b).

Among psychologists as well as among the public, a controversy has raged about whether such "recovered" memories can be trusted and whether such belated accusations should be believed. As with the issue of children's testimony, much is at stake: finding justice and safety for people who have been abused, while also protecting adults from false charges that can destroy their lives

(Banks & Pezdek, 1994; Schooler, 1994). It's no wonder that emotions run high on this matter.

On one side of the issue (let's call it the *recovered-memory school*), many therapists believe that virtually all memories recovered in therapy should be accepted as true (Harvey & Herman, 1994; Terr, 1994). In their view, false memories occur but are rare compared to the many valid ones. Advocates of this position fear that people who raise doubts about recovered memories are betraying children and supporting adult molesters. On the other side (let's call it the *false-memory school*), many research psychologists argue that false memories of abuse are being manufactured by naïve, poorly trained, or unscrupulous therapists, and are supported by a mood of sexual hysteria and feelings of victimization in the culture at large. These researchers know that many cases of abuse occur, but they also fear that there is a rising tide of spurious accusations (Loftus, 1993a, 1993b; McHugh, 1993a).

There are researchers on the recovered-memory side, and psychiatrists and clinical psychologists on the false-memory side, but in general mental-health practitioners are overrepresented in the first group and research psychologists in the second. The polarization between the two schools results in part from their respective assumptions about scientific research and clinical evidence. Here are just a few:

• *Memory and repression.* In the clinical view, forgetting occurs because of repression: the person intentionally, if unconsciously, blots out a traumatic event; but later, if the anxiety about the event is removed, an accurate memory of the traumatic event will return. Many clinicians believe, as Freud did, that repression explains why we can't remember anything from the first two or three years of life. They insist that it is common for patients to show total or partial amnesia for abusive experiences, and that artificial laboratory studies are irrelevant because they do not deal

part because they are far less emotionally aroused than they were at the time of the crime (Clark, Milberg, & Erber, 1987).

Some researchers have proposed that retrieval of a memory is also more likely when a person's *mood* is the same as it was when the memory was first encoded and stored, presumably because mood serves as a retrieval cue. Findings on this notion, however, have been frustratingly inconsistent (Bower &

with real-life traumas (Harvey & Herman, 1994; Terr, 1994; Wylie, 1993).

But research on memory, as we have seen in this chapter, disputes the belief that memories can be stored in a pristine state of "repression," uncontaminated for years. The evidence indicates that all memories, including traumatic ones, are subject to the normal processes of decay, influence, and distortion (Loftus & Coan, in press). Cognitive researchers agree that people can and do forget details of traumatic experiences, but they doubt that people forget the fact that they experienced the trauma *at all;* no one forgets that they were in a concentration camp or a war. Moreover, as we discuss in this chapter (on pages 366–367), forgetting events from the first few years of life is a *normal* result of physiological and cognitive immaturity (Howe, Courage, & Peterson, 1994).

- *The accuracy of hypnotic recall.* Increasing numbers of therapists are using hypnosis and other suggestive techniques to try to "retrieve" their patients' repressed memories, without knowing much about the limitations of hypnosis (Poole et al., 1995). In Chapter 5, we described a study of 869 family therapists, many of whom were ignorant of the research on hypnosis and memory (Yapko, 1994). Half mistakenly thought that "hypnosis can be used to recover memories from as far back as birth"; a third agreed that "the mind is like a computer, accurately recording events that actually occurred"; one-fourth agreed that "someone feeling certain about a memory means the memory is likely to be correct."

- *The aftermath of abuse.* The recovered-memory school accepts the clinical assumption that childhood sexual abuse inevitably causes long-term trauma and predictable symptoms. As we will see in Chapter 13, empirical research disputes this assumption. Like any other trauma—say, being

orphaned or having alcoholic parents—sexual abuse has many possible long-term outcomes (including *no* symptoms), depending on what else happens to the child and the emotional support the child gets from adults (Kendall-Tackett, Williams, & Finkelhor, 1993).

How, then, should a person evaluate claims of recovered memory? We think the answer lies somewhere between "believe all of them" and "believe none of them," and it depends on the specific evidence in each case. For example, here are some indications that skepticism is warranted and that a person may be having false memories (Schooler, 1994): (1) The person says that, thanks to therapy, he or she now clearly remembers being molested in the first year or two of life. (2) Over time, the memories of abuse become more implausible—for instance, that every member of the family was also a perpetrator, or that the abuse continued day and night for 15 years without ever being remembered and without anyone else in the household noticing. (3) The therapist's diagnosis of sexual abuse was made quickly, based on problems a client could have for many other reasons, such as depression, low self-esteem, or an eating disorder. (4) The therapist used hypnosis or pseudoscientific techniques such as guided imagery to "help" a patient recall unremembered abuse.

In contrast to these indications of possible false memories, is it possible to find corroborating evidence from school or medical records or the recollections of other family members? Did the person show signs of trauma when the abuse originally occurred, such as nightmares and disturbed behavior? In such cases, the person's recollections would be more trustworthy. This issue demands our best efforts to avoid either–or thinking, summon all the rules of critical thinking and empirical evidence, and retain compassion both for abused children and unjustly accused adults. ■

Mayer, 1989). Better support exists for the idea that what really counts is the match between your current mood and the *kind of material being remembered.* This effect seems to occur mainly when people are feeling happy: That is, you are likely to remember happy events or ideas better when you are feeling happy than when you are feeling sad (Mayer et al., 1990; McCormick & Mayer, 1991).

*Q*uick QUIZ

If you haven't repressed what you just read, try these questions.

1. Willard was a fan of Judy Garland in the 1950s and 1960s. Later, he became a fan of Garland's daughter, singer/actress Liza Minnelli. Now Willard often mistakenly refers to Ms. Minnelli as "Judy." Why doesn't he remember her name correctly?
2. When a woman at her twentieth high school reunion sees her old friends, she recalls incidents she had thought were long forgotten. Why?

Answers:

1. proactive interference 2. The sight of her friends provides retrieval cues for the incidents.

■ AUTOBIOGRAPHICAL MEMORIES: THE WAY WE WERE

Memory provides each of us with a sense of identity that evolves and changes as we build up a store of episodic memories about events we have experienced firsthand. For most of us, the memories we have of our own lives are by far the most fascinating. We use them as entertainment ("Did I ever tell you about the time . . . ?"); we manipulate them—some people even publish them—in order to create a certain image; we analyze them to learn more about who we are (Ross, 1989).

Childhood Amnesia: The Missing Years

She may be having a great birthday party, but this toddler will be unable to recall it when she grows up. Like the rest of us, she will fall victim to "childhood amnesia."

■ **childhood (infantile) amnesia**

The inability to remember events and experiences that occurred during the first two or three years of life.

One curious aspect of autobiographical memory is that most people cannot recall any events from earlier than the third or fourth year of life. A few people apparently can recall momentous experiences that occurred when they were as young as 2 years old, such as the birth of a sibling, but not earlier (Usher & Neisser, 1993). Of course, we all retain procedural memories from the toddler stage, when we first learned to use a fork, drink from a cup, and pull a wagon. We also retain semantic memories acquired early in life: the rules of counting, the names of people and things, knowledge about all manner of objects in the world. But as adults, we can no longer remember being fed in infancy by our parents, taking our first steps, or uttering our first halting sentences. We are victims of **childhood amnesia** (sometimes called *infantile amnesia*).

People often find childhood amnesia difficult to accept. There is something deeply disturbing about the fact that our early years are beyond recall—so disturbing that some people adamantly deny it, claiming to remember events from the second or even the first year of life. But most psychologists believe these memories are merely reconstructions based on photographs, family stories, and imagination. The "remembered" event may not even have taken place.

Swiss psychologist Jean Piaget (1951) once reported a very early memory of nearly being kidnapped at the age of 2. Piaget remembered sitting in his pram, watching his nurse as she bravely defended him from the kidnapper. He remembered the scratches she received on her face. He remembered a police officer with a short cloak and white baton who finally chased the kidnapper away. There was only one small problem: None of it happened. When Piaget was 15 years old, his nurse wrote to his parents confessing that she had made up the entire story. Piaget noted, "I therefore must have heard, as a child, the account of this story . . . and projected it into the past in the form of a visual memory, which was a memory of a memory, but false."

Some biological researchers believe that childhood amnesia occurs because hippocampal or cortical areas involved in the formation or long-term storage of events are not well developed for some years after birth (McKee & Squire, 1993; Nadel & Zola-Morgan, 1984; Schacter & Moscovitch, 1984). Cognitive scientists emphasize the cognitive reasons behind the amnesia of the first years. In reviewing theories of this phenomenon, Mark Howe and Mary Courage (1993) conclude that "it is the emergence of the cognitive self that is pivotal to the establishment of autobiographical memory." As this hypothesis would predict, age differences in the emergence of self-recognition, not chronological age per se, are related to the age at which autobiographical memories begin (Howe, Courage, & Peterson, 1994).

Other cognitive processes also seem to be involved in childhood amnesia (Usher & Neisser, 1993). As adults, we use very different cognitive schemas from those we use in early childhood, schemas that are not useful for reconstructing early events from the memory fragments we stored at the time (Howe & Courage, 1993). Only after we enter school do we learn to think as adults do, using language to organize our memories and storing not only events but also what we think about them. In addition, as preschoolers, we may encode our experiences far less elaborately than we do as adults because our information-processing abilities are still limited. As a result, we may have few cues for retrieving our early memories later on in life (White & Pillemer, 1979).

Longitudinal research with children suggests still other explanations for the puzzling loss of early memories. It turns out that preschoolers, even toddlers younger than 2, can often remember past events; and four-year-olds can often remember experiences that occurred before age 2½ (Bauer & Dow, 1994; Bauer & Fivush, 1992; Bauer & Hertsgaard, 1993). But preschoolers are still trying to figure out how the world works, and they tend to focus on the routine, familiar aspects of an experience (eating lunch, going to sleep, playing with toys) rather than the distinctive aspects that make the event more memorable in the long run. Also, young children have not yet mastered the social conventions for reporting events; they do not know what is important and interesting to others. Instead, they tend to rely on adults' questions to provide retrieval cues ("Where did we go for breakfast?" "Who did you go trick-or-treating with?"), and this dependency on adults may prevent them from building up a stable core of remembered material that will be available when they are older (Fivush & Hamond, 1991).

Whatever the explanation for childhood amnesia, our first memories may provide some useful insights into our personalities. Some psychologists believe that these memories are not random but instead reflect our basic concerns, ambitions, and attitudes toward life (Kihlstrom & Harackiewicz, 1982). What are your own earliest memories? Do you think the kinds of events and experiences you recall reveal anything important about you? The early psychologist Lloyd Morgan once wrote that an autobiography "is a story of oneself in the past, read in the light of one's present self." That is just what our private memories are.

Memory and Narrative: The Stories of Our Lives

In the first chapter of this book, we noted George Gerbner's observation that our species is unique because we tell stories and live by the stories we tell. This view of human beings as the "storytelling animal" is sweeping cognitive psychology and related fields (Sarbin, 1986). Researchers find that the narratives we compose to make sense of our lives have a profound influence on us: Our plans, memories, love affairs, hatreds, ambitions, and dreams are all guided by plot outlines. "Understanding one's past, interpreting one's actions, evaluating

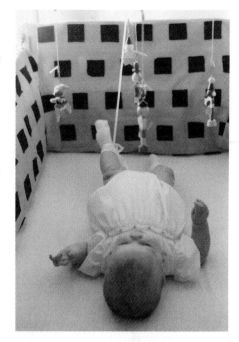

How do you study memory in infants who can't talk? One clever method is to attach a string from the baby's leg to a colorful mobile hanging overhead; every time the baby kicks her leg, the mobile moves. Since babies find this movement deeply fascinating, within a few minutes they will double or triple their kick rates—an example, by the way, of operant learning (Rovee-Collier, 1993). Up to a week later, when tested without the string attached to their feet, 3-month-olds will still kick vigorously, showing that they remember what they learned. But the memory is probably procedural and not episodic; in any case, they will not be able to remember the experience itself when they are older.

What do our memories about our own lives tell us? Do they reveal actual events that occurred—or events that we wish had occurred? Do they tell us what we were like then—or what we are like now?

future possibilities—each is filtered through these stories," writes Mary Gergen (1992). "Events 'make sense' as they are placed in the correct story form."

Thus we say, "I am this way because, as a small child, this happened to me, and then my parents. . . ." We say, "Let me tell you the story of how we fell in love." We say, "When you hear what happened, you'll understand why I felt entitled to take such cold-hearted revenge." These stories are not necessarily *fictions,* as in the child's meaning of "tell me a story." Rather, they are narratives that provide a unifying theme to organize the events of our lives and give them meaning.

But because our life narratives rely heavily on memory, and because memories are constructed and dynamic, constantly shifting in response to present needs and experiences, our stories are also, to some degree, works of interpretation and imagination. Adult memories thus reveal as much about the present as they do about the past. From his own research and that of others, Michael Ross (1989) concludes that even when we appear to remember what we said, did, or believed months or years ago, many of our memories are actually based on our present traits and beliefs, and also on our *implicit theories* about how much certain traits or beliefs can change. The theories are "implicit" because we may never have expressed them to anyone, even ourselves.

For example, Ross finds that most people have an implicit theory that their feelings and attitudes are consistent over time. As a result, whether recalling their past opinions of a dating partner, their past drug use, or their past incomes, they tend to think they have not changed much—even when the evidence shows they have. In one study, 91 percent of people who had recently changed their political affiliation reported that they had *not* changed (Niemi, Katz, & Newman, 1980). Remarkably, if they were currently Republicans, they forgot that they had only recently voted Democratic, and vice versa!

Conversely, when people's implicit theories do predict change, they are likely to forget evidence that they haven't really changed much at all. An implicit theory predicting change, Ross observes, seems to explain why (as we saw in Chapter 5) many women "remember" mood changes associated with their menstrual cycles, even though their own daily diaries fail to confirm their memories. Implicit theories of change also raise a problem in evaluating self-help programs: Because most people have an implicit theory that these programs will change their lives, they tend to remember themselves as having been worse off before the program than they really were (Conway & Ross, 1984).

Human beings are, above all, story-telling animals, and they have many ways to construct, preserve, and relate stories about the past. The Hmong of Laos have created needlework narratives that tell of their long, dangerous flight from their homeland to Thai refugee camps in the early 1970s, at the end of the war in Southeast Asia. The Hmong have also created tapestries that recount the celebrations and daily events of their former villages. (Many artisans make these tapestries for sale abroad and include English inscriptions.) If you had the sewing skills of the Hmong, what kind of tapestry would you create of your own life?

An understanding of the importance of narrative helps us appreciate some features of how autobiographical memory works and why it sometimes fails. As we age, certain periods of our lives stand out; old people remember more from adolescence and early adulthood than from midlife, a phenomenon known as the "reminiscence bump" (Fromholt & Larsen, 1991; MacKavey, Malley, & Stewart, 1991). Perhaps the younger years are especially memorable because they are full of memorable transitions. Or perhaps, as narrative research suggests, people are especially likely to weave events from their youth into a coherent story, and thus remember them better ("After I graduated from college I met the love of my life, who dumped me in the most cruel and heartless fashion, and before I knew it . . . ") (Fitzgerald, 1988).

Yet, as we have seen throughout this chapter, many of the details of our memories, even those we are sure we remember so clearly, probably are added after the event, as we try to tie our own life stories to the broader saga of history (Neisser, 1982). By now, you should not be surprised that memory can be as fickle as it can be accurate. As cognitive psychologists have shown repeatedly, we are not merely actors in our personal life dramas. We also write the scripts.

*T*aking Psychology with You

How to . . . Uh . . . Remember

Someday, drugs may help people with memory deficiencies and increase normal memory performance. For the time being, however, those of us who hope to improve our memories must rely on mental strategies. As we saw in this chapter, some simple mnemonics can be useful, but complicated ones are often more bother than they're worth. A better route to a good memory is to follow some general guidelines based on the principles in this chapter:

- *Pay attention!* It seems obvious, but often we fail to remember because we never encoded the information in the first place. For example, which of these is the real Lincoln penny?

Most people have trouble recognizing the real penny because they have never attended carefully to the details of a penny's design (Nickerson & Adams, 1979). We are not advising you to do so, unless you happen to be a coin collector or a counterfeiting expert. Just keep in mind that when you do have something to remember, you will do better if you encode it well. (The real penny, by the way, is the left one in the bottom row.)

- *Encode information in more than one way.* The more elaborate the encoding of information, the more memorable it will be. Use your imagination! In addition to remembering a telephone number by the sound of the individual digits, you might note the spatial pattern they make as you punch them in on a push-button phone.

- *Add meaning.* The more meaningful material is, the more likely it is to link up with information already in long-term memory. Meaningfulness also reduces the number of chunks of information you have to learn. Thus, if your license plate happens to be 236MPL, you might think of 236 maples.

- *Make up a story.* A narrative can provide a cognitive schema into which separate items of information fit. If you need to remember dates and facts about the civil rights movement in the United States, for example, you can weave them into a story. What were the conditions that provoked civil rights protests and demonstrations? How did the movement get underway, and what events were critical? How did authorities respond to the movement? What part did court rulings play in desegregating schools and public facilities?

• *Use visual imagery.* Memory for pictures is often better than memory for words. You can make up your own mental "pictures" when you have to memorize verbal information. If you are in the import–export business and need to remember the main exports of several different countries, instead of trying to store, say, "Brazil: coffee," you might imagine a map of Brazil with a big coffee mug superimposed on it. Some people find that the odder the image, the better.

• *Take your time.* If you must remember large amounts of verbal material, leisurely learning, spread out over several sessions, will probably produce better results than harried cramming. (*Reviewing* material just before you are tested on it, however, can be helpful because it places the information at the top of your "cognitive deck.") In terms of hours spent, distributed (spaced) learning sessions are more efficient than trying to learn everything in one day. Thus, you may find that you retain information better after three separate one-hour sessions than after one session of three hours.

• *Take time out.* If possible, minimize interference by using study breaks for rest or recreation. Sleep is the ultimate way to reduce interference. In a classic study, students who slept for eight hours after learning lists of nonsense syllables retained them better than students who went about their usual business (Jenkins & Dallenbach, 1924). Sleep is not always possible, of course, but periodic mental relaxation usually is.

• *Overlearn.* You can't remember something you never learned well in the first place. Overlearning—studying information even after you think you know it—is one of the best ways to ensure that you'll remember it.

• *Monitor your learning.* People who remember well tend to score well on tests of *metamemory,* the ability to monitor and be aware of one's own retention. By testing yourself frequently, rehearsing, and reviewing periodically, you will have a better idea of how you are doing. Don't try to evaluate your own learning immediately after reading the material, though; because the information is still in short-term memory, you are likely to feel a false sense of confidence about your ability to recall it later. If you delay making a judgment for at least a few minutes, your evaluation will probably be more accurate (Nelson & Dunlosky, 1991).

Whatever strategies you use, you will find that active learning produces more retention than passive reading or listening. The mind does not gobble up information automatically; you must make the material digestible. Even then, you should not expect to remember everything you read or hear. Nor should you want to. Piling up facts without distinguishing the important from the trivial is just confusing. Books about the workings of memory may help you improve improve recall, but books or courses that promise a "perfect," "photographic," or "instant" memory fly in the face of what psychology knows about the way the mind operates. Our advice: Forget them.

Summary

1. *Memory,* the capacity to retain and retrieve information, confers competence and personal identity. Unlike a tape recorder or videocamera, it is highly selective. The process of remembering is *reconstructive:* People add, delete, and change elements in ways that help them make sense of information and events.

2. People who hold the mistaken belief that all memories are permanently stored with perfect accuracy often cite studies of recall under hypnosis, studies of electrical brain stimulation, and studies of emotionally powerful memories (*flashbulb memories*) that seem permanent. All three lines of evidence however, fail to support such a belief. Under hypnosis, people confabulate, and the same is true in studies of electrical brain stimulation. Even flashbulb memories may be embellished or distorted, and they tend to change over time.

3. The reconstructive nature of memory raises problems in legal cases involving eyewitness testimony. Errors are especially likely when the suspect's race differs from that of the witness and when leading questions are put to witnesses. Findings on memory help clarify the issues in the debate about whether children are capable of making up accounts of sexual abuse. Children, like

adults, are often able to remember the essential factors about an important event with great accuracy. However, like adults, they can also be suggestible, especially when they are very young, are influenced by other children's stories, have a desire to please the interviewer, or are pressured by adults to give a particular account.

4. The ability to remember depends in part on the type of performance being called for. In tests of *explicit memory* (conscious recollection), *recognition* is usually better than *recall*. In tests of *implicit memory*, which is measured by indirect methods such as *priming*, past experiences may affect current thoughts or actions, even when these experiences are not consciously and intentionally remembered.

5. Cognitive psychologists have constructed *information-processing models* of memory, in which memory is viewed as the encoding, storage, and retrieval of information. In these models, sensory information is changed in form almost as soon as it is detected, as a person integrates the information into existing *cognitive schemas* and simplifies it by storing it in the form of propositions, images, or sets of instructions. Some kinds of information require effortful, as opposed to automatic, encoding.

6. The "three-box model" has dominated research on memory for three decades, but it does not explain all the findings on memory, and competing models also exist. Some cognitive scientists have rejected the traditional information-processing approach and computer metaphors for the mind in favor of a *parallel distributed processing (PDP)* or *connectionist* model. In PDP models, knowledge is represented as connections among numerous interacting processing units, distributed in a vast network and all operating in parallel. Computer scientists are now designing machines called *neural networks* that attempt to imitate the brain's grid of densely connected neurons, and researchers in the field of *artificial intelligence* have been writing programs that simulate the way PDP theorists believe the human mind works. Nonetheless, the "three-box model" continues to offer a convenient way to organize the major findings on memory, and it fits the known biological facts about memory.

7. In most information-processing models of memory, incoming sensory information makes a brief stop in *sensory memory,* which temporarily retains it in the form of literal sensory images, such as *icons* and *echoes,* so that it can be further processed. Pattern recognition occurs during the transfer of information from sensory memory to short-term memory. Sensory memory acts as a filter, keeping out extraneous and unimportant information.

8. *Short-term memory (STM)* retains new information for up to 30 seconds by most estimates (unless rehearsal takes place) and also acts as a *working memory* for the processing of information retrieved from long-term memory for temporary use. The capacity of STM is extremely limited but can be extended if information is organized into larger units by *chunking.* Items that are meaningful, have an emotional impact, or link up to something already in long-term memory may enter long-term storage easily with only a brief stay in STM.

9. *Long-term memory (LTM)* contains a vast amount of information that must be organized and indexed. For example, words (or the concepts they represent) seem to be organized in part by semantic categories. Many models of LTM represent its contents as a network of interrelated concepts. The way people use these networks depends on experience and education. Words are also indexed in LTM in terms of sound and form.

10. *Procedural memories* ("knowing how") are memories for how to perform specific actions; *declarative memories* ("knowing that") are memories for abstract or representational knowledge. Declarative memories include *semantic memories* and *episodic memories.*

11. The three-box model has often been invoked to explain the *serial-position effect* in memory, but it cannot explain why a *recency effect* sometimes occurs when it shouldn't and why even rats show the serial-position effect.

12. Rehearsal is a technique for keeping information in short-term memory and increasing the chances of long-term retention. *Elaborative rehearsal* is more likely to result in transfer to long-term memory than is *maintenance rehearsal,* and *deep processing* is usually a more effective retention strategy than shallow processing. *Mnemonics* can also enhance retention by promoting elaborate encoding and making material meaningful, but complex mnemonics are often ineffective or even counterproductive.

13. Short-term memory appears to involve temporary changes within neurons that alter their ability to release neurotransmitters. In contrast, long-term memory involves permanent structural changes in neurons and synapses. *Long-term potentiation,* an increase in the strength of synaptic responsiveness, seems to be an important mechanism of long-term memory. Neural changes associated with long-term potentiation take time to develop, which may explain why long-term memories require a period of *consolidation.*

14. The different components of a memory are probably stored at different sites distributed across wide areas of the brain, with all these sites participating in the representation of the event as a whole. The initial formation of declarative memories involves the hippocampus and adjacent parts of the temporal-lobe cortex, whereas the formation of procedural memories involves other brain areas, including the cerebellum. Long-term storage of declarative memories may take place in the same cortical areas that were involved in the original perception of the information. Studies of patients with amnesia suggest that different brain systems may be involved in explicit and implicit memory tasks.

15. Hormones released by the adrenal glands during stress or emotional arousal, including *epinephrine* and certain steroids, may enhance memory at low or moderate levels. Epinephrine causes the level of glucose to rise in the bloodstream, and glucose may enhance memory either directly or by altering the effects of neurotransmitters. Hormonal effects may explain why moderate emotional arousal is an essential ingredient in learning and memory.

16. There are several theories of why forgetting occurs. Information may simply decay (although this explanation cannot account for all forgetting in long-term memory). New information may "erase" old information. *Proactive* and *retroactive interference* may occur. Some lapses in memory may be due to *motivated forgetting.* (However, the validity of "repressed" memories of past abuse that are "recovered" in therapy is the subject of bitter debate, as we discuss in "Psychology and Popular Culture.") Finally, *cue-dependent forgetting* may occur when retrieval cues are inadequate. The most effective retrieval cues are those that were present at the time of the initial experience. A person's mood or physical state may also act as a retrieval cue, evoking a *state-dependent memory,.*

17. Because of *childhood (infantile) amnesia,* most people cannot recall any events from earlier than the third or fourth year of life. The reason may be biological, but cognitive explanations have also been proposed: the lack of a "cognitive self" in the first few years of life; the child's reliance on cognitive schemas that differ from those used later; the fact that young children encode experiences less elaborately; and children's focus on routine rather than distinctive aspects of an experience.

18. A person's narrative or "life story" organizes the events of his or her life and gives it meaning. Narratives change as people build up a store of episodic memories. Many memories seem to be based on people's current traits and beliefs, and also on their *implicit theories* of how much particular traits or beliefs can change. Life stories are, to some degree, works of interpretation and imagination.

Key Terms

memory *328*
reconstruction in memory *328*
anterograde amnesia *329*
flashbulb memories *330*
leading questions *333*
explicit memory *336*
recall *336*
recognition *337*
implicit memory *337*
priming *337*
relearning method *338*
information-processing models *338*
encoding *338*
cognitive schema *338*
proposition *339*
effortful/automatic encoding *339*
storage *340*
retrieval *340*
"three-box model" *340*
parallel distributed processing (PDP) models *341*
neural networks *341*
artificial intelligence *341*
sensory memory *343*
sensory registers *343*
icons *343*
echoes *343*
pattern recognition *343*
short-term memory (STM) *344*
working memory *344*
chunks *345*

long-term memory (LTM) *346*
semantic categories *346*
tip-of-the-tongue state *347*
procedural memories *348*
declarative memories *348*
semantic memories *348*
episodic memories *349*
serial-position effect *349*
primacy and recency effects *349*
rehearsal *350*
maintenance rehearsal *351*
elaborative rehearsal *351*
deep versus shallow processing *352*
mnemonics *352*
long-term potentiation *354*
long-term depression *354*
consolidation *354*
decay theory *361*
retroactive interference *361*
proactive interference *362*
motivated forgetting/repression *362*
retrograde amnesia *362*
cue-dependent forgetting *363*
retrieval cues *363*
state-dependent memory *363*
childhood (infantile) amnesia *366*
narratives *367*
implicit theory *368*
"reminiscence bump" *369*

10
Emotion

Some of these drawings of emotional expressions, from a 1749 French book on natural history, are easily recognized today; others are not. The reason is that some aspects of emotion are universal across time and place, whereas others vary with culture and circumstance.

*The beauty of the world has two edges,
one of laughter, one of anguish,
cutting the heart asunder.*

■ VIRGINIA WOOLF ■

On Sunday, April 25, in the year 1227, a knight named Ulrich von Lichtenstein disguised himself as the goddess Venus. Wearing an ornate white gown, waist-length braids, and heavy veils, and bedecked with pearls, Ulrich began a pilgrimage from Venice to Bohemia. As he traveled, he invited any and all local warriors to challenge him to a duel. By his own count (which may have been exaggerated), Ulrich broke 307 lances, unhorsed four opponents, and completed his five-week journey with an undefeated record. The reason for this extravagant performance was his passion for a highborn princess, nameless to history, whom he adored but who barely gave poor Ulrich the time of day. Ulrich trembled in her presence, suffered in her absence, and constantly endured feelings of longing, misery, and melancholy—a state of love that apparently made him very happy (M. Hunt, 1959/1967).

How would Ulrich's story sound with the emotion removed? Suppose Ulrich endured his hardships and tribulations because he was somewhat fond of the lady. Suppose he was bored in her presence and only vaguely aware of her absence. Suppose, in short, that she meant nothing more to him than his wife (oh, yes, Ulrich was married), and that theirs was merely an economic union, a practical arrangement for the purpose of begetting children and managing the serfs. How would we evaluate Ulrich's knightly performance then?

Let's try another story, from this century. In the wealthy community of Scarsdale, New York, 23-year-old Richard Herrin murdered his sleeping girlfriend, Bonnie Garland. Herrin was depressed because Garland had told him she was too young to marry and wanted to date other men. In a rage over her decision, he battered her to death with a claw hammer. The jury did not convict Herrin of murder, but of the lesser crime of manslaughter, believing that he had acted under "extreme emotional disturbance." Herrin's supporters thought even this sentence too harsh, arguing that he had loved Bonnie deeply and passionately and was desperately unhappy because of her death. This defense did not persuade the prosecution. One psychiatrist said it reminded him of the old story of the man who murdered his parents and then pleaded for mercy because he was an orphan.

How would Herrin's story sound with the emotion removed? Suppose Herrin murdered Garland calmly, barely flinching as he slaughtered her. Suppose he wasn't depressed about losing her, but indifferent. He wasn't enraged that she rejected him, only mildly sorry. He didn't love her "deeply and passionately"; he just liked her a little. He didn't grieve over her loss; he barely noticed it. What sentence do you think Herrin would have received? Would his friends still have defended him?

As these stories show, emotions are the heart and soul of human life. They give life color, intensity, excitement—and misery. If you could wave a magic wand and eliminate them, you would never again worry about a test result, a job interview, or a first date. You would never feel angry, even if your roommate

What we do for love: Ulrich von Lichtenstein disguised as Venus.

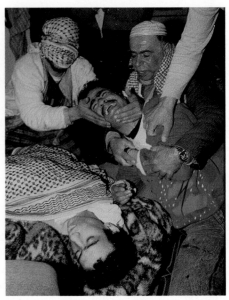

Israeli parents (left) and an Arab father (right) react to the deaths of their children in the Middle Eastern conflict. Their grief involves both a physiological response to loss and the cognition that a young life has been unfairly cut short. In turn, culture affects the display of emotion—whether, say, you should "let it out" or "keep a stiff upper lip." Your own culture may affect how you are reacting to these two photos: Is the Israeli father "cold and uptight" or "mature and manly"? Is the Arab father being too "hysterical" or "humanly expressive"?

called you an idiot or you were arrested on false charges. You wouldn't be afraid to jump out of an airplane, with or without a parachute. You would never feel the grief of losing someone you love, not only because you wouldn't know sadness but also because you wouldn't know love. You would never laugh, because nothing would strike you as funny.

Psychologists today recognize that emotions are a key factor in virtually every domain of human experience: motivation, stress, development, personality, abnormal behavior, prejudice, perception, you name it. In their research and theories they are trying to integrate three elements that the full experience of **emotion** involves: *physiological* changes in the face and body, *cognitive* processes such as interpretations of events, and *cultural* influences that shape the experience and expression of emotion.

▪ ELEMENTS OF EMOTION 1: THE BODY

Early philosophers thought our emotional personalities depended on mixes of four basic body fluids, or "humors": blood, phlegm, yellow bile (choler), and black bile. If you were an angry, irritable sort of person, you supposedly had an excess of choler; even now, the word *choleric* describes a hothead. If you were slow-moving and unemotional, you supposedly had an excess of phlegm, and the word for such people is *phlegmatic*. The theory of the four humors is farfetched, and yet the basic questions it was trying to answer remain with us. What is the physiology of emotion? Where in the body does an emotion occur?

One of the first modern answers to these questions came from William James (1884), who challenged everyone who thought the chicken comes first to think about the egg. Common sense, then as now, assumed that (1) something happens, (2) you feel an emotion, (3) you do something. In James's own examples, you lose your fortune, you feel miserable, you cry; or your rival insults you, you feel angry, you hit him. But James argued that this seemingly logical sequence was out of order, and he turned it around. The correct sequence, he said, should be (1) something happens, (2) your body reacts with a specific set of physiological responses, (3) you interpret and experience those responses as an emotion. If a slimy alien appeared in your room as you were reading this, your heart would start pounding and you would escape as fast as you could; *then* you would realize you were feeling fear. "We feel sorry *because* we cry," James wrote, "angry *because* we strike, afraid *because* we tremble." At about the same

▪ **emotion**
A state of arousal involving facial and bodily changes, brain activation, cognitive appraisals, subjective feelings, and tendencies toward action.

time that James was writing, a Danish researcher named Carl Lange came up with a similar theory, and the two names were soon linked in the **James-Lange theory of emotion:** the idea that events trigger specific bodily changes and responses—for example, running away if you are frightened—and that emotion follows from your awareness of those physical changes.

The James-Lange theory was not quite right, but it produced animated debate and spurred a wave of research. During the past few decades, psychologists, armed with new ways to study the physiology of emotion, have explored the contributions to emotion of facial expressions, brain processes, and the autonomic nervous system.

The Face of Emotion

The most obvious place to look for emotion is on the face, where its expression is usually most visible. "There are characteristic facial expressions which are observed to accompany anger, fear, erotic excitement, and all the other passions," wrote Aristotle. Centuries later, in his classic book *The Expression of the Emotions in Man and Animals* (1872/1965), Charles Darwin argued that certain human facial expressions—the smile, the frown, the grimace, the glare—are as "wired in" as the wing flutter of a frightened bird, the purr of a contented cat, and the snarl of a threatened wolf. Such expressions may have evolved because they allowed animals and our human forebears to tell the difference immediately between a stranger who was friendly and one who was about to attack.

Modern psychologists have supported Darwin's idea by showing that certain emotional expressions are recognized the world over (see Figure 10.1). For more than 20 years, Paul Ekman and his colleagues have been gathering evidence for the universality of six basic facial expressions of emotion: anger, happiness, fear, surprise, disgust, and sadness—pretty much the same ones that have been observed in infants (Ekman, 1994; Ekman, Friesen, & Ellsworth, 1972; Ekman et al., 1987). In the late 1980s they also found evidence of a seventh universal expression, contempt (Ekman & Heider, 1988). In every culture they have studied—in Brazil, Chile, Estonia, Germany, Greece, Hong Kong, Italy, Japan, New Guinea, Scotland, Sumatra, Turkey, and the United States—a large majority has recognized the emotional expressions portrayed by people in other cultures. Even most members of isolated tribes that have never watched a movie or read *People* magazine, such as the Foré of New Guinea or the Minangkabau of West Sumatra, can recognize the emotions expressed in pictures of people who are entirely foreign to them, and we can recognize theirs.

These findings do not mean, however, that everybody in a society can recognize the same expressions in all situations. Ekman and Friesen called their theory *neuro-cultural* to emphasize that there are two important determinants of facial expression: a universal neurophysiology in the facial muscles associated with certain emotions and culture-specific variations in the expression of emotion. Thus, while most people in most cultures *do* recognize basic emotions as portrayed in photographs, sometimes a large minority does *not*. Across 20 studies of Western cultures, for example, fully 95 percent of the participants agreed in their judgments of happy faces, but only 78 percent agreed on expressions of sadness and anger; and across 11 non-Western societies, 88 percent recognized happiness, but only 74 percent agreed on sadness and 59 percent on anger (Ekman, 1994). Further, often the ability to recognize a person's facial expression depends on the *context* in which an observer sees it. For example, a neutral expression is typically judged as "happy" when it is shown in a set of happy faces, but as "sad" when it is embedded in a set of sad faces. Likewise, in some contexts people will judge an "angry" expression to be sad or an expression of "contempt" to be disgust (Russell, 1994).

One emotion that nicely illustrates how physiology and culture both contribute to facial expression is disgust. Make an expression of disgust and notice

■ **James-Lange theory of emotion**
The theory, proposed independently by William James and Carl Lange, that emotion results from the perception of one's own bodily reactions.

■ **Figure 10.1 Some Universal Expressions**

Can you tell what feelings are being conveyed here? Most people around the world can readily identify facial expressions of surprise, disgust, happiness, sadness, anger, and fear—no matter what the age, culture, or historical epoch of the person conveying the emotion, and even when the "person" is a work of art. This suggests that universal facial expressions of emotion evolved to play an important role in communication.

what you are doing: You are probably wrinkling your nose, dropping the corners of your mouth, or retracting your upper lip. These universal reactions may have originated in the "distaste" response of infants to bitter tastes and may serve as a warning against eating tainted food. But the *content* of what produces disgust changes as the infant matures, and it varies from culture to culture. In the course of growing up, people may acquire feelings of disgust in response to certain foods as well as to bugs, sex, gore, dirt, and death; "contamination" by contact with undesirable strangers; or violations of moral rules, such as those governing incest (Rozin, Lowery, & Ebert, 1994).

All in all, the evidence is overwhelming that certain emotions are registered on the face, and they probably evolved to help us communicate with others. This communication starts in infancy; a baby's expressions of misery, angry frustration, happiness, and disgust are apparent to most parents (Izard, 1994b; Stenberg & Campos, 1990)—and babies, in turn, react to the facial expressions of their parents. American, German, Greek, Japanese, Trobriand Island, and Yanomamo mothers all "infect" their babies with happy moods by displaying happy expressions (Keating, 1994). A baby's ability to recognize facial expressions of emotion has survival value. Perhaps you recall the visual cliff studies described in Chapter 6 (see p. 230), studies that were originally designed to test the development of depth perception. It turns out that if the baby's mother is on the far side of the cliff and warns the baby against crossing by assuming an expression of fear or anger, the baby will not cross. If, however, the mother smiles at the baby warmly, the baby will cross to her, even though the baby is aware of the "cliff" (Sorce et al., 1985).

Interestingly, facial expressions of emotion may also help people communicate with themselves, so to speak, by enabling them to identify their own emotions. Like William James, some psychologists argue that people don't frown because they are angry; rather, they feel angry because they are frowning. According to this **facial-feedback hypothesis,** the facial muscles send messages to the brain, identifying each basic emotion (Izard, 1990; Laird, 1984; Tomkins, 1962, 1981b). When people are asked to contort their facial muscles into various patterns, they often report changed emotions to fit the pattern. As one young man put it, "When my jaw was clenched and my brows down, I tried not to be angry but it just fit the position" (Laird, 1974). Voluntary facial expressions even seem to affect the involuntary nervous system. If you put on an "angry" face, your heart rate will rise faster than if you put on a "happy" face (Levenson, Ekman, & Friesen, 1990). When people are told to contract the facial muscles involved in smiling (though not actually instructed to smile) and then to look at cartoons, they find the cartoons funnier than if they are contracting their muscles in a way that is incompatible with smiling (Strack, Martin, & Stepper, 1988).

Findings like these suggest that the facial muscles are somehow tied to the autonomic nervous system, which controls heart rate, breathing, and other vital functions. But what might link the muscles of the face with a subjective emotional state? One imaginative line of research suggests that facial expressions change the pattern of blood flow to the brain, thereby altering temperature in certain parts of the brain, which in turn affects the release of neurotransmitters (Zajonc, Murphy, & Inglehart, 1989). Experiments find that lowering the temperature of the brain seems to cause pleasant feelings; raising the temperature seems to cause unpleasant ones. One action that helps cool a fevered brain, apparently, is smiling, which allows more air to enter the nasal passages and thus cools the blood flowing through the sinuses to the brain. The breathing techniques in yoga apparently have the same effect, which may be why yoga, meditation, and smiling can all improve a person's mood.

There are limits, however, to the effects of facial feedback. Obviously, smiling won't overcome the grief of hearing that a friend has died of cancer. Moreover, people do not always wear their emotions on their faces. They do not go around scowling and clenching their jaws whenever they are angry. They can grieve and feel enormously sad without weeping. They can feel worried and tense, yet put on a happy face. They can use facial expressions to lie about a "real" feeling. Judging another person's mood just from his or her facial expression is not always a simple task.

■ **facial-feedback hypothesis**
The notion that the facial muscles send messages to the brain, identifying the emotion a person feels.

Facial expressions don't always convey the emotion that is felt. A posed, social smile (left) may have nothing to do with true feelings of happiness. Conversely, even a face that seems to convey utter anguish (right) may be misleading. This young woman is weeping for joy: She has just won the "Best Young Actress of the Year" award.

To get around the human ability to mask emotions, Paul Ekman and his associates have developed a way to peek under the mask. The Facial Action Coding System (FACS) allows researchers to analyze and identify each of the nearly 80 muscles of the face, as well as the combinations of muscles that are associated with various emotions. When people try to hide their real emotions, Ekman (1985) finds, they use different groups of muscles. For example, when people try to pretend that they feel grief, only 15 percent manage to get the eyebrows, eyelids, and forehead wrinkle exactly right, mimicking the way grief is expressed spontaneously. Authentic smiles last only two seconds; false smiles may last ten seconds or more. Moreover, the muscle changes associated with the real emotion—anger, contempt, sadness—can be identified beneath the smiling mask (Ekman, 1994; Ekman, Friesen, & O'Sullivan, 1988).

Nevertheless, facial expressions of emotion are only part of the emotional picture. For one thing, some widely experienced feelings that many people would call "emotions," such as hope, shame, regret, guilt, sympathy, or dislike, do not have typical facial expressions (Roseman, Wiest, & Swartz, 1994). Of course, facial expressions communicate more than emotion; they also reveal boredom, pain, interest, sleepiness, confusion, worry, puzzlement, and countless other states. Even Ekman, who has been studying emotions for years, concludes, "There is obviously emotion without facial expression and facial expression without emotion." In Shakespeare's play *Henry VI*, the villain who will become the evil King Richard III says,

> Why, I can smile, and murder while I smile;
> And cry content to that which grieves my heart;
> And wet my cheeks with artificial tears,
> And frame my face to all occasions.

Emotion and the Brain

Another line of physiological research seeks to identify parts of the brain responsible for the many different aspects of emotional experience: recognizing another person's emotion, feeling intensely aroused, labeling the emotion, deciding what to do about it, and so on. Take something as apparently simple as recognizing a face. You can recognize your mother's face any old time. You can even recognize a picture of her taken ten years ago. You can recognize her when she is crying and when she is smiling. If you had a rare disease called *prosopagnosia*, though, you would lose the ability to recognize all faces, including your own (Sacks, 1985). Yet people with this problem are often able to recognize facial *expressions* even when they can't identify *faces*, suggesting that different parts of the brain are involved in each process (Damasio, 1994; Tranel, Damasio, & Damasio, 1988).

The source of our basic emotions lies in the limbic system and hypothalamus, evolutionarily old parts of the brain that human beings share with other species (see Chapter 4). The *amygdala*, a small structure in the limbic system, appears to be responsible for evaluating sensory information and quickly determining its emotional importance, and also for the initial decision to approach or withdraw from a person or situation.

The amygdala quickly assesses danger or threat, which is a good thing, because otherwise you could be standing in the street asking, "Is it wise to cross now, while that very large truck is coming toward me?" The amygdala also plays an important role in mediating anxiety and depression; PET scans find that depressed and anxious patients show increased activation of the amygdala (Schulkin, 1994). According to studies by neurobiologist Joseph LeDoux (1989), pathways in the limbic system prompt the amygdala to trigger an emo-

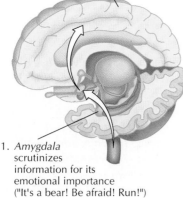

2. *Cerebral cortex* generates more complete picture; can override signals sent by amygdala ("It's only Mike in a down coat")

1. *Amygdala* scrutinizes information for its emotional importance ("It's a bear! Be afraid! Run!")

tional response to incoming sensory information, which may then be "overridden" by a more accurate appraisal from the cerebral cortex. This is why you jump with fear when you suddenly feel a hand on your back in a dark alley, and why your fear evaporates when the cortex registers that the hand belongs to a friend. If either the amygdala or critical areas of the cortex are damaged, emotional abnormalities result. That is, if you damage a rat's amygdala it "forgets" to be afraid when it should be; and people with damage to the amygdala often have difficulty recognizing fear in themselves or others (Damasio, 1994). But rats or people with damage to certain areas of the cortex often lose the capacity to "override" their fear when it is no longer necessary.

Research suggests that the two cerebral hemispheres play different roles in the generation of positive and negative emotions, and that this specialization is already apparent in infants (Davidson et al., 1990; Fox & Davidson, 1988; Tucker, 1989). Certain regions of the left hemisphere appear to be specialized for the processing of such positive emotions as happiness, whereas certain regions of the right hemisphere are specialized for such negative emotions as anger, fear, and depression. Damage to the left hemisphere tends to produce excessive anger, tears, and pessimism. "Well," you might say, "wouldn't brain damage make anyone angry, sad, and pessimistic?" But damage to the right hemisphere is associated with excessive displays of joking and laughing.

This research shows that it is possible to differentiate the components of emotional processing in the brain. However, in real life, all parts of the brain operate interdependently to generate what feels like a single emotional experience (Lazarus, 1991).

The Energy of Emotion

A third line of physiological research focuses on hormones, which produce the energy of emotion. In particular, the inner part of the adrenal gland, the *medulla,* sends out two hormones, *epinephrine* and *norepinephrine* (see Chapter 4). These hormones activate the sympathetic division of the autonomic nervous system and thus produce a state of *arousal,* a level of alertness that allows the body to respond quickly. During arousal the pupils dilate, widening to allow in more light; the heart beats faster; breathing speeds up; blood sugar rises, providing the body with more energy to act; and digestion slows down, so that blood flow can be diverted from the stomach and intestines to the muscles and surface of the skin. This is why, when you are excited, scared, furious, or wildly in love, you may not want to eat. In addition, your memory, concentration, and performance improve—up to a point. If hormone levels become too high and you are too agitated, concentration and performance can worsen. This is why a little nervousness when you take an exam is a good thing but hand-trembling anxiety is not.

The adrenal glands produce epinephrine and norepinephrine in response to many challenges in the environment. These hormones will surge if you are laughing at a funny movie or playing a video game, if you are worried about an exam, if you are cheering at a game, or if you are responding to an insult. They will also rise in response to nonemotional conditions, such as heat, cold, pain, injury, burns, and physical exercise; in response to some drugs, such as caffeine, nicotine, and alcohol; and in response to stress and pressure.

Epinephrine in particular provides the *feeling* of an emotion—that familiar tingle, excitement, and sense of energy. At high levels, it can create the sensation of being "seized" or "flooded" by an emotion that is out of one's control. In a sense, the release of epinephrine does cause us to "lose control," because few people can consciously alter their heart rates, blood pressures, and digestive tracts. (But people can learn to control their actions when they are emotionally aroused, as we discuss in "Taking Psychology with You.") As arousal subsides, a

Why does the driver of a car usually feel angrier than the passenger when another car cuts them off? One reason may be that the driver is physiologically aroused by the tension of coping with traffic.

"hot" emotion usually turns into its "cool" counterpart (Frijda, 1988; Reisenzein, 1994). Anger may pale into annoyance, ecstasy into contentment, fear into suspicion, past emotional whirlwinds into calm breezes.

It was once thought that the autonomic nervous system responded to events in a "one-reaction-fits-all-emotions" manner. However, neuropsychological research has shown that although most emotions do involve similar changes that mobilize the body to cope with the environment, some emotions are physiologically distinct from one another. Depending on which emotion is being experienced, arousal can take several forms, involving one or the other hemisphere of the brain and differing hormone levels (Neiss, 1988; Tucker & Williamson, 1984).

In one series of experiments, subjects were induced, in a variety of ways, to experience fear, disgust, anger, sadness, surprise, and happiness. Each emotion was associated with a somewhat different pattern of autonomic activity, involving such measures as heart rate, electrical activity of the skin (galvanic skin responses, or GSR), and finger temperature. Indeed, the researchers found 14 distinctions among emotions in autonomic nervous system activity (Levenson, 1992; Levenson, Ekman, & Friesen, 1990). These distinctive patterns may be why people say they feel "hot and bothered" when they are angry, but "cold and clammy" when they are afraid.

Arousal is not a single, global phenomenon, produced as simply as switching on the engine of a car. It's as if one switch turns on the car, another activates it into movement, and a third coordinates the whole operation, making the car move forward. Indeed, some psychologists believe that the ultimate *purpose* of emotion is to "make the car move forward": that is, to produce a response. In other words, the nervous system changes associated with emotion do not occur in order to allow you to sit there and contemplate your internal state. Most emotions involve some change in *action readiness* (Frijda, 1988); they prepare the body to cope with danger or threat, excitement or opportunity. Studies find that when you feel an emotion, you will feel motivated to do something specific to that state: embrace the person who instills joy in you, yell at the person who is angering you, run from the situation that is frightening you, or punish yourself for doing something stupid or shameful (Roseman, Wiest, & Swartz, 1994).

This disposition to approach or withdraw, so closely linked with emotional states, is evident in infancy. In one study, ten-month-old babies were briefly separated from their mothers, then monitored during the happy reunion. The babies' reactions were recorded in three physiological measures: unmistakable smiles of happiness, left-hemisphere activation, and literally reaching out to their moms (Fox & Davidson, 1988). But when the babies were only smiling socially at strangers, there was no increased left-hemispheric activation and no reaching out.

Psychologists who are interested in the physiology of emotion have approached their task from many different directions. As we have seen, they are mapping the interconnections among facial expressions, blood flow in the hypothalamus and limbic system (especially the amygdala), activity in the two cerebral hemispheres during positive or negative emotions, and sympathetic nervous system activity that prepares the body to take action during an emotional state. Most of these researchers believe that certain primitive emotions occur independently of higher cognitive processes, which is why people can be afraid for no "rational" reason or have pleasant feelings about a familiar object without knowing why (Izard, 1994a; Murphy & Zajonc, 1993).

Even so, physiological processes are not the entire emotional experience. The physical changes caused by the autonomic nervous system cannot explain why of two students about to take an exam, one feels psyched up and the other feels overwhelmed by anxiety. They also cannot explain why the intensity of physical changes can be unrelated to emotional experience—why, for example, injecting people with ephedrine, a powerful stimulant, has no effect on how frightened they feel about being threatened with electric shock; and why, conversely, drugs that lower heart rate have no effect on people's subjective reports of anxiety (Neiss, 1988).

One consequence of the mistaken assumption that physiological changes tell the whole story of emotion has been the widespread use of "lie detectors" designed to read a person's "true" feelings (see "Think About It"). But physiological arousal itself, which can be produced by many events in the environment, may not have a specific emotional meaning. Are you thrilled or frightened? Sick or just in love? Your hormones alone won't tell you.

Quick QUIZ

Which aspects of the physiology of emotion—hormones, cerebral hemispheres, or a specific part of the brain—are involved in the following reactions to events?

1. A three-year-old sees her dad dressed as a gorilla and runs away in fear. What structure in the limbic system is probably involved in her withdrawal from him?
2. Casey is watching *Hatchet Murders in the Dorm: Sequel XVII.* What hormones cause his heart to pound and his palms to sweat when the murderer is stalking an unsuspecting victim?
3. Melissa is watching an old Laurel and Hardy film, which makes her chuckle and puts her in a good mood. Which hemisphere of her brain is likely to be most activated?

Answers:

1. the amygdala 2. epinephrine, norepinephrine 3. left

▪ ELEMENTS OF EMOTION 2: THE MIND

Put your finger on the dot in the margin, and smile. How do you feel at this moment, amused or irritated? If you followed our instructions and touched the dot, you probably feel more amused than angry. You may be laughing at yourself for doing such a silly thing, and that will make you feel happy—remember the facial-feedback hypothesis. If you didn't put your finger on the dot, you probably feel more angry than amused. "Why are the authors of this book asking me to play stupid games?" you may be asking yourself.

Notice that it is not what we wrote that produced your emotion; it is your *interpretation* of what we asked you to do. Such interpretations are critical to all emotions. Let's say that you have had a crush for weeks on a fellow student in your history class. Finally you get up the nerve to start a conversation. Heart pounding, palms sweating, you cheerfully say, "Hi, there!" Before you can continue, the student has walked past you without even a nod. What emotion do you feel? Your answer will depend on how you explain the student's behavior:

> **Angry:** "What a rude thing to do, to ignore me like that!"
> **Sad:** "I knew it; I'm no good. No one will ever like me."
> **Embarrassed:** "Oh, no! Everyone saw how I was humiliated!"
> **Relieved:** "Thank goodness; I wasn't sure I wanted to get involved, anyway."

*T*hink About It

*C*an Lies Be "Detected"?

■ "The truth will out," goes an old saying, but the truth is that most human beings are not very good at detecting the lies of others. Many people think that liars won't smile or look you in the eye, for instance, but plenty of liars do exactly that. Many people assume that some body signs (such as facial animation) reflect truthfulness, whereas other signals (such as nervous gestures) indicate deception, but neither assumption is true. Even professionals thought to be skilled at detecting lies—customs officers, police, polygraphers, judges, psychiatrists, lawyers, and members of the U.S. Secret Service—are no better than amateurs at detecting deceit . . . which is to say, they aren't very good at it (Ekman & O'Sullivan, 1991). Of these groups, only the Secret Service does particularly well.

Is it possible to design a test that would let you know for sure if a person is lying? In Asia, for many centuries, the "rice" method of lie detection was used on people suspected of a crime. The suspect had to chew on a handful of dry rice and then spit it out. The belief was that an innocent person would be able to do this easily, while a guilty person would have grains of rice stuck to the tongue and the roof of the mouth.

The rice method may seem primitive, but its rationale is not much removed from that of the modern polygraph machine, commonly called the *lie detector.* Both methods are based on the belief that a person who is guilty and fearful will have increased activity in the autonomic nervous system. In the case of the guilty rice-eater, such arousal should dry the saliva in the mouth and cause grains to stick to the tongue. In the case of the guilty suspect taking a polygraph test, a lie should be revealed by increased heart rate, respiration, and GSR as the person responds with incriminating answers to questions.

The appeal of the lie detector is that it is supposed to do better than people at finding out who is innocent of a crime or of lying and who is not. However, psychologists have found that polygraph tests are not reliable *because no physiological patterns of responses are specific to lying* (Lilienfeld, 1993; Saxe, 1994). Machines cannot tell whether you are feeling guilty, angry, nervous, amused, or revved up from an exciting day. Innocent people may be tense and nervous about the whole procedure. They may react to a certain word ("bank") not because they robbed it, but because they recently bounced a check. In either case, the machine will record a "lie." The reverse mistake is also common. Some suave, practiced liars can lie without flinching, and others learn to "beat the machine" by tensing muscles or thinking about an exciting experience during neutral questions (Lykken, 1981). A few years ago, for example, Aldrich Ames, a high-level CIA official, was con-

As we noted in Chapter 1, in the first century A.D., the Stoic philosophers suggested that people do not become angry or sad or anxious because of actual events, but because of their explanations of those events. Modern psychologists have been testing the Stoics' ideas experimentally and identifying the specific mental processes involved in emotions.

How Thoughts Create Emotions

If emotion were the result of physiological changes alone, it would be possible to generate emotions in the laboratory simply by injecting people with epinephrine. In 1924, Spanish physician Gregorio Marañon tried this, and he happened on an unexpected result (see Cornelius, 1991). Nearly 30 percent of the 210 people in his research reported feeling genuine emotions, usually sadness, often accompanied by weeping. But more than 70 percent merely reported physical changes ("My heart is beating fast," "My throat feels tight") or what

victed of spying for the former Soviet Union over a period of ten years and selling national secrets. During the investigation, Ames passed two polygraph tests designed to detect his treasonous acts.

Moreover, the people who administer the polygraph test often make many errors in reading the results. They do not reliably agree with one another's judgments, and, worst of all, they are more likely to accuse the innocent of lying than to let the guilty go free (Saxe, 1994; Kleinmuntz & Szucko, 1984). Because of such findings, in 1988 the U.S. Congress passed a law prohibiting employers from using lie detectors to screen job applicants or randomly test employees, and most courts do not admit polygraph evidence in trials. However, police departments continue to use them for various purposes, and polygraph tests are still used for obtaining security clearances in the U.S. government even though test accuracy is very low. In experiments in which federal employees were given knowledge of acts of mock espionage and told to try to hide this knowledge from investigators, many of the "guilty" respondents were able to pass polygraph tests with flying colors (Honts, 1994).

Nevertheless, efforts to measure physiological signs of lying continue unabated. The Guilty Knowledge Test (Lykken, 1991) is based on the assumption that autonomic arousal will be higher in guilty subjects who are asked about aspects of a crime that only they could know about. Some researchers are using measures of brain electrical activity, commonly called *event-related brain potentials,* to see if they can infer whether a person possesses guilty knowledge of a crime or is lying (Bashore & Rapp, 1993). But because of the normal variability among people in their autonomic reactivity, innocent but highly reactive people are still likely to be misdiagnosed as "guilty" by these tests.

Paul Ekman, who has studied emotions and deception for many years, offers some thoughtful questions to consider when thinking about lie detection: "What would life be like if we couldn't lie? If we had something that was the equivalent of the dog's tail? Everyone would know when we were happy, when we weren't. What a terrible life; there would be no privacy! On the other hand, imagine a world in which everyone could lie perfectly; [in which] anyone could mislead you without your knowing it. Basically, the world we live in—where we can lie, but not perfectly—is probably the best" (quoted in Howell, 1993).

Do you agree? When would it be desirable or disastrous to detect another person's lies—and would you want everyone to be able to detect yours? How reliable does a test need to be before its widespread use can be justified: Is it acceptable if it misidentifies "only" one innocent person in ten? a hundred? a thousand? What do you think? ■

Marañon called "as if" emotions: "I feel *as if* I were angry," "I feel *as if* I were happy."

What caused the difference between the two groups? Marañon reported that he was able to induce "genuine" emotions by asking the first group to think about their sick children or their deceased parents. In short, the people who reported genuine emotions had a reason for them! Marañon concluded that emotions involve a *physical* component, consisting of the bodily changes that accompany arousal, and a psychological or *mental* component, consisting of the context in which those changes occur and the interpretation the individual gives them.

Marañon's research languished in a French journal of endocrinology until the 1960s, when Stanley Schachter and Jerome Singer advanced similar ideas with their **two-factor theory of emotion** (Schachter, 1971; Schachter & Singer, 1962). Like Marañon, they argued that bodily changes are necessary to experience an emotion, but they are not enough. Emotion, they said, depends on two factors: *physiological arousal* and the *cognitive interpretation* of that

■ **two-factor theory of emotion**
The theory that emotions depend on both physiological arousal and a cognitive interpretation of that arousal.

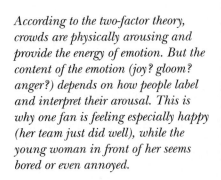

According to the two-factor theory, crowds are physically arousing and provide the energy of emotion. But the content of the emotion (joy? gloom? anger?) depends on how people label and interpret their arousal. This is why one fan is feeling especially happy (her team just did well), while the young woman in front of her seems bored or even annoyed.

arousal. Your body may be churning away in high gear, but unless you can interpret, explain, and label those changes, you won't feel an "emotion." Conversely, if all your friends are worried about an upcoming exam, you may decide that the pounding of your heart is a sign that you are nervous, too. You may not realize that your heart is pounding because you have been partying late, losing sleep, and drinking too much coffee.

Schachter and Singer's own experiments, which were widely cited, were not successfully replicated. Their idea that arousal was necessary to feel an emotion proved to be overstated. Also, subsequent research, as we just saw, has found that the physiology of emotion involves more than the activation of hormones. But their work was important for two major reasons. First, it helped explain why people often mislabel their own physical states. For example, when people are aroused and they don't know why (perhaps, as in one study, because of residual arousal following exercise), they are more emotionally affected by cues in the environment than they are when they have an obvious explanation for their arousal (Sinclair et al., 1994). Second, Schachter and Singer's work launched scores of studies designed to identify the kinds of cognitions that are involved in the experience of emotion. Psychologists went on to study the thought patterns and perceptions that are typical of many emotions, from gradations of joy to degrees of sadness.

For example, most people assume that success on a project brings happiness, and failure brings unhappiness. In fact, research shows that people's emotions depend on how they *explain* their success or failure. In a series of experiments, students reported times when they had done well on or failed an exam for a particular reason, such as help from others or lack of effort, and described the emotions they felt on each of these occasions. Their emotions were more closely associated with their explanations than with the outcome of the test (Weiner, 1986). Students who believed they did well because of their own efforts and abilities tended to feel proud, competent, and satisfied. Those who believed they did well because of a lucky fluke or chance tended to feel gratitude, surprise, or guilt ("I don't deserve this"). Those who believed their failures were their own fault tended to feel regret, guilt, or resignation. And those who blamed others for their failures tended to feel angry or hostile.

In general, psychologists have found that negative emotions differ from positive ones in the kinds of perceptions and explanations that generate them. We observed this phenomenon for ourselves when some friends returned from a mountain-climbing trip to Nepal. One said, "It was wonderful! The crystal-clear skies, the millions of stars, the friendly people, the majestic mountains, the harmony of the universe!" The other said, "It was horrible! The bedbugs, the millions of fleas, the lack of toilets, the yak-butter tea, the horrible food, the unforgiving mountains!" Guess which traveler was ecstatic while traveling and which was unhappy?

To understand the mental processes involved in emotion, let's consider the feelings of sadness involved in loneliness and depression. National surveys show that the loneliest people in the United States are adolescents and college students; fortunately, loneliness declines as people get older (Perlman, 1990). Loneliness, however, is not the same thing as solitude or being alone. Many people live alone and do not feel lonely, because they have close ties to good friends and family. Others live in large families and feel desperately lonely, because they think that no one understands them or cares about them. Feelings of loneliness, therefore, cannot be understood by studying only *actual* isolation. Similarly, certain events may set the stage for depression: the breakup of a dating relationship or a marriage, the death of a loved one, moving away from home, being fired from a job. But the course of depression also depends on how a person interprets and reacts to these events over time (Anderson et al., 1994; Forgas, 1994; Snodgrass, 1987; Weiner, 1986). Three aspects of a person's cognitions—internality, stability, and control—are especially important with regard to depression:

Being alone is not the same as being lonely. Why?

1. *Internality.* Do you believe the reason for your sad feelings is internal (something in you, an entrenched aspect of your personality) or external (something in the outside world)? Internal reasons for loneliness include "I'm unattractive" and "I don't know how to make friends." External explanations look outward: "The people I work with are unfriendly," "I'm having a run of bad luck," "This school is so big and impersonal it's hard to meet new people." People who attribute their failures and woes to internal causes are sadder and more lonely than those who do not (Anderson et al., 1994).

2. *Stability.* Do you believe the reason for your feelings is permanent and unchangeable ("This is just an unfriendly place and always will be") or temporary and changeable? People who think their negative emotions are hopelessly stable create a vicious cycle for themselves. Expecting nothing to improve, they do nothing to improve their circumstances, and therefore remain lonely and sad.

3. *Control.* Do you believe you have control over the causes of your feelings? The belief that there is absolutely nothing one can do to change the situation ("I'm ugly and horrible and there is nothing I can do about it") often prolongs loneliness, depression, and despair.

These three dimensions help account for people's emotional reactions in a wide variety of situations. For example, in a recent series of laboratory and field studies, Joseph Forgas (1994) found that when happy or sad people were asked to describe and account for conflicts in their close relationships, the sad people's explanations for the conflicts were more internal, stable, and global—leading them to feel more negative and pessimistic about their relationships—than the happy people's.

Emotions occur, cognitive researchers explain, because people are constantly appraising the events that befall them for their personal implications: Do I care about what is happening? Is it good or bad for me? Can I do anything about it? Is this matter going to get better or worse? According to Craig Smith and his colleagues (1993), these appraisals provide the emotional "heat" in our encounters. If you decide that being stuck in a traffic jam is not important and you can't do anything about it anyway, you may take it calmly. If you are on the way to, say, your wedding, and you see that the traffic is getting worse, and being late is *really* going to be bad for you, you are likely to feel hopping mad at those stupid cars that are blocking your way.

Many emotions are distinguished by the particular thoughts and perceptions that generate them. For example, most people tend to think that envy and jealousy are much alike; but when students were asked to write about their actual experiences with either of them, the two emotions proved to be cognitively different (Parrott & Smith, 1993). *Envy* was characterized by thoughts of inferiority, longing, and resentment; *jealousy* was characterized by fear of rejection or loss, distrust, anxiety, and anger. And some people might feel "jealous envy" of the admirable qualities of a rival who steals their sweetheart.

Even feelings of happiness can be distinguished by the cognitions involved in them. One kind of happiness, which has been called "personal expressiveness," is associated with perceptions of feeling challenged, competent, and assertive, having clear goals, and knowing how well one is doing. Another kind, "pleasurable enjoyment," is associated with the ability to put negative cognitions aside—feeling relaxed, content, losing track of time, and forgetting one's personal problems (Waterman, 1993).

One of the challenges of studying emotion is the sheer complexity of emotional experiences. Psychologists usually study one emotion *or* another, but most people feel one emotion *and* another; emotions occur in bunches, like grapes. People's perceptions, beliefs, expectations, and appraisals of a situation can help explain the reason for such mixed emotions. In one study, college students described their thoughts and feelings just before taking a midterm exam and again after they got their grades (Smith & Ellsworth, 1987). At both times, students often reported mixed feelings, such as hope and fear before the exam or anger and guilt after the exam. These emotional blends were reliably related to the students' appraisals of their performance, the importance of the test, their own effort in studying, their degree of certainty about how well they would do, and so on. The students who felt angriest about their poor grades, for example, interpreted the exam as being unfair. This anger, though, was often combined with guilt ("I should have studied harder"), fear ("What if I don't pass?"), or apathy ("I don't care about this course anyway").

In addition, people differ in how intensely they experience their emotions. Of two people who do well on a test, one may feel mildly pleased whereas the other is ecstatic; of two people who read about a crook who has cheated victims out of their life's savings, one may feel annoyed but the other enraged. Cognitive appraisals help explain why these different reactions occur. People who feel emotions intensely have typical ways of thinking (Larsen, Diener, & Cropanzano, 1987). They *personalize* events ("I thought about how I would feel if my friends, family, or I were in that situation"); they *pay selective attention* to the emotion-provoking aspects of events ("I focused on the worst part of the situation"); and they *overgeneralize*, taking a single event as a sign of a general state of the world. They make mountains out of molehills, whether the molehills are good or bad.

Intensity of emotion also depends on the *frame of reference* against which people interpret an event (Frijda, 1988). Let's say you win a car in a lottery. If you already have four cars, you will probably be merely pleased. If you have always struggled to make ends meet and have been driving a clunker for years, you will probably be ecstatic. Likewise, people who place a great deal of value and significance on reaching a particular goal may feel intensely happy if they succeed, but intensely unhappy if they fail. Other people prefer not to invest so much energy in having brief moments of peak happiness, because they won't then suffer the depths of sadness in contrast—what has been called the "psychic cost" of extreme joy (Diener et al., 1991). Which type are you?

Studies of the cognitive element in emotion suggest that depressed or anxious people can learn how their thinking affects their emotions and change their thinking accordingly (Beck, 1991; see Chapter 16). They can ask themselves what the evidence is for their belief that the world will collapse if they get a C in biology, that no one loves them, or that they will be lonely forever. In

Evelyn Ashford, winner of the 100-meter dash at the 1984 Olympics in spite of nearly being sidelined by injuries, shows blends of emotion on her face: joy, pride, relief, exhaustion.

such cases, it is not emotional reasoning that prevents critical thinking; it is the failure to think critically that creates the emotion!

As you see, the cognitions that are involved in emotion range from your immediate perceptions of a specific event to your basic philosophy of life. If you believe that winning is everything and trying your best counts for nothing, you may feel depressed rather than happy if you "only" come in second. If you think a friend's criticism is intentionally mean rather than well meaning, you may respond with anger rather than gratitude. If you believe that intense emotions are what life is all about, you may ride a roller coaster of ups and downs; if you follow a Zen philosophy that an ideal life requires the mastery of feeling, you may seek a path of emotional calm. This is why almost all theories of emotion agree that cognitive appraisals, the *meanings* people give to events, are essential to the creation of emotion (Frijda, 1988; Lazarus, 1991; Oatley & Johnson-Laird, 1987; Ortony, Clore, & Collins, 1988). Our emotions cannot be separated from our mental lives.

Quick QUIZ

Test your understanding of the cognitive components of emotion.

1. Chronically lonely and depressed people tend to believe that the reasons for their unhappiness are (a) controllable, (b) temporary, (c) internal, (d) caused by the situation.
2. People who react intensely to events tend to (a) take them personally, (b) be oversensitive, (c) have abnormal arousal levels, (d) focus on the larger meaning of the event.
3. At a party, you see your date flirting with your best friend. Suddenly you are flooded with jealousy. What cognitions might be causing this emotion? *Be specific.* What alternative thoughts might reduce the jealousy?

Answers:

1. c 2. a 3. Possible thoughts causing jealousy are "My date finds other people more attractive," "My best friend is trying to steal my date," "My date's behavior is humiliating me." But you could be saying, "It's a compliment to me that other people find my date attractive" or "It pleases me that my date is getting such deserved attention."

The Mind-Body Connection

For many centuries in Western civilization, emotion was regarded as the opposite of thinking, and an inferior opposite at that. The heart (emotion) was said to go its own way, in spite of what the head (reason) wanted. The division between thinking and feeling has provoked some of the longest-running "either-or" debates in intellectual history. Are emotions and cognitions two separate processes that often conflict with each other, or are they inextricably connected? Can we control our emotions, or do they control us? Is thinking always "rational" and emotion "irrational"?

Today, as their understanding of emotion increases, researchers are finding new ways of thinking about feeling and of understanding how physiological and cognitive processes interact (Izard, 1994a). Some findings and research directions help to resolve the historic conflict between mind and body:

1. *Emotions and cognitions evolve and change in the course of human development, and so do their interconnections.* Infant emotion is not cognitively sophisticated,

Many people believe that emotions are the downfall of our species because emotions are the opposite of reason. But are emotion and rationality really independent of each other? How can we avoid thinking about reason and emotion in either-or ways?

This baby will not feel an ounce of remorse for keeping her parents up all night—or gratitude for their care. Remorse and gratitude require the capacity for complex appraisals.

but infants certainly notice *something* that distresses them—gas pains, frustrations in the environment, discomfort. Their early "appraisals" and responses are fairly primitive: good or bad, approach it or avoid it. As the baby and the cerebral cortex develop, cognitive appraisals, and therefore emotions, become more complex (Malatesta, 1990; Oatley & Jenkins, 1992). Indeed, some emotions depend entirely on cognitive development. Infants don't feel shame or guilt, for example, because these "self-conscious" emotions require the emergence of a sense of self and the perception that one has behaved badly and let down another person (Baumeister, Stillwell, & Heatherton, 1994; Tangney & Fischer, 1995).

2. *Relationships between cognition and emotion work in both directions.* Emotion results from appraisals and other thoughts; but emotions themselves can impair or interfere with subsequent thoughts and feelings. For example, you decide that a friend has intentionally stood you up for lunch, so you feel angry. But once you feel angry, you may be unwilling to listen to anyone who tries to correct your way of thinking about your friend's tardiness.

Similarly, a perception such as "This person is out to hurt me" can produce emotional arousal; but being physiologically aroused for nonemotional reasons—exercise, stress, crowds, noise—can make emotions more intense. If you are at a noisy, crowded concert and you believe that someone has insulted you, you are likely to feel very angry, very quickly. You will feel angrier than if you had been listening to a quiet clarinet, lying on the sofa, or watching a romantic comedy when the "insult" occurred (Averill, 1982; Zillmann, 1983).

3. *Cognitions need not be conscious and voluntary to create emotions; there are different levels of cognitive processing and awareness.* As we saw in previous chapters, some modes of cognitive activity operate nonconsciously and without voluntary control. Some emotions, too, involve only simple nonconscious reactions, such as a conditioned emotional response to a symbol of patriotism. Others require complex cognitive capacity, such as the ability to appreciate wordplay or subtle puns before finding them funny. Some emotions are almost instantaneous, processed quickly by the amygdala, but others require the cerebral cortex, the center of reason, symbols, and logic. This part of the brain gives us the capacity for deciding we have been betrayed, for reanalyzing our fears, for interpreting someone else's actions—in short, for generating complex emotions. Appraisals may conflict at these different levels, which is why you can simultaneously believe that airplanes are safe *and* feel worried about getting in one.

4. *Both emotion and cognition can be "rational" or "irrational."* As we saw in the chapters on thinking (Chapter 8) and memory (Chapter 9), thinking is not always rational. There are many "irrational" biases in normal human cognition, such as the confirmation bias, biases due to cognitive dissonance, and biases in the construction of memories. Conversely, emotions are not always irrational. They bind people together, regulate relationships, and motivate people to achieve their goals. Without the capacity to feel emotion, as we saw in Chapters 4 and 8, people have difficulty making ethical decisions and planning for the future (Damasio, 1994). "The appropriate way to see emotions is not as irrational elements in our lives," observes emotion researcher Keith Oatley (1990), "but as a clever biological solution to problems . . . that have no fully rational solutions." When you are faced with a decision between two appealing and justifiable career alternatives, for example, your sense of which one "feels right" emotionally may help you make the best personal choice.

An individual's experience of emotion, then, combines mind and body. But all individuals live in a social world. Thoughts may influence emotion, but where do these thoughts come from? You may decide you are wildly jealous, but where do you get your ideas of jealousy? You may feel angry enough to punch the walls, but where do you learn what to do when you are that enraged? To answer these questions, we turn to the third major aspect of emotional experience: the role of culture.

■ ELEMENTS OF EMOTION 3: THE CULTURE

A young wife leaves her house one morning to draw water from the local well as her husband watches from the porch. On her way back from the well, a male stranger stops her and asks for some water. She gives him a cupful and then invites him home to dinner. He accepts. The husband, wife, and guest have a pleasant meal together. The husband, in a gesture of hospitality, invites the guest to spend the night—with his wife. The guest accepts. In the morning, the husband leaves early to bring home breakfast. When he returns, he finds his wife again in bed with the visitor.

The question is: At what point in this story does the husband feel angry? The answer is: It depends on the culture to which he belongs (Hupka, 1981, 1991). A North American husband would feel rather angry at a wife who had an extramarital affair, and a wife would feel rather angry at being offered to a guest as if she were a lamb chop. But these reactions are not universal:

- A Pawnee husband of the nineteenth century would be enraged at any man who dared ask his wife for water.

- An Ammassalik Inuit husband finds it perfectly honorable to offer his wife to a stranger, but only once. He would be angry to find his wife and the guest having a second encounter.

- A Toda husband at the turn of the century in India would not be angry at all. The Todas allowed both husband and wife to take lovers, and women were even allowed to have several husbands. Both spouses might feel angry, though, if one of them had a *sneaky* affair, without announcing it publicly.

People in most cultures experience anger as a response to insult and the violation of social rules. It's just that they disagree about what an insult or the correct rule is. In this section, we will explore some cultural influences on emotion.

The Varieties of Emotion

Are emotions universal, or do some of them have national boundaries? One problem in answering this question is that some languages have words for emotional states that other languages lack (Mesquita & Frijda, 1993). The Germans have *schadenfreude,* a feeling of joy at another's misfortune. The Japanese have *ijirashii,* a feeling associated with seeing an admirable person overcoming an obstacle, and *hagaii,* helpless anguish tinged with frustration. *Litost* is a Czech word that combines grief, sympathy, remorse, and longing; the Czech writer Milan Kundera used it to describe "a state of torment caused by a sudden insight into one's own miserable self." On the island of Java, *isin* is a complex anxiety and shame reaction involving fear and lowered self-esteem. Interestingly, a number of languages lack a word for *emotion* itself (Russell, 1991a).

Anthropologist Robert Levy (1984) reports that Tahitians lack the Western concept of and word for sadness. If you ask a Tahitian who is grieving over the loss of a lover what is wrong, he will say, "A spirit has made me ill." In contrast, Tahitians have a word for an emotion that most Westerners do not experience: *mehameha* reflects "a sense of the uncanny," a trembling sensation that Tahitians feel when ordinary categories of perception are suspended: at twilight, in the brush, watching fires glow without heat. To Westerners, an event that cannot be categorized and identified is usually greeted with fear. Yet *mehameha* does not describe what Westerners call fear or terror.

Cultures everywhere determine the rules for expressing emotions. The rule for a formal Japanese wedding portrait is "no expressions"—but not every member of this family has learned that rule yet.

Do these interesting examples mean that Germans are more likely than others actually to feel *schadenfreude*, the Japanese to feel *hagaii*, the Javanese to feel *isin*, and the Czechs to feel *litost*—or are they just more willing to give these emotions a single name? And do the Tahitians experience sadness the way we do even though they identify it as illness?

One way to examine the problem of cultural universals is to take a *prototype* approach to the concept of emotion (Russell, 1991b; Shaver, Wu, & Schwartz, 1992). We saw in Chapter 8 that a prototype is the best representative of a certain class of things. For example, most people will say that anger and sadness are more representative of an emotion than irritability and nostalgia are. According to the prototype approach, basic emotions are those that people everywhere consider the core examples of the category "emotion," and these basic emotions are reflected in the emotion words that young children learn first: *happy, sad, mad,* and *scared*. As children develop, they begin to draw emotional distinctions that are less prototypical and more specific to their language and culture, such as *ecstatic, depressed, hostile,* or *anxious* (Russell, 1991b; Russell & Fehr, 1994; Storm & Storm, 1987). They may learn that *indignation* is a kind of anger, or that *pride* is a kind of happiness.

Many psychologists believe that it is possible to identify a number of **primary emotions** that are experienced universally. Depending on the method of measuring emotion, the list of the primary ones varies somewhat, but it typically includes fear, anger, sadness, joy, surprise, disgust, and contempt. The evidence for primary emotions comes from physiological research on the brain; universally recognized facial expressions; the fact that there are emotion prototypes in most languages; and the predictable appearance of these emotions in child development. Some researchers define an emotion as basic if it cannot be reduced to other component emotions and if it is linked with specific tendencies to act, as in running from something fearful (Fox, 1991; Johnson-Laird & Oatley, 1992). In contrast, **secondary emotions** are more culture-specific. They include cultural variations such as *schadenfreude* or *hagaii;* blends of feeling such as *litost* or *isin;* and degrees of intensity and nuance.

Other psychologists think that the effort to find basic or universal emotions is misleading. They point out that most people don't really think of surprise, disgust, or contempt as true emotions, although all three are registered on the face (Ortony & Turner, 1990; Shaver et al., 1987). Conversely, these researchers note, shame, hope, guilt, pride, pity, and empathy are as much a part of human emotional experience as sadness and anger, but these feelings fail to make the

■ **primary emotions**
Emotions that are considered to be universal and biologically based. They generally include fear, anger, sadness, joy, surprise, and disgust.

■ **secondary emotions**
Emotions that are either "blends" of primary emotions or that are specific to certain cultures.

This father is clearly proud of his family. Is pride just a variation of happiness, or is it a distinct emotion?

list of primary emotions because they can't be measured in the brain or identified on the face.

Cultural psychologists argue that the effort to find biological universals in emotion masks the profound influence of culture on *every* aspect of emotional experience, including those considered basic. For example, anger may be a basic emotion in the United States, which emphasizes independence and personal rights, but it is caused and experienced quite differently in community-oriented cultures, where shame and loss of face are more central and basic emotions (Kitayama & Markus, 1994). And most Westerners would say that love is a basic, positive emotion, even though it doesn't have a typical facial expression (except perhaps the mooning gaze of new sweethearts). In a study of Chinese adults in the People's Republic of China, however, "sad love" turned out to be a basic and *negative* emotion prototype, consisting of a cluster of feelings such as unrequited love, infatuation, nostalgia, and sorrow (Shaver, Wu, & Schwartz, 1992). The researchers describe this emotion as "the fleeting passion you feel for an attractive person you see on a train and will never meet again." Most Westerners would surely recognize this feeling, but they would consider it, along with other forms of love, to be more positive than the Chinese do. What, then, would theories of primary emotions look like from a non-Western perspective?

As a result of such problems, a few psychologists are ready to abandon the whole idea of trying to identify primary emotions. Some argue that it may be useful to classify emotions for research purposes, but we should not infer that some emotions are therefore more *fundamental* or universal than others (Ortony & Turner, 1990).

As you can see, answers to the question "Are emotions universal?" depend on whether researchers are focusing on the common elements in all emotions or on cultural differences. In the most general sense, for instance, emotions are evoked by the same situations (Mesquita & Frijda, 1993; Oatley & Duncan, 1994). In a massive cross-cultural research project involving 37 countries on five continents, the researchers found remarkable commonalities in people's reported experiences with fear, anger, joy, sadness, disgust, shame, and guilt (Scherer & Wallbott, 1994). For people everywhere, sadness follows perception of loss, fear follows perception of threat and bodily harm, anger follows perception of insult or injustice, and so forth. Moreover, in all of these cultures, people's subjective descriptions of these emotions were quite similar. So were their descriptions of physical symptoms, such as feeling hot in response to anger and a "lump in the throat" in response to sadness.

Nevertheless, psychologists do agree that cultures determine much of what people feel angry, sad, lonely, happy, or ashamed *about*. Among the Bedouins, shame is produced by any violations of a complex code of honor; on Bali and Java, shame and embarrassment are generated by perceived challenges to one's status (Mesquita & Frijda, 1993). On the Micronesian atoll of Ifaluk, it is cause for anger if someone next to you is smoking without offering you the cigarette; it means the smoker is unwilling to share—a terrible offense (Lutz, 1988). Increasingly in the United States, of course, it is cause for anger if someone is smoking at all. To nonsmokers, it means an infringement on their right to clean air.

The Communication of Emotion

When Brian Boitano won the gold medal in men's figure skating in the 1988 Olympics, he burst into tears of joy. But when he was actually given the award, he accepted it without expression. Why did he put on a stone face? "I almost felt guilty," Boitano explained later. "I had to hold back. My facial expression could only make him [rival Brian Orser] feel worse. I was not going to gloat" (in Friedman & Miller-Herringer, 1991).

As Boitano's story illustrates, once you feel an emotion, how you express it is rarely a simple matter of "I say (or show) what I feel." You may be obliged to disguise what you feel. You may wish you could feel what you say. You may convey an emotional message unintentionally, through nonverbal signals.

Whatever the emotion, every society has **display rules** that govern how and when emotions may be expressed (Ekman et al., 1987). In some cultures, grief is expressed by noisy wailing and weeping; in others, by stoic, tearless resignation; in still others, by merry dance, drink, and song. In some traditions, love is supposed to be expressed by extravagant gesture, like the one Ulrich made in his Venus suit; in others, love is expressed by sustained, understated action. Imagine, then, the conflict that can occur between people from different cultures.

Even biologically based expressions have many cultural interpretations. For example, the smile seems simple and unmistakable; it is, as we saw, generally recognized the world over as a sign of friendliness. Yet it has many meanings and uses that are not universal. Americans smile more frequently than Germans; this does not mean that Americans are friendlier than Germans, but that they differ in their notions of when a smile is appropriate. After a German-American business session, Americans often complain that their German counterparts are cold and aloof. Meanwhile, Germans often complain that the Americans are excessively cheerful, hiding their real feelings under the mask of a smile (Hall & Hall, 1990). The Japanese smile even more than Americans, to disguise embarrassment, anger, or other negative emotions whose public display is considered rude and incorrect.

People learn their culture's display rules as effortlessly as they learn its language. Just as they can speak without knowing the rules of grammar, most people express or suppress their emotions without being aware of the rules they are following (Keating, 1994). Consider the display rules for the stages of an angry dispute (Hall, 1976). Suppose your neighbor builds a fence on what you believe is your property. If you are an American or Canadian, your anger is likely to move from small steps to large ones. You start by dropping hints ("Gee, Mort, are you sure that fence is on your side of the line?"). Next, you talk to friends. Then you get a third person to intervene. Eventually you confront Mort directly. If none of this works, you may go to court and sue him. If that strategy fails, you may burn the fence down.

What are good manners and dignified restraint to a European may seem "cold" or "unfeeling" to the average American. Can you imagine the unfortunate consequences of overlooking the effects of culture on the display of emotions?

■ **display rules**
Social and cultural rules that regulate when, how, and where a person may express (or suppress) emotions.

There is, however, nothing "natural" about this course of action. Worldwide, it isn't even very typical. In many cultures, especially those of the Middle East and Latin America, the first thing you do when your neighbor builds a fence that angers you is . . . nothing. You think about it. You brood over your grievances and decide what to do. This brooding may last for weeks, months, or even years. The second step is . . . you burn the fence down. This is only to draw your neighbor's attention to the fact that you two have a problem, and now you are ready for negotiations, lawyers, third-party interventions, and so on. Notice how cultures misunderstand the same action: Burning the fence down is the last resort in one, but the start of the conversation in another.

Display rules not only tell us what to do when we *are* feeling an emotion; they also tell us how and when we should show an emotion we do *not* feel. Acting out an emotion we don't really feel, or trying to create the right emotion for the occasion, has been called **emotion work.** People are expected to demonstrate sadness at funerals, happiness at weddings, and affection toward relatives. If they don't really feel such emotions, they may playact to convince others that they do.

Sometimes emotion work is a job requirement, as a study of flight attendants and bill collectors found (Hochschild, 1983). Flight attendants must "put on a happy face" to convey cheerfulness, even if they are angry about a rude or drunken passenger. Bill collectors must put on a stern face to convey threat; they must withhold sympathy, even if they are feeling sorry for the poor person in debt. Other employees do emotion work when they express agreement with an employer's infuriating decision or when they display cheerfulness to annoying customers. But not all emotion work is negative. The effort to interpret a situation in a positive light, and to generate real feelings of warmth and friendliness toward others, not only makes social relations more pleasurable but also makes feeling positive emotions more likely.

Smiling and friendliness are part of the job description for flight attendants—but not necessarily for the executives who are among the passengers they serve.

Quick QUIZ

The following example of cultural miscommunication occurred in an English class for foreign students. An Arab student was describing a tradition of his home country, when he inadvertently said something that embarrassed a Japanese student. To disguise his shame, the Japanese student smiled, and the Arab demanded to know what was so funny about Arab customs. The Japanese, now feeling publicly humiliated, giggled. The Arab, enraged, hit him. What concepts from the previous section explain this misunderstanding?

Answers:

Arab and Japanese cultures have different display rules regarding the expression of anger, the appropriate response to feeling shamed, and the management of embarrassment in public. The two students also misread each other's nonverbal communication. To the Arab, the Japanese student's smile meant he was being laughed at, but the Japanese intended merely to disguise his discomfort.

■ PUTTING THE ELEMENTS TOGETHER: THE CASE OF EMOTION AND GENDER

"Women are too emotional," men often complain. "Men are too repressed," women often reply. People hold strong beliefs about gender differences in emotion and about whether the male or female style is better (Fischer, 1993;

■ **emotion work**
Expression of an emotion, often because of a role requirement, that one does not really feel.

Why is it "arguing" when he does it but "getting emotional" when she does it? On emotional subjects, people often fail to define their terms. What, for example, does emotional *mean?*

Shields, 1991). But what do they mean by "emotional"? As we have seen, "being emotional" can refer to an internal emotional state, to the cognitive tendency to make mountains out of molehills, to the way an emotion is displayed, or to emotion work. Because emotion has so many aspects, it is necessary to define our terms before we can understand whether or how the sexes differ.

The Experience of Emotion.   To begin with, there is not much evidence that, around the world, one sex experiences emotions more often than the other (Baumeister, Stillwell, & Wotman, 1990; Fischer et al., 1993; Oatley & Duncan, 1994; Shaver & Hazan, 1987; Shields, 1991). Both sexes are equally likely, on the average, to feel anxious in new situations; to feel jealousy, love, and loneliness; to feel angry when they are frustrated or believe they have been insulted or treated unfairly; to feel embarrassed when they make goofy mistakes; and to grieve when attachments break up. So it seems we must look elsewhere for gender differences in emotion.

The Physiology of Emotion.   If we define emotionality in terms of physiological reactivity to provocation, it seems that men are more emotional than women. John Gottman and his colleagues (Gottman & Krokoff, 1989; Gottman & Levenson, 1986), in longitudinal studies of hundreds of married couples, have found that conflict and dissension are physiologically more upsetting for men than for women, which may be why many men try to avoid conflict entirely. They fear they will overreact by losing control. The researchers monitored the heart rates of husbands and wives before and during actual quarrels, and found that the men's heart rates, unlike the women's, soared to a very fast rate as soon as signs of conflict began—and stayed high longer. Other studies too have found that hostility and anger are more closely linked with marital distress and conflict for husbands than for wives (Smith, Sanders, & Alexander, 1990).

Gottman (1994) suggests two possible explanations for the physiological differences between men and women in response to conflict. One is that the male's autonomic nervous system may be more sensitive and hyperreactive than the female's. Indeed, in field and laboratory studies of stress, males show a more pronounced elevation in the secretion of epinephrine than do females (Polefrone & Manuck, 1987). Gottman suspects that another reason, however, is that men are more likely than women to rehearse negative thoughts—such as "I don't have to take this" or "It's all her fault"—that keep them riled up. This explanation brings us to the next factor that might produce gender differences in emotion.

Cognitions That Generate Emotion.   Men and women often differ in the perceptions and expectations that generate certain emotions, within particular situations (Lakoff, 1990; Stapley & Haviland, 1989). As we have seen, two interpretations of the same event can create two different emotional responses to it. If a male teacher compliments a female student on her new outfit, is that a sign of flattery or sexual harassment? If a woman affectionately touches a male friend on his arm, is she signaling affection or sexual interest? Under such circumstances, it is not that one sex is more emotional, but that the same situation may be interpreted differently by the two parties, producing an emotional response in one partner that the other does not share or understand.

Nonverbal Communication.   Sometimes women are considered more emotional because of their supposed sensitivity to other people's emotional states. This idea has been studied using a test called the Profile of Nonverbal Sensitivity (PONS), which measures a person's ability to detect emotions revealed in tones of voice, movements of the body, and facial expressions (Rosenthal et al., 1979). Women have scored slightly better on this test than men (J. Hall, 1987). But research finds that being sensitive to another person's

Men and women often disagree on the meaning of a touch: Does it signify affection, dominance, harassment, sexual interest, sympathy, or simple friendliness? Depending on their perceptions, men and women may react to a touch with anger, happiness, disgust, fear, or desire.

emotional state often depends more on the *context* in which the two people are interacting than on their gender. In particular, sensitivity to emotional signals depends on:

1. *The sex of the sender and of the receiver.* People do better reading their own sex's signals than those of the other sex (Buck, 1984).

2. *How well the two people know each other.* Dating couples and married couples can interpret each other's facial expressions and other emotional signs better than strangers can (Hatfield, Cacioppo, & Rapson, 1992).

3. *Who has the power.* Less powerful people learn to read the powerful person's signals, usually for self-protection (Fiske, 1993; Henley, 1995; Lakoff, 1990). For example, in two experiments, Sara Snodgrass (1985, 1992) found that "women's intuition" should more properly be called "subordinate's intuition." In male-female pairs, the person in the subordinate (follower) position was more sensitive to the leader's nonverbal signals than the leader was to the follower's cues. This difference occurred whether a man or a woman was the leader or the follower. The social positions that people are in, Snodgrass found, almost totally overrode any gender differences.

The Display Rules for Emotional Expression. Finally, we come to a significant gender difference that contributes to the stereotype of women's greater emotionality. In North America, women are encouraged and permitted to express certain emotions and men are expected to control them. In numerous studies, women say that they express their feelings more often than men

Both sexes feel emotionally attached to their friends and loved ones, but often they learn to express their feelings of closeness differently. From childhood on, girls tend to prefer face to face friendships, based on shared feelings; boys tend to prefer side by side friendships, based on shared activities.

do, and they also report a greater tendency to talk about their emotions—especially emotions that reveal vulnerability and helplessness, such as fear, sadness, loneliness, shame, and guilt (Fischer, 1993; Grossman & Wood, 1993; Nolen-Hoeksema, 1990).

In contrast, most North American men are permitted to express only one emotion more freely than women, and that is anger in public. Men are more likely than women to reveal anger to strangers, especially other men, when they believe they have been challenged or insulted. Men are also more likely to express anger, fear, or hurt pride in the form of aggressive action (Fischer, 1993). Otherwise, men are expected to control negative feelings that might reveal weakness, such as fear and loneliness. If they express "unmanly" emotions at all, many men tend to do so only to their intimate partners, and rarely to casual male friends (Gottman, 1994). Two psychologists, reviewing 39 studies, found that both sexes were equally liosly to feel lonely but women were much more likely to admit it. One reason, the researchers discovered, was that both sexes are more likely to reject a lonely male than a lonely female. There are greater negative consequences to men than to women, it seems, of revealing unhappiness (Borys & Perlman, 1985).

One consequence of the social taboo on male expression of vulnerability and hurt may be difficulty in recognizing when men are unhappy. In fact, some researchers believe that many boys and men fail to be diagnosed as depressed because the tests for depression are based on typically female reactions such as crying, staying in bed, and talking about one's unhappiness (Riessman, 1990; Stapley & Haviland, 1989). Because many men do not express grief this way, some people wrongly infer that men suffer less than women when relationships end or that they are somehow incapable of deep feeling.

Catherine Riessman (1990) began to question this assumption while she was interviewing a large sample of wives and husbands about their divorces. The men were suffering as much as the women, Riessman learned; they just didn't say so. In fact, most of the men claimed they felt sad only "some or a little of the time" and that they felt depressed or lonely "none of the time." However, Riessman found, these men were expressing grief in ways that are acceptably masculine: "frantic work," heavy drinking, driving too fast, singing sentimental songs. Many of the men reported trouble concentrating at work, difficulties on the job, restlessness and hyperactivity, and numerous physical ailments and stress symptoms. One man confessed that for four months after his separation he "threw up every morning," but he firmly denied that he was actually depressed. Another denied feeling sad, but in the six months since his divorce he had racked up a long list of criminal charges.

Research suggests that gender differences in emotional expressiveness are a learned result of social roles and cultural norms (Grossman & Wood, 1993). Across cultures the display rules for women and men are highly variable. In many Asian cultures, both sexes are taught to control emotional expression (Buck & Teng, 1987). In cultures throughout Europe, the Middle East, and South America, the display rules for women and men often depend on the emotion in question. In the international study mentioned earlier, for example, Israeli and Italian men were much more likely than women to control feelings of sadness, but British, Spanish, Swiss, and German women were more likely than their male counterparts to inhibit this emotion. Overall, European women were not more emotionally expressive than men; the differences were greater between cultures than between genders (Wallbott, Ricci-Bitti, & Bänninger-Huber, 1986).

Moreover, even within a culture, the influence of a particular situation often overrides gender rules. An American man will be as likely as an American woman to control his temper when the target of anger is someone with higher status or power; few people, no matter how angry, will readily sound off at a professor, police officer, or employer. But in the home, when men and women feel angry they are both likely to express it by sulking, discussing matters outright, or being verbally abusive (Averill, 1982; Gelles & Straus, 1988). Although many men are reluctant to express vulnerable feelings to their friends, men in happy marriages are as likely as their wives to express feelings of worry, fear, anger, and joy to their spouse (Gottman, 1994). And you won't find gender differences in emotional expressiveness at a football game!

So if emotionality is defined in terms of display rules, we find that North American women tend to be more emotional than men in revealing and talking about their negative feelings, to friends as well as husbands; men are more emotional than women in displaying negative feelings in aggressive or self-destructive ways. And in some situations—such as a happy marriage, an exciting sports event, or a conflict with one's employer—neither sex is more emotionally expressive than the other.

Emotion Work. Both sexes know the experience of having to hide emotions they feel and pretend emotions they do not feel. Yet their emotion work, on the job and at home, is often different. On the whole, women tend to be involved in the flight-attendant side of emotion work, persuading others that they are friendly, happy, and warm, and making sure others are happy. Men tend to be involved in the bill-collection side, persuading others that they are stern, aggressive, and unemotional. Care-oriented emotion work—tending to other people's feelings as well as managing or disguising one's own—is typically part of the woman's role more than the man's (Fischer, 1993; Grossman & Wood, 1993).

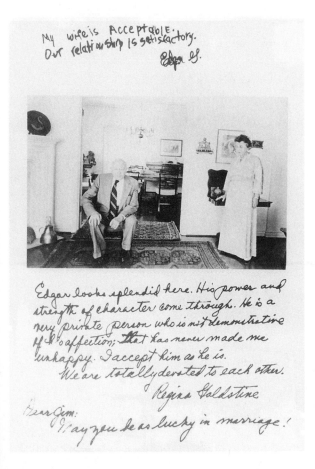

Photographer Jim Goldberg took photos of couples and asked them to write their comments on the prints. What do you think about the marriage portrayed in this picture? Do Edgar and Regina have different feelings about each other or do they just express their feelings differently?

Perhaps as part of their emotion work, women in North America smile more often than men do—not necessarily because they feel happier, but to pacify, nurture, and convey deference (Henley, 1995). If women don't smile when others expect them to, they are often disliked, even if they are actually smiling as often as men would. Children learn this lesson early. Carolyn Saarni (1989) found that 6- to 10-year-olds show a steady increase in knowledge about where and when they should disguise feelings and put on a "polite smile" (for instance, when they are given a gift they don't like). From childhood on, girls are more likely than boys to mask their negative feelings with positive expressions. As adults, women often express anger with a smile, a mixed message that can be puzzling to their friends, spouses, and children (Deutsch, LeBaron, & Fryer, 1987). The smile requirement for women is not universal, though. In Taiwan and China, for example, women do not differ from men in facial expressiveness (Buck & Teng, 1987).

Thus, with regard to emotion work and display rules, it appears that, in some cultural groups at least, women are expected to be more emotional than men, in terms of managing their own and other people's feelings. But if we define emotionality in terms of physiological reactivity, emotion-generating perceptions, expressiveness, or nonverbal sensitivity, we see that the answer to "who is more emotional" is sometimes men, sometimes women, and sometimes neither. It depends on the individual, the situation, the particular emotion, and the culture.

As we have seen in this chapter, the full experience and expression of emotion involves physiology, cognitive processes, and cultural rules. The case of gender and emotion shows that if we look at just one component, we come up with an incomplete or misleading picture. Human emotions can be compared to a tree: The biological capacity for emotion is the trunk; thoughts and explanations create the many branches; and culture is the gardener that shapes the tree and prunes it, cutting off some limbs and cultivating others.

Emotions have many purposes in human life. They allow us to establish close bonds, threaten and warn, get help from others, reveal or deceive. The many varieties and expressions of emotion suggest that although we feel emotions physically, we use them socially. As we explore further issues in motivation, personality, development, well-being, and mental disorders, we will see again and again how emotions involve thinking and feeling, perception and action—head and heart.

Taking Psychology with You

"Let It Out" or "Bottle It Up"? The Dilemma of Anger

What do you do when you feel angry? Do you tend to brood and sulk, collecting your righteous complaints like acorns for the winter, or do you erupt, hurling your wrath upon anyone or anything at hand? Do you discuss your feelings when you have calmed down? Does "letting anger out" get rid of it for you, or does it only make it more intense? The answer is crucial for how we get along with our families, neighbors, employers, and strangers. Increasingly, it seems, people are freely venting their anger in the home and in public with rude gestures and insulting remarks, and the level of public

debate about serious issues seems to have degenerated into name-calling and the exchange of hostilities.

Although some schools of therapy once advised people to "get it out of your system," psychologists have found that this advice often backfires. Chronic feelings of anger and an inability to control anger can be as emotionally devastating and unhealthy as chronic problems with depression or anxiety (Deffenbacher, 1994; Williams, 1989). In contrast to much pop-psych advice, research shows that expressing anger does not always get rid of anger; often it prolongs it. When people talk about their anger or act on that feeling, they tend to rehearse their grievances, create a hostile disposition, and pump up their blood pressure (Averill, 1982; Tavris, 1989). Conversely, when people learn to control their tempers and express anger constructively, they usually feel better, not worse; calmer, not angrier. Charles Darwin (1872/1965) observed this fact more than a century ago. "The free expression by outward signs of an emotion intensifies it," he wrote. "On the other hand, the repression, as far as this is possible, of all outward signs softens our emotions. He who gives way to violent gestures will increase his rage."

Some people behave aggressively when they are angry, but others behave in a friendly, cooperative way to try to solve the problem that is causing their anger. When people are feeling angry, after all, they can do many things: write letters, play the piano, jog, bake bread, kick the sofa, abuse their friends or family, or yell. If a particular action soothes their feelings or gets the desired response from other people, they are likely to acquire a habit. Soon that habit feels "natural," as if it could never be changed; indeed, many people justify their violent tempers by saying "I just couldn't help myself." But they can. If you have learned an abusive or aggressive habit, the research in this chapter offers practical suggestions for relearning constructive ways of managing anger:

- *Don't sound off in the heat of anger; let bodily arousal cool down.* Whether your arousal comes from background stresses such as heat, crowds, or loud noise, or from conflict with another person, take time to relax (Gottman, 1994). Time allows you to decide if you are "really" angry or just tired and tense. This is the reason for that age old advice to count to 10, count to 100, or sleep on it. Other "cooling-off" strategies include taking a time-out in the middle of an argument, meditating or relaxing, and calming yourself with a distracting activity.

- *Remember that anger depends on the perception of insult; check your perceptions for accuracy, and then see if you can rethink the problem.* People who are quick to feel anger tend to interpret other people's actions as intentional offenses. People who are slow to anger tend to give others the benefit of the doubt and they are not as focused on their own injured pride. Empathy ("Poor guy, he's feeling rotten") is usually incompatible with anger, so practice seeing the situation from the other person's perspective (Miller & Eisenberg, 1988; Tangney, 1992).

- *If you decide that expressing anger is appropriate, think carefully about how to do it so that you will get the results you want.* As we saw, different cultures have different display rules. Be sure the recipient of your anger understands what you are feeling and what complaint you are trying to convey—and this is true whether the recipient is your parent, friend, annoying neighbor, employer, or city hall.

Ultimately, the decision about whether to express anger depends not only on whether you will feel good if you do, but also on what you hope to accomplish. Do you want to restore your rights, change the other person, improve a bad situation, or achieve justice? If those are your goals, then learning how to express anger so the other person will listen and respond is essential. People who have been the targets of injustice have learned that outbursts of anger may draw society's attention to a problem—but real change requires sustained political effort, challenges to unfair laws, and the use of tactics that persuade rather than alienate the opposition.

Of course, if you just want to "blow off steam," go right ahead; but you risk becoming a hothead.

Summary

1. The complex experience of *emotion* involves physiological changes in the brain, face, and body; cognitive processes; and culture. In the late nineteenth century, the *James-Lange theory of emotion* proposed that awareness of bodily reactions to an event gives rise to the experience of emotion. "We feel sorry *because* we cry, angry *because* we strike," wrote James. His work inspired modern efforts to study the relationship between physiology and cognition in emotion.

2. Some basic facial expressions—anger, fear, sadness, happiness, disgust, surprise, contempt—are widely recognized across cultures. Different facial expressions are apparent in infancy, and infants recognize adult expressions of fear, anger, and happiness. But culture interacts with physiology to influence when and how emotions are displayed, as the example of disgust illustrates. Facial expressions probably evolved to foster communication and survival, but according to the *facial-feedback hypothesis*, they also send messages to the brain identifying our own emotional states; facial expressions may also affect positive and negative moods by regulating blood flow in the brain. Because people can disguise their emotions, however, facial expressions do not always communicate accurately.

3. Some researchers study structures of the brain in order to identify biological components of emotion: particularly the *amygdala*, which is part of the limbic system and responsible for immediate processing of incoming stimuli that are perceived as dangerous or threatening, and the *cerebral cortex*, which provides the ability to assess incoming information and evaluate danger. Biological research is identifying the different areas of the brain that are involved in various aspects of emotional experience; for example, the right hemisphere seems to be specialized for the processing of negative emotions, the left hemisphere for positive emotions. Parts of the brain also specialize in recognizing faces and facial expressions.

4. *Epinephrine* and *norepinephrine* are hormones that produce physiological *arousal* to prepare the body to cope with environmental stimuli, nonemotional but physically taxing events, and all emotional states. These hormones produce changes in heart rate, respiration, pupil dilation, blood sugar levels, digestion, memory, and performance. Arousal takes several forms, which involve different areas of the brain; arousal itself does not cause an emotional state. The autonomic nervous system produces different patterns of physiological changes that correspond to different emotions.

5. Schachter and Singer's *two-factor theory of emotion* holds that emotions result from *arousal* and the *labeling* or interpretation of that arousal. Their research launched many studies designed to identify the cognitive processes involved in emotion, such as the way people interpret and evaluate events. For example, people who feel depressed and lonely tend to think that the reasons for their unhappiness are *internal, stable, and uncontrollable.* People who feel emotions intensely tend to personalize events, pay selective attention, and overgeneralize. Intensity of emotion also depends on a person's *frame of reference* against which an event is interpreted.

6. New approaches help resolve the age-old "reason-versus-emotion" debate in philosophy, showing how physiological and cognitive processes interact in the experience of emotion. Developmental research shows that emotions and cognitions change and become more complex with age; cognition and emotion influence each other; the cognitions involved in emotion can be nonconscious as well as conscious, and involve different degrees of cognitive complexity; both emotion and cognition can be rational or irrational, and both are necessary for wise reasoning and planning.

7. Some researchers distinguish *primary* emotions, which are thought to be universal, from *secondary* emotions, which include variations and blends that are specific to cultures. Research on facial expressions and brain physiology, emotion *prototypes*, and child development supports the view that the primary emotions are fear, anger, sadness, joy, surprise, disgust, and contempt. Other psychologists disagree with the effort to find primary emotions. They doubt that surprise and disgust are true emotions; they also think this list omits such universal emotions as love, hope, empathy, shame, and pride, which are difficult to measure physiologically.

8. Although cross-cultural research does find remarkable commonalities in the general causes of the basic emotions and in people's subjective descriptions of them, it is also true that cultures profoundly influence the experience and expression of emotions. They determine what their members feel emotional about and what people do when they feel an emotion. *Display rules* are the culture's way of regulating how, when, and where a person may express or must suppress an emotion. *Emotion work* is the effort a person makes to display an emotion he or she doesn't really feel but feels obliged to convey.

9. Women and men are equally likely to feel a wide array of emotions, from love to anger. Men seem to be more physiologically reactive to conflict than women are, however, and the sexes sometimes differ in the perceptions and expectations that generate emotion and emotional intensity. Although women are said to be better than men at reading another person's emotional state, this ability depends on whether the two individuals are of the same gender, their familiarity with each other, and, most of all, which one has more power.

10. Men and women differ primarily in the display rules that govern the expression of emotions, a reason for the stereotype of female "emotionality." Women are more likely to talk about feelings of fear, sadness, guilt, and loneliness than men are; men are more likely to deny they have such feelings or to reveal them in aggressive acts. But these gender differences are in turn affected by cultural norms and the influence of a particular situation. Role requirements often specify different emotion work for the two sexes.

Key Terms

emotion *376*

James-Lange theory of emotion *377*

facial-feedback hypothesis *379*

amygdala *380*

epinephrine *381*

norepinephrine *381*

arousal *381*

two-factor theory of emotion *385*

cognitions and depression (internality, stability, control) *387*

prototypes and emotion *392*

primary emotions *392*

secondary emotions *392*

display rules *394*

emotion work *395*

11
Motivation

THE·HARE AND THE·TORTOISE

THEY STARTED TOGETHER, AND THE TORTOISE KEPT JOGGING ON STILL, TILL HE CAME TO THE END OF THE COURSE. THE HARE LAID HIMSELF DOWN MIDWAY AND TOOK A NAP; "FOR," SAYS HE, "I CAN CATCH UP WITH THE TORTOISE WHEN I PLEASE"

In Aesop's fable The Hare and the Tortoise, *the slow but determined tortoise outraces the swift hare because he keeps plodding along while the overconfident rabbit stops for a nap. Moral: In the race of life, motivation and persistence are as important as ability.*

The essential [conditions] of everything you do
. . . must be choice, love, passion.

■ NADIA BOULANGER ■

All Jim Abbott ever wanted to do was play baseball. This is not an unusual ambition, perhaps, but Jim Abbott was born with a condition that might have dampened the motivation of most others: He has no right hand. You'd never know it to watch him pitch in the majors, though (he's currently with the Angels). What would motivate a young man to pursue a goal that everyone told him was impossible?

All Dian Fossey ever wanted to do was study mountain gorillas. This was not an unusual ambition, considering the varied interests that people have, but Dian Fossey's methods might have dampened the motivation of most others. Fossey lived in the wilderness with "her" gorillas, fought fiercely against the human poachers who were paid to kill or capture the animals, endured countless hardships and physical assaults, and was eventually murdered by unknown assailants. Many people have lived temporarily under staggering conditions of hardship to advance knowledge, by, say, traveling to the North Pole or outer space. What would motivate a young woman to choose such hardship as a way of life, forgoing all comforts, family, and human love?

The words *motivation* and *emotion* both come from the Latin root meaning "to move," and the psychology of motivation is indeed the study of what moves us, why we do what we do. Like emotion, motivation involves physiological processes, cognitive processes, and social and cultural processes that shape its expression. Emotion can motivate us to behave in particular ways: Anger can move us to shout, fear can move us to run, and love moves us to do all sorts of things. But emotion is only one kind of motivating force.

In general, **motivation** refers to an inferred process within a person or animal that causes that organism to move toward a goal. The goal may be to satisfy a biological need, as in eating a sandwich to reduce hunger. The goal may be to fulfill a psychological ambition, such as discovering a vaccine for AIDS or winning a Nobel Prize. But psychologists who study motivation, like those who study emotion, often disagree about what the phenomenon is, what causes it, and how to identify it. If you see a woman eating a doughnut, you don't necessarily know her motive for doing so. Perhaps she is ravenously hungry and would eat anything you put in front of her; perhaps she has an insatiable passion for doughnuts and will eat one even if she has just consumed a five-course meal; perhaps she hates doughnuts but is being polite because a friend brought her one as a surprise. Moreover, just as several emotions usually cluster together, so several motives may operate together, sometimes in different directions. A man may be motivated to achieve financial success and to be a good father, but what happens when one motive conflicts with the other?

For many decades, the study of motivation was dominated by *drive theory* (Hull, 1943). In drive theory, biological *needs* result from states of physical deprivation, such as a lack of food or water. Such needs create a physiological *drive*, a state of tension that motivates an organism to satisfy the need. We have

Pitcher Jim Abbott at work.

■ **motivation**
An inferred process within a person or animal that causes that organism to move toward a goal.

405

only a few primary (unlearned) drives, including hunger, thirst, excessive cold, and pain. Although physical energy fuels most human motives (Biner, 1991), it soon became apparent that drive theory could not account for the complexity and variety of human motivations. As drive theory went out of fashion, so did the field of motivation as a major topic in psychology.

Recently, however, research on motivation has been reinvigorated by the "cognitive revolution"—the emphasis throughout psychology on the fact that people are conscious creatures who think and plan ahead, who set goals for themselves and plot strategies to reach them (Dweck, 1992; Pervin, 1992). Modern motivational research tends to emphasize what is unique in human aspirations—such as the pursuit of fame, romantic love, athletic perfection, or a seemingly impossible goal such as rowing across the ocean. These *social motives* (in contrast to biological drives) are learned, some in childhood, some in later life, and they are called "social" because they develop in the context of family, environment, and culture. In this chapter, we have chosen to focus on three domains of adult life that we think best illustrate the cognitive and biological complexities of human social motivation: love, sex, and work. We will then turn to the difficulties that can arise when motives conflict.

▪ THE SOCIAL ANIMAL: MOTIVES FOR CONNECTION

The **need for affiliation** refers to the motive to be with others, to make friends, to cooperate, to love. Our lives would be impossible without connection to others. Human development depends on the child's ability to form attachments and to learn from adults and peers, and on the adult's ability to form relationships with intimate partners, family, friends, and colleagues. No one doesn't need someone.

Of course, individuals vary in their need for affiliation; some like "lots of space" and "breathing room," and others like to be surrounded by friends and family every minute of the day. Cultures, too, vary in the value they place on affiliation. American culture emphasizes independence and self-reliance, but Latino and Asian cultures emphasize family cohesiveness, group interdependence, and teamwork (LeVine & Padilla, 1980; Pascale & Athos, 1981; Spence, 1985a). In the United States "dependence" is almost a dirty word, but in Japan the need for dependence is assumed to be powerful and necessary (Doi, 1973). In reality, all individuals are dependent; but they often depend on one another for different things at different ages.

Attachment

In developmental psychology, *attachment* refers to the deep emotional tie that babies and children develop for their primary caregivers and their distress at being separated from them. But attachments—the sense of physical connection with a loved one and of loss when a loved one leaves—are important all through life. Most adults, no less than babies, find it painful and difficult to endure repeated, temporary separations from a loved partner because of war or job obligations (Vormbrock, 1993). Once people are emotionally attached, separation is a wrenching experience.

Emotional attachment begins with physical attachment: touching and cuddling between infant and parent. Babies who are given adequate food, water, and warmth but who are deprived of being touched and held show retarded emotional and physical development (Bowlby, 1969). The need for and pleasure in physical contact continues throughout life. Emotional and physical symptoms also occur in adults who are "undertouched," such as the sick and the aged. In hospital settings, even the mildest touch by a nurse or physician on the arm, forehead, or shoulder of a sick person reassures and comforts, and reassurance and comfort are half the battle in getting well (Lynch, 1985; Thomas, 1983).

▪ **need for affiliation**
The motive to associate with other people, as by seeking friends, moral support, contact comfort, or companionship.

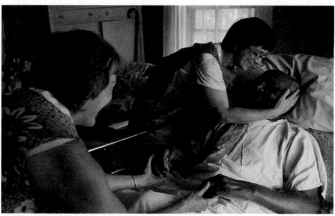

Human beings respond to contact comfort, whether from the reassuring presence of a loved pet or from the reassuring touch of a caretaker.

Margaret and Harry Harlow first demonstrated the primate need for touching, or *contact comfort,* by raising infant rhesus monkeys with two kinds of artificial mothers (Harlow, 1958; Harlow & Harlow, 1966). The first was a forbidding construction of wires and warming lights, with a milk bottle attached. The second was constructed of wire and covered in foam rubber and cuddly terry cloth (see Figure 11.1). At the time, psychologists (but not many mothers) thought that babies become attached to their mothers because mom provides food and warmth. But Harlow's baby monkeys ran to the terry cloth "mother" when they were frightened or startled, and cuddling it calmed them down.

Infants become attached to their mothers or other caregivers for the contact comfort the adults provide, but infant attachment also has other purposes. According to John Bowlby (1969, 1973), it provides a secure base from which

■ **Figure 11.1   The Comfort of Contact**

Infants need cuddling as much as they need food. In Margaret and Harry Harlow's studies, infant rhesus monkeys were raised with a terry cloth "mother" that was cuddly to cling to and with a bare wire "mother" that provided milk. The infants preferred clinging to the terry "mother" when they weren't being fed, and when they were frightened or startled, it was the terry "mother" they ran to. The basis of infant love, concluded the Harlows, is contact comfort, not food.

the child can explore the environment, and it provides a haven of safety to which the child can return when he or she is afraid. A sense of security, said Bowlby, allows children to develop cognitive skills. A sense of safety allows them to develop trust. Severe social deprivation and continued separations from loved ones prevent children from forming attachments, with tragic results.

Between 7 and 9 months, many babies become wary or fearful of strangers, a reaction called *stranger anxiety*. They wail if they are put in an unfamiliar setting or are left with an unfamiliar person. They have become attached to the mother or the primary caregiver and show *separation anxiety* if she or he temporarily leaves the room. This reaction usually continues until the middle of the second year, but many children show signs of distress at parental separation until they are about 3. Virtually all children go through this phase, though cultural child-rearing practices influence how strongly the anxiety is felt and how long it lasts (see Figure 11.2).

To determine the nature of the attachment between mothers and babies, Mary Ainsworth (1973, 1979; Ainsworth et al., 1978) devised a method called the *strange situation*. A mother brings her baby into an unfamiliar room containing lots of toys. After a while a stranger comes in and attempts to play with the child. The mother leaves the baby with the stranger. She then returns, plays with the child, and the stranger leaves. Finally, the mother leaves the baby alone for three minutes and returns. In each case, observers carefully note how the baby behaves—with the mother, with the stranger, and when the baby is alone.

Ainsworth and her associates divided children into three categories on the basis of the children's reactions to the strange situation. Some babies are *securely attached:* They cry or protest if the parent leaves the room; they welcome her back and then play happily again; they are clearly more attached to the mother than to the stranger. But others are insecurely attached. They may be detached or *avoidant*, not caring if the mother leaves the room, making little effort to seek contact with her on her return, and treating the stranger about the same as the mother; or they may be *anxious* or *ambivalent*, resisting contact with the mother at reunion but protesting loudly if she leaves. Insecurely attached children may cry to be picked up and then demand to be put down. Some behave as if they are angry with the mother and resist her efforts to give comfort.

Ainsworth argued that the difference between secure, avoidant, and anxious attachment lies primarily in the way mothers treat their babies in the first few months. Mothers of securely attached babies, she believes, are sensitive to their babies' needs and the meanings of their cries; they are affectionate and demonstrative. Mothers of avoidant babies are irritated by their infants, express con-

■ **Figure 11.2   The Development of Separation Anxiety**

This graph shows the percentage of children in four different cultures who cried when their mothers left the "strange situation." Notice that the babies' attachment typically does not develop until the ages of 7 to 9 months, peaks at about a year of age, and then steadily declines. Notice, too, how the proportion of children responding to their mother's departure varies across cultures, from a high among the African children to a low among the Israelis (from Kagan, Kearsley, & Zelazo, 1978).

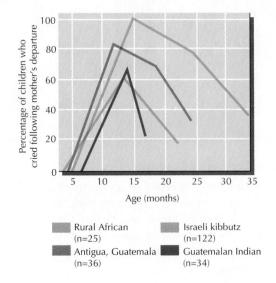

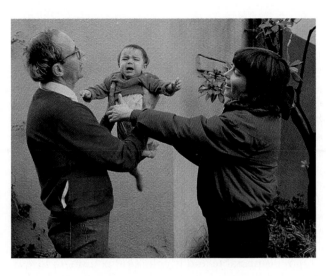

At around 8 months of age, most babies show separation anxiety when their main source of attachment tries handing them over to a stranger.

trolled anger toward them, and are rejecting; they dislike or are uncomfortable with close physical contact with their children. Mothers of anxious-ambivalent babies are insensitive and inept but not rejecting. They don't know what to do to relieve their babies' distress and are "out of sync" in handling their babies.

It is true that mothers and fathers who are abusive, neglectful, or "out of sync" are more likely to have insecurely attached children. Longitudinal studies have found that maternal unresponsiveness to an infant's emotional needs and demands for attention is related to the child's later disruptive and aggressive behavior at ages 2 and 3, and this is especially true for boys (Shaw, Keenan, & Vondra, 1994). However, some babies may become insecurely attached because they are temperamentally difficult, and anyone would have trouble dealing with them (Campos et al., 1984). Moreover, the stability of a particular pattern of attachment also depends on the stability of a child's circumstances: Children are likely to shift from secure to insecure attachment patterns if their families are undergoing a period of chronic stress or illness. And mothers are not the only source of healthy attachment. As we will see in Chapter 13, depending on their culture and environment, babies become attached to their fathers, siblings, regular baby-sitters, and grandparents as well (Tronick, Morelli, & Ivey, 1992).

Behaviorists also point out that babies may learn, through a process of operant conditioning, to fuss and cry when their parents leave the room. In a series of experiments, Jacob Gewirtz and Martha Peláez-Nogueras (1991a, b) showed that when a mother who is about to leave responds to her child's protests by stopping, hesitating, speaking to the child, or returning to pick the child up, or when she comes back into the room while the child is still complaining, the child's protests and crying increase. (Of course, this is precisely what many parents do in real life, leading one to wonder whether it is the child or the parent who has the separation anxiety.) When, in contrast, the mother responds to anything the child does that is *not* crying and protesting, such as laughing or playing with toys, the child's protests soon stop. The researchers were able to condition the child to cry while the mother was leaving the room but not during her brief absence itself—or vice versa—simply by manipulating the mother's behavior.

Regardless of how much of an infant's attachment style is learned, though, everyone agrees that babies need the care, attention, and affection of adults. When infants are consistently deprived of social contact, affection, and cuddling, the effects can be disastrous and long-lasting. Insecurely attached infants often grow into children who have a number of behavioral problems (Speltz, Greenberg, & Deklyen, 1990) and problems in cognitive functioning, such as deductive reasoning (Jacobson, Edelstein, & Hofmann, 1994). And they may grow into adults who are anxious or avoidant in their own close relationships, as we will see next.

Love

"How do I love thee? Let me count the ways," wrote Elizabeth Barrett Browning in a love sonnet to Robert Browning. Social scientists have also counted the ways of loving, although not as eloquently as Browning did. How do people differ in their styles of love? The first step in our understanding, as usual, is to define our terms.

The Varieties of Love. Perhaps the oldest distinction between kinds of love is that between *passionate ("romantic") love,* characterized by a turmoil of intense emotions, and *companionate love,* characterized by affection and trust (Hatfield, 1988). Passionate love is emotionally intense, *the* focus of one's life and highly sexualized; it often feels unstable and fragile. Companionate love is calmer, *a* focus of one's life and not necessarily sexualized; it feels stable and reliable—more like liking. Passionate love is the stuff of crushes, infatuations, "love at first sight," and the early stage of love affairs. It may "burn out" completely or subside into companionate love.

But many researchers maintain that love comes in many more varieties than two. Years ago, John Alan Lee (1973, 1988), after interviewing hundreds of people, proposed that there are six distinct *styles of loving,* which he labeled with Greek names. These styles are *ludus* (game-playing love); *eros* (romantic, passionate love); *storge* [pronounced stor-gay] (affectionate, friendly love); *mania* (possessive, dependent, "crazy" love); *pragma* (logical, pragmatic love); and *agape* [ah-GAH-pay] (unselfish love).

To validate Lee's six types of love, Clyde and Susan Hendrick designed a Love Attitudes Scale that has been given to thousands of adults in such ethnically and culturally diverse cities as Miami (Hendrick & Hendrick, 1986, 1992) and Toronto (Dion & Dion, 1993). People who score high on eros believe in true love, instant chemistry, and abiding passion; they would agree, for example, that "My lover and I were attracted to each other immediately after we first met." Those who score high on ludic love like to play the game of love with several partners at once; they enjoy the chase more than the catch, agreeing that "I try to keep my lover a little uncertain about my commitment to him/her." Those who score high on storge believe that true love grows out of friendship; they value companionship and trust, and agree that "It is hard for me to say exactly when our friendship turned into love." Pragmatic lovers choose partners on the basis of a shopping list of compatible traits; for example, they agree that "I considered what my lover was going to become in life before I commit-

The gaze of love is unmistakable, even after years together.

A "ludic lover" in action. Do you think that gender differences in this style of love are fading?

"Sorry, Eric, but before I commit to anybody I still need about three years of fun."

ted myself to him/her." People who score high on mania yearn desperately for love but suffer from jealously and worry when they find it: "When things aren't right with my lover and me," they would agree, "my stomach gets upset." And those who score high on agape think of love as a selfless, almost spiritual form of giving to the partner: They will say, "I always try to help my lover through difficult times."

Yet another way of conceptualizing styles of love is based on the universal need for attachment. In their *attachment theory of love,* Cindy Hazan and Phillip Shaver (1987) argue that adult styles of love originate in a person's first and most important "love relationship," the infant-parent attachment. Just like Ainsworth's babies, their research suggests, adult lovers can be secure, avoidant, or anxious/ambivalent. Securely attached couples aren't jealous, nervous, or worried about being abandoned. Anxious or ambivalent lovers are always fretting about their relationship; they want to be close but worry that their partners will leave them. Avoidant people distrust and avoid all intimate attachments. To use Lee's terms, we might say that erotic and storgic lovers are likely to be securely attached; manic lovers are anxious and ambivalent; and ludic lovers are avoidant. According to Shaver (1994) and others, people learn these styles in part from how their parents cared for them. Was the parent sensitive or insensitive, accepting or rejecting? Was the parent a "compulsive" caregiver—excessively attending to and overprotecting the child, controlling and intrusive—or a normally supportive caregiver?

The theory that adult forms of love have their roots in the security or insecurity of infant attachment has sparked a wave of interesting research. Although no one as yet has followed a sample of infants from birth to marriage, numerous studies find that adult attachment styles do correspond to Ainsworth's three types of attachment. These adult styles are in turn related to both partners' levels of trust, love, satisfaction, and commitment to the relationship (Collins & Read, 1990; Feeney & Noller, 1990; Kirkpatrick & Davis, 1994). Anxiously attached partners report less satisfaction and more conflict and ambivalence in their relationships than securely attached partners do. Moreover, people's current forms of attachment are associated with what they report about their parents' attachment, although their recall may be biased by their current relationships with their parents. For example, securely attached individuals report relatively positive perceptions of their early family relationships, whereas avoidant individuals are most likely to report childhood separation from their mothers (Feeney & Noller, 1990).

The general overlap among these theories suggests that they are describing the same things. All imply that some styles of love are better suited to satisfying relationships than others, or to having a stable relationship at all (Hendrick & Hendrick, 1992). Most people choose partners who share their fundamental approach to love; individuals who endorse eros, storge, pragma, or agape are likely to marry others who have the same love style (Waller & Shaver, 1994). But certain combinations of love styles rarely or never turn up in studies of dating or married couples: avoidant-avoidant, anxious-anxious, ludic-ludic, or manic-manic (Hendrick, Hendrick, & Adler, 1988; Kirkpatrick & Davis, 1994; Waller & Shaver, 1994). This is hardly surprising; two people who are busy avoiding one another, or who are equally desperate and jealous and possessive, are unlikely to stay together for very long! Stability does not always depend on similarity of love style, however. Longitudinal studies have found that avoidant men and anxious women can have remarkably stable and successful relationships if they find secure partners (Kirkpatrick & Davis, 1994).

All in all, the research on love suggests that when someone says "I love you," perhaps you should reply, "What, exactly, do you mean by that?" But this research also shows that a person's reply can change—that most people can, and do, change their styles of love over time and with new partners. People who are in love for the first time are apt to be especially romantic and idealistic, but by their third love relationship they tend to be more realistic and even a touch cynical (Carducci & McGuire, 1990). The most pragmatic person can have an "erotic" interlude. The most game-playing ludic lover may become committed to an affectionate relationship. Older couples are far less likely to show signs of mania than younger couples are, suggesting that the desperation of mania subsides with time and experience (Waller & Shaver, 1994). And lovers who are insecurely attached as young adults may find secure attachments later on. Nevertheless, at any particular time, people are likely to feel strongly about which style of love is the "right" one, as we discuss in "Think About It."

The stereotype holds that men avoid and women seek love and intimacy. Yet the research evidence indicates that both sexes need and enjoy love. What are some reasons for the gap between the stereotype and the reality?

Gender, Culture, and Love. Do men and women differ in their typical styles of love, and if so, does this difference apply cross-culturally? The stereotypes suggest that men are more ludic and avoidant than women, and that women are more romantic and anxious than men; but like all stereotypes, these oversimplify. There is no evidence that one sex loves more than the other in terms of "love at first sight," manic (possessive) love, erotic (passionate) love, selfless love, or companionate love over the long haul (Dion & Dion, 1993; Fehr & Russell, 1991; Hatfield & Sprecher, 1986; Hendrick & Hendrick, 1992). Both sexes become equally attached and both suffer when a love relationship ends.

The stereotype of the avoidant male and the pursuing female often blinds people to greater evidence of the similarities between men and women in their needs for attachment and love. For example, one popular theory, posed by Carol Gilligan (1982), holds that many men regard attachment as a source of danger and threat, whereas many women regard attachment as a source of safety and intimacy. As evidence, Gilligan cited research in which she asked college students to tell stories in response to ambiguous pictures of a couple sitting together. She reported that men were more likely than women to see danger and threat in such pictures. "The men in the class, considered as a group, projected more violence into situations of personal affiliation than they did into impersonal situations of achievement," she wrote. *The men?* This statement was true for 25 percent of 88 college men—a higher percentage than for the women, but not even close to a majority. Other researchers, too, have exagger-

Think About It

What Is a Good Love Story?

■ As we have seen earlier in this book, the stories we tell to describe our lives have become a key metaphor in understanding human behavior (see Chapter 9). According to Robert Sternberg (1994), love too is a story: an implicit narrative about what love means, what a love relationship should be like, and how it should work. "Each relationship is a different story," he observes. "We choose the person who presents us with the love story we like best, even though that person might not be the most compatible partner for us." The reason people don't fall in love with someone who is otherwise their best friend, or who is objectively "right," says Sternberg, is that the friend fits their story of friendship, but not their story of love.

Relationships may come to an end, says Sternberg, if the two partners have different stories about what love is and should be. For example, Dan's love story is that a loving relationship should be calm and free of conflict. If two people love each other, in his view, they accept each other as they are and try to avoid confrontation. Susan's love story is that two people in love *do* confront their differences and together find a solution. So, because she loves him, Susan confronts Dan when she feels they have a problem—and he regards these confrontations as evidence that she does not love him! "The relationship is deteriorating," says Sternberg, but "not because the two people don't love each other. Rather, they have different stories about love, which lead them to interpret events in opposite ways. The relationship may fall apart simply because neither partner has understood the other partner's story about love."

Are some love stories better or healthier than others? Many philosophers and social critics believe that by defining love as a passionate emotion instead of as a relationship or an experience, people set themselves up for disappointment. For example, Robert Solomon (1994) argues that "We conceive of [love] falsely—as a feeling, as novelty, as bound up with youth and beauty. We fall into domestic habits and routine relationships and assume that love will take care of itself, which, of course, it will

not. We expect an explosion at the beginning powerful enough to fuel love through all of its ups and downs instead of viewing love as a process over which we have control, a process that tends to *increase* with time rather than wane."

As Solomon's remarks suggest, the way we define love, and the love stories we choose to guide our lives, deeply affect our feelings and satisfaction with relationships. If you believe that love "just happens," that you have no control over it, that love is defined by sexual passion and hot emotion, then you may decide you are "out of love" when the initial phase of attraction fades, as it eventually must. Worse yet, critics argue, maladaptive stories about romantic love can lead women and men to behave in irrational and self-defeating ways. Writer Bonnie Kreps (1990) worries especially about the many women, who, she feels, are too quick to sacrifice their self-interest, talents, and achievements when romantic love comes along. They become what she calls a reverse Sleeping Beauty: They kiss the prince and promptly fall asleep.

Critics of romantic love maintain that it is a relatively modern, Western invention. It is a love story that people in community-oriented cultures tend to distrust (Dion & Dion, 1993) and that people in postmodern cultures tend to regard with cynicism and skepticism (Gergen & Gergen, 1994). But evolutionary psychologists believe that passionate love is universal, even if it takes different forms, and that we could no more eliminate it than we could eliminate the need for food and water. In their view, romantic love sees to it that couples bond together, reproduce, look after each other, and stay together in spite of illness, mortgages, and housework (Buss, 1994).

Why do the popular love stories in Western culture almost exclusively celebrate romantic, passionate love rather than the kinds of love that abide for decades? How can people cultivate a more realistic view of what it takes to sustain love over the long haul? What are the ingredients essential to a loving relationship, and what is *your* ideal love story? Think about it. ■

ated small findings. One study claimed that men were "more than twice as likely as women" to see danger in attachment, but the numbers in question were 18 percent of the men and 8 percent of the women (Helgeson & Sharpsteen, 1987). Most important, numerous studies have found no gender differences at all in the desire for attachment or autonomy (Benton et al., 1983; Cochran & Peplau, 1985; Cohn, 1991).

Yet women and men do differ, on the average, in certain respects. Young women are somewhat more pragmatic and less ludic than men in their characteristic love styles and sexual behavior (Dion & Dion, 1993). And they sometimes differ in how they express love. In contemporary Western society, many women express feelings of love in words, whereas many men express these feelings in actions—doing things for the partner, supporting the family financially, or simply sharing the same activity, such as watching TV or reading together (Cancian, 1987; Gilmore, 1990; Tavris, 1992). Similarly, many women tend to define intimacy as shared revelations of private feelings; but many men define intimacy as simply being together comfortably. As one young man in a study of male friendship explained, his most intimate experiences with other men consisted of "a lot of outdoor-type things—fishing, hunting, Tom Sawyer–type things" (Swain, 1989).

These differences between the sexes are in turn related to male and female roles and cultural norms. As we saw in Chapter 10, males in many cultures learn early that revelations of emotion can be construed as evidence of vulnerability and weakness—terribly unmasculine qualities. Cultural factors, in turn, affect people's notions of proper male and female behavior. Asians of both sexes are less likely than people of other ethnicities to endorse romantic love as their ideal; they are more friendship-oriented in their love relationships (Dion & Dion, 1993).

Gender differences in people's ideas about love also depend on social and economic factors. For many years studies found that Western men were more romantic than women, who were in turn far more pragmatic than men. One reason was that, until quite recently, a woman didn't just marry a man; she married a standard of living (Waller, 1938). Therefore she could not afford to marry someone "unsuitable" or waste her time in a relationship that was "not going anywhere," even if she loved him. In contrast, a man could afford to be sentimental in his choice of partner. In the 1960s, two-thirds of a sample of college men said they would not marry someone they did not love, but only a fourth of the women ruled out the possibility (Kephart, 1967). As women entered the workforce and as two incomes became necessary in most families, the gender difference in romantic love waned. Nowadays most Canadian and American women are as romantic and "erotic" as men (Dion & Dion, 1993) and just as likely to say that love is essential in marriage.

Thus, even our most private beliefs about love, and the kind of love we feel, are influenced by the culture we live in, the historical era that shapes us, and something as unromantic as economic self-sufficiency. How do these influences affect your own style of love?

Quick QUIZ

A. Of Lee's six styles of loving, which kind does each example below illustrate?

1. St. Paul tells the Corinthians to love others whether or not they deserve it.
2. Jane Welsh and Thomas Carlyle enjoy exchanging ideas and confidences for years before realizing they love each other.
3. In choosing his last four wives, Henry VIII makes sure they are likely to bear children and are of suitably high status for his court.
4. Romeo and Juliet think only of each other and hate to be separated for even an hour.
5. Casanova tries to seduce every woman he meets for the thrill of the conquest.

B. Tiffany is wildly in love with Timothy, and he with her, but she can't stop worrying about him and doubting his love. She wants to be with him constantly, but when she feels jealous she pushes him away. According to the attachment theory of love, which style of attachment does Tiffany have? In terms of the six styles of love, which style does she have?

Answers:

A. 1. selfless love (agape) 2. friendship; companionate love (storge) 3. pragmatic love (pragma) 4. romantic, passionate love (eros) 5. game-playing love (ludus) B. anxious/ambivalent; mania

■ THE EROTIC ANIMAL: MOTIVES FOR SEX

Many people believe that sex is a matter of doing what comes naturally; that, in contrast to love, sex is a simple biological drive like hunger. In fact, people often use the same words in describing food and sex: "She has a strong sexual appetite," someone will say, or "I'm lusting for a hamburger." But psychologists do not agree on whether human sexuality is a primary drive or even whether it is a drive at all. After all, a person will not live long without food and water, but people can live long, healthy lives without sex.

In lower species, sexual behavior is genetically programmed: A male stickleback fish knows exactly what to do with a female stickleback, and a whooping crane knows when to whoop without instruction. But human beings must learn from experience and cultural standards what they are supposed to *do* with their sexual desires. They learn what "turns them on," what parts of the body and what activities are erotic, and even how to have sexual relations. As we will see in this section, the answer to the question "Why do people have sex?" is not just "Because it's natural" or "Because it feels good." Many motives are involved in human sexuality, and not all of them are obvious.

The Biology of Desire

How much of sexual motivation is influenced by physiology? The answer seems to be: some, but not as much as you think. Biological factors, particularly having a minimum level of the hormone testosterone, may promote sexual desire in both sexes (McCauley & Ehrhardt, 1980; Sherwin, 1988). Many different kinds of studies have implicated the role of testosterone in sexual motivation: studies of men who have been chemically castrated (given synthetic hormones that suppress the production or functioning of testosterone); of men who have abnormally low testosterone levels; of women who are taking androgens after having their ovaries removed; and of women who kept diaries of their sexual activity while also having their hormone levels measured (Wade & Cirese, 1991). But it is important to understand that hormones and behavior influence each other: Testosterone contributes to sexual arousal, but sexual stimulation also produces higher levels of testosterone (Knussmann, Christiansen, & Couwenbergs, 1986).

Physiological research has dispelled a lot of the nonsense that has been written about female sexuality. Freud, for example, believed that when women reach puberty their locus of sexual sensation shifts from the "childish" clitoris to the "mature" vagina, and women can then have healthy "vaginal" orgasms instead of immature "clitoral" orgasms. (Freud's theory was at least an improvement on the Victorian notion, still held in some cultures, that normal or "good"

Desire and sensuality are lifelong pleasures.

women don't have orgasms at all.) Freudian ideas caused countless women to worry that they were mentally disturbed and sexually repressed if they were not having the "correct" kind of orgasm (Ehrenreich, 1978).

The first modern attack on these beliefs came from Alfred Kinsey and his associates (1948, 1953), in their pioneering books on male and female sexuality in America. In *Sexual Behavior in the Human Female,* they observed that "males would be better prepared to understand females, and females to understand males, if they realized that they are alike in their basic anatomy and physiology." For example, the penis and the clitoris develop from the same embryonic tissues; they differ in size, of course, but not in sensitivity.

Such an idea was extremely shocking and progressive in 1953, when many people believed that women were not as sexually motivated as men—that orgasm wasn't as important to them, that female sexuality was more "diffuse" than men's, and that women cared far more about affection than sexual satisfaction. Yet Kinsey also tended to attribute the sex differences he *did* find, in frequency of masturbation and orgasm, primarily to biology—specifically, to women's lesser "sexual capacity." Although he acknowledged throughout his books that women are systematically taught to avoid, dislike, or feel ambivalent about sex, he didn't connect these psychological lessons with women's physiological responses.

Kinsey's survey findings were replicated and expanded in the 1960s in the laboratory research of physician William Masters and his associate Virginia Johnson (1966). In studies of physiological changes during sexual arousal and orgasm, they confirmed that male and female arousal and orgasms are indeed remarkably similar and that all orgasms are physiologically the same, regardless of the source of stimulation. But Masters and Johnson disagreed with Kinsey's assertion that women have a lesser sexual capacity than men. On the contrary, they argued, women's capacity for sexual response "infinitely surpasses that of men," because a woman, unlike most men, can have repeated orgasms until exhaustion or a persistent telephone makes her stop.

Masters and Johnson's work advanced the understanding of human sexual motivation and behavior, but it too had limitations (Tiefer, 1995). Perhaps most important, Masters and Johnson did not do research to find out how sexual response might vary among individuals according to age, experience, and culture. They accepted as research subjects only those volunteers who met their predetermined notions of normalcy—for instance, who were readily orgasmic. But not all women, or even all men, are easily orgasmic. Moreover, people's *subjective* experience of orgasm does not always correlate strongly with their *physiological* responses (Irvine, 1990; Levin & Wagner, 1985).

Nevertheless, biological researchers have made a major contribution to our understanding of sexual motivation by sweeping away the cobwebs of superstition and ignorance about how the body works. They have disproved the idea that the sexes are physically "opposite"; they have dispelled the myth that there is a "right" kind of orgasm for women to have; and they have documented the capacity for sexual arousal, orgasm, and pleasure in both sexes.

The Psychology of Desire

Many people assume that sex is "just doing what comes naturally." What does the variety of motives that people bring to sexual relations tell us about this assumption?

For most people in close relationships, the primary motive for sexuality is to express love and intimacy and to experience erotic pleasure (Hatfield & Rapson, 1993). But people have sex for many other reasons: to have children, to feel spiritual transcendence, to feel desirable, to raise their self-esteem, to exact revenge on a previous partner, to get money or other benefits, to dominate or bind the other person to them, or because they feel obligated.

When psychologists study the motives for sex, they find many reasons that people have sex even when they don't want to. On college campuses, large numbers of women *and* men say they have had unwanted sex because of psychological pressures. The percentages vary from school to school but are consistently high. In one survey of 275 undergraduate women, more than 50 percent said they had been pressured into kissing, fondling, oral sex, and intercourse (Christopher, 1988). For their part, many men feel obliged to "make a move" despite a lack of desire. In a survey of 993 undergraduates, 63 percent of the men reported having had unwanted intercourse (Muehlenhard & Cook, 1988). The main reasons for doing so, the men said, were peer pressure, inexperience, a desire for popularity, and a fear of seeming homosexual or "unmasculine." Women too said they "gave in" for various motives: because it was easier than having an argument; because they didn't want to lose the relationship; because they felt obligated, once the partner has spent time and money on them; or because the partner made them feel guilty or inhibited.

The two sexes differ, then, in the reasons they give for having unwanted sex. But nowhere do they differ more dramatically than in their perceptions of outright sexual coercion. In 1994, researchers at the University of Chicago published the results of their national, random sex survey of more than 3,000 Americans ages 18 to 59 (Laumann et al., 1994). They reported that 22.8 percent of the women said they had been forced by men to do something sexually that they did not want to do, usually by a boyfriend or husband, not a stranger. But only 2.8 percent of the men said they had ever forced a woman into a sexual act. Obviously, what many women experience as coercion is not seen as such by many men.

The most extreme form of sexual coercion, of course, is rape. Although the public image of the rapist tends to be one of a menacing stranger, in most cases the rapist is known to the victim. They may have dated once or a few times; they may have been friends for years; they may even be married (Koss et al., 1988;

In a famous scene from Gone with the Wind *(left), Rhett Butler (Clark Gable) forcibly carries a protesting Scarlett O'Hara (Vivien Leigh) to bed; she awakes the next morning with a smile on her face and love in her heart. Many similar scenes in film and TV convey the false impression that women want to be forced into sex and will be happy afterward. To help counteract this message, an antirape poster of* The Rape of the Sabine Women *(right) was created by men at a fraternity and distributed to other fraternity houses around the country.*

Russell, 1990). According to a study of a nationally representative sample of 4,008 women in the United States, at least 12 million American women have been the victims of forcible rape at least once in their lives, most before the age of 18. Only 22 percent were assaulted by strangers (National Victim Center, 1992). The survey did not include children or adult men, so the actual number of people who have been raped is much higher.

What motivates men to rape? Studies of convicted rapists find a mixture of motives: anger at women or the world, the expression of power, contempt for women, acting out a sexual fantasy, and sometimes sexual sadism (Knight, Prentky, & Cerce, 1994; Prentky & Knight, 1991). Rape is not only a matter of crossed signals or sexual desire; by its very nature, it implies hostility and a devaluing of the victim. Thus researchers who surveyed nearly 3,000 male college students found that sexually aggressive males had two characteristics: *hostile attitudes and personality* (hostility to women, violent tendencies, arousal to depictions of sexual aggression, and a need to control and dominate women) and *sexual promiscuity* (early sex with many partners, using sex as a way to prove masculinity) (Malamuth et al., 1991). Evidence that rape is primarily an act of dominance and aggression comes also from studies of male victims: Men can be and are raped, usually by anal penetration committed by other men. This typically occurs in youth gangs, when the rape is intended to humiliate rival gang members, and in prison, again with the intention of conquering and degrading the victim (Wade & Cirese, 1991).

Perhaps you can begin to see that the answer to the question "Why do people have sex?" is not simple after all. In addition to pleasure, passion, procreation, and love, the psychological motives involved can include intimidation, insecurity, and the desire to prove oneself a real man or a desirable woman.

The Culture of Desire

Consider kissing. Westerners *like* to consider kissing, and to do it, too. But if you think it is "natural," try to remember your first serious kiss—and all you had to learn about noses, breathing, position of teeth and tongue, and whatnot. Indeed, the sexual kiss is so complicated that some cultures have never gotten around to it. They think that kissing another person's mouth—the very place that food enters!—is disgusting (Tiefer, 1978/1995).

As the kiss illustrates, merely having the physical equipment to perform a sexual act is not all there is to sexual motivation. Men and women acquire their notions of "proper," "normal" sexual behavior from cultural norms and parental lessons (Lottes & Kuriloff, 1994). They learn what to consider erotic or

Whether to convey tender affection, playfulness, or passionate desire, kissing is an "acquired taste" and a learned skill.

sexy. They learn whether sex itself is supposed to be good or bad, healthy or sinful. Even the physiological responses of sexual arousal and orgasm are profoundly affected by learning. The cultural variations in sexual motivation and response are remarkable:

- Among Sambian males of New Guinea, boys are expected to have temporary homosexual relationships with older males as a normal part of growing up, a rite of passage on the route to manhood and marriage (Herdt, 1984).

- Cultures differ in what parts of the body and what style of clothing, if any, are considered erotic. To men of the Victorian era, the sight of an ankle, let alone an entire leg, was highly arousing; to men of the modern era, an ankle doesn't do it.

- Cultures differ in the specific sexual acts and sexual positions that are considered erotic or repulsive. In some, for example, oral sex is considered a bizarre sexual deviation; in others, oral sex is considered not only normal but also supremely desirable.

Such findings remind us that sexual motivation and behavior always take place in a social and cultural context. Sexual behavior is further shaped by a society's **gender roles**—collections of rules that determine the "proper" attitudes and behavior for men and women. As we will see in Chapter 17, people play many roles in society. During childhood and adolescence, people learn the "scripts" that fit each role.

According to John Gagnon and William Simon (1973), *sexual scripts* teach boys and girls what to consider erotic or sexy, and how to behave in dating and sex (see also Laumann et al., 1994). In this view, biology influences sexuality only indirectly. Adolescent males have spontaneous erections and eventually orgasms, so boys often talk and joke about masturbation with their friends. Female anatomy, however, makes the discovery of masturbation and orgasm less certain. Male sexuality is often learned in a competitive atmosphere where the goal is to impress other males. While boys are learning about physical sex, girls are learning to value the emotional aspects of relationships and to make themselves attractive. They are taught that their role is to be sexually desirable (which is "good"), but not to indulge in their own sexual pleasures (which would be "bad"). As one psychologist, summarizing her research findings, said, "'nice women' don't say yes and 'real men' don't say no" (Muehlenhard, 1988).

As a result of these differing lessons about the value and purpose of sexuality, say Simon and Gagnon (1969), male sexuality becomes more genitally focused and emotionally detached, compared to that of females. Female sexuality becomes more closely connected to love and attachment. Thus the sexual scripts for heterosexual couples are almost guaranteed to create conflicting motives for sexuality and misreadings of one another's behavior. For example, what is a "sexual signal"? How do you know if a person is conveying sexual interest in you? Men and women often answer these questions differently: A woman's intent might be to look sexy and attractive, and a man may interpret her dress and demeanor as indicating sexual interest. In one study of 400 teenagers ages 14 to 17, researchers found that, in general, boys thought almost everything was a sexual signal! They were more likely to regard tight clothing, certain situations (such as being alone in a room), and affectionate actions (such as a girl's playing with her date's hair or gazing into his eyes) as signs of willingness for sex. The girls were more likely to regard tight clothing as a sign of being fashionable, and being alone with a date or behaving affectionately simply as signs of—well, affection (Zellman & Goodchilds, 1983).

Gay men and lesbians follow sexual scripts, too. In terms of number of sexual partners, sexual behavior, and acceptance of casual sex, gay men are gener-

Is she dressing provocatively or comfortably? Boys and girls often disagree on the answer.

■ **gender role**
A set of rules and norms that defines socially approved attitudes and behavior for men and women.

ally similar to heterosexual men and lesbians are similar to heterosexual women. But most gay men and lesbians do not follow the scripts of traditional gender roles and tend to be more idiosyncratic and innovative in establishing rules for their relationships (Peplau, 1991; Rose, Zand, & Cini, 1993). An American study of lesbian courtship scripts—as revealed by analysis of lesbian romance novels, "how-to" books on dating and relationships, first-person accounts, and empirical research on lesbian sexuality—found that emotional intimacy, rather than physical attraction or sexuality, is the basis for most lesbian courtship scripts. These scripts are more ambiguous and varied than heterosexual dating and sexual scripts, for there is no clear role for the "pursuer" and the "pursued" or who makes the sexual overtures. "Whereas heterosexual women generally make the decision about when to 'let' sex happen," the researchers found, "lesbians indicated a more mutual decision-making process for initiating physical intimacy" (Rose, Zand, & Cini, 1993).

Simon and Gagnon (1986) have argued that people follow three different kinds of sexual scripts. *Cultural* scripts describe the larger culture's requirements for proper sexual behavior. Are women, for example, supposed to be sexually adventurous and assertive or sexually modest and passive? The answers vary from culture to culture. However, although people may know what their culture expects of them in general, not everyone follows its rules specifically. Sexual behavior also depends on *interpersonal* scripts, the rules of behavior that a couple develops in the course of their relationship. For example, will one be dominant and one passive? The answers differ depending on the relationship, and may change as the relationship changes. Finally, individuals follow their own *intrapsychic* scripts, scenarios for ideal or fantasized sexual behavior that develop out of a person's unique history.

Role theory maintains that most of the differences in the sexual behavior of heterosexuals occur as a result of the different role requirements of the two sexes, which in turn are a result of the economic and social arrangements of a particular society. Because women have traditionally been concerned with finding and keeping a secure relationship, in this view, they have regarded sex as a bargaining chip. It is an asset to be rationed rather than an activity to be enjoyed for its own sake. But for many men, sex is an expected part of the male role, so men are free to enjoy sexuality without social condemnation. (Think of all the negative words you know to describe "promiscuous" women, and then try to think of a single male equivalent.) But the demands of the male role can also be oppressive to both sexes: In a study of 71 college men who admitted to having coerced their dates into having sex with them, Eugene Kanin (1985) found that these young men had, from early adolescence, been pressured by male friends to "prove their masculinity" by "scoring."

Understanding sexual motives and behavior as part of a larger pattern of gender roles helps explain why, in many, but by no means all, societies, many men are likely to pressure women for sex, women tend to reject casual sex, and women "give in" and men "make a move" when they don't really want to (Oliver & Hyde, 1993). Women cannot afford to "let themselves go" and enjoy sex in cultures in which such behavior means they will lose the economic safety of marriage, their reputations in society, or their physical safety. But when roles change, when women become more economically independent, and when women's nonmarital sexual behavior does not invoke extreme social sanctions, women are as likely as men to want sex for pleasure rather than as a means to another goal.

The Riddle of Sexual Orientation

Why do some people become exclusively heterosexual, others exclusively homosexual, and still others bisexual? The subject of sexual orientation illus-

Many heterosexual people think that all gay people live unconventional, flamboyant lives. In reality, there is as much diversity among gay men and lesbians as among straights, and just about everyone, regardless of sexual orientation, seeks the pleasures of love and companionship.

trates how all the elements of sexual motivation—biology, learning, and culture—interact in any given individual's experience. It also illustrates how beliefs and values affect research and how people respond to the findings of research. It is difficult for most people to separate studies about homosexuality from their feelings about it, pro or con, and from their political or religious beliefs.

Although same-sex sexual behavior has existed throughout history in various forms, the words *homosexual* and *heterosexual* were not invented until the mid-nineteenth century (Katz, 1995; Trumbach, 1989). Only then did homosexuality become a "problem" to be studied, an entity distinct from heterosexuality. Today the question of whether these two sexual orientations are essentially, fundamentally different, determined once and for all by biology or early learning—or whether sexual identity is socially and psychologically created by experience and opportunity—is still hotly debated (Baumrind, 1995).

Many researchers are persuaded that human sexual orientation has a genetic basis, and that certain brain areas, hormones, and neuroendocrine processes differ in homosexual and heterosexual men and women (Gladue, 1994). For example, Heino Meyer-Bahlburg and his colleagues (1995) find that women with a history of prenatal exposure to synthetic estrogen are more likely than others to become bisexual or lesbian. Simon LeVay (1991) made national headlines when he announced that he had found a difference in certain brain structures of homosexual and heterosexual men (see also Allen & Gorski, 1992). Michael Bailey and his associates have reported evidence that sexual orientation is moderately heritable in men (Bailey & Pillard, 1991) and women (Bailey & Benishay, 1993; Bailey et al., 1993). And Dean Hamer and his team (1993) caused a stir when they reported a genetic linkage study that found a shared stretch of DNA on the X chromosome in 33 of 40 pairs of gay brothers—a rate significantly above what one would expect in siblings by chance.

These scientists are excited about biological findings because exclusively *psychological* theories of homosexuality have never been supported. Of course, as we saw in discussing cultural scripts and cultural norms, the specific forms of homosexual and heterosexual behavior vary so much across culture and history that psychological factors must be profoundly involved in the *expression* of sexual orientation—gay or straight (Katz, 1995). But contrary to psychological the-

422 PART FOUR ■ MOTIVATION, PERSONALITY, AND DEVELOPMENT

ories, having a homosexual orientation is unrelated to bad mothering, absent fathering, or individual psychopathology (Bell, Weinberg, & Hammersmith, 1981; Garnets & Kimmel, 1993). Nor is it related to socialization practices or parental role models; gay and lesbian parents are no more likely to have homosexual children than heterosexuals are (Bailey et al., 1995; Patterson, 1992).

Other researchers are skeptical of biological explanations (Baumrind, 1995; Byne & Parsons, 1993). Some argue that the sexual "fluidity" of women's experiences—that is, the fact that most lesbians have had heterosexual relationships—can best be explained in terms of psychological processes by which such women decide that they are lesbian and want to be identified this way (Kitzinger and Wilkinson, 1995). Other critics point out that studies claiming to find differences in the brain and evidence of heritability have important limitations. Dean Hamer's genetics study, for example, was based on a sample of gay brothers; but the vast majority of gay men and lesbians do *not* have a close gay relative. And a key problem in LeVay's study was that all of the gay men in his sample had died of AIDS. AIDS itself, and also some of the medical treatments given for the disease, creates endocrine abnormalities that can affect brain structures. The differences LeVay observed, therefore, might have been a result of AIDS rather than a cause of sexual orientation (Byne, 1993).

The evidence suggests, in sum, that sexual identity and behavior involve an interaction of biology, culture, experiences, and opportunities; and, most important, *that the route to sexual identity for one person may not be the same for another* (Gladue, 1994; Patterson, 1995). As Dean Hamer told *The New York Times,* "Sexual orientation is too complex to be determined by a single gene. The main value of this work is that it opens a window into understanding how genes, the brain and the environment interact to mold human behavior" (July 16, 1993).

What is your response to these findings? The chances are that your reactions to the research are affected by your feelings about homosexuality and gay rights. Many gay men and lesbians themselves welcome the new biological research on the grounds that it supports what they have been saying all along: Sexual orientation is not a matter of choice, but a fact of nature. But people who are prejudiced against homosexuals regard the same research as evidence that gay people have a biological "defect" that should be eradicated or "cured" (Bailey, 1993; Gagnon, 1987). Other gay men and lesbians strongly oppose biological arguments and their implication of essential differences between gays and straights (Kitzinger & Wilkinson, 1995); and so do many anti-gay people, who argue that homosexuality is a "preference" or "choice" that can and should be "unchosen."

Similarly, evidence about the rates of homosexuality in the general population has been interpreted differently by pro- and anti-gay groups, for different reasons. The Chicago survey we described earlier, confirming studies done in Europe, reported that gay men did not constitute 10 percent of the total population, as Kinsey had estimated, but more like 2 to 4 percent, and the percentage of lesbians was smaller yet (Laumann et al., 1994). (The percentages are significantly higher in big cities, where gay men and lesbians feel safer.) If you ask people if they have same-sex *fantasies* and *attraction,* you get higher numbers: about 7.5 percent of both sexes. And if you ask people if they have ever engaged in any sexual activities with a member of the same sex, you get higher numbers yet: 4 percent of the women and 9 percent of the men. For many of those men, however, the same-sex activity occurred only between the ages of 13 and 18.

These statistics, like evidence of biological factors in sexual orientation, can be used for different purposes. Gay-rights activists welcomed the 10 percent estimate as evidence that homosexuality is a rather common sexual variation and should therefore be accepted as such; thus they tend to discount the new statistics, fearing the loss of power that a loss of numbers might produce. Anti-

Why do you think so many people react emotionally to research on possible biological contributions to homosexuality? How does the definition of homosexuality or heterosexuality affect the kind of research that is done? And what is, or should be, the relationship between research and social policy?

gay people used the 10 percent estimate to lament the decline of morality, and they tend to welcome the lower numbers as evidence that homosexuality is such an aberration that gay people should be denied their civil rights.

Whatever research eventually reveals about the origins and prevalence of homosexuality, it is important to understand that there is no logical relationship between the *scientific question of the origins of homosexuality* and *political and moral questions of the rights of gay men and lesbians* (Strickland, 1995). In a democracy, civil rights do not depend on whether one's beliefs or practices are a matter of choice, nor do they depend on how popular those beliefs are. A person's religion is not biologically inherited, yet America and Canada guarantee freedom of religion to everyone—whether your religion is shared by 75 percent of the population or 2 percent.

As you can see, research findings on sexuality can be used for many contradictory purposes and political goals, depending on the values and attitudes of the popular culture in which such findings emerge. As long as a society is uncomfortable about homosexuality, its reactions to research on sexual orientation are likely to be clouded by preconceptions and prejudice.

Quick QUIZ

1. Why do people have sex? As the previous section suggests, sexual behavior has many motives. List as many of them as you can think of.
2. Now look over your list and decide which motives are primarily *physiological*, which *psychological*, and which *social or cultural*.

Answers:

1. Physiological motives include sexual arousal and release, reproduction, and sensual pleasure. Psychological motives include expressing intimacy, revenge, or anger; raising self-esteem; and preserving the relationship. Social and cultural motives include conforming to peer group norms, using sex to live up to cultural ideals of masculinity or femininity, and following the sexual dating script for one's culture. 2. If you found it difficult to categorize motives, that's the point: they all interact. For example, having sex in order to feel masculine is a psychological motive, but it is culture that teaches men that sex is a way of proving one's masculinity. Likewise, reproduction is a physiological motive, but the desire to reproduce is influenced by social ideologies and pressures.

■ THE COMPETENT ANIMAL: MOTIVES TO WORK

Almost every adult works. Most people spend more time at work than they do at play or with their families. "Work" does not mean only paid employment. Students work at studying. Homemakers work, often more hours than salaried employees, at running a household. Artists, poets, and actors work, even if they are paid erratically. What keeps everybody doing it? The obvious answer, of course, is the need for food and shelter. Yet survival does not explain what motivates LeRoy to work for caviar on his table and Duane to work for peanut butter on his. It doesn't explain why some people want to do their work well and others want just to get it done. It doesn't explain the difference between Aristotle's view ("All paid employments absorb and degrade the mind") and Noël Coward's ("Work is more fun than fun").

Psychologists, particularly those in the field of *industrial/organizational psychology,* have studied work motivation in the laboratory, where they have measured internal motives such as the desire for achievement, and in organizations, where they study the conditions that influence productivity and satisfaction. Their results give us a fuller answer to "what keeps everybody working?"

The Effects of Motivation on Work

Several independent forces keep you working toward a goal: your expectation of success, your need to achieve, opportunities in the environment, and the nature of your work (McClelland, 1985). These factors apply to any form of achievement, from running a household to running a marathon.

Expectations and Values. How hard you work for something depends partly on what you expect to accomplish. If you are fairly certain of success, you will work much harder to reach your goal than if you are fairly certain of failure.

A classic experiment showed how quickly experience affects these expectations. Young women were asked to solve 15 anagram puzzles. Before working on each one, they had to estimate their chances of solving it. Half of the women started off with very simple anagrams, but half began with insoluble ones. Sure enough, those who started with the easy ones increased their estimates of success on later ones. Those who began with the impossible ones decided they would *all* be impossible. These expectations, in turn, affected the young women's ability to actually solve the last 10 anagrams, which were the same for everyone. The higher the expectation of success, the more anagrams the women solved (Feather, 1966).

Once acquired, therefore, expectations can create a **self-fulfilling prophecy,** in which a person predicts how he or she will do and then behaves in such a way as to make the prediction come true (Jones, 1977). You expect to do well, so you study hard, and then you do well. You expect to fail, so you don't do much work, and then you do poorly. In either case, you have fulfilled your expectation of yourself.

How hard you work for something, of course, also depends on how much you want it, which in turn depends on your general value system (Feather, 1982). A *value* is a central motivating belief, reflecting the fundamental goals and ideals that are important to the person: freedom, beauty, equality, friendship, fame, wisdom, and so on (Rokeach & Ball-Rokeach, 1989). The values that motivate people can themselves have psychological consequences. For example, American culture puts a high value on wealth and financial success. But psychologists have found that there is a dark side to the pursuit of material wealth for its own sake. In studies with hundreds of young adults, people for whom the acquisition of wealth is the central value and goal have poorer overall emotional adjustment and lower well-being than do people whose primary aspirations and values are self-acceptance, affiliation with others, or "community feeling" (wanting to make the world a better place for others) (Kasser & Ryan, 1993).

Goals and Competence. Why do some people give up when a goal seems to become difficult, whereas others become even more determined to succeed? Why do some people sink into helplessness, doing poorly at solving the problem and eventually giving up, whereas others keep going to master the problem and avoid failure? The crucial fact about these alternatives—helplessness or mastery—is that *they are unrelated to ability.* When people are faced with a frustrating problem, talent or ambition alone does not predict who will push on and who will give up. What does predict success is the way in which people think about the goals they set for themselves and how competent they feel about reaching them.

■ **self-fulfilling prophecy**
An expectation that comes true because of the tendency of the person holding it to act in ways to confirm it.

According to Carol Dweck (1990, 1992), people who are motivated by *performance* goals are concerned with doing well, being judged highly, and avoiding criticism. When such people are focused on how well they are performing and then do poorly, they often decide the fault is theirs and they stop trying to improve. Because their goal is to demonstrate their abilities, they set themselves up for grief when they temporarily fail—as all of us must if we are to learn anything new. In contrast, those who are motivated by *learning and mastery* goals are concerned with increasing their competence and skills. Therefore, they regard failure as a source of useful information that will help them improve. Failure and criticism do not discourage them because they know that learning takes time (Elliott & Dweck, 1988).

The distinction between performance and learning goals, however, applies primarily to people who are not highly achievement oriented. For them, focusing on mastery rather than performance raises the intrinsic pleasure of the task they are working on or the goal they are pursuing. But for people who are driven to achieve, focusing on specific ways of improving their performance raises their intrinsic motivation and satisfaction (Elliot & Harackiewicz, 1994; Harackiewicz & Elliot, 1993).

In either case, the successful attainment of one's goals enhances feelings of competence, and competence is known to be one of the most important motivating forces in human psychology (Sternberg & Kolligian, 1990; White, 1959). Albert Bandura (1990, 1994) argues that competence is based on **self-efficacy,** the conviction that you can accomplish what you set out to do. Dozens of studies to date have found that self-efficacy affects how well people do on a task, how persistently they pursue their goals, the kind of career choices they make, their ability to solve complex problems at work, and even their health habits (Bandura, 1992, 1994; Betz & Hackett, 1986; Hackett et al., 1992). Fortunately, self-efficacy can be acquired through programs and experiences that provide skills and a sense of mastery (Ozer & Bandura, 1990). We will discuss self-efficacy further in Chapter 12.

The Need for Achievement. In the early 1950s, David McClelland and his associates (1953) speculated that some people have a **need for achievement** (often abbreviated *nAch*) that motivates them as much as hunger motivates people to eat. How could this motive be identified? McClelland (1961) later wrote that he and his colleagues sought the "'psychic x-ray' that would permit us to observe what was going on in a person's head in the same way that we can observe stomach contractions or nerve discharges in a hungry organism."

The solution came in the form of a method developed by Henry Murray and Christiana Morgan in the 1930s. The *Thematic Apperception Test* (TAT) consists of a series of ambiguous pictures and drawings; all you have to do is make up a story about each scene. What is happening in the picture? What are the characters thinking and feeling? What will happen next? Your behavior, said McClelland (1961), may be influenced by many things, but the strength of your internal motive to achieve is best captured in the fantasies you tell. "In fantasy anything is at least symbolically possible," he explained. "A person may rise to great heights, sink to great depths, kill his grandmother, or take off for the South Sea Islands on a pogo stick."

Needless to say, people with high achievement motivation do not fantasize about taking off for the South Seas or sinking to great depths. They tell stories about working hard, becoming rich and famous, and clobbering the opposition with their wit and brilliance. These achievement-related themes increase when high achievers are in situations that arouse their competitiveness and desire to succeed—when, for example, they believe that the TAT is measuring their intelligence and leadership ability (Atkinson, 1958). Studies of the achievement motive in the laboratory and in real life have found numerous differences

People with high self-efficacy pursue their goals even in the face of great obstacles.

■ **self-efficacy**
The belief that one is capable of producing, through one's own efforts, desired results (such as mastering new skills and reaching goals).

■ **need for achievement**
A learned motive to meet personal standards of success and excellence in a chosen area (often abbreviated nAch).

The Many Motives of Accomplishment

Productivity
*ISAAC ASIMOV
(1920–1992)*
SCIENTIST, WRITER

"If my doctor told me I had only six minutes to live, I wouldn't brood. I'd type a little faster."

Knowledge
*MARGARET MEAD
(1901–1978)*
ANTHROPOLOGIST

"I was brought up to believe that the only thing worth doing was to add to the sum of accurate information in the world."

Justice
*MARTIN LUTHER
KING, JR.
(1929–1968)*
CIVIL RIGHTS ACTIVIST

"I have a dream . . . that my four little children will one day live in a nation where they will not be judged by the color of their skin but by the content of their character."

Autonomy
*GEORGIA O'KEEFFE
(1887–1986)*
ARTIST

"[I] found myself saying to myself—I can't live where I want to, go where I want to, do what I want to. . . . I decided I was a very stupid fool not to at least paint as I wanted to."

between people who score high on the need for achievement and those who score low. High scorers are more likely, for example, to start their own businesses. They set high personal standards, and prefer to work with capable colleagues who can help them succeed rather than with co-workers who are merely friendly (McClelland, 1987).

However, the measurement of achievement motivation turned up an interesting problem: The motive revealed by the TAT is unrelated to a person's conscious need for achievement. Achievement motives apparently come in two varieties: an *implicit (unconscious) motive* and an *explicit (self-aware) motive* (McClelland, Koestner, & Weinberger, 1989). Thus, a person may express a desire to be successful but never seem "motivated" to carry it out. Explicit and implicit achievement motives are acquired in different ways at different times of life, respond differently to different incentives, have different physiological correlates with stress and arousal, and predict different behaviors. For example, the implicit motive predicts sustained achievement over time, because of the pleasure derived from achievement itself; whereas the explicit achievement motive predicts how a person will behave in a specific situation, because of immediate incentives and rewards.

The Need for Power.   Using the TAT, McClelland (1975) also found that some people are motivated by a **need for power**—the desire to dominate others and to influence people. The methods they use to win power may be aggressive and manipulative, or inspirational, charismatic, and persuasive (Winter, 1993).

■ **need for power**
A learned motive to dominate or influence others.

Power

*HENRY KISSINGER
(b. 1923)*
FORMER SECRETARY OF
STATE

*"Power is the ultimate
aphrodisiac."*

Duty

*ELEANOR ROOSEVELT
(1884–1962)*
HUMANITARIAN, LEC-
TURER, STATESWOMAN

*"As for accomplishments,
I just did what I had to
do as things came along."*

Excellence

*FLORENCE GRIFFITH
JOYNER
(b. 1959)*
OLYMPIC GOLD
MEDALIST

*"When you've been second
best for so long, you can
either accept it, or try to
become the best. I made
the decision to try and be
the best."*

Money

*SALVADOR DALI
(1904–1988)*
SURREALIST ARTIST

*"Liking money like I like
it, is nothing less than
mysticism. Money is a
glory."*

Although there are gender differences in the distribution of *actual* power, studies have consistently failed to find any *motivational* differences: Men and women who have high power motivation seek prestige and visibility, enter powerful careers, and run for office (Winter, 1988). For example, in a longitudinal study that followed women for 14 years after their college graduation, women who had high power motivation were more likely than women with low power motivation to plan, enter, and remain in careers requiring the exercise of power and influence (Jenkins, 1994).

Considerable research now suggests that the need for power, interacting with other motives, spurs some people to become leaders. But the kind of power that drives them distinguishes effective leaders from ineffective ones. Great leaders are motivated to use power for social goals rather than personal ambition (the difference between, say, Abraham Lincoln and Adolf Hitler). William Spangler and Robert House (1991) systematically examined the speeches, letters, and biographies of 39 Presidents, from George Washington to Ronald Reagan. Using complex measures of presidential performance, effectiveness, and greatness, they found that great presidents fit a pattern of motives. They had a lower need for affiliation and for achievement, but a higher need for power and a higher motivation to use power for social rather than personal objectives.

In an innovative series of studies linking individual motives to national events, David Winter (1993) has measured power and achievement motivation in secret government documents and official speeches by leaders. His work suggests that power motivation may be an important psychological cause of war. "When it rises," Winter reports, "war is likely; when it falls, war is less likely and ongoing wars are likely to end." The affiliation motive works in just the opposite fashion: When it rises, wars are averted.

This research raises fascinating questions. What causes power, achievement, and affiliation motives to rise and fall within a culture? Do we have any control over them? The evidence that these motives can be scored and measured on a national level—using historical documents, speeches, popular books, and indicators of achievement such as patents and discoveries—suggests not only that people's motivations can change historical events, but also that historical events can change people's motivations.

The Effects of Work on Motivation

If someone isn't working hard, people tend to ask, "What's the matter with that person's motivation?" What do we learn by asking, instead, "What's the matter with that person's job?"

Like the motives for affiliation and sexuality, the motives for achievement or power are embedded in cultural contexts. At one time, for example, many people believed that women had an internalized "fear of success"; but as opportunities for women improved, this apparent motive faded. Similarly, when the proportion of men and women in an occupation changes, so do people's motivations to work in that field (Kanter, 1977/1993). As a result of such findings, some psychologists have criticized the whole idea that achievement depends on internal "motives"—enduring, unchanging qualities of the individual. This notion, they say, leads to the incorrect inference that if people don't succeed, it's their own fault because they lack the internal drive to make it (Morrison & Von Glinow, 1990). In fact, research finds that accomplishment depends not only on internal motives and cognitive processes; it can be nurtured or reduced by the work you do and the conditions under which you do it.

Working Conditions. In an important longitudinal study, researchers interviewed a random sample of American workers over a period of ten years (Kohn & Schooler, 1983). Comparing results of the first interviews with later ones, they found that aspects of the work (such as fringe benefits, complexity of daily tasks, pace, pressure, and how routine or varied the work was) significantly changed the workers' self-esteem, job commitment, and motivation. The degree of job flexibility was especially important. People who have a chance to set their own hours, make decisions, vary their tasks, and solve problems are likely to rise to the challenge. They tend to become more flexible in their thinking and feel better about themselves and their work than if they feel stuck in a routine, boring job that gives them no control over what they do. As a result, their work motivation rises and stress drops (Karasek & Theorell, 1990; Locke & Latham, 1990). Conversely, when people with high power or achievement motivation are put in situations that frustrate their desire and ability to express

Students can have poor working conditions too, such as having to study in crowded quarters or having small siblings who pester them.

these motives, they become dissatisfied and stressed, and their power and achievement motives decline (Jenkins, 1994).

American culture emphasizes money as the great motivator, but actually the research shows that having a high income does *not* increase work motivation. Motivation is not related to money per se, but to how and when the money is paid. The strongest motivator is *incentive pay*, that is, bonuses that are given upon completion of a goal and not as an automatic part of salary (Locke et al., 1981). If you think about it, you can see why this might be so. Incentive pay increases people's feelings of self-efficacy and sense of accomplishment ("I got this raise because I deserved it"). This doesn't mean that people should accept low pay so they will like their jobs better, or that they should not demand cost-of-living raises!

Similarly, the "working conditions" of marriage can produce either highly motivated homemakers or apathetic ones (Strasser, 1982). Motivated home-makers tend to have extended families whom they see regularly and friends in the neighborhood who drop in frequently. They set specific goals ("I'm cleaning closets today and devoting tomorrow to the kids"). They get feedback from the family ("This meal is fabulous!"). Apathetic homemakers tend to lack social contacts and to be physically isolated. They have no clear standards for a job well done, so they don't feel they have done their jobs well. None of this, by the way, applies only to women. When men are "househusbands," their motivation rises or falls according to the same circumstances (Beer, 1983).

Teamwork.   One way to improve working conditions and work motivation is by creating cohesive, independent work teams. For example, an alternative to the standard boring assembly line is to have factory employees work in groups and handle different aspects of assembling the product instead of one repeated routine, an approach that has been tried successfully by Volvo, Sherwin-Williams, General Foods, and Saab (Sundstrom, De Meuse, & Futrell, 1990). Although some groups can be oppressive and stifle innovation, as we will see in Chapter 17, teamwork often raises workers' motivation and job satisfaction. Organizational psychologists have identified some of the conditions of the group that create these benefits: giving employees clarity of purpose and auton-omy, prompt feedback on their performance, an environment that permits informal interaction, and rewards and recognition in which the benefits to indi-vidual members depend on the whole team's performance (Sundstrom, De Meuse, & Futrell, 1990).

Gender, Culture, and Ambition.   Ultimately, achievement ambitions are related to people's *chances* of achieving. Reviewing dozens of studies of oppor-tunity and ambition, Rosabeth Kanter (1977/1993) found that men and women who work in dead-end jobs with no prospect of promotion behave the same way. They play down the importance of achievement, fantasize about quit-ting, and emphasize the social benefits of their jobs instead of the intellectual benefits. Consider some comments from a man who realized in his mid-30s that he was never going to be promoted to top management and who scaled down his ambitions accordingly (Scofield, 1993). As organizational psychologists would predict, he began to emphasize the benefits of not achieving: "I'm freer to speak my mind," "I can choose not to play office politics," and "I don't vol-unteer for lousy assignments." He had time, he learned, for coaching Little League and could stay home when the kids were sick. "Of course," he wrote, "if I ever had any chance for upward corporate mobility it's gone now. I couldn't take the grind. Whether real or imagined, that glass ceiling has become an invisible shield."

Studies show that women and members of minority groups encounter that "glass ceiling" in management—a barrier to promotion that is so subtle as to be transparent, yet strong enough to prevent advancement. For example, in a study of the banking industry, the three most significant problems that African-Americans reported were (1) not being "in the network," and therefore not being told what was going on; (2) racism; and (3) an inability to find a mentor (Irons & Moore, 1985). And a study of Asian-Americans in professional and managerial positions found that their education and work experience did not predict advancement as they do for white American men (Cabezas et al., 1989).

Many people believe that women are underrepresented in leadership positions because of something about women—their style of managing is different from men's, or they have lower self-esteem and feelings of competence than men, or they have less commitment to the job than men. None of these popular beliefs has been supported by research. For example, after conducting a field study of 2,000 male and female managers, two researchers concluded that "the disproportionately low numbers of women in management can no longer be explained away by the contention that women practice a different brand of management from that practiced by men" (Donnell & Hall, 1980). And marketing researcher Robert Snyder (1993) found that "there is absolutely no reliable empirical evidence based on truly comparable samples of men and women that women's attitudes [e.g., their commitment to work and their self-esteem] are lower than men's." In fact, reports Snyder, when you compare women and men who are at the same organizational level, women's self-esteem and organizational commitment are usually *higher* than those of men. It is true that women managers are about twice as likely as men to leave an organization—but the reason, Snyder found, is not that they are leaving the workplace: They leave for better jobs, often because of lack of career advancement at the first one!

Work motivation and satisfaction, in sum, depend on the right fit between qualities of the individual and conditions of the work. Such evidence raises a host of questions about how best to structure work so that the increasing diversity of workers will result in worker satisfaction, achievement, and effectiveness rather than conflict, bitterness, and prejudice (Morrison & Von Glinow, 1990). When should people be required to fit in to the dominant culture, and when should companies become more multicultural, changing themselves to fit their diverse employees?

Quick QUIZ

Work on your understanding of work motivation.

1. Expecting to fail at work and then making no effort to do well can result in a _____.
2. Ramon and Ramona are learning to ski. Every time she falls, Ramona says, "This is the most humiliating experience I've ever had! Everyone is watching me behave like a clumsy dolt!" When Ramon falls, he says, "&*!!@$@! I'll show these dratted skis who's boss!" Why is Ramona more likely than Ramon to give up? (a) She *is* a clumsy dolt. (b) She is less competent at skiing. (c) She is focused on performance. (d) She is focused on learning.
3. Which of these factors significantly increase work motivation? (a) specific goals (b) regular pay (c) feedback (d) general goals (e) being told what to do (f) being able to make decisions (g) the chance of promotion (h) having routine, predictable work (i) having mentors

4. Phyllis is an employee at an umbrella company. Her work is always perfectly competent, but she rarely arrives on time, she doesn't seem as motivated to do well as others, and she has begun to take an unusual number of "sick days." Phyllis's employer is irritated by this behavior and is thinking of firing her. What guidelines of critical thinking is the boss overlooking, and what research should the boss consider before taking this step?

Answers:

1. self-fulfilling prophecy 2. c 3. a, c, f, g, i 4. The boss is jumping to the conclusion that Phyllis has low achievement motivation. This may be true, but because her work is competent, the boss should consider other explanations and examine the evidence. Perhaps the work conditions are unsatisfactory; there may be few opportunities for promotion; she may get no feedback; perhaps the company does not provide day care, so Phyllis arrives late because she has child-care obligations. What other possible explanations come to mind?

■ WHEN MOTIVES CONFLICT

As we have seen, human beings are motivated by physical needs for food, water, and contact comfort, as well as by psychological needs for achievement, power, or success. But motives rarely coexist in perfect harmony. Two motives are in conflict when the satisfaction of one leads to the inability to act on the other—when, that is, you want to have your cake and eat it, too. Researchers have identified four kinds of motivational conflicts (Lewin, 1948):

1. *Approach-approach* conflicts occur when you are equally attracted to two or more possible activities or goals. For example, you would like to go out with Tom, Dick, *and* Harry; you would like to be a veterinarian *and* a cowboy; you would like to go out with friends (an affiliation motive) *and* study like mad for an exam (an achievement motive).

2. *Avoidance-avoidance* conflicts, which require you to choose between "the lesser of two evils," occur when you dislike two alternatives. Novice parachute jumpers, for example, must choose between the fear of jumping and the fear of losing face if they don't jump.

3. *Approach-avoidance* conflicts occur when one activity or goal has both a positive and a negative aspect. For example, you want to be a powerful executive but worry about losing your friends if you succeed. You want power and fear it at the same time. In ethnically diverse nations, differing cultural values produce many approach-avoidance conflicts, such as the following, which our students have described:

- A Chicano student said he wants to succeed and do well in "white" culture, but the community he grew up in values family closeness. His parents worry that if he goes to college, he will eventually leave them behind.

- A Filipina student said she wants an education more than anything else, but she also doesn't want to be disobedient to her parents, who have arranged a marriage for her back home.

- An African-American student from an impoverished neighborhood is in college on a prestigious scholarship. He is torn between wanting to leave his ghetto background behind him forever and returning to help the family and community who have supported him.

- A white student wants to be a marine biologist, but her friends tell her that only nerds and dweebs go into science.

"C'mon, c'mon—it's either one or the other."

A classic avoidance-avoidance conflict.

In an approach-avoidance conflict, both attraction and repulsion are strongest when you are nearest the goal. The closer you are to something appealing, the stronger your desire to approach; the closer you are to something unpleasant, the stronger your desire to flee. However, as you step away from the goal, the two motives change in strength. The attractive aspects of the goal still seem appealing, but the negative ones seem less unpleasant. This may be one reason people often have trouble resolving their ambivalence in these situations. When they leave a situation that has some benefits but many problems, and consider it from a distance, they see its positive aspects and overlook the negative ones. So they approach it again. Up close, the problems appear more clearly, motivating them to avoid the situation once more.

4. *Multiple approach-avoidance* conflicts occur in situations that offer several possible choices, each containing advantages and disadvantages. For example, you might want to marry and settle down while you're still in school, and you think you have found the right person. On the other hand, you also may want to establish a career and have some money in the bank, and lately you and the right person have been quarreling a lot.

Internal conflict is inevitable unless you are a garden slug. But over time, unresolved conflicts have a physical and mental cost. In a series of studies, students listed their main "personal strivings": *approach* goals such as "trying to be attractive" or "trying to seek new experiences," and *avoidance* goals such as "trying to avoid being noticed by others" or "trying to avoid being dependent on my boyfriend." Students rated these objectives on the amount of conflict they caused and on how ambivalent they felt about them; striving "to appear more intelligent than I am" conflicts with striving "to always present myself in an honest light." High levels of conflict and ambivalence were associated with anxiety, depression, headaches and other symptoms, and more visits to the student health center (Emmons & King, 1988).

Humanist psychologist Abraham Maslow (1954/1970) arrayed people's "motivational strivings" on a pyramid that he called a *hierarchy of needs,* with basic survival needs at the bottom and "self-actualization" and "self-transcendence" at the top. Maslow argued that your needs must be met at each level before you can even think of the matters posed by the level above it. You can't worry about achievement, for instance, if you are hungry, cold, and poor. You can't become self-actualized if you haven't satisfied your need for self-esteem and love. Human beings behave badly, he argued, only when their lower needs are frustrated, especially those for love, belonging, and self-esteem.

This theory, which is intuitively logical and optimistic about human nature, became immensely popular, but it has not been supported by research (Howell & Dipboye, 1982; Smither, 1988). One reason is that people may have *simultaneous* needs for comfort and safety *and* for attachments, self-esteem, and competence. Another is that people who have met their "lower" needs do not inevitably seek "higher" ones, nor is it the case that antisocial behavior results only from frustrated lower needs. And a third reason is that "higher" needs may overcome "lower" ones. Human history is full of examples of people who would rather starve than be humiliated; rather die of torture than sacrifice their convictions; rather explore, risk, or create new art than be safe and secure at home.

Think of Jim Abbott, Dian Fossey, and the men and women portrayed on pages 426–427. All were surely "self-actualized," but not necessarily because they had overcome lower needs or reached a resolution of all conflicts. Perhaps the safest conclusion, therefore, is that each of us develops an individual hierarchy of motives in the course of our development from childhood to old age. For some, the need for love, security, and safety will dominate. For others, the need for achievement or power will rule. Some will wrestle with conflicting motives; for others, certain motives will hold sway over all others. This diversity is an inevitable part of human personality and cultural experience.

It seems intuitively right that motives can be ranked from basic physical needs to higher psychological ones. What is wrong with this intuitive assumption? What are other ways of looking at the diversity of human motives?

Taking Psychology with You

Improving Your Work Motivation

Why are you in school? What do you hope to accomplish in your life? Are you motivated primarily by the intrinsic goals of a job well done and the satisfaction of the work itself or by extrinsic goals such as getting a degree, a job, and a salary, or by both? Do you have a burning ambition that drives you or are you burned out? If you are feeling "unmotivated" these days, research on work motivation suggests some steps you might take:

- *Seek activities that are intrinsically pleasurable, even if they don't "pay off."* If you really, really want to study Swahili or Swedish even though these languages are not in your pre-law requirements, try to find a way to do it! You might also ask yourself whether your major in school or the kind of work you do is right for you. Are you in this field because you are drawn to it, or because others think you should be in it? Remember, though, that even when people are doing the work they want to do, there will be difficult or boring days.

- *Focus on learning goals rather than performance goals.* As studies of success and self-efficacy repeatedly find, you will be better able to cope with inevitable setbacks if your goal is to learn rather than to show off how good you are. It is important to be able to regard failure as a "learning experience" rather than as a sure sign of incompetence. Ironically, the more you are able to focus on learning, mastery, and improvement, the better your performance will be.

- *Set realistic but challenging goals.* One of the most important influences on motivation is the nature of the goal you are working toward. Given two people of equal ability, the one who sets specific and moderately difficult goals (not painfully difficult ones) will work longer and achieve more than the one who sets vague, easy goals or none at all (Locke & Latham, 1990; Smither, 1988).

- *Get accurate feedback on your performance.* Once you have specified a goal, continued motivation depends in part on getting feedback about your performance. Your employer needs to tell you that you are almost number one in sales. Your piano teacher needs to tell you that your playing has improved. Your statistics instructor needs to tell you what you need to do to raise a grade. When people work or study in environments that do not provide constructive feedback, their motivation to do well is often weakened. If you are not getting enough feedback, ask for it.

- *Assess your working conditions.* How is your job or academic situation structured? Are you getting support from co-workers, employers, or instructors? Do you have opportunities to develop ideas and vary your routine, or are you expected to toe the line and do the same thing day after day? Do you perceive a "glass ceiling" that might limit your advancement in your chosen field, and are you accurate in your perceptions? If you have entered school or a job with enthusiasm, optimism, and expectations of success, only to have these feelings slowly dwindle and dissipate, you might want to consider whether your working conditions are causing your burnout. And then you might consider whether changing some of those conditions could recharge your batteries.

- *Take steps to resolve motivational conflicts.* Many students in an approach-avoidance conflict tend to *think* a great deal about their conflicts but not *do* anything to resolve them (Emmons & King, 1988). A student in one study, for instance, remained unhappily stuck between his goal of achieving independence and his desire to be cared for by his parents. The reconciliation of motivational conflicts, the researchers found, is "a premier goal of human development" and a cornerstone of well-being.

What psychology cannot tell you, of course, is which goals and values to choose in the first place: love, wealth, security, freedom, fame, the desire to improve the world, or any other goal of your choosing. In a commencement address some years ago, Mario Cuomo, the former governor of New York, had these words of wisdom for the graduating students: "When you've parked the second car in the garage, and installed the hot tub, and skied in Colorado, and wind-surfed in the Caribbean, when you've had your first love affair and your second and your third, the question will remain: Where does the dream end for me?"

Summary

1. *Motivation* refers to an inferred process within a person or animal that causes that organism to move toward a goal—satisfy a biological need or achieve a psychological ambition. A few basic motivating drives are based on

physiological needs, but people are also motivated by cognitive processes that permit them to plan and work for goals. These *social motives* are learned.

2. People are motivated to *affiliate* with others for contact comfort, reassurance, and friendship. As with all social motives, individuals and cultures differ in how much affiliation they seek and in the importance they place on attachments. *Contact comfort* is essential in human development from birth and early childhood, where it provides a secure base, throughout life. Infants and caregivers become *attached* to each other after a few months; by the age of 7 to 12 months, babies often feel *stranger anxiety* and *separation anxiety*. Studies of the "strange situation" find three kinds of infant attachment: secure, avoidant, and anxious/ambivalent. Some aspects of attachment are learned by parental reinforcements, but everyone agrees that healthy attachment is necessary to development.

3. There have been several efforts to describe varieties of love: *passionate* ("romantic") versus *companionate* love; the *six styles of love;* and the *attachment theory of love* (love as secure, avoidant, or anxious/ambivalent). Adults' attachment styles are related to how their parents cared for them and predict whom they will have close relationships with. Men and women are equally likely to feel love and need attachment, but gender roles affect how they experience and express love.

4. Psychologists disagree about whether any aspect of human sexuality can be considered a "primary drive." Biological research finds that testosterone influences sexual desire in both sexes, that there is no "right" kind of orgasm for women to have, and that both sexes are capable of sexual arousal and response. Kinsey and, later, Masters and Johnson were the first modern researchers to show that physiologically, male and female sexuality are more similar than "opposite," but human sexual desire and behavior are more influenced by learning, cultural standards, and social roles than by biology.

5. Although most men and women have sex for reasons of intimacy and pleasure, they often have other motives as well: to feel desirable, for revenge, for personal gain, to raise self-esteem. Both sexes may agree to intercourse for nonsexual motives: Men sometimes feel obligated to "make a move" to prove their masculinity, and women sometimes feel obliged to "give in" to preserve the relationship. The major gender difference in sexuality has to do with sexual coercion and rape. Men rape for a variety of motives, including anger at women, sadism, and opportunity. Sexually aggressive males typically combine hostile attitudes toward women with a need for sexual promiscuity to prove masculinity.

6. Sexual attitudes and behavior are affected by cultural norms and different *gender role* expectations for men and women, whether they are straight or gay, including the *sexual scripts* that dictate how people should behave during courtship, intimacy, and sex. The scripts for heterosexual women and men often lead to misunderstandings over the meaning of "sexual signals" and the purpose of sex. There are cultural, interpersonal, and intrapsychic scripts.

7. Explanations of the origins of sexual orientation are contradictory. Traditional psychological explanations (such as bad mothers or absent fathers) do not account for why some people become homosexual, and growing evidence suggests that genetic and hormonal factors are involved. However, biology, culture, learning, and circumstance interact in complex ways to produce a given person's orientation. This research is politically sensitive because people often confuse scientific questions about the origins of homosexuality with political and moral questions about the rights of gays and lesbians.

8. The motivation to work depends on a person's *expectations* of success, which can create self-fulfilling prophecies of success or failure, and the *value* the person places on the goal. Success or failure depend not only on ability, but on whether people set *learning goals,* which can lead to mastery, or *performance goals,* which can lead to helplessness if the person temporarily fails. People are also motivated by a need to feel competent at what they do and to have *self-efficacy* about their abilities to reach their goals.

9. People who are motivated by a high *need for achievement* set their own standards for success and excellence; this motive may be implicit (unconscious) or explicit (self-aware). People who are motivated by a *need for power* seek to dominate and influence others. They may use a variety of methods to gain this power, from persuasion to aggression. Patterns of social motives can predict individual behavior, including presidential greatness, and national events, such as the outbreak of war.

10. Work motivation also depends on having the right *working conditions*, such as job flexibility, control, incentive pay, and teamwork, and on the *opportunity* to be promoted and have one's good work rewarded and recognized.

11. Human motives often conflict. In an *approach-approach* conflict, a person is equally attracted to two goals. In an *avoidance-avoidance* conflict, a person is equally repelled by two goals. An *approach-avoidance* conflict is the most difficult to resolve, because the person is both attracted to and repelled by the same goal. Prolonged conflict can lead to physical symptoms and reduced well-being.

12. Abraham Maslow believed that human motives could be ranked from basic biological needs to higher psychological needs, but this popular theory remains unproven. People can have simultaneous motives; "higher" motives can outweigh "lower" ones; and people do not always become kinder or more self-actualized when their needs for safety and love are met. The diversity of motives, and the combinations they take in any individual, are the hallmark of human variation.

Key Terms

motivation *405*

social motives *406*

need for affiliation *406*

attachment *406*

contact comfort *407*

stranger anxiety *408*

separation anxiety *408*

the "strange situation" *408*

secure/avoidant/anxious attachment *408*

passionate and companionate love *410*

six "styles of love" *410*

attachment theory of love *411*

gender roles *419*

sexual scripts *419*

cultural, interpersonal, intrapsychic scripts *420*

self-fulfilling prophecy *424*

value *424*

performance and learning goals *425*

self-efficacy *425*

need for achievement (nAch) *425*

Thematic Apperception Test (TAT) *425*

implicit vs. explicit achievement motives *426*

need for power *426*

working conditions *428*

incentive pay *429*

teamwork *429*

approach and avoidance conflicts *431*

Maslow's hierarchy *432*

12
Theories of Personality

Think About It
  Can You Change Your
  Personality—and Would You if
  You Could?

Taking Psychology with You
  How to Avoid the Barnum
  Effect

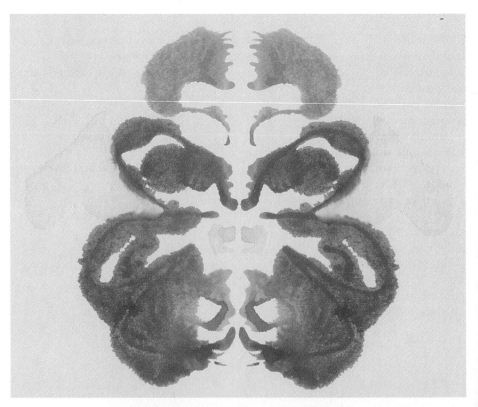

How can personality be captured? Psychodynamic clinicians and research psychologists offer different answers. The former use projective tests that they believe identify unconscious processes; the Rorschach test, for example, asks people to interpret abstract patterns similar to this one. But most personality researchers prefer methods that are more valid and reliable.

Selfness is an essential fact of life.
The thought of nonselfness, precise
sameness, is terrifying.

■ LEWIS THOMAS ■

A psychologist we know once gave a lecture to the faculty of the first school she ever attended—her nursery school. Her topic was an optimistic report on adult life. "People are not prisoners of childhood," she said. "They change their attitudes, philosophies of life, self-esteem, ambitions, values, and looks. They have new experiences that change their outlook. Most recover from early traumas." In the audience was one of her first teachers, now 96 years old and as clear-minded as ever. "A nice speech, dear," she said when it was over, "but as far as I'm concerned, you haven't changed a bit since you were 3. You're a bit taller, is all."

What made our friend appear unchanged to her nursery-school teacher was, undoubtedly, her "personality." In psychology, the word doesn't refer to enthusiasm or a set of positive qualities, as in "he has a great personality." **Personality** is a distinctive and stable pattern of behavior, thoughts, motives, and emotions that characterizes an individual over time. This pattern reflects a particular constellation of **traits,** characteristics that are assumed to describe the person across many situations: shy, brave, reliable, friendly, hostile, confident, sullen, and so on.

Psychologists differ, however, in which traits they consider the most important, and in their views of the origins and permanence of personality. Biological psychologists seek evidence for genetically influenced qualities that remain entrenched throughout life. Psychodynamic psychologists look for personality in the dark, unconscious motives of the mind. Behaviorists argue that personality is an illusion because people are far more influenced by their immediate circumstances than by any individual qualities. And humanists regard personality as the private self, the "true self," behind the masks that people wear in daily life. In this chapter we will describe the major approaches to the study of personality and the two questions that guide researchers: How can we describe the astonishing variety among individuals, and what is it that makes a person's personality distinctive?

Does personality really change, or only superficial qualities? Marilyn Monroe changed significantly when she became a star—or did she?

■ THE ELEMENTS OF PERSONALITY

Personality consists of a complex interaction of traits, habits, tendencies, preferences, and moods, so no one test can possibly summarize a person's entire personality. But tests and assessment methods do provide information about aspects of personality, such as needs, values, interests, and typical ways of responding to situations. Using objective tests, psychologists have identified many fascinating traits, from "sensation seeking" (the enjoyment of risk) to "erotophobia" (the fear of sex). Some researchers have tried to

■ **personality**
A distinctive and relatively stable pattern of behavior, thoughts, motives, and emotions that characterizes an individual throughout life.

■ **trait**
A descriptive characteristic of an individual, assumed to be stable across situations and time.

The four basic personality types.

identify the many individual traits that make up personality. Other researchers, unhappy with this piece-by-piece approach, look for a few organizing traits of personality.

One of the most influential trait theorists in this century was Gordon Allport (1897–1967). Allport observed that most members of a society share certain common traits that their culture expects and rewards. To understand why two people differ, said Allport (1937, 1961), we must look at the individual traits that make each of them unique. *Cardinal traits* are of overwhelming importance to an individual and influence almost everything the person does. We might say that Mohandas Gandhi (called *Mahatma,* or "wise one") and Martin Luther King, Jr., had the cardinal trait of nonviolence. But few people, said Allport, have cardinal traits. Instead, most of us have five to ten *central (or global) traits* that reflect a characteristic way of behaving, dealing with others, and reacting to new situations. Allport (1961) wrote: "For some the world is a hostile place where men are evil and dangerous; for others it is a stage for fun and frolic. It may appear as a place to do one's duty grimly; or a pasture for cultivating friendship and love." *Secondary traits,* in contrast, are more changeable aspects of personality. They include preferences (for foods, colors, movies), habits, casual opinions, and the like.

Another important theorist, Raymond B. Cattell, advanced the study of personality traits by applying a statistical method called *factor analysis,* which we discussed in Chapter 8. Performing a factor analysis on traits is like adding water to flour: It causes the material to clump up into little balls. Using questionnaires, life descriptions, and observations, Cattell (1965, 1973) measured dozens of personality traits in hundreds of people. He called these descriptive qualities *surface traits* because they are visible in a person's words or deeds. He believed that factor analysis, which identifies traits that are correlated with each other, would identify *source traits,* the bedrock of personality, the underlying causes of surface qualities. A person might have the surface traits of assertiveness, courage, and ambition; the source trait, linking all three, might be dominance. Cattell and his associates investigated many aspects of personality, including humor, music preferences, intelligence, creativity, leadership, and emotional disorder. His method of conducting large-scale research and describing the connections between traits has had an important influence on research in personality.

Cattell maintained that there are 16 factors necessary to describe the complexities of personality, and today many still agree with him (Mershon & Gorsuch, 1988). Other psychologists, however, using longitudinal studies and factor analysis, have boiled surface traits down into even fewer clusters. A consensus is emerging among researchers that personality can be described according to five "robust factors," sometimes called the *Big Five* (Costa & McCrae, 1994; Digman, 1990; Goldberg, 1993; McCrae & Costa, 1991; Zuckerman, Kuhlman, & Camac, 1988):

1. *Introversion versus extroversion* describes the extent to which people are outgoing or shy. It includes such personality traits as being talkative or silent, sociable or reclusive, adventurous or cautious, eager to be in the limelight or preferring to stay in the shadows.

2. *Neuroticism,* or emotional instability, includes such traits as being anxious and unable to control impulses; a tendency to have unrealistic ideas; and generally being emotionally unstable and negative. Neurotic individuals are complainers and defeatists. They complain about different things at different ages, but they are always ready to see the sour side of life and none of its sweetness.

Neuroticism is sometimes called *negative affectivity* (emotionality), or NA, because of the neurotic person's tendency to feel anger, scorn, revulsion, guilt, anxiety, sadness, and other negative moods (Watson & Clark, 1984). People with high NA frequently feel worried and tense, even in the absence of real problems. They complain more about their health and report more physical symptoms than people with low NA do, yet they are not actually in poorer health (Brett et al., 1990; Watson & Pennebaker, 1989).

   3. *Agreeableness* describes the extent to which people are good-natured or irritable, gentle or headstrong, cooperative or abrasive, not jealous or jealous. It reflects the capacity for friendly relationships or the tendency to have hostile ones.

   4. *Conscientiousness* describes the extent to which individuals are responsible or undependable; are persevering or quit easily; are steadfast or fickle; are tidy or careless; are scrupulous or unscrupulous.

   5. *Openness to experience,* which in some personality measures is called *intellect* or *imagination,* describes the extent to which people are original, imaginative, questioning, artistic, and capable of divergent (creative) thinking—or are conforming, unimaginative, and predictable (Goldberg, 1993).

According to research on the "Big Five" traits, extroversion or introversion is a basic dimension of personality.

   Not everyone agrees with the the Big Five model. Cattell still thinks that five factors are too few, and another personality researcher, Hans Eysenck (1994), argues that there are only the "Giant Three"—psychoticism (the extent to which a person lacks empathy and is disposed to crime and mental illness), extroversion, and neuroticism. Some agree that there are five basic factors, but disagree on what exactly they are (Saucier, 1994; Zuckerman et al., 1993). And some psychologists object to the effort to reduce the shifting complexities of personality to any such simple dimensions (Church & Burke, 1994; Kroger & Wood, 1993).

   However, evidence for the Big Five is turning up from many different sources, such as studies of children and adults in other cultures, including Australian, Chinese, Filipino, German, Hawaiian, and Japanese samples (Digman & Inouye, 1986; Johnson & Ostendorf, 1993; Noller, Law, & Comrey, 1987). Moreover, longitudinal studies find that the Big Five traits are as persistent as crabgrass. You might think (and hope) that people would become more open-minded and agreeable and less neurotic as they mature. But Paul Costa and Robert McCrae (1988), having conducted longitudinal studies of men and women aged 21 to 96, concluded that no matter how you measure them, these traits are "still stable after all these years."

   Researchers on the Big Five traits are investigating the way each personality trait interacts with circumstances to foster or inhibit well-being. For example, the qualities of openness to experience, agreeableness, and extroversion are positively related to well-being (Magnus et al., 1993; McCrae & Costa, 1991). One reason seems to be that when individuals with these traits are under stress or have problems, they respond by seeking help from others, by trying new solutions, and by maintaining optimism. In contrast, people who are high in neuroticism react by indulging in wishful thinking ("the problem will go away soon") or self-blame—two strategies that further increase their anxiety and other negative feelings (Bolger, 1990). A 7-year longitudinal study of 296 adults concluded that "temperamental dispositions are more powerful than environmental factors in predicting psychological distress" (Ormel & Wohlfarth, 1991). Emotional difficulties and crises occur for everyone, of course, but people high in neuroticism bring their pessimism and negativity with them, making the situation worse.

   Measures of the essential dimensions of personality are useful in probing the origins of human diversity, and psychologists have identified some of the key qualities that form the foundation of an individual's character. The logical next question is this: Where do those traits come from? Are they inherited, learned, motivated by the unconscious, or based on an individual's subjective interpretation of current circumstances? We turn now to the major theories and the answers they offer.

> *Quick* QUIZ
>
> **1.** Raymond Cattell advanced the study of personality by his method of (a) case study analysis (b) factor analysis
> **2.** Which of the following traits are *not* among the five "robust factors" in personality? (a) introversion (b) agreeableness (c) psychoticism (d) openness to experience (e) intelligence (f) neuroticism (g) conscientiousness
>
> **Answers:**
>
> 1.b 2. c, e

■ THE BIOLOGICAL TRADITION: YOU ARE WHAT YOU'RE BORN

A student we know was describing her lifelong problem with her bad temper. "I was *born* angry," she said. "I hissed at passersby when I was carried home from the hospital." People do talk this way, but is it possible to be "born angry"? What aspects of personality might have an inherited component? And if any of them do, does that mean that people are stuck with those traits forever?

Heredity, Temperament, and Traits

One way to study the origins of personality differences is to look at **temperaments,** which are relatively stable, characteristic styles of responding to the environment that appear in infancy or early childhood and have some genetic basis (Kagan, 1994). Indeed, even in the first weeks after birth, infants differ in activity level, mood, responsiveness, and attention span. Some are irritable and cranky. Others are placid and sweet-natured. Some cuddle up in any adult's arms and snuggle. Others squirm and fidget, as if they can't stand being held. Babies differ in activity level (squirming and kicking), smiling and laughing, fussing and showing signs of distress, soothability (the time it takes a baby to calm down after distress), emotionality and expressiveness, cooing and burbling in reaction to people or things, and amount of crying (Field, 1989; Kagan, 1994; Thomas & Chess, 1982).

Jerome Kagan and his colleagues have been studying the physiological correlates of two specific temperamental styles, which they call "inhibited" and "uninhibited." (These temperaments are extremes; most children fall somewhere in between.) Inhibited and uninhibited temperaments are detectable in infancy and, in the absence of intervention, tend to remain stable throughout childhood (Kagan, 1994; Kagan & Snidman, 1991). Inhibited children are shy and timid; they react negatively to novel situations, such as being introduced to a group of unfamiliar children. In contrast, uninhibited children are talkative and spontaneous. Kagan's group has found that shy, socially inhibited 5-year-olds are more likely than uninhibited children to show signs of sympathetic nervous system activity during mildly stressful mental tasks. These signs include increased heart rate, dilation of the pupils, and a rise in norepinephrine. Inhibited children also have higher-than-average levels of cortisol, a hormone associated with physiological arousal during stress. In white children (most of the children studied have been white), inhibition is associated to some extent with having blue eyes and allergies, or having close relatives with these characteristics (Kagan & Snidman, 1991; Kagan et al., 1991).

■ **temperaments**
Characteristic styles of responding to the environment that are present in infancy and are assumed to be innate.

Interestingly, Stephen Suomi (1987, 1991) has found exactly the same physiological attributes in shy, anxious infant rhesus monkeys (except for the blue eyes). Suomi calls the inhibited monkeys "uptight" and the uninhibited ones "laid back." Starting early in life, uptight monkeys, like Kagan's inhibited children, respond with anxiety to novelty and challenge. Like Kagan's human subjects, Suomi's monkeys have high heart rates and elevated levels of cortisol, and they are more likely to have allergic reactions starting in infancy. When uptight rhesus monkeys grow up, they usually continue to be anxious when challenged. They act traumatized even though they have experienced no traumas. When they are under stress, like humans, they tend to turn to alcohol (which the researchers make available) and they drink more than other monkeys do (Higley et al., 1991).

Some aspects of temperament may lead to characteristic habits and mannerisms in adults. Separated identical twins have some unnerving similarities in gestures, movements, and speech. In a review of twin studies, Susan Farber (1981) remarked on two male twins who both nodded their heads while speaking, two other male twins who both flicked their fingers when unable to think of an answer, and two female twins who both rubbed their noses and rocked when tired. Identical twins reared apart also tended to have similar characteristic moods. If one twin was optimistic, excitable, or glum, so was the other. If one had frequent mood changes, the other was apt to have them as well. The Minnesota Twins project, described in Chapter 3, has found the same resemblances in mood and personal style (Bouchard et al., 1986).

Another way to explore the genetic basis of personality is to estimate the **heritability** of adult personality traits, by comparing identical and fraternal twins reared apart with twins reared together (see Chapter 3). Researchers using this method report that whether the trait in question is altruism, aggression, one of the Big Five, or even religious attitudes, heritability is typically around .50 (Bouchard et al., 1990; Loehlin, 1988; Pedersen et al., 1988; Tellegen et al., 1988; Waller et al., 1990). This means that within a group of people about 50 percent of the variance in such traits is usually attributable to genetic differences. Some researchers have even reported high heritability estimates for such specific behaviors as getting divorced (McGue & Lykken, 1992) and watching a lot of television in childhood (Plomin et al., 1990).

■ **heritability**
A statistical estimate of the proportion of the total variance in some trait within a group that is attributable to genetic differences among individuals within the group.

Identical twins often unconsciously arrange their arms and legs in the same way and assume similar expressions. Research suggests that such physical mannerisms probably have a genetic basis.

These results are surprising; how can religious attitudes, divorce, and TV watching be heritable? Our prehistoric ancestors didn't have marriage, let alone divorce, and they certainly didn't watch TV. What are the personality traits or temperaments underlying these behaviors? But even more startling and controversial is the finding that the only environmental effects on personality come from *nonshared* experiences, such as having had a particular teacher in the fourth grade or having won the lead in the school play. Study after study has found that *shared environment and parental child-rearing practices seem to be not at all related to adult personality traits* (Plomin & Daniels, 1987).

Understandably, researchers doing this research are excited about their findings. They believe the evidence for the heritability of personality traits represents an overwhelming attack on the conventional wisdom that child-rearing practices are central to personality development. "Our retrospective study showed only meager associations between parent-child relations and adult personality," wrote McCrae and Costa (1988a). "It will doubtless seem incredible to many readers that variables such as social class, educational opportunities, religious training, and parental love and discipline have no substantial influence on adult personality, but imagine for a moment that it is correct. What will it mean for research in developmental psychology? How will clinical psychology and theories of therapy be changed?"

Think About It

Can You Change Your Personality—and Would You if You Could?

■ Which of your personality traits, if any, would you like to change? And what would you be willing to do to change them?

More than a decade ago, a book called *Mind, Mood, and Medicine* predicted that research in the biology of personality would transform psychology (Wender & Klein, 1981). Thanks to the success of research in behavioral genetics and drug treatments, the authors said, people would no longer be doomed to suffer from unpleasant personality traits or emotional disorders such as depression and anxiety. In 1993, a book called *Listening to Prozac* reinforced these predictions. Its author, psychiatrist Peter Kramer, had begun administering Prozac—an antidepressant that we will discuss in more detail in Chapter 16—to his patients. "Spending time with patients who responded to Prozac had transformed my views about what makes people the way they are," Kramer wrote. "I had come to see inborn, biologically determined temperament where before I had seen slowly acquired, history-laden character."

Kramer reported the seemingly miraculous effects of Prozac on all sorts of traits: compulsion, perfectionism, low self-esteem, shyness, irritability, anxiety, hypersensitivity to rejection, need for attention, lack of assertiveness and inability to take risks, inhibition of pleasure, sluggishness of thought, and *dysthymia,* a condition of chronic melancholy. While admitting that scientists really don't know much about the brain, depression, or drugs at the

moment, Kramer endorsed the biological model of personality and its prediction that drugs will one day "modify inborn predisposition" and "repair traumatic damage to personality." "As we have access to yet more specific drugs," he says, "our accuracy in targeting individual traits will improve."

As we discuss in this chapter, some key traits in personality are partly heritable. Suppose that drugs can be developed that would make a genetically shy person more extroverted, a neurotic person more positive and optimistic, or a melancholy person happier. If you could take a pill to correct some part of your personality that you don't like, would you take it? And where would you draw the line? Would you take the pill if you were just mildly unhappy, or only if you were devastatingly depressed?

Before you answer, consider a few troubling issues. Kramer himself admits that the possibility of reaching into the personality to alter a single trait—to perk up low self-esteem, perhaps, or mental agility—"has worrisome implications." One is that doctors are already inclined to overprescribe medication for even mild or transitory personality problems, without considering alternative explanations and treatments. Another is what Kramer calls the "coercive power of convention." If most people in your social circle are extroverts and you are not, will you feel undue pressure to be like them? Why should you be?

Good questions! What would these findings, if true, mean for education, for raising children, for the treatment of personality problems? Is the key to personality change biological and medical rather than environmental? (See "Think About It.") McCrae and Costa (1988a) believe that these findings are simply too threatening for most psychologists to accept, because they challenge the optimistic view that human nature can be improved by altering experiences. However, while it is wise to keep an open mind about the challenge of genetic theories of personality, we also need to consider their limitations and some problems in interpreting their results.

Evaluating Genetic Theories

Before we can conclude that differences in personality are based almost entirely on differences in heredity, we need to consider some of the complexities of measuring heritability.

One problem, as we saw in Chapter 3, is that measures of environmental factors are still quite crude and probably fail to detect some important environmental influences. Because heritability tells us only the relative impact of genetics and the environment on behavior or personality, underestimating the influence of the environment inevitably means overestimating the influence of

There is clear evidence for the heritability of some personality traits, such as shyness and aggressiveness. Does that mean that shy 5-year-olds will inevitably grow up to become wallflowers, or that aggressive 8-year-olds will become criminals? What is a better way to think about the impact of heredity on personality?

Another issue concerns the social and cultural context of personality. A trait such as "perfectionism" might be normal and desirable in one society or relationship, but a problem or liability in another. Which should be fixed—the person or the environment? "Should a person with a personality style that might succeed in a different social setting," Kramer asks, "have to change her personality (by means of drugs!) in order to find fulfillment?" Suppose a person has a cooperative, agreeable way of getting along with others, but works in a company or goes to a school that rewards aggressive, combative, and competitive behavior. Is it a good idea for such a person to take a drug to help him or her succeed in such a setting? Or would it be better to change the institution to make it possible for people with diverse personality traits to succeed?

As this example suggests, people will disagree about which traits are desirable and which should be "fixed." It isn't always easy to tell, again because *traits always interact with situations*. For instance, the most common behavioral disorder diagnosed in American children is something called Attention Deficit Hyperactivity Disorder (ADHD), a condition describing children (and adults) who are full of energy, can't sit still, have trouble concentrating, and are messy and impulsive. The usual treatment for ADHD is Ritalin, a drug that helps modify these symptoms. Many people with ADHD and many parents of children with ADHD regard the drug as a

life-saver. But is the problem always in the children, or is it sometimes in the situations that require energetic children to sit still too long? In America, ADHD is diagnosed at ten times the rate that it is in Europe, leading some critics to wonder whether America is less tolerant of normally obstreperous children who won't accommodate to boring surroundings (Armstrong, 1993). Further, where do we draw the line between the positive and negative aspects of ADHD? "Kids with ADHD are wild, funny, effervescent," a psychiatrist told *Time* magazine (July 18, 1994). "They have a love of life. The rest of us sometimes envy them." Are those traits "cured" along with the rest of the disorder?

Finally, it is essential to consider the unforeseen *social* consequences of thousands of otherwise rational *individual* decisions to improve one's personality through medication. Do we want a world in which no one ever feels miserable or has chronic complaints? At first glance the answer might seem yes. But as Kramer points out, "Much of the insight and creative achievement of the human race is due to the discontent, guilt, and critical eye of dysthymics." Will people be able to resist a pill that eliminates their discontent, guilt, and critical observations? Who will want to make the effort to fix institutions, protest injustice, create art, and spend years working on new inventions if they can take a drug to help them adjust to the world as it is? Think about it. ■

heritability. Another problem is that most separated twins have grown up in fairly similar environments. When subjects in heritability studies share similar environments—in terms of opportunities, stimulation, affluence, and experiences—there may be too few environmental differences among them to explain their personality differences. This means that heritability estimates will automatically be inflated, and the impact of the environment will again be underestimated.

In evaluating genetic influences on personality, we must also keep in mind that although temperaments appear early in life and can influence later personality traits, they do not provide a fixed, unchangeable blueprint. Consistency in a given temperament depends in part on how extreme that trait is in infancy. Jerome Kagan (1994) found that children who are exceptionally shy at age 2 tend to be quiet, cautious, and inhibited at age 7; those who are extremely sociable and uninhibited at 2 are usually talkative and sociable five years later. But most children fall somewhere between the extremes and show far less consistency over time.

Even children at the extremes of a temperament may change as they grow older, and such change seems to depend on how parents and others respond to the child. In his work with monkeys, Stephen Suomi (1989) has shown that a highly inhibited infant is likely to overcome its timidity if it is reared by an extremely nurturant foster mother (see Figure 12.1). In human beings, the "fit" between a child's nature and the parents' is critical (Thomas & Chess, 1980). Not only do parents affect the baby, but the baby affects the parents. Imagine a high-strung parent with a child who is difficult and sometimes slow to respond to affection. The parent may begin to feel desperate, angry, or rejected. Over time, the parent may withdraw from the child or use excessive punishment, which in turn makes the child even more difficult to live with. In contrast, a more easygoing parent may have a calming effect on a difficult child or may persist in showing affection even when the child holds back, causing the child to become more responsive.

Finally, we must consider the diminishing effect of genes over time. A meta-analysis of 103 studies of twins found that over the years, correlations

Some children are temperamentally disposed to shyness and timidity in new situations.

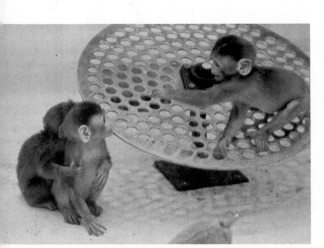

■ Figure 12.1 Don't Be Shy

On the left, a timid infant rhesus monkey cowers behind a friend in the presence of a more outgoing stranger. Such socially inhibited behavior seems to be a biologically based disposition, both in monkeys and in human beings (Suomi, 1987, 1989; Kagan, 1994). But a nurturant adult monkey (center, a foster mother) can help an infant overcome its initial timidity. At first, the infant clings to her, but a few days later (right) the same young monkey has become more adventurous.

between twins in most personality traits tended to decrease. "In other words," concluded the researchers, "as twins grow up, they grow apart" (McCartney, Harris, & Bernieri, 1990). For some traits, experiences at certain periods in life become particularly important. For example, a recent analysis of data from nearly 15,000 Finnish twins, ages 18 to 59, found that the heritability of extroversion decreases (and thus the impact of the environment *increases*) from the late teens and early 20s to the late 20s—a time when young people tend to leave home, marry, and establish independent adult lives (Viken et al., 1994).

In sum, even if some traits have a heritable component, this does not mean that all human qualities are rigidly fixed. As developmental psychologist Jerome Kagan (1994) observes of his own research with temperamentally inhibited children, "a fearful child can learn to control the urge to withdraw from a stranger or a large dog. . . . The role of the environment is more substantial in helping a child overcome the tendency to withdraw than in making that child timid in the first place." Every child, he reminds us, is always part of a context in which biology and experience are inextricably intertwined.

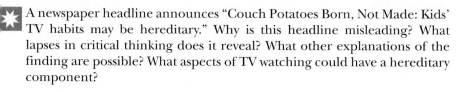

Quick QUIZ

A newspaper headline announces "Couch Potatoes Born, Not Made: Kids' TV habits may be hereditary." Why is this headline misleading? What lapses in critical thinking does it reveal? What other explanations of the finding are possible? What aspects of TV watching could have a hereditary component?

Answers:

The headline implies that TV habits are directly inherited. The writer is jumping to conclusions and failing to consider other explanations. There is no "TV-watching gene," but perhaps some temperaments dispose people to be sedentary or passive, and this disposition may lead to a lot of TV watching.

■ THE LEARNING TRADITION: YOU ARE WHAT YOU DO

On a hot summer day, James Peters shot and killed his next-door neighbor, Ralph Galluccio. Peters had reached the end of his patience in a ten-year dispute with Galluccio over their common property line. Shocked friends said that this feud was not predictable from the men's personalities. Galluccio, his employer reported, was "a likable person with a good, even disposition." Peters, said his employer, was a "very mild-mannered, cooperative" man, "an all-around good guy."

A biological psychologist might say that this violent episode demonstrates the aggressive capacity of human nature in general and of violence-prone personalities in particular. A learning theorist, however, would emphasize each man's past learning and present environment. Within the learning tradition, some *radical behaviorists* take the extreme view that "personality" is an illusion. To understand human behavior, they say, we do not need to consider mental processes or biological factors; we need only consider the environment in which the behavior occurs. In contrast, *cognitive social-learning theorists* argue that we acquire personality patterns as we learn to deal with the environment, and that personality and situation are constantly influencing each other in an unending chain of interaction.

Puzzles of Personality #1

Is Personality Stable Over a Lifetime?

In the view of biological psychologists, the basic ingredients of personality are pretty well ingrained and do not change much throughout life. Psychodynamic psychologists agree, and also believe that unconscious elements of personality are set during a child's first five years. Other schools of psychology maintain that personality traits are flexible and can change in adulthood depending on experiences. Research finds that the truth lies somewhere in between; some traits do seem to be stable across the life span, whereas others are more influenced by circumstances.

Chance events—losing a job, being injured, getting divorced—can affect people's personalities in unexpected ways. Many individuals lose self-esteem and achievement motivation when they are fired from jobs or work in environments that give them no feedback or support.

Not all traits are lifelong aspects of personality. Although aggressive children are more likely than their calmer peers to be aggressive as adults, many children and teenagers outgrow early aggressiveness.

Extroversion and introversion are among the more stable of traits, and have a genetic component. This merry dancer kicking up her heels has probably been outgoing and demonstrative since childhood.

Shyness and timidity also seem to be relatively stable. Although everyone feels shy on occasion, some people feel shy on most occasions; they are uncomfortable in new situations and slow to reveal themselves.

The Behavioral School

In 1913, while Sigmund Freud was busy formulating psychoanalysis in Vienna, John B. Watson was founding the behavioral tradition in the United States. The two men, as we will see, represented the north and south poles of personality theory, with Freud talking about instincts and unconscious motives and Watson dismissing these concepts as being vague and unscientific. To Watson, all elements of personality were classically conditioned responses, just as salivation was in Pavlov's dogs.

The best-known American behaviorist, B. F. Skinner, shared with Watson a belief that behavior is primarily learned, but he rejected Watson's emphasis on classical conditioning as the major form of learning. Noting that many kinds of behavior were not classically conditioned, he turned to operant (instrumental) conditioning as the fundamental form of learning. (To refresh your memory on these terms, see Chapter 7.) For Skinner, personality was a collection of behavioral patterns, and labels such as "aggressive," "extroverted," or "conscientious" were merely shorthand descriptions of responses in particular situations.

This doesn't mean that all situations produce the same responses in all individuals. Imagine two people at a party of strangers—one who is extroverted and friendly, another who is withdrawn and shy. Skinner would say that if we looked into the behavioral histories of these two people, we would find different patterns of reinforcement. For one, friendliness was reinforced; for the other, shyness was reinforced and assertiveness punished. What could possibly reward painful shyness? Experiments have found that shyness and anxiety are encouraged when they serve as a *self-handicapping strategy*. When shy people or people with low self-esteem are in situations in which they believe they will be evaluated, they learn to use their anxiety as an excuse for poor performance (Snyder, 1990). Self-handicappers place obstacles in the path of their own success. If they then fail, they can blame the failure on the handicap ("I'm shy" or "I have writer's block") instead of a lack of ability. If they succeed anyway, they can claim additional credit for doing well despite the handicap. In this way apparently self-defeating habits are acquired as learned strategies to protect self-esteem.

Behaviorists do not deny that people have feelings, thoughts, or values. However, they believe that these mental states are as subject to the laws of learning as, say, nail biting is. Skinner believed that the study of values is essentially the study of reinforcers. It is unscientific and imprecise, he said, to say that "Pat values fame." Rather, fame is positively reinforcing to Pat, which is why Pat continues to strive for it. Someone else might find fame unpleasantly punishing, and thus hold different "values." If we want a peaceful world, behaviorists say, we had better not wait around for people's personalities to change. We had better change circumstances so that cooperation is rewarded, cheaters don't win, and aggressors don't stay in power.

The Cognitive Social-Learning School

As we saw in Chapter 7, modern cognitive social-learning theories of personality depart from classic behaviorism in their emphasis on three phenomena: (1) observational learning and the role of models; (2) cognitive processes such as perceptions and interpretations of events; and (3) motivating beliefs, such as enduring expectations of success or failure and confidence (or lack of it) in one's ability to master new skills and achieve goals. Where behaviorists see personality as a set of habits and beliefs that have been rewarded over a person's lifetime, cognitive social-learning theorists maintain that these habits and beliefs eventually acquire a life of their own, coming to exert their own effects on behavior. They may even supersede the power of reinforcers, which is why some people persist in their pursuit of fame, glory, or other goals without ever receiving external reinforcement of their efforts.

According to cognitive social-learning theorists, then, much of human behavior and personality is *self-regulated*—shaped by thoughts, values, self-reflections, and intentions. As Albert Bandura (1994) puts it, people motivate themselves and evaluate their actions by setting goals, anticipating results, and planning courses of action. Two of the most important personality traits that influence behavior are the extent to which people believe they have control over their lives and how much confidence they have in their own abilities.

Locus of Control. Much of the work on people's sense of control has been done by Julian Rotter (1966, 1982, 1990), who started out as a behaviorally oriented experimentalist. During the 1950s, Rotter was working both as a psychotherapist and a researcher. He noticed that his patients weren't behaving according to behavioral principles; they kept having troubling emotions and irrational beliefs (Hunt, 1993).

Rotter initially framed his observations of his clients' problems in behavioral terms. Over time, he concluded, people learn that some acts will be rewarded and others punished. He then noticed that they develop *generalized expectancies* about which situations and acts will be rewarding. A child who studies hard and gets good grades, attention from teachers, admiration from friends, and loving praise from parents will come to expect that hard work in other situations will also pay off. A child who studies hard and gets poor grades, is ignored by teachers, is rejected by friends for being a grind, or earns no support or praise from parents will come to expect that hard work isn't worth it. One child may learn that if she speaks her mind, she can expect praise and attention. Another may learn that if she speaks her mind, she can expect to irritate her parents, who want her to be quiet and obedient. Once acquired, as we saw in Chapter 11, these expectations often create a *self-fulfilling prophecy*.

Rotter and his colleagues demonstrated the power of expectancies in many experiments. At the same time, both in his private practice and in his studies, Rotter was observing people whose expectations of success never went up *even when they were actually successful*. "Oh, that was just a fluke," they would say, or "I was lucky; it will never happen again." Rotter concluded that people's feelings or beliefs about the factors that govern their behavior are as important as the actual reinforcers and punishers in the environment. He chose the term **locus of control** to refer to people's general expectations about whether or not the results of their actions are under their own control. People who have an *internal* locus of control ("internals") tend to believe they are responsible for what happens to them, that they control their own destiny. People who have an *external* locus of control ("externals") tend to believe they are victims (or sometimes beneficiaries) of luck, fate, or other people. To measure these traits, Rotter (1966) developed an *Internal/External (I/E) scale* consisting of pairs of statements. People had to choose the statement in each pair with which they most strongly agreed, as in these two items:

1. a. Many of the unhappy things in people's lives are partly due to bad luck.
   b. People's misfortunes result from mistakes they make.

2. a. Becoming a success is a matter of hard work; luck has little or nothing to do with it.
   b. Getting a good job depends mainly on being in the right place at the right time.

Research on locus of control took off like a hot rod, and over the years more than 2,000 studies based on the I/E scale have been published (Hunt, 1993). For example, dozens of studies conducted in different cultures and ethnic

A person's locus of control—internal or external—often depends on events and experiences. These members of the Communications Workers Union have an internal locus of control with regard to New York City's budget cuts: They believe their collective protest will have an effect. What social forces might increase people's sense of efficacy and internal locus of control, and what might extinguish them?

▪ **locus of control**
A general expectation about whether the results of one's actions are under one's own control (internal locus) or beyond one's control (external locus).

groups, with people of different ages, have confirmed that internal locus of control is strongly related to academic achievement and political activism. And more than 700 studies using a children's version of the I/E scale find that internal control and its effects emerge at an early age (Nowicki & Strickland, 1973; Strickland, 1989). We will discuss locus of control again in relation to health—its benefits and some of its drawbacks—in Chapter 14.

Self-efficacy.   In the previous chapter we discussed the importance of having a sense of competence, particularly *self-efficacy*—the belief that you can accomplish what you set out to do. According to Bandura (1994), self-efficacy, as an integral aspect of personality, derives from four sources:

1. *Experiences in mastering new skills and overcoming obstacles on the path to achievement.* Occasional failures are necessary for a robust sense of self-efficacy, because people who experience only success learn to expect quick results and tend to be easily discouraged by normal difficulties.

2. *Vicarious experiences provided by successful and competent people (models) who are similar to oneself.* For example, if an African-American boy learns that a black man, Garrett Morgan, invented the traffic light, his belief that he too could be an engineer might be strengthened. By observing the competence of a person similar to oneself, an individual learns both that the task is possible and how to do it. But negative modeling can undermine self-efficacy: If other people in their group seem to keep failing, people may come to doubt that they can succeed.

3. *Encouragement and persuasion from others.* People acquire a sense of self-efficacy when they are in an environment in which other people persuade them that they have what it takes to "make it," reward their capabilities, allow them to succeed, and do not subject them to repeated failure.

4. *Judgments of one's own physiological state.* People feel more competent when they are calm and relaxed than when they are tense or under extreme stress. People who have high self-efficacy are also able to use states of arousal and tension productively. For example, instead of interpreting normal feelings of stage fright as "evidence" that they are going to bomb when they give a talk, they regard these jitters as a source of energy that will help them perform better.

Bandura (1994) observes that because ordinary life is "full of impediments, adversities, setbacks, frustrations, and inequities," having an "optimistic sense of personal efficacy" is needed to sustain the effort to persist and succeed. Such a sense lies somewhere between having unrealistic delusions that all things are possible, and cynical expectations that nothing can ever be done.

Evaluating Learning Theories

Why did James Peters kill Ralph Galluccio? Instead of assuming that Galluccio and Peters were driven by biologically determined temperaments or genes for aggressiveness, cognitive social-learning psychologists would investigate the environmental conditions of their quarrel and each man's perceptions about it. The two men found themselves in an increasingly difficult situation that seemed to offer no way out. Learning psychologists would investigate why these two men lacked the skills to negotiate their differences, and how each had learned over time that aggressive actions would make other people knuckle under.

Learning approaches emphasize the ways in which personality and situation interact. In the learning view, you may have a skill, such as pie baking or hog calling, and find yourself in a place that never gives you the chance to reveal it. On the other hand, you may find yourself in a new environment that gives you an opportunity to learn skills you never dreamed you could master. Likewise, specific situations either allow us to express aspects of our personalities or prevent us from doing so. If George is assertive at home but meek at work, or if Georgina is independent at work but clings to her friends, it is because they are reinforced differently in different situations.

Some psychologists criticize behaviorism for implying that individuals are as soft as jellyfish, and that with the right environment, anyone can become anything. They also criticize behaviorism for its implication that people are entirely passive recipients of environmental events. These common charges are not really fair. Skinner, for instance, stated frequently that people have limits because of their genetic constitutions and temperaments, and he argued that people can choose to change their environments to provide themselves with different reinforcers.

A more important criticism is that learning approaches to personality sometimes attribute behavior to a vague category called "environment" without defining its contents or the process by which the environment affects people, just as biological approaches sometimes attribute behavior to a vague category called "heredity." For example, many people assume that images of women and men in the popular media strongly influence what people learn about femininity and masculinity. Principles of observational learning would seem to dictate that this is so. Yet not everyone reacts to the same images in the same way. Therefore it is difficult to specify *which* media images are having an effect, and on whom; and it is difficult to disentangle the effects of the media from all the other events that influence people's ideas about "correct" gender behavior.

Learning researchers tend to study one influence on learning at a time: a parental model, a teacher's reactions, the pattern of reinforcers in a given situation, media images, self-efficacy, locus of control, and so forth. In real life, however, people are surrounded by hundreds of interacting influences. This fact poses a serious problem for learning theories of personality: When nearly anything *can* have an influence on behavior, it can be frustratingly difficult to show that any one thing actually *is* having an influence. It's like trying to grab a fistful of fog; you know it's there, but somehow it keeps getting away from you.

Nevertheless, the learning approach to personality makes an essential point: that in the most general sense, people must learn by observation and reinforcement what the rules of their culture and community are, how their parents expect them to behave, and which personality traits are encouraged and which disparaged.

We turn now to approaches to personality that depart from mainstream empirical psychology, both in theory and methods. Psychodynamic and humanist views of the person regard the objective measurement of traits and the piece-by-piece approach of biological and behavioral theories of personality as being too cold, mechanical, and incomplete. Instead, they propose global theories of personality that emphasize the development of the whole person.

■ THE PSYCHODYNAMIC TRADITION: YOU ARE WHAT YOU WERE

Of all the theories of personality, the psychodynamic approach is the one most embedded in popular culture, particularly in people's ways of talking and thinking. A man apologizes for "displacing" his frustrations at work onto his family. A woman suspects that she is "repressing" a childhood trauma. An alcoholic reveals that he is no longer "in denial" about his dependence on drinking. A newspaper columnist advises readers to "sublimate" their anger or risk becoming ill. A teacher informs a divorcing couple that their 8-year-old child is "regressing" to immature behavior.

Puzzles of Personality #2

What Is the "Nature" of Human Nature?

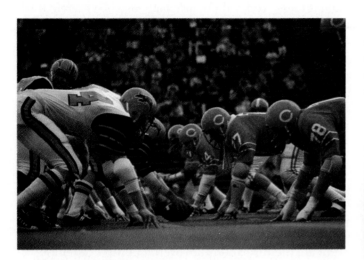

To Freudians, human nature reflects an eternal war between the aggressive or death instincts and the sexual or life instincts. The modern football game, in this view, represents the displacement of aggressive energy into a socially accepted activity.

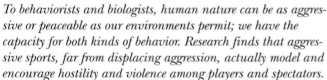

Karen Horney argued that human nature is basically social and cooperative; individuals who row together, so to speak, grow together. When people are prevented from expressing their needs for attachment and connection, however, they feel a basic anxiety and insecurity that may be expressed in destructiveness and hostility.

To behaviorists and biologists, human nature can be as aggressive or peaceable as our environments permit; we have the capacity for both kinds of behavior. Research finds that aggressive sports, far from displacing aggression, actually model and encourage hostility and violence among players and spectators.

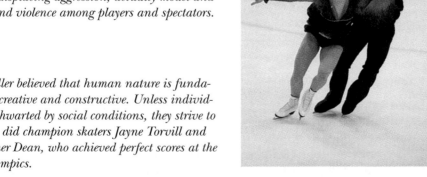

Alfred Adler believed that human nature is fundamentally creative and constructive. Unless individuals are thwarted by social conditions, they strive to excel—as did champion skaters Jayne Torvill and Christopher Dean, who achieved perfect scores at the 1984 Olympics.

All of this language—about displacing, repressing, denying, sublimating, and regressing; about the unconscious—can be traced to the first psychodynamic theory of personality, Sigmund Freud's **psychoanalysis.** Freud's theory and the theories of his followers are called **psychodynamic** because they are based on the movement of psychological energy within the person, in the form of attachments, conflicts, and motivations. (As we saw in Chapter 1, *dynamics* is a term from physics that refers to the motion and balance of systems under the action of outside or inside forces.) Today there are many psychodynamic theories, differing from Freudian theory and from one another, but they all share five general elements:

1. An emphasis on unconscious **intrapsychic** dynamics, the movement of psychic forces within the mind.

2. An assumption that adult behavior and ongoing problems are determined primarily by experiences in early childhood.

3. A belief that psychological development occurs in fixed stages, during which predictable mental events occur and unconscious issues or crises must be resolved.

4. A focus on fantasies and symbolic meanings of events as the unconscious mind perceives them—a person's *psychic reality*—as the main motivators of personality and behavior.

5. A reliance on subjective rather than objective methods of getting at the truth of a person's life: for example, through analysis of dreams, myths, folklore, symbols, and, most of all, the revelations uncovered in psychotherapy.

In this section, we will introduce you to Freud's ideas, to the variations of Freudian theory offered by some of his dissenting colleagues during his lifetime, and to some of the contemporary psychodynamic approaches that have added new rooms and levels to the original Freudian edifice.

Freud and Psychoanalysis

No one disputes the profound influence that Sigmund Freud (1856–1939) had on this century. But there is plenty of dispute about the lasting significance of his work, reflected in three current attitudes toward Freud and his ideas. The first, held by Freud himself and by his most devoted followers to this day, is that Freud was one of the great geniuses of history, an intellectual revolutionary like Copernicus, Darwin, and Newton. The second view, probably the most common among clinical psychologists today, is that Freud was a great thinker and that many of his ideas have lasting value, but some are dated and others are plain wrong. The third view, held by many scientists and researchers in other areas of psychology, is that Freud was a fraud. The British scientist and Nobel Laureate Peter Medawar (1982) once called psychoanalysis a dinosaur in the history of ideas, doomed to extinction. For good measure, he added that it is "the most stupendous intellectual confidence trick of the twentieth century."

In order to understand the kind of theory that could produce such wildly different reactions, let us enter the world of Freud—a realm of unconscious motives, conflicts, and fears. These unseen forces, Freud believed, have far more power over human behavior than consciousness does, so the true study of psychology must probe beneath the surface of a person's mental life. The unconscious reveals itself, said Freud, in dreams, "free association"—talking about anything that pops into your head, without worrying about what anyone will think of you—and slips of the tongue. A slip of the tongue was no random flub to Freud. The British member of Parliament who referred to the "honourable member from Hell" when he meant to say "Hull," said Freud (1920/1960), was revealing his actual, unconscious appraisal of his colleague.

■ **psychoanalysis**
A theory of personality and a method of psychotherapy developed by Sigmund Freud; it emphasizes unconscious motives and conflicts.

■ **psychodynamic theories**
Theories that explain behavior and personality in terms of unconscious energy dynamics within the individual.

■ **intrapsychic**
Within the mind (psyche) or self.

The Structure of Personality. In Freud's theory, personality is made up of three major systems: the *id*, the *ego*, and the *superego*. Although each system has its own functions and elements, human behavior is nearly always a result of the interaction among them (Freud, 1905b, 1920/1960, 1923/1962).

The **id** is the reservoir of all psychological energies and inherited instincts. To Freud, the id was the true psychic reality because it represents the inner world of subjective experience. It is unconcerned with objective reality and is unaffected by the environment. The id operates according to the *pleasure principle*, seeking to reduce tension, avoid pain, and obtain pleasure. It contains what Freud considered to be two competing groups of instincts: the life, or sexual, instincts (fueled by psychic energy called the **libido**) and the death, or aggressive, instincts. As instinctive energy builds up in the id, the result is an uncomfortable state of tension. The id may discharge this tension in the form of reflex actions, physical symptoms, or wishful thinking—uncensored mental images and unbidden thoughts.

The **ego,** the second system to emerge, is a referee between the needs of instinct and the demands of society. It obeys the *reality principle*, putting a rein on the id's desire for pleasure until a suitable outlet can be found. The ego, said Freud, represents "reason and good sense." Freud (1923/1962) described the relationship between ego and id this way: "In relation to the id, [the ego] is like a man on horseback, who has to hold in check the superior strength of the horse. . . . Often a rider, if he is not to be parted from his horse, is obliged to guide it where it wants to go; so in the same way the ego constantly carries into action the wishes of the id as if they were its own."

The **superego,** the last system of personality to develop, represents morality, the rules of parents and society, and the power of authority. The superego consists of the *ego ideal*, those moral and social standards you learn are right, and the *conscience*, the inner voice that says you did something wrong. The superego judges the activities of the id, handing out good feelings (pride, satisfaction) when you do something well and handing out miserable feelings (guilt, shame) when you break the rules.

An old joke summarizes the role of the id, ego, and superego this way: The id says, "I want, and I want it now"; the superego says, "You can't have it; it's bad for you"; and the ego, the rational mediator, says, "Well, maybe you can have some of it—later." According to Freud, the healthy personality must keep all three systems in balance. Someone who is too controlled by the id is governed by impulse and selfish desires. Someone who is too controlled by the superego is rigid, moralistic, and bossy. Someone who has a weak ego is unable to balance personal needs and wishes with social duties and realistic limitations.

If a person feels anxious or threatened when the wishes of the id conflict with social rules, the ego has weapons at its command to relieve the tension. These weapons, called **defense mechanisms,** have two characteristics: They deny or distort reality, and they operate unconsciously. According to Freud, ego defenses are necessary to protect us from uncomfortable conflict; they become unhealthy only when they cause self-defeating behavior and emotional problems. Freud described 17 defense mechanisms; later, other psychoanalysts expanded and modified his list. Here are some of the primary defenses described by Freud's daughter Anna (1946), who became a psychoanalyst herself, and by most contemporary psychodynamic psychologists (Horowitz, 1988; Vaillant, 1992a,b):

1. In *repression*, a threatening idea, memory, or emotion is blocked from becoming conscious. "Repression" doesn't mean that you consciously bite your tongue rather than reveal a guilty secret. It refers to the mind's effort to keep a lid on unacceptable feelings and thoughts in the unconscious, so that you aren't even aware of them.

■ **id**
In psychoanalysis, the part of personality containing inherited psychological energy, particularly sexual and aggressive instincts.

■ **libido**
In psychoanalysis, the psychic energy that fuels the life or sexual instincts of the id.

■ **ego**
In psychoanalysis, the part of personality that represents reason, good sense, and rational self-control.

■ **superego**
In psychoanalysis, the part of personality that represents conscience, morality, and social standards.

■ **defense mechanisms**
Methods used by the ego to prevent unconscious anxiety or threatening thoughts from entering consciousness.

"I'm sorry, I'm not speaking to anyone tonight.
My defense mechanisms seem to be out of order."

2. In *projection,* one's own unacceptable feelings are attributed to someone else. A boy who dislikes his father, for instance, may feel anxious about disliking someone he depends on. So he may project his feelings onto his father, concluding that "he hates me." A person who has uncomfortable sexual feelings about members of a different ethnic group may project this discomfort onto them, saying, "those people are dirty-minded and oversexed."

3. In *displacement,* people direct their emotions (especially anger) toward things, animals, or other people that are not the real object of their feelings. People use displacement when they perceive the real target as being too threatening to confront directly. A boy who is forbidden to express anger at his father, for example, may "take it out" on his toys or his sister.

Freud believed that energy from the id that is blocked from direct expression would be displaced onto a substitute. Thus the "aggressive instinct" might be displaced in sports competition instead of directly expressed in war. When displacement serves a higher cultural or socially useful purpose, as in the creation of art or inventions, it is called *sublimation.* Freud himself thought that for the sake of civilization and survival, sexual and aggressive energies could and should be displaced or sublimated into socially appropriate and constructive forms.

4. In *reaction formation,* the feeling that causes unconscious anxiety is transformed into its opposite in consciousness. A woman who is afraid to admit she doesn't love her husband may consciously believe she loves him. A person who is aroused by erotic images may angrily assert that pornography is disgusting. How does such a transformed emotion differ from the true emotion? Usually, a reaction formation gives itself away by being excessive: The person asserts the feeling too insistently and is compulsive about demonstrating it. ("*Of course* I love him! I *never* have any bad thoughts about him! He's perfect!")

5. *Regression.* As we will see, Freud believed that personality develops in a series of stages, from birth to maturity. Each new step, however, produces a certain amount of frustration and anxiety. If these become too great, normal development may be briefly or permanently halted and the child may remain *fixated* at the current stage; for instance, he or she may not outgrow clinging dependence. Children may also regress to an earlier stage if they suffer a traumatic experience in a later one. An 8-year-old child who is anxious about family fights may regress to earlier habits of thumbsucking or clinging. Adults may reveal "partial fixations" that they never outgrew, such as biting nails, or regress to immature behavior when they are under pressure.

Is she "regressing" to the oral stage?

Table 12.1	Summary of Freud's Model of the Mind	
Id	**Ego**	**Superego**
Location of the aggressive and sexual instincts; follows the pleasure principle	Relies on the reality principle to mediate between desires of the id and the demands of the superego. Uses defense mechanisms to protect against unconscious anxiety, including: repression projection displacement reaction formation regression denial	Location of conscience and the ego ideal

6. In *denial,* people simply refuse to admit that something unpleasant is happening or that they are experiencing a forbidden emotion. A woman may deny that she is angry with her boyfriend; an alcoholic may deny that he depends on liquor. In the psychodynamic view, people who assert that they *never* have negative feelings or never feel disgusted by anything are revealing denial, for these are normal emotions. Denial protects the illusion of invulnerability—"It will never happen to me"—which is why people often behave in self-destructive and risky ways.

These defense mechanisms, Freud maintained, protect the ego and allow the person to cope with reality (see Table 12.1). Different personalities emerge because people differ in the defenses they use, in how rigid their defenses are, and in whether their defenses lead to healthy or disturbed functioning.

The Development of Personality. Freud maintained that personality develops in a fixed series of five stages. He called these stages *psychosexual* because he believed that psychological development depends on the changing expression of sexual energy in different parts of the body as the child matures.

1. *The oral stage* marks the first year of life. Babies take in the world, as well as their nourishment, through their mouths, so the mouth, said Freud, is the focus of sensation at this stage. People who remain fixated at the oral stage may, as adults, seek constant oral gratification in smoking, drinking, overeating, chewing on pencils, and the like.

2. *The anal stage,* at about ages 2 to 3, marks the start of ego development, as the child becomes aware of the self and of the demands of reality. The major issue at this stage, said Freud, is control of bodily wastes, a lesson in self-control that the child learns during toilet training. People who remain fixated at this stage, he thought, become "anal retentive," holding everything in, obsessive about neatness and cleanliness. Or they become just the opposite, "anal expulsive," that is, messy and disorganized.

3. *The phallic (or Oedipal) stage* lasts roughly from ages 3 to 5. Now sexual sensation is located in the penis, for boys, and in the clitoris, for girls. The child, said Freud, unconsciously wishes to possess the parent of the opposite sex and get rid of the parent of the same sex. Children of this age often announce proudly that "I'm going to marry Daddy (or Mommy) when I grow up" and reject the same-sex "rival." Freud (1924a, 1924b) labeled this phenomenon the **Oedipus complex,** after the Greek legend of King Oedipus, who unwittingly killed his father and married his mother.

Boys and girls, Freud believed, go through the Oedipal stage differently. Boys at this stage are discovering the pleasure and pride of having a penis.

■ **Oedipus complex**
In psychoanalysis, a conflict in which a child desires the parent of the other sex and views the same-sex parent as a rival; this is the key issue in the phallic stage of development.

When they see a naked girl for the first time, they are horrified. Their unconscious exclaims (in effect), "Her penis has dropped off! Who could have done such a thing to her? Why, it must have been her powerful father. And if he could do it to her, mine could do it to me!" This realization, said Freud, causes the boy to repress his desire for his mother, accept the authority of his father, and identify with him. **Identification** is the process by which boys take in, as their own, the father's standards of conscience and morality. The superego has emerged.

Freud admitted that he didn't quite know what to make of girls, who, lacking the penis, couldn't go through the same steps. He speculated that a girl, upon discovering male anatomy, would panic that she had only a puny clitoris instead of a stately penis. She would conclude, said Freud, that she already had lost her penis. As a result, girls don't have the powerful motivating fear to give up their Oedipal feelings; they have only a lingering sense of "penis envy." Thus, Freud concluded, women do not develop the strong moral superegos that men do.

By about ages 5 or 6, when the Oedipus complex is resolved, said Freud, the child's personality patterns are formed. Unconscious conflicts with parents, unresolved fixations and guilts, and attitudes toward the same and the other sex will continue to replay themselves throughout life.

4. *The latency stage* lasts from the end of the phallic stage to puberty. The child settles down, goes to school, makes friends, develops self-confidence, and learns the social rules for appropriate male or female behavior. Sexual feeling subsides.

5. *The genital stage* begins at puberty and marks the beginning of what Freud considered mature adult sexuality. Sexual energy is now located in the genitals and eventually is directed toward sexual intercourse.

As you might imagine, Freud's ideas were not exactly received with yawns. Sexual feelings in infants and children! Repressed longings in the most respectable adults! Unconscious meanings in dreams! Penis envy! Sexual sublimation! This was strong stuff, and before long psychoanalysis had captured the public imagination in Europe and America. And it produced a sharp rift with the emerging schools of empirical psychology (Hornstein, 1992).

This rift continues to divide psychologists today. Many of Freud's followers revere Freud as they would the founder of a new religion, regarding him as a man who bravely battled public censure and ridicule in his unwavering pursuit of scientific truth (Gay, 1988). They think that even if some of his ideas have proved faulty, the overall framework of his theory is timeless and brilliant. Others think psychoanalysis is, frankly, nonsense, and that Freud himself was nothing like the brilliant theoretician and clinician he claimed to be. They cite new scholarship on Freud, based on previously unpublished papers, revealing that Freud himself manufactured the myth that he was a poor misunderstood genius in order to gain sympathy and credibility; that he was jealous and vengeful toward those who criticized his ideas; that, far from being an impartial scientist, he often pressured his patients into accepting his explanations of their symptoms; and even that he was an incompetent therapist whose most famous patients would today have every ground to sue him for incompetence and malpractice (Cioffi, 1974; Crews, 1993; Esterson, 1993; Powell & Boer, 1994).

A particularly chilling example is the famous case of "Dora" (Ida Bauer) (Lakoff & Coyne, 1993). Eighteen-year-old Dora had been spurning the explicit sexual advances made by her father's friend, "Herr K," since she was 14, and finally complained to her father. But her father wanted her to accept Herr K's overtures, perhaps because he himself was having an affair with Herr K's wife; so he sent her off to Freud, who attempted to cure Dora of her "hysterical" refusal to have sex with Herr K. Freud tried to convince Dora that it was not the ugly situation involving her father and his friend that was distressing her, but

■ **identification**

A process by which the child adopts an adult's standards of morality, values, and beliefs as his or her own; in psychoanalysis, identification with the same-sex parent is said to occur at resolution of the Oedipus complex.

her own *repressed desires for sex.* "I should without question consider a person hysterical," Freud (1905a) wrote, "in whom an occasion for sexual excitement elicited feelings that were preponderantly or exclusively unpleasurable." Dora angrily left treatment after three months, and Freud was never able to accept her "obstinate" refusals to believe his analysis of her symptoms. If only Herr K had learned, said Freud, "that the slap Dora gave him by no means signified a final 'No' on her part," and if he had resolved "to press his suit with a passion which left room for no doubts, the result might very well have been a triumph of the girl's affection for him over all her internal difficulties."

Sigmund Freud was thus a man of contradictions—a mix of vision and blindness, sensitivity and stubbornness (Hunt, 1993). In his provocative ideas, his approach to therapy, and his own complicated personality, Freud left a powerful legacy to psychology. And it was one that others began to tinker with immediately.

Quick QUIZ

Which Freudian concepts do these events suggest?

1. A 4-year-old girl wants to snuggle on Daddy's lap but refuses to kiss her mother.
2. A celibate priest writes poetry about sexual passion.
3. A man who is angry at his boss shouts at his kids for making noise.
4. A woman who was molested by her stepfather for many years assures her friends that she adores him and thinks he is perfect.
5. A racist justifies segregation by saying that black men are only interested in sex with white women.
6. A 9-year-old boy who moves to a new city starts having tantrums.

Answers:

1. Oedipus complex 2. sublimation 3. displacement 4. reaction formation 5. projection 6. regression

Freud's Descendants

Some of Freud's followers stayed in the psychoanalytic tradition and modified Freud's theories from within. One of the most notable of these early dissenters was *Karen Horney* [HORN-eye] (1885–1952), who was one of the first analysts to challenge Freud's notions of penis envy and female inferiority. Horney (1967) argued that it is insulting philosophy and bad science to claim that half the human race is dissatisfied with its gender. When women feel inferior to men, she said, we should look for explanations in the disadvantages that women live with and their second-class status. Freudian theory, she feared, would be used to justify discrimination against women by making it seem that inferiority was in their nature and not in the conditions of their lives. In fact, said Horney, if anyone has an envy problem, it is men. Men have "womb envy": They envy women's ability to bear and nurse children. Men glorify their genitals, she said, because they are unable to give birth and unconsciously fear women's sexual power over them. Later psychoanalysts, such as Bruno Bettelheim (1962), agreed, but argued that both sexes envy the reproductive abilities of the other.

Other members of Freud's circle broke away completely from Freud, or were actively rejected by him, and went off to start their own schools. One was *Alfred Adler* (1870–1937), who had a more positive view of the human condition than

In Adler's view, everyone would strive for perfection if given the chance.

Freud did. Whereas Freud held that personality development pretty much stops after the resolution of the Oedipal complex, Adler was one of the first psychologists to emphasize growth and change over the entire life span. Unlike Freud, Adler thought we are the directors of our lives, not merely victims of unconscious forces. He believed that people have a drive for superiority, which is not the desire to dominate others but a desire for self-improvement, an "upward drive" for perfection. This impulse, said Adler (1927/1959), stems from the natural feelings of inferiority that all of us have, first as children, when we are weak and powerless compared to adults, and then later, when we have to recognize limitations on our abilities. But some individuals, he wrote, are unable to accept their limits and try to mask them by pretending to be strong and capable. They develop an *inferiority complex,* becoming overly concerned with protecting their self-esteem.

Adler's work contains many valuable insights, but today few psychoanalysts identify themselves as "Adlerians," though they may draw on aspects of his theories. In this section we will consider three other psychodynamic approaches that continue to have theoretical and therapeutic influence: the work of Carl Jung, Erik Erikson, and the object-relations school.

Jungian Theory.   Carl Jung (1875–1961) was originally one of Freud's closest friends, but by 1914 he had left Freud's inner circle. His greatest difference with Freud concerned the nature of the unconscious. In addition to the individual's own unconscious, said Jung (1967), a **collective unconscious** contains the universal memories and history of humankind. From his study of myths, folklore, and art in cultures all over the world, Jung was impressed by common, repeated images, which he called **archetypes.** An archetype can be a picture, such as the "magic circle," called a *mandala* in Eastern religions, which symbolizes the unity of life. It can be a mythical figure, such as the Hero, the Nurturing Mother, the Powerful Father, or the Wicked Witch. Other powerful archetypes are the *persona* and the *shadow.* The persona is the public personality, the aspects of yourself that you reveal to others, the role that society expects you to play. The shadow archetype reflects the prehistoric fear of wild animals and represents the animal side of human nature. In the late 1940s, Joseph Campbell gathered evidence that a few archetypes—such as the Hero, the Evil Beast, and the Earth Mother—appear in virtually every society (Campbell, 1949/1968).

According to Jung, the circle is an archetypal image that conveys the cycle of life and death, as in this Hindu mandala showing the god Vishnu surrounded by lesser deities.

Two of the most important archetypes, in Jung's view, are those of men and women themselves. Jung (like Freud) recognized that human beings are psychologically bisexual, that is, that "masculine" and "feminine" qualities are to be found in both sexes. The *anima* represents the feminine archetype in men; the *animus* represents the masculine archetype in women. Problems can arise, however, if a person tries to repress his or her internal, opposite archetype: that is, if a man totally denies his softer "feminine" side or if a woman denies her "masculine" aspects. People also create problems in relationships when they expect their partner to behave like the ideal archetypal man or woman, instead of a real human being (Young-Eisendrath, 1993).

Although Jung shared with Freud a fascination with the unconscious side of the personality, he shared with Adler a belief in the positive, forward-moving strengths of the ego. For Jung, people are motivated not only by past conflicts, as Freud thought, but also by their future goals and by their desire to fulfill themselves. This emphasis anticipated the humanist movement in psychology by several decades. Jung also accurately anticipated modern trait research by many years when he identified *introversion* and *extroversion* as central personality orientations.

Some Jungians, drawing on the cognitive concepts of schema and narrative (see Chapters 8 and 9), are interested in how images and stories affect the way people see their own lives. When Dan McAdams (1988) asked 50 people to tell

▪ **collective unconscious**
To Carl Jung, the universal memories and experiences of humankind, represented in the unconscious images and symbols of all people.

▪ **archetypes [AR-ki-tipes]**
To Carl Jung, universal, symbolic images that appear in myths, art, dreams, and other expressions of the collective unconscious.

their life stories in a two-hour session, he found that people tended to report a common archetype, a mythic character, at the heart of their life narratives. For example, many individuals told stories that could be symbolized by the myth of the Greek god Dionysus, the pleasure seeker who escapes responsibility. Archetypes, says McAdams, represent "the main characters in the life stories we construct as our identities."

Erikson's Psychosocial Theory.   Freud believed that the personality is formed by age 5 or 6, when the Oedipus complex is resolved. A fuller theory of personality development, stretching from birth to death, was proposed by psychoanalyst Erik H. Erikson (1902–1994). Erikson called his theory *psychosocial,* instead of "psychosexual" as Freud had, because he believed that people are propelled by many kinds of psychological and social forces, not just by sexual motives. There are eight stages of life, said Erikson, each resulting from a combination of biological drives and societal demands. At each one, there is a "crisis" that must be resolved (Erikson, 1950/1963, 1982, 1987):

1. The first stage, during the baby's first year, produces the crisis of *trust versus mistrust.* A baby depends on others to provide food, comfort, cuddling, and warmth. If these needs are not met, the child may never develop the essential trust necessary to get along in the world, especially in relationships.

2. The second stage, as the baby becomes a toddler, sees the crisis of *autonomy (independence) versus shame and doubt.* The young child is learning to "stand on his own feet," said Erikson, and must do so without feeling ashamed of his behavior or too doubtful of his growing abilities.

3. The third stage, as the child enters school, is marked by the crisis of *initiative versus guilt.* The child is acquiring new physical and mental skills, setting goals, and enjoying newfound talents. At the same time, the child must learn to control impulses and energies. The danger lies in developing too strong a sense of guilt over his or her fantasies, newfound power, and childish instincts.

4. The fourth stage, the crisis of *competence versus inferiority,* teaches the school-age child, said Erikson, "to be a worker and potential provider." The child now is learning to make things, use tools, and acquire the skills for adult life. Children who fail these lessons of mastery and competence, Erikson argued, risk feeling inadequate and inferior.

5. The fifth stage, puberty, sets off the crisis of *identity versus role confusion.* You must decide what you are going to be and what you hope to make of your life. If you succeed, you will come out of this stage with a strong identity, ready to plan for the future. Otherwise, you will sink into confusion, unable to make decisions. The term *identity crisis* describes what Erikson considered to be the major conflict of adolescence.

6. The sixth stage sees the crisis of *intimacy versus isolation.* Once you have decided who you are, you must share yourself with another and learn to make commitments. No matter how successful you are in work, said Erikson, you are not complete until you are capable of intimacy.

7. The seventh stage involves the crisis of *generativity versus stagnation.* Now that you know who you are and have an intimate relationship, will you sink into complacency and selfishness, or will you experience generativity, the pleasure of creativity and renewal? Parenthood is the most common means for the successful resolution of this stage, but people can be productive, creative, and nurturant in other ways, in their work or their relationships with the younger generation.

8. The eighth and final crisis is that of *ego integrity versus despair.* As they age, people strive to reach the ultimate goal—wisdom, spiritual tranquility, an acceptance of one's life and one's role in the world. Just as the healthy child will not fear life, said Erikson, the healthy adult will not fear death.

Erikson recognized, more than Freud did, that cultural and economic factors affect psychological development. Some societies, for example, make the

According to Erikson, children must master a sense of competence and older adults must meet the need for generativity and nurturance. But do these challenges occur only during one stage of life?

transition between stages relatively easy. If you know you are going to be a farmer like your mother and father and you have no alternative, then moving from adolescence into young adulthood is not a very painful or passionate step (unless you hate farming). If you have many choices, however, as adolescents in urban societies often do, the transition can become prolonged. Some people put off making choices indefinitely and never resolve their "identity crisis." Similarly, cultures that place a high premium on independence and individualism will make it difficult for many of their members to resolve Erikson's sixth crisis, that of intimacy versus isolation.

Erikson was correct in observing that in Western societies adolescence and the college years are a time of confusion about identity and aspirations (Adams et al., 1985). However, modern research in adult development suggests that his lock-step sequence of stages is far from universal. An "identity crisis" is not limited to adolescence. A man who has worked in one job all his life, and then is laid off and must find an entirely new career, may have an identity crisis too. Likewise, competence is not mastered once and for all in childhood. People learn new skills and lose old ones throughout their lives, and their sense of competence rises and falls accordingly. Erikson omitted women from his original work, and when they were later studied they seemed to be doing things out of order—for example, going through "generativity" by having families before they faced the matter of professional "identity" (Peterson & Stewart, 1993). For these reasons, theories of adult development today emphasize the transitions and milestones that mark adult life instead of a rigid developmental sequence (Baltes, 1983; Schlossberg, 1984). In these theories, *having* a child has stronger effects on you than *when* you have a child. Entering the workforce affects self-esteem and ambition regardless of when you start work (Kanter, 1977/1993; Stewart et al., 1982).

Despite the problems with his theory, Erikson (like Adler before him) showed that development is never finished; it is an ongoing process, and the unconscious crises or issues of one stage may be reawakened during another. Erikson was also the first psychodynamic theorist to look at changes in the functioning of the ego throughout the life cycle. Erikson made his most important contributions, however, by considering the individual in the context of family and society, and by identifying the essential concerns of adulthood: trust, identity, competence, love and nurturance, the ability to enjoy life and accept death.

The Object-Relations School. In the late 1950s, John Bowlby (1958), a British psychoanalyst, contested the Freudian view that explained the infant's attachment to the mother solely in terms of her ability to gratify the baby's oral needs. Bowlby had found that infants who were deprived of normal contact with parents and other adults suffered catastrophically, and he argued for the primacy of attachment needs—for stimulation, warmth, and contact. Bowlby's work influenced other psychoanalysts to acknowledge the fundamentally *social* nature of human development (Benjamin, 1988). Although the need for social contact now seems obvious, this change in emphasis was a significant departure from the classic Freudian view, for Freud essentially regarded the baby as if it were an independent little organism ruled by its own instinctive desires.

Today an emphasis on relationships is associated most closely with the **object-relations school,** which was developed in Great Britain by Melanie Klein, W. Ronald Fairbairn, and D. W. Winnicott (Horner, 1991; Hughes, 1989). In contrast to Freud's emphasis on the Oedipal period, object-relations theorists hold that the first two years of life are the most critical for development of the inner core of personality. Freud emphasized the child's fear of the powerful father; object-relations analysts emphasize the child's need for the powerful mother, who is usually the baby's caregiver in the first critical years. Freud's theory was based on the dynamics of inner drives and impulses; object-relations theory holds that the basic human drive is not impulse gratification but the need to be in relationships.

The reason for the clunky word "object" in object-relations theory (instead of the warmer word "human" or even "parent") is to indicate that the infant's attachment isn't really to a person but to the infant's evolving *perception* of the person. In this theory, the child "takes in" or *introjects* a representation of the mother—someone who is kind or fierce, protective or rejecting—that is not literally the same as the woman herself. A "representation" is a complex cognitive schema that is constructed by the child. Object relations reflect the nature of the inner representational world, the numerous representations of the self and others, and the psychodynamic and emotional interplay among them (Horner, 1991). These representations may unconsciously affect the individual throughout his or her life.

In Freudian theory, as we saw, the central dynamic tension is the shifting of psychic energy—sexual and aggressive drives in particular—within the individual. Other people are relevant only insofar as they gratify our drives or block them. But to object-relations theorists, other people are important as *sources of attachment.* Therefore, the central dynamic tension is the constantly changing balance between independence and connection to others. This balance requires constant adjustment to separations and losses, from small ones that occur during quarrels, to moderate ones such as leaving home for the first time, to major ones such as divorce or death. In object-relations theory, the way we react to these separations is largely determined by our experiences in the first two years of life.

Whereas Freud thought that female development was the problem to be explained, many proponents of the object-relations school regard male development as the problem (Chodorow, 1978; Dinnerstein, 1976; Sagan, 1988; Winnicott, 1957/1986). In their view, children of both sexes identify first with the mother. Girls, who are the same sex as the mother, do not need to separate from her; the mother treats a daughter as an extension of herself. But boys, if they are to develop a masculine identity, must break away from the mother; the mother encourages a son to be independent and separate. To some object-relations theorists, this process is inevitable because women are biologically suited to be the primary caregivers and nurturers. But others, such as Nancy Chodorow (1978, 1992), believe the process is culturally determined, and that

■ **object-relations school**
A psychodynamic approach that emphasizes the importance of the infant's first two years of life and the baby's formative relationships.

if men played a greater role in the nurturing of infants and small children, the sex difference in the need for separation from the mother would fade.

In either case, in the object-relations view, a man's identity is more insecure than a woman's identity, because it is based on *not* being like women. Men develop more rigid *ego boundaries* between themselves and other people, whereas women's boundaries are more permeable. Later in life, runs this argument, the typical psychological problem for women is how to increase their autonomy and independence, so they can assert their own abilities in their close relationships. In contrast, the typical problem for men is permitting close attachments (Gilligan, 1982).

Quick QUIZ

Match each idea with the analyst or school who proposed it:

1. Sigmund Freud	**a.** collective unconscious
2. Karen Horney	**b.** inferiority complex
3. Erik Erikson	**c.** womb envy
4. Carl Jung	**d.** Oedipus complex
5. object-relations	**e.** identity crisis
6. Alfred Adler	**f.** archetype
	g. introjection of mother
	h. superego
	i. psychosocial stages

Answers:

1. d, h 2. c 3. e, i 4. a, f 5. g 6. b

Evaluating Psychodynamic Theories

Psychodynamic theories are provocative. But how would you test them? What errors can arise in generalizing from patients to all humanity and in using retrospective histories to create theories of development?

■ **projective tests**
Psychological tests used to infer a person's motives, conflicts, and unconscious dynamics on the basis of the person's interpretations of ambiguous stimuli.

■ **Thematic Apperception Test (TAT)**
A projective personality test that asks respondents to interpret a series of drawings showing ambiguous scenes of people.

There are few true-blue Freudians any more. Modern neo- ("new") Freudians, such as those in the object-relations school, have modified many aspects of Freud's original theories (Horowitz, 1988; Hughes, 1989). Yet they continue to use the same language and assumptions of unconscious dynamics.

Most of the criticism of psychodynamic theories comes from other schools of psychology, which hold that psychodynamic ideas may be interesting but they are *untestable hypotheses* that cannot be evaluated with traditional empirical methods; they are descriptive metaphors, more poetic than scientific. Because so many psychodynamic claims depend on the subjective interpretation of the analyst, there is no scientific way to decide which view is right. Freud saw penis envy; Horney saw womb envy. Freud thought the Oedipal period was most important in determining personality; object-relations theorists think the first two years are critical. Freud thought personality development ended in childhood; Erikson saw personality development as a life-long process.

Some psychologists have tried to validate psychodynamic ideas by using psychodynamic concepts to design personality tests. For example, the concept of projection provided the basis for the development of **projective tests** that attempt to measure unconscious motives, thoughts, perceptions, and conflicts—aspects of personality that may not be apparent in a person's overt behavior. The tests present ambiguous pictures, patterns, or stories for the test-taker to interpret or complete. There is no correct answer or interpretation; each person is free to respond as he or she likes. The assumption is that the person's unconscious thoughts and feelings will be "projected" onto the test materials and revealed in the person's interpretations (see Figure 12.2). One widely

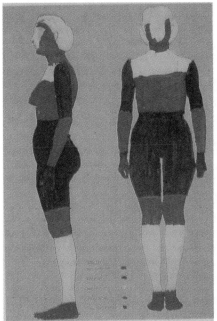 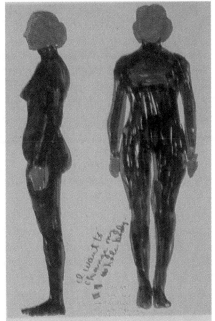

■ **Figure 12.2 A Projective Test For Body Satisfaction**

The Color-A-Person Test is a projective test for evaluating a person's body image and the emotions associated with it. Test-takers use different colors to indicate their degree of satisfaction with parts of their bodies. Scoring takes into account not only which colors were used, but differentiation of body parts, distortions from reality, and comments made during the test. These drawings were made by two women with eating disorders. Notice that one makes fine distinctions—she uses yellow, for "neutral," on her lower legs, hair, and upper torso—but the other hates everything about herself. On the drawing she has written, "I want to change my whole body." (Wooley & Wooley, 1985)

used projective test, the **Thematic Apperception Test (TAT),** consists of a series of drawings or photographs showing people in ambiguous situations (see Figure 12.3). The test-taker must make up a story about each scene. A scoring system takes into account the issues raised in each story, the characters the test-taker identifies with, the motives and emotions attributed to the characters, and the endings given to the stories. As we saw in Chapter 11, the TAT has been used to assess achievement motivation.

However, projective tests often turn out to have serious flaws as methods of identifying people's personality problems, because of reliability and validity issues. Just as these tests depend on the test-takers' unconscious "projections," they depend on how the clinician interprets them; there is therefore subjectivity on both sides. Different clinicians often interpret the same test differently,

■ **Figure 12.3 The Thematic Apperception Test**

On the left, a woman taking the TAT makes up stories for a set of ambiguous pictures. The picture on the right, similar to one included in an adaptation of the test, has been used to study people's unconscious feelings about intimacy. When you look at this picture, what sort of "story" do you think of? Who are the people and what are they thinking and saying? What will happen to them?

"Rorschach! What's to become of you?"

and the clinicians themselves may be "projecting" when they decide what a specific response means (Dawes, 1994).

Such problems are apparent in the **Rorschach Inkblot Test,** which was devised by Swiss psychiatrist Hermann Rorschach in 1921. It consists of ten cards with symmetrical abstract patterns, originally formed by spilling ink on paper and folding the paper in half. The test-taker reports what he or she "sees" in the inkblots, and clinicians interpret the answers subjectively, taking into account the symbolic meanings emphasized by psychodynamic theories. Unfortunately, although the Rorschach is enormously popular among clinicians, efforts to confirm its reliability and validity have failed (Wood et al., in press). As early as 1959, Lee Cronbach, one of the world's leading experts on testing, observed that "The test has repeatedly failed as a prediction of practical criteria"; and another testing expert, Raymond McCall, said, "Though tens of thousands of Rorschach tests have been administered . . . and while many relationships to personality dynamics and behavior have been hypothesized, the vast majority of these relationships *have never been validated empirically*, despite the appearance of more than 2,000 publications about the test" (emphasis in original; quoted in Dawes, 1994). Similarly, research on another test based on Jung's theory of personality types, the Myers-Briggs Type Indicator, fails to confirm the test's premise that knowledge of a person's alleged "type" can predict that person's behavior (Pittenger, 1993).

Clinicians reply that projective techniques are a rich source of information because test-takers cannot fake answers or lie as easily as on objective tests. The tests can help a clinician establish rapport with a client and encourage a person to open up about anxieties, conflicts, and problems. And projective tests may help clinicians determine when someone is defensively attempting to hide worries or mental problems (Shedler, Mayman, & Manis, 1993).

But the difference between objective and subjective approaches to personality continues to divide empirical and psychodynamic psychologists. To empirical psychologists, psychodynamic theories are guilty of three other scientific failings:

1. *Violating the principle of falsifiability.* As we saw in Chapter 2, a theory that is impossible to disconfirm in principle is not a scientific theory. Many psychodynamic ideas about unconscious motivations are, in fact, impossible to confirm or disprove. If your experience seems to support these ideas, it is taken as evidence of their correctness; but if you doubt their veracity, you must be "revealing defensiveness" or have "faulty observational skills" or (a favorite accusation) you are "in denial." This is why arguing with some psychodynamic theorists can be exasperating: If you agree with them, fine; but if you don't agree, something is the matter with you.

2. *Drawing universal principles from the experiences of selected patients.* Freud and most of his followers generalized from a very few individuals, often patients in therapy, to all human beings. Of course, the problem of overgeneralizing from small samples occurs in other areas of psychology too, and sometimes valid insights about human behavior can be obtained from observations of limited numbers of people. The problem occurs when the observer fails to confirm these observations by studying other samples, and incorrectly infers that what applies to some individuals or groups must apply to all.

For example, to confirm Freud's ideas about penis envy, you would need to observe or talk to many young children. Freud himself did not do this; however, when research psychologists interview preschool-age children, they typically find that many children of *both* sexes envy one another. In one study of 65 preschool-age boys and girls, Linda Linday (1994) found that although 45 percent of the girls had fantasized about having a penis or being male in other ways, it was also the case that 44 percent of the boys had fantasized about being pregnant.

▪ **Rorschach Inkblot Test**
A projective personality test that asks respondents to interpret abstract, symmetrical inkblots.

3. *Basing theories of development on the retrospective accounts of patients.* Most psychodynamic theorists have not observed random samples of children at different ages, as modern cognitive and child psychologists do, to construct their theories of development. Instead they have worked backward, creating theories based on themes in adults' recollections.

Retrospective analysis can be a useful and illuminating way to achieve insights about a person's life, but it contains an inherent problem: Looking backward at the events of our lives can create an illusion of causality between events. We assume that if A came before B, then A must have *caused* B. For example, if your mother spent three months in the hospital when you were an infant and today you are having trouble in school, you might draw a connection between the two facts. (An object-relations analyst would.) Perhaps these events are connected, but a lot of other things in your present circumstances might be causing your school difficulties. Freud himself was aware of this problem. "So long as we trace the development from its final stage backwards," he wrote, "the connection appears continuous, and we feel we have gained an insight which is completely satisfactory or even exhaustive. But if we proceed the reverse way [if we start at the beginning and try to predict the result], then we no longer get the impression of an inevitable sequence of events" (Freud, 1920/1963). Indeed, when researchers have done *prospective* studies in which people are followed from childhood to adulthood, they find that psychological development is far more gradual and varied than psychodynamic theories maintain (as we will see in Chapter 13). The assumption that development consists of predictable stages leading to predictable outcomes has not been supported by research.

In spite of these problems, researchers have been able to translate some psychodynamic assumptions into testable hypotheses, and are finding support for some of them. For example, Ernest Hartmann (1991) has developed a theory of personality based on the psychoanalytic and object-relations idea of ego boundaries. Using an objective test that has been given to about 2,000 people, he has found that people differ in terms of how "thick" or "thin" their boundaries are—both with other people ("I expect other people to keep a certain distance") and even with their own internal states ("Sometimes I don't know whether I'm thinking or feeling").

Other psychodynamic psychologists are using empirical methods and research findings to formulate and refine their theories. Some draw on cognitive findings on schemas, narratives, consciousness, and infant mental abilities (Horowitz, 1988; Schafer, 1992; Stern, 1985); sociocultural findings on gender roles and the impact of culture (Young-Eisendrath, 1993); and biological findings on the hereditary aspects of personality traits and the physiology of emotions (Plutchik, 1988). For their part, some scientific psychologists are investigating psychodynamic concepts. Cognitive psychologists, for example, are integrating the psychodynamic notion of the unconscious with research on nonconscious processes (Epstein, 1994; Greenwald, 1992; Kihlstrom, Barnhardt, & Tataryn, 1992). Other researchers have developed objective tests of defense mechanisms to study the ways in which defenses protect self-esteem and reduce anxiety (Plutchik et al., 1988).

Such research finds that people are indeed often unaware of the motives behind their own puzzling actions. Some childhood experiences can have a lasting effect on personality. Rational thoughts and behavior can be distorted by guilt, anxiety, and shame. The mind does defend itself against information that is threatening, unpleasant, or shocking. Prolonged emotional conflict may indeed play itself out in physical symptoms, immature habits, and self-defeating actions. Thus psychodynamic ideas have contributed to psychology in many respects.

Quick QUIZ

For each situation, match each explanation with the appropriate theorist: psychoanalyst, object-relations analyst, behaviorist, or cognitive social-learning theorist.

1. A 6-year-old boy is behaving aggressively in class, hitting other children and refusing to obey the teacher.
   a. The boy is being positively reinforced for aggressive behavior by getting attention from the teacher and the other children.
   b. The boy is expressing the aggressive energy of the id and has not developed enough ego control.
   c. The boy's behavior is due to an interaction between his own high energy level and what he believes, from his own experience and observation, about the consequences of aggression.
   d. The boy is having unusual difficulty separating emotionally from his mother.

2. A 6-year-old girl is clinging to her teacher in the classroom, afraid to do anything on her own.
   a. The girl has learned to expect that any independent action she tries will be ignored or punished, so she is reluctant to work on her own.
   b. The girl may have suffered repeated separations from her mother or father in the first two years of life, and thus is overreacting to any signs of separation from significant adults.
   c. The girl gets attention from the teacher only when she is in close range. When she goes off to do work on her own, the teacher ignores her.
   d. The girl has developed passivity and dependency as a normal resolution of her Oedipus complex, in preparation for her adult roles of wife and mother.

Answers:

1. a. behaviorist b. psychoanalyst c. cognitive social-learning theorist d. object-relations theorist 2. a. cognitive social-learning theorist b. object-relations analyst c. behaviorist d. psychoanalyst

■ THE HUMANIST AND EXISTENTIAL TRADITIONS: YOU ARE WHAT YOU CAN BECOME

Biological and learning psychologists seek the measurable traits that constitute personality and affect people's behavior; psychodynamic psychologists seek the unconscious motivations that they believe determine personality and affect behavior. A very different way to look at personality, however, is not from the outside, observing what a person does or says, but from the inside, concentrating on a person's own sense of self and experience. This approach, sometimes called **phenomenology,** does not seek to predict behavior or to uncover hidden motivations. It focuses on the person's subjective interpretation of what is happening right now. Psychologists who adopt this view, humanists and existentialists, believe that personality is defined by the human abilities that separate us from other animals: freedom of choice and free will.

The Inner Experience

Humanistic psychology was launched as a movement within psychology in the early 1960s. Its chief leaders, Abraham Maslow (1908–1970), Rollo May

■ **phenomenology**
The study of events and situations as individuals experience them; in personality, the study of an individual's qualities from the person's own point of view.

Puzzles of Personality #3

To What Extent Is Personality Available to Consciousness?

To Freudians, conscious awareness is only the tip of the mental iceberg; most motives and conflicts are hidden in the unconscious and are revealed only in symbols (such as the phallic symbol of the snake), dreams, slips of the tongue, and free associations.

Carl Jung believed that besides having a private unconscious, individuals share a collective unconscious containing the images and themes (archetypes) that unite human history and experience. One such archetype is the "shadow," the monster or evil creature. From dragons to Dracula to Darth Vader, the shadow represents the primordial fear of animals and the bestial side of humanity.

Radical behaviorists regard the unconscious as an "explanatory fiction" that is unnecessary for explaining human behavior. A woman who bites her nails is not revealing unconscious anxiety or oral needs; she has simply acquired a bad habit that is maintained by reinforcement.

Some psychoanalysts, such as Karen Horney, have argued that men's efforts to participate in the births of their children reveal unconscious "womb envy." To social-learning theorists, these efforts reflect a conscious desire to be involved, and are a result of changing social rules, reinforcements, and attitudes about the father's role.

Cognitive social-learning theorists hold that conscious perceptions and learned behaviors generate arguments and conflicts. In contrast, psychodynamic theorists, such as members of the object-relations school, would say that in every quarrel there are many unconscious issues going on; each partner may be projecting his or her childhood anxieties and expectations onto the other.

Self-actualization is a lifelong process. Hulda Crooks, shown here at the age of 91 climbing Mt. Fuji, began mountain climbing in her sixties.

(1909–1994), and Carl Rogers (1902–1987), argued that it was time for a "third force" in psychology. They rejected the psychoanalytic emphasis on hostility, biological instincts, and conflict. They also rejected the fragmented approach of behaviorism, with its emphasis on pieces of the person. Mainstream psychology, they said, was not dealing with people's real problems or drawing a full picture of human potential.

The trouble with psychology, said Maslow (1971), was that it had forgotten that human nature includes some good things, such as joy, laughter, love, happiness, and *peak experiences* (rare moments of rapture caused by the attainment of excellence or the drive toward higher values). The traits that Maslow thought most important to personality were not the Big Five, but rather the qualities of the self-actualized person—the person who strives for a life that is meaningful, challenging, and exciting. Personality development could be viewed, ideally, as a gradual progression toward a state of self-actualization.

Carl Rogers, like Freud, derived many of his ideas from observing his clients in therapy. As a clinician, Rogers (1951, 1961) was interested not only in why some people cannot function well, but also in what he called the fully functioning individual. Rogers's theory of personality is based on the relationship between the *self* (your conscious view of yourself, the qualities that make up "I" or "me") and the *organism* (the sum of all of your experiences, including unconscious feelings, perceptions, and wishes). This experience is known only to you, through your own frame of reference. How you behave depends on your own subjective reality, Rogers said, not on the external reality around you. Fully functioning people show a *congruence,* or harmony, between self and organism. Such people are trusting, warm, and open. They aren't defensive or intolerant. Their beliefs about themselves are realistic. When the self and the organism are in conflict, the person is said to be in a state of incongruence.

To become fully functioning people, Rogers maintained, we all need **unconditional positive regard,** love and support for the people we are, without strings (conditions) attached. This doesn't mean that Winifred should be allowed to kick her brother when she is angry with him or that Wilbur may throw his dinner out the window because he doesn't like pot roast. In these cases, a parent can correct the child's behavior without withdrawing love from the child. The child can learn that the behavior, not the child, is what is bad. "House rules are 'no violence,' Winifred," is a very different message from "You are a horrible person, Winifred."

Unfortunately, Rogers observed, many children are raised with *conditional* positive regard. The condition is "I'll love you if you behave well, and I won't love you if you behave badly." Adults often treat each other this way, too. People treated with conditional regard begin to suppress or deny feelings or actions that they believe are unacceptable to those they love. The result, said Rogers, is incongruence. The suppression of feelings and parts of oneself produces low self-regard, defensiveness, and unhappiness. Incongruence creates the sensation of being "out of touch with your feelings," of not being true to your "real self." The result is an individual who scores high on neuroticism—who is bitter, unhappy, and negative.

Not all humanists have been cheerful about human nature. Rollo May emphasized some of the fundamentally difficult and tragic aspects of the human condition, including loneliness, anxiety, and alienation. In books such as *The Meaning of Anxiety, Existential Psychology,* and *Love and Will,* May brought to American psychology elements of the European philosophy of **existentialism.** This doctrine holds that human beings have freedom of choice, but this freedom carries a price in anxiety and despair, which is why so many people try to escape from freedom into narrow certainties and blame others for their misfortunes.

Existential psychologists argue that mainstream psychology overlooks the important dilemmas of human existence—such as the universal struggle to find

■ **unconditional positive regard**
To Carl Rogers, love or support given to another person with no conditions attached.

■ **existentialism**
The doctrine, which influenced the psychodynamic approach of existential psychology, that people have free will, and that they struggle with the anxieties of existence such as the need to find meaning in life and accept death.

meaning in life, to live by moral standards, and to come to an understanding of suffering and death (Becker, 1973; Schneider & May, 1995; Vandenberg, 1993). According to Irvin Yalom (1989), the primal conflicts and concerns of life do not stem, as Freud thought, from repressed instinctual desires or traumatic childhood experiences. Rather, he argues, anxiety emerges from a person's efforts, conscious and unconscious, to cope with the harsh realities of life, "the 'givens' of existence." Those "givens" are "the inevitability of death for each of us and those we love; the freedom to make our lives as we will; our ultimate aloneness; and, finally, the absence of any obvious meaning or sense to life. However grim these givens may seem, they contain the seeds of wisdom and redemption." Perhaps the most remarkable example of a man able to find seeds of wisdom in a barren landscape was Victor Frankl (1955), who developed a form of existential therapy after surviving a Nazi concentration camp. In that pit of horror, he observed, some people maintained their sanity because they were able to find meaning in the experience, shattering though it was.

Existential and humanist psychologists depart from many other schools of psychology in maintaining that our lives are not inevitably determined by our parents, our pasts, or our present circumstances; we have the power to choose our own destinies, even when fate delivers us into tragedy.

To humanists and existentialists, the essence of personality is the inner sense of self that exists beneath the external masks we present to the world.

Evaluating Humanistic and Existential Theories

As you might imagine, the major criticism of these approaches is that many of their assumptions cannot be tested. How can we know if existential anxiety characterizes everyone just by virtue of being human? How would you tell if a person is "self-fulfilled" or "self-actualized"? "Unconditional positive regard" certainly sounds like a good thing, but can people really be expected to give it to their children and relatives at all times, no matter what the loved ones do? Humanists tend to use warm, intuitively appealing terms like this one, but critical thinkers would want to know how they are defining their terms and how these concepts would be translated into actual practice. If defined as unquestioned support of a child's efforts at mastering a new skill or as assuring the child that he or she is loved in spite of making mistakes, "unconditional positive regard" is a good idea. If it is defined as an unwillingness ever to say no to a child, offer constructive criticism, or set limits, then, as we will see in Chapter 13, research suggests it is not such a good idea after all.

Critics also say that humanistic and existential psychologies are closer to philosophy than science. Humanism happens to be a nicer view of human nature than, say, Freud's vision, but it is just as difficult to verify. Freud looked at humanity and saw conflict, destructive drives, selfishness, and lust. Maslow and Rogers looked at humanity and saw cooperation, altruism, and love. Existentialists look at humanity and see fear of death, loneliness, and the struggle for meaning. These differences may tell us more about the observers than about the observed.

Despite such concerns, the issues raised by humanistic and existential psychology have added balance to psychology's view of personality. Influenced by humanism, psychologists now study the happier emotions and positive experiences, such as love, altruism, cooperation, and creativity, along with the troubling ones. Stress researchers have discovered the healing powers of humor and hope. Developmental psychologists have shown how parental treatment can foster or crush a child's empathy and creativity. Psychologists are even incorporating existential ideas about anxiety and the fear of death into their theories of behavior. Jean Lipman-Blumen (1994), for example, argues that existential anxiety—"our human inability either to know or control our destiny"—is at the root of power relationships: People try to reduce such anxiety either by domination of others or through submission to individuals or institu-

✴ *Unconditional positive regard sounds like a good thing, but what does it mean? Can people really be expected to give their loved ones such regard no matter what the loved ones do? Would the results always be beneficial, or might there be unforeseen negative effects?*

tions. Finally, the idea that personality contains a deep well of "potential" has spawned an interest in the further reaches of consciousness and capability.

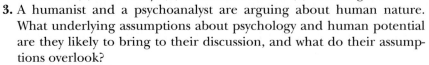

*Q*uick QUIZ

1. According to Carl Rogers, a man who loves his wife only when she is looking her best is giving her (a) *conditional* or (b) *unconditional* positive regard.
2. The humanist who described the importance of having peak experiences was (a) Rollo May, (b) Abraham Maslow, (c) Carl Rogers.
3. A humanist and a psychoanalyst are arguing about human nature. What underlying assumptions about psychology and human potential are they likely to bring to their discussion, and what do their assumptions overlook?

Answers:

1. a 2. b 3. Assumptions: the analyst, that human nature is basically selfish and destructive; the humanist, that it is basically loving and life-affirming. Their assumptions overlook the fact that (1) human beings have both capacities, and (2) that the situation often determines which capacity is expressed.

The need to feel consistent can blind us to the fact that how we actually behave is often unrelated to our conceptions of ourselves. Are we being guilty of emotional reasoning, or are our feelings of consistency justified in some ways?

■ THE PRIVATE PERSONALITY

Whatever personality is, most psychologists (apart, perhaps, from radical behaviorists) believe it is fairly stable. Biologically oriented researchers think that the essential qualities of personality are part of a person's genetic heritage. Even social-learning theorists think that people are pretty much shaped for life in their formative years by the rewards, punishments, and parental treatment they get. At the same time we know that people do not behave the same way across all situations or throughout their lives. Indeed, the *consistency paradox* refers to the gap between the belief that people are stable in their traits and the fact that their behavior often varies (Bem & Allen, 1974; Mischel, 1984). How flexible is personality?

One reason that our personalities seem so consistent is that we *feel* the same across situations. Each of us has a sense of self, an identity, through which we process and absorb experiences, thoughts, and emotions. Each of us is a unique repository of memories, dreams, wishes, and experiences. The result, that inner sense of continuity and perception that we all have, has been called the *private personality* (Singer, 1984). The private personality allows us to draw links across situations and explain away behavior we think is out of character. We even rewrite personal history if necessary—that is, we correct our memories—to maintain the sense of consistency (Greenwald, 1980).

Of course, as we have seen in this chapter, some qualities are indeed consistent throughout life, especially temperaments, mannerisms, and the Big Five personality traits. But others are more susceptible to change and experience: attitudes, self-efficacy, locus of control, ambitions, and interests (McCrae, 1993). In truth, every personality is a mixture of stability and change. The particular balance in a person's life will depend on genetic predispositions, defenses, emotional needs, and experience. For some, personality change is like a sunrise; you can't pinpoint the single moment when the sky turns color. For others, the steady nature of their personalities contributes to the belief that they don't really change; they just become more like themselves.

Puzzles of Personality #4

Which Has More Influence on Behavior: One's Personality or the Situation?

Some societies, such as China, are highly situation-oriented; others, such as the United States, are more individual-oriented. Chinese workers in Beijing do their morning T'ai Chi exercises in identical fashion; individualistic Americans exercise by running or walking in different directions, in different ways, in different clothes.

Many psychologists believe that behavior is more strongly influenced by the situation you are in than by your personality. Numerous situations, from working in an office to playing in a marching band, require us to set aside personal preferences and feelings and behave in socially specified ways. Other psychologists reply that even in situations which demand a certain uniformity, individuals manage to put their unique marks on their environments. This office setting, for instance, is stamped with the personality of its occupant.

Taking Psychology with You

How to Avoid the Barnum Effect

ow well does the following paragraph describe you?

> Some of your aspirations tend to be pretty unrealistic. At times you are extroverted, affable, sociable, while at other times you are introverted, wary, and reserved. You have found it unwise to be too frank in revealing yourself to others. You pride yourself on being an independent thinker and do not accept others' opinions without satisfactory proof. You prefer a certain amount of change and variety, and become dissatisfied when hemmed in by restrictions and limitations. At times you have serious doubts as to whether you have made the right decision or done the right thing.

When people believe that this description was written just for them—the result of a personalized horoscope, personality profile, or handwriting analysis—they all say the same thing: "It's me! It describes me *exactly!*" The reason is that this description is vague enough to apply to almost everyone, positive enough to please almost everyone, and flattering enough to get almost anyone to accept it (French et al., 1991; Snyder & Shenkel, 1975). People are not so quick to accept this "profile," however:

> You are a sullen, hateful slob. You dislike people and most people dislike you too. You are usually nasty, cruel, and calculating. You never think for yourself but steal other people's ideas. Once you've made a decision you stick with it, even when it's wrong.

Studies repeatedly find that *people are more willing to believe flattering statements about themselves than statements that are scientifically accurate* (Thiriart, 1991). In addition, the more effort people invest in getting a horoscope or profile, the more likely they are to believe the results, even when the identical results are given to everyone. If they must pay money for a profile, take the time to write away for it, or give detailed information about themselves, they are more likely to believe the profile is "eerily accurate." A French psychologist once advertised himself as an astrologer. In reply to the hundreds of people who wrote to him for his services, he sent out the same vague horoscope. More than 200 recipients sent him thank-you notes praising his accuracy and perceptiveness (Snyder & Shenkel, 1975).

This is why many psychologists worry about people who fall prey to the "P. T. Barnum effect." Barnum was the great circus showman who said "There's a sucker born every minute." He knew that the formula for success was to "have a little something for everybody"—which is what unscientific personality profiles, horoscopes, and handwriting tests have in common. To help you avoid the Barnum effect, research offers a few strategies:

- *Beware of all-purpose descriptions that could apply to anyone.* We know a couple who were terribly impressed when an astrologer told them that "each of you needs privacy and time to be independent" along with "but don't become too independent or you will lose your bond." Such observations, which play it safe by playing it both ways, apply to just about all couples.

- *Beware of your own selective perceptions.* Most of us are so impressed when a palm reader or horoscope gets something right that we overlook all the descriptions that are plain wrong.

- *Resist flattery.* This is the hard one. Most of us would reject a profile that described us as being nasty, sullen, and stupid. But many of us fall for profiles that tell us how wonderful and smart we are, especially if they seem "scientific."

If you keep your critical faculties with you, you won't end up paying hard cash for soft answers, pawning the piano because Leos should invest in gold this month, or taking a job you despise because it fits your "type." In other words, prove Barnum wrong.

I see you being less gullible in the future.

Summary

1. *Personality* is usually defined as an individual's distinctive and relatively stable pattern of behavior, motives, thoughts, and *traits,* characteristics that describe a person across situations.

2. Gordon Allport argued that personality consists of three kinds of traits: cardinal, central, and secondary. Raymond Cattell used *factor analysis* to distinguish surface traits from source traits, which he considered the basic components of personality. Research suggests that there are five "robust (stable) factors" in personality: extroversion, neuroticism, agreeableness, conscientiousness, and openness to experience.

3. Some personality characteristics appear to be heritable to some degree. Individual differences in *temperaments* or ways of reacting to the environment emerge early in life and can influence subsequent development. Temperamental differences in shyness and inhibition, found in children and monkeys, may be due to variations in the responsiveness of the sympathetic nervous system to change and novelty. Data from twin studies suggest that the heritability of some adult personality traits is around .50. But caution is warranted in drawing conclusions about the heritability of traits because of the vagueness with which "environment" has been measured, the similarity of environments of even separated twins, the interaction of a child's temperament and the environment, and the diminishing effect of genes over time.

4. Learning theories of personality emphasize the behavioral principles by which traits are acquired. Radical behaviorists argue that personality is a convenient fiction, since behavior depends on environmental reinforcers and punishers. Cognitive social-learning theorists also believe that personality consists of learned patterns, but they have added cognitive factors and social learning principles, such as observation and self-reinforcement. They emphasize how learned expectations, habits, and beliefs come to influence and regulate behavior, even when external reinforcers are no longer present.

5. In cognitive social-learning views, two of the most important traits that influence and motivate behavior are the extent to which people believe they have control over their lives (*locus of control*) and how much confidence they have in their own abilities (*self-efficacy*). Self-efficacy comes from experience in mastering new skills, having successful role models, encouragement from others, and constructive judgments of one's own physiological state. One problem with learning theories of personality is that behavior is sometimes attributed to a vague category called "the environment" without specifying which aspects of the environment are having effects; another problem is that there are so many situational influences on people's behavior that it can be difficult to single out the impact of any one of them.

6. Sigmund Freud was the founder of *psychoanalysis,* which emphasizes unconscious aspects of personality; it was the first *psychodynamic* theory, based on the movement of energy within the person. Modern psychodynamic theories share an emphasis on intrapsychic dynamics; the formative role of childhood experiences and conflicts; the idea that psychological development occurs in stages; a person's "psychic reality" as determined by the unconscious; and subjective methods of understanding a person's life and personality.

7. To Freud, the personality consists of the *id* (the source of *libido* or sexual energy and the aggressive instinct), *ego* (the source of reason), and *superego* (the source of conscience). *Defense mechanisms* protect the ego from unconscious anxiety. They include repression, projection, displacement (one form of which is sublimation), reaction formation, regression, and denial.

8. Freud believed that personality develops in a series of *psychosexual stages:* oral, anal, phallic (Oedipal), latency, and genital. During the phallic stage, Freud believed, the *Oedipus complex* occurs, in which the child desires the par-

ent of the other sex and feels rivalry with the same-sex parent. When the complex is resolved, the child will *identify* with the same-sex parent and settle into the latency stage, but females retain a lingering sense of inferiority and "penis envy." At puberty, the genital stage of adult sexuality begins.

9. Karen Horney dissented from Freud's notion of inherent female inferiority and envy of the male, countering that men envied women's ability to bear children. Alfred Adler, another early dissenter, emphasized psychological development over the life span, self-determination, and the need for self-improvement, which if thwarted can become an inferiority complex.

10. Carl Jung believed that people share a *collective unconscious* that contains universal human memories and history. There are many universal *archetypes* in personality, including the persona and shadow, and anima and animus. Jung also identified extroversion-introversion as a key personality trait.

11. Erik Erikson expanded Freud's theory of five developmental stages into an eight-stage *psychosocial* approach to development, from birth to death. Each stage is characterized by a psychological *crisis* that must be resolved, such as an *identity crisis* in adolescence. Although modern research disputes the idea that psychological development occurs in such predictable stages, Erikson made an important contribution by considering the individual in the context of family and society and by recognizing the essential concerns of adulthood—including identity, competence, nurturance, and the ability to accept death.

12. The contemporary *object-relations* school differs from classical Freudian theory by emphasizing the importance of the first two years of life, rather than the Oedipal phase; the infant's relationships to important figures, especially the mother, rather than sexual needs and drives; and the problem in male development of breaking away from the mother.

13. Psychodynamic theories have been criticized on many scientific grounds: for their untestable hypotheses and subjective methods, such as *projective tests* (including the Rorschach Inkblot Test) that are low in reliability and validity; for violating the principle of falsifiability; for overgeneralizing from selected patients to all humanity; and for basing theories on the unreliable and retrospective memories of patients, rather than on prospective studies. But some psychodynamic ideas, especially about nonconscious processes and defense mechanisms, have influenced experimental research.

14. Humanistic and existential psychologists take a *phenomenological* approach to personality, focusing on the person's sense of self, perceptions of the world, and free will to change. Humanists emphasize human potential and the strengths of human nature, as in Abraham Maslow's concepts of peak experiences and self-actualization. Carl Rogers stressed the importance of *unconditional positive regard* in creating a "fully functioning" person. Rollo May and other existentialists emphasize the inherent dilemmas of the human condition, including loneliness, anxiety, the search for meaning in life, and the fear of death. Critics observe that these ideas are subjective, elusive, and difficult to measure, but they have added depth to the study of psychology.

15. Personality is a mixture of some traits that are stable, such as the Big Five, and others that are more flexible, such as self-efficacy. The sense of consistency is enhanced by the *private personality,* the inner sense of the continuity of self that we carry across situations.

Key Terms

personality   *437*
trait   *437*
Gordon Allport   *438*
Raymond Cattell   *438*
factor analysis   *438*

"Big Five" personality traits (extroversion, neuroticism, agreeableness, conscientiousness, openness to experience)   *438*
temperaments   *440*

13

Child and Adolescent Development

In some societies and eras, children have been regarded as "little adults," as this painting of Sir Walter Raleigh and his son shows. The idea of childhood as a special time of development is a relatively new invention.

In automobile terms, the child supplies the power but the parents have to do the steering.

■ BENJAMIN SPOCK ■

In 1618, a Puritan minister advised parents that all children have "a stubbornness, and stoutness of mind arising from natural pride, which must, in the first place, be broken and beaten down" (Demos, 1970). Today, most parents want to help their children develop pride and self-esteem by building them up instead of beating them down. But people continue to differ in their beliefs about what children are like and how they should be brought up. Do babies need their mothers around all the time? Do they need their fathers around all the time? Should society worry about unwed mothers, and if so, which ones? What about unwed fathers? How early can babies start learning, and how much can we teach them? Can you create the child you want, or does the child have something to say about it?

Against this background of social issues and practical concerns, child psychologists study many facets of children's physical, cognitive, social, emotional, and moral development. *Child development* includes the processes by which an organism grows from a fetus in the womb to an adult, processes that include predictable changes in biological **maturation,** physical structure, behavior, and thinking. Some researchers think of *development* as a series of small, gradual, continuous steps that blend into each other, just as the babbling sound "maa, maa" becomes a call for "Mama." Others think of development as a series of distinct stages that are qualitatively different from each other, just as walking is significantly different from crawling. These two ways of thinking about development have shaped research and theory about children and adolescents, as we will see in this chapter.

Psychologists study *universal* aspects of development, the changes that occur in all children as they mature; *cultural* differences in development, the patterns that occur in some cultures and ethnic groups but not in others; and *individual* differences in development, the changes that occur in some children but not in others. In this chapter we will consider some of their discoveries. Then we will ask you to step back, put what you have read into perspective, and consider a controversial question: What is the connection between childhood and adulthood?

Children can have fun with anything—even a bath.

■ FROM CONCEPTION TO THE FIRST YEAR

A baby's development, before and after birth, is an astonishing process, a marvel of maturation. In only 9 months of a mother's pregnancy, a cell grows from a dot this big (.) to a squalling bundle of energy that looks just like Aunt Sarah. In roughly another 15 months, that bundle of energy grows into a babbling toddler who is curious about everything. No other time in human development brings so many changes, so fast.

■ **maturation**
The sequential unfolding of genetically influenced behavior and physical characteristics.

Prenatal Development

Prenatal development is divided into three stages: the *germinal,* the *embryonic,* and the *fetal.* The germinal stage begins at conception, when the male sperm unites with the female ovum (egg). A day or so after conception, the fertilized egg, or *zygote,* begins to divide into two parts and, in 10 to 14 days, it attaches itself to the wall of the uterus. The outer portion of the zygote will form part of the placenta and umbilical cord, and the inner portion becomes the *embryo.* The placenta will be the growing embryo's food and supply link from the mother, connected to the embryo itself through the umbilical cord. The placenta allows nutrients to enter the embryo and wastes to exit, and it screens out some, but not all, harmful substances.

Once implantation of the zygote is completed, about two weeks after conception, the germinal stage is over and the *embryonic* stage begins, lasting until the eighth week after conception. The embryo develops webbed fingers and toes, a tail, eyes, ears, a nose, a mouth, a heart and circulatory system, and a spinal cord—although at eight weeks, the embryo is only 1½ inches long. Sometime during the fourth to eighth week, the male hormone testosterone is secreted by the rudimentary testes in embryos that are genetically male; without this hormone, the embryo will develop as a female.

After eight weeks, the *fetal* stage begins. The organism, now called a *fetus,* further develops the organs and systems that existed in rudimentary form during the embryonic stage. By 28 weeks, the nervous and respiratory systems are developed enough to allow some fetuses to live if born prematurely. (New technology allows some prematures to survive if born even earlier, but the risks are much higher.) The greatest gains in brain and nervous system development, length, and weight occur during the last 12 weeks before birth.

Although the womb is a fairly sturdy protector of the growing fetus, some harmful influences, collectively called **teratogens,** can cross the placental barrier. For example:

■ **teratogen**
An external agent, such as a disease or chemical, that increases the risk of abnormalities in prenatal development.

■ **fetal alcohol syndrome (FAS)**
A pattern of physical and intellectual abnormalities in infants whose mothers drank an excessive amount of alcohol during pregnancy.

- *German measles* (rubella), especially early in the pregnancy, often affects the fetus's eyes, ears, and heart. The most common consequence is deafness. Rubella is preventable if the mother has been vaccinated, which can be done in adulthood, up to three months before pregnancy.

- *X-rays* or other radiation, or *toxic chemicals* such as lead, can cause fetal abnormalities and deformities.

- *Sexually transmitted diseases,* such as syphilis, can cause mental retardation, blindness, and other physical disorders. Genital herpes can affect the fetus only if the mother has an outbreak at the time of delivery, which exposes the newborn to the virus in the birth canal. This risk can be avoided by having a Caesarean section, in which the baby is removed surgically through the uterus. Although the AIDS virus can be transmitted to the fetus, not all babies born to HIV-infected mothers themselves become infected; estimates range from 13 percent in a European study to 30 percent in U.S. studies (Bee, 1995).

- *Cigarettes.* Pregnant women who smoke increase the likelihood of miscarriage, premature birth, abnormal fetal heartbeat, and underweight babies. The negative effects of smoking during pregnancy can last long after the child's birth, showing up in increased rates of infant sickness, Sudden Infant Death Syndrome, and, in later childhood, hyperactivity and difficulties in school.

- *Alcohol.* Pregnant women who drink alcohol heavily—that is, who have several drinks a day—increase by 30 percent the risk of their babies having **fetal alcohol syndrome (FAS).** FAS infants are smaller than normal, have smaller brains, are more uncoordinated, and have some degree of mental retardation. The more that women drink during pregnancy, the worse the effects on their children's mental abilities and concentration (Streissguth et al., 1991). Because these results are so tragic, some people have inferred that a pregnant woman should not drink at all, but the studies on how much alcohol is "too much" have been inconclusive. One reason is that the effects of alcohol on the fetus are different at different stages of pregnancy; the most dangerous stage is the first trimester (12 weeks), but a *little* alcohol later in pregnancy is sometimes recommended as a way to prevent premature contractions. Another problem is that drinking in binges is more harmful to the fetus than an occasional drink.

One study of 592 British women who were interviewed and examined during their pregnancies, and whose children were examined three years later, found that the children of mothers who did not drink at all during pregnancy were no different from those of mothers who had had fewer than 10 drinks a week during pregnancy (Forrest et al., 1991). In contrast, a similar study, in which more than 500 American women and their children were followed from the mothers' pregnancies to when the children were 11 years old, found small but significant differences in the children's intellectual performance even when the mothers had had only a drink or two of alcohol per day during their pregnancies (Streissguth, Barr, & Sampson, 1990; Streissguth et al., 1991). So American researchers are divided on the question of whether pregnant women should drink at all, with most concluding that the safest course of action is total abstention.

- *Drugs.* The effects of morphine, cocaine, and heroin can be transmitted to the fetus and do harm, as can commonly used drugs such as antibiotics, antihistamines, tranquilizers, acne medication, diet pills, coffee, and excessive amounts of vitamins. Women should also guard against prescribed drugs that have not been adequately tested. In the 1960s, pregnant women who took the tranquilizer Thalidomide gave birth to fetuses with missing or deformed limbs. Between the 1940s and 1971, many women were given the hormone diethylstilbestrol (DES) to prevent miscarriages. Daughters of these women had an unusually high risk of developing vaginal cancer during adolescence, and sons were prone to testicular problems.

The lesson is clear. A pregnant woman does well to quit smoking completely, to avoid or drink very little alcohol, and to take no drugs of any kind unless they are medically necessary and tested for safety (and then to accept the fact that her child will never be properly grateful for all that sacrifice!). But what if she doesn't take this advice? Should the fetus be protected from its own mother? We discuss the ethical and political issues surrounding these questions in "Think About It."

What about positive prenatal experiences? Should a pregnant woman be reading Shakespeare to her fetus, playing classical music, and preparing the fetus for college entrance exams? The fetus can certainly hear sounds in the last few months of pregnancy—its mother's voice, music, startling sounds from television, hair dryers, and vacuum cleaners—and some even develop preferences for various sounds. Two psychologists asked 16 pregnant women to read Dr. Seuss's classic story *The Cat in the Hat* aloud twice a day for the last six weeks of their pregnancies. When the babies were born, they had a choice of sucking on one of two nipples. Sucking on the first brought a recording of their mothers reading the Seuss story. Sucking on the other nipple produced a recording of the mothers reading *The King, the Mice and the Cheese*, a story with a different rhythm and pace. The newborns preferred—you guessed it—*The Cat in the Hat* (DeCasper & Spence, 1986).

This is fascinating work on two counts. First, it shows the amazing ability of psychologists to find ways to "interview" newborn babies who cannot talk and who don't even know what a hat is, let alone a cat. Second, it shows the amazing

Think About It

Who Should Protect the Fetus?

■ In his moving book *The Broken Cord,* Michael Dorris told of his and his wife Louise Erdrich's struggles raising an adopted child who was born profoundly retarded as a result of fetal alcohol syndrome (FAS). "Adam's birthdays are reminders for me," wrote Dorris. "For each celebration commemorating that he was born, there is the pang, the rage, that he was not born whole."

It is indeed enraging to learn about the suffering of children born to women who seem to have been entirely unconcerned about the fetus they were carrying. Many people are justifiably worried about the growing number of babies who are born with FAS or the damaging effects of other drugs. What will happen to them? Who will pay for their care? Supporters of a movement on behalf of "fetal rights" argue that fetuses have rights to legal protection, including protection from their mothers. Shouldn't the fetus be protected from a pregnant woman who is unable or unwilling to care for it properly by following safe prenatal practices? Before you answer, consider these issues:

1. *Where do we draw the line between abuse and use?* It may seem easy to identify addicts and alcoholics, but many people readily confuse abusers with users. For example, in 1991, a Seattle woman who was eight months pregnant went into a local restaurant, where she ordered a salad and a glass of wine. The waiter told the woman he didn't think she should have the drink, and she politely told him to mind his own business. Still, the waiter refused to serve her. He was fired the next day and the woman had her perfectly healthy baby a month later.

As we noted in the text, researchers do not know precisely how much alcohol it takes to cause problems in development. Moreover, not all babies of women who use other drugs moderately, even cocaine, show detrimental effects.

2. *Which maternal practices should we protect the fetus from?* What about women with chronic medical conditions, such as diabetes, who get pregnant and do not follow their doctors' advice? What about a woman who cannot afford to "protect" her fetus by quitting work and staying in bed for three months as her doctor recommends? Obstetrical advice over the years has been full of errors and continues to be an uncertain art (Rothman, 1989). Years ago, doctors might have wanted to "protect" a fetus from being miscarried by requiring a pregnant woman to take DES, when it was mistakenly believed that this drug was safe; or to "protect" the fetus's development by requiring the mother to lose 20 pounds, when it was mistakenly believed that pregnant women should not gain "too much" weight. Today doctors recommend that women have Caesarean sections—major surgery that is costly and not without risks—if they think a vaginal birth could result in the slightest chance of damage to the fetus. As a consequence, the United States

ability of the human brain to learn as soon as it develops. But it does not necessarily mean that a pregnant woman should rush out to buy a "prega-phone" in order to read novels to her fetus. As we will see, it's good to have some respect for what a newborn knows, but without going overboard. That newborn still has a lot to learn.

The Newborn Child

Newborn babies could never survive on their own, but they are far from being passive and inert. As Table 13.1 shows, they have a number of *motor reflexes,* automatic behaviors that are necessary for survival. They can see, hear, touch, smell, and taste (bananas and sugar water are in, rotten eggs are out). They even have rudimentary "conversations" with the adults who tend them.

Reflexes.   Babies will turn their heads toward a touch on the cheek or corner of the mouth and search for something to suck on, a handy "rooting reflex" that allows them to find the breast or bottle. They suck vigorously on a nipple, finger, or pacifier placed in their mouths. They grasp tightly a finger pressed on

has the highest rate of unnecessary Caesarean surgeries in the world. Should physicians be able to override the decision of a pregnant woman if she chooses to have a vaginal delivery?

3. *Is maternal drug abuse the only or even major contributor to the child's later problems?* Sociologist Barbara Rothman (1989), who has been studying the social effects of changes in reproductive technology, fears that pregnant woman are fast becoming viewed as "the unskilled workers on a reproductive assembly line." They are blamed, she argues, for producing "flawed products," that is, damaged newborns or fetuses with defects. Indeed, several dozen women in the United States have been prosecuted for taking drugs during pregnancy. But scientists are also learning that *fathers'* drug use can cause fetal defects; cocaine, for example, does so by binding to sperm (Yazigi, Olem, & Polakoski, 1991). And many people overlook other environmental causes of damage to the fetus that are far more common than maternal or paternal drug abuse, such as the lack of prenatal services for poor women and exposure to toxins in the workplace or home, which can affect the reproductive systems of *both* sexes.

As Lucile Newman and Stephen Buka (1991) observe, many of the learning problems that are caused by prenatal exposure to drugs are greatly worsened by poverty and parental neglect; conversely, they can be overcome if the child lives in a good environment. In fact, research has found that children who live with cocaine-abusing parents are almost twice as likely to have behavioral problems such as aggressiveness, hyperactivity, and bedwetting as children who were exposed to cocaine in the womb but who then were placed in healthy homes (Meyers & Dennis, 1991).

4. *Is money best spent on incarcerating addicted pregnant women, treating their addictions, or caring for their children?* At present, only a small percentage of pregnant addicts get treatment; many detoxification programs specifically reject pregnant women because prenatal services are not provided. Meanwhile, the cost of providing *post*natal care and special educational programs for children born with FAS and drug-related deficits is skyrocketing.

Ultimately, the question, "Who protects the fetus?" is inseparable from the question, "Who protects the mother?" Why, if society is concerned about the welfare of the fetus, has it allotted so few public resources to the health and care of the pregnant woman? What is the best way to respond to addicted women who become pregnant—leave them alone, punish them, or treat them? How can drug-related birth defects be reduced and at the same time the rights of pregnant women to control their own bodies be respected? These are tough issues. What do you think? ■

Table 13.1   *Reflexes of the Newborn Baby*

Reflex	Description
Rooting	An infant touched on the cheek or corner of the mouth will turn toward the touch and search for something to suck on.
Sucking	An infant will suck on anything suckable, such as a nipple or finger.
Swallowing	An infant can swallow, though this reflex is not yet well coordinated with breathing.
Moro or "startle"	In response to a loud noise or physical shock, an infant will throw its arms outward and arch back.
Babinski	In response to a touch on the bottom of the foot, the infant's toes will splay outward and then curl in. (In adults, the toes curl in.)
Grasp	In response to a touch on the palm of the hand, an infant will grasp.
Stepping	If held so the feet just touch the ground, an infant will show "walking" movements, alternating the feet in steps. This reflex vanishes in a couple of weeks.

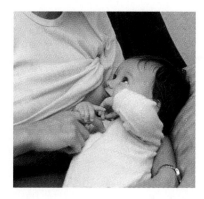

The sucking and grasping reflexes at work.

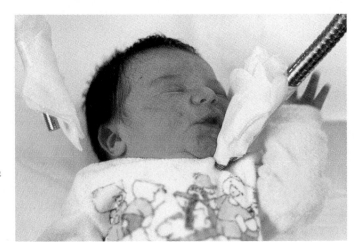

Using imaginative methods, researchers can now study the remarkable abilities of newborn babies. Infants as young as 3 days old are calmer when they get a whiff of gauze worn by their mothers than when they smell gauze worn by other women (Montagner, 1985).

their palms. They are startled by loud noises or shocks. They follow a moving light with their eyes and turn toward a familiar sound, such as the mother's voice or the thump-thump of a heartbeat (both of which they heard in the womb). Many of these reflexes eventually disappear, but others, such as the knee-jerk, eye-blink, and sneeze reflexes, remain.

Vision. At birth, a baby is very, very nearsighted. The focus range is about 8 inches, the average distance between the baby and the face of the person holding the baby. But visual ability develops rapidly. Newborns open their eyes wide to investigate what is around them, even in the dark. They can distinguish contrasts, shadows, and edges. They can discriminate their mother or other primary caregiver on the basis of smell, sight, or sound almost immediately (Bee, 1995).

By observing what infants look at, given a choice, and how long they gaze at it, psychologists have identified many infant preferences. For instance, infants are primed to respond to faces. Babies who are only nine minutes old will turn their heads to watch a drawing of a face if it moves in front of them, but they will not turn if the "face" consists of scrambled features or is just the outline of a face (Goren, Sarty, & Wu, 1975). Within a few months of birth, they develop depth perception (see Chapter 6).

Social Skills. Newborns are sociable from the first. The first "conversation" a baby has is with the mother or primary caregiver, and like most human conversations, it often takes place over a good meal. Babies and their mothers play little games with each other, exchanging signals in a rhythmic pattern (see Figure 13.1). Whether on breast or bottle, babies nurse in a pattern of sucks and pauses. During the pauses, the mother often jiggles the baby, who then starts to suck again. The pattern between them has the back-and-forth rhythm of spoken conversation: suck, pause, jiggle, pause, suck, pause, jiggle, pause (Kaye, 1977).

This early rhythmic conversation illustrates a crucial aspect of all human exchanges: the importance of **synchrony,** the adjustment of one person's nonverbal behavior to coordinate with another's (Bernieri et al., 1994; Condon, 1982). As we will see in Chapter 18, people unconsciously adjust their rhythms of speech, their gestures, and their expressions to be "in sync" with each other, and this synchrony begins at birth. Newborn infants will synchronize their behavior and attention to adult speech but not to other sounds, such as street noise or tapping (Beebe et al., 1982). Synchrony has three aspects: *simultaneous movement* (e.g., the mother turns her head just as the baby lifts an arm), *similar tempo* (the parent and baby move at the same pace and rhythm), and *coordina-*

■ **synchrony**
The adjustment of one person's nonverbal behavior to coordinate with another's.

■ Figure 13.1   Look Who's Talking

This mother and infant illustrate synchrony in action, exchanging giggles, gestures, coos, and smiles. Some infants are able to imitate adult facial expressions even as newborn: most develop the ability to do so within a few weeks.

tion and smoothness (the responses of parent and baby mesh smoothly, like those of well-matched dance partners). Mothers show more synchrony with their own infants than with others, and parents learn how to tune in to their babies' rhythms early on (Bernieri, Reznick, & Rosenthal, 1988).

The Older Infant

Babies grow as fast as weeds during their first two years. Most infants double their birth weight in five months. By 1 year of age, on the average, they have tripled their birth weight and grown 10 to 12 inches in length. (The custom of talking about a baby's "length" but a child's "height" is charming; the language changes as soon as the baby is upright!) By age 2, most toddlers are half the height they will be as adults. The baby not only grows in height and weight, but also changes proportion. An infant's head is nearly one-third of the whole body; a 2-year-old's head is about one-fourth; an adult's head is only one-eighth to one-tenth of total height.

A baby's motor skills develop accordingly. At about 1 month, infants can hold their chins up when lying on their stomachs. At about 2 months, they can raise the upper body. At 4 months, they can sit if someone supports them. At about 7 months, they can sit upright without support. From then on, parents have to look sharp. Babies soon crawl and stand with help (9 months), walk with help (10 months), and toddle off on their own (13 months). These milestones are only averages, however; some babies develop more quickly, others more slowly.

Although babies and infants everywhere develop according to the same maturational sequence, many aspects of their development depend on cultural customs. Parents in different cultures treat their babies differently right from the start, in how often they hold, touch, feed, or talk to them (Super & Harkness, 1994). For example, infant sleep patterns vary according to a culture's rules for sleeping arrangements. In the United States, babies are expected to sleep for eight uninterrupted hours by the age of 4 or 5 months. This milestone is considered a sign of neurological maturity, although many babies weep and wail when the parent puts them in the crib at night and leaves the room. Yet for people in many cultures, including Mayan Indians, rural Italians, African villagers, and urban Japanese, this nightly clash of wills never occurs because the infant sleeps with the mother for the first few years of life. Mothers have no incentive to get their babies to sleep through the night, and infants continue to wake and nurse about every four hours. Cultural differences in babies' sleep arrangements in turn reflect cultural values. Mayan mothers believe it is important to sleep with the baby in order to forge a close bond with the child; American par-

✳ *Most child-rearing manuals advise parents to teach their 5-month-old infants to sleep through the night by not responding to the babies' cries for attention. What assumptions about babies and about the parent-child relationship are these books making? Are these assumptions the same everywhere?*

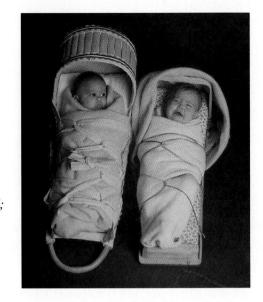

A good example of the intersection between maturation and culture is the case of the cradleboard. Most Navaho babies (left) calmly accept the Navaho custom of being strapped to a cradleboard until they are about 6 months old; Caucasian babies (right) protest vigorously when strapped in one. Yet despite cultural differences in such practices, babies in every culture sit, crawl, and walk eventually.

ents believe it is important to foster the child's independence as soon as possible (Morelli et al., 1992).

Similarly, as we saw in Chapter 11, attachment between infant and caregiver is a universal human need; but cultures differ in whether they expect that attachment to be between mother and infant, parents and infant, or extended-family and infant. Among the Efe of Africa, researchers found, babies spend about half their time, and 3-year-olds spend fully 70 percent of their time, away from their mothers, in the care of older children and other adults (Tronick, Morelli, & Ivey, 1992). The researchers concluded that an Efe child does not experience the one-on-one intense attachment that American children do, and thus, unlike most American children, develops a sense of self that incorporates other people. In another example, infants in many African cultures routinely

Table 13.2 Developmental Milestones During the First Year

Average Age	Motor	Cognitive	Emotional
0–2 months	Turns head; lifts chin when lying on stomach	Prefers looking at faces; likes familiar sounds; is interested in novelty; tracks *where* things are	Can imitate adult facial expressions; cries when distressed
3–4 months	Lifts chest; holds head erect; reaches for an object; sits with support	Becomes interested in *what* things are; recognizes different faces and details of objects	Smiles and shows interest in slightly unfamiliar objects; may be distressed by objects that are too unfamiliar
5–6 months	Holds head steady; transfers an object from one hand to another	Develops depth perception; understands object identity (that a thing is the same each time it is encountered)	Apparent fear at visual cliff (see Chapter 6); facial expressions of anger may appear in response to frustration
7–8 months	Sits alone; gets into sitting position	Develops retrieval memory (can recall a familiar face) and larger "working memory"; understands object permanence	Shows first signs of stranger and separation anxiety
9–10 months	Stands with help; crawls	Understands some words and concepts	
11–12 months	Pulls self to standing position; walks with support	Begins symbolic play; utters first meaningful words	Shows sadness at loss of an attachment figure

surpass American infants in their rate of learning to sit and to walk, but not in learning to crawl or climb stairs. The reason is that the African parents routinely bounce babies on their feet, exercise the newborn's walking reflex, prop young infants in sitting positions, and discourage crawling (Cole & Cole, 1993).

As these examples show, biological capacities and needs are affected by interacting elements of the child's environment: the physical and social settings of everyday life; the traditional customs of child care and child rearing; and the common beliefs, values, and psychological traits of the child's caregivers (Super & Harkness, 1994). By the end of the first year, infants everywhere have made tremendous progress in their physical abilities (see Table 13.2). Now the story becomes even more interesting.

Quick QUIZ

Is your understanding of early development developing normally?

1. Name as many potentially harmful influences on fetal development as you can.
2. Almost all newborn babies can (a) focus at about 16 inches, (b) identify scrambled features of a face, (c) synchronize their behavior with that of a caretaker.
3. True or false: Neurologically normal children will sleep through the night by age 4 or 5 months.

Answers:

1. German measles early in pregnancy; exposure to radiation or toxic chemicals; sexually transmitted diseases; the mother's use of cigarettes, alcohol, or other drugs. 2. c 3. false; it depends on the culture.

■ COGNITIVE DEVELOPMENT

Our friend Joel reports how thrilled he was when his 13-month-old daughter Alison looked at him one day and said, for the first time, "Daddy! Daddy!" His delight was deflated somewhat, though, when the doorbell rang and she ran to the door, calling, "Daddy! Daddy!" And his delight was completely shattered when the phone rang and Alison ran to it, shouting, "Daddy! Daddy!" Later Joel learned that there was a 2-year-old child in Alison's day-care group whose father would call her on the telephone during the day and ring the doorbell when he picked her up in the evening. Alison acquired her little friend's enthusiasm for doorbells and phones, but didn't quite get the hang of "Daddy." She will soon enough, though, and that is the mystery of language. Further, she will eventually be able to imagine, reason, and see the world from Daddy's viewpoint, and that is the mystery of thought.

The Ability to Think

In the 1920s, the Swiss psychologist Jean Piaget [Zhan Pea-ah-ZHAY] (1896–1980) developed a new theory of cognitive development in children. Piaget's great insight was that children's errors are as interesting as their correct responses. He observed that children understand concepts and reason differently at different stages. The strategies children use to solve problems, said

Piaget, are not random; rather, they reflect an interaction between the child's developmental stage and their experience in the world. Although many of his ideas have since been challenged and modified, they caused a revolution in thinking about how thinking develops.

Piaget's Cognitive Stages.   Piaget (1929/1960, 1952, 1984) proposed that mental functioning depends on two basic biological processes. One is *organization:* All human beings are designed to organize their observations and experiences into a coherent set of meanings. The other is *adaptation* to new observations and experiences. Adaptation, said Piaget, takes two forms, which he called assimilation and accommodation.

Assimilation is what you do when you fit new information into your present system of knowledge and beliefs or into your mental *schemas* (categories of things and people). Suppose that little Harry learns the schema for "dog" by playing with the family schnauzer. If he then sees the neighbor's chihuahua and says "doggie!" he has assimilated the new information about the neighbor's pet into his schema for dogs. **Accommodation** is what you do when, as a result of undeniable new information, you must change or modify your existing schemas. If Harry sees the neighbor's Siamese cat and still says "doggie!" his parents are likely to laugh and correct him. Harry will have to modify his schema for *dogs* to exclude cats, and he will have to create a schema for *cats*. In this way, he accommodates the new information that a Siamese cat is not a dog.

Using these basic concepts, Piaget proposed that all children go through four stages of cognitive development:

1. During the *sensory-motor stage* (birth to age 2), the infant learns through concrete actions: looking, touching, hearing, putting things in the mouth, sucking, grasping. "Thinking" consists of coordinating sensory information with bodily movements. Soon these movements become more purposeful, as the child actively explores the environment and learns that specific movements will produce specific results. Swatting a cloth away will reveal a hidden toy; releasing one's grasp of a fuzzy duck will cause the duck to drop out of reach; banging on the table with a spoon will produce dinner (or Mom, taking the spoon away).

One of the baby's major accomplishments at this stage, said Piaget, is **object permanence,** the understanding that something continues to exist even if you can't see it or touch it. In the first few months of life, he observed, infants seem to follow the motto "out of sight, out of mind." They will look intently at a little toy, but if you hide it behind a piece of paper they will not look behind the paper or make an effort to get the toy. By about 6 months, infants begin to grasp the idea that a toy exists and the family cat exists, whether they can see the toy, or the cat, or not. If a baby of this age drops a toy from her playpen, she will look for it; she also will look under a cloth for a toy that is partially hidden. By 1 year of age, most babies have developed an awareness of the permanence of (some) objects. This is when they love to play peek-a-boo.

Object permanence, said Piaget, represents the beginning of *representational thought,* the capacity for using mental imagery and other symbolic systems. The child is able for the first time to hold a concept in mind, to learn that the word *fly* represents an annoying, buzzing creature, and that *Daddy* represents a friendly, playful one.

2. During the *preoperational stage* (ages 2 to 7) the use of symbols and language accelerates, in play and in imitation of adult behavior. A 2-year-old is able to pretend, for instance, that a large box is a house, table, or train. Piaget described this stage largely in terms of what (he thought) the child cannot do. Children can think, said Piaget, but they cannot reason. They do not yet have the kinds of mental abilities that allow them to understand abstract principles or cause and effect. Piaget called these missing abilities **operations,** by which he meant reversible actions that the child performs in the mind. An operation is a sort

▪ **assimilation**
In Piaget's theory, the process of absorbing new information into existing cognitive structures, modifying them if necessary to fit.

▪ **accommodation**
In Piaget's theory, the process of modifying existing cognitive structures in response to experience and new information.

▪ **object permanence**
The understanding, which develops in the first year of life, that an object continues to exist even when you can't see it or touch it.

▪ **operations**
In Piaget's theory, mental actions that are cognitively reversible.

▪ Figure 13.2 Piaget's Principle of Conservation

These children are taking part in experiments designed to measure their understanding of conservation. In a typical test of conservation of number (right), the child shows whether he understands that two sets of seven blocks contain the same number—even though the blocks in one set are larger and take up more space. In a test of conservation of quantity (left), the child shows whether she understands that pouring liquid from a short fat glass into a tall narrow glass does not change the amount of liquid.

of "train of thought" that can be run backward or forward. Multiplying 2 times 6 to get 12 is an operation; so is the reverse operation, dividing 12 by 6 to get 2.

Children at the preoperational stage, Piaget believed, rely on primitive or "magical" reasoning based on the evidence of their own senses, which can be misleading. If a tree moves in the wind, it must be alive. If the wind blows while the child is walking, then walking must make the wind blow. Piaget also believed—mistakenly, as we will see—that children of this age cannot take another person's point of view because their thinking is **egocentric.** They see the world only from their own frame of reference. They cannot imagine that you see things differently, that events happen to others that do not happen to them, that the world does not exist solely for them. "Why are there mountains [with lakes]?" Piaget asked a preoperational Swiss child. "So that we can skate," answered the child.

Further, said Piaget, preoperational children cannot grasp the concept of **conservation**—the notion that physical properties do not change when their forms or appearances change. They are unable to understand that an amount of liquid, a number of pennies, or a length of rope remains the same even if you pour the liquid from one glass to another, stack the pennies, or coil the rope (see Figure 13.2). If you pour liquid from a short, fat glass into a tall, narrow glass, preoperational children will say there is more liquid in the second glass. They attend to the appearance of the liquid (its height in the glass) instead of its fixed quantity.

3. During the *concrete operations stage* (about age 6 or 7 to 11), the nature and quality of children's thought changes significantly. According to Piaget, during these years children come to understand the principles of conservation, reversibility, and cause and effect. They understand the nature of *identity;* they know that a girl doesn't turn into a boy by wearing a boy's hat, and that a brother will always be a brother, even if he grows up. They learn mental operations, such as addition, subtraction, multiplication, division, and categorization—not just of numbers, but of people, events, and actions. They learn a few abstract concepts such as *serial ordering,* the idea that things can be ranked from smallest to largest, lightest to darkest, shortest to tallest. But, according to Piaget, children's thinking at this age is "concrete" because it is still grounded primarily in concrete experiences and concepts, rather than in abstractions or logical deductions.

4. The *formal operations stage* (age 12 to adulthood), said Piaget, marks the beginning of abstract reasoning. Teenagers understand that ideas can be

▪ **egocentric thinking**
Seeing the world from only one's own point of view; the inability to take another person's perspective.

▪ **conservation**
The understanding that the physical properties of objects—such as the number of items in a cluster or the amount of liquid in a glass—can remain the same even when their appearances change.

compared and classified, just as objects can. They are able to reason deductively, using premises common to their culture and experience. They apply reasoning to situations they have not experienced firsthand. They can think about future possibilities and search systematically for answers to problems.

Evaluating Piaget.   Most researchers today accept Piaget's major point, that new reasoning abilities depend on the emergence of previous ones; you can't study algebra before you can count. However, research has called into question several aspects of Piaget's theory. For example, the changes from one stage to another are neither as clear-cut nor as sweeping as Piaget implied; in particular, there seems to be no major or abrupt shift from preoperational to concrete-operational thought. Further, children's (and adults') reasoning abilities have as much to do with what they are reasoning *about* as with the stage they are in. And, as we saw in Chapter 8, not all adolescents and adults develop the ability for formal reasoning and reflective judgment; many continue to show the "magical thinking" typical of preoperational children (such as "If X precedes Y, then X must have caused Y").

Here are three other challenges to Piagetian theory:

1. *Children can understand more than Piaget gave them credit for.* Taking advantage of the well-documented fact that infants look longer at novel than at familiar stimuli (see Chapter 3), researchers have designed delightfully imaginative studies to test what babies know. In a typical experiment, infants are shown a possible event and an impossible event that violates expectations of reality (see Figure 13.3). The idea is that if infants possess the belief or expectation being tested—for example, "it is impossible for a box to float on air"—they will perceive the impossible event as being more unusual and surprising than the possible event and, thus, will look at it longer. And so they do.

Using this method, Elizabeth Spelke and her colleagues (1992) are finding that infants as young as 4 months seem to understand some basic principles of physics! The babies look longer at a ball if it seems to roll through a solid barrier, or leap between two platforms, or hang in midair, than they do when an action obeys the laws of physics. Spelke believes that babies are biologically programmed with a certain "core knowledge" about how the world works. Similarly, Renee Baillargeon (1994) has found that infants as young as 2½ to 3½ months understand some of the physical properties of objects. Even at this age, she summarizes, babies "are aware that objects continue to exist when masked by other objects, that objects cannot remain stable without support, that objects move along spatially continuous paths, and that objects cannot move through the space occupied by other objects."

Children also advance rapidly in their symbolic abilities much earlier than Piaget thought—between the ages of 2½ and 3. Within that six-month period, as one experiment showed, toddlers become able to think of a miniature model of a room in two ways at once: as a room in its own right and as a symbol of the larger room it represents (DeLoache, 1987). This ability is a big step toward adult symbolic thought, in which anything can stand for anything else—a flag for a country, a logo for a company.

2. *Preschoolers are not as egocentric as Piaget thought, nor as fooled by appearances.* A large body of evidence shows that most 3- and 4- year-olds *can* take another person's perspective. When 4-year-olds play with 2-year-olds, for example, they modify and simplify their speech so the younger child will understand (Shatz & Gelman, 1973). As we will see later, even very young children are capable of astonishing acts of empathy.

John Flavell (1992, 1993) has proposed that children go through two levels of perspective-taking ability: at level one, about age 2 to 3, the child knows *that* another person experiences things differently. At level two, about age 4 to 5,

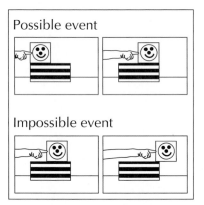

■ Figure 13.3   Testing Infants' Knowledge

In this paradigm for studying infants' understanding of whether an object needs physical support, a gloved hand pushes a colorful box from left to right along a striped platform. In the possible event (top), the box is pushed until its edge reaches the end of the platform. In the impossible event (bottom), the box is pushed until only a bit of its bottom surface rests on the platform. Babies look longer at the impossible event, suggesting that it surprises and startles them (Baillargeon, 1994).

Are children really egocentric? This 3-year-old girl was asked to place the boy doll where the police officer could not find him. According to Piaget, she should be "egocentric," and therefore hide the boy doll from herself as well (left). On several occasions, however, she placed the doll where she, but not the police officer, could see him, suggesting that she could take the police officer's point of view (right).

the child begins to figure out *what* another person is seeing or experiencing (Flavell, Green, & Flavell, 1990). One 5-year-old showed her teacher a picture she had drawn of a cat and an unidentifiable blob. "The cat is lovely," said the teacher, "but what is this thing here?" "That has nothing to do with you," said the child. "That's what the *cat* is looking at."

This shift in perspective-taking, says Flavell, is part of a broader change in how the child understands appearance and reality. Two- and 3-year-olds judge by appearance: If you put a dog mask on a cat, they will say it's a dog. By age 5, children know it's "really" a cat. Even more important, at 4 or 5 they understand that someone else might be fooled into thinking it's a dog and even act on that false belief. They understand that you can't predict what a person will do just by observing the actual situation or the "facts"; you have to know what the person is feeling and thinking. In short, they have developed a **theory of mind,** a theory about how one's own and other people's minds work and how people are affected by their beliefs and feelings (Astington & Gopnik, 1991; Flavell, Green, & Flavell, 1990).

There has been an explosion of research on the 4- and 5-year-old child's emerging theory of mind, as psychologists debate how and why this development takes place. The accumulating evidence shows that Piaget was clearly wrong in assuming that children of this age are egocentric and literal-minded; they are capable of forms of logic and inference about other people's behavior that Piaget thought impossible.

3. Children's cognitive development, like their biological development, occurs in a social and cultural context. The development of concrete operations, for example, varies in timing and content from one culture to another. Pierre Dasen (1994) spent years testing Piaget's theory in different cultures: among the Aborigines in Australia, the Inuit in Canada, the Ebri and the Baoulé in the Ivory Coast, and the Kikuyu in Kenya. Dasen found that traditional nomadic hunting peoples, such as the Inuit and the Aborigines, do not quantify things and do not need to. The Aborigines have number words only up to "five"; after that, all quantities are described as "many." In such cultures, the cognitive ability to understand the conservation of quantity or number develops late, if at all. But nomadic hunting tribes rely on their spatial orientation—knowing where water holes and successful hunting routes are—and so spatial abilities develop rapidly. In contrast, children who live in settled agricultural communities, such as the Baoulé, develop rapidly in the domain of quantification and much more slowly in spatial reasoning. Experiences with school affect cognitive development too: Many unschooled children of the Wolof, a rural group in Senegal, do not acquire an understanding of conservation, as do their peers who attend school, but brief training can speed its development (Greenfield, 1976).

▪ **theory of mind**
A theory held by a child or adult about the way one's own mind and other people's minds work, and how people are affected by their beliefs and feelings. Children develop a theory of mind by age 4 or 5.

Experience affects cognitive development. This young potter in India and other children who work with materials such as clay understand the concept of conservation of quantity sooner than children who do not have this practical experience.

These important findings have required significant modifications of Piaget's original theory. However, the general sequence of cognitive development that Piaget described does hold up across cultures. And even Piaget's critics agree with him on a most important point: Children are not passive vessels into which education and experience are poured. Children bring to their experiences their own perceptions and modes of thought and actively interpret their worlds.

The Ability to Speak

In Chapter 3 we saw that the ability to use language is an evolutionary adaptation of the human species. In only a few years of life, children are able to understand thousands and thousands of words; use rules of syntax to string them together in meaningful sentences; and produce and understand an infinite number of new word combinations.

In the first months, babies cry and coo. They are highly responsive to the pitch, intensity, and sound of language. They are responsive to emotions in the voice before they respond to facial expressions. Anne Fernald (1990) finds that for a baby, "the melody is the message." When most people speak to babies, their pitch is higher and more varied and the intonation is more exaggerated, a habit of speech that linguists call *motherese* (although fathers and other adults tend to speak it too). Babies as young as two days old prefer to hear motherese to normal adult talk. Speaking motherese to infants is not a universal phenomenon, but it is widespread, as studies in France, Italy, Japan, rural South Africa, Britain, Canada, and China have found.

By 4 to 6 months, babies have learned many of the basic sounds of their native language, even before they can utter a word of it. They can recognize their own names and other words that regularly get spoken with emotion, such as "mommy" and "daddy." As a study of 64 infants in Sweden and the United States found, 6-month-olds can distinguish the typical consonant and vowel sounds (phonemes) of their parents' language from those of a foreign language (Kuhl et al., 1992). Over time, exposure to the baby's native language reduces his or her ability to perceive speech sounds in other languages. Thus Japanese infants can hear the difference between the English sounds "la" and "ra," but Japanese adults cannot because this contrast does not exist in their language.

Between 6 months and one year, infants become increasingly familiar with the sound structure of their native language, and soon they are able to distinguish words from the flow of speech. They will listen longer to native words that violate their expectations of what words should sound like (Jusczyk, 1993; Jusczyk et al., 1993). They start making many "ba-ba" and "goo-goo" sounds, endlessly repeating sounds and syllables. This *babbling phase* lasts until about 1 year of age, when the child begins to name things. One-year-olds already have some concepts in their minds—they can recognize favorite objects and people—and their first words are those that represent familiar concepts ("mama," "doggie," "bug").

By 12 to 14 months of age, babies have also developed a repertoire of symbolic *gestures,* another important tool of communication. They use gestures to refer to objects (sniffing to indicate "flower"), to request something (smacking the lips for "food," moving the hands up and down for "play the piano"), to describe an object (blowing or waving a hand for "hot," raising the arms for "big"), and to reply to questions (opening the palms or shrugging the shoulders for "I don't know"). One baby baseball fan used a clapping sign in response to baseball games—real or pictured (Acredolo & Goodwyn, 1988).

Between the ages of 18 months and 2 years, toddlers begin to produce words in two- or three-word combinations ("Mama here," "go 'way bug," "my toy").

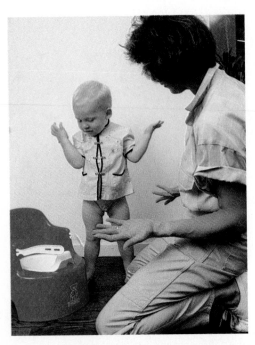

Symbolic gestures emerge early! This mother and her son are clearly having a conversation.

The child's first combinations of words have a common quality in many (but not all) languages: They are **telegraphic.** When you have to pay for every word in a telegram, you quickly learn to drop unnecessary articles (*a, an,* or *the*) and auxiliary verbs (such as *is* or *are*), but you still convey your message. Similarly, the two-word sentences of toddlers omit lots of articles, auxiliary verbs, other parts of speech, and word endings, but are remarkably accurate in conveying many messages. Here are some functions and examples of children's two-word "telegrams" (Slobin, 1979, 1985):

- *To locate or name something:* there toy, that chair, see doggie
- *To demand something:* more milk, give candy
- *To negate an action:* no wet, no want, not hungry, allgone milk
- *To describe an event:* Bambi go, mail come, hit ball
- *To show possession:* my shoe, Mama dress
- *To modify an object:* pretty dress, big boat
- *To question:* where ball, where Daddy

Pretty good for a little kid, don't you think? At about this age, children reveal another impressive talent. As we saw in Chapter 3, they begin to acquire new words at a rapid rate, a phenomenon called the *naming explosion.* Obviously, they are doing this without word-by-word training. They absorb the new words as they encounter them in conversation, and they are able to do this on the basis of hearing only one or two uses of the word in context (Rice, 1989). They seem to form quick impression of the likely meaning of the word, using their growing knowledge of grammatical contexts and the rules for formulating words. Recent studies suggest that the cognitive ability to understand meanings of words seems to precede the rapid acquisition of vocabulary: Even 13-month-old infants, who have 6 to 8 months to go before the naming explosion begins, are able to comprehend new names for objects after hearing them only 9 times in a 5-minute training session (Woodward, Markman, & Fitzsimmons, 1994). This process of understanding new words continues throughout childhood (see Figure 13.4).

■ **telegraphic speech**
A child's first combination of words, which omit (as a telegram did) unnecessary words.

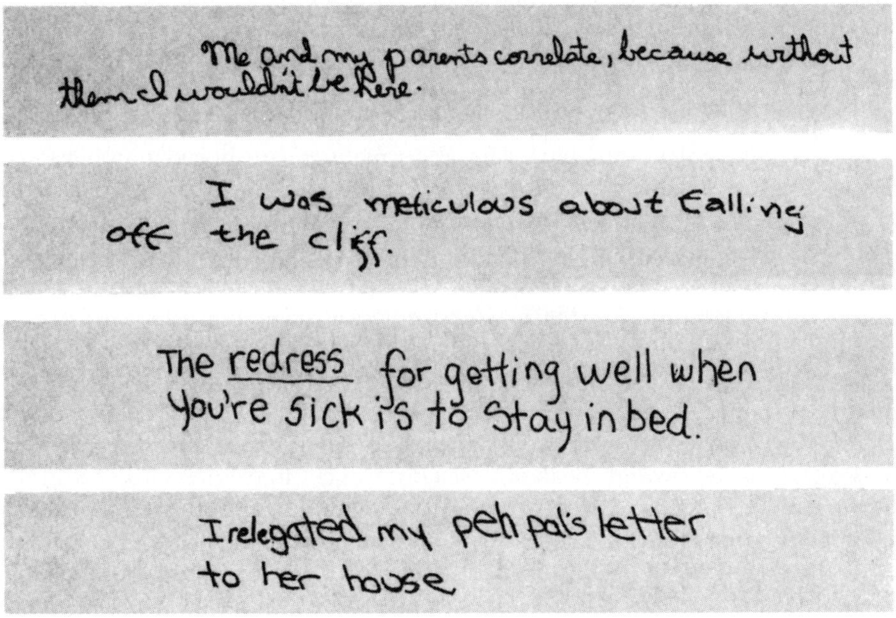

■ **Figure 13.4 How Children Learn Words**

Me and my parents correlate, because without them I wouldn't be here.

I was meticulous about falling off the cliff.

The <u>redress</u> for getting well when you're sick is to stay in bed.

I relegated my pen pal's letter to her house.

Schoolchildren often produce mystifying sentences when they are trying to learn a new word. The reason is that they extract one element of a word's definition and then apply it inappropriately: If "correlate" means related to, you must be "correlated" with your parents. Similarly, "meticulous" involves being careful about small details; to "redress" a grievance means to find a remedy for it; and to "relegate" means to send away. Children learn words faster when they are given sentences that use the word correctly than when they are given only definitions of it (Miller & Gildea, 1987).

Quick QUIZ

Please use language (and thought) to answer these questions.

1. Understanding that two rows of six pennies are equal in number, even if one row is flat and the other is stacked up, is an example of _____.

2. Understanding that a toy exists even after Mom puts it in her purse is an example of _____, which develops during the _____ stage.

3. The belief that a car moves because you are riding in it shows _____ thinking.

4. Name three modifications of Piaget's theory.

5. "More cake!" and "Daddy here" are examples of _____ speech.

6. True or false: Children acquire most new words without explicit training.

Answers:

1. conservation 2. object permanence, sensory-motor 3. egocentric 4. Children know more and earlier than Piaget thought; they are less egocentric than Piaget thought; and their cognitive development is affected by the demands of their culture 5. telegraphic 6. true

■ GENDER DEVELOPMENT

If you woke up tomorrow and found that you had been transformed into a member of the other sex, how would your life change? What would be different about your attitudes, behavior, habits, experiences, choices, preferences, and feelings? By the time they are in the first grade, most boys will tell you the transformation would be disastrous. They couldn't do as much or be as active. They would have to wash more often. They would have to be polite and pretty. Most girls, however, will say that the transformation would be beneficial. They could do more and be more assertive. People would like them more. They would be more confident (Baumgartner, 1983). Where do children get these ideas? How is it that little kids know "for sure" what boys and girls can and cannot do, what they are or are not like?

Most babies, unless they have rare abnormalities, are born unambiguously male or female—a biological distinction. But developmental psychologists want to know how they learn to be masculine or feminine—a psychological distinction. This learning starts at the moment of birth, when the newborn is enveloped in the clothes, colors, and toys the parents think are appropriate for its sex (Pomerleau et al., 1990). No parent ever excitedly calls a relative to exclaim, "It's a baby! It's a seven-and-a-half-pound, black-haired baby!"

To distinguish what is anatomically given from what is learned, many psychologists distinguish "sex" from "gender" (Deaux, 1985; Lott & Maluso, 1993; Unger, 1990). *Sex* refers to the anatomical and physiological attributes of, well, the sexes; thus they would speak of a "sex difference" in frequencies of baldness and color blindness. But they use *gender* to refer to the cultural and psychological attributes that children learn are appropriate for the sexes. Thus they would speak of a "gender difference" in sexual attitudes, dishwashing, and fondness for romance novels. (In Chapter 18 we will take up this distinction again, in considering how culture shapes the rules of gender.)

cathy®  **by Cathy Guisewite**

Sex typing starts early.

By the age of 4 or 5, children have developed a secure **gender identity,** a fundamental sense of maleness or femaleness that exists regardless of what one wears or does. They understand that a girl remains a girl even if she can climb a tree, and a boy remains a boy even if he has a ponytail. **Gender socialization,** sometimes called **sex typing,** is the psychological process by which boys and girls learn what it means to be masculine or feminine, including the abilities, interests, personality traits, actions, and self-concepts that their culture says are appropriate for males or females. A person can have a strong gender identity and not be sex typed: A man may be confident in his maleness and not feel threatened by doing "nonmasculine" things such as needlepointing a pillow; a woman may be confident in her femaleness and not feel threatened by doing "unfeminine" things such as serving in combat.

Developmental psychologists account for the emergence of gender identity and for gender socialization by considering biological factors, principles of learning, cognitive processes, and situational influences.

Biological Factors. Biological psychologists and sociobiologists, as we saw in Chapter 3, hold that some differences between the sexes are wired in at birth. In this view, differences between the sexes in levels of aggression, in

■ **gender identity**
The fundamental sense of being male or female, regardless of whether or not one conforms to the rules of sex typing.

■ **gender socialization (sex typing)**
The process by which children learn the behaviors, attitudes, and expectations associated in their culture with being masculine or feminine.

In many places you would never see a man or his son in the kitchen, but gender roles are affected by history and culture and therefore keep changing. By their actions, parents convey all sorts of sex-typed lessons to their children. This group effort to make dinner is teaching the children that (1) both sexes belong in the kitchen, (2) group cooking may be messy but it's fun, and (3) the person who frosts the cake gets to lick the spoon.

occupational interests (such as math or nursing), and in various skills (such as flying planes or knitting sweaters) are largely a matter of hormones, genes, and possibly brain lateralization. Several studies have found that girls who were exposed to prenatal androgens (masculinizing hormones) in the womb were later more likely than nonexposed girls to prefer "boys' toys" such as cars, fire engines, and Lincoln logs (Berenbaum & Snyder, 1995). And in all primate species, including human beings, young males are more likely than females to go in for physical roughhousing. This difference in styles of play may result from an average difference in a biological disposition for rough-and-tumble play.

Biologically oriented researchers are critical of learning theories of gender socialization, which emphasize the rewards and punishments that children get for behaving appropriately or inappropriately for their sex. For one thing, they argue, some sex differences emerge regardless of what parents and teachers do; parents may treat their sons and daughters equally (or try to), yet their sons will still prefer mechanical toys while their daughters will want teddy bears. Parents say they are merely *responding* to their children's interests and behavior when they give their children sex-typed toys, and indeed, children express preferences for what they want to do and play with at a very early age (Snow, Jacklin, & Maccoby, 1983). In a meta-analysis of 172 studies, Hugh Lytton and David Romney (1991) found that in 18 domains of parental treatment of children—including warmth and responsiveness, encouragement of achievement or dependency, restrictiveness, use of reasoning, and amount of interaction—there was no evidence that parents treated sons and daughters differently. Yet the children often acted out gender stereotypes anyway, leading the researchers to conclude that there is a "biological substrate for toy and play preferences."

Learning Influences.   Behavioral and social-learning theorists agree that traditional learning principles cannot account for all aspects of gender socialization, but they have identified many of the subtle reinforcers that do affect behavior. For example, sociobiologists (and many parents) believe that males are naturally more aggressive than females, and that this difference appears too early to be a result of systematic patterns of reinforcement. But even at 1 year of age, boys and girls *whose behavior is the same* are treated differently by adults. Beverly Fagot and her colleagues (1985) observed the reactions of teachers to "assertive acts" and "communicative acts" of 12- to 16-month-old children. Although there were no differences between the boys and girls in the frequency of these acts, the teachers responded far more often to assertive boys and to verbal girls. When the researchers observed the same children a year later, a gender difference was now apparent, with boys behaving more assertively and girls talking more to teachers.

Similarly, the aggressiveness of boys gets more attention and other rewards from teachers and peers than does aggressiveness in girls, again even when the children start out being equally aggressive. In one observational study of preschool children, peers or teachers paid attention to the aggression of boys 81 percent of the time, compared to only 24 percent of the time for the girls' aggression. When girls and boys behaved dependently, however, such as by calling for help from the teacher, the girls got attention far more often (Fagot, 1984).

The hidden messages conveyed by parents, teachers, and other adults affect older children as well. Janis Jacobs and Jacquelynne Eccles (1985) conducted a longitudinal study of seventh- and ninth-grade children's math achievement. At the start of the study, the children were equal in math ability, as determined by test scores and teachers' evaluations. The researchers found that parents who believed that boys have a "natural" superiority in math were unintentionally communicating this message to their children. For instance, parents would say

Is this a "mailman"? Learning theorists study subtle influences on gender socialization, such as the way masculine nouns and pronouns promote the unconscious assumption that certain jobs are best suited to men (Henley, 1989). As a result of their findings, many organizations now use gender-neutral terms, such as police officer and mail carrier.

of their sons' good math grades, "You're a natural math whiz, Johnny!" But if their daughters got identically good grades, the parents would say, "Boy, you really worked hard in math, Janey, and it shows!" The implication, not lost on the children, was clear: When girls do well, it is because of concerted effort; when boys do well, it is because they have a natural gift. Over time, this attitude was related to the reduced likelihood that the girls would take further math courses, remain interested in math, and value math in general. Why should they, if the subject is going to be so hard and isn't natural to females anyway? In subsequent longitudinal studies, Eccles has found that parents' stereotypical expectations about their children's talents in math, English, and sports strongly influence their children's performance and feelings of competence in these areas (Eccles, 1993; Eccles, Jacobs, & Harold, 1990).

Gender Schemas.   Another approach to gender socialization examines the role of children's unfolding cognitive abilities. In this view, once a boy has a concept of himself as male, he automatically values "boy things" and dislikes "girl things," without being taught (Kohlberg, 1966). As children mature, they develop a **gender schema;** that is, they begin to divide people into the categories of male or female (Archer & Lloyd, 1982; Bem, 1985; Fagot, 1985; Spence, 1985b). Gender schemas begin to form early in life—indeed, well before children can speak! By the age of only 9 months, most babies can discriminate male and female faces, even if they vary according to clothing, hair style, and facial expression (Fagot & Leinbach, 1993), and they can match female faces with female voices (Poulin-Dubois et al., 1994).

Once children acquire the ability to distinguish male and female, it is not long before they can label themselves as "boy" or "girl." And once they can do that, they begin to prefer same-sex playmates and sex-typed toys (Fagot, 1993). In Beverly Fagot's studies, 18-month-old children *did not differ* on several behavioral measures in which sex differences are often taken for granted: "large motor activity" (running, jumping, climbing), play with sex-typed toys (such as trucks for boys, dolls for girls), aggression, and verbal skills. Nine months later, at age 27 months, half of the children could correctly distinguish boys from girls on a test in which they had to assign gender labels to pictures of boys and girls, men and women. That is, they had acquired a gender schema. These "early-labeling" children were now more sex-typed in their toy play and the other categories than were children who still could not consistently label males and females. Most notably, early-labeling girls showed less aggression than late-labeling girls. It was as if the girls were going along, behaving like the boys, until they knew they were girls. At that moment, but not until that moment, they seemed to decide: "Girls don't do this; I'm a girl; I'd better not either." The late-labeling children eventually caught up in their ability to distinguish males and females, and then their behavior, too, became more sex-typed.

The period between ages 2 and 4 is especially important for the development of gender schemas. Later, schemas expand far beyond preferences for dolls or jungle gyms to include all sorts of meanings and associations (Fagot & Leinbach, 1993). Children between the ages of 4 and 7, for instance, will usually say that the following things are "masculine": bears, fire, anger, the color black, spiky and angular shapes, dogs, and rough textures. "Feminine" things are butterflies, hearts, the color pink, flowers, cats, birds, rabbits, and soft textures. (Crayons, maple trees, cameras, and telephones are neutral.) Children at this age are learning the *metaphors* of gender, associating qualities such as strength or dangerousness with males, and gentler qualities with females (Fagot, 1993). By age 5 all children can differentiate male from female solely on the basis of these qualities.

With increasing experience, knowledge, and cognitive sophistication, children construct their own standards of what boys and girls may or may not do.

■ **gender schema**
A cognitive schema (mental network) of knowledge, beliefs, metaphors, and expectations about what it means to be male or female.

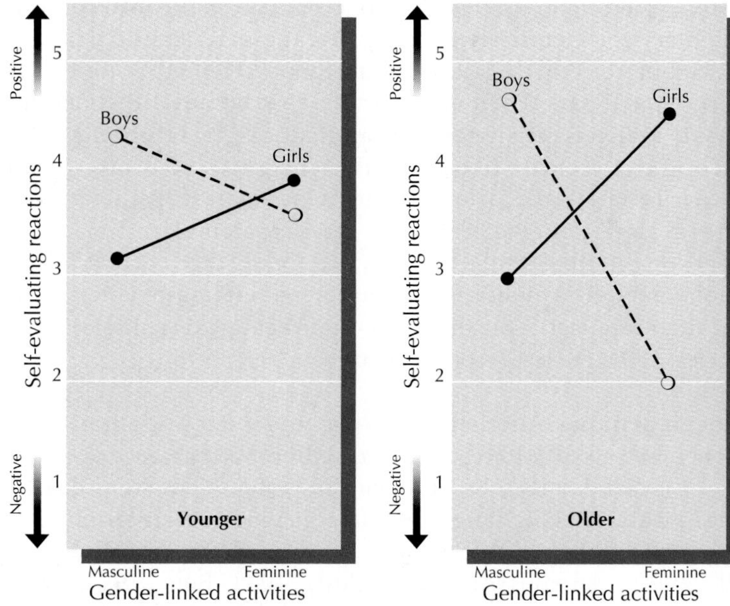

Figure 13.5   The Internalization of Sex Typing

In this experiment, 3-year-old children did not significantly differ in how they expected to feel—approving or critical—if they played with "masculine" or "feminine" toys. But the 4-year-olds, especially the boys, anticipated that they would feel much better about playing with "boy's toys" and much worse about playing with toys associated with girls. These self-evaluations, the researchers found, accurately predicted which toys the children played with (Bussey & Bandura, 1992).

However, numerous studies find that boys express stronger preferences for "masculine" toys and activities than girls do for "feminine" ones, and boys are harsher on themselves if they fail to behave in sex-typed ways (see Figure 13.5). Some researchers think that this gender difference reflects the fact that "masculine" activities, occupations, and traits hold more value in society than "feminine" ones, so that it is a loss of status for boys to behave like (or play with) girls and a rise in status for girls to behave like boys (Serbin, Powlishta, & Gulko, 1993). Indeed, 4- and 5-year-old preschoolers are already aware of gender differences in status: When asked to observe two furry rabbit puppets acting out a story, the children thought the rabbit that was deferent, had its opinions overruled, and was less likely to have its advice followed was a female (Ward, 1994).

As their abilities mature, children understand the exceptions to their gender schemas—for instance, that women can be engineers and men can be cooks. From middle childhood through adolescence, they become more flexible both about what they can do as women or men, and about people who are nontraditional, especially if they have friends of the other sex and if their environments encourage such flexibility (Katz & Ksansnak, 1994). But internalized beliefs about gender continue to have an effect throughout adulthood. When a man or a woman behaves in a way or takes a job that violates an observer's gender schema, the observer is often uncomfortable and reacts negatively (Eagly, Makhijani, & Klonsky, 1990). Gender schemas can and do change throughout our lives as they accommodate to new experiences, but they continue to influence us.

The Specific Situation.   Although most people think of "feminine" and "masculine" qualities as being stable aspects of personality, most boys and girls, like adult men and women, often behave in feminine ways *and* in masculine ways (Deaux & Major, 1987, 1990). This observation has led researchers to study a fourth key influence on gender socialization: a person's *social context*. Some situations, such as a date, evoke sex-typed behavior: Which partner pays? Who asks whom out? Who makes the sexual overtures? In other situations, such as working on an assembly line, gender is irrelevant, and sex-typed behavior disappears.

The effects of the situation on sex-typed behavior are apparent in early childhood. Eleanor Maccoby (1990), reviewing many studies, found that boys and girls do not consistently differ in the traits of passivity or activity; *their behavior depends on the gender of the child they are playing with*. Among preschoolers, girls are seldom passive with each other; however, when paired with boys, girls typically stand on the sidelines and let the boys monopolize the toys. This behavior, Maccoby found, is unrelated to the individual traits or temperaments of the children. Instead, it is related to the fact that when a boy and girl compete for a shared toy, the boy dominates—unless there is an adult in the room. Girls in mixed classrooms stay nearer to the teacher, Maccoby found, not because they are more dependent but because they want a chance at the toys! Girls play just as independently as boys when they are in all-girl groups, and they will actually sit farther from the teacher than boys in all-boy groups do.

Because of the importance of situations in evoking or minimizing sex-typed behavior, gender differences in personality and behavior that are acquired in childhood do not necessarily last (Lott & Maluso, 1993). Consider the fascinating results of a meta-analysis of 65 studies, involving more than 9,000 people (Cohn, 1991). The researcher wanted to determine the extent of gender differences in personality, moral reasoning, "maturity of thought," conformity, and other characteristics throughout adolescence and adulthood. He found that differences were greatest among junior- and senior-high-school students, largely because girls mature earlier than boys. But most of these differences, he found, declined significantly among college-age adults, and disappeared entirely among older men and women. The reason, it seems, is that as people have new experiences, their behavior changes. This is why children can grow up in an extremely sex-typed family and, as adults, find themselves in careers or relationships they might never have imagined for themselves.

Quick QUIZ

Are you socialized yet into the habit of answering quizzes?

1. A 7-year-old girl who is quiet and passive in class, but active and independent in her all-girl Brownie troop, illustrates which type of influence on gender development? (a) gender schemas (b) cognitive (c) situational (d) biological
2. Which statement about gender schemas is *false?* (a) They are present in early form by age 1, (b) They are permanent conceptualizations of what it means to be masculine or feminine, (c) They eventually expand to include metaphors associated with male and female
3. Herb really wants to be a doctor, but he doesn't get in to medical school. A friend suggests he become a nurse. "Yipes!" says Herb. "Real men aren't nurses!" Herb (a) has a strong gender identity and is sex typed, (b) has a strong gender identity but isn't sex typed, (c) is strongly sex-typed but has a weak gender identity, (d) isn't sex typed and has a weak gender identity.

Answers:

1. c 2. b 3. a

▪ MORAL DEVELOPMENT

Do you think it is morally acceptable to steal something you desperately need if you can't afford to pay for it? If you visit your 95-year-old aunt, but only because you hope to inherit her estate, would your act be moral? If you could help a friend cheat on a test, would you do it? How would you feel about it? As these questions suggest, "morality" is a complex phenomenon involving empathy for others, the cognitive ability to evaluate moral dilemmas, the inner voice of conscience, and behaving in considerate and responsible ways (Kurtines & Gewirtz, 1991).

The study of moral development in children focuses on three areas: (1) how children make moral judgments (is stealing candy right or wrong?); (2) how children develop moral emotions (how will they feel if they steal that candy?); and (3) how children learn to behave morally (they may know it is wrong to steal, and even feel guilty if they do, but will they do it anyway?).

Moral Judgments: Reasoning About Morality

How do children learn to resist temptation and eventually follow social rules?

Piaget (1932) was the first psychologist to divide the development of moral reasoning into stages. Children's moral reasoning, said Piaget, follows the increasing cognitive complexity of their reasoning in general. Young children, he said, see right and wrong in terms of results rather than intention. They might tell you that a child who accidentally breaks two dishes is naughtier than a child who intentionally breaks one. They think that rules are set by a higher authority and are inflexible: You can't change the rules of a game, of family tradition, or of life, and if you break the rules, punishment will be swift and sure. Not until about age 7, said Piaget, do children begin to understand that rules are social contracts that can be changed. Older children believe that good intentions, fair play, and reciprocity ("you do for me and I do for you") are the standards of moral action.

In the 1960s, Lawrence Kohlberg outlined a new theory of stages in moral reasoning that became highly influential both for the research it generated and for its applications (Darley, 1993). Like Piaget, Kohlberg focused on moral reasoning, not behavior. Your moral stage, said Kohlberg, can be determined by the answers you give to hypothetical moral dilemmas. For example, a man's wife is dying and needs a special drug. The man can't afford the drug and the druggist won't lower his price. Should the man steal the drug? What if he no longer loves his wife? If the man is caught, should the judge be lenient? To Kohlberg and Piaget, the reasoning behind the answers was more important than the decisions themselves.

Kohlberg (1964, 1976, 1984) proposed three levels of moral development, each divided into two stages. He believed that the stages were universal and occurred in invariant order; a person would not reach the highest stages, however, without having certain key experiences. At Kohlberg's first level, *preconventional morality*, young children obey rules because they fear being punished if they disobey (stage 1), and later because they think it is in their best interest to obey (stage 2). Stage 2 reasoning is also hedonistic, self-centered, and lacking in empathy; what is "right" is what feels good. At about ages 10 or 11, according to Kohlberg, children shift to the second level, the *conventional morality* of adult society. At stage 3, conventional morality is based on trust, conformity, and loyalty to others; morality means "don't hurt others; don't rock the boat." Most people then advance to stage 4, a "law-and-order orientation," based on understanding the social order, law, justice, and duty.

Late in adolescence and early adulthood, said Kohlberg, some people realize that there is a level of moral judgment that transcends human laws. They see that some laws—such as those that segregate ethnic groups or that legitimize the systematic mistreatment of minorities—are themselves immoral. Such awareness moves them to the highest moral level, *postconventional ("principled") morality*. At stage 5, they realize that values and laws are relative, that people hold different standards, that laws are important but can be changed. A few great individuals reach stage 6, and develop a moral standard based on universal human rights. When faced with a conflict between law and conscience, such people follow conscience, even at personal risk.

Hundreds of studies have been done, on samples all over the world, to test Kohlberg's theory (Eckensberger, 1994; Shweder, Mahapatra, & Miller, 1990; Snarey, 1985). The results show that stages 5 and 6 are rare, but the others indeed develop sequentially in many cultures. Some developmental psychologists are persuaded therefore that children's moral reasoning does evolve according to Kohlberg's stages (Bee, 1995; Walker, 1989).

But others find important limitations to his stage theory. One researcher, studying people in Iceland and Germany, found that concern for others was far more important among children supposedly at only a "stage 2" level than the theory would predict, and that because stage 4 is heavily based on formal legal conceptions, unschooled members of many cultures do not achieve it (Eckensberger, 1994). Others argue that stage 4 reasoning reflects *verbal* rather than moral development and thus favors educated, middle-class people in Western society (Shweder, Mahapatra, & Miller, 1990). College-educated people give "higher-level" explanations of moral decisions than people who have not attended college, but all that shows, say Kohlberg's critics, is that they are more verbally sophisticated. Likewise, adults have greater understanding of law than children do, but this knowledge does not necessarily make their moral reasoning "better." A child who says "The judge should be lenient because [the husband] acted unselfishly" will score lower than the adult who says "The judge should be lenient because he or she can find a precedent or rule that reflects what is right." As two psychologists noted, in Kohlberg's system the cruelest lawyer will get a higher score than the kindest 8-year-old (Schulman & Mekler, 1994).

Some developmental psychologists agree with Kohlberg's notion that stages of moral reasoning reflect a child's expanding mental abilities, but they question the overall significance of this approach. As Jerome Kagan (1993) points out, a 7-year-old, when asked why he should not steal, will typically reply that he wants to avoid punishment, whereas a 15-year-old will typically say that the stability of society would be destroyed if everyone stole. Yet, says Kagan, fear of punishment is not the main reason that 7-year-olds don't steal; as we will see, dozens of research studies show that very young children are capable of moral feelings, of behaving kindly and considerately, of understanding that their actions have consequences. Conversely, adolescents are by no means indifferent to being punished by their parents or the police! Furthermore, says Kagan, "although the quality of moral reasoning increases dramatically from school entrance to high school graduation, so, too, do cheating and cruelty." This observation suggests that Kohlberg could just as well have proposed a stage theory of "immoral development," based on the child's increasing cognitive abilities to rationalize immoral acts.

In addition, many critics have pointed to a fundamental error in stage theories of moral reasoning: the assumption that people's moral reasoning is the same across situations, and that once people reach a higher level, they stay there. In most people's lives, however, moral reasoning depends on the situation (Colby et al., 1983; Kagan, 1993). You might show conventional morality by overlooking a racial slur at a dinner party (you don't want to upset everyone else), but postconventional reasoning by protesting a war you regard as immoral. And although adults aren't supposed to "regress" once they reach a higher stage based on principles of justice and fair play, about one-third of American and Canadian college men say they would force a woman into sexual acts if they could "get away with it" (Malamuth & Dean, 1990), an admission that reveals the lowest form of moral reasoning.

✴ *As their cognitive abilities mature, children become able to make more sophisticated moral decisions. What are the benefits and limitations of stage theories of moral reasoning? At what "stage" is a person who works for human rights around the world, but treats his or her own family in a callous manner?*

Finally, other psychologists have pointed out that Kohlberg's theory is limited to reasoning about *justice,* and that there are other bases of moral assessment. Carol Gilligan (1982) argues that men tend to base their moral choices on abstract principles, such as "Whose rights should take precedence here?" whereas women tend to base their moral decisions on principles of compassion and care, such as "Who will be hurt least?"

Some studies have supported Gilligan's view, finding that men care more about justice and women care more about compassion (Bussey & Maughan, 1982; Gilligan & Wiggins, 1987). Most research, however, finds no gender differences in moral reasoning, especially when people are allowed to rank *all* the reasons behind their moral judgments (Clopton & Sorell, 1993; Cohn, 1991; Friedman, Robinson, & Friedman, 1987; Thoma, 1986; Walker, 1989). Both men and women say that they base their moral decisions on compassion *and* on abstract principles of justice; they worry about feelings *and* fairness. How they reason also depends significantly on the *situation they are reasoning about.* Women and men tend to use "justice" reasoning when they are thinking about highly abstract ethical dilemmas and "care" reasoning when they are thinking about intimate dilemmas in their own lives (Clopton & Sorell, 1993; Walker, de Vries, & Trevethan, 1987).

Nevertheless, Gilligan's approach has an important virtue. Rather than ranking moral reasoning skills one above the other, perhaps we should consider how they can coexist—and why they vary across situations. To Kohlberg, Mohandas Gandhi was a man at the highest moral stage because of his commitment to universal principles of peace, justice, and nonviolence. But as Gandhi's biographers have pointed out, Gandhi was *also* a man who was aloof from his family and followers, whom he often treated harshly and even cruelly. Do you agree with Kohlberg that people can be ranked on a scale of moral reasoning, with individuals like Gandhi at the top stage? Or do you agree with the critics who believe that moral principles depend on the situation, even for principled people like Gandhi?

Moral Emotions: Acquiring Empathy, Guilt, and Shame

A different approach to studying moral development concentrates on the emergence of conscience and the development of a "moral sense" based on empathy, shame, and guilt. The capacity for moral feeling, like that for language, seems to be inborn. As Jerome Kagan (1984) says, "Without this fundamental human capacity, which nineteenth-century observers called a *moral sense,* the child could not be socialized." The "moral sense" stems from children's attachment to their parents, which motivates them to adopt the parents' standards of good and bad behavior. Children shift from obeying rules for external reasons, such as fear of punishment, to obeying rules for internal reasons, because they will feel guilty or ashamed of behaving badly or disappointing the loved parent (Bandura, 1991).

The internalization of moral standards begins with *empathy,* the ability to feel bad about another person's unhappiness and to feel good about another's joy. According to research by Martin Hoffman (1987, 1990), empathy takes different forms, depending on a child's age and cognitive abilities. In the first year, before they even have a sense of themselves as distinct from others, infants feel *global empathy,* general distress at another person's misery. At times, they act as though what happened to the other happened to themselves. One 11-month-old girl in Hoffman's research, seeing an older child fall and cry, behaved as if *she* had been hurt. She looked about to cry, put her thumb in her mouth, and buried her head in her mother's lap.

As toddlers develop a sense of self (ages 1 to 2), they also develop *egocentric empathy.* Children now understand that someone else is in distress, but they

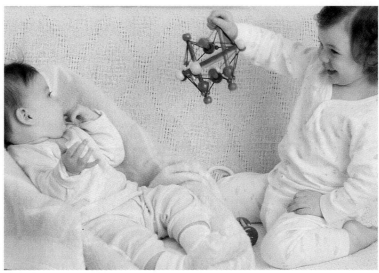

Children have an innate ability to form attachments, but experience determines whether they will develop empathy for or rivalry with others. In the photo on the right, 21-month old Shifra is obviously pleased to offer a toy to her 4-month-old sister. A child who learns how to care for a new sibling, as in the photo on the left, is likely to acquire feelings of protectiveness and concern instead of rivalry and distance.

assume that the other person must feel as they do. Two-year-olds are sometimes impulsive and egocentric, but they also are able to feel sad when another child or adult is unhappy and are capable of trying to make the person feel better. In one touching instance, a 13-month-old child offered her beloved doll to a sad adult (Hoffman, 1977). In another, an 18-month-old boy fetched his own mother to comfort a crying friend, although the friend's mother was also there!

By the age of 2 or 3, children are capable of *empathy for another's feelings* that are different from their own. For example, they can empathize with another child's feelings of shame, and they know when the child wants to be left alone. They are able to feel angry on someone else's behalf. One little boy, seeing a doctor give another child a painful injection, swatted the doctor in protest. A toddler in one study said, "You sad, Mommy. What Daddy do?" (Bretherton & Beeghly, 1982).

The final stage of empathy, *empathy for another's life condition*, emerges by late childhood. Children are able to understand that people have different experiences and histories and to feel empathy toward whole groups of individuals who are less fortunate than they.

Although people might like a life without shame or guilt, these emotions, too, are essential to the social learning of morality (Bandura, 1991). They help maintain rules and standards, and encourage moral action. *Shame* is a wound to the self-concept. It comes from perceiving that others have seen you doing something wrong and that they will like you less for having done it. As soon as the toddler has a sense of self, shame is quick to follow (Lewis, 1992). *Guilt*, in contrast, is the emotion you feel when you have not lived up to your own internal standard; it is remorse for real or imagined wrongdoings, a kind of self-inflicted punishment. Of course, guilt can also be maladaptive and self-defeating. Studies of children who live with a chronically depressed or deeply troubled parent, for example, find that these children often develop unhealthy patterns of empathy and guilt. Their feelings of empathy for the parent tend to be infused with guilt and frustration, a result of overinvolvement with the unhappy parent and an unrealistic feeling that they are somehow responsible for the parent's misery (Zahn-Waxler et al., 1990).

By the age of 2, children are aware of standards of behavior, and at this tender age they react with anxious concern or distress when a standard has been violated. By the age of 3 or 4, children associate a bad act with being a "bad boy" or "bad girl," and they begin to regulate their own behavior. In every culture around the world, children at this age judge their thoughts, feelings, and behavior against the standards they know are "right" (Edwards, 1987; Kagan & Lamb, 1987). In turn, adults begin to treat children differently, expecting them to do the right thing.

Moral Action: Learning to Behave Morally

Unfortunately, moral reasoning and emotions are not always related to moral behavior. "We can reach high levels of moral reasoning," said Thomas Likona (1983), "and still behave like scoundrels." We can feel really miserable about treating each other horribly, and do it anyway. In Chapter 17 we will look at some social forces, such as conformity and obedience, that affect moral behavior. Here we want to consider how children become helpful members of society. How do they learn to avoid the temptations to steal, lie, cheat, and otherwise behave as they might like to?

Learning theorists answer that children's moral actions depend on the rewards, punishments, and examples they get as they grow up. When children are rewarded for aggressive and competitive acts, such behavior will prevail over cooperation and altruism (Kohn, 1992; Maccoby, 1980). Children also learn about moral behavior by observing the behavior of public figures—what they do, and what they "get away with." Does a person commit an illegal act and then earn a fortune from movie deals? Does a sports hero get away with cheating because it helped the team win?

Although role models and cultural norms set standards for the moral behaviors a culture values, children also learn as much from *how* their parents interact with them as from the content of their parents' lessons. When you did something wrong as a child, for example, what did the adults in your family do about it? Did they shout at you, punish you, or explain the error of your ways?

One of the commonest methods that parents use to enforce standards is **power assertion,** which includes threats, physical punishment, depriving the child of privileges, and generally taking advantage of being bigger, stronger, and more powerful ("because I say so"). Yet power assertion, which is based on the child's fear of punishment, is associated with a *lack* of moral feeling and behavior in children; as we saw in Chapter 7, fear of punishment often interferes with the learning of self-control, empathy, and internalized values. The

■ **power assertion**
A method of child rearing in which the parent uses punishment and authority to correct the child's misbehavior.

Power assertion may seem to work as a way to get a child to obey, but it usually leaves the child feeling resentful and rebellious.

child may feel guilty about his or her own desires and impulses, but not guilty about harming others.

But perhaps aggressive, self-absorbed children are simply hard to discipline consistently, so the parent must respond with efforts to assert power. For many years, Gerald Patterson and his colleagues have been conducting longitudinal and observational studies of parents and children, often in the family's home, to try to separate cause and effect of parental practices (Patterson, 1986, 1994; Patterson, DeBaryshe, & Ramsey, 1989; Patterson, Reid, & Dishion, 1992). They find that parents of aggressive children use a great deal of punishment (shouting, scolding, spanking), yet fail to make the punishment contingent on the child's behavior. They do not state clear rules, require compliance, consistently punish violations, or praise good behavior. Instead, they nag and shout at the child, occasionally and unpredictably tossing in a slap or loss of privileges. This combination of power assertion with a pattern of intermittent discipline causes the children's aggressiveness to increase and eventually get out of hand. The child becomes withdrawn, manipulative, and difficult to control, which causes the parents to try to assert their power even more forcefully, which makes the child angrier, . . . and a vicious cycle is generated.

Across numerous longitudinal studies, child-rearing practices based on power assertion have been linked to a wide variety of negative outcomes for children's moral behavior (Hoffman, 1994). In a large study designed to investigate the origins of male delinquency, for example, the researchers found many factors that predicted which inner-city, high-risk boys would avoid a life of crime. These included consistent discipline, parental affection, a low level of aggressiveness in the father, restrictions on the son's behavior, and high parental standards and expectations (McCord, 1990). In the families that scored below the median on these factors, 58 percent of the sons eventually went on to commit serious crimes, compared to only 15 percent of those who came from families above the median. (Lately there has been extensive public discussion about the consequences of having only one parent in the home to discipline and socialize the children; we discuss this issue in "Psychology and Popular Culture.")

In contrast to power assertion, a far more successful method for teaching moral behavior is **induction,** in which the parent appeals to the child's own resources, affection for others, and sense of responsibility. For example, a mother may tell her child that the child's actions will harm, inconvenience, or disappoint another person. Induction tends to produce children who have moral feelings and who behave morally on five different measures. They feel guilty if they hurt others; they internalize standards of right and wrong, instead of just following orders; they confess rather than lie if they misbehave; they accept responsibility for their misbehavior; and they are considerate of others (Hoffman & Saltzstein, 1967; Schulman & Mekler, 1994).

In a study of children ages 15 to 20 months, some were already more helpful than others. If their behavior caused a friend to feel unhappy, afraid, or hurt, they would bring comfort by offering a toy, hugging the friend, or going to get help. It turned out that the mothers of these little Samaritans were using induction to reprimand their children in a particular way. They would *moralize* ("You made Doug cry; it's not nice to bite") or prohibit bad behavior with *explanations* or *statements of principle* ("You must never poke anyone's eyes because that could hurt them seriously"). Other ways of reprimanding were ineffective, and so were neutral explanations ("Tina is crying because you pushed her"). The reprimands that produced the lowest rates of helping were unexplained prohibitions ("Stop that!") and punishment, such as spanking and hitting (Zahn-Waxler, Radke-Yarrow, & King, 1979). Another study found that the only effective punishments are forceful reprimands or time-outs—again, accompanied by an explanation ("You can't play with that toy for a half-hour because you hit people with it") (Schulman & Mekler, 1994).

Parents can teach their children to be responsible by explaining the reasons for rules and limits, instead of asserting "because I said so!"

■ **induction**

A method of child rearing in which the parent appeals to the child's own resources, abilities, sense of responsibility, and feelings for others in correcting the child's misbehavior.

Psychology and Popular Culture

The Great Single-Mom Debate

■ When former Vice-President Dan Quayle criticized the television character Murphy Brown for having a baby out of wedlock, he set off a firestorm of argument that revealed how much the culture has changed since Quayle was a boy. Not long ago, "unwed mothers" were considered deviant and shameful; today, many women choose to have children before or without marriage—indeed, without living with a man at all. Not long ago, divorce, another cause of single parenting, was rare and shameful. Now, divorce is as common as the flu; a child born today in the United States has a 40 percent chance of living through a *second* parental divorce by age 18.

Amid the political debate about whether unmarried mothers should be "blamed" or "congratulated" for trying to raise children on their own, social scientists have been trying to answer a different question: What is the psychological effect on children of living in a single-parent household? (Usually the "single parent" is the mother.) Many psychologists and social observers are worried. They argue that many if not most of these children suffer negative effects and that these effects are long-lasting. Children in single-parent families are six times as likely as children in two-parent families to be poor, and they remain poor longer; they are more likely to drop out of school, commit crimes, have children as teenagers, and to abuse drugs; and they are more likely to have unstable jobs and relationships (Wallerstein & Blakeslee, 1989; Whitehead, 1993).

Other observers point out that although these statistics are very serious, we should not jump to the conclusion that all single-parent families are the same. A poor woman with several children on welfare, or a mother struggling alone to keep her sons from joining a gang, lives in drastically different circumstances than an affluent woman who has chosen to adopt or conceive children without marriage. And not all single-parent households are single *adult* households. When a divorce occurs, its effects can be cushioned for children who live with other relatives as well as the custodial parent (Hetherington, 1989; Wilson, 1989). Finally, these observers worry about the common tendency to focus on mothers who are single by choice or by circumstance, and ignore or exonerate fathers who fail to support their children financially or psychologically.

What about children who grow up in single-parent households because of divorce? What are the effects on the children's well-being, achievement, conduct, social adjustment, and relations with parents? To find out, Paul Amato and Bruce Keith (1991) analyzed the results of 92 studies, representing more than 13,000 children of all ages. The bad news is that children of divorce do, in general, have lower well-being than do children living in two-parent families; the argument that children adapt readily and recover quickly after parental divorce was not supported. The better news is that most children do not suffer irreparably.

Amato and Keith examined three hypotheses that account for the negative effects of divorce: the

In a program of research spanning three decades, Diana Baumrind (1966, 1971, 1973, 1989, 1991), expanding on the concepts of induction and power assertion, has identified three overall styles of child-rearing and their results:

1. *Authoritarian parents* exercise too much power and give too little nurturance. Communication is all one way: The parent issues orders ("Stop that!" "Do it because I say so!") and the child is expected to listen and obey. The children of these parents tend to be less socially skilled than other children, have lower self-esteem, and do more poorly in school. Some are overly timid and others are overly aggressive.

2. *Permissive parents* are nurturant, but they exercise too little control and don't make strong demands for mature and responsible behavior on the part of their children. They fail to state rules clearly and consistently and they have poor communication with their kids. Their children, compared to the offspring

"father absence" explanation; the "economic disadvantage" explanation; and the "family conflict" explanation. Surprisingly, the father-absence explanation was not as strong as anticipated; some studies even found that contact with fathers was associated with *increased* problems in children. The outcome clearly depends on the quality of fathering. However, most boys did better when they lived either in the custody of their fathers or with stepfathers, in contrast to seeing their fathers intermittently or not at all. Economic disadvantage does reduce the well-being of children of divorce, particularly if the children are shifted into poverty when the father leaves. But children of divorce continue to have lower well-being than children of nondivorced parents even when their families have equal incomes.

By far the strongest explanation for the negative impact of divorce was family conflict. Divorcing parents are often bitter and angry with each other, and their anger often catches the children in the middle. But parental conflict has negative effects on children in two-parent families as well. Children in high-conflict families are more likely to have conduct problems, poor adjustment, and low self-esteem than children in families with low levels of discord (Gottman & Katz, 1989). When researchers have compared children in these "fighting families" with children of divorced parents, they find a similar incidence of depression and reduced well-being (Nolen-Hoeksema, Girgus, & Seligman, 1991). In contrast, the children of divorce usually adjust eventually, unless their parents continue to quarrel, take each other to court, fight with each other at every visit, or make the children choose sides.

Thus there is no single answer to the question "What are the effects of living with only one parent?" The effects, for any child, will depend on the child's sex, temperament, age, and needs; the financial security and psychological well-being of the custodial parent; the level of conflict between the parents; the family's extended support system; and whether the child lives in a world of poverty, drugs, and crime, or a stable and supportive environment.

The research findings, along with troubling statistics on the rates of poverty among single mothers and their children, raise provocative concerns for individuals and society. For some groups of women, such as white women in their 40s and young black women, a demographic fact of life is that there aren't enough men to go around; should these women forgo motherhood? Moreover, many women no longer have to stay, for economic reasons, with violent, abusive, or merely incompatible partners; should bad marriages stay together "for the sake of the children"?

Given today's society, where single parenthood will be a fact of life for many adults, perhaps the question is no longer "Is single parenthood good or bad for children?" but rather "What factors enable single parents to do well by their children, and which factors are harmful to parent and child?" ■

of other kinds of parents, are likely to be impulsive, immature, irresponsible, and academically unmotivated.

3. *Authoritative parents* travel a middle road: They know when and how to discipline their children. They set high but reasonable expectations and teach their children how to meet them. They also give their children emotional support and encourage two-way communication; they use induction. Their children tend to have good self-control, high self-esteem, and high self-efficacy, be independent yet cooperative, be socially mature, do better than average in school, and be cheerful, thoughtful, and helpful.

Parental techniques, however, can have different results in different social and economic contexts. A parent may seem harsh and "authoritarian" in an impoverished or dangerous community, but the child may interpret the parent's behavior as evidence of love and concern (Baumrind, 1991). This is why many developmental psychologists have been focusing on the *interaction* between the parent's methods of discipline and the child's temperament, cognitive abilities (such as an understanding of rules and another person's feelings), and perceptions of the parent's intentions (Fabes et al., 1994; Grusec & Goodnow, 1994). (We discuss methods of child rearing further in "Taking Psychology with You.")

Ultimately, the greatest influence on children's moral behavior is what others expect of them. In a large-scale study of children in Kenya, India, Mexico, the Philippines, Okinawa, and the United States, Beatrice and John Whiting (1975) measured how often children behaved altruistically (offering help, support, or unselfish suggestions) or egoistically (seeking help and attention or wanting to dominate others). This study was later reanalyzed and five new cultures were added to it (Whiting & Edwards, 1988). American children were the least altruistic on all three measures and the most egoistic. The most altruistic children came from societies in which:

- Children are assigned many tasks, such as caring for younger children, helping with gathering food, and preparing it.
- Children know that their work makes a genuine contribution to the well-being or economic survival of the family.
- Parents depend on the children's contributions.
- Mothers have many responsibilities inside and outside the home.
- Children respect parental authority.

In summary, in accounting for how children learn to become (or fail to become) kind, helpful, and responsible members of society, developmental psychologists direct us to the importance of children's emerging cognitive capacities to evaluate complex moral issues; the "moral emotions" of empathy, shame, and guilt; the styles of child rearing that foster or inhibit moral standards and behavior; and the importance of the behavior that is expected and required of children in everyday situations.

In many cultures around the world, children are expected to work to contribute to the family income, do family chores, and take care of their younger siblings. These experiences encourage helpfulness and empathy.

Quick QUIZ

A. To raise children who are kind and helpful, parents and parents-to-be should be able to answer the following questions.

1. LaVerne, age 14 months, feels sad when she sees her mother crying during a tearjerker, and she starts to cry too. LaVerne has developed (a) global empathy, (b) egocentric empathy, (c) empathy for another's feelings.

2. Shame and guilt are (a) unconscious emotions in infancy, (b) necessary in internalizing moral standards, (c) destructive emotions that should be stamped out as soon as possible.

3. Which method of parental discipline tends to create children who have internalized values of helpfulness and empathy? (a) induction, (b) punishment, (c) power assertion

4. Which form of family life tends to create helpful children? (a) every family member "does his or her own thing," (b) parents are appropriate role models, (c) children contribute to the family welfare, (d) parents remind children often about the importance of being helpful

B. In Chapter 12 you read that the Big Five personality traits have a genetic component, are resistant to change, and emerge almost regardless of what parents do. Now here we are offering evidence that what parents do *does* make a difference. How might these two lines of research be reconciled?

Answers:

A. 1. b 2. b 3. a 4. c B. We can avoid either–or thinking by asking which qualities may be due largely to temperament (such as extroversion) and which are strongly affected by parental lessons (such as aggressiveness and empathy). Also, how a child turns out depends on the interactions between a child's temperament and the parents' reactions. And perhaps the relative impact of temperament and parental techniques changes as the child matures.

■ ADOLESCENCE

Adolescence refers to the period of development between **puberty,** the age at which a person becomes capable of sexual reproduction, and adulthood. In some cultures, the time span between puberty and adulthood is only a few months; a sexually mature boy or girl is expected to marry and assume adult tasks. In modern Western societies, adolescence lasts several years. Teenagers are not considered emotionally mature enough to be full-fledged adults with all the rights, responsibilities, and roles of adulthood. The long span of adolescence is new to this century. In the past, societies needed the labor of young people and could not afford to have them spend a decade in school or in "self-discovery."

The Physiology of Adolescence

Until puberty, both boys and girls produce roughly the same amount of male hormones (androgens) and female hormones (estrogens). At puberty, the pituitary gland begins to stimulate hormone production in the adrenal and other endocrine glands and in the reproductive glands. In boys, the reproductive glands are the testes (testicles), which produce sperm; in girls, the reproductive

■ **puberty**
The age at which a person becomes capable of sexual reproduction.

glands are the ovaries, which release eggs, or ova. Now boys have a higher level of androgens than girls do, and girls have a higher level of estrogens than boys do.

During puberty, the sex organs mature and the individual becomes capable of reproduction. In girls, the onset of menstruation, called **menarche,** and the development of breasts are major signs of sexual maturity. In boys, the major signs are the onset of nocturnal emissions and the growth of the testes, scrotum, and penis. Hormones are also responsible for the emergence of *secondary sex characteristics,* such as a deepened voice and facial and chest hair in boys and pubic hair in both sexes.

The dramatic physical changes of puberty are part of the last "growth spurt" on the child's road to adulthood. For girls, the adolescent growth spurt begins, on the average, at age 10, peaks at 12 or 13, and stops at about age 16, by which time most girls are sexually mature. For boys, the average adolescent growth spurt starts at about age 12 and ends at about age 18. This difference in the rates of development is often a source of misery to adolescents, for most girls mature sooner than most boys.

The timing of the changes of puberty depends on both genetic and environmental factors. The onset of menarche, for example, can be affected by nutrition, stress, and exercise; indeed, better nutrition may be one reason that the average age of menarche has been declining in Europe and North America for the last 150 years. The onset of puberty seems to be occurring earlier for males, too. Decades ago, the average American man did not reach his maximum height until the age of 26; today this marker of the end of puberty occurs, on the average, at 18 (Cole & Cole, 1993).

There is, however, enormous individual variation in the onset and length of puberty. Some girls menstruate as early as age 8 and others do not begin until age 15. One 15-year-old male may be as developed as an adult man and another will still be a boy. In addition, just to be mischievous, nature has seen fit to make growth a jumpy, irregular, uneven business, with different parts of the body maturing at different rates. A girl may have undeveloped breasts but adult-sized hands and feet. A boy may be tall and gangly but have no trace of a longed-for beard. Eventually, everything catches up.

If you entered puberty before most of your classmates, or if you matured much later than they did, you know that your experience of adolescence was different from that of the average teenager. Some psychologists believe that the *timing* of puberty is more important in an adolescent's development than the specific biological events themselves. Early-maturing boys generally have a more positive view of their bodies, and their relatively greater size and strength gives them a boost in sports and the prestige that being a good athlete brings young men. But they are also more likely to smoke, drink, use drugs, and break the law than later-maturing boys, and to have less self-control and emotional stability (Duncan et al., 1985). Late-developing boys feel the worst about themselves in the 7th grade, but by the 12th grade they usually end up as the healthiest group (Petersen, 1989).

Likewise, some early-maturing girls have the prestige of being socially popular, but, partly because others regard them as being sexually precocious, they are also more likely to have conflict with their parents, have behavioral problems, drop out of school, have a negative body image, and have emotional problems (Caspi & Moffitt, 1991; Stattin & Magnusson, 1990). Girls who go through puberty relatively late, in contrast, have a more difficult time at first, but by the end of adolescence many are happier with their appearance and more popular than their early-maturing classmates (Petersen, 1989).

Are these effects a result of (1) hormonal changes alone, (2) being out of sync with one's classmates (early or late), or (3) the specific effects of entering puberty early? In a longitudinal study of 501 girls in New Zealand, the first two

■ **menarche [men-ARE-kee]**

The onset of menstruation at puberty.

Boys and girls typically reach puberty at different times, often to their embarrassment. These girls are all the same age, but differ considerably in physical maturity.

hypotheses were not supported (Caspi & Moffitt, 1991). As in other studies, late-maturing girls, who began menarche at 14 or 15, had the fewest behavioral problems, whereas girls who entered menarche before the age of 12 subsequently had the most problems. Because the researchers had been observing these teenagers since childhood, they were able to find out why this was so. Although early menarche created certain stresses for many of the early-maturing girls, it did not do so for all of them. Instead, early menarche tended to accentuate the *existing* behavioral problems and family conflicts the girls had had in childhood. The group with the most troubles throughout adolescence were early maturers who had a history of behavioral problems in childhood.

The researchers conclude that during times of transition—whether a biological change such as puberty or a social change such as going to college—existing personality traits and problems are magnified. Biological changes alone, even the hormonal changes of adolescence, do not inevitably lead to specific psychological consequences. Recent theories of adolescent development, therefore, emphasize the fit between the individual and the situation, between maturational stage and social context (Eccles et al., 1993; Jessor, 1993).

The Psychology of Adolescence

The biological storms of puberty are reputed to carry over into psychological storms: insecurity about oneself in relation to friends, a fierce and unhappy struggle for self-identity, and a distrust and dislike of parents. Many older theories of adolescent development held that adolescent anguish and rebellion are necessary and inevitable, the means by which teenagers separate themselves psychologically from their parents and form their own identities (Blos, 1962).

It is certainly true that adolescence can be difficult for teenagers, who must learn the rules of adult sexuality, morality, work, and family. Teenagers are beginning to develop their own standards and values, and often they do so by trying on the styles, actions, and attitudes of their peers in contrast to those of their parents. They are questioning adult life, even as they are rehearsing for it. For some teenagers, these changes can feel overwhelming and lead to loneliness and depression (Garland & Zigler, 1994). Indeed, rates of depression and suicide are a serious and growing problem among the young (see Chapter 15).

Rebellious-teenager movies and studies of troubled teens depict adolescence as a time of turmoil and misery, conflict and hostility toward parents, and a desire for separation. What is missing from this portrait of adolescence? How is "separation" best defined?

The Varieties of Adolescence

The stereotype of adolescence emphasizes teenage turmoil and rebellion (left). But most teens feel good about themselves and their communities, as do the students (center) at a volunteer trash clean-up day on the Texas coast, and many hold jobs to earn income (right).

Yet studies of representative samples of teenagers find that extreme turmoil and unhappiness are the exception, not the rule. For instance, a study of more than 20,000 teenagers surveyed between 1962 and 1982 found that adolescents travel one of three routes to adulthood, depending on their temperament, childhood experiences, opportunities, coping skills, and social life (Offer & Sabshin, 1984). More than half have few emotional upsets. They have supportive families, a sense of purpose and self-confidence, good friends, and the skill to cope with problems. Others have a bumpier ride, having suffered parental divorce, the death of a close relative, or serious illness. Their self-esteem wavers; they are more dependent on the positive evaluation of peers and parents and often feel discouraged. A third group, about 20 percent of all teenagers, have a tumultuous time. They report more difficulties than satisfactions in their lives. Their backgrounds tend to be less stable, more fraught with conflicts and problems, and less advantageous than those of the other two groups. They feel less happy and secure.

One important explanation for the increased unhappiness and misconduct among some adolescents holds that the problem has less to do with the adolescents themselves than with their schools and families (Eccles et al., 1993). The Michigan Study of Adolescent Life Transitions followed some 1,500 adolescents as they moved from the sixth grade (elementary school) to the seventh (junior high). The researchers found that the preteens who showed reduced motivation and increased misconduct were reacting to specific changes in their environments: Their teachers were no longer encouraging active classroom participation and decision making as they had in elementary school, but rote learning; and their parents, perhaps worried about their maturing children's sexuality and possible drug use, were using increasingly punitive measures of controlling them. Thus, the researchers conclude, just when adolescents want more say in making their own rules, and just when their cognitive abilities are maturing to enable them to do more complex academic tasks and make personal decisions, some teachers and parents are stifling these needs. Several studies have found that when adolescents are given a say in family decisions and in classroom activities they feel better about themselves and are more enthusiastic about their schoolwork (Eccles et al., 1993).

A need for autonomy, however, doesn't mean total separation from or rejection of the parent. Early theories of adolescent development assumed that a child who did not separate sufficiently, who maintained a close bond with the parents, was "immature." Psychologists now believe that separation is an issue for only a small stratum of society and does not reflect the pattern that is common in most cultures: continued love and connection between child and parent. Terri Apter (1990) argues that two meanings of "separation" have been confused: *individuation,* the process of becoming a distinct individual with your own values and needs; and a complete *rift,* a severing of affection and an effort to replace the parent with other mentors and influences. Most adolescents learn to become individuals in the former sense, not by rejecting their parents but by striking a different balance with them.

Most teenagers, of course, do have some conflicts with their parents. In one large study, adolescents listed complaints like these: "Why my mother manipulates the conversation to get me to hate her"; "How much of a bastard my father is to my sister"; "How ugly my mom's taste is"; "How pig-headed my mom and dad are" (Csikszentmihalyi & Larson, 1984). But fights—over what is important, who should set the rules, differences of opinion and taste, and the like—did not usually reflect a profound split between parent and adolescent. Likewise, in a study of 65 ethnically diverse mother–daughter pairs in Britain and the United States, Terri Apter (1990) found that most of the teenage girls said the person they felt closest to, who offered them the greatest support, was their mother. There were plenty of quarrels—over clothes, school, chores—but these were, said Apter, "little puff balls" that did not indicate a serious break in the relationship, but an effort to get the mother to *understand.* For young men and women in Western societies, the familiar quarrels they have with their parents tend to signify a change from one-sided parental authority to a more reciprocal, adult relationship (Laursen & Collins, 1994; Paikoff & Brooks-Gunn, 1991; Steinberg, 1990). Feelings of attachment to parents are not an indication of a young person's "immaturity" or "dependence." On the contrary, researchers have found that attachment to parents is related to assertiveness, self-confidence, and ease in same- and other-sex friendships (Kenny, 1989).

Quick QUIZ

If you're not feeling rebellious, try these questions.

1. The onset of menstruation is called _____.

2. In boys, a deepening voice and a new mustache are examples of

_____.

3. Extreme turmoil and rebellion in adolescence are (a) nearly universal, (b) the exception rather than the rule, (c) rare.

4. A TV reporter asserts that teenagers must "separate" from their parents and develop "independent selves." What assumption is implicit in this claim, and can it be challenged? What are some possible definitions of "separation"?

Answers:

1. menarche 2. secondary sex characteristics 3. b 4. The reporter assumes that independence from parents is normal, universal, and good. But many people hold other values, such as continued attachment to one's family and respect for elders. The reporter also assumes that it is always economically feasible for adolescents to break away from their families; this is not always so! Finally, it is important to define terms like "separation": Does it mean a complete severing of connection, putting oneself first, or developing one's own identity and wishes?

Childhood is not just a time of happy innocence. Like adults, children have many troubling experiences with humiliation, loss, fear, pain, and unhappiness. But, also like adults, most are resilient.

✴ *What assumptions underlie the belief that we are "prisoners of childhood"? If you suffered a trauma in your early years, must you endure its effects for the rest of your life? What accounts for the resilience of most children?*

■ CAN CHILDREN SURVIVE CHILDHOOD?

The study of child development is often the study of controversies. Can children's cognitive development be hurried? Is sex typing a necessary stage in social development or can it be eliminated? Can moral reasoning and behavior be taught? By generating studies to answer these questions, psychologists narrow the gap between the laboratory and real life. This is how science advances.

Of all the controversial issues in child development, perhaps the most controversial is this: How straight is the path from childhood to adolescence to adulthood? All of us acquire attitudes, habits, and deep emotional feelings from our families, and many adults carry with them the scars of abuse they suffered as children. Some psychologists argue that no year of life is as important as the first; if the baby doesn't start out well, they warn, if the parents (especially the mother) do not tend to the baby's every need in the "right" way, the baby's whole life may be influenced for the worse. But do all of the experiences of childhood lead in a straight and inflexible line to the future? And how important is that first year?

Certainly, if newborns start off on the wrong foot, with sickness, premature birth, or social deprivation, they don't do as well as babies who start off healthy and loved. But study after study shows that the events of the first year do not necessarily have permanent effects. For example, researchers who followed the development of 643 poor and biologically vulnerable children, from birth to age 32, found that supportive home environments totally overcame any initial biological weakness. Problems that emerged were related more to stressful home environments than to biological vulnerabilities in infancy, and even those problems proved temporary. "As we watched these children grow from babyhood to adulthood," the researchers reported, "we could not help but respect the self-righting tendencies within them that produced normal development under all but the most persistently adverse circumstances" (Werner & Smith, 1982; see also Werner, 1989).

Given adequate stimulation, attention, and nourishment, normal babies will develop normally. But "adequate" covers considerable territory. Babies get along just fine on cradleboards or unbound, in good child-care centers or at home with caregivers (Clarke-Stewart, 1991; Mott, 1991). It's good to give them the very best stimulation, attention, and nourishment possible. But parents need not fear that one wrong step will cost their baby a place in graduate school or will later require 17 years of therapy.

What about the effects of prolonged difficulties in childhood? Many adults today account for their current problems in terms of the traumatic experiences of their early years. Certainly, it is indisputable that children who are beaten or neglected, or who live in continuous risk of violence from their parents, strangers, or gangs, are more likely than nonabused children to become delinquent and violent themselves, to commit crimes, to have lower IQs, and to attempt suicide (Malinosky-Rummell & Hansen, 1993; Widom, 1989). Remarkably, however, prospective studies, which follow people from childhood to adulthood, do not confirm the widespread belief that childhood traumas have specific and inevitable effects:

- After World War II, many European children, made homeless by the war, were adopted by American families. A group of these orphans, ages 5 months to 10 years, was followed and their adjustment observed. About 20 percent of the children initially showed many signs of anxiety (such as overeating, insomnia, and nightmares), but over the years these symptoms vanished. All of the children made good progress in school; none had psychiatric problems; and all established happy, affectionate relationships with their new parents (Rathbun, DiVirgilio, & Waldfogel, 1958).

- In a study of 53 children who had had psychological disorders ranging from delinquency to depression, 35 had recovered completely by late adolescence. The researchers concluded, "The emotionally traumatized child is not doomed, the parents' early mistakes are not irrevocable" (Thomas & Chess, 1984).

- Another study followed 200 disturbed children who had been referred to a child guidance clinic for treatment when they were, on the average, 9 years old. But as young adults, ages 18 to 27, most of those children had improved enormously. Except for the most seriously disturbed children, the researchers said, "there seems to be little continuity between child and adult disturbances" (Cass & Thomas, 1979).

- A review of 45 studies of children who had been sexually abused found that these children had more emotional and behavioral symptoms than nonabused children, including fears, poor self-esteem, and oversexualized behavior; the more severe and prolonged the abuse, the more severe the child's symptoms. Yet a third of the children had no symptoms at all, and about two-thirds recovered during the first 12 to 18 months after the abuse, especially if they had a supportive family environment (Kendall-Tackett, Williams, & Finkelhor, 1993).

- Although *more* children of alcoholic or abusive parents become alcoholic or abusive as adults than do children of nondisturbed parents, *most* of them do not. After reviewing ten years of studies of children of alcoholic parents, two researchers concluded that "parental alcoholism is undoubtedly disruptive to family life" but that "neither all nor a major portion of the population of children from alcoholic homes are inevitably doomed to psychological disorder" (West & Prinz, 1987). Similarly, as we noted in Chapter 2, being physically beaten in childhood makes a person more likely to be an abusive parent, but fully 70 percent do not repeat their parents' cruelties (Kaufman & Zigler, 1987).

Because of these heartening studies, some psychologists are pinpointing the origins of *resilience* in the children of violent, abusive, or alcoholic parents (Cowen et al., 1990; Garmezy, 1985, 1991; Werner, 1989). Many of these resilient children get love and attention from the nondisturbed parent or another doting adult. They have an informal support network for advice and aid. They have good experiences in school. They have found activities and hobbies that they do well at, that provide solace and self-esteem. They have acquired a sense of meaning about life. Most of all, they are determined not to repeat their histories.

We do not wish to imply, in reporting this optimistic news, that a painful or traumatic childhood is easy to recover from. Although this chapter has emphasized the joys and challenges of child development, there is a more serious issue to consider: whether children themselves are valued by the culture in which they develop. Unlike Canada, Sweden, and most European nations, the United States places a low priority on child-care services and education; one in five American children lives in poverty, more than in any other industrialized nation (see Figure 13.6). American professionals who work with children earn less than people who work with adults, even within the same field (pediatricians earn less than internists, elementary school teachers earn less than college teachers). And, most tragically, the physical and emotional abuse and victimization of children continues to be widespread (Finkelhor & Dziuba-Leatherman, 1994).

Keep in mind, therefore, that although some children are able to survive early traumas, this doesn't mean that childhood experiences are insignificant or that society can afford to be indifferent to children's welfare. But as children develop, they are subject to other influences, too. They outgrow certain habits

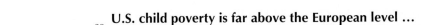

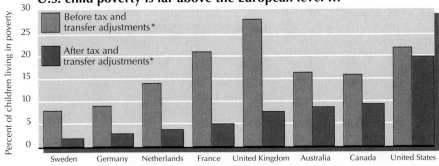

*Includes all income tax policies and transfers, such as cash benefits, food stamps, etc.

■ **Figure 13.6   Living Conditions for Children Around the World**

According to the United Nations Children's Fund Progress of Nations report, children in the United States are more likely to live in poverty than children in any other industrialized nation. Only the United Kingdom has a higher child poverty rate than the United States, but its social welfare programs for the poor sharply reduce that rate to less than 1 in 10. (Graph adapted from the San Francisco Chronicle, *September 23, 1993.)*

and attitudes, even as they cling to others that have been rewarded and encouraged. Things happen to children and adults that *can* overturn the effects of earlier experiences. Perhaps the most powerful reason for the breaks between childhood and adulthood is that children actively interpret their experiences, a point we have emphasized. This is the reason for the gap between what parents try to teach and what children learn, and between what children learn and what they take with them into adulthood.

Taking Psychology with You

Bringing Up Baby

How should you treat your children? Should you be strict or lenient, powerful or permissive? Should you require your child to stop having tantrums, to clean up his or her room, to be polite? How can parents learn to rear children who are competent, kind, responsible, and emotionally healthy? According to many research studies, the following guidelines are effective in teaching children to control aggressive impulses; have good self-control, high self-esteem, and confidence; and be cheerful, thoughtful, and helpful (Schulman & Mekler, 1994):

• *Be consistent in enforcing specific rules and demands.* Do not give in to the child's whining or tantrums or let the child break rules behind your back. Inconsistency—letting the child draw on the walls on Tuesday but not on Thursday—encourages the undesirable behavior by rewarding it intermittently.

• *Set high expectations that are appropriate to the child's age, and teach the child how to meet them.*

Some parents make few demands on their children, either unintentionally or because they believe a parent should not impose standards. Others have many demands, such as requiring children to be polite, help with chores, control their anger, be thoughtful of others, and do well in school. The children of parents who make few demands tend to be aggressive, impulsive, and immature. The children of parents who have high expectations tend to be helpful and above average in competence and self-confidence. Of course, the demands must be appropriate for the child's age. You can't expect 2-year-olds to dress themselves, and before you can expect children to get up on time by themselves they have to know how to work an alarm clock.

• *Explain, explain, explain.* Induction—telling a child *why* you have applied a rule—is an essential guideline. Punitive methods ("do it because I say so") may result in compliance, but the child will tend to disobey as soon as you are out of sight. Explanations also teach children how to reason and understand; they reward curiosity and open-mindedness. This doesn't mean you have to argue with a 4-year-old about the merits of table manners. But, while setting standards for your children, you can also allow them to express disagreements and feelings.

- *Notice, approve of, and reward good behavior.* Many parents tend to punish the behavior they dislike, a form of attention that may actually be rewarding to the child (see Chapter 7). It is much more effective to praise the behavior you *do* want, which teaches the child what is right.

- *Use induction and empathy.* Call the child's attention to the effect of his or her actions on others, and teach the child to take another person's point of view. Vague orders, such as "Don't fight!", are less effective than showing the child how his fighting disrupts and hurts others. For boys especially, there is a strong negative relationship between aggres-sion and empathy: The higher the one, the lower the other (Feshbach et al., 1983).

We know that many people get huffy at the notion of using induction with their children, saying "My parents hit me and I turned out okay, so why shouldn't I do the same with my kids?" Some people scoff at the idea of explaining family rules to a 6-year-old. People often care deeply for even the most authoritarian of parents, and therefore they may equate criticisms of the authoritarian approach with criticisms of their parents who, after all, may only have been doing their best. But if we are willing to examine the evidence and question some assumptions, we will be open to the lessons that developmental psychology has to offer.

Finally, all of these guidelines depend on how the child reacts to them and how the child interprets your actions. You cannot create the "ideal child," that is, one who is an exact replica of you. But you *can* expect the best from your children—their best, not yours.

Summary

1. Prenatal development consists of the *germinal, embryonic,* and *fetal* stages. Certain drugs and diseases can cross the placental barrier and affect the fetus's development, including measles, toxic chemicals, some sexually transmitted diseases, cigarettes, alcohol (which in excess can cause *fetal alcohol syndrome*), illegal drugs, and even over-the-counter medications.

2. Babies are born with basic motor reflexes that are necessary for survival, including the grasping, startle, sucking, and rooting reflexes. At first, babies can see only a distance of 8 inches, but within a few weeks they can distinguish where something is and what it is. Babies also develop *synchrony* of pace and rhythm with their caretakers.

3. Physical development is very rapid during the first year. On the average, babies sit without support at 7 months, crawl at 9 months, and take their first steps at 13 months. But many aspects of maturation depend on cultural practices, such as whether the baby sleeps alone or with the mother and the sources of the infant's attachment.

4. Jean Piaget proposed that children's cognitive development depends on their current developmental stage and their experience in the world. Children's thinking changes and adapts through two processes, *assimilation* and *accommodation.* Piaget proposed four stages of cognitive development: *sensory-motor* (birth to age 2), during which the child learns *object permanence; preoperational* (ages 2 to 7), during which language and symbolic thought develop; *concrete operations* (ages 6 or 7 to 11); and *formal operations* (age 12 to adulthood). These age brackets are only guidelines; Piaget emphasized the sequence of the stages rather than their pace.

5. In evaluating Piaget's theory, researchers find that young children have more cognitive abilities, at earlier ages, than Piaget thought; they are not always egocentric in their thinking, and by the age of 4 or 5 they have developed a *theory of mind* to account for their own and other people's behavior; and cultural practices affect the pace and content of cognitive development. But the sequence of development that Piaget observed does hold up.

6. Infants are responsive to the pitch, intensity, and sound of language, which may be why adults in many cultures speak to babies in *motherese.* At 4 to 6 months they begin to recognize the sounds of their own language; and they

go through a "babbling phase" from age 6 months to a year. At about 1 year, one-word utterances begin, as do symbolic gestures. At age 2, children speak in two- or three-word *telegraphic* sentences that convey a variety of messages, and they begin to acquire new words rapidly.

7. *Gender socialization* (or *sex typing*) is the process by which boys and girls learn what it means to be "masculine" or "feminine," as distinct from acquiring a *gender identity,* which is the cognitive understanding that one is biologically male or female.

8. Biological psychologists account for gender differences in behavior and sex-typed activities in terms of genetics, hormones, and brain lateralization. Learning theorists study the subtle rewards, punishments, and models that cause children to become sex typed. Cognitive psychologists study how children develop *gender schemas* of "male" and "female" categories and qualities, which in turn shape their sex-typed behavior. Gender schemas tend to be inflexible at first but often assimilate new information as the child cognitively matures. A fourth important influence on gender socialization is the child's *context and situation.*

9. Lawrence Kohlberg's theory of moral development proposes three levels of moral reasoning, each with two stages: *preconventional morality* (based on rules, punishment, and self-interest), *conventional morality* (based on relationships and rules of justice and law), and *postconventional ("principled") morality* (based on higher principles of human rights).

10. Evidence supports the universality of Kohlberg's middle three stages, but the approach itself has been criticized on several grounds: It reflects verbal sophistication rather than moral reasoning, and thus is biased in favor of educated individuals; moral reasoning is often unrelated to people's behavior; and people's moral reasoning is not consistent across situations or ages—people often "regress" to a lower stage. Carol Gilligan's theory, that men and women have equally valuable but different forms of moral reasoning, has been popular but unsupported by most research.

11. Moral development also depends on the emergence of the "moral emotions"—empathy, shame, and guilt. Empathy takes different forms, depending on the child's age and cognitive abilities: *global* empathy, *egocentric* empathy, *empathy for another's feelings,* and *empathy for another's life condition.* Shame develops with the sense of self, around age 2; guilt develops when children have an internal standard of behavior, about age 3 or 4.

12. Parental methods of discipline, such as *power assertion* and *induction,* have different consequences for a child's moral behavior. Power assertion is associated with children who have a sense of external control, are aggressive and destructive, and show a lack of empathy and moral behavior. Induction is associated with children who develop empathy and internalized moral standards and who can resist temptation. In general, *authoritative* parents have better results with their children than do *authoritarian* or *permissive* parents. Altruistic (helpful) children tend to come from families in which they contribute to the family's well-being, carry out many tasks, and respect parental authority, and in which parents set limits without being arbitrary.

13. Adolescence begins with *puberty.* In girls, puberty is signaled by *menarche* and the development of breasts; in boys, it begins with the onset of nocturnal emissions and the development of the testes and scrotum. Hormones are responsible for *secondary sex characteristics.* Boys and girls who enter puberty early tend to have a more difficult later adjustment than those who enter puberty later than average. One reason may be that early puberty exacerbates existing problems of childhood.

14. Most adolescents do not go through extreme emotional turmoil. Most have a relatively calm adolescence, some face specific difficulties, and some

have serious problems. New research questions the universality and meaning of "separation" from the parent.

15. With the exception of serious disorders, many infant and childhood problems are outgrown by late adolescence or adulthood, and most children of alcoholic or abusive parents do not repeat their parents' problems. Psychologists now study the origins of such children's resilience as well as the consequences of childhoods of poverty and trauma.

Key Terms

maturation *477*

germinal, embryonic, fetal stages *478*

teratogens *478*

fetal alcohol syndrome *478*

motor reflexes *480*

synchrony *482*

Jean Piaget *485*

assimilation *486*

accommodation *486*

sensory-motor stage *486*

object permanence *486*

representational thought *486*

preoperational stage *486*

operations *486*

egocentric thought *487*

conservation *487*

concrete operations stage *487*

formal operations stage *487*

theory of mind *489*

motherese *490*

telegraphic speech *491*

sex vs. gender *492*

gender identity *493*

gender socialization (sex typing) *493*

gender schema *495*

preconventional, conventional, postconventional stages of moral reasoning (Kohlberg) *498*

empathy *500*

shame and guilt *501*

power assertion *502*

induction *503*

authoritarian, permissive, and authoritative styles *504*

puberty *507*

menarche *508*

secondary sex characteristics *508*

14

Health, Stress, and Coping

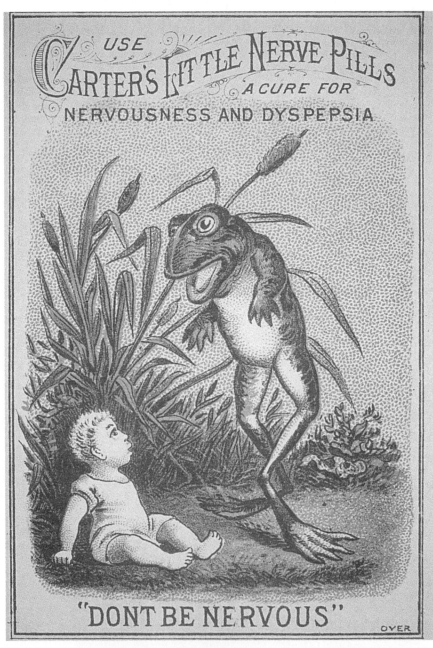

A century ago, people took Carter's Little Nerve Pills to cure stress and indigestion. Our age has its own pills and potions, but psychologists find that stress, illness, and well-being reflect complex interactions between mind and body.

Rule No. 1 is don't sweat the small stuff.
Rule No. 2 is it's all small stuff.
And, if you can't fight and you can't flee, flow.

■ Physician Robert Eliot ■

- Bill and his father have been battling for years. Bill feels that his father is always ready to criticize him for the slightest flaw. After Bill left home he gained some perspective on their relationship, but one thing hasn't changed. Every time his father comes to visit, Bill breaks out in a rash.

- Tanya lost her apartment and most of her possessions in the Northridge earthquake in southern California. A year later, she finds it difficult to talk about her continuing anxieties, sure that no one will understand or sympathize.

- Josh and Jenny are quarreling more and more lately, and their fights have become increasingly abusive and unpleasant. In the aftermath of every argument, they both feel bitter, depressed, and resentful.

- Lucy gets stuck in a massive traffic jam and is late for class. As she walks in the door, her instructor reprimands her for being late. Later, rushing to get her notes together for an overdue research paper, Lucy spills coffee all over herself and the documents. By noon she has a splitting headache and feels exhausted.

Like a bolt from the blue, a stressful event can strike at any time.

All of these people are certainly under "stress," but, as you see, their experiences are far from the same. Stress can be caused by occasional but recurring conflicts (Bill and his father), a traumatic experience that shatters your sense of safety (Tanya), recurrent arguments with someone you are close to (Josh and Jenny), or a collection of small irritations that wear you down (Lucy). Is there a link between these stressors and health or illness? In this chapter, we will explore this question by looking at findings from two fields. *Health psychology* addresses psychological factors that influence how people stay healthy, why they become ill, and how they respond when they do get ill. A related field, *behavioral medicine,* takes an interdisciplinary approach to health and illness, drawing on findings from medicine, nutrition, physiology, psychology, and other fields.

Psychology and medicine have typically taken a *pathogenic* approach to the topic of health (from *patho-,* "disease" or "suffering," and -*genic,* "producing"). The pathogenic approach focuses on why people get sick. It divides the world into the healthy and the unhealthy, even though many healthy people sometimes feel poorly and many sick people are able to function fairly well. It emphasizes people who are at high risk of becoming ill, ignoring the majority who, although at risk, stay well. It asks, "How can we eradicate this or that stressor?" But health psychologists also want to know what generates health, and so they take a *salutogenic* approach (from *salut,* "health") (Antonovsky, 1987). The salutogenic approach studies not only those who become ill but also the exceptions—the people who theoretically should become sick but don't, the people who transcend difficult problems instead of giving in to them. It asks, "How can we learn to live, and live well, with stressors, and possibly even turn them to our advantage?" It seeks to understand both wellness and illness.

Modern research in health psychology is extremely promising. But unfortunately some of its findings have been misused to foster two common misconceptions: that illness is "all in the mind" and that curing illness just requires the right attitude of "mind over matter." In this chapter we will try to show how the study of health psychology can give us a better appreciation of the complexities of mind and body and of the ways in which mind and body influence one another.

■ THE NATURE OF STRESS

Throughout history, stress has been one of those things that everyone has experienced but few can define. Why has it been so difficult to agree on something that all of us have felt?

Alarm and Adaptation

In his 1956 book *The Stress of Life,* Canadian physician Hans Selye (1907–1982) greatly advanced the study of stress. Selye noted that many environmental factors—heat, cold, pain, toxins, viruses, and so on—can throw the body out of balance. These factors, called *stressors,* force the body to respond by mobilizing its resources and preparing the individual to fight or flee. Citing data from many animal studies, Selye concluded that "stress" consists of a series of physiological reactions that occur in three phases:

1. In the *alarm phase,* the organism mobilizes to meet the threat with a basic package of biological responses that allow the person or animal to escape from danger no matter what the stressor is: crossing a busy street or avoiding a cross rattlesnake.

2. In the *resistance phase,* the organism attempts to resist or cope with a threat that cannot be avoided. During this phase, the body's physiological responses are in high gear—a response to the original stressor—but this very mechanism makes the body more susceptible to other stressors. For example, when your body has mobilized to fight off the flu, you may find that you are more easily annoyed by minor frustrations. In most cases, the body will eventually adapt to the stressor and return to normal.

3. In the *exhaustion phase,* which occurs if the stressor persists, the body's resources are overwhelmed. Depleted of energy, the body becomes vulnerable to fatigue, physical problems, and eventually illness. The same reactions that allow the body to resist short-term stressors—a boost in energy, tensed muscles, reduced sensitivity to pain, the shutting down of digestion, elevated blood pressure—are unhealthy as long-range responses. Tense muscles can cause headache and neck pain. Increased blood pressure can become chronic hypertension. The closing off of digestion can eventually lead to digestive disorders.

Stress is a bane of modern civilization because our physiological alarm mechanism now chimes too often. Today, when the typical stressor is a mammoth traffic jam and not a mammoth mammal, the fight-or-flight response often gets revved up with nowhere to go. When your teacher announces an unexpected quiz, you don't really need to respond as if you were fighting for your life, but your body will still sweat to dispose of excess body heat. When you see your former sweetheart with someone else, you don't really need to breathe hard to get oxygen to your muscles, as you would if you were fleeing to safety.

Not all stress is bad, however. Some stress, which Selye called **eustress,** is positive and feels good, even if it also requires the body to produce short-term

■ **eustress [YOU-stress]**
Positive or beneficial stress.

Who has more stress, and whose stress counts? Many media stories emphasize the stress faced by white-collar workers and managers of companies. They are less concerned with the stress faced by assembly-line workers and blue-collar laborers. Why do you think this might be so? Which group do you suppose is under more stress: people in highly competitive and complicated jobs, or people in boring and predictable jobs? Actually, researchers find that "it is not the bosses but the bossed who suffer most from job stress" (Karasek & Theorell, 1990).

energy: competing in an athletic event, falling in love, working hard on a project you enjoy. Selye did not believe that all stress could be avoided or that people should aim for a stress-free life, which is an impossible goal anyway. The goal is to minimize wear and tear on the system, not get rid of it.

Selye recognized that psychological stressors, such as emotional conflict or grief, can be as important as physical stressors, such as heat, toxic chemicals, or noise. He also observed that some factors *mediate* between the stressor and the stress. A comfortable climate or a nutritious diet, for example, can soften the impact of an environmental stressor such as pollution. Conversely, a harsh climate or a poor diet can make such stressors worse. But by and large, Selye concentrated on the biological responses that result from a person's attempt to adapt to environmental demands. A diagram of his view would look like this:

Stressor → Physiological stress reactions → Illness or healthy adaptation

Later studies, however, found that stress is not a purely biological condition that leads directly to illness (Cohen & Williamson, 1991). First, between the stressor and physiological reactions to it are *qualities of the individual,* such as personality traits and perceptions: An event that is stressful or enraging for one person may be challenging for another and boring for a third. Losing a job, traveling to China, or having "too much" work to do is stressful to some people and not to others.

Second, between the stress and its consequences is *how the individual behaves when under stress and how he or she copes with it.* Not all individuals who are under stress behave in the same way. Some drink too much, drive recklessly, or fail to take care of themselves, all of which can increase their risk of illness or accident. Some cope well to reduce the effects of stress, and others seem not to manage well at all.

For these reasons, most psychologists prefer a definition of stress that includes aspects of the environment, aspects of the individual, and how the two interact. In this view, **psychological stress** is the result of an exchange between the person and the environment, in which the person believes that the situation strains or overwhelms his or her resources and is endangering his or her

■ **psychological stress**
The result of a relationship between the person and the environment, in which the person believes the situation is overwhelming and threatens his or her ability to cope.

well-being (Lazarus & Folkman, 1984). Some researchers probe the physiological mechanisms in the immune system that transform stress into illness; some try to specify which stressors are particularly risky; and some study the qualities of the person and the person's life that make some stressors worse than others.

Illness and Immunology

An early approach to the psychological origins of illness came from the field of *psychosomatic medicine,* which developed in psychiatry at the turn of the century. The word **psychosomatic** refers to the interaction of mind (*psyche*) and body (*soma*). Sigmund Freud promoted the view that physical symptoms are often the result of unconscious conflicts, and other psychodynamic theorists maintained that many disorders—such as rheumatoid arthritis, hypertension, asthma, ulcers, and migraine headaches—are caused by neurotic personality patterns. (We now know they aren't.) These early theories led to the popular but mistaken view that a "psychosomatic" illness is one that is "all in the mind." The modern field of psychosomatic medicine, however, recognizes the reciprocal nature of the mind-body relationship—not only how mind affects body, but also how body affects mind. Researchers today, therefore, define a psychosomatic illness as a physical disorder that is affected by emotional and psychological factors, but not necessarily caused by them.

In the 1980s, scientists interested in exploring the links between the psychological and physical processes involved in illness created an interdisciplinary field with the cumbersome name **psychoneuroimmunology,** sometimes referred to as PNI: "psycho" for psychological processes such as emotions and perceptions, "neuro" for the nervous and endocrine systems, and "immunology" for the immune system (Andersen, Kiecolt-Glaser, & Glaser, 1994; Kiecolt-Glaser & Glaser, 1989). These researchers hope to explain, for example, why, of two people who are exposed to a flu virus, one is sick all winter and the other doesn't even get the sniffles.

The immune system is designed to do two things: recognize foreign substances (*antigens*), such as flu viruses, bacteria, and tumor cells, and destroy or deactivate them. Basically, the immune system has two types of white blood cells: *lymphocytes,* whose primary job is to recognize and destroy foreign cells, and *phagocytes,* whose job is to ingest and eliminate those cells.

To defend the body against foreign invaders, the immune system deploys different cells as weapons, sometimes together and sometimes alone, depending on the nature of the enemy. Several kinds of lymphocytes aid in this attack. *Natural killer cells* are important in tumor detection and rejection. *B cells* (so called because they are released from the bone marrow) are responsible for producing antibodies, highly specific molecules that recognize a target antigen. After the initial response to a specific antigen, "memory B cells" are created to produce a faster and more efficient attack on subsequent exposures to it; this is why inoculations against chicken pox and flu are effective. Finally, *T cells* (so called because they mature in the thymus) make direct contact with the antigen. They too come in several versions. *Killer T cells* help destroy antigens that they have been exposed to previously. *Helper T cells* enhance and regulate the immune response; they are the primary target of the HIV virus that causes AIDS. Prolonged stress can suppress some or many of these cells that fight disease and infection.

For example, researchers have found that herpes outbreaks are more likely to occur among medical students with herpes when the students are feeling lonely or are under exam pressure. Loneliness and tension apparently suppress the immune system's capabilities, permitting the existing herpes virus to erupt (Kiecolt-Glaser et al., 1985a). In another study, 420 people heroically volun-

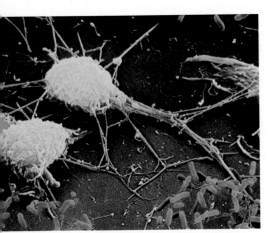

Like a fantastical Hollywood creature, a phagocyte reaches out with extended "arms" to ensnare unwitting bacteria.

■ **psychosomatic**
A term that describes the interaction between a physical illness or condition and psychological states; literally, mind (psyche) and body (soma).

■ **psychoneuroimmunology (PNI)**
The study of the relationships among psychology, the nervous system, and the immune system.

teered to fight in the war against the common cold. Some were given nose drops containing viruses known to cause a cold's miserable symptoms and others received uncontaminated nose drops. Everyone was then quarantined for a week. The results: People who were under high stress, who felt their lives were "unpredictable, uncontrollable, and overwhelming," were twice as likely to develop colds as those reporting low levels of stress (Cohen, Tyrrell, & Smith, 1991).

Some Sources of Stress

We have seen that stressors do not lead directly to illness. But are some stressors more likely than others to affect the immune system and thus lead eventually to poor health? To find out, some psychologists study the significant events that disrupt our lives; some count the irritating nuisances; and others emphasize continuing pressures in the environment.

Bereavement and Tragedy. One of the most powerful stressors in anyone's life is the loss of a loved one or close relationship, especially through divorce or the death of a spouse. In the two years following bereavement, widowed people are more susceptible to illness and physical ailments, and their mortality rate is higher than expected (Stroebe, Stroebe, & Domittner, 1988). Divorce also often takes a long-term health toll: Divorced adults have higher rates of heart disease, pneumonia, and other diseases than comparable adults who are not divorced (Jacobson, 1983).

Bereaved and divorced people may be vulnerable to illness because, feeling unhappy, they don't sleep well, they stop eating properly, and they consume more drugs and cigarettes. However, animal and human studies suggest that separation *itself* also creates cardiovascular changes, a lowered white blood cell count, and other abnormal responses of the immune system (Laudenslager, 1988). You may recall that attachment is a biological need of the species; indeed, broken attachments affect us at a basic cellular level. But the quality of the attachment is as important as its presence. Unhappily married individuals show the same decline in immune function as unhappy divorced people (Kiecolt-Glaser et al., 1987a, 1993).

These findings do not mean that everyone who loses a loved one gets sick or has an impaired immune system. In a study of 202 women who had breast cancer and who were interviewed about stressful events in their lives at 4, 24, and 42 months after the initial diagnosis and treatment, there was *no* relationship between stress and recurrence of the cancer. Half of the women had experienced a painful emotional event, but many of these women remained well, including all 13 who had suffered the death of a husband, child, or grandchild. And many women who did have a relapse of cancer had not experienced a traumatic event (Barraclough et al., 1992).

Daily Hassles. Some psychologists argue that we handle most big problems, even the occasional tragedies, relatively well. It's the daily hassles that get us down—everyday irritations such as thoughtless friends, traffic jams, bad weather, loud noise, crowds, quarrels, broken plumbing, lost keys, and sick cats. One significant hassle that is hard to escape is loud noise, which impairs the ability to think and work even when people believe they have adjusted to it. Children in noisy schools, such as those near airports, tend to have higher blood pressure, be more distractable, and have more difficulty with puzzles and math problems than do children in quieter schools, even when factors such as social class are taken into account (Cohen et al., 1980). In adults, noise contributes to cardiovascular problems, ulcers, irritability, fatigue, and aggressiveness, probably because of overstimulation of the autonomic nervous system

(Taylor, 1991). The noise that is most stressful to people, however, is noise *they cannot control*. The rock song that you choose to listen to at jackhammer loudness may be pleasurable to you but intolerable—stressful—to anyone who does not share your musical taste.

A similar pattern of findings is true of crowding. As with noise, crowds become most stressful when they curtail your sense of freedom and control. They are detrimental to health and intellectual performance not when you *are* crowded but when you *feel* crowded or trapped. Thus people who work without interruptions in a densely packed room feel less crowded and are less stressed than those who work with fewer people but lots of interruptions (Taylor, 1991). Chronic residential crowding—whether in prisons, dorms, or households—is associated with psychological distress, but this link occurs primarily when people feel they are having too many interactions that are *unwanted,* intrusive, and inescapable (Evans & Lepore, 1993). Reactions to crowding also depend in part on culture. At one time, environmental psychologists thought that crowding was a direct cause of crime, juvenile delinquency, and other urban ills. But this theory did not hold up when researchers controlled for income, class, ethnicity, and cultural differences. In Tokyo, where population density exceeds that of any U.S. city, people are accustomed to crowding, and it is not associated with urban problems such as crime.

Any major event can increase the number of hassles a person must contend with, thus making a person more intolerant of small irritants. Divorce, for instance, often entails the upsetting experience of moving and selling a home, and perhaps financial worries and custody questions. When a person must cope with such major concerns, nuisances that would otherwise seem trivial, such as a leaky faucet, can suddenly seem "too much." By and large, however, people's reports of being hassled are independent of specific events. Among police officers, for instance, the greatest stressors are not dramatic dangers but daily paperwork, annoyance with the press, and the snail-like pace of the judicial system (Grier, 1982).

Of course, when people report that something is a hassle, they are really reporting their feelings about it. The activity itself might be neutral: Cooking, weeding the garden, or running errands can be a burdensome chore to some

These airplane passengers, frustrated about a canceled flight, show the many possible responses to life's hassles: amused friendliness, sullen acceptance, efforts to get information, and just plain gloom.

and a refreshing change of pace to others, depending on the circumstances. So the effect of hassles, like that of stressful events generally, will depend on the person's reaction to them. Research finds that hassles are hazardous to health primarily for people who tend to be very anxious and quick to overreact (Kohn, Lafreniere, & Gurevich, 1991). Every little thing, to them, feels like the last straw.

Continuing Problems. People at the lower end of the socioeconomic ladder have worse health and higher mortality rates for almost every disease and medical condition than do those on the upper rungs (Adler et al., 1994). One obvious reason is that poor people cannot afford good medical care and preventive examinations. But another has to do with the kinds of stressors they live with.

Most stress researchers believe that the most serious threat to health occurs when stress becomes *interminable and uncontrollable:* living in a war zone or a high-crime neighborhood; being chronically unemployed; living with a violent parent; having repeated experiences of discrimination; feeling caught in a situation you can't escape. Thus the workers who most suffer from job stress and who are at greatest risk of a variety of illnesses are not executives and managers, but those who have no say in job-related decisions, who have little opportunity to exercise initiative, and who are trapped doing repetitive tasks (Karasek & Theorell, 1990). The women who are most at risk of heart disease are female clerical workers who feel they have no support from their bosses, who are stuck in low-paying jobs without hope of promotion, and who have financial problems at home (Haynes & Feinleib, 1980). And a recent Swedish study, which compared 569 colorectal cancer patients with 510 matched but cancer-free controls, found that those who reported a history of severe workplace problems over the past decade had 5.5 times the risk of developing colon or rectal cancers. This finding held even when the researchers controlled for diet and other factors linked to these malignancies (Courtney et al., 1993).

Prolonged stress is also associated with hypertension (high blood pressure), which can lead to kidney disease, strokes, and heart attacks. Hypertension and heart disease have been called "diseases of civilization" because they occur largely in people living in high-pressure urban environments. Hypertension, which in the United States is far more likely to occur among blacks than whites, is partly a result of living in neighborhoods characterized by poverty, poor housing, drug use, high divorce and unemployment rates, crime, and greater exposure to chemical contamination (Anderson, 1991). But the environment interacts with diet, such as fast foods that are high in sodium, and a genetic susceptibility to the negative effects of salt. African-Americans are more likely to be salt sensitive, possibly, as one leading theory holds, because over many centuries their ancestors adapted to living in a hot African climate. (When people sweat, they lose salt, which is necessary for the regulation of body systems. A mechanism that would permit retention of salt would therefore be evolutionarily adapative in a hot climate.) When people with such a genetic vulnerability are then placed in a high-stress environment, the result is high blood pressure (Weder & Schork, 1994).

In general, these kinds of stressors—bereavement and tragedy, daily hassles, and continuing problems—are related to health. But they are not the whole story. Individuals differ considerably in how their immune systems respond to such stressors. Some people show impaired immune function as a result of bereavement, marital fighting, and school exams, yet many individuals show no immune changes at all (Manuck et al., 1991). Something else, as we will see next, is going on between the stressful event and the physical response to it.

Middle-class stress might seem a luxury to people whose health is chronically jeopardized by poverty, exposure to toxic materials, malnutrition, and lack of access to medical care.

Quick QUIZ

We hope these questions are not sources of stress for you.

1. Steve is unexpectedly called on in class to discuss a question. He hasn't the faintest idea of the answer, and he feels his heart start to pound and his palms to sweat. According to Selye, he is in the _____ phase of his stress response.

2. Which of these stressors has the strongest relationship to immune problems and illness? (a) listening to loud music in your room, (b) listening to your roommate's rotten choice of loud music in your room, (c) being swept up in a crowd of people celebrating New Year's Eve, (d) having a high-paying job that requires you to make many important decisions.

3. Maria has worked as a file clerk for 17 years. Which aspect of the job is likely to be *most* stressful for her? (a) the speed of the work, (b) the predictable routine, (c) feeling trapped, (d) the daily demands from her boss.

Answers:

1. alarm 2. b 3. c

■ THE INDIVIDUAL SIDE OF HEALTH AND WELL-BEING

We have seen that stressors themselves are only part of the stress-illness story. How does personality fit in? Certainly it seems that some people manufacture their own misery. Send them to a beach for a week to escape the pressures of civilization, and they bring along a suitcase full of worries and irritations. We now turn to four aspects of personality that affect how people respond to stressors: negative emotions, pessimism or optimism, healthy habits, and a sense of control.

Personality and Emotions

If sick people are angrier than others, does that mean that anger caused their illnesses? Can you think of other explanations for a relationship between emotions and disease?

Many people believe that certain emotions are hazardous to health, which is why we often hear remarks like "She was so depressed, it's no wonder she got cancer" or "He worried himself into an ulcer over that job." Before we can conclude that negative emotions directly lead to illness, however, we must consider four other possible links between emotion and disease (Friedman & Booth-Kewley, 1987):

• *The disease may cause the emotion.* Many physicians see patients who are angry, depressed, or anxious; it is easy to conclude that the anger, depression, or anxiety must have *caused* the sickness. But the reverse may actually be true: Being sick may have caused the negative emotion. Likewise, people often jump to the comparable conclusion that happiness causes wellness. In one study of women with cancer, those who had expressed higher levels of joy at the start of the research were likely to live longer than less joyful patients (Levy et al., 1988). That sounds like a recipe for joy, which can't hurt anyone! One reason the women were more joyful, however, was that they had fewer cancerous sites and their doctors were more optimistic. In short, it is likely that the slow course of the disease was causing the women's joy and their extended survival, and not that joy slowed the cancer.

- *Unhealthy habits may cause the disease.* Before we can conclude that "an anxious person gets ulcers," we must rule out the possibility that people who worry a lot are also more likely to smoke or drink. Unfortunately, many studies that examine the links between emotion and disease do not take health habits into account.

- *Something else entirely may cause both the emotion and the disease.* Many risk factors may combine, over time, to produce illness. Perhaps an overresponsive nervous system leads to feelings of frequent anger and, independently, to the development of heart disease.

- *Mind and body interact.* Chronic anxiety or depression often lead to unhealthy practices, which could cause physical changes, which could make one's negative emotions worse, which could keep one from taking care of oneself, which could speed up the course of the disease . . . you get the idea.

Among health psychologists, there are currently two opposing views about the relationship between negative emotion and disease. One side says that the way people manage and express anger, sadness, and fear *predicts with great accuracy* whether they will become ill—in fact, whether they will get cancer, heart disease, or some other disease (Eysenck, 1990, 1993; Grossarth-Maticek et al., 1991). The other side says, in essence, that the way people manage emotion *has almost nothing to do* with becoming ill or surviving serious illness (Angell, 1985; Greenwald, 1992). They point out that peptic ulcers, for example, which were thought for many years to be caused by worry or suppressed anger, are caused by a bacterium and have nothing to do with emotion (Monmaney, 1993).

Because of all the possible links between emotion and illness, this debate has been difficult to resolve. Consider the story of the *Type A behavior pattern,* a set of qualities proposed two decades ago as a predictor of heart disease, the nation's leading cause of death (Friedman & Rosenman, 1974). Although the Type A pattern has been measured in different, often inconsistent ways, it basically describes people who are constantly struggling to achieve, have a sense of time urgency, are irritable, and are impatient at anyone who gets in their way. Type B people are calmer and less intense. At the time, it seemed logical that Type As would be at greater risk of heart trouble than Type Bs.

It turned out, however, that different tasks and situations produce different physiological responses in the same people, and being highly reactive to stress and challenge is *not* in itself a risk factor in heart disease (Krantz & Manuck, 1984). Type A people do set themselves a fast work pace and a heavy workload, but many cope better than Type B people who have a lighter workload, and without paying a high physiological price. Further, people who are highly involved in their jobs, even if they work hard, have a low incidence of heart disease. "There'd be nothing wrong with us fast-moving Type As," said a friend of ours, "if it weren't for all those slow-moving Type Bs."

These findings led to more research, which revealed that something about Type A behavior is indeed dangerous to health: hostility. Having your heart rate shoot up in response to a challenging task is far less risky to your health than having your heart rate shoot up because you are quick to anger or fight a lot with your friends and family (Ewart & Kolodner, 1994; Lassner, Matthews, & Stony, 1994). In a major longitudinal study, men who were chronically angry and resentful and who had a hostile attitude toward others were five times as likely as nonhostile men to get coronary heart disease and other ailments, even after controlling for other risk factors such as smoking (Williams, 1989; Williams, Barefoot, & Shekelle, 1985). (See Figure 14.1.)

The next step was to find out what kind of hostility was hazardous. *Neurotic hostility,* the kind felt by people who are complaining and irritable, is not related to heart disease. But *antagonistic hostility,* which characterizes those who

Which is more stressful for this Type A man—his workload or his emotional reaction to it?

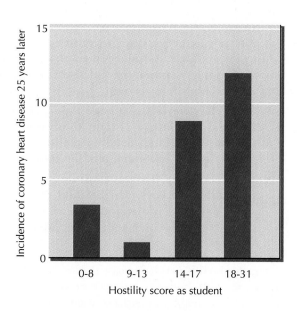

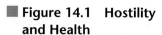

▪ **Figure 14.1 Hostility and Health**

Men who had the highest hostility scores as young medical students were the most likely to have coronary heart disease 25 years later (Williams, Barefoot, & Shekelle, 1985).

are aggressive, confrontational, rude, cynical, and uncooperative, seems to be the "toxic" variety that is linked to heart disease (Dembroski & Costa, 1988; Marshall et al., 1994; Smith, Sanders, & Alexander, 1990). At least this is true for men; the relationship between hostility and heart disease in women is less clear because women have been omitted from many of the longitudinal studies of anger and heart disease. Men are more likely than women to have higher rates of cynical, antagonistic hostility at all ages, however, and there is as yet little evidence that hostility alone is related to heart disease in women (Thomas, 1993).

If the relationship between anger and illness is complex, the relationship between depression and illness is even more so. Some studies find that chronic depression is associated with aberrations in the immune system, presumably the precursor to illness (Herbert & Cohen, 1993; Weisse, 1992). Yet a review of 22 studies found that most reported *no* immune-system differences between people with major depressive disorders and control subjects (Stein, Miller, & Trestman, 1991). Moreover, a ten-year study of a nationally representative sample of 6,403 women and men found that those who had depressive symptoms or even clinical depression were *not* more likely to develop cancer (Zonderman, Costa, & McCrae, 1989). To confuse the picture further, some studies find that depressed men who are infected with the HIV virus lose certain disease-fighting cells in the immune system and thus become vulnerable to infection and AIDS-related diseases more quickly than HIV-infected men who are not depressed (Burack et al., 1993). Yet other large-scale studies have found no links among depression, psychological distress, immune function, and outbreaks of illness among men with HIV (Lyketsos et al., 1993; Rabkin et al., 1991).

Some researchers believe that depression is not as dangerous to health as is having a *repressive* personality style: denying normal feelings of anxiety, anger, or fear and pretending that everything is fine. Howard Friedman (1991) calls repressors "phony Type Bs"—people who *say* that pressure doesn't bother them and who seem unaggressive, but who, just under the surface, actually are competitive, angry, and tense. Other researchers call them "defensive deniers" (Shedler, Mayman, & Manis, 1993). By whatever name, they may be at greater risk of serious illness than true type Bs or even volatile Type As. And there is controversial evidence from some studies that once deniers contract a disease, they die sooner, on average, than people who are able to acknowledge and express their feelings (Burgess, Morris, & Pettingale, 1988).

Thus the connection between negative emotions and disease remains elusive. Howard Friedman and Stephanie Booth-Kewley (1987), summarizing the results of 101 studies, failed to find any significant links between specific emotions and specific diseases. They did find evidence for what they called a generic, "disease-prone personality" in people who are chronically depressed, angry and hostile, worried and anxious, but the evidence was not strong.

Perhaps, then, the most reasonable conclusion at present is that extremes of emotional expression—both denial of negative emotions and constant ventilation of such emotions—are probably involved in illness, but they are unlikely to be the only cause. "Personality may function like diet," Friedman and Booth-Kewley concluded. "Imbalances can predispose one to all sorts of diseases." Personality traits may determine how you react to a stressor or to becoming sick—with anger and belligerence, with resignation, with denial, with constructive action—and these responses affect the cardiovascular and immune systems in general (Andersen, Kiecolt-Glaser, & Glaser, 1994). But the occurrence of a *specific* illness depends on other factors, such as whether you drink excessively or smoke or have genetic vulnerabilities; the nature of the stressful events you are experiencing; and the biology of the disease itself.

Optimism and Pessimism

As we saw in Chapter 10, different ways of thinking are associated with different emotions. Lonely or depressed people tend to explain uncontrollable negative events as internal ("It's all my fault"), stable ("This misery is going to last forever"), and global ("It's going to affect everything I do"). Cheerful people regard the same events as external ("I couldn't have done anything about it"), unstable ("Things will improve"), and limited in impact ("Well, at least the rest of my life is OK").

Martin Seligman (1991) calls these two characteristic responses to bad events pessimistic and optimistic *explanatory styles*. A pessimistic explanatory style is associated with less self-esteem, less achievement, more illness, and slower emotional recovery from trauma. When researchers followed a sample of people in Florida who had suffered devastating losses as a result of Hurricane Andrew, they found that pessimism was a significant predictor of continued distress six months after the disaster, whereas loss of resources was not (Carver et al., 1993a). It's not how much you lose, apparently, but how you think about that loss that makes the most difference to your state of mind.

Pessimists will probably complain that optimism is just a result of good health or good fortune; it's easy to think positively when you feel good. But there is growing evidence that optimism may produce good health as well as reflect it. In one imaginative study of baseball Hall-of-Famers who had played between 1900 and 1950, 30 players were rated according to their explanatory style. A pessimistic remark would be internal, stable, and global, as in "We didn't win because my arm is shot, it'll never get better, and it affects my performance every time." An optimistic version would be external, unstable, and specific: "We didn't win because we got a couple of lousy calls, just bad luck in this game, but we'll be great tomorrow." The optimists were significantly more likely to have lived well into old age than were the pessimists (Seligman, 1991). Another study followed 1,719 men and women with heart disease who had undergone a procedure to check the arteries for clogging. Twelve percent of the pessimists—people who doubted they would recover enough to lead normal lives—died within a year, compared to only 5 percent of the optimists (Mark, 1994). This difference was not related to differences in severity of the disease: Some of the people with the mildest heart disease were the most pessimistic.

One reason for the link between pessimism and illness may have to do with how people cope with stress. When faced with a problem, such as a risky operation or a serious continuing struggle with alcoholism, optimists focus on what

Studies suggest that explanatory style affects longevity. One example, from a study of baseball players, is Zack Wheat, an outfielder for the Brooklyn Dodgers. Wheat had an optimistic explanatory style: "I'm a better hitter than I used to be because my strength has improved and my experience has improved." Wheat lived to be 83.

they can do about it. They have a higher expectation of being successful, so they don't give up at the first sign of a setback. They keep their senses of humor, plan for the future, and reinterpret the situation in a positive light (Carver, Scheier, & Weintraub, 1989; Carver et al., 1993a). Note that optimists do not deny their anxieties, cheerfully asserting (like those phony Type Bs) that "everything will be fine." Rather, they acknowledge their problems and illnesses, but have confidence that they will overcome them (Schwartz, 1990). Pessimists, in contrast, may be more likely to become ill because they give in to negative emotions, or just give up, instead of acting constructively.

Can pessimism be "cured"? Optimists, naturally, think so! In fact, cognitive therapy has been successful in teaching depressed people new explanatory styles (see Chapter 16). Psychologist Rachel Hare-Mustin told us how her mother cured her childhood pessimism—with humor. "Nobody likes me," Rachel lamented. "Don't say that," her mother said. "Everybody hasn't met you yet."

Healthy Habits

We bet you $100 that you already know the rules for protecting your health: get enough sleep, get regular exercise, eat a nutritious diet, drink alcohol only in moderation, do not overeat or go on starvation diets, and do not smoke cigarettes. A ten-year longitudinal study of nearly 7,000 people in Alameda County, California, found that each of these practices was independently related to good health and a lack of stress symptoms (Matarazzo, 1984; Wiley & Camacho, 1980). The more of these practices people followed, the better their mental and physical health.

So, why aren't you following all of them? Why, when people know what is good for them, don't they always do it? An important goal of health psychology is to help people reduce or eliminate the risk factors for illness before the illness has a chance to develop. But health psychologists have found several obstacles in their pursuit of prevention (Taylor, 1991):

- Many health habits become entrenched during childhood. Parents play a powerful role in determining a child's health habits. For example, they determine what a child learns about alcohol and about nutrition. It will be hard for you to give up a high-cholesterol diet if you associate it with love and hearty home-cooked meals.

Walter Johnson, a star pitcher for the Washington Senators, had a pessimistic explanatory style: "I can't depend on myself to pitch well. I'm growing old. I have had my day." Johnson died at the age of 59.

- People often have little incentive to change unhealthy habits. Smoking, eating rich food, and not exercising have few immediate negative consequences; their effects do not become apparent for years. Many people in good health therefore feel invulnerable.

- Health habits are largely independent of one another. Some people exercise every day and continue to smoke. Some people eat nutritious meals and take a lot of drugs.

- Health habits are unstable over time. Some people quit smoking for a year, and then take it up again. Others lose 50 pounds, and then gain 60.

Health psychologists have identified many factors that influence your ability to overcome these obstacles to good health. Some are in your *social system:* Do all your friends smoke and drink themselves into a stupor on weekends? Chances are that you will join them. Some are in your larger *cultural environment:* Does your culture think it is appropriate for women to exercise or for men to stop eating red meat? Some are in your *access to health care services* and information: In the United States, unlike Canada, Europe, and Japan, many people lack medical insurance and cannot afford to visit a doctor. Finally, as we will see next, some are in your *beliefs:* Do you feel fatalistic about illness or in charge of your health?

The Question of Control: Fight or Flow?

All of the factors we have discussed so far—negative emotions, pessimism, and poor health habits—may in turn be related to one critical factor: Having a sense of personal control over a troubling event, chronic problem, or illness (Cohen & Edwards, 1989; Marshall, 1991). As we saw in discussing Albert Bandura's cognitive social-learning theory (Chapters 7 and 12), people who feel in control have a belief in their own *self-efficacy,* a conviction that they can successfully accomplish what they set out to do. Self-efficacy is in fact an important predictor of good health practices (Bandura, 1992; Hackett et al., 1992).

Locus of control, described in Chapter 12, refers to the general expectation of whether or not the results of your actions are under your own control (Rotter, 1966). People who have an *internal* locus of control ("internals") tend to believe that they are responsible for what happens to them; those who have an *external* locus of control ("externals") tend to believe that they are the victims of

■ **locus of control**
A general expectation about whether the results of one's actions are under one's own control (internal locus) or beyond one's control (external locus).

These people, setting up sandbags during the 1993 floods that devastated so many midwestern cities, are taking constructive action in the face of adversity. Other people respond by feeling overwhelmed by events or accepting them fatalistically.

✳ *In general, it's good to feel in control of your life, but what does that mean exactly? Control over what? How much of your life? How do the events in your life affect your sense of control?*

circumstance. When a team of researchers conducted a factor analysis of many personality inventories and measures of psychological and physical health, they found that the first key factor was "optimistic control": a sense of optimism, hope, faith in one's abilities (self-efficacy), self-esteem, and an internal locus of control (Marshall et al., 1994).

The Benefits of Control.

As we noted earlier, the most debilitating aspect of chronically stressful situations is a feeling of powerlessness, of having no control over what happens. People can tolerate years of difficulty if they believe they can control events or at least predict them (Laudenslager, 1988). You may not be able to control when an exam will be given, but you can usually predict and prepare for it. When people know that they will be going through a hard time, they can take steps to reduce their stress.

Feeling in control of events has important advantages. It helps to reduce chronic pain, improve psychological adjustment to surgery and illness, and speed up recovery from some diseases (Taylor, 1991). In a study of patients recovering from heart attack, those who thought their illness was due to bad luck or fate—factors outside their control—were less likely to generate active plans for recovery and more likely to resume their old unhealthy habits. In contrast, those who thought the heart attack occurred because they smoked, didn't exercise, or had a stressful job were more likely to change their bad habits and recover more quickly (Affleck et al., 1987).

A sense of control affects the neuroendocrine and immune systems. This fact may explain why an improved sense of control is so beneficial to old people, whose immune systems normally decline (Rodin, 1988). When elderly residents of nursing homes are given more choices over their activities and environment and given more control over day-to-day events—even small but engrossing activities such as tending plants—the results are dramatic: They become more alert, more active, happier, and even less likely to die (Langer, 1983; Langer et al., 1979).

Research on the importance of control and self-efficacy has provided important practical benefits. For example, studies find that media campaigns to encourage people to eat healthier meals, wear seat belts, take needed medication, practice safe sex, and so forth are most likely to succeed when they enhance people's perceptions of their self-efficacy in managing their own health. In contrast, campaigns based only on providing factual information, scaring the public, or trying to persuade people of the risks of some activity are far less effective (Bandura, 1992; Meyerowitz & Chaiken, 1987).

Cultures differ in their degree of fatalism and in their beliefs about whether it is possible to take control of one's health. Might these cultural attitudes be related to mortality rates? The answer, remarkably, is yes. Researchers examined the deaths of 28,169 adult Chinese-Americans and 412,632 randomly selected, matched control subjects whose death certificates identified them as "white." In traditional Chinese astrology, certain birth years are considered bad luck, and people born in those years often acquire a fatalistic attitude toward bad fortune. This expectation can become a self-fulfilling prophecy. Chinese-Americans died significantly earlier than whites who had the same disease—by a margin of one to five years!—if they were born in a year traditionally considered to be ill-fated. The more strongly traditional the Chinese were, the more years of life they lost. These results held for nearly all causes of death studied, even when the researchers controlled for the behavior of the patients (how well they took care of themselves) and the doctors (which kinds of treatments they administered) (Phillips, Ruth, & Wager, 1993).

Some Problems with Control.

Overall, then, a sense of control is a good thing. But believing that an event is controllable does not always lead to a reduction in stress, and believing that an event is uncontrollable does not always lead to an increase in stress. The question must always be asked: Control over what?

If an unrealistically confident person tries to control the uncontrollable ("I'm going to be a movie star in 60 days!"), the inevitable failure may lead to a sense of helplessness or incompetence. It also doesn't help people to believe they had control over a past traumatic event if they then feel unable to cope with it. Victims of rape or other crimes, for example, often suffer because they blame themselves for having "provoked" their attackers, as if they could have controlled the criminal's behavior (Janoff-Bulman, 1989).

Some psychologists maintain that the very notion of being in control of your destiny reflects a middle-class and Western view of life: Work hard enough and anything is possible (Markus & Kitayama, 1991). This attitude, however, does not reflect reality for everyone. Poor people and minorities often have a less optimistic view of what is possible for them than affluent whites do, and being "external" is one way for them to preserve self-esteem and cope with the difficulties and barriers they face. They say, in effect, "I am a good and worthy person; my lot in life is a result of prejudice, fate, or society" (Crocker & Major, 1989).

"Control," therefore, has different meanings, and not all of them are related to health (Marshall, 1991). In one study that dissected the varieties of control, the only one that was related to health was self-efficacy: the belief that you are basically in charge of your own life and well-being, and that if you become sick you have the power to make yourself well again. Other, more unrealistic kinds of control were not related to health and well-being, such as self-blame ("Whatever goes wrong with my health is my fault") and the illusion that all disease can be prevented by doing the right thing ("If I eat right, I can avoid all illness").

Ideas about control, as we have seen, are strongly influenced by culture. Eastern and Western cultures hold different attitudes toward the ability and desirability of controlling one's life. In general, the Western approach celebrates **primary control,** in which people try to influence existing reality by changing other people, events, or circumstances: If you don't like the way it is, change it, fix it, or fight it. The Eastern approach emphasizes **secondary control,** in which people try to accommodate to reality by changing their own perceptions, goals, or desires: If you have a problem, learn to live with it or act in spite of it (Rothbaum, Weisz, & Snyder, 1982). Studies that have compared the United States and Japan find that these two perspectives influence practices in child rearing, socialization, religion, work, and psychotherapy (Weisz, Rothbaum, & Blackburn, 1984).

▪ **primary control**
An effort to modify reality by changing other people, the situation, or events; a "fighting back" philosophy.

▪ **secondary control**
An effort to accept reality by changing one's own attitudes, goals, or emotions; a "learn to live with it" philosophy.

Sometimes life serves up a disaster, as it has for many farm families who have lost their lands and livelihoods because of the changing economy. How can people in such situations strike a healthful balance between primary and secondary control?

A Japanese psychologist offered some examples of Japanese proverbs that teach the benefits of yielding to the inevitable (Azuma, 1984): *To lose is to win* (giving in, to protect the harmony of a relationship, demonstrates the superior trait of generosity); *Willow trees do not get broken by piled up snow* (no matter how many problems pile up in your life, flexibility will help you survive them); and *The true tolerance is to tolerate the intolerable* (some "intolerable" situations are facts of life that no amount of protest will change). Perhaps you can imagine how long "to lose is to win" would survive on an American football field, or how long most Americans would be prepared to tolerate the intolerable!

Both primary and secondary control have lessons to offer. One way that people who are ill or under stress can combine these two forms of control is to take responsibility for future actions, while not blaming themselves for past ones. People who use *both* forms of control in this way show better adjustment than people who are ill who believe they can control everything—or nothing—about their disease (Thompson, Nanni, & Levine, 1994). In a study of women coping with cancer, for instance, adjustment was related to a woman's belief that she was not to blame for getting sick but that she was in charge of taking care of herself from now on (Taylor, Lichtman, & Wood, 1984). "I felt that I had lost control of my body somehow," said one woman, "and the way for me to get back some control was to find out as much as I could." This way of thinking about illness allows people to avoid guilt and self-blame while gaining mastery and self-efficacy. Indeed, most problems require us to choose between trying to change what we can and accepting what we cannot. Perhaps the secret of healthy control lies in knowing the difference, as the subject of coping with terminal illness painfully illustrates (see "Think About It").

Quick Quiz

You can increase your sense of control over the material in this section by answering these questions:

1. Which of the following aspects of Type A behavior seems most hazardous to men's health? (a) working hard (b) being in a hurry (c) antagonistic hostility (d) high physical reactivity to work (e) neurotic hostility
2. "I'll never find anyone else to love because I'm not good-looking; that one romance was a fluke" illustrates a(n) _____ explanatory style.
3. Adapting yourself to the reality that you are getting older is an example of (primary/secondary) control.
4. Joining a protest against sexual harassment on the job is an example of (primary/secondary) control.
5. On television, a health expert describes the case of a woman who was the victim of assault and then suffered the death of her mother. "No wonder," said the expert, "that she soon developed cancer." What can we conclude from this case about the causes of cancer, and what other explanations are possible?

Answers:

1. c 2. pessimistic 3. secondary 4. primary 5. From this one case we cannot conclude anything; the expert is just arguing by anecdote. What about all the people who live with extreme stressors and don't get cancer? Some other possible explanations: The woman's stressful experiences may have weakened her immune system, which made an already existing cancer begin to grow; the stress and the cancer may have been coincidental events; the stressful events may have caused her

*T*hink About It

*H*ow Long Should We Prolong Life, and When Should We Accept Death?

- In 1991, physician Timothy Quill revealed that he had helped a dying leukemia patient to commit suicide, which was her carefully considered wish. A grand jury in New York was summoned to determine whether Quill should be indicted for his role in his patient's death. They decided no.
- A 76-year-old Florida man shot and killed his beloved wife who was dying of Alzheimer's disease. He was convicted of first-degree murder.
- In 1994, Oregon became the first state to permit doctors to help terminally ill patients end their lives—a law overturned by a federal judge in 1995. In Michigan, Dr. Jack Kevorkian has been repeatedly arrested for doing the same thing, although no jury has yet convicted him.

As these conflicting examples illustrate, people are extremely divided in their opinions about *euthanasia,* the act of painlessly putting to death someone who is suffering an incurable and agonizing disease. (Euthansia means "easy death"—from the Greek *eu,* "good" or "well," as in *euphoria;* and *thanatos,* "death.") Some people think it is only humane and merciful to help a person who is dying in pain to end life quickly. Others fear that such license will be abused; for example, that it will open the door to the unnecessary deaths of people who are not dying, but who are depressed, disabled, or a financial burden to their families. As a result of new technologies that can prolong life, individuals and society must struggle with difficult questions:

- *What is legal death?* Once, death was simple to determine: the cessation of heartbeat and breathing. But today patients can "live" for weeks, even years, unconscious and in a coma, while machines keep the vital organs going. Is a person dead if he or she could not survive without machine support? New definitions of "death" include irreversible brain damage, total brain death, and the inability of the heart to beat on its own.
- *When is it time to "pull the plug," and who decides?* Doctors, lawyers, families, and clergy often disagree with each other on the "right" time to let an ailing person die. Doctors, trained to prolong life, often want to keep the dying person alive as long as possible, even when that goal produces pain and suffering. They also fear malpractice suits that may occur if they let someone die who the family thinks could have lived longer. Religious groups differ too. Some believe that death is natural and inevitable and that doctors and

lawyers should not interfere with its course. Others believe that death is to be fought with all the weapons of modern medicine.

- *How can prejudice against old people be kept out of these decisions?* Is a person ever "too old" to be given an emergency appendectomy? How can we determine whether an old person wants to die because he or she is clinically depressed or because the decision is a "rational" one?
- *Which kinds of euthanasia, if any, are justified?* "Passive" euthanasia means allowing a person to die without using heroic measures, such as intravenous feeding, to keep the person alive. In "active" euthanasia, or "mercy killing," a physician or relative intentionally causes death to come sooner to spare the patient suffering.
- *Who cares for the dying?* Dying of protracted illnesses, such as Alzheimer's disease, AIDS, or cancer, can last months or even years. Thus the issue of who will care for the terminally ill is becoming more urgent. Hospitals are often cold institutions that deprive a dying person of dignity and individuality, the company of friends and family, and choices about life-prolonging techniques. One alternative is the *hospice,* a center for the dying person and his or her family. Hospices offer the medical care of hospitals, but they are homier, allow families to live with the patient, and help the patient die with little pain. Some hospice services are provided in the patient's home.
- *Who pays for the dying, and do only the wealthy live?* The costs of life-sustaining equipment, long-term hospital or hospice care, and organ transplants are growing rapidly, a result of new technology. Who will pay the costs? Families? Government? If someone else can afford an organ transplant and you can't, should that person be allowed to live and you to die?

These issues reflect one abiding psychological theme: How much control do we have over illness and death, and when is it time to let go? Is the American belief in primary control—fighting back against unfortunate or sad events—beneficial or harmful in this case? In *What Kind of Life: The Limits of Medical Progress,* Daniel Callahan (1989) argues that Americans must curb their insatiable appetite for a longer life. They should, he says, be "creatively and honorably accepting aging and death, not struggling to overcome them." Do you agree? Should a society set limits on life, and, if so, how? ▪

■ COPING WITH STRESS

Remarkably, most people who are "under stress"—even those living in the toxic environments of war and poverty, or living through long episodes of anger or grief—do not become ill. Why not? What helps people manage endless hassles and recover from the most awful adversity? How, in short, do they cope?

Coping consists of constantly changing cognitive and behavioral efforts to manage demands, in the environment or in oneself, that one feels or believes to be stressful (Lazarus & Folkman, 1984). Coping is not a single strategy that applies to all circumstances; people cope differently with hassles, losses, dangers, and challenges. And the techniques they use change over time and circumstance, depending on the nature of the stressor and the particular situation they are in (Carver & Scheier, 1994; Terry, 1994). These techniques fall into three general categories: (1) solving the problem, (2) rethinking the problem, and (3) learning to live with the problem. The first deals with the stressor, the second involves the person's interpretation of the stressor, and the third addresses the physical effects of stress.

Solving the Problem

A woman we know, whom we will call Nancy, was struck by tragedy when she was 22. She and her new husband were driving home one evening when a car ran out of control and crashed into them. When Nancy awoke in a hospital room, she learned that her husband had been killed and that she herself had permanent spinal injury and would never walk again. For many months, Nancy reacted with understandable rage and despair. "Get it out of your system," her friends said. "You need to get in touch with your feelings." "But I *know* I'm miserable," Nancy lamented. "What do I *do?*"

What should Nancy do, indeed? Her friends' advice and her reply illustrate the difference between *emotion-focused* and *problem-focused* coping (Lazarus & Folkman, 1984). Emotion-focused coping concentrates on the emotions the problem has caused, whether anger, anxiety, or grief. For a period of time after any personal tragedy or traumatic natural disaster, it is normal to give in to these emotions and feel overwhelmed by them. In this stage, people often need to talk obsessively about the event in order to come to terms with it, make sense of it, and decide what to do about it (Pennebaker & Harber, 1993). (We further discuss the importance of talking about traumatic events in "Taking Psychology with You.") Eventually, though, most people become ready to move beyond their emotional state and concentrate on the problem itself. The specific steps in problem-focused coping depend on the nature of the problem: whether it is a pressing but one-time decision; a continuing difficulty, such as living with a disability; or an anticipated event, such as having an operation.

"Defining the problem" may seem obvious, especially when the problem is standing there yelling at you. However, people often define a problem incorrectly and then set off down a wrong coping road. For example, unhappy couples often blame each other for their misery. Sometimes, of course, they are right. But a study of several hundred couples found that marital unhappiness is often a result of misdiagnosis. A husband who is under great pressure at his office may decide that his problem is an unsupportive wife. A wife who is feeling too many conflicting demands may decide that her problem is her lazy husband. If this couple tries to cope with their unhappiness by attacking each other, they merely increase their misery. If they correctly diagnose the problem ("I'm worried about my job"; "I don't have enough leisure time to myself"), different coping solutions become apparent (Pines, 1986).

Once the problem is identified, the coper can learn as much as possible about it from professionals, friends, books, and others in the same boat. In Nancy's case, she can begin by learning more about her medical condition and prognosis. What can she do for herself? What kind of exercise will help her?

How do you cope with continuing stresses? If you were in this single mother's place, would you usually be amused and charmed by your small children's demands, or annoyed and harassed?

■ **coping**
Cognitive and behavioral efforts to manage demands in the environment or oneself that one feels to be stressful.

How do other accident victims cope? Many people in stressful situations divide their options into "stay here and suffer" versus "leave here and die." But usually there is a middle course. What are Nancy's options? She could give up and feel sorry for herself forever. She could return home to live with her parents. She could learn to care for herself. She could go into the wheelchair business. She could. . . . (In fact, Nancy stayed in school, remarried, got a Ph.D. in psychology, and now does research and counseling with disabled people.)

Problem-focused coping has a large psychological benefit: It tends to increase a person's sense of self-esteem, control, and effectiveness (D'Zurilla & Sheedy, 1991). Sometimes, of course, emotions get in the way of assessing a problem accurately. When people are agonizing over a decision, they may, to relieve their anguish, make a fast, impulsive choice. They may say or do something in anger that worsens their predicament, or become so anxious that they cannot evaluate the situation carefully. That is why it is often best to use a combination of emotion- and problem-focused coping (Carver & Scheier, 1994). Problem-focused coping requires components of critical thinking, such as considering alternatives and resisting emotional reasoning. When under stress, people who think creatively and constructively about their problems are better able to solve them, avoid negative emotions such as anger and anxiety, and even reduce physiological arousal (Katz & Epstein, 1991).

Rethinking the Problem

A second way of coping with problems is to think about them in new ways. Shelley Taylor (1989), who has worked with cancer and cardiac patients, women who have been raped, and other victims of disaster or disease, finds that rethinking strategies have three goals. First, they help the person find meaning in the experience: Why did this event happen to me? What does it mean for my life now? Second, they help the person regain a sense of mastery over the event and the future: What can I do about it now? How can I keep this from happening again? And third, they help the person regain self-esteem after a devastating setback. Let's consider some of the most effective cognitive strategies that people use.

Reappraisal: "It's Not So Bad."   When people cannot eliminate a stressor, they can choose to reassess its meaning. Problems can be turned into challenges, losses into unexpected gains. You lost your job; maybe it wasn't such a good job, but you were too afraid to quit to look for another, and now you can do so. Even life-shattering events can be viewed in more than one light. A study of 100 spinal-cord-injured people found that two-thirds of them felt the disability had had positive side effects (Schulz & Decker, 1985). Benefits included becoming "a better person," "seeing other people as more important," and having an "increased awareness of self" and a new appreciation of "brain, not brawn." People can also reappraise the actions of others. Instead of becoming enraged at someone's distressing behavior, for example, the empathic person tries to see the situation from the other person's standpoint in order to avoid misunderstandings (Miller & Eisenberg, 1988).

Social Comparisons: "I'm Better Off Than Some People, and I Can Learn From Those Who Are Doing Better Than I Am."   When they are sick or in a difficult situation, successful copers often compare themselves to others who are (they feel) less fortunate. No matter how bad off they are, they are able to find someone who is even worse off (Taylor & Lobel, 1989). This is true even of people who know they have fatal diseases. For example, one AIDS sufferer said in an interview, "I made a list of all the other diseases I would rather not have than AIDS. Lou Gehrig's disease, being in a wheelchair; rheumatoid arthritis, when you are in knots and in terrible pain. So I said, 'You've got to get some perspective on this, and where you are on the Great Nasty Disease List.' " Another said: "I really have an advantage in a sense over other people. I know

The ultimate example of rethinking your problems.

there is a possibility that my life may not go on for as many years as other people's. I have the opportunity to look at my life, to make changes, and to deeply appreciate the time that I have" (Reed, 1990).

Sometimes successful copers also compare themselves to those who are doing *better* than they are (Aspinwall & Taylor, 1993; Taylor & Lobel, 1989). Such comparisons are beneficial when they provide a person with information about ways of coping or managing the illness, and when the person feels able to take advantage of such information. Comparisons in either direction can be inspiring or detrimental, depending on what the coper is looking for and what lesson he or she draws from the experiences of others. People with low self-esteem, for example, seem to feel insecure when they compare themselves to others who are doing better than they; they cope better with setbacks when they compare themselves to others who are worse off (Aspinwall & Taylor, 1993).

⭐ *Where would you draw the line between "healthy illusions" that maintain self-esteem and optimism and self-destructive ones? How would you know which is which?*

Vigilance Versus Avoidance: "Tell Me Everything" Versus "It's Not Important; Let's Go to the Movies."

Suppose you are going to the hospital for surgery. Should you get as much information as you can about every detail and risk of the procedure, or, having decided to go ahead, should you avoid thinking about it?

Many studies have now been done on the difference between people who are vigilant, who scan all information for evidence of threat, and those who avoid threatening information by distracting themselves. There are benefits and disadvantages in both styles of coping. Vigilant individuals, for example, are overly sensitive to their bodily symptoms and take longer to recover from them (Miller, Brody, & Summerton, 1988). But there is also evidence that a moderate amount of preoperative anxiety actually protects against the stressfulness of surgery and speeds recovery, perhaps by helping the person mentally prepare for the operation (Manyande et al., 1992). Several studies have found that women who used cognitive avoidance or other "escape" tactics to cope with anxiety before a biopsy later had higher levels of distress after receiving a diagnosis of breast cancer than did women who coped by accepting the possibility that the test might prove positive (Carver et al., 1993b; Stanton & Snider, 1993). In such cases, vigilant individuals may do well because they face the situation, get information about what to do, and then do it.

Vigilance during a crisis or illness may also prevent feelings of hopelessness and fatalism (recall the traditional Chinese-Americans whose fatalism about their unlucky birth year was associated with an earlier death). In a study of 178 women diagnosed with breast cancer, the patients were divided according to their style of coping with the illness: positive/confronting, fatalistic, hopeless/helpless, and denial/avoidance (Burgess, Morris, & Pettingale, 1988). The "positive/confronting" style was associated with the greatest longevity, even after controlling for severity of the illness.

Vigilance is called for when action is possible and necessary, but once you have all the necessary information to make a decision and that decision is out of your hands, avoidance and distraction are excellent coping tactics. Both strategies can work together. In a hospital, patients do best if they refuse to dwell on every little thing that could go wrong and distract themselves as much as possible. They also get well faster—and protect themselves—when they are vigilant about the care they are getting, and when they protest incorrect or thoughtless treatment. The benefits of distraction do not mean you should lie there like a flounder and passively accept every decision made for you.

Of course, some people do more than distract themselves when they cope with a stressful situation; they deny it altogether. "This isn't happening to me," they say, or "It is happening to me, but it isn't important," or perhaps "If I ignore it, the problem will go away." As we saw in our discussion of people who repress all negative feelings, such denial can be stressful to the body. Since Freud, many psychologists have regarded denial as a primitive, dangerous defense mechanism that means a person is out of touch with reality—one of the hallmarks of mental illness. In this view, emotionally healthy people are good at "reality testing"; they can face the truth about themselves and honestly appraise their abilities and limitations (Colvin & Block, 1994).

But after reviewing the mental health research, Shelley Taylor and Jonathon Brown (1988, 1994) have concluded that denial is not always bad. Well-being, they maintain, often depends on "overly positive self-evaluations, exaggerated perceptions of control or mastery, and unrealistic optimism." These "positive illusions," Taylor argues, are not only characteristic of normal human thought, but also necessary for meeting the usual criteria of mental health: the ability to care about others, the ability to be contented, and the ability to work productively.

Why should this be so? The mind tends to filter all incoming information, distorting it in a positive direction to enhance self-esteem and ward off bad news. Positive illusions may be useful when people are threatened with illness, crisis, or attacks to their self-esteem, because they allow people to respond with hope for the future rather than giving up (Snyder, 1989). On the other hand, health psychologists, including Taylor and Brown themselves, know that denial and illusions permit people to do self-destructive things: drink too much, smoke, fail to wear seat belts, refuse to take medication for chronic illness. So this research raises some provocative choices: When do positive illusions help us, and when are they risky? Is it better to maintain illusions if they protect your feelings of hope, or to think critically about them and risk losing optimism?

Humor: "People Are Funny." "A merry heart doeth good like a medicine," says Proverbs, and researchers now agree. Once thought too frivolous a topic for serious study, humor has made its way into the laboratory. "Sense of humor" includes the ability to respond with humor in real situations, to like humor and witty people, and to use humor in coping with stress.

What's so funny about misery? "He who laughs," thundered the German poet and dramatist Bertolt Brecht, "has not heard the terrible news." But people who can transform the "terrible news" into a sense of the absurd or the whimsical are less prone to depression, anger, tension, and fatigue than are people who give in to gloom. In studies of college students coping with unfortunate events, those who respond with humor feel fewer negative emotions and unhappiness than do students who don't have a sense of humor or who instead succumb to moping and tears (Nezu, Nezu, & Blissett, 1988). And studies of people with serious illnesses also find that humor reduces distress, improves immune functioning, and hastens recovery from surgery (Berk et al., 1988; Carver et al., 1993b; Martin & Dobbin, 1988).

Some theories of laughter emphasize its ability to reduce tension and emotion. You have probably been in a tense group situation when someone suddenly made exactly the right crack to make everyone laugh and defuse the mood. Laughter seems to produce some beneficial biological responses, possibly stimulating the immune system or starting a flow of endorphins, the painkilling chemicals in the brain (Martin & Dobbin, 1988). Other theories emphasize the cognitive components of humor. When you laugh at a problem, you are putting it in a new perspective—seeing its silly or absurd aspects—and gaining control over it (Dixon, 1980). Humor also allows you to express indirectly feelings that are hazardous to express directly, which is why it is so often the weapon of minorities. An old joke tells of a Jewish man who accidentally bumped into a Nazi on a street. "Swine!" bellowed the Nazi. "And I'm Cohen," replied the Jew, "pleased to meet you."

Having a sense of humor, however, is not the same as smiling all the time or "putting on a happy face." For humor to be effective in coping with stress, a person must actually use it during a stressful situation—seeing or inventing funny aspects of serious events and having the ability to laugh at them (Crawford & Gressley, 1991; Nezu, Nezu, & Blissett, 1988). Hostile humor therefore misses

Many comedians use humor as a way to cope with problems. The actor Bert Lahr, shown here as the lovable Cowardly Lion in The Wizard of Oz, *began using humor as a shield against stress early in life.*

the point: Vicious, rude jokes at another person's expense are not stress reducers. Indeed, they often create more tension and anger.

Living with the Problem

In modern life, we often cannot escape changes, ongoing conflicts, or the hassles of traffic, noise, or job or school pressure. A third approach to coping concentrates on reducing the physical effects of stress itself.

Relaxation. The simplest way to reduce signs of stress, such as high blood pressure and rapid breathing, is to relax. Relaxation training—learning to alternately tense and relax certain muscles, to lie or sit quietly, to banish worries of the day—has beneficial effects on the immune system. In a study of 45 elderly people living in retirement homes, those who reduced stress with relaxation techniques showed significantly improved immune activity (Kiecolt-Glaser et al., 1985b). And in a study of 13 women with first-stage breast cancer, the women who received relaxation training during a nine-week intervention study showed no decline in their white blood cell count and a beneficial increase in natural killer cell activity, in contrast to the control subjects (Gruber et al., 1993).

Some people learn to relax through systematic *meditation*, a practice aimed at focusing one's attention and eliminating all distracting thoughts. Meditation does not produce a unique physiological or emotional state; most studies find no difference between meditation and simple resting (Holmes, 1984). This does not mean that meditation has no benefits. In Eastern religions such as Hinduism and Buddhism, meditation is much more than a relaxation or stress-reduction technique. The goal is not to unwind but to attain wisdom, acceptance of reality, emotional detachment, and transcendence of the self—states of mind not measurable on an EEG machine.

Exercise. Physical exercise, such as walking, jogging, dancing, biking, and swimming, is an important buffer between stressors and physiological symptoms. A low level of physical activity is associated with decreased life expectancy for both sexes and contributes independently to the development of many chronic diseases (Dubbert, 1992). As you can see in Figure 14.2, people who are physically fit show less physiological arousal to stressors and pay fewer visits to the doctor than people who are less fit, even when both groups are under the same objective pressures (Brown, 1991). These benefits of exercise have been shown in studies of adults, adolescents, and even preschoolers. Preschoolers who did aerobic exercises daily for eight weeks, compared to children who spent the same time each day in free play, had better cardiovascular fitness and agility, and their self-esteem improved (Alpert et al., 1990).

Exercise also combats anxiety, depression, and the blues (Dubbert, 1992; Plante & Rodin, 1990). In a study of 43 college women, all moderately to severely depressed, researchers assigned the students to one of three groups. One group did aerobic exercise three times a week, another practiced relaxation and took leisurely walks four times a week, and a control group did neither. After five weeks and again after ten weeks, the women took tests of their aerobic capacity and level of depression. Those who exercised vigorously showed improved fitness and sharp declines in depression; the relaxation and control groups didn't reduce their depression levels (McCann & Holmes, 1984). Similarly, studies of workers have found that the more that employees exercise, the fewer physical symptoms, colds, and stresses, and the less anxiety, depression, and irritability, they report (Hendrix et al., 1991).

Many popular books and magazines therefore advocate exercise as the all-purpose coping strategy. There is no doubt that regular exercise is an excel-

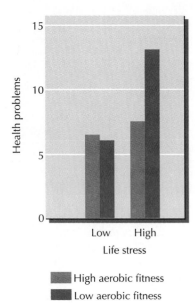

■ Figure 14.2 Fitness and Health

In one study, when people were under low stress, their fitness levels were unrelated to the number of their current health problems. But when under high stress, people who were aerobically fit had fewer health problems than did people who were less fit (Roth & Holmes, 1985).

Exercise has many all-around health benefits, which is why some American companies are adopting the Japanese practice of scheduling exercise breaks for workers. Do you think that exercise should be a formal and required part of the workday?

lent health tonic. Yet people who exercise in order to *avoid* their problems are not necessarily reducing their stress load, especially if they have to go back to the same old problem tomorrow. A study of 230 working women found that the strongest predictor of depression, anxiety, and stress was difficulty at work. The form of coping that helped best was dealing with the job problems directly (O'Neill & Zeichner, 1985). You can't, it seems, jog away from everything.

Looking Outward

Julius Segal (1986), a psychologist who worked with Holocaust survivors, prisoners of war, hostages, refugees, and other survivors of catastrophe, wrote that a key element in their recovery is compassion, "healing through helping." People gain strength, he said, by giving it to others. This observation echoes Alfred Adler's theory of *social interest:* the ability to understand other people's problems and needs, to feel empathy and attachment, and to cooperate with others for the common welfare (Adler, 1938/1964). Adler believed that people who are involved with others are better able to cope with problems, have higher self-esteem, and are psychologically stronger than people who are self-involved.

Adler's ideas have been supported by research (Rareshide & Kern, 1991). One large study used two measures of social interest: a scale of moral values and an index of cooperation in love, work, and friendship. People who were high in social interest, compared to others, had fewer stressful experiences and were better able to cope with the stressful episodes they did have. Among people low in social interest, stress was more likely to be associated with anxiety, depression, and hostility (Crandall, 1984).

Why is social interest healthy? The ability to look outside of oneself, to be concerned with others, is related to virtually all of the successful coping mechanisms we have discussed so far. It tends to lead to solving problems instead of blaming others. It helps you reappraise a conflict by trying to see the conflict as others do, instead of taking it personally. It allows you to get perspective on a problem instead of exaggerating its importance. Because of its elements of forgiveness, tolerance, and empathy, it helps you live with situations that are facts of life.

Quick QUIZ

Can you cope with these refresher questions?

1. You accidentally broke your glasses. Which response is an example of cognitive reappraisal? (a) "I am such a stupid clumsy idiot!" (b) "I never do anything right." (c) "What a shame, but I've been wanting new frames anyway." (d) "I'll forget about it in aerobics class."

2. Finding out what your legal and financial resources are when you have been victimized by a crime is an example of (a) problem-focused coping, (b) emotion-focused coping, (c) distraction (d) reappraisal.

3. Learning deep-breathing techniques to reduce anxiety in taking exams is an example of (a) problem-focused coping, (b) emotion-focused coping, (c) avoidance, (d) reappraisal.

4. "This class drives me crazy, but it's better than not being in school" is an example of (a) distraction, (b) social comparison, (c) denial, (d) empathy.

5. Your roommate has turned your room into a garbage dump, filled with rotten leftover food and unwashed clothes. Assuming that you don't like living with rotting food and dirty clothes, what coping strategies described in this section might be beneficial to you?

Answers:

1. c 2. a 3. b 4. b 5. You might attack the problem by trying to find a compromise (clean the room together). You might reappraise the seriousness of the problem ("I only have to live with this person until the end of the term") or compare your roommate to others ("at least my roommate is generous and friendly"). You might also apply a sense of humor (pile everything into a heap, put a flag on top, and add a sign: "Monument to the Battle of the Bilge").

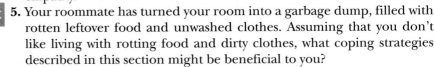

■ THE SOCIAL SIDE OF HEALTH AND WELL-BEING

Thus far we have been looking at individual factors involved in stress and illness. But health and well-being are not just up to you as an individual. They also depend on the people around you.

The Alameda County health study that we mentioned earlier, which followed nearly 7,000 adults for a decade, also investigated the importance of social relationships to health. The researchers considered four kinds of social ties: marriage, contact with friends and relatives, church membership, and participation in other groups. The people who had few social networks were more likely to have died at the time of the ten-year follow-up than those who had many (Berkman & Syme, 1979).

Perhaps the people who died were sicker to begin with or had poorer health habits, which kept them from socializing? No. The importance of social networks was unrelated to physical health at the time the study began, to socioeconomic status, and to such risk factors as smoking.

Perhaps the people who died had some undiagnosed illness at the beginning of the study? This interpretation was possible because the study was based on the participants' self-reports. So the research was repeated with nearly 3,000 people in Tecumseh, Michigan, and this time the investigators collected everyone's medical exams. Ten years later, those who had few social relationships were more likely to have died than the people who had many, even after age, health, and other risk factors were taken into account (House, Landis, & Umberson, 1988; House, Robbins, & Metzner, 1982).

One possible explanation for these findings is that social support somehow affects the immune system. In fact, studies find that lonely people have poorer immune function than people who are not lonely; students in a network of friends have better immune function before, during, and after exam periods than students who don't have enough social support; and spouses of cancer patients, although under considerable stress themselves, do not show a drop in immune function if they have high levels of social support (Baron et al., 1990). Social support speeds recovery from illness when it does occur (Kulik & Mahler, 1989), and it can increase survival time among people with serious illnesses. In a study of 194 older men and women who had had heart attacks, only 27 percent of those who said they had two or more people they could count on died within the year—compared to 58 percent of those who reported having no close contacts (Berkman, Leo-Summers, & Horwitz, 1992).

As psychologists have explored the benefits of friends and family, they have noticed something else. Sometimes friends and family are themselves the source of hassles, headaches, and conflicts. There are, therefore, two sides to the human need for social support.

When Friends Help You Cope . . .

Everyone lives in a social network of family, friends, neighbors, co-workers, and extended relations. Members of this network provide support in many ways—what one psychologist calls "assisted coping" (Thoits, 1986). They provide emotional support, such as concern and affection. They offer cognitive guidance, helping you evaluate problems and plan a course of action. They offer tangible support, with resources and services such as loaning money or the car, or taking notes in class for you when you have to go to the doctor. They offer companionship. Perhaps most of all, they are sources of attachment and connection, which people need throughout their lives; indeed, people who score high on the need for affiliation (see Chapter 11) actually have higher levels of natural killer cell activity (Jemmott et al., 1990). Old people who have dogs as companions visit medical clinics less often than their comparable peers who have no pets—or who have cats! Dogs provide companionship and attachment, the two ingredients of a truly best friend (Siegel, 1990).

The effect of friends on your health depends on what the friends are doing for you and how much stress you are under. In studying a representative sample of more than 2,000 adults, Karen Rook (1987) found that for people with average levels of stress, social support had no effect on health one way or the other. Among people who had above-average levels of stress, support from friends did help reduce their physical and emotional symptoms. But among people who had below-average levels of stress, such support was actually harmful. It was associated with more symptoms! Why might this be so? When people are going through a series of disasters, Rook believes, they need friends for advice, assistance, and reassurance. But talking too much about daily, trivial nuisances may simply reward people's distress rather than helping them manage it.

Parents are particularly important sources of support. In a two-year prospective study of 175 college students, students who felt they could rely on their parents for understanding and emotional support showed better psychological adjustment and lower emotional distress in coping with the stresses of school and of relationships—especially unpredictable ones (Valentiner, Holahan, & Moos, 1994). Conversely, students who described their parents as being unsupportive or involved in their own marital conflicts were less able to cope and were less well adjusted.

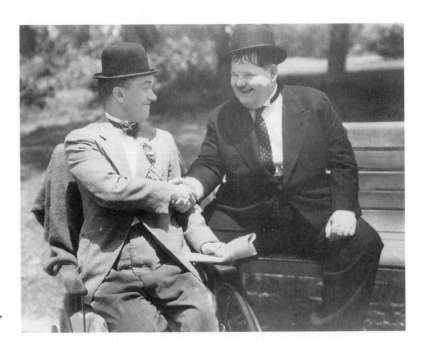

Friends can be our greatest source of warmth, support, and fun . . .

Of course, individuals and cultures differ in how many friends and relations are needed for well-being and in what they define as "support." Mexican-Americans, for example, tend to rely on their extended families for emotional support much more than Anglo-Americans do, and they feel more anxiety when separated from them. (Perhaps for this reason, rates of homelessness are very low among Mexican-Americans.) Anglos have more casual networks than do Mexican-Americans, even listing co-workers among those they depend on (Griffith & Villavicencio, 1985). In France, older people are more likely than American whites or blacks to feel satisfied with the amount of support provided by friends and family. Older Americans are more likely to complain that they give more than they receive (Antonucci, Fuhrer, & Jackson, 1990).

Cultures also differ in the value they place on friends and family. Many Americans value quick friendliness and sociability, a result perhaps of frequent moves and life changes, but in many European and Asian cultures friendship develops slowly. It takes a long time to flower but then it blooms for life. The difference between Japanese and American culture shows clearly in the reactions to the proverb "A rolling stone gathers no moss." To Americans, it means keep moving; don't let anything cling to you. To the Japanese, it means stay where you are; if you keep moving you will never acquire the beauty of stability.

. . . And Coping with Friends

Your neighbor tells you that your closest friend has betrayed your confidence. You ask a friend for help, and he says, "Sorry—I'm too busy." You're describing your most recent unhappy date, and your friend says, "Oh, quit whining." You're in the hospital recovering from major surgery, and your closest friend never visits. Your relationship with your partner has dwindled into constant arguing, which makes you feel belittled and misunderstood.

As most of us learn, friends and loved ones can be stress-producing as well as stress-reducing, undermining one's mental health as well as bolstering it. They are often sources of hassles and conflicts. When disaster or serious illness strikes, friends and family members may blunder around, not knowing what to do or say. Cancer victims report that they are often upset by the well-meaning but unhelpful reassurances from their families and friends that "all will be

. . . and also sources of exasperation, headaches, and pressure.

fine." They often feel better talking to other cancer patients (Dunkel-Schetter, 1984). A study of more than 1,000 people who had recently lost their jobs found that "social undermining" had a strong, adverse effect on mental health. Laid-off workers who felt that their spouses or significant others made their life difficult, made them feel unwanted, criticized them, or acted in an unpleasant or angry manner were in worse mental health than those who felt their spouses offered useful advice and emotional support (Vinokur & van Ryn, 1993).

Moreover, relationships often impose *the burdens of care*. If too many people in your life require your energy and support, you can become exhausted. The work of caring for a chronically sick child, partner, or parent, a task that disproportionately falls on women in mid-life, can become extremely stressful (Shumaker & Hill, 1991). In a study of 34 people who were taking care of a relative with Alzheimer's disease, the caregivers had lower percentages of T cells than the control group and showed other abnormalities of the immune system (Kiecolt-Glaser et al., 1987b).

Do the benefits of friendship outweigh these costs, or do they balance each other out? Several factors affect whether support helps or not (Dakof & Taylor, 1990):

1. *Amount of support.* Too much help and sympathy offered to someone in trouble can backfire, creating dependency and low self-esteem. For example, cancer patients who say they are receiving lots of support and that people are doing many things for them tend to have lower self-esteem and less sense of mastery than cancer patients who grumble about having to rely on themselves (Revenson, Wollman, & Felton, 1983).

2. *Timing of support.* After bereavement, divorce, or loss, a person needs lots of understanding. Friends who try to stem grief prematurely are not helping the sufferer. Later, however, they can prove helpful by trying to get the friend back into a social life.

3. *Type of support.* For a friend's advice and sympathy to be effective, the sufferer must feel that the friend understands and has been in the same boat. That is, the friend's support must match what the sufferer needs. People who are under stress at work, for example, feel better if they can talk their problems over with their employers or co-workers. Their spouses generally lack the experience to offer useful advice (Kobasa & Puccetti, 1983).

4. *Density of support.* In dense social networks, friends all know one another. Dense networks are good for your sense of stability and identity, and in a crisis everybody in the network pitches in. Women in particular seem to benefit from living in dense networks, which provide a form of social support they enjoy (Shumaker & Hill, 1991). But being in such a web can get sticky if you want to get out. Among women going back to school, those who were in a tight group of friends showed worse adjustment, more physical symptoms, and lower self-esteem than women who were not in dense networks (Hirsch, 1981). "Good old friends" tend to want you to stay put. They can make you feel guilty for wanting to change.

In close relationships, the person who is the source of support can also become the source of stress, especially when the relationship has deteriorated into frequent fighting and conflict. Researchers have long known that constant marital fights can elevate both partners' blood pressures, but now it seems that hostile fighting can affect the immune system, too. In a study of 90 married couples, those who behaved in a negative and hostile fashion during a 30-minute discussion of marital problems (criticizing, interrupting, or insulting the other person, and becoming angry and defensive) showed significant elevations of stress hormones and impairments on four measures of immune function over the next 24 hours. Couples who argued in a positive fashion (trying to find common ground, compromising, listening to the other's concerns, and using humor to defuse tension) did not show these impairments (Kiecolt-Glaser et al., 1993; Malarkey et al., 1994). As one student of ours observed, "This study gives new meaning to the accusation 'You make me sick'!" It also suggests that learning to argue fairly and constructively may have physical as well as psychological benefits, and may even turn a person who is a source of stress into a source of support.

Quick QUIZ

Match each of these stressful aspects of friendship with the correct description:

1. Your friends let you rage too long about an unfair experience.
2. You want to go away to graduate school, but your circle of friends wants you to stay with them.
3. Two friends are breaking up and each wants you to take his or her side.
4. You try to explain to your parents your conflicts about choosing a major, but they don't "get it."

a. wrong kind of support
b. conflicting demands
c. badly timed support
d. dense network

Answers:

1. c 2. d 3. b 4. a

News reports often imply that health is mostly "mind over matter." What is the matter with overemphasizing the power of the mind—and, conversely, what's wrong with ignoring the mind's influence?

■ THE MIND-BODY CONNECTION

Sometimes it seems that people don't have problems any more; they only have "stress." If someone says, "Gee, I've been under a lot of stress lately," everyone immediately advises the person to relax, meditate, watch funny movies, or take a nap. But if the person is about to be evicted for not paying the rent, is advice to relax and reduce stress really going to help? This question raises a thorny issue: In studying the factors that contribute to health and illness, are researchers overestimating psychological factors such as optimism, humor, and attitude, and underestimating economic and biological conditions such as unemployment or disease?

As we have seen, psychological factors are links in a long chain that connects stressors and illness (see Figure 14.3). But researchers disagree about how strong these links are (Andersen, Kiecolt-Glaser, & Glaser, 1994; Cohen & Williamson, 1991). As we noted in discussing emotion and illness, some researchers think that psychology counts for almost nothing. Disease is a biological matter, they say, and personality cannot influence a germ or a tumor. An editorial in the *New England Journal of Medicine* lashed out against the "psychologizing" of illness. "At a time when patients are already burdened by disease," the editor wrote, "they should not be further burdened by having to accept the responsibility for the outcome" (Angell, 1985). At the other extreme, numerous popular books state or imply that health is largely mind over matter and that the worst diseases can be cured with jokes, papaya juice, and positive thinking.

So caution and critical thinking are called for. We need, in particular, to avoid either–or thinking; to resist the temptation to jump to wished-for conclusions; to avoid oversimplifying; and to think of other possible explanations for provocative research results. This is difficult, especially when some findings are so encouraging and when so many people want to believe that "mind" can really overcome disease. Consider an exciting longitudinal study that made the news some years ago, suggesting that social support groups can extend the survival

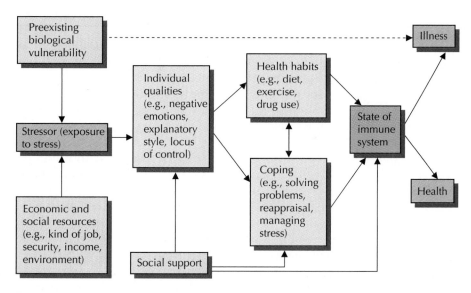

▪ Figure 14.3 A Model of Stress and Illness

Psychologists have found that the link between stressors and illness is not a simple straight line. As this diagram shows, many factors intervene between the stressors that strike a person and whether he or she becomes sick or remains healthy: predisposing biological factors; attitudes and feelings (such as emotions, optimism, and feelings of being in control); health habits (smoking, exercising, diet); and the individual's ways of coping. But even this complicated model, which summarizes the topics discussed in this chapter, shows only some pieces of the picture. Can you fill in some connecting lines that have been omitted? For example, being ill can affect how people cope and the negative emotions they feel; friends and family, instead of providing social support, can become sources of stress themselves; and practicing good health habits may counteract an existing biological vulnerability to disease.

Many commercial techniques promise to help people reduce stress. Here, a person tries an electronic route to relaxation by wearing goggles that flash lights in the eyes and headphones that play tones and songs. Based on the information in this chapter, what would you predict about the long-term success of such methods?

time of women with terminal breast cancer. The research team, led by psychiatrist David Spiegel, compared the survival rates of 84 women, some of whom had had cancer treatment plus weekly group therapy with other patients, and some of whom had had cancer treatment alone. Four years after the study's start, all of the women in the control group had died, but a third of the women in the support group were still alive; three were still alive ten years later. Overall, a striking survival difference was found between the women in the control group, who lived an average of 18.9 months from the start of the study, and those in the support group, who lived an average of 36.6 months (Spiegel et al., 1989).

Then, as is so often the case in research, other explanations of the data emerged (Andersen, Kiecolt-Glaser, & Glaser, 1994). One researcher compared the survival rates of the women in the Spiegel study with national survival rates for women with breast cancer, and found that the survival of the social support group was actually slightly *worse* than that of the national sample (Fox, 1992). This fact suggests that the findings in the Spiegel study may have been due to chance and to the small size of the sample.

Yet other well-controlled studies have gotten promising results: Interventions that provide social support, improve the patients' coping skills, and increase their optimism and self-efficacy *may* be able to prolong the length of remissions in some kinds of cancer (Fawzy et al., 1993). So what should a critical thinker conclude from these findings and from health psychology research in general?

1. *Social support is a fundamental human need.* Even if social support does not, by itself, prolong the lives of all individuals suffering from terminal illnesses, few dispute that it affects their quality of life: It lessens their suffering and pain, and it enhances their ability to come to terms with death. And sometimes, under some conditions, with some diseases but not all, it can prolong remissions.

2. *In terms of action, one should follow "good old-fashioned motherly advice" and practice those habits associated with health.* These include not smoking, not drinking excessively or in binges, eating a healthful diet, and so on. Healthful habits are not only important for prevention of illness, but for its treatment. When people become ill, they often stop taking care of themselves. They drink too much, don't exercise, misuse medication, and don't eat well, which in turn can speed the course of the disease.

3. *The effects of stress are worsened when a person feels helpless.* Many things happen that are out of our control: exams, accidents, being born to certain parents, flu epidemics, natural disasters, and countless other events. But we do have control over how we cope with them. Programs that build self-efficacy—by teaching people to monitor the behavior they wish to change, set incentives for success, and find social support—can help people increase control over their health and emotional well-being.

4. *Once a person is in a stressful situation, some ways of coping are better than others.* If the situation requires action, problem-solving techniques are more helpful than wallowing around indecisively or simply venting emotions. But if the situation is a fact of life, people who can use humor, hope, reappraisal, and constructive social comparisons will be better off than those who are overcome by depression and pessimism.

Even if we follow all these guidelines, however, successful coping does not mean eliminating all stress. It does not mean constant happiness or a life without pain. The healthy person faces problems, deals with them, and gets beyond them, but the problems are necessary if the person is to acquire coping skills that endure. To wish for a life without stress would be like wishing for a life without friends. The result might be calm, but it would be joyless and ultimately hazardous to your health. The stresses of life—the daily hassles and the occasional tragedies—force us to grow, and to grow up.

*T*aking Psychology with You

Why Confession Is Good for the Soul—and the Body

ow pay attention: *Don't think of a white bear.* Are you not thinking of it? Anyone who has ever tried to banish an uninvited thought knows how hard it can be to erase the mental tape of worries, unhappy memories, or unwished-for longings: We stay awake, worried that we can't get to sleep; we fantasize about chocolate and hamburgers when we are trying to cut down on sweets and fast food; we obsess about a relationship that is definitely over (Wegner, 1994).

In an actual study, people who were told not to think of a white bear mentioned it nine times in a five-minute stream-of-consciousness session (Wegner et al., 1987). The reason seems to be that when you are trying to avoid a thought, you are in fact processing the thought frequently—rehearsing it and making it more accessible to consciousness. When the subject of your obsession involves an old flame whom you still desire, trying *not* to think of him or her actually prolongs your emotional responsiveness to the person (Wegner & Gold, 1995).

According to James Pennebaker and his associates, the prolonged inhibition of thoughts and emotions requires physical effort that is stressful to the body (Pennebaker & Harber, 1993; Pennebaker, Hughes, & O'Heeron, 1987). Yet many people try to inhibit secret thoughts and feelings that make them ashamed or depressed. The inability or unwillingness to confide important or traumatic events places continuing stress on the system and can lead to long-term health problems. Such individuals prove to be at greater risk of illness than people who are able to talk about their tragedies, even though disclosures of traumatic events are often painful and unpleasant at first.

This information poses a problem: If an event is stressful and trying to stop thinking about the event is stressful, what should you do? Research from psychoneuroimmunology suggests some answers. First, when you realize that you are not being successful at controlling unwanted thoughts, do not blame yourself or feel distressed; just change your usual strategies. For example, instead of having scattershot distracting thoughts of anything but the thing that is bothering you, focus on one distracting idea or topic of concentration (Kelly & Kahn, 1994). Second, sometimes it is necessary to let go of the effort to suppress a thought: Instead of furiously trying to sleep when you have insomnia, suggests Daniel Wegner (1994), decide *not* to try to sleep. Instead of trying repeatedly to escape or suppress feelings of worry, sadness, or anger, accept them—and then try to understand and reduce them.

Pennebaker's research suggests how this might be done. In one of his studies, college students were assigned to write about either personal, traumatic experiences or trivial topics for 20 minutes a day, four days in a row. Those who were asked to reveal "their deepest thoughts and feelings" about a traumatic event all had something to talk about. Many told stories of sexual abuse, physical beatings, emotional humiliation, and parental abandonment. Yet most had never discussed these feelings with anyone. The researchers took blood samples from the students to test for the immune activity of lymphocytes. They also measured the students' physical symptoms, emotions, and visits to the health center. On every measure, the students who wrote about traumatic experiences were better off than those who did not (Pennebaker, Kiecolt-Glaser, & Glaser, 1988). Some of them showed *short-term* increases in anger and depression; writing about an unpleasant experience was not fun. But as months passed, their health and well-being improved.

The researchers believe that "the failure to confront a trauma forces the person to live with it in an unresolved manner." Actively writing or talking about it helps people assimilate the experience and come to a sense of completion about it. But confession must not turn to obsession. Confessing your deepest thoughts and feelings is not therapeutic if you keep rehearsing and confessing them endlessly to all who will listen. The key is physiological release *and* a new cognitive perspective.

Writing about the same experience for several days can produce insight and distance. One woman, who had been molested at the age of 9 by a boy a year older, at first wrote about her feelings of embarrassment and guilt. By the third day, she was writing about how angry she felt at the boy. By the last day, she had begun to see the whole event differently; he was young too, after all. When the study was over, she said, "Before, when I thought about it, I'd lie to myself. . . . Now, I don't feel like I even have to think about it because I got it off my chest. I finally admitted that it happened."

Confession even seems able to speed up the normal coping process associated with major life changes. In one study, freshmen wrote either about their feelings associated with going to college or their feelings on superficial topics. The experimental group reported higher feelings of homesickness and anxiety in the short run, but by the end of the school year they had had far fewer bouts of flu and visits to the infirmary than the control group (Pennebaker, Colder, & Sharp, 1990).

To see if this research will benefit you, why not keep a diary this year? All you have to do is jot down, from time to time, your "deepest thoughts and feelings" about school, your past, your future, anything. Pennebaker predicts that you will have fewer colds, headaches, and trips to the medical clinic next year.

Summary

1. Hans Selye argued that environmental *stressors* such as heat, pain, and toxins cause the body to respond with fight-or-flee responses, occurring in stages: alarm, resistance, exhaustion. If a stressor persists, it may overwhelm the body's ability to cope, and fatigue and illness may result. Current theories, however, emphasize the psychological factors that mediate between the stressor and the stress, especially qualities of the individual (personality traits and perceptions) and how the individual copes with problems.

2. The immune system consists of several types of blood cells that are designed to recognize and destroy foreign substances, such as viruses. Researchers in the field of *psychoneuroimmunology* are studying how psychological factors, the nervous and endocrine systems, and the immune system interact to produce illness.

3. Certain major events, such as divorce or the death of a loved one, are known to be extremely stressful. Daily hassles, such as traffic jams, loud noise, and crowding, are also stressful but primarily for people who believe they cannot control these annoyances. Continuing, uncontrollable situations of powerlessness are far more stressful than one major event.

4. Researchers have sought possible links between personality traits (such as being chronically hostile or having a tendency to repress all negative emotions) and illness. But there are several possible connections between emotion and disease: Disease may cause emotional changes; some emotions, such as worry, may cause unhealthy habits, which cause disease; a third factor may affect both emotionality and disease; and emotion and illness may affect each other in a complex feedback loop.

5. Although evidence for the influence of *Type A personality* on heart disease is mixed, studies indicate that antagonistic hostility increases the risk. However, the link between depression and illness, and between repressing emotions and becoming ill, remains unclear. It may be that negative emotions in general can lead to a "disease-prone personality." Another important personality factor that affects health is *optimistic or pessimistic explanatory style*.

6. An important goal of health psychology is prevention—encouraging people to eat nutritious meals, to quit or never start smoking, not to abuse drugs, and the like. Some problems in prevention are that health habits are often entrenched in childhood, people have little incentive to change their patterns, and health habits are independent of one another and are unstable.

7. Feelings of personal control and self-efficacy affect a person's ability to tolerate pain, live with ongoing illness and stress, and recover from disease. People who have an *internal locus of control* believe that events are largely under their control, in contrast to people who have an *external locus of control*. However, control and health influence each other, and control is also affected by one's circumstances. People can sometimes have too strong a sense of control; the healthiest balance is taking responsibility for getting well without blaming oneself for getting sick. Health and well-being seem to depend on the right combination of *primary control*, trying to change the stressful situation, and *secondary control*, learning to accept the stressful situation. Cultures differ in the kind of control they emphasize and value.

8. *Coping* involves a person's active and adaptive efforts to manage demands that he or she feels are stressful. Methods of coping include *solving the problem; rethinking the problem* (reappraising the situation to find meaning in the experience, comparing oneself to others with the problem, finding the right balance between vigilance and distraction in attending to the problem, and seeing the humor in the situation); and *living with the problem* (reducing the physical effects of stress through relaxation, meditation, or exercise). Healthy coping also involves *social interest* in other people.

9. Friends, family, and other sources of *social support* are important in maintaining physical health and emotional well-being. They provide emotional support, cognitive guidance, tangible support, companionship, and the sense of attachment. The need for social support is universal, but cultures differ in the value they place on the amount and kind of support. Parents and friends can also be stressful, a source of hassles, conflicts, burdens, and betrayals. They sometimes provide the wrong kind of support or too much support or they offer support at the wrong time. A *dense network,* in which many friends know each other, is good for stability and identity but can make change difficult if one member wants to break away. In close relationships, a partner can be both a source of support and of stress. Couples who fight in a hostile and negative way, in contrast to those who argue with the goal of understanding and compromise, show impaired immune function.

10. Psychological factors are only one link in a long chain that connects stress and illness; illness is not "all in your mind" or easily cured with "the right attitude." Still, psychologists agree on the importance to good health of social support, practicing good health habits, developing control and self-efficacy, and of acquiring good coping skills. Coping with stress does not mean trying to live without pain, problems, or nuisances. It means learning how to live with them.

Key Terms

health psychology   *519*
behavioral medicine   *519*
pathogenic   *519*
salutogenic   *519*
alarm/resistance/exhaustion phases of stress   *520*
eustress   *520*
psychological stress   *521*
psychosomatic   *522*
psychoneuroimmunology   *522*
hassles   *523*
Type A behavior pattern   *527*
neurotic versus antagonistic hostility *527*
"disease-prone personality"   *529*

pessimistic and optimistic explanatory styles   *529*
locus of control (internal versus external)   *531*
primary control   *533*
secondary control   *533*
coping   *536*
emotion-focused coping   *536*
problem-focused coping   *536*
reappraisal   *537*
social comparisons   *537*
avoidance and vigilance   *538*
social interest   *541*
dense network   *546*

15

Psychological Disorders

In Alice's Adventures in Wonderland *the Mad Hatter is a comic character. But the origins of the expression "mad as a hatter" aren't funny: A century ago, many hatmakers suffered mental impairment as a result of inhaling mercury vapors where they worked.*

Who in the rainbow can draw the line where the violet tint ends and the orange tint begins? . . . So with sanity and insanity. In pronounced cases there is no question about them. But in [less obvious cases, few people are willing] to draw the exact line of demarcation . . . though for a fee some professional experts will.

■ HERMAN MELVILLE, *BILLY BUDD* ■

You don't have to be a psychologist to recognize extreme forms of abnormal behavior. A homeless woman stands on a street corner every night between midnight and 3:00 A.M., screaming obscenities and curses; by day, she is calm. A man in a shop tells you confidentially that his shoes have been bugged by the FBI, his phone is wiretapped, and his friends are spying on him for the CIA. An old man has kept every one of his daily newspapers going back to 1945, and, although there is no room in his house for anything else, he panics at the thought of giving them up.

When most people think of "abnormal behavior," they think of odd individuals like these whose bizarre stories fill the newspapers. They assume that "abnormal" is the same as "insane," "crazy," or "sick." But most episodes of abnormal behavior are far less dramatic and would never make the nightly news. They occur when an individual cannot cope effectively with the stresses and problems of life. The person may become so anxious and worried that work is impaired, or become severely depressed for months, or begin to abuse drugs. In most cases, as the novelist Melville knew, there is no "exact line of demarcation" that indicates when normalcy ends and madness begins.

You will have noticed by now that we have tried to avoid traps of either–or thinking in this book, whether the subject is right-brain versus left-brain differences or health versus illness. It is the same with *normal* and *abnormal*, terms that describe a rainbow of behaviors, with many shadings of color and brightness. A particular problem is not a fixed point on the rainbow. It may shift over time; a person may go through episodes of inability to function and then be fine between them. Problems also vary in intensity; they may be mildly uncomfortable, serious but endurable, or completely incapacitating. Psychologists and psychiatrists diagnose and treat a wide range of "abnormal" problems.

One of the most common worries that people have is "Am I normal?" It is normal to fear being abnormal. Everyone on occasion has difficulties that seem too much to handle, that make us feel we can't cope. It is also normal to experience Medical Students' Syndrome: deciding that you suffer from whatever disorder you are reading about. Precisely because many psychological disorders are so common, differing from "normal" problems only by a shade of intensity on the rainbow, it is often easy to conclude that you have them all. (We are tempted to add that this faulty conclusion is a pigment of the imagination.)

Joan of Arc heard voices that inspired her to martyrdom. Was she sane and saintly or mad?

▪ DEFINING DISORDER

Members of a sect believe that they are being persecuted by nonbelievers, that a secret cabal controls the world, and that World War III is imminent. They are stockpiling weapons and building bunkers to protect themselves. This behavior is "normal" to all members of the group, but would you call it a sign of mental disorder? Why or why not?

Many people tend to confuse the terms *abnormal behavior* with *mental disorder,* but the two are not the same. A person may behave in ways that are statistically rare or that deviate from the norm without having a mental illness. Some "abnormal" behavior is destructive, such as murder; some is charmingly unique, such as collecting ceramic pigs; and some is desirable, such as genius. Conversely, some mental disorders, such as depression or anxiety, can be widespread in a society; and some thoughts or behaviors that would usually be called disordered, such as paranoid delusions or sadism, may even be considered "normal" or desirable qualities in certain cults and organizations, such as the neo-Nazi Aryan Nation.

Nevertheless, defining mental disorder is not easy, because it depends in part on who is doing the defining and for what purpose. Here are several definitions in current use:

1. *Violation of cultural standards.* One definition of a mental disorder is that it involves behavior that violates the standards of a group. Every society sets up its own standards of appropriate behavior and cultural rules that people are expected to follow. Some kinds of behavior are shared by many cultures, such as wearing clothes and not committing murder. But others might be normal in one culture and abnormal in another. For example, seeing visions might be interpreted as a sign of schizophrenia in a twentieth-century farmer, but as a sign of healthy religious fervor in a thirteenth-century monk. In North America, hallucinations of a deceased spouse or other relative are thought to be abnormal. Actually, this experience is not uncommon during bereavement; it is just that grieving spouses don't talk about it much because they fear being considered "crazy." In some cultures, however, such as those of the Chinese and the Hopi, hallucinations are regarded as normal expressions of grief and therefore are more prevalent and acceptable (DePaola & DePaola, 1988). The "line on the rainbow" between normal and abnormal hallucinations is often very fuzzy indeed (Bentall, 1990).

2. *Maladaptive behavior.* Many psychologists define mental disorder in terms of behavior that is maladaptive for the individual or society. This definition would apply to the behavior of a woman who is so afraid of crowds that she can-

People all over the world paint their bodies or parts of their bodies, but what is perfectly normal in one culture often is abnormal or eccentric in another. Hiromi Nakano (left), whose body has been completely tattooed by her husband Choshiro, has taken body painting to an extreme rare in most societies, but the Samburu tribesman of Kenya (center) is painted and adorned in ways typical of his culture. And the tattoos of the American bikers (right) are abnormal to most Americans but perfectly normal in the biking subculture. How are you reacting to these examples of body painting? Do you think they are beautiful, amusing, disgusting, or creepy?

not leave her house, the behavior of a man who drinks so much he cannot keep a job, and the behavior of a student who is so anxious about failure that he cannot write term papers or take exams. It also covers the actions of individuals who say they feel fine and deny that anything is wrong but who behave in ways that are disruptive or dangerous to the community: the child who sets fires, the compulsive gambler who loses the family savings.

3. *Emotional distress.* A third definition identifies mental disorder in terms of a person's suffering. A person may conform to all the rules of his or her community, working and getting along adequately, yet privately feel unreasonably anxious, afraid, angry, depressed, or guilty. By these criteria, according to a nationwide study of 20,000 randomly selected adults, about 28 percent of all Americans have one or more disorders in a given year—such as depression, anxiety, incapacitating fears, and alcohol or other drug problems (Regier et al., 1993; see also Kessler et al., 1994). The benefit of this definition is that it takes the person's own distress as a measure of disorder instead of imposing a single standard for everyone. A behavior that is unendurable or upsetting for one person, such as lack of interest in sex, may be acceptable and thus no problem to another.

4. *The legal definition: impaired judgment and lack of self-control.* In law, the definition of mental disorder rests primarily on whether a person is aware of the consequences of his or her actions and can control his or her behavior. If not, the person may be declared insane—that is, incompetent to stand trial. But *insanity* is a legal term only; psychologists and psychiatrists do not use the terms *sanity* or *insanity* in relation to mental disorders.

Each of these definitions is useful, and no one of them is enough. In this chapter we will define **mental disorder** broadly, as any behavior or emotional state that causes an individual great suffering or worry; is self-defeating or self-destructive; or is maladaptive and disrupts the person's relationships or the larger community. Many people will have some mental-health problem in the course of their lives. This is normal.

▪ DILEMMAS OF DIAGNOSIS

Even armed with a broad definition of mental disorder, psychologists have found that agreeing on a specific diagnosis is easier said than done. As George Albee (1985), a past president of the American Psychological Association, put it, "Appendicitis, a brain tumor and chicken pox are the same everywhere, regardless of culture or class; mental conditions, it seems, are not." In this section we will examine the difficulties of measuring and diagnosing some abnormal "mental conditions."

Measuring Mental Disorders

Clinical and personality psychologists often use psychological tests to help them decide if a person has a mental disorder. In Chapter 12 we discussed *projective* tests, which are based on the assumption that the test-taker will project his or her unconscious conflicts and motivations onto the stimulus materials. (You may recall the problems with reliability and validity of these tests; see pages 463–464.) Most clinicians also rely on *objective tests,* or **inventories,** to diagnose their patients' problems. These tests are standardized questionnaires that require written responses, typically to multiple-choice or true-false items. Usually the test-taker is asked to report how she or he feels or acts in certain circumstances. For example, the Beck Depression Inventory is widely used to diagnose the severity of depression and distress; and the Spielberger State-Trait Anger Inventory and the Taylor Manifest Anxiety Scale assess degrees and expressions of anger and anxiety. In general, objective tests have better reliability (they are more consistent over time) and validity (they actually measure

▪ **mental disorder**
Any behavior or emotional state that causes an individual great suffering or worry, is self-defeating or self-destructive, or is maladaptive and disrupts the person's relationships or the larger community.

▪ **inventories**
Standardized objective questionnaires requiring written responses; they typically include scales on which people rate themselves.

what they say they measure) than projective methods or clinicians' subjective judgment (Dawes, 1994).

The most famous and widely used objective test of normal personality and mental disorders is the **Minnesota Multiphasic Personality Inventory (MMPI).** The MMPI was developed in the 1930s by Starke Hathaway and J. Charnley McKinley, who wanted a way to screen people with psychological disorders. A thousand potential test items were given to approximately 200 mental patients and 1,500 nonpatients in Minneapolis. The items took the form of statements about symptoms, moods, attitudes, and behavior, and test-takers had to indicate whether the statements applied to themselves by responding "true," "false," or "cannot say." Of the initial test items, 550 were answered differently on the average by the disturbed and nondisturbed sample groups; these items were retained. The various items were assigned to ten clinical categories, or *scales,* that identified such problems as depression, paranoia, schizophrenia, and introversion. Four *validity scales* indicated whether a test-taker was lying, careless, defensive, or evasive while answering the items. For example, if a person tried to present an overall favorable but unrealistic image on nearly every item, the person's score on the lie scale would be high.

Since the original MMPI was devised, hundreds of additional scales have been added, and more than 8,000 books and articles have been written on the test (Butcher & Finn, 1983; Cronbach, 1990). The inventory has been used in some 50 countries, on everyone from ordinary job applicants to Russian cosmonauts, and it is increasingly used to assess normal personality traits rather than emotional disorders. In 1989, a major revision of the MMPI was released, the MMPI-2, with norms based on a sample that was more representative in terms of region, ethnicity, age, and gender (Butcher et al., 1989).

Despite its popularity, the MMPI has many critics. Some have observed that the test may be ethnically and culturally biased because its standards of "normalcy" do not reflect cultural differences. Although the sample used for establishing test norms in the MMPI-2 was an improvement, it still underrepresented minorities, the elderly, the poor, and the poorly educated. Some of the scales overlap; some are still based on inadequate and outdated norms; and some items are affected by the respondent's tendency to give the socially appropriate answer rather than an honest one (Edwards & Edwards, 1991; Helmes & Reddon, 1993).

The validity and reliability of the test also have come under fire. One review of studies concluded that the MMPI is adequate if the test is used for its original purpose—identifying people with personality or emotional disorders (Parker, Hanson, & Hunsley, 1988). Yet in practice, the MMPI, along with other objective tests, is often used in business, industry, and education for inappropriate reasons by persons who are not well trained in testing. Two psychologists who reviewed the entire history and validity of both MMPIs concluded that these tests are "outmoded" and "inefficient," and that their interpretation requires "substantial experience and sophistication" by the clinician who administers them (Helmes & Reddon, 1993). Many clinicians, for their part, swear by the MMPI as a diagnostic tool. Others find it useful, but believe that any objective test is limited. They argue that only skilled clinicians can detect the self-protective defenses and the denial of distress that some people bring to test-taking ("Me, unhappy? Never") (Shedler, Mayman, & Manis, 1993).

The debate about the MMPI illustrates a deeper issue: whether mental disorder can be assessed objectively at all. The debate about testing is a whisper compared to the noisy controversy about the diagnosis of mental disorder itself.

Diagnosis: Art or Science?

In the early years of the nineteenth century, a physician named Samuel Cartwright argued that many slaves were suffering from two forms of mental illness: *drapetomania,* an uncontrollable urge to escape from slavery, and *dysathesia*

■ **Minnesota Multiphasic Personality Inventory (MMPI)**

A widely used objective personality test.

aethiopica, the symptoms of which included destroying property on the plantation, being disobedient, talking back, refusing to work, and fighting back when beaten. "Sanity for a slave was synonymous with submission," notes Hope Landrine (1988), "and protest and seeking freedom were the equivalent of psychopathology." Thus doctors could assure slaveowners that a mental illness, not the intolerable condition of slavery, made slaves seek freedom.

Today, "drapetomania" sounds foolish and cruel, and most people assume that the bad old days of psychiatric misdiagnosis are past. Yet many psychologists realize that cultural factors and subjective interpretations still affect the process of diagnosis, which raises many important issues for those who define and treat mental disorders.

In theory, diagnostic categories must meet a set of solid scientific criteria to be included in the "bible" of psychological and psychiatric diagnosis, the *Diagnostic and Statistical Manual of Mental Disorders* (DSM), which is published by the American Psychiatric Association. The first edition of the DSM, in 1952, was only 128 pages long and listed a few types of mental "illness." The second edition, the DSM-II, appeared in 1968; it too was short and contained brief descriptions of organic brain disorders, severe mental disorders, and personality problems. The third edition, DSM-III, published in 1980, began to include normal difficulties (such as tobacco dependence, marital conflicts, and sexual problems) along with serious disorders such as schizophrenia. The revised third edition, DSM-III-R, in 1987, was 567 pages long and listed more than 200 kinds of mental disorder. The fattest edition yet, the DSM-IV, published in 1994, is nearly 900 pages long and contains more than 300 mental disorders.

The primary aim of the DSM is *descriptive:* to provide clear criteria of diagnostic categories, so that clinicians and researchers can agree on the disorders they are talking about, study them, and treat them. (For a list of its major categories, see Table 15.1.) The DSM makes few assumptions about the causes of the disorders it describes; in many cases, the causes are not known. Each disorder is identified by its behavioral signs. Where possible, information is also provided about typical age of onset, predisposing factors, course of the disorder, prevalence (rare or common), sex ratio of those affected, and cultural issues that might affect diagnosis. The DSM also classifies each disorder on five *axes,* or factors:

- The primary diagnosis of the problem, such as depression.
- Ingrained aspects of the individual's personality that are likely to affect the patient's behavior and ability to be treated, such as narcissism or dependency.
- General medical conditions that are relevant to the disorder, such as respiratory or digestive problems.
- "Psychosocial and environmental problems" that can make the disorder worse, such as job and housing troubles or loss of a support group.
- A global assessment of the patient's overall level of functioning in work, relationships, and leisure time. This factor indicates whether the problem is of recent origin or of long duration, and how incapacitating it is.

The DSM has had an extraordinary impact worldwide. It has standardized the categories of what is, and what is not, a mental disorder. Its categories and terminology have become the common language of most clinicians and researchers. Virtually all textbooks in psychiatry and psychology base their discussions of mental disorders on the DSM. Insurance companies require clinicians to assign their patients the appropriate DSM code number of the diagnosed disorder, which puts pressure on compilers of the manual to add more diagnoses and refinements so that physicians and psychologists will be compensated. Attorneys and judges often refer to the manual's list of mental

Table 15.1   Major Diagnostic Categories in the DSM-IV

Disorders usually first diagnosed in infancy, childhood, or adolescence include mental retardation, attention deficit disorders (such as hyperactivity or an inability to concentrate), eating disorders, and developmental problems.

Delirium, dementia, amnesia, and other cognitive disorders are those resulting from brain damage, degenerative diseases such as syphilis or Alzheimer's, toxic substances, or drugs.

Substance-related disorders are problems associated with excessive use of or withdrawal from alcohol, amphetamines, caffeine, cocaine, hallucinogens, nicotine, opiates, or other drugs.

Schizophrenia and other psychotic disorders are disorders characterized by delusions, hallucinations, and severe disturbances in thinking and emotion.

Mood disorders include major depression, bipolar disorder (manic depression), and dysthymia (chronic depressed mood).

Anxiety disorders include generalized anxiety disorder, phobias, panic attacks with or without agoraphobia, posttraumatic stress disorder, and obsessive thoughts or compulsive rituals.

Somatoform disorders involve individual reports of physical symptoms (such as paralysis, heart palpitations, dizziness) for which no organic cause can be found. This category includes *hypochondria,* the extreme preoccupation with one's health and the unfounded conviction that one is ill, and *conversion disorder,* in which a physical symptom (such as a paralyzed arm or blindness) serves a psychological function.

Dissociative disorders include dissociative *amnesia,* in which important events cannot be remembered after a traumatic event, and *dissociative identity disorder* (formerly "multiple personality disorder"), characterized by the presence of two or more distinct identities or personality states.

Sexual and gender identity disorders include problems of sexual (gender) identity, such as transsexualism (wanting to be the other gender); sexual performance (such as premature ejaculation, lack of orgasm, or lack of desire); and paraphilias, which involve unusual or bizarre imagery or acts that are necessary for sexual arousal, as in fetishism, sadomasochism, or exhibitionism.

Impulse control disorders involve an inability to resist an impulse to perform some act that is harmful to the individual or to others, as in pathological gambling, stealing (*kleptomania*), setting fires (*pyromania*), or violent rages.

Personality disorders are inflexible and maladaptive patterns that cause distress to the individual or impair the ability to function; they include *paranoid, narcissistic,* and *antisocial* personality disorders.

Additional conditions that may be a focus of clinical attention include "problems in living" such as bereavement, academic difficulties, religious or spiritual problems, acculturation problems, and "phase of life" problems.

---

disorders, even though the DSM warns that its categories "may not be wholly relevant to legal judgments."

Because of the power of the DSM to define mental disorders, it is important to know its limitations. Critics point to the following concerns about the scientific basis of diagnosis in general and the DSM in particular:

1. *The fostering of overdiagnosis and self-fulfilling prophecies.* It has been commonly observed that when people have a tool, they will use it; Abraham Kaplan (1967) called this tendency "The Law of the Instrument." "If you give a small boy a hammer," Kaplan wrote, "it will turn out that everything he runs into needs pounding." So it is, some say, with clinicians. Give them the instruments to diagnose disorders, and everything they run into will need treatment. For example, before 1980 fewer than 200 cases of dissociative identity disorder (commonly known as "multiple personality disorder") had ever been diag-

nosed. Since 1980, when the DSM-III included new criteria for this diagnosis, more than *thirty thousand* cases have been reported (Nathan, 1994). Does this mean that the disorder is being better identified, or that it is being overdiagnosed because clinicians are looking for it (Holmes, 1994; McHugh, 1993a)? Clinicians are also more likely to diagnose a particular disorder once a treatment seems to be successful for it. As medication was promoted to treat obsessive-compulsive disorder, for example, the rate of diagnosis of this problem rose significantly (Stoll, Tohen, & Baldessarini, 1993).

Many clinicians and social critics are also concerned that the act of diagnosing someone can create a self-fulfilling prophecy in which a person then tries to conform to the assigned diagnosis (Robitscher, 1980; Rosenhan, 1973). Moreover, once a person has acquired a label ("borderline schizophrenic"), other people often become oblivious to changes in the person's behavior, continuing to see him or her in terms of the diagnosis (see Chapter 17).

2. *Confounding serious "mental disorders" with normal problems in living.* The DSM is not called "The Diagnostic and Statistical Manual of Mental Disorders and a Whole Bunch of Everyday Problems." Some critics fear that by lumping together normal problems, such as the grief following bereavement, with true mental illness, such as having delusions, the DSM implies that everyday problems are comparable to true disorders—and equally likely to require professional treatment (Dumont, 1987; Maddux, 1993; Szasz, 1961/1967). Yet the compilers of the DSM keep adding everyday problems to its roster. The latest version actually contains "disorder of written expression" (having trouble writing clearly), "mathematics disorder" (not doing well in math), and "caffeine-induced sleep disorder."

3. *Misusing diagnoses for social and political purposes.* Some critics of the DSM system of categorization are concerned that once people are given a formal diagnosis for their problems, they may feel absolved of responsibility for their actions—or at least be able to use the label to claim diminished responsibility for their actions. This concern was a major reason that the task force revising the DSM-III decided to drop a proposed diagnosis called "paraphilic coercive disorder," describing the behavior of men who rape. The task force agreed with women who were concerned that rapists diagnosed as having such a "disorder" would not be held responsible.

The subjective nature of diagnosis raises critical questions for society: If people have a disorder, are they still responsible for their actions? Which disorders described in this chapter merit the legal defense of "diminished responsibility"? Where would you draw the line between labeling or explaining people's problems and excusing the behavior they attribute to their problems?

4. *Implying that the subjective art of diagnosis can be made objectively scientific.* Finally, some critics argue that the whole enterprise of the DSM is a foolhardy effort to impose a veneer of science on what is ultimately an art form. This is why, they say, the reliability in tests of most DSM categories has consistently been poor: That is, even when clinicians use the DSM's criteria for diagnosing disorders, many still fail to agree with one another on a given person's problem (Kirk & Kutchins, 1992).

Such critics maintain that the DSM wants to look like a purely objective set of disorders, as if no bias or choice were involved. Yet the DSM is by its very nature subjective, both in terms of what it defines as a mental disorder and what it does not (Dumont, 1987; Maddux, 1993; Tiefer, 1992, 1995). Many of the decisions about which categories of mental disorder to include or exclude are based not on empirical evidence, but on group consensus or the pressure to have more diagnosable categories that insurance companies will compensate (Kirk & Kutchins, 1992).

Thus, when the American Psychiatric Association decided in the early 1970s to remove homosexuality from the DSM, it did not base its decision on the research showing that homosexuals were no more disturbed than heterosexuals. Rather, it *took a vote of its members* (Bayer, 1981). Over the years, psychiatrists have quite properly rejected many other "disorders" that reflected earlier cultural prejudices, such as drapetomania, lack of vaginal orgasm, childhood masturbation disorder, masochism, and nymphomania (Wakefield, 1992). But they have also voted in new "disorders" that reflect today's prejudices and values, such as hypoactive sexual desire disorder—not wanting to have sex often "enough." Compilers of the DSM-III-R, amid much controversy, voted in a diagnosis called "self-defeating personality disorder," which described the extreme self-sacrificing qualities of the female role; compilers of the DSM-IV voted it out. But they kept, in an appendix, premenstrual dysphoric disorder, even though, as we saw in Chapter 5, there is no coherent definition of this alleged syndrome and men have as many symptoms and mood changes over the course of a month as women do.

The point to underscore is that *as times change, so do ideas about many mental disorders.* And that, in turn, means that clinicians must be aware of how their own beliefs and leanings affect their clinical judgments, even if they are trying to follow objective criteria. In one study, for example, 47 therapists were randomly assigned to view one of two versions of a videotaped simulation of a depressed male client. The tapes were identical except for the man's job and family roles: He was portrayed as either a traditional breadwinner or a nontraditional "househusband" whose wife earned the family income. Later, when the therapists evaluated the man's mental health, assigned a diagnosis, and outlined a proposed treatment, they judged nontraditional men as being more disturbed than traditional men (Robertson & Fitzgerald, 1990).

Advocates of the DSM argue that when the manual is used correctly, diagnoses are more accurate and bias is reduced, and that new field studies are improving the empirical basis of the clinical categories (Barlow, 1991; Spitzer & Williams, 1988). A study of psychiatric patients in Maryland, for instance, found better accuracy in the diagnosis of schizophrenia and mood disorders than other studies had, apparently because the physicians were more closely following DSM criteria (Pulver et al., 1988). Other advocates argue that the correct labeling of a disorder helps people identify the source of their unhappiness and leads them to proper treatment (Kessler et al., 1994). They respond to the criticisms of subjectivity in diagnosis by pointing out that some mental disorders, such as schizophrenia, anxiety, and depression, occur in all societies. The fact, they say, that *some* diagnoses reflect society's biases, such as drapetomania, doesn't mean that *all* diagnoses do (Wakefield, 1992). Anthropologist Jane Murphy (1976), who lived with the Inuit of Alaska and the Yorubas of Nigeria, expected that their ideas of mental illness would be different from those held in Western culture; but she found many commonalities. In every society, individuals who have delusions, who are severely depressed, or who can't control their behavior are considered to have mental illnesses (Kleinman, 1988).

We will return to these controversies as we examine some of the major categories of disorder in the DSM.

Quick QUIZ

1. What is the advantage of inventories, compared to projective tests and clinical judgment, in diagnosing mental disorders?
2. The Minnesota Multiphasic Personality Inventory (MMPI) (a) has norms based on a sample that is culturally and socioeconomically representative of most people; (b) is useful for assessing normal personality traits; (c) requires the test-giver to have substantial experience and training.
3. The primary purpose of the DSM is to (a) provide descriptive criteria for diagnosing mental disorders; (b) help psychologists assess normal as well as abnormal personality traits; (c) describe the causes of common mental disorders; (d) keep the number of diagnostic categories of mental disorders to a minimum.
4. True or false: The DSM considers the psychosocial and environmental problems that can make a disorder worse.
5. What four concerns do critics have about the DSM and its use?

Answers:

1. In general, they have better reliability and validity. 2. c 3. a 4. true 5. Fostering overdiagnosis and self-fulfilling prophecies; confounding normal problems in living with mental disorders; using diagnoses for undesirable social and political purposes; and using scientific-sounding categories to disguise the essentially subjective process of diagnosis.

Is this woman feeling normal fear or unreasonable panic? (Turn the page.)

▪ ANXIETY DISORDERS

The body, sensibly, prepares us to feel anxiety (a general state of apprehension or psychological tension) or fear (apprehension about a specific threat) when we are facing dangerous, unfamiliar, or stressful situations, such as making a first parachute jump or waiting for important news. In the short run, these are adaptive emotions that prepare us to cope with danger. But some individuals are more prone than others to irrational fear or to a chronic state of anxiety. In clinical terms, fear and anxiety can take several forms: *generalized anxiety disorder,* marked by long-lasting, continuous feelings of apprehension and doom; *phobias,* unrealistic fears of specific things or situations; and *obsessive-compulsive disorder,* in which people develop irrational thoughts and rituals designed to ward off anxious feelings.

Anxiety and Phobias

The sign of **generalized anxiety disorder** is continuous, uncontrollable anxiety or worry—feelings of foreboding and dread—that occurs more days than not in a six-month period and is not brought on by physical causes such as disease, drugs, or drinking too much coffee. Symptoms include restlessness or

▪ **generalized anxiety disorder**
A continuous state of anxiety marked by feelings of worry and dread, apprehension, difficulties in concentration, and signs of motor tension.

It is normal to feel afraid when you jump out of a plane for the first time. But people with anxiety disorders feel as if they are jumping out of planes all the time.

■ **phobia**
An unrealistic fear of a specific situation, activity, or object.

■ **agoraphobia**
"Fear of fear"; a set of phobias, often set off by a panic attack, involving the basic fear of being away from a safe place or person.

■ **panic attack**
A brief feeling of intense fear and impending doom or death, accompanied by intense physiological symptoms such as rapid breathing and pulse, and dizziness.

feeling "keyed up"; being easily fatigued; difficulty concentrating; irritability; muscle tension and jitteriness; and sleep disturbance.

Chronic anxiety has no single cause. *Predisposing factors* include hereditary predisposition, inadequate coping mechanisms, traumatic events, and psychological dispositions, such as having unrealistic goals or unreasonable beliefs (Beck, 1988; Clark, 1988). There are also many *precipitating factors* that produce anxiety and keep it going. You are likely to feel anxious when you are in a situation in which others continually express their disapproval of you, or when you have to adapt yourself to an environment that doesn't fit your personality, such as being a slow-paced person in a fast-moving job.

When anxiety results from experiencing an uncontrollable and unpredictable danger or a natural disaster, it may produce *posttraumatic stress disorder* (PTSD) or *acute stress disorder* (Cardeña et al., 1994; Foa, Zinbarg, & Rothbaum, 1992). PTSD consists of emotional symptoms that are common in people who have suffered traumatic experiences such as war and combat, rape, other assaults, and natural disasters such as hurricanes, fire, or earthquake. The reaction might occur immediately or it might be delayed for months. In contrast, acute stress disorder typically occurs right after the traumatic event and subsides within several months. In both disorders, typical symptoms include reliving the trauma in recurrent, intrusive thoughts or dreams; "psychic numbing," a sense of detachment from others and an inability to feel happy or loving; and increased physiological arousal, reflected in difficulty concentrating, insomnia, and irritability.

A **phobia** is an unrealistic fear of a specific situation, activity, or thing. There are many common phobias, such as fear of heights (acrophobia); fear of closed spaces (claustrophobia); fear of dirt and germs (mysophobia); and fear of such animals as snakes, dogs, insects, and mice (zoophobia). There are also idiosyncratic fears such as porphyrophobia (fear of purple), triskaidekaphobia (fear of the number 13), and brontophobia (fear of thunder).

People who have a *social phobia* have a persistent, irrational fear of situations in which they will be observed by others. They fear that they will do or say something that will humiliate or embarrass them. Common examples of social phobias are fears of speaking or performing in public, using public restrooms, eating in public, and writing in the presence of others.

By far the most disabling fear disorder is **agoraphobia,** which accounts for more than half of the phobia cases for which people seek treatment. Disregard the dictionary and popular definition of agoraphobia as "fear of open spaces." The Greek *agora* was the social, political, business, and religious center of town. It was the public meeting place away from home. The essential feature in what agoraphobics fear is being alone in a public place from which escape might be difficult or help unavailable. They may report a great variety of specific fears—of public buses, driving in traffic or tunnels, eating in restaurants, or going to parties—but the underlying fear is of being away from a safe place, usually home, or a safe person, usually a parent or spouse.

Agoraphobia may begin with a series of **panic attacks** that seem to come out of the blue. A panic attack is a sudden onset of intense fear or terror, with feelings of impending doom. It may last from a few minutes to (more rarely) several hours, and involves such intense symptoms as trembling and shaking; dizziness; chest pain or discomfort; feelings of unreality; hot and cold flashes; sweating; tingling in hands or feet; and a fear of dying, going crazy, or losing control. The attack is so unexpected and so scary that the agoraphobic-to-be begins to avoid situations that he or she thinks may provoke another one. After a while, any sort of emotional arousal, from whatever source, feels too much like anxiety, and the person with agoraphobia will try to avoid it. Because so many of the actions associated with this phobia are designed to help the person avoid a panic attack, researchers often describe agoraphobia as a "fear of fear" rather than a fear of places (Chambless, 1988).

People who have panic attacks are found throughout the world, both in industrial and nonindustrial societies (Barlow, 1990). The common symptoms are heart palpitations, dizziness, and faintness, but culture influences the likelihood of other telltale signs. Feelings of choking or being smothered, numbness, and fear of dying are most common in Latin America and southern Europe; fear of public places is most common in northern Europe and America; and a fear of going crazy is more common in the Americas than in Europe. In Greenland, some fishermen suffer from "kayak-angst": a sudden attack of dizziness and fear that occurs while they are fishing in small, one-person kayaks (Amering & Katschnig, 1990).

Some investigators believe that panic attacks may be caused by biological abnormalities, because they tend to run in families. Studies of twins suggest a heritable component in this disorder, a tendency for the body to respond to stress with a sudden "alarm" reaction. (For other people, the response may be headaches or hives.) During a stressful time, the individual has a panic attack that seems to come from nowhere. In fact, the attack is often related to the physical arousal of stress, prolonged emotion, exercise, drugs such as caffeine or cigarettes, or specific worries (Barlow, 1990; Beck, 1988).

Panic attacks are not uncommon. The essential difference between people who go on to develop a disorder and those who don't lies in *how the person interprets this bodily reaction* (Barlow, 1990; McNally, 1994). Healthy people who have occasional panic attacks dismiss them as being unimportant—a result of some passing crisis, something they ate at lunch, or a difficult day at work. But people who develop a full-fledged panic disorder begin to worry about possible future attacks. They regard the attack as a sign of impending death or disaster instead of a passing moment of agitation. Agoraphobia develops when they begin to avoid any situation that they fear will set off another attack.

Obsessions and Compulsions

Obsessive-compulsive disorder (OCD) is characterized by recurrent, persistent, unwished-for thoughts or images (*obsessions*) and repetitive, ritualized, stereotyped behaviors that the person feels must be carried out to avoid disaster (*compulsions*). The disorder can begin in childhood and it occurs in both sexes; many psychologists believe it has a biological basis. People with this disorder usually realize their thoughts and behaviors are abnormal, but they feel helpless to stop. For one young man, stairs became a treadmill: "At first I'd walk up and down the stairs only three to four times," he recalls. "Later I had to run up and down 63 times in 45 minutes. If I failed, I had to start all over again from the beginning. Then other weird behaviors, such as compulsive washing, started to kick in. . . . They took on a life of their own and became the enemy. I led two lives—one a hidden nightmare, the other normal" (quoted in King, 1989).

A person with obsessive-compulsive disorder often finds his or her obsessions frightening and sometimes repugnant. For example, the person may have repetitive thoughts of killing a child, of becoming contaminated by shaking hands, or of having unknowingly hurt someone in a traffic accident. Obsessive thoughts take many forms, but they are alike in reflecting maladaptive ways of reasoning and processing information. Some people may develop obsessive thoughts because they have difficulty managing anger. In one case, a man had repeated images of hitting his 3-year-old son with a hammer. Unable to explain his horrible thoughts about his beloved son, he assumed he was going insane. Most parents, in fact, have occasional negative feelings about their children and may even entertain a fleeting thought of murder, but they recognize that these brief feelings are not the same as actions. The man, it turned out, felt that his son had usurped his place in his wife's affections, but he was unable to reveal his anger and hurt to his wife directly (Carson & Butcher, 1994).

■ **obsessive-compulsive disorder**
An anxiety disorder in which a person feels trapped in repetitive, persistent thoughts (obsessions) and repetitive, ritualized behaviors (compulsions) designed to reduce anxiety.

The Disease Germ Is
More Dangerous
Than the Mad Dog

Cultural compulsions? A normal concern with hygiene in one culture could seem abnormal in another. This Lysol ad played on Americans' fears of disease by warning about the "unseen menace—more threatening, more fatal, more cruel than a million mad dogs—. . . the disease germ"!

People who suffer from compulsions do not feel they have any control over them. For example, a woman *must* check the furnace, lights, locks, oven, and fireplace three times before she can sleep; a man *must* wash his hands and face precisely eight times before he leaves the house. The most common compulsions are hand washing, counting, touching, and checking. Most sufferers of OCD do not enjoy these rituals and even realize that the behavior is senseless. But if they try to break the ritual, they feel mounting anxiety that is relieved only by giving in to the compulsion. They are like the man who constantly snaps his fingers to keep tigers away. "But there aren't any tigers here," says a friend. "You see! It works!" answers the man.

Many people have trivial compulsions and superstitious rituals; as we noted in Chapter 7, baseball players are famous for them. Obsessions and compulsions become serious when they trouble the individual and interfere with his or her life. But they also become serious when they interfere with the life of the target of a person's preoccupation. Some states have passed "antistalking" laws to prohibit people with obsessions about celebrities or lovers who spurned them from compulsively following or threatening them.

Anxiety disorders, uncomfortable or painful as they can be, are at least a sign of commitment to the future. They mean a person can anticipate the future enough to worry about it. But sometimes people's hopes for the future become extinguished. They are no longer anxious that something *may* go wrong; they are convinced it *will* go wrong, so there is no point in trying. This belief is a sign of the disorder of depression.

Quick QUIZ

A. We hope you don't feel anxious about matching the term on the left with its description on the right:

1. social phobia	**a.** need to perform ritual
2. generalized anxiety disorder	**b.** fear of fear; of being trapped in public
3. posttraumatic stress disorder	**c.** continuing sense of doom and worry
4. agoraphobia	**d.** repeated, unwanted thoughts
5. compulsion	**e.** fear of meeting new people
6. obsession	**f.** anxiety state following severe shock

B. Two psychologists are debating the case of an anxious and depressed Japanese-American man who, with 112,000 other Japanese-Americans in World War II, lost his job and home and was forcibly sent to a U.S. internment camp. Dr. Smith diagnoses posttraumatic stress disorder. Dr. Jones believes that because the man's symptoms result from an act of governmental injustice, the diagnosis should be something like "post-oppression disorder" (Loo, 1991). Can you identify the main *assumption* in the kind of label each psychologist is using and the solution it implies?

Answers:

A. 1. e 2. c 3. f 4. b 5. a 6. d **B.** Dr. Smith assumes that the origins of the man's unhappiness lie within him, in his own personal reaction to the trauma of imprisonment; the implied solution is psychotherapy. Dr. Jones assumes that the man's unhappiness is a result of a specific miscarriage of justice; the implied solution, in addition to psychotherapy, might involve a social remedy, such as reparations.

■ MOOD DISORDERS

Many people use the word *depression* to describe normal sadness, gloom, and loss of pep, and they mistake these normal states for an abnormal condition. Of course, everyone feels depressed at times. Severe forms of depression, however, go beyond normal sadness over life's problems, and even beyond the wild grief that may accompany tragedy or bereavement. Serious depression is so wide-spread that it has been called the common cold of psychiatric disturbances.

Depression and Mania

Major depression is severe enough to disrupt a person's ordinary function-ing. It differs from chronic depressed mood, a condition called *dysthymia* [dis-THIGH-me-a], in the intensity and duration of symptoms. In dysthymia, the depressive symptoms are milder, and they *are* the person's customary way of functioning.

Major depression brings emotional, behavioral, and cognitive changes. Depressed people report despair and hopelessness. They are tearful and weepy. They think often of death or suicide. They lose interest or pleasure in their usual activities. They feel unable to get up and do things; it takes an enormous effort just to get dressed. Their thinking patterns feed their bleak moods. They exaggerate minor failings, ignore or discount positive events ("She didn't mean that compliment; she was only being polite"), and focus on anything that goes wrong ("Just my luck to miss that train"). Unlike normal sadness or grief, major depression involves low self-esteem. Emotionally healthy grieving people do not see themselves as completely worthless and unlovable, and they know at some level that grief will pass. Depressed people interpret all losses as signs of per-sonal failure and conclude that they will never be happy again.

Depression is accompanied by physical changes as well. The depressed per-son may stop eating or overeat, have difficulty falling asleep or sleeping through the night, lose sexual desire, have trouble concentrating, and feel tired all the time. Some sufferers have other physical reactions, such as inexplicable pain or headaches. (Because these symptoms can also be signs of physical ill-ness, people should have a thorough medical exam before depression is diag-nosed.) About half of all people who go through a period of major depression will do so only once. Others have recurrent bouts. Some people have episodes that are many years apart, while others have clusters of depressive episodes over a few years. Alarmingly, depression and suicide rates among young people have increased rapidly in recent years. (See "Taking Psychology with You.")

At the opposite pole from depression is *mania,* an abnormally high state of exhilaration. You might think it's impossible to feel *too* good, but mania is not the normal joy of being in love or winning the Pulitzer Prize. Someone in a manic phase is expansive to an extent that is out of character. The symptoms are exactly the opposite of those in depression. Instead of feeling fatigued and listless, the manic person is full of energy. Instead of feeling unambitious, hope-less, and powerless, the manic person feels full of ambitions, plans, and power. The depressed person speaks slowly, monotonously, with no inflections. The manic person speaks rapidly, dramatically, often with many jokes and puns. The depressed person has no self-esteem. The manic person has inflated self-esteem. Although people may experience major depressions without manic episodes, it is extremely rare for a person to experience only manic episodes. Most manic episodes are a sign of **bipolar disorder** (formerly called manic-depressive disorder), in which depression alternates with mania.

Although bipolar disorder is equally common in both sexes, women of all ethnicities and nationalities are overrepresented in statistics on major depres-sion (McGrath et al., 1990). Some think that women actually are more likely to

In his book Darkness Visible, *novelist William Styron described his descent into depression and his recovery. ". . . mysteriously and in ways that are totally remote from normal experience," he wrote, "the gray drizzle of horror induced by depression takes on the quality of physical pain."*

■ **major depression**
A mood disorder involving distur-bances in emotion (excessive sad-ness), behavior (loss of interest in usual activities), cognition (distorted thoughts of hopelessness and low self-esteem), and body function (fatigue, loss of appetite).

■ **bipolar disorder**
A mood disorder in which depression alternates with mania (excessive euphoria).

become depressed than men are, but others think the difference is more apparent than real. For example, women seek treatment more often than men do; when researchers interview random samples of people who are not in treatment, they often find no significant differences between women and men. Some researchers argue that the apparent difference occurs because a few women score higher at the *extreme* end of depression measures, bringing up the average depression scores for all women (Golding, 1988). It also seems likely, as we saw in Chapter 10, that the sexes *express* feelings of depression differently, and that men's depression is thus often overlooked or misdiagnosed. Men, for instance, have higher rates of drug abuse and violent behavior than women do, and some researchers believe that this behavior masks depression or anxiety (Canetto, 1992; Kessler et al., 1994).

Causes of Depression

There are many studies of depression and many contradictory findings. What does this suggest about the search for a single cause or theory of the disorder? How can we make the most sense of conflicting results and points of view?

Many different hypotheses about the origins of depression have been advanced, which roughly fall into four categories: biological, social, attachment, and cognitive.

1. *Biological explanations* account for depression in terms of genetics and brain chemistry (see Figure 15.1). As we saw in Chapter 4, neurotransmitters permit messages to be transmitted from one neuron to another in the brain. Two neurotransmitters that seem to be implicated in depressive disorders are norepinephrine and serotonin. In the view of some, depression is caused by a deficient production of one or both of these neurotransmitters, and manic moods are caused by an excessive production. Biological theories seem especially applicable in cases of depression that do not involve reactions to real-life crises or losses, but which instead seem to "come from nowhere" or occur in response to minor stresses.

Biological theories are supported by studies showing that when animals are given drugs that diminish the body's ability to produce serotonin, the animals become sluggish and inactive—a symptom of depression (Kramer, 1993; Wender & Klein, 1981). Conversely, drugs that increase the levels of serotonin and norepinephrine sometimes alleviate symptoms of depression; hence they are called "antidepressants." The early success of these drugs provoked great inter-

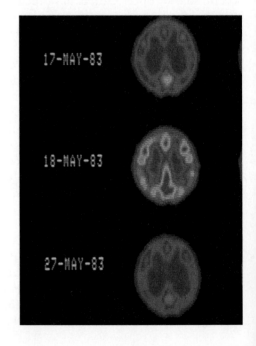

■ Figure 15.1   The Depressed Brain

These PET scans show changes in the metabolism of glucose, the brain's energy supply, in a patient with bipolar disorder. On May 17, the patient was depressed, and glucose metabolism throughout most of the brain was lower than normal. The next day, the patient became manic, and metabolic activity increased to near normal levels. By May 27, the patient was once again depressed, as reflected in glucose changes. Nevertheless, keep in mind that such changes do not show the direction of cause and effect: A drop in glucose might bring on depression, but depression might also cause a drop in brain activity.

est in the search for the biological origins of depression. However, as we will discuss further in the next chapter, drugs are not universally effective, and even when they help some individuals, this does not necessarily mean that the depression had an organic basis.

Studies of twins and adopted children suggest that there may be a genetic component in major depression and bipolar disorder, but the search for the gene or genes involved has so far proved fruitless. Some years ago, several highly publicized studies raised the possibility that a specific gene might be linked with bipolar disorder (Baron et al., 1987; Egeland et al., 1987), but subsequent research failed to confirm these results (Faraone, Kremen, & Tsuang, 1990; Kelsoe et al., 1989).

2. *Social explanations* of depression consider the conditions of people's lives. In this view, the reason that women are more likely than men to suffer from depression is that women are more likely to lack fulfilling jobs or family relations. Men are nearly twice as likely as women to be married and working full time, a combination of activities that is strongly associated with mental health (Brown, 1993; Golding, 1988). In a random sample of 1,111 men and women in Boston, virtually all of the differences between men and women in their reported levels of depression could be accounted for by their different states of marriage and employment (Gore & Mangione, 1983). Mothers are especially vulnerable to depression: The more children they have, the more likely women are to become depressed (McGrath et al., 1990). Social-economic explanations may also help account for the rise of depression among young people all over the world, many of whom are struggling economically and have delayed marriage.

Another social factor in the origins of adult depression may be childhood sexual abuse. In a study of female patients in a psychiatric inpatient hospital, over half of the women reported a history of such abuse. The number and severity of their depressive symptoms were greater than those of patients who reported no sexual trauma (Bryer et al., 1987). A community survey of 3,125 white, Latino, and black women found that depression, anxiety, panic attacks, and phobias were significantly more frequent among women who had been sexually mistreated as children or adolescents (Burnam et al., 1988).

Social analyses, though, fail to explain why some people who lose their jobs or spouses or have traumatic experiences do not become clinically depressed, while others stay locked in the grip of despair. Nor do they explain why some people become depressed even though they seem to have it all.

3. *Attachment explanations* emphasize the fundamental importance to well-being of affiliation and attachment. In this view, depression results from disturbed relationships and separations, both past and present. One attachment theory, the *interpersonal theory of depression,* includes biological, psychodynamic, and cognitive factors, but emphasizes the depressed person's disputes, losses, anxieties, feelings of incompetence, and problems with relationships (Klerman et al., 1984).

A large-scale review of studies of depression indeed found that the one thing that most often sets off a depressive episode is "disruption of a primary relationship," which is hardest on people who lack social support and coping skills (Barnett & Gotlib, 1988). However, attachment theories raise an interesting cause-and-effect problem. Disturbed or broken relationships may make some people severely depressed; but depressed people are also demanding and "depressing" to family and friends, who often feel angry or sad around them and may eventually break away (Gotlib & Hooley, 1988).

4. *Cognitive explanations* propose that depression results from particular habits of thinking and interpreting events, as we saw in Chapter 10 (Beck, 1987; Margo et al., 1993). Two decades ago, Martin Seligman (1975) proposed a "theory of learned helplessness," which held that people become depressed when their efforts to control the environment fail. But it soon became apparent that not all depressed people have actually failed in their lives; many merely believe that nothing they do will be successful (Abramson, Seligman, & Teasdale, 1978). Today Seligman (1991) thinks that some depression results from having a hopeless and pessimistic explanatory style (see Chapter 14)—the beliefs that nothing good will ever happen and that the person is helpless to change this bleak future (Abramson, Metalsky, & Alloy, 1989).

Psychologists have been trying to pinpoint other cognitive styles that are associated with depression. For example, when people feel depressed, what they do about it affects the course and duration of their misery. Susan Nolen-Hoeksema (1992) has found that people who focus inward and brood endlessly about their negative feelings—she calls this a "ruminating response style"—tend to have longer and more intense periods of depression than do those who are able to distract themselves, look outward, and seek solutions to problems. Considerable evidence suggests that women are more likely than men to develop this introspective style, beginning in adolescence, which may contribute to longer-lasting depressions in women (Nolen-Hoeksema & Girgus, 1994).

One problem with cognitive theories of depression is that it is not always clear whether distorted thinking *causes* depression, *accompanies* depression, or *follows* depression. When you are feeling sad, negative thoughts come more easily (Lewinsohn et al., 1981). Two researchers set themselves the awesome task of reviewing dozens of studies based on different theories of depression (Barnett & Gotlib, 1988). They concluded that there are many "cognitive abnormalities that wax and wane with the onset and remission of depression," but these cognitions do not necessarily precede depression, do not predict the severity of its symptoms, and tend to vanish during remission. Studies that follow people over time find that negative thinking is sometimes a cause of depression, sometimes a result, and sometimes a two-way street (Robins, 1988).

In assessing these different approaches, we should keep in mind that depression comes in degrees of severity, from tearful tiredness to an inability to get out of bed, and psychologists study many different groups of depressed people. Yet researchers sometimes speak of the "depression" of clinical patients, college students, children, and married couples as if it were the same thing. Further, it seems clear that depression can have different causes in different people. One person may have been abandoned in childhood; another may have a pessimistic cognitive style that fosters depressive interpretations of events; a third may have a biological predisposition to respond to stress with depression. The same precipitating event, therefore—such as the loss of a loved one or even a minor setback—might produce different degrees of depression in different people. All of these explanations are important pieces in the puzzle of depression.

Quick QUIZ

 A newspaper headline announces that a single gene has been identified as the cause of depression, but when you read the fine print you learn that other studies have failed to support this research. What explanations can you think of to explain these contradictory findings?

Answers:

The conflicting evidence may mean, among other possibilities, that if a genetic predisposition for depression does exist, it is not due to a single specific gene, but involves several genes working in the context of environmental events. It may mean that the right gene has not yet been identified. And it may mean that genes are not a factor in *all* forms of depression.

■ PERSONALITY DISORDERS

Personality disorders involve rigid, maladaptive traits that cause great distress or an inability to get along with others. The DSM-IV describes a personality disorder as "an enduring pattern of inner experience and behavior that deviates markedly from the expectations of the individual's culture." This pattern is not caused by depression, a drug reaction, or a particular situation that temporarily induces a person to behave in ways that are out of character.

Problem Personalities

One common personality disorder—one that is often the subject of novels and movies—is characterized by **paranoia,** a pervasive, unfounded suspiciousness and mistrust of other people, irrational jealousy, secretiveness, and doubt about the loyalty of others. Another personality disorder is **narcissism,** an exaggerated sense of self-importance and self-absorption. Narcissism is named after the Greek myth of Narcissus, a beautiful boy who fell in love with his own image. Individuals with narcissistic personality disorder are preoccupied with fantasies of unlimited success, power, brilliance, or ideal love. They require constant attention and admiration and feel entitled to special favors, without being willing to reciprocate. They fall in love quickly and out of love just as fast, when the beloved proves to have some human flaw.

Notice that these descriptions are both specific and vague. They are specific in that they evoke flashes of recognition ("I know that type!") but vague in that they involve general qualities that depend on subjective labels and value judgments. Culture influences the decision to classify an individual as having one of these personality disorders. For example, American society often encourages people to have fantasies of unlimited success and ideal love. But an individual who in this culture might be regarded as normal might be considered seriously disturbed in a more group-oriented society. Where would you draw the line between having a "narcissistic personality disorder" and being a normal member of a group or culture that encourages "looking out for number one" and places supreme emphasis on youth and physical beauty?

One personality disorder in particular has provoked interest and study because of its consequences for society: the disorder of the individual who lacks conscience, morality, and emotional attachments. In the 1830s this disorder was called "moral insanity." By 1900 it became the "psychopathic personality," a phrase that some researchers and most newspapers still use. More recently the word "sociopath" was coined. The DSM now uses the term *antisocial personality disorder.* By any name, this disorder, which has been around forever, has troubling symptoms.

Narcissus fell in love with his own image; now he has a personality disorder named after him.

The Antisocial Personality

- Two teenage boys held a teacher down while a third poured gasoline over him and set him on fire. Fortunately, another teacher intervened in time for a rescue, but the boys showed no remorse, did not consider their actions wrong, and were disappointed that they had not actually murdered the teacher (whom they did not know). "Next time we'll do it right," said the ringleader, "so there won't be nobody left around to identify us."

- Giovanni Vigliotto was, by all accounts, warm and charming; by too many accounts, in fact. Vigliotto married 105 women in 33 years in an elaborate con game. He would find a wealthy woman, charm her into marriage, steal her assets, and vanish. Finally, one wife charged him with fraud, and he was convicted. Vigliotto admitted the many marriages, but

■ **personality disorders**
Rigid, maladaptive personality patterns that cause personal distress or an inability to get along with others.

■ **paranoia**
Unreasonable and excessive suspiciousness, jealousy, or mistrust. It may occur as a type of personality disorder or, with more severe symptoms of psychosis, as a type of schizophrenic disorder.

■ **narcissism**
An exaggerated sense of self-importance and self-absorption.

People with antisocial personalities are not necessarily violent. Some manipulate and deceive others through the use of charm and elaborate con tricks. Giovanni Vigliotto, for example, who admitted to marrying 105 women over 33 years, allegedly seized their assets and then vanished. He was convicted of defrauding one of his wives; many of the others said he was charming, friendly, and warm.

▪ **antisocial personality disorder**

A disorder characterized by antisocial behavior such as lying, stealing, manipulating others, and sometimes violence; a lack of social emotions (guilt, shame, and empathy); and impulsivity. (Sometimes called psychopathy or sociopathy.)

not deception or theft. He didn't think he had done anything wrong (Carson & Butcher, 1994).

People like these, who have **antisocial personality disorder,** are fascinating and frightening because they lack the emotions that link people to one another: empathy, the ability to take another person's perspective; shame for actions that hurt others; and guilt, the ability to feel remorse or sorrow for immoral actions. They have no conscience. They can lie, charm, seduce, and manipulate others, and then drop them without a qualm. If caught in a lie or a crime, they may seem sincerely sorry and promise to make amends, but it is all an act. They are often sexually promiscuous, unable to maintain attachments, and irresponsible in their obligations to others. Some antisocial persons, like the teenagers who set a teacher on fire, are sadistic, with a history of criminal or cruel behavior that began in childhood. They can kill anyone—an intended victim, a child, a bystander—without a twinge of regret. Others direct their energies into con games or career advancement, abusing other people emotionally rather than physically. Understandably, more attention is devoted to the antisocial individuals who commit violent crimes than to those who gain power and fortune while wreaking devastation on their families or employees, although the latter do great harm.

For unknown reasons, this disorder is far more common in males than in females; according to the DSM-IV and survey evidence, it is estimated to occur among 3 to 5 percent of all males and less than 1 percent of all females (Robins, Tipp, & Przybeck, 1991). Although these percentages are small, antisocial individuals create a lot of havoc: They are believed to account for many of the serious crimes committed in the United States (Hare, 1993). And their crimes are scary: In 1994, Robert Sandifer, an 11-year-old boy who already had a long record of crimes, shot another child to death on instructions from his gang. He was himself murdered by the gang so he wouldn't talk.

It is important to distinguish antisocial *behavior* from antisocial *personalities.* Most kinds of antisocial behavior, as defined by crime statistics on homicide, rape, robbery, assault, burglary, and auto theft, are carried out by young men whose criminal activities peak in late adolescence and drop off sharply by their late twenties. Their behavior is more a matter of their age, situation, and peer group than their personalities. But a much smaller number of males begin displaying antisocial behavior in early childhood, are drawn to criminal environments, and end up with confirmed antisocial personalities. In reviewing longitudinal research, Terrie Moffitt (1993) observes that the behavior of such antisocial personalities might include "biting and hitting at age 4, shoplifting and truancy at age 10, selling drugs and stealing cars at age 16, robbery and rape at age 22, and fraud and child abuse at age 30 . . . [such] persons lie at home, steal from shops, cheat at school, fight in bars, and embezzle at work."

Some people with antisocial personality disorder can be very "sociable," charming everyone around them, but they have no emotional connection to others or guilt about their wrongdoing. Their inability to feel emotional arousal—empathy, guilt, fear of punishment, anxiety under stress—implies some abnormality in the central nervous system. Antisocial individuals do not respond to punishments that would affect other people, such as threat of physical harm or loss of approval. It is as if they aren't "wired" to feel the anxiety necessary for avoidance learning (see Figure 15.2). This fact may explain why antisocial persons fail to learn that their actions will have unpleasant consequences (Hare, 1993).

A fascinating finding about antisocial personalities is that after age 40, about half of them "burn out"—at least in terms of their likelihood of committing further criminal acts. In one study of 521 men, the researchers used longitudinal and cross-sectional methods to follow the criminal histories of male psy-

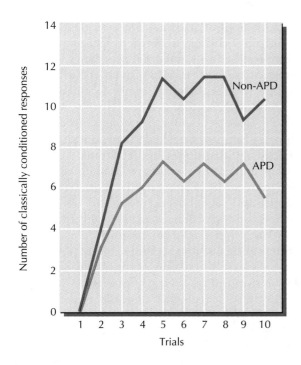

■ Figure 15.2 The Antisocial Personality: Immune to Anxiety?

Normally, when a person is anticipating danger, pain, or shock, the electrical conductance of the skin changes—a classically conditioned response that indicates anxiety. But in several experiments such as this one, people with antisocial personality disorder were slow to develop such responses. This deficit seems to be related to their ability to behave in destructive ways without remorse or regard for the consequences (Hare, 1965, 1993).

chopaths and nonpsychopaths (the researchers' terms) between the ages of 16 and 45. Both types of analysis indicated that the criminal activities of nonpsychopaths were relatively constant over the years, whereas those of psychopaths remained extremely high until around age 40, after which they declined dramatically (Hare, 1993; Hare, McPherson, & Forth, 1988). Researchers are unsure why this burnout occurs—experience? exhaustion? maturation of the nervous system?—and why it happens only in some cases.

One theory, based on animal and human studies, maintains that people who are antisocial, hyperactive, addicted, or impulsive have a common inherited disorder (Luengo et al., 1994; Newman, Widom, & Nathan, 1985). All of these conditions involve problems in *behavioral inhibition*—the ability to control responses to frustration or to inhibit a pleasurable action that may have unpleasant repercussions. For such individuals, the momentary attraction of an activity blocks out all thought of consequences. Behavioral-genetics research finds that both the adopted and the biological children of parents with antisocial personality disorder, substance-abuse problems, or impulsivity disorders are at greater than normal risk of developing these disorders themselves (Nigg & Goldsmith, 1994).

There is also good evidence that many children who become violent and antisocial have suffered neuropsychological impairments, a result not of genetics but of physical battering and subsequent brain injury (Milner & McCanne, 1991; Moffitt, 1993). Consider the chilling results of a study that compared two groups of delinquents: violent boys who had been arrested for repeated incidents of vicious assault, rape, or murder; and boys whose violence was limited to fistfights. Nearly all of the extremely violent boys (98.6 percent) had at least one neurological abnormality, and many had more than one, compared to 66.7 percent of the less violent boys. More than three-fourths of the violent boys had suffered head injuries as children, had had serious medical problems, or had been beaten savagely by their parents, compared to "only" one-third of the others (Lewis, 1981). In addition, numerous studies have found various EEG abnormalities in people with antisocial personality disorder (Holmes, 1994).

Other research suggests that brain damage can interact with social deprivation and other factors to produce individuals who are impulsively violent. A study based on a sample of 4,269 boys, followed from birth to age 18, found that many of those who became violent offenders had had a *combination* of birth complications (damaging the prefrontal cortex, as noted in Chapter 4) *and* early maternal rejection. Their mothers hadn't wanted the pregnancy, and the babies were put in public institutional care for at least four months during their first year (Raine, Brennan, & Mednick, 1994). Although only 4.4 percent of the boys had both risk factors, they accounted for 18 percent of all violent crimes committed by the sample as a whole. Robert Sandifer, the violent boy we mentioned earlier, fit this profile. He was known to have been scarred with lit cigarettes as a toddler, beaten, and eventually abandoned by his parents.

On the other hand, it is also clear that cultures and environments can make some kinds of antisocial behavior more or less likely (Moffitt, 1993; Patterson, 1994; Persons, 1986). Some societies and subcultures cultivate the qualities of selfishness, professional ruthlessness, and emotional hard-heartedness; small, close-knit cultures that depend on each member's cooperation and consideration for others would find selfishness and emotional coldness intolerable.

It seems, then, that several routes lead to the development of antisocial personality disorder: Having a genetic disposition toward impulsivity, addiction, hyperactivity or other qualities that lead to rule-breaking and crime; being neglected or rejected by parents; having brain damage as a result of birth complications or being beaten throughout childhood; and living in a culture or environment that rewards and fosters certain antisocial traits. These multiple origins may explain why the incidence of antisocial personality disorder varies within and across societies and history.

Quick QUIZ

Can you diagnose each of the following disorders?

1. Ann can barely get out of bed in the morning. She feels life is hopeless and despairs of ever feeling good about herself.
2. Brad lacks guilt, empathy, and moral standards.
3. Connie constantly feels a sense of impending doom; for many weeks, her heart has been beating rapidly and she can't relax.
4. Damon is totally absorbed in his own feelings and wishes.
5. Edna believes that everyone is out to get her and no one can be trusted.

Answers:

1. major depression 2. antisocial personality disorder 3. generalized anxiety disorder 4. narcissistic personality disorder 5. paranoid personality disorder.

▪ DISSOCIATIVE DISORDERS

▪ **dissociative disorders**
Conditions in which normally integrated consciousness or identity is split or altered, as in psychogenic amnesia.

Stress or shock can make any of us feel temporarily *dissociated*—that is, cut off from ourselves, feeling strange, dazed, or "unreal." In **dissociative disorders,** consciousness, behavior, and identity are split or altered. Unlike normal, short-lived states of dissociation, these disorders are extremely intense, last a long time, and appear to be out of one's control. Like posttraumatic stress disorder, dissociative disorders are often responses to shocking events. But in the former case, people can't get the trauma out of their minds and waking thoughts. In the latter, people apparently escape the trauma by putting it out of their minds, erasing it from memory (Cardeña et al., 1994).

Amnesia and Fugue

Amnesia, a sudden inability to remember important personal information that cannot be explained by ordinary forgetfulness, is the most common dissociative disorder. Amnesia can result from organic conditions, such as head injury; when no organic causes are apparent it is called *psychogenic*. Psychogenic amnesia is highly selective; the person "forgets" only information that is threatening to the self. In one case, for example, a young man appeared at a hospital complaining that he did not know who he was. After a few days, he awoke in great distress, eventually remembering that he had been in an automobile accident in which a pedestrian was killed. The shock of the experience and his fear that he might have been responsible set off the amnesia.

Psychogenic fugue states are even more fascinating. A person in a *fugue state* not only forgets his or her identity, but gives up customary habits and wanders far from home. The person may take on a new identity, remarry, get a new job, and live contentedly until he or she suddenly "wakes up"—puzzled and often with no memory of the fugue experiences. The fugue state may last anywhere from a few days to many years. James McDonnell, Jr., left his family in New York in 1971 and wandered to New Jersey, where he took a new name (James Peters), a new job (short-order cook), and new friends. Fifteen years later, he "woke up" and made his way back to his wife—who (apparently) greeted him with open arms.

As you might imagine, it is often difficult for clinicians to determine when people in fugue states have a true disorder and when they are faking (Schacter, 1986). This problem is also apparent in the remarkable disorder of multiple personality.

Dissociative Identity Disorder ("Multiple Personality")

The DSM-IV has dropped the familiar term "multiple personality disorder" (MPD) in favor of **dissociative identity disorder** to describe the appearance, within one person, of two or more distinct identities. (In our discussion, however, we will retain the more commonly used term.) In this disorder, each identity appears to have its own memories, preferences, handwriting, and medical problems (Braun, 1988). In a case study of one person with four identities, for example, the researcher concluded that it was "as if four different people had been tested" (Larmore et al., 1977).

Cases of multiple personality are extremely dramatic: Those portrayed in the films *The Three Faces of Eve* and *Sybil* fascinated audiences for years, and so do the legal cases that make the news. A woman charges a man with rape, claiming that only one of her personalities consented to have sex with him while another objected; a man kills his wife and claims his "other personality" did it. Among mental health professionals, however, there are two competing and *totally incompatible* views of MPD. Some think it is a real disorder, all too common but often underdiagnosed. Others are skeptical: They think that most cases are concocted by psychiatrists and psychologists who believe in it, in unwitting collusion with vulnerable and suggestible patients, and that if it exists at all it is extremely rare.

Those in the MPD-is-real camp believe the disorder originates in childhood, as a means of coping with unspeakable, continuing traumas such as torture (Herman, 1992; Kluft, 1993). In this view, the trauma produces a mental "splitting" or dissociation; one "personality" emerges to handle everyday experiences and another "personality" emerges to cope with the bad ones. MPD patients are frequently described as having lived for years with several personalities of which they were unaware, until hypnosis and other techniques in therapy revealed them. Clinicians who endorse MPD argue that the disorder is often misdiagnosed, but that diagnoses can be made more accurately today because the

✴ *A man charged with murder claims that one of his "other personalities" committed the crime. You are on the jury, and you know that psychologists disagree about the validity of his defense. What questions would you want to ask about this man's claim, and how would you reach a decision about it?*

■ **amnesia (psychogenic)**
When no organic causes are present, a dissociative disorder involving partial or complete loss of memory for threatening information or past events.

■ **dissociative identity disorder**
A rare dissociative disorder marked by the appearance within one person of two or more distinct personalities, each with its own name and traits; also called multiple personality disorder.

physiological changes that occur within each "personality" cannot be faked. One patient, for example, had a blood pressure of 150/110 when one personality appeared to be in control and a blood pressure of 90/60 when another personality took over (Braun, 1988).

Those who are skeptical about MPD, however, have shown that most of the research used to support the diagnosis is seriously flawed. Indeed, a review of the claims that MPD patients have different physiological patterns associated with each "personality" finds that most of these studies are anecdotal, involve many methodological problems, and have failed to be replicated (Brown, 1994). For instance, can you spot a problem with the blood pressure study? It's that familiar research mistake, the Missing Control Group. When one research team compared the EEG activity of two MPD patients with that of a normal person who merely role-played different personalities, they found EEG differences between "personalities" to be *greater* in the normal person (Coons et al., 1982)! Other studies comparing MPD patients with control subjects who are merely role-playing have not found any reliable differences (Miller & Triggiano, 1992). Because normal people can create EEG changes by changing their moods, energy levels, and concentration, brain wave activity cannot be used to verify the existence of MPD. Clinicians and researchers who are doubtful about this diagnosis point out that cases of MPD only seem to turn up in patients who go to therapists who believe in it and are looking for it (Holmes, 1994; McHugh, 1993a; Nathan, 1994; Spanos, 1994). They fear that clinicians who are convinced of the widespread existence of MPD may actually be creating the disorder in their patients through the power of suggestion (see Chapter 16). For example, here is the way one psychologist questioned the "Hillside Strangler," Kenneth Bianchi, a man who killed more than a dozen young women:

> I've talked a bit to Ken, but I think that perhaps there might be another part of Ken that I haven't talked to, another part that maybe feels somewhat differently from the part that I've talked to. . . . And I would like that other part to come to talk to me. . . . Part, would you please come to communicate with me? (Quoted in Holmes, 1994.)

Kenneth Bianchi, the Hillside Strangler, tried to claim he was a multiple personality whose other personality was the killer. Under astute questioning by a skeptical psychologist, Bianchi revealed that he had only one personality—a violent, antisocial one.

Notice that the psychologist repeatedly asked Bianchi to produce another "part" of himself and even addressed the "part" directly. Before long, Bianchi was maintaining that the murders were really committed by another personality called Steve Walker. Did the psychologist in this case *permit* another personality to reveal itself or did he actively *create* such a personality by planting the suggestion that one existed? Proponents of the view that MPD is real and widespread often seem unaware of the difference. One of the best-known advocates of the MPD diagnosis, Richard Kluft (1987), maintains that efforts designed to determine the presence of MPD—that is, to get the patient to reveal a dissociated personality—may require "between 2½ and 4 hours of continuous interviewing. Interviewees must be prevented from taking breaks to regain composure, averting their faces to avoid self-revelation, etc. In one recent case of singular difficulty, the first sign of dissociation was noted in the 6th hour, and a definitive spontaneous switching of personalities occurred in the 8th hour." After eight hours of "continuous interviewing" without a single break, how many of us wouldn't do what the interviewer wanted?

An alternative, *sociocognitive* explanation of multiple personality disorder is that it is an extreme form of a normal human process: the ability we all have to present different aspects of our personalities to others (Spanos, 1994). In this view, the diagnosis of multiple personality disorder provides a way for some troubled people to understand and legitimize their problems—and to account for embarrassing, regretted, or even criminal behavior that they commit ("My other personality did it"). In turn, therapists who believe in MPD reward such patients by paying a lot of attention to their various "symptoms" and "personalities," thus further influencing the patients to reorganize their memories and make them consistent with the diagnosis (Ofshe & Watters, 1994). Canadian psychiatrist Harold Mersky (1992) reviewed several famous cases of MPD, including those of Eve and Sybil, and was unable to find a single case in which a patient's "other personalities" developed without being shaped or influenced by external factors, such as the therapist's suggestions or reports about the disorder in the media. Sybil's psychiatrist, for example, first diagnosed Sybil as being schizophrenic, but later encouraged her to produce multiple personalities and memories of having endured severe sexual abuse in childhood (reports that were never corroborated). Some investigators who looked into the case think that this change of diagnosis was part of a marketing strategy for the psychiatrist's book (see Nathan, 1994).

Psychiatrist Paul McHugh (1993c) concludes that the solution to the growing number of multiple personality cases is simple: "Ignore the alters [other personalities]," he advises therapists. "Stop talking to them, taking notes on them, and discussing them in staff conferences. Pay attention to real present problems and conflicts rather than fantasy. If these simple, familiar rules are followed, multiple personalities will soon wither away and psychotherapy can begin."

Of course, the fact that MPD is a controversial diagnosis with little empirical evidence to support it does not mean that no legitimate cases exist (Holmes, 1994). It does mean that caution is warranted, especially because diagnoses of MPD have implications regarding responsibility for criminal acts. In the case of the Hillside Strangler, a determined and skeptical prosecutor discovered that Bianchi had read numerous psychology textbooks on multiple personality and had modeled "Steve" on a student he knew! When another psychologist purposely misled Bianchi by telling him that "real" multiple personalities come in packages of at least three, Bianchi suddenly produced a third personality. Bianchi was convicted of murder and sentenced to life in prison. But Paul Miskamen, who battered his wife to death, convinced psychiatrists and a jury that the man who killed his wife was a separate personality named Jack Kelly. Judged insane, Miskamen was committed to a mental hospital and released after 14 months. (For further discussion of the relationship between mental illness and legal responsibility for one's crimes, see "Think About It.")

■ DRUG ABUSE AND ADDICTION

Perhaps no topic in this chapter better illustrates the problem of finding the "shade of the spectrum" in which normal blurs into abnormal than that of drug abuse and addiction. Most people use drugs—legal, illegal, or prescription—in moderation, for short-lived effects. But some people overuse them, and the consequences of their drug abuse for society are costly in loss of productive work, high rates of violence and crime, and family disruption. The consequences for individuals and their families are tragic: unhappiness, illness, and the increased likelihood of early death from accident or disease.

From Use to Abuse

Every drug—including aspirin, cough medicine, and coffee—can be dangerous and even lethal if taken in excess. The problem lies in defining excess. When does moderate use of a drug become abuse? As we saw in Chapter 5, there are many medical and psychological differences between moderate use of any drug and overuse. (You might want to refer to Chapter 5 to refresh your memory about stimulant and depressant drugs and how people learn to react to them.) In fact, a surprising longitudinal study that followed a large sample of children from preschool through age 18 found that adolescents who had experimented moderately with alcohol and marijuana were the *best* adjusted in the sample. Those who had never experimented with any drug were the most

When and why does drug use become abuse?

Think About It

When Does a Mental Disorder Cause Diminished Responsibility?

■ No one disputes the fact that Lyle and Erik Menendez shot their parents to death in a barrage of gunfire, as their parents sat watching television and eating ice cream. After the initial volley, Lyle reloaded his gun and shot their mother several more times because, he later told his therapist, "She was trying to sneak away." At first the brothers maintained their innocence, while spending extravagant amounts of their $14 million inheritance; then, faced with incontrovertible evidence, they confessed. Many months later they explained why they had committed this crime: They were victims of sexual molestation by their father and believed they were in imminent danger of being killed by him. Their first trial ended in two separate hung juries; at this writing, they are due to be retried.

Were the Menendez brothers responsible for murdering their parents? "No," say some people, "not if they were abused and humiliated by their parents; no wonder they eventually broke down and lost control of their rage. Society must be sympathetic to children who are treated brutally." "Yes," say others; "because that sex-abuse excuse seems awfully unlikely, and everything about their actions was premeditated. And even if they were abused, so are plenty of people who don't commit murder. These young men had all the resources of wealth and class to have simply left home."

The Menendez case raises some fascinating questions for law and psychology. What mental conditions and disorders warrant a defense of diminished responsibility or exoneration of one's actions? What is the proper penalty for someone who temporarily or habitually cannot control his or her actions: treatment or prison? If someone is sentenced to spend time in a mental institution, how can we know when he or she is "cured"? How do we know if someone is "insane" or faking?

Insanity is a legal term, not a psychological one. In 1834, a Scot named Daniel M'Naghten tried to assassinate the prime minister of England, killing the prime minister's secretary by mistake. M'Naghten was acquitted of murder on the grounds that he had a "mental defect" that prevented him from understanding what he was doing at the time of the act. The "M'Naghten Rule" meant that people could be acquitted "by reason of insanity" and sentenced not to prison, but to mental institutions (or set free). In the United States, the 1954 *Durham* decision specified that "an accused is not criminally responsible if his unlawful act was the product of a mental disease or defect."

Today, because of sensational cases that make the headlines, the public has the impression that hordes of crazed and violent criminals are "getting off" by reason of insanity. Public outrage has caused some states to abolish the insanity defense altogether or to permit only a defense of "insane but guilty." Actually, public perceptions are not accu-

anxious, emotionally constricted, and lacking in social skills. And those who overused and abused drugs were maladjusted, alienated, impulsive, and emotionally distressed (Shedler & Block, 1990). We'll have more to say about the direction of cause and effect here in a moment.

The DSM-IV definition of *substance abuse* is "a maladaptive pattern of substance use leading to clinically significant impairment or distress." Symptoms of such impairment include the failure to fulfill role obligations at work, home, or school (the person cannot hold a job, care for children, or complete course work because of excessive drug use); use of the drug in hazardous situations (such as driving a car or operating machinery); recurrent arrests for drug use; and persistent conflicts with other people about use of the drug or caused by the drug.

Addiction: Disease or Social Problem?

Why are some people able to use drugs moderately, while others become addicts? One explanation looks to personality: Drug abusers may be sensation seekers who crave lots of excitement and stimulation. Another considers family history: Some drug abusers have had deprived childhoods, antisocial parents,

rate. The public thinks the insanity defense is raised in 37 percent of all felony cases; in fact, it is raised in only 0.9 percent. The public believes that 44 percent of all those who claim this defense are acquitted; the actual rate is 26 percent. The public believes that only about half of those acquitted actually spend time in mental hospitals; in fact, about 81 percent do (Silver, Cirincione, & Steadman, 1994). And it is getting tougher to claim an insanity defense at all. Federal statutes enacted in 1984 shifted the burden of proof to the defense, which must show "clear and convincing evidence" that the defendant had a severe, abnormal mental condition and not just a personality defect.

Nevertheless, many defense attorneys, aided by the testimony of psychiatrists and psychologists, keep trying to expand the legal grounds for diminished responsibility, searching for "the mental disease or defect" that might mitigate the sentence a guilty person receives. Because of the differing views within psychology and psychiatry—and because, as we have seen, of the subjective nature of most diagnoses—many trials end up as a battle of the experts, and the jury must decide which side to believe. Some psychologists think that the Menendez brothers were suffering from a form of posttraumatic stress disorder resulting from years of abuse. Others think that if the brothers have any mental disorder at all, their coldbloodedness indicates psychopathy—antisocial personality disorder.

How can a jury decide between such competing views when the experts can't?

In a sizzling indictment of the ability of psychologists to determine legal insanity or to predict the future behavior of individuals, psychologists David Faust and Jay Ziskin (who is also a lawyer) reviewed hundreds of studies (Faust & Ziskin, 1988). They found that clinicians were wrong more often than they were right. In one study, for example, military recruits who were kept in the service, despite psychiatrists' recommendations that they be discharged for "severe psychiatric liabilities," turned out to be as successful and adjusted as the control group. In study after study, clinicians were not very good at detecting malingering or efforts to fake insanity, and they were dismal at predicting future violence.

Most legal and mental health professionals believe that in a humane society, people who are mentally incompetent, delusional, or disturbed should not be held entirely responsible for their actions. But where do we draw the line of responsibility? Should being physically beaten or sexually abused, having experiences with racism, or living in a violent subculture be treated as legitimate reasons for taking violent revenge? If so, under what conditions? What should the treatment or punishment for such individuals be? And if psychologists cannot agree on the answers, how should juries do so? Think about it. ▪

and a lifetime of rejection. A third explanation holds that peer pressure is the reason: If all your friends smoke or use drugs, you are more likely to do so too. But these factors are only part of the story.

In longitudinal studies that followed three groups of people for more than 40 years, researchers were able to observe the course of alcohol use and abuse over time in people's lives (Vaillant, 1983). The first surprising discovery was that many people went through a period of problem drinking but eventually healed themselves. For such persons, alcoholism was not progressive, permanently incapacitating, or a downward spiral to skid row. They outgrew alcoholism, cutting back to social drinking levels.

Second, the study found that many of the factors thought to *cause* alcoholism were instead a *result* of alcoholism. It had long been argued, from retrospective studies, that alcoholism was a result of an unstable or dependent personality. Alcoholics were supposed to have lower self-esteem and be more depressed, paranoid, aggressive, and impulsive than social drinkers. However, the longitudinal evidence showed that these traits, along with differences in social class, unemployment, and educational achievement, all tended to develop *after* the emergence of alcoholism. As adults, problem drinkers had personality disorders and were socially inadequate. But as children they were no less privileged than peers who became normal social drinkers, were no less intelligent, and had no more emotional problems (Vaillant & Milofsky, 1982). Likewise, in that longitudinal study that followed children from preschool to age 18, problem drug use among adolescents proved to be largely a result, not a cause, of their maladjustment and other personal problems (Shedler & Block, 1990). Conversely, the best-adjusted students were able to use drugs moderately *because* they were well adjusted.

Then why do people become alcoholic? One clue comes from history. In colonial America, the average person drank two to three times the amount of liquor that is consumed today, yet alcoholism was not the serious social problem it is now. Drinking was a universally accepted social activity. Families drank and ate together. Alcohol was believed to produce pleasant feelings and relaxation. The Puritan minister Cotton Mather even called liquor "the good creature of God." If a person committed a crime or became violent while drunk, the colonials did not conclude that liquor was to blame. Rather, it was the person's own immoral tendencies that led to drunkenness *and* crime (Critchlow, 1986).

Between 1790 and 1830, when the American frontier was expanding, drinking came to symbolize masculine independence, high-spiritedness, and toughness. The saloon became the typical setting for drinking away from home. Alcoholism rates rose rapidly. The temperance movement, which followed, argued that drinking inevitably led to drunkenness, and drunkenness to crime. The solution it proposed, and won for the Prohibition years (1920 to 1933), was national abstinence.

By the mid-twentieth century, drunkenness came to be seen not as an inevitable property of alcohol but as a characteristic of some people who have an inbred vulnerability to alcoholism. In *The Disease Concept of Alcoholism* (1960), E. M. Jellinek argued that alcoholism is a disease over which an individual has no control and from which he or she never recovers. Again, complete abstinence was the only solution. Today the *disease model of addiction* is still widely accepted by researchers and the public. The disease model holds that addiction, whether to alcohol or any other drug, is a biochemical process. The individual acquires a tolerance for the drug, meaning that greater and greater amounts are required to produce the same effect. Withdrawal produces severe physiological reactions, including, in the case of alcohol, "the shakes," nervousness, anxiety, nightmares, and delirium.

Proponents of the disease model believe that alcoholism involves an inherited predisposition, because having biological relatives who are alcoholic contributes to a person's risk of becoming alcoholic. As with so many other disorders, medical researchers are trying to identify the key gene or genes that might be involved (Blum, 1991; Cloninger, 1987; Kendler et al., 1992; Polich, Pollock, & Bloom, 1994).

Yet, again, one study's positive results are often contradicted by another study's negative ones. Several studies have found that a specific gene, which affects the function of key dopamine receptors on brain cells, is more likely to be present in the DNA of alcoholics than of nonalcoholics (Noble et al., 1991). Dopamine helps regulate pleasure-seeking actions, so researchers suspect that this gene might help explain why alcoholics drink. However, other studies, using different measurements, have found no difference between alcoholics and controls in the presence of this gene (Baron, 1993; Bolos et al., 1990; Gelernter et al., 1991). Similarly, some researchers, comparing alcoholism rates among identical and fraternal twins, conclude that genetic factors play a part in alcoholism in women (Kendler et al., 1992); but other studies find evidence of genetic factors only in men (McGue, Pickens, & Svikis, 1992). To further complicate the picture, some studies suggest that genes may play a role only in certain kinds of alcoholism in men: one kind, which appears relatively early, and another that is implicated in antisocial behavior and violent criminality (Bohman et al., 1987; McGue, Pickens, & Svikis, 1992).

At present, then, we cannot conclude that a single gene "causes" alcoholism in any direct way. Two psychologists who reviewed the research in this area reported that "on critical examination . . . the evidence [of a hereditary component in alcoholism] appears less strong" (Newlin & Thomson, 1990). Perhaps several genes in combination affect the body's response to alcohol and other mood-altering drugs or contribute to personality traits that predispose some people to become alcoholics. Perhaps, though, genes have nothing to do with alcoholism, and alcoholism results, basically, from alcohol! Heavy drinking alters brain function, reduces the level of painkilling endorphins, produces nerve damage, shrinks the cerebral cortex, and wrecks the liver. In the view of some researchers, these changes in turn create a biological dependence, an inability to metabolize alcohol, and psychological problems.

The disease model, popular though it is, has an additional problem: It cannot adequately account for the often rapid rise and fall in addiction rates. Between 1942 and 1976 there was a 20-fold increase in the number of alcoholics in treatment (Peele, 1989), and more and more people are becoming addicted to other drugs as well. Further, people can become "addicted" to activities and to television as well as to drugs; what "disease" are they catching? A growing number of television addicts compulsively watch TV the way drug addicts compulsively use drugs—to relieve loneliness, sadness, or anger (Jacobvitz, 1990). "Exercise addicts" have a compulsion to exercise that far exceeds any health benefits (Chan & Grossman, 1988). Some of them cannot stop exercising even when their muscles and joints have been seriously injured. Like alcoholics who organize their lives around drink, addicted athletes put exercise above everything else, including their jobs or relationships. And they have major withdrawal symptoms, such as depression and anxiety, when they are unable to exercise.

Amid much argument, therefore, some researchers want to replace the disease model of addiction with a *learning model*, which holds that alcoholism is a result of physical, personal, and social factors. It is neither a sin nor a disease but "a central activity of the individual's way of life" (Fingarette, 1988). Similarly, Stanton Peele and his associates want to replace the disease model of addiction and treatment with a "life-process" model (Peele & Brodsky, 1991). Some of the underlying assumptions of the disease and life-process models of addiction are shown in Table 15.2.

✳ *It's time to think critically about the popular disease model of addiction. People can become "addicted" to jogging, love, and rock and roll. What "disease" are they catching?*

Table 15.2 — The Disease versus "Life-Process" Models of Addiction

Disease Model	Life-Process Model
Addiction is genetic, biological.	Addiction is a way of coping.
A person is always an addict.	A person can grow beyond the need for alcohol or other drugs.
An addict must abstain from the drug forever.	Most problem drinkers can learn to drink in moderation.
A person is either addicted or not.	The degree of addiction will vary depending on the situation.
Therapy focuses on the addiction.	Therapy focuses on a person's problems and environment.
An addict needs the same treatment and group support forever.	The treatment or group support lasts only as long as necessary.
A person must accept his or her identity as an addict.	A person focuses on problems, not permanent labels.

Source: Adapted from Peele and Brodsky, 1991.

Rates of alcoholism depend on when and where people drink. In cultures in which people drink moderately with meals, and children learn the rules of drinking with their families, alcoholism rates are much lower than in cultures in which drinking occurs in bars, in binges, or in privacy.

Opponents of the disease model of addiction marshal three lines of support for their argument:

1. *Addiction patterns vary according to culture and learning.* Study after study has found that alcoholism is much more likely to occur in cultures that forbid children to drink but condone drunkenness in adults (such as Ireland) than in cultures that teach children how to drink responsibly but condemn adult drunkenness (such as Italy, Greece, France, and colonial America). In cultures with low rates of alcoholism, adults demonstrate correct drinking habits to their children, gradually introducing them to alcohol in safe family settings. These lessons are maintained by adult customs. Alcohol is not used as a rite of passage into adulthood, nor is it associated with masculinity and power (Peele, 1989; Vaillant, 1983). Drinking is considered neither a virtue nor a sin. Abstainers are not sneered at and drunkenness is not considered charming, comical, or manly; it's considered stupid or obnoxious.

2. *Not all drug users go through withdrawal symptoms when they stop taking the drug.* During the Vietnam War, nearly 30 percent of American soldiers were taking heroin in doses far stronger than those available on the streets of U.S. cities. These men believed themselves to be addicted. Experts predicted a drug-withdrawal disaster among the returning veterans. It never materialized (see Figure 15.3). Over 90 percent of the men simply gave up the drug, without withdrawal pain, when they came home (Robins, Davis, & Goodwin, 1974). Studies find that the majority of people who are addicted to alcohol, cigarettes, tranquilizers, or painkillers are also able to stop taking these drugs, without outside help and without withdrawal symptoms (Lee & Hart, 1985).

Addicts use drugs to escape from the real world, but as we saw in Chapter 5, people living with chronic pain use some of the same drugs, including opiates, in order to function in the real world—and they don't become addicted (Portenoy, 1994). In a study of 100 hospital patients who had been given strong doses of narcotics, 99 had no withdrawal symptoms upon leaving the hospital. They left postoperative pain behind them, along with the drug (Zinberg, 1974). And in a study of 10,000 burn patients who received narcotics as part of their hospital care, *not one* became an addict (Perry & Heidrich, 1982).

3. *Policies of total abstinence tend to increase rates of alcoholism rather than reduce them.* Further compelling evidence for a learning explanation of alcoholism is that when people do not learn how to drink moderately, they are more likely to drink irresponsibly and in binges (unless they are committed to a culture or religion that forbids all drugs). Research suggests that Prohibition itself, which was a national effort to eliminate alcoholism and problem drinking, actually

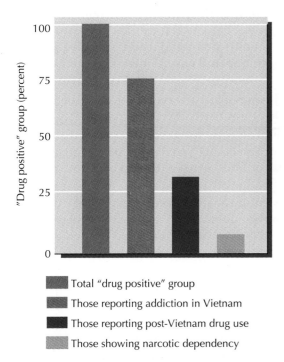

■ **Figure 15.3   Drugs and Vietnam Veterans: Failure of the Addiction Prediction**

U.S. soldiers who tested "drug positive" when they were in Vietnam showed a dramatic drop in drug use when they returned to civilian life—contrary to prediction and to the "disease model" of addiction (Robins, Davis, & Goodwin, 1974).

Legend:
- Total "drug positive" group
- Those reporting addiction in Vietnam
- Those reporting post-Vietnam drug use
- Those showing narcotic dependency

Y-axis: "Drug positive" group (percent) — 0, 25, 50, 75, 100

increased rates of alcoholism. Sociologist Joan McCord (1989) found that men who were teenagers at the time of Prohibition were far and away more likely to become serious problem drinkers in adulthood than were older men, who had learned how to drink alcohol before it became illegal. Similarly, the Inuit of British Columbia were forbidden alcohol until 1951, and then permitted to drink only in licensed bars. As a result, the Inuit would drink as much as they could while in the bar. It was a policy virtually guaranteed to create drunkenness.

The differences between the disease and learning models of addiction become apparent in the heated debate over controlled drinking: Is it possible for former alcoholics to drink moderately without showing signs of dependence and intoxication and without causing harm to themselves or others? To those who hold the disease model, controlled drinking is impossible; once an addict has even a single drink, he or she cannot stop. To those who hold a learning model, controlled drinking is possible; once an addict no longer needs to become drunk, he or she can learn to drink socially and in moderation. Because alcoholism and problem drinking occur for many and varied reasons, neither model has a lock on the truth. Many alcoholics, perhaps most, simply cannot learn to drink moderately, especially if they have had drinking problems for many years (Vaillant, 1993). But some problem drinkers can learn new responses to alcohol and are able to keep their drinking under control (Rosenberg, 1993).

In a major review of the factors that predict whether an addict or problem drinker will be able to learn to control excessive drinking, Harold Rosenberg (1993) found that the most important predictors were these: previous severity of dependence on the drug; social stability (not having a criminal record, having a stable work history, being married); and beliefs about the necessity of maintaining abstinence. Alcoholics who believe that one drink will set them off—those who accept the alcoholics' creed, "first drink, then drunk"—are in fact more likely to behave that way, compared with those who believe that controlled drinking is possible. Ironically, then, the course that alcoholism takes may reflect, in part, a person's belief in the disease model or the learning model.

All of this evidence suggests that drug abuse and addiction reflect an interaction of physiology *and* psychology, person *and* culture. They occur when an individual who is emotionally vulnerable to abusing drugs, and who perhaps has a genetic susceptibility, finds a culture and environment that support drug abuse. In particular:

- Addiction and drug abuse are more likely to occur when the drug is taken in its most potent and distilled form (such as crack), and possibly when a person has a biological vulnerability to certain drugs.

- Addiction is more likely to occur among people who believe the drug is stronger than they are—that is, who believe they are addicted and will always be addicted.

- Addiction and drug abuse are more likely to occur when people learn (or when laws or customs encourage them) to take a drug in binges rather than in moderation, and when they learn that drugs can be used to justify behavior that would not otherwise be socially tolerated.

- Addiction occurs when people come to rely on a drug or an experience as a way of coping with problems, relieving pain, or avoiding stress; and when it provides a sense of power, control, and self-esteem that the individual lacks without it.

- Drug abuse is more likely to occur when the drug becomes a permanent part of a person's life instead of an occasional experience; when "everyone" in one's peer group drinks heavily or uses other drugs; and when moderate use is neither taught nor encouraged.

The disease model of addiction was important historically because it transformed the moral condemnation of the addict as a "bad" person into concern for someone who is "sick." If the disease model is inadequate, this is no reason to abandon sympathy for people with serious problems or to abandon the search for solutions. It may mean, though, that the time has come to quit hoping for the perfect, nonaddictive drug and to look instead at the human qualities that make a drug seem perfect.

Quick QUIZ

If you are not yet addicted to studying, try these questions:

1. Longitudinal studies find that the personality problems of adult alcoholics are often a result of (a) childhood trauma, (b) low self-esteem, (c) broken marriages, (d) alcoholism.

2. Which cultural practice is associated with *low* rates of alcoholism? (a) drinking in family or group settings, (b) infrequent but binge drinking, (c) drinking as a rite of passage, (d) regarding alcohol as a sinful drink

3. What seems to be the most reasonable conclusion about the role of genes in alcoholism? (a) Without a key gene, a person cannot become alcoholic; (b) the presence of a key gene or genes will almost always cause a person to become alcoholic; (c) genes may work in combination to increase a person's vulnerability to some kinds of alcoholism.

 4. For a century, people have been searching for a magic drug that can be used recreationally but is not addictive. Heroin, cocaine, barbiturates, methadone, and tranquilizers were all, at first, thought to be nonaddictive. But, in each case, some people became addicted and abuse of the drug became a social problem. Based on what you've read, what are some possible reasons for the failure to find a mood-altering but non-addictive drug?

Answers:

■ SCHIZOPHRENIA

To be schizophrenic is best summed up in a repeating dream that I have had since childhood. In this dream I am lying on a beautiful sunlit beach but my body is in pieces. This fact causes me no concern until I realize that the tide is coming in and that I am unable to gather the parts of my dismembered body together to run away. The tide gets closer and just when I am on the point of drowning I wake up screaming in panic. This to me is what schizophrenia feels like; being fragmented in one's personality and constantly afraid that the tide of illness will completely cover me. (Quoted in Rollin, 1980)

In 1911, Swiss psychiatrist Eugen Bleuler coined the term **schizophrenia** to describe cases in which the personality loses its unity: words are split from meaning, actions from motives, perceptions from reality. Schizophrenia is *not* the same as "split" or "multiple personality." As the above quotation illustrates, schizophrenia refers to a fragmented condition, not the coexistence of several different personalities. It is an example of a **psychosis,** a mental condition that involves distorted perceptions of reality and an inability to function in most aspects of life.

The Nature of the "Schizophrenias"

If depression is the common cold of psychological disorder, says psychiatrist Donald Klein (1980), schizophrenia is its cancer: a baffling and complex problem. Schizophrenia produces *active* or *positive symptoms* that involve an exaggeration or distortion of normal thinking processes and behavior, and more subtle *negative symptoms* that involve the loss of former traits and abilities. The most common active symptoms include the following:

1. *Bizarre delusions,* such as the belief that dogs are anthropologists from another planet, disguised as pets to infiltrate human families. Some people with schizophrenia have paranoid delusions, taking innocent events—a stranger's cough, a helicopter overhead—as evidence that the world is plotting against them. Some have "delusions of identity," believing that they are Moses, Jesus, Joan of Arc, or some other famous person.

2. *Hallucinations* that usually take the form of voices and consist of garbled, odd words; a running conversation in the head; or two or more voices conversing with each other. Unlike the hallucinations that might occur in a normal person on a drug high, schizophrenic hallucinations feel intensely real and believable to the sufferer (Bentall, 1990). Most are voices but some are tactile (such as feeling insects crawling over the body) or visual (such as seeing Elizabeth Taylor in the mirror).

3. *Disorganized, incoherent speech* consisting of an illogical jumble of ideas and symbols, linked by meaningless rhyming words or by remote associations called *word salads.* A patient of Bleuler's wrote: "Olive oil is an Arabian liquorsauce which the Afghans, Moors and Moslems use in ostrich farming. The Indian plantain tree is the whiskey of the Parsees and Arabs. Barley, rice and

■ **schizophrenia**
A psychotic disorder or disorders marked by some or all of these symptoms: delusions, hallucinations, disorganized and incoherent speech, severe emotional abnormalities, and withdrawal into an inner world.

■ **psychosis**
An extreme mental disturbance involving distorted perceptions and irrational behavior. It may have psychological or organic causes.

sugar cane called artichoke, grow remarkably well in India. The Brahmins live as castes in Baluchistan. The Circassians occupy Manchuria and China. China is the Eldorado of the Pawnees" (Bleuler, 1911/1950). The story goes that the great novelist James Joyce once asked Carl Jung to explain the difference between his own stream-of-consciousness writing and the odd associations of his schizophrenic daughter. Jung supposedly replied, "You dive—she falls" (Wender & Klein, 1981).

4. *Grossly disorganized and inappropriate behavior* that may range from child-like silliness to unpredictable and violent agitation. The person may wear three overcoats and gloves on a hot day, start collecting garbage, or hoard scraps of food. Some people with schizophrenia completely withdraw into a private world, sitting for hours without moving, a condition called *catatonic stupor*. In *Autobiography of a Schizophrenic Girl*, Marguerite Sechehaye wrote, "A wall of brass separates me from everybody and everything. In the midst of desolation, in indescribable distress, in absolute solitude, I am terrifyingly alone. . . ."

Negative symptoms may appear months before these active symptoms and often persist when the active symptoms are in remission. They include loss of motivation (an inability to pursue goals); poverty of speech (making only brief, empty replies in conversation, reflecting diminished thought rather than unwillingness to speak); and, most notably, *emotional flatness:* unresponsive facial expressions, poor eye contact, and diminished emotionality (see Figure 15.4). One man set fire to his house, and then sat down calmly to watch TV.

Schizophrenia varies in the severity and duration of these symptoms. In some individuals, the symptoms appear abruptly and eventually disappear with the passage of time, with or without treatment. In others, the onset is more gradual and insidious. Friends and family report a change in personality. The person may stop working or bathing, become isolated and withdrawn, and start behaving in peculiar ways.

As for prognosis, again schizophrenia is unpredictable. Psychiatrists often speak of the "rule of thirds": Of all people diagnosed and hospitalized with

■ **Figure 15.4   Emotions and Schizophrenia**

When people with schizophrenia are asked to draw a picture, their drawings are typically distorted, lack color, include words, and reveal flat emotion. One patient diagnosed as schizophrenic was asked to copy a picture of flowers from a magazine (left). The initial result is shown in the center. The picture on the right shows how much the patient improved after several months of treatment.

schizophrenia, one-third will recover completely, one-third will improve significantly, and one-third will not get well. The more breakdowns and relapses the individual has had, the poorer the chances for complete recovery (Eaton et al., 1992a, b). Yet many people suffering from this illness learn to live with it, are able to work and have warm family relationships, and eventually outgrow their symptoms (Eaton et al., 1992a; Harding, Zubin, & Strauss, 1992; Ram et al., 1992).

The mystery of schizophrenia is that we could go on listing symptoms and variations all day and not finish. Some people with schizophrenia are almost completely impaired in all spheres; others do extremely well in certain areas. Some have normal moments of lucidity in otherwise withdrawn lives. One adolescent crouched in a rigid catatonic posture in front of a television for the month of October; later, he was able to report on all the highlights of the World Series he had seen. A middle-aged man, hospitalized for 20 years, believing he was a prophet of God and that monsters were coming out of the walls, was able to interrupt his ranting to play a good game of chess (Wender & Klein, 1981). People with brain damage usually cannot interrupt their "madness" to watch the World Series or play chess. How can those with schizophrenia do so?

Theories of Schizophrenia

As you might imagine, any disorder that has so many variations and symptoms will pose many problems for diagnosis and explanation. Some psychologists have concluded that there is really no such entity as "schizophrenia" and that everyone would be better off to drop the label entirely (Sarbin, 1992). A review of 374 studies found "a persisting failure of research to establish schizophrenia as a stable, determinate, diagnostic entity," much less one that has an identifiable cause (Mancuso & Sarbin, 1984). Robert Carson (1989), pointing to the failure of clinicians to agree reliably on what they are diagnosing and to predict the outcome for the patient, concluded that the concept of schizophrenia is "almost hopelessly in tatters."

Of course, these critics recognize that some people do behave in bizarre ways and that *something* is wrong with them. In their view, "schizophrenia" is a lot of different somethings, and its name is a grab-bag term for rule-breaking actions and disorders that must be understood by the context in which they occur. For example, Carson (1989) points out that it is impossible to define the term "delusion" without reference to a culture's norms. In every society, he reminds us, perfectly sane individuals hold patently "false or absurd beliefs" with great conviction and zeal. Why do we think a person has schizophrenia if he believes he is the Prophet Ezekiel now, but not if he believes he was the Prophet Ezekiel in a past life?

Other psychologists (and the DSM) reply to these criticisms by arguing that in cultures around the world, the same core signs of schizophrenia appear: hallucinations, delusions, inappropriate behavior, and disorders of thought. That is why almost everyone studying this disorder believes that schizophrenia is a brain disease of some sort (Heinrichs, 1993; Torrey et al., 1994). But to date no single brain abnormality can account for all of schizophrenia's many symptoms.

Some studies have found that some individuals with schizophrenia (but not all) have decreased brain weight, a decrease in the volume of the temporal lobe or limbic regions, and reduced numbers of neurons in specific layers of the prefrontal cortex (Meltzer, 1987). Another promising clue is the discovery that spaces in the brain filled with cerebro-spinal fluid are enlarged, which may indicate cerebral damage (Andreasen et al., 1994; Heinrichs, 1993; Raz & Raz, 1990). (See Figure 15.5 on the next page.) There is also evidence of eye movement abnormalities in people who have schizophrenic symptoms, leading some researchers to suggest that these abnormalities are actually a biological marker of the disease (Clementz & Sweeney, 1990). And a recent MRI study comparing the brains of healthy men and men with schizophrenia found that the latter

When most people think of schizophrenia, they imagine the lonely suffering of someone like this woman. But many individuals with schizophrenia learn to control their symptoms and lead productive lives.

Joseph Rogers recovered from schizophrenia and became director of the National Mental Health Consumers' Association. Other people with schizophrenia learn to recognize signs of an oncoming breakdown and manage it, just as people with diabetes learn to live with their disease.

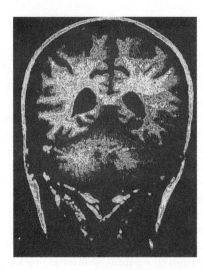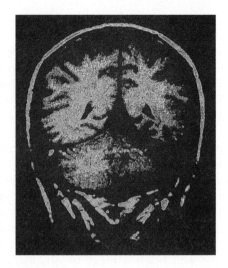

▪ **Figure 15.5   Schizophrenia and the Brain**
Magnetic resonance imaging (MRI) shows that people with schizophrenia (left) are more likely than normals (right) to have enlarged spaces (ventricles) in the brain (Andreasen et al., 1994).

had abnormalities in the thalamus, the traffic-control center for incoming sensations (Andreasen et al., 1994). This finding might explain why the brains of some people with schizophrenia are overly sensitive to everyday stimuli, causing them to retreat into an inner world.

Biological research has also focused on abnormalities in neurotransmitters. Early studies reported that some people with schizophrenia had more dopamine receptors than other people, but today the evidence for a possible link between dopamine and schizophrenia is inconsistent and inconclusive (Heinrichs, 1993). Abnormalities in dopamine transmission may be a minor element in the origins of this disorder or a result of the medication often given to people with schizophrenia.

Brain abnormalities in schizophrenia could be the result of damage to the brain at birth or during childhood (Cannon, Mednick, & Parnas, 1989; Torrey et al., 1994). Or they could occur because of genetic problems. Children have a greater risk of schizophrenia if an identical twin develops the disorder, if one parent has the disorder, and especially if both parents are schizophrenic—even if the child is reared apart from the affected relative (Gottesman, 1991, 1994). Compared to a risk of 1 to 2 percent in the general population, children with one schizophrenic parent have a lifetime risk of 12 percent; for children with two schizophrenic parents, the risk jumps to 35 to 46 percent (Goldstein, 1987). Even so, nearly 90 percent of all persons who develop schizophrenia do *not* have a schizophrenic parent, and nearly 90 percent of all children with such a parent do *not* develop the disorder.

Just as with alcoholism and bipolar disorder, it has been hard to track down specific genes or determine the extent of their influence (Holzman & Matthysse, 1990). There was great excitement when a research team found a link between schizophrenic symptoms and abnormalities on chromosome 5 (Sherrington et al., 1988). This discovery was followed by disappointment when other research failed to confirm it (Kennedy et al., 1988). One problem is that even in studies of identical twins, when one twin develops schizophrenia, the chances that the other will do so range from 28 percent to 40 percent—not even half of them (Torrey et al., 1994).

Lately there has been a surge of support for the possibility, long argued by E. Fuller Torrey, that an infectious virus during prenatal development is the main culprit in schizophrenia (Torrey, 1988; Torrey et al., 1994). Viruses are known to attack very specific areas of the brain, leaving other areas untouched, and they can remain latent for many years before symptoms appear. The infectious disease theory fits many aspects of schizophrenia, such as the odd fact that there are seasonal patterns in the births of schizophrenic children (viruses are seasonal). A longitudinal study that began decades ago found a significant association between exposure to influenza virus during the second trimester of gestation and adult schizophrenia 20 to 30 years later (Barr, Mednick, & Munk-Jorgensen, 1990; Mednick, Huttunen, & Machon, 1994). Other studies have supported this finding.

The second trimester of prenatal development is critical because the brain is forming crucial connections during this time. Working with Torrey, neurologist H. Stefan Bracha reasoned that if a viral infection or other prenatal trauma (such as lack of oxygen) affected the fetal brain and the subsequent development of schizophrenia, its effects should appear elsewhere in the body as well. Bracha's team conducted an ingenious study of 24 pairs of identical twins in which only one twin suffered from schizophrenia. They discovered that the twins who had schizophrenia, unlike their healthy counterparts, were significantly more likely to have deformities in their hands, such as fewer ridges in their fingerprints (Bracha et al., 1991). Of course, hand abnormalities do not cause schizophrenia! But hands are formed during the second trimester, so the same environmental accident that can affect the brain's development might also affect the hands. These findings, although preliminary, may explain why sometimes only one twin of a genetically identical pair later becomes schizophrenic: Only one was affected prenatally by a virus (Torrey et al., 1994).

Many researchers conclude that the onset and course of the schizophrenias depend on a combination of genetic factors, abnormal neurobiology, and family or other pressures (Gottesman, 1991). According to the *vulnerability-stress model,* a combination of biological vulnerability (because of genes or brain damage) and stress is necessary to produce the varieties of schizophrenia. In this view, genes or brain damage alone will not inevitably produce the disorder, and a vulnerable person who lives in a good environment may never show signs of it. As David Holmes (1994) puts it, "Humpty Dumpty had a fragile shell, but he didn't break until he fell." But what makes a person with schizophrenia fall? Torrey (1988) has noted that stress theories of schizophrenia raise many questions: Why don't we have epidemics of schizophrenia in prisons and concentration camps? Why did the schizophrenia rate go down during World War II rather than up? Why is the schizophrenia rate low in warring Northern Ireland, and much higher in the peaceful western part of Ireland?

The answers to Torrey's provocative questions do not lie in the kind of environmental causes that have been blamed in the past, such as parents who give children mixed messages or who abuse them. Some parents of people with schizophrenia have treated their children in cruel or eccentric ways, but many others have given their children love and support. The Copenhagen High-Risk Project has followed 207 children at high risk for schizophrenia (because of having a schizophrenic parent) and a control group of 104 low-risk children. The project directors have identified several factors that, *working in interaction,* increase the likelihood of a schizophrenic breakdown: the existence of schizophrenia in the family; physical trauma during childbirth that might damage the brain; exposure to the flu virus or other prenatal trauma during the second trimester of gestation; unstable, stressful environments in adulthood; and having emotionally disturbed parents (Mednick, Parnas, & Schulsinger, 1987).

Some researchers hope that a common source of all the schizophrenias may yet be discovered. They note that rheumatic fever can appear as a disease of the nervous system, of the heart, of the joints, or of the skin. It seemed to be four different diseases until bacteriologists identified the common source. But other investigators, faced with all the contradictory findings, believe that the "schizophrenias" include several disorders with different causes and that no single culprit is likely to be found. "The likelihood that researchers are studying different illnesses without being able to specify these differences," concludes researcher Walter Heinrichs (1993), ". . . is the major obstacle to scientific progress."

We have come to the end of a long walk along the spectrum of mental disorders. The writer William Styron, who recovered from severe and debilitating depression, used the beginning of Dante's beautiful classic poem, *The Inferno*, to convey his experience of mental illness:

> In the middle of the journey of our life
> I found myself in a dark wood.
> For I had lost the right path.

"For those who have dwelt in depression's dark wood," wrote Styron, "and known its inexplicable agony, the return from the abyss is not unlike the ascent of the poet, trudging upward and upward out of hell's black depths and at last emerging into what he saw as 'the shining world.'" Dante wrote:

> And so we came forth, and once again beheld the stars.

*T*aking Psychology with You

When a Friend Is Suicidal

Suicide is a scary subject, surrounded by mystery and myth. It can be frightening to those who find themselves fantasizing about it, and it is devastating to the family, friends, and acquaintances of those who go through with it. In the United States, most people who commit suicide are over the age of 45, but suicide rates are rapidly increasing among young people. Between 1960 and 1988, the suicide rate among adolescents rose by more than 200 percent, especially among white males (Garland & Zigler, 1994).

People who attempt suicide have different motives. Some believe they have no reason to live; some feel like failures in a world where they think everyone else is happy and successful; some want revenge against those who they think have made them suffer. But they all share the belief that life is unendurable and that suicide is the only solution. This belief may be rational in the case of people who are terminally ill and in pain, but more often it reflects the distorted thinking of someone suffering from depression. Often, the suicidal person doesn't really want to *die;* rather, he or she wants to escape intolerable emotions and self-consciousness (Baumeister, 1990).

Friends and family members can help prevent a suicide by knowing the difference between fact and fiction and by recognizing the danger signs.

• *There is no "suicidal type."* Most adolescents who try to commit suicide are isolated and lonely. Many are children of divorced or alcoholic parents. Some have problems in school and feel like failures. But others who are vulnerable to suicide attempts are college students who are perfectionistic, self-critical, and highly intelligent. The former may feel like ending their lives because they can foresee no future. The latter may feel suicidal because they do not like the futures they foresee.

• *Take all suicide threats seriously.* Many people fail to take action when a friend talks about committing suicide. Some believe the friend's intentions but assume there is nothing they can do. "He'll just do it at another place, another time," they think. In fact, most suicides occur during an acute crisis. Once the person gets through the crisis, the desire to commit suicide fades. One researcher tracked down 515 people who had attempted suicide by jumping off the Golden Gate Bridge many years earlier. After those attempts, fewer than 5 percent had actually committed suicide in the subsequent decades (Seiden, 1978).

• Some people believe that if a friend is talking about suicide, he or she won't really do it. This belief is also false. Few people commit suicide without signaling their intentions. Most are ambivalent: "I want to kill myself, but I don't want to be dead—at least not forever." Most suicidal people want relief from the terrible pain of feeling that nobody cares, that life is not worth living. Getting these thoughts and fears out in the open is an important first step.

- *Know the danger signs.* A depressed person may be at risk of trying to commit suicide if he or she has tried to commit suicide before; has become withdrawn, apathetic, and isolated, or has a history of depression; reveals specific plans for carrying out the suicide or begins to give away cherished possessions; expresses no concern about the usual deterrents to suicide, such as consideration for one's family, adherence to religious rules, or the fact that suicide is irreversible; and has access to a lethal method, such as a gun (Garland & Zigler, 1994).

- *Take constructive action.* If you believe a friend is in danger of suicide, trust your judgment. Do not be afraid to ask, "Are you thinking of suicide?" This question does not "put the idea" in anyone's mind. If your friend is contemplating the action, he or she will probably be relieved to talk about it, and you will know that it is time to find help. Let your friend talk without argument or disapproval. Don't try to talk your friend out of it by debating whether suicide is right or wrong, and don't put on phony cheerfulness. If your friend's words or actions scare you, say so. By listening nonjudgmentally, you are showing that you care. By allowing your friend to unburden his or her grief, you help the person get through the immediate crisis.

Most of all, don't leave your friend alone. If necessary, get the person to a counselor, health professional, or emergency room of a hospital; or call a local suicide hot line. Don't worry about "doing the wrong thing." In an emergency, the worst thing you can do is nothing at all.

Summary

1. "Mental disorder" is not necessarily the same as behavior that is statistically abnormal. Mental disorder has been defined as a violation of cultural standards; as maladaptive or destructive behavior; as emotional distress; and as "insanity," the legal term for incompetence to stand trial.

2. Diagnosing psychological disorders is a complicated process. Clinicians typically use *projective tests* and also *objective tests* or *inventories* such as the MMPI. Reliability and validity are better with objective tests than projective tests. The *Diagnostic and Statistical Manual of Mental Disorders* (DSM) tries to provide objective criteria for the diagnosis of mental disorder. But some critics argue that the manual fosters overdiagnosis and creates self-fulfilling prophecies; inflates normal "problems in living" into "disorders"; can be misused for social and political purposes, such as by absolving people of responsibility for their actions; and implies that diagnosis is scientific when really it is a subjective process. Because of human bias and judgment, reliability in diagnosing most mental disorders is low. Supporters of the DSM reply that when the DSM criteria are used correctly, reliability in diagnosis improves; and that although some diagnoses are subjective and culture-specific, certain mental illnesses are found in all societies.

3. *Generalized anxiety disorder* is a condition of continuous anxiety, with signs of nervousness, worry, and physiological arousal. Other anxiety disorders include *posttraumatic stress disorder* and *acute stress disorder, phobia, panic attack, agoraphobia,* and *obsessive-compulsive disorder.*

4. *Mood disorders* include *major depression, dysthymia,* and *bipolar disorder.* Symptoms of major depression include distorted thinking patterns, low self-esteem, physical ailments such as fatigue and loss of appetite, and prolonged grief and despair. Dysthymia is chronic depressed mood. In bipolar disorder, depression alternates with mania or euphoria. Although women are more likely than men to be treated for depression, it is not known if the sex difference is real or a

result of differences in reporting depression, willingness to be treated, or ways of expressing it.

5. Biological explanations of depression emphasize a depletion of neurotransmitters in the brain and the role of specific genes in mood disorders. Social explanations consider the conditions of people's lives that might generate depression (and cause gender differences), such as work and family life, motherhood, and sexual abuse. Attachment or interpersonal theories argue that depression results from broken or conflicted relationships. Cognitive explanations, such as having a pessimistic explanatory style, emphasize distorted thoughts and habits of brooding or rumination that cause depressions to last.

6. *Personality disorders* are characterized by rigid, self-destructive traits that cause distress or an inability to get along with others. They include *paranoid, narcissistic,* and *antisocial* personality disorders. A person with antisocial personality disorder (sometimes also called a psychopath or sociopath) shows extreme forms of antisocial behavior; lacks guilt, shame, and empathy; and is impulsive and lacks self-control. The disorder may involve a neurological defect caused by genetics or by damage at birth or during childhood to the brain and central nervous system; parental rejection and abuse; and living in certain environments that reward some antisocial traits and behaviors.

7. *Dissociative disorders* involve a split in consciousness or identity. They include *amnesia, fugue* states, and *dissociative identity disorder (multiple personality disorder, or* MPD), in which two or more distinct personalities and identities appear within one person. However, considerable controversy surrounds the validity and nature of MPD. Some clinicians think it is a common but often undiagnosed disorder, originating in childhood trauma; others hold a *sociocognitive* explanation, arguing that most cases of MPD are manufactured in unwitting collusion by therapists who believe in the disorder and suggestible patients who find it a congenial explanation for their problems.

8. The effects of drugs depend on whether they are used moderately or are abused. Signs of *substance abuse* include impaired ability to work or get along with others, use of the drug in hazardous situations, recurrent arrests for drug use, and conflicts with others caused by drug use. According to the *disease model of addiction,* some people have a biological vulnerability to addictions such as alcoholism. The vulnerability may result from a genetic factor or from years of heavy drinking or other drug use. The *learning model of addiction* points out that addiction patterns vary according to culture, learning, and accepted practice; that many people can stop taking a drug, even narcotics, with no withdrawal symptoms; and that drug abuse increases when people are not taught moderate use. Addiction and abuse appear to reflect an interaction of physiology and psychology, person and culture, vulnerability and opportunity.

9. *Schizophrenia* is a psychotic disorder involving positive or "active" symptoms—delusions, hallucinations, disorganized speech ("word salads"), and grossly inappropriate behavior—and negative symptoms—loss of motivation, poverty of speech, and emotional flatness. The "schizophrenias" vary in severity, duration, and prognosis. According to the *vulnerability-stress model,* they result from a combination of biological vulnerability (due to genetic defects, viral infection during the second trimester of prenatal development, or brain damage during birth), and an unstable, stressful, or abusive environment in childhood or young adulthood.

Key Terms

insanity *555*

mental disorder *555*

objective tests (inventories) *555*

Minnesota Multiphasic Personality
  Inventory (MMPI) *556*

DSM *557*

generalized anxiety disorder *561*

posttraumatic stress disorder
  (PTSD) *562*

acute stress disorder *562*

phobia *562*

social phobia *562*

agoraphobia *562*

panic attack *562*

obsessive-compulsive disorder *563*

major depression *565*

dysthymia *565*

mania *565*

bipolar disorder *565*

personality disorders *569*

paranoid personality disorder *569*

narcissistic personality disorder
  569

antisocial personality disorder *570*

dissociative disorders *572*

amnesia (psychogenic) *573*

fugue state *573*

dissociative identity disorder (multiple personality disorder) *573*

substance abuse disorder *576*

disease model of addiction *578*

learning model of addiction *579*

schizophrenia *583*

psychosis *583*

word salads *583*

vulnerability-stress model (of schizophrenia) *587*

16

Approaches to Treatment and Therapy

Two hundred years ago, this circulating swing was used as an "antimaniacal remedy," along with such other crude "cures" as bleeding and purging. Today's mental health professionals have a wide array of biological and psychological treatments at their disposal.

No form of therapy has ever been initiated without a claim that it had unique therapeutic advantages. And no form of therapy has ever been abandoned because of its failure to live up to these claims.

■ MORRIS B. PARLOFF ■

- Murray is a smart fellow with just one problem: He procrastinates. He can't seem to settle down and write his term papers. He keeps getting incompletes, swearing he'll do those papers soon, but before long the incompletes turn to Fs. Why does Murray do this, manufacturing his own misery? What kind of therapy might help him?

- Sally complains of anxieties, irritability, and continuing problems in her marriage. Although she is successful at work, she feels like a fraud, a useless member of society, and a burden to her family. She weeps often. Why is Sally so unhappy, and what can she do about it?

- Jerry, a college student, is brought to the hospital by the campus police, who found him wandering around, dazed and confused. He is anxious and talkative, and reports hearing angry voices that accuse him of being a spy. What treatment can help Jerry?

- Margaret's parents were drug addicts who abandoned her when she was a baby. She lived in four foster homes before finding a family that truly cared for her. Margaret is married and loves her husband, but she has many inhibitions and insecurities. What can Margaret do to recover from her unhappy childhood?

Psychotherapists use many techniques to help people resolve their problems, including the use of art. In this drawing, a child expresses her grief over a classmate's suicide.

People seek professional help for many difficulties and disorders. These range from "problems in living," such as family conflicts and procrastination, to the delusions of schizophrenia. Today there is an equally large array of programs that promise help for personal problems. In this chapter we will evaluate three major approaches to treatment. *Medical treatments* include drugs or direct intervention in brain function, with or without additional therapy; they are prescribed by psychiatrists or other physicians in a hospital or on an outpatient basis. *Psychotherapy* covers an array of psychological approaches to treating mental problems, including psychodynamic therapies, cognitive-behavioral therapies, family therapy, group therapy, and humanistic therapies. Finally, *self-help and community alternatives* include support groups, skills training, rehabilitation counseling, and community interventions.

Each of these approaches can successfully treat some problems but not others. Each can help some individuals but may harm others. Finding the right treatment depends not only on having a good practitioner but also on being an educated consumer. What does research show about the effectiveness of drugs, psychotherapy, counseling, and self-help? What works best and for what problem? When do therapies fail, and when do they do harm?

■ MEDICAL TREATMENTS

Over the centuries, approaches to psychological disorders have alternated between the medical or *organic model,* which regards mental problems as having

Centuries ago, people suffering from physical and mental problems were often "diagnosed" as being possessed by the devil or being witches. The "cure" was to be hanged or burned at the stake.

biological causes, and the *psychological model,* which views mental problems as having psychological causes. Treatments likewise have varied from physical interventions, such as drugs and surgery, to psychological ones. Today the organic model is enjoying a resurgence partly because of new research on the brain, drugs, and genetics, and partly because of the failure of traditional psychotherapies to help chronic sufferers of many disorders.

The Question of Drugs

Two primary lines of evidence support the view that there is a biological basis to certain emotional disorders and psychoses: (1) the evidence, discussed in Chapter 15, that some disorders may have a genetic component or involve a biochemical or neurological abnormality, and (2) the finding that some medications affect people with disorders but have no effect on others who lack the disorders, which suggests that the drugs may be compensating for an organic deficiency. The main classes of drugs used in the treatment of mental and emotional disorders are these:

1. Antipsychotic drugs, or *major tranquilizers,* include chlorpromazine (Thorazine), haloperidol (Haldol), clozapine (Clozaril), and risperidone. These drugs have transformed the treatment of schizophrenia and other psychoses. Before they were introduced, hospital staffs controlled patients with physical restraints, including straitjackets, or put them in padded cells to keep them from hurting others or themselves during states of extreme agitation and delusion. When given to people who are acutely ill with schizophrenia and likely to improve spontaneously within a few weeks or months, antipsychotic drugs can reduce agitation and panic, and shorten the schizophrenic episode (Kane, 1987). Some people on clozapine have "awakened" after a decade of illness and resumed their former lives.

Unfortunately, antipsychotic drugs can have some potentially dangerous effects if they are taken over many years. One is the development of a neurological disorder called *tardive* (late-appearing) *dyskinesia,* which is characterized by involuntary muscle movements. About one-fourth of all adults who take antipsychotics develop this disorder, and fully one-third of elderly patients do (Saltz et al., 1991). In a small percentage of cases, antipsychotic drugs cause *neuroleptic malignant syndrome,* which produces fever, delirium, coma, and sometimes death (Pope, Keck, & McElroy, 1986). Clozapine has produced, in about 2 percent of cases, a potentially fatal condition in which there is a dangerous decrease in certain white blood cells. To avoid these dangers, researchers are trying to develop safer antipsychotic drugs and prescribing lower doses of existing ones. Yet doses that are too low increase the chance that schizophrenic symptoms will worsen, particularly after a year of treatment (Marder et al., 1987).

Thus antipsychotic drugs are a double-edged sword in the treatment of schizophrenia. For some patients, they remove or lessen the most dramatic symptoms, such as word salads and hallucinations, but they usually cannot restore normal thought patterns or relationships. They allow many people to be released from hospitals, but often these individuals cannot care for themselves or they fail to take their medication because of its unpleasant unintended effects. The overall success of these drugs is modest, and some individuals diagnosed as schizophrenic deteriorate when they take them (Breggin, 1991; Karon, 1994; Smith, Glass, & Miller, 1980).

2. Antidepressant drugs, which are classified as stimulants, alter mood by affecting the levels of neurotransmitters in the brain. One type, called *monoamine oxidase (MAO) inhibitors,* elevates the level of norepinephrine and serotonin by blocking or inhibiting the enzyme that deactivates these neuro-

■ **antipsychotic drugs**
Major tranquilizers primarily used in the treatment of schizophrenia and other psychotic disorders.

These photos show the effects of antipsychotic drugs on the symptoms of a young man with schizophrenia. In the photo on the left, he was unmedicated; in the photo on the right, he had taken medication. However, because drugs carry risks and do not help all people with schizophrenia, the public should be wary of claims of miracle cures.

transmitters. A second, more commonly used type, called *tricyclic antidepressants,* prevents reabsorption, or "reuptake," of norepinephrine and serotonin by the cells that have released them. A third kind of antidepressant is fluoxetine (Prozac), which works on the same principle as the tricyclics but specifically targets serotonin. Antidepressants are prescribed not only for depression but also for anxiety, agoraphobia, and obsessive-compulsive disorder. For example, one tricyclic, clomipramine, has successfully reduced such symptoms as endless hand-washing and hair-pulling in many people with obsessive-compulsive disorder (Swedo & Rapoport, 1991). Antidepressants are nonaddictive, but they can produce unpleasant physical reactions. Tricyclics can cause dry mouth, headaches, constipation, nausea, weight gain, and blurry vision. Prozac has fewer disagreeable effects, but it does make some people headachy, nauseated, or restless.

3. "Minor" tranquilizers, such as Valium or Xanax, are classified as depressants. These drugs are the ones most often prescribed by physicians for patients who complain of unhappiness or anxiety, but, unfortunately, they are the least effective in treating emotional disorders. A small but significant percentage of people who take tranquilizers overuse the drugs and develop problems with tolerance (they need larger and larger doses) and withdrawal (Lader, 1989; Lader & Morton, 1991). Xanax can also result in "rebound" panic attacks if it is not taken exactly on schedule. In general, antidepressants are preferable to tranquilizers in treating mood disorders.

4. A special category of drug, a salt called *lithium carbonate,* is often successful in calming people who suffer from bipolar disorder (depression alternating with manic euphoria) (Klerman et al., 1984). It must be given in exactly the right dose, because too little won't help and too much is toxic; the patient's blood levels of lithium must be carefully monitored.

There is no doubt that drugs have helped many people who have gone from therapy to therapy without relief (Shuchman & Wilkes, 1990). The increasing popularity of drugs as a method of treatment poses a problem for clinical psychologists, who, unlike psychiatrists, are not currently licensed to prescribe medication. Many psychologists are now lobbying for prescription rights, arguing that they should have access to the full range of treatment possibilities. But

■ **antidepressant drugs**
Stimulants that influence neurotransmitters in the brain; they are used in the treatment of mood disorders, usually depression and anxiety.

■ **"minor" tranquilizers**
Depressants commonly but often inappropriately prescribed for patients who complain of unhappiness or worry.

they have run into resistance from the medical profession, which argues that even with increased training psychologists will not be qualified to prescribe medication, and from other psychologists who are concerned about the medicalizing of their field and who want psychology to remain a distinct alternative to psychiatry (DeNelsky, 1990; Sanua, 1994).

Although medication cannot magically eliminate people's real-life problems, it can be a useful first step in treatment. By improving sleep patterns, appetite, and energy, it may help people concentrate on solving their problems. Yet, despite these benefits, some words of caution are in order:

1. *The placebo effect and other research problems.* New drugs, like new therapies, often promise quick and effective cures, as was the case with the arrival of clozapine, Xanax, and Prozac. Yet the placebo effect ensures that some people will respond positively to new drugs just because of the enthusiasm surrounding them. After a while, when placebo effects decline, many drugs turn out to be neither as effective as promised nor as widely applicable. This has happened repeatedly with each new generation of tranquilizer, and is happening again with antidepressants. A meta-analysis of 22 studies that compared new antidepressants to older kinds of antidepressants *and* to placebos found that although clinicians thought the drugs were helpful, the patients did not: "Patient ratings revealed no advantage for antidepressants beyond the placebo effect," the researchers reported, and this was true for men and women regardless of their age, dosage level of the drug, and length of treatment. With some understatement, the researchers noted that these findings "highlight the fragility of the antidepressant effect" (Greenberg et al., 1992). New studies of the much-heralded Prozac show that it, too, is no more effective than the older generation of antidepressants.

Even when drugs do show a positive effect, there is another problem: In supposedly double-blind studies of new drugs, patients can usually tell if they are being given an active drug or a placebo. The reason is that virtually all of the drugs we have described produce physical effects, whereas inert placebos do not (Fisher & Greenberg, 1993). Patients and researchers therefore often figure out who is getting a genuine drug and who is getting a placebo, and this knowledge can affect the patients' responses and the researchers' expectations—and judgments of the treatment's success (Carroll et al., 1994a). When true double-blind studies are done, using *active placebos* that mimic the physical effects of real drugs, researchers have found, again, little difference in effectiveness between the placebos and the antidepressants (Fisher & Greenberg, 1989, 1993).

Another important research limitation on drug testing, which the general public and even many physicians do not recognize, is that new drugs are often tested on only a few hundred people for only a few weeks—even when the drug is one that patients might take for many years. For example, the Food and Drug Administration (FDA) warns that "Because clomipramine [for obsessive-compulsive disorder] has not been systematically evaluated for long-term use (more than ten weeks), physicians should periodically reevaluate the long-term usefulness of the drug for individual patients." Clozapine, the neuroleptic now often prescribed for people with schizophrenia, was tested in controlled trials that lasted only six weeks (FDA Drug Bulletin, 1990). Many psychiatrists, relying on these short-term tests, overlook the possibility of negative long-term effects. Peter Kramer (1993) does not mention until the very last page of his best-seller *Listening to Prozac* that "concern over unforeseen or tardive [late-appearing] effects" is realistic because the effects of taking Prozac indefinitely are unknown.

2. *The therapeutic window.* The challenge with drugs is to find the "therapeutic window," the amount that is enough but not too much. Some people have

Newsweek announces that Prozac is "a breakthrough drug for depression." Other media herald the news that clozapine helps thousands of people with schizophrenia. Why should the public be cautious before concluding that these drugs are miracle cures?

been given antidepressants in doses too weak to make a difference. Others have been given doses that are too strong, causing harmful or even dangerous effects (Breggin, 1991). Some people have taken drugs for years without improvement, which is as useless as staying in a "talk therapy" for years without improvement. Some critics are concerned that drug therapy creates a "delusion of precision" in treatment, when in fact many questions remain about which drug best suits which problem, what the proper dose should be, how long the drug should and can be taken, and so forth (Gutheil, 1993).

3. *Relapse and drop-out rates.* A person may have short-term success with antipsychotic or antidepressant drugs. However, in part perhaps because these medications have some unpleasant effects, the percentage of people who stop taking them is very high—between 50 and 67 percent (McGrath et al., 1990; Torrey, 1988). People who take antidepressants without learning how to cope with their problems are also more likely to relapse; that is, the depression is more likely to return.

4. *Race, gender, age, and dosage.* The same dose of a drug may not be suitable for men and women, for all age groups, or for all racial groups. When psychiatrist Keh-Ming Lin moved from Taiwan to the United States, he was amazed to learn that the dosage of antipsychotic drugs given to American patients with schizophrenia was often 10 times higher than the dose for Chinese patients with the same illness. In subsequent research comparing 13 white and 16 Asian schizophrenics, Lin and his colleagues confirmed that the Asian patients required significantly lower doses of the medication for optimal treatment (Lin et al., 1989; Lin, Poland, & Lesser, 1986). The reason may involve differences in metabolic rates, amount of body fat, the number or type of drug receptors in the brain, or cultural practices such as smoking and eating habits. And within a culture, men and women, and old people and young people, may not metabolize antidepressants and other drugs the same way (McGrath et al., 1990).

As we will see later in this chapter, many psychotherapies work as well as drugs, or even better, for many people who have panic attacks, phobias, anxiety, or depression that is not extremely severe (Barlow, 1990; Dobson, 1989; Lambert & Bergin, 1994; Lipsey & Wilson, 1993; Robinson, Berman, & Neimeyer, 1990). Moreover, unlike drug treatment, psychotherapies teach people how to cope with recurrences of their disorder, so the relapse rate for people in psychotherapy is much lower than for people who take medication exclusively.

In this respect it is important to emphasize that *the fact that a disorder may have biological origins does not mean that the only appropriate treatment is medical.* Researchers in one study used PET scans to examine cerebral glucose metabolism in 18 patients with obsessive-compulsive disorder, before and after treating them with either fluoxetine (Prozac) or behavior therapy. They found that glucose metabolic rates changed in response to *both* treatments (Baxter et al., 1992)—another reminder that the brain affects behavior, but behavior also affects the brain.

There is no doubt that drugs can be miraculous, rescuing some people from institutions, emotional despair, or suicide. But many psychologists are worried about the *routine* prescription of medications, which are often dispensed without accompanying therapy for the person's problems. At one conference we attended, a psychiatrist warned that because of the ease of prescribing antidepressants and tranquilizers, "It is not unusual for [psychiatrists] to see anywhere from six to eight patients per client hour. This is not being involved with your patient in any meaningful way." The proper use of drugs depends on the individual, the problem, the practitioner, and whether drugs are combined with therapy.

Probing the Brain: Surgery and Electroshock

Some physicians attempt to treat mental illness by changing brain function directly. **Psychosurgery** is an operation designed to destroy selected areas of the brain thought to be responsible for emotional disorders or disturbed behavior. It should not be confused with brain surgery to remove an abnormal organic condition, such as a tumor, or with "split-brain" surgery to control life-threatening epileptic seizures (see Chapter 4).

The first attempts to do psychosurgery occurred in 1935, when a Portuguese neurologist, Egas Moniz, drilled two holes into the skull of a mental patient and used a specially designed instrument to cut or crush the nerve fibers in its path to the frontal lobes of the brain. The operation, called a leucotomy or prefrontal *lobotomy,* was supposed to reduce the patient's emotional symptoms without impairing intellectual ability. This procedure, *which was never assessed scientifically or validated,* was performed on tens of thousands of people in its heyday. In America, a version of the lobotomy was popularized by Walter Freeman, who personally performed more than 3,500 operations. Tragically, lobotomies left many patients apathetic, withdrawn, and unable to care for themselves (Valenstein, 1986). Moniz won a Nobel Prize for his work.

With the advent of antipsychotic drugs in the 1950s, the number of lobotomies declined, but other forms of psychosurgery took their place. Some neurosurgeons tried to reduce violent rages by removing parts of the amygdala, a structure in the limbic system that, as we saw in Chapter 10, is involved in emotion. But such procedures to "fix" the brain have been found to be unreliable, have unpredictable results, and cause unintended brain damage (Breggin, 1991; Valenstein, 1986). Because of the legal and ethical problems involved in psychosurgery, it is rarely used today.

An equally controversial procedure is **electroconvulsive therapy (ECT),** or "shock treatments." An electrode is placed on one or both sides of the head, and a brief current is turned on. The current triggers a seizure that typically lasts one minute, causing the body to convulse intensely. A colleague told us about a man who was given ECT in the early 1950s: The convulsions sent him flying off the table and shattered his legs. Cases such as this reinforce the public impression of ECT as a barbaric and painful practice, akin to electrocution. The method lost favor as a result, especially when drugs seemed to be so promising. When drugs proved to have limited effectiveness and to take time to

▪ **psychosurgery**

Any surgical procedure that destroys selected areas of the brain believed to be involved in emotional disorders or violent, impulsive behavior.

▪ **electroconvulsive therapy (ECT)**

A procedure occasionally used for cases of prolonged major depression, in which a brief brain seizure is induced to alter brain chemistry.

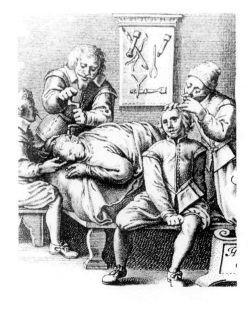

Throughout history, healers have tried literally to root out behavior they considered abnormal. An engraving from 1634 shows trepanning, an ancient method of drilling holes in the skull to release psychic pressures supposedly causing mental illness.

work, and when new ways of measuring brain activity appeared, researchers began to reexamine ECT.

Today, the technique has been vastly modified and the voltage reduced. Patients are given muscle relaxants and anesthesia, so their convulsions are minimized and they can sleep through the procedure (Malitz & Sackeim, 1986). Advocates maintain that ECT is a faster and more effective way to treat severe depression than drugs. ECT affects every aspect of brain activity, including blood flow, neuroendocrine levels, and neurotransmitters, but supporters point out that MRI studies of patients given ECT find no evidence that the treatment causes brain damage (Coffey, 1993; Endler, 1991).

ECT is most effective with suicidally depressed people, for whom there is a risk in waiting until antidepressants or psychotherapy can take effect. It is not effective with other disorders, such as schizophrenia or alcoholism. Its main drawback is that it produces memory loss and other cognitive impairments, sometimes briefly but sometimes permanently. That is why some former patients call it "a crime against humanity," and a psychiatrist has called the use of ECT "like hitting [someone] with a two-by-four" (Fisher, 1985). ECT continues to inspire passion, pro and con.

Quick QUIZ

A. Match the treatment with the problem(s) for which it is most typically used.

1. antipsychotic drugs   **a.** suicidal depression
2. antidepressant drugs   **b.** bipolar disorder
3. lithium carbonate   **c.** schizophrenia
4. electroconvulsive therapy   **d.** depression and anxiety
     e. obsessive-compulsive disorder

B. Mildred has had episodes of major depression throughout her life, and antidepressants are helping her feel better. So when her daughter Jezebel complains of feeling blue, Mildred sends her to her own psychiatrist. The psychiatrist listens briefly, thinks, "Like mother, like daughter," and then prescribes the same antidepressant for Jezebel. Before taking it, what questions should Jezebel ask herself—and the doctor?

Answers:

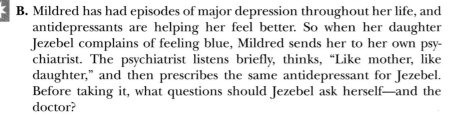

A. 1. c 2. d, e 3. b 4. a **B.** Is Jezebel as seriously depressed as her mother, or is the doctor seeing a superficial similarity between them? What is Jezebel *depressed about?* Has the doctor taken Jezebel's full medical and psychological history? Are there other forms of therapy that might be tried first?

The Hoofbeats of a Zebra

One rainy afternoon a young woman named Sheila Allen went to a community hospital and asked for psychiatric help. Sheila Allen had virtually no strength left. She couldn't walk; she could barely sit up. For years she had been going to doctors, getting sicker and sicker. The doctors didn't take her physical complaints seriously, and finally she agreed to enter the "kook hospital." Her diagnosis upon admission was "bizarre behavior, with looseness of thought associations and severe depression associated with suicidal thoughts."

Psychologically minded experts and medically minded experts often interpret the same behavior differently. How can we avoid the diagnostic errors that occur because of this either–or thinking?

Sheila Allen was lucky. She met a neurologist who suspected, correctly, that she had an uncommon disease called myasthenia gravis, which weakens the muscles. Fortunately, there is a treatment for this illness and Sheila Allen recovered. Why had no doctor accurately diagnosed her problem? Her neurologist said, "There is a saying about diagnosis—about why doctors often fail to recognize one of the less common diseases. It goes, 'When you hear hoofbeats, you don't necessarily think of a zebra.' I recognized the hoofbeats of a zebra" (Roueché, 1984).

All researchers learn to recognize the hoofbeats that make the most noise in their profession. "Mind"-oriented people listen for one beat, "body"-oriented people for another. Throughout history, both sides have made terrible errors. In the nineteenth century, people thought that tuberculosis was caused by a "tubercular personality" until the bacillus that causes the disease was discovered (Sontag, 1978). A British medical historian, Elizabeth Thornton (1984), believes that many of Freud's patients were suffering from physical illnesses that were unidentified in his day, such as tuberculous meningitis and temporal lobe epilepsy. Thornton collected cases of dozens of patients who were subjected to months or years of psychoanalytic therapy when their real problem was a brain tumor, a disease, or another organic condition.

But psychologists are also concerned about reducing complex psychological problems to matters of biochemistry. As we noted, some physicians prescribe drugs indiscriminately, without finding out why the patient is distressed and without helping the patient learn to cope with adversities. As long as people think that hoofbeats indicate only one animal, disagreements about medical and psychological models of mental illness will continue.

▪ KINDS OF PSYCHOTHERAPY

All psychotherapists have one thing in common: They want to help clients think about their lives in new ways in order to find solutions to the problems that plague them. In this section we will consider the major schools of psychotherapy and some of their offshoots. To describe the basic philosophy and methods of each of the therapeutic schools that follow, we will use the example of our procrastinating friend Murray, whom we met at the start of this chapter. But keep in mind that these therapies can be applied to many problems, including emotional disorders, difficult decisions, conflicts in relationships, and traumatic experiences.

Psychodynamic Therapy

Sigmund Freud was the father of the "talking cure," as one of his patients called it. He believed that intensive probing of the past and of the mind would produce insight—the patient's moment of truth, the awareness of the reason for his or her symptoms and anguish. With insight and emotional release, the symptoms would disappear. Freud's original method of *psychoanalysis* has evolved into many different forms, which are called *psychodynamic therapies* because they share the goal of exploring the unconscious dynamics of personality, such as defenses and conflicts. These approaches are considered by their proponents to be "depth" therapies because the goal is to delve for unconscious processes rather than "superficial" symptoms and conscious beliefs.

Traditional, orthodox psychoanalysis is a method for those who have money and time. The client usually meets with the analyst three to five times a week, often for many years. One such analyst, John Gedo (1979), reported that in 20 years he treated only 36 people, each one requiring "more than 600 sessions,

Freud (1910) believed that Leonardo da Vinci's paintings of Madonnas were a sublimated expression of his longing for his mother, from whom he had been separated early in life. One goal of psychoanalysis is to help clients sublimate their energies constructively instead of expressing them neurotically.

sometimes as many as 1,000, spread over 3 to 7 years." (In the film *Sleeper,* Woody Allen's character was in suspended animation for two centuries. When he awakes, his first thought is: "I haven't seen my analyst in 200 years! He was a strict Freudian—if I'd been going all this time I'd probably almost be cured by now.")

In analysis and some other psychodynamic therapies, the client lies on a couch, facing away from the analyst, and uses **free association** to say whatever comes to mind. For example, by free associating to his dreams, his fantasies about work, and his early memories, Murray might gain the insight that he procrastinates as a way of expressing anger toward his parents. He might realize that he is angry because they insist that he study for a career he dislikes. Ideally, Murray will come to this insight by himself. If the analyst suggests it, Murray might feel too defensive about displeasing his parents to accept it.

The second major element of psychodynamic therapy is **transference,** the patient's transfer (displacement) of emotional elements of his or her inner life—usually feelings about the parents—outward onto the analyst. Have you ever found yourself responding to a new acquaintance with unusually quick affection or dislike, and later realized it was because the person reminded you of a loved or loathed relative? That experience is similar to transference. A woman who failed to resolve her Oedipal love for her father might seem to fall in love with the analyst. A man who is unconsciously angry at his mother for rejecting him might now become furious with his analyst for going on vacation. Through transference, psychodynamic therapists believe, patients resolve their emotional conflicts.

Psychodynamic therapy, and especially psychoanalysis, does not expressly aim to solve an individual's immediate problem. In fact, a person may come in complaining of a symptom such as anxiety or headaches, and the therapist may not get around to that symptom for months or even years. The therapist views the symptom as only the tip of the mental iceberg. Some traditional analysts don't attempt "cures" at all. The goal, they say, is understanding, not change.

Many psychodynamic therapists use Freudian principles but reject traditional psychoanalytic methods. They face the client; they participate more; they are more goal-directed. Time-limited or *brief psychodynamic therapy* consists of 15, 20, or 25 sessions. Without delving into the client's entire history, the therapist listens to the client's problems and formulates the main issue or *dynamic focus* (Strupp & Binder, 1984). The rest of the therapy focuses on the person's self-defeating habits and repetitive problems. The therapist looks for clues in the client's behavior in therapy to identify and change these patterns.

Behavioral and Cognitive Therapy

Psychologists who practice behavioral or cognitive therapy (or a combination of the two) would focus on helping Murray change his current behavior and attitudes rather than striving for insight. "Mur," they would say, "you have lousy study habits. And you have a set of beliefs about studying, writing papers, and success that are woefully unrealistic." Such therapists would not worry much about Murray's past, his parents, or his unconscious anxieties.

In Chapter 7 we discussed the major principles of learning theory and some of their applications. *Behavior therapies* are based on techniques derived from behavioral principles:

1. *Behavioral records and contracts* are used to help clients identify the rewards that keep an unwanted habit going and make commitments to better forms of behavior. For example, a man who wants to curb his overeating may not be aware of how much he eats throughout the day; a behavioral record

■ **free association**
In psychoanalysis, a method of recovering unconscious conflicts by saying freely whatever comes to mind.

■ **transference**
In psychodynamic therapies, a critical step in which the patient transfers emotional feelings for his or her parents to the therapist.

Two therapists assist a phobic woman who is afraid of stairs. In this form of behavior therapy, the therapists take the client directly into the feared situation in order to extinguish her fear.

might show that he eats more junk food than he realized in the late afternoon. Once the unwanted behavior is identified, along with the reinforcers that keep it going, a treatment program can be designed to establish a new set of reinforcers. The therapist can help the person set *behavioral goals,* small step by small step. A husband and wife who fight over housework, for instance, might be asked to draw up a contract indicating who will do what, with specified rewards for carrying out their duties. With such a contract, they can't fall back on mutual accusations, such as "You never do anything around here!"

2. *Systematic desensitization* is a step-by-step process of "desensitizing" a client to a feared object or experience. It combines relaxation training with a systematic hierarchy of stimuli, sometimes in imagined situations and sometimes in real ones, leading gradually to the one that is most feared. The sequence for a person who is terrified of flying might be: Read about airplane safety, visit an airport, sit in a plane while it is on the ground, take a short flight, take a long flight. At each step the person must become comfortable before going on.

3. *Aversive conditioning* substitutes punishment for the positive reinforcement that has perpetuated a bad habit. Suppose a woman who bites her nails is reinforced each time she does so by relief of anxiety and a brief good feeling. A behavior therapist might have her wear a rubber band around her wrist and ask her to snap it (hard!) each time she bites her nails or feels the desire to do so. The goal is to make sure that there are no continuing rewards for the undesirable behavior.

4. *Flooding or exposure treatments* take the client right into a feared situation, but the therapist goes along to show that the situation isn't going to kill either of them. For example, a person suffering from agoraphobia would be taken into the very situation that he or she fears most—a procedure called "in vivo" exposure—and remain there, with the therapist, until the panic and anxiety decline. Notice how different this approach is from a psychodynamic one, in which the goal would be to uncover the presumably unconscious reason the agoraphobic fears going out.

5. *Skills training* provides practice in specific acts that are necessary for achieving the person's goals. It's not enough to tell someone "Don't be shy" if the person doesn't know how to make companionable small talk when meeting other people. Countless skills-training programs are available—for parents who don't know how to discipline children, for people with social anxieties, for children and adults who don't know how to express themselves, and so on.

A behaviorist would treat Murray's procrastination in several ways. Murray might not be aware of how he actually spends his time when he is avoiding his studies. Afraid he hasn't time to do everything, he does nothing. Keeping a behavioral diary would let Murray know exactly how he spends his time, and how much time he should realistically allot to a project. (Procrastinators often are poor judges of how much time it takes to do things.) Instead of having a vague, impossibly huge goal, such as "I'm going to reorganize my life," Murray would establish specific small goals, such as reading the two books necessary for an English paper and writing one page of an assignment. The therapist might also offer skills training to make sure Murray knows how to reach those goals.

Of course, people's thoughts, feelings, and motivations can influence their behavior. In discussing emotion (Chapter 10) and emotional disorders (Chapter 15), we saw that distorted thoughts and perceptions are related to mood problems. In *cognitive therapy* the aim is to help clients identify the thoughts, beliefs, and expectations that might be unnecessarily prolonging their unhappiness, loneliness, conflicts, and other problems (Beck, 1976, 1991; Ellis & Dryden, 1987). Albert Ellis founded one of the earliest and still best-known forms of cognitive therapy (Rational Emotive Therapy), which he now calls

Rational Emotive Behavior Therapy (Ellis, 1993). In this approach, the therapist challenges the client's illogical beliefs directly with rational arguments. Other forms of cognitive therapy are usually less direct, instead encouraging a person to formulate the beliefs as hypotheses and test them against the evidence. For example, clients would be told to ask themselves what the evidence is for their belief that no one loves them, that a co-worker is intentionally sabotaging their work, or that they will always be lonely. They would be encouraged to see how their thoughts create self-fulfilling prophecies ("I'm ugly and unlikable and that's just the way it is"; "My office is an unfriendly place and always will be").

In cognitive therapy, clients may be asked to write down their negative thoughts, read the thoughts as if someone else had said them, and then write a rational response to each one. This technique is useful because many people have unrealistic notions of what they "must" or "should" do in their lives, and often they do not examine the validity of these notions. Thus a cognitive therapist might treat Murray's procrastination problem by having Murray write down his thoughts and feelings about his work. Many procrastinators are perfectionists. If they can't do something perfectly, they won't do it at all. Unable to accept their human limitations, they set impossible standards and "catastrophize":

> *Negative thought:* "This paper isn't good enough; I'd better rewrite it for the twentieth time."
>
> *Rational response:* "Good enough for what? It won't win a Pulitzer Prize, but if I look at it objectively, I see it is a pretty good paper."
>
> *Negative thought:* "If I don't get an A+ on this paper, my life will be ruined."
>
> *Rational response:* "My life will be a lot worse if I keep getting incompletes. It's better to get a B or even a C than to do nothing at all."
>
> *Negative thought:* "My professor is going to think I'm an idiot when he reads this. I'll feel humiliated by his criticism."
>
> *Rational response:* "He's never accused me of being an idiot before. If he makes some criticisms, I can learn from them and do better next time."

Strict behaviorists consider thoughts to be "behaviors" that are modifiable by learning principles, rather than explanations of behavior. But most psychologists believe that thoughts and behavior influence each other, which is why "cognitive-behavior" therapy is more common than either method alone.

Humanistic and Existential Therapy

Humanistic therapies, like their parent philosophy humanism, start from the assumption that people seek self-actualization and self-fulfillment. These therapies generally do not delve into past conflicts, but aim to help people feel better about themselves and free themselves from self-imposed limits. To do this, they explore what is going on "here and now," not the issues of "why and how."

In *client-centered* or *nondirective therapy,* developed by Carl Rogers, the therapist's role is to listen sympathetically, to offer what Rogers called *unconditional positive regard,* to be an "ideal parent." The goal is to build the client's self-esteem and help the client feel that he or she is loved and respected no matter what. To Rogerians, it almost doesn't matter what the client's specific complaint is. Thus a Rogerian might assume that Murray's procrastination masks his low self-regard, and that Murray is out of touch with his real feelings and wishes.

Although client-centered therapy has no specific techniques, Rogers (1961) believed that effective therapists must have three qualities. They must be warm, providing unconditional positive regard for the client. They must be genuine and honest in expressing their feelings. And they must show accurate empathic

The poet Michael Casey described the first daffodil that bravely rises through the snow as "a gleam of laughter in a sullen face." Are you more inclined to focus on the lingering icy clutch of winter or the early sunny signs of spring?

understanding of the client's problems. The therapist's support for the client, according to Rogers, is eventually adopted by the client, who will become more self-accepting. Once that is accomplished, the person can accept the limitations of others too.

Existential therapy helps clients explore the meaning of existence, facing with courage the great questions of life such as death, freedom, free will, alienation from oneself and others, loneliness, and meaninglessness. Existential therapists believe that our lives are not inevitably determined by our pasts or our circumstances; instead, we have the power to choose our own destinies. As Irvin Yalom (1989) explains, "the crucial first step in therapy is the patient's assumption of responsibility for his or her life predicament. As long as one believes that one's problems are caused by some force or agency outside oneself, there is no leverage in therapy." Victor Frankl (1955) developed a form of existential therapy after surviving a Nazi concentration camp. In that pit of horror, he observed, some people maintained their dignity and sanity because they were able to find meaning in the experience, shattering though it was.

Some observers believe that ultimately, all therapies are existential. In different ways, therapy helps people determine what is important to them, what values guide them, and what changes they will have the courage to make. An existential therapist might help Murray think about the significance of his procrastination, what his ultimate goals in life are, and how he might find the strength to carry out his ambitions.

Beyond the Person: Family and Group Therapy

Murray's situation is getting worse. His father has begun to call him Mr. Tomorrow, which upsets his mother, and his brother the math major has been

Family psychologist Alan Entin uses photographs to help people identify important themes in their family histories and trigger memories or insights that may help them put their feelings in new perspective. For example, when one woman was asked to talk about a photo of her parents (left), she began to cry; she realized that in every photo she had of her family, she and her brother were touching their mother and their father was always standing apart—distant and remote, as if alienated from them. Does the photo on the right convey a happy cohesive family to you, or one split in half? Shortly after it was taken, the couple divorced; the father took custody of the children . . . and the mother kept the dog (Entin, 1992).

calculating how much tuition money Murray's incompletes are costing. His older sister Isabel, the biochemist who never had an incomplete in her life, now proposes that all of them go to a family therapist. "Murray's not the only one in this family with complaints," she says.

Family therapists maintain that Murray's problem is not *in him*. It developed in a social context, it is sustained by a social context, and any change he makes will affect that context.

The Family Kaleidoscope.   Salvador Minuchin (1984) compares the family to a kaleidoscope, a changing pattern of mosaics in which the pattern is larger than any one piece. Efforts to isolate and "therapize" one piece, one member of the family without the others, are, in this view, doomed. For one thing, each member has his or her own perceptions about the others, which may be entirely wrong. For another, family members are usually unaware of how they influence one another. By observing the entire family together (or, in the case of couple problems, both partners) the therapist can discover the family's tensions and imbalances in power and communication (Satir, 1983).

In "psychosomatic families," only one member, usually a child, actually gets an illness or psychological symptoms, but that condition plays a role in the workings of the whole family. Minuchin believes that psychosomatic families have a common feature: They avoid conflict. The child gets sick as a way of expressing anger, keeping the parents together, or asserting control (Minuchin, Rosman, & Baker, 1978).

Some family therapists use a *multigenerational* approach, helping clients identify repetitive patterns of behavior across generations in their families (Kerr & Bowen, 1988). The therapist and client create a *genogram*, a family tree of psychologically significant events across as many generations as the client can determine (Carter & McGoldrick, 1988). Sometimes the genogram highlights the origins of current problems and conflicts. The genogram of the playwright Eugene O'Neill, for instance, shows a pattern of estrangement between father and children for three generations (see Figure 16.1). Sometimes the genogram reveals positive patterns. The genogram of Alexander Graham Bell, who invented the telephone, reveals a three-generation preoccupation with solving problems in hearing and speaking.

Although many family therapists treat the whole family, others will treat individuals in a *family systems* perspective (Bowen, 1978; Carter & McGoldrick, 1988). Clients learn that if they change in any way, even in getting rid of their problem or unhappiness, their families will usually protest noisily. They will send explicit and subtle messages that read, "Change back!" The family systems view recognizes that if one family member changes, the others must change too: If I won't tango with you, you can't tango with me. But most people don't like change. They are comfortable with old patterns and habits, even those that cause them trouble. They *want* to keep tangoing, even if their feet hurt.

In general, family therapists would observe how Murray's procrastination fits his family dynamics. Perhaps it allows Murray to get his father's attention and his mother's sympathy. Perhaps it keeps Murray from facing his greatest fear: that if he does finish his work, it won't measure up to his father's high standards. The therapist will not only help Murray change, but will help his family deal with a changed Murray.

One contemporary approach in family therapy is *solution focused* (or "strategic"). Its advocates approach family problems with minimal emphasis on learning the family's history, generating insights, or fostering self-fulfillment. Rather, they help clients specify their goals and find ways of achieving them. They try to figure out how a person's problem works in that person's life, and then to determine what particular tactics might undo it (de Shazer, 1993; Walter & Peller, 1993).

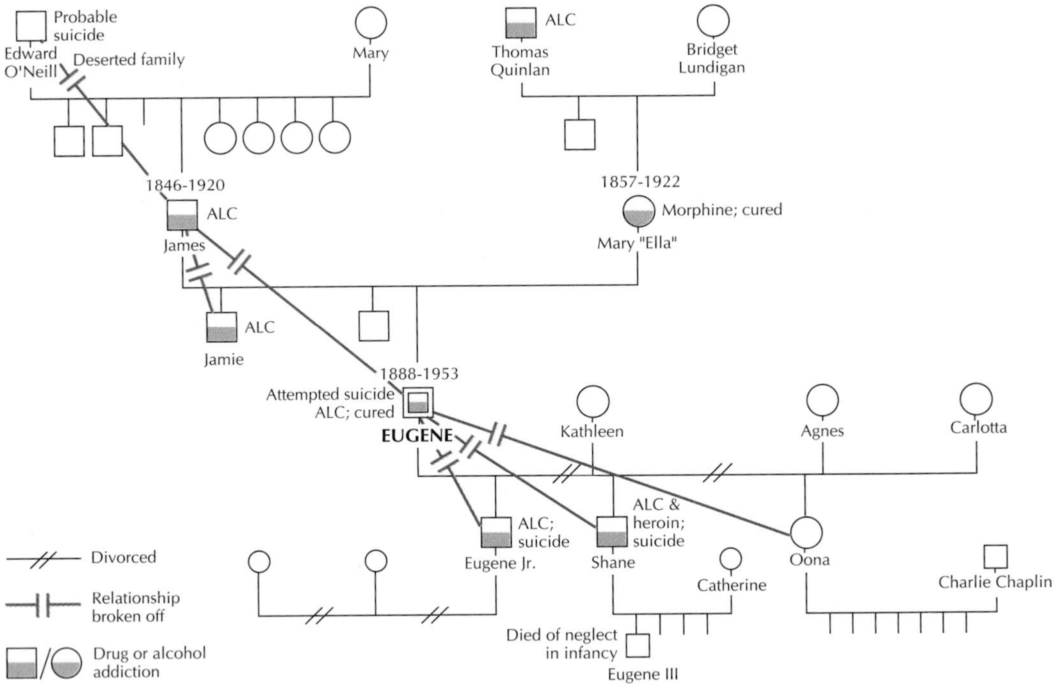

Figure 16.1 **The Family Genogram of Playwright Eugene O'Neill**

The O'Neill family shows multigenerational patterns of estrangement between father and children, multiple marriages, and addiction. Both Eugene and his older brother Jamie felt alienated from their father; in turn, Eugene was totally estranged from his two sons, and he never spoke to his daughter Oona again after she married Charlie Chaplin. Eugene attempted suicide; both of his sons did commit suicide. Eugene's grandfather, father, older brother, and sons were alcoholics; his mother, a morphine addict for 26 years, was later cured. Eugene, who had had problems with alcohol as well, quit drinking at age 37.

Constructing a genogram allows family therapists and their clients to observe patterns across generations that often illuminate current conflicts and concerns. By recognizing patterns that are destructive, family members can begin to change them (McGoldrick & Gerson, 1985).

One famous practitioner of solution-focused family therapy was Milton Erickson, who was known for his unconventional methods. Erickson was one of the first to emphasize the importance of narratives—the stories that people tell about their lives—in generating therapeutic change, and he devised ingenious methods tailored to his clients' particular problems. For example, he used "paradoxical" techniques, in which he would instruct a person to do *more* of what he or she was trying to eliminate. Erickson once treated an old man who had insomnia by telling him to get up at 2 A.M. and scrub the kitchen floor. This technique showed them both that the man's insomnia was not a symptom of anxiety but simply of having excess energy (Haley, 1984).

Group Therapy. Murray could also meet weekly with a group of procrastinators who already know every one of his excuses and habits. Group therapies are as diverse as their leaders. Psychodynamic therapists, cognitive-behaviorists, family therapists, and humanists all may run group therapy sessions. Some groups consist of people who share a problem; others consist of people with different problems. Only the basic format, self-revelation in a group, is the same. In group therapy, ideally, members learn that their problems are not unique. They learn to speak up and become more assertive with other people in (presumably) a safe setting. They learn that they cannot get away with their usual excuses because others in the group have tried them all (Yalom, 1995). Group therapies are commonly used in institutions, such as prisons and mental hospitals. But they are also popular among people who have a range of social difficulties, such as shyness and anxiety, or who share a common traumatic experience, such as sexual assault (Becker et al., 1984).

Group therapy, however, is not the same as encounter groups, which are designed for "personal growth" rather than psychotherapy. Encounter groups exist today in dozens of different forms, none regulated by law or by professional standards. Generally, they promise increased awareness, unconditional regard from others, and self-fulfillment. But they vary widely in their philosophy and in the kinds of encounters they offer. Some of the programs are mild in method and intention, offering support, cohesiveness, and a search for spiritual meaning. Others are based on breaking people down by putting them through isolation, stress, fatigue, and hunger, and then "reconstructing" them in the group's image. The psychological casualties are high in such settings (Galanter, 1989; Mithers, 1994). (In Chapter 17 we will look at methods of coercive persuasion that such groups use.)

Quick QUIZ

Match each method with the therapy most likely to use it.

1. free association
2. systematic desensitization
3. facing the fear of death
4. reappraisal of thoughts
5. unconditional positive regard
6. revelation with others
7. genogram
8. contract specifying duties

a. cognitive therapy
b. psychoanalysis
c. humanistic therapies
d. behavior therapy
e. group therapy
f. family therapy
g. existential therapy

Answers:

1. b 2. d 3. g 4. a 5. c 6. e 7. f 8. d

Psychotherapy in Practice

The four general approaches to psychotherapy that we have discussed may seem entirely different. In theory, they are, and so are the techniques resulting from those approaches. Yet in practice, most psychotherapists are *eclectic*, borrowing a method from here, an idea from there, and avoiding strong allegiances to narrow theories or schools of thought (Lambert & Bergin, 1994). This flexibility suits their own styles and enables them to treat many different clients with whatever methods are appropriate and effective. In a survey of 800 therapists trained in clinical psychology, marriage and family therapy, social work, or psychiatry, 68 percent said they were eclectic in orientation, drawing on psychodynamic, cognitive-behavioral, humanistic, and family systems techniques as necessary (Jensen, Bergin, & Greaves, 1990).

Thus some cognitive therapists integrate psychodynamic ideas into their practice, such as the importance of dealing with the client's defenses, transference, and motivations (Safran & Segal, 1990). Some psychoanalytic therapists borrow methods from the family systems approach. Some humanistic therapists are more directive than the theory recommends and some behaviorists are less

Successful therapists are flexible in their methods.

"I UTILIZE THE BEST FROM FREUD, THE BEST FROM JUNG AND THE BEST FROM MY UNCLE MARTY, A VERY SMART FELLOW."

directive. Because of this overlap among these approaches, researchers who study the effectiveness of therapy are trying to find the common processes in all of them, even those as apparently different as psychoanalysis and behavior therapy (Lambert & Hill, 1994; Mahony, 1991; Orlinsky & Howard, 1994).

One such common process in therapy has to do with the stories, or narratives, that people tell about themselves. All good therapies try to replace a client's self-defeating, pessimistic, or unrealistic life story with one that is more hopeful and attainable. As George Howard (1991) puts it, therapy is an exercise in "story repair." Sometimes this "story repair" is implicit, but many therapists today are making it an explicit focus of treatment.

For example, some therapists use *the narrative method* as a tool to help clients form new stories about themselves. (Mahony, 1991; White & Epston, 1990). The therapist may write a letter to the client, reframing the problem as the therapist sees it and inviting the client to write a reply. Letter writing allows people to identify their problems more clearly and see their own behavior in new ways. One proponent of the narrative method, David Epston, wrote a long letter to Marisa, an immigrant woman who had been abused and rejected all her life. It said, in part: ". . . telling me, a virtual stranger, your life story, which turned out to be a history of exploitation, frees you to some extent from it. To tell a story about your life turns it into a history, one that can be left behind, and makes it easier for you to create a future of your own design" (quoted in O'Hanlon, 1994). Marisa replied that his letter helped her to tell a new story about her life and future. Instead of seeing the tragedies that had befallen her as evidence that she was a worthless victim, as she always had, she now saw the same events as evidence of her strength and endurance. In short, she transformed her victim narrative into a story of triumph. "My life has a future now," she wrote back to him. "It will never be the same again."

■ ALTERNATIVES TO PSYCHOTHERAPY

Psychotherapy is popular for people with all sorts of problems, but sometimes it is not enough and sometimes it is too much. *Community programs* aim to help people who are seriously mentally ill or who have disabilities and need more than individual therapy. *Self-help groups* are designed for people who have problems that do not require individual or group therapy.

The Community and Rehabilitation Movements

Many people assume that individuals who are seriously mentally ill are in hospitals and other institutions, but this is not so. The vast majority of those

with mental disorders spend most of their lives in the community. However, they usually cannot live with their families. Instead, most of them live in boarding houses, hotel rooms, hostels, jails, hallways, abandoned buildings, halfway houses, or the streets (Torrey, 1988). The question of how best to treat them is critical to these individuals, their families, and society (see "Think About It").

Rehabilitation psychologists are concerned with the assessment and treatment of people who are physically or mentally disabled, either temporarily or permanently—for instance, people with mental retardation, epilepsy, chronic pain, severe physical injuries, arthritis, cancer, addictions, and psychiatric problems. They conduct research to find the best ways to teach disabled people to work and live independently, overcome motivational slumps, improve their sex lives, and follow healthy regimens. Rehabilitation psychologists' approach to treatment is eclectic, often including behavior therapy, group counseling, job training, and community intervention. Because more people are surviving traumatic injuries and living long enough to develop chronic medical conditions, rehabilitation is one of the fastest-growing areas of health care (Frank, Gluck, & Buckelew, 1990).

Community programs have proven highly successful in helping many people who are mentally ill and who have disabilities (Dion & Anthony, 1987). In a follow-up study of people with schizophrenia who had been hospitalized 20 years earlier, researchers found that the greatest predictor of successful functioning was community support, including outpatient services of local clinics and close contact with family and friends (Harding et al., 1987). The course of schizophrenia, they found, has less to do with "any inherent natural outcome" and more to do with the individual's family and support systems (Harding, Zubin, & Strauss, 1987).

But what kind of community support? People with schizophrenia need a comprehensive program. Traditional "talk" therapies are not effective for most of them (Kane, 1987). Although drugs are helpful, even essential, they are not sufficient; a drug can reduce symptoms but not teach a person how to get a job. Psychologists have experimented with many different solutions. For a while, "halfway houses," places for people who had been discharged from hospitals but who were unable to go home, were popular. Halfway houses vary in the services they provide for their residents; in their primary emphasis (work, social activities, companionship); in the strictness of their rules (e.g., about visitors or alcohol); and in the length of stay of their residents, from six months to indefinitely (Torrey, 1988).

A successful method is the *clubhouse model,* a program for mentally ill people that provides rehabilitation counseling, job and skills training, and a support network. Members may live at the clubhouse until they are ready to be on their own, and they may visit the clubhouse at any time. New York City's Fountain

At halfway houses such as Fountain House in New York City, people with various mental disorders live halfway between hospitalization and complete independence. They learn to take care of themselves and others, they get job training, and they receive some therapy until they are able to live on their own.

Think About It

Mental Illness and the Limits of Liberty

■ You have seen them on the streets. They aren't violent, but they are distressing. They live in alleys and on sidewalks, carrying all their possessions with them. They may mumble to themselves or shout to the heavens. They are emotionally disturbed or psychotic, and they are homeless. What should be done with them? Should people who have obvious signs of mental illness be forced to receive treatment, or do they have an absolute right to refuse therapy and medication if they have committed no crime? If you think society can and should impose treatment on the mentally ill, what behaviors would warrant such intrusion on personal liberty: if the person is dangerous to others, or "only" dangerous to himself or herself? What if the person is annoying, dirty, and unpleasant in manner, but is breaking no law and is insisting on his or her right to live on the street?

Once, disturbed people were involuntarily committed to mental hospitals. But in the 1960s and 1970s, three trends resulted in the closing of many institutions and the release of most patients:

1. New antipsychotic medications calmed most of the extreme symptoms, so people were released with the expectation that they would be able to return to their families and communities.

2. Civil-rights and patients'-rights movements protested the abuses of institutionalization. Many mentally ill people were being warehoused without treatment; people were being committed without sufficient cause; and there were no review procedures to enable a person to get out of the hospital. Many disturbed individuals were spending far longer in mental hospitals for committing minor crimes than they would have spent in prison. Some people were confined by mistake, because they could not speak English or were mildly retarded. A woman named Gladys Burr was involuntarily confined in 1936, with an incorrect diagnosis of mental retardation and psychosis. No one paid attention to her pleas for freedom for 42 years.

3. The federal government began a program of deinstitutionalizing mentally disturbed people, sending them back to their communities for treatment. The public, wanting more cuts in taxes, supported this effort. In 1963, Congress passed the Community Mental Health Centers Act, designed to set up a nationwide network of mental health centers that would provide inpatient and outpatient services for the mentally ill.

Sadly, efforts to eliminate the warehousing of the mentally ill backfired. Hospital administrators, anxious to avoid legal charges of violating patients' rights, began discharging patients as soon as possible without regard for where they might go. Some state regulations made it very difficult to hospitalize people involuntarily for longer than a few weeks, even those who were dangerous to themselves or others. Although this meant that hospitals couldn't make the mistake they did with Gladys Burr, it created other problems. A woman who had been hospitalized 12 times in ten years for violent attacks was let out (again) after a four-month confinement for stabbing someone. She then killed two people with a semiautomatic rifle. Her parents and psychiatrists had been unable to commit her against her will.

House, one of the oldest such programs in the country, has an excellent track record, helping its members find work, return to school, and establish friendships (Beard, Propst, & Malamud, 1982; Foderaro, 1994). Other community approaches include the establishment of support systems, family therapy, foster care and family home alternatives, and family support groups (Hatfield & Lefley, 1987). The success of these programs often depends on the dedication of the people running them, which is why it can be difficult to transplant a program from one place to another. To solve this problem, some psychologists are developing ways of teaching the staff who work with psychiatric patients how to set rehabilitation goals, how to teach skills, and how to evaluate patients' progress (Anthony, Cohen, & Kennard, 1990).

Rehabilitation psychologists do not work only with the mentally ill. We know a secretary who permanently injured her back and was no longer able to sit long hours at a desk. She entered a program run by rehabilitation psychologists who were helping people find new careers when they could no longer

Further, having pressured the states to close their mental hospitals and release disturbed people, the government then cut financial aid for local and state mental health care and for housing the poor and homeless. The Community Mental Health Centers Act, which had seemed such a promising idea, was never funded. Thousands of patients were simply "dumped" onto the streets. Between 1955 and 1992 the number of people in mental institutions plummeted from 559,000 to 90,000 (Shogren, 1994).

Today the care of chronic mental patients has shifted to profit-making, private nursing homes and board-and-care homes, which are often unregulated and poorly staffed. For the most part, mental patients are no better off in these facilities than they were in state institutions (Shadish, Lurigio, & Lewis, 1989). General hospitals have been burdened with people who have mental problems (Kiesler & Simpkins, 1991). Many patients are given medication and released with no services and families to care for them. Back on the street, patients stop taking their medication because of its negative effects and long-term risks, or because they don't see a need for it. Their psychotic symptoms return, they are rehospitalized, and the revolving-door cycle continues.

For all these reasons, the pendulum is swinging back toward some forms of involuntary commitment, particularly if a person is dangerous to him- or herself or to others. About 35 states in the United States have policies of *involuntary outpatient commitment,* which permit the courts to compel patients to take part in community treatment programs if they meet certain standards of being dangerous or have a "grave disability" (Mulvey, Geller, & Roth, 1987). Some states in the United States—including Arizona, Hawaii, Iowa, Oklahoma, Delaware, and South Carolina—allow courts to commit a person based on other factors, including the patient's psychiatric history and evidence of being "obviously ill" (Shogren, 1994). The idea behind involuntary outpatient commitment is that patients can be monitored regularly so that they don't slip through the cracks; only if they violate the regimen are they committed to an institution. However, there is little agreement on what should be done when a patient contests involuntary commitment.

Opponents of any form of involuntary treatment argue that, in practice, patients often end up being policed, like parolees from prison, without actually getting treatment. They worry about granting the state too much power to invade the privacy of the mentally ill. To make sure a person is taking medication, for example, would you require drug tests? Exactly what aspects of the person's life would you monitor for treatment—the patient's family life? Sexual relationships? Friends? Drinking?

You are the public. What services should governments provide for disturbed people? How can communities protect the rights of the mentally ill while responding to the public's desire to be shielded from disturbed people who can be aggressive but who more often are merely unpleasant or upsetting to see on the street? How can a community balance the values of compassion and individual liberty? What do you think? ▨

work at their old ones. Today this former secretary has a new career; she's a rehabilitation psychologist.

The Self-Help Movement

Long before there were psychotherapists, there were sympathetic advisers. Long before there were psychologists, there was psychological help. Nowadays, there are literally thousands of books and programs designed to help people help themselves. More than 2,000 self-help books are published every *year,* and estimates of people in self-help groups range from 7 to 15 million adults (Christensen & Jacobson, 1994; Jacobs & Goodman, 1989). (See "Psychology and Popular Culture.")

Self-help groups are organized around a common concern. Name it, and there is a group for it: Alcoholics Anonymous, groups for the children or spouses of alcoholics, Overeaters Anonymous, Parents Anonymous (for abusive parents), Depressives Anonymous, Schizophrenics Anonymous. There are countless nonanonymous groups such as those for gay fathers, divorced people, women who have had mastectomies, parents of murdered children, rape victims, widows, stepparents, cancer patients, and relatives of patients.

By uniting people with common problems, support groups offer their members three ingredients of feeling better: understanding, empathy, and advice. Others in the group have been there, know what you are going through, and may have found solutions you never would have imagined. For people who fear that no one else has ever suffered what they have or felt what they feel, such groups can be reassuring in ways that family, friends, and even psychotherapists are not (Dunkel-Schetter, 1984; Wyatt & Mickey, 1987). Although self-help groups can be immensely therapeutic, however, they are not the same as psychotherapy that focuses on specific problems. They do not search for "underlying problems." They are not designed to help people with serious psychological difficulties.

▪ EVALUATING PSYCHOTHERAPY AND ITS ALTERNATIVES

Poor Murray! He's getting a little tired by now, having tried so many therapies. That last weekend with the Nature Walk "Trek to Truth" Encounter was especially fun, but now he's *really* behind. All of these choices are enough to make a person procrastinate about getting help. Which therapy is the "right" one?

Psychology and Popular Culture

The Self-Help Society

▪ If you were to wander through the psychology section of your local bookstore (perhaps called "psychology and self-help" or "personal growth") you might conclude that . . .

- psychology is only about psychotherapy and fixing yourself.

- psychology is for helping people who suffer from syndromes, of which there seems to be one for every life experience, from the "Superwoman Syndrome" for women who have too many commitments to the "Peter Pan Syndrome" for men who can't commit at all.

- psychology is full of contradictory advice. You can find a book called *Goodbye to Guilt* and also *What's So Bad About Guilt?* You can *Learn to Love Again* as long as you don't join the *Women Who Love Too Much*. You can find books praising *The Art of Selfishness* and *The Art of Love*.

- psychology can fix anything that ails you. It will tell you how to stop procrastinating, how to fix your relationships, how to make money, how to use your mind to cure your body, how to shape up your intuitive "right brain," how to recover from heartbreak, and how to think your way to a stress-free life.

America and Canada, cultures with long historical traditions of self-improvement and do-it-yourself attitudes, consume self-help books like peanuts—by

the handful. These books offer solutions for any problem a person could have. Which are helpful, harmful, or just innocuous? How should a person read a self-help book?

Self-help books, if they propose a specific program of treatment for the reader to follow, can be effective, in some cases as effective as treatment administered by a therapist (Christensen & Jacobson, 1994; Scogin et al., 1990). The major drawback to self-help books and programs is that many individuals, on their own, don't follow through, or do better with the assistance of a therapist. For example, one study found that procedures for teaching parents to toilet-train their children were more effective and had fewer "emotional side effects" when a therapist was involved than when the parents got the same advice from a self-help book (Matson & Ollendick, 1977).

Gerald Rosen (1993) cautions consumers that the fact that a book has been written by a psychologist or even endorsed by the American Psychological Association is no guarantee of the book's merit. After serving as chair of the APA's Task Force on Self-Help Therapies, which investigated the proliferation and promises of self-help books and tapes, Rosen (1981) concluded: "Unfortunately, the involvement of psychologists in the development, assessment, and marketing of do-it-yourself treatment programs has often been less than responsible. Psychologists have published untested materials, advanced exag-

The Scientist–Practitioner Gap

Is it possible to measure the effectiveness of therapy, or is this human exchange too varied and complex to be captured by the researcher's empirical arsenal? Many psychotherapists believe that measuring psychotherapy is a futile task. Psychotherapy is an art, not a science, they say, and research is simply irrelevant to what they do. Most believe that clinical experience is more valuable and accurate than the methods of traditional research, and that laboratory and survey studies capture only a small and shadowy image of the real person. They wish that academic psychologists would pay more attention to *clinical* evidence and observations in the research they do (Edelson, 1994). A survey of 400 clinical psychologists found that the great majority paid little attention to empirical research at all, stating that they gained their most useful information from "clinical work with clients." The majority also believed that research on therapy's effectiveness fails to incorporate the complexities of psychotherapy, obscures essential differences among therapies, and ignores the importance of the relationship between therapist and client (Elliott & Morrow-Bradley, 1994).

For their part, scientific psychologists maintain that *assertions* of the effectiveness of therapy must not substitute for *demonstrations* of effectiveness (Dawes, 1994; Orlinsky, 1994). They are concerned that when therapists fail to keep up with empirical findings in the field—not only about beneficial or potentially harmful techniques in therapy, but also about basic psychological research on topics relevant to their practice, such as memory, hypnosis, and

Some psychotherapists think that it is impossible to measure the effectiveness of therapy; researchers disagree. What assumptions does each side bring to this debate? How can it be resolved?

---

gerated claims, and accepted the use of misleading titles that encourage unrealistic expectations regarding outcome." Rosen recognizes that self-help books and programs can be truly effective in helping people, however, and thus offers consumers some research-based criteria for evaluating a self-help book:

- The authors must be qualified, either because they have conducted careful research or are thoroughly versed in the field. Personal testimonials by people who have survived trauma and tragedy can be helpful and inspirational, of course, but an author's own experience is not grounds for generalizing to everyone. This criterion would exclude one of the most popular self-help books in North America, *The Courage to Heal,* whose authors admit that their book is "not based on any psychological theories" and that they are neither researchers nor scholars.

- The book's advice must be based on sound scientific theory, not on the author's hunches, pseudoscientific theories, or armchair observations. This criterion lets out, among other books, all the weight-loss manuals based on crash diets or goofy nutritional advice ("Eat popcorn and watermelon for a week").

- The book must include evidence of the program's effectiveness and not simply the author's assertions of its success. Many self-help books offer

programs that have not been tested for efficacy; they are just the author's idea of what sounds good.

- The book must not promise the impossible. This lets out books that promise to bring the reader thin thighs, perfect sex, total love, or high self-esteem in 30 days, and anything with "instant" in the title, such as *The Doctor's Guide to Instant Stress Relief* (Koocher, 1990). And it lets out books, programs, or tapes that promote techniques whose effectiveness has been disconfirmed by psychological research, such as "subliminal" tapes, discussed in Chapter 5 (Moore, 1995).

- The advice should be organized in a systematic program, step by step, not as a vague pep talk to "take charge of your life" or "find love in your heart"; and the reader must be told how to evaluate his or her progress.

Of course, in one sense the best self-help books aren't written in a "how-to" format at all. They don't offer simplistic advice, but candid and complex analysis of an issue. They don't talk down to the reader, but instead invite the reader to talk back. They offer useful information that readers can apply to their lives. Yet as long as people yearn for a magic bullet to cure their problems—a pill, a book, a subliminal tape—quick-fix solutions will continue to sell. Perhaps it's time for someone to write *How to Break Your Addiction to Self-Help Books.* ▪

normal child development—their clients may pay the price. Over the years, the breach between scientists and therapists has widened on just this issue of the relevance and importance of research findings, leading to what some psychologists call the *scientist–practitioner gap* (Persons, 1991). It is a gap that can have powerful individual and social consequences, as we saw in Chapter 9, in our discussion of the controversy about repressed memories of sexual abuse, and in Chapter 13, in our discussion of the varied outcomes of childhood trauma.

Nevertheless, economic pressures and the rise of managed-care health programs are forcing psychotherapists to justify what they do, and to produce clear guidelines for which therapies are most effective, which therapies are best for which disorders, and which therapies are ineffective or potentially harmful (Barlow, 1994; Chambless, 1995). To develop these guidelines, researchers conduct *controlled clinical trials,* in which patients with a given problem or disorder are randomly assigned to one or more treatment groups or to a control group. To date, hundreds of studies have been designed to test the effectiveness of different kinds of therapy, counseling, and self-help groups (Lambert & Hill, 1994). Although much remains to be learned, here are the overall results, which contain some good news and some bad news for therapists:

1. *Psychotherapy is better than doing nothing at all.* People who receive almost any professional treatment improve more than people who do not get help (Lambert & Bergin, 1994; Lipsey & Wilson, 1993; Maling & Howard, 1994; Robinson, Berman, & Neimeyer, 1990; Smith, Glass, & Miller, 1980; Weisz et al., 1995).

2. *The people who do the best in psychotherapy have less serious problems and are motivated to improve.* Emotional disorders, self-defeating habits, and problems coping with life crises are more successfully treated by psychotherapy than are long-standing personality problems and psychotic disorders (Kopta et al., 1994). The people who make best use of therapy tend to have more adaptive levels of mental and behavioral functioning to begin with, are prepared for treatment, and are ready to change (Orlinsky & Howard, 1994; Strupp, 1982).

3. *For many common mild disorders and everyday problems, paraprofessional therapists may be as effective as professional therapists.* Numerous meta-analyses of studies of therapist effectiveness find no difference in overall success rates between professional and paraprofessional therapists—that is, people without graduate training in any mental-health field (Christensen & Jacobson, 1994; Dawes, 1994; Shapiro & Shapiro, 1982; Smith, Glass, & Miller, 1980; Strupp, 1982; Weisz et al., 1987, 1995). A meta-analysis of 150 psychotherapy studies with children and adolescents, for example, found no overall difference in effectiveness between professional therapists, graduate-student therapists, and paraprofessional therapists (Weisz et al., 1995).

4. *In a significant minority of cases, psychotherapy is harmful because of the therapist's incompetence, bias against the client, or unethical behavior* (Brodsky, 1982; Garnets et al., 1991; Lambert & Bergin, 1994; López, 1989; McHugh, 1993b; Peterson, 1992; Pope & Bouhoutsos, 1986). Individual therapists can do great harm by behaving unethically or prejudicially. Some psychologists are concerned that therapeutic malpractice may be increasing because of the recent surge in the number of poorly trained, unlicensed therapists who use unvalidated pop-psych methods (Dawes, 1994).

Given this pattern of findings, most of the new research on psychotherapy is directed toward three questions: What are the common ingredients in all therapies that make them successful? Which kinds of therapy are best suited for which problems? Under what conditions can therapy be harmful?

THE SEVEN DWARFS AFTER THERAPY

How much can therapy change a person, and how can we evaluate that change?

When Therapy Helps

Psychotherapy is a social exchange. Like all relationships, its success depends on qualities of both participants and on the "fit" between the two people (Frank, 1985; Lambert & Hill, 1994; Orlinsky & Howard, 1994).

The clients who are most likely to do well in therapy have a strong sense of self and also sufficient distress to motivate them to change. For example, one study of depressed elderly people found that cognitive, behavioral, and brief dynamic therapy were equally likely to be successful. What made the difference between good outcomes and poor ones were the clients' *commitment* to the therapy, *willingness* to work on their problems, and their *expectations* of success. In turn, the people who were committed and willing had support from their families and a personal style of dealing actively with problems instead of avoiding them (Gaston et al., 1988, 1989).

As we saw in Chapter 12, some people are temperamentally negative and bitter; others, even in the midst of emotional crises, are temperamentally more agreeable and positive. These personality differences often influence the success of therapy and how much a person can be expected to change (Costa & Widiger, 1994). The strongest predictors of successful therapy, in terms of the client's qualities, are the client's cooperativeness with suggested interventions and positive feelings during the therapy session. Hostile, negative individuals are more resistant to treatment and less likely to benefit from it (Orlinsky & Howard, 1994).

The personality of the therapist is also important to the success of any therapy, particularly the qualities that Carl Rogers praised: empathy, warmth, genuineness, and imagination. The great teachers who establish new schools of therapy often have high success rates because of their own "healing power" and charisma. They make their clients feel respected, accepted, and understood. Therapists whose efforts are most successful tend to be empathic, expressive, and actively invested in the interaction with the client—as opposed to being an "impartial," detached observer in the manner of Freud (Orlinsky & Howard, 1994). These qualities are not limited to professional psychologists, which may be one reason for the finding that paraprofessionals are often as effective as trained psychologists in treating most everyday problems.

Finally, apart from the individual qualities of the client and the therapist, there is the **therapeutic alliance,** the bond they establish between them. (For an example of such an alliance in action, see Figure 16.2.) The therapeutic alliance describes a relationship in which both parties respect and understand one another, feel reaffirmed, and work toward a common goal. "The patient and therapist who are not well attuned to each other—who are not 'on the

■ **therapeutic alliance**
The bond of confidence and mutual understanding established between therapist and client that allows them to work together to solve the client's problems.

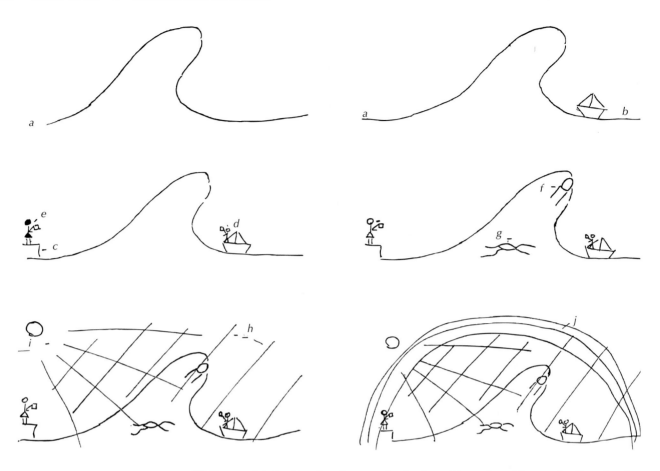

■ **Figure 16.2 Psychotherapy in Action: How One Therapist Reached a Withdrawn Boy**

Robert Hobson (1985) spent many weeks trying to communicate with Stephen, a 15-year-old boy who refused to speak or look at him. One day, in frustration, Hobson took an envelope and drew a squiggly line (a) and invited Stephen to add to the picture. Stephen drew a ship (b) thereby turning Hobson's line into a "terrifying tidal wave." Was the boy, Hobson wondered, afraid of being emotionally "drowned"?

Hobson next drew (c), a landing pier, representing safety. Stephen was not interested in safety. He responded with (d), a person waving goodbye.

Hobson, suspecting that Stephen's problem might stem from emotional separation from his mother, drew (e), a woman waving goodbye. Stephen drew (f), and spoke for the first time: "A flying fish." Hobson drew (g) and said "An octopus." Stephen, shoulders drooping in sadness, marked up the entire sketch with lines (h), adding, "It's raining."

Hobson, hoping to convey optimism, drew the sun (i), its rays conflicting with the rain. Stephen paused, and looked at Hobson intently for the first time. He drew large arcs embracing the whole illustration (j). "A rainbow," said Stephen. He smiled.

same wavelength' but, instead, 'talk at' or 'talk past' each other," observes David Orlinsky (1994), "are likely to produce rather unfavorable outcomes."

Establishing a successful therapeutic alliance does not mean that the therapist and client must be the same race, gender, sexual orientation, or religion (Howard, 1991). It does mean that both parties must try to identify and avoid potential misunderstandings that might result from ignorance, dissimilar qualities, or prejudice on either side (Comas-Díaz & Greene, 1994; Franklin, 1993; McGoldrick, Pearce, & Giordano, 1982). For example, some white therapists misread their black clients' body language. They regard lack of eye contact and frequent glancing around as the client's attempt to "size up what can be ripped off," instead of as signs of discomfort and an effort to get oriented (Brodsky, 1982). For their part, African-American clients often misunderstand or distrust the white therapist's demand for self-disclosure. A lifetime of experience with

Some psychologists are developing forms of therapy that fit the client's cultural back-ground. "Cuento" (folktale) therapy, for example, was developed for Puerto Rican chil-dren who have behavioral problems. It makes use of traditional Puerto Rican stories, such as the tales of Juan Bobo (left), to teach children to control aggression, understand right from wrong, and delay gratification. The photo on the right shows a therapy ses-sion conducted by Giuseppe Costantino and Migdalia Coubertier, in which the children and their mothers watch a videotape of the folktale, discuss it together, and later role-play its major themes. The method has been more successful than traditional therapies in reducing children's anxieties and improving their attention spans and imaginations (Costantino, Malgady, & Rogler, 1986).

the white therapist's demand for self-disclosure. A lifetime of experience with racism often makes them reluctant to reveal feelings that they believe a white person wouldn't understand or accept. As for black therapists, they frequently have to deal with clients who are bigoted or uncomfortable with them; and with clients and co-workers who fail to understand or accept them (Boyd-Franklin, 1989; Markowitz, 1993; Ridley, 1984).

In establishing a bond with clients, therapists must distinguish normal cul-tural patterns from individual psychological problems (Sue, 1991). Monica McGoldrick and John Pearce (1982), Irish-American clinicians who edited a book on therapy with ethnic Americans of all kinds, describe some problems that are typical of Irish-American families. These problems arose from Irish history and religious beliefs, and are deeply ingrained. "In general, the thera-pist cannot expect the family to turn into a physically affectionate, emotion-ally intimate group, or to enjoy being in therapy very much," they observe. "The notion of Original Sin—that you are guilty before you are born—leaves them with a heavy sense of burden. Someone not sensitized to these issues may see this as pathological. It is not. But it is also not likely to change and the therapist should help the family tolerate this inner guilt rather than try to get rid of it."

More and more psychotherapists are becoming "sensitized to the issues" caused by cultural differences. For example, Latino and Asian clients are likely to react to a formal interview with a therapist with relative passivity, deference, and inhibited silence, leading some therapists to diagnose a shyness "problem" that is only a cultural norm. Latinos may respond to catastrophic stress with an *ataque nervioso,* a nervous attack of screaming, swooning, and agitation. It is a culturally determined response, but an uninformed clinician might label it as a sign of pathology (Malgady, Rogler, & Costantino, 1987).

Being aware of cultural differences, however, doesn't mean that the therapist should stereotype all clients from a particular culture or tailor the therapy to fit a stereotype of cultural rules (Sue, 1991). Some Asians, after all, *do* have prob-

Table 16.1	*Factors Common Across Therapies That Are Associated with Positive Outcomes*

Support factors	Learning factors	Action factors
Trust	Advice	Behavioral change
Identification with the therapist	Experiencing emotion in a safe context	Encouragement of facing fears
Reduced sense of isolation	Assimilating problems	Cognitive mastery
Positive relationship	Feedback	Success experiences
Reassurance	Changing expectations	Taking risks
Release of tension	Cognitive learning	Modeling
Therapist expertise	Corrective emotional experience	Practice
Therapeutic alliance	Exploring internal frames of reference	Reality testing
Therapist warmth, respect, empathy, genuineness, acceptance	Insight	Working through problems in relationships

Source: Lambert & Bergin, 1994.

lems with excessive shyness, some Latinos *do* have emotional disorders, and some Irish *don't* feel the burden of guilt! It does mean that therapists must do what is necessary to ensure that the client will find the therapist to be trustworthy and effective, and clients must be aware of their prejudices too (Sue & Zane, 1987).

Table 16.1 summarizes the common factors in psychotherapy that are associated with positive results (Lambert & Bergin, 1994): *support factors,* which allow the client to feel secure and safe in therapy; *learning factors,* which allow the client to see and experience his or her problems in a new light and think about how to solve them; and *action factors,* which allow the client to reduce fears, take risks, and make necessary changes.

Which Therapy for Which Problem?

Murray has found a therapist who is sympathetic, he's motivated to change, and he thinks that he and the therapist will form a nice therapeutic alliance. But which therapeutic approach, if any, will be best for him? Research finds that the success of therapy depends in part on the nature of the problem being treated.

Depth Therapies Versus Solution-Oriented Therapies.   One major difference among therapies is that some, such as psychoanalysis and humanism, encourage depth of understanding and focus on the emotional process of the therapy itself, whereas others, such as behaviorism, focus on action for change. Depth therapies are as helpful as any other kind in helping people cope with general problems. However, they have been shown to be significantly less effective for many specific disorders (Prioleau, Murdock, & Brody, 1983). In particular, they are not highly successful in treating major depression (McGrath et al., 1990); anxiety, fears, panic, and agoraphobia (Chambless, 1985); sex problems and sex offenders (Abel et al., 1988); personality disorders (Strupp, 1982); or drug abuse (Vaillant, 1983). These therapies seem to be best suited to people who are introspective about their motives and feelings, who want to explore their pasts and examine their current lives.

In contrast, hundreds of controlled studies have demonstrated the effectiveness of behavior therapies and cognitive-behavioral therapies, in contrast to doing nothing at all or to being in exclusively psychodynamic therapy (Chambless, 1995; Lambert & Bergin, 1994; Lazarus, 1990; Rachman & Wilson, 1980; Weisz et al., 1995). Exposure therapy has proved particularly effective with agoraphobia and other anxiety disorders; a meta-analysis of 88 studies found that exposure techniques for reducing fear were more effective than any other treatment (Kaplan, Randolph, & Lemli, 1991). And researchers who conducted a meta-analysis of more than 100 outcome studies of children and adolescents reported that "Behavioral treatments proved more effective than non-behavioral treatments regardless of client age, therapist experience, or treated problem" (Weisz et al., 1987). Cognitive therapy's greatest success has been in the treatment of mood disorders, particularly panic attacks, anxiety, and moderate depression (Black et al., 1993). Reviews and meta-analyses find that cognitive therapy is often more effective than antidepressant drugs in preventing relapses of depression and panic (Barlow, 1994; Chambless, 1995; McNally, 1994; Robinson, Berman, & Neimeyer, 1990; Whisman, 1993). Finally, cognitive-behavioral therapies have also been effective in helping people live with pain (J. Skinner et al., 1990) and chronic fatigue syndrome (Butler et al., 1991), and in treating eating disorders (Wilson & Fairburn, 1993).

Yet in spite of their successes, behavior therapy and cognitive therapies too have their failures, especially with personality disorders and psychoses (Brody, 1990; Foa & Emmelkamp, 1983). They are not particularly helpful for people in severe depression or recovering from trauma. They are not highly effective with people who do not really want to change and who are not motivated to carry out a behavioral or cognitive program (Woolfolk & Richardson, 1984).

Most psychodynamic therapists believe that the longer therapy goes on, the more successful it will be. Research does not support this claim: About half of all people in therapy improve within eight to 11 sessions (according to their self-reports and on objective measures of improvement) and 76 percent improve within six months to a year; after that, further change is minimal (Howard et al., 1986; Kopta et al., 1994). (See Figure 16.3.) Of course, people who have severe mental disorders often require and benefit from continued therapeutic care. But for people who have one or another of the common emotional problems of life, short-term treatment is usually all that is necessary (Strupp & Binder, 1984).

"Pure" Versus Combined Approaches. Some problems, and some clients, are immune to any single kind of therapy but may respond to combined methods, which, as we have noted, are what most therapists use anyway. For example, people who have continuing, difficult problems—such as recovering from a traumatic experience, living with pain, or coping with a disturbed family member—often are best helped by a combination approach (Lazarus, 1989). One eclectic therapist has combined cognitive, behavioral, and psychoanalytic methods in an effective treatment for survivors of coercive cults (Solomon, 1991). Many children with obsessive-compulsive disorder been have helped

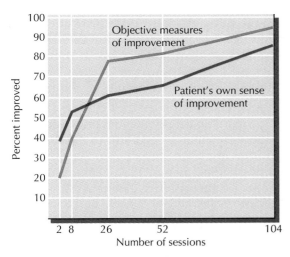

■ Figure 16.3 Is More Therapy Better?

In this study, about half of all patients improved in only eight sessions and about three-fourths improved by the twenty-sixth session; after that, only a few percent were helped by further treatment (Howard et al., 1986). More recent research confirms that the benefits of therapy occur within eight to eleven sessions for half of all clients, especially those suffering from emotional distress rather than personality disorders. Three-fourths benefit from treatment lasting up to a year (Kopta et al., 1994).

with a combination of antidepressant medication and behavior therapy (Leonard et al., 1993). The most promising treatment for sex offenders combines cognitive therapy, aversive conditioning, sex education, group therapy, reconditioning of sexual fantasies, and social skills training (Abel et al., 1988; Kaplan, Morales, & Becker, 1993).

Some people who have mood disorders respond better to a combination of antidepressants and cognitive-behavioral therapy than to either method alone (Bowers, 1990; Carroll et al., 1994b; Conte et al., 1986). For these reasons, some psychiatrists and psychologists are collaborating in what they call the *split treatment* model: The psychiatrist prescribes medication while the psychologist focuses on the psychological aspects of treatment (Wiggins, 1991).

When Therapy Harms

- After "Susan B." committed suicide, her distraught husband discovered a letter she had left for her psychotherapist. In it, she implored the therapist not to feel guilty for "using me for your own pleasure"—for the sexual intercourse he required as part of her therapy for the five months she had been seeing him. She chided him for his waning sexual interest in her that caused her final depressive episode, but begged him not to blame himself for her death.

- A man entered therapy for help in dealing with his family relationships, steadily increasing his involvement until he was going four times a week. He spent much time preparing for his sessions and reflecting on them afterwards, growing more and more intolerant of his wife and children's efforts to get his attention. One day he said, "I wish my wife and kids would just go away. They're interfering with my analysis."

As these cases illustrate, some people in therapy are not helped by it; instead, they are seriously harmed or unduly influenced by the treatment or by the therapist. Their emotional state may deteriorate and their symptoms may worsen (Lambert & Bergin, 1994). Some clients become excessively dependent, relying on the therapist for all decisions. Some therapists actively foster this dependency for financial or psychological motives (Johnson, 1988). Therapists can also harm or unduly influence a client because of the following factors:

- *Coercion* by the therapist to accept the therapist's advice, sexual intimacies, or other unethical behavior (Gabbard, 1989; Peterson, 1992; Pope & Bouhoutsos, 1986). Some therapists abuse their clients' trust, convincing them that the therapy requires them to behave in ways they find reprehensible. Coercion can be subtle as well as overt. Some therapy groups acquire cult-like attributes, persuading their members that their mental health depends on staying in the group (Mithers, 1994). One study found that such "psychotherapy cults" are created by the therapist's use of techniques that foster the client's dependency and isolation, prevent the client from terminating therapy, and—as you might expect by now—reduce the client's ability to think critically (Temerlin & Temerlin, 1986).

- *Bias* on the part of a therapist who doesn't understand the client because of the client's gender, race, religion, sexual orientation, or ethnic group. The therapist may try to induce the client to conform to the therapist's standards and values, even if they are not appropriate to the client or in the client's best interest (Brodsky, 1982; López, 1989). For example, for many years gay men and lesbians who entered therapy were told that homosexuality is a mental illness that should be "cured," and some of the treatments were quite savage (Garnets et al., 1991).

- *Therapist-induced disorders.* In a healthy therapeutic alliance, therapists and clients seek a common explanation for the client's problems. Of course the therapist will influence this explanation, according to his or her training and philosophy. This is why Freudian patients have dreams of phallic symbols, and patients in Jungian therapy have dreams of archetypes! It is also why people in primal scream therapy "remember" being born, people in fetal therapy "remember" their lives in the womb, and people in past-lives therapy "remember" being Julius Caesar (or whomever) (Spanos et al., 1991).

However, some therapists so zealously believe in the prevalence of certain problems that, sometimes consciously but more often unconsciously, they induce the client to produce the symptoms they are looking for (Ganaway, 1991; Holmes, 1994; McHugh, 1993b). Indeed, recent fascinating evidence suggests that Freud himself, in his conviction of the truth of psychoanalytic theory, induced his patients to report memories and symptoms that confirmed his beliefs, without subjecting his patients' reports to independent verification (Powell & Boer, 1994). In Chapter 15 we discussed how such unintended therapist influence might be one reason for the growing number of patients diagnosed with multiple personality disorder, but it is also the mechanism by which people create *pseudomemories*—constructed fantasies shaped by the suggestions and expectations of the therapist (Spanos, 1994; Spanos et al., 1991). The risk of therapist influence is increased when a therapist uses hypnosis, sodium amytal (a barbiturate misleadingly called "truth serum"), guided imagery, story fabrication, and other techniques that enhance the client's suggestibility.

For all of these reasons, it is important for people to become educated consumers of psychotherapeutic services (see "Taking Psychology with You").

Quick QUIZ

Refresh your understanding of psychotherapy.

1. The most important predictor of successful therapy is (a) how long it lasts, (b) the insight it provides the client, (c) the bond between therapist and client, (d) whether the therapist and client are matched according to gender, race, and culture.
2. The most important attribute of a good therapist is (a) years of training, (b) warmth and empathy, (c) objective detachment, (d) intellectual ability.
3. What are three possible sources of harm in psychotherapy?

4. Ferdie, who spends all his free time playing softball, joins a self-help group called "Sportaholics Anonymous" (SA). The group tells him he is suffering from sport addiction and that the only cure is SA. After a few months, Ferdie announces that the group doesn't seem to be helping him and he's going to quit. The other members reply with personal testimonials of how SA has helped them. They tell Ferdie that he is "in denial," and that his very doubts about the group are a sign that it's working. What are some problems with their argument?

Answers:

1. c 2. b 3. coercion, bias, and therapist-induced disorders 4. The group members have violated the principle of *falsifiability* (see Chapter 2): that is, they will accept no evidence that disproves their claims. If a person is helped by the group, they say it works; if a person is *not* helped by the group, they still say it works but the person doesn't know it yet or is "denying" its benefits. They are also arguing by anecdote: Ferdie is not hearing testimonials from people who have dropped out of the group and were not helped by it. Arguing by anecdote is not scientific reasoning, nor is it a way to determine a group's or therapy's effectiveness.

The language and goals of psychotherapy have made their way into many programs designed to expand human potential. This woman, for example, is hoping to learn to relax and trust others by being thrown into the air and caught. The exercise is probably fun, but is it likely to have lasting effects?

▪ THE VALUE AND VALUES OF PSYCHOTHERAPY

✴ *What are the benefits and disadvantages of psychotherapy? Can a culture be too therapy-oriented?*

On radio, in the newspapers, on television, in countless popular books, media psychologists offer free thera ... well, free advice. There is nothing unethical about advice. Neighbors, relatives, and friends hand it out all the time. Indeed, some observers have argued that psychotherapy is, in reality, paid friendship. As North Americans become more and more geographically mobile, as families grow smaller, as city life becomes more impersonal, the professional support of psychotherapy has replaced the informal support of friends and relations.

Is there anything wrong with that? In *The Shrinking of America,* Bernie Zilbergeld (1983), himself a psychotherapist, argued that psychotherapy, while often very helpful, promotes three myths that also increase dissatisfaction: that people should always be happy, and if they aren't they need fixing; that almost any change is possible; and that change is relatively easy. As we have seen in previous chapters, however, some aspects of personality are resistant to change, and most changes do not happen overnight.

In addition, some critics are concerned about modern psychotherapy's undue emphasis on fixing the self. In their book *We've Had a Hundred Years of Psychotherapy—And the World's Getting Worse,* family therapists James Hillman and Michael Ventura (1992) argue that therapy's emphasis on the self is a holdover from nineteenth-century individualism, and that it is inappropriate in modern societies that also demand active social involvement in one's community and world.

In contrast, as you may remember from Chapter 14, Eastern cultures have a somewhat less optimistic view of change; they are more tolerant of events they regard as being outside of human control. In the Japanese practice of Morita therapy, clients are taught to live with their most troubling emotions, instead of trying to eradicate these psychological weeds from the lawn of life. Some Western psychotherapists have been borrowing ideas from the Japanese, attempting to teach greater self-acceptance instead of constant self-improvement (Reynolds, 1987; Welwood, 1983).

Psychotherapy warrants neither extravagant claims nor total rejection. There are many things it cannot do, and many things it can do. It cannot transform you into someone you're not. It cannot cure you overnight. It cannot provide a life without problems. But it can help you make decisions. It can get you through bad times when no one seems to care or understand. It can improve morale and restore the energy to cope. Psychotherapy is not intended to substitute for experience—for work that is satisfying, relationships that are sustaining, activities that are enjoyable. As Socrates knew, the unexamined life is not worth living. But as an anonymous philosopher added, the unlived life is not worth examining.

Taking Psychology with You

Becoming a Smart Therapy Consumer

In North America today a vast and bewildering array of therapies fills the marketplace. The word *therapy* is unregulated; anyone can set up any kind of program and call it "therapy." To protect themselves as well as to get the best possible help, consumers need to be informed and know how to choose wisely. Some people spend more time looking for a good dentist than a good therapist. They fail to remember that their consumer rights apply to buying mental health services as well as to buying any other professional service. You would not be likely to keep going to a dentist, year after year, if your toothache got worse and the dentist merely kept promising to make it go away. Yet some people stay in therapy, year after year, with no resolution of their problems. They become "therapy junkies."

In order for consumers to make the best use of therapy, research suggests the following guidelines:

- *Knowing when to start.* In general, if you have a persistent problem that you do not know how to solve, one that causes you considerable unhappiness and that has lasted six months or more, it may be time to look for help. Everyone gets caught in an emotional maze from time to time. It may take the clear-eyed observations of a perceptive bystander to see a way out.

- *Setting goals.* Try to identify exactly what you expect from therapy, and discuss your goals with the therapist. Do you want to solve a problem in your relationships or in your emotional life? Are your goals realistic? Some therapies, as we discussed in this chapter, are designed not for solving problems but for exploring ideas. People often seek help in making important decisions. Others want to explore a philosophy of life to guide their future actions. Still others want to understand themselves better. If you know what you want from therapy, you are less likely to feel disappointed later. You will also be better able to select a therapist who can meet your needs.

- *Choosing a therapist.* As we saw in Chapter 1, a person must have a professional degree and a period of supervised training to become a licensed psychologist, psychiatrist, counselor, or social worker. Unfortunately, the fact that someone has a license does not guarantee that he or she is competent, reputable, or ethical. Your school counseling center is a good place to start if you are looking for a reputable therapist. Your local mental health association or psychological association chapter (check your phone book) can also provide information on nearby therapists.

- A therapist or counselor should be someone you trust and like; remember that empathy between client and counselor, and the warmth of the counselor, are two of the most important factors in predicting success of treatment. Never trust anyone who suggests that a sexual relationship will help your problem. This is unethical conduct and illegal in many states. The basic rule is this: If the therapist does not treat you with the same attention and respect that you give him or her, find someone else.

- *The question of fees.* Freud thought that patients should pay for treatment, enough to make it hurt. Only then, he said, would patients be motivated to improve. This theory, to put it kindly, serves therapists more than it does clients. *There is no evidence that the amount of payment affects the success of the therapy* (Orlinsky, 1994). In one study, in fact, college students in paid versus free therapy did not differ in self-reports of improvement, but the students who paid no fee had *lower* levels of distress when the therapy ended (Yoken & Berman, 1984). As a consumer, you can often negotiate a fee depending on what you can afford. If you have medical insurance that covers psychotherapy, find out whether your policy covers the kind of therapist you are seeking. Most insurance companies pay only for treatments by psychiatrists or licensed psychologists.

- *Knowing when to stop.* If you are in time-limited treatment, such as 12 sessions of brief therapy or a 7-session plane-phobia program, you ought to try to stick with it to the end. In an unlimited therapy program, however, you have the right to determine when enough is enough. Breaking with a therapist or self-help group can be painful and difficult, like leaving home for the first time, but it can also be a sign that the treatment has been successful (Johnson, 1988). You may need to consider ending therapy, changing therapists, or leaving a group if therapy dominates your life and nothing else seems important; the therapist keeps finding new reasons for you to stay, although the original problems were solved long ago; you have become so dependent on the therapist that you won't make a move without consulting him or her; or your therapist has been unable to help you cope with the problem that brought you there.

As we saw in this chapter, not all therapies are appropriate for all problems. If you are not improving, the reason could be as much in the treatment as in you. If you have made a real effort to work with a therapist and there has been no result after ample time and effort, it is time to think about alternatives.

Summary

1. Diagnoses and treatments of psychological problems have alternated throughout history from the medical (organic) model to the psychological (mental) model. Recent research has sparked renewed interest in medical treatments of mental disorder, but there is still much controversy.

2. The drugs most in use for mental disorders are *antipsychotic drugs,* used in treating schizophrenia and other psychotic disorders; *antidepressants,* used in treating depression and anxiety disorders; *minor tranquilizers,* often prescribed for emotional problems; and *lithium,* a salt used to treat bipolar disorder. Antipsychotics reduce symptoms and allow many people with schizophrenia to be released from hospitals, but if taken for many years they can have dangerous effects. Antidepressants are more effective for mood disorders than minor tranquilizers, which have little or no effect and can become addictive.

3. Some issues in drug treatment include the problem of the placebo effect, including the need to use *active* placebos in double-blind studies, and the problem of testing new drugs for only a few weeks when patients may take them for years; finding the *therapeutic window* (correct dose) for each individual; the high drop-out and relapse rates among people who take medications without also learning how to cope with problems; and the effects of gender, age, and race on the effectiveness of the dosage. Also, nondrug therapies can work as well as drugs for many mood and behavioral problems. Medication can be helpful, even life-saving, but it should not be prescribed mindlessly and routinely.

4. When drugs or psychotherapy fail to help seriously disturbed people, some psychiatrists intervene directly in the brain. *Psychosurgery,* one form of which was the *lobotomy,* destroys an area of the brain thought to be responsible for the problem; it is rarely done today. *Electroconvulsive therapy* (ECT), in which a brief current is sent through the brain, has been used successfully to treat suicidal depressives. However, its effects do not last and it has unpredictable effects on memory.

5. Errors of diagnosis and treatment occur on both sides of the mind-body debate. Some people with organic disorders have been mistakenly treated with psychotherapy; some people with psychological problems have been mistakenly treated with drugs.

6. There are hundreds of psychotherapies, but they basically fall into four schools: (a) *Psychodynamic ("depth") therapies* include Freudian psychoanalysis and its modern variations, which explore unconscious dynamics. *Brief psychodynamic therapy* is a time-limited version that focuses on one major dynamic issue. (b) *Behavioral therapies* are based on learning principles, and include such methods as behavioral contracts, systematic desensitization, aversive conditioning, flooding or exposure, and skills training. *Cognitive therapies* aim to change the irrational thoughts involved in negative emotions and self-defeating actions. In practice, many therapists combine cognitive and behavioral techniques. (c) *Humanistic therapies,* such as Carl Rogers' *client-centered* therapy, aim to help people feel better about themselves and reach "self-actualization" by focusing on here-and-now issues. *Existential* therapy helps people cope with philosophic dilemmas, such as the meaning of life and the fear of death. (d) *Family therapies* share the view that individual problems do not exist by themselves but are part of the whole family network. Family therapists may use a *genogram* to document generational patterns in a family or *solution-focused* techniques to solve a client's problems. Therapists from any of these schools sometimes work with clients in *group therapy.* In practice most therapists are *eclectic,* using many methods and ideas, and good therapies share certain features, such as helping clients form better "life narratives."

7. People who have severe mental disorders, such as schizophrenia, or who have physical disabilities resulting from disease or injury, may benefit from alternatives to individual psychotherapy. *Rehabilitation psychologists* offer job

training, support, and community treatment programs such as the *clubhouse model*. The growing *self-help movement* provides support groups organized around a specific problem.

8. The *scientist–practitioner gap* refers to the different assumptions held by researchers and many clinicians on the value of research in assessing psychotherapy. Efforts to evaluate the effectiveness of psychotherapy show that overall, psychotherapy is better than no treatment at all; it is most effective with people who have the least serious disorders and who are motivated to improve; for many everyday problems, paraprofessionals are as effective as professionals; and sometimes therapy can be harmful.

9. Successful therapy requires a good relationship between therapist and client. Good clients are motivated to solve their problems and are willing to take responsibility for them. Good therapists are empathic, inspirational, and teach constructive lessons. A *therapeutic alliance* between client and therapist depends on their ability to understand each other and work together. They do not need to be perfectly matched in terms of gender, culture, or ethnicity, but it is important for both sides to avoid bias and stereotyping.

10. Some therapies are better than others for specific problems. Cognitive-behavioral therapies have a higher success rate than psychodynamic or humanist therapies; for most problems, short-term treatment is as effective as long, indefinite therapy; and therapies that combine techniques are able to solve some problems that one technique alone cannot.

11. In some cases, therapy is harmful. The therapist may foster the client's dependency; be coercive, biased, or unethical; or create therapist-induced disorders—delusions, other symptoms of mental disorder, and pseudomemories—through the process of suggestion.

12. Some psychologists believe that North Americans have come to expect too much from therapy and incorrectly assume that change is always easy and desirable. Therapy can help people in many ways, but it cannot transform them into something they are not.

Key Terms

antipsychotic drugs (major tranquilizers) *594*
antidepressant drugs *594*
"minor" tranquilizers *595*
lithium carbonate *595*
active placebo *596*
therapeutic window *596*
psychosurgery *598*
lobotomy *598*
electroconvulsive therapy (ECT) *598*
psychoanalysis *600*
psychodynamic ("depth") therapies *600*
free association *601*
transference *601*
brief psychodynamic therapy *601*
behavior therapies *601*
behavioral records and contracts *601*
systematic desensitization *602*
aversive conditioning *602*

flooding (exposure) *602*
skills training *602*
cognitive therapies *602*
rational-emotional behavior therapy *603*
humanistic therapies *603*
client-centered therapy *603*
unconditional positive regard *603*
existential therapy *604*
family therapy *605*
family systems approach *605*
genogram *605*
solution-focused (strategic) family therapy *605*
group therapy *606*
eclectic approaches *607*
narrative method *608*
rehabilitation psychology *609*
support, self-help groups *611*
scientist–practitioner gap *614*
therapeutic alliance *615*
pseudomemories *621*

17
Principles of Social Life

On May 14, 1884, thousands of people panicked and rioted on Wall Street when the stock market crashed. Social psychologists have shown that individuals will often behave quite differently when in a mob or a crowd than they ever would when alone.

> *. . . to hurt innocent people whom I knew many years ago in order to save myself is, to me, inhuman and indecent and dishonorable. I cannot and will not cut my conscience to fit this year's fashions.*
>
> ■ LILLIAN HELLMAN ■

In 1942, Wladyslaw Misiuna, a young man from Radom, Poland, was ordered by the Germans to supervise inmates at a concentration camp. Misiuna would stuff his pockets with bread, milk, and potatoes and smuggle the food to the 30 women in his charge. One day, one of his workers, Devora Salzberg, came to see him about an infection that had covered her arms with open lesions. Misiuna knew that if the Germans discovered her illness, they would kill her; but of course there was no way he could get a doctor to the camp to treat her. So Misiuna did the only thing he could think to do: He infected himself with her blood, contracted the lesions himself, and went to a doctor. Then he shared with Devora the medication he was given. Both were cured, and both survived the war (Fogelman, 1994).

Why do some people behave so generously? Before the outbreak of the Gulf War in 1991, many anonymous Kuwaitis risked their lives to help Westerners get out of the country, moving them from house to house, disguised in Arab dress (Fogelman, 1994). Thanks to the much-publicized story of Oskar Schindler, the Polish entrepreneur who used his economic resources to save more than 1,100 Jews who worked for him (Keneally, 1982/1993), people are becoming aware of those remarkable individuals who, in times of adversity, put themselves in danger in order to rescue others. In these cases, rescuers rise above the temptation to walk away and save their own skins, choosing instead to rescue fellow human beings in trouble.

Rescuers always raise our hopes for humanity, but the fact is that they are a minority. The historical record shows, sadly, that most people will go along with the crowd, even when the crowd is performing immoral or brutal acts. The Nazis, for good reason, have come to symbolize the evil potential in "human nature"; the Holocaust was unique because the Nazis so systematically used technology and ideology to exterminate 6 million Jews as well as millions of Catholics, blacks, Gypsies, homosexuals, disabled people, and anyone else not of the "pure" Aryan "race." But the Nazis are not an aberration that can safely be buried in the past; no nation can claim to have bloodless hands. The practices of torture, genocide, and massacre are all too common in human history: the slaughter of Native Americans in the United States, the slaughter of Armenians by the Turks, the slaughter of millions of Cambodians by their own Khmer Rouge, the slaughter of Mexicans by the invading Spaniards, Idi Amin's reign of terror against his own people in Uganda, the slaughter of Koreans and Chinese by the Japanese, the slaughter of Kurds by the Iraqis, the slaughter of members of the Baha'i religion by the Iranians, the mass killings ("disappearances") in Argentina and Chile by despotic political regimes, . . . Far from being rare, the systematic destruction of people defined as "the enemy" was and is a widespread practice (Staub, 1989). In 1994, a bloodbath in Rwanda left hundreds of thousands of Tutsis murdered—shot or hacked to death by machetes—by members of the rival Hutu tribe; and in the former Yugoslavia,

During the Nazi occupation of France, people living in the impoverished Protestant village of Le Chambon, led by their pastor André Trocmé and his wife Magda, rescued some 5,000 Jewish children from being sent to their deaths.

Bosnian Serbs have exterminated entire villages of Bosnian Muslims in the name of "ethnic cleansing."

Why do so many human beings commit such atrocities, and why do some individuals behave bravely, even at the risk of their lives? The fields of *social psychology* and *cultural psychology* explore these and many other questions by examining the individual in a social and cultural context. In the next chapter, we will consider findings from cultural psychology that illuminate some of the reasons for group conflict, prejudice, and war. In this chapter, we will examine some of the major areas of research in social psychology: roles, attitudes, and the behavior of groups, including the conditions under which people conform or dissent. The "psychology" part of social psychology concerns the person's perceptions, attitudes, emotions, and behavior. The "social" part concerns the person's group, situation, and relationships. In previous chapters, we have already reported on many topics and studies in social psychology, including love and attachment; how "set and setting" affect the use of drugs; how roles and scripts affect sexual behavior; how emotions communicate; why friends are necessary for health; and social processes in psychotherapy. Social psychology covers a lot of territory, from first impressions on meeting a stranger to international diplomacy.

▪ ROLES AND RULES

"We are all fragile creatures entwined in a cobweb of social constraints," said social psychologist Stanley Milgram. This cobweb snares people in two ways. First, people are expected to follow social **norms,** or rules. Norms are the conventions of everyday life that make our interactions with other people predictable and orderly. Some are matters of law, such as, "A person may not beat up another person, except in self-defense." Some come from a group's cultural values and standards, such as, "A man may beat up another man who insults his masculinity." Some rules are tiny, invisible regulations that people learn to follow unconsciously, such as, "You may not sing at the top of your lungs on a public bus."

Second, people fill a variety of social **roles.** A role is a position in society that is regulated by norms about how a person in that position should behave. In modern life, most people play many roles. Gender roles define the "proper" behavior for a man and a woman. Occupational roles determine "correct" behavior for a manager and an employee, a professor and a student. Family roles set tasks for parent and child, husband and wife, brother and sister. Certain aspects of every role must be carried out. As a student, for instance, you know just what you have to do to pass your psychology course.

How might you identify a role requirement? One way is simply by violating it. For instance, in your family, whose job is it to buy gifts for parents, send greeting cards to friends, organize parties and prepare the food, remember an aunt's birthday, and call friends to see how they're doing? Chances are you are thinking of a woman. These activities are considered part of the woman's role in most cultures. Therefore, it will be the woman in the family, not the man, who is blamed if these responsibilities are not carried out (di Leonardo, 1987; Lott & Maluso, 1993). Similarly, what is likely to happen to a man who reveals his fears and worries when his culture's male gender role requires the suppression of signs of "weakness" or "vulnerability"? In North America, men who deviate from the masculine role by disclosing their emotions and private fears are frequently regarded by both sexes as being "too feminine" and "poorly adjusted" (Peplau & Gordon, 1985; Taffel, 1990).

Of course, people bring their own personalities and interests to the roles they play. Although two actresses who play the role of Cleopatra must follow the same

▪ **norms**
Social conventions that regulate human life, including explicit laws and implicit cultural standards.

▪ **role**
A given social position that is governed by a set of norms for proper behavior.

Many roles in modern life require us to give up individuality, as conveyed by this dazzling image of white-suited referees at the Seoul Olympics. If each referee decided to behave out of role, the games could not continue. When is it justified to yield our personal styles and preferences for the role, and when is it not?

script, you can bet that Glenn Close and Madonna will have different interpretations. Yet, as we will see next, the requirements of a role can cause a person to behave in ways that violate his or her deeply held feelings, personal wishes, and fundamental sense of self. We now turn to three classic and controversial studies that illuminate the power of social roles to influence people's behavior.

The Prison Study

One day, as you are walking home from school, a police car pulls up. Two uniformed officers get out, arrest you, and take you to a prison cell. There you are stripped of your clothes, sprayed with a delousing fluid, assigned a prison uniform, photographed with your prison number, and put behind bars. You feel a little queasy but you are not panicked, because you have agreed to play the part of prisoner in an experiment for two weeks, and your "arrest" is part of the script. Your prison cell, while apparently authentic, is located in the basement of a university building.

So began an effort to study what happens when ordinary college students take on the roles of prisoners and guards (Haney, Banks, & Zimbardo, 1973). The students who volunteered for this experiment were paid a nice daily sum of money. They were randomly assigned to be prisoners or guards, but other than that, they were given no instructions about how to behave. Within a very short time, the prisoners became distressed, helpless, and panicky. They developed emotional symptoms and psychosomatic ailments. Some became depressed, tearful, and apathetic. Others became rebellious and angry. After a few days, half of the prisoners begged to be let out. Most were more than willing to forfeit their pay for an early release.

Within an equally short time, the guards adjusted to their new power. Some tried to be nice, helping the prisoners and doing little favors for them. Some were "tough but fair," holding strictly to "the rules." But about a third of them became tyrannical. Although they had complete freedom to use any method to

Prisoners and guards quickly learn their respective roles, as they have done at this correctional facility.

maintain order, they almost always chose to be abusive, even when the prisoners were not resisting in any way. One guard, unaware that he was being observed by the experimenters, paced the yard while the prisoners were sleeping, pounding his nightstick into his hand. Another put a prisoner in solitary confinement (a small closet) and tried to keep him there all night. He concealed this information from the experimenters, who, he thought, were "too soft" on the prisoners. Many guards were willing to work overtime without additional pay.

The researchers ended this experiment after only six days. They had not expected such a speedy and terrifying transformation of normal students. The prisoners were relieved by this decision, but most of the guards were disappointed. They had not only become bullies, but also enjoyed it.

Critics of this study maintain that you can't learn much from such an artificial setup. In their view, the volunteers knew very well—from movies, TV, and games—how they were supposed to behave. They acted their parts to the hilt, in order to have fun and not disappoint the experimenters. Their behavior was no more surprising than if young men had been dressed in football gear and then had been found to be willing to bruise each other. The critics agree that the prison study makes a great story, but they maintain that it isn't *research*. That is, it does not carefully investigate relationships between factors; for all its drama, the study provides no new information. "It's just staging a 'happening,'" argued Leon Festinger (1980).

Philip Zimbardo, who designed the study, believes that these criticisms make his point: People's behavior depends to a large extent on the roles they are asked to play. *Real* prisoners and guards know their parts, too. Moreover, if the students were having so much fun, why did the prisoners beg for early release? Why did the guards lose sight of the "game" and behave as if it were a real job? Even if the prison study was a dramatization, Zimbardo said, it illustrates the power of roles in a way that a short-lived experiment cannot.

The Hospital Study

In another famous study, conducted by David Rosenhan (1973), eight normal, healthy adults—a housewife, a painter, a pediatrician, a graduate student in psychology, a psychiatrist, and three psychologists, including Rosenhan himself—appeared at 12 different hospitals in five states with the same complaint. They said that they had heard voices, mostly unclear, but they could make out the words *hollow, empty,* and *thud.* Apart from this lie, they all gave honest personal histories, which contained not a trace of abnormal problems. All eight were quickly admitted to the hospitals; one was diagnosed as manic-depressive and the rest as schizophrenic. Once in the hospital, the pseudopatients immediately stopped faking any symptoms. All behaved normally and "sanely." Nevertheless, they were kept in the hospital from 7 to 52 days, an average of 19 days. When they were released, it was with the same diagnosis: "in remission."

This study is usually cited to illustrate the problems of psychiatric diagnosis, but it also shows the impact on behavior of being in the role of patient or attendant. Once the pseudopatients were diagnosed as disturbed and assigned the role of patient, the hospital staff regarded everything they did as further signs of emotional disorder. For example, all of the pseudopatients took frequent notes about their experiences. Several nurses noted this act in the records without asking them what they were writing about. One nurse wrote "patient engages in writing behavior," as if writing were an odd thing to do.

The powerless role of patient and the label "mentally ill," Rosenhan found, confer invisibility and encourage **depersonalization,** the loss of someone's distinctive individuality as a human being. In all 12 hospitals, the staff avoided eye contact and conversation with patients as much as possible. The pseudopatients attempted to speak a total of 185 times to staff psychiatrists, but 71 percent of the time, the psychiatrist moved on without replying or even looking at the person. Only 4 percent of the attempts succeeded in getting the psychiatrist to stop and talk. Of 1,283 attempts to talk to nurses and attendants, only half of 1 percent succeeded. The usual response to a pseudopatient's effort to communicate was the staff member's equal effort to avoid discussion. The result was often a bizarre exchange, such as this:

> **Pseudopatient:** Pardon me, Dr. X. Could you tell me when I am eligible for grounds privileges?
> **Psychiatrist:** Good morning, Dave. How are you today? [moves off without waiting for a response]

The role of attendant confers a power that often causes well-meaning individuals to treat patients badly. Rosenhan personally observed real patients being beaten by staff members for trying to talk to them. One patient was hit for approaching an attendant and saying, "I like you." A staff member might abuse a patient in front of a dozen other patients and stop only if another staff member appeared. To the staff, Rosenhan explains, patients are not full human beings. Their disorders somehow turn them into robots who lack feelings and perceptions.

There are problems with Rosenhan's study, as there are with the prison study. Critics point out that it was not necessarily wrong to hospitalize people who complained of hearing voices. They also dislike the deceptiveness of the infiltrators and argue that Rosenhan wasn't sympathetic enough to an overworked staff suffering from financial cutbacks. Emotionally disturbed people, they add, often *do* behave in unpleasant, unpredictable, and difficult ways. It is not surprising that even trained staff would feel ambivalent about them or would impose control.

Rosenhan is sympathetic to the problems of mental-health professionals. He knows that they are not monsters and that most of them enter their jobs with good motives. The heartless or depersonalizing behavior of staff members arises from the roles they are required to play. Even in times of financial hardship, he adds, hospitals set priorities for what a person in each role is expected to do. Staffs are still required to keep records and to have lengthy meetings, so time with patients becomes a low priority. The result is less attention to the people whom the staff is there to help.

■ **depersonalization**
Treating another person without regard for the person's individuality as a human being.

The Obedience Study

In the early 1960s, Stanley Milgram (1963, 1974) designed a study that was to become one of the most famous in all of psychology. Milgram wanted to know how many people would obey an authority figure when ordered to violate their own ethical standards. Participants in the study, however, thought they were part of an experiment on the effects of punishment on learning. Each was assigned, apparently at random, to the role of "teacher." Another person, introduced as a fellow volunteer, was the "learner." Whenever the learner, seated in an adjoining room, made an error in reciting a list of word pairs he was supposed to have memorized, the teacher was expected to give him an electric shock by depressing a lever on an ominous-looking machine (see Figure 17.1). With each error, the voltage—marked from 0 to 450—was to be increased by another 15 volts. The shock levels on the machine were labeled from SLIGHT SHOCK to DANGER—SEVERE SHOCK and, finally, XXX. In reality, the learners were confederates of Milgram and did *not* receive any shocks, but none of the teachers ever realized this. The actor–victims played their parts convincingly: As the study continued, they shouted in pain and pleaded to be released, all according to a prearranged script.

When Milgram first designed this experiment, he asked a number of psychiatrists, students, and middle-class adults how many people they thought would "go all the way" to XXX on orders from the experimenter. The psychiatrists predicted that most people would refuse to go beyond 150 volts, when the learner first demanded to be freed, and that only one person in a thousand, someone who was emotionally disturbed and sadistic, would administer the highest voltage. The nonprofessionals agreed with this prediction, and all of them said that they personally would disobey early in the experiment.

In fact, however, every subject in the study administered some shock to the learner, and about two-thirds of them, of all ages and from all walks of life, obeyed the experimenter to the fullest. They obeyed no matter how much the victim shouted for them to stop and no matter how painful the shocks seemed to be. They obeyed even when they themselves were anguished about the pain they believed they were causing. They obeyed even as they wept, implored the experimenter to release them, and argued with themselves. Milgram (1974) noted that many would "sweat, tremble, stutter, bite their lips, groan, and dig their fingernails into their flesh"; yet they continued.

More than 1,000 participants at several universities eventually went through the Milgram experiment. Most of them, men and women equally, inflicted what they thought were dangerous amounts of shock to another person. (Seven of eight subsequent replications of the study also found the obedience rates of

■ **Figure 17.1   The Milgram Obedience Experiment**
On the left is Milgram's shock machine. On the right, you see the "learner" being strapped into his chair by the experimenter and the "teacher" (the subject).

men and women to be identical [Blass, 1993].) Many protested to the experimenter, but their doubts were usually overcome when he simply responded, "The experiment requires that you continue."

Milgram and his team next set up several variations of the basic experiment to determine the conditions under which people might disobey the experimenter. They found that virtually *nothing the victim did or said changed the likelihood of the person's compliance*—even when the victim said he had a heart condition, screamed in agony, or stopped responding entirely as if he had collapsed. However, people were more likely to disobey under the following conditions:

- When the experimenter left the room. Many people then subverted authority by giving low levels of shock but reporting that they were following orders.

- When the victim was right there in the room, and the teacher had to administer the shock directly to the victim's body.

- When two experimenters issued conflicting demands to continue the experiment or to stop at once. In this case, no one kept inflicting shock.

- When the person ordering them to continue was an ordinary man, apparently another volunteer, instead of the authoritative experimenter.

- When the subject worked with peers who refused to go further. Seeing someone else rebel gave subjects the courage to disobey.

In the "touch-proximity" variation of Milgram's experiment, the "teacher" had to administer shock directly to the learner. Here, a subject continues to obey, although most in this condition did not.

Obedience, then, was more a function of the situation than of the particular personalities of the participants. "The key to the behavior of subjects," Milgram (1974) summarized, "lies not in pent-up anger or aggression but in the nature of their relationship to authority. They have given themselves to the authority; they see themselves as instruments for the execution of his wishes; once so defined, they are unable to break free."

The Milgram experiment, too, has had its critics. Some believe it was unethical, both because of Milgram's deception in not telling subjects what was really happening until after the session was over (of course, such honesty in advance would have invalidated the study) and because the study caused so many of the subjects such emotional pain (Milgram countered that the subjects wouldn't have felt pain if they had disobeyed instructions). Others argue that there are plenty of examples of obedience to immoral authority in history without having to set up such an unreal laboratory scenario. Still others question Milgram's assertion that the situation always overrules personality. Subsequent studies find that certain personality traits, such as hostility and authoritarianism, do increase obedience to authority in real life (Blass, 1991, 1993). Nevertheless, this experiment had a tremendous influence on public awareness of the dangers of uncritical obedience.

The Power of Roles

In spite of their limitations, the three imaginative studies we have described demonstrate the power of social roles and obligations to influence the behavior of individuals. The behavior of the prisoners and guards varied; some prisoners were more rebellious than others, some guards were more abusive than others. But, ultimately, what people did depended on the roles they were assigned. Regardless of their personal feelings, staff members at the mental hospitals had to adapt to the structure of the institution, from psychiatrists at the top to ward attendants at the bottom. And whatever their personal traits, when people in the Milgram study believed they had to follow the legitimate orders of authority, most of them put their private values aside.

Obedience, of course, is not always harmful or bad; a certain amount of routine compliance with rules is necessary for any group to succeed. All societies impose penalties, from a mild fine to life in prison, on those who fail to obey the law. All groups impose consequences, from mild censure to outright banishment, on those who fail to obey the group's everyday norms and rules. A nation could not function if all its citizens ignored traffic signals, cheated on their taxes, dumped garbage wherever they chose, or assaulted each other. An organization could not function if its members "did their own thing," working only when they felt like it. But obedience also has a darker aspect. Throughout history, the plea "I was only following orders" has been offered to excuse actions carried out on behalf of orders that were foolish, destructive, or illegal. The writer C. P. Snow observed that "more hideous crimes have been committed in the name of obedience than in the name of rebellion."

Most people follow orders because of the obvious consequences of disobedience: They can be suspended from school, fired from their jobs, or arrested. In addition, they obey because they respect the authority who is giving the orders; because they want to be liked; or because they hope to gain personal advantages. They obey without thinking critically about the authority's right to issue orders or in the confidence that the authority knows more than they do. But what about those obedient people in Milgram's experiment who felt they were doing wrong, who wished they were free, but who could not untangle themselves from the cobweb of social constraints? Why do people obey when it is not in their interests, or when obedience requires them to ignore their own values or even commit a crime?

Social psychologists Herbert Kelman and Lee Hamilton (1989) have studied "crimes of obedience," ranging from military massacres of civilians to bureaucratic crimes such as Watergate and the Iran-Contra fiasco. They and other researchers draw our attention to several factors that cause people to obey when they would rather not:

1. *Legitimization of the authority,* which allows people to feel absolved of the responsibility for their actions. In Milgram's experiment, many people who administered the highest levels of shock gave up their own accountability to the demands of the experiment. A 37-year-old welder explained that the experimenter was responsible for any pain the victim might suffer "for the simple reason that I was paid for doing this. I had to follow orders. That's how I figured it." In contrast, the people who refused to give high levels of shock took credit for their actions and refused to grant the authority legitimacy. "One of the things I think is very cowardly," said a 32-year-old engineer, "is to try to shove the responsibility onto someone else. See, if I now turned around and said, 'It's your fault . . . it's not mine,' I would call that cowardly" (Milgram, 1974).

2. *Routinization,* the process of defining the activity in terms of routine duties and roles so that one's behavior becomes normalized, a job to be done, and there is little opportunity to raise doubts or ethical questions. In the Milgram study, some people became so fixated on the "learning task" that they shut out any moral concerns about the learner's demands to be let out.

3. *The rules of good manners.* Good manners, of course, are the honey of relationships and the grease of civilization; they smooth over the rough spots of interaction and protect good feelings. Once people are caught in what they perceive to be legitimate roles and obeying a legitimate authority, good manners further ensnare them into obedience. Most people don't like to rock the boat, appear to doubt the experts, or be rude, because they know they will be disliked for doing so (Sabini & Silver, 1985). Indeed, when students watch a videotape of the Milgram procedure, they are much more favorably inclined toward dissenters who politely disobey than those who get furiously riled up and morally indignant. The psychologist who got these findings, Barry Collins (1993), observes that they dispel the typical fantasy that people have about "What *I* would have liked to have done as a Milgram subject."

Because of good manners, many people literally *lack a language of protest*. To have gotten up from your chair in the Milgram study and walked out would have been embarrassing, and you would have had to explain and justify your "rudeness." Many literally lacked the words to do so. One woman kept apologizing to the experimenter, trying not to offend him with her worries for the victim: "Do I go right to the end, sir? I hope there's nothing wrong with him there." (She did go right to the end.) A man repeatedly protested and questioned the experimenter, but he too obeyed, even when the victim had apparently collapsed in pain. "He thinks he is killing someone," Milgram (1974) commented, "yet he uses the language of the tea table."

4. *Entrapment*. Although obedience often seems to be an either–or matter—you obey or you do not—the fact is that obedience usually escalates through a process called **entrapment.** In entrapment, individuals escalate their commitment to a course of action in order to justify their investment in it (Brockner & Rubin, 1985). You are trapped at the point at which you are heavily invested in an activity and it costs too much to get out. The first steps of entrapment pose no difficult choices. But one step leads to another, and before the person realizes it, he or she has become committed to a course of action that does pose problems. In Milgram's study, once subjects had given a 15-volt shock, they had committed themselves to the experiment. The next level was "only" 30 volts. Before they knew it, they were administering what they believed were dangerously high shocks. At that point, it was difficult to explain a sudden decision to quit.

Everyone is vulnerable to the process of entrapment. A job requires, at first, only a "little" cheating, and, besides, "everyone else is doing it," and before long, you are enmeshed in the company's dishonest policies. You start dating someone you like moderately. Before you know it, you have been together so long that you can't break up, although you don't want to become committed, either. Or you visit Las Vegas and quickly lose the $50 you allotted yourself for gambling, so you decide to keep going "just a little longer" in hopes of recovering the lost money. Before long, you're out $500 and have to go home early.

Entrapment can lead to aggressive and violent actions by individuals and nations, and examples of it appear frequently in the news. A young man decides to ride along with some gang members but does not intend to do anything illegal. Soon he is scrawling graffiti, then stealing tires, then dealing drugs, although he would rather not be doing any of these things. Government leaders start a war they think will end quickly. Years later, the nation has lost so many soldiers and so much money that the leaders believe they cannot retreat without losing face.

▪ **entrapment**
A gradual process in which individuals escalate their commitment to a course of action to justify their investment of time, money, or effort.

Slot machines are a classic example of entrapment: The person vows to spend only a few dollars, but then says, "Well, maybe another couple of tries" or "I've spent so much, now I really have to win something to get back my loss."

A chilling example of entrapment comes from a study of 25 men who had served in the Greek military police during the authoritarian regime that ended in 1974 (Haritos-Fatouros, 1988). A psychologist who interviewed the men identified the steps used in training them to use torture in questioning prisoners. First, the men were ordered to stand guard outside the interrogation and torture cells. Then they stood guard in the detention rooms, where they observed the torture of prisoners. Then they "helped" beat up prisoners. Once they had obediently followed these orders and became actively involved, the torturers found their actions easier to carry out.

Many people expect the solutions to moral problems to fall into two clear categories, with right on one side and wrong on the other. Yet in real life, as in the Milgram study, people often set out on a path that is morally ambiguous, only to find that they have traveled a long way toward violating their own principles (Sabini & Silver, 1985). From Greece's "bad" torturers to Milgram's "good" subjects, people share the difficult task of drawing a line beyond which they will not go. To draw that line, they need to understand the difference between the demands of their role and the demands of their conscience.

Quick Quiz

A. 1. About what percentage of the people in Milgram's obedience study administered the highest levels of shock? (a) two-thirds, (b) one-half, (c) one-third, (d) one-tenth
   2. Which of the following actions by the "learner" reduced the likelihood of being shocked by the "teacher"? (a) protesting noisily, (b) screaming in pain, (c) complaining of having a heart ailment, (d) nothing he did made a difference
   3. In the Zimbardo, Rosenhan, and Milgram studies, people's behavior was predicted most strongly by (a) their personality traits, (b) the dictates of their consciences, (c) their assigned roles, (d) norms codified in law.
B. What social-psychological concepts does each story illustrate?
   1. A friend of yours, who is moving, asks you to bring over a few boxes. Since you are there anyway, he asks you to fill them with books. Before you know it, you have packed up his entire kitchen, living room, and den.
   2. Sam is having dinner with a group of fellow students when one of his friends tells a joke about how dumb women are. Sam is angry and disgusted but doesn't say anything. Later, in the shower, he thinks of what he should have said.

Answers:

A. 1. a **2.** d **3.** c **B. 1.** entrapment **2.** rules of manners and lacking a language of protest

■ SOCIAL COGNITION: ATTRIBUTIONS AND ATTITUDES

■ **social cognition**
An area in social psychology concerned with social influences on thought, memory, perception, and other cognitive processes.

Social psychologists are interested not only in what people do in social situations, but also in what goes on in their heads while they are doing it. Researchers in the area of **social cognition** examine how the social environment influences thoughts, perceptions, and beliefs (Fiske & Taylor, 1991). Two of the most important topics they study are the importance of explanations about behavior and the formation and change of attitudes.

Explanations and Excuses

One theme of this book has been that human beings are active, problem-solving creatures, forever trying to make sense of the world and understand what is going on around them. According to **attribution theory,** people are motivated to make sense of their own and others' behavior in order to predict and control events (Cheng & Novick, 1990; Ross & Fletcher, 1985). "To attribute" means "to consider as caused by." Caused by what? Generally, there are two kinds of causes. When you make a *situational attribution,* you identify the cause of an action as something in the environment: "Joe stole the money because his family is starving." When you make a *dispositional attribution,* you identify the cause of an action as something in the person, such as a trait or a motive: "Joe stole the money because he is a born thief."

In other chapters, we have already noted the psychological effects of certain attributions: In Chapter 10, for example, we saw that attributions influence emotions (did that man intend to insult you or not?), and in Chapter 14, we saw that attributions about the locus of control affect how much influence people think they have over their health and their future. Longitudinal studies find that attributions even affect the happiness of marriage partners and the long-term success of their marriages. Unhappy spouses are more likely than happy ones to attribute marital problems to their partner's stable *dispositions,* blaming the person's selfishness, meanness, or "intentional" acts of thoughtlessness. Happy spouses, in contrast, are more likely to attribute marital problems to the *situation,* blaming the stress the partner is under, not having enough time together because of work and family obligations, and so forth (Fincham & Bradbury, 1993; Karney et al., 1994).

Through experimental research, social psychologists have specified some of the conditions under which people prefer certain attributions to others. For example, when people try to find reasons for someone else's behavior, they tend to overestimate personality factors and underestimate the influence of the situation (Nisbett & Ross, 1980). This tendency has been called the **fundamental attribution error.** Were the student guards in the prison study basically mean and the prisoners basically cowardly? Were the staff members in the hospital study lazy, thoughtless, or selfish? Were the hundreds of people who obeyed Milgram's experimenters sadistic by nature? People who think so are committing the fundamental attribution error. This kind of mistake is most likely to occur when people are distracted or mentally preoccupied and don't have time to stop and ask themselves, "Why, exactly, *is* Aurelia behaving like a dope today?" Instead, they leap to the easiest attribution, which is dispositional: Aurelia simply has a dopey personality (Gilbert, Pelham, & Krull, 1988). Often, people discount the power of roles to affect behavior even when they know that a person has had no choice in a particular setting (Taylor, Peplau, & Sears, 1994).

The fundamental attribution error is prevalent in Western nations, where middle-class people tend to believe that individuals are responsible for their own actions. But this error by no means universal (Fletcher & Ward, 1988). In countries such as India, for example, where everyone is embedded in caste and family networks, and China, where people are more group oriented than they are in the West, people are more likely to recognize situational constraints on behavior (J. G. Miller, 1984; Morris & Peng, 1994). If someone is behaving oddly, therefore, an Indian or Chinese is likely to make a situational attribution of the problem rather than a dispositional one.

When it comes to explaining their *own* behavior, most Westerners tend to choose attributions that are favorable to them (Markus & Kitayama, 1991). This

Have you ever called someone else's error a "stupid clumsy mistake," yet excused an identical blunder on your part as "something that couldn't be helped"? Why? Why do people need excuses anyway?

■ **attribution theory**
The theory that people are motivated to explain their own and other people's behavior by attributing causes of that behavior to a situation or a disposition.

■ **fundamental attribution error**
The tendency, in explaining other people's behavior, to overestimate personality factors and underestimate the influence of the situation.

self-serving bias means that people like to take credit for their good actions and let the situation account for their bad ones. For instance, most of us will say, "I am furious for good reason—this situation is intolerable!" We are less likely to say, "I am furious because I am an ill-tempered grinch." If we do something admirable, though, such as donating $100 to charity, we attribute our motives to personality ("I'm the generous type") instead of to the situation ("The fund-raiser pressured me into it").

The self-serving bias is also apparent in the excuses people make to justify their mistakes. C. R. Snyder, Raymond Higgins, and Rita Stucky (1983) have observed that self-protecting excuses have been part of human life since Adam blamed Eve for giving him the apple—and Eve blamed the serpent. The researchers identified several categories of excuses: "I didn't do it"; "I did it, but it wasn't so bad"; "I didn't mean to"; and "I couldn't help it." A psychotherapy client of one of the researchers put it best. "It's like this," she said. "If it's not my fault, it's her fault, and if it's not her fault, it's still not my fault."

Excuses have several social purposes. They allow people to assert their good qualities, reduce their responsibility, and minimize the badness of the action itself (Snyder, 1989). Excuses also make it possible for people to maintain self-esteem, soften the other person's anger, and change the other person's attributions about their own actions (Weiner, Figueroa-Muñoz, & Kakihara, 1991). Unfortunately, excuses are also used to justify the destructive things that people do and to rationalize their failure to take helpful action.

Culture affects not only the fundamental attribution error, but also self-serving attributions and excuses. In Japan, for example, heads of companies are expected to take responsibility not only for their own failings, but also for the failings of their employees or products—and they do (Hall & Hall, 1987; Pascale & Athos, 1981). In the United States, in contrast, the common practice is for heads of corporations to get huge salaries and bonuses even when the company is doing poorly, and to blame the economy, government policies, or their employees if something goes wrong (Crystal, 1991). Of course, many Americans refuse to take responsibility for their mistakes because they fear lawsuits.

People also make attributions for events that have little to do with their self-esteem or even their own behavior. According to the **just-world hypothesis,** people all over the world need to believe that the world is fair, that good people are rewarded and villains punished (Lerner, 1980). The belief in a just world helps people make sense out of senseless events and feel safe in the presence of threatening events. If a friend loses his job, if a woman is raped, if a prisoner is tortured, it is reassuring to believe that they all must have done something to deserve what happened or at least to cause it. The need to believe in a just world often leads to a dispositional attribution called *blaming the victim.* When

■ **self-serving bias**
The tendency, in explaining one's own behavior, to take credit for good actions and to rationalize mistakes.

■ **just-world hypothesis**
The notion that many people need to believe that the world is fair, that justice is served, and that bad people are punished and good people rewarded.

Calvin and Hobbes   by Bill Watterson

Children learn the value of excuses at an early age.

there is no question in anyone's mind that A did something to harm B, A can argue that B deserved the treatment, provoked the treatment, or wanted the treatment. "Many subjects harshly devalue the victim *as a consequence* of acting against him," wrote Milgram (1974). "Such comments as, 'He was so stupid and stubborn he deserved to get shocked,' were common."

By now, you might be wondering where, in all these attributions, the truth is. Most human actions are determined both by personality and by environment. In that case, is the fundamental attribution error always an error? Maybe we make dispositional attributions about another person because they are more accurate in predicting that person's future actions (Fiske & Taylor, 1991). Moreover, is the self-serving bias always a bias? Maybe we know more about our own behavior and intentions than we do about the actions of others. Researchers are still debating these questions. But they all agree that attributions, whether accurate or not, have major consequences for emotions and actions, for the legal system, and for everyday relations.

Quick QUIZ

A. What kind of attribution is being made in each case, situational (S) or dispositional (D)?

1. A jury decides that a congressman accepted a bribe because FBI agents set up a sting operation to trap him.
2. A jury decides that a congressman accepted a bribe because he is dishonest.
3. A man says, "My wife has sure become a grouchy person."
4. The same man says, "I'm grouchy because I've had a bad day at the office."
5. A woman reads that unemployment is very high in inner-city communities. "Well, if those people weren't so lazy, they would find work," she says.

B. What principles of attribution theory are suggested by items 3, 4, and 5 in the preceding question?

Answers:

A. 1. S 2. D 3. D 4. S 5. D B. 3 illustrates the fundamental attribution error; 4, the self-serving bias; and 5, blaming the victim, because of the just-world hypothesis.

The Social Origins of Attitudes

People have attitudes about all sorts of things—politics, people, food, children, movies, sports heroes, you name it. An *attitude* is a relatively stable opinion containing a cognitive element (perceptions and beliefs about the topic, including any stereotypes about it) and an emotional element (feelings about the topic, which may range from negative and hostile to positive and loving). Attitudes range from shallow, changeable opinions to major convictions. Many public-opinion polls do not discriminate between these two extremes; they just ask for a person's attitude, not how strongly it is felt. The results, therefore, may be misleading; public opinion often seems easily swayed.

Most people tend to think that their attitudes are based on thinking—that is, on reasoned conclusions about how things work. Sometimes, of course, that's

The "cohort effect" refers to psychological characteristics that arise out of the shared experiences and values of a generation. Many people who came of age during the political protests of the 1960s, such as this couple, have continued their political activism throughout their lives.

true. But social psychologists have found that attitudes are also affected by conformity, habit, rationalization, economic self-interest, and many subtle social and environmental influences. For example, some attitudes arise by virtue of "the cohort effect." Each generation, or age *cohort,* has its own experiences and economic concerns, and therefore its own characteristic viewpoints and perspectives. The ages of 16 to 24 appear to be especially critical for the formation of a *generational identity* that lasts throughout adulthood (Inglehart, 1990). In one survey of a cross-section of the American population, researchers found that the major political events and social changes that occur during these years make deeper impressions and exert more lasting influence than those that happen later (Schuman & Scott, 1989). Some of the key events that have affected generational cohorts in this century include the Great Depression (1930s), World War II (1940s), the dropping of the atomic bomb on Hiroshima (1945), the rise of the civil rights movement (1950s–1960s), the assassination of John F. Kennedy (1963), the Vietnam War (1965–1973), the rebirth of the women's rights movement (1970s), and the legalization of abortion (1973). People who were between 16 and 24 when these events occurred regard them as "peak memories" that have shaped their political philosophy, values, and attitudes about life. What do you think might be the critical generational events affecting the attitudes of your cohort?

Psychologists have argued for years about which comes first, attitudes or behavior, and whether they need even be related. All too often, attitudes and behavior are as unrelated as grapefruit and shoes. For example, studies of college students find that many sexually active students believe that they should use condoms and that they are at risk of contracting AIDS and other sexually transmitted diseases, but they do not practice what is being preached to them (Biglan et al., 1990). In a study of 5,500 Canadian college students, the majority knew which sexual acts increase the risk of AIDS transmission and also knew about safe sexual practices. Yet that knowledge, the researchers reported, "was not typically translated into safer behavior" (MacDonald et al., 1990).

Of course, attitudes do dispose people to act in certain ways (Kraus, 1995). If you have a positive attitude about the game of soccer, you may try to get to every game you can. If you have a negative attitude, you may refuse every invitation to go to one. However, cause and effect can also work in the other direction: A change of behavior may change attitudes because of new information and experiences. For example, your friends drag you, kicking and screaming, to the World Cup, and you become a devoted soccer fan. Naturally, serious convictions are more strongly related to behavior than garden-variety attitudes are.

People who are emotionally committed to an issue are more likely to work on its behalf (Abelson, 1988).

Attitudes and behavior can also be brought into harmony by the wish for consistency. In Chapter 8, we discussed how the desire to avoid **cognitive dissonance** can affect a person's thinking and beliefs. As we saw, when two attitudes, or when an attitude and behavior, are in conflict (are dissonant), people are often motivated to resolve the conflict by changing an attitude or their behavior (Aronson, 1992). One group of researchers recently applied cognitive-dissonance theory in an effort to prevent AIDS transmission among sexually active young adults whose behavior—unprotected sex—was dissonant with their knowledge of the risks of getting a sexually transmitted disease (Stone et al., 1994). Students who were asked to publicly advocate the importance of safe sex, and then list the reasons for their own past failure to use condoms, were in a state of dissonance, aware of their hypocrisy in failing to practice what they preached. They were nearly twice as likely as all other students in the experiment to buy condoms later.

Many influences on attitudes, however, are external; they result from the intentional efforts of others, not always benign, to get us to change our minds. Changing attitudes is not, in and of itself, good or bad, but people need to know why they are doing so. When persuasive tactics go beyond the use of reasoned argument, people become vulnerable to manipulation. The best protection is not rigid thinking and the refusal to accept new ideas; it is critical thinking, and the ability to identify some of the social forces that influence the formation and change of attitudes. (In "Taking Psychology with You," we discuss some ways to protect yourself from manipulation.)

Friendly Persuasion.   All around you, every day, advertisers, politicians, and friends are trying to get you to change your attitudes. One weapon they use is to repeat, and repeat, and repeat the message. Research shows that repeated exposure even to a nonsense syllable like *zug* is enough to make a person feel more positive toward it (Zajonc, 1968). And the effectiveness of familiarity has long been known to politicians and advertisers: Repeat something often enough, even the basest lie, and eventually the public will believe it.

The formal name for this phenomenon is the **validity effect.** In a series of experiments, Hal Arkes and his associates demonstrated how the validity effect operates (Arkes, 1991; Arkes, Boehm, & Xu, 1991). In one typical study, people read a list of statements, such as "Mercury has a higher boiling point than copper" or "Over 400 Hollywood films were produced in 1948." They had to rate each statement for its validity, where "1" meant the rater thought the statement was definitely false and "7" that it was definitely true. A week or two later, subjects again rated the validity of some of these statements and also rated others that they hadn't seen previously. The result: Mere repetition increased the perception that the familiar statements were true. The validity effect also occurred for other kinds of statements, including unverifiable opinions (such as "At least 75 percent of all politicians are basically dishonest"), opinions that subjects initially felt were true, and those they initially felt were false. "Note that no attempt has been made to persuade," wrote Arkes (1991). "No supporting arguments are offered. We just have subjects rate the statements. Mere repetition seems to increase rated validity. This is scary." Further experiments have ruled out competing explanations, confirming that the simple familiarity of an argument is sufficient to make many people believe it is valid (Boehm, 1994).

When Arkes discussed this research with a student from the People's Republic of China, she was not surprised. She told him how her government made use of the validity effect by distributing posters claiming, for example, that the protest for democracy in Tiananmen Square had been organized by a small

■ **cognitive dissonance**
A state of tension that occurs when a person holds two cognitions that are psychologically inconsistent, or when a person's belief is incongruent with his or her behavior.

■ **validity effect**
The tendency of people to believe that a statement is true or valid simply because it has been repeated many times.

band of traitors. At first, no one believed these lies; but over time, with repetition, the government's assertions became more plausible.

Closer to home, here is another example of the validity effect. Over and over during former president Ronald Reagan's term of office, the press claimed that he was the most popular president in history. Yet when two political scientists actually examined the evidence of public-opinion polls, they found that Reagan's approval rating averaged 50 percent, lower than the averages of Eisenhower (69), Kennedy (71), Johnson (52), and Nixon (56), and not much above Carter's (47). His highest rating, early in his presidency, was 68 percent—lower than that of the five previous presidents at the same point in their terms. It is true that Reagan's ratings for personal appeal were much higher than his ratings for job performance, but Americans have always given higher approval to their president's personal qualities than to his political skills (Ferguson & Rogers, 1986). Nevertheless, the effect of the repeated assertion of Reagan's unique popularity was to get the country to believe it.

Another effective way to influence people's attitudes is to expose them to arguments from someone they admire or think is attractive or trustworthy, which is why advertisements are full of beautiful models, sports heroes, and "experts" (Pratkanis & Aronson, 1992). Persuaders will also try to link their message with a good feeling. In one classic study, students who were given peanuts and Pepsi while listening to an argument were more likely to be convinced than were students who listened to the same words without the pleasant munchies and soft drinks (Janis, Kaye, & Kirschner, 1965). Perhaps this is why so much business is conducted over lunch, and so many courtships over dinner!

The emotion of fear, in contrast, can cause people to resist arguments that are in their own best interest (Pratkanis & Aronson, 1992). Fear tactics are often used to try to persuade people to quit smoking or abusing other drugs, to drive only when sober, to use condoms, to check for signs of cancer, and to prepare for earthquakes. However, fear works only if people are moderately anxious, not scared to death; and if the message is combined with information about what a person can do to avoid the danger (Leventhal, 1970; Leventhal & Nerenz, 1982). When messages about a future disaster are too terrifying and when people believe that there is nothing they can do to avoid it, they tend to deny the danger.

Coercive Persuasion.

Sometimes, efforts to change attitudes go beyond exposing people to a new idea and persuading them to accept it. The manipulator uses harsh tactics, not just hoping that people will change their minds, but attempting to force them to. These tactics are sometimes referred to as *brainwashing*, a term that was first used during the Korean War to describe techniques used on American prisoners of war to get them to collaborate with their Chinese Communist captors and to endorse anti-American propaganda. Most psychologists, however, prefer to use the phrase "undesired social influence" or *coercive persuasion*. "Brainwashing," they argue, implies that a person has a sudden change of mind and is unaware of what is happening. It sounds mysterious and powerful. In fact, the methods involved are neither mysterious nor unusual. The difference between "persuasion" and "brainwashing" is often only a matter of degree and the observer's bias, just as a group that is a "crazy cult" to one person is a group of "devoutly religious" people to another (Boyer, 1992).

Persuasion techniques become coercive when they suppress an individual's ability to reason and make choices in his or her own best interests. Studies of religious, political, and other cults have identified some of the processes by which individuals, whether singly or in groups, can be coerced (Galanter, 1989; Ofshe & Watters, 1994; Singer, Temerlin, & Langone, 1990; Zimbardo & Leippe, 1991):

1. *The person is put under physical or emotional distress.* The individual may not be allowed to eat, sleep, or exercise. He or she may be isolated in a dark room with no stimulation or food prior to joining the group. In the group, the person may be induced into a trancelike state through repetitive chanting, hypnosis, deep relaxation, or fatigue. If a participant is already under stress, perhaps feeling lonely or troubled, he or she is especially likely to be primed to accept the ideas of the leader or group.

2. *The person's problems are defined in simplistic terms, and simple answers are offered repeatedly.* There are as many of these answers as there are persuasive groups, but here are some real examples: Do you have problems with your marriage? A long-term marriage is an "addiction"; better break the habit. Are you afraid or unhappy? It all stems from the pain of being born. Are you worried about homeless earthquake victims? It's not your problem; victims are responsible for everything that happens to them. Are your parents giving you a hard time? Reject them completely. Are you struggling financially? It's your fault for not wanting to be rich fervently enough.

3. *The leader offers unconditional love, acceptance, and attention.* The new recruit may be given a "love bath" from the group—constant praise, support, applause, and affection. Positive emotions of euphoria and well-being are generated. In exchange, the leader demands everyone's attachment, adoration, and idealization.

4. *A new identity based on the group is created.* The recruit is told that he or she is part of the chosen, the elite, the redeemed. To foster this new identity, many cults require a severe initiation rite; require their members to wear identifying clothes or eat special diets; and assign each new member a new name. All members of the Philadelphia group MOVE were given the last name "Africa"; all members of the Church of Armageddon took the last name "Israel." Conversely, members are taught to hate certain "evil" enemies: parents, capitalists, blacks, whites, nonbelievers.

5. *The person is subjected to entrapment.* "There is no contract up front that says 'I agree to become a beggar and give up my family,'" says Philip Zimbardo. Instead, the person agrees to small things: to spend a weekend with the group, then another weekend, then take weekly seminars, then advanced courses. During the Korean War, the Chinese first got the American POWs to agree with mild remarks, such as "The United States is not perfect." Then the POWs had to add their own examples of the imperfections. At the end, they were signing their names to anti-American broadcasts (Schein, Schneier, & Barker, 1961).

6. *Once a person accepts the new philosophy, his or her access to information is severely controlled.* As soon as a person is a committed believer or follower, the group limits his or her choices, denigrates critical thinking, makes fun of doubts, defines the outside world as evil, and insists that any private distress is due to lack of belief in the group. The person may be isolated from the outside world and antidotes to the leader's ideas. Total conformity is demanded.

All of these techniques were apparent in the Branch Davidian cult led by David Koresh. By moving his group to a virtually self-sufficient compound in Waco, Texas, Koresh physically isolated his followers from their families and from other people who would have offered them a different interpretation of Koresh's paranoid beliefs. He subjected them to exhausting all-night vigils and lectures. He offered them simple answers for their complex lives: "Believe in

David Koresh used standard principles of coercive persuasion to entrap his followers into leaving their homes, jobs, and often their families and persuade them to follow him to a remote location for the promise of salvation.

me; you will be saved; you will no longer be unhappy; I will take care of you." He entrapped them in an escalating series of obligations and commitments. Koresh never said to new recruits, "Follow me, and you will have to give up your marriages, your homes, your children, and your lives"; but by the end, that is just what they did.

Some people may be more vulnerable than others to coercive tactics. But these techniques are powerful enough to overwhelm even strong individuals. Unless people understand how these methods work, few can resist their effects.

Quick QUIZ

1. Candidate A spends 3 million dollars to make sure his name is seen and heard frequently, and to repeat unverified charges that his opponent is a thief. What psychological process is he relying on to win?

 2. Your best friend urges you to join a "life-renewal" group called "The Feeling Life." Your friend has been spending increasing amounts of time with her fellow Feelies, and you have some doubts about them. What questions would you want to have answered before joining up?

Answers:

1. the validity effect 2. A few things to consider: Is there a single autocratic leader who tolerates no dissent or criticism, while rationalizing this practice as a benefit for members? ("Doubt and disbelief are signs that your feeling side is being repressed.") Have long-standing members given up their friends and families, their interests and ambitions, for this group? Does the leader offer simple but unrealistic promises to repair your life and all that troubles you? Are members required to make extreme personal sacrifices by donating large amounts of money and breaking off their outside relationships? You might also examine the dissonance you are feeling between loyalty to your friend and doubts about your friend's enthusiasm for this group.

▪ INDIVIDUALS AND GROUPS

Something happens to individuals when they collect in groups. They act differently than they would on their own; this is true for every social species. It is true when the group exists to solve problems and make decisions; when it has gathered to have fun, as at a soccer game; when it consists of anonymous bystanders; or when it is just a loose collection of individuals in a room. A group's actions, research suggests, depend less on the personalities of its members than on the structure and dynamics of the group itself.

Conformity

One thing that happens in groups is that people conform; that is, they take action or adopt attitudes as a result of real or imagined group pressure.

Suppose that you are required to appear at your professor's laboratory for an experiment on perception. You join seven other students seated in a room, and the study begins. You are shown a 10-inch line and asked which of three other lines is identical to it. The correct answer, line A, is obvious, so you are amused when the first person in the group chooses line B. "Bad eyesight," you say to yourself. "He's off by 2 whole inches!" The second person also chooses line B. "What a dope," you think. But by the time the fifth person has chosen line B, you are beginning to doubt yourself. The sixth and seventh students also choose line B, and now you are worried about *your* eyesight. The experimenter looks at you. "Your turn," he says. Do you follow the evidence of your own eyes or the collective judgment of the group?

This was the basic design for a series of classic studies of conformity conducted by Solomon Asch (1952, 1965). The seven supposedly nearsighted students were actually Asch's confederates. Asch wanted to know what people would do when a group unanimously contradicted an obvious fact. He found that when people made the line comparisons on their own, they were almost always accurate. But in the group, only 20 percent of the students remained completely independent on every trial, often being apologetic for not agreeing with the group. One-third conformed to the group's incorrect decision more than half the time, and the rest conformed at least some of the time. Conformers and independents often felt uncertain regardless of their decision. As one participant later said, "I felt disturbed, puzzled, separated, like an outcast from the rest."

Like obedience, conformity has both its positive and its negative sides. It allows people to feel connected to one another. Society runs more smoothly when people know how to behave in a given situation, when they go along with the rules of dress and manners. But conformity can also suppress critical thinking and creativity. People often do destructive and even self-destructive things because "everyone else does it." As decades of research now confirm, many people will, in a group, deny their private beliefs, agree with silly notions, and violate their own values (Aronson, 1995). Some do so because they identify with group members and want to be like them in dress, attitudes, or behavior. Some conform because they believe the group has knowledge or abilities that are superior to their own (Insko et al., 1985). Some conform in order to keep their jobs, win promotions, or win votes. Some conform for the same reason they obey; they wish to be liked and know that disagreeing with a group can make them unpopular. For their part, groups are often uncomfortable with nonconformists, and their members will try to persuade a deviant to conform. If pleasant persuasion fails, the group may punish, isolate, or reject the deviant altogether (Shaver & Buhrmester, 1983).

People who have a strong need for social approval, who are highly rigid, or who have low self-esteem are all more likely to conform than people who are more self-assured and flexible (Taylor, Peplau, & Sears, 1994). Most instances of

Sometimes people like to conform in order to feel part of the group . . .

conformity, however, depend heavily on the group situation and on the reasons behind the person's need to adapt to it.

The Anonymous Crowd

Many years ago, in a case that received much public attention, a woman named Kitty Genovese was stabbed repeatedly in front of her apartment building. She screamed for help for more than half an hour, but not one of the 38 neighbors who heard her, who came to their windows to watch, even called the police.

Kitty Genovese was a victim of a group process called the **diffusion of responsibility,** in which responsibility for an outcome is diffused, or spread, among many people. Individuals fail to take action because they believe that someone else will do so. The many reports of bystander apathy in the news—people watching as a woman is attacked, as a man burns himself to death, as a car hits a child and drives away—reflect the diffusion of responsibility on a large scale.

In work groups, the diffusion of responsibility sometimes takes the form of *social loafing:* Each member of a team slows down, letting others work harder (Karau & Williams, 1993; Latané, Williams, & Harkins, 1979). This slowdown of effort and abdication of personal responsibility does not happen in all groups. It occurs primarily when individual group members are not accountable for the work they do, when people feel that working harder would only duplicate their colleagues' efforts, or when the work itself is uninteresting. Members of a group need to feel that they are making unique contributions, even if their contributions are anonymous. When the challenge of the job is increased or when each member of the group has a different, important job to do, the sense of individual responsibility rises, and loafing declines (Harkins & Petty, 1983). Loafing also declines when people know they will have to evaluate their own performance privately, or when they know their group's performance will be evaluated against that of another group (Harkins & Szymanski, 1989). And if people are working on a group project that really matters to them, they may even work harder than they would on their own in order to compensate for some of their loafing buddies (Williams & Karau, 1991)!

The most extreme instances of the diffusion of responsibility occur in groups in which people lose all awareness of their individuality and sense of self, a state called **deindividuation** (Festinger, Pepitone, & Newcomb, 1952). Deindividuated people do not take responsibility for their own actions; they forget themselves in responding to the immediate situation. They are more likely to act mindlessly, and their behavior becomes disconnected from their attitudes. They may do destructive things: break store windows, loot, get into fights, riot at a sports event, commit rape and torture. But sometimes deindi-

▪ **diffusion of responsibility**
In organized or anonymous groups, the tendency of members to avoid taking responsibility for actions or decisions, assuming that others will do so.

▪ **deindividuation**
In groups or crowds, the loss of a person's awareness of her or his own individuality and the abdication of mindful action.

. . . and sometimes they like to rebel a little in order to assert their individuality.

viduated people become more friendly; think of all the chatty people on buses and planes who reveal things to their seatmates they would never tell anyone they knew. Deindividuation increases under conditions of anonymity. It is more likely to occur, for instance, when a person is in a large city rather than a small town, in a faceless mob rather than an intimate group; when signs of individuality are covered by uniforms or masks; or in a large and impersonal class of hundreds of students rather than a small class of only 15.

The power of the situation to influence what deindividuated people do has been demonstrated repeatedly in experiments. In one, women who were dressed in Ku Klux Klan–like white disguises delivered twice as much apparent electric shock to another woman as did women who were not only undisguised but also wore large name tags (Zimbardo, 1970; see Figure 17.2). In a second study, women who were wearing nurses' uniforms gave *less* shock than women in regular dress (Johnson & Downing, 1979). Evidently, the KKK disguise was a signal to behave aggressively; the nurses' uniforms were a signal to behave nurturantly.

As these studies suggest, deindividuated women are perfectly capable of behaving aggressively, in spite of the stereotype that women are less aggressive than men. Indeed, two recent experiments found that the commonly observed sex difference in aggressiveness has more to do with *gender roles* than with "natural" male and female inclinations—and that being in a state of deindividuation can overrule the influence of those roles (Lightdale & Prentice, 1994). In these studies, men behaved more aggressively than women in a competitive video war game when they were individuated—that is, when their names and background information about them were spoken aloud, heard by all subjects, and recorded publicly by the experimenter. But when the subjects believed they were anonymous to their fellow students and to the experimenter—deindividu-

■ **Figure 17.2   Anonymity and Cruelty**

Women covered in Ku Klux Klan–like disguises gave more shocks to another woman than did women who were not disguised or who were identified with name tags (Zimbardo, 1970).

ated—there were no gender differences in how aggressively they played the game. (The social consequences of deindividuation, and the problem of individual responsibility, are the subject of "Psychology and Popular Culture.")

Individuation can be involuntary, a result of circumstances over which the person has no control, such as being the only Korean in a group of Swiss, or it can be a voluntary result of a personal desire to be different. Christina Maslach and her associates have developed a scale that assesses a person's willingness to be distinguished from others—for example, to give your opinion on a controversial subject to a group of strangers, to publicly challenge a speaker with whom you disagree, or to raise your hand to ask a question in a large class. In a series of studies, they find that some people are more willing than others to be the center of attention, to be seen as different. These high "individuators" are more creative in dress, attitudes, and abilities; more likely to seek leadership roles in a group; and more willing to express original ideas and make controversial statements (Maslach, Stapp, & Santee, 1985; Whitney, Sagrestano, & Maslach, 1994).

Psychology and Popular Culture

Swept Away: Mob Violence and the Law

■ The research on people's behavior in crowds poses an interesting moral and legal issue: What is the personal responsibility of individuals who are swept away by mob violence and group pressure? Should the law treat them as harshly as it would treat individuals, or is their responsibility diminished by virtue of being in a crowd? The psychology of mob violence made the news during the 1992 Los Angeles riots that followed the acquittal of four police officers who had beaten the black motorist Rodney King. In the ensuing violence and looting, Damian Williams and three other black men attacked and nearly killed a white man, Reginald Denny. Did their anger at the acquittal of the police officers, and the understandable community outrage that followed, justify their loss of self-control? The jury that served at the men's trial seemed to think so.

In the late 1980s, British social psychologist Andrew Colman (1991a, 1991b) appeared as an expert witness in two murder trials in South Africa. In one, eight black railway workers had pleaded guilty to the murder of four black strike-breakers during a bitter industrial dispute. In the other, six black residents of an impoverished township were accused of the murder of an 18-year-old black woman who was having an affair with a hated black police officer. She was "necklaced"—a tire was placed around her neck and set afire—during a community protest against the police that got out of control. The crowd danced and sang as she burned to ashes.

Colman testified about the social-psychological processes that he believed should be considered extenuating circumstances in these cases, including conformity, obedience to authority, deindividuation, and other aspects of crowd psychology. "Each of these social forces on its own," he wrote

(1991b), "is powerful and can lead people to behave in ways that are not characteristic of their normal behaviour. . . . Anything that helps to explain a person's behaviour could potentially have a bearing on the moral blameworthiness of that behaviour."

Colman's testimony was not intended to acquit the defendants, who had all been found guilty, but to keep them from being executed. In this, he was successful. In the first case, only four of the eight were sentenced to death, and an appeals court commuted those sentences on the grounds that the psychological evidence of extenuating circumstances had not been disproved by the prosecutor. In the second case, all six had their death sentences commuted to 20 months of imprisonment.

Colman regards the successful use of social-psychological findings as a major breakthrough for law and justice, but other psychologists and social critics are worried that such findings could also be used to exonerate the guilty. Pumla Gobodo-Madikizela (1994), an African social scientist, interviewed some of the men accused of the necklacing and didn't find them quite so "deindividuated" after all. Some were tremendously upset, were well aware of their actions and choices, actively debated the woman's guilt, thought about running away, and consciously tried to rationalize their behavior. More important, she adds, "If nobody can be held culpable, it would be an open invitation to resort to vigilante justice. Surely, the thugs of the world who prefer to act in groups should be found guilty when they knowingly and willingly kill their declared 'enemies.'"

This issue alerts us to the problem, raised in various places throughout this book, between under-

Just as extreme deindividuation has its hazards, however, so does extreme individuation. People can become *too* self-aware and self-focused, and forget their dependence on others. The whole notion of whether deindividuation is good or bad is strongly influenced by culture. Some cultures emphasize the importance of individual action; others emphasize the importance of social harmony. Asians are on the average less individuated than whites, blacks, and Latinos, reflecting the Asian cultural emphasis on social harmony (Maslach, Stapp, & Santee, 1985).

Groupthink and Group Thinking

Group members who like each other and share attitudes often enjoy working together. But all groups face the problem of getting the best ideas and efforts of their members while reducing the risk of social loafing and conformity. In particular, they must avoid a problem called **groupthink,** the tendency for all members of the group to think alike and to suppress dissent.

▪ **groupthink**
In close-knit groups, the tendency for all members to think alike for the sake of harmony and to suppress disagreement.

standing behavior and excusing it. Deindividuation certainly helps us understand why people in crowds do things they would never do on their own, but should they therefore be exempt from punishment? If not, what punishment is appropriate? Before you answer, you might consider that if you support a "deindividuation defense" because you sympathize with the defendants, you will need to support the same defense when you are unsympathetic to the defendants. Deindividuation may characterize a mob of oppressed people rioting to protest living conditions, but it also characterizes members of the Ku Klux Klan out on a raid, soldiers committing mass rapes in Bosnia, and the South African whites who went on bloody rampages before the 1994 elections, shooting black civilians.

As Gobodo-Madikizela (1994) says, "Psychologists must separate scientific findings from our political preferences, no matter how distasteful the political consequences."

Finally, remember that in every crowd, there are always people who don't go along, who remain individuated. During the same riot in which Reginald Denny was attacked, two African-Americans, Terri Barnett and Gregory Alan Williams, rescued a white man from the same fate, and many other black people came to the aid of white and Latino passersby. Does that information affect your reaction to the deindividuation defense? We can be sure that the issue of personal responsibility and psychological understanding will return frequently in the news. ▪

Millions remember the sight on television of Reginald Denny being bludgeoned by Damian Williams during the 1992 Los Angeles riots. Yet even under conditions of anonymity, many people retain their individuality and moral courage. Terri Barnett and Gregory Alan Williams, along with other African-Americans, were honored at City Hall for rescuing whites who were in danger.

How not to lead a group.

■ **group polarization**

The tendency for a group's decision to be more extreme than its members' individual decisions.

According to Irving Janis (1982, 1989), groupthink occurs when a group's need for total agreement overwhelms its need to make the wisest decision, and when the members' needs to be liked and accepted overwhelm their ability to disagree with a bad decision. Two instances of groupthink in American history resulted in disastrous military decisions. In 1961, President John F. Kennedy, after meeting with his advisers, approved a CIA plan to invade Cuba at the Bay of Pigs and overthrow the government of Fidel Castro; the invasion was a humiliating disaster. In the mid-1960s, President Lyndon Johnson and his cabinet escalated the war in Vietnam in spite of obvious signs that further bombing and increased troops were not bringing the war to an end.

To study groupthink, Janis (1982) examined the historical records pertaining to these two decisions. He argued that groupthink has several identifiable features. First, to preserve harmony and to stay in the leader's good graces, group members avoid thinking of alternatives to the leader's initial preference. Instead of generating as many solutions to a problem as possible, they stick with the first one. Second, members don't want to disagree with each other or make their friends look bad, so they don't examine this initial preference closely for errors or flaws. They suppress their own misgivings, which creates an illusion of unanimity. Third, the group avoids getting any outside information from experts that might challenge its views, and it suppresses dissent within the group. (President Johnson, who favored increased bombing of North Vietnam, ridiculed his adviser Bill Moyers by greeting him with "Well, here comes Mr. Stop-the-Bombing.") The result is that everyone remains in a "tight little ship," even if the ship is about to sink. Groupthink can sometimes be counteracted, however, under conditions that explicitly encourage and reward the expression of doubt and dissent (Janis, 1989); if group members are not worried about how they are being evaluated by others (Paulus & Dzindolet, 1993); and if the group's decision is based on majority rule instead of a demand for unanimity (Kameda & Sugimori, 1993).

Some researchers today dislike the term *groupthink* because, catchy and compelling though it is, they believe it oversimplifies the complexities of group decision making and implies that conformity and group cohesiveness are always bad. Ramon Aldag and Sally Fuller (1993) argue that it is easy to see *retrospectively* how conformity contributes to making a bad decision, as Janis did in studying disastrous political decisions. It is harder to specify the complex conditions under which a group will make good or bad decisions in the future. Conformity and cohesion are not the only contributions to such decisions. In reviewing the decade of research since Janis's classic study, Aldag and Fuller consider the many factors that affect a group's decision. These include its history; its cohesiveness and homogeneity; the nature of the decision to be made; the characteristics of the leader; the context in which the group is making the decision; whether the group is permanent or temporary; whether the group is subject to outside pressures; the members' political agendas; organizational politics and policies; and so forth. Nevertheless, Janis certainly put his finger on a phenomenon that many people have experienced in groups: individual members suppressing their real opinions and doubts so as to be a good team player.

Another influence on group decisions is a phenomenon called **group polarization.** Polarization does not mean that a group becomes split between two poles. It means that the group's *average* decision is more extreme than its members' individual decisions would be (Lord, Ross, & Lepper, 1979; Miller et al., 1993). Here is an example. Suppose a man with a serious heart ailment is offered an operation that could cure him or kill him. Should the man have the operation if his chances of dying are one in ten, three in ten, nine in ten? Years ago, a graduate student was studying the effects of group discussion on decisions such as this one (Stoner, 1961). He found that on their own, people tended to be cautious about recommending surgery, but when they discussed the matter in a group, they made riskier recommendations. This result came to be called "the risky shift." It was invoked to explain irrational company decisions, mob madness, and the Bay of Pigs invasion. Since then, researchers have learned that the direction of the group's decision depends, in part, on the topic being debated. Some topics bring out the risky side, but others, such as marriage or one's own illness, tend to bring out caution. The direction of polarization also depends on how many people in the group were *initially* leaning toward risky or conservative decisions.

Once the group starts talking, polarization occurs for several reasons. First, some people intensify their opinions once they realize that others not only agree with them but also are even stronger in their convictions. Second, people are likely to start thinking of arguments that will support their views. As arguments increase in favor of risk or caution, the shift toward the extreme appears to be the only rational or logical choice (Kaplan & Miller, 1983). Third, as people talk in a group, they may become aware of inconsistencies in their own thinking and resolve them in favor of a stronger, more polarized position (Chaiken & Yates, 1985). Nevertheless, certain topics seem immune to group polarization, particularly when group members are experiencing a conflict about values (Liberman & Chaiken, 1991). For example, in an experiment in which students debated affirmative action, no polarization occurred. The researchers speculate that the topic evoked conflicting values: The students favored justice for minorities that had suffered discrimination, but they also were opposed to "discriminating" against deserving members of the majority (Miller et al., 1993).

One kind of group whose decisions have especially important consequences is the jury, 12 individuals who must agree on conviction or acquittal. What are the effects of group discussion on their collective decision? Usually, the verdict initially favored by a majority of the members is the one that eventually wins, as group polarization would predict. When the group is equally split, however, most juries show a *leniency bias:* The more the group talks, the more lenient its verdict. One reason is that jurors who favor acquittal are more influential than jurors who favor conviction. Why might this be so? The "reasonable doubt" standard—a person is innocent unless proven guilty beyond a reasonable doubt—favors acquittal; it is easier to raise one doubt than to refute all doubts. But when juries are instructed to arrive at a verdict based on "a preponderance of evidence that the defendant committed the crime," the leniency bias vanishes (MacCoun & Kerr, 1988). If you ever serve on a jury, you might keep these findings in mind!

Other researchers remind us that just as groups influence individuals, individuals influence groups (Wood et al., 1994). Group members who hold minority opinions do not have the same power as the majority, but they can sometimes persuade and change the majority. Considering, as Serge Moscovici (1985) puts it, that the minority starts off being viewed as "deviant, incompetent, unreasonable, unappealing, and unattractive," how *does* it influence the group?

One strategy is repetition. Repeated minority arguments are like drops of water eroding a rock. Eventually, as such arguments become familiar, they seem less outrageous—an instance of the validity effect, perhaps, but also, sometimes, a sign that the idea does have validity! Recycling, for example, was once thought to be a weirdo radical extremist proposal, but today it is practiced by countless households and is an integral part of many cities' waste-management programs. A second strategy for making deviant opinions more persuasive is by expressing such views firmly, consistently, and articulately. A third strategy is to find allies in the group, which makes minority members seem less deviant or rebellious and their ideas more legitimate. Dissenters are disruptive to a group, but they force the group to become aware of other ideas and solutions (Wood et al., 1994). By undermining the majority's complacency, dissenters may move the group to more independent and innovative ideas.

✳ *In the United States, most people assume that competition, in everything from Little League to big business, is a good thing. Why, then, do some psychologists think that "healthy competition" is a contradiction in terms?*

Competition and Cooperation

If you want to make some money, play the dollar auction with a few friends. Everyone must bid for your dollar in 5-cent increases, and the auction is over when there is no new bid for 30 seconds. The catch is this: The second-highest bidder must also pay you, although he or she will get nothing in return. Usually, the bidding soon narrows to two competitors. After one of them has bid $1.00, the other decides to bid $1.05, because she would rather pay $1.05 for your dollar than give you $.95 for nothing. Following the same logic, the person who bid $1.00 decides to go to $1.10. By the time they quit, you may have won $5 or $6. Your bidders will have been trapped by the nature of competition—and of entrapment. Both will want to win; both will fear losing; both will try to save face. Had they thought of cooperation, however, they would both have won. The bidders could have agreed to set a limit on the bidding, say 45 cents, and split the profits.

During a competitive game, participants and spectators are involved and energized, and they have a good time. Competition in business and science can lead to better services and products and new inventions. Yet there are some psychological hazards to competition, whether between individuals or between groups. When winning is everything, competitors may find no joy in being second or even being in the activity at all.

After reviewing the huge number of studies on the effects of competition, Alfie Kohn (1992) concluded that "the phrase *healthy competition* is a contradiction in terms." Competition, research shows, often decreases work motivation. It makes people feel insecure and anxious, even if they win; it fosters jealousy and hostility; and it can stifle achievement. Because competition is "the common denominator of American life," Kohn maintains, we rarely pause to notice its negative effects. And we rarely notice that in practice, most businesses depend on cooperation among employees, and that cooperation is often economically beneficial to all participants. In 1993, the three rival companies that had been competing for the right to develop high-definition television (HDTV) agreed to join forces to design a single approach. With that decision, they avoided litigation and disputes that would have delayed HDTV for years.

Years ago, Muzafer Sherif and his colleagues used a natural setting, a Boy Scout camp called Robbers Cave, to conduct an experiment on the effects of cooperation and competition (Sherif, 1958; Sherif et al., 1961). Sherif randomly assigned 11- and 12-year-old boys to two groups, the Eagles and the Rattlers. To build team spirit, each group worked on communal projects, such as making a rope bridge and building a diving board. Sherif then put the teams in competition for prizes. During fierce games of football, baseball, and tug-of-war, the boys whipped up a competitive fever that spilled off of the playing fields. They began to raid each other's cabins, call each other names, and start fistfights. No one dared to have a friend from the opposite gang. Before long, the Rattlers and the Eagles were as hostile toward each other as any two rival gangs fighting for turf, any two siblings fighting for a parent's attention, and any two nations fighting for dominance. Their hostility continued even when they were just sitting around together watching movies.

So far, Sherif had done nothing more than a typical Little League competition might do. But then he determined to undo the hostility he had created and to make peace between the Eagles and Rattlers. The experimenters set up situations in which both groups needed to work together to reach a desired goal. The boys had to cooperate to get the water supply system working. They had to pool their resources to get a movie they all wanted to see. When the staff truck broke down on a camping trip, they all had to join forces to pull the truck up a steep hill and get it started again. This policy of *interdependence in reaching mutual goals* was highly successful in reducing the boys' competitiveness and hostility. The boys eventually made friends among their former enemies.

Interdependence has a similar effect in adult groups. When adults work together in a cooperative group in which teamwork is rewarded, they often like each other better and are less hostile than when they are competing for individual success (Deutsch, 1949, 1980). Cooperation causes people to think of themselves as members of one big group instead of two opposed groups, *us* and *them* (Gaertner et al., 1990). Organizational psychologists have found that in many companies, employees do better, and their motivation is higher, when they work in cooperative teams than when they work competitively or alone. For example, an alternative to the standard boring assembly line is to have factory employees work in groups and handle different aspects of assembling the product instead of one repeated routine. This approach has been tried successfully by Volvo, General Foods, Sherwin-Williams, and Saab (Sundstrom, De Meuse, & Futrell, 1990).

In the first stage of the Robbers Cave study, a harmonious atmosphere was created through cooperation and teamwork. In the photo on the left, the Rattlers build solidarity carrying canoes to the lake. In the second stage, rivalry was created through competitive games such as tug-of-war (middle photo), which fostered stereotyping and hostility between the Rattlers and the Eagles. Finally, in stage three, cooperation was again established when the two groups had to work together to solve various problems, such as repairing the camp's water supply system (right).

Quick QUIZ

A. Identify which phenomenon—deindividuation, group polarization, diffusion of responsibility, or groupthink—is represented in each of the following four situations.

1. The president's closest advisers are afraid to disagree with his views on arms negotiations.
2. You are at a Halloween party wearing a silly gorilla suit. When you see a chance to play a practical joke on the host, you do it.
3. You invite four friends out for pizza to help you decide the merits of a new job offer. After talking things over with them, you agree to quit your safe job for a new one that offers greater challenge but has a risk of failure.
4. Walking down a busy street, you see that fire has broken out in a store window. "Someone must have called the fire department," you say.

B. What strategy does the Robbers Cave study suggest for reducing hostility between groups?

Answers:

A. 1. groupthink 2. deindividuation 3. group polarization 4. diffusion of responsibility B. the fostering of interdependence in reaching mutual goals

Sometimes a lone dissenter can change history. In 1956 in Montgomery, Alabama, Rosa Parks, weary after a hard day's work, refused to give up her seat and move to the back of a bus as the segregation laws of the time required. She was arrested, fingerprinted, and convicted of violating the law. Her calm defiance touched off a boycott in which the black citizens of Montgomery refused to ride city buses. It took them over a year, but they won—and the civil rights movement began.

▪ ALTRUISM AND DISSENT: THE CONDITIONS OF INDEPENDENT ACTION

Throughout history, men and women have often obeyed orders or conformed to ideas that they believed to be misguided or immoral; sometimes, however, people have disobeyed such orders or gone against prevailing beliefs. Many blacks and whites disobeyed the laws of segregation. Many individuals have stopped conforming to traditional gender roles. Many men and women "blow the whistle" on practices they consider immoral or unfair, risking their jobs and friendships to do so (Glazer & Glazer, 1990).

Altruism, the willingness to take selfless or dangerous action on behalf of others, is in part a matter of personal belief and conscience. The Quakers and other white abolitionists who risked their lives to help blacks escape their captors before the Civil War did so because they believed in the inherent evil of slavery. In the former Soviet Union, a KGB officer named Viktor Orekhov began to secretly inform political dissidents of planned KGB action against them, thereby saving hundreds of people from arrests and grueling interrogations. Orekhov was eventually caught and spent eight years in a Soviet jail. On his release, he explained why he felt he had to help the protesters: "I was afraid that [unless I acted] my children would be ashamed of me" (Fogelman, 1994).

Studies of individuals who have saved the lives of others find that two motives sustain the rescuers: deeply held moral values or personal feelings for the victim (Fogelman, 1994; Oliner & Oliner, 1988). The second motive is obviously at work when someone rescues a friend or colleague whom they know and like. Sometimes, however, rescuers are willing to save people whom they consider boring, demanding, or otherwise unpleasant! In such cases, the rescuers' moral values—their belief in the importance of saving a human being in danger—supersede their personal feelings. Do you think that you could ever be a hero? (For a discussion of this question, see "Think About It" on page 656.)

However, just as there are many social and situational reasons for obedience and conformity, so there are many social and situational influences on a person's decision to dissent, speak up for an unpopular opinion, or help a stranger in trouble. Instead of condemning bystanders and conformists for their "laziness" or "cowardice," social psychologists investigate these social and situational predictors of independent action. They have used a variety of methods to do so.

For example, some have set up experimental situations in which they can vary the conditions under which a bystander observes another person in trouble: alone or with other people, when the victim is anonymous or when the bystander empathizes with the victim, and so forth (Dovidio, Allen, & Schroeder, 1990; Latané & Darley, 1976). Others have gone into the field and interviewed people in actual work settings. In one study of 8,587 federal government employees, employees were asked whether they had observed any wrongdoing at work, whether they told anyone about it, and what happened if they told (Graham, 1986). Nearly half of the sample had personally observed some serious cases of wrongdoing, such as someone stealing federal funds, accepting bribes, or creating a situation that was dangerous to public safety. Of that half, 72 percent had done nothing at all. What made the rest different?

According to evidence from many field and laboratory studies, several factors predict independent action such as whistle-blowing and altruism:

1. *The individual perceives the need for intervention or help.* Many bystanders see no need to help someone in trouble. Sometimes this willful blindness is used to justify inaction. During World War II, the German citizens of Dachau didn't "see" the local concentration camp, although it was in plain view. Similarly, many employees choose not to see flagrant examples of bribery and other illegal actions.

Sometimes, however, the blindness is an inevitable result of screening out too many demands on attention. People who live in a big city cannot stop to help everyone who seems to need it; people who have many demands on their time at work cannot stop to correct every problem they notice. Indeed, a study of 36 small, medium, and large American cities found that the strongest predictor of whether people would help strangers with small favors (such as making change for a quarter or helping a person with a leg brace pick up a heavy stack of spilled magazines) was not population *size,* but population *density* (Levine et al., 1994). Density both increases the sensory overload on people and makes them more deindividuated.

Whether people interpret a situation as requiring their aid also depends on cultural rules. In northern European nations and in the United States, husband–wife disputes are considered strictly private; neighbors intervene at their peril. In one field study, bystanders observed a (staged) fight between a man and a woman. When the woman yelled, "Get away from me; I don't know you!" two-thirds of the bystanders went to help her. When she shouted, "Get away from me; I don't know why I ever married you!" only 19 percent tried to help (Shotland & Straw, 1976). In Mediterranean and Latin cultures, however, a dispute between any two people is considered fair game for anyone who is passing by. In fact, two people in a furious dispute might even *rely* on bystanders to intervene (Hall & Hall, 1990).

2. *The individual decides to take responsibility.* In a large crowd of observers or in a large organization, it is easy for people to avoid action. Crowds of anonymous people encourage the diffusion of responsibility because everyone assumes that someone else will take charge. When people are alone and hear someone call for help, they usually do intervene (Latané & Darley, 1976). Bystanders are also more likely to take responsibility when they are in a good mood—and when they are thinking of themselves as kind people (Brown & Smart, 1991). Similarly, whistle-blowers take personal responsibility for doing something about the ethical violations they have observed (Glazer & Glazer, 1990).

3. *The individual decides that the costs of doing nothing outweigh the costs of getting involved.* The cost of helping or protesting might be embarrassment and wasted time or, more seriously, lost income, loss of friends, and even personal danger. The cost of not helping or remaining silent might be guilt, blame from others, loss of honor, or, in some tragic cases, responsibility for the injury or death of others. Although three courageous whistle-blowers from Rockwell International tried to inform NASA that the space shuttle *Challenger* was not safe, the NASA authorities remained silent. No one was prepared to take responsibility for the unpopular and expensive decision to postpone the launch. The cost of their silence was a disastrous explosion and the deaths of the entire crew.

Three courageous whistle-blowers from Rockwell International—Ria Solomon, Sylvia Robins, and Al Bray—tried to inform NASA that the space shuttle Challenger *was not safe.*

Some psychologists believe that all acts of helpfulness and moral protest are ultimately selfish, even if one person helps another in order to feel like a moral and decent soul. Others argue that life is full of countless illustrations of true altruism, in which people help others out of empathy and concern, without weighing costs or benefits at all (Batson, 1990). Bystanders who feel a moral obligation to the victim or who empathize with the victim are more likely to take responsibility for helping (Batson et al., 1988; Dovidio, Allen, & Schroeder, 1990). Likewise, whistle-blowers believe that loyalty to their company or country is best expressed by correcting its mistakes, not by ignoring them (Glazer & Glazer, 1990).

4. *The individual has an ally.* In Asch's experiment, the presence of one other person who gave the correct answer was enough to overcome conformity to the incorrect majority. In Milgram's experiment, too, the presence of a peer who disobeyed sharply increased the number of subjects who also disobeyed. One dissenting member of a group may be viewed as a troublemaker, but two dissenting members are a coalition, and enough dissenting members can become a majority. Having an ally reassures a person of the rightness of the protest, and their combined efforts may eventually persuade others (Moscovici, 1985).

5. *The individual feels competent.* People who intervene to help others or to blow the whistle feel that they have the skills and knowledge to do so. This sense

Think About It

Could You Be a Hero—and Should You Be?

- You are working for an organization that you like very much. Your job is to supervise the safe installation of toxic-waste cleanup systems. But after a while, you learn that your immediate supervisor is taking bribes from companies that do not want to pay the cost of cleaning up their wastes. What would you do?
- You are witness to a violent crime in a grocery store. The robber sees you and threatens your life if you identify him. When the police arrive to question witnesses, what would you do?
- You are home one evening and hear a commotion in the street outside. You look outside, and see a man attacking a woman. What would you do?

In truth, none of us really knows how we would behave in an emergency or when faced with a moral dilemma. The lesson of social psychology is that group pressure, conformity, and the power of social roles will influence people's behavior in many situations more than their attitudes or preferences will. This is why psychiatrists and laypeople alike were so wildly wrong in their predictions about how many people would "go all the way" in the Milgram experiment: They overlooked the compelling nature of social roles and obedience to authority. If you were to predict your behavior based on the statistics for most people, you would keep quiet about your employer's illegal behavior, lie to the police, and go back to watching television without even calling 911.

Perhaps for this reason, many people are suspicious of rescuers, Good Samaritans, whistle-blowers, and others who take action in a crisis. When Eva Fogelman (1994) began lecturing on the non-Jewish rescuers of Jews during the Holocaust, she noticed that her stories "had a disquieting effect on many listeners. Rescuers' altruistic behavior throws people off balance by calling into question their own vision of themselves as good people. As they listen, they cannot help but wonder: What would I have done? Would I have had the courage to defy authority? Would I have risked my life? My family's lives?" She added,

General audiences listened, they wondered, and they doubted their own capacity for selfless action. This discomfort, in turn, led to a disbelief that anyone could engage in altruistic behavior.

of competence turns up in studies of people who rescue others from political persecution, who protest wrongdoing on the job, and who help in street emergencies. Of 32 people who had directly intervened in real criminal episodes, for example, all said they felt certain they could handle the dangerous situation. Many had been trained in police work, first aid, or self-defense (Huston et al., 1981).

6. *The individual becomes entrapped.* Once having taken the initial step of getting involved, most people will increase their commitment. In the study of federal employees who had witnessed wrongdoing, 28 percent reported the problem to their immediate supervisors. Once they had taken that step, nearly 60 percent eventually took the matter to higher authorities (Graham, 1986). Many non-Jewish rescuers of Jews said that once they had taken action to aid one person, even in a small way, they could not avoid helping others. Because they could be arrested or shot for helping one Jew, they reasoned, they might as well rescue as many as possible (Fogelman, 1994).

As you can see, independent action is not only a spontaneous or selfless expression of a desire to do the right thing. There are social conditions that make altruism and dissent more likely to occur, just as there are conditions that suppress them. How do you think you would behave if you were faced with a conflict between social pressure and conscience?

People looked for ulterior motives. . . . "What's the angle?" they want to know. Many young people simply do not believe that there were then, or are today, individuals who do not put their own concerns first.

The decision to intervene to rescue someone in trouble, blow the whistle on wrongdoing, or help the needy is not an easy matter of right or wrong. In big cities across the nation and increasingly in small towns, helping strangers in trouble can sometimes be dangerous, even fatal. A Good Samaritan in San Francisco intervened in an angry dispute between two men in the street and was stabbed to death as a consequence; he had interrupted a quarrel between drug dealers. In cities where homeless persons number in the thousands, many people are feeling "compassion fatigue": How many can they help? What kind of help is best? It is easier to be a whistle-blower or to protest a company policy when you know it will be easy to find another job, but what if jobs in your field are scarce and you have a family to support?

As research in this chapter shows, people can end up doing all sorts of harmful things they would never have predicted doing, and then call on self-serving attributions, excuses, and belief in a just world to rationalize their behavior. On the other hand, research also shows that people can end up doing all sorts of helpful and courageous things they would never have imagined doing. What anyone does in a given situation depends on a particular constellation of personal beliefs and perceptions, personality traits, and aspects of the situation itself. This is why a man may leap into a frozen river to rescue a child on Monday and embezzle money from his company on Friday.

So: *Would* you blow the whistle on your boss, tell the truth to the police although worried about your safety, and call 911 when you see a fight? What aspects of the situation would influence your responses, and what aspects of your own personality and beliefs? Can you imagine situations in which you could not live with yourself if you failed to help, and if so, what are they? Do you agree with Eva Fogelman that some people truly are humanitarian and selfless in their willingness to rescue others in distress, or do you side with the skeptics who want to know "What's the angle?" Think about it. ■

Quick QUIZ

Imagine that you are chief executive officer of a new electric-car company. You want your employees to feel free to offer their suggestions and criticisms to improve productivity and satisfaction, and to inform managers if they find any evidence that your cars are unsafe, even if that means delaying production. What concepts from this chapter could you use in setting company policy?

Answers:

Some possibilities: Set up cooperative production teams based on teamwork rather than competition; reward individual innovation and suggestions by paying attention to them and implementing the best ones; encourage and acknowledge deviant ideas; stimulate commitment to the task (building a car that will solve the world's pollution problem!); establish a written policy to protect whistle-blowers. What else can you think of?

▪ THE QUESTION OF HUMAN NATURE

Adolf Eichmann at his trial. Was he a "monster"?

A man was on trial for murder, although he personally had never killed anyone. Six psychiatrists examined him and found him sane. His family life was normal and he had deep feelings of love for his wife, children, and parents. Two observers, after reviewing transcripts of his 275-hour interrogation, described him as "an average man of middle class origins and normal middle class upbringing, a man without identifiable criminal tendencies" (Von Lang & Sibyll, 1984).

The man was Adolf Eichmann, a high-ranking officer of the Nazi SS (an elite military unit of storm troopers). Eichmann supervised the deportation and death of millions of Jews during World War II. He was proud of his efficiency at his work and his ability to resist the temptation to feel pity for his victims. But he insisted he was not anti-Semitic: He had had a Jewish mistress, and he personally arranged for the protection of his Jewish half-cousin—two dangerous crimes for an SS officer. Shortly before his execution by hanging, Eichmann said, "I am not the monster I am made out to be. I am the victim of a fallacy" (Brown, 1986).

The fallacy to which Eichmann referred was the widespread belief that a person who does monstrous deeds must be a monster—someone sick, insane, evil, cruel. But as we have seen, otherwise good people can and do behave in monstrous ways. When philosopher Hannah Arendt (1963) wrote about the trial of Adolph Eichmann, she used the phrase "the banality of evil" to describe this phenomenon. (*Banal* means "commonplace" or "unoriginal.") Eichmann and his fellow Nazis were ordinary men, Arendt wrote, just doing their jobs.

This is, perhaps, the hardest lesson in psychology. Most people want to believe that harm to others is done only by evil people who are bad down to their bones. It is reassuring to divide the world into those who are good or bad, kind or mean, moral or immoral. Yet the evidence is overwhelming that perfectly nice people can behave in brutal, conforming, and mindless ways if the situation demands. From the standpoint of social psychology, such universal problems as mob violence, bystander apathy, and groupthink are not a result of human nature but of human social organization. They are a result of the *normal psychological processes* discussed in this chapter, such as adherence to roles, obedience to authority, vulnerability to self-serving biases, conformity, entrapment, deindividuation, and competition.

This is good news and bad news. The bad news is that bad behavior cannot be eliminated by getting rid of a few "bad" people or nations, because the conditions that produce deindividuation, groupthink, and war will always be with us. The good news is that situations can be created that encourage considerate and helpful behavior, independent action, and constructive dissent. If social conditions have created the banality of evil, others can be used to foster the "banality of virtue"—everyday acts of kindness, selflessness, and generosity.

✹ *People often disagree about whether human beings are basically cooperative and good or basically selfish and cruel. With the question stated that way, the only answer is both—or neither. What would be a better question, and a more useful answer?*

Taking Psychology with You

Swimming in a Sea of Ads

From time to time, we ask our classes to do a seemingly simple field study: From the time you get up to the time you go to sleep, count the number of ads you see or hear. This includes television, radio, and newspaper ads, of course, but also hidden ads such as giant product names on T-shirts and on the walls surrounding sports arenas, or the names of product sponsors of various events. If you try this assignment, chances are that you won't finish it: There are just too many ads to count. Indeed, in a single year, the average American watches more than 37,000 TV commercials, gets more than 200 pieces of direct-mail ads, and hears from at least 50 telemarketers by phone (Aronson, Wilson, & Akert, 1994).

In a nation dominated by advertising, where so many are trying to get you to buy their product—whether their product is soap, cereal, a candidate for political office, a ballot proposition, or support for a cause—how can you determine which ads are useful and which are manipulative? Social psychologists have discovered not only which kinds of ads are effective and for which people, but also how you can resist manipulation (Aronson, Wilson, & Akert, 1994; Pratkanis & Aronson, 1992):

- *Beware of the validity effect.* Are you feeling favorably inclined toward a product or candidate simply because you have heard the name a zillion times? Test yourself by asking what you actually know about the product's unique benefits or the candidate's actual voting record. For example, is there any difference in the ingredients of generic drugs and brand-name drugs? Are you as informed about the voting record and political goals of candidates who don't have as much money to spend on their campaigns as the most familiar candidate does?

- *Assess your actual need for the product.* Early in this century, a man named Gerald Lambert inherited a

company that made an antiseptic for treating throat infections. The product was called Listerine. Lambert decided to expand the market for Listerine by promoting it as a mouthwash. Trouble was, nobody used mouthwash in those days, so Lambert had to invent a reason for them to do it. He made up a medical-sounding term to describe bad breath— "halitosis"—and advertised Listerine as the cure for it. His ads played on people's insecurities about their personal hygiene, health, and attractiveness. So do many ads today. For example, ads for "rejuvenation" creams, which often claim to contain miracle ingredients with scientific-sounding labels, play to people's fears of aging.

- *Beware of emotion-based advertising and political campaigns.* Many ads for practical products such as computers, air conditioners, and cameras are useful; they tell you about the product's price, reliability, and quality. But choosing a particular brand of jeans, perfume, athletic shoes, or cola is mostly a matter of personal taste. So, to win your allegiance, advertisers associate these products with happy emotions, a cool lifestyle, sexiness, sex appeal, and good looks. In other words, they try to generate emotional responses in you that have nothing to do with the product itself. One ad campaign was designed to get young men to drink diet cola. This was a challenge: Diet cola is not a macho drink! So the ad showed a handsome, suitably macho construction worker with an officeful of women ogling him as he took his diet-cola break.

  Many political campaigns increasingly are based on invoking emotions—fear of crime, fear and hatred of "outsiders," passionate reactions to hot-button topics such as the death penalty—rather than providing information. Often, these ads tell a single inflammatory story, such as one about a paroled felon who commits rape or murder, to accuse the opposition of being "soft on crime." But critical thinkers should be wary of arguing by anecdote and should not be swayed by one story, no matter how sensational or infuriating it is.

- *Think critically about conformity and peer pressure.* As we have seen, the desire to feel part of a group is universal and necessary in human societies. Some ads, however, play on people's insecurities about being outsiders. The result is that many people buy products they don't need or can't afford in the hopes that the product will help them fit in.

- *Be mindful.* The bottom line in evaluating any message designed to persuade you to change your mind, buy a product, or vote for a candidate is to keep your wits about you. In *The Age of Propaganda,* Anthony Pratkanis and Elliot Aronson (1992) suggest the kinds of mindful questions people can ask that will help inoculate them against manipulative messages: "What does the source of communication have to gain? Why are these choices being presented to me in this manner? Are there other options and other ways of presenting those options? What would happen if I chose something other than the recommended option? What are the arguments for the other side?"

We do not wish to imply that all advertising is misleading or fraudulent, and that you should believe nothing you hear. On the contrary, many ads contain useful information. Without ads, new products could never get a foothold in the noisy marketplace, and unknown candidates could never become visible to voters. Like obedience, conformity, and groupthink, the effort to persuade is itself neither good nor bad. Persuasive tactics can be used to twist the facts or to expose the facts. The goal is to use ads wisely, and not to let them use you.

Summary

1. Social psychology is the study of people in social context, including the influences of *norms, roles,* and groups on behavior and cognition. Three studies illustrate the power of roles to affect individual personality and values. In Zimbardo's prison study, college students quickly fell into the role of "prisoner" or "guard." In Rosenhan's mental-hospital study, the role of staff member caused nurses and psychiatrists to *depersonalize* patients and sometimes treat them harshly. In Milgram's obedience study, people in the role of "teacher" inflicted what they thought was extreme shock to another person in the role of "learner" because of the authority of the experimenter.

2. Obedience to authority has many important positive functions for the smooth running of society, but obedience can lead to actions that are deadly, foolish, or illegal. People obey orders not only because they may be punished for disobedience, but also because they believe the authority is legitimate; because the role is routinized into duties that are performed mindlessly; because they are embarrassed to break the rules of good manners and lack a language of protest to do so; or because they have been *entrapped.*

3. According to *attribution theory,* people are motivated to explain their own and other people's actions. They may attribute actions to the *situation* or to a person's *disposition* (qualities in the person). The *fundamental attribution error* occurs when people overestimate personality traits as a cause of behavior and underestimate the situation. A *self-serving bias* allows people to excuse their own mistakes by blaming the situation. According to the *just-world hypothesis,* people need to believe that the world is fair and that people get what they deserve. To preserve this belief, they may *blame the victim* for inviting injustice.

4. People have many *attitudes,* which include cognitions and feelings about a subject. Some attitudes are casual opinions; others are based on carefully elaborated convictions. One important influence on attitudes is a person's age *cohort* and the corresponding experiences that shape the person's *generational identity.* Another influence is the *validity effect:* Simply hearing a statement over and over again makes it seem more believable. Techniques of attitude change include associating a product or message with someone who is famous, attractive, or expert, and linking the product with good feelings. Fear tactics tend to backfire. Attitudes dispose people to behave in certain ways, but sometimes a change of behavior causes attitudes to change.

5. Some methods of attitude change are intentionally manipulative rather than persuasive. Tactics of such *coercive persuasion* include putting a person under extreme distress; defining problems simplistically; offering the appearance of unconditional love and acceptance in exchange for unquestioning loyalty; creating a new identity for the person; using entrapment; and controlling access to outside information.

6. In groups, individuals often behave differently than they would on their own. They *conform* to social pressure because they identify with a group, trust the group's judgment or knowledge, hope for personal gain, or wish to be liked. But they also may conform mindlessly and self-destructively, violating their own preferences and values because "everyone else is doing it."

7. The *diffusion of responsibility* causes group members to work less hard ("social loafing") and to avoid taking responsibility for their decisions and actions. *Deindividuation* is the loss of self- awareness and sense of individuality in a group or crowd; when people are deindividuated and anonymous, they are more inclined to behave aggressively than when they are self-aware. Excessive conformity to a group can produce *groupthink,* the tendency of group members to think alike and to suppress disagreement. In *group polarization,* the group's collective decision is more extreme than its members' private decisions. These group processes have been used to explain foolhardy group decisions, mindless mob violence, and the unwillingness of bystanders to help a stranger in trouble. However, groups can be structured to counteract all of these processes. Also, people who hold minority opinions can influence the larger group by repeating their arguments, expressing their views persuasively, and finding allies.

8. Cooperation and competition have strong effects on attitudes and behavior. Competition often increases hostility, stereotyping, and aggression between groups. Conflict and hostility between groups can be reduced by teamwork and by *interdependence* in working for mutual goals.

9. Dissent, nonconformity, and independent action to help people in danger occur because of qualities of the individual (such as moral values and empathy) and of the situation. Several factors increase *altruistic* behavior: the individual perceives the need to intervene; takes responsibility for helping; has an ally; weighs the costs of doing nothing versus intervening; feels competent to help; and is entrapped.

10. Although it is commonly believed that only bad people do bad deeds, the principles of social psychology show that under certain conditions, good people can be induced to do bad things. By themselves, roles, obedience, conformity, self-serving biases, entrapment, deindividuation, groupthink, and competition are neutral; they can be used positively or negatively.

Key Terms

social psychology *628*
cultural psychology *628*
norms *628*
role *628*
depersonalization *631*
entrapment *635*
social cognition *636*
attribution theory *637*
situational attributions *637*
dispositional attributions *637*
fundamental attribution error
  637
self-serving bias *638*
just-world hypothesis *638*

blaming the victim *638*
attitude *639*
cohort *640*
generational identity *640*
cognitive dissonance *641*
validity effect *641*
coercive persuasion *642*
diffusion of responsibility *646*
social loafing *646*
deindividuation *646*
groupthink *649*
group polarization *650*
altruism *654*
banality of evil *658*

18

The Cultural Context

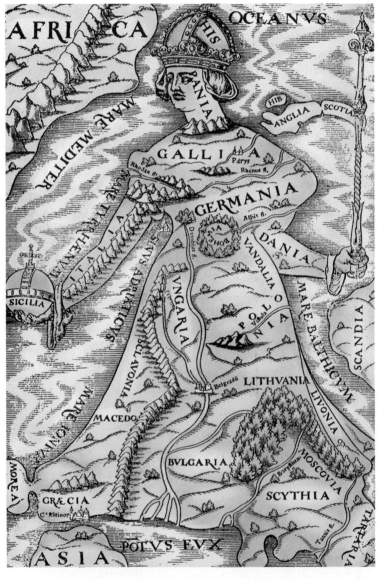

This 1457 map shows Spain as the head and crown of Europe, reflecting the mapmaker's belief that Spain was the most important country in Europe. Ethnocentrism—the belief that one's own culture or ethnic group is superior to all others—is probably universal.

As the traveler who has once been from home is wiser than he who has never left his own doorstep, so a knowledge of one other culture should sharpen our ability to scrutinize more steadily, to appreciate more lovingly, our own.

■ MARGARET MEAD ■

In a suburb of Baton Rouge, Louisiana, in October 1992, Yoshihiro Hattori, a 16-year-old Japanese exchange student, went along with his friend Webb Haymaker to a Halloween party. They mistakenly stopped in front of a house covered in Halloween decorations and rang the bell. Hearing no answer, Yoshihiro went around the side of the house to see if the party might be in the back yard. The home owner, Bonnie Peairs, opened the front door, saw Webb (in a Halloween costume), and then saw Yoshihiro running back toward her waving an object (which turned out to be a camera). She panicked and called for her husband to get his gun. Rodney Peairs grabbed a loaded .44 Magnum and shouted at Yoshihiro to "freeze." Yoshi, not understanding the word, did not stop. Peairs shot him in the heart, killing him instantly. Little more than a minute passed between the time that Yoshi Hattori rang the doorbell and the time that Rodney Peairs shot him to death.

Yoshihiro Hattori and his friends.

When the case came to trial, the jury acquitted Rodney Peairs of manslaughter after only three hours of deliberation.

If ever a tragic misunderstanding illustrated the power of cultural differences, this one is it. To the Japanese news media, the story illustrated everything that is wrong with America. In their view, it is a nation rife with guns and violence—a "developing nation," as one commentator put it, that is still growing out of its wild-west past. Japanese television reporters, in amazement, showed their viewers American gun stores, restaurants that display guns on the walls, and racks of gun magazines. The Japanese cannot imagine a nation in which private individuals are allowed to keep guns. In the entire nation of Japan in 1991, 74 people were killed with guns, almost all of them members of organized crime; in the United States, a person is fatally shot every 16 minutes.

"I think for Japanese the most remarkable thing is that you could get a jury of Americans together, and they could conclude that shooting someone before you even talked to him was reasonable behavior," Masako Notoji, a professor of American cultural studies in Tokyo, told *The New York Times* (May 25, 1993). "We are more civilized. We rely on words." Yet the citizens of Baton Rouge were surprised that the case came to trial at all. What is more right and natural, they said, than protecting oneself and one's family from intruders? "A man's home is his castle," said one potential juror, expressing puzzlement that Peairs had even been arrested. "That's my question—why [was he arrested]?" A local man, joining the many sympathizers of Rodney Peairs, said, "It would be to me what a normal person would do under those circumstances."

Bonnie Peairs wept on the witness stand. "There was no thinking involved," she said. "I wish I could have thought. If I could have just thought."

The clash of American and Japanese cultures, which is so clear in this sad case, shows why it is important to understand what "culture" means and how it influences us. Although we have been describing research on culture throughout this book—for example, in discussions of thinking and intelligence

(Chapter 8), emotion (Chapter 10), child development (Chapter 13), and psychotherapy (Chapter 16)—actually defining it is easier said than done. As cross-cultural psychologist Walter Lonner (1995) observes, "It ranks right up there with truth, beauty, justice, and intelligence as abstract and fuzzy constructs whose precise definitions challenge even the most insightful thinkers."

Lonner himself and most other researchers, however, would agree that **culture** can be generally described as (1) a program of shared rules that govern the behavior of members of a community or society, and (2) a set of values, beliefs, and attitudes shared by most members of that community. Every culture includes a system of rules, passed from one generation to another, for just about everything in the human-made environment: for getting along with other people, for raising children, for making decisions, and for using artifacts (e.g., an ax or a computer) and symbols (e.g., written words or painted images) (Cole, 1990; Lonner, 1995; Lonner & Malpass, 1994; Shweder, 1990).

Cultural psychologists study the many ways in which people are affected by the rules of the culture in which they live. *Cross-cultural psychologists* compare members of different societies, searching both for their commonalities and their specific cultural differences. As we noted in Chapter 1, cultural psychology overlaps somewhat with anthropology, which also studies human groups cross-culturally, and indeed we will be reporting some research from anthropologists. But whereas anthropologists tend to study the economy and customs of a cultural unit as a whole, cultural psychologists are more interested in how culture affects individual psychological and physiological processes, such as the motivation to achieve.

Until recently, most Western psychologists were uninterested in the influence of culture on psychological processes. In contrast to physiology, which they treated as real and tangible, they regarded culture as if it were merely a light veneer on human behavior, or perhaps a source of information for tourist travel ("In Spain, people eat dinner at 10 P.M."). As a result, students and teachers knew little about the psychological characteristics of people living in other societies, and they assumed that they could generalize from studies of people in their own culture to people everywhere (Betancourt & López, 1993; Cole, 1984).

Today, most psychologists recognize that culture is just as powerful an influence on human behavior as any biological process. In fact, culture affects biological processes. Everyone needs to eat, for instance, but culture affects how often people eat, what they eat, and with whom they eat. Depending on your culture, you might eat lots of little meals throughout the day or only one large meal. You will eat food that your culture calls delicious—whale meat in Inuit communities, lizards in South America, locusts in Africa, horses in France, dogs in Asia—and you are likely to find everyone else's food preferences disgusting. You won't eat animals that your culture calls taboo: pigs among Muslims and orthodox Jews, cows in India, horses in America, deer among the Tapirapé (Harris, 1985). And your culture will affect your choice of dining companions. People don't eat with those they consider their social inferiors, such as servants; in some cultures, men do not eat with children or women.

These cultural influences on a process as essential as eating can cause people to eat when they *aren't* hungry (to be sociable) or not to eat when they *are* hungry (because the company or food is culturally "unappetizing"). Sometimes, cultural pressures are in direct conflict with biological dispositions. Evolution has programmed women to maintain a reserve of fat necessary for healthy childbearing, nursing, and, after menopause, the production and storage of the hormone estrogen. And, as we saw in Chapter 3, genes influence body shape and weight. Yet the contemporary cultural ideal for many American women is the boyishly slim body, an ideal that is by no means universal across cultures or across historical epochs. The result of the battle between biological design and cultural standards is that many women are obsessed with weight, continually dieting, excessively exercising, or suffering from eating disorders such as

■ **culture**

A program of shared rules that govern the behavior of members of a community or society, and a set of values, beliefs, and attitudes shared by most members of that community.

Studying a culture other than your own poses many interesting problems. You are by definition an outsider, with different clothes, customs, and attitudes. How can you overcome the distance between you and the people you are studying, while retaining some objective detachment?

anorexia nervosa (self-starvation) or *bulimia* (bingeing and vomiting) (Rodin, Silberstein, & Striegel-Moore, 1990; Silverstein, Peterson, & Perdue, 1986).

If culture can so powerfully affect a person's belief in what is proper behavior, you can imagine why misunderstandings between cultures are so frequent. "Many people have the well-meaning delusion that if they could only get to know people in another culture, they would realize how alike they are," says anthropologist Edward T. Hall. "The truth is that the more you get to know people from another culture, the more you realize how *different* they are" (quoted in Tavris, 1987). In this chapter, we will try to show you what Hall means.

We begin with a discussion of some unique difficulties that the study of culture poses for psychologists. We will then consider some studies that illustrate the influence of culture on certain psychological processes and behaviors not already discussed in this book, ranging from the gestures you make to support your favorite football team to your very identity. These topics, however, create what anthropologist Marvin Harris (1974) calls the "potato chip" problem: Individual cultural customs are fascinating, but there is a tendency to treat them like unconnected chips to munch on. So we will also give you an idea of how cultural psychologists explain cultural practices—where these practices come from, why they change, and what purpose they serve for the society as a whole.

■ STUDYING CULTURE

The study of culture is challenging both for methodological and psychological reasons. Four issues in particular make this kind of research different from other methods and approaches in psychology.

1. *The problem of methods and samples.* Devising good methods and getting good samples is difficult enough when you are studying just one culture; these tasks are even more daunting when you are dealing with many societies and hope to make cultural comparisons. Cross-cultural psychologists must consider many different criteria in selecting their samples: societal (how many societies or cultures should I have?), community (how many groups within each society do I need?), individual (how many individuals within each community shall I select?), and behavioral (which specific actions or attitudes should I measure?) (Lonner & Malpass, 1994).

Some cultural differences can be measured indirectly, by drawing inferences from data about collective behavior such as the frequency of domestic violence, traffic accidents, or suicides (Hofstede & Bond, 1988). In New York, for example, almost everyone jaywalks, but in German cities almost no one jaywalks, a finding that implies a cultural difference in attitudes toward breaking a law governing public behavior. However, indirect measurements permit different interpretations: Perhaps the jaywalking difference doesn't reflect attitudes toward the law but the density of pedestrians and the number of cars per clogged street.

For this reason, many cross-cultural psychologists prefer to use direct measures, such as questionnaires or observations of *matched samples* of respondents from different countries. Matching means that an effort is made to study samples of individuals who are similar in all aspects of their lives except their nationality, including age, socioeconomic status, and education. For example, two researchers, Michael Bond (a psychologist and cross-cultural management trainer for multinational corporations in Hong Kong) and Geert Hofstede (an anthropologist and director of the Institute for Research on International Cooperation in the Netherlands), were able to make use of a remarkable databank of directly obtained cross-cultural information. The IBM corporation had been surveying its employees worldwide, in 53 different cultures and in 20 languages, using standardized questionnaires. Analyzing this rich mine of data on matched samples of IBM employees, Hofstede and Bond (1988) found that members of these 53 cultures differ across four key dimensions: the extent to which they accept and expect an unequal distribution of power in organizations and families; the extent to which they are integrated into groups or are expected to be individualistic; the extent to which they endorse "masculine" values of assertiveness or "feminine" values of nurturance; and, most interesting, the extent to which they can tolerate uncertainty. Cultures that try to minimize or avoid uncertainty, say Hofstede and Bond, tend to adhere to strict laws, rules, and safety and security measures; and, philosophically and religiously, they tend to believe that "There can be only one truth, and we have it." People in cultures that are more tolerant of uncertainty are more accepting of differing behavior, opinions, and religious views.

These differences in values, attitudes toward life and institutions, and beliefs about one's place in society, Hofstede and Bond learned, had implications for business practices (such as whether group loyalty or individual ambition is rewarded, and what style of leadership is most effective) and people's motivations (competition is more effective in "masculine" cultures). By identifying and measuring the precise components of cultural beliefs and practices, they were able to show how "culture" translates into behavior.

2. *The problem of interpreting results.* A second concern in cross-cultural research is linguistic and functional equivalence: You must make sure that your questionnaires and interviews convey the same meanings in every language. This is hard to do. The meaning of "Mary had a little lamb" is obvious to an English speaker, who knows that she owned the lamb and did not give birth to it, eat it, or have an affair with it! But translations can be difficult. Sometimes a concept that is tremendously important in one culture cannot easily be translated into an equivalent term in another culture. In many parts of American society, "dependence" is practically a dirty word, especially for men, but in Japan the need for dependence and nurturing concern for others (*amae*) is assumed to be a powerful and lifelong motive for both sexes, and the word has no real equivalent in English (Doi, 1973). The Chinese Value Survey contains items that seem strange to many Westerners, such as "filial piety," defined as "honoring of ancestors and obedience to, respect for, and financial support of parents" (Bond, 1988; Hofstede & Bond, 1988).

Moreover, a custom in one culture might not have the same meaning or purpose as the same practice elsewhere. For example, the circumcision of male babies has a religious purpose among Jews and serves to strengthen identification with the group, but the same practice became widespread in Europe and

The same behavior may have different functions in different cultures. For the Yanomamo Indians, nose piercing is a part of normal facial decoration and display, but a Westerner might do it to be unusual, rebellious, or shocking.

America during the Victorian era for a very different reason: It was (mistakenly) believed that circumcised boys wouldn't masturbate and thus succumb to "masturbatory insanity" (Paige, 1978; Szasz, 1970). In addition, a custom may persist long after its original function or intention has been abandoned. Circumcision continued in North America, but not in Europe, decades after masturbatory insanity was forgotten as its rationale, because the medical establishment endorsed the procedure in the name of hygiene.

3. *The problem of stereotyping.* A third problem in studying culture is how to identify and describe average differences across societies without stereotyping. As one student of ours put it, "How come when we students speak of 'the' Japanese or 'the' blacks or 'the' whites or 'the' Latinos, it's called stereotyping, and when you do it, it's called 'cross-cultural psychology'?" This question shows excellent critical thinking! The study of culture does not rest on the assumption, implicit in stereotypes, that *all* members of a culture behave the same way. (Later in this chapter, we will discuss the functions and consequences of stereotypes.) As we have seen in this book, individuals vary according to their temperaments, beliefs, and learning histories, and this variation occurs within every culture. Just as people play their social roles differently, they read their cultural scripts differently. But the fact that people carry out their roles in individual ways does not negate the reality of role requirements in general. Likewise, the fact that individuals vary within a culture does not negate the existence of cultural rules that, overall, make Swedes different from Bedouins or Cambodians different from Italians.

Stereotyping affects everyone, including researchers. When she was doing fieldwork with Bedouin women, Lila Abu-Lughod (1992) found considerable divergence among them. She warned that the scientist who strives for general descriptions of behavior "risks smoothing over contradictions, conflicts of interest, doubts and arguments, not to mention changing motivations and historical circumstances." "Smoothing over" contradictions within groups is the essence of stereotyping, and it is important to resist the temptation to do so.

Moreover, if researchers set out to study a culture with a preexisting set of stereotypes, what they expect to find may be what they get (Geis, 1993). In the case of gender, for example, the belief that men are aggressive and women are nurturant has caused numerous researchers to overlook the many examples of male nurturance and female aggression around the world. When David Gilmore (1990) examined how cultures define manhood, he expected to find

Cultural psychologists often use terms such as "the" Japanese or "the" Canadians. What is the difference, if any, between such convenient generic labels and stereotyping?

masculinity equated with selfishness and hardness. Yet by resisting this stereotype, he was able to see that masculinity frequently entails selfless generosity and sacrifice. Men nurture their families and society, he observed, by "bringing home food for both child and mother . . . and by dying if necessary in faraway places to provide a safe haven for their people." Conversely, the fact that men are more likely than women to behave aggressively does not mean that all men, or even most men, are aggressive. Nor does it mean that all women, or even most women, are *not* aggressive. On the average, women are as aggressive as men when "aggression" is defined as saying intentionally cruel and hurtful things; slapping, kicking, biting, or throwing objects during domestic disputes; abusing and humiliating their children; having bellicose attitudes toward their perceived enemies; and supporting and participating in war, in whatever ways their societies have permitted (Campbell, 1993; Elshtain, 1987; Gelles & Straus, 1988).

The moral is that we can study and talk about average differences between groups, but we should try to do so without implying that the groups are as different as chocolate and cheese—or, as one pop-psych book title grandiosely asserts, that *Men Are from Mars, Women Are from Venus.*

4. *The reification of culture.* To *reify* means to regard an intangible process, such as a feeling, as if it were a literal object. For example, when people say, "I have a lot of anger buried in me," they are reifying anger—treating it as a thing that sits inside them like a kidney, instead of as an emotion that comes and goes. In this respect, a fourth concern in the study of cultural psychology is the tendency to reify culture—that is, to regard it as an explanation without identifying the specific mechanisms or aspects of culture that influence behavior (Betancourt & López, 1993). To say "The Japanese work hard because of their culture" or "The Americans are violent because of their culture" shows circular reasoning. "Using a label as an explanation doesn't help our understanding very much," observe Lonner and Malpass (1994). It is, they say, like telling a man with a leg injury that he can't walk because he is lame. We may observe that Culture A behaves more aggressively than Culture B, but we don't get to say that Culture A frequently attacks its neighbors because it is a warlike culture! Instead, we need to ask what is going on in Culture A that makes it different from Culture B. "To say that the difference is cultural," say Lonner and Malpass, "just means that we have to look for the explanation in the details of how people live." Some people reduce behavior to culture in a quite literal way, speaking as if there were "cultural genes" that make people behave a certain way, just as genes cause eye color. The concept of culture is extremely useful, but it is not a static concept. When people use it as an explanatory label, they often lose sight of the fact that cultures evolve and change.

As if these methodological problems in the study of culture were not enough, we then have to deal with the political and emotional sensitivity of many cross-cultural findings. It is often difficult for people to talk about cultural differences when they feel uncomfortable and suspicious about other groups and defensive about their own. Emotions run high. For example, some time ago, we were talking with students about average differences in the kinds of questions that southern African-American adults and white adults ask children (Heath, 1983). (This interesting study was discussed in Chapter 8.) Later, a white student came up to us and asked why we had "trashed" the white parents. Not long after that conversation, we got a letter from a black student arguing that the study was invalid because no one *she* knew in *her* southern community talked to children that way. Both of these students were letting their feelings and tensions about race get in the way of their ability to hear the point of the research. Of course we weren't trashing the white parents, or the black parents either; neither was the study's author. She merely wanted to find what might be going on in families that would cause black children to score differently on tests designed by whites, and she wants school systems to make use of black children's strengths. However, the students were unable to distinguish an *objective* difference between these two groups of parents from a *value* judgment. No one said that one parental style was better than the other, but these students heard it that way.

Social and cultural psychologists have studied why discussions of culture so often deteriorate into judgmental and emotional language. As we will see, these psychologists have also explored the reasons for the universal habit of assuming that one's own culture is the best. Must cultural differences always be sources of conflict and misunderstanding, or can people learn to accept their differences? And must differences always be evaluated in terms of better and worse, or can they just be . . . differences?

Quick QUIZ

1. Dr. Livingston does research on Americans' habit of making frequent moves and how it affects their attitudes toward friendship and sociability. Dr. Livingston can best be described as a (cultural/cross-cultural) psychologist.
2. Like eating, sleeping is a biological process that is influenced in many ways by culture. Can you think some of these ways?
3. Several decades ago, a study compared arranged marriages in Japan with marriages for love in the United States; after ten years of married life there were no differences between the two groups in their self-rankings of marital satisfaction and marital love. What might be a problem in interpreting these findings?

Answers:

1. cultural 2. Culture affects what time people go to sleep and get up in the morning; the kind of bed, cot, or mat they sleep on; what they wear (if anything); whether they rely on an artificial signal (e.g., an alarm clock) to wake them up; whether they permit their infants or older children to sleep with them; and whether they take afternoon naps. (This list is not exhaustive.) 3. One problem is that "satisfaction" and "love" might have had different meanings in the two cultures, or been measured in different ways.

■ THE RULES OF CULTURE

People learn their culture's rules as effortlessly as they learn its language. Just as they can speak without being able to state the rules of grammar, most people follow their culture's prescriptions without being consciously aware of them. In this section, we will consider some of those invisible rules.

Context and Communication

Fiorello LaGuardia, who was mayor of New York from 1933 to 1945, was fluent in three languages: English, Italian, and Yiddish. LaGuardia knew more than the words of those languages; he also knew the gestures that went along with each one. Researchers who studied films of his speeches could tell which language he was speaking with the sound turned off! They could do so by reading his *body language,* the nonverbal signals of body movement, posture, gesture, and gaze that people constantly express (Birdwhistell, 1970). Italians and

Culture influences many kinds of body language. Arabs stand much closer to each other in conversation than Westerners do, close enough to feel one another's breath and "read" one another's eyes. In many societies, men greet men with an embrace and a kiss, behavior that is uncustomary in most of the United States and Canada. And gestures that are harmless or fun in one culture, such as the Texas longhorn sign, can be seriously insulting in another—be careful!

Jews embellish their speech with circular movements of their arms and hands, and by measuring the radius of those movements you can actually predict whether a speaker is of Italian or Jewish descent: The larger the radius, the more likely the speaker is Italian (Keating, 1994).

Some signals of body language, like some facial expressions, seem to be "spoken" universally. Across cultures, people generally recognize body movements that reveal pleasure or displeasure, liking or dislike, tension or relaxation, high status or low status, and the basic emotions described in Chapter 10 (Buck, 1984; Keating, 1994). When people are depressed, it shows in their walk, stance, and head position. However, most aspects of body language are specific to particular spoken languages and cultures, which makes even the simplest gesture subject to misunderstanding and offense. The sign of the University of Texas football team, the Longhorns, is to extend the second finger and the pinkie. In Italy and other parts of Europe, this gesture means a man's wife has been unfaithful to him—a serious insult! Anita Rowe, a consultant who advises businesses on cross-cultural customs, tells of a newly hired Asian engineer in a California company who left his office to lead the first meeting of his project team. His secretary crossed her fingers and wished him luck. Instead of reassuring him, her gesture left him thoroughly confused: In his home country, crossing one's fingers is a sexual proposition (Gregor, 1993).

When a nonverbal rule is broken, a person is likely to feel extremely uncomfortable without knowing why. One such rule governs *conversational distance:* how close people normally stand to one another when they are speaking (Hall, 1959, 1976). Arabs like to stand close enough to feel your breath, touch your arm, and see your eyes—a distance that makes white North Americans and northern Europeans uneasy, unless they are talking intimately with a lover. The average distance between two conversing people that most black Americans consider comfortable is 22 inches; white Americans prefer to stand 27 inches apart (Connolly, 1974). Cross-cultural researchers have found that white North Americans, the English, and the Swedes stand farthest apart when they converse; southern Europeans stand closer; and Latin Americans and Arabs stand the closest (Keating, 1994; Sommer, 1969).

Knowing about cultural differences, though, doesn't make it easy to change one's own rules. Caroline Keating (1994), an American cross-cultural psychologist, tells of walking with a Pakistani colleague: "I found myself clumsily stepping off the sidewalk. Without realizing it, the closer my Muslim colleague moved toward me (seeking the interpersonal closeness he was comfortable with) the more I moved over streetside (seeking the interpersonal distance I was comfortable with)....I would suddenly disappear from his view, having fallen into the street; perhaps not 'the ugly American,' but a clumsy one!"

Body language seems to be important in the communication of emotion. Have you ever been in a cheerful mood, had lunch with a depressed friend, and come away feeling vaguely depressed yourself? Have you ever stopped to have a chat with a friend who was nervous about an upcoming exam, and ended up feeling jumpy and anxious yourself? Research confirms what you may have suspected: Moods can be highly contagious, especially when two people's body languages are in harmony (see Figure 18.1). In a study of 96 pairs of college roommates, roommates of depressed students became more depressed themselves over the course of the three-week study, even when the researchers controlled for upsetting life events that might be affecting them (Joiner, 1994). An ability to synchronize moods through nonverbal gestures is crucial to smooth interaction between people (Bernieri et al., 1994; Hatfield, Cacioppo, & Rapson, 1992). Conversely, a mismatch of body languages makes conversation feel "out of sync"; it can be as confusing and upsetting as verbal misunderstandings. Synchrony seems to be essential in establishing rapport between people, and its absence has been observed in people who have learning disabilities and emotional problems such as depression (Tronick, 1989).

People from different cultures differ in how attentive they are to body language and other nonverbal signals, and they differ in how much attention they pay to the context of a conversation (Gudykunst & Ting-Toomey, 1988; Hall, 1976, 1983; Triandis, 1994). In **high-context cultures,** which are generally homogeneous and close-knit, people pay close attention to nonverbal signs such as posture and distance between speakers. They assume a shared knowledge and history, so things don't have to be spelled out directly. In Japan, for instance, people will rarely say "No, I can't do that" right to your face; it would be considered too direct and too insulting. They are more likely to say, "That is difficult" or "We will see."

In **low-context cultures,** such as Germany and most regions of the United States, people pay far more attention to words than to nonverbal language. They assume little shared knowledge and history, so everything has to be

▪ **high-context cultures**
Cultures in which people pay close attention to nonverbal forms of communication and assume a shared context for their interactions—a common history and set of attitudes.

▪ **low-context cultures**
Cultures in which people do not take a shared context for granted and instead emphasize direct verbal communication.

▪ **Figure 18.1   The Contagion of Moods and Gestures**

As these scenes from an actual videotaped study show, volunteers who have never previously met each other are obviously "in sync" in their nonverbal gestures. In turn, the degree to which people's movements are synchronized determines how much emotional rapport they will feel. Such physical synchrony paves the way for the "contagion" of moods (Bernieri et al., 1991).

explained and stated directly. When a low-context American talks to a high-context Japanese, both may come away dissatisfied. The American will have difficulty knowing what the Japanese was getting at, why he meandered around the subject instead of getting to the point. The Japanese, who thinks that intelligent human beings should be able to discover the point of a conversation from its context, will think the direct-speaking American is talking down to him.

The importance of knowing the difference between high- and low-context cultures cannot be overestimated: Misunderstandings between them can lead to war (Triandis, 1994). On January 9, 1991, the Foreign Minister of Iraq, Tariq Aziz, met with the American Secretary of State, James Baker, to discuss Iraq's invasion of Kuwait. Seated next to Aziz was the half-brother of Iraq's president, Saddam Hussein. Baker said, "If you do not move out of Kuwait we will attack you." An unmistakable statement, right? But his *nonverbal* language was that of a low-context American diplomat, moderate and polite. He didn't roar, stamp his feet, or wave his hands. Saddam Hussein's brother, for his part, behaved like a normal, high-context Iraqi. He paid attention to Baker's nonverbal language, which he considered the important form of communication. He reported to Saddam Hussein that Baker was "not at all angry. The Americans are just talking, and they will not attack." Saddam therefore instructed Aziz to be inflexible and to yield nothing. This misunderstanding contributed to the outbreak of a bloody war in which untold thousands of people died.

The Organization of Time

Imagine that you have arranged to meet a friend for lunch at noon. The friend has not arrived at 12:15, 12:30, or even 12:45. Please answer these questions: What time would *you* have arrived? Would you have been "on time"? How long would you wait for your friend before you started to feel annoyed or worried? When would you leave?

In most parts of the United States and Canada, the answers are obvious. You would have been there pretty close to noon, and not waited much past 12:30. That is because these countries, along with northern European nations, are **monochronic cultures:** Time is organized into linear segments in which people do one thing "at a time" (Hall, 1983; Hall & Hall, 1990). The day is divided into appointments, schedules, and routines, and because time is a precious commodity, people don't like to "waste" time or "spend" too much time on any one activity. In such cultures, therefore, it is considered the height of rudeness (or high status) to keep someone waiting. But the further south you go in Europe, South America, and Africa, the more likely you are to find **polychronic cultures.** Here, time is organized along parallel lines. People do many things at once, and the demands of friends and family supersede those of the appointment book. People in Latin America and the Middle East think nothing of waiting all day, or even a week, to see someone. The idea of having to be somewhere "on time," as if time were more important than a person, is unthinkable. Table 18.1 is a summary of the differences between the two cultural styles.

The Japanese have one of the few cultures to combine elements of both systems. With the American occupation that followed World War II, they started being monochronic as a way of creating harmony with the *gaijin* (foreigners). Today, they are extremely monochronic about appointments and schedules, but in every other way they are high context and polychronic. For instance, they are loyal to long-term relationships and customers, and employees and managers share office space and information freely (Hall & Hall, 1990).

In diverse North America, the two time systems keep bumping into each other. Business, government, and other institutions are organized monochronically, but Native Americans, Latinos, and African-Americans (among others) tend to operate on polychronic principles. The result is repeated misunder-

■ **monochronic cultures**
Cultures in which time is organized sequentially; schedules and deadlines are valued over people.

■ **polychronic cultures**
Cultures in which time is organized horizontally; people tend to do several things at once and to value relationships over schedules.

| Table 18.1 | Cross-cultural Differences in the Uses and Structure of Time |

Monochronic People	Polychronic People
Are low context	Are high context
Do one thing at a time	Do many things at once
Concentrate on the job	Are highly distractible and subject to interruptions
Take time commitments seriously	Consider time commitments an objective to be achieved if possible
Give the job first priority	Give people first priority
Adhere religiously to plans	Change plans often and easily
Are concerned about not disturbing others; value privacy	Are more concerned with relationships than with privacy; may not even have a word for privacy
Like "own space" or private office to work in	Freely share working space, which increases flow of information
Show great respect for private property; seldom borrow or lend	Borrow and lend things often
Emphasize promptness	Care less about own promptness than other people's needs; are almost never "on time"
Develop many short-term relationships	Build lifetime relationships

Source: Hall & Hall, 1990

standings. A white judge in Miami got into hot water when he observed that "Cubans always show up two hours late for weddings"—late in his culture's terms, that is. The judge was accurate in his observation; the problem was his implication that there was something wrong with Cubans for being "late." And "late" compared to what, by the way? The Cubans were perfectly on time for Cubans.

A culture's way of organizing time does not develop arbitrarily. It stems from the culture's economic system, social organization, political history, and ecology. The monochronic structure of time emerged as a result of the Industrial Revolution in England (Hall, 1983). That makes sense: When thousands of people began working in factories and assembly lines, their efforts had to

North Americans and northern Europeans from "monochronic" cultures often feel like fish out of water when they are in "polychronic" cultures such as those of the Middle East. A tourist from one kind of culture may have fun visiting another, but often the two sets of rules lead to clashes and misunderstandings.

become coordinated. Moreover, factories have no intrinsic rhythms; people can and do work day or night in them.

But in rural economies, where work is based on the rhythms of nature, people think of time differently. When Hall (1983) worked on a Hopi reservation many decades ago, he found that the Hopi were behaving in ways that were mysterious and silly to the whites. The Hopi were always leaving work undone; they would start to build a dam, a house, or a road, and stop in the middle. To the whites, the Hopi were shiftless and lazy. To the Hopi, the whites were rigid, arbitrary, and compulsive. What was so important about building dams, houses, and roads? Unlike the maturing of a sheep or the ripening of corn, said the Hopi, building a house had no inherent timetable. What did matter to the Hopi was working in their fields and completing religious ceremonies, activities that indeed had to be done "on time"—nature's time, not human time.

The Self and Self-identity

Who are you? Take as much time as you like to complete this projective test: "I am _____."

One of the most important ways in which cultures differ has to do with whether the individual or the group is given the greater emphasis (Hofstede & Bond, 1988; Markus & Kitayama, 1991; Triandis, 1990, 1994). This difference, in turn, affects people's concepts of the self and personality. (See Figure 18.2.) The idea of defining the "self" as a collection of stable personality traits ("I am extroverted, agreeable, and ambitious") is inherent in *individual-centered* cultures. In *collectivist* or *group-centered* cultures, the "self" is seen as something embedded in a community and is defined that way ("I am the descendant of Jimmy Joe and Ginny Mae Jones, who came to Iowa in 1908, opened a grain-supply store, and soon had 5 children and 13 grandchildren, one of whom ran for the state Senate. . . ").

In one interesting study comparing Japanese and Americans, the Americans reported that their sense of self changes only 5 to 10 percent in different situations, whereas the Japanese said that 90 to 99 percent of their sense of self

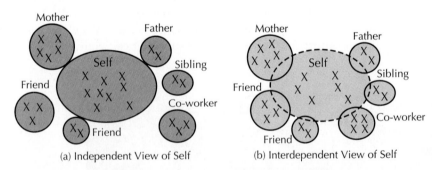

(a) Independent View of Self   (b) Interdependent View of Self

▪ **Figure 18.2   Conceptions of the Self in Individualist and Collectivist Cultures**

The Western, independent view of the self is illustrated in (a), and the Eastern interdependent view of the self is illustrated in (b). The large circle represents the self; the smaller circles represent other people. The Xs represent various aspects of the self or others, such as "I am creative" or "my friend is kind." Notice that in non-Western cultures, the self is seen as interacting with others; the boundaries are more permeable and shifting. Xs on the boundaries represent the self in relation to others or in a particular social situation, as in "I am very polite in front of my professor" (from Markus & Kitayama, 1991).

changes (de Rivera, 1989). For the Japanese, it is important to enact *tachiba,* to perform one's social roles correctly so that there will be harmony with others. (As we just noted, this was one reason they adopted the American monochronic system of time after World War II.) Americans, in contrast, tend to value "being true to your self" and having a "core identity." Similarly, in cross-cultural studies of how people respond to the "I am . . ." cue, people from collectivist cultures typically answer in terms of family (e.g., "I am an uncle, a cousin, a son"), gender, or nation, whereas people from individualist cultures tend to answer in terms of personality traits or occupation (Triandis, 1990). The way that people define the self affects many aspects of individual psychology, including people's personalities, emotions, and relationships (Markus & Kitayama, 1991; Trafimow, Triandis, & Goto, 1991).

The perception of the self also affects how people perceive their need for relationships. As we saw in Chapter 11, all human beings are dependent on others, but just as individuals vary—some like solitude and others like to be surrounded by friends—cultures also vary in the value they place on this dependency. An African proverb says "It takes a whole village to raise a child," but in white American culture, child rearing is considered a private parental matter, and neighbors and friends intervene at their peril.

In collectivist cultures, the strongest human bond is usually not between husband and wife, but between parent and child or among siblings (Triandis, 1990). In China, the most valued and celebrated relationship is the father–son bond; in India, Mexico, Ireland, and Greece, it is mother–son; in parts of Africa, it is older brother–younger brother; among the Tiwi of North Australia, it is mother-in-law and son-in-law (no mother-in-law jokes among the Tiwi!). In addition, child rearing in collectivist cultures is a communal matter; everyone has a say in correcting the child's behavior. The idea of privacy for children is unknown, and the goal is to raise children who are obedient, hardworking, and dutiful toward their parents. Can you predict what will happen if a collectivist man marries an individualist woman? The chances are high that the husband will regard his relationship with one or both of his parents as being most important, whereas his wife will expect his relationship to her to be most important. And they are likely to disagree intensely, without knowing why, about such matters as letting their children have their own rooms, speak their minds, make their own choices, talk back, and become independent.

Everyone develops a *personal* identity—a sense of who one is—that is based on the person's individual traits and unique history. But people also develop **social identities** based on their nationality, ethnicity, religion, and other roles in society (Brewer, 1991; Hogg & Abrams, 1988; Tajfel & Turner, 1986). Social identities are important because they give people a feeling of place and position in the world. Without social identities, most people would feel like loose marbles rolling around in an unconnected universe. The social identity that comes from belonging to a distinctive group satisfies two important motives: the individual's need for inclusion in a larger collective, and the individual's need to feel differentiated from others (Brewer, Manzi, & Shaw, 1993).

In modern societies, many social identities are possible. Their members face the dilemma of balancing an **ethnic identity,** a close identification with one's own religious or ethnic group, with **acculturation,** identifying with and feeling part of the dominant culture (Cross, 1971; Helms, 1990; Spencer & Dornbusch, 1990). Research suggests that ethnic-identity formation and acculturation are separate processes. Some people learn to alternate easily between their culture of origin and the majority culture, slipping into the customs and language of each as circumstances dictate. They are comfortable and competent in both cultures, just as bilingual people are in two languages, without feeling that they must choose one culture over another (LaFromboise, Coleman, & Gerton,

■ **social identity**
The part of a person's self-concept that is based on his or her identification with a nation, culture, or ethnic group or with gender or other roles in society.

■ **ethnic identity**
Having a close identification with one's own racial, religious, or ethnic group.

■ **acculturation**
The process by which members of groups that are minorities in a given society come to identify with and to feel part of the mainstream culture.

 These young people—Mexican-American, Chinese-American, and African-American—are celebrating the traditions of their respective ethnic groups, and having a good time doing it. Does an overemphasis on acculturation erase cultural differences that are an important part of identity? On the other hand, might an overemphasis on ethnic identity lead to a different problem: a society of small, separate, competing cultures? Where is the balance between preserving your own ethnic heritage and becoming an integral part of the larger society?

1993). Others, however, struggle to find a balance between their culture of origin and the dominant culture of the society.

For any individual, four outcomes are possible, depending on whether ethnic identity is strong or weak, and whether identification with the larger culture is strong or weak (Berry, 1994; Phinney, 1990). People who are truly *bicultural* have strong ties both to their ethnicity and to the larger culture: They say, "I am proud of my own ethnic heritage, but I identify just as much with my country." People who choose *assimilation* have weak feelings of ethnicity but a strong sense of acculturation: They might say, for example, "I'm an American, period." People who are *ethnic separatists* have a strong sense of ethnic identity but weak feelings of acculturation: They might say, "My ethnicity comes first; if I join the mainstream, I'm betraying my origins." And some people feel *marginal,* connected to neither their ethnicity nor the dominant culture: They may say, "I'm an individual and don't identify with any group" or "I don't belong anywhere." (See Table 18.2.)

Some of the conflicts between cultural groups in North America, as well as within these groups, arise because people have different ideas about the relative benefits of acculturation versus ethnic identity and how their different identities should be balanced. This tension is reflected in the touchy subject of what groups should be called, and why these labels change (as we discuss in "Psychology and Popular Culture").

For example, *Hispanic* is a label used by the U.S. government to include all Spanish-speaking groups. But many "Hispanics" dislike the term, pointing out that Spaniards, Cubans, Mexican-Americans (Chicanos), Latin-Americans (Latinos), and Puerto Ricans differ in their culture and history, and therefore in their ethnic identity (Vasquez & Barón, 1988). Other "Hispanics," however, dislike the term "Latino." The 1992 Latino National Political Survey, a major random-sample survey, found that most Latinos don't think of themselves as such, preferring national-origin labels such as Mexican-American or just "American" (de la Garza et al., 1992). Likewise, Koreans, Japanese, Chinese,

Table 18.2 *Patterns of Ethnic Identity and Acculturation*

		Ethnic Identity is	
		Strong	Weak
Acculturation is	**Strong**	Bicultural	Assimilated
	Weak	Separatist	Marginal

and Vietnamese are all Asian, but many individuals in these groups resent being lumped into a single category. For that matter, not all white Americans are WASPs—white Anglo-Saxon Protestants. And not all want to be called Anglos, which refers to a British heritage, or European-American, as if all European countries, from Greece to Norway, France to Poland, were the same.

The tension between personal identity and social identity is likely to continue, as ethnic groups in America struggle to define their place and to raise their status in a medley of cultures.

An appreciation of the rules of culture expands our understanding of human behavior. Among other things, culture affects a person's sense of time, the priorities given to people and schedules, how people process information and communicate meaning, their nonverbal language and even whether they pay much attention to nonverbal language, their notions of the self and their relationships, and their fundamental identities.

Quick QUIZ

1. Provide the term that describes each of the following cultural characteristics:
   a. Cultures whose members pay close attention to nonverbal signs and often don't spell things out directly.
   b. Cultures whose members do things one at a time and consider time a precious commodity.
   c. Cultures whose members regard the "self" as a collection of stable personality traits.
2. Which of the terms in Item 1 applies to the majority culture in the United States?
3. Frank, an African-American college student, finds himself caught between two philosophies on his campus. One holds that blacks should shed their identity as victims of racism and move toward full integration into American culture. The other favors Afrocentric education, holding that blacks should immerse themselves in the history, values, and contributions of African culture. Frank is caught between his _____ and _____.

Answers:

1. a. high context b. monochronic c. individual-centered 2. Terms *b* and *c* apply to the majority culture in the United States. 3. ethnic identity, acculturation

Psychology and Popular Culture

What's in a Name? The Debate over "Political Correctness"

▪ Across the United States and Canada, many universities, companies, government agencies, and newspapers have tried to come up with regulations regarding what different groups should be called. When does a term become offensive, and why? One college, in a leaflet distributed to all students, defined "ableism" as "oppression of the differently abled by the temporarily able." Was that a wise effort to make people think about the terms they use to describe people with disabilities, or was it plain silliness? "Sexual preference," with its implication that people can choose to be homosexual or heterosexual, has been widely replaced by "sexual orientation," but some homosexuals now prefer the term "affectional orientation" so that they will not be labeled solely according to their sexual behavior. Will such a change in terms affect straight people's prejudices?

The question of what various groups should be called and what terms are offensive evokes much controversy. One side argues that because language shapes attitudes and prejudices, we must be ever vigilant about the mindless use of labels or phrases that offend or perpetuate untruths. Although most Americans do not realize the derivation of the term "to welsh" on a bet, for example, the term is as offensive to people from Wales as the expression "to Jew him down" is to Jews.

The opposing side argues that efforts to legislate "political correctness" in language produce tedious or comical gobbledegook, impede clear thinking, and don't change anyone's prejudices anyway. Moreover, in this view, when everyone is focused on the correct word and quick to take offense if someone uses the "wrong" one, it becomes easy to forget the bottom line: How people are actually being treated. Nancy Mairs (1986), a writer who suffers from multiple sclerosis, says:

I am a cripple. I choose this word to name me. . . . "cripple" seems to me a clean word, straightforward and precise. . . . As a lover of words, I like the accuracy with which it describes my condition: I have lost the full use of limbs. "Disabled," by contrast, suggests any incapacity, physical or mental . . . Most remote is the recently coined euphemism "differently abled," which partakes of the same semantic hopefulness that transformed countries from "undeveloped" to "underdeveloped," then to "less developed," and finally to "developing" nations. People have continued to starve in those countries during the shift. Some realities do not obey the dictates of language.

The one thing everyone can agree on is that labels have great symbolic and emotional significance. As social-identity theory suggests, the name a group chooses for itself has an important symbolic function. Around the world, many ethnic groups are rejecting names that were imposed on them by the majority culture, insisting instead on a name that reflects their own cultural identity. This is why the Eskimos of Canada are now called the Inuit, their own name for themselves. In addition, a group's name reflects its history, status, and self-concept. In the early 1970s, William Cross (1971) analyzed "The Negro-to-Black conversion experience," arguing that this change was critical for "the psychology of Black liberation." In the 1980s, Halford Fairchild (1985) analyzed the significance of labels that are based on skin color ("black"), race ("Negro"), or national origin ("Afro-American"), for each term has different historical and emotional connotations. Only a few years after that article appeared, African-American became a popular term to identify people of African descent

▪ THE ORIGINS OF CULTURE

When most people read about the customs of other cultures, they are inclined to say, "Oh, boy, I like the attitudes of the Gorks but I hate the habits of the Zorks." But a culture's practices cannot easily be exported elsewhere, like cheese, or surgically removed, like a tumor. The reason is that a culture's attitudes and practices are deeply embedded in its history, environment, economy, and survival needs.

living in the Americas; those who like the term argue that it is analogous to Polish-American or Italian-American.

Nevertheless, as psycholinguist Stephen Pinker (1994a) observes, there is a difference between changing a word or phrase that is blatantly incorrect or offensive and changing a word in the hopes of *changing its connotations.* Pinker argues that when terms that are acceptable are nearly synonymous with those that are now offensive—such as colored people versus people of color; Afro-American versus African-American; Negro (which is Spanish for "black") versus black—something else is going on besides identity politics. Pinker calls this something the "euphemism treadmill." As linguistic studies show, people invent new words to try to escape emotional associations with the old words. In the absence of social change, the new word acquires the same emotional association, and soon another word must be found (as in the case of evolving terms for "developing" nations). "We will know we have achieved equality and mutual respect," Pinker concludes, "when names for minorities stay put."

Moreover, says Pinker, cognitive research demonstrates that

> words are not thoughts. Despite the appeal of the theory that language determines thought, no cognitive scientist believes it. People coin new words, grapple for le mot juste [the right word], translate from other languages and ridicule or defend P.C. terms. None of this would be possible if the ideas expressed by the words were identical to the words themselves. This should alleviate anxiety on both sides, reminding us that we are talking about style manuals, not brain programming.

Psychological research also reminds us that because language and ethnic identities are dynamic, constantly changing processes, it is impossible to designate a single P.C. term that everyone will know about immediately, let alone agree on. Many blacks, feeling no special kinship to Africa, do not consider themselves African-American. The Supreme Court Justice Thurgood Marshall preferred the word Negro for most of his life, and social critic Henry Louis Gates, Jr., called his autobiography *Colored People,* the term he grew up with and still likes. A decade ago, activist American Indian groups sought to replace the term *American Indian* with *Native American,* and the latter term caught on with colleges and other organizations wanting to support a group's right to self-designation. Ironically, according to Joseph Trimble and Beatrice Medicine (1993), Indian political groups then decided to keep the term *American Indian*—as in the American Indian Movement and the National Congress of American Indians. Today, despite the stance of American Indian groups themselves, it is *non*-Indians who tend to prefer the term Native American!

This story contains a lesson for people on both sides of the debate about being P.C. Words do matter, but words are not everything. Pinker worries about people who, unaware of the current "correct" term (because they are older or do not travel in university, media, and government circles), find themselves accused of being bigots when they innocently use the "wrong" word. But if Nancy Mairs considers herself a cripple, and Thurgood Marshall favored the word Negro, and members of the American Indian Movement call themselves Indians, how rigid should we all be about names? And if the goal is tolerance for all groups, how can we make sure that a focus on words does not replace a commitment to deeds? ▪

To explain the origins of cultural customs, cultural researchers study a culture's political system and its economy, and how that economy is affected by geography, natural resources, and even the weather. They observe who controls and distributes the resources, and how safe a society is from interlopers. They study the kinds of work that people do. They observe whether there is environmental pressure on a group to produce more children or to have fewer of them.

To illustrate this approach, we will take a look at explanations for the origins of gender roles and why those roles often vary across cultures. Let's start with a story: A young boy notices, at an early age, that he seems different from other boys. He prefers playing with girls. He is attracted to the work adult women do, such as cooking and sewing. He often dreams at night of being a girl, and he even likes to put on the clothes of girls. As the boy enters adolescence, people begin to whisper that he's "different," that he seems feminine in his movements, posture, and language. One day, the boy can hide his secret feelings no longer and reveals them to his parents.

How do his parents respond? It depends on their culture. In the United States today, many parents would react with tears, anger, or guilt. They might haul their son off to a psychiatrist, who would diagnose him as having a "gender identity disorder" and begin intensive treatment (American Psychiatric Association, 1994). But these reactions are not universal. Until the late 1800s, in a number of Plains Indians and western American Indian tribes, parents and other elders reacted with sympathy and understanding when a young man wanted to live the life of a woman. He was often given an honored status as a shaman, a person with the power to cure illness and to act as an intermediary between the natural and spiritual worlds, and he was permitted to dress as and perform the duties of a woman. In some tribes, he was even permitted to marry another man (Williams, 1986).

In the Sambian society of Papua New Guinea, parents would react still differently (Herdt, 1984). In Sambia, all adolescent boys are *required* to engage in oral sex with older males as part of their initiation into manhood. Sambians believe that a boy cannot mature physically or emotionally unless he ingests another man's semen over a period of several years. However, Sambian parents would react with shock and disbelief if a son said he wanted to live as a woman. Every man and woman in Sambian society marries someone of the other sex and performs the work assigned to his or her own sex. There are no exceptions.

These diverse reactions support the view of social-learning theorists and cultural psychologists that although anatomical *sex* is universal and unchangeable (unless extraordinary surgical procedures are used), *gender*—which encompasses all the duties, rights, and behaviors a culture considers appropriate for males and females—is learned, or *socially constructed* (Hare-Mustin & Marecek, 1990; Rhode, 1990; West & Zimmerman, 1991). (As we discussed in Chapter 2, **social constructionism** is the theory that there are no universal truths about human nature because people construct reality differently, depending on their culture, the historical moment, and power arrangements within their society.) In contrast, sociobiologists and evolutionary psychologists believe that sex heavily influences gender—that is, that the biological fact of being male or female constrains the fundamental tasks and gender roles that men and women will play. By comparing and contrasting different cultures around the world, cross-cultural psychologists are trying to identify which aspects of gender roles seem to be universally male or female, as well as those that differ.

First, the commonalities. In general, men have had, and continue to have, more status and more power than women, especially in public affairs. Men have fought the wars and, on the average, are more aggressive and violent than women. If a society's economy includes hunting large game, traveling a long way from home, or making weapons, men typically handle these activities. Women have had the primary responsibility for cooking, cleaning, and taking care of children. Corresponding with this division of tasks, in many cultures around the world masculinity is regarded as something that boys must achieve through strenuous effort. Males must pass physical tests, endure pain, confront danger, and separate themselves psychologically and even physically from their mothers and the world of women. Sometimes they have to prove their self-reliance and courage in harsh initiation rites. Femininity, in contrast, tends to be associated with responsibility, obedience, and child care, and it is seen as something that develops without any special intervention from others.

■ **social constructionism**
The view that there are no universal truths about human nature because people construct reality differently depending on their culture, the historical moment, and the power arrangements within their society.

Throughout history, a person's anatomical sex and the culturally assigned duties of gender have not always corresponded. Some men have chosen to wear the clothes and play the roles of women, as in the case of the Native American berdache. In the photo at left, taken about 1885, We-wha, a Zuni Indian, wears the traditional earrings, jewelry, and dress of a woman. Likewise, some women have worn the clothes and played the roles of men, as did the eighteenth-century pirate Mary Read (right).

Those are the common themes. Now consider the variations:

- The status of women worldwide is not uniformly low (di Leonardo, 1991); it is highest in Scandinavian countries and lowest in Bangladesh, with tremendous variation in between. Women's status has been assessed by measures of economic security, educational opportunities, access to birth control and medical care, degree of self-determination, participation in public and political life, power to make decisions in the family, and physical safety. In some places, women are completely under the rule of men. Women in Saudi Arabia are not allowed to drive a car; many girls in India submit to arranged marriages as early as age 9. Yet elsewhere, women are attaining greater power, influence, education, and independence. In this century, women have been elected heads of state in Israel, India, Norway, England, Iceland, Pakistan, Nicaragua, Bangladesh, Poland, Turkey, . . . the list keeps growing.

- The content of what is considered "men's work" and "women's work" varies from culture to culture. In some places, dentistry and teaching are men's work; in others, they are women's work. In many cultures, women do the shopping and marketing, but in others, marketing is men's work.

- Cultures differ in the degree of daily contact that is permitted between the sexes. In many farm communities and in most modern occupations in North America and Europe, men and women work together closely. At the other end of the continuum, some Middle Eastern societies have a tradition of *purdah*, the custom of veiling women and secluding them from all male eyes except those of their relatives.

- In some cultures, particularly those of East Asia, Southeast Asia, and Muslim societies, female chastity is highly prized. Women are expected to suppress all sexual feeling and behavior until marriage, and premarital or extramarital sex is cause for the woman's ostracism from the community or even her death. In other cultures, such as those of Polynesia, Scandinavia, and northern Europe, female chastity is considered unimportant (Buss, 1989). Women are expected to have sex before marriage and even extramarital sex is not necessarily cause for alarm.

- In some cultures, men and women regard one another as opposite in nature, ability, and personality, a view that reflects their separate domains. In other cultures, such as those of the Ifaluk, the Tahitians, and people who live on Sudest Island southeast of New Guinea, men and women do not regard each other as opposites or even as being very different (Gilmore, 1990; Lepowsky, 1994; Lutz, 1988). When Robert Levy (1973) lived in Tahiti, he found that Tahitian men were no more aggressive than women, nor were women gentler or more nurturant than men. To Tahitians, Levy found, gender was no big deal.

✳ *Around the world, men tend to be more aggressive than women. Many people assume that the universality of this difference means that the difference must be biologically based. What are some alternative explanations?*

Cultural researchers argue that biological differences cannot account for the wide variation in gender roles around the world. They have examined instead two other fundamental factors: *production* (matters pertaining to the economy and the creation of food, clothing, and shelter) and *reproduction* (matters pertaining to the bearing, raising, and nurturing of children).

One important finding is that rigid concepts of manhood tend to exist wherever there is a great deal of competition for resources—which is to say, in most places (Gilmore, 1990). For the human species, life has usually been harsh. Consider a tribe trying to survive in the wilds of a South American forest; or in the dry and unforgiving landscape of the desert; or in an icy Arctic terrain that imposes limits on the number of people who can survive by fishing. When conditions such as these exist, men are taught to hunt for large game, compete with each other for work, and fight off enemies. (This division of labor may originally have occurred because of men's relatively greater upper-body muscular strength and the fact that they do not become pregnant or nurse children.) Men are socialized to face confrontation and to resist the impulse to retreat from danger. They are "toughened up" and pushed to take risks, even with their lives.

How do you get men to wage war and risk death, go off on long treks for food, and be willing to get bloodied defending the homestead? Far from being natural to men, some researchers argue, aggressiveness has to be constantly rewarded (Gilmore, 1990). To persuade men to wage war and risk death, societies have to give them something; and the something is prestige, power—and women (Harris, 1974). That in turn means you have to raise obedient women;

In most cultures, men are required to do the dangerous, life-threatening work . . . but it's not always easy to get all of them to do it.

if the king is going to offer his daughter in marriage to the bravest warrior, she has to agree to be handed over. In contrast, in societies such as Tahiti and Sudest Island, where resources are abundant and there are no serious hazards or enemies to worry about, men don't feel they have to prove themselves or set themselves apart from women (Lepowsky, 1994).

A culture's economy and social structure also help account for the variations in how aggressive men are required and expected to be. In a fascinating analysis of the rates of violence in different regional cultures of the United States, Richard Nisbett (1993) set out to explain why the American south, and some western regions of the country originally settled by southerners, have much higher rates of white homicide than the rest of the country. Southerners are more likely to endorse the use of violence for protection (recall the reactions to Rodney Peairs' shooting of the Japanese exchange student) and as the proper response to perceived insults. "Violence has been associated with the South since the time of the American Revolution," begins an essay in the *Encyclopedia of Southern Culture,* and it goes on to devote 39 pages to bloodcurdling accounts of feuds, duels, lynchings, violent sports, and murder.

Nisbett ruled out explanations based on poverty. Although poverty is associated with violence, "southernness" remains a predictor of homicide even when you control for regional differences in poverty. Nisbett also ruled out explanations based on racial tensions; the counties with the smallest African-American populations have the highest white homicide rates. And he ruled out the southern tradition of slavery as an explanation; regions of the south that had the highest concentrations of slaves in the past have the lowest homicide rates today.

Nisbett argues that the south "is heir to a culture, deriving ultimately from economic determinants, in which violence is a natural and integral part." The New England and the middle Atlantic states were settled by Puritans, Quakers, and Dutch farmers and artisans who had an advanced agricultural economy. For them, the most adaptive policy was one of cooperation with others for the common good. In contrast, the south was settled largely by immigrants from Scotland and Ireland, whose economies were based on herding and hunting, activities that continued to provide their economic base in America.

Why should herding, as opposed to farming, make such a difference in rates of violence? People who depend economically on their herds are extremely vulnerable; their livelihoods can be lost in an instant by the theft of their animals. To reduce the likelihood of theft, says Nisbett, herders "cultivate a posture of extreme vigilance toward any act that might be perceived as threatening in any way, and respond with sufficient force to frighten the offender and the community into recognizing that they are not to be trifled with." This is why cattle rustling and horse thievery were capital crimes in the old west, and why Mediterranean and Middle Eastern herding cultures, as well as those of the southern United States, place a high value on male aggressiveness. When Nisbett examined agricultural practices within the south, he found that homicide rates were more than twice as high in the hills and dry plains regions (where herding occurs) than in the farming regions. As you can see, male biology does not automatically dictate aggressive behavior. Aggressiveness occurs primarily when it is useful for protecting a society's economic interests.

In terms of the kinds of gender roles they promote, cultures fall along a continuum from traditional to modern (egalitarian). In a major cross-cultural study of 100 men and women from each of 14 countries in North and South America, Europe, and Asia, Deborah Best and John Williams (1993) asked people to fill out an inventory concerning ideal role relationships between women and men. Sample items included, "The husband should be regarded as the legal representative of the family group in all matters of law" (a traditional atti-

According to one theory, cultures based on herding rather than agriculture foster male aggressiveness as a means of protecting livestock and economies. That is why cattle rustlers and horse thieves were often summarily hanged, as this one was in Colorado in 1888.

tude) and "A woman should have exactly the same freedom of action as a man" (a modern attitude). Best and Williams found that gender-role ideologies are significantly related to a culture's social and economic development. As countries become industrialized and urban, their gender roles also become more modern. Why might this be so?

One answer is that industrialization eliminates the traditional reasons for a sexual division of labor. Most jobs in industrial nations, including military jobs, now involve service skills and brainwork that both sexes can do—a situation that has never existed before in human history. And another profound change has also occurred in this century for the first time: Reproduction has been revolutionized. Although women in many countries still lack access to safe and affordable contraceptives, it is now technologically possible for women to limit reliably the number of children they will have and to plan when to have them. Along with these changes, ideas about the "natural" qualities of men and women are being transformed. It is no longer news that a woman can be a Supreme Court justice or a miner, walk in space or run a country. And it is no longer news that many men, whose own fathers would no more have diapered a baby than jumped into a vat of boiling oil, now want to be involved fathers (Gerson, 1993).

What cross-cultural studies show, then, is that many of our gender arrangements, and the qualities associated with being male and female, are affected by

Think About It

Are There Limits to Tolerance?

■ Alice Walker's haunting novel *Possessing the Secret of Joy* is about the tradition, practiced in more than 25 countries throughout Africa, the Middle East, and Indonesia, of the genital mutilation of girls. Performed on an estimated 2 million female children every year, ranging in age from infancy to adolescence, the operation takes one of three forms: in *circumcision,* part of the clitoris is removed; in *excision,* the entire clitoris and all or part of the vaginal lips (labia) are removed; and in *infibulation,* the clitoris and the inner and outer labia are removed and the sides of the vaginal opening are stitched together, leaving only a small hole for urination and menstruation. These operations, usually performed without anesthesia or even an antiseptic, are excruciatingly painful and hazardous; some girls bleed to death. Most women who have been incised or infibulated develop lifelong medical problems, and an estimated 20 percent die in childbirth (Bardach, 1993).

People in cultures that practice infibulation believe that it will ensure a girl's chastity before marriage and her fidelity afterward. Most people in other cultures believe it is barbaric; hence their insistence on calling it "genital mutilation." But what, if anything, should outsiders do? Should they say, "Well, it's their custom, and it's up to them to change it; we must be tolerant," or "It is a violation of human rights, and we should do what we can to eradicate it"? This is not just an intellectual matter in countries such as France and England, which have growing numbers of immigrants who subject their daughters to the surgery. The result is a clash between the law of the majority that forbids the practice and the immigrants' determination to continue their tradition. French and British doctors have been confronting the moral dilemma of whether they should perform the surgery: If they do, they are condoning the practice; but if they do not, the child may be infibulated without anesthesia or antiseptic. If you were a physician faced with such a choice, what would you do?

Cultural psychologists have described problems with both "absolutist" and "relativist" positions on such issues (Adamopoulos & Lonner, 1994). In reacting to the absolutist assumptions of traditional psychology, which holds that there are universal truths and a common human nature, relativists conclude that every culture differs from every other and that each can be judged only on its own terms. Extreme relativists take a nonjudgmental view of all cultural practices, even those that cause suffering and death.

It is not necessary to be utterly relativist, but it is important to prevent moral indignation from get-

Many cultural theorists hold that gender differences in traits and occupations will decline in response to changes in technology and production (as jobs that both sexes can perform become commonplace) and changes in reproduction (as more people have access to fertility control). And so they have.

economic, ecological, and other practical conditions. This research also suggests that no matter how entrenched our own cultural habits and attitudes are, they change depending on the kind of work we do, technological advances, and the needs of society. Understanding the forces that generate and sustain cultural practices may even help us better evaluate customs we think are morally reprehensible, in our own culture or elsewhere (see "Think About It").

ting in the way of understanding why and how certain practices emerged or eventually faded. Cultural psychologists try to find out why certain customs have survived and what their adaptive consequences might be. This does *not* mean that any custom that survives must therefore be right and good. It *does* mean that because cultural customs are embedded in the larger structure of society, efforts to outlaw them often fail. In the case of infibulation, for example, social scientists have found that the custom works like a marriage contract, guaranteeing a woman a place in society (Paige & Paige, 1981). Outsiders who want to barge in and make it illegal (assuming they could), ignoring the system of kinship and economic arrangements that support the practice, might actually condemn countless women to even more hardship. African women who are working to eliminate female genital mutilation know this (Dawit & Mekuria, 1993). They know that the custom cannot simply be outlawed without making other changes to raise the status and security of women.

The study of culture does not require us to abandon the concern for human rights, but it does alert us to the dangers of climbing up on an ethnocentric high horse, galloping off in the certainty that our own ways are always right and normal and

everyone else's are wrong. Alice Walker herself, who regards infibulation as a horrific crime against women, pointed out in a television interview that plenty of American women mutilate themselves with breast implants, plastic surgery, and liposuction to fit their culture's standards of being beautiful. How would we like it if outsiders pressured the U.S. government to make plastic surgery for cosmetic purposes illegal? Or consider this: Among the developed nations of the world, only the United States continues to execute criminals in increasing numbers. To most other nations, the death penalty is barbaric, a violation of human rights. But many Americans would counter that it's our cultural custom, and no one has the right to interfere (Stephens, 1993).

Obviously, then, emotional reasoning should not be our only guide in evaluating practices we find reprehensible or immoral. What criteria would you use in deciding when to be tolerant of other cultures' practices and when to take a stand against them? If you take an opposing stand, what actions would you be willing to ask your own country to take—moral persuasion, education, military intervention, sanctions, or something else? And when might it be wise to let yourself be influenced by another culture's customs? Think about it. ■

Will your gender affect your answers to these questions?

1. Which of the following is most common in cultures around the world? (a) Women do the weaving, marketing, and teaching, (b) men have more status and power in public affairs than women do, (c) men and women are physically separated while working.
2. What two general factors do cultural researchers emphasize in explaining variations in gender roles around the world?
3. Nisbett's analysis of regional differences in violence showed that an important factor in predicting male aggressiveness is (a) poverty, (b) racial tensions, (c) how people earn their livings, (d) male biology.

Answers:

1. b 2. production and reproduction 3. c

■ CROSS-CULTURAL RELATIONS

By now, you should be persuaded that cultures differ in countless ways and that a culture's customs do not arise for some arbitrary or foolish reason. But it has probably also been difficult for you to turn off your mental moral evaluator, the little voice that says, "Boy, a culture that does *that* must really be dumb." That little voice, which everyone hears to one degree or another, is the echo of **ethnocentrism,** the belief that one's own culture or ethnic group is superior to all others.

Ethnocentrism is so pervasive that it is even embedded in some languages: The Chinese word for China means "the center of the world" and the Navajo call themselves simply "the People." Ethnocentrism is probably universal because it aids survival by making people feel attached to their groups and willing to work on the group's behalf. But does the fact that people feel good about their own ethnic group, race, or nationality mean that prejudice toward other groups is inevitable? Does it mean we are destined to a world of ethnic separatism? Can't people say, "Well, I'm really happy being an Agfloyp, and I love our customs, but I also am grateful to the people who invented jazz, small cars, chicken soup, movies, paper, the tango, democracy, penicillin. . ."?

Ethnocentrism and Stereotypes

Ethnocentrism rests on a fundamental social identity: Us. As soon as people have created a category called "us," however, they invariably perceive everybody else as "not-us." In the last chapter, in discussing the experiment at Robbers Cave, we saw how easy it is to activate *us–them thinking* when any two groups perceive themselves to be in competition. Although competition is sufficient to stimulate ethnocentrism, however, it isn't necessary. Just being a member of an in-group will do it (Brewer, 1986).

Ethnocentrism can be manufactured in a minute in a laboratory, as Henri Tajfel and his colleagues (1971) first demonstrated in a classic experiment with British schoolboys. Tajfel showed the boys slides with varying numbers of dots on them and asked the boys to guess how many dots there were. The boys were arbitrarily told they were "overestimators" or "underestimators" and were then asked to work on another task. In this phase, they had the chance to allocate points to other boys who were known to be overestimators or underestimators. The researchers had created in-group favoritism: Although each boy worked

■ **ethnocentrism**
The belief that one's own ethnic group, nation, or religion is superior to all others.

Who is the chemical engineer and who is the assistant? The Western stereotype holds that (1) women aren't engineers in the first place but (2) if they are, they are Western. Actually, the engineer at this refinery is the Kuwaiti woman on the left.

alone in a private cubicle, almost every single one assigned far more points to other boys he thought were like him, an overestimator or an underestimator. As the boys emerged from their rooms, they were asked, "Which were you?"—and the answer received a mix of cheers and boos.

Even the collective pronouns that apply to *us* and *them* are powerful emotional signals. In one experiment, which students believed was testing their verbal skills, nonsense syllables such as *xeh, yof, laj* or *wuh* were randomly paired with either an in-group word (*us, we,* or *ours*), an out-group word (*them, they,* or *theirs*), or, for a control measure, another pronoun (such as *he, hers,* or *yours*). The students then had to rate the nonsense syllables on how pleasant or unpleasant they were. Why, you might ask, would anyone have an emotional reaction to the syllable *yof*? Yet, in fact, students liked the nonsense syllables significantly more when they had been paired with in-group words. Not one student guessed why; none was aware of how the words had been paired (Perdue et al., 1990).

Ethnocentric thinking is especially common during war, when enemies regard each other as inhuman and deserving of destruction. "We" are good, noble, and human; "they," the enemy, are bad, stupid, and beastly. But you can see everyday examples of ethnocentric thinking at a football game, during an election, or in discussions of controversial issues.

Us–them thinking both creates and reflects stereotyping. A **stereotype** is a summary impression of a group of people in which a person believes that all members of that group share a common trait or traits. Stereotypes are among the cognitive schemas by which we map the world. They may be negative, positive, or neutral. There are stereotypes of people who drive Volkswagens or BMWs, of men who wear earrings and of women who wear business suits, of engineering students and art students, of feminists and fraternities.

The fact that everyone occasionally thinks in stereotypes is itself neither good nor bad. Stereotypes help us process new information and retrieve old memories. They allow us to organize experience, make sense of the differences among individuals and groups, and predict how people will behave. They are, as some psychologists have called them, useful "tools in the mental toolbox"— energy-saving devices that allow us to make efficient decisions (Gilbert & Hixon, 1990; Macrae, Milne, & Bodenhausen, 1994). For example, as one study found, people remember the qualities associated with stereotypes such as "prude" or "politician" better than they remember a list of specific traits ("reserved"; "extroverted"). The researchers concluded that "categorization by stereotype provides a virtually instantaneous, detailed, and memorable portrait of an individual" (Andersen, Klatzky, & Murray, 1990).

■ **stereotype**
A cognitive schema or a summary impression of a group, in which a person believes that all members of the group share a common trait or traits (positive, negative, or neutral).

Faces of the Enemy

In every country, propaganda posters stereotype "them," the enemy, as ugly, aggressive, brutish, and greedy; "we," the heroes, are beautiful and virtuous. Some examples, clockwise starting from upper left: an American depiction of the German enemy in World War I as a "mad brute"; the Soviet view of the United States in the 1930s as a greedy capitalist; an Iraqi view of a barbaric Iran in 1985, in the midst of their long war; a Nicaraguan mural of the enemy as "chicken-footed Death"; an IRA poster of bloody "English pigs"; and a southeast Asian portrayal of Richard Nixon as a vampire devouring the region.

One cognitive process that contributes to stereotyping is the phenomenon of *illusory correlation:* When two variables that are unusual or distinct in some way become linked on one occasion (for example, if a member of a minority group commits a crime), people tend to expect them to *always* be linked, overestimating the strength of the actual relationship between the two events (Hamilton & Sherman, 1989; Mullen & Johnson, 1990; Taylor & Porter, 1994). One recent example of an illusory correlation in popular culture is that between eating disorders and sexual abuse. It seemed that so many women with eating disorders were also reporting having been sexually molested that some psychotherapists inferred that eating disorders were actually a symptom of abuse. But after reviewing six studies that used proper control groups of women who had not been abused, two researchers found no support for the idea that sexual abuse is a risk factor for bulimia (Pope & Hudson, 1992). Eating disorders are widespread among women who have not been abused, and in some cases, the correlation works in the opposite direction: Some women are sexually abused in adolescence *after* they become bulimic.

Although stereotypes do help us put the world together, the illusory correlations on which they are based lead to three distortions of reality. First, *stereotypes accentuate differences between groups.* They emphasize the ways in which groups are different and overlook the common features. So the stereotyped group may seem odd, unfamiliar, or dangerous—"not like us." Second, *stereotypes produce selective perception.* People tend to see only what fits the stereotype and to reject any perceptions that do not fit. Third, *stereotypes underestimate differences within other groups.* People realize that their own groups are heterogeneous—that is, made up of all kinds of individuals. But stereotypes create the impression that all members of other groups (say, all Texans or all teenagers) are the same. One rude French waiter means that all French people are rude; one Greek thief means that all Greeks are thieves. But if someone in their own group is rude or steals, most people draw no such conclusions. This cognitive habit starts early. Social psychologist Marilynn Brewer (1993) reports that her daughter returned from kindergarten one day with the observation that "Boys are crybabies." The child's evidence was that she had seen two boys crying on their first day away from home. Brewer asked whether there hadn't been little girls who cried also. Oh yes, said her daughter. "But," she insisted, "only some girls cry; I didn't cry."

Stereotypes are not always entirely wrong. Many have a grain of truth, capturing with some accuracy something about the group (Allport, 1954/1979). The problems occur when people assume that the grain of truth is the whole seashore. For example, the stereotype that most American whites have about blacks is based on the troubling statistics that are in the news, such as the number of young black men who are in prison. But the stereotype causes many whites to overlook the fact that there has also been a striking expansion of blacks into the middle class and into integrated occupations and communities. From 1950 to 1990, the black population doubled, but the number of blacks holding white-collar jobs jumped 920 percent (Edsall & Edsall, 1991). Many whites, however, have not assimilated these positive statistics into their racial stereotypes (Jones, 1991).

When people like a group, their stereotype of the group's behavior tends to be positive. When they dislike a group, their stereotype of the same behavior tends to be negative. In a study that asked people to evaluate the traits associated with members of six cultures (English, Russian, German, American, French, and Italian), people strongly agreed in their judgments of their own and the others' typical national traits (Peabody, 1985). But the terms they used to describe the traits depended on whether they liked the country or not. For example, if you like a woman who is careful with money, you might call her *thrifty,* but if you dislike her, you will probably call her *stingy.* Likewise, someone who is friendly toward strangers could be *trusting* or *gullible;* someone who enjoys spending time with the relatives could be *family-loving* or *clannish.*

Positive and negative stereotypes, in turn, depend on the values and cultural norms of the observer. People from different cultures will see and evaluate the same social event differently (Taylor & Porter, 1994). Is coming late to class good, bad, or neutral? Is it good or bad to argue with your parents about grades? Chinese students in Hong Kong, where communalism and respect for elders are highly valued, and white students in Australia, where individualism is highly valued, give entirely different interpretations of these two events (Forgas & Bond, 1985). It is a small step from different interpretations to negative stereotypes: "Australians are selfish and disrespectful of adults"; "The Chinese are mindless slaves of authority." And it is a small step from negative stereotyping to prejudice.

Prejudice

A *prejudice* is an unreasonable negative feeling toward a category of people or a cultural practice. Prejudice consists of a negative stereotype of a group and a strong emotional discomfort with, dislike of, or outright hatred of its members. Feelings of prejudice violate the spirit of critical thinking and the scientific method because they resist rational argument and evidence. In his classic book *The Nature of Prejudice*, social psychologist Gordon Allport (1954/1979) described the responses characteristic of a prejudiced person when confronted with evidence contradicting his or her beliefs:

> **Mr. X:** The trouble with Jews is that they only take care of their own group.
> **Mr. Y:** But the record of the Community Chest campaign shows that they give more generously, in proportion to their numbers, to the general charities of the community, than do non-Jews.
> **Mr. X:** That shows they are always trying to buy favor and intrude into Christian affairs. They think of nothing but money; that is why there are so many Jewish bankers.
> **Mr. Y:** But a recent study shows that the percentage of Jews in the banking business is negligible, far smaller than the percentage of non-Jews.
> **Mr. X:** That's just it; they don't go in for respectable business; they are only in the movie business or run night clubs.

Notice that Mr. X doesn't respond to Mr. Y's evidence; he just moves along to another reason for his dislike of Jews. That is the nature of prejudice. As Elliot Aronson (1995) observes, suppose Mr. Y tried to persuade you to eat boiled insects. "Ugh," you might say, "they are so ugly." "But so are lobsters," he says, "and lots of people love lobsters." "Well, insects have no food value," you say. "Actually, they are a good source of protein," he answers. He might try other arguments, but the fact is that you have a food prejudice against eating insects, a reaction that exists in some cultures but by no means all.

The Sources of Prejudice. Psychodynamic psychologists hold that much of the emotional heat in prejudice stems from unconscious mechanisms. Prejudice, they say, allows a person to ward off feelings of inadequacy, doubt, and fear by projecting them onto the target group and using it as a *scapegoat*. Prejudice also reduces anxiety in uncertain times by allowing people to reduce complex problems to one cause: "Those people are the source of all my troubles." Most important, as research on samples from many nations has repeatedly confirmed, prejudice is related to low self-esteem: By disliking or hating certain groups, people are able to puff up their own low feelings of self-worth (Islam & Hewstone, 1993; Stephan et al., 1994; Tajfel & Turner, 1986).

In a demonstration of the link between low self-esteem and prejudice, 60 students participated in what they believed were two separate studies (Fein & Spencer, 1993). In the first, they got positive or negative feedback about their performance on a test of "social perceptiveness" and verbal skills. In the second, they were asked to evaluate the résumé of a woman who had applied for a job as personnel manager. All the subjects were shown the same résumé and photograph of the candidate, but half were told her name was "Julie Goldberg," and that she did volunteer work for a Jewish organization, and half were told her name was "Maria D'Agostino," and that she volunteered at a Catholic organization. The researchers found that the students who were feeling good about their test scores did not evaluate the "Jewish" woman differently from the

"Italian" woman. But those who had received a blow to their self-esteem evaluated the woman they believed to be Jewish more harshly than the Italian candidate. Their denigration of her, in turn, had the effect of raising their own self-esteem.

Social and cultural psychologists do not deny the importance of such psychological functions of prejudice. However, they have identified some social and economic factors that also contribute to the persistence of prejudice and discrimination:

1. *Socialization.* Many prejudices are passed along from parents to children, in messages that say "We don't associate with people like that," sometimes without either generation having ever met the object of their dislike. Advertising, entertainment shows, and news reports also perpetuate derogatory images and stereotypes of various groups, such as old people, women, gay men and lesbians, fat people, disabled people, and ethnic minorities.

2. *Social benefits.* Prejudices often bring support from others who share them—and the threat of losing that support if the prejudice is abandoned. The pressures to conform make it difficult for most people to break away from the prejudices of their friends, families, and associates.

3. *Economic benefits and justification of discrimination.* Many studies have found that prejudice rises when groups are in direct competition for jobs. In the nineteenth century, when Chinese immigrants were working in the gold mines, they were described by the local whites as being depraved and vicious, bloodthirsty and inhuman (Aronson, 1995). Just a decade later, when the Chinese began working on the transcontinental railroad across the United States—doing difficult and dangerous jobs that few white men wanted—prejudice against them declined. They were considered hard-working, industrious, and law-abiding. But after the railroad was finished, jobs dwindled. The Chinese had to compete with Civil War veterans for scarce jobs, and white attitudes toward the Chinese changed again. Chinese workers were considered criminal, crafty, conniving, and stupid (Aronson, 1995). Thus prejudice served to justify the whites' treatment of the Chinese, as it serves in general to justify any majority group's ill treatment of a minority. For example, in a series of experiments in Bangladesh, Muslims (who are the majority there) and Hindus (a minority) both revealed strong in-group favoritism, but only the Muslims also denigrated the minority Hindus (Islam & Hewstone, 1993).

Years ago, a classic study demonstrated the chilling link between economic conditions and scapegoating in America. Using data from 14 states in the American south, the researchers found a strong negative correlation between the number of black lynchings and the economic value of cotton: that is, the poorer the economic conditions for whites, the greater the number of lynchings (Hovland & Sears, 1940). These data were later reanalyzed to assess other possible explanations, but the correlation remained (Hepworth & West, 1988). Another research project used many different measures of economic threat and social insecurity (such as the unemployment rate, the rate of serious crimes, the number of work stoppages, and personal income levels) and of prejudice (the number of anti-Semitic incidents, activities by the Ku Klux Klan, and attitudes toward other groups). The researchers found that during times of high social and economic threat, prejudice increases significantly (Doty, Peterson, & Winter, 1991).

In the late 1980s and early 1990s, tough economic conditions in the United States (and around the world) meant that ethnic groups found themselves competing once again for portions of a shrinking pie. The violence and looting that occurred in Los Angeles in 1992 made the economic underpinnings of group conflict and racism explicit, casting a harsh spotlight on the competition for jobs among African-Americans, Koreans, and Latinos.

WANTS, &c.

WANTED A COOK—She must not be an Irish woman, and must bring unexceptionable recommendations. Apply at 33 Grove street, Greenwich.   j5 3t

WANTED—A FARM in Westchester county, with a good water prospect. One in the vicinity of Throg's Neck would be preferred. Apply at 250 Pearl-street.   d20 d&ctf

WANTED—Young Ladies as apprentices wanted at the Mantua-making Establishment of A. C. SMETS & CO. 258 Broadway.   n30

BOARD WANTED—by a gentleman and lady in a private family, in the vicinity of Cliff-street. A family where there are no other boarders would be preferred. Address A. B. at this Office.   J6 3t*

WANTED—Immediately, a respectable woman, as Nurse, who has been accustomed to the care of children. None need apply without the best of references, at No. 2 Bond-street.   d28 tf

WANTED—by a young lady educated in France, and who also possesses a good knowledge of the English— a situation as Instructress to small children in a private family. Satisfactory references will be given. Direct to M. R. at this Office.   d30

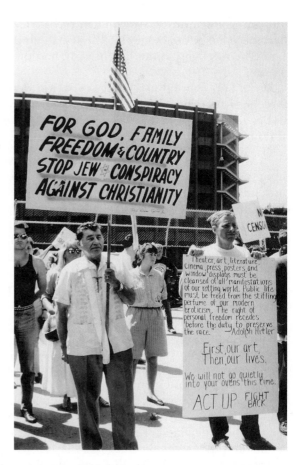

These signs reveal the history of prejudice in the United States. In 1831, a newspaper boldly reflected the then-popular dislike of the Irish. Job ads and hotels used to make it clear that "Christians only" were wanted, and anti-Semitism is on the rise again today. Anti-Japanese feelings ran high in the 1920s, during World War II, and returned in the 1990s with America's economic recession. Iranians and other "aliens" have been the targets of political hostilities and movements to restrict "colored" immigration. Native Americans have been targets of hatred since Europeans arrived on the continent. Animosity toward blacks resulted in segregated facilities, a legal practice until the 1950s, and today many neighborhoods and schools remain separate and unequal. Prejudice against women also remains widespread, as shown by a male-only club in Virginia. And virulent anger against gay men and lesbians continues today. Why do new prejudices keep emerging, and why do some old ones persist?

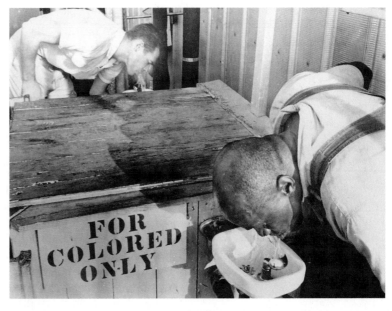

✳ *How would you define a racist? Are people racist if they privately dislike members of another group, but never actually treat them unfairly? Are people racist if they are intellectually opposed to racism but feel uncomfortable being around a member of another group?*

The Varieties of Prejudice. One problem in studying prejudice is that not all prejudiced people are prejudiced in the same way or to the same extent. Gordon Allport (1954/1979) once astutely observed that "defeated intellectually, prejudice lingers emotionally." That is, a person might want to lose a prejudice against a certain group and realize that his or her feelings are unwarranted, yet still feel uncomfortable with members of the group. Should we put this person in the same category as one who is outspokenly bigoted? Should we label the person as prejudiced because of his or her discomfort, or use the label only if the person actually acts on those feelings, perhaps by being rude or by actively discriminating against a person by virtue or his or her gender, culture, sexual orientation, or skin color? Do good intentions count? What if a person is ignorant of another culture and mindlessly blurts out a remark that reflects that ignorance ("Gee, I was always told that Jews had little horns on their heads")? Does that count as prejudice or merely as ignorance?

According to Patricia Devine, people who are actively trying to break their "prejudice habit" should not be accused of being bigots. Devine and her colleagues (1991) have studied white heterosexuals' responses to being in situations with blacks or gay men. The researchers found that most people hold remnants of emotional prejudices that were acquired in childhood but that, as adults, they consciously try to eradicate. They are caught between what they know they *should* do when they meet a target of their old prejudice and what they fear they *would* do. Highly prejudiced people feel little guilt or conflict about their biases, so they feel no conflict between "should" and "would." Less prejudiced whites and heterosexuals may feel uncomfortable when they are with blacks or gays, but they also feel guilty about having these feelings and struggle to overcome them. Research such as Devine's suggests that individuals might feel uncomfortable with one another without being prejudiced. Their discomfort could reflect simple unfamiliarity with one another person's ways; a tourist in a Turkish bazaar may feel like a fish out of water, but that discomfort does not make the tourist anti-Turkish. Or the discomfort could reflect an honest effort to put old prejudices aside; as Devine and Julia Zuwerink (1994) have noted, reducing prejudice is a *process,* not something that can happen overnight.

A similar argument holds that the main problem dividing blacks and whites is not prejudice but differing cultural values. Surveys find that many white Americans place a high value on equality but also on individualism and self-reliance (Katz & Hass, 1988). Their support of equality leads many whites to feel sympathy toward blacks because of the disadvantages and discrimination that they know that blacks have suffered. But the values of individualism and self-reliance lead many of the same whites to accuse blacks of not taking enough responsibility for solving their problems. Most African-Americans, however, place their highest value on equality and justice. They argue that their lower status and income are not a result of a failure of self-reliance but of the systematic injustice they have suffered at the hands of whites. The gap in perceptions of racism and injustice in America is growing (Edsall & Edsall, 1991), and it confirms to many blacks that whites just "don't get it."

Other social scientists and observers of North American society strongly assert that racial prejudice and animosity are not declining. Derrick Bell (1992), an African-American legal scholar, argues that progress against racism is an illusion. Those who agree with him maintain that publicly stated attitudes—what people will say to an interviewer—are not an accurate measure of racism because too many people know that revealing overtly prejudiced attitudes is inappropriate and unfashionable. These observers maintain that old prejudices lurk behind a mask of *symbolic racism,* in which whites focus not on dislike of black individuals but on racial symbols and issues such as "forced bus-ing," "welfare abuse," "reverse discrimination," or "hard-core criminals." In their view, these issues have become code words for the continuing animosity and resentment that most whites have for blacks.

The way to measure racism, according to this argument, is by observing how people actually behave when they are with the object of their discomfort (Jones, 1991). In an experiment in which students administered shock to confederates in an apparent study of biofeedback, whites showed *less* aggression toward blacks than toward whites. But as soon as the whites were angered by overhearing derogatory remarks about themselves, they showed *more* aggression toward blacks than toward whites (Rogers & Prentice-Dunn, 1981). This finding implies that whites may be willing to control their negative feelings toward blacks (or, if you recall the "Julie Goldberg" study, toward Jews or other targets of prejudice) under normal conditions. But as soon as they are angry, stressed, provoked, or suffer a blow to their self-esteem, their real prejudice reveals itself.

As if these complexities of prejudice were not enough, there is another. Peter Glick and Susan Fiske (in press) argue that sexism is "a special case of prejudice" that is often marked by "a deep ambivalence, rather than a uniform antipathy, toward women." Using a questionnaire they call the Ambivalent Sexism Inventory, which has been administered to more than 2,000 individuals of both sexes, they have identified two kinds of sexism that are empirically distinct. The first is *hostile sexism,* which involves strongly negative feelings about women, such as anger, hatred, and contempt; this kind of sexism is comparable to any other negative prejudice toward an entire group. The second is *benevolent sexism,* which involves positive feelings about women, along with paternalistic, protective, and stereotyped attitudes toward them—a prejudice that says "I like women, as long as they stay in their proper place."

As you can see, defining and studying racism and other forms of prejudice are not easy. How does covert discomfort or a patronizing sense of superiority differ from explicit hostility? Can a woman hold sexist attitudes toward men, or should sexism refer only to prejudice and discrimination against women? Is an African-American who dislikes all whites a racist, or is racism an attribute only of institutions and of whites with power? Because people differ in their basic premises, such as the definitions of *racist* and *sexist,* and because they differ in their values, such as equality or self-reliance, their conclusions about prejudice will also differ.

Reducing Prejudice.   Over the years, various solutions have been proposed for reducing prejudice and conflict between groups. One view holds that indi-

How do you react to this cartoon, which is a warning about being too quick to assume that other people are prejudiced against you? Do you see it as a trivializing of people's real experiences with discrimination, or a plea for empathy and shared understanding?

viduals must have the right education, develop more self-esteem, or have a religious or spiritual conversion; then their prejudices will fade. A second view, the *contact hypothesis,* holds that the best solution is to bring members of both sides together and let them get acquainted; in this way, they will discover their shared humanity. A third view is that prejudice can be eradicated with the right set of laws; once prejudiced behavior is illegal, people's hearts and minds will follow. And a fourth approach holds that groups in conflict need to put aside their individual interests and work together for a common goal.

Solutions to prejudice that focus on the individual have not, alas, been terribly successful at a group or national level, as history amply documents. On the contrary, research shows repeatedly that formerly unprejudiced people can, under conditions of economic competition or the inflamed nationalism of wartime, become enraged haters of their new enemies.

The contact hypothesis had a moment of glory during the 1950s and 1960s; in some settings, such as integrated housing projects, contact between blacks and whites did reduce hostility (Deutsch & Collins, 1951; Wilner, Walkley, & Cook, 1955). However, as is apparent at most big-city high schools today, desegregation and opportunities to socialize are often unsuccessful (Stephan, 1985). In many integrated schools, ethnic groups form cliques and gangs, fighting other groups and defending their own ways.

As for the legal approach, changes in the law have been essential in achieving justice and in changing some prejudiced attitudes. Integration of public facilities in the American south would never have occurred if civil-rights advocates had waited around for segregationists to have a change of heart. Women would never have gotten the right to vote, attend college, or become physicians without persistent challenges to the laws that permitted discrimination. But laws do not necessarily change attitudes if all they do is produce unequal contact between two former antagonists or if economic competition for jobs continues. Even with legal reforms, de facto segregation of schools and neighborhoods is still the rule in the United States.

Finally, although cooperative learning is unquestionably beneficial to students of all ages, it, too, is not enough to reduce hostility between groups. Elliot Aronson and his colleagues (1978) tried to apply the research on cooperation to reducing ethnic conflict among white, Chicano, and black children in elementary schools. Aronson's team designed a "jigsaw method" to build cooperation. Classes were divided into groups of six students of mixed ethnicities, and every group worked together on a shared task that was broken up like a jigsaw puzzle. Each child needed the contributions of the others to put the assignment together; for instance, each child might be given one paragraph of a six-paragraph biography and asked to learn the whole story. The jigsaw students, in comparison to classmates in regular classes, did show greater self-esteem, liked their classmates better, and improved their grades . . . but only slightly. The differences were statistically significant, but so small as to be socially insignificant (R. Brown, 1986).

The reason for this result highlights a difficulty in all attempts to apply research findings to complex social problems: The intervention is usually too narrow and too brief to overcome all the influences on a person's behavior. In this case, children were in the jigsaw classroom only three times a week, for a 45-minute class period. That was not much time to overturn entrenched habits and conflicting customs outside the classroom.

It seems, then, that all single-arrow efforts to hit the bull's-eye of prejudice are bound to miss their target. Researchers have spent many decades working on ways to apply what they know about ethnocentrism and prejudice to the serious problem of cultural conflicts. While recognizing that there are numerous psychological sources of prejudice, they have also identified the conditions necessary to reduce prejudice and conflict (Amir, 1994; Brewer, 1986; Kohn, 1992; Stephan & Brigham, 1985; Stephan & Stephan, 1992). The zinger is that for any of them to be effective, you have to have all of them:

1. Both sides must cooperate, working together for a common goal, an enterprise that reduces us–them thinking and creates an encompassing social identity. Competition, which can create animosities where none existed, is likely to make existing animosities worse.

2. Both sides must have equal status and equal economic standing. If one side has more power or greater economic opportunity, prejudice can continue. Thus, simply putting blacks and whites in the same situation won't necessarily reduce conflict if the whites have all the decision-making authority and higher status. Indeed, in such cases, white stereotypes about blacks tend to be reinforced rather than weakened (Amir, 1994). But when blacks have equal or higher status, white attitudes typically change in a much more favorable direction.

3. Both sides must believe they have the moral, legal, and economic support of authorities, such as teachers, employers, the judicial system, government officials, and the police. In other words, the larger culture must support the goal of equality in its laws and in the actions of its officials.

4. Both sides must have opportunities to work and socialize together, formally and informally, if they are ever going to get used to one another's food, music, customs, attitudes, and everyday human qualities.

Perhaps one reason that cultural conflicts have been so persistent around the world is that these four conditions are rarely met all at the same time.

Quick QUIZ

A. Identify which concept—ethnocentrism, stereotyping, or prejudice—is illustrated by the following three statements.

1. Juan believes that all Anglos are uptight and cold, and he won't listen to any evidence that contradicts his belief.
2. John knows and likes the Mexican minority in his town, but he privately believes that Anglo culture is superior to all others.
3. Jane believes that Honda owners are thrifty and practical. June believes that Honda owners are stingy and dull.

B. Jemma vacations in Spain, where her handbag is snatched. "All Spanish men are thieves," she fumes. Jemma has formed a(n) _____ between being a Spanish man and being a criminal.

 C. A 1994 Louis Harris survey found that large percentages of African-Americans, Asian-Americans, and Latinos hold negative stereotypes of one another and resent other minorities almost as much as they resent whites. What are some of the reasons that people who have themselves been victims of stereotyping and prejudice would hold the same attitudes toward others?

Answers:

A. 1. prejudice 2. ethnocentrism 3. stereotypes B. illusory correlation C. socialization by parents and the larger society; peer pressure from friends who share these prejudices; and economic competition for jobs and resources

■ CAN CULTURES GET ALONG?

The whole world is festering with unhappy souls—
The French hate the Germans, the Germans hate the Poles,
Italians hate Yugoslavs, South Africans hate the Dutch;
And I don't like anybody very much.

■ SHELDON HARNICK, "MERRY LITTLE MINUET" ■

★ *Given all the cultural and economic sources of group conflict and ethnocentrism, how should we define the goals of a multicultural society? Should we aim for true understanding and acceptance of differences, or merely peaceful coexistence?*

Sometimes the possibility of harmonious relations between cultures looks bleak indeed. All over world, animosities erupt in bloody battles, and new wars emerge even where groups had been living together companionably. When cultures with different customs, values, and nonverbal gestures collide, misunderstandings can even be fatal. In Stockton, California, a driver used a hand signal to alert a car behind him at a stoplight that his headlights were off. The driver of the second car, taking this gesture as a sign of disrespect, shot at the first car, killing a passenger.

Cultural psychology, which has identified the continuing reasons for international and multicultural conflict, also gives us hope for reducing it. The knowledge of how cultures differ, even in the smallest rules of time management and eye contact, benefits everyone who has to deal with another culture—which, on this shrinking planet, is all of us: neighbor, tourist, diplomat, business executive. The study of culture suggests that conflict and aggression are not determined solely by human biology, but also by our circumstances. Therefore, as circumstances change, so does the need for violence; and indeed, throughout history, societies have changed from being warlike to being peaceful, and vice versa. The Swedes were once one of the most warlike nations on earth, but today they are among the most pacifistic (Groebel & Hinde, 1989).

So it is ironic and sad that cultural research, which has done so much to make people aware of the dangers of ethnocentrism and reasons for differences among groups, can be used to inflame intolerance rather than reduce it. Celebrations of difference can lead to ethnic, societal, and gender separatism, in which people glorify only their own group and regard other cultures or the other gender as inherently inferior—or so hopelessly different that there's no point in trying to get along with them.

As groups that were once excluded from psychological research and theory have become aware of the injustice of this omission, they have done much to remedy matters. But some psychologists and social critics are concerned about tendencies to replace old biases with new ones (Appiah, 1994; Crawford & Marecek, 1989; Gates, 1992; Hughes, 1993; Yoder & Kahn, 1993). Thus, some women want to replace the view that women are the deficient sex with the view that women are the better sex, the sex that will save the world (Eisler, 1987); some African-Americans argue that Africans are the "sun people" who have a "humanistic, spiritualistic value system," whereas Europeans are the "ice people" who are "egoistic, individualistic, and exploitative" (Traub, 1993). However, as Kwame Appiah (1994), a professor of Afro-American studies who is himself from Ghana, writes, "Cruelty and kindness are not Western prerogatives, any more than intelligence and creativity. . . . The proper response to Eurocentrism is surely not a reactive Afrocentrism, but a new understanding that humanizes all of us by learning to think beyond race."

Indeed, cultural psychology shows that no cultural or ethnic group has always and everywhere been superior to every other in its dealings with humanity. This is because as human beings, all of us are subject to the psychological processes that social and cultural psychology have identified, from obedience to ethnocentrism. The fact that groups differ in certain practices and attitudes does not mean that they have no shared human needs and qualities.

In Hawaii, many different ethnic and racial groups coexist, and no single group is a majority. This group of Hawaiian musicians provides a metaphor for a question that cultural psychologists hope to answer: Can people harmonize in spite of their differences, or do they inevitably end up singing different songs?

Perhaps research will never yield a definite answer to the question of how different cultures can get along better. (The last guideline of critical thinking: Tolerate uncertainty.) One reason is that people differ in their goals for a culturally diverse world. At one unrealistic extreme, some people would persuade or force every other group and religion to become just like them. At the other unrealistic extreme, some people dream of all cultures living together in perfect harmony, respecting their differences. Cultural research suggests, on the contrary, that we would do better to recognize that conflicts will always occur, because of economic inequities and because of cultural misunderstandings, and then turn our attention to finding nonviolent ways of resolving these conflicts. Ethnocentrism may always be with us, as long as people exist in different cultural groups. But if we can think of ways of reducing the payoffs of prejudice, perhaps we can reduce the tendency for good feelings about our own culture to create hostile feelings toward others. That would be the best way of all to "take psychology with us."

*T*aking Psychology with You

Travels Across the Cultural Divide

A French salesman worked for a company that was bought by Americans. When the new American manager ordered him to step up his sales within the next three months, the employee quit in a huff, taking his customers with him. Why? In polychronic France, it takes years to develop customers; in family-owned businesses, relationships with customers may span generations. The monochronic American wanted instant results, as Americans usually do, but the French salesman knew this was impossible and quit. The American view was, "He wasn't up to the job; he's lazy and disloyal, so he stole my customers." The French view was, "There is no point in explaining anything to a person who is so stupid as to think you can acquire loyal customers in three months" (Hall & Hall, 1987).

As this story shows, when monochronic and polychronic people try to do business with one another, they often make unintentional mistakes. Many corporations are beginning to realize that such cultural differences are not trivial and that their business success depends on understanding them. You, too, can benefit from the psychological research on cultures, whether you plan to do business abroad, visit as a tourist, or simply want to get along better in our own increasingly diverse society.

● *Be sure you understand the other culture's rules, not only of manners and customs but also of nonverbal gestures and methods of communication.* If you find yourself getting angry over something a person from another culture is doing, you should try to find out whether your expectations and perceptions of that person's behavior are appropriate. For example, in Los Angeles there is tension between Koreans, who typically do not shake hands when greeting strangers, and African-Americans and whites, who do. A person who is used to shaking hands as a gesture of friendship and courtesy is likely to feel insulted if another person refuses to do the same, unless he or she understands that what is going on is a cultural difference and not a personal affront.

- *When in Rome, do as the Romans do—as much as possible.* Most of the things you really need to know about a culture are not to be found in the guidebooks or travelogues, but in the kinds of research results found in this chapter. To learn the unspoken rules of a culture, it is wise to keep your eyes open and your mouth shut: Look, listen, and observe. What is the pace of life like? Which is more valued in this culture, relationships or schedules? Are business transactions based on bargaining and negotiation or on a fixed exchange? When customers enter a shop, do they greet and chat with the shopkeeper or ignore the person as they browse?

Of course, knowing another culture's ways of doing things doesn't mean that it will always be easy for you to pick them up. If you are not used to bargaining, shopping in Turkey or Mexico will be exasperating. You won't know the unstated rules, you won't know whether you got "taken" or got "a great buy," and you will probably walk away wishing for a system of fixed prices. If you *are* used to bargaining, you will be just as exasperated when a seller offers you a flat price. "Where's the fun in this?" you'll say. "The whole human experience of shopping is gone!" It will help to find a cultural "translator" who can show you the ropes.

Remember, though, that even when you know the rules, you may find it difficult to carry them out. For example, cultures differ in their tolerance for prolonged gazes (Keating, 1994). In the Middle East, two men will typically gaze at one another for extended periods of conversation, but such direct gazes would be deeply uncomfortable to most Japanese or white Americans, and a sign of insult to some African-Americans. Knowing this fact about gaze rules can help people accept the reality of different customs, but most of us will still feel uncomfortable trying to change our own ways.

- *Nevertheless, avoid stereotyping.* Try not to let your awareness of cultural differences cause you to exaggerate differences between groups and to overlook variation within them. During a dreary Boston winter, social psychologist Roger Brown (1986) went to the Bahamas for a vacation. To his surprise, he found the people he met unfriendly, rude, and sullen. He decided that the reason was that Bahamians had to deal with spoiled, critical foreigners, and he tried out this hypothesis on a cab driver. The cab driver looked at Brown in amazement, smiled cheerfully, and told him that Bahamians don't mind tourists; just *unsmiling* tourists.

And then Brown realized what had been going on. "Not tourists generally, but this tourist, myself, was the cause," he wrote. "Confronted with my unrelaxed wintry Boston face, they had assumed I had no interest in them and had responded noncommittally, inexpressively. I had created the Bahamian national character. Everywhere I took my face it sprang into being. So I began smiling a lot, and the Bahamians changed their national character. In fact, they lost any national character and differentiated into individuals."

Finally, perhaps the best advice is to *use cultural explanations to expand your understanding of human behavior, not to reduce behavior to culture.* Any one-factor explanation can lead to an abdication of individual responsibility, which is why "The system made me do it" or "My culture made me do it" is no more valid than "My hormones made me do it" or "My upbringing made me do it." Social and cultural research teaches us to appreciate the power of circumstances, situations, roles, and working conditions in influencing behavior, but we should not forget Roger Brown's lesson that there is an individual person rattling around in there: one who not only reflects his or her culture, but who shares the common concerns of all humanity.

Summary

1. *Culture* is a program of shared rules that govern the behavior of members of a community or society, and a set of values, beliefs, and attitudes shared by most members of that community. The study of culture is challenging because of difficulties in devising good methods and getting samples from many societies in order to make valid cultural comparisons; the difficulty of interpreting results when the same custom may have different meanings and functions across cultures; the risk of stereotyping; the common tendency to *reify* "culture" as an explanation without identifying the mechanisms or aspects of culture that influence behavior; and the political sensitivity of many findings.

2. Some signals of *body language* seem to be universal, but most, such as *conversational distance* and notions of when a smile is appropriate, are specific to particular cultures. This fact creates many possibilities for misunderstanding and offense. Body language is especially important in communicating emotion, which can be "contagious," and in regulating smooth social interactions. In *high-context cultures,* people pay close attention to nonverbal signs; they assume a shared knowledge and history, so things need not be spelled out. In *low-context cultures,* people pay more attention to words than to nonverbal language; everything must be explained and stated directly.

3. *Monochronic cultures* organize time into linear segments in which people do one thing at a time and value promptness. *Polychronic cultures* organize time along parallel lines; people do many things at once, and the demands of friends and family supersede those of the appointment book. A culture's way of organizing time stems from its economic system, social organization, political history, and ecology.

4. *Individual-centered cultures* define the "self" as a collection of personality traits; *collectivist* or *group-centered cultures* see the "self" as embedded in a community. The way that people define the self affects many aspects of individual psychology, including people's personalities, emotions, and relationships. In collectivist cultures, the strongest human bond is usually not between husband and wife but between parent and child, and child rearing is communal.

5. People develop *social identities* based on their nationality, ethnicity, religion, and other roles in society. One important social identity is an *ethnic identity.* In culturally diverse societies, many people face the problem of balancing their ethnic identity with *acculturation.* Depending on whether ethnic identity and identification with the larger culture are strong or weak, a person may become *bicultural;* choose *assimilation;* become an *ethnic separatist;* or feel *marginal.* Ethnic labels have great symbolic and emotional significance, which is why they are so politically volatile (as discussed in "Psychology and Popular Culture").

6. In the cultural view, a culture's attitudes and practices are embedded in its history, environment, economy, and survival needs and thus are *socially constructed.* For example, although some gender differences appear to be universal, there are many variations in women's status, the work that men and women do, the degree of male–female contact, the value placed on female chastity, and the salience of gender differences. Factors pertaining to *production* (the economy and ecology) and *reproduction* (availability of birth control and the need for many or few children) help explain these variations.

7. Economic and social factors are also involved in the variations among men in aggressiveness and in the status of women. High rates of male violence and white homicide in the American south and west are related to a history of reliance on herding rather than on farming. As countries become industrialized and urban, their gender roles also become more egalitarian; access to reliable birth control and the growth of jobs involving service skills and brainwork are eliminating the traditional reasons for a sexual division of labor.

8. *Ethnocentrism,* the belief that one's own group or nation is superior to all others, promotes "us–them" thinking and is especially common in war. *Stereotypes* help people rapidly process new information, retrieve memories, organize experience, and predict how others will behave. But they often create *illusory correlations* in which people overestimate the link between two variables, such as sexual abuse and eating disorders. Stereotypes distort reality in three ways: (1) They emphasize differences between groups; (2) they underestimate the differences within groups; (3) and they produce selective perception. The values and rules of culture determine how people see and interpret the same event. When they like a group, their stereotypes of the group's behavior are positive; when they dislike a group, their stereotypes of the same behavior are often negative.

9. A *prejudice* is an unreasonable negative feeling toward a category of people or a cultural practice. Prejudice has several psychological functions: It reduces anxiety by allowing people to feel superior; it bolsters self-esteem when a person feels threatened; and it provides a simple explanation of complex problems. But prejudice also has social and financial functions. People acquire prejudices through childhood socialization, the social support they receive, and the economic benefits they gain as a result. During times of economic difficulty, prejudice rises significantly.

10. Prejudice occurs in many varieties and degrees, a fact that causes debates about definitions of racism, sexism, and other prejudices. Blacks and whites often disagree on their definitions of racism and on the question of whether racism is declining or has taken new forms (such as *symbolic racism*). Similarly, *hostile sexism*—dislike of and contempt for women—is different from *benevolent sexism*—an attitude of "I like women, as long as they stay in their place."

11. Social and cultural psychologists have studied many efforts to reduce prejudice and conflict between groups. Approaches that focus solely on individual change or increased contact between groups (the *contact hypothesis*) have not been very successful. Changes in the law have been essential in achieving justice, but laws do not inevitably change attitudes, especially if economic competition continues. Prejudice decreases when people from different groups work together for a common goal; have equal status and economic standing; have the support of authorities; and have opportunities to work and socialize together.

12. Cross-cultural psychologists have identified many reasons for cultural conflicts and have sought solutions for reducing them. But they also are concerned that cultural research, which has done much to make people aware of the dangers of ethnocentrism and the differences among groups, can be used to foster ethnocentrism and ethnic separatism and to inflame intolerance rather than reduce it.

Key Terms

culture *664*
cultural psychologists *664*
cross-cultural psychologists *664*
reification *668*
body language *669*
conversational distance *670*
high-context and low-context cultures *671*
monochronic and polychronic cultures *672*
individual-centered and collectivist cultures *674*
social identity *675*
ethnic identity *675*
acculturation *675*
bicultural identity *676*

assimilation *676*
ethnic separatism *676*
marginal identity *676*
sex versus gender *680*
social constructionism *680*
production *682*
reproduction *682*
ethnocentrism *686*
us–them thinking *686*
stereotype *687*
illusory correlation *688*
prejudice *690*
symbolic racism *694*
hostile vs. benevolent sexism *695*
contact hypothesis *696*

Taking Psychology with You

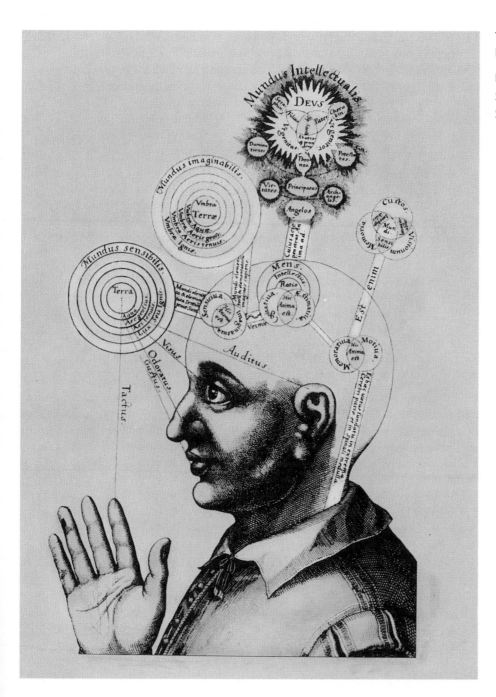

THE FIVE STRANDS OF HUMAN EXPERIENCE

PSYCHOLOGY IN YOUR LIFE
Situation 1: When Love Has Gone
Situation 2: Job Stress

You've come a long way since the beginning of this book. It is now time to stand back and ask yourself where you've been and what you've learned from the many studies, topics, and controversies that have been covered. What fundamental principles emerge, and how can you take them with you into your own life? You probably won't be surprised that different psychologists would answer these questions differently; as we noted back in Chapter 1, psychology is a patchwork quilt of ideas. Still, even a patchwork quilt has an overall pattern. We believe that there exists a "big picture" in the study of psychology, one that reveals five fundamental determinants of human behavior.

■ THE FIVE STRANDS OF HUMAN EXPERIENCE

If you look back at the chapters in this book, you will see that our focus began within the individual—with neurons and hormones—and gradually expanded to include the physical environment, the social environment, and entire cultures. In Chapter 1, we saw that there are five general perspectives on human behavior that guide the assumptions and methods of psychologists. Each of these perspectives on human experience offers different questions to ask when you are trying to understand or change a particular aspect of your own life:

1. *Biological influences.* As physical creatures, we are influenced by our bodies and our brains. Physiology affects the rhythms of our lives, our perceptions of reality, our ability to learn, the intensity of our emotions, our temperaments, and, in some cases, our vulnerability to emotional disorder.

Thus, when you are distressed, you might want to ask: What is going on in your body? Do you have a physical condition that might be affecting your behavior? Do you have a temperamental tendency to be easily aroused or to be

"I still don't have all the answers, but I'm beginning to ask the right questions."

calm? Are alcohol or other drugs altering your ability to make decisions or behave as you would like? Might an irregular schedule be disrupting your physical functions and impairing your efficiency? Are you under unusual pressures that increase physical stress?

2. *Cognitive influences.* Our species is, above all, the animal that explains things. These explanations may not always be realistic or sensible, but they continually influence our actions and choices. To solve problems, you need to ask yourself how you are framing the situation you are in. Are your explanations of what is causing the problem reasonable? Have you tested them? Are you wallowing in negative thoughts? Do you attribute your successes to luck but take all the blame for your failures—or do you take credit for your successes and blame everyone else for your failures? Do you assume the worst about others? Do you make external attributions or internal ones? Are you responding to other people's expectations or rules in a mindless way?

3. *Learning influences.* From the moment of birth, human beings begin learning and are exquisitely sensitive to their environments. What we do and how we do it are often a result of our learning histories and the specific situation we are in. We respond to the environment, and, in turn, our acts have consequences that influence future behavior. The right environment and rewards can help us cope better with disabilities, get along better with others, and even become more creative and happy. The wrong kind can foster boredom, hostility, and discontent.

So, as you analyze a situation, you would want to ask: What are the contingencies and consequences governing your behavior and that of others? What rewards are maintaining your behavior? Of the many messages being aimed at you by television, books, parents, and teachers, which have the greatest influence? Who are your role models, the people you most admire and wish to emulate?

4. *Psychodynamic influences.* People are often unaware of the reasons they are getting themselves in trouble, just as they are unaware of the defense mechanisms they use to rationalize mistakes and protect self-esteem. If you find that you are repeating self-defeating patterns, expectations, and emotional reactions that you acquired in childhood, you might want to consider the reasons. Do other people "push your buttons" for reasons you cannot explain? Are you displacing feelings about your parents onto your friends or intimates? Are you carrying around "unfinished business" from childhood losses and hurts?

5. *Social and cultural influences.* Although most Westerners think of themselves as independent creatures, everyone conforms, to one extent or another, to the expectations and demands of others. Spouses, lovers, friends, bosses, parents, and perfect strangers "pull our strings" in ways we may not recognize. We conform to group pressures, obey authorities, and blossom or wilt in close relationships. Throughout life, we need "contact comfort"—sometimes in the literal touch or embrace of others and sometimes in shared experience or conversation. Although there are many universals of behavior that unite humanity, "human nature" also varies from one culture to another. Culture dictates a set of norms and roles for how employers and employees, strangers and friends, and men and women are supposed to act. Whenever you find yourself wondering irritably why "*those* people are behaving that way," chances are that a cultural difference is at work.

So, in solving problems, you might ask: Who are the people in your life who affect your attitudes and behavior? Do your friends and relatives support you or hinder you in achieving your goals? How do your ethnicity and nationality affect you? What gender roles do they specify for you and your partners in close relationships? What would happen if you ignored the norms of your role? Are your conflicts with other people a result of cultural misunderstandings—due, for instance, to differing rules for expressing emotion?

Keep in mind, though, that *no single one of these factors operates in isolation from the others*. The forces that govern our behavior are as intertwined as strands of ivy on a wall, and it can be hard to see where one strand begins and another ends. This message, if enough people believed it, would probably put an end to the pop-psych industry, which promotes single, simple answers to real-life complexities. (Anxious about the state of the world? Just jog some more, or fix your diet. Not doing so well at work? Just learn to dress for success.) Some simplifiers of psychology try to reduce human problems to biochemical imbalances or genetic defects. Others argue that anyone can "fulfill any potential," regardless of biology or environment, and that solving problems is merely a matter of being determined.

In this book, we have tried to show that the concerns and dilemmas of life do not divide up neatly according to the chapters of an introductory psychology text (even ours). For example, to understand shyness or loneliness, you might need to consider your personal learning history; childhood experiences and what you observed from adult role models; temperamental tendencies; the autobiographical memories that make up your personal story; how stress, diet, drugs, and sleep patterns might be affecting your mood; and whether you come from a culture that encourages or prohibits assertiveness. It may seem daunting to keep so many factors in mind. But once you get into the habit of seeing a situation from many points of view, relying on single-answer approaches will feel like wearing blinders. And it's a habit that will inoculate you against the temptations of psychobabble—pop-psych ideas that are unsupported by evidence.

■ PSYCHOLOGY IN YOUR LIFE

If the theories and findings in this book are to be of long-lasting personal value to you, they must jump off the printed page and into your daily life. In previous chapters, we have tried to point out ways in which you can apply what you have learned. However, *you* must do the actual work of selecting those aspects of psychological knowledge that can be of benefit to you.

To give you some practice in doing so, we will take two common problems and offer some ideas about where to look in this book for principles and findings that may shed light on them. If you are serious about wanting to use psychology, we recommend that you turn to the specified pages and think about how the information there can best be applied, even if you don't have the particular problems we have selected. Our brief lists of hints are far from exhaustive, and we have not attempted to touch on every topic in this book that might be relevant to each problem. You should feel free to make the remote associations that are the heart of creativity and come up with additional ideas that could be brought to bear on a particular problem. There is no single correct solution in these hypothetical situations, any more than there is a single solution to the problems you encounter in your life.

Situation 1: When Love Has Gone

You have been romantically involved with someone for a year. When the relationship began, you felt very much in love, and you thought your feelings were returned. But for a long time now, your partner's treatment of you has been anything but loving. In fact, your partner makes fun of your faults in front of others, yells at you about the slightest annoyance, and insults and humiliates you. Sometimes you are ignored for days on end, as if your partner wants to punish you for some imagined wrong. All of your friends advise you to leave the relationship. Yet you can't shake the feeling that your partner must really love you. You still occasionally have a great time together, and your partner seems to become very distressed whenever you threaten to leave. You wish you could either improve the relationship or get out, and your inability to act leaves you feeling angry and depressed.

How might each of the following topics help you resolve this problem? We suggest that you try to come up with your own answers, aided by these text references, before you look at ours:

- Approach–avoidance conflicts (Chapter 11, page 431)
- Intermittent reinforcement (Chapter 7, page 262)
- Observational learning (Chapter 7, page 276)
- Locus of control (Chapter 12, page 448, and Chapter 14, page 531)
- Cognitive-dissonance theory (Chapter 8, page 303)
- Gender differences in emotion and love (Chapter 10, page 395, and Chapter 11, page 412)
- Attribution theory (Chapter 17, page 637)

Here are a few reasons why these topics might apply, but feel free to think of others:

- Research on *approach–avoidance conflicts* may help explain why you are both attracted to and repelled by this relationship, and why the closer you approach, the more you want to leave (and vice versa). When a goal is both attractive and painful, it is not unusual to feel uncertain and to vacillate about the possible courses of action.

- *Intermittent reinforcement* may explain why you persist in apparently self-defeating behavior. If staying in the relationship brought only punishment or if your partner always ignored you, it would be easier to leave. But your partner intermittently gives you good times, and when behavior is occasionally rewarded, it becomes resistant to extinction.

- Past *observational learning* may help account for your present behavior. Perhaps your parents have a dominant/submissive relationship, and their way of interacting is what you have learned to expect in your own relationships.

- If you have an *external locus of control*, you may feel that you cannot control what is happening to you, that you are merely a victim of fate, chance, or the whims and wishes of others. People with an internal locus of control feel more in charge of their lives and are less inclined to blame outside circumstances for their difficulties.

- *Cognitive-dissonance theory* suggests that you may be trying to keep your attitudes and behavior consistent. The cognition "I am in this relationship and choose to be with this person" is dissonant with "This person ignores and mistreats me." Because you are still unable to break up and alter the first cognition, you are working on the second cognition, hoping that your partner will change for the better.

- Research on *gender differences* finds that men and women often have different unstated rules about expressing emotion and different definitions of love. Perhaps traditional gender roles are preventing you and your partner from communicating your true preferences and feelings.

- *Attribution theory* addresses the consequences of holding dispositional explanations of another person's behavior (something about the person) or situational explanations (something about the circumstances). Unhappy couples tend to make dispositional attributions when the partner does something wrong or thoughtless ("My partner is mean"); happy couples look for situational attributions ("My partner is under a lot of pressure at work"). You might want to look for evidence to test different reasons that your partner is treating you badly. Is the behavior characteristic of your partner in many situations, or might it be a result of stress, particular problems with you, or other difficulties?

Understanding your situation, of course, does not lead automatically to a solution. Depending on the circumstances, you might choose to cope with the ongoing stress of the situation (Chapter 14); change your perceptions of the situation and your attributions about your partner (Chapter 17); use learning principles to try to alter your own or your partner's behavior (Chapter 7); find a support group of people in the same situation (Chapter 16); seek psychological therapy or counseling, with or without your partner (Chapter 16); or leave the relationship.

Situation 2: Job Stress

You are an up-and-coming computer programmer. You like your job, but you feel overwhelmed by the amount of work you have to do. You never seem to be able to meet your deadlines, and you find yourself worrying about work at night and on weekends; you are unable to relax. Your friends accuse you of being a grind and a workaholic, though you would like to work less if you could. You believe you deserve a promotion, but your boss is curt and abrupt, rarely accepts your good ideas, and never gives you any feedback about your work, let alone praise. You assume that your boss dislikes you and has some grudge against you. You are beginning to feel isolated from your co-workers, too. Lately, you find that your motivation is sagging, and creative ideas are slow in coming. The occasional evening drink to calm your nerves has turned into steady drinking at home and several belts during the day, too, as you try to blot out your worries. What can you do to improve this situation? Here are some psychological topics that may yield insights:

- Sources of stress (Chapter 14, page 523)
- Work motivation (Chapter 11, page 423)
- Attributions (Chapter 17, page 637)
- Defense mechanisms (Chapter 12, page 453)
- Drug use and abuse (Chapter 5, page 176, and Chapter 15, page 575)
- Conformity and dissent (Chapter 17, pages 645 and 654)

Again, here are a few reasons why these topics might apply:

- Research on *sources of stress* may alert you to the reasons for your harried condition. You may need to analyze how much of the pressure you feel is due to the demands of the job and how much is a product of your own internal standards. You can't cope with stress appropriately until you know what is causing it.

- Research on *work motivation* shows that achievement motivation can be a part of personality but is also affected by the work environment. "Burnout," for instance, often occurs because of the way a job is structured; there may be little support from co-workers or employers, infrequent feedback, and few opportunities for developing innovative ideas. Workers are most productive when the conditions of the job—such as flexibility, variation in routine, and the power to make decisions—encourage intrinsic motivation.

- *Attribution theory* states that attributions, whether accurate or not, guide our responses to a situation. Your assumption that your employer dislikes you and holds a grudge may not be valid. Perhaps he or she is under unusual pressure and is therefore distracted. Perhaps he or she is unaware of your contributions. A talk with the boss may be in order.

- Some clinicians would say your overwork is a *defense mechanism*, a way to channel thoughts away from some other area of your life that is troubling you. Would you really work less if you could, or is your constant preoccupation with your job a sign of denial—an unwillingness to face problems at home?

- Research on *drug use* shows that drug effects and the likelihood of abuse depend on mental set and situational setting, your physical tolerance, your cultural experience with the use of the drug, and your social environment when taking the drug. You may also have a vulnerability to alcohol's physical effects, which may explain your gradual slide into a serious alcohol problem. Or alcohol may offer you a convenient excuse for relaxing your standards of performance on the job ("I can't help it; it's the booze"). Because excessive drinking affects brain function and judgment, it probably does impair your performance, creating a vicious cycle of drug use and excuse.

- Finally, research on *conformity* and *dissent* suggests that you may not be alone in your problems at work. Perhaps your co-workers share your problems and would like to make improvements, but they fear rocking the boat. There may be a solution you could accomplish with the aid of others that would be difficult to achieve on your own.

Our two examples have been personal problems, but the applications of psychology extend beyond personal concerns to social ones, as we have seen throughout this book: disputes between neighbors and nations; prejudice and cross-cultural relations; the best ways to rear moral, considerate, and competent children; the application of research to social policy; and countless other issues.

On the other hand, it is also true that research findings often change as new questions are asked, new methods become available, and new theories evolve. Indeed, some "findings" become dated in a year, thanks to the speed of the information explosion. That is why the one chapter that may ultimately be most useful to you is the one you may have assumed to be least useful: Chapter 2, "How Psychologists Know What They Know." The best way to take psychology with you is to understand its basic ways of approaching problems and questions—that is, its principles of critical and scientific thinking. Old theories give way to new ones, dated results yield to contemporary ones, dead-end investigations halt, and new directions are taken. But the method of psychology continues, and critical thinking is its hallmark.

Statistical Methods

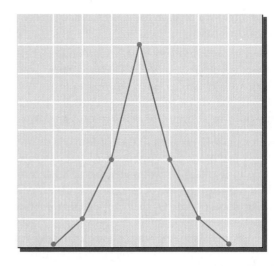

Nineteenth-century English statesman Benjamin Disraeli reportedly once named three forms of dishonesty: "lies, damned lies, and statistics." It is certainly true that people can lie with the help of statistics. It happens all the time: Advertisers, politicians, and others with some claim to make either use numbers inappropriately or ignore certain critical ones. (When hearing that "four out of five doctors surveyed" recommended some product, have you ever wondered just how many doctors were surveyed and whether they were representative of all doctors?) People also use numbers to convey a false impression of certainty and objectivity when the true state of affairs is uncertainty or ignorance. But it is people, not statistics, that lie. When statistics are used correctly, they neither confuse nor mislead. On the contrary, they expose unwarranted conclusions, promote clarity and precision, and protect us from our own biases and blind spots.

If statistics are useful anywhere, it is in the study of human behavior. If human beings were all alike, and psychologists could specify all the influences on behavior, there would be no need for statistics. But any time we measure human behavior, we are going to wind up with different observations or scores for different individuals. Statistics can help us spot trends amid the diversity.

This appendix will introduce you to some basic statistical-calculations used in psychology. Reading the appendix will not make you into a statistician, but it will acquaint you with some ways of organizing and assessing research data. If you suffer from a "number phobia," relax: You do not need to know much math to understand this material. However, you should have read Chapter 2, which discussed the rationale for using statistics and described various research methods. You may want to review the basic terms and concepts covered in that chapter. Be sure that you can define *hypothesis, sample, correlation, independent variable, dependent variable, random assignment, experimental group, control group, descriptive statistics, inferential statistics* and *test of statistical significance*. (Correlation coefficients, which are described in some detail in Chapter 2, will not be covered here.)

To read the tables in this appendix, you will also need to know the following symbols:

N = the total number of observations or scores in a set

X = an observation or score

Σ = the Greek capital letter sigma, read as "the sum of"

$\sqrt{}$ = the square root of

(*Note:* Boldfaced terms in this appendix are defined in the glossary at the end of the book.)

■ ORGANIZING DATA

Before we can discuss statistics, we need some numbers. Imagine that you are a psychologist and that you are interested in that most pleasing of human qualities, a sense of humor. You suspect that a well-developed funny bone can protect people from the negative emotional effects of stress. You already know that in the months following a stressful event, people who score high on sense-of-humor tests tend to feel less tense and moody than more sobersided individuals do. You realize, though, that this correlational evidence does not prove cause and effect. Perhaps people with a healthy sense of humor have other traits, such as flexibility or creativity, that act as the true stress buffers. To find out whether humor itself really softens the impact of stress, you do an experiment.

First, you randomly assign subjects to two groups, an experimental group and a control group. To keep our calculations simple, let's assume there are only 15 people per group. Each person individually views a silent film that most North Americans find fairly stressful, one showing Australian aboriginal boys undergoing a puberty rite involving physical mutilation. Subjects in the experimental group are instructed to make up a humorous monologue while watching the film. Those in the control group are told to make up a straightforward narrative. After the film, each person answers a mood questionnaire that measures current feelings of tension, depression, aggressiveness, and anxiety. A person's overall score on the questionnaire can range from 1 (no mood disturbance) to 7 (strong mood disturbance). This procedure provides you with 15 "mood disturbance" scores for each group. Have people who tried to be humorous reported less disturbance than those who did not?

Constructing a Frequency Distribution

Your first step might be to organize and condense the "raw data" (the obtained scores) by constructing a **frequency distribution** for each group. A frequency distribution shows how often each possible score actually occurred. To construct one, you first order all the possible scores from highest to lowest. (Our mood disturbance scores will be ordered from 7 to 1.) Then you tally how often each score was actually obtained. Table A.1 gives some hypothetical "raw data" for the two groups, and Table A.2 shows the two frequency distributions based on these data. From these distributions you can see that the two groups differed. In the experimental group, the extreme scores of 7 and 1 did not occur at all, and the most common score was the middle one, 4. In the control group, a score of 7 occurred four times, the most common score was 6, and no one obtained a score lower than 4.

Because our mood scores have only seven possible values, our frequency distributions are quite manageable. Suppose, though, that your questionnaire had yielded scores that could range from 1 to 50. A frequency distribution with 50 entries would be cumbersome and might not reveal trends in the data clearly. A solution would be to construct a *grouped frequency distribution* by grouping adjacent scores into equalsized *classes* or *intervals*. Each interval could cover, say, five scores (1–5, 6–10, 11–15, and so forth). Then you could tally the frequencies within each *interval*. This procedure would reduce the number of entries in each distribution from 50 to only 10, making the overall results much easier to grasp. However, information would be lost. For example, there would be no way of knowing how many people had a score of 43 versus 44.

Graphing the Data

As everyone knows, a picture is worth a thousand words. The most common statistical picture is a **graph,** a drawing that depicts numerical relationships. Graphs appear at several points in this book, and are routinely used by psycholo-

Table A.1	Some Hypothetical Raw Data

These scores are for the hypothetical humor-and-stress study described in the text.

Experimental group	4,5,4,4,3,6,5,2,4,3,5,4,4,3,4
Control group	6,4,7,6,6,4,6,7,7,5,5,5,7,6,6

Table A.2	Two Frequency Distributions

The scores are from Table A.1

Experimental Group			Control Group		
Mood Disturbance Score	Tally	Frequency	Mood Disturbance Score	Tally	Frequency
7		0	7	////	4
6	/	1	6	///// /	6
5	///	3	5	///	3
4	///// //	7	4	//	2
3	///	3	3		0
2	/	1	2		0
1		0	1		0
		N = 15			N = 15

gists to convey their findings to others. From graphs, we can get a general impression of what the data are like, note the relative frequencies of different scores, and see which score was most frequent.

In a graph constructed from a frequency distribution, the possible score values are shown along a horizontal line (the *x-axis* of the graph) and frequencies along a vertical line (the *y-axis*), or vice versa. To construct a **histogram,** or **bar graph,** from our mood scores, we draw rectangles (bars) above each score, indicating the number of times it occurred by the rectangle's height (Figure A.1 on page 712).

A slightly different kind of "picture" is provided by a **frequency polygon,** or **line graph.** In a frequency polygon, the frequency of each score is indicated by a dot placed directly over the score on the horizontal axis, at the appropriate height on the vertical axis. The dots for the various scores are then joined together by straight lines, as in Figure A.2. When necessary an "extra" score, with a frequency of zero, can be added at each end of the horizontal axis, so that the polygon will rest on this axis instead of floating above it.

A word of caution about graphs: They may either exaggerate or mask differences in the data, depending on which units are used on the vertical axis. The two graphs in Figure A.3, although they look quite different, actually depict the same data. Always read the units on the axes of a graph; otherwise, the shape of a histogram or frequency polygon may be misleading.

■ DESCRIBING DATA

Having organized your data, you are now ready to summarize and describe them. As you will recall from Chapter 2, procedures for doing so are known as *descriptive statistics*. In the following discussion, the word *score* will stand for any numerical observation.

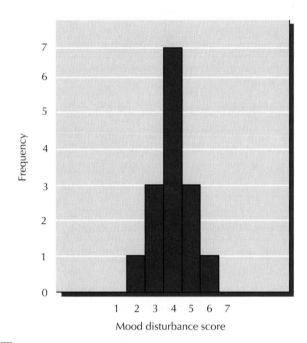

Figure A.1 A histogram

This graph depicts the distribution of mood disturbance scores shown on the left side of Table A.2.

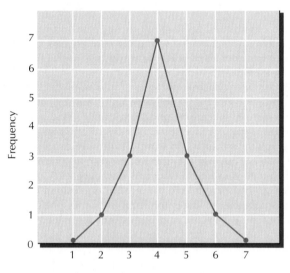

Figure A.2 A frequency polygon

This graph depicts the same data as Figure A.1.

Measuring Central Tendency

Your first step in describing your data might be to compute a **measure of central tendency** for each group. Measures of central tendency characterize an entire set of data in terms of a single representative number.

The Mean. The most popular measure of central tendency is the *arithmetic mean*, usually called simply the **mean.** It is often expressed by the symbol *M*. Most people are thinking of the mean when they say "average." We run across means all the time: in grade point averages, temperature averages, and batting averages. The mean is valuable to the psychologist because it takes all the data into account

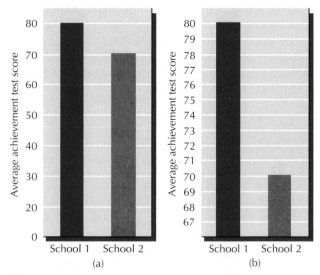

Figure A.3 Same data, different impressions

These two graphs depict the same data, but have different units on the vertical axis.

and it can be used in further statistical analyses. To compute the mean, you simply add up a set of scores and divide the total by the number of scores in the set. Recall that in mathematical notation, Σ means "the sum of," *X* stands for the individual scores, and *N* represents the total number of scores in a set. Thus the formula for calculating the mean is:

$$M = \frac{\Sigma X}{N}$$

Table A.3 shows how to compute the mean for our experimental group. Test your ability to perform this calculation by computing the mean for the control group yourself. (You can find the answer, along with other control group statistics, on page 716.) Later, we will describe how a psychologist would compare the two means statistically to see if there is a significant difference between them.

The Median. Despite its usefulness, sometimes the mean can be misleading, as we noted in Chapter 2. Suppose you piled some children on a seesaw in such a way that it was perfectly balanced, and then a 200-pound adult came and sat on one end. The center of gravity would quickly shift toward the adult. In the same way, one extremely high score can dramatically raise the mean (and one extremely low score can dramatically lower it). In real life, this can be a serious problem. For example, in the calculation of a town's mean income, one millionaire would offset hundreds of poor people. The mean income would be a misleading indication of the town's actual wealth.

When extreme scores occur, a more representative measure of central tendency is the **median,** or midpoint in a set of scores or observations ordered from highest to lowest. In any set of scores, the same *number* of scores falls above the median as below it. The median is not affected by extreme scores. If you were calculating the *median* income of that same town, the one millionaire would offset only one poor person.

When the number of scores in the set is odd, calculating the median is a simple matter of counting in from the ends to the middle. However, if the number of scores is even,

Table A.3 *Calculating a Mean and a Median*

The scores are from the left side of Table A.1.

Mean (M)

$$M = \frac{4+5+4+4+3+6+5+2+4+3+5+4+4+3+4}{15}$$

$$= \frac{60}{15}$$

$$= 4$$

Median

Scores, in order: 2, 3, 3, 3, 4, 4, 4, 4, 4, 4, 5, 5, 5, 6

Median

---

there will be two middle scores. The simplest solution is to find the mean of those two scores and use that number as the median. (When the data are from a grouped frequency distribution, a more complicated procedure is required, one beyond the scope of this appendix.) In our experimental group, the median score is 4 (see Table A.3). What is it for the control group?

The Mode. A third measure of central tendency is the **mode,** the score that occurs most often. In our experimental group, the modal score is 4. In our control group, it is 6. In some distributions, all scores occur with equal frequency, and there is no mode. In others, two or more scores "tie" for the distinction of being most frequent. Modes are used less often than other measures of central tendency. They do not tell us anything about the other scores in the distribution; they often are not very "central"; and they tend to fluctuate from one random sample of a population to another more than either the median or the mean.

Measuring Variability

A measure of central tendency may or may not be highly representative of other scores in a distribution. To understand our results, we also need a **measure of variability** that will tell us whether our scores are clustered closely around the mean or widely scattered.

The Range. The simplest measure of variability is the **range,** which is found by subtracting the lowest score from the highest one. For our hypothetical set of mood disturbance scores, the range in the experimental group is 4 and in the control group it is 3. Unfortunately, though, simplicity is not always a virtue. The range gives us some information about variability but ignores all scores other than the highest and lowest ones.

The Standard Deviation. A more sophisticated measure of variability is the **standard deviation (SD).** This statistic takes every score in the distribution into account. Loosely speaking, it gives us an idea of how much, on the average, scores in a distribution differ from the mean. If the scores were all the same, the standard deviation would be zero. The higher the standard deviation, the more variability there is among scores.

To compute the standard deviation, we must find out how much each individual score deviates from the mean. To

do so we simply subtract the mean from each score. This gives us a set of *deviation scores.* Deviation scores for numbers above the mean will be positive, those for numbers below the mean will be negative, and the positive scores will exactly balance the negative ones. In other words, the sum of the deviation scores will be zero. That is a problem, since the next step in our calculation is to add. The solution is to *square* all the deviation scores (that is, to multiply each score by itself). This step gets rid of negative values. Then we can compute the average of the *squared* deviation scores by adding them up and dividing the sum by the number of scores (N). Finally, we take the square root of the result, which takes us from squared units of measurement back to the same units that were used originally (in this case, mood disturbance levels).

The calculations just described are expressed by the following formula:

$$SD = \sqrt{\frac{\Sigma (X - M)^2}{N}}$$

Table A.4 shows the calculations for computing the standard deviation for our experimental group. Try your hand at computing the standard deviation for the control group.

Remember, a large standard deviation signifies that scores are widely scattered, and that therefore the mean is not terribly typical of the entire population. A small standard deviation tells us that most scores are clustered near the mean, and that therefore the mean is representative. Suppose two classes took a psychology exam, and both classes had the same mean score, 75 out of a possible 100. From the means alone, you might conclude that the classes were similar in performance. But if Class A had a standard deviation of 3 and Class B had a standard deviation of 9, you would know that there was much more variability in performance in Class B. This information could be useful to an instructor in planning lectures and making assignments.

Transforming Scores

Sometimes researchers do not wish to work directly with raw scores. They may prefer numbers that are more manageable, such as when the raw scores are tiny fractions. Or they may want to work with scores that reveal where a person stands relative to others. In such cases, raw scores can be transformed to other kinds of scores.

Percentile Scores. One common transformation converts each raw score to a *percentile score* (also called a *centile rank*). A percentile score gives the percentage of people who scored at or below a given raw score. Suppose you learn that you have scored 37 on a psychology exam. In the absence of any other information, you may not know whether to celebrate or cry. But if you are told that 37 is equivalent to a percentile score of 90, you know that you can be pretty proud of yourself; you have scored as well as, or higher than, 90 percent of those who have taken the test. On the other hand, if you are told that 37 is equivalent to a percentile score of 50, you have scored only at the median—only as well as, or higher than, half of the other students. The highest possible percentile rank is 99, or more precisely, 99.99, because you can never do better than 100 percent of a group when you are a member of the group. (Can you say what the lowest possible percentile score is? The answer is on page 716.) Standardized tests such as those described in previous chapters often come with tables that allow for the easy conversion of any

Table A.4 *Calculating a Standard Deviation*

Scores (X)	Deviation scores (X – M)	Squared deviation scores (X – M)²
6	2	4
5	1	1
5	1	1
5	1	1
4	0	0
4	0	0
4	0	0
4	0	0
4	0	0
4	0	0
4	0	0
3	–1	1
3	–1	1
3	–1	1
2	–2	4
	0	14

$$SD = \sqrt{\frac{\Sigma(X - M)^2}{N}} = \sqrt{\frac{14}{15}} = \sqrt{.93} = .97$$

Note: When data from a sample are used to estimate the standard deviation of the population from which the sample was drawn, division is by $N-1$ instead of N, for reasons that will not concern us here.

raw score to the appropriate percentile score, based on data from a larger number of people who have already taken the test.

Percentile scores are easy to understand and easy to calculate. However, they also have a drawback: They merely rank people and do *not* tell us how far apart people are in terms of raw scores. Suppose you scored in the 50th percentile on an exam, June scored in the 45th, Tricia scored in the 20th, and Sean scored in the 15th. The difference between you and June may seem identical to that between Tricia and Sean (five percentiles). But in terms of *raw* scores you and June are probably more alike than Tricia and Sean, because exam scores usually cluster closely together around the midpoint of the distribution and are farther apart at the extremes. Because percentile scores do not preserve the spatial relationships in the original distribution of scores, they are inappropriate for computing many kinds of statistics. For example, they cannot be used to calculate means.

Z-scores. Another common transformation of raw scores is to **z-scores,** or **standard scores.** A z-score tells you how far a given raw score is above or below the mean, using the standard deviation as the unit of measurement. To compute a z-score, you subtract the mean of the distribution from the raw score and divide by the standard deviation:

$$z = \frac{X - M}{SD}$$

Unlike percentile scores, z-scores preserve the relative spacing of the original raw scores. The mean itself always corresponds to a z-score of zero, since it cannot deviate from itself. All scores above the mean have positive z-scores and all scores below the mean have negative ones. When the raw scores form a certain pattern called a *normal distribution* (to be described shortly), a z-score tells you how high or low the corresponding raw score was, relative to the other scores. If your exam score of 37 is equivalent to a z-score of +1.0, you

have scored 1 standard deviation above the mean. Assuming a roughly normal distribution, that's pretty good, because in a normal distribution only about 16 percent of all scores fall at or above 1 standard deviation above the mean. But if your 37 is equivalent to a z-score of –1.0, you have scored 1 standard deviation below the mean—a poor score.

Z-scores are sometimes used to compare people's performance on different tests or measures. Say that Elsa earns a score of 64 on her first psychology test and Manuel, who is taking psychology from a different instructor, earns a 62 on his first test. In Elsa's class, the mean score is 50 and the standard deviation is 7, so Elsa's z-score is $(64 - 50)/7 = 2.0$. In Manuel's class, the mean is also 50, but the standard deviation is 6. Therefore, his z-score is also 2.0 $[(62 - 50)/6]$. Compared to their respective classmates, Elsa and Manuel did equally well. *But be careful:* This does *not* imply that they are equally able students. Perhaps Elsa's instructor has a reputation for giving easy tests and Manuel's for giving hard ones, so Manuel's instructor has attracted a more industrious group of students. In that case, Manuel faces stiffer competition than Elsa does, and even though he and Elsa have the same z-score, Manuel's performance may be more impressive.

You can see that comparing z-scores from different people or different tests must be done with caution. Standardized tests, such as IQ tests and various personality tests, use z-scores derived from a large sample of people assumed to be representative of the general population taking the tests. When two tests are standardized for similar populations, it is safe to compare z-scores on them. But z-scores derived from special samples, such as students in different psychology classes, may not be comparable.

Curves

In addition to knowing how spread out our scores are, we need to know the *pattern* of their distribution. At this point we come to a rather curious phenomenon. When researchers make a very large number of observations, many of the physical and psychological variables they study have a distribution that approximates a pattern called a **normal distribution.** (We say "approximates" because a *perfect* normal distribution is a theoretical construct and is not actually found in nature.) Plotted in a frequency polygon, a normal distribution has a symmetrical, bell-shaped form known as a **normal curve** (see Figure A.4).

A normal curve has several interesting and convenient properties. The right side is the exact mirror image of the left. The mean, median, and mode all have the same value and are at the exact center of the curve, at the top of the "bell." Most observations or scores cluster around the center of the curve, with far fewer out at the ends, or "tails" of the curve. Most important, as Figure A.4 shows, when standard deviations (or z-scores) are used on the horizontal axis of the curve, the percentage of scores falling between the mean and any given point on the horizontal axis is always the same. For example, 68.26 percent of the scores will fall between plus and minus 1 standard deviation from the mean; 95.44 percent of the scores will fall between plus and minus 2 standard deviations from the mean; and 99.74 percent of the scores will fall between plus and minus 3 standard deviations from the mean. These percentages hold for any normal curve, no matter what the size of the standard deviation. Tables are available showing the percentages of scores in a normal distribution that lie between the mean and various points (as expressed by z-scores).

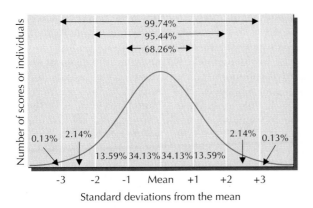

Figure A.4 A normal curve

When standard deviations (or z-scores) are used along the horizontal axis of a normal curve, certain fixed percentages of scores fall between the mean and any given point. As you can see, most scores fall in the middle range (between +1 and −1 standard deviations from the mean).

The normal curve makes life easier for psychologists when they want to compare individuals on some trait or performance. For example, since IQ scores from a population form a roughly normal curve, the mean and standard deviation of a test are all the information you need in order to know how many people score above or below a particular score. On a test with a mean of 100 and a standard deviation of 15, about 68.26 percent of the population scores between 85 and 115—1 standard deviation below and 1 standard deviation above the mean (see Chapter 8).

Not all types of observations, however, are distributed normally. Some curves are lopsided, or *skewed,* with scores clustering at one end or the other of the horizontal axis (see Figure A.5). When the "tail" of the curve is longer on the right than on the left, the curve is said to be positively, or right, skewed. When the opposite is true, the curve is said to be negatively, or left, skewed. In experiments, reaction times typically form a right-skewed distribution. For example, if people must press a button whenever they hear some signal, most will react quite quickly; but a few will take an unusually long time, causing the right "tail" of the curve to be stretched out.

Knowing the shape of a distribution can be extremely valuable. Paleontologist and biologist Stephen Jay Gould (1985) has told how such information helped him cope with the news that he had a rare and serious form of cancer. Being a researcher, he immediately headed for the library to learn all he could about his disease. The first thing he found was that it was incurable, with a median mortality of only eight months after discovery. Most people might have assumed that a "median mortality of eight months" means "I will probably be dead in eight months." But Gould realized that although half of all patients died within eight months, the other half survived longer than that. Since his disease had been diagnosed in its early stages, he was getting top-notch medical treatment, and he had a strong will to live, Gould figured he could reasonably expect to be in the half of the distribution that survived beyond eight months. Even more cheering, the distribution of deaths from the disease was right-skewed: The cases to the left of the median of eight months could only extend to zero months, but those to the right could stretch out for years. Gould saw no reason why he should not expect to be in the tip of that right-hand tail.

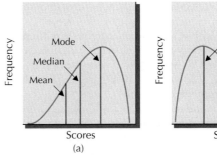

Figure A.5 Skewed curves

Curve (a) is skewed negatively, to the left. Curve (b) is skewed positively, to the right. The direction of a curve's skewness is determined by the position of the long tail, not by the position of the bulge. In a skewed curve, the mean, median, and mode fall at different points.

For Stephen Jay Gould, statistics, properly interpreted, were "profoundly nurturant and life-giving." They offered him hope and inspired him to fight his disease. Today, Gould is as active professionally as he ever was. The initial diagnosis was made in July of 1982.

ANSWERS:

Control group statistics:

$$\text{Mean} = \frac{\Sigma X}{N} = \frac{87}{15} = 5.8$$

Median = 6

$$\text{Standard Deviation} = \sqrt{\frac{\Sigma(X - M)^2}{N}} = \sqrt{\frac{14.4}{15}}$$

$$= \sqrt{.96} = .98$$

Lowest possible percentile score: 1 (or, more precisely, .01)

■ DRAWING INFERENCES

Once data are organized and summarized, the next step is to ask whether they differ from what might have been expected purely by chance (see Chapter 2). A researcher needs to know whether it is safe to infer that the results from a particular sample of people are valid for the entire population from which the sample was drawn. *Inferential statistics* provide this information. They are used in both experimental and correlational studies.

The Null Versus the Alternative Hypothesis

In an experiment, the scientist must assess the possibility that his or her experimental manipulations will have no effect on the subjects' behavior. The statement expressing this possibility is called the **null hypothesis.** In our stress-and-humor study, the null hypothesis states that making up a funny commentary will not relieve stress any more than making up a straightforward narrative will. In other words, it predicts that the difference between the means of the two groups will not deviate significantly from zero. Any obtained difference will be due solely to chance fluctuations. In contrast, the **alternative hypothesis** (also called the experimental or research hypothesis) states that on the average the experimental group will have lower mood disturbance scores than the control group.

The null hypothesis and the alternative hypothesis cannot both be true. Our goal is to reject the null hypothesis. If our results turn out to be consistent with the null hypothesis, we will not be able to do so. If the data are inconsistent with the null hypothesis, we will be able to reject it with some degree of confidence. Unless we study the entire population, though, we will never be able to say that the alternative hypothesis has been proven. No matter how impressive our results are, there will always be some degree of uncertainty about the inferences we draw from them. Since we cannot prove the alternative hypothesis, we must be satisfied with showing that the null hypothesis is unreasonable.

Students are often surprised to learn that it is the null hypothesis, not the alternative hypothesis, that is tested. After all, it is the alternative hypothesis that is actually of interest. But this procedure does make good sense. The null hypothesis can be stated precisely and tested directly. In the case of our fictitious study, the null hypothesis predicts that the difference between the two means will be zero. The alternative hypothesis does not permit a precise prediction because we don't know how much the two means might differ (if, in fact, they do differ). Therefore, it cannot be tested directly.

Testing Hypotheses

Many computations are available for testing the null hypothesis. The choice depends on the design of the study, the size of the sample, and other factors. We will not cover any specific tests here. Our purpose is simply to introduce you to the kind of *reasoning* that underlies inferential statistics. With that in mind, let us return once again to our data. For each of our two groups we have calculated a mean and a standard deviation. Now we want to compare the two sets of data to see if they differ enough for us to reject the null hypothesis. We wish to be reasonably certain that our observed differences did not occur entirely by chance.

What does it mean to be "reasonably certain"? How different from zero must our result be to be taken seriously? Imagine, for a moment, that we had infinite resources and could somehow repeat our experiment, each time using a new pair of groups, until we had "run" the entire population through the study. It can be shown mathematically that if only chance were operating, our various experimental results would form a normal distribution. This theoretical distribution is called "the sampling distribution of the difference between means," but since that is quite a mouthful, we will simply call it the *sampling distribution* for short. If the null hypothesis were true, the mean of the sampling distribution would be zero. That is, on the average, we would find no difference between the two groups. Often, though, because of chance influences or *random error,* we would get a result that deviated to one degree or another from zero. On rare occasions, the result would deviate a great deal from zero.

We cannot test the entire population, though. All we have are data from a single sample. We would like to know whether the difference between means that we actually obtained would be close to the mean of the theoretical sampling distribution (if we *could* test the entire population) or far away from it, out in one of the "tails" of the curve. Was our result highly likely to occur on the basis of chance alone or highly unlikely?

Before we can answer that question, we must have some precise way to measure distance from the mean of the sampling distribution. We must know exactly how far from the mean our obtained result must be to be considered "far away." If only we knew the standard deviation of the sampling distribution, we could use it as our unit of measurement. We don't know it, but fortunately, we can use the standard deviation of our *sample* to estimate it. (We will not go into the reasons that this is so.)

Now we are in business. We can look at the mean difference between our two groups and figure out how far it is (in terms of standard deviations) from the mean of the sampling distribution. As mentioned earlier, one of the convenient things about a normal distribution is that a certain fixed percentage of all observations falls between the mean of the distribution and any given point above or below the mean. These percentages are available from tables. Therefore, if we know the "distance" of our obtained result from the mean of the theoretical sampling distribution, we automatically know how likely our result is to have occurred strictly by chance.

To give a specific example, if it turns out that our obtained result is 2 standard deviations above the mean of the theoretical sampling distribution, we know that the probability of its having occurred by chance is less than 2.3 percent. If our result is 3 standard deviations above the mean of the sampling distribution, the probability of its having occurred by chance is less than .13 percent—less than 1 in 800. In either case, we might well suspect that our result did not occur entirely by chance after all. We would call the result *statistically significant.* (Psychologists usually consider any highly unlikely result to be of interest, no matter which direction it takes. In other words, the result may be in either "tail" of the sampling distribution.)

To summarize: Statistical significance means that if only chance were operating, our result would be highly improbable, so we are fairly safe in concluding that more than chance was operating—namely, the influence of our independent variable. We can reject the null hypothesis, and open the champagne. As we noted in Chapter 2, psychologists usually accept a finding as statistically significant if the likelihood of its occurring by chance is 5 percent or less (see Figure A.6). This cutoff point gives the researcher a reasonable chance of confirming reliable results as well as reasonable protection against accepting unreliable ones.

Some cautions are in order, though. As noted in Chapter 2, statistically significant results are not always psychologically interesting or important. Further, statistical significance is related to the size of the sample. A large sample increases the likelihood of reliable results. But there is a trade-off: The larger the sample, the more probable it is that a small result having no practical importance will reach statistical significance. For this reason, it is always useful to know how much of the total variability in scores was accounted for by the independent variable. (The computations are not discussed here.) If only 3 percent of the variance was accounted for, then 97 percent was due either to chance factors or to systematic influences of which the researcher was unaware. Because human behavior is affected by so many factors, the amount of variability accounted for by a single psychological variable is often modest.

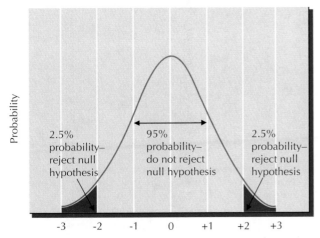

Probability

2.5% probability—reject null hypothesis

95% probability—do not reject null hypothesis

2.5% probability—reject null hypothesis

-3   -2   -1   0   +1   +2   +3

Distance from the mean (in standard deviations)

■ Figure A.6   Statistical significance

This curve represents the theoretical sampling distribution discussed in the text. The curve is what we would expect by chance if we did our hypothetical stress-and-humor study many times, testing the entire population. If we used the conventional significance level of .05, we would regard our obtained result as significant only if the probability of getting a result that far from zero by chance (in either direction) totaled 5 percent or less. As shown, the result must fall far out in one of the tails of the sampling distribution. Otherwise, we cannot reject the null hypothesis.

Oh, yes, about those humor findings: Our fictitious study is similar to two more complicated ones done by Herbert M. Lefcourt and Rod A. Martin (1986). Women who tried to be funny reported less mood disturbance than women who merely produced a straightforward narrative. They also grimaced and fidgeted less during the film, suggesting that they really did feel less stress. The results were not statistically significant for men, possibly because men did not find the film all that stressful. Other findings, however, suggest that humor can shield both sexes from stress (see Chapter 14). *The moral:* When gravity gets you down, try a little levity.

■ KEY TERMS

frequency distribution *711*
graph *711*
histogram/bar graph *711*
frequency polygon/line graph *711*
measure of central tendency *711*
mean *712*
median *713*
mode *713*
range *713*
standard deviation *713*

deviation score *713*
percentile score *714*
z-score (standard score) *714*
normal distribution *715*
normal curve *715*
right- and left-skewed distributions *715*
null hypothesis *716*
alternative hypothesis *716*
sampling distribution *717*
statistically significant *717*

■ SUMMARY

1. When used correctly, statistics expose unwarranted conclusions, promote precision, and help researchers spot trends amid diversity.

2. Often, the first step in data analysis is to organize and condense data in a *frequency distribution,* a tally showing how often each possible score (or interval of scores) occurred. Such information can also be depicted in a *histogram* (bar graph) or a *frequency polygon* (line graph).

3. Descriptive statistics summarize and describe the data. *Central tendency* is measured by the *mean, median,* or, less frequently, the *mode.* Since a measure of central tendency may or may not be highly representative of other scores in a distribution, it is also important to analyze variability. A large *standard deviation* means that scores are widely scattered about the mean; a small one means that most scores are clustered near the mean.

4. Raw scores can be transformed into other kinds of scores. *Percentile scores* indicate the percentage of people who scored at or below a given raw score. Z-scores (standard scores) indicate how far a given raw score is above or below the mean of the distribution.

5. Many variables have a distribution approximating a *normal distribution,* depicted as a *normal curve.* The normal curve has a convenient property: When standard deviations are used as the units on the horizontal axis, the percentage of scores falling between any two points on the horizontal axis is always the same. Not all types of observations are distributed normally, however. Some distributions are *skewed* to the left or right.

6. Inferential statistics are used to test the *null hypothesis.* They tell a researcher whether a result differed significantly from what might have been expected purely by chance. Basically, hypothesis testing involves estimating where the obtained result would have fallen in a theoretical *sampling distribution* based on studies of the entire population in question. If the result would have been far out in one of the "tails" of the distribution, it is considered statistically significant. A statistically significant result may or may not be psychologically interesting or important.

GLOSSARY

absolute threshold The smallest quantity of physical energy that can be reliably detected by an observer.

accommodation In Piaget's theory, the process of modifying existing cognitive structures in response to experience and new information.

acculturation The process by which members of groups that are minorities in a given society come to identify with and to feel part of the mainstream culture.

activation-synthesis theory The theory that dreaming results from the cortical synthesis and interpretation of neural signals triggered by activity in the lower part of the brain.

agoraphobia "Fear of fear"; a set of phobias, often set off by a panic attack, involving the basic fear of being away from a safe place or person.

algorithm A problem-solving strategy guaranteed to produce a solution even if the user does not know how it works.

alpha waves Relatively large, slow brain waves characteristic of relaxed wakefulness.

altered state of consciousness A state of consciousness that differs from ordinary wakefulness or sleep.

amnesia (psychogenic) When no organic causes are present, a dissociative disorder involving partial or complete loss of memory for threatening information or past events.

amygdala A brain structure involved in the arousal and regulation of emotion; it may also play a role in the association of memories formed in different senses.

anterograde amnesia The inability to form lasting memories for new events and facts.

antidepressant drugs Stimulants used in the treatment of mood disorders, usually depression and anxiety.

antipsychotic drugs Major tranquilizers used primarily in the treatment of schizophrenia and other psychotic disorders.

antisocial personality disorder A disorder characterized by antisocial behavior such as lying, stealing, manipulating others, and sometimes violence; a lack of social emotions (guilt, shame, and empathy); and impulsivity. (Sometimes called *psychopathy* or *sociopathy*.)

applied psychology The study of psychological issues that have direct practical significance and the application of psychological findings.

archetypes [AR-ki-tipes] To Carl Jung, universal, symbolic images that appear in myths, art, dreams, and other expressions of the collective unconscious.

arithmetic mean An average that is calculated by adding up a set of quantities and dividing the sum by the total number of quantities in the set.

assimilation In Piaget's theory, the process of absorbing new information into existing cognitive structures, modifying them if necessary to fit.

attribution theory The theory that people are motivated to explain their own and other people's behaviors by attributing causes of those behaviors to a situation or a disposition.

autonomic nervous system The subdivision of the peripheral nervous system that regulates the internal organs and glands.

availability heuristic The tendency to judge the probability of a type of event by how easy it is to think of examples or instances.

axon The extending fiber of a neuron that conducts impulses away from the cell body and transmits them to other neurons.

basic concepts Concepts that have a moderate number of instances and that are easier to acquire than those having few or many instances.

basic psychology The study of psychological issues in order to seek knowledge for its own sake rather than for its practical application.

behavioral genetics An interdisciplinary field of study concerned with the genetic bases of behavior and personality.

behaviorism An approach to psychology that emphasizes the study of observable behavior and the role of the environment as a determinant of behavior.

behavior modification The application of conditioning techniques to teach new responses or to reduce or eliminate maladaptive or problematic behavior.

binocular cues Visual cues to depth or distance requiring two eyes.

biofeedback A technique for controlling bodily functions by attending to an instrument that monitors the function and signals changes in it.

biological perspective A psychological approach that emphasizes bodily events and changes associated with actions, feelings, and thoughts.

biological rhythm A periodic, more or less regular fluctuation in a biological system; may or may not have psychological implications.

bipolar disorder A mood disorder in which depression alternates with mania (excessive euphoria).

brain stem The part of the brain at the top of the spinal cord; it is responsible for automatic functions such as heartbeat and respiration.

brightness Lightness or luminance; the dimension of visual experience related to the amount of light emitted from or reflected by an object.

case study A detailed description of a particular individual under study or treatment.

cell body The part of the neuron that keeps it alive and determines whether it will fire.

central nervous system (CNS) The portion of the nervous system consisting of the brain and spinal cord.

cerebellum A brain structure that regulates movement and balance.

cerebral cortex A collection of several thin layers of cells covering the cerebrum; it is largely responsible for higher mental functions; *cortex* is Latin for "bark" or "rind."

cerebral hemispheres The two halves of the cerebrum.

cerebrum [suh-REE-brum] The largest brain structure, consisting of the upper part of the forebrain; it is in charge of most sensory, motor, and cognitive processes in human beings; from the Latin for "brain."

childhood (infantile) amnesia The inability to remember events and experiences that occurred during the first two or three years of life.

chromosomes Within every body cell, rod-shaped structures that carry the genes.

chunk A meaningful unit of information; it may be composed of smaller units.

circadian [sur-CAY-dee-un] rhythm A biological rhythm with a period (from peak to peak or trough to trough) of about 24 hours; from the Latin *circa*, "about," and *dias*, "a day."

classical conditioning The process by which a previously neutral stimulus acquires the capacity to elicit a response through association with a stimulus that already elicits a similar or related response; also called *Pavlovian* and *respondent conditioning*.

cochlea [KOCK-lee-uh] A snail-shaped, fluid-filled organ in the inner ear, containing the receptors for hearing.

coefficient of correlation A measure of correlation that ranges in value from −1.00 to +1.00.

cognitive dissonance A state of tension that occurs when a person simultaneously holds two cognitions that are psychologically inconsistent, or when a person's belief is incongruent with his or her behavior.

cognitive ethology The study of cognitive processes in nonhuman animals.

cognitive map A mental representation of the environment.

cognitive perspective A psychological approach that emphasizes mental processes in perception, memory, language, problem solving, and other areas of behavior.

cognitive schema An integrated mental network of knowledge, beliefs, and expectations concerning a particular topic or aspect of the world.

collective unconscious To Carl Jung, the universal memories and experiences of humankind, represented in the unconscious images and symbols of all people.

complexity (of light) Refers to the number of different wavelengths contained in light from a particular source.

concept A mental category that groups objects, relations, activities, abstractions, or qualities having common properties.

conditioned response (CR) The classical-conditioning term for a response that is elicited by a conditioned stimulus; it occurs after the conditioned stimulus is associated with an unconditioned stimulus.

conditioned stimulus (CS) The classical-conditioning term for an initially neutral stimulus that comes to elicit a conditioned response after being associated with an unconditioned stimulus.

cones Visual receptors involved in color vision.

confirmation bias The tendency to look for or pay attention only to information that confirms one's belief.

consciousness The awareness of the environment and of one's own existence, sensations, and thoughts.

conservation The understanding that the physical properties of objects—such as the number of items in a cluster or the amount of liquid in a glass—can remain the same even when their appearances change.

consolidation The process by which a long-term memory becomes durable and stable.

continuous reinforcement A reinforcement schedule in which a particular response is always reinforced.

control condition In an experiment, a comparison condition in which subjects are not exposed to the same treatment or manipulation of the independent variable as in the experimental condition.

coping Cognitive and behavioral efforts to manage demands in the environment or oneself that one feels to be stressful.

corpus callosum The bundle of nerve fibers connecting the two cerebral hemispheres.

correlation A measure of how strongly two variables are related to one another.

correlational study A descriptive study that looks for a consistent relationship between two phenomena.

counterconditioning In classical conditioning, the process of pairing a conditioned stimulus with a stimulus which elicits a response that is incompatible with an unwanted conditioned response.

critical thinking The ability and willingness to assess claims and to make objective judgments on the basis of well-supported reasons.

cross-sectional study A study in which groups of subjects of different ages are compared at a given time.

cue-dependent forgetting The inability to retrieve information stored in memory due to a lack of sufficient cues for recall.

culture A program of shared rules that govern the behavior of members of a community or society, and a set of values, beliefs, and attitudes shared by most members of that community.

dark adaptation A process by which visual receptors become maximally sensitive to dim light.

decay theory (of forgetting) The theory that information in memory eventually disappears if it is not reactivated; it appears to apply more to short-term than to long-term memory.

declarative memories Memories of facts, rules, concepts, and events ("knowing that"); they include semantic and episodic memories.

deductive reasoning A form of reasoning in which a conclusion follows necessarily from certain premises; if the premises are true, the conclusion must be true.

deep processing In the encoding of information, the processing of meaning rather than simply the physical or sensory features of a stimulus.

defense mechanisms Methods used by the ego to prevent unconscious anxiety or threatening thoughts from entering consciousness.

deindividuation In groups or crowds, the loss of a person's awareness of her or his own individuality and the abdication of mindful action.

delta waves Slow, regular brain waves characteristic of stage 3 and stage 4 sleep.

dendrites Branches on a neuron that receive information from other neurons and transmit it toward the cell body.

dependent variable A variable that an experimenter predicts will be affected by manipulations of the independent variable.

depersonalization Treating another person without regard for the person's individuality as a human being.

depressants Drugs that slow down activity in the central nervous system.

descriptive methods Methods that yield descriptions of behavior but not necessarily causal explanations.

descriptive statistics Statistics that organize and summarize research data.

dialectical reasoning A process in which opposing facts or ideas are weighed and compared, with a view to determining the best solution or to resolving differences.

difference threshold The smallest difference in stimulation that can be reliably detected by an observer when two stimuli are compared; also called *just noticeable difference (jnd)*.

diffusion of responsibility In organized or anonymous groups, the tendency of members to avoid taking responsibility for actions or decisions, assuming that others will do so.

discriminative stimulus A stimulus that signals when a particular response is likely to be followed by a certain type of consequence.

display rules Social and cultural rules that regulate when, how, and where a person may express (or suppress) emotions.

dissociation Separation of consciousness into distinct parts.

dissociative disorders Conditions in which normally integrated consciousness or identity is split or altered, as in psychogenic amnesia.

dissociative identity disorder A rare dissociative disorder marked by the appearance within one person of two or more distinct personalities, each with its own name and traits; also called *multiple personality disorder*.

dizygotic twins *See* **fraternal twins.**

DNA (deoxyribonucleic acid) The chromosomal molecule that transfers genetic characteristics by way of coded instructions for the structure of proteins.

double-blind study An experiment in which neither the subjects nor the researchers know which subjects are in the control group(s) and which in the experimental group(s) until after the results are tallied.

ego In psychoanalysis, the part of personality that represents reason, good sense, and rational self-control.

egocentric thinking Seeing the world from only one's own point of view; the inability to take another person's perspective.

elaborative rehearsal Association of new information with already stored knowledge and analysis of the new information to make it memorable.

electroconvulsive therapy (ECT) A procedure occasionally used for cases of prolonged major depression, in which a brief brain seizure is induced to alter brain chemistry.

electroencephalogram (EEG) A recording of neural activity detected by electrodes.

emotion A state of arousal involving facial and bodily changes, brain activation, cognitive appraisals, subjective feelings, and tendencies to action.

emotion work Expression of an emotion, often because of a role requirement, that one does not really feel.

empirical Relying on or derived from observation, experimentation, or measurement.

encoding The conversion of information into a form that can be stored in and retrieved from memory.

endocrine glands Internal organs that produce hormones and release them into the bloodstream.

endorphins [en-DOR-fins] Neuromodulators that are similar in structure and action to opiates. They are involved in pain reduction, pleasure, and memory and are known technically as *endogenous opioid peptides*.

entrapment A gradual process in which individuals escalate their commitment to a course of action to justify their investment of time, money, or effort.

epinephrine, norepinephrine Hormones produced by the adrenal glands that provide the body with energy to respond to environmental events.

episodic memories Memories for personally experienced events and the contexts in which they occurred.

equilibrium The sense of balance.

ethnic identity Having a close identification with one's own racial, religious, or ethnic group.

ethnocentrism The belief that one's own ethnic group, nation, or religion is superior to all others.

eustress [YOU-stress] Positive or beneficial stress.

evoked potentials Patterns of brain activity produced in response to specific events.

evolution A change in gene frequencies within a population over many generations; a mechanism by which genetically influenced characteristics of a population change.

evolutionary psychology A field of psychology emphasizing evolutionary mechanisms that may help explain human commonalities in cognition, development, emotion, social practices, and other areas of behavior.

existentialism The doctrine, which influenced the psychodynamic approach of existential psychology, that people have free will, and that they struggle with the anxieties of existence such as the need to find meaning in life and accept death.

experiment A controlled test of a hypothesis in which the researcher manipulates one variable to discover its effect on another.

experimenter effects Unintended changes in subjects' behaviors due to cues inadvertently given by the experimenter.

explicit memory Conscious, intentional recollection of an event or of an item of information.

extinction The weakening and eventual disappearance of a learned response. In classical conditioning, it occurs when the conditioned stimulus is no longer paired with the unconditioned stimulus. In operant conditioning, it occurs when a response is no longer followed by a reinforcer.

extrinsic reinforcers Reinforcers that are not inherently related to the activity being reinforced, such as money, prizes, and praise.

facial-feedback hypothesis The notion that the facial muscles send messages to the brain, identifying the emotion a person feels.

factor analysis A statistical method for analyzing the intercorrelations among various measures or test scores. Clusters of measures or scores that are highly correlated are assumed to measure the same underlying trait, ability, or aptitude (factor)

feature detectors Cells in the visual cortex that are sensitive to specific features of the environment.

feminist psychology A psychological approach that analyzes the influence of social inequities on gender relations and the behavior of the two sexes.

fetal alcohol syndrome (FAS) A pattern of physical and intellectual abnormalities in infants whose mothers drank an excessive amount of alcohol during pregnancy.

fixed-interval (FI) schedule An intermittent schedule of reinforcement in which a reinforcer is delivered for the first response made after a fixed period of time has elapsed since the last reinforcer.

fixed-ratio (FR) schedule An intermittent schedule of reinforcement in which reinforcement occurs only after a fixed number of responses.

flashbulb memory A vivid, detailed recollection of a significant or startling event, or of the circumstances in which a person learned of such an event.

fraternal (dizygotic) twins Twins that develop from two separate eggs fertilized by different sperm; they are no more alike genetically than any other pair of siblings.

free association In psychoanalysis, a method of recovering unconscious conflicts by saying freely whatever comes to mind.

frequency (of a sound wave) The number of times per second a sound wave cycles through a peak and low point.

functionalism An early psychological approach that stressed the function or purpose of behavior and consciousness.

fundamental attribution error The tendency in explaining other people's behavior to overestimate personality factors and underestimate the influence of the situation.

ganglion cells Neurons in the retina of the eye that gather information from receptor cells (by way of intermediate bipolar cells); their axons make up the optic nerve.

gate-control theory The theory that the experience of pain depends in part on whether pain impulses get past a neurological "gate" in the spinal cord and thus reach the brain.

gender identity The fundamental sense of being male or female, regardless of whether or not one conforms to the rules of sex typing.

gender role A set of rules and norms that defines socially approved attitudes and behavior for men and women.

gender schema A cognitive schema (mental network) of knowledge, beliefs, metaphors, and expectations about what it means to be male or female.

gender socialization (sex typing) The process by which children learn the behaviors, attitudes, and expectations associated in their culture with being masculine or feminine.

generalized anxiety disorder A continuous state of anxiety marked by feelings of worry and dread, apprehension, difficulties in concentration, and signs of motor tension.

genes The functional units of heredity; they are composed of DNA and specify the structure of proteins.

genome The full set of genes in each cell of an organism.

g factor A general intellectual ability assumed by some theorists to underlie various specific mental abilities and talents.

glial cells Cells that hold neurons in place, insulate neurons, and provide them with nutrients.

group polarization The tendency for a group's decision to be more extreme than its members' individual decisions.

groupthink In close-knit groups, the tendency for all members to think alike for the sake of harmony and to suppress disagreement.

heritability A statistical estimate of the proportion of the total variance in some trait within a group that is attributable to genetic differences among individuals within the group.

heuristic A rule of thumb that suggests a course of action or guides problem solving but does not guarantee an optimal solution; heuristics are often used as shortcuts in solving complex problems.

high-context cultures Cultures in which people pay close attention to nonverbal forms of communication and assume a shared context for their interactions—a common history and set of attitudes.

higher-order conditioning In classical conditioning, a procedure in which a neutral stimulus becomes a conditioned stimulus through association with an already established conditioned stimulus.

hindsight bias The tendency to overestimate one's ability to have predicted an event once the outcome is known; the "I knew it all along" phenomenon.

hippocampus A brain structure thought to be involved in the storage of new information in memory.

hormones Chemical substances, secreted by organs called glands, that affect the functioning of other organs.

hue The dimension of visual experience specified by color names and related to the wavelength of light.

humanistic psychology A psychological approach that emphasizes personal growth and the achievement of human potential more than the scientific understanding, prediction, and control of behavior.

hypnosis A condition in which attention is focused and a person is extremely responsive to suggestion.

hypothalamus A brain structure involved in emotions and drives vital to survival, such as fear, hunger, thirst, and reproduction; it regulates the autonomic nervous system.

hypothesis A statement that attempts to predict or to account for a set of phenomena. Scientific hypotheses specify relationships among events or variables and are supported or disconfirmed by empirical investigation.

id In psychoanalysis, the part of personality containing inherited psychological energy, particularly sexual and aggressive instincts.

identical (monozygotic) twins Twins born when a fertilized egg divides into two parts that develop into separate embryos.

identification A process by which the child adopts an adult's standards of morality, values, and beliefs as his or her own; in psychoanalysis, identification with the same-sex parent is said to occur at resolution of the Oedipus complex.

implicit memory Unconscious retention in memory, as evidenced by the effect of a previous experience or previously encountered information on current thoughts or actions.

independent variable A variable that an experimenter manipulates.

induction A method of child rearing in which the parent appeals to the child's own resources, abilities, sense of responsibility, and feelings for others in correcting the child's misbehavior.

inductive reasoning A form of reasoning in which the premises provide support for a certain conclusion, but it is still possible for the conclusion to be false.

infantile amnesia *See* **childhood amnesia.**

inferential statistics Statistical tests that allow researchers to assess how likely it is that their results occurred merely by chance.

infradian [in-FRAY-dee-un] rhythm A biological rhythm that occurs less frequently than once a day; from the Latin for "below a day."

insight A form of learning that occurs in problem solving and appears to involve the (often sudden) understanding of how elements of a situation are related or can be reorganized to achieve a solution.

instinctive drift The tendency of an organism to revert to an instinctive behavior over time; it can interfere with learning.

intelligence An inferred characteristic of an individual, usually defined as the ability to profit from experience, acquire knowledge, think abstractly, act purposefully, or adapt to changes in the environment; different theorists weigh the components differently.

intelligence quotient (IQ) A measure of intelligence originally computed by dividing a person's mental age by his or her chronological age and multiplying the result by 100; it is now derived from norms provided for standardized intelligence tests.

intermittent (partial) schedule of reinforcement A reinforcement schedule in which a particular response is sometimes but not always reinforced.

intrapsychic Within the mind (*psyche*) or self.

intrinsic reinforcers Reinforcers that are inherently related to the activity being reinforced, such as enjoyment of the task and the satisfaction of accomplishment.

introspection *See* **trained introspection.**

inventories Standardized objective questionnaires requiring written responses; they typically include scales on which people are asked to rate themselves.

James-Lange theory of emotion The theory proposed independently by William James and Carl Lange that emotion results from the perception of one's own bodily reactions.

just-world hypothesis The notion that many people need to believe that the world is fair, that justice is served, and that bad people are punished and good people rewarded.

kinesthesis [KIN-es-THEE-sis] The sense of body position and movement of body parts; also called *kinesthesia*.

language A system that combines meaningless elements such as sounds or gestures to form structured utterances that convey meaning.

latent learning A form of learning that is not immediately expressed in an overt response; occurs without obvious reinforcement.

lateralization Specialization of the two cerebral hemispheres for particular psychological operations.

learning A relatively permanent change in behavior (or behavioral potential) due to experience.

learning disability A difficulty in the performance of a specific mental skill, such as reading or arithmetic; sometimes linked to perceptual or memory problems.

libido In psychoanalysis, the psychic energy that fuels the life or sexual instincts of the id.

limbic system A group of brain areas involved in emotional reactions and motivated behavior.

linkage studies Genetic studies that look for patterns of inheritance of genetic markers in large families in which a particular condition is common; the markers consist of DNA segments that vary considerably among individuals and that have known locations on the chromosomes.

localization of function Specialization of particular brain areas for particular functions.

locus of control A general expectation about whether the results of one's actions are under one's own control (*internal locus*) or beyond one's control (*external locus*).

longitudinal study A study in which subjects are followed and periodically reassessed over a period of time.

long-term memory (LTM) In the three-box model of memory, the memory system involved in the long-term storage of information; theoretically, it has an unlimited capacity.

long-term potentiation A long-lasting increase in the strength of synaptic responsiveness, thought to be a biological mechanism of long-term memory.

loudness The dimension of auditory experience related to the intensity of a pressure wave.

low-context cultures Cultures in which people do not take a shared context for granted and instead emphasize direct verbal communication.

lucid dream A dream in which the dreamer is aware of dreaming.

magnetic resonance imaging *See* **MRI.**

maintenance rehearsal Rote repetition of material in order to maintain its availability in memory.

major depression A mood disorder involving disturbances in emotion (excessive sadness), behavior (loss of interest in usual activities), cognition (distorted thoughts of hopelessness and low self-esteem), and body function (fatigue, loss of appetite).

maturation The sequential unfolding of genetically influenced behavior and physical characteristics.

mean *See* **arithmetic mean.**

medulla A structure in the brain stem responsible for certain automatic functions such as breathing and heart rate.

melatonin A hormone secreted by the pineal gland; it is involved in the regulation of circadian rhythms.

memory The capacity to retain and retrieve information; also, the mental structure or structures that account for this capacity and the material that is retained.

menarche [men-ARE-kee] The onset of menstruation at puberty.

mental age (MA) A measure of mental development expressed in terms of the average mental ability at a given age. A child with a mental age of 8 performs on a test of mental ability at the level of the average 8-year-old.

mental disorder Any behavior or emotional state that causes an individual great suffering or worry, is self-defeating or self-destructive, or is maladaptive and disrupts the person's relationships or the larger community.

mental image A mental representation that mirrors or resembles the thing it represents. Mental images can occur in many and perhaps all sensory modalities.

meta-analysis A statistical procedure for combining and analyzing data from many studies; it determines how much of the variance in scores across all studies can be explained by a particular variable.

metacognition The knowledge or awareness of one's own cognitive processes.

Minnesota Multiphasic Personality Inventory (MMPI) A widely used objective personality test.

"minor" tranquilizers Depressants commonly but often inappropriately prescribed for patients who complain of unhappiness or worry.

mnemonics Strategies and tricks for improving memory, such as the use of a verse or a formula.

monochronic cultures Cultures in which time is organized sequentially; schedules and deadlines are valued over people.

monocular cues Visual cues to depth or distance that can be used by one eye alone.

monozygotic twins *See* **identical twins.**

motivated forgetting Forgetting because of a desire to eliminate awareness of painful, embarrassing, or otherwise unpleasant experiences.

motivation An inferred process within a person or animal that causes that organism to move toward a goal.

motor nerves Nerves in the peripheral nervous system that carry messages from the central nervous system to muscles, glands, and internal organs.

MRI (magnetic resonance imaging) A method for studying body and brain tissue using magnetic fields and special radio receivers.

multiple personality disorder A rare dissociative disorder marked by the appearance within one person of two or more distinct personalities, each with its own name and traits; now called *dissociative identity disorder*.

myelin sheath A fatty insulating sheath surrounding many axons.

narcissism An exaggerated sense of self-importance and self-absorption.

natural selection The evolutionary process in which individuals with genetically influenced traits that are adaptive in a particular environment tend to survive and to reproduce in greater numbers than other individuals; as a result, their traits become more common in the population over time.

need for achievement A learned motive to meet personal standards of success and excellence in a chosen area (often abbreviated *nAch*).

need for affiliation The motive to associate with other people, as by seeking friends, moral support, contact comfort, or companionship.

need for power A learned motive to dominate or influence others.

negative correlation An association between increases in one variable and decreases in another.

negative reinforcement A reinforcement procedure in which a response is followed by the removal, delay, or decrease in intensity of an unpleasant stimulus; as a result, the response becomes stronger or more likely to occur.

nerve A bundle of nerve fibers (axons and sometimes dendrites) in the peripheral nervous system.

neuromodulators Chemical messengers in the nervous system that increase or decrease the action of specific neurotransmitters.

neuron A cell that conducts electrochemical signals; the basic unit of the nervous system; also called a *nerve cell.*

neuropsychology The field of psychology concerned with the neural and biochemical bases of behavior and mental processes.

neurotransmitter A chemical substance that is released by a transmitting neuron at the synapse and that alters the activity of a receiving neuron.

nonconscious processes Mental processes occurring outside of and not available to conscious awareness.

norepinephrine *See* **epinephrine, norepinephrine.**

norms In test construction, established standards of performance.

norms (social) *See* **social norms.**

object permanence The understanding, which develops in the first year of life, that an object continues to exist even when you can't see it or touch it.

object-relations school A psychodynamic approach that emphasizes the importance of the infant's first two years of life and the baby's formative relationships.

observational learning A learning process in which an individual learns new responses by observing the behavior of another (a model) rather than through direct experience; sometimes called *vicarious conditioning.*

observational study A study in which the researcher carefully and systematically observes and records behavior without interfering with the behavior; it includes naturalistic and laboratory observations.

obsessive-compulsive disorder An anxiety disorder in which a person feels trapped in repetitive, persistent thoughts (obsessions) and repetitive, ritualized behaviors (compulsions) designed to reduce anxiety.

Oedipus complex In psychoanalysis, a conflict in which a child desires the parent of the other sex and views the same-sex parent as a rival; it is the key issue in the phallic stage of development.

operant conditioning The process by which a response becomes more or less likely to occur, depending on its consequences.

operational definition A precise definition of a term in a hypothesis, which specifies the operations for observing and measuring the process or phenomenon being defined.

operations In Piaget's theory, mental actions that are cognitively reversible.

opiates Drugs derived from the opium poppy that relieve pain and commonly produce euphoria.

opponent-process theory (of color) A theory of color perception which assumes that the visual system treats pairs of colors as opposing or antagonistic.

panic attack A brief feeling of intense fear and impending doom or death, accompanied by intense physiological symptoms such as rapid breathing and pulse, and dizziness.

papillae [pa-PILL-ee] Knoblike elevations on the tongue containing the taste buds (singular: *papilla*).

parallel distributed processing (PDP) An alternative to the information-processing model of memory, in which knowledge is represented not as propositions or images but as connections among thousands of interacting processing units, distributed in a vast network and all operating in parallel.

paranoia Unreasonable and excessive suspiciousness, jealousy, or mistrust; it may occur as a type of personality disorder or, with more severe symptoms of psychosis, as a type of schizophrenic disorder.

parapsychology The study of purported psychic phenomena, such as ESP and mental telepathy.

parasympathetic nervous system The subdivision of the autonomic nervous system that operates during relaxed states and that conserves energy.

perception The process by which the brain organizes and interprets sensory information.

perceptual constancy The accurate perception of objects as stable or unchanged despite changes in the sensory patterns they produce.

perceptual illusion An erroneous or misleading perception of reality.

perceptual set A habitual way of perceiving, based on expectations.

peripheral nervous system (PNS) All portions of the nervous system outside the brain and spinal cord; it includes sensory and motor nerves.

personality A distinctive and relatively stable pattern of behavior, thoughts, motives, and emotions that characterizes an individual throughout life.

personality disorders Rigid, maladaptive personality patterns that cause personal distress or inability to get along with others.

PET scan (positron-emission tomography) A method for analyzing biochemical activity in the brain, using injections of a glucoselike substance containing a radioactive element.

phenomenology The study of events and situations as individuals experience them; in personality, the study of an individual's qualities from the person's own point of view.

phobia An unrealistic fear of a specific situation, activity, or object.

pitch The dimension of auditory experience related to the frequency of a pressure wave; height or depth of a tone.

pituitary gland A small endocrine gland at the base of the brain that releases many hormones and regulates other endocrine glands.

placebo An inactive substance or fake treatment used as a control in an experiment or given by a medical practitioner to a patient.

polychronic cultures Cultures in which time is organized horizontally; people tend to do several things at once and to value relationships over schedules.

pons A structure in the brain stem involved in, among other things, sleeping, waking, and dreaming.

positive correlation An association between increases in one variable and increases in another.

positive reinforcement A reinforcement procedure in which a response is followed by the presentation of or increase in intensity of a reinforcing stimulus; as a result, the response becomes stronger or more likely to occur.

positron-emission tomography *See* **PET scan.**

power assertion A method of child rearing in which the parent uses punishment and authority to correct the child's misbehavior.

primacy effect The tendency for items at the beginning of a list to be well recalled.

primary control An effort to modify reality by changing other people, the situation, or events; a "fighting back" philosophy.

primary emotions Emotions that are considered to be universal and biologically based; they generally include fear, anger, sadness, joy, surprise, and disgust.

primary punisher A stimulus that is inherently punishing; an example is electric shock.

primary reinforcer A stimulus that is inherently reinforcing, typically satisfying a physiological need; an example is food.

priming A method for measuring implicit memory in which a person reads or listens to information and is later tested to see whether the information is "activated" on another type of task.

principle of falsifiability The principle that a scientific theory must make predictions that are specific enough to expose the theory to the possibility of disconfirmation—that is, the theory must predict not only what will happen, but also what will not happen.

proactive interference Forgetting that occurs when previously stored material interferes with the ability to remember similar, more recently learned material.

procedural memories Memories for the performance of actions or skills ("knowing how").

projective tests Psychological tests used to infer a person's motives, conflicts, and unconscious dynamics on the basis of the person's interpretations of ambiguous or unstructured stimuli.

proposition A unit of meaning that is made up of concepts and that expresses a unitary idea.

psychedelic drugs Consciousness-altering drugs that produce hallucinations, change thought processes, or disrupt the normal perception of time and space.

psychiatry The medical specialty concerned with mental disorders, maladjustment, and abnormal behavior.

psychoactive drug A drug capable of influencing perception, mood, cognition, or behavior.

psychoanalysis A theory of personality and a method of psychotherapy originally developed by Sigmund Freud; it emphasizes unconscious motives and conflicts.

psychodynamic theories Psychological approaches that emphasize unconscious energy dynamics within the individual, such as inner forces, conflicts, or the movement of instinctual energy.

psychological stress The result of a relationship between the person and the environment, in which the person believes the situation is overwhelming and threatens his or her ability to cope.

psychological tests Procedures used to measure and evaluate personality traits, emotional states, aptitudes, interests, abilities, and values.

psychology The scientific study of behavior and mental processes and how they are affected by an organism's physical state, mental state, and external environment; the term is often represented by ψ, the Greek letter *psi* (usually pronounced SY).

psychometrics The measurement of mental abilities, traits, and processes.

psychoneuroimmunology (PNI) [psycho-neuro-immun-ology] The study of the relationships among psychology, the nervous system, and the immune system.

psychophysics The area of psychology concerned with the relationship between physical properties of stimuli and sensory experience.

psychosis An extreme mental disturbance involving distorted perceptions and irrational behavior; it may have psychological or organic causes.

psychosomatic A term that describes the interaction between a physical illness or condition and psychological states; literally, mind (*psyche*) and body (*soma*).

psychosurgery Any surgical procedure that destroys selected areas of the brain believed to be involved in emotional disorders or violent, impulsive behavior.

puberty The age at which a person becomes capable of sexual reproduction.

punishment The process by which a stimulus or event weakens or reduces the probability of the response that it follows.

random assignment A procedure for assigning people to experimental and control groups in which each individual has the same probability as any other of being assigned to a given group.

range A measure of the spread of scores, calculated by subtracting the lowest score from the highest score.

rapid eye movement (REM) sleep Sleep periods characterized by eye movement, loss of muscle tone, and dreaming.

reasoning The drawing of conclusions or inferences from observations, facts, or assumptions.

recall The ability to retrieve and reproduce from memory previously encountered material.

recency effect The tendency for items at the end of a list to be well recalled.

recognition The ability to identify previously encountered material.

reflex An automatic response to a stimulus.

reinforcement The process by which a stimulus or event strengthens or increases the probability of the response that it follows.

relearning method A method for measuring retention that compares the time required to relearn material with the time used in the initial learning of the material.

reliability In test construction, the consistency from one time and place to another of scores derived from a test.

REM sleep *See* **rapid eye movement sleep.**

representative sample A sample that matches the population in question on important characteristics such as age and sex.

reticular activating system (RAS) A dense network of neurons found in the core of the brain stem; arouses the cortex and screens incoming information.

retina Neural tissue lining the back of the eyeball's interior, which contains the receptors for vision.

retinal disparity The slight difference in lateral separation between two objects as seen by the left eye and the right eye.

retroactive interference Forgetting that occurs when recently learned material interferes with the ability to remember similar material stored previously.

retrograde amnesia Loss of the ability to remember events or experiences that occurred before some particular point in time.

rods Visual receptors that respond to dim light but are not involved in color vision.

role A given social position that is governed by a set of norms for proper behavior.

Rorschach Inkblot Test A projective personality test that asks respondents to interpret abstract, symmetrical inkblots.

sample A group of subjects selected from a population for study in order to estimate characteristics of the population.

saturation Vividness or purity of color; the dimension of visual experience related to the complexity of light waves.

schizophrenia A psychotic disorder or disorders marked by some or all of these symptoms: delusions, hallucinations, disorganized and incoherent speech, severe emotional abnormalities, and withdrawal into an inner world.

secondary control An effort to accept reality by changing one's own attitudes, goals, or emotions; a "learn to live with it" philosophy.

secondary emotions Emotions that are either "blends" of primary emotions or that are specific to certain cultures.

secondary punisher A stimulus that has acquired punishing properties through association with other punishers.

secondary reinforcer A stimulus that has acquired reinforcing properties through association with other reinforcers.

selective attention The focusing of attention on selected aspects of the environment and the blocking out of others.

self-efficacy The belief that one is capable of producing, through one's own efforts, desired results (such as mastering new skills and reaching goals).

self-fulfilling prophecy An expectation that comes true because of the tendency of the person holding it to act in ways to confirm it.

self-serving bias The tendency in explaining one's own behavior to take credit for one's good actions and to rationalize one's mistakes.

semantic memories Memories of general knowledge, including facts, rules, concepts, and propositions.

semicircular canals Sense organs in the inner ear that contribute to equilibrium by responding to rotation of the head.

sensation The detection or direct experience of physical energy in the external or internal environment due to stimulation of receptors in the sense organs.

sense receptors Specialized cells that convert physical energy in the environment into electrical energy that can be transmitted as nerve impulses to the brain.

sensory adaptation The reduction or disappearance of sensory responsiveness that occurs when stimulation is unchanging or repetitious.

sensory deprivation The absence of normal levels of sensory stimulation.

sensory memory A memory system that momentarily preserves extremely accurate images of sensory information.

sensory nerves Nerves in the peripheral nervous system that carry sensory messages toward the central nervous system.

sensory registers Subsystems of sensory memory; most memory models assume a separate register for each sensory modality.

serial-position effect The tendency for recall of the first and last items on a list to surpass recall of items in the middle of the list.

set point According to one theory, the genetically influenced weight range for an individual, thought to be maintained by a biological mechanism that regulates food intake, fat reserves, and metabolism.

sex hormones Hormones that regulate the development and functioning of reproductive and sex organs and that stimulate the development of male and female sexual characteristics; they include estrogens, progesterone, and testosterone.

sex typing *See* **gender socialization.**

shaping An operant-conditioning procedure in which successive approximations of a desired response are reinforced; used when the desired response has a low probability of occurring spontaneously.

short-term memory (STM) In the three-box model of memory, a limited capacity memory system involved in the retention of information for brief periods; it is also used to hold information retrieved from long-term memory for temporary use.

signal-detection theory A psychophysical theory that divides the detection of a sensory signal into a sensory process and a decision process.

single-blind study An experiment in which subjects do not know whether they are in an experimental or a control group.

social cognition An area in social psychology concerned with social influences on thought, memory, perception, and other cognitive processes.

social constructionism The view that there are no universal truths about human nature because people construct reality differently depending on their culture, the historical moment, and the power arrangements within their society.

social identity The part of a person's self-concept that is based on his or her identification with a nation, culture, or ethnic group or with gender or other roles in society.

social-learning theories Theories of learning that typically emphasize a person's reciprocal interaction with the environment and that involve observational learning, cognitive processes, expectations, and motivating beliefs.

social norms Social conventions that regulate human life, including explicit laws and implicit cultural standards.

sociobiology An interdisciplinary field of study that emphasizes evolutionary explanations of social behavior in animals, including human beings; unlike most evolutionary psychologists, sociobiologists generally assume a motive for reproductive fitness.

sociocultural perspective A psychological approach that emphasizes social and cultural influences on behavior.

somatic nervous system The subdivision of the peripheral nervous system that connects to sensory receptors and skeletal muscles; sometimes called the *skeletal nervous system.*

spinal cord A collection of neurons and supportive tissue running from the base of the brain down the center of the back, protected by a column of bones (the spinal column).

spontaneous recovery The reappearance of a learned response after its apparent extinction.

standardize In test construction, to develop uniform procedures for giving and scoring a test.

state-dependent memory The tendency to remember something when one is in the same physical or mental state as during the original learning or experience.

states of consciousness Distinctive and discrete patterns in the functioning of consciousness, characterized by particular modes of perception, thought, memory, or feeling.

statistically significant A term used to refer to a result that is extremely unlikely to have occurred by chance.

stereotype A cognitive schema or a summary impression of a group, in which a person believes that all members of the group share a common trait or traits (positive, negative, or neutral).

stimulants Drugs that speed up activity in the central nervous system.

stimulus control Control over the occurrence of a response by a discriminative stimulus.

stimulus discrimination The tendency to respond differently to two or more stimuli that are similar but that differ from one another in some way. In classical conditioning, it occurs when a stimulus similar to the conditioned stimulus fails to evoke the conditioned response. In operant conditioning, it occurs when an organism learns to make a response in the presence of one stimulus but not in the presence of other, similar stimuli.

stimulus generalization After conditioning, the tendency to respond to a stimulus that resembles one involved in the original conditioning. In classical conditioning, it occurs when a stimulus that resembles the conditioned stimulus elicits the conditioned response. In operant conditioning, it occurs when a response that has been reinforced (or punished) in the presence of one stimulus occurs (or is suppressed) in the presence of other, similar stimuli.

stress *See* **psychological stress.**

structuralism An early psychological approach that stressed analysis of immediate experience into basic elements.

subconscious processes Mental processes occurring outside of conscious awareness but accessible to consciousness when necessary.

sublimation In psychoanalysis, a type of displacement that serves a higher cultural or social useful purpose; for example, the creation of art or music as a sublimation of sexual energy.

successive approximations In the operant-conditioning procedure of shaping, behaviors that are ordered in terms of increasing similarity or closeness to the desired response.

superego In psychoanalysis, the part of personality that represents conscience, morality, and social standards.

surveys Questionnaires and interviews that ask people directly about their experiences, attitudes, or opinions.

sympathetic nervous system The subdivision of the autonomic nervous system that mobilizes bodily resources and increases the output of energy during emotion and stress.

synapse The site where transmission of a nerve impulse from one nerve cell to another occurs; it includes the synaptic end bulb, synaptic cleft, and receptor sites in the membrane of the receiving cell.

synchrony The adjustment of one person's nonverbal behavior to coordinate it with another's.

taste buds Nests of taste-receptor cells.

telegraphic speech A child's first combination of words, which omit (as a telegram did) unnecessary words.

temperaments Characteristic styles of responding to the environment that are present in infancy and are assumed to be innate.

teratogen An external agent such as a disease or chemical that increases the risk of abnormalities in prenatal development.

thalamus The brain structure that relays sensory messages to the cerebral cortex.

Thematic Apperception Test (TAT) A projective personality test that asks respondents to interpret a series of drawings showing ambiguous scenes of people.

theory An organized system of assumptions and principles that purports to explain a specified set of phenomena and their interrelationships.

theory of mind A theory held by a child or adult about the way one's own mind and other people's minds work, and how people are affected by their beliefs and feelings. Children develop a theory of mind by age 4 or 5.

therapeutic alliance The bond of confidence and mutual understanding established between therapist and client that allows them to work together to solve the client's problems.

thinking The mental manipulation of information stored in the form of concepts, images, or propositions.

timbre The distinguishing quality of a sound; the dimension of auditory experience related to the complexity of the pressure wave.

token economy A behavior-modification technique in which secondary reinforcers called *tokens,* which can be collected and exchanged for primary or other secondary reinforcers, are used for shaping behavior.

tolerance Increased resistance to a drug's effects brought about by continued use; as tolerance develops, larger doses are required to produce effects once made by smaller ones.

trained introspection A form of self-observation in which individuals examine and report the contents of their own consciousnesses.

trait A descriptive characteristic of an individual, assumed to be stable across situations and time.

transduction The conversion of one form of energy to another; sensory receptors are biological transducers.

transference In psychodynamic therapies, a critical step in which the patient transfers emotional feelings, usually involving his or her parents, to the therapist.

trichromatic theory A theory of color perception that proposes three mechanisms in the visual system, each sensitive to a certain range of wavelengths; their interaction is assumed to produce all the different experiences of hue.

two-factor theory of emotion The theory that emotions depend on both physiological arousal and a cognitive interpretation of that arousal.

ultradian [ul-TRAY-dee-un] rhythm A biological rhythm that occurs more frequently than once a day; from the Latin for "beyond a day."

unconditional positive regard To Carl Rogers, love or support given to another person with no conditions attached.

unconditioned response (UR) The classical-conditioning term for a reflexive response elicited by a stimulus in the absence of learning.

unconditioned stimulus (US) The classical-conditioning term for a stimulus that elicits a reflexive response in the absence of learning.

validity The ability of a test to measure what it was designed to measure.

validity effect The tendency of people to believe that a statement is true or valid simply because it has been repeated many times.

variable-interval (VI) schedule An intermittent schedule of reinforcement in which a reinforcer is delivered for a response made after a variable period of time has elapsed since the last reinforcer.

variable-ratio (VR) schedule An intermittent schedule of reinforcement in which reinforcement occurs after a variable number of responses.

variables Characteristics of behavior or experience that can be measured or described by a numeric scale; variables are manipulated and assessed in scientific studies.

variance A measure of the dispersion of scores around the mean.

volunteer bias A shortcoming of findings derived from a sample of volunteers instead of a representative sample.

Weber's law A law of psychophysics stating that the change necessary to produce a just noticeable difference is a constant proportion of the original stimulus.

withdrawal symptoms Physical and psychological symptoms that occur when someone addicted to a drug stops taking it.

BIBLIOGRAPHY

Bulleted entries indicate reference new to the fourth edition of Psychology.

• **Abel, Gene G.; Mittelman, Mary; Becker, Judith V.; Rathner, Jerry; et al.** (1988). Predicting child molesters' response to treatment. Conference of the New York Academy of Sciences: Human sexual aggression: Current perspectives. *Annals of the New York Academy of Sciences, 528,* 223–234.

Abelson, Robert P. (1988). Conviction. *American Psychologist, 43,* 267–275.

Abrams, David B., & Wilson, G. Terence (1983). Alcohol, sexual arousal, and self-control. *Journal of Personality and Social Psychology, 45,* 188–198.

Abramson, Lyn Y.; Metalsky, Gerald I.; & Alloy, Lauren B. (1989). Hopelessness depression: A theory-based subtype of depression. *Psychological Review, 96,* 358–372.

Abramson, Lyn Y.; Seligman, Martin E. P.; & Teasdale, John (1978). Learned helplessness in humans: Critique and reformulation. *Journal of Abnormal Psychology, 87,* 49–74.

• **Abu-Lughod, Lila** (1992). *Writing women's worlds: Bedouin stories.* Berkeley: University of California Press.

Acredolo, Linda, & Goodwyn, Susan (1988). Symbolic gesturing in normal infants. *Child Development, 59,* 450–466.

• **Adamopoulos, John, & Lonner, Walter J.** (1994). Absolutism, relativism, and universalism in the study of human behavior. In W. J. Lonner & R. S. Malpass (eds.), *Psychology and culture.* Needham Heights, MA: Allyn & Bacon.

Adams, Gerald R.; Ryan, John H.; Hoffman, Joseph J.; Dobson, William R.; & Nielsen, Elwin C. (1985). Ego identity status, conformity behavior, and personality in late adolescence. *Journal of Personality and Social Psychology, 47,* 1091–1104.

• **Adams, M. J.** (1990). *Learning to read: Thinking and learning about print.* Cambridge, MA: MIT Press.

• **Ader, Robert, & Cohen, Nicholas** (1993). Psychoneuroimmunology: Conditioning and stress. *Annual Review of Psychology, 44,* 53–85.

Adler, Alfred (1927/1959). *Understanding human nature.* New York: Premier.

Adler, Alfred (1938/1964). *Social interest: A challenge to mankind.* New York: Capricorn.

• **Adler, Nancy E.; Boyce, Thomas; Chesney, Margaret A.; Cohen, Sheldon; Folkman, Susan; Kahn, Robert L.; & Syme, S. Leonard** (1994). Socioeconomic status and health: The challenge of the gradient. *American Psychologist, 49,* 15–24.

Affleck, Glenn; Tennen, Howard; Croog, Sydney; & Levine, Sol (1987). Causal attribution, perceived control, and recovery from a heart attack. *Journal of Social and Clinical Psychology, 5,* 339–355.

Ainsworth, Mary D. S. (1973). The development of infant-mother attachment. In B. M. Caldwell & H. N. Ricciuti (eds.), *Review of child development research,* Vol. 3. Chicago: University of Chicago Press.

Ainsworth, Mary D. S. (1979). Infant-mother attachment. *American Psychologist, 34,* 932–937.

Ainsworth, Mary D. S.; Blehar, Mary L.; Waters, Everett; & Wall, Sally (1978). *Patterns of attachment.* Hillsdale, NJ: Erlbaum.

Alagna, Sheryle W., & Hamilton, Jean A. (1986). Science in the service of mythology: The psychopathologizing of menstruation. Paper presented at the American Psychological Association, Washington, DC.

Albee, George W. (1977). The Protestant ethic, sex, and psychotherapy. *American Psychologist, 32,* 150–161.

Albee, George W. (1985, February). The answer is prevention. *Psychology Today,* 60–64.

• **Aldag, Ramon J., & Fuller, Sally R.** (1993). Beyond fiasco: A reappraisal of the groupthink phenomenon and a new model of group decision processes. *Psychological Bulletin, 113,* 533–552.

• **Allen, Laura S., & Gorski, Robert A.** (1992). Sexual orientation and the size of the anterior commissure in the human brain. *Proceedings of the National Academy of Sciences, 89,* 7199–7202.

• **Allison, David B., & Heshka, Stanley** (1993). Emotion and eating in obesity? A critical analysis. *International Journal of Eating Disorders, 13,* 289–295.

• **Allison, David B.; Heshka, Stanley; Neale, Michael C.; Lykken, David T.; et al.** (1994). A genetic analysis of relative weight among 4,020 twin pairs, with an emphasis on sex effects. *Health Psychology, 13,* 362–365.

Allport, Gordon W. (1937). *Personality: A psychological interpretation.* New York: Holt, Rinehart and Winston.

Allport, Gordon W. (1954/1979). *The nature of prejudice.* Reading, MA: Addison-Wesley.

Allport, Gordon W. (1961). *Pattern and growth in personality.* New York: Holt, Rinehart and Winston.

Alpert, Bené; Field, Tiffany; Goldstein, Sheri; & Perry, Susan (1990). Aerobics enhances cardiovascular fitness and agility in preschoolers. *Health Psychology, 9,* 48–56.

Amabile, Teresa M. (1983). *The social psychology of creativity.* New York: Springer-Verlag.

Amabile, Teresa M. (1985). Motivation and creativity: Effects of motivational orientation on creative writers. *Journal of Personality and Social Psychology, 48,* 393–399.

• **Amabile, Teresa M.; Hill, Karl G.; Hennessey, Beth A.; & Tighe, Elizabeth M.** (1994). The work preference inventory: Assessing intrinsic and extrinsic motivational orientations. *Journal of Personality and Social Psychology, 66,* 950–967.

• **Amabile, Teresa M.; Phillips, Elise D.; & Collins, Mary Ann** (1993). Creativity by contract: Social influences on the creativity of professional artists. Paper presented at the annual meeting of the American Psychological Association, Toronto.

Amato, Paul R., & Keith, Bruce (1991). Parental divorce and the well-being of children: A meta-analysis. *Psychological Bulletin, 110,* 26–46.

• **American Psychiatric Association** (1994). *Diagnostic and statistical manual of mental disorders, fourth edition: DSM-IV.* Washington, DC: American Psychiatric Association.

Amering, Michaela, & Katschnig, Heinz (1990). Panic attacks and panic disorder in cross-cultural perspective. *Psychiatric Annals, 20,* 511–516.

• **Amir, Yehuda** (1994). The contact hypothesis in intergroup relations. In W. J. Lonner & R. Malpass (eds.), *Psychology and culture.* Needham Heights, MA: Allyn & Bacon.

Anastasi, Anne (1988). *Psychological testing* (6th ed.). New York: Macmillan.

• **Andersen, Barbara L.; Kiecolt-Glaser, Janice K.; & Glaser, Ronald** (1994). A biobehavioral model of cancer stress and disease course. *American Psychologist, 49,* 389–404.

Andersen, Susan M.; Klatzky, Roberta L.; & Murray, John (1990). Traits and social stereotypes: Efficiency differences in social information processing. *Journal of Personality and Social Psychology, 59,* 192–201.

• **Anderson, Craig A.; Miller, Rowland S.; Riger, Alice L.; Dill, Jody C.; & Sedikides, Constantine** (1994). Behavioral and characterological attributional styles as predictors of depression and loneliness: Review, refinement, and test. *Journal of Personality and Social Psychology, 66,* 549–558.

Anderson, James A., & Rosenfeld, Edward (eds.) (1988). *Neurocomputing: Foundations of research.* Cambridge, MA: MIT Press.

Anderson, John R. (1983). Retrieval of information from long-term memory. *Science, 220,* 25–30.

• **Anderson, John R.** (1990). *The adaptive nature of thought.* Hillsdale, NJ: Erlbaum.

Anderson, John R., & Bower, Gordon H. (1973). *Human associative memory.* Washington, DC: Winston.

Anderson, Norman B. (1991). Addressing ethnic minority health issues: Behavioral medicine at the forefront of research and practice. Paper presented at the annual meeting of the Society of Behavioral Medicine, Washington, DC.

• **Andreasen, Nancy C.; Arndt, Stephan; Swayze, Victor, II; Cizadlo, Ted; et al.** (1994). Thalamic abnormalities in schizophrenia visualized through magnetic resonance image averaging. *Science, 266,* 294–298.

Angell, Marcia (1985, June 13). Disease as a reflection of the psyche. *New England Journal of Medicine, 312,* 1570–1572.

• **Anliker, J. A.; Bartoshuk, L. M.; Ferris, A. M.; & Hooks, L. D.** (1991). Children's food preferences and genetic sensitivity to the bitter taste of PROP. *American Journal of Clinical Nutrition, 54,* 316–320.

Anthony, William A.; Cohen, Mikal; & Kennard, William (1990). Understanding the current facts and principles of mental health systems planning. *American Psychologist, 45,* 1249–1252.

Antonovsky, Aaron (1987). *Unraveling the mystery of health: How people manage stress and stay well.* San Francisco: Jossey-Bass.

Antonucci, Toni C.; Fuhrer, Rebecca; & Jackson, James S. (1990). Social support and reciprocity: A cross-ethnic and cross-national perspective. *Journal of Social and Personal Relationships, 7,* 519–530.

Antrobus, John (1991). Dreaming: Cognitive processes during cortical activation and high afferent thresholds. *Psychological Review, 98,* 96–121.

• **APA Commission on Violence and Youth** (1993). *Violence and youth: Psychology's response.* Washington, DC: American Psychological Association.

• **Appiah, Kwame A.** (1994). Beyond race: Fallacies of reactive Afrocentrism. *Skeptic, 2*(4), 104–107.

Apter, Terri (1990). *Altered loves: Mothers and daughters during adolescence.* New York: St. Martin's Press.

• **Archer, J., & Lloyd, B.** (1982). *Sex and gender.* Cambridge, England: Cambridge University Press.

Arendt, Hannah (1963). *Eichmann in Jerusalem: A report on the banality of evil.* New York: Viking.

Arendt, Josephine; Aldhous, Margaret; & Wright, John (1988, April 2). Synchronization of a disturbed sleep-wake cycle in a blind man by melatonin treatment. *Lancet, 1*(8588), 772–773.

Arkes, Hal R. (1991). Some practical judgment/decision making research. Paper presented at the annual meeting of the American Psychological Association, Boston.

• **Arkes, Hal R.; Boehm, Lawrence E.; & Xu, Gang** (1991). The determinants of judged validity. *Journal of Experimental Social Psychology, 27,* 576–605.

Arkes, Hal R.; Faust, David; Guilmette, Thomas J.; & Hart, Kathleen (1988). Eliminating the hindsight bias. *Journal of Applied Psychology, 73,* 305–307.

• **Armstrong, Louise** (1978/1987). *Kiss daddy goodnight: Ten years later.* New York: Pocket Books.

• **Armstrong, Louise** (1993). *And they call it help: The psychiatric policing of America's children.* Reading, MA: Addison-Wesley.

• **Aronson, Elliot** (1992). The return of the repressed: Dissonance theory makes a comeback. *Psychological Inquiry, 3,* 303–311.

• **Aronson, Elliot** (1995). *The social animal* (7th ed.). New York: Freeman.

Aronson, Elliot, & Mills, Judson (1959). The effect of severity of initiation on liking for a group. *Journal of Abnormal and Social Psychology, 59,* 177–181.

Aronson, Elliot; Stephan, Cookie; Sikes, Jev; Blaney, Nancy; & Snapp, Matthew (1978). *The jigsaw classroom.* Beverly Hills, CA: Sage.

• **Aronson, Elliot; Wilson, Timothy D.; & Akert, Robin** (1994). *Social psychology: The heart and the mind.* New York: HarperCollins.

Asch, Solomon E. (1952). *Social psychology.* Englewood Cliffs, NJ: Prentice-Hall.

Asch, Solomon E. (1965). Effects of group pressure upon the modification and distortion of judgments. In H. Proshansky & B. Seidenberg (eds.), *Basic studies in social psychology.* New York: Holt, Rinehart and Winston.

Aschoff, Jürgen, & Wever, Rutger (1981). The circadian system of man. In J. Aschoff (ed.), *Handbook of behavioral neurobiology, Vol. 4: Biological rhythms.* New York: Plenum.

Aserinsky, Eugene, & Kleitman, Nathaniel (1955). Two types of ocular motility occurring in sleep. *Journal of Applied Physiology, 8,* 1–10.

• **Aspinwall, Lisa G., & Taylor, Shelley E.** (1993). Effects of social comparison direction, threat, and self-esteem on affect, self-evaluation, and expected success. *Journal of Personality and Social Psychology, 64,* 708–722.

• **Astington, J. W., & Gopnik, Alison** (1991). Theoretical explanations of children's understanding of the mind. In G. E. Butterworth, P. L. Harris, A. M. Leslie, & H. M. Wellman (eds.), *Perspectives on the child's theory of mind.* New York: Oxford University Press.

Atkinson, John W. (ed.) (1958). *Motives in fantasy, action, and society.* Princeton, NJ: Van Nostrand.

• **Atkinson, Richard C., & Shiffrin, Richard M.** (1968). Human memory: A proposed system and its control processes. In K. W. Spence & J. T. Spence (eds.), *The psychology of learning and motivation. Vol. 2: Advances in research and theory.* New York: Academic Press.

Atkinson, Richard C., & Shiffrin, Richard M. (1971, August). The control of short-term memory. *Scientific American, 225*(2), 82–90.

Averill, James R. (1982). *Anger and aggression.* New York: Springer-Verlag.

Azrin, Nathan H., & Foxx, Richard M. (1974). *Toilet training in less than a day.* New York: Simon & Schuster.

Azuma, Hiroshi (1984). Secondary control as a heterogeneous category. *American Psychologist, 39,* 970–971.

• **Bahill, A. Terry, & Karnavas, William J.** (1993). The perceptual illusion of baseball's rising fastball and breaking curveball. *Journal of Experimental Psychology: Human Perception & Performance, 19,* 3–14.

Bahrick, Harry P. (1984). Semantic memory content in permastore: Fifty years of memory for Spanish learned in school. *Journal of Experimental Psychology: General, 113,* 1–29.

Bahrick, Harry P.; Bahrick, Phyllis O.; & Wittlinger, Roy P. (1975). Fifty years of memory for names and faces: A cross-sectional approach. *Journal of Experimental Psychology: General, 104,* 54–75.

Bahrke, Michael S.; Yesalis, Charles E., III; & Wright, James E. (1990). Psychological and behavioral effects of endogenous testosterone levels and anabolic-androgenic steroids among males: A review. *Sports Medicine, 10,* 303–337.

• **Bailey, J. Michael** (1993, March 25). Science and the fear of knowledge. *Chicago Tribune,* opinion page.

• **Bailey, J. Michael, & Benishay, Deana S.** (1993). Familial aggregation of female sexual orientation. *American Journal of Psychiatry, 150,* 272–277.

• **Bailey, J. Michael; Bobrow, David; Wolfe, Marilyn; & Mikach, Sarah** (1995). Sexual orientation of adult sons of gay fathers. *Developmental Psychology, 31,* 124–129.

• **Bailey, J. Michael; Gaulin, Steven; Agyei, Yvonne; & Gladue, Brian A.** (1994). Effects of gender and sexual orientation on evolutionarily relevant aspects of human mating psychology. *Journal of Personality and Social Psychology, 66,* 1081–1093.

• **Bailey, J. Michael, & Pillard, Richard C.** (1991). A genetic study of male sexual orientation. *Archives of General Psychiatry, 48,* 1089–1096.

• **Bailey, J. Michael; Pillard, Richard C.; Neale, Michael C.; & Agyei, Yvonne** (1993). Heritable factors influence sexual orientation in women. *Archives of General Psychology, 50,* 217–223.

• **Baillargeon, Renée** (1994). How do infants learn about the physical world? *Current Directions in Psychological Science, 5,* 133–140.

• **Baker, Robert A.** (1992). *Hidden memories: Voices and visions from within.* Buffalo, NY: Prometheus.

Baltes, Paul B. (1983). Life-span developmental psychology: Observations on history and theory revisited. In R. M. Lerner (ed.), *Developmental psychology: Historical and philosophical perspectives.* Hillsdale, NJ: Erlbaum.

Baltes, Paul B.; Dittmann-Kohli, Freya; & Dixon, Roger A. (1984). New perspectives on the development of intelligence in adulthood: Toward a dual-process conception and a model of selective optimization with compensation. In P. B. Baltes & O. G. Brim, Jr. (eds.), *Life-span development and behavior,* Vol. 6. New York: Academic Press.

Bandura, Albert (1973). *Aggression: A social learning analysis.* Englewood Cliffs, NJ: Prentice-Hall.

Bandura, Albert (1977). *Social learning theory.* Englewood Cliffs, NJ: Prentice-Hall.

Bandura, Albert (1986). *Social foundations of thought and action: A social cognitive theory.* Englewood Cliffs, NJ: Prentice-Hall.

Bandura, Albert (1990). Self-regulation of motivation through goal systems. In R. A. Dienstbier (ed.), *Nebraska Symposium on Motivation,* Vol. 38. Lincoln: University of Nebraska Press.

• **Bandura, Albert** (1991). Social cognitive theory of moral thought and action. In W. M. Kurtines & J. L. Gewirtz (eds.), *Theory.* Vol. 1 of *Handbook of moral behavior and development.* Hillsdale, NJ: Erlbaum.

• **Bandura, Albert** (1992). Self-efficacy mechanism in psychobiologic functioning. In R. Schwarzer (ed.), *Self-efficacy: Thought control of action.* Washington, DC: Hemisphere.

• **Bandura, Albert** (1994). Self-efficacy. In *Encyclopedia of Human behavior,* Vol. 4. Orlando, FL: Academic Press.

Bandura, Albert; Ross, Dorothea; & Ross, Sheila A. (1963). Vicarious reinforcement and imitative learning. *Journal of Abnormal and Social Psychology, 67,* 601–607.

Banks, Martin S. (in collaboration with Philip Salapatek) (1984). Infant visual perception. In P. Mussen (ed.), *Handbook of child psychology* (4th ed.). Vol. II, M. M. Haith & J. J. Compos (eds.), *Infancy and developmental psychobiology.* New York: Wiley.

• **Banks, William P., & Pezdek, Kathy** (1994). The recovered memory/false memory debate [introductory remarks]. *Consciousness and Cognition* (Special issue: The recovered memory/false memory debate), 3(3/4), 265–268.

Bányai, Éva I., & Hilgard, Ernest R. (1976). Comparison of active-alert hypnotic induction with traditional relaxation induction. *Journal of Abnormal Psychology, 85,* 218–224.

Barber, Theodore X. (1979). Suggested ("hypnotic") behavior: The trance paradigm versus an alternative paradigm. In E. Fromm & R. E. Shor (eds.), *Hypnosis: Developments in research and new perspectives* (2nd ed.). New York: Aldine.

Barber, Theodore X., & Wilson, Sheryl C. (1977). Hypnosis, suggestions, and altered states of consciousness: Experimental evaluation of a new cognitive-behavioral theory and the traditional trance-state therapy of "hypnosis." *Annals of the New York Academy of Sciences, 296,* 34–47.

• **Bardach, Ann Louise** (1993, August). Tearing the veil. *Vanity Fair,* 123–127, 154–158.

• **Barinaga, Marcia** (1992). Challenging the "no new neurons" dogma. *Science, 255,* 1646.

• **Barinaga, Marcia** (1994, May 6). Neurotrophic factors enter the clinic. *Science, 264,* 772–774.

• **Barkow, Jerome H.; Cosmides, Leda; & Tooby, John (eds.)** (1992). *The adapted mind: Evolutionary psychology and the generation of culture.* New York: Oxford University Press.

Barlow, David H. (1990). Disorders of emotion. Paper presented at the annual meeting of the American Psychological Association, Boston.

Barlow, David H. (ed.) (1991). Special issue on diagnoses, dimensions, and DSM-IV: The science of classification. *Journal of Abnormal Psychology, 100,* 243–412.

• **Barlow, David H.** (1994). Empirically validated psychological procedures. Paper presented at the annual meeting of the American Psychological Association, Los Angeles.

Barnett, Peter A., & Gotlib, Ian H. (1988). Psychosocial functioning and depression: Distinguishing among antecedents, concomitants, and consequences. *Psychological Bulletin, 104,* 97–126.

• **Baron, Miron** (1993). The D2 dopamine receptor gene and alcoholism: A tempest in a wine cup? *Biological Psychiatry, 34,* 821–823.

Baron, Miron; Risch, Neil; Hamburger, Rahel; Mandel, Batsheva; et al. (1987, March 19). Genetic linkage between X-chromosome markers and bipolar affective illness. *Nature, 326,* 289–292.

Baron, Robert S.; Cutrona, Carolyn E.; Hicklin, Daniel; Russell, Daniel W.; & Lubaroff, David M. (1990). Social support and immune function among spouses of cancer patients. *Journal of Personality and Social Psychology, 59,* 344–352.

Barr, Christopher E.; Mednick, Sarnoff A.; & Munk-Jorgensen, Poul (1990). Exposure to influenza epidemics during gestation and adult schizophrenia: A 40-year study. *Archives of General Psychiatry, 47,* 869–874.

• **Barraclough, J.; Pinder, P.; Cruddas, M.; Osmond, C.; Taylor, I.; & Perry, M.** (1992). Life events and breast cancer prognosis. *British Medical Journal, 304*(6834), 1078–1081.

Barron, Frank, & Harrington, David M. (1981). Creativity, intelligence, and personality. *Annual Review of Psychology, 32,* 439–476.

Bartlett, Frederic C. (1932). *Remembering.* Cambridge, England: Cambridge University Press.

Bartoshuk, Linda (1990, August/September). Psychophysical insights on taste. *APA Science Agenda,* 12–13.

• **Bartoshuk, Linda M.** (1993). Genetic and pathological taste variation: What can we learn from animal models and human disease? In D. J. Chadwick, J. Marsh, & J. Goode (eds.), *The molecular basis of smell and taste transduction.* CIBA Foundation Symposia Series, No. 179. New York: Wiley.

• **Bartoshuk, Linda M., & Beauchamp, Gary K.** (1994). Chemical senses. *Annual Review of Psychology, 45,* 419–449.

• **Bashore, Theodore R., & Rapp, Paul E.** (1993). Are there alternatives to traditional polygraph procedures? *Psychological Bulletin, 113,* 3–22.

Batson, C. Daniel (1990). How social an animal? The human capacity for caring. *American Psychologist, 45,* 336–346.

Batson, C. Daniel; Dyck, Janine; Brandt, J. Randall; Batson, Judy; et al. (1988). Five studies testing two new egoistic alternatives to the empathy-altruism hypothesis. *Journal of Personality and Social Psychology, 55,* 52–77.

• **Bauer, Patricia J., & Dow, Gina Annunziato** (1994). Episodic memory in 16- and 20-month-old children: Specifics are generalized but not forgotten. *Developmental Psychology, 30,* 403–417.

• **Bauer, Patricia J., & Fivush, Robyn** (1992). Constructing event representations: Building on a foundation of variation and enabling relations. *Cognitive Development, 7,* 381–401.

• **Bauer, Patricia J., & Hertsgaard, Louise A.** (1993). Increasing steps in recall of events: Factors facilitating immediate and long-term memory in 13.5- and 16.5-month-old children. *Child Development, 64,* 1204–1223.

• **Baum, William M.** (1994). *Understanding behaviorism: Science, behavior, and culture.* New York: HarperCollins.

Baumeister, Roy F. (1990). Suicide as escape from self. *Psychological Review, 97,* 90–113.

• **Baumeister, Roy F.; Stillwell, Arlene M.; & Heatherton, Todd F.** (1994). Guilt: An interpersonal approach. *Psychological Bulletin, 115,* 243–267.

Baumeister, Roy F.; Stillwell, Arlene M.; & Wotman, Sara R. (1990). Victim and perpetrator accounts of interpersonal conflict: Autobiographical narratives about anger. *Journal of Personality and Social Psychology, 59,* 994–1005.

Baumgartner, Alice (1983). "My daddy might have loved me": Student perceptions of differences between being male and being female. Paper published by the Institute for Equality in Education, Denver.

• **Baumrind, Diana** (1966). Effects of authoritative parental control on child behavior. *Child Development, 37,* 887–907.

• **Baumrind, Diana** (1971). Current patterns of parental authority. *Developmental Psychology Monograph, 4* (1, Part 2).

• **Baumrind, Diana** (1973). The development of instrumental competence through socialization. In A. D. Pick (ed.), *Minnesota Symposium on Child Psychology,* Vol. 7. Minneapolis: University of Minnesota Press.

• **Baumrind, Diana** (1989). Rearing competent children. In W. Damon (ed.), *Child development today and tomorrow.* San Francisco: Jossey-Bass.

• **Baumrind, Diana** (1991). Parenting styles and adolescent development. In R. Lerner, A. C. Petersen, & J. Brooks-Gunn (eds.), *The encyclopedia of adolescence.* New York: Garland.

• **Baumrind, Diana** (1995). Commentary on sexual orientation: Research and social policy implications. *Developmental Psychology, 31,* 130–136.

• **Baxter, Lewis R.; Schwartz, Jeffrey M.; Bergman, Kenneth S.;**

Szuba, Martin P.; et al. (1992). Caudate glucose metabolic rate changes with both drug and behavior therapy for obsessive-compulsive disorder. *Archives of General Psychiatry, 49,* 681–689.

Bayer, Ronald (1981). *Homosexuality and American psychiatry.* New York: Basic Books.

Beard, John H.; Propst, Rudyard N.; & Malamud, T. J. (1982). The Fountain House model of psychiatric rehabilitation. *Psychosocial Rehabilitation Journal, 5,* 47–54.

• Bechtel, William, & Abrahamsen, Adele (1990). *Connectionism and the mind: An introduction to parallel processing in networks.* Cambridge, MA: Basil Blackwell.

Beck, Aaron T. (1976). *Cognitive therapy and the emotional disorders.* New York: International Universities Press.

Beck, Aaron T. (1987). Cognitive models of depression. *Journal of Cognitive Psychotherapy, An International Quarterly, 1,* 5–37.

Beck, Aaron T. (1988). Cognitive approaches to panic disorder: Theory and therapy. In S. Rachman & J. D. Maser (eds.), *Panic: Psychological perspectives.* Hillsdale, NJ: Erlbaum.

Beck, Aaron T. (1991). Cognitive therapy: A 30-year retrospective. *American Psychologist, 46,* 368–375.

• Becker, Ernest (1973). *The denial of death.* New York: Free Press.

• Becker, Judith V.; Skinner, Linda J.; Abel, Gene G.; & Cichon, Joan (1984). Time-limited therapy with sexually dysfunctional sexually assaulted women. *Journal of Social Work and Human Sexuality, 3,* 97–115.

Beckwith, Leila, & Cohen, Sarale E. (1984). Home environment and cognitive competence in preterm children during the first 5 years. In A. W. Gottfried (ed.), *Home environment and early cognitive development: Longitudinal research.* Orlando, FL: Academic Press.

• Bee, Helen (1995). *The developing child* (7th ed.). New York: HarperCollins.

• Bee, Helen; Barnard, Kathryn E.; et al. (1982). Prediction of IQ and language skill from perinatal status, child performance, family characteristics, and mother-infant interaction. *Child Development, 53,* 1134–1156.

Beebe, B.; Gerstman, L.; Carson, B.; et al. (1982). Rhythmic communication in the mother-infant dyad. In M. Davis (ed.), *Interaction rhythms: Periodicity in communicative behavior.* New York: Human Sciences Press.

Beer, William R. (1983). *Househusbands: Men and housework in American families.* South Hadley, MA: J. F. Bergin/Praeger.

• Begg, Ian M.; Needham, Douglas R.; & Bookbinder, Marc (1993). Do backward messages unconsciously affect listeners? No. *Canadian Journal of Experimental Psychology, 47,* 1–14.

• Bekenstein, Jonathan W., & Lothman, Eric W. (1993). Dormancy of inhibitory interneurons in a model of temporal lobe epilepsy. *Science, 259,* 97–100.

• Bell, Alan P.; Weinberg, Martin S.; & Hammersmith, Sue K. (1981). *Sexual preference: Its development in men and women.* Bloomington: Indiana University Press.

• Bell, Derrick (1992). *Faces at the bottom of the well: The permanence of racism.* New York: Basic Books.

Bellah, Robert N.; Madsen, Richard; Sullivan, William M.; Swidler, Ann; & Tipton, Steven M. (1985). *Habits of the heart: Individualism and commitment in American life.* Berkeley: University of California Press.

• Bellugi, Ursula; Bihrle, Amy; Neville, Helen; Doherty, Sally; & Jernigan, Terry L. (1992). Language, cognition, and brain organization in a neurodevelopmental disorder. In M. Gunnar & C. Nelson (eds.), *Developmental behavioral neuroscience: The Minnesota symposia on child psychology.* Hillsdale, NJ: Erlbaum.

Belmont, Lillian, & Marolla, Frands A. (1973). Birth order, family size, and intelligence. *Science, 182,* 1096–1101.

Bem, Daryl, & Allen, Andrea (1974). On predicting some of the people some of the time: The search for cross-cultural consistencies in behavior. *Psychological Review, 81,* 506–520.

• Bem, Daryl J., & Honorton, Charles (1994). Does psi exist? Replicable evidence for an anomalous process of information transfer. *Psychological Bulletin, 115,* 4–18.

Bem, Sandra L. (1985). Androgyny and gender schema theory: A conceptual and empirical integration. In T. B. Sonderegger (ed.), *Nebraska Symposium on Motivation: Psychology and Gender, 1984.* Vol. 32. Lincoln: University of Nebraska Press.

• Bem, Sandra L. (1993). *The lenses of gender.* New Haven, CT: Yale University Press.

Benbow, Camilla P., & Stanley, Julian C. (1983). Sex differences in mathematical reasoning: More facts. *Science, 222,* 1029–1031.

• Benedek, E. P., & Schetky, D. H. (1987). Problems in validating allegations of sexual abuse: Parts 1 and 2. Factors affecting perception and recall of events. *Journal of the American Academy of Child and Adolescent Psychiatry, 26,* 915–922.

Benjamin, Jessica (1988). *The bonds of love: Psychoanalysis, feminism, and the problem of domination.* New York: Pantheon.

Bennett, Henry L. (1988). Perception and memory for events during adequate general anesthesia for surgical operations. In H. M. Pettinati (ed.), *Hypnosis and memory.* New York: Guilford Press.

Bennett, Neil G.; Blanc, Ann Klimas; & Bloom, David E. (1988). Commitment and the modern union: Assessing the link between premarital cohabitation and subsequent marital stability. *American Sociological Review, 53,* 127–138.

• Benoit, Stephen, & Thomas, Roger L. (1992). The influence of expectancy in subliminal perception experiments. *Journal of General Psychology, 119,* 335–341.

Bentall, R. P. (1990). The illusion of reality: A review and integration of psychological research on hallucinations. *Psychological Bulletin, 107,* 82–95.

Benton, Cynthia; Hernandez, Anthony; Schmidt, Adeny; Schmitz, Mary; Stone, Anna; & Weiner, Bernard (1983). Is hostility linked with affiliation among males and with achievement among females? A critique of Pollak and Gilligan. *Journal of Personality and Social Psychology, 45,* 1167–1171.

• Bereiter, Carl, & Bird, Marlene (1985). Use of thinking aloud in identification and teaching of reading comprehension strategies. *Cognition and Instruction, 2,* 131–156.

• Berenbaum, Sheri A., & Snyder, Elizabeth (1995). Early hormonal influences on childhood sex-typed activity and playmate preferences: Implications for the development of sexual orientation. *Developmental Psychology, 31,* 31–42.

• Berk, L. S.; Tan, S. A.; Nehlsen-Cannarella, S. L.; Napier, B. J.; et al. (1988). Humor associated laughter decreases cortisol and increases spontaneous lymphocyte blastogenesis. *Clinical Research, 36,* 435A.

• Berkman, L. F.; Leo-Summers, L.; & Horwitz, R. I. (1992). Emotional support and survival after myocardial infarction: A prospective, population-based study of the elderly. *Annals of Internal Medicine, 117,* 1003–1009.

Berkman, Lisa, & Syme, S. Leonard (1979). Social networks, host resistance, and mortality: A nine-year follow-up study of Alameda County residents. *American Journal of Epidemiology, 109,* 186–204.

• Bernieri, Frank J.; Davis, Janet M.; Rosenthal, Robert; & Knee, C. Raymond (1994). Interactional synchrony and rapport: Measuring synchrony in displays devoid of sound and facial affect. *Personality and Social Psychology Bulletin, 20,* 303–311.

Bernieri, Frank J.; Reznick, J. Steven; & Rosenthal, Robert (1988). Synchrony, pseudosynchrony, and dissynchrony: Measuring the entrainment process in mother-infant interactions. *Journal of Personality and Social Psychology, 54,* 243–253.

Bernstein, Ilene L. (1985). Learning food aversions in the progression of cancer and treatment. *Annals of the New York Academy of Sciences, 443,* 365–380.

• Berry, John W. (1994). Acculturative stress. In W. J. Lonner & R. S. Malpass (eds.), *Psychology and culture.* Needham Heights, MA: Allyn & Bacon.

Besalel-Azrin, V.; Azrin, N. H.; & Armstrong, P. M. (1977). The student-oriented classroom: A method of improving student conduct and satisfaction. *Behavior Therapy, 8,* 193–204.

• Best, Deborah L., & Williams, John E. (1993). Cross-cultural viewpoint. In A. E. Beall & R. J. Sternberg (eds.), *The psychology of gender.* New York: Guilford Press.

• Betancourt, Hector, & López, Steven Regeser (1993). The study of culture, ethnicity, and race in American psychology. *American Psychologist, 48,* 629–637.

Bettelheim, Bruno (1962). *Symbolic wounds.* New York: Collier.

Bettelheim, Bruno (1967). *The empty fortress.* New York: Free Press.

• Betz, Nancy E., & Hackett, Gail (1986). Applications of self-efficacy theory to understanding career choice behavior. *Journal of Social and Clinical Psychology, 4,* 279–289.

Biederman, Irving (1987). Recognition-by-components: A theory of human image understanding. *Psychological Review, 94,* 115–147.

• Biglan, A.; Metzler, C. W.; Wirt, R.; Ary, D.; Noell, J.; et al. (1990). Social and behavioral factors associated with high-risk sexual behavior among adolescents. *Journal of Behavioral Medicine, 13,* 245–262.

Biner, Paul M. (1991). Effects of lighting-induced arousal on the magnitude of goal valence. *Personality and Social Psychology Bulletin, 17,* 219–226.

Birdwhistell, Ray L. (1970). *Kinesics and context: Essays on body motion communication.* Philadelphia: University of Pennsylvania Press.

• **Bjork, Daniel W.** (1993). *B. F. Skinner: A life.* New York: Basic Books.

• **Black, Donald W.; Wesner, Robert; Bowers, Wayne; & Cabel, Janelle** (1993). A comparison of fluoxatine, cognitive therapy, and placebo in the treatment of panic disorder. *Archives of General Psychiatry, 50,* 44–50.

• **Black, J. E.; Isaacs, K. R.; Anderson, B. J.; Alcantara, A. A.; & Greenough, W. T.** (1990). Learning causes synaptogenesis, whereas motor activity causes angiogenesis, in cerebellar cortex of adult rats. *Proceedings of the National Academy of Science, 87,* 5568–5572.

Blakemore, Colin, & Cooper, Grahame F. (1970). Development of the brain depends on the visual environment. *Nature, 228,* 477–478.

Blass, Thomas (1991). Understanding behavior in the Milgram obedience experiment: The role of personality, situations, and their interactions. *Journal of Personality and Social Psychology, 60,* 398–413.

• **Blass, Thomas** (1993). What we now know about obedience: Distillations from 30 years of research on the Milgram paradigm. Paper presented at the annual meeting of the American Psychological Association, Toronto.

Bleuler, Eugen (1911/1950). *Dementia praecox or the group of schizophrenias.* New York: International Universities Press.

• **Bliss, T. V., & Collingridge, G. L.** (1993). A synaptic model of memory: Long-term potentiation in the hippocampus. *Nature, 361* (6407), 31–39.

Bloom, Benjamin S. (ed.) (1985). *Developing talent in young people.* New York: Ballantine.

• **Bloom, Lois M.** (1970). *Language development: Form and function in emerging grammars.* Cambridge, MA: MIT Press.

Blos, Peter (1962). *On adolescence.* New York: Free Press.

• **Blum, Deborah** (1994). *The monkey wars.* New York: Oxford University Press.

• **Blum, Kenneth, with James E. Payne** (1991). *Alcohol and the addictive brain.* New York: Free Press/Science News Press.

• **Boehm, Lawrence E.** (1994). The validity effect: A search for mediating variables. *Personality and Social Psychology Bulletin, 20,* 285–293.

• **Boesch, Cristophe** (1991). Teaching among wild chimpanzees. *Animal Behavior, 41,* 530–532.

Bogen, Joseph (1978, October). The giant walk-through brain. *Human Nature, 1*(10), 40–47.

Bohannon, John N. (1988). Flashbulb memories for the space shuttle disaster: A tale of two theories. *Cognition, 29,* 179–196.

Bohannon, John N., & Stanowicz, Laura (1988). The issue of negative evidence: Adult responses to children's language errors. *Developmental Psychology, 24,* 684–689.

Bohannon, John N., & Symons, Victoria (1988). Conversational conditions of children's imitation. Paper presented at the biennial Conference on Human Development, Charleston.

• **Bohman, Michael; Cloninger, R.; Sigvardsson, S.; & von Knorring, Anne-Liis** (1987). The genetics of alcoholisms and related disorders. *Journal of Psychiatric Research, 21,* 447–452.

Bolger, Niall (1990). Coping as a personality process: A prospective study. *Journal of Personality and Social Psychology, 59,* 525–537.

Bolles, Robert C. (1972). Reinforcement, expectancy and learning. *Psychological Review, 79,* 394–409.

Bolles, Robert C.; Holtz, Rolf; Dunn, Thomas; & Hill, Wendy (1980). Comparisons of stimulus learning and response learning in a punishment situation. *Learning and Motivation, 11,* 78–96.

Bolos, Annabel M.; Dean, M.; Lucas-Derse, S.; Ramsburg, M.; Brown, G. L.; Goldman, D. (1990, December 26). Population and pedigree studies reveal a lack of association between the dopamine D2 receptor gene and alcoholism. *Journal of the American Medical Association, 264,* 3156–3160.

• **Bolshakov, Vadim Y., & Siegelbaum, Steven A.** (1994). Postsynaptic induction and presynaptic expression of hippocampal long-term depression. *Science, 264,* 1148–1152.

• **Bond, Michael H.** (1988). Finding universal dimensions of individual variation in multicultural studies of values: The Rokeach and Chinese value surveys. *Journal of Personality and Social Psychology, 55,* 1009–1015.

Bonnet, Michael H. (1990). The perception of sleep onset in insomniacs and normal sleepers. In R. R. Bootzin, J. F. Kihlstrom, & D. L. Schacter (eds.), *Sleep and cognition.* Washington, DC: American Psychological Association.

Bootzin, Richard R.; Epstein, Dana; & Wood, James M. (1991). Stimulus control instruction. In P. Hauri (ed.), *Case studies in insomnia.* New York: Plenum.

Boring, Edwin G. (1953). A history of introspection. *Psychological Bulletin, 50,* 169–187.

Bornstein, Robert F.; Leone, Dean R.; & Galley, Donna J. (1987). The generalizability of subliminal mere exposure effects: Influence of stimuli perceived without awareness on social behavior. *Journal of Personality and Social Psychology, 53,* 1070–1079.

Borys, Shelley, & Perlman, Daniel (1985). Gender differences in loneliness. *Personality and Social Psychology Bulletin, 11,* 63–74.

Bouchard, Claude; Tremblay, A.; Despres, J. P.; Nadeau, A.; et al. (1990, May 24). The response to long-term overfeeding in identical twins. *New England Journal of Medicine, 322,* 1477–1482.

Bouchard, Thomas J., Jr. (1984). Twins reared together and apart: What they tell us about human diversity. In S. W. Fox (ed.), *Individuality and determinism.* New York: Plenum.

• **Bouchard, Thomas J., Jr.** (1995). Nature's twice-told tale: Identical tins reared apart—what they tell us about human individuality. Paper presented at the annual meeting of the Western Psychological Association, Los Angeles.

• **Bouchard, Thomas J., Jr.** (in press). IQ similarity in twins reared apart: Findings and responses to critics. In R. J. Sternberg & E. L. Grigorenko (eds.), *Intelligence: Heredity and environment.* New York: Cambridge University Press.

Bouchard, Thomas J., Jr.; Lykken, David T.; McGue, Matthew; Segal, Nancy L.; et al. (1990). Sources of human psychological differences: The Minnesota Study of Twins Reared Apart. *Science, 250,* 223–228.

• **Bouchard, Thomas J., Jr.; Lykken, David T.; McGue, Matthew; Segal, Nancy L.; et al.** (1991). "Sources of human psychological differences: The Minnesota Study of Twins Reared Apart": Response. *Science, 252,* 191–192.

Bouchard, Thomas J., Jr.; Lykken, David T.; Segal, Nancy L.; & Wilcox, Kimerly J. (1986). Development in twins reared apart: A test of the chronogenetic hypothesis. In A. Demirjian (ed.), *Human growth: A multidisciplinary review.* London: Taylor & Francis.

Bousfield, W. A. (1953). The occurrence of clustering in the recall of randomly arranged associates. *Journal of General Psychology, 49,* 229–240.

Bowen, Murray (1978). *Family therapy in clinical practice.* New York: Jason Aronson.

Bower, Gordon H., & Clark, M. C. (1969). Narrative stories as mediators of serial learning. *Psychonomic Science, 14,* 181–182.

Bower, Gordon H., & Mayer, John D. (1989). In search of mood-dependent retrieval. *Journal of Social Behavior and Personality, 4,* 121–156.

Bowers, Kenneth S.; Regehr, Glenn; Balthazard, Claude; & Parker, Kevin (1990). Intuition in the context of discovery. *Cognitive Psychology, 22,* 72–110.

Bowers, Wayne A. (1990). Treatment of depressed in-patients: Cognitive therapy plus medication, relaxation plus medication, and medication alone. *British Journal of Psychiatry, 156,* 73–78.

• **Bowlby, John** (1958). The nature of the child's tie to his mother. *International Journal of Psycho-Analysis, 39,* 350–373.

Bowlby, John (1969). *Attachment and loss. Vol. I: Attachment.* New York: Basic Books.

Bowlby, John (1973). *Attachment and loss. Vol. II: Separation.* New York: Basic Books.

• **Boyd-Franklin, Nancy** (1989). *Black families in therapy: A multisystems approach.* New York: Guilford Press.

• **Boyer, Paul** (1992). *When time shall be no more: Prophecy belief in modern American culture.* Cambridge: Harvard University Press.

• **Boysen, Sarah T., & Berntson, Gary G.** (1989). Numerical competence in a chimpanzee *(Pan troglodytes). Journal of Comparative Psychology, 103,* 23–31.

Bracha, H. Stefan; Torrey, E. Fuller; Bigelow, Llewellyn B.; Lohr, James B.; & Linington, Beverly B. (1991). Subtle signs of prenatal maldevelopment of the hand ectoderm in schizophrenia: A preliminary monozygotic twin study. *Biological Psychiatry, 30,* 719–725.

• **Braddock, Oliver; Atkinson, Janette; Hood, Bruce; Harkness, William; et al.** (1992). Possible blindsight in infants lacking one cerebral hemisphere. *Nature, 360,* 461–463.

Bradley, Robert H., & Caldwell, Bettye M. (1984). 174 children: A study of the relationship between home environment and cognitive development during the first 5 years. In Allen W. Gottfried (ed.), *Home environment and early cognitive development: Longitudinal research.* Orlando, FL: Academic Press.

Braun, Bennett G. (1988). *The treatment of multiple personality disorder.* Washington, DC: American Psychiatric Press.

Breggin, Peter R. (1991). *Toxic psychiatry.* New York: St. Martin's Press.

• **Brehm, Sharon S.** (1992). Intimate relationships (2nd ed.). New York: McGraw-Hill.

Breland, Keller, & Breland, Marian (1961). The misbehavior of organisms. *American Psychologist, 16,* 681–684.

Bretherton, Inge, & Beeghly, Marjorie (1982). Talking about internal states: The acquisition of an explicit theory of mind. *Developmental Psychology, 18,* 906–921.

Brett, Joan F.; Brief, Arthur P.; Burke, Michael J.; George, Jennifer M.; & Webster, Jane (1990). Negative affectivity and the reporting of stressful life events. *Health Psychology, 9,* 57–68.

• **Brewer, Marilynn B.** (1986). The role of ethnocentrism in intergroup conflict. In S. Worchel & W. G. Austin (eds.), *Psychology of intergroup relations.* Chicago: Nelson-Hall.

• **Brewer, Marilynn B.** (1991). The social self: On being the same and different at the same time. *Personality and Social Psychology Bulletin, 17,* 475–482.

• **Brewer, Marilynn B.** (1993). Social identity, distinctiveness, and ingroup homogeneity. *Social Cognition, 11,* 150–164.

• **Brewer, Marilynn B.; Manzi, Jorge M.; & Shaw, John S.** (1993). Ingroup identification as a function of depersonalization, distinctiveness, and status. *Psychological Science, 4,* 88–92.

Briggs, Jean (1970). *Never in anger: Portrait of an Eskimo family.* Cambridge: Harvard University Press.

Briggs, John (1984, December). The genius mind. *Science Digest, 92*(12), 74–77, 102–103.

Brigham, John C., & Malpass, Roy S. (1985, Fall). The role of experience and contact in the recognition of faces of own- and other-race persons. *Journal of Social Issues, 41,* 139–155.

Brockner, Joel, & Rubin, Jeffrey Z. (1985). *Entrapment in escalating conflicts: A social psychological analysis.* New York: Springer-Verlag.

• **Brodie-Scott, Cheryl, & Hobbs, Stephen H.** (1992). Biological rhythms and publication practices: A follow-up survey, 1987–1991. Paper presented at the Southeastern Psychological Association, Knoxville, Tennessee.

Brodsky, Annette M. (1982). Sex, race, and class issues in psychotherapy research. In J. H. Harvey & M. M. Parks (eds.), *Psychotherapy research and behavior change.* The Master Lecture Series, Vol. 1. Washington, DC: American Psychological Association.

• **Brody, D. J.; Pirkle, J. L.; Kramer, R. A.; et al.** (1994). Blood lead levels in the US population. Phase 1 of the Third National Health and Nutrition Examination Survey (NHANES III, 1988 to 1991). *Journal of the American Medical Association, 272,* 277–283.

Brody, Nathan (1990). Behavior therapy versus placebo: Comment on Bowers and Clum's meta-analysis. *Psychological Bulletin, 107,* 106–109.

Brown, Alan S. (1991). A review of the tip-of-the-tongue experience. *Psychological Bulletin, 109,* 204–223.

• **Brown, George W.** (1993). Life events and affective disorder: Replications and limitations. *Psychosomatic Medicine, 55,* 248–259.

Brown, Jonathon D. (1991). Staying fit and staying well. *Journal of Personality and Social Psychology, 60,* 555–561.

Brown, Jonathon D., & Smart, S. April (1991). The self and social conduct: Linking self-representations to prosocial behavior. *Journal of Personality and Social Psychology, 60,* 368–375.

• **Brown, Paul** (1994). Toward a psychobiological study of dissociation. In S. J. Lynn & J. Rhue (eds.), *Dissociation: Clinical, theoretical and research perspectives.* New York: Guilford Press.

Brown, Roger (1986). *Social psychology* (2nd ed.). New York: Free Press.

Brown, Roger; Cazden, Courtney; & Bellugi, Ursula (1969). The

child's grammar from I to III. In J. P. Hill (ed.), *Minnesota Symposium on Child Psychology,* Vol. 2. Minneapolis: University of Minnesota Press.

• **Brown, Roger, & Fraser, C.** (1964). The acquisition of syntax. In U. Bellugi & R. Brown (eds.), The acquisition of language. *Monographs of the Society for Research in Child Development, 29* (Serial No. 92), 43–79.

• **Brown, Roger, & Hanlon, C.** (1970). Derivational complexity and order of acquisition in child speech. In J. R. Hayes (ed.), *Cognition and the development of language.* New York: Wiley.

Brown, Roger, & Kulik, James (1977). Flashbulb memories. *Cognition, 5,* 73–99.

Brown, Roger, & McNeill, David (1966). The "tip of the tongue" phenomenon. *Journal of Verbal Learning and Verbal Behavior, 5,* 325–337.

Brown, Robert, & Middlefell, Robert (1989). Fifty-five years of cocaine dependence [letter]. *British Journal of Addiction, 84,* 946.

• **Brownell, Kelly D., & Rodin, Judith** (1994a). Medical, metabolic, and psychological effects of weight cycling and weight variability. *Archives of Internal Medicine, 154,* 1325–1330.

• **Brownell, Kelly D., & Rodin, Judith** (1994b). The dieting maelstrom: Is it possible and advisable to lose weight? *American Psychologist, 49,* 781–791.

• **Brunner, H. G.; Nelen, M. R.; & van Zandvoort, P.** (1993). X-linked borderline mental retardation with prominent behavioral disturbance: Phenotype, genetic localization, and evidence for disturbed monoamine metabolism. *American Journal of Human Genetics, 52,* 1032–1039.

Bryant, Richard A., & McConkey, Kevin M. (1990). Hypnotic blindness and the relevance of cognitive style. *Journal of Personality and Social Psychology, 59,* 756–761.

Bryer, Jeffrey; Nelson, Bernadette; Miller, Jean; & Krol, Pamela (1987). Childhood sexual and physical abuse as factors in adult psychiatric illness. *American Journal of Psychiatry, 144,* 1426–1430.

Buck, Linda, & Axel, Richard (1991). A novel multigene family may encode odorant receptors: A molecular basis for odor recognition. *Cell, 65,* 175–187.

Buck, Ross (1984). *The communication of emotion.* New York: Guilford Press.

Buck, Ross, & Teng, Wan-Cheng (1987). Spontaneous emotional communication and social biofeedback: A cross-cultural study of emotional expression and communication in Chinese and Taiwanese students. Paper presented at the annual meeting of the American Psychological Association, New York.

• **Burack, J. H.; Barrett, D. C.; Stall, R. D.; Chesney M. A.; Ekstrand, M. L.; & Coates, T. J.** (1993). Depressive symptoms and CD4 lymphocyte decline among HIV-infected men. *Journal of the American Medical Association, 270,* 2568–2573.

• **Burgess, C.; Morris, T.; & Pettingale, K. W.** (1988). Psychological response to cancer diagnosis—II. Evidence for coping styles (coping styles and cancer diagnosis). *Journal of Psychosomatic Research, 32,* 263–272.

Burke, Deborah M.; Burnett, Gayle; & Levenstein, Peggy (1978). Menstrual symptoms: New data from a double-blind study. Paper presented at the annual meeting of the Western Psychological Association, San Francisco.

Burke, Deborah M.; MacKay, Donald G.; Worthley, Joanna S.; & Wade, Elizabeth (1991). On the tip of the tongue: What causes word finding failures in young and older adults? *Journal of Memory and Language, 30,* 237–246.

Burnam, M. Audrey; Stein, Judith; Golding, Jacqueline; Siegel, Judith; & Sorenson, Susan (1988). Sexual assault and mental disorders in a community population. *Journal of Counseling and Clinical Psychology, 56,* 843–850.

• **Bushman, Brad J.** (1993). Human aggression while under the influence of alcohol and other drugs: An integrative research review. *Psychological Science, 2,* 148–152.

• **Buss, David M.** (1989). Sex differences in human mate preferences: Evolutionary hypotheses tested in 37 cultures. *Behavioral and Brain Sciences, 12,* 1–49.

• **Buss, David M.** (1994). *The evolution of desire: Strategies of human mating.* New York: Basic Books.

• **Buss, David M.** (1995). Evolutionary psychology: A new paradigm for psychological science. *Psychological Inquiry, 6,* 1–30.

Bussey, Kay, & Maughan, Betty (1982). Gender differences in moral reasoning. *Journal of Personality and Social Psychology, 42,* 701–706.

Butcher, James N.; Dahlstrom, W. Grant; Graham, John R.; Tellegen, Auke; & Kaemmer, Beverly (1989). *Minnesota Multiphasic Personality Inventory-II: Manual for administration and scoring.* Minneapolis: University of Minnesota Press.

Butcher, James N., & Finn, Stephen (1983). Objective personality assessment in clinical settings. In M. H. Hersen, A. E. Kazdin, & A. S. Bellack (eds.), *The clinical psychology handbook.* New York: Pergamon.

• Butler, S.; Chalder, T.; Ron, M.; Wessely, S.; et al. (1991). Cognitive behaviour therapy in chronic fatigue syndrome. *Journal of Neurology, Neurosurgery and Psychiatry, 54,* 153–158.

Butterfield, E. C., & Belmont, J. M. (1977). Assessing and improving the executive cognitive functions of mentally retarded people. In I. Bialer & M. Sternlict (eds.), *Psychological issues in mental retardation.* New York: Psychological Dimensions.

• Byne, William (1993). Sexual orientation and brain structure: Adding up the evidence. Paper presented at the annual meeting of the International Academy of Sex Research, Pacific Grove, California.

• Byne, William, & Parsons, Bruce (1993). Human sexual orientation: The biologic theories reappraised. *Archives of General Psychiatry, 50,* 228–239.

Cabezas, A.; Tam, T. M.; Lowe, B. M.; Wong, A.; & Turner, K. (1989). Empirical study of barriers to upward mobility of Asian Americans in the San Francisco Bay area. In G. Nomura (ed.), *Frontiers of Asian American studies.* Pullman: Washington State University Press.

Callahan, Daniel (1989). *What kind of life: The limits of medical progress.* New York: Simon & Schuster.

Camel, J. F.; Withers, G. S.; & Greenough, William T. (1986). Persistence of visual cortex dendritic alterations induced by post-weaning exposure to a "superenriched" environment in rats. *Behavioral Neuroscience, 100,* 810–813.

• Camera, Wayne J., & Schneider, Dianne L. (1994). Integrity tests: Facts and unresolved issues. *American Psychologist, 49,* 112–119.

Campbell, Anne (1993). *Men, women, and aggression.* New York: Basic Books.

Campbell, Joseph (1949/1968). *The hero with 1,000 faces* (2nd ed.). Princeton, NJ: Princeton University Press.

Campos, Joseph J.; Barrett, Karen C.; Lamb, Michael E.; Goldsmith, H. Hill; & Stenberg, Craig (1984). Socioemotional development. In P. Mussen (ed.), *Handbook of child psychology* (4th ed.). Vol. II, M. M. Haith & J. J. Campos (eds.), *Infancy and developmental psychobiology.* New York: Wiley.

• Cancian, Francesca M. (1987). *Love in America: Gender and self-development.* Cambridge, England: Cambridge University Press.

• Canetto, Silvia S. (1992). Suicide attempts and substance abuse: Similarities and differences. *Journal of Psychology, 125,* 605–620.

Cannon, Tyrone D.; Mednick, Sarnoff A.; & Parnas, Josef (1989). Genetic and perinatal determinants of structural brain deficits in schizophrenia. *Archives of General Psychiatry, 46,* 883–889.

• Cantor, Nancy (1994). Life task problem solving: Situational affordances and personal needs. *Personality and Social Psychology Bulletin, 20,* 235–243.

Caramazza, Alfonso, & Hillis, Argye E. (1991, February 28). Lexical organization of nouns and verbs in the brain. *Nature, 349,* 788–790.

• Cardeña, Etzel; Lewis-Fernández, Roberto; Bear, David; Pakianathan, Isabel; & Spiegal, David (1994). Dissociative disorders. In DSM-IV *Sourcebook.* Washington, DC: American Psychiatric Press.

Carducci, Bernardo J., & McGuire, Jay C. (1990). Behavior and beliefs characteristic of first-, second-, and third-time lovers. Paper presented at the annual meeting of the American Psychological Association, Boston.

• Carli, Linda L.; Michelsen, Caroline C.; Schineller, Karen S.; Shamma, Negar; & Sharma, Sheena (1993). Gender differences in mate selection. Paper presented at the annual meeting of the American Psychological Association, Toronto.

Carpenter, William T., Jr.; Sadier, John H.; et al. (1983). The therapeutic efficacy of hemodialysis in schizophrenia. *New England Journal of Medicine, 308*(12), 669–675.

• Carr, Edward G., & Durand, V. Mark (1985). Reducing behavior problems through functional communication training. *Journal of Applied Behavior Analysis, 18,* 111–126.

• Carroll, Kathleen M.; Rounsaville, Bruce J.; & Nich, Charla (1994a). Blind man's bluff: Effectiveness and significance of psychotherapy and pharmacotherapy blinding procedures in a clinical trial. *Journal of Consulting and Clinical Psychology, 62,* 276–280.

• Carroll, Kathleen M.; Rounsaville, Bruce J.; Gordon, Lynn T.; Nich, Charla; et al. (1994b). Psychotherapy and pharmacotherapy for ambulatory cocaine abusers. *Archives of General Psychiatry, 51,* 177–187.

Carskadon, Mary A.; Mitler, Merrill M.; & Dement, William C. (1974). A comparison of insomniacs and normals: Total sleep time and sleep latency. *Sleep Research, 3,* 130 [Abstract].

Carson, Robert C. (1989). What happened to schizophrenia? Reflections on a taxonomic absurdity. Paper presented at the annual meeting of the American Psychological Association, New Orleans.

• Carson, Robert C., & Butcher, James N. (1994). *Abnormal psychology and modern life* (10th ed.). New York: HarperCollins.

Carter, Betty, & McGoldrick, Monica (eds.) (1988). *The changing family life cycle: A framework for family therapy* (2nd ed.). New York: Gardner Press.

Cartwright, Rosalind D. (1989). Sleep and dreams in depressed men and women undergoing divorce. Paper presented at the annual meeting of the American Psychological Association, New Orleans.

Cartwright, Rosalind D. (1990). A network model of dreams. In R. R. Bootzin, J. F. Kihlstrom, & D. L. Schacter (eds.), *Sleep and cognition.* Washington, DC: American Psychological Association.

Cartwright, Rosalind D. (1991). Dreams that work: The relation of dream incorporation to adaptation to stressful events. *Dreaming, 1,* 3–9.

• Carver, Charles S.; Ironson, G.; Wynings, C.; Greenwood, D.; et al. (1993a). Coping with Andrew: How coping responses relate to experience of loss and symptoms of poor adjustment. Paper presented at the annual meeting of the American Psychological Association, Toronto.

• Carver, Charles S.; Pozo, Christina; Harris, Suzanne D.; Noriega, Victoria; et al. (1993b). How coping mediates the effect of optimism on distress: A study of women with early stage breast cancer. *Journal of Personality and Social Psychology, 65,* 375–390.

• Carver, Charles S., & Scheier, Michael F. (1994). Situational coping and coping dispositions in a stressful transaction. *Journal of Personality and Social Psychology, 66,* 184–195.

Carver, Charles S.; Scheier, Michael F.; & Weintraub, Jagdish K. (1989). Assessing coping strategies: A theoretically based approach. *Journal of Personality and Social Psychology, 56,* 267–283.

Caspi, Avshalom, & Moffitt, Terrie E. (1991). Individual differences are accentuated during periods of social change: The sample case of girls at puberty. *Journal of Personality and Social Psychology, 61,* 157–168.

Cass, Loretta K., & Thomas, Carolyn (1979). *Childhood pathology and later adjustment.* New York: Wiley-Interscience.

• Cassel, W. S., & Bjorklund, D. F. (1992). Age differences and suggestibility of eyewitnesses. Symposium paper presented at the annual meeting of the Conference on Human Development, Atlanta.

• Casswell, Sally (1993). Public discourse on the benefits of moderation: Implications for alcohol policy development. *Addiction, 88,* 459–465.

Cattell, Raymond B. (1965). *The scientific analysis of personality.* Baltimore: Penguin.

Cattell, Raymond B. (1973). *Personality and mood by questionnaire.* San Francisco: Jossey-Bass.

• Ceci, Stephen J., & Bruck, Maggie (1993). Suggestibility of the child witness: A historical review and synthesis. *Psychological Bulletin, 113,* 403–439.

Ceci, Stephen J., & Liker, Jeffrey K. (1986). Academic and nonacademic intelligence: An experimental separation. In R. J. Sternberg & R. K. Wagner (eds.), *Practical intelligence: Nature and origins of competence in the everyday world.* New York: Cambridge University Press.

• Celis, William, III (1993, August 1). Down from the self-esteem high. *New York Times,* Education Section.

Cermak, Laird S., & Craik, Fergus I. M. (eds.) (1979). *Levels of processing in human memory.* Hillsdale, NJ: Erlbaum.

• **Chaiken, Shelly, & Yates, Suzanne** (1985). Affective-cognitive consistency and thought-induced attitude polarization. *Journal of Personality and Social Psychology, 49,* 1470–1481.

Chambless, Dianne L. (1988). Cognitive mechanisms in panic disorder. In S. Rachman & J. D. Maser (eds.), *Panic: Psychological perspectives.* Hillsdale, NJ: Erlbaum.

• **Chambless, Dianne L.** (1995). Training in and dissemination of empirically validated psychological treatments: Report and recommendations. *The Clinical Psychologist, 48,* 3–24.

Chan, Connie S., & Grossman, Hildreth Y. (1988). Psychological effects of running loss on consistent runners. *Perceptual & Motor Skills, 66,* 875–883.

• **Chance, June E., & Goldstein, Alvin G.** (1995). The other-race effect in eyewitness identification. In S. L. Sporer, G. Koehnken, & R. S. Malpass (eds.), *Psychological issues in eyewitness identification.* Hillsdale, NJ: Erlbaum.

Chance, Paul (1994). *Learning and behavior* (3rd ed.). Belmont, CA: Wadsworth.

Chance, Paul (1988, October). Knock wood. *Psychology Today,* 68–69.

• **Chance, Paul** (1992, November). The rewards of learning. *Phi Delta Kappan, 74,* 200–207.

• **Chaves, J. F.** (1989). Hypnotic control of clinical pain. In N. P. Spanos & J. F. Chaves (eds.), *Hypnosis: The cognitive-behavioral perspective.* Buffalo, NY: Prometheus Books.

• **Checkley, Stuart A.; Murphy, D. G.; Abbas, M.; Marks, M.; et al.** (1993). Melatonin rhythms in seasonal affective disorder. *British Journal of Psychiatry, 163,* 332–337.

Cheney, Dorothy L., & Seyfarth, Robert M. (1985). Vervet monkey alarm calls: Manipulation through shared information? *Behavior, 94,* 150–166.

• **Cheney, Dorothy L., & Seyfarth, Robert M.** (1990). *How monkeys see the world: Inside the mind of another species.* Chicago: University of Chicago Press.

Cheng, Patricia W., & Novick, Laura R. (1990). A probabilistic contrast model of causal induction. *Journal of Personality and Social Psychology, 58,* 545–567.

• **Chipuer, Heather M.; Rovine, Michael J.; & Plomin, Robert** (1990). LISREL modeling: Genetic and environmental influences on IQ revisited. *Intelligence, 14,* 11–29.

Chodorow, Nancy (1978). *The reproduction of mothering.* Berkeley: University of California Press.

• **Chodorow, Nancy** (1992). *Feminism and psychoanalytic theory.* New Haven, CT: Yale University Press.

Chomsky, Noam (1957). *Syntactic structures.* The Hague, Netherlands: Mouton.

Chomsky, Noam (1980). Initial states and steady states. In M. Piatelli-Palmerini (ed.), *Language and learning: The debate between Jean Piaget and Noam Chomsky.* Cambridge: Harvard University Press.

• **Chrisler, Joan C.; Johnston, Ingrid K; Champagne, Nicole M.; & Preston, Kathleen E.** (1994). Menstrual joy: The construct and its consequences. *Psychology of Women Quarterly, 18,* 375–387.

• **Christensen, Andrew, & Jacobson, Neil S.** (1994). Who (or what) can do psychotherapy: The status and challenge of nonprofessional therapies. *Psychological Science, 5,* 8–14.

Christensen, Larry, & Burrows, Ross (1990). Dietary treatment of depression. *Behavior Therapy, 21,* 183–194.

Christopher, F. Scott (1988). An initial investigation into a continuum of premarital sexual pressure. *Journal of Sex Research, 25,* 255–266.

• **Church, A. Timothy, & Burke, Peter J.** (1994). Exploratory and confirmatory tests of the Big Five and Tellegen's three- and four-dimensional models. *Journal of Personality and Social Psychology, 66,* 93–114.

• **Cioffi, Delia, & Holloway, James** (1993). Delayed costs of suppressed pain. *Journal of Personality and Social Psychology, 64,* 274–282.

• **Cioffi, Frank** (1974, February 7). Was Freud a liar? *The Listener, 91,* 172–174.

Clark, David M. (1988). A cognitive model of panic attacks. In S. Rachman & J. D. Maser (eds.), *Panic: Psychological perspectives.* Hillsdale, NJ: Erlbaum.

• **Clark, Margaret S.; Milberg, Sandra; & Erber, Ralph** (1987). Arousal state dependent memory: Evidence and some implications for understanding social judgments and social behavior. In K. Fiedler & J. P. Forgas (eds.), *Affect, cognition and social behavior.* Toronto: Hogrefe.

Clarke-Stewart, K. Alison (1991). A home is not a school: The effects of child care on children's development. In S. L. Hofferth & D. A. Phillips (eds.), *Child care policy research. Journal of Social issues, 47*(2), 105–124.

Clarke-Stewart, K. Alison; VanderStoep, Laima P.; & Killian, Grant A. (1979). Analyses and replication of mother-child relations at two years of age. *Child Development, 50,* 777–793.

Clementz, Brett A., & Sweeney, John A. (1990). Is eye movement dysfunction a biological marker for schizophrenia? A methodological review. *Psychological Review, 108,* 77–92.

• **Cloninger, C. Robert** (1987, April). Neurogenetic adaptive mechanisms in alcoholism. *Science, 236,* 410–416.

• **Clopton, Nancy A., & Sorell, Gwendolyn T.** (1993). Gender differences in moral reasoning: Stable or situational? *Psychology of Women Quarterly, 17,* 85–101.

• **Cochran, Susan D., & Peplau, Letitia A.** (1985). Value orientations in heterosexual relationships. *Psychology of Women Quarterly, 9,* 477–488.

Coe, William C., & Sarbin, Theodore R. (1977). Hypnosis from the standpoint of a contextualist. *Annals of the New York Academy of Sciences, 296,* 2–13.

• **Coffey, C. E.** (1993). Structural brain imaging and ECT. In C. E. Coffey (ed.), *The clinical science of electroconvulsive therapy.* Washington, DC: American Psychiatric Association.

Cohen, Sheldon, & Edwards, Jeffrey R. (1989). Personality characteristics as moderators of the relationship between stress and disorder. In R. W. J. Neufeld (ed.), *Advances in the investigation of psychological stress.* New York: Wiley.

Cohen, Sheldon; Evans, Gary W.; Krantz, David S.; & Stokols, Daniel (1980). Physiological, motivational, and cognitive effects of aircraft noise on children. *American Psychologist, 35,* 231–243.

Cohen, Sheldon; Tyrrell, D. A.; & Smith, A. P. (1991, August 29). Psychological stress and susceptibility to the common cold. *New England Journal of Medicine, 325*(9), 606–612.

Cohen, Sheldon, & Williamson, Gail M. (1991). Stress and infectious disease in humans. *Psychological Bulletin, 109,* 5–24.

Cohn, Lawrence D. (1991). Sex differences in the course of personality development: A meta-analysis. *Psychological Bulletin, 109,* 252–266.

Colby, Anne; Kohlberg, Lawrence; Gibbs, J.; & Lieberman, M. (1983). A longitudinal study of moral judgment. *Monographs of the Society for Research in Child Development, 48* (1–2, Serial No. 200).

• **Cole, Michael** (1984). The world beyond our borders: What might our students need to know about it? *American Psychologist, 39,* 998–1005.

Cole, Michael (1990). Cultural psychology: A once and future discipline? In J. J. Berman (ed.), *Cross-cultural perspectives: Nebraska Symposium on Motivation, 1989.* Lincoln: University of Nebraska Press.

• **Cole, Michael, & Cole, Sheila R.** (1993). *The development of children* (2nd ed.). New York: Freeman.

Collins, Allan M., & Loftus, Elizabeth F. (1975). A spreading-activation theory of semantic processing. *Psychological Review, 82,* 407–428.

• **Collins, Barry** (1993). Using person perception methodologies to uncover the meanings of the Milgram obedience paradigm. Paper presented at the annual meeting of the American Psychological Association, Toronto.

• **Collins, Nancy L., & Read, Stephen J.** (1990). Adult attachment, working models, and relationship quality in dating couples. *Journal of Personality and Social Psychology, 58,* 644–663.

• **Collins, Robert L.** (1985). On the inheritance of degree and direction of asymmetry. In S. D. Glick (ed.), *Cerebral lateralization in nonhuman species.* New York: Academic Press.

• **Collins, Robert L.** (1991). Reimpressed selective breeding for lateralization of handedness in mice. *Brain Research, 564,* 194–202.

• **Colman, Andrew** (1991a). Crowd psychology in South African murder trials. *American Psychologist, 46,* 1071–1079.

• **Colman, Andrew** (1991b, November). Psychological evidence in South African murder trials. *The Psychologist, 4,* 482–486.

- **Colvin, C. Randall, & Block, Jack** (1994). Do positive illusions foster mental health? An examination of the Taylor and Brown formulation. *Psychological Bulletin, 116,* 3–20.
- **Comas-Díaz, Lillian, & Greene, Beverly** (1994). *Women of color: Integrating ethnic and gender identities in psychotherapy.* New York: Guilford Press.
- **Comstock, George; Chaffee, Steven; Katzman, Natan; McCombs, Maxwell; & Roberts, Donald** (1978). *Television and human behavior.* New York: Columbia University Press.
- **Condon, William** (1982). Cultural microrhythms. In M. Davis (ed.), *Interaction rhythms: Periodicity in communicative behavior.* New York: Human Sciences Press.
- **Connolly, Patrick R.** (1974). An investigation of the perception of personal space and its meaning among Black and White Americans. Unpublished dissertation, University of Iowa.
- **Conte, Hope; Plutchik, Robert; Wild, Katherine; & Karasu, Toksoz** (1986). Combined psychotherapy and pharmacotherapy for depression. *Archives of General Psychiatry, 43,* 471–479.
- **Conway, Michael, & Ross, Michael** (1984). Getting what you want by revising what you had. *Journal of Personality and Social Psychology, 47,* 738–748.
- **Coons, Philip M.; Milstein, Victor; & Marley, Carma** (1982). EEG studies of two multiple personalities and a control. *Archives of General Psychiatry, 39,* 823–825.
- **Copi, Irving M., & Burgess-Jackson, Keith** (1992). *Informal logic* (2nd ed.). New York: Macmillan.
- **Corkin, Suzanne** (1984). Lasting consequences of bilateral medial temporal lobectomy: Clinical course and experimental findings in H. M. *Seminars in Neurology, 4,* 249–259.
- **Cornelius, Randolph R.** (1991). Gregorio Maraûon's two-factor theory of emotion. *Personality and Social Psychology Bulletin, 17,* 65–69.
- **Cornell-Bell, A. H.; Finkbeiner, S. M.; Cooper, M. S.; & Smith, S. J.** (1990). Glutamate induces calcium waves in cultured astrocytes: Long-range glial signaling. *Science, 247,* 470–473.
- **Cose, Ellis** (1994). The rage of a privileged class. New York: HarperCollins.
- **Cosmides, Leda; Tooby, John; & Barkow, Jerome H.** (1992) Introduction: Evolutionary psychology and conceptual integration. In J. H. Barkow, L. Cosmides, & J. Tooby (eds.), *The adapted mind: Evolutionary psychology and the generation of culture.* New York: Oxford University Press.
- **Costa, Paul T., Jr., & McCrae, Robert R.** (1988). Personality in adulthood: A six-year longitudinal study of self-reports and spouse ratings on the NEO personality inventory. *Journal of Personality and Social Psychology, 54,* 853–863.
- **Costa, Paul T., Jr., & McCrae, Robert R.** (1994). "Set like plaster"? Evidence for the stability of adult personality. In R. Heatherton & J. Weinberger (eds.), *Can personality change?* Washington, DC: American Psychological Association.
- **Costa, Paul T., Jr., & Widiger, Thomas A.** (eds.) (1994). *Personality disorders and the five-factor model of personality.* Washington, DC: American Psychological Association.
- **Courtney, J. G.; Longnecker, M. P.; Theorell, T.; & Gerhardsson de Verdier, M.** (1993). Stressful life events and the risk of colorectal cancer. *Epidemiology, 4,* 407–414.
- **Cowen, Emory L.; Wyman, Peter A.; Work, William C.; & Parker, Gayle R.** (1990). The Rochester Child Resilience Project (RCRP): Overview and summary of first year findings. *Development and Psychopathology, 2,* 193–212.
- **Cowen, Ron** (1989). Receptor encounters: Untangling the threads of the serotonin system. *Science News, 136,* 248–250, 252.
- **Craik, Fergus I. M., & Tulving, Endel** (1975). Depth of processing and the retention of words in episodic memory. *Journal of Experimental Psychology: General, 104,* 268–294.
- **Crain, Stephen** (1991). Language acquisition in the absence of experience. *Behavioral & Brain Sciences, 14,* 597–650.
- **Crandall, Christian S.** (1994). Prejudice against fat people: Ideology and self-interest. *Journal of Personality and Social Psychology, 66,* 882–894.
- **Crandall, James E.** (1984). Social interest as a moderator of life stress. *Journal of Personality and Social Psychology, 47,* 164–174.
- **Crawford, Mary, & Gressley, Diane** (1991). Creativity, caring, and context: Women's and men's accounts of humor preferences and practices. *Psychology of Women Quarterly, 15,* 217–231.
- **Crawford, Mary, & Marecek, Jeanne** (1989). Psychology constructs the female: 1968–1988. *Psychology of Women Quarterly, 13,* 147–165.
- **Crews, Frederick** (1993, November 18). The unknown Freud. *The New York Review of Books,* 55–66.
- **Critchlow, Barbara** (1983). Blaming the booze: The attribution of responsibility for drunken behavior. *Personality and Social Psychology Bulletin, 9,* 451–474.
- **Critchlow, Barbara** (1986). The powers of John Barleycorn: Beliefs about the effects of alcohol on social behavior. *American Psychologist, 41,* 751–764.
- **Crocker, Jennifer, & Major, Brenda** (1989). Social stigma and self-esteem: The self-protective properties of stigma. *Psychological Review, 96,* 608–630.
- **Cronbach, Lee J.** (1990). *Essentials of psychological testing* (5th ed.). New York: Harper & Row.
- **Crook, John H.** (1987). The nature of conscious awareness. In C. Blakemore & S. Greenfield (eds.), *Mindwaves: Thoughts on intelligence, identity, and consciousness.* Oxford: Basil Blackwell.
- **Cross, A. J.** (1990). Serotonin in Alzheimer-type dementia and other dementing illnesses. *Annals of the New York Academy of Science, 600,* 405–415.
- **Cross, William E.** (1971). The Negro-to-Black conversion experience: Toward a psychology of Black liberation. *Black World, 20,* 13–27.
- **Crystal, David S.; Chen, Chuansheng; Fuligni, Andrew J.; Stevenson, Harold W.; et al.** (1994). Psychological maladjustment and academic achievement: A cross-cultural study of Japanese, Chinese, and American high school students. *Child Development, 65,* 738–753.
- **Crystal, Graef S.** (1991). *In search of excess: The overcompensation of the American executive.* New York: Norton.
- **Csikszentmihalyi, Mihaly, & Larson, Reed** (1984). *Being adolescent: Conflict and growth in the teenage years.* New York: Basic Books.
- **Cubelli, Roberto** (1991, September 19). A selective deficit for writing vowels in acquired dysgraphia. *Nature, 353,* 209–210.
- **Cummins, Robert A., & Prior, Margot P.** (1992). Autism and facilitated communication: A reply to Biklen. *Harvard Educational Review, 62,* 228–241.
- **Curtin, Brian J.** (1985). *The myopias.* New York: Harper & Row.
- **Curtiss, Susan** (1977). *Genie: A psycholinguistic study of a modern-day "wild child."* New York: Academic Press.
- **Curtiss, Susan** (1982). Developmental dissociations of language and cognition. In L. Obler & D. Fein (eds.), *Exceptional language and linguistics.* New York: Academic Press.
- **Cutler, Brian, & Penrod, Steven D.** (1988). Improving the reliability of eyewitness identification: Lineup construction and presentation. *Journal of Applied Psychology, 73,* 281–290.

- **Dabbs, James M., Jr., & Morris, Robin** (1990). Testosterone, social class, and antisocial behavior in a sample of 4,462 men. *Psychological Science, 1,* 209–211.
- **Dagenbach, Dale; Carr, Thomas H.; & Wilhelmsen, AnneLise** (1989). Task-induced strategies and near-threshold priming: Conscious influences on unconscious perception. *Journal of Memory and Language, 28,* 412–443.
- **Dahl, K.; Avery, D. H.; Lewy, A. J.; Savage, M. V.; et al.** (1993). Dim light melatonin onset and circadian temperature during a constant routine in hypersomnic winter depression. *Acta Psychiatrica Scandinavica, 88,* 60–66.
- **Dahmer, Lionel** (1994). *A father's story.* New York: Morrow.
- **Dakof, Gayle A., & Taylor, Shelley E.** (1990). Victims' perceptions of social support: What is helpful from whom? *Journal of Personality and Social Psychology, 58,* 80–89.
- **Daly, Martin, & Wilson, Margo** (1983). Sex, evolution, and behavior (2nd ed.). Belmont, CA: Wadsworth.
- **Damasio, Antonio R.** (1990). Category-related recognition defects as a clue to the neural substrates of knowledge. *Trends in Neurosciences, 13,* 95–98.
- **Damasio, Antonio R.** (1994). *Descartes' error: Emotion, reason, and the human brain.* New York: Grosset/Putnam.
- **Damasio, Hanna; Grabowski, Thomas; Frank, Randall; Galaburda, Albert M.; & Damasio, Antonio R.** (1994). The return of Phineas Gage: Clues about the brain from the skull of a famous patient. *Science, 264,* 1102–1105.
- **Danish, Paul** (1994, February 13). Legalizing marijuana would allow regulation of its potency. *New York Times,* letters page.

• **Darley, John M.** (1993). Research on morality: Possible approaches, actual approaches [review of *Handbook of moral behavior and development*]. *Psychological Science, 4,* 353–357.

• **Darwin, Charles** (1859). *On the origin of species.* [A facsimile of the first edition, edited by Ernst Mayer, 1964.] Cambridge: Harvard University Press.

Darwin, Charles (1872/1965). *The expression of the emotions in man and animals.* Reprinted by the University of Chicago Press.

• **Dasen, Pierre R.** (1994). Culture and cognitive development from a Piagetian perspective. In W. J. Lonner & R. S. Malpass (eds.), *Psychology and culture.* Needham Heights, MA: Allyn & Bacon.

Davidson, Richard; Ekman, Paul; Saron, Clifford D.; Senulis, Joseph A.; & Friesen, Wallace V. (1990). Approach-withdrawal and cerebral asymmetry: Emotional expression and brain physiology I. *Journal of Personality and Social Psychology, 58,* 330–341.

Davis, Joel (1984). *Endorphins: New waves in brain chemistry.* Garden City, NY: Dial Press (Doubleday).

• **Dawes, Robyn M.** (1994). *House of cards: Psychology and psychotherapy built on myth.* New York: Free Press.

• **Dawit, Seble, & Mekuria, Salem** (1993, December 7). The West just doesn't get it (Let Africans fight genital mutilation). *New York Times,* A13.

• **Dawson, Drew; Lack, Leon; & Morris, Mary** (1993). Phase resetting of the human circadian pacemaker with use of a single pulse of bright light. *Chronobiology International, 10,* 94–102.

Dawson, Neal V.; Arkes, Hal R.; Siciliano, C.; et al. (1988). Hindsight bias: An impediment to accurate probability estimation in clinicopathologic conferences. *Medical Decision Making, 8*(4), 259–264.

Dean, Geoffrey (1986–1987, Winter). Does astrology need to be true? Part I: A look at the real thing. *Skeptical Inquirer, 11,* 166–184.

Dean, Geoffrey (1987, Spring). Does astrology need to be true? Part II: The answer is no. *Skeptical Inquirer, 11,* 257–273.

• **Deaux, Kay** (1985). Sex and gender. *Annual Review of Psychology, 36,* 49–81.

• **Deaux, Kay, & Major, Brenda** (1987). Putting gender into context: An interactive model of gender-related behavior. *Psychological Review, 94,* 369–389.

• **Deaux, Kay, & Major, Brenda** (1990). A social-psychological model of gender. In D. L. Rhode (ed.), *Theoretical perspectives on sexual difference.* New Haven, CT: Yale University Press.

de Bono, Edward (1985). *De Bono's thinking course.* New York: Facts on File.

DeCasper, Anthony J., & Spence, Melanie J. (1986). Prenatal maternal speech influences newborns' perception of speech sounds. *Infant Behavior and Development, 9,* 133–150.

Deci, Edward L. (1975). *Intrinsic motivation.* New York: Plenum.

Deci, Edward L., & Ryan, Richard M. (1987). The support of autonomy and the control of behavior. *Journal of Personality and Social Psychology, 53,* 1024–1037.

• **Defebvre, Philippe P.; Malgrange, Brigitte; Staecker, Hinrich; Moonen, Gustave; & Van De Water, Thomas R.** (1993). Retinoic acid stimulates regeneration of mammalian auditory hair cells. *Science, 260,* 692–695.

• **Deffenbacher, Jerry L.** (1994). Anger and diagnosis: Where has all the anger gone? Paper presented at the annual meeting of the American Psychological Association, Los Angeles.

de Lacoste-Utamsing, Christine, & Holloway, Ralph L. (1982). Sexual dimorphism in the human corpus callosum. *Science, 216,* 1431–1432.

• **de la Garza, Rodolfo O.; DeSipio, Luis; Garcia, F. Chris; Garcia, John; & Falcon, Angelo** (1992). *Latino voices: Mexican, Puerto Rican, & Cuban perspectives on American politics.* Boulder, CO: Westview Press.

DeLoache, Judy S. (1987, December 11). Rapid change in the symbolic functioning of very young children. *Science, 238,* 1556–1557.

Dembroski, Theodore M., & Costa, Paul T., Jr. (1988). Assessment of coronary-prone behavior: A current overview. *Annals of Behavioral Medicine, 10,* 60–63.

Dement, William (1955). Dream recall and eye movements during sleep in schizophrenics and normals. *Journal of Nervous and Mental Disease, 122,* 263–269.

Dement, William (1978). *Some must watch while some must sleep.* New York: Norton.

• **Dement, William** (1992). *The sleepwatchers.* Stanford, CA: Stanford Alumni Association.

Dement, William, & Kleitman, Nathaniel (1957). The relation of eye movements during sleep to dream activity: An objective method for the study of dreaming. *Journal of Experimental Psychology, 53,* 339–346.

Demos, John (1970). *A little commonwealth.* New York: Oxford University Press.

DeMyer, Marian K. (1975). Research in infantile autism: A strategy and its results. *Biological Psychiatry, 10,* 433–452.

DeNelsky, Garland Y. (1990). The case against prescription privileges for psychologists. Paper presented at the annual meeting of the American Psychological Association, Boston.

• **Denmark, Florence; Russo, Nancy F.; Frieze, Irene H.; & Sechzer, Jeri A.** (1988). Guidelines for avoiding sexism in psychological research. *American Psychologist, 43,* 582–585.

Dennett, Daniel C. (1991). *Consciousness explained.* Boston: Little, Brown.

DePaola, Laura, & DePaola, Steve (1988). Hallucinations during widowhood. Paper presented at the annual meeting of the Western Psychological Association, San Francisco.

• **de Rivera, Joseph** (1989). Comparing experiences across cultures: Shame and guilt in America and Japan. *Hiroshima Forum for Psychology, 14,* 13–20.

• **de Shazer, Steve** (1993). *Putting difference to work.* New York: Norton.

• **Desimone, Robert** (1991). Face-selective cells in the temporal cortex of monkeys. *Journal of Cognitive Neuroscience, 3,* 1–8.

Deutsch, Francine M.; LeBaron, Dorothy; & Fryer, Maury M. (1987). What is in a smile? *Psychology of Women Quarterly, 11,* 341–352.

Deutsch, Morton (1949). An experimental study of the effects of cooperation and competition among group processes. *Human Relations, 2,* 199–231.

Deutsch, Morton (1980). Fifty years of conflict. In L. Festinger (ed.), *Retrospections on social psychology.* New York: Oxford University Press.

Deutsch, Morton, & Collins, Mary Ellen (1951). *Interracial housing: A psychological evaluation of a social experiment.* Minneapolis: University of Minnesota Press.

DeValois, Russell L. (1960). Color vision mechanisms in the monkey. *Journal of General Physiology, 43,* 115–128.

DeValois, Russell L., & DeValois, Karen K. (1975). Neural coding of color. In E. C. Carterette & M. P. Friedman (eds.), *Handbook of perception,* Vol. 5. New York: Academic Press.

Devine, Patricia G.; Monteith, Margo J.; Zuwerink, Julia R.; & Elliot, Andrew J. (1991). Prejudice with and without compunction. *Journal of Personality and Social Psychology, 60,* 817–830.

• **Devine, Patricia G., & Zuwerink, Julia R.** (1994). Prejudice and guilt: The internal struggle to overcome prejudice. In W. J. Lonner & R. Malpass (eds.), *Psychology and culture.* Needham Heights, MA: Allyn & Bacon.

• **Devolder, Patricia A., & Pressley, Michael** (1989). Metamemory across the adult lifespan. *Canadian Psychology, 30,* 578–587.

Diamond, Jared (1987, August). Soft sciences are often harder than hard sciences. *Discover, 8*(8), 34–35, 38–39.

• **Diamond, Jared** (1994, November). Race without color. *Discover,* 82–89.

Diamond, Marian; Johnson, Ruth E.; Young, Daniel; & Singh, S. Sukhwinder (1983). Age related morphologic differences in the rat cerebral cortex and hippocampus: Male-female; right-left. *Experimental Neurology, 81,* 1–13.

Dickson, W. Patrick; Hess, Robert D.; Miyake, Naomi; & Azuma, Hiroshi (1979). Referential communication accuracy between mother and child as a predictor of cognitive development in the United States and Japan. *Child Development, 50,* 53–59.

Diener, Ed; Colvin, C. Randall; Pavot, Wiliam G.; & Allman, Amanda (1991). The psychic costs of intense positive affect. *Journal of Personality and Social Psychology, 61,* 492–503.

DiFranza, Joseph R.; Winters, Thomas H.; Goldberg, Robert J.; Cirillo, Leonard; et al. (1986). The relationship of smoking to motor vehicle accidents and traffic violations. *New York State Journal of Medicine, 86,* 464–467.

Digman, John M. (1990). Personality structure: Emergence of the five-factor model. In M. R. Rosenzweig & L. W. Porter (eds.), *Annual Review of Psychology.* Palo Alto, CA: Annual Reviews.

Digman, John M., & Inouye, Jillian (1986). Further specification of the five robust factors of personality. *Journal of Personality and Social Psychology, 50,* 116–123.

• di Leonardo, Micaela (1987). The female world of cards and holidays: Women, families, and the work of kinship. *Signs, 12,* 1–20.

• di Leonardo, Micaela (1991). Introduction. In M. di Leonardo (ed.), *Gender at the crossroads of knowledge.* Berkeley: University of California Press.

• Dillon, Kathleen M. (1993, Spring). Facilitated communication, autism, and Ouija. *Skeptical Inquirer, 17,* 281–287.

Dinges, David F.; Whitehouse, Wayne G.; Orne, Emily C.; Powell, John W.; Orne, Martin T.; & Erdelyi, Matthew H. (1992). Evaluating hypnotic memory enhancement (hypermnesia and reminiscence) using multitrial forced recall. *Journal of Experimental Psychology: Learning, Memory, and Cognition, 18,* 1139–1147.

• Dinnerstein, Dorothy (1976). *The mermaid and the Minotaur: Sexual arrangements and human malaise.* New York: Harper & Row.

Dion, George L., & Anthony, William A. (1987). Research in psychiatric rehabilitation: A review of experimental and quasi-experimental studies. *Rehabilitation Counseling Bulletin, 30,* 177–203.

• Dion, Kenneth L., & Dion, Karen K. (1993). Gender and ethnocultural comparisons in style of love. *Psychology of Women Quarterly, 17,* 463–474.

Dixon, N. F. (1980). Humor: A cognitive alternative to stress? In I. G. Sarason & C. D. Spielberger (eds.), *Stress and anxiety,* Vol. 7. Washington, DC: Hemisphere.

• Doblin, R., & Kleiman, M. A. R. (1991). Marihuana as anti-emetic medicine: A survey of oncologists' attitudes and experiences. *Journal of Clinical Oncology, 9,* 1275–1280.

Dobson, Keith S. (1989). A meta-analysis of the efficacy of cognitive therapy for depression. *Journal of Consulting and Clinical Psychology, 57,* 414–419.

Doering, Charles H.; Brodie, H. K. H.; Kraemer, H. C.; Becker, H. B.; & Hamburg, D. A. (1974). Plasma testosterone levels and psychologic measures in men over a 2-month period. In R. C. Friedman, R. M. Richard, & R. L. Vande Wiele (eds.), *Sex differences in behavior.* New York: Wiley.

Doering, Charles H., et al. (1975). Negative affect and plasma testosterone: A longitudinal human study. *Psychosomatic Medicine, 37,* 484–491.

Doi, L. T. (1973). *The anatomy of dependence.* Tokyo: Kodansha International.

Dollard, John, & Miller, Neal E. (1950). *Personality and psychotherapy: An analysis in terms of learning, thinking, and culture.* New York: McGraw-Hill.

Dolnick, Edward (1990, July). What dreams are (really) made of. *The Atlantic Monthly, 226,* 41–45, 48–53, 56–58, 60–61.

Donnell, S. M., & Hall, J. (1980, Spring). Men and women as managers: A significant case of no significant difference. *Organizational Dynamics, 8,* 60–76.

Doty, Richard M.; Peterson, Bill E.; & Winter, David G. (1991). Threat and authoritarianism in the United States, 1978–1987. *Journal of Personality and Social Psychology, 61,* 629–640.

Dovidio, John F.; Allen, Judith L.; & Schroeder, David A. (1990). Specificity of empathy-induced helping: Evidence for altruistic motivation. *Journal of Personality and Social Psychology, 59,* 249–260.

Druckman, Daniel, & Swets, John A. (eds.) (1988). *Enhancing human performance: Issues, theories, and techniques.* Washington, DC: National Academy Press.

• Dubbert, Patricia M. (1992). Exercise in behavioral medicine. *Journal of Consulting and Clinical Psychology, 60,* 613–618.

Dumont, Matthew P. (1987, December). A diagnostic parable (first edition—unrevised) [Review of DSM-III-R]. *Readings: A Journal of Reviews and Commentary in Mental Health,* 9–12.

Duncan, Paula D.; Ritter, Philip L.; Dornbusch, Sanford M.; Gross, Ruth T.; & Carlsmith, J. Merrill (1985). The effects of pubertal timing on body image, school behavior, and deviance. *Journal of Youth and Adolescence, 14,* 227–235.

Dunford, Franklyn; Huizinga, David; & Elliott, Delbert S. (1990). The role of arrest in domestic assault: The Omaha police experiment. *Criminology, 28,* 183–206.

Dunkel-Schetter, Christine (1984). Social support and cancer: Findings based on patient interviews and their implications. *Journal of Social Issues, 40*(4), 77–98.

Dunn, Judy, & Plomin, Robert (1990). *Separate lives: Why siblings are so different.* New York: Basic Books.

du Verglas, Gabrielle; Banks, Steven R.; & Guyer, Kenneth E. (1988). Clinical effects of fenfluramine on children with autism: A review of the research. *Journal of Autism and Developmental Disorders, 18,* 297–308.

Dweck, Carol (1990). Toward a theory of goals: Their role in motivation and personality. In R. A. Dienstbier (ed.), *Nebraska Symposium on Motivation,* Vol. 38. Lincoln: University of Nebraska Press.

• Dweck, Carol S. (1992). The study of goals in psychology [Commentary to feature review]. *Psychological Science, 3,* 165–167.

Dworkin, Barry R., & Dworkin, Susan (1988). The treatment of scoliosis by continuous automated postural feedback. In R. Ader, H. Weiner, & A. Baum (eds.), *Experimental foundations of behavioral medicine: Conditioning approaches.* Hillsdale, NJ: Erlbaum.

Dywan, Jane, & Bowers, Kenneth (1983). The use of hypnosis to enhance recall. *Science, 222,* 184–185.

D'Zurilla, Thomas J., & Sheedy, Collette F. (1991). Relation between problem-solving ability and subsequent level of psychological stress in college students. *Journal of Personality and Social Psychology, 61,* 841–846.

Eagly, Alice H., & Carli, Linda L. (1981). Sex of researchers and sex-typed communications as determinants of sex differences in influencibility: A meta-analysis of social influence studies. *Psychological Bulletin, 90,* 1–20.

Eagly, Alice H.; Makhijani, M. G.; & Klonsky, B. G. (1990). Gender and the evaluation of leaders: A meta-analysis. *Psychological Bulletin, 111,* 3–22.

• Eaton, William W.; Bilker, Warren; Haro, Josep M.; Herrman, Helen; et al. (1992b). Long-term course of hospitalization for schizophrenia: II. Change with passage of time. *Schizophrenia Bulletin, 18,* 229–241.

• Eaton, William W.; Mortensen, Preben B.; Herrman, Helen; Freeman, Hugh; et al. (1992a). Long-term course of hospitalization for schizophrenia: I. Risk for rehospitalization. *Schizophrenia Bulletin, 18,* 217–228.

Ebbinghaus, Hermann M. (1885/1913). *Memory: A contribution to experimental psychology.* (H. A. Ruger & C. E. Bussenius, trans.) New York: Teachers College, Columbia University.

• Eberlin, Michael; McConnachie, Gene; Ibel, Stuart; & Volpe, Lisa (1993). Facilitated communication: A failure to replicate the phenomenon. *Journal of Autism and Developmental Disorders, 23,* 507–530.

• Eccles, Jacquelynne S. (1993). Parents and gender-role socialization during the middle childhood and adolescent years. In S. Oskamp & M. Costanzo (eds.), *Gender issues in contemporary society* (The Claremont Symposium on Applied Social Psychology). Newbury Park, CA: Sage.

• Eccles, Jacquelynne S.; Jacobs, Janis E.; & Harold, Rena D. (1990). Gender role stereotypes, expectancy effects, and parents' socialization of gender differences. *Journal of Social Issues, 46,* 183–201.

• Eccles, Jacquelynne S.; Midgley, Carol; Wigfield, Allan; Buchanan, Christy M.; et al. (1993). Development during adolescence: The impact of stage-environment fit on young adolescents' experiences in schools and in families. *American Psychologist, 48,* 90–101.

Eccles, John C. (1981). In praise of falsification. In R. D. Tweney, M. E. Doherty, & C. R. Mynatt (eds.), *On scientific thinking.* New York: Columbia University Press.

• Eckensberger, Lutz H. (1994). Moral development and its measurement across cultures. In W. J. Lonner & R. Malpass (eds.), *Psychology and culture.* Needham Heights, MA: Allyn & Bacon.

• Edelson, Marshall (1994). Can psychotherapy research answer this psychotherapist's questions? In P. F. Talley, H. H. Strupp, & S. F. Butler (eds.), *Psychotherapy research and practice: Bridging the gap.* New York: Basic Books.

Edsall, Thomas B., & Edsall, Mary D. (1991). *Chain reaction: The impact of race, rights, and taxes on American politics.* New York: Norton.

Edwards, Betty (1986). *Drawing on the artist within: A guide to innovation, invention, imagination and creativity.* New York: Simon & Schuster.

Edwards, Carolyn P. (1987). Culture and the construction of moral values. In J. Kagan & S. Lamb (eds.), *The emergence of morality in young children.* Chicago: University of Chicago Press.

Edwards, Lynne K., & Edwards, Allen L. (1991). A principal-components analysis of the Minnesota Multiphasic Personality Inventory Factor Scales. *Journal of Personality and Social Psychology, 60,* 766–772.

Egeland, Janice A.; Gerhard, Daniela; Pauls, David; Sussex, James; et al. (1987, February 26). Bipolar affective disorders linked to DNA markers on chromosome 11. *Nature, 325,* 783–787.

• **Ehrenreich, Barbara** (1978). *For her own good: 150 years of the experts' advice to women.* New York: Doubleday.

• **Eich, E., & Hyman, R.** (1992). Subliminal self-help. In D. Druckman & R. A. Bjork (eds.), *In the mind's eye: Enhancing human performance.* Washington, DC: National Academy Press.

• **Eisenberger, Robert, & Selbst, Michael** (1994). Does reward increase or decrease creativity? *Journal of Personality and Social Psychology, 66,* 1116–1127.

• **Eisler, Riane** (1987). *The chalice and the blade.* San Francisco: HarperCollins.

• **Ekman, Paul** (1994). Strong evidence for universals in facial expressions: A reply to Russell's mistaken critique. *Psychological Bulletin, 115,* 268–287.

Ekman, Paul; Friesen, Wallace V.; & Ellsworth, Phoebe (1972). *Emotion in the human face: Guidelines for research and an integration of findings.* New York: Pergamon.

Ekman, Paul; Friesen, Wallace V.; & O'Sullivan, Maureen (1988). Smiles when lying. *Journal of Personality and Social Psychology, 54,* 414–420.

Ekman, Paul; Friesen, Wallace V.; O'Sullivan, Maureen; et al. (1987). Universals and cultural differences in the judgments of facial expression of emotion. *Journal of Personality and Social Psychology, 53,* 712–717.

Ekman, Paul, & Heider, Karl G. (1988). The universality of a contempt expression: A replication. *Motivation and Emotion, 12,* 303–308.

Ekman, Paul, & O'Sullivan, Maureen (1991). Who can catch a liar? *American Psychologist, 46,* 913–920.

• **Elliot, Andrew J., & Harackiewicz, Judith M.** (1994). Goal setting, achievement orientation, and intrinsic motivation: A mediational analysis. *Journal of Personality and Social Psychology, 66,* 968–980.

Elliott, Elaine S., & Dweck, Carol S. (1988). Goals: An approach to motivation and achievement. *Journal of Personality and Social Psychology, 54,* 5–12.

• **Elliott, Robert, & Morrow-Bradley, Cheryl** (1994). Developing a working marriage between psychotherapists and psychotherapy researchers: Identifying shared purposes. In P. F. Talley, H. H. Strupp, and S. F. Butler (eds.), *Psychotherapy research and practice: Bridging the gap.* New York: Basic Books.

• **Ellis, Albert** (1993). Changing rational-emotive therapy (RET) to rational emotive behavior therapy (REBT). *Behavior Therapist, 16,* 257–258.

Ellis, Albert, & Dryden, Windy (1987). *The practice of rational emotive therapy.* New York: Springer.

• **Elshtain, Jean B.** (1987). *Women and war.* New York: Basic Books.

Emmons, Robert A., & King, Laura A. (1988). Conflict among personal strivings: Immediate and long-term implications for psychological and physical well-being. *Journal of Personality and Social Psychology, 54,* 1040–1048.

• **Endler, Norman S.** (1991). Electroconvulsive therapy: Myths and realities. Paper presented at the annual meeting of the American Psychological Association, San Francisco.

Englander-Golden, Paula; Whitmore, Mary R.; & Dienstbier, Richard A. (1978). Menstrual cycle as focus of study and self-reports of moods and behavior. *Motivation and Emotion, 2,* 75–86.

Englund, C., & Naitoh, P. (1980). An attempted validation study of the birthdate-based biorhythm (BBB) hypothesis. *Aviation, Space, and Environmental Medicine, 51,* 583–590.

Ennis, Robert H. (1985). Critical thinking and the curriculum. *National Forum, 65*(1), 28–30.

• **Entin, Alan D.** (1983). The family photo album as icon: Photographs in family psychotherapy. In D. Krauss & J. L. Fryrear (eds.), *Phototherapy in mental health.* Springfield, IL: Charles C. Thomas.

• **Entin, Alan D.** (1992). Family photographs: Visual icons and emotional history. Paper presented at the annual meeting of the American Psychological Association, Washington, DC.

• **Epstein, Robert** (1990). Generativity theory and creativity. In M. A. Runco & R. S. Albert (eds.), *Theories of creativity.* Newbury Park, CA: Sage.

Epstein, Robert; Kirshnit, C. E.; Lanza, R. P.; & Rubin, L. C.

(1984, March 1). "Insight" in the pigeon: Antecedents and determinants of an intelligent performance. *Nature, 308,* 61–62.

• **Epstein, Seymour** (1994). Integration of the cognitive and the psychodynamic unconscious. *American Psychologist, 49,* 709–724.

• **Ericsson, K. Anders, & Chase, William G.** (1982). Exceptional memory. *American Scientist, 70,* 607–615.

Erikson, Erik H. (1950/1963). *Childhood and society* (2nd ed.). New York: Norton.

• **Erikson, Erik H.** (1982). *The life cycle completed.* New York: Norton.

Erikson, Erik H. (1987). *A way of looking at things: Selected papers from 1930 to 1980* (edited by Stephen Schlein). New York: Norton.

Ernsberger, Paul, & Nelson, D. O. (1988). Refeeding hypertension in dietary obesity. *American Journal of Physiology, 154,* R47–55.

Eron, Leonard D. (1980). Prescription for reduction of aggression. *American Psychologist, 35,* 244–252.

• **Eron, Leonard D.** (1982). Parent-child interaction, television violence, and aggression of children. *American Psychologist, 37,* 197–211.

• **Eron, Leonard D., & Huesmann, L. Rowell** (1987). Television as a source of maltreatment of children. *School Psychology Review, 16,* 195–202.

Ervin-Tripp, Susan (1964). Imitation and structural change in children's language. In E. H. Lenneberg (ed.), *New directions in the study of language.* Cambridge, MA: MIT Press.

• **Escera, Carles; Cilveti, Robert; & Grau, Carles** (1992). Ultradian rhythms in cognitive operations: Evidence from the P300 component of the event-related potentials. *Medical Science Research, 20,* 137–138.

• **Esterson, Allen** (1993). *Seductive mirage: An exploration of the work of Sigmund Freud.* New York: Open Court.

Evans, Christopher (1984). *Landscapes of the night.* (Edited and completed by Peter Evans.) New York: Viking.

• **Evans, Gary W., & Lepore, Stephen J.** (1993). Household crowding and social support: A quasiexperimental analysis. *Journal of Personality and Social Psychology, 65,* 308–316.

• **Ewart, Craig K., & Kolodner, Kenneth B.** (1994). Negative affect, gender, and expressive style predict elevated ambulatory blood pressure in adolescents. *Journal of Personality and Social Psychology, 66,* 596–605.

Eyferth, Klaus (1961). [The performance of different groups of the children of occupation forces on the Hamburg-Wechsler Intelligence Test for Children.] *Archiv für die Gesamte Psychologie, 113,* 222–241.

• **Eysenck, Hans J.** (1990). The prediction of death from cancer by means of personality/stress questionnaire: Too good to be true? *Perceptual and Motor Skills, 71,* 216–218.

• **Eysenck, Hans J.** (1993). Prediction of cancer and coronary heart disease mortality by means of a personality inventory: Results of a 15-year follow-up study. *Psychological Reports, 72,* 499–516.

• **Eysenck, Hans J.** (1994). The "Big Five" or "Giant 3"? Criteria for a paradigm. In C. F. Halverson, G. A. Kohnstamm, & R. P. Martin (eds.), *The developing structure of temperament and personality from infancy to adulthood.* Hillsdale, NJ: Erlbaum.

• **Eysenck, Hans J., & Grossarth-Maticek, Ronald** (1991). Creative novation behaviour therapy as a prophylactic treatment for cancer and coronary heart disease: Part II—effects of treatment. *Behavior Research and Therapy, 29,* 17–31.

• **Fabes, Richard A.; Eisenberg, Nancy; Karbon, Mariss; Bernzweig, Jane; Speer, Anna Lee; & Carlo, Gustavo** (1994). Socialization of children's vicarious emotional responding and prosocial behavior: Relations with mothers' perceptions of children's emotional reactivity. *Developmental Psychology, 30,* 44–55.

• **Fagot, Beverly I.** (1984). Teacher and peer reactions to boys' and girls' play styles. *Sex Roles, 11,* 691–702.

• **Fagot, Beverly I.** (1985). Beyond the reinforcement principle: Another step toward understanding sex role development. *Developmental Psychology, 2,* 1097–1104.

• **Fagot, Beverly I.** (1993, June). Gender role development in early childhood: Environmental input, internal construction. Invited address, International Academy of Sex Research, Monterey, California.

• **Fagot, Beverly I.; Hagan, R.; Leinbach, Mary D.; & Kronsberg, S.** (1985). Differential reactions to assertive and communicative acts of toddler boys and girls. *Child Development, 56,* 1499–1505.

• **Fagot, Beverly I., & Leinbach, Mary D.** (1993). Gender-role development in young children: From discrimination to labeling. *Developmental Review, 13,* 205–224.

Fairchild, Halford H. (1985). Black, Negro, or Afro-American? The differences are crucial! *Journal of Black Studies, 16,* 47–55.

Faraone, Stephen V.; Kremen, William S.; & Tsuang, Ming T. (1990). Genetic transmission of major affective disorders: Quantitative models and linkage analyses. *Psychological Bulletin, 108,* 109–127.

Farber, Susan L. (1981). *Identical twins reared apart: A reanalysis.* New York: Basic Books.

Faust, David, & Ziskin, Jay (1988, July 1). The expert witness in psychology and psychiatry. *Science, 241,* 31–35.

• Fawzy, Fawzy I.; Fawzy, Nancy W.; Hyun, Christine S.; Elashoff, Robert; et al. (1993). Malignant melanoma: Effects of an early structured psychiatric intervention, coping, and affective state on recurrence and survival six years later. *Archives of General Psychiatry, 50,* 681–689.

• *FDA Drug Bulletin* (1990, April). Two new psychiatric drugs. *20*(1), 9.

Feather, N. T. (1966). Effects of prior success and failure on expectations of success and subsequent performance. *Journal of Personality and Social Psychology, 3,* 287–298.

Feather, N. T. (ed.) (1982). *Expectations and actions: Expectancy-value models in psychology.* Hillsdale, NJ: Erlbaum.

Feeney, Dennis M. (1987). Human rights and animal welfare. *American Psychologist, 42,* 593–599.

• Feeney, Judith A., & Noller, Patricia (1990). Attachment style as a predictor of adult romantic relationships. *Journal of Personality and Social Psychology, 58,* 281–291.

Fehr, Beverly, & Russell, James A. (1991). The concept of love viewed from a prototype perspective. *Journal of Personality and Social Psychology, 60,* 425–438.

• Fein, Steven, & Spencer, Steven J. (1993). Self-esteem and stereotype-based downward social comparison. Paper presented at the annual meeting of the American Psychological Association, Toronto.

Feingold, Alan (1988). Cognitive gender differences are disappearing. *American Psychologist, 43,* 95–103.

• Fendrich, Robert; Wessinger, C. Mark; & Gazzaniga, Michael S. (1992). Residual vision in a scotoma: Implications for blindsight. *Science, 258,* 1489–1491.

Ferguson, Thomas, & Rogers, Joel (1986, May). The myth of America's turn to the right. *Atlantic,* 43–53.

Fernald, Anne (1990). Emotion in the voice: Meaningful melodies in mother's speech to infants. Paper presented at the annual meeting of the American Psychological Association, Boston.

Fernald, L. D. (1984). *The Hans legacy: A story of science.* Hillsdale, NJ: Erlbaum.

• Fernandez, Ephrem, & Turk, Dennis C. (1992). Sensory and affective components of pain: Separation and synthesis. *Psychological Bulletin, 112,* 205–217.

Feshbach, Norma; Feshbach, Seymour; Fauvre, Mary; & Ballard-Campbell, Michael (1983). *Learning to care: A curriculum for affective and social development.* Glenview, IL: Scott, Foresman.

Festinger, Leon (1957). *A theory of cognitive dissonance.* Evanston, IL: Row, Peterson.

Festinger, Leon (1980). Looking backward. In L. Festinger (ed.), *Retrospections on social psychology.* New York: Oxford University Press.

Festinger, Leon; Pepitone, Albert; & Newcomb, Theodore (1952). Some consequences of deindividuation in a group. *Journal of Abnormal and Social Psychology, 47,* 382–389.

Festinger, Leon; Riecken, Henry W.; & Schachter, Stanley (1956). *When prophecy fails.* Minneapolis: University of Minnesota Press.

Field, Tiffany (1989, Summer). Individual and maturational differences in infant expressivity. *New Directions for Child Development, 44,* 9–23.

Fields, Howard (1991). Depression and pain: A neurobiological model. *Neuropsychiatry, Neuropsychology, and Behavioral Neurology, 4,* 83–92.

• Fincham, Frank D., & Bradbury, Thomas N. (1993). Marital satisfaction, depression, and attributions: A longitudinal analysis. *Journal of Personality and Social Psychology, 64,* 442–452.

Fingarette, Herbert (1988). *Heavy drinking: The myth of alcoholism as a disease.* Berkeley: University of California Press.

• Finkelhor, David, & Dziuba-Leatherman, Jennifer (1994). Victimization of children. *American Psychologist, 49,* 173–183.

• Fiore, Edith (1989). *Encounters: A psychologist reveals case studies of abductions by extraterrestrials.* New York: Doubleday.

• Fischer, Agneta H. (1993). Sex differences in emotionality: Fact or stereotype? *Feminism & Psychology, 3,* 303–318.

• Fischer, Pamela C.; Smith, Randy J.; Leonard, Elizabeth; Fuqua, Dale R.; et al. (1993). Sex differences on affective dimensions: Continuing examination. *Journal of Counseling and Development, 71,* 440–443.

Fischhoff, Baruch (1975). Hindsight is not equal to foresight: The effect of outcome knowledge on judgment under uncertainty. *Journal of Experimental Psychology: Human Perception and Performance, 1,* 288–299.

Fisher, Kathleen (1985, March). ECT: New studies on how, why, who. *APA Monitor, 16,* 18–19.

• Fisher, Seymour, & Greenberg, Roger P. (1993). How sound is the double-blind design for evaluating psychotropic drugs? *The Journal of Nervous and Mental Disease, 181,* 345–350.

Fisher, Seymour, & Greenberg, Roger P. (eds.) (1989). *A critical appraisal of biological treatments for psychological distress: Comparisons with psychotherapy and placebo.* Hillsdale, NJ: Erlbaum.

• Fiske, Susan T. (1993). Controlling other people: The impact of power on stereotyping. *American Psychologist, 48,* 621–628.

Fiske, Susan T., & Taylor, Shelley E. (1991). *Social cognition* (2nd ed.). New York: McGraw-Hill.

Fitzgerald, Joseph M. (1988). Vivid memories and the reminiscence phenomenon: The role of a self narrative. *Human Development, 31,* 261–273.

Fivush, Robyn, & Hamond, Nina R. (1991). Autobiographical memory across the school years: Toward reconceptualizing childhood amnesia. In R. Fivush & J. A. Hudson (eds.), *Knowing and remembering in young children.* New York: Cambridge University Press.

• Flavell, John H. (1992). Cognitive development: Past, present, and future. *Developmental Psychology, 28,* 998–1005.

• Flavell, John H. (1993). Young children's understanding of thinking and consciousness. *Current Directions in Psychological Science, 2,* 40–43.

• Flavell, John H.; Green, F. L.; & Flavell, E. R. (1990). Developmental changes in young children's knowledge about the mind. *Cognitive Development, 5,* 1–27.

Fletcher, Garth J., & Ward, C. (1988). Attribution theory and processes: Cross-cultural perspective. In M. H. Bond (ed.), *The cross-cultural challenge to social psychology.* Newbury Park, CA: Sage.

Flor, Herta; Kerns, Robert D.; & Turk, Dennis C. (1987). The role of spouse reinforcement, perceived pain, and activity levels of chronic pain patients. *Journal of Psychosomatic Research, 31,* 251–259.

Foa, Edna, & Emmelkamp, Paul (eds.) (1983). *Failures in behavior therapy.* New York: Wiley.

• Foa, Edna; Zinbarg, Richard; & Rothbaum, Barbara O. (1992). Uncontrollability and unpredictability in post-traumatic stress disorder: An animal model. *Psychological Bulletin, 112,* 218–238.

• Foderaro, Lisa W. (1994, November 8). 'Clubhouse' helps mentally ill find the way back. *New York Times,* B1, B3.

• Fogelman, Eva (1994). *Conscience and courage: Rescuers of Jews during the Holocaust.* New York: Anchor Books.

• Foreyt, John P.; Goodrick, G. Ken; Reeves, Rebecca S.; Raynaud, A. Scott; et al. (1993). Response of free-living adults to behavioral treatment of obesity: Attrition and compliance to exercise. *Behavior Therapy, 24,* 659–669.

• Forgas, Joseph (1994). Sad and guilty? Affective influences on the explanation of conflict in close relationships. *Journal of Personality and Social Psychology, 66,* 56–68.

Forgas, Joseph, & Bond, Michael H. (1985). Cultural influences on the perception of interaction episodes. *Personality and Social Psychology Bulletin, 11,* 75–88.

Forrest, F.; Florey, C. du V.; Taylor, D.; McPherson, F.; & Young, J. A. (1991, July 6). Reported social alcohol consumption during pregnancy and infants' development at 18 months. *British Medical Journal, 303,* 22–26.

• Forsyth, G. Alfred; Arpey, Stacie H.; & Stratton-Hess, Caroline L. (1992). Correcting errors in the interpretation of research. Poster session paper presented at the annual meeting of the American Psychological Association, Washington, DC.

Foulkes, David (1990). Dreaming and consciousness. *European Journal of Cognitive Psychology, 2,* 39–55.

Foulkes, David; Hollifield, Michael; Sullivan, Brenda; Bradley, Laura; et al. (1990). REM dreaming and cognitive skills at ages 5–8: A cross-sectional study. *International Journal of Behavioral Development, 13,* 447–465.

Fouts, Roger S.; Fouts, Deborah H.; & Van Cantfort, Thomas E. (1989). The infant Loulis learns signs from cross-fostered chimpanzees. In R. A. Gardner, B. T. Gardner, & T. E. Van Cantfort (eds.), *Teaching sign language to chimpanzees.* Albany: State University of New York Press.

Fouts, Roger S., & Rigby, Randall L. (1977). Man-chimpanzee communication. In T. A. Seboek (ed.), *How animals communicate.* Bloomington: University of Indiana Press.

• Fox, B. H. (1992). LeShan's hypothesis is provocative, but is it plausible? *Advances, the Journal of Mind-Body Health, 8*(2), 82–84.

Fox, Nathan A. (1991). If it's not left, it's right: Electroencephalograph asymmetry and the development of emotion. *American Psychologist, 46,* 863–872.

Fox, Nathan A., & Davidson, Richard J. (1988). Patterns of brain electrical activity during facial signs of emotion in 10-month-old infants. *Developmental Psychology, 24,* 230–236.

• Fox, Ronald E. (1994). Training professional psychologists for the twenty-first century. *American Psychologist, 49,* 200–206.

Frank, Jerome D. (1985). Therapeutic components shared by all psychotherapies. In M. J. Mahony & A. Freeman (eds.), *Cognition and psychotherapy.* New York: Plenum.

Frank, Robert G.; Gluck, John P.; & Buckelew, Susan P. (1990). Rehabilitation: Psychology's greatest opportunity? *American Psychologist, 45,* 757–761.

Frankl, Victor E. (1955). *The doctor and the soul: An introduction to logotherapy.* New York: Knopf.

• Franklin, Anderson J. (1993, July/August). The invisibility syndrome. *The Family Therapy Networker,* 33–39.

• Freed, C. R.; Breeze, R. E.; Rosenberg, N. L.; & Schneck, S. A. (1993). Embryonic dopamine cell implants as a treatment for the second phase of Parkinson's disease. Replacing failed nerve terminals. *Advances in Neurology, 60,* 721–728.

• Freed, C. R.; Breeze, R. E.; Rosenberg, N. L.; et al. (1992). Survival of implanted fetal dopamine cells and neurologic improvement 12 to 46 months after transplantation for Parkinson's disease. *New England Journal of Medicine, 327,* 1549–1555.

Freedman, Jonathan L. (1988). Television violence and aggression: What the evidence shows. In S. Oskamp (ed.), *Television as a social issue* (*Applied Social Psychology Annual,* Vol. 8). Newbury Park, CA: Sage.

Freeman, Ellen; Rickels, Karl; Sondheimer, S. J.; & Polansky, M. (1990). Ineffectiveness of progesterone suppository treatment for premenstrual syndrome. *Journal of the American Medical Association, 264,* 349–353.

French, Christopher C.; Fowler, Mandy; McCarthy, Katy; & Peers, Debbie (1991, Winter). Belief in astrology: A test of the Barnum effect. *Skeptical Inquirer, 15,* 166–172.

Freud, Anna (1946). *The ego and the mechanisms of defence.* New York: International Universities Press.

• Freud, Sigmund (1900/1953). The interpretation of dreams. In J. Strachey (ed.), *The standard edition of the complete psychological works of Sigmund Freud,* Vols. IV and V. London: Hogarth Press.

Freud, Sigmund (1905a). Fragment of an analysis of a case of hysteria. In J. Strachey (ed. and trans.), *Standard edition of the complete psychological works of Sigmund Freud,* Vol. VII. London: Hogarth Press and the Institute of Psycho-Analysis (1964 edition).

Freud, Sigmund (1905b). Three essays on the theory of sexuality. In *Standard edition,* Vol. VII.

Freud, Sigmund (1920/1960). *A general introduction to psychoanalysis* (Joan Riviere, trans.). New York: Washington Square Press.

Freud, Sigmund (1923/1962). *The ego and the id* (Joan Riviere, trans.). New York: Norton.

Freud, Sigmund (1924a). The dissolution of the Oedipus complex. In *Standard edition,* Vol. XIX.

Freud, Sigmund (1924b). Some psychical consequences of the anatomical distinction between the sexes. In *Standard edition,* Vol. XIX.

Friedman, Howard S. (1991). *The self-healing personality.* New York: Henry Holt.

Friedman, Howard S., & Booth-Kewley, Stephanie (1987). The disease-prone personality: A meta-analytic view of the construct. *American Psychologist, 42,* 539–555.

Friedman, Howard S., & Miller-Herringer, Terry (1991). Nonverbal display of emotion in public and private: Self-monitoring, personality, and expressive cues. *Journal of Personality and Social Psychology, 61,* 766–775.

Friedman, Meyer, & Rosenman, Ray (1974). *Type A behavior and your heart.* New York: Knopf.

Friedman, William; Robinson, Amy; & Friedman, Britt (1987). Sex differences in moral judgments? A test of Gilligan's theory. *Psychology of Women Quarterly, 11,* 37–46.

Frijda, Nico H. (1988). The laws of emotion. *American Psychologist, 43,* 349–358.

Fromholt, Pia, & Larsen, Steen F. (1991). Autobiographical memory in normal aging and primary degenerative dementia (dementia of Alzheimer type). *Journal of Gerontology, 46,* P85–P91.

Frye, Richard E.; Schwartz, B. S.; & Doty, Richard L. (1990). Dose-related effects of cigarette smoking on olfactory function. *Journal of the American Medical Association, 263,* 1233–1236.

Fussell, Paul (1989). *Wartime.* New York: Oxford University Press.

• Gabbard, Glen O. (ed.) (1989). *Sexual exploitation within professional relationships.* Washington, DC: American Psychiatric Association.

Gaertner, Samuel L.; Mann, Jeffrey A.; Dovidio, John F.; Murrell, Audrey J.; & Pomare, Marina (1990). How does cooperation reduce intergroup bias? *Journal of Personality and Social Psychology, 59,* 692–704.

Gagnon, John (1987). Science and the politics of pathology. *Journal of Sex Research, 23,* 120–123.

Gagnon, John, & Simon, William (1973). *Sexual conduct: The social sources of human sexuality.* Chicago: Aldine.

Galanter, Eugene (1962). Contemporary psychophysics. In R. Brown, E. Galanter, H. Hess, and G. Mandler (eds.), *New directions in psychology.* New York: Holt, Rinehart and Winston.

Galanter, Marc (1989). *Cults: Faith, healing, and coercion.* New York: Oxford University Press.

• Gallant, Jack L.; Braun, Jochen; & Van Essen, David C. (1993). Selectivity for polar, hyperbolic, and Cartesian gratings in macaque visual cortex. *Science, 259,* 100–103.

• Gallo, Linda C., & Eastman, Charmane I. (1993). Circadian rhythms during gradually delaying and advancing sleep and light schedules. *Physiology and Behavior, 53,* 119–126.

Galotti, Kathleen (1989). Approaches to studying formal and everyday reasoning. *Psychological Bulletin, 105,* 331–351.

Ganaway, George K. (1991). Alternative hypotheses regarding satanic ritual abuse memories. Paper presented at the annual meeting of the American Psychological Association, San Francisco.

• Gannon, Linda, & Ekstrom, Bonnie (1993). Attitudes toward menopause: The influence of sociocultural paradigms. *Psychology of Women Quarterly, 17,* 275–288.

Garcia, John, & Koelling, Robert A. (1966). Relation of cue to consequence in avoidance learning. *Psychonomic Science, 4,* 23–124.

Gardner, Howard (1983). *Frames of mind: The theory of multiple intelligences.* New York: Basic Books.

• Gardner, Howard (1985). *The mind's new science: A history of the cognitive revolution.* New York: Basic Books.

• Gardner, Howard (1992). Scientific psychology: Should we bury it or praise it? *New Ideas in Psychology, 10,* 179–190.

Gardner, R. Allen, & Gardner, Beatrice T. (1969). Teaching sign language to a chimpanzee. *Science, 165,* 664–672.

Garfield, Patricia (1974). *Creative dreaming.* New York: Ballantine.

• Garland, Ann F., & Zigler, Edward (1994). Adolescent suicide prevention: Current research and social policy implications. *American Psychologist, 48,* 169–182.

Garmezy, Norman (1985). Stress-resistant children: The search for protective factors. In J. E. Stevenson (ed.), *Recent research in developmental psychopathology.* New York: Pergamon.

Garmezy, Norman (1991). Resilience and vulnerability to adverse developmental outcomes associated with poverty. *American Behavioral Scientist, 34,* 416–430.

• Garner, David M., & Wooley, Susan C. (1991). Confronting the failure of behavioral and dietary treatments for obesity. *Clinical Psychology Review, 11,* 729–780.

Garnets, Linda; Hancock, Kristin A.; Cochran, Susan D.; Goodchilds, Jacqueline; & Peplau, Letitia A. (1991). Issues in psychotherapy with lesbians and gay men: A survey of psychologists. *American Psychologist, 46,* 964–972.

• **Garnets, Linda, & Kimmel, Douglas C. (eds.)** (1993). *Psychological perspectives on lesbian and gay male experiences.* New York: Columbia University Press.

Gaston, Louise; Marmar, Charles R.; Gallagher, Dolores; & Thompson, Larry W. (1989). Impact of confirming patient expectations of change processes in behavioral, cognitive, and brief dynamic psychotherapy. *Psychotherapy, 26,* 296–302.

Gaston, Louise; Marmar, Charles R.; Thompson, Larry W.; & Gallagher, Dolores (1988). Relation of patient pretreatment characteristics to the therapeutic alliance in diverse psychotherapies. *Journal of Consulting and Clinical Psychology, 56,* 483–489.

• **Gates, Henry Louis** (1992, July 20). Black demagogues and pseudo-scholars. *New York Times,* opinion page.

• **Gay, Peter** (1988). *Freud: A life for our time.* New York: Norton.

Gazzaniga, Michael S. (1967). The split brain in man. *Scientific American, 217*(2), 24–29.

Gazzaniga, Michael S. (1983). Right hemisphere language following brain bisection: A 20-year perspective. *American Psychologist, 38,* 525–537.

Gazzaniga, Michael S. (1985). *The social brain: Discovering the networks of the mind.* New York: Basic Books.

Gazzaniga, Michael S. (1988). *Mind matters.* Boston: Houghton Mifflin.

Gedo, John (1979). A psychoanalyst reports at mid-career. *American Journal of Psychiatry, 136,* 646–649.

Geen, Russell G. (1978). Some effects of observing violence upon the behavior of the observer. In B. A. Maher (ed.), *Progress in experimental personality research.* New York: Academic Press.

• **Geis, Florence L.** (1993). Self-fulfilling prophecies: A social psychological view of gender. In A. E. Beall & R. J. Sternberg (eds.), *The psychology of gender.* New York: Guilford Press.

Geiselman, R. Edward (1988). Improving eyewitness memory through mental reinstatement of context. In G. M. Davies and D. M. Thomson (eds.), *Memory in context: Context in memory.* New York: Wiley.

Gelernter, Joel; O'Malley, S.; Risch, N.; Kranzler, H. R.; et al. (1991, October 2). No association between an allele at the D2 dopamine receptor gene (DRD2) and alcoholism. *Journal of the American Medical Association, 266,* 1801–1807.

Geller, E. Scott, & Lehman, Galen R. (1988). Drinking-driving intervention strategies: A person-situation-behavior framework. In M. D. Laurence, J. R. Snortum, & F. E. Zimring (eds.), *The social control of drinking and driving.* Chicago: University of Chicago Press.

Gelles, Richard J., & Straus, Murray A. (1988). *Intimate violence: The causes and consequences of abuse in the American family.* New York: Simon & Schuster/Touchstone.

Gerbner, George (1988). Telling stories in the information age. In B. D. Ruben (ed.), *Information and behavior,* Vol. 2. New Brunswick, NJ: Transaction Books.

Gergen, Kenneth J. (1985). The social constructionist movement in modern psychology. *American Psychologist, 40,* 266–274.

• **Gergen, Kenneth J.** (1994). Exploring the postmodern: Perils or potentials? *American Psychologist, 49,* 412–416.

Gergen, Mary M. (1992). Life stories: Pieces of a dream. In G. Rosenwald & R. Ochberg (eds.), *Storied lives.* New Haven, CT: Yale University Press.

• **Gergen, Mary M., & Gergen, Kenneth J.** (1994). What is this thing called love? Emotional scenarios in historical perspective. Paper presented at the annual meeting of the American Psychological Association, Los Angeles.

• **Gerson, Kathleen** (1993). *No man's land: Men's changing commitments to family and work.* New York: Basic Books.

• **Gevins, A. S.; Le, J.; Martin, N.; et al.** (1994). High resolution EEG: 124-channel recording, spatial enhancement and MRI integration methods. *Electroencephalographic Clinical Neurophysiology, 90,* 337–358.

Gewirtz, Jacob L. (1991). An analysis of infant social learning. Paper presented at the annual meeting of the American Psychological Association, San Francisco.

Gewirtz, Jacob L., & Peláez-Nogueras, Martha (1991a). The attachment metaphor and the conditioning of infant separation protests. In J. L. Gewirtz & W. M. Kurtines (eds.), *Intersections with attachment.* Hillsdale, NJ: Erlbaum.

Gewirtz, Jacob L., & Peláez-Nogueras, Martha (1991b). Infants' separation difficulties and distress due to misplaced maternal con-

tingencies. In T. Field, P. McCabe, & N. Schneidennan, *Stress and coping in infancy and childhood.* Hillsdale, NJ: Erlbaum.

Gibbons, Frederick X.; McGovern, Paul G.; & Lando, Harry A. (1991). Relapse and risk perception among members of a smoking cessation clinic. *Health Psychology, 10,* 42–45.

Gibson, Eleanor, & Walk, Richard (1960). The "visual cliff." *Scientific American, 202,* 80–92.

• **Gilbert, D. T.; & Hixon, J. G.** (1990). The trouble of thinking: Activation and application of stereotypic beliefs. *Journal of Personality and Social Psychology, 60,* 509–517.

Gilbert, Daniel T.; Pelham, Brett W.; & Krull, Douglas S. (1988). On cognitive busyness: When person perceivers meet persons perceived. *Journal of Personality and Social Psychology, 54,* 733–739.

Gilligan, Carol (1982). *In a different voice.* Cambridge: Harvard University Press.

Gilligan, Carol, & Wiggins, Grant (1987). The origins of morality in early childhood relationships. In J. Kagan & S. Lamb (eds.), *The emergence of morality in young children.* Chicago: University of Chicago Press.

Gillin, J. Christian; Sitaram, N.; Janowsky, D.; et al. (1985). Cholinergic mechanisms in REM sleep. In A. Wauquier, J. M. Gaillard, J. M. Monti, & M. Radulovacki (eds.), *Sleep: Neurotransmitters and neuromodulators.* New York: Raven Press.

• **Gilmore, David D.** (1990). *Manhood in the making: Cultural concepts of masculinity.* New Haven, CT: Yale University Press.

• **Giordano, Magda; Ford, Lisa M.; Shipley, Michael T.; et al.** (1990). Neural grafts and pharmacological intervention in a model of Huntington's disease. *Brain Research Bulletin, 25,* 453–465.

• **Gladue, Brian A.** (1994). The biopsychology of sexual orientation. *Current Directions in Psychological Science, 3,* 150–154.

Glanzer, Murray, & Cunitz, Anita R. (1966). Two storage mechanisms in free recall. *Journal of Verbal Learning and Verbal Behavior, 5,* 351–360.

Glazer, Myron P., & Glazer, Penina M. (1990). *The whistleblowers: Exposing corruption in government and industry.* New York: Basic Books.

• **Glick, Peter, & Fiske, Susan T.** (in press). The ambivalent sexism inventory: Differentiating hostile and benevolent sexism. *Journal of Personality and Social Psychology.*

• **Gobodo-Madikizela, Pumla** (1994). The notion of the "collective" in South African "political" murder cases: The "deindividuation" argument revisited. Paper presented to the biennial conference of the American Psychology and Law Society, Santa Fe, New Mexico.

Goddard, Henry H. (1917). Mental tests and the immigrant. *Journal of Delinquency, 2,* 243–277.

• **Gold, Paul E.** (1987). Sweet memories. *American Scientist, 75,* 151–155.

• **Goldberg, Lewis R.** (1993). The structure of phenotypic personality traits. *American Psychologist, 48,* 26–34.

Golding, Jacqueline M. (1988). Gender differences in depressive symptoms. *Psychology of Women Quarterly, 12,* 61–74.

Goldstein, Michael J. (1987). Psychosocial issues. *Schizophrenia Bulletin, 13*(1), 157–171.

• **Goldstein, Richard** (1980, September 30). Getting real about getting high: An interview with Andrew Weil, M.D. *The Village Voice.*

Goleman, Daniel (1982, March). Staying up: The rebellion against sleep's gentle tyranny. *Psychology Today,* 24–25, 27–28, 31–32, 35.

Golub, Sharon (1988). A developmental perspective. In L. H. Gise, N. G. Kase, & R. L. Berkowitz (eds.), *The premenstrual syndrome.* New York: Churchill Livingstone.

Goodenough, Donald R.; Shapiro, Arthur; Holden, Melvin; & Steinschriber, Leonard (1959). A comparison of dreamers and nondreamers: Eye movements, electroencephalograms and the recall of dreams. *Journal of Abnormal and Social Psychology, 59,* 295–302.

• **Goodman, Gail S.; Qin, Jianjian; Bottoms, Bette L.; & Shaver, Phillip R.** (1995). Characteristics and sources of allegations of ritualistic child abuse. Final report to the National Center on Child Abuse and Neglect, Washington, DC. [Executive summary and complete report available from NCCAN, 1-800-394-3366.]

• **Gopnik, Myrna** (1990). Feature-blind grammar and dysphasia. *Nature, 344*(6268), 715.

• **Gopnik, Myrna** (1991). Familial aggregation of a developmental language disorder. *Cognition, 39,* 1–50.

• **Gorassini, Donald R., & Spanos, Nicholas P.** (1986). A social cognitive skills training program for the successful modification of hypnotic susceptibility. *Journal of Personality and Social Psychology, 50,* 1004–1012.

Gore, Susan, & Mangione, Thomas W. (1983). Social roles, sex roles and psychological distress. *Journal of Health and Social Behavior, 24,* 300–312.

Goren, C. C.; Sarty, J.; & Wu, P. Y. (1975). Visual following and pattern discrimination of face-like stimuli by newborn infants. *Pediatrics, 56,* 544–549.

Gotlib, Ian H., & Hooley, J. M. (1988). Depression and marital functioning. In S. Duck (ed.), *Handbook of personal relationships: Theory, research and interventions.* Chichester, England: Wiley.

Gottesman, Irving I. (1991). *Schizophrenia genesis: The origins of madness.* New York: Freeman.

• **Gottesman, Irving I.** (1994). Perils and pleasures of genetic psychopathology. Distinguished Scientist Award address presented at the annual meeting of the American Psychological Association, Los Angeles.

• **Gottman, John** (1994, May/June). Why marriages fail. *The Family Therapy Networker,* 40–48.

Gottman, John M., & Katz, Lynn F. (1989). Effects of marital discord on young children's peer interaction and health. *Developmental Psychology, 25,* 373–381.

• **Gottman, John M.; Katz, Lynn F.; & Hooven, Carole** (in press). Parental meta-emotion structure predicts family and child outcomes. *Cognition and Emotion.*

Gottman, John M., & Krokoff, Lowell J. (1989). Marital interaction and satisfaction: A longitudinal view. *Journal of Consulting and Clinical Psychology, 57,* 47–52.

Gottman, John M., & Levenson, Robert W. (1986). Assessing the role of emotion in marriage. *Behavioral Assessment, 8,* 31–48.

• **Gould, Stephen Jay** (1981). *The mismeasure of man.* New York: Norton.

• **Gould, Stephen Jay** (1987). *An urchin in the storm.* New York: Norton.

• **Gould, Stephen Jay** (1990, April). The war on (some) drugs. *Harper's,* 24.

• **Gould, Stephen Jay** (1994, November 28). Curveball. [Review of *The Bell Curve,* by Richard J. Herrnstein and Charles Murray.] *The New Yorker,* 139–149.

• **Gould, Stephen Jay, & Eldredge, Niles** (1977). Punctuated equilibria: The tempo and mode of evolution reconsidered. *Paleobiology, 3,* 115–151.

Graf, Peter, & Schacter, Daniel A. (1985). Implicit and explicit memory for new associations in normal and amnesic subjects. *Journal of Experimental Psychology: Learning, Memory, and Cognition, 11,* 501–518.

Graham, Jill W. (1986). Principled organizational dissent: A theoretical essay. *Research in Organizational Behavior, 8,* 1–52.

• **Green, Gina** (1994). Facilitated communication: Mental miracle or sleight of hand? *Skeptic, 2*(3), 68–76.

• **Greenberg, Roger P.; Bornstein, Robert F.; Greenberg, Michael D.; & Fisher, Seymour** (1992). A meta-analysis of antidepressant outcome under "blinder" conditions. *Journal of Consulting and Clinical Psychology, 60,* 664–669.

Greene, Robert L. (1986). Sources of recency effects in free recall. *Psychological Bulletin, 99,* 221–228.

Greenfield, Patricia (1976). Cross-cultural research and Piagetian theory: Paradox and progress. In K. F. Riegel & J. A. Meacham (eds .), *The developing individual in a changing world, Vol.1: Historical and cultural issues.* The Hague, Netherlands: Mouton.

Greenfield, Patricia, & Beagles-Roos, Jessica (1988). Radio vs. television: Their cognitive impact on children of different socioeconomic and ethnic groups. *Journal of Communication, 38,* 71–92.

Greenough, William T. (1984). Structural correlates of information storage in the mammalian brain: A review and hypothesis. *Trends in Neurosciences, 7,* 229–233.

Greenough, William T. (1991). The animal rights assertions: A researcher's perspective. *Psychological Science Agenda* (American Psychological Association), *4*(3), 10–12.

Greenough, William T., & Anderson, Brenda J. (1991). Cerebellar synaptic plasticity: Relation to learning vs. neural activity. *Annals of the New York Academy of Sciences, 627,* 231–247.

Greenough, William T., & Black, James E. (1992). Induction of brain structure by experience: Substrates for cognitive development. In M. Gunnar & C. A. Nelson (eds.), *Behavioral developmental neuroscience, Vol. 24, Minnesota Symposia on Child Psychology.* Hillsdale, NJ: Erlbaum.

Greenwald, Anthony G. (1980). The totalitarian ego: Fabrication and revision of personal history. *American Psychologist, 35,* 603–618.

Greenwald, Anthony G. (1992). New Look 3: Unconscious cognition reclaimed. *American Psychologist, 47,* 766–779.

Greenwald, Anthony G.; Spangenberg, Eric R.; Pratkanis, Anthony R.; & Eskenazi, Jay (1991). Double-blind tests of subliminal self-help audiotapes. *Psychological Science, 2,* 119–122.

• **Greenwald, Howard P.** (1992). *Who survives cancer?* Berkeley: University of California Press.

• **Gregor, Anne** (1993, June 1). Getting to root of cultural gaffes. *Los Angeles Times,* D3, D10.

Gregory, Richard L. (1963). Distortion of visual space as inappropriate constancy scaling. *Nature, 199,* 678–679.

Gregory, Richard L., & Wallace, Jean G. (1963). Recovery from early blindness: A case study. *Monograph Supplement 2, Quarterly Journal of Experimental Psychology, No. 3.* (Reprinted in R. L. Gregory, *Concepts and mechanisms of perception.* New York: Scribners.)

Greven, Philip (1991). *Spare the child: The religious roots of punishment and the psychological impact of physical abuse.* New York: Knopf.

Grier, Kenneth (1982). A study of job stress in police officers and high school teachers. Unpublished doctoral dissertation, University of South Florida, Tampa.

• **Griffin, Donald R.** (1984). *Animal thinking.* Cambridge: Harvard University Press.

• **Griffin, Donald R.** (1992). *Animal minds.* Chicago: University of Chicago Press.

Griffith, James E., & Villavicencio, Sandra (1985). Relationships among acculturation, sociodemographic characteristics and social supports in Mexican American adults. *Hispanic Journal of Behavioral Sciences, 7,* 75–92.

• **Grinspoon, Lester, & Bakalar, James B.** (1993). *Marihuana, the forbidden medicine.* New Haven, CT: Yale University Press.

Groebel, Jo, & Hinde, Robert (eds.) (1989). The Seville statement on violence. *Aggression and war: Their biological and social bases.* Cambridge, England: Cambridge University Press.

• **Grossarth-Maticek, Ronald; Eysenck, Hans J.; Gallasch, G.; Vetter, H.; & Frentzel-Beyme, R.** (1991). Changes in degree of sclerosis as a function of prophylactic treatment in cancer-prone and CHD-prone probands. *Behavior Research and Therapy, 29,* 343–351.

• **Grossman, Michele, & Wood, Wendy** (1993). Sex differences in intensity of emotional experience: A social role interpretation. *Journal of Personality and Social Psychology, 65,* 1010–1022.

• **Gruber, Barry L.; Hersh, Stephen P.; Hall, Nicholas R.; Waletzky, Lucy R.; et al.** (1993). Immunological responses of breast cancer patients to behavioral interventions. *Biofeedback and Self-Regulation, 18,* 1–22.

• **Grusec, Joan E., & Goodnow, Jacqueline J.** (1994). Impact of parental discipline methods on child's internalization of values: A reconceptualization of current points of view. *Developmental Psychology, 30,* 4–19.

• **Grusec, Joan E.; Saas-Kortsaak, P.; & Simutis, Z. M.** (1978). The role of example and moral exhortation in the training of altruism. *Child Development, 49,* 920–923.

Guba, Egon G. (1990). The alternative paradigm dialog. In E. G. Guba (ed.), *The paradigm dialog.* Newbury Park, CA: Sage.

• **Gudykunst, W. B., & Ting-Toomey, S.** (1988). *Culture and interpersonal communication.* Newbury Park, CA: Sage.

Guilford, J. P. (1950). Creativity. *American Psychologist, 5,* 444–454.

• **Gusella, J. F.; MacDonald, M. E.; Ambrose, C. M.; & Duyao, M. P.** (1993). Molecular genetics of Huntington's disease. *Archives of Neurology, 50,* 1157–1163.

• **Gutheil, Thomas G.** (1993). The psychology of pharmacology. In M. Schacter (ed.), *Psychotherapy and medication.* Worthvale, NJ: Jason Aronson.

• **Gwiazda, Jane; Thorn, Frank; Bauer, Joseph; & Held, Richard** (1993). Emmetropization and the progression of manifest refraction in children followed from infancy to puberty. *Clinical Vision Sciences, 8,* 337–344.

Haber, Ralph N. (1970, May). How we remember what we see. *Scientific American, 222,* 104–112.

• **Hackett, Gail; Betz, Nancy E.; Casas, J. Manuel; & Rocha-Singh, Indra A.** (1992). Gender, ethnicity, and social cognitive factors predicting the academic achievement of students in engineering. *Journal of Counseling Psychology, 39,* 527–538.

Haier, Richard J.; Siegel, Benjamin V., Jr.; MacLachlan, Andrew; Soderling, Eric; et al. (1992). Regional glucose metabolic changes after learning a complex visuospatial/motor task: A positron emission tomographic study. *Brain Research, 570,* 134–143.

Haier, Richard J.; Siegel, Benjamin V., Jr.; Nuechterlein, Keith H.; Hazlett, Erin; et al. (1988). Cortical glucose metabolic rate correlates of abstract reasoning and attention studied with positron emission tomography. *Intelligence, 12,* 199–217.

Haley, Jay (1984). *Ordeal therapy.* San Francisco: Jossey-Bass.

• **Hall, Edward T.** (1959). *The silent language.* Garden City, NY: Doubleday.

Hall, Edward T. (1976). *Beyond culture.* New York: Anchor Press/Doubleday.

Hall, Edward T. (1983). *The dance of life: The other dimension of time.* Garden City, NY: Anchor Press/Doubleday.

• **Hall, Edward T., & Hall, Mildred R.** (1987). *Hidden differences: Doing business with the Japanese.* Garden City, NY: Anchor Press/Doubleday.

Hall, Edward T., & Hall, Mildred R. (1990). *Understanding cultural differences.* Yarmouth, ME: Intercultural Press.

Hall, G. Stanley (1899). A study of anger. *American Journal of Psychology, 10,* 516–591.

Hall, Judith A. (1987). On explaining gender differences: The case of nonverbal communication. In P. Shaver & C. Hendrick (eds.), *Sex and gender: Review of Personality and Social Psychology* (Vol. 7). Beverly Hills, CA: Sage.

Hallin, Daniel (1991). *Sound bite news: Television coverage of elections, 1968–1988.* Occasional paper, Woodrow Wilson International Center for Scholars, Media Studies Project, Washington, DC.

• **Halpern, Diane** (1989). The disappearance of cognitive gender differences: What you see depends on where you look. *American Psychologist, 44,* 1156–1157.

• **Halpern, Diane** (1995). *Thought and knowledge: An introduction to critical thinking* (3rd ed.). Hillsdale, NJ: Erlbaum..

Hamilton, David L., & Sherman, Steven J. (1989). Illusory correlations: Implications for stereotype theory and research. In D. Bar-Tal, C. F. Graumann, A. W. Kruglanski, & W. Stroebe (eds.), *Stereotypes and prejudice: Changing conceptions.* New York: Springer-Verlag.

• **Hamilton, Sandra, & Fagot, Beverly** (1988). Chronic stress and coping styles: A comparison of male and female undergraduates. *Journal of Personality and Social Psychology, 55,* 819–823.

Haney, Craig; Banks, Curtis; & Zimbardo, Philip (1973). Interpersonal dynamics in a simulated prison. *International Journal of Criminology and Penology, 1,* 69–97.

• **Harackiewicz, Judith M., & Elliot, Andrew J.** (1993). Achievement goals and intrinsic motivation. *Journal of Personality and Social Psychology, 65,* 904–915.

Harding, Courtenay; Brooks, George W.; Ashikaga, Takamaru; Strauss, John S.; & Breier, Alan (1987). The Vermont longitudinal study of persons with severe mental illness. I. Methodology, study sample, and overall current status. II. Long-term outcome for DSM-III schizophrenia. *American Journal of Psychiatry, 144,* 718–735.

Harding, Courtenay M.; Zubin, Joseph; & Strauss, John S. (1987). Chronicity in schizophrenia: Fact, partial fact, or artifact? *Hospital and Community Psychiatry, 38,* 477–486.

• **Harding, Courtenay M.; Zubin, Joseph; & Strauss, John S.** (1992). Chronicity in schizophrenia: Revisited. *British Journal of Psychiatry, 161* (Suppl. 18), 27–37.

• **Hare, Robert D.** (1993). *Without conscience: The disturbing world of the psychopaths among us.* New York: Pocket Books.

Hare, Robert D.; McPherson, Leslie M.; & Forth, Adelle E. (1988). Male psychopaths and their criminal careers. *Journal of Consulting and Clinical Psychology, 56,* 710–714.

• **Hare-Mustin, Rachel T.** (1991). Sex, lies, and headaches: The problem is power. In T. J. Goodrich (ed.), *Women and power: Perspectives for therapy.* New York: Norton.

Hare-Mustin, Rachel T., & Maracek, Jeanne (1990). Gender and the meaning of difference: Postmodernism and psychology. In R. Hare-Mustin & J. Maracek (eds.), *Psychology and the construction of gender.* New Haven, CT: Yale University Press.

Haritos-Fatouros, Mika (1988). The official torturer: A learning model for obedience to the authority of violence. *Journal of Applied Social Psychology, 18,* 1107–1120.

Harkins, Stephen G., & Petty, Richard E. (1983). Social context effects in persuasion. In P. Paulus (ed.), *Basic group processes.* New York: Springer-Verlag.

Harkins, Stephen G., & Szymanski, Kate (1989). Social loafing and group evaluation. *Journal of Personality and Social Psychology, 56,* 934–941.

Harlow, Harry F. (1958). The nature of love. *American Psychologist, 13,* 673–685.

Harlow, Harry F., & Harlow, Margaret K. (1966). Learning to love. *American Scientist, 54,* 244–272.

Harlow, Harry F.; Harlow, Margaret K.; & Meyer, D. R. (1950). Learning motivated by a manipulation drive. *Journal of Experimental Psychology, 40,* 228–234.

Harris, Ben (1979). Whatever happened to little Albert? *American Psychologist, 34,* 151–160

• **Harris, Marvin** (1974). *Cows, pigs, wars, and witches: The riddles of culture.* New York: Simon & Schuster.

Harris, Marvin (1985). *Good to eat: Riddles of food and culture.* New York: Simon & Schuster.

Hart, John, Jr.; Berndt, Rita S.; & Caramazza, Alfonso (1985, August 1). Category-specific naming deficit following cerebral infarction. *Nature, 316,* 339–340.

• **Harter, Susan, & Jackson, Bradley K.** (1992). Trait vs. nontrait conceptualizations of intrinsic/extrinsic motivational orientation. *Motivation and Emotion, 16,* 209–230.

Hartmann, Ernest (1991). *Boundaries in the mind: A new psychology of personality differences.* New York: Basic Books.

• **Harvey, Mary R., & Herman, Judith L.** (1994). Amnesia, partial amnesia and delayed recall among adult survivors of childhood trauma. *Consciousness and Cognition* (Special issue: The recovered memory/false memory debate), *3,* 295–306.

Hasher, Lynn, & Zacks, Rose T. (1984). Automatic processing of fundamental information: The case of frequency of occurrence. *American Psychologist, 39,* 1372–1388.

Hastorf, Albert H., & Cantril, Hadley (1954). They saw a game: A case study. *Journal of Abnormal and Social Psychology, 49,* 129–134.

Hatfield, Agnes B., & Lefley, Harriet P. (eds.) (1987). *Families of the mentally ill: Coping and adaptation.* New York: Guilford Press.

Hatfield, Elaine (1988). Passionate and companionate love. In R. J. Sternberg & M. L. Barnes (eds.), *The psychology of love.* New Haven, CT: Yale University Press.

Hatfield, Elaine; Cacioppo, John T.; & Rapson, Richard (1992). The logic of emotion: Emotional contagion. In M. S. Clark (ed.), *Review of Personality, and Social Psychology,* Vol. 12. Newbury Park, CA: Sage.

• **Hatfield, Elaine, & Rapson, Richard L.** (1993). *Love, sex, and intimacy.* New York: HarperCollins.

Hatfield, Elaine, & Sprecher, Susan (1986). Measuring passionate love in intimate relationships. *Journal of Adolescence, 9,* 383–410.

Hawkins, Scott A., & Hastie, Reid (1990). Hindsight: Biased judgments of past events after the outcomes are known. *Psychological Bulletin, 107,* 311–327.

Haynes, Suzanne, & Feinleib, Manning (1980). Women, work, and coronary heart disease: Prospective findings from the Framingham heart study. *American Journal of Public Health, 70,* 133–141.

Hazan, Cindy, & Shaver, Phillip (1987). Romantic love conceptualized as an attachment process. *Journal of Personality and Social Psychology, 52,* 511–524.

Heath, Shirley B. (1983). *Ways with words: Language, life, and work in communities and classrooms.* New York: Cambridge University Press.

• **Heinrichs, R. Walter** (1993). Schizophrenia and the brain: Conditions for a neuropsychology of madness. *American Psychologist, 48,* 221–233.

Helgeson, Vicki S., & Sharpsteen, Don J. (1987). Perceptions of danger in achievement and affiliation situations: An extension of the Pollak and Gilligan versus Benton et al. debate. *Journal of Personality and Social Psychology, 53,* 727–733.

• **Helmes, Edward, & Reddon, John R.** (1993). A perspective on developments in assessing psychopathology: A critical review of the MMPI and MMPI-2. *Psychological Bulletin, 113,* 453–471.

• **Helms, Janet E.** (1990). *Black and White racial identity theory, research, and practice.* Westport, CT: Greenwood Press.

Hendrick, Clyde, & Hendrick, Susan S. (1986). A theory and method of love. *Journal of Personality and Social Psychology, 50,* 392–402.

• **Hendrick, Susan S., & Hendrick, Clyde** (1992). *Romantic love.* Newbury Park, CA: Sage.

Hendrick, Susan S.; Hendrick, Clyde; & Adler, Nancy L. (1988). Romantic relationships: Love, satisfaction, and staying together. *Journal of Personality and Social Psychology, 54,* 980–988.

Hendrix, William H.; Steel, Robert P.; Leap, Terry L.; & Sum-

mers, Timothy P. (1991). Development of a stress-related health promotion model: Antecedents and organizational effectiveness outcomes. Special Issue: Handbook on job stress. *Journal of Social Behavior and Personality, 6,* 141–162.

• Henley, Nancy (1995). Body politics revisited: What do we know today? In P. J. Kalbfleisch & M. J. Cody (eds.), *Gender, power, and communication in human relationships.* Hillsdale, NJ: Erlbaum.

Hepworth, Joseph T., & West, Stephen G. (1988). Lynchings and the economy: A time-series reanalysis of Hovland and Sears (1940). *Journal of Personality and Social Psychology, 55,* 239–247.

• Herbert, Tracy B., & Cohen, Sheldon (1993). Depression and immunity: A meta-analytic review. *Psychological Bulletin, 113,* 472–486.

Herdt, Gilbert (1984). *Ritualized homosexuality in Melanesia.* Berkeley: University of California Press.

Herman, John H. (1992). Transmutative and reproductive properties of dreams: Evidence for cortical modulation of brainstem generators. In J. Antrobus & M. Bertini (eds.), *The neuropsychology of dreaming.* Hillsdale, NJ: Erlbaum.

Herman, Louis M. (1987). Receptive competencies of language-trained animals. In J. S. Rosenblatt, C. Beer, M. C. Busnel, & P. J. B. Slater (eds.), *Advances in the study of behavior, Volume 17.* Petaluma, CA: Academic Press.

• Herman, Louis M.; Kuczaj, Stan A.; & Holder, Mark D. (1993). Responses to anomalous gestural sequences by a language-trained dolphin: Evidence for processing of semantic relations and syntactic information. *Journal of Experimental Psychology: General, 122,* 184–194.

Herman, Louis M.; Morrel-Samuels, Palmer; & Pack, Adam A. (1990). Bottlenosed dolphin and human recognition of veridical and degraded video displays of an artificial gestural language. *Journal of Experimental Psychology: General, 119,* 215–230.

Heron, Broodburn (1957). The pathology of boredom. *Scientific American, 196*(1), 52–56.

• Herrnstein, Richard J., & Murray, Charles (1994). *The bell curve: Intelligence and class structure in American life.* New York: Free Press.

Hetherington, E. Mavis (1989). Coping with family transitions: Winners, losers, and survivors. *Child Development, 60,* 1–14.

Hicks, Robert D. (1991). The police model of Satanism crime. In J. T. Richardson, J. Best, & D. G. Bromley (eds.), *The Satanism scare.* New York: Aldine de Gruyter.

• Higley, J. D.; Hasert, M. L.; Suomi, S. J.; & Linnoila, M. (1991). A nonhuman primate model of alcohol abuse: Effects of early experience, personality, and stress on alcohol consumption. *Proceedings of the National Academy of Science, 88,* 7261–7265.

• Hilgard, Ernest R. (1977). *Divided consciousness: Multiple controls in human thought and action.* New York: Wiley-Interscience.

• Hilgard, Ernest R. (1986). *Divided consciousness: Multiple controls in human thought and action* (2nd ed.). New York: Wiley.

• Hilgard, Ernest R. (1991). Psychology as an integrative science versus a unified one. Invited address, presented at the annual meeting of the American Psychological Association, San Francisco.

Hilgard, Ernest R., & Hilgard, Josephine R. (1975). *Hypnosis in the relief of pain.* Los Altos, CA: William Kaufmann.

Hilgard, Josephine R. (1979). *Personality and hypnosis: A study of imaginative involvement* (2nd ed.). Chicago: University of Chicago Press.

Hill, Harlan F.; Chapman, C. Richard; Kornell, Judy A.; Sullivan, Keith M.; et al. (1990). Self-administration of morphine in bone marrow transplant patients reduces drug requirement. *Pain, 40,* 121–129.

• Hillman, James, & Ventura, Michael (1992). *We've had a hundred years of psychotherapy—and the world's getting worse.* San Francisco: HarperCollins.

Hirsch, Barton (1981). Social networks and the coping process: Creating personal communities. In B. H. Gottlieb (ed.), *Social networks and social support.* Beverly Hills, CA: Sage.

Hirsch, Helmut V. B., & Spinelli, D. N. (1970). Visual experience modifies distribution of horizontally and vertically oriented receptive fields in cats. *Science, 168,* 869–871.

Hirschel, J. David; Hutchinson, Ira W., III; Dean, Charles; et al. (1990). *Charlotte spouse assault replication project: Final report.* Washington, DC: National Institute of Justice.

Hirst, William; Neisser, Ulric; & Spelke, Elizabeth (1978, January). Divided attention. *Human Nature, 1,* 54–61.

Hite, Shere (1987). *Women and love: A cultural revolution in progress.* New York: Knopf.

Hobson, J. Allan (1988). *The dreaming brain.* New York: Basic Books.

Hobson, J. Allan (1990). Activation, input source, and modulation: A neurocognitive model of the state of the brain-mind. In R. R. Bootzin, J. F. Kihlstrom, & D. L. Schacter (eds.), *Sleep and cognition.* Washington, DC: American Psychological Association.

Hobson, J. Allan, & McCarley, Robert W. (1977). The brain as a dream state generator: An activation-synthesis hypothesis of the dream process. *American Journal of Psychiatry, 134,* 1335–1348.

Hochschild, Arlie (1983). *The managed heart.* Berkeley: University of California Press.

Hockett, Charles F. (1960). The origins of speech. *Scientific American, 203,* 89–96.

Hoffman, Martin L. (1977). Empathy, its development and prosocial implications. In C. B. Keasey (ed.), *Nebraska Symposium on Motivation,* Vol. 25. Lincoln: University of Nebraska Press.

Hoffman, Martin L. (1987). The contribution of empathy to justice and moral judgment. In N. Eisenberg & J. Strayer (eds.), *Empathy and its development.* New York: Cambridge University Press.

Hoffman, Martin L. (1989). Empathy, social cognition, and moral action. In W. Kurtines & J. Gewirtz (eds.), *Moral behavior and development: Advances in theory, research, and application,* Vol. 1. Hillsdale, NJ: Erlbaum.

• Hoffman, Martin L. (1994). Discipline and internalization. *Developmental Psychology, 30,* 26–28.

Hoffman, Martin L., & Saltzstein, Herbert (1967). Parent discipline and the child's moral development. *Journal of Personality and Social Psychology, 5,* 45–57.

• Hofstede, Geert, & Bond, Michael H. (1988). The Confucius connection: From cultural roots to economic growth. *Organizational Dynamics,* 5–21.

Hogg, Michael A., & Abrams, Dominic (1988). *Social identifications: A social psychology of intergroup relations and group processes.* New York: Routledge.

Holmes, David (1984). Meditation and somatic arousal reduction: A review of the experimental evidence. *American Psychologist, 39,* 1–10.

Holmes, David S. (1994). *Abnormal psychology* (2nd ed.). New York: HarperCollins.

• Holt, Jim (1994, October 19). Anti-social science? *New York Times,* op-ed page.

Holzman, Philip S., & Matthysse, Steven (1990). The genetics of schizophrenia: A review. *Psychological Science, 1,* 279–286.

• Honts, Charles R. (1994). Psychophysiological detection of deception. *Current Directions in Psychological Science, 3,* 77–82.

• Hoptman, Matthew J., & Davidson, Richard J. (1994). How and why do the two cerebral hemispheres interact? *Psychological Bulletin, 116,* 195–219.

• Horm, J., & Anderson, K. (1993). Who in America is trying to lose weight? *Annals of Internal Medicine, 119,* 672–676.

• Horn, G., & Hinde, R. A. (eds.) (1970). *Short-term changes in neural activity and behaviour.* New York: Cambridge University Press.

Horn, John L., & Donaldson, Gary (1980). Cognitive development in adulthood. In O. G. Brim, Jr. & J. Kagan (eds.), *Constancy and change in human development.* Cambridge: Harvard University Press.

Horne, J. A. (1988). Sleep loss and "divergent" thinking ability. *Sleep, 11,* 528–536.

• Horner, Althea J. (1991). *Psychoanalytic object relations therapy.* New York: Jason Aronson.

• Hornstein, Gail (1992). The return of the repressed: Psychology's problematic relations with psychoanalysis, 1909–1960. *American Psychologist, 47,* 254–263.

Horowitz, Mardi J. (1988). *Introduction to psychodynamics: A new synthesis.* New York: Basic Books.

House, James S.; Landis, Karl R.; & Umberson, Debra (1988, July 19). Social relationships and health. *Science, 241,* 540–545.

House, James S.; Robbins, Cynthia; & Metzner, Helen (1982). The association of social relationships and activities with mortality: Prospective evidence from the Tecumseh Community Health Study. *American Journal of Epidemiology, 116,* 123–140.

Houston, John P. (1981). *Fundamentals of learning and memory* (2nd ed.). New York: Academic Press.

Hovland, Carl I., & Sears, Robert R. (1940). Minor studies of aggression: Correlation of lynchings with economic indices. *Journal of Psychology, 9,* 301–310.

Howard, George S. (1991). Culture tales: A narrative approach to thinking, cross-cultural psychology, and psychotherapy. *American Psychologist, 46,* 187–197.

Howard, Kenneth; Kopta, S. Mark; Krause, Merton S.; & Orlinsky, David (1986). The dose-effect relationship in psychotherapy. *American Psychologist, 41,* 159–164.

• Howe, Mark L., & Courage, Mary L. (1993). On resolving the enigma of infantile amnesia. *Psychological Bulletin, 113,* 305–326.

• Howe, Mark L.; Courage, Mary L.; & Peterson, Carole (1994). How can I remember when "I" wasn't there? Long-term retention of traumatic experiences and emergence of the cognitive self. *Consciousness and Cognition* (Special issue: The recovered memory/false memory debate), *3,* 327–355.

• Howell, Debi (1993, August 8). Detecting the dirty lie [Interview with Paul Ekman]. *San Francisco Examiner and Chronicle, This World,* 7.

Howell, William C., & Dipboye, Robert L. (1982). *Essentials of industrial and organizational psychology.* Homewood, IL: Dorsey Press.

Hrdy, Sarah B. (1988). Empathy, polyandry, and the myth of the coy female. In R. Bleier (ed.), *Feminist approaches to science.* New York: Pergamon.

Hubbard, Ruth (1990). *The politics of women's biology.* New Brunswick, NJ: Rutgers University Press.

• Hubbard, Ruth, & Wald, Elijah (1993). *Exploding the gene myth.* Boston: Beacon Press.

Hubel, D. H., & Wiesel, T. N. (1962). Receptive fields, binocular interaction and functional architecture in the cat's visual cortex. *Journal of Physiology* (London), *160,* 106–154.

Hubel, D. H., & Wiesel, T. N. (1968). Receptive fields and functional architecture of monkey striate cortex. *Journal of Physiology* (London), *195,* 215–243.

• Huesmann, L. Rowell (ed.) (1994). *Aggressive behavior: Current perspectives.* New York: Plenum.

Hughes, Judith M. (1989). *Reshaping the psychoanalytic domain: The work of Melanie Klein, W. R. D. Fairbairn, & D. W. Winnicott.* Berkeley: University of California Press.

• Hughes, Robert (1993). *The culture of complaint: The fraying of America.* New York: Oxford University Press.

Huizinga, Johan (1950). *Homo ludens: A study of the play element in culture.* Boston: Beacon Press.

Hull, Clark (1943). *Principles of behavior.* New York: Appleton-Century-Crofts.

Hunt, Morton M. (1959/1967). *The natural history of love.* New York: Minerva Press.

• Hunt, Morton M. (1993). *The story of psychology.* New York: Doubleday.

• Huntington's Disease Collaborative Research Group (1993). A novel gene containing a trinucleotide repeat that is expanded and unstable on Huntington's disease chromosomes. *Cell, 72,* 971–983.

Hupka, Ralph (1981). Cultural determinants of jealousy. *Alternative Lifestyles, 4,* 310–356.

• Hupka, Ralph B. (1991). The motive for the arousal of romantic jealousy: Its cultural origin. In P. Salovey (ed.), *The psychology of jealousy and envy.* New York: Guilford Press.

Hurvich, Leo M., & Jameson, Dorothea (1974). Opponent processes as a model of neural organization. *American Psychologist, 29,* 88–102.

Huston, Ted L.; Ruggiero, Mary; Conner, Ross; & Geis, Gilbert (1981). Bystander intervention into crime: A study based on naturally-occurring episodes. *Social Psychology Quarterly, 44,* 14–23.

Hyde, Janet S. (1981). How large are cognitive gender differences? A meta-analysis using ω^2 and d. *American Psychologist, 36,* 892–901.

Hyde, Janet S. (1984). How large are gender differences in aggression? A developmental meta-analysis. *Developmental Psychology, 20,* 722–736.

Hyde, Janet S.; Fennema, Elizabeth; & Lamon, Susan J. (1990). Gender differences in mathematics performance: A meta-analysis. *Psychological Bulletin, 107,* 139–155.

Hyde, Janet S., & Linn, Marcia C. (1988). Gender differences in verbal ability: A meta-analysis. *Psychological Bulletin, 104,* 53–69.

• Hyman, Irwin A. (1994). Is spanking child abuse? Conceptualiza-

tions, research and policy implications. Paper presented at the annual meeting of the American Psychological Association, Los Angeles.

• Hyman, Ray (1994). Anomaly or artifact? Comments on Bem and Honorton. *Psychological Bulletin, 115,* 25–27.

Infant Health and Development Program (1990). Enhancing the outcomes of low-birth-weight, premature infants: A multisite, randomized trial. *Journal of the American Medical Association, 263,* 3035–3042.

• Inglehart, Ronald (1990). *Culture shift in advanced industrial society.* Princeton, NJ: Princeton University Press.

Inglis, James, & Lawson, J. S. (1981). Sex differences in the effects of unilateral brain damage on intelligence. *Science, 212,* 693–695.

Insko, Chester A.; Smith, Richard; Alicke, Mark; Wade, Joel; & Taylor, Sylvester (1985). Conformity and group size: The concern with being right and the concern with being liked. *Personality and Social Psychology Bulletin, 11,* 41–50.

Irons, Edward D., & Moore, Gilbert W. (1985). *Black managers: The case of the banking industry.* New York: Praeger/Greenwood.

• Irvine, Janice M. (1990). *Disorders of desire: Sex and gender in modern American sexology.* Philadelphia: Temple University Press.

Isen, Alice M.; Daubman, Kimberly A.; & Nowicki, Gary P. (1987). Positive affect facilitates creative problem solving. *Journal of Personality and Social Psychology, 52,* 1122–1131.

• Islam, Mir Rabiul, & Hewstone, Miles (1993). Intergroup attributions and affective consequences in majority and minority groups. *Journal of Personality and Social Psychology, 64,* 936–950.

Izard, Carroll E. (1990). Facial expressions and the regulation of emotions. *Journal of Personality and Social Psychology, 58,* 487–498.

• Izard, Carroll E. (1994a). Four systems for emotion activation: Cognitive and noncognitive processes. *Psychological Review, 100,* 68–90.

• Izard, Carroll E. (1994b). Innate and universal facial expressions: Evidence from developmental and cross-cultural research. *Psychological Bulletin, 115,* 288–299.

• Jacobs, Janis E., & Eccles, Jacquelynne S. (1985). Gender differences in math ability: The impact of media reports on parents. *Educational Researcher, 14,* 20–25.

• Jacobs, Marion K., & Goodman, Gerald (1989). Psychology and self-help groups: Predictions on a partnership. *American Psychologist, 44,* 536–545.

Jacobson, Gerald (1983). *The multiple crises of marital separation and divorce.* New York: Grune & Stratton.

• Jacobson, John W.; Eberlin, Michael; Mulick, James A.; Schwartz, Allen A.; Szempruch, Allen A. (1993). An experimental assessment of facilitated communication. *Mental Retardation, 31,* 49–59.

• Jacobson, Teresa; Edelstein, Wolfgang; & Hofmann, Volker (1994). A longitudinal study of the relation between representations of attachment in childhood and cognitive functioning in childhood and adolescence. *Developmental Psychology, 30,* 112–124.

Jacobvitz, Robin N. S. (1990). Defining and measuring TV addiction. Paper presented at the annual meeting of the American Psychological Association, Boston.

James, William (1902/1936). *The varieties of religious experience.* New York: Modern Library.

Janis, Irving L. (1982). *Groupthink: Psychological studies of policy decisions and fiascoes* (2nd ed.). Boston: Houghton Mifflin.

• Janis, Irving L. (1989). *Crucial decisions: Leadership in policymaking and crisis management.* New York: Free Press.

Janis, Irving L.; Kaye, Donald; & Kirschner, Paul (1965). Facilitating effects of "eating-while-reading" on responsiveness to persuasive communications. *Journal of Personality and Social Psychology, 1,* 181–186.

Janoff-Bulman, Ronnie (1989). The benefits of illusions, the threat of disillusionment, and the limitations of inaccuracy. Special Issue: Self-illusions: When are they adaptive? *Journal of Social and Clinical Psychology, 8,* 158–175.

Jaynes, Julian (1973). Introduction: The study of the history of psychology. In M. Henle, J. Jaynes, & J. J. Sullivan (eds.), *Historical conceptions of psychology.* New York: Springer.

• Jemmott, John B.; Hellman, Caroline; McClelland, David C.; Locke, Steven E.; et al. (1990). Motivational syndromes associated with natural killer cell activity. *Journal of Behavioral Medicine, 13,* 53–73.

Jenkins, John G., & Dallenbach, Karl M. (1924). Oblivescence during sleep and waking. *American Journal of Psychology, 35,* 605–612.

• **Jenkins, Sharon Rae** (1994). Need for power and women's careers over 14 years: Structural power, job satisfaction, and motive change. *Journal of Personality and Social Psychology, 66,* 155–165.

Jensen, Arthur R. (1969). How much can we boost IQ and scholastic achievement? *Harvard Educational Review, 39,* 1–123.

Jensen, Arthur R. (1981). *Straight talk about mental tests.* New York: Free Press.

• **Jensen, J. P.; Bergin, Allen E.; & Greaves, D. W.** (1990). The meaning of eclecticism: New survey and analysis of components. *Professional Psychology: Research and Practice, 21,* 124–130.

Jessel, T. M., & Iversen, L. L. (1979). Opiate analgesics inhibit substance P release from rat trigeminal nucleus. *Nature, 268,* 549–551.

• **Jessor, Richard** (1993). Successful adolescent development among youth in high-risk settings. *American Psychologist, 48,* 117–126.

John, E. Roy (1976, May). How the brain works' a new theory. *Psychology Today,* 48–52.

John, E. R.; Tang, Y.; Brill, A. B.; Young, R.; & Ono, K. (1986). Double-labeled metabolic maps of memory. *Science, 233,* 1167–1175.

Johnson, Catherine (1988). *When to say goodbye to your therapist.* New York: Simon & Schuster.

• **Johnson, John A., & Ostendorf, Fritz** (1993). Clarification of the five-factor model with the Abridged Big Five dimensional circumplex. *Journal of Personality and Social Psychology, 65,* 563–576.

Johnson, Robert, & Downing, Leslie (1979). Deindividuation and valence of cues: Effects of prosocial and antisocial behavior. *Journal of Personality and Social Psychology, 37,* 1532–1538.

• **Johnson-Laird, Philip N.** (1988). *The computer and the mind: An introduction to cognitive science.* Cambridge: Harvard University Press.

• **Johnson-Laird, Philip N., & Oatley, Keith** (1992). Basic emotions, rationality, and folk theory. *Cognition and Emotion, 6,* 201–223.

• **Joiner, Thomas E.** (1994). Contagious depression: Existence, specificity to depressed symptoms, and the role of reassurance seeking. *Journal of Personality and Social Psychology, 67,* 287–296.

Jones, James M. (1991). Psychological models of race: What have they been and what should they be? In J. Goodchilds (ed.), *Psychological perspectives on human diversity in America.* Washington, DC: American Psychological Association.

Jones, Lyle V. (1984). White-black achievement differences: The narrowing gap. *American Psychologist, 39,* 1207–1213.

Jones, Mary Cover (1924). A laboratory study of fear: The case of Peter. *Pedagogical Seminary, 31,* 308–315.

Jones, Russell A. (1977). *Self-fulfilling prophecies.* Hillsdale, NJ: Erlbaum.

• **Jones, Steve** (1994). *The language of genes.* New York: Anchor/Doubleday.

Jung, Carl (1967). *Collected works.* Princeton, NJ: Princeton University Press.

• **Jusczyk, Peter W.** (1993). From general to language-specific capacities: The WRAPSA model of how speech perception develops. Special Issue: Phonetic development. *Journal of Phonetics, 21,* 3–28.

• **Jusczyk, Peter W.; Friederici, Angela D.; Wessels, Jeanine M.; Svenkerud, Vigdis Y.; et al.** (1993). Infants' sensitivity to the sound patterns of native language words. *Journal of Memory and Language, 32,* 402–420.

Kagan, Jerome (1984). *The nature of the child.* New York: Basic Books.

Kagan, Jerome (1989). *Unstable ideas: Temperament, cognition, and self.* Cambridge: Harvard University Press.

• **Kagan, Jerome** (1993). The meanings of morality. *Psychological Science, 4,* 353, 357–360.

• **Kagan, Jerome** (1994). *Galen's prophecy: Temperament in human nature.* New York: Basic Books.

Kagan, Jerome; Kearsley, Richard B.; & Zelazo, Philip R. (1978). *Infancy: Its place in human development.* Cambridge, MA: Harvard University Press.

Kagan, Jerome, & Lamb, Sharon (eds.) (1987). *The emergence of morality in young children.* Chicago: University of Chicago Press.

Kagan, Jerome, & Snidman, Nancy (1991). Infant predictors of inhibited and uninhibited profiles. *Psychological Science, 2,* 40–44.

Kahneman, Daniel, & Treisman, Anne (1984). Changing views of attention and automaticity. In R. Parasuraman, D. R. Davies, & J. Beatty (eds.), *Varieties of attention.* New York: Academic Press.

Kalmijn, Ad. J. (1982). Electric and magnetic field detection in elasmobranch fishes. *Science, 218,* 916–918.

• **Kameda, Tatsuya, & Sugimori, Shinkichi** (1993). Psychological entrapment in group decision making: An assigned decision rule and a groupthink phenomenon. *Journal of Personality and Social Psychology, 65,* 282–292.

Kandel, Eric R. (1981). Visual system III: Physiology of the central visual pathways. In E. R. Kandel & J. H. Schwartz (eds.), *Principles of neural science.* New York: Elsevier-North Holland.

Kandel, Eric R., & Schwartz, James H. (1982). Molecular biology of learning: Modulation of transmitter release. *Science, 218,* 433–443.

Kane, John M. (1987). Treatment of schizophrenia. *Schizophrenia Bulletin, 13,* 133–156.

Kanin, Eugene J. (1985). Date rapists: Differential sexual socialization and relative deprivation. *Archives of Sexual Behavior, 14,* 219–231.

Kanter, Rosabeth (1977/1993). *Men and women of the corporation.* New York: Basic Books.

Kaplan, Abraham (1967). A philosophical discussion of normality. *Archives of General Psychiatry, 17,* 325–330.

Kaplan, Martin F., & Miller, Charles E. (1983). Group discussion and judgment. In P. Paulus (ed.), *Basic group processes.* New York: Springer-Verlag.

• **Kaplan, Meg S.; Morales, Miguel; & Becker, Judith V.** (1993). The impact of verbal satiation of adolescent sex offenders: A preliminary report. *Journal of Child Sexual Abuse, 2,* 81–88.

• **Kaplan, Stephen L.; Randolph, Stephen W.; & Lemli, James M.** (1991). Treatment outcomes in the reduction of fear: A meta-analysis. Paper presented at the annual meeting of the American Psychological Association, San Francisco.

Karasek, Robert, & Theorell, Tores (1990). *Healthy work: Stress, productivity, and the reconstruction of working life.* New York: Basic Books.

• **Karau, Steven J., & Williams, Kipling D.** (1993). Social loafing: A meta-analytic review and theoretical integration. *Journal of Personality and Social Psychology, 65,* 681–706.

• **Karney, Benjamin R.; Bradbury, Thomas N.; Fincham, Frank D.; & Sullivan, Kieran T.** (1994). The role of negative affectivity in the association between attributions and marital satisfaction. *Journal of Personality and Social Psychology, 66,* 413–424.

• **Karni, Avi; Tanne, David; Rubenstein, Barton S.; Askenasy, Jean J. M.; & Sagi, Dov** (1994). Dependence on REM sleep of overnight improvement of a perceptual skill. *Science, 265,* 679–682.

• **Karon, Bertram P.** (1989). Psychotherapy vs. medication for schizophrenia: Empirical considerations. In S. Fisher & R. P. Greenberg (eds.), *The limits of biological treatments for psychological distress: Comparisons with psychotherapy and placebo.* Hillsdale, NJ: Erlbaum.

• **Karon, Bertram P.** (1994). Psychotherapy: The appropriate treatment of schizophrenia. Paper presented at the annual meeting of the American Psychological Association, Los Angeles.

• **Kasser, Tim, & Ryan, Richard M.** (1993). A dark side of the American dream: Correlates of financial success as a central life aspiration. *Journal of Personality and Social Psychology, 65,* 410–422.

Katz, Irwin, & Hass, R. Glen (1988). Racial ambivalence and American value conflict: Correlational and priming studies of dual cognitive structures. *Journal of Personality and Social Psychology, 55,* 893–905.

Katz, Joel, & Melzack, Ronald (1990). Pain "memories" in phantom limbs: Review and clinical observations. *Pain, 43,* 319–336.

• **Katz, Jonathan Ned** (1995). *The invention of heterosexuality.* New York: Dutton.

• **Katz, Lilian G.** (1993, Summer). All about me. *American Educator, 17*(2), 18–23.

Katz, Lori, & Epstein, Seymour (1991). Constructive thinking and coping with laboratory-induced stress. *Journal of Personality and Social Psychology, 61,* 789–800.

• **Katz, Phyllis A., & Ksansnak, Keith R.** (1994). Developmental aspects of gender role flexibility and traditionality in middle childhood and adolescence. *Developmental Psychology, 30,* 272–282.

• **Katz, Stuart; Blackburn, A. Boyd; & Lautenschlager, Gary J.** (1991). Answering reading comprehension items without passages on the SAT when items are quasi-randomized. *Educational and Psychological Measurement, 51,* 747–754.

• **Katz, Stuart, & Lautenschlager, Gary J.** (1994). Answering reading comprehension items without passages on the SAT-I, the ACT, and the GRE. *Educational Assessment, 2,* 295–308.

Kaufman, Joan, & Zigler, Edward (1987). Do abused children become abusive parents? *American Journal of Orthopsychiatry, 57,* 186–192.

Kaye, Kenneth (1977). Toward the origin of dialogue. In H. R. Schaffer (ed.), *Studies in mother-infant interaction.* New York: Academic Press.

Keane, M. M.; Gabrieli, J. D. E.; & Corkin, S. (1987). Multiple relations between fact-learning and priming in global amnesia. *Society for Neuroscience Abstracts, 13,* 1454.

• **Keating, Caroline F.** (1994). World without words: Messages from face and body. In W. J. Lonner & R. Malpass (eds.), *Psychology and culture.* Needham Heights, MA: Allyn & Bacon.

Keefe, Francis J., & Gil, Karen M. (1986). Behavioral concepts in the analysis of chronic pain syndromes. *Journal of Consulting and Clinical Psychology, 54,* 776–783.

Keesey, Richard E. (1980). A set-point analysis of the regulation of body weight. In A. Stunkard (ed.), *Obesity.* Philadelphia: Saunders.

Keirstead, Susan A.; Rasminsky, Michael; Fukuda, Y.; et al. (1989). Electrophysiologic responses in hamster superior colliculus evoked by regenerating retinal axons. *Science, 246,* 255–257.

• **Kelly, Anita E., & Kahn, Jeffrey H.** (1994). Effects of suppression of personal intrusive thoughts. *Journal of Personality and Social Psychology, 66,* 998–1006.

Kelly, Dennis D. (1981a). Disorders of sleep and consciousness. In E. Kandel & J. Schwartz (eds.), *Principles of neural science.* New York: Elsevier-North Holland.

Kelly, Dennis D. (1981b). Physiology of sleep and dreaming. In E. Kandel & J. Schwartz (eds.), *Principles of neural science.* New York: Elsevier-North Holland.

Kelman, Herbert C., & Hamilton, V. Lee (1989). *Crimes of obedience: Toward a social psychology of authority and responsibility.* New Haven, CT: Yale University Press.

Kelsoe, John R.; Ginns, Edward I.; Egeland, Janice A.; Gerhard, Daniela S.; et al. (1989). Re-evaluation of the linkage relationship between chromosome 11p loci and the gene for bipolar affective disorder in the Old Order Amish. *Nature, 342,* 238–243.

• **Kendall-Tackett, Kathleen A.; Williams, Linda Meyer; & Finkelhor, David** (1993). Impact of sexual abuse on children: A review and synthesis of recent empirical studies. *Psychological Bulletin, 113,* 164–180.

• **Kendler, K. S.; Heath, A. C.; Neale, M. C.; Kessler, R. C.; & Eaves, L. J.** (1992, October 14). A population-based twin study of alcoholism in women. *Journal of the American Medical Association, 268,* 1877–1882.

• **Keneally, Thomas** (1982/1993). *Schindler's list.* New York: Simon & Schuster.

Kennedy, James; Giuffra, Luis; Moises, Hans; Cavalli-Sforza, L. L.; et al. (1988, November 10). Evidence against linkage of schizophrenia to markers on chromosome 5 in a northern Swedish pedigree. *Nature, 336*(6195), 167–169.

Kenny, Maureen W. (1989). The assessment of parental attachment among college seniors. Paper presented at the annual meeting of the American Psychological Association, New Orleans.

• **Kenrick, Douglas T., & Trost, Melanie R.** (1993). The evolutionary perspective. In A. E. Beall & R. J. Sternberg (eds.), *The psychology of gender.* New York: Guilford Press.

Kephart, William M. (1967). Some correlates of romantic love. *Journal of Marriage and the Family, 29,* 470–474.

Kerr, Michael E., & Bowen, Murray (1988). *Family evaluation: An approach based on Bowen theory.* New York: Norton.

Kesner, Raymond P.; Measom, Michael O.; Forsman, Shawn L.; & Holbrook, Terry H. (1984). Serial-position curves in rats: Order memory for episodic spatial events. *Animal Learning and Behavior, 12,* 378–382.

• **Kessler, Ronald C.; McGonagle, Katherine A.; Zhao, Shanyang; Nelson, Christopher B.; et al.** (1994). Lifetime and 12-month prevalence of DSM-III-R psychiatric disorders in the United States: Results from the National Comorbidity Study. *Archives of General Psychiatry, 51,* 8–19.

Kiecolt-Glaser, Janice; Garner, Warren; Speicher, Carl; Penn, Gerald; Holliday, Jane; & Glaser, Ronald (1985a). Psychosocial modi-

fiers of immunocompetence in medical students. *Psychosomatic Medicine, 46,* 7–14.

Kiecolt-Glaser, Janice; Glaser, Ronald; Williger, D.; Stout, J. C; et al. (1985b). Psychosocial enhancement of immunocompetence in a geriatric population. *Health Psychology, 4,* 25–41.

Kiecolt-Glaser, Janice; Fisher, L. D.; Ogrocki, P.; Stout, J. C.; et al. (1987a). Marital quality, marital disruption, and immune function. *Psychosomatic Medicine, 49,* 13–34.

Kiecolt-Glaser, Janice; Glaser, Ronald; Shuttleworth, Edwin; Dyer, Carol; et al. (1987b). Chronic stress and immunity in family caregivers of Alzheimer's disease victims. *Psychosomatic Medicine, 49,* 523–535.

Kiecolt-Glaser, Janice, & Glaser, Ronald (1989). Behavioral influences on immune function: Evidence for the interplay between stress and health. In T. Field, P. McCabe, & N. Schneiderman (eds.), *Stress and coping,* Vol. 2. Hillsdale, NJ: Erlbaum.

• **Kiecolt-Glaser, Janice; Malarkey, William B.; Chee, MaryAnn; Newton, Tamara; et al.** (1993). Negative behavior during marital conflict is associated with immunological down-regulation. *Psychosomatic Medicine, 55,* 395–409.

Kiesler, Charles A., & Simpkins, Celeste (1991). The de facto national system of psychiatric inpatient care. *American Psychologist, 46,* 579–584.

Kihlstrom, John F., & Harackiewicz, Judith M. (1982). The earliest recollection: A new survey. *Journal of Personality, 50,* 134–148.

• **Kihlstrom, John F.; Barnhardt, Terrence M.; & Tataryn, Douglas J.** (1992). The psychological unconscious: Found, lost, and regained. *American Psychologist, 47,* 788–791.

Kihlstrom, John F.; Schacter, Daniel L.; Cork, Randall C.; Hurt, Catherine A.; and Behr, Steven E. (1990). Implicit and explicit memory following surgical anesthesia. *Psychological Science, 1,* 303–306.

Kimble, Gregory A. (1990). Mother Nature's bag of tricks is small. *Psychological Science, 1,* 36–41.

• **Kimble, Gregory A.** (1993). A modest proposal for a minor revolution in the language of psychology. *Psychological Science, 4,* 253–255.

King, Pamela (1989, October). The chemistry of doubt. *Psychology Today, 58,* 60.

• **King, Patricia M., & Kitchener, Karen S.** (1994). *Developing reflective judgment: Understanding and promoting intellectual growth and critical thinking in adolescents and adults.* San Francisco: Jossey-Bass.

Kinsbourne, Marcel (1982). Hemispheric specialization and the growth of human understanding. *American Psychologist, 37,* 411–420.

Kinsey, Alfred C.; Pomeroy, Wardell B.; & Martin, Clyde E. (1948). *Sexual behavior in the human male.* Philadelphia: Saunders.

Kinsey, Alfred C.; Pomeroy, Wardell B.; Martin, Clyde E.; & Gebhard, Paul H. (1953). *Sexual behavior in the human female.* Philadelphia: Saunders.

• **Kirk, Stuart A., & Kutchins, Herb** (1992). *The selling of DSM: The rhetoric of science in psychiatry.* Hawthorne, NY: Aldine de Gruyter.

• **Kirkpatrick, Lee A., & Davis, Keith A.** (1994). Attachment style, gender, and relationship stability: A longitudinal analysis. *Journal of Personality and Social Psychology, 66,* 502–512.

• **Kirsch, Irving; Silva, Christopher E.; Carone, James E.; Johnston, J. Dennis; & Simon, B.** (1989). The surreptitious observation design: An experimental paradigm for distinguishing artifact from essence in hypnosis. *Journal of Abnormal Psychology, 98,* 132–136.

• **Kitayama, Shinobu, & Markus, Hazel R.** (1994). Introduction to cultural psychology and emotion research. In S. Kitayama & H. R. Markus (eds.), *Emotion and culture: Empirical studies of mutual influence.* Washington, DC: American Psychological Association.

• **Kitchener, Karen S., & King, Patricia M.** (1981). Reflective judgment: Concepts of justification and their relationship to age and education. *Journal of Applied Developmental Psychology, 2,* 89–116.

• **Kitchener, Karen S., & King, Patricia M.** (1990). The Reflective Judgment Model: Ten years of research. In M. L. Commons (ed.), *Adult development.* Vol. 2 of *Models and methods in the study of adolescent and adult thought.* Westport, CT: Greenwood Press.

• **Kitchener, Karen S.; Lynch, Cindy L.; Fischer, Kurt W.; & Wood, Phillip K.** (1993). Developmental range of reflective judgment: The effect of contextual support and practice on developmental stage. *Developmental Psychology, 29,* 893–906.

• **Kitzinger, Celia, & Wilkinson, Sue** (1995). Transitions from heterosexuality to lesbianism: The discursive production of lesbian identities. *Developmental Psychology, 31,* 95–104.

Klein, Donald F. (1980). Psychosocial treatment of schizophrenia, or psychosocial help for people with schizophrenia? *Schizophrenia Bulletin, 6,* 122–130.

Klein, Raymond, & Armitage, Roseanne (1979). Rhythms in human performance: 1 1/2-hour oscillations in cognitive style. *Science, 204,* 1326–1328.

Kleinman, Arthur (1988). *Rethinking psychiatry: From cultural category to personal experience.* New York: Free Press.

Kleinmuntz, Benjamin, & Szucko, Julian J. (1984, March 29). A field study of the fallibility of polygraph lie detection. *Nature, 308,* 449–450.

Klerman, Gerald L.; Weissman, Myrna M.; Rounsaville, Bruce J.; & Chevron, Eve S. (1984). *Interpersonal psychotherapy of depression.* New York: Basic Books.

• Klima, Edward S., & Bellugi, Ursula (1966). Syntactic regularities in the speech of children. In J. Lyons & R. J. Wales (eds.), *Psycholinguistics papers.* Edinburgh, Scotland: Edinburgh University Press.

• Kluft, Richard P. (1987). The simulation and dissimulation of multiple personality disorder. *American Journal of Clinical Hypnosis, 30,* 104–118.

• Kluft, Richard P. (1993). Multiple personality disorders. In D. Spiegel (ed.), *Dissociative disorders: A clinical review.* Lutherville, MD: Sidran.

• Knight, Raymond A.; Prentky, Robert A.; & Cerce, David D. (1994). The development, reliability, and validity of an inventory for the multidimensional assessment of sex and aggression. Special Issue: The assessment and treatment of sex offenders. *Criminal Justice and Behavior, 21,* 72–94.

Knussmann, Rainer; Christiansen, Kerrin; & Couwenbergs, Catharina (1986). Relations between sex hormone levels and sexual behavior in men. *Archives of Sexual Behavior, 15,* 429–445.

Kobasa, Suzanne C., & Puccetti, Mark C. (1983). Personality and social resources in stress resistance. *Journal of Personality and Social Psychology, 45,* 839–850.

• Koch, Sigmund (1992). "Psychology" or "The psychological studies"? *American Psychologist, 48,* 902–904.

Koegel, Robert L.; Schreibman, Laura; O'Neill, Robert E.; & Burke, John C. (1983). The personality and family-interaction characteristics of parents of autistic children. *Journal of Consulting and Clinical Psychology, 51,* 683–692.

• Koeske, Randi D. (1987). Premenstrual emotionality: Is biology destiny? In M. R. Walsh (ed.), *The psychology of women: Ongoing debates.* New Haven, CT: Yale University Press.

Kohlberg, Lawrence (1964). Development of moral character and moral ideology. In M. Hoffman & L. W. Hoffman (eds.), *Review of child development research.* New York: Russell Sage Foundation.

Kohlberg, Lawrence (1966). A cognitive-developmental analysis of children's sex-role concepts and attitudes. In E. E. Maccoby (ed.), *The development of sex differences.* Stanford, CA: Stanford University Press.

Kohlberg, Lawrence (1976). Moral stages and moralization: The cognitive-developmental approach. In T. Lickona (ed.), *Moral development and behavior.* New York: Holt, Rinehart and Winston.

Kohlberg, Lawrence (1984). *Essays on moral development, Vol. 2. The psychology of moral development: The nature and validity of moral stages.* San Francisco: Harper & Row.

Köhler, Wolfgang (1925). *The mentality of apes.* New York: Harcourt, Brace.

Köhler, Wolfgang (1959). Gestalt psychology today. Presidential address to the American Psychological Association, Cincinnati. [Reprinted in E. R. Hilgard (ed.), *American psychology in historical perspective: Addresses of the presidents of the American Psychological Association, 1892–1977.* Washington, DC: American Psychological Association, 1978.]

• Kohn, Alfie (1992). *No contest: The case against competition* (rev. ed.). Boston: Houghton Mifflin.

• Kohn, Alfie (1993). *Punished by rewards.* Boston: Houghton Mifflin.

Kohn, Melvin, & Schooler, Carmi (1983). *Work and personality: An inquiry into the impact of social stratification.* Norwood, NJ: Ablex.

Kohn, Paul M.; Lafreniere, Kathryn; & Gurevich, Maria (1991). Hassles, health, and personality. *Journal of Personality and Social Psychology, 61,* 478–482.

Kohout, Jessica, & Wicherski, Marlene (1991). *1989 Doctorate Employment Survey.* Washington, DC: American Psychological Association (Office of Demographic, Employment and Educational Research).

Koocher, Gerald (1990). Self-help or hype? Paper presented at the annual meeting of the American Psychological Association, Boston.

• Kopta, Stephen M.; Howard, Kenneth I.; Lowry, Jenny L.; & Beutler, Larry E. (1994). Patterns of symptomatic recovery in psychotherapy. *Journal of Consulting and Clinical Psychology, 62,* 1009–1016.

• Koshland, Daniel E., Jr. (1988–1989). The future of biological research: What is possible and what is ethical? *MBL Science, 3,* 10–15.

Koss, Mary P.; Dinero, Thomas E.; Seibel, Cynthia A.; & Cox, Susan L. (1988). Stranger and acquaintance rape: Are there differences in the victim's experience? *Psychology of Women Quarterly, 12,* 1–24.

Kosslyn, Stephen M. (1980). *Image and mind.* Cambridge: Harvard University Press.

Kosslyn, Stephen M. (1983). *Ghosts in the mind's machine: Creating and using images in the brain.* New York: Norton.

Kosslyn, Stephen M.; Seger, Carol; Pani, John R.; & Hillger, Lynn A. (1990). When is imagery used in everyday life? A diary study. *Journal of Mental Imagery, 14,* 131–152.

• Kramer, Peter (1993). *Listening to Prozac.* New York: Viking.

Krantz, David S., & Manuck, Stephen B. (1984). Acute psychophysiologic reactivity and risk of cardiovascular disease: A review and methodological critique. *Psychological Bulletin, 96,* 435–464.

• Kraus, Stephen J. (1995). Attitudes and the prediction of behavior: A meta-analysis of the empirical literature. *Personality and Social Psychology Bulletin, 21,* 58–75.

• Krechevsky, Mara, & Gardner, Howard (1990). Approaching school intelligently: An infusion approach. *Contributions to Human Development, 21,* 79–94.

• Kreps, Bonnie (1990). *Authentic passion.* Toronto, Ontario: McClelland & Stewart.

Kripke, Daniel F. (1974). Ultradian rhythms in sleep and wakefulness. In E. D. Weitzman (ed.), *Advances in sleep research,* Vol. 1. Flushing, NY: Spectrum.

Kripke, Daniel F., & Sonnenschein, David (1978). A biologic rhythm in waking fantasy. In K. S. Pope & J. L. Singer (eds.), *The stream of consciousness: Scientific investigations into the flow of human experience.* New York: Plenum.

Krippner, Stanley, & Hillman, Deborah (1990). Social aspects of grassroots experiential dream groups. Paper presented at the annual meeting of the American Psychological Association, Boston.

• Kroger, Rolf O., & Wood, Linda A. (1993). Reification, "faking," and the Big Five. *American Psychologist, 48,* 1297–1298.

• Kroll, Barry M. (1992). *Teaching hearts and minds: College students reflect on the Vietnam War in literature.* Carbondale: Southern Illinois University Press.

• Krupa, David J.; Thompson, Judith K.; & Thompson, Richard F. (1993). Localization of a memory trace in the mammalian brain. *Science, 260,* 989–991.

Kubey, Robert, & Csikszentmihalyi, Mihaly (eds.) (1990). *Television and the quality of life: How viewing shapes everyday experiences.* Hillsdale, NJ: Erlbaum.

• Kuczmarski, R. J.; Flegal, K. M; Campbell, S. M.; & Johnson, C. L. (1994). Increasing prevalence of overweight among US adults. The National Health and Nutrition Examination Surveys, 1960 to 1991. *Journal of the American Medical Association, 272,* 205–211.

• Kuhl, Patricia K.; Williams, Karen A.; Lacerda, Francisco; Stevens, Kenneth N.; et al. (1992, January 31). Linguistic experience alters phonetic perception in infants by 6 months of age. *Science, 255,* 606–608.

• Kuhn, Deanna; Weinstock, Michael; & Flaton, Robin (1994). How well do jurors reason? Competence dimensions of individual variation in a juror reasoning task. *Psychological Science, 5,* 289–196.

Kuhn, Thomas (1981). Unanswered questions about science. In R. D. Tweney, M. E. Doherty, & C. R. Mynatt (eds.), *On scientific thinking.* New York: Columbia University Press.

Kulik, James A.; & Mahler, Heike I. (1989). Social support and recovery from surgery. *Health Psychology, 8,* 221–238.

Kunda, Ziva (1990). The case for motivated reasoning. *Psychological Bulletin, 108,* 480–498.

• Kurtines, William M., & Gewirtz, Jacob L. (eds.) (1991). *Handbook of moral behavior and development,* Vols. 1–3. Hillsdale, NJ: Erlbaum.

LaBerge, Stephen (1986). *Lucid dreaming.* New York: Ballantine Books.

LaBerge, Stephen (1990). Lucid dreaming: Psychophysiological studies of consciousness during REM sleep. In R. R. Bootzin, J. F. Kihlstrom, & D. L. Schacter (eds.), *Sleep and cognition.* Washington, DC: American Psychological Association.

Lader, Malcolm (1989). Benzodiazepine dependence. Special Issue: Psychiatry and the addictions. *International Review of Psychiatry, 1,* 149–156.

Lader, Malcolm, & Morton, Sally (1991). Benzodiazepine problems. *British Journal of Addiction, 86,* 823–828.

• **LaFromboise, Teresa; Coleman, Hardin L. K.; & Gerton, Jennifer** (1993). Psychological impact of biculturalism: Evidence and theory. *Psychological Bulletin, 114,* 395–412.

Laird, James D. (1974). Self-attribution of emotion: The effects of expressive behavior on the quality of emotional experience. *Journal of Personality and Social Psychology, 29,* 475–486.

Laird, James D. (1984). The real role of facial response in the experience of emotion: A reply to Tourangeau and Ellsworth, and others. *Journal of Personality and Social Psychology, 47,* 909–917.

Lakoff, Robin T. (1990). *Talking power.* New York: Basic Books.

• **Lakoff, Robin T., & Coyne, James C.** (1993). *Father knows best: The use and abuse of power in Freud's case of "Dora."* New York: Teachers College Press.

• **Lambert, Michael J., & Bergin, Allen E.** (1994). The effectiveness of psychotherapy. In A. E. Bergin & S. L. Garfield (eds.), *Handbook of psychotherapy and behavior change* (4th ed.). New York: Wiley.

• **Lambert, Michael J., & Hill, Clara E.** (1994). Assessing psychotherapy outcomes and processes. In A. E. Bergin & S. L. Garfield (eds.), *Handbook of psychotherapy and behavior change* (4th ed.). New York: Wiley.

Lancaster, Jane (1975). *Primate behavior and the emergence of human culture.* New York: Holt, Rinehart and Winston.

Land, Edwin H. (1959). Experiments in color vision. *Scientific American, 200*(5), 84–94, 96, 99.

Landrine, Hope (1988). Revising the framework of abnormal psychology. In P. Bronstein & K. Quina (eds.), *Teaching a psychology of people.* Washington, DC: American Psychological Association.

• **Lane, Charles** (1994, December 1). The tainted sources of "The Bell Curve." *The New York Review,* 14–18.

Langer, Ellen J. (1983). *The psychology of control.* Beverly Hills, CA: Sage.

Langer, Ellen J. (1989). *Mindfulness.* Cambridge, MA: Addison-Wesley.

Langer, Ellen J.; Blank, Arthur; & Chanowitz, Benzion (1978). The mindlessness of ostensibly thoughtful action: The role of placebic information in interpersonal interaction. *Journal of Personality, and Social Psychology, 36,* 635–642.

Langer, Ellen J., & Piper, Alison I. (1988). Television from a mindful/mindless perspective. In S. Oskamp (ed.), *Television as a social issue* (*Applied Social Psychology Annual,* Vol. 8). Newbury Park, CA: Sage.

Langer, Ellen J.; Rodin, Judith; Beck, Pearl; Weinman, Cynthia; & Spitzer, Lynn (1979). Environmental determinants of memory improvement in late adulthood. *Journal of Personality and Social Psychology, 37,* 2003–2013.

Larmore, Kim; Ludwig, Arnold M.; & Cain, Rolene L. (1977). Multiple personality: An objective case study. *British Journal of Psychiatry, 131,* 35–40.

Larsen, Randy J.; Diener, Ed; & Cropanzano, Russell (1987). Cognitive operations associated with individual differences in affect intensity. *Journal of Personality and Social Psychology, 53,* 767–774.

Lashley, Karl S. (1950). In search of the engram. In *Symposium of the Society for Experimental Biology,* Vol. 4. New York: Cambridge University Press.

• **Lassner, Jason B.; Matthews, Karen A.; & Stoney, Catherine M.** (1994). Are cardiovascular reactors to asocial stress also reactors to social stress? *Journal of Personality and Social Psychology, 66,* 69–77.

Latané, Bibb, & Darley, John (1976). Help in a crisis: Bystander response to an emergency. In J. Thibaut, J. Spence, & R. Carlson (eds.), *Contemporary topics in social psychology.* Morristown, NJ: General Learning Press.

Latané, Bibb; Williams, Kipling; & Harkins, Stephen (1979). Many hands make light the work: The causes and consequences of social loafing. *Journal of Personality and Social Psychology, 37,* 822–832.

Laudenslager, Mark L. (1988). The psychobiology of loss: Lessons from humans and nonhuman primates. *Journal of Social Issues, 44*(3), 19–36.

• **Laumann, Edward O.; Gagnon, John H.; Michael, Robert T.; & Michaels, Stuart** (1994). *The social organization of sexuality.* Chicago: University of Chicago Press.

• **Laursen, Brett, & Collins, W. Andrew** (1994). Interpersonal conflict during adolescence. *Psychological Bulletin, 115,* 197–209.

Lave, J.; Murtaugh, M.; & de la Roche, O. (1984). The dialectic of arithmetic in grocery shopping. In B. Rogoff & J. Lave (eds.), *Everyday cognition: Its development in social context.* Cambridge: Harvard University Press.

Lavie, Peretz (1976). Ultradian rhythms in the perception of two apparent motions. *Chronobiologia, 3,* 21–218.

Lazarus, Arnold A. (1989). *The practice of multi-modal therapy.* Baltimore, MD: Johns Hopkins University Press.

Lazarus, Arnold A. (1990). If this be research.... *American Psychologist, 58,* 670–671.

Lazarus, Richard S. (1991). Cognition and motivation in emotion. *American Psychologist, 46,* 352–367.

Lazarus, Richard S., & Folkman, Susan (1984). *Stress, appraisal, and coping.* New York: Springer.

Lee, Jerry W., & Hart, Richard (1985). Techniques used by dividuals who quit smoking on their own. Paper presented at the annual meeting of the American Psychological Association, Los Angeles.

Lee, John Alan (1973). *The colours of love.* Ontario, Canada: New Press.

Lee, John Alan (1988). Love-styles. In R. J. Sternberg & M. L. Barnes (eds.), *The psychology of love.* New Haven, CT: Yale University Press.

Lehman, Adam K., & Rodin, Judith (1989). Styles of self-nurturance and disordered eating. *Journal of Consulting and Clinical Psychology, 57,* 117–122.

Lehman, Darrin R.; Lempert, Richard O.; & Nisbett, Richard E. (1988). The effects of graduate training on reasoning. *American Psychologist, 43,* 431–442.

• **Leibel, Rudolph L.; Rosenbaum, Michael; & Hirsch, Jules** (1995). Changes in energy expenditure resulting from altered body weight. *New England Journal of Medicine, 332,* 621–628.

Lenhardt, Martin L.; Skellett, Ruth; Wang, Peter; & Clarke, Alex M. (1991). Human ultrasonic speech perception. *Science, 253,* 82–85.

Lent, James R. (1968, June). Mimosa cottage: Experiment in hope. *Psychology Today,* 51–58.

• **Leonard, Henrietta L.; Swedo, Susan E.; Lenane, Marge C.; Rettew, David C.; et al.** (1993). A 2- to 7-year follow-up study of 54 obsessive-compulsive children and adolescents. *Archives of General Psychiatry, 50,* 429–439.

• **Lepowsky, Maria** (1994). *Fruit of the motherland: Gender in an egalitarian society.* New York: Columbia University Press.

Lepper, Mark R.; Greene, David; & Nisbett, Richard E. (1973). Undermining children's intrinsic interest with extrinsic rewards. *Journal of Personality and Social Psychology, 28,* 129–137.

Lerner, Melvin J. (1980). *The belief in a just world: A fundamental delusion.* New York: Plenum.

• **LeVay, Simon** (1991). A difference in hypothalamic structure between heterosexual and homosexual men. *Science, 253,* 1034–1037.

• **Levenson, Robert W.** (1992). Autonomic nervous system differences among emotions. *Psychological Science, 3,* 23–27.

Levenson, Robert W.; Ekman, Paul; & Friesen, Wallace V. (1990). Voluntary facial action generates emotion-specific autonomic nervous system activity. *Psychophysiology, 27,* 363–384.

Leventhal, Howard (1970). Findings and theory in the study of fear communications. In L. Berkowitz (ed.), *Advances in experimental social psychology,* Vol. 5. New York: Academic Press.

• **Leventhal, Howard, & Nerenz, D. R.** (1982). A model for stress research and some implications for the control of stress disorders. In D. Meichenbaum & M. Jaremko (eds.), *Stress prevention and management: A cognitive behavioral approach.* New York: Plenum.

• **Levin, R. J., & Wagner, G.** (1985). Orgasm in women in the laboratory—Quantitative studies on duration, intensity, latency, and vaginal blood flow. *Archives of Sexual Behavior, 11,* 367–386.

Levine, Daniel S. (1990). *Introduction to cognitive and neural modeling.* Hillsdale, NJ: Erlbaum.

Levine, Elaine S., & Padilla, Amado M. (1980). *Crossing cultures in therapy: Pluralistic counseling for the Hispanic.* Monterey, CA: Brooks/Cole.

• Levine, Joseph, & Suzuki, David (1993). *The secret of life: Redesigning the living world.* Boston: WBGH Educational Foundation.

• Levine, Robert V.; Martinez, Todd S.; Brase, Gary; & Sorenson, Kerry (1994). Helping in 36 U.S. cities. *Journal of Personality and Social Psychology, 67,* 69–82.

• Levinthal, Charles F. (1988). *Messengers of paradise: Opiates and the brain.* New York: Doubleday/Anchor Press.

Levitan, Alexander A., & Ronan, William J. (1988). Problems in the treatment of obesity and eating disorders. *Medical Hypnoanalysis Journal, 3,* 131–136.

Levy, Jerre (1985, May). Right brain, left brain: Fact and fiction. *Psychology Today,* 38–39, 42–44.

Levy, Jerre; Trevarthen, Colwyn; & Sperry, Roger W. (1972). Perception of bilateral chimeric figures following hemispheric deconnection. *Brain, 95,* 61–78.

• Levy, Robert I. (1973). *Tahitians: Mind and experience in the Society Islands.* Chicago: University of Chicago Press.

Levy, Robert I. (1984). The emotions in comparative perspective. In K. R. Scherer & P. Ekman (eds.), *Approaches to emotion.* Hillsdale, NJ: Erlbaum.

Levy, Sandra M.; Lee, Jerry; Bagley, Caroline; & Lippman, Marc (1988). Survival hazards analysis in first recurrent breast cancer patients: Seven-year follow-up. *Psychosomatic Medicine, 50,* 520–528.

Lewin, Kurt (1948). *Resolving social conflicts.* New York: Harper.

Lewinsohn, Peter; Steinmetz, Julia; Larson, Douglass; & Franklin, Judith (1981). Depression-related cognitions: Antecedent or consequence? *Journal of Abnormal Psychology, 90,* 213–219.

Lewis, Dorothy O. (ed.) (1981). *Vulnerabilities to delinquency.* New York: Spectrum Medical and Scientific Books.

• Lewis, Michael (1992). *Shame: The exposed self.* New York: Free Press.

Lewontin, Richard C. (1970). Race and intelligence. *Bulletin of the Atomic Scientists, 26*(3), 2–8.

Lewontin, Richard C. (1982). *Human diversity.* New York: Scientific American Library.

• Lewontin, Richard C. (1993). *Biology as ideology: The doctrine of DNA.* New York: HarperPerennial.

Lewontin, Richard C.; Rose, Steven; & Kamin, Leon J. (1984). *Not in our genes: Biology, ideology, and human nature.* New York: Pantheon.

• Lewy, Alfred J.; Ahmed, Saeeduddin; Jackson, Jeanne L.; & Sack, Robert L. (1992). Melatonin shifts human circadian rhythms according to a phase-response curve. *Chronobiology International, 9,* 380–392.

Lewy, Alfred J.; Sacks, Robert L.; Miller, L. Steven; & Hoban, Tana M. (1987). Antidepressant and circadian phase-shifting effects of light. *Science, 235,* 352–354.

• Li, Deming; Wu, Zhenyun; Shao, Daosheng; & Liu, Shanxun (1991). The relationship of sleep to learning and memory. *International Journal of Mental Health, 20,* 41–47.

• Liberman, Akiva, & Chaiken, Shelly (1991). Value conflict and thought-induced attitude change. *Journal of Experimental Social Psychology, 27,* 203–216.

Libet, Benjamin (1985). Unconscious cerebral initiative and the role of conscious will in voluntary action. *Behavioral and Brain Sciences, 8,* 529–566.

Lichstein, Kenneth L., & Fanning, John (1990). Cognitive anxiety in insomnia: An analogue test. *Stress Medicine, 6,* 47–51.

Lichtenstein, Sarah; Slovic, Paul; Fischhoff, Baruch; Layman, Mark; & Combs, Barbara (1978). Judged frequency of lethal events. *Journal of Experimental Psychology: Human Learning and Memory, 4,* 551–578.

Lieberman, David A. (1979). Behaviorism and the mind: A (limited) call for a return to introspection. *American Psychologist, 34,* 319–333.

• Lightdale, Jenifer R., & Prentice, Deborah A. (1994). Rethinking sex differences in aggression: Aggressive behavior in the absence of social roles. *Personality and Social Psychology Bulletin, 20,* 34–44.

Lightfoot, Lynn O. (1980). Behavioral tolerance to low doses of alcohol in social drinkers. Unpublished doctoral dissertation, University of Waterloo, Waterloo, Ontario.

• Likona, Thomas (1983). *Raising good children.* New York: Bantam.

• Lilienfeld, Scott O. (1993, Fall). Do "honesty" tests really measure honesty? *Skeptical Inquirer, 18,* 32–41.

Lin, Keh-Ming; Poland, Russell E.; & Lesser, Ira M. (1986). Ethnicity and psychopharmacology. *Culture, Medicine, and Psychiatry, 10,* 151–165.

Lin, Keh-Ming; Poland, Russell E.; Nuccio, Inocencia; Matsuda, Kazuko; et al. (1989). A longitudinal assessment of haloperidol doses and serum concentrations in Asian and Caucasian schizophrenic patients. *American Journal of Psychiatry, 146,* 1307–1311.

• Linday, Linda A. (1994). Maternal reports of pregnancy, genital, and related fantasies in preschool and kindergarten children. *Journal of the American Academy of Child and Adolescent Psychiatry, 33,* 416–423.

Linton, Marigold (1978). Real-world memory after six years: An in vivo study of very long-term memory. In M. M. Gruneberg, P. E. Morris, & R. N. Sykes (eds.), *Practical aspects of memory.* London: Academic Press.

Linz, Daniel; Donnerstein, Edward; & Penrod, Steven (1988). The effects of long-term exposure to violent and sexually degrading depictions of women. *Journal of Personality and Social Psychology, 55,* 758–767.

• Lipman-Blumen, Jean (1994). The existential bases of power relationships: The gender role case. In H. L. Radtke & H. J. Stam (eds.), *Power/gender social relations in theory and practice.* London: Sage.

Lipscomb, David (1972). The increase in prevalence of high frequency hearing impairment among college students. *Audiology, 11,* 231–237.

• Lipsey, Mark W., & Wilson, David B. (1993). The efficacy of psychological, educational, and behavioral treatment: Confirmation from meta-analysis. *American Psychologist, 48,* 1181–1209.

• Lipstadt, Deborah E. (1993). *Denying the holocaust: The growing assault on truth and memory.* New York: Free Press.

• Lipstadt, Deborah E. (1994, Spring). Denying the Holocaust: The fragility of memory. *Brandeis Review,* 30–33.

Lissner, L.; Odell, P. M.; D'Agostino, R. B.; Stokes, J., III; et al. (1991, June 27). Variability of body weight and health outcomes in the Framingham population. *New England Journal of Medicine, 324* (26), 1839–1844.

Locke, Edwin A., & Latham, Gary P. (1990). Work motivation and satisfaction: Light at the end of the tunnel. *Psychological Science, 1,* 240–246.

Locke, Edwin A., & Latham, Gary P. (1991). The fallacies of common sense "truths": A reply to Lamal. *Psychological Science, 2,* 131–132.

Locke, Edwin A.; Shaw, Karyll; Saari, Lise; & Latham, Gary (1981). Goal-setting and task performance: 1969–1980. *Psychological Bulletin, 90,* 125–152.

Loehlin, John C. (1988). Partitioning environmental and genetic contributions to behavioral development. Invited address at the annual meeting of the American Psychological Association, Atlanta.

• Loehlin, John C.; Horn, J. M.; & Willerman, L. (in press). Heredity, environment, and IQ in the Texas adoption study. In R. J. Sternberg & E. L. Grigorenko (eds.), *Intelligence: Heredity and environment.* New York: Cambridge University Press.

• Loewen, James W. (1995). *Lies my teacher told me: Everything your American history textbook got wrong.* New York: New Press.

Loftus, Elizabeth F. (1980). *Memory.* Reading, MA: Addison-Wesley.

• Loftus, Elizabeth F. (1993a). The reality of repressed memories. *American Psychologist, 48,* 518–537.

• Loftus, Elizabeth F. (1993b, March). Repressed memories of childhood trauma: Are they genuine? *The Harvard Mental Health Letter, 9,* 4–5.

• Loftus, Elizabeth F., & Coan, James (in press). The construction of childhood memories. In D. Peters (ed.), *The child witness in context: Cognitive, social, and legal perspectives.* Norwell, MA: Kluwer.

• Loftus, Elizabeth F., & Greene, Edith (1980). Warning: Even memory for faces may be contagious. *Law and Human Behavior, 4,* 323–334.

Loftus, Elizabeth F.; Miller, David G.; & Burns, Helen J. (1978). Semantic integration of verbal information into a visual memory. *Journal of Experimental Psychology: Human Learning and Memory, 4,* 19–31.

Loftus, Elizabeth F., & Palmer, John C. (1974). Reconstruction of automobile destruction: An example of the interaction between language and memory. *Journal of Verbal Learning and Verbal Behavior, 13,* 585–589.

Loftus, Elizabeth F., & Zanni, Guido (1975). Eyewitness testimony: The influence of the wording of a question. *Bulletin of the Psychonomic Society, 5,* 86–88.

• **Lombardo, John A., & Sickles, R. Trent** (1992). Medical and performance-enhancing effects of anabolic steriods. *Psychiatric Annals, 22,* 19–23.

• **Lonner, Walter J.** (1995). Culture and human diversity. In E. Trickett, R. Watts, & D. Birman (eds.), *Human diversity: Perspectives on people in context.* San Francisco: Jossey-Bass.

• **Lonner, Walter J., & Malpass, Roy S.** (1994). When psychology and culture meet: An introduction to cross-cultural psychology. In W. J. Lonner & R. S. Malpass (eds.), *Psychology and culture.* Needham Heights, MA: Allyn & Bacon.

Loo, Chalsa M. (1991). An integrative-sequential treatment model for post-traumatic stress disorder: A case study of the Japanese American internment and redress. Paper presented at the annual meeting of the American Psychological Association, San Francisco.

López, Steven R. (1989). Patient variable biases in clinical judgment: Conceptual overview and methodological considerations. *Psychological Bulletin, 106,* 184–203.

• **Lord, C. G.; Ross, L.; & Lepper, M. R.** (1979). Biased assimilation and attitude polarization: The effects of prior theories on subsequently considered evidence. *Journal of Personality and Social Psychology, 37,* 2098–2109.

• **Lott, Bernice, & Maluso, Diane** (1993). The social learning of gender. In A. E. Beall & R. J. Sternberg (eds.), *The psychology of gender.* New York: Guilford Press.

• **Lottes, Ilsa L., & Kuriloff, Peter J.** (1994). Sexual socialization differences by gender, Greek membership, and religious background. *Psychology of Women Quarterly, 18,* 203–219.

Louis, Arthur M. (1978, April). Should you buy biorhythms? *Psychology Today,* 93–96.

Lovaas, O. Ivar (1977). *The autistic child: Language development through behavior modification.* New York: Halsted Press.

Lovaas, O. Ivar; Schreibman, Laura; & Koegel, Robert L. (1974). A behavior modification approach to the treatment of autistic children. *Journal of Autism and Childhood Schizophrenia, 4,* 111–129.

Luce, Gay Gaer, & Segal, Julius (1966). *Current research on sleep and dreams.* Bethesda, MD: U.S. Department of Health, Education, and Welfare.

Luce, Terrence S. (1974, November). Blacks, whites and yellows, they all look alike to me. *Psychology Today,* 105–106, 108.

• **Luengo, M. A.; Carrillo-de-la-Peña, M. T.; Otero, J. M.; & Romero, E.** (1994). A short-term longitudinal study of impulsivity and antisocial behavior. *Journal of Personality and Social Psychology, 66,* 542–548.

Lugaresi, Elio; Medori, R.; Montagna, P.; et al. (1986, October 16). Fatal familial insomnia and dysautonomia with selective degeneration of thalamic nuclei. *New England Journal of Medicine, 315,* 997–1003.

Luria, Alexander (1968). *The mind of a mnemonist.* (L. Soltaroff, trans.) New York: Basic Books.

Luria, Alexander (1980). *Higher cortical functions in man* (2nd rev. ed.). New York: Basic Books.

Lutz, Catherine (1988). *Unnatural emotions.* Chicago: University of Chicago Press.

• **Lyketsos, C. G.; Hoover, D. R.; Guccione, M.; Senterfitt, W.; et al.** (1993). Depressive symptoms as predictors of medical outcomes in HIV infection: Multicenter AIDS Cohort Study. *Journal of the American Medical Association, 270,* 2563–2567.

Lykken, David T. (1981). *A tremor in the blood: Uses and abuses of the lie detector.* New York: McGraw-Hill.

• **Lykken, David T.** (1991). The lie detector controversy: An alternative solution. In J. R. Jennings, P. K. Ackles, & M. G. H. Coles (eds.), *Advances in psychophysiology.* London: Jessica Kingsley Publishers.

• **Lynch, James J.** (1985). *Language of the heart: The body's response to human dialogue.* New York: Basic Books.

Lynn, Steven Jay; Rhue, Judith W.; & Weekes, John R. (1990). Hypnotic involuntariness: A social cognitive analysis. *Psychological Review, 97,* 69–184.

Lytton, Hugh, & Romney, David M. (1991). Parents' differential socialization of boys and girls: A meta-analysis. *Psychological Bulletin, 109,* 267–296.

McAdams, Dan P. (1988). *Power, intimacy, and the life story: Personological inquiries into identity.* New York: Guilford Press.

McCann, I. Lisa, & Holmes, David S. (1984). Influence of aerobic exercise on depression. *Journal of Personality and Sodal Psychology, 46,* 1142–1147.

McCartney, Kathleen; Harris, Monica J.; & Bernieri, Frank

(1990). Growing up and growing apart: A developmental meta-analysis of twin studies. *Psychological Bulletin, 107,* 226–237.

McCauley, Elizabeth, & Ehrhardt, Anke (1980). Female sexual response. In D. D. Youngs & A. Ehrhardt (eds.), *Psychosomatic obstetrics and gynecology.* New York: Appleton-Century-Crofts.

• **McClearn, Gerald E.** (1993). Behavioral genetics: The last century and the next. In R. Plomin & G. E. McClearn (eds.), *Nature, nurture, and psychology.* Washington, DC: American Psychological Association.

McClelland, David C. (1985). How motives, skills, and values determine what people do. *American Psychologist, 40,* 812–825.

McClelland, David C. (1987). Characteristics of successful entrepreneurs. *Journal of Creative Behavior, 3,* 219–233.

McClelland, David C.; Koestner, Richard; & Weinberger, Joel (1989). How do self-attributed and implicit motives differ? *Psychological Review, 96,* 690–702.

• **McCloskey, Michael, & Cohen, Neal J.** (1989). Catastrophic interference in connectionist networks: The sequential learning problem. *The Psychology of Learning and Motivation, 24,* 109–165.

McCloskey, Michael; Wible, Cynthia G.; & Cohen, Neal J. (1988). Is there a special flashbulb-memory mechanism? *Journal of Experimental Psychology: General, 117,* 171–181.

Maccoby, Eleanor E. (1980). *Social development.* New York: Harcourt Brace Jovanovich.

Maccoby, Eleanor E. (1990). Gender and relationships: A developmental account. *American Psychologist, 45,* 513–520.

McConnell, James V. (1962). Memory transfer through cannibalism in planarians. *Journal of Neuropsychiatry, 3,* Monograph Supplement 1.

McCord, Joan (1989). Another time, another drug. Paper presented at conference, Vulnerability to the Transition from Drug Use to Abuse and Dependence, Rockville, Maryland.

McCord, Joan (1990). Crime in moral and social contexts. *Criminology, 28,* 1–26.

• **McCord, Joan** (1991). Questioning the value of punishment. *Social Problems, 38,* 167–179.

McCormick, Laura J., & Mayer, John D. (1991). Mood-congruent recall and natural mood. Poster presented at the annual meeting of the New England Psychological Association, Portland, Maine.

MacCoun, Robert J., & Kerr, Norbert L. (1988). Asymmetric influence in mock jury deliberation: Jurors' bias for leniency. *Journal of Personality and Social Psychology, 54,* 21–33.

McCrae, Robert R. (1987). Creativity, divergent thinking, and openness to experience. *Journal of Personality and Social Psychology, 52,* 1258–1265.

• **McCrae, Robert R.** (1993). Moderated analyses of longitudinal personality stability. *Journal of Personality and Social Psychology, 65,* 577–585.

McCrae, Robert R., & Costa, Paul T., Jr. (1988). Do parental influences matter? A reply to Halverson. *Journal of Personality, 56,* 445–449.

McCrae, Robert R., & Costa, Paul T., Jr. (1991). Adding *Liebe und Arbeit:* The full five-factor model and well-being. *Personality and Social Psychology Bulletin, 17,* 227–232.

MacDonald, N. E.; Wells, G. A.; Fisher, W. A.; Warren, W. K; et al. (1990). High risk STD/HIV behavior among college students. *Journal of the American Medical Association, 263,* 3155–3159.

McEwen, Bruce S. (1983). Gonadal steroid influences on brain development and sexual differentiation. *Reproductive Physiology IV (International Review of Physiology), 27,* 99–145.

McFarlane, Jessica; Martin, Carol Lynn; & Williams, Tannis M. (1988). Mood fluctuations: Women versus men and menstrual versus other cycles. *Psychology of Women Quarterly, 12,* 201–223.

McGaugh, James L. (1990). Significance and remembrance: The role of neuromodulatory systems. *Psychological Science, 1,* 15–25.

• **McGinnis, Michael, & Foege, William** (1993, November 10). Actual causes of death in the United States. *Journal of the American Medical Association, 270,* 2207–2212.

McGlone, Jeannette (1978). Sex differences in functional brain asymmetry. *Cortex, 14,* 122–128.

McGlynn, Susan M. (1990). Behavioral approaches to neuropsychological rehabilitation. *Psychological Bulletin, 108,* 420–441.

• **McGoldrick, Monica, & Pearce, John K.** (1982). Family therapy with Irish Americans. In M. McGoldrick, J. K. Pearce, & J. Giordano (eds.), *Ethnicity and family therapy.* New York: Guilford Press.

McGoldrick, Monica; Pearce, John K.; & Giordano, J. (eds.) (1982). *Ethnicity and family therapy.* New York: Guilford Press.

McGrath, Ellen; Keita, Gwendolyn P.; Strickland, Bonnie; &

Russo, Nancy F. (eds.) (1990). *Women and depression: Risk factors and treatment issues.* Washington, DC: American Psychological Association.

• **McGue, Matt, & Lykken, David T.** (1992). Genetic influence on risk of divorce. *Psychological Science, 3,* 368–373.

• **McGue, Matt; Pickens, Roy W.; & Svikis, Dace S.** (1992). Sex and age effects on the inheritance of alcohol problems: A twin study. *Journal of Abnormal Psychology, 101,* 3–17.

• **McGuinness, Diane** (1993). Sex differences in cognitive style: Implications for math performance and achievement. In L. A. Penner, G. M. Batsche, & H. Knoff (eds.), *The challenge in mathematics and science education: Psychology's response.* Washington, DC: American Psychological Association.

• **McHugh, Paul R.** (1993a). History and the pitfalls of practice. Unpublished paper, Johns Hopkins University.

• **McHugh, Paul R.** (1993b, December). Psychotherapy awry. *American Scholar,* 17–30.

• **McHugh, Paul R.** (1993c, September). Multiple personality disorder. *The Harvard Mental Health Letter, 10,* 4–6.

MacKavey, William R.; Malley, Janet E.; & Stewart, Abigail J. (1991). Remembering autobiographically consequential experiences: Content analysis of psychologists' accounts of their lives. *Psychology and Aging, 6,* 50–59.

Mackenzie, Brian (1984). Explaining race differences in IQ: The logic, the methodology, and the evidence. *American Psychologist, 39,* 1214–1233.

• **McKee, Richard D., & Squire, Larry R.** (1992). Equivalent forgetting rates in long-term memory for diencephalic and medical temporal lobe amnesia. *Journal of Neuroscience, 12,* 3765–3772.

• **McKee, Richard D., & Squire, Larry R.** (1993). On the development of declarative memory. *Journal of Experimental Psychology: Learning, Memory, and Cognition, 19,* 397–404.

McKinlay, John B.; McKinlay, Sonja M.; & Brambilla, Donald (1987). The relative contributions of endocrine changes and social circumstances to depression in mid-aged women. *Journal of Health and Social Behavior, 28,* 345–363.

MacKinnon, Donald W. (1962). The nature and nurture of creative talent. *American Psychologist, 17,* 484–495.

MacKinnon, Donald W. (1968). Selecting students with creative potential. In P. Heist (ed.), *The creative college student: An unmet challenge.* San Francisco: Jossey-Bass.

McLeod, Beverly (1985, March). Real work for real pay. *Psychology Today,* 42–44, 46, 48–50.

• **McNally, Richard J.** (1994). *Panic disorder: A critical analysis.* New York: Guilford Press.

McNaughton, B. L., & Morris, R. G. M. (1987). Hippocampal synaptic enhancement and information storage within a distributed memory system. *Trends in Neuroscience, 10,* 408–415.

McNeill, David (1966). Developmental psycholinguistics. In F. L. Smith & G. A. Miller (eds.), *The genesis of language: A psycholinguistic approach.* Cambridge, MA: MIT Press.

• **Macrae, C. Neil; Milne, Alan B.; & Bodenhausen, Galen V.** (1994). Stereotypes as energy-saving devices: A peek inside the cognitive toolbox. *Journal of Personality and Social Psychology, 66,* 37–47.

• **Maddux, James E.** (1993, Summer). The mythology of psychopathology: A social cognitive view of deviance, difference, and disorder. *The General Psychologist, 29,* 34–45.

• **Magnus, Keith; Diener, Ed; Fujita, Frank; & Pavot, William** (1993). Extraversion and neuroticism as predictors of objective life events: A longitudinal analysis. *Journal of Personality and Social Psychology, 65,* 1046–1053.

Mahony, Michael J. (1991). *Human change processes: The scientific foundations of psychotherapy.* New York: Basic Books.

• **Mairs, Nancy** (1986). *Plaintext: Deciphering a woman's life.* New York: Harper & Row.

• **Maki, Ruth H., & Berry, Sharon L.** (1984). Metacomprehension of text material. *Journal of Experimental Psychology: Learning, Memory, and Cognition, 10,* 663–679.

Malamuth, Neil, & Dean, Karol (1990). Attraction to sexual aggression. In A. Parrot & L. Bechhofer (eds.), *Acquaintance rape: the hidden crime.* Newark, NJ: Wiley.

• **Malamuth, Neil M.; Sockloskie, Robert J.; Koss, Mary P.; & Tanaka, J. S.** (1991). Characteristics of aggressors against women: Testing a model using a national sample of college students. Special Section: Theories of sexual aggression. *Journal of Consulting and Clinical Psychology, 59,* 670–681.

• **Malarkey, William B.; Kiecolt-Glaser, Janice K.; Pearl, Dennis; & Glaser, Ronald** (1994). Hostile behavior during marital conflict alters pituitary and adrenal hormones. *Psychosomatic Medicine, 56,* 41–51.

Malatesta, Carol Z. (1990). The role of emotions in the development and organization of personality. In R. A. Thompson (ed.), *Socioemotional development. Nebraska Symposium on Motivation, 1988.* Lincoln: University of Nebraska Press.

Malgady, Robert G.; Rogler, Lloyd; & Costantino, Giuseppe (1987). Ethnocultural and linguistic bias in mental health evaluation of Hispanics. *American Psychologist, 42,* 228–234.

• **Maling, Michael S., & Howard, Kenneth I.** (1994). From research to practice to research to. . . . In P. F. Talley, H. H. Strupp, and S. F. Butler (eds.), *Psychotherapy research and practice: Bridging the gap.* New York: Basic Books.

• **Malinosky-Rummell, Robin, & Hansen, David J.** (1993). Long-term consequences of childhood physical abuse. *Psychological Bulletin, 114,* 68–79.

Malitz, Sidney, & Sackeim, Harold A. (eds.) (1986). *Electroconvulsive therapy: Clinical and basic research issues.* New York: New York Academy of Sciences.

Mancuso, James C., & Sarbin, Theodore (1984). Illusion and reality in the science of schizophrenia. *Contemporary Psychology, 29,* 992–993.

Manning, Carol A.; Hall, J. L.; & Gold, Paul E. (1990). Glucose effects on memory and other neuropsychological tests in elderly humans. *Psychological Science, 1,* 307–311.

• **Manning, Carol A.; Ragozzino, Michael E.; & Gold, Paul E.** (1993). Glucose enhancement of memory in patients with probable senile dementia of the Alzheimer's type. *Neurobiology of Aging, 14,* 523–528.

• **Manyande, Anne; Chayen, Susan; Priyakumar, Pooma; Smith, Christopher C.; et al.** (1992). Anxiety and endocrine responses to surgery: Paradoxical effects of preoperative relaxation training. *Psychosomatic Medicine, 54,* 275–287.

• **Marcus, Gary F.; Pinker, Steven; Ullman, Michael; Hollander, Michelle; et al.** (1992). Overregularization in language acquisition. *Monographs of the Society for Research in Child Development, 57*(Serial No. 228), 1–182.

Marder, Stephen; Van Putten, T.; Mintz, J.; LeBell, M.; et al. (1987). Low- and conventional-dose maintenance therapy with fluphenazine decanoate. Two-year outcome. *Archives of General Psychiatry, 44,* 518–521.

• **Margo, Geoffrey M.; Greenberg, Roger P.; Fisher, Seymore; & Dewan, Mantosh** (1993). A direct comparison of the defense mechanisms of nondepressed psychiatric inpatients. *Comprehensive Psychiatry, 34,* 65–69.

• **Mark, Daniel** (1994). Paper presented to the annual meeting of the Society of Behavioral Medicine, Boston.

• **Markowitz, Laura M.** (1993, July/August). Walking the walk. *The Family Therapy Networker,* 19–31.

Marks, Gary, & Miller, Norman (1987). Ten years of research on the false-consensus effect: An empirical and theoretical review. *Psychological Bulletin, 102,* 72–90.

Markus, Hazel R., & Kitayama, Shinobu (1991). Culture and the self: Implications for cognition, emotion, and motivation. *Psychological Review, 98,* 224–253.

Marlatt, G. Alan, & Rohsenow, Damaris J. (1980). Cognitive processes in alcohol use: Expectancy and the balanced placebo design. In N. K. Mello (ed.), *Advances in substance abuse,* Vol. 1. Greenwich, CT: JAI Press.

• **Marriott, Bernadette M. (ed.)** (1994). *Food components to enhance performance.* Washington, DC: National Academy Press.

Marshall, Grant N. (1991). A multidimensional analysis of internal health locus of control beliefs: Separating the wheat from the chaff? *Journal of Personality and Social Psychology, 61,* 483–491.

• **Marshall, Grant N.; Wortman, Camille B.; Vickers, Ross R., Jr.; Kusulas, Jeffrey W.; & Hervig, Linda K.** (1994). The five-factor model of personality as a framework for personality-health research. *Journal of Personality and Social Psychology, 67,* 278–286.

• **Martin, Emily** (1987). *The woman in the body: A cultural analysis of reproduction.* Boston: Beacon Press.

• **Martin, Rod A.; & Dobbin, James P.** (1988). Sense of humor, hassles, and immunoglobulin A: Evidence for a stress-moderating effect of humor. *International Journal of Psychiatry in Medicine, 18,* 93–105.

Maslach, Christina; Stapp, Joy; & Santee, Richard T. (1985). Individuation: Conceptual analysis and assessment. *Journal of Personality and Social Psychology, 49,* 729–738.

Maslow, Abraham H. (1954/1970). *Motivation and personality* (1st and 2nd eds.). New York: Harper & Row.

Maslow, Abraham H. (1971). *The farther reaches of human nature.* New York: Viking.

Masters, William H., & Johnson, Virginia E. (1966). *Human sexual response.* Boston: Little, Brown.

Matarazzo, Joseph (1984). Behavioral immunogens and pathogens in health and illness. In B. L. Hammonds & C. J. Scheirer (eds.), *Psychology and health: The master lecture series,* Vol. 3. Washington, DC: American Psychological Association.

Matson, Johnny L., & Ollendick, Thomas H. (1977). Issues in toilet training normal children. *Behavior Therapy, 8,* 549–553.

Matthews, Karen A.; Wing, Rena R.; Kuller, Lewis H.; Meilahn, Elaine N.; et al. (1990). Influences of natural menopause on psychological characteristics and symptoms of middle-aged healthy women. *Journal of Consulting and Clinical Psychology, 58,* 345–351.

Mawhinney, T. C. (1990). Decreasing intrinsic "motivation" with extrinsic rewards: Easier said than done. *Journal of Organizational Behavior Management, 11,* 175–191.

• **May, Cynthia P.; Hasher, Lynn; & Stoltzfus, Ellen R.** (1993). Optimal time of day and the magnitude of age differences in memory. *Psychological Science, 4,* 326–330.

Mayer, John D.; Gayle, Michael; Meehan, Mary Ellen; & Haarman, Anna-Kristina (1990). Toward better specification of the mood-congruency effect in recall. *Journal of Experimental Social Psychology, 26,* 465–480.

Mayer, John D., & Salovey, Peter (1993). The intelligence of emotional intelligence. *Intelligence, 17*(3).

Mazur, Allen, & Lamb, Theodore A. (1980). Testosterone, status, and mood in human males. *Hormones and Behavior, 14,* 236–246.

• **Mealey, Linda** (in press). Evolutionary psychology: The search for evolved mental mechanisms underlying complex human behavior. In J. P. Hurd (ed.), *The biology of morality.* Lewiston, NY: Edwin Mellen Press.

Medawar, Peter B. (1979). *Advice to a young scientist.* New York: Harper & Row.

Medawar, Peter B. (1982). *Pluto's Republic.* Oxford, England: Oxford University Press.

• **Mednick, Martha T.** (1989). On the politics of psychological constructs: Stop the bandwagon, I want to get off. *American Psychologist, 44,* 1118–1123.

Mednick, Sarnoff A. (1962). The associative basis of the creative process. *Psychological Review, 69,* 220–232.

• **Mednick, Sarnoff A.; Huttunen, Matti O.; & Machón, Ricardo** (1994). Prenatal influenza infections and adult schizophrenia. *Schizophrenia Bulletin, 20,* 263–267.

Mednick, Sarnoff A.; Parnas, Josef; & Schulsinger, Fini (1987). The Copenhagen High-Risk Project, 1962–86. *Schizophrenia Bulletin, 13,* 485–495.

Meltzer, Herbert Y. (1987). Biological studies in schizophrenia. *Schizophrenia Bulletin, 13,* 77–111.

• **Meltzoff, Andrew N., & Gopnik, Alison** (1993). The role of imitation in understanding persons and developing a theory of mind. In S. Baron-Cohen, H. Tager-Flusberg, & D. Cohen (eds.), *Understanding other minds.* New York: Oxford University Press.

Melzack, Ronald (1973). *The puzzle of pain.* New York: Basic Books.

Melzack, Ronald (1990). Phantom limbs and the concept of a neuromatrix. *Trends in Neurosciences, 13,* 88–92.

Melzack, Ronald, & Dennis, Stephen G. (1978). Neurophysiological foundations of pain. In R. A. Sternback (ed.), *The psychology of pain.* New York: Raven Press.

Melzack, Ronald, & Wall, Patrick D. (1965). Pain mechanisms: A new theory. *Science, 13,* 971–979.

Mercer, Jane (1988, May 18). Racial differences in intelligence: Fact or artifact? Talk given at San Bernardino Valley College.

• **Merikle, Philip M., & Skanes, Heather E.** (1992). Subliminal self-help audiotapes: A search for placebo effects. *Journal of Applied Psychology, 77,* 772–776.

Mershon, Bryan, & Gorsuch, Richard L. (1988). Number of factors in the personality sphere: Does increase in factors increase predictability of real life criteria? *Journal of Personality and Social Psychology, 55,* 675–680.

• **Mersky, Harold** (1992). The manufacture of personalities: The production of MPD. *British Journal of Psychiatry, 160,* 327–340.

• **Mesquita, Batja, & Frijda, Nico H.** (1993). Cultural variations in emotions: A review. *Psychological Bulletin, 112,* 179–204.

• **Meyer-Bahlburg, Heino F. L.; Ehrhardt, Anke A.; Rosen, Laura R.; Gruen, Rhoda S.; Veridiano, Norma P.; Vann, Felix H.; & Neuwalder, Herbert F.** (1995). Prenatal estrogens and the development of homosexual orientation. *Developmental Psychology, 31,* 12–21.

Meyerowitz, Beth E., & Chaiken, Shelley (1987). The effect of message framing on breast self-examination attitudes, intentions, and behavior. *Journal of Personality and Social Psychology, 52,* 500–510.

Meyers, Raymond C., & Dennis, Barbara (1991). Health, behavioral and developmental ramifications for children exposed to "crack" cocaine. Unpublished manuscript, Department of Human Services, Philadelphia.

• **Middlebrooks, John C.; Clock, Ann E.; Xu, Li; & Green, David M.** (1994). A panoramic code for sound location by cortical neurons. *Science, 264,* 842–844.

Milavsky, J. Ronald (1988). Television and aggression once again. In S. Oskamp (ed.), *Television as a social issue* (*Applied Social Psychology Annual,* Vol. 8). Newbury Park, CA: Sage.

Milgram, Stanley (1963). Behavioral study of obedience. *Journal of Abnormal and Social Psychology, 67,* 371–378.

Milgram, Stanley (1974). *Obedience to authority: An experimental view.* New York: Harper & Row.

• **Miller, Arthur G.; McHoskey, John W.; Bane, Cynthia M.; & Dowd, Timothy G.** (1993). The attitude polarization phenomenon: Role of reponse measure, attitude extremity, and behavioral consequences of reported attitude change. *Journal of Personality and Social Psychology, 64,* 561–574.

Miller, George A. (1956). The magical number seven, plus or minus two: Some limits on our capacity for processing information. *Psychological Review, 63,* 81–97.

Miller, George A. (1969, December). On turning psychology over to the unwashed. *Psychology Today,* 53–55, 66–68, 70, 72, 74.

Miller, George A., & Gildea, Patricia M. (1987, September). How children learn words. *Scientific American, 257*(6), 94–99.

Miller, Inglis J., & Reedy, Frank E. (1990). Variations in human taste bud density and taste intensity perception. *Physiology and Behavior, 47,* 1213–1219.

Miller, Joan G. (1984). Culture and the development of everyday social explanation. *Journal of Personality and Social Psychology, 46,* 961–978.

Miller, Jonathan (1983). *States of mind.* New York: Pantheon.

• **Miller, Keith, & Watkinson, Neal** (1983). Recognition of words presented during general anaesthesia. *Ergonomics, 26,* 585–594.

Miller, Neal E. (1978). Biofeedback and visceral learning. *Annual Review of Psychology, 29,* 421–452.

Miller, Neal E. (1985). The value of behavioral research on animals. *American Psychologist, 40,* 423–440.

Miller, Paul A., & Eisenberg, Nancy (1988). The relation of empathy to aggressive and externalizing/antisocial behavior. *Psychological Bulletin, 103,* 324–344.

• **Miller, Scott D., & Triggiano, Patrick J.** (1992). The psychophysiological investigation of multiple personality disorder: Review and update. *American Journal of Clinical Hypnosis, 35,* 47–61.

Miller, Suzanne M.; Brody, David; & Summerton, Jeffrey (1988). Styles of coping with threat: Implications for health. *Journal of Personality and Social Psychology, 54,* 142–148.

Miller-Jones, Dalton (1989). Culture and testing. *American Psychologist, 44,* 360–366.

Milner, Brenda (1970). Memory and the temporal regions of the brain. In K. H. Pribram & D. E. Broadbent (eds.), *Biology of memory.* New York: Academic Press.

• **Milner, J. S., & McCanne, T. R.** (1991). Neuropsychological correlates of physical child abuse. In J. S. Milner (ed.), *Neuropsychology of aggression.* Norwell, MA: Kluwer Academic.

Minuchin, Salvador (1984). *Family kaleidoscope.* Cambridge: Harvard University, Press.

Minuchin, Salvador; Rosman, Bernice L.; & Baker, Lester (1978). *Psychosomatic families: Anorexia nervosa in context.* Cambridge: Harvard University Press.

Mischel, Walter (1973). Toward a cognitive social learning reconceptualization of personality. *Psychological Review, 80,* 252–253.

Mischel, Walter (1984). Convergences and challenges in the search for consistency. *American Psychology, 39,* 351–364.

• **Mischel, Walter** (1990). Personality dispositions revisited and revised: A view after three decades. In L. A. Pervin (ed.), *Handbook of personality.* New York: Guilford Press.

Mishkin, Mortimer, & Appenzeller, Tim (1987). The anatomy of memory. *Scientific American, 256,* 80–89.

• **Mistlberger, Ralph E.** (1991). Scheduled daily exercise or feeding alters the phase of photic entrainment in Syrian hamsters. *Physiology and Behavior, 50,* 1257–1260.

• **Mistry, Jayanthi, & Rogoff, Barbara** (1994). Remembering in cultural context. In W. J. Lonner & R. Malpass (eds.), *Psychology and culture.* Needham Heights, MA: Allyn & Bacon.

• **Mitchell, D. E.** (1980). The influence of early visual experience on visual perception. In C. S. Harris (ed.), *Visual coding and adaptability.* Hillsdale, NJ: Erlbaum.

• **Mithers, Carol L.** (1994). *Reasonable insanity: A true story of the seventies.* Reading, MA: Addison-Wesley.

• **Moffitt, Terrie E.** (1993). Adolescence-limited and life-course-persistent antisocial behavior: A developmental taxonomy. *Psychological Review, 100,* 674–701.

Monk, Timothy H., & Aplin, Lynne C. (1980). Spring and Autumn daylight saving time changes: Studies of adjustment in sleep timings, mood, and efficiency. *Ergonomics, 23,* 167–178.

• **Monmaney, Terence** (1993, September 20). Marshall's hunch: Annals of medicine. (Barry J. Marshall, discoverer of ulcer-causing bacterium.) *The New Yorker, 69,* 64ff.

• **Monteith, Margo J.** (1993). Self-regulation of prejudiced responses: Implications for progress in prejudice-reduction efforts. *Journal of Personality and Social Psychology, 65,* 469–485.

• **Moore, Timothy E.** (1982, Spring). Subliminal advertising: What you see is what you get. *Journal of Marketing, 46,* 38–47.

• **Moore, Timothy E.** (1989). Subliminal psychodynamic activation and the establishment of thresholds. *American Psychologist, 44,* 1420–1421.

• **Moore, Timothy E.** (1992, Spring). Subliminal perception: Facts and fallacies. *Skeptical Inquirer, 16,* 273–281.

• **Moore, Timothy E.** (1994, June). Scientific consensus and expert testimony: Lessons from the Judas Priest trial. Paper presented at the meeting of the Committee for the Scientific Investigation of Claims of the Paranormal, Seattle.

• **Moore, Timothy E.** (1995). Subliminal self-help auditory tapes: An empirical test of perceptual consequences. *Canadian Journal of Behavioural Science, 27,* 9–20.

Moore-Ede, Martin C.; Sulzman, Frank M.; & Fuller, Charles A. (1984). *The clocks that time us: Physiology of the circadian timing system.* Cambridge: Harvard University Press.

• **Morelli, Gilda A.; Rogoff, Barbara; Oppenheim, David; & Goldsmith, Denise** (1992). Cultural variation in infants' sleeping arrangements: Questions of independence. Special Section: Cross-cultural studies of development. *Developmental Psychology, 28,* 604–613.

• **Morris, Michael W., & Peng, Kaiping** (1994). Culture and cause: American and Chinese attributions for social and physical events. *Journal of Personality and Social Psychology, 67,* 949–971.

Morrison, Ann M., & Von Glinow, Mary Ann (1990). Women and minorities in management. *American Psychologist, 42,* 200–208.

Moscovici, Serge (1985). Social influence and conformity. In G. Lindzey & E. Aronson (eds.), *Handbook of social psychology,* Vol. II (3rd ed.). New York: Random House.

• **Moss, Howard B.; Panzak, George L.; Tarter, Ralph, E.** (1993). Personality, mood, and psychiatric symptoms among anabolic steriod users. *American Journal on Addictions, 1,* 315–324.

• **Moston, S.** (1987). The suggestibility of children in interview studies. *First Language, 2,* 67–78.

Mott, Frank L. (1991). Developmental effects of infant care: The mediating role of gender and health. In S. L. Hofferth & D. A. Phillips (eds.), *Child care policy, research. Journal of Social Issues, 47*(2), 139–158.

Mozell, Maxwell M.; Smith, Bruce P.; Smith, Paul E.; Sullivan, Richard L.; & Swender, Philip (1969). Nasal chemoreception in flavor identification. *Archives of Otolaryngology, 90,* 367–373.

• **Muehlenhard, Charlene L.** (1988). "Nice women" don't say yes and "real men" don't say no: How miscommunication and the double standard can cause sexual problems. *Women & Therapy* (Special Issue: Women and sex therapy), *7,* 95–108.

Muehlenhard, Charlene, & Cook, Stephen (1988). Men's self-reports of unwanted sexual activity. *Journal of Sex Research, 24,* 58–72.

• **Mulick, James** (1994, November/December). The non-science of facilitated communication. *Science Agenda* (APA newsletter), 8–9.

Mullen, Brian, & Johnson, Craig (1990). Distinctiveness-based illusory correlations and stereotyping: A meta-analytic integration. *British Journal of Social Psychology, 29,* 11–28.

Mulvey, Edward P.; Geller, Jeffrey L.; & Roth, Loren H. (1987). The promise and peril of involuntary outpatient commitment. *American Psychologist, 42,* 571–584.

Murphy, Jane (1976). Psychiatric labeling in cross-cultural perspective. *Science, 191,* 1019–1028.

• **Murphy, Sean (ed.)** (1993). *Astrocytes: Pharmacology and function.* San Diego, CA: Academic Press.

• **Murphy, Sheila T., & Zajonc, R. B.** (1993). Affect, cognition, and awareness: Affective priming with optimal and suboptimal stimulus exposures. *Journal of Personality and Social Psychology, 64,* 723–739.

Myers, David G. (1980). *The inflated self.* New York: Seabury.

Myers, Ronald E., & Sperry, R. W. (1953). Interocular transfer of a visual form discrimination habit in cats after section of the optic chiasm and corpus callosum. *Anatomical Record, 115,* 351–352.

• **Nadel, Lynn, & Zola-Morgan, Stuart** (1984). Infantile amnesia: A neurobiological perspective. In M. Moscovitch (ed.), *Infantile memory: Its relation to normal and pathological memory in humans and other animals.* New York: Plenum.

• **Nadon, Robert; Hoyt, Irene, P.; Register, Patricia A.; & Kihlstrom, John** (1991). Absorption and hypnotizability: Context effects reexamined. *Journal of Personality and Social Psychology, 60,* 144–153.

Nash, Michael R. (1987). What, if anything, is regressed about hypnotic age regression? A review of the empirical literature. *Psychological Bulletin, 102,* 42–52.

• **Nathan, Debbie** (1994, Fall). Dividing to conquer? Women, men, and the making of multiple personality disorder. *Social Text, 40,* 77–114.

• **National Academy of Sciences (National Research Council).** (1989). *Diet and health: Implications for reducing chronic disease risk.* Washington, DC: National Academy Press.

National Victim Center & Crime Victims Research and Treatment Center (1992). *Rape in America: A report to the nation.* Fort Worth, TX: National Victim Center.

• **Nedergaard, Maiken** (1994). Direct signaling from astrocytes to neurons in cultures of mammalian brain cells. *Science, 263,* 1768–1771.

Needleman, Herbert L.; Leviton, Alan; & Bellingen, David (1982). Lead-associated intellectual deficit. *New England Journal of Medicine, 306,* 367.

Needleman, Herbert L.; Schell, Alan; Bellinger, David; Leviton, Alan; et al. (1990). The long-term effects of exposure to low doses of lead in childhood: An 11-year follow-up report. *New England Journal of Medicine, 322,* 83–88.

Neiss, Rob (1988). Reconceptualizing arousal: Psychobiological states in motor performance. *Psychological Bulletin, 103,* 345–366.

Neisser, Ulric (1982). Snapshots or benchmarks? In U. Neisser (ed.), *Memory observed: Remembering in natural contexts.* San Francisco: Freeman.

Neisser, Ulric, & Harsch, Nicole (1992). Phantom flashbulbs: False recollections of hearing the news about Challenger. In E. Winograd & U. Neisser (eds.), *Affect and accuracy in recall: Studies of "flashbulb memories."* New York: Cambridge University Press.

Neisser, Ulric; Winograd, Eugene; & Weldon, Mary Sue (1991). Remembering the earthquake: "What I experienced" vs. "How I heard the news." Paper presented at the annual meeting of the Psychonomic Society, San Francisco.

Nelson, Thomas O., & Dunlosky, John (1991). When people's judgments of learning (JOLs) are extremely accurate at predicting subsequent recall: The "delayed JOL effect." *Psychological Science, 2,* 267–270.

• **Nelson, Thomas O., & Leonesio, R. Jacob** (1988). Allocation of self-paced study time and the "labor in vain effect." *Journal of Experimental Psychology: Learning, Memory, and Cognition, 14,* 676–686.

Newlin, David B., & Thomson, James B. (1990). Alcohol challenge with sons of alcoholics: A critical review and analysis. *Psychological Bulletin, 108,* 383–402.

Newman, Eric A., & Hartline, Peter H. (1982). The infrared "vision" of snakes. *Scientific American, 246*(3), 116–127.

Newman, Joseph P.; Widom, Cathy S.; & Nathan, Stuart (1985). Passive avoidance in syndromes of disinhibition: Psychopathy and extraversion. *Journal of Personality and Social Psychology, 48,* 1316–1327.

• **Newman, Leonard S., & Baumeister, Roy F.** (1994). "Who would wish for the trauma?" Explaining UFO abductions. Paper presented at the annual meeting of the American Psychological Association, Los Angeles.

Newman, Lucille F., & Buka, Stephen (1991, Spring). Clipped wings. *American Educator,* 27–33, 42.

Nezu, Arthur M.; Nezu, Christine M.; & Blissett, Sonia E. (1988). Sense of humor as a moderator of the relation between stressful events and psychological distress: A prospective analysis. *Journal of Personality and Social Psychology, 54,* 520–525.

Nickerson, Raymond A., & Adams, Marilyn Jager (1979). Long-term memory for a common object. *Cognitive Psychology, 11,* 287–307.

Niemi, G.; Katz, R. S.; & Newman, D. (1980). Reconstructing past partisanship: The failure of party identification recall questions. *American Journal of Political Science, 24,* 633–651.

• **Nigg, Joel T., & Goldsmith, H. Hill** (1994). Genetics of personality disorders: Perspectives from personality and psychopathology research. *Psychological Bulletin, 115,* 346–380.

Nisbett, Richard E. (1988). Testimony on behalf of the American Psychological Association before the U.S. House of Representatives Committee on Armed Services, October 6.

• **Nisbett, Richard E.** (1993). Violence and U.S. regional culture. *American Psychologist, 48,* 441–449.

Nisbett, Richard E., & Ross, Lee (1980). *Human inference: Strategies and shortcomings of social judgment.* Englewood Cliffs, NJ: Prentice-Hall.

Noble, Ernest P.; Blum, Kenneth; Ritchie, T.; Montgomery, A.; & Sheridan, P. J. (1991). Allelic association of the D2 dopamine receptor gene with receptor-binding characteristics in alcoholism. *Archives of General Psychiatry, 48,* 648–654.

Noelle-Neumann, Elisabeth (1984). *The spiral of silence.* Chicago: University of Chicago Press.

Nolen-Hoeksema, Susan (1990). *Sex differences in depression.* Stanford, CA: Stanford University Press.

Nolen-Hoeksema, Susan (1991). Responses to depression and their effects on the duration of depressive episodes. *Journal of Abnormal Psychology, 100,* 569–582.

• **Nolen-Hoeksema, Susan, & Girgus, Joan S.** (1994). The emergence of gender differences in depression during adolescence. *Psychological Bulletin, 115,* 424–443.

Nolen-Hoeksema, Susan; Girgus, Joan S.; & Seligman, Martin E. (1991). Sex differences in depression and explanatory style in children. Special Issue: The emergence of depressive symptoms during adolescence. *Journal of Youth and Adolescence, 20,* 233–245.

Noller, Patricia; Law, Henry; & Comrey, Andrew L. (1987). Cattell, Comrey, and Eysenck personality factors compared: More evidence for the five robust factors? *Journal of Personality and Social Psychology, 53,* 775–782.

Norman, Donald A. (1988). *The psychology of everyday things.* New York: Basic Books.

Nowicki, Stephen, & Duke, Marshall P. (1989). A measure of nonverbal social processing ability in children between the ages of 6 and 10. Paper presented at the annual meeting of the American Psychological Society, Alexandria, VA.

Nowicki, Stephen, & Strickland, Bonnie R. (1973). A locus of control scale for children. *Journal of Consulting Psychology, 40,* 148–154.

• **Oatley, Keith** (1990). Do emotional states produce irrational thinking? In K. J. Gilhooly, M. T. G. Keane, R. H. Logie, & G. Erdos (eds.), *Lines of thinking,* Vol. 2. New York: Wiley.

• **Oatley, Keith, & Duncan, Elaine** (1994). The experience of emotions in everyday life. *Cognition and Emotion, 8,* 369–381.

• **Oatley, Keith, & Jenkins, Jennifer M.** (1992). Human emotions: Function and dysfunction. *Annual Review of Psychology, 43,* 55–85.

Oatley, Keith, & Johnson-Laird, P. N. (1987). Towards a cognitive theory of emotions. *Cognition and Emotion, 1,* 29–50.

Offer, Daniel, & Sabshin, Melvin (1984). Adolescence: Empirical perspectives. In D. Offer & M. Sabshin (eds.), *Normality and the life cycle.* New York: Basic Books.

• **Ofshe, Richard J., & Watters, Ethan** (1994). *Making monsters: False memory, psychotherapy, and sexual hysteria.* New York: Scribners.

Ogden, Jenni A., & Corkin, Suzanne (1991). Memories of H. M. In W. C. Abraham, M. C. Corballis, and K. G. White (eds.), *Memory mechanisms: A tribute to G. V. Goddard.* Hillsdale, NJ: Erlbaum.

• **Ogletree, Billy T.; Hamtil, Anne; Solberg, Larry; & Scoby-Schmelzle, Shelly** (1993). Facilitated communication: Illustration of a naturalistic validation method. *Focus on Autistic Behavior, 8,* 1–10.

• **O'Hanlon, Bill** (1994, November/December). The third wave. *The Family Therapy Networker,* 18–29.

Oliner, Samuel P., & Oliner, Pearl M. (1988). *The altruistic personality: Rescuers of Jews in Nazi Europe.* New York: Free Press.

• **Oliver, Mary Beth, & Hyde, Janet S.** (1993). Gender differences in sexuality: A meta-analysis. *Psychological Bulletin, 114,* 29–51.

• **Olsen, Bonnie J.; Starr, Arnold; & Parker, Elizabeth S.** (in preparation). Learning in a patient with profound memory loss.

O'Neill, Colleen, & Zeichner, Amos (1985). Working women: A study of relationships between stress, coping and health. *Journal of Psychosomatic Obstetrics & Gynaecology, 4,* 105–116.

• **Orlinsky, David E.** (1994). Research-based knowledge as the emergent foundation for clinical practice in psychotherapy. In P. F. Talley, H. H. Strupp, and S. F. Butler (eds.), *Psychotherapy research and practice: Bridging the gap.* New York: Basic Books.

• **Orlinsky, David E., & Howard, Kenneth I.** (1994). Unity and diversity among psychotherapies: A comparative perspective. In B. Bongar & L. E. Beutler (eds.), *Foundations of psychotherapy: Theory, research, and practice.* New York: Oxford University Press.

Ormel, Johan, & Wohlfarth, Tamar (1991). How neuroticism, long-term difficulties, and life situation change influence psychological distress: A longitudinal model. *Journal of Personality and Social Psychology, 60,* 744–755.

• **Orne, Martin T., & Evans, Frederick J.** (1965). Social control in the psychological experiment: Antisocial behavior and hypnosis. *Journal of Personality and Social Psychology, 1,* 189–200.

Ortar, G. (1963). Is a verbal test cross-cultural? *Scripts Hierosolymitana* (Hebrew University, Jerusalem), *13,* 219–235.

Ortony, Andrew; Clore, Gerald L.; & Collins, Allan (1988). *The cognitive structure of emotions.* Cambridge, England: Cambridge University Press.

Ortony, Andrew, & Turner, Terence J. (1990). What's basic about basic emotions. *Psychological Review, 97,* 315–331.

• **Oskamp, Stuart (ed.)** (1988). *Television as a social issue.* Newbury Park, CA: Sage.

• **Oyserman, Daphna, & Saltz, Eli** (1993). Competence, delinquency, and attempts to attain possible selves. *Journal of Personality and Social Psychology, 65,* 360–374.

Ozer, Elizabeth M., & Bandura, Albert (1990). Mechanisms governing empowerment effects: A self-efficacy analysis. *Journal of Personality and Social Psychology, 58,* 472–486.

• **Page, Gayle G.; Ben-Eliyahu, Shamgar; Yirmiya, Raz; & Liebeskind, John C.** (1993). Morphine attenuates surgery-induced enhancement of metastatic colonization in rats. *Pain, 54,* 21–28.

Page, J. Bryan; Fletcher, Jack; & True, William R. (1988). Psychosociocultural perspectives on chronic cannabis use: The Costa Rican follow-up. *Journal of Psychoactive Drugs, 20,* 57–65.

Paige, Karen (1978, May). The ritual of circumcision. *Human Nature, 1,* 40–49.

• **Paige, Karen E., & Paige, Jeffery M.** (1981). *The politics of reproductive ritual.* Berkeley: University of California Press.

Paikoff, Roberta L., & Brooks-Gunn, Jeanne (1991). Do parent-child relationships change during puberty? *Psychological Bulletin, 110,* 47–66.

Paivio, Allan (1983). The empirical case for dual coding. In J. C. Yuille (ed.), *Imagery, memory and cognition.* Hillsdale, NJ: Erlbaum.

Palmer, Stephen; Schreiber, Charles; & Fox, Craig (1991). Remembering the earthquake: "Flashbulb" memory for experienced vs. reported events. Paper presented at the annual meeting of the Psychonomic Society, San Francisco.

Panksepp, J.; Herman, B. H.; Vilberg, T.; Bishop, P.; & DeEskinazi, F. G. (1980). Endogenous opioids and social behavior. *Neuroscience and Biobehavioral Reviews, 4,* 473–487.

Papini, Mauricio R., & Bitterman, M. E. (1990). The role of contingency in classical conditioning. *Psychological Review, 97,* 396–403.

• **Park, Denise C.; Smith, Anderson D.; & Cavanaugh, John C.**

(1990). Metamemories of memory researchers. *Memory and Cognition, 18,* 321–327.

Parker, Elizabeth S.; Birnbaum, Isabel M.; & Noble, Ernest P. (1976). Alcohol and memory: Storage and state dependency. *Journal of Verbal Learning and Verbal Behavior, 15,* 691–702.

Parker, Keven C. H.; Hanson, R. Karl; & Hunsley, John (1988). MMPI, Rorschach, and WAIS: A meta-analytic comparison of reliability, stability, and validity. *Psychological Bulletin, 103,* 367–373.

Parks, Randolph W.; Loewenstein, David A.; Dodrill, Kathryn L.; Barker, William W.; et al. (1988). Cerebral metabolic effects of a verbal fluency test: A PET scan study. *Journal of Clinical & Experimental Neuropsychology, 10,* 565–575.

Parlee, Mary Brown (1982). Changes in moods and activation levels during the menstrual cycle in experimentally naive subjects. *Psychology of Women Quarterly, 7,* 119–131.

Parlee, Mary Brown (1989). The science and politics of PMS research. Paper presented at the annual meeting of the Association for Women in Psychology, Newport, Rhode Island.

• **Parrott, W. Gerrod, & Smith, Richard H.** (1993). Distinguishing the experiences of envy and jealousy. *Journal of Personality and Social Psychology, 64,* 906–920.

• **Parsons, Michael W., & Gold, Paul E.** (1992). Glucose enhancement of memory in elderly humans: An inverted-U dose–response curve. *Neurobiology of Aging, 13,* 401–404.

Pascale, Richard, & Athos, Anthony G. (1981). *The art of Japanese management.* New York: Simon & Schuster.

• **Patterson, Charlotte J.** (1992). Children of lesbian and gay parents. *Child Development, 63,* 1025–1042.

• **Patterson, Charlotte J.** (1995). Sexual orientation and human development: An overview. *Developmental Psychology, 31,* 3–11.

Patterson, Francine, & Linden, Eugene (1981). *The education of Koko.* New York: Holt, Rinehart and Winston.

Patterson, Gerald R. (1986). Performance models for antisocial boys. *American Psychologist, 41,* 432–444.

• **Patterson, Gerald R.** (1994). Developmental perspectives on violence. Invited address presented at the annual meeting of the American Psychological Association, Los Angeles.

Patterson, Gerald R.; DeBaryshe, Barbara D.; & Ramsey, Elizabeth (1989). A developmental perspective on antisocial behavior. *American Psychologist, 44,* 329–335.

• **Patterson, Gerald R.; Reid, John; & Dishion, Thomas** (1992). *Antisocial boys.* Eugene, OR: Castalia.

Paul, Richard W. (1984, September). Critical thinking: Fundamental to education for a free society. *Educational Leadership,* 4–14.

• **Paulus, Paul B., & Dzindolet, Mary T.** (1993). Social influence processes in group brainstorming. *Journal of Personality and Social Psychology, 64,* 575–586.

• **Peabody, Dean** (1985). *National characteristics.* Cambridge, England: Cambridge University Press.

• **Pedersen, Nancy L.; Plomin, Robert; McClearn, G. E.; & Friberg, Lars** (1988). Neuroticism, extraversion, and related traits in adult twins reared apart and reared together. *Journal of Personality and Social Psychology, 55,* 950–957.

Peele, Stanton (1989). *Diseasing of America: Addiction treatment out of control.* Lexington, MA: Lexington Books.

• **Peele, Stanton** (1993). The conflict between public health goals and the temperance mentality. *American Journal of Public Health, 83,* 805–810.

• **Peele, Stanton, & Brodsky, Archie, with Mary Arnold** (1991). *The truth about addiction and recovery.* New York: Simon & Schuster.

• **Pellegrini, Anthony D., & Galda, Lee** (1993). Ten years after: A reexamination of symbolic play and literacy research. *Reading Research Quarterly, 28,* 163–175.

Penfield, Wilder, & Perot, Phanor (1963). The brain's record of auditory and visual experience: A final summary and discussion. *Brain, 86,* 595–696.

Pennebaker, James W.; Colder, Michelle; & Sharp, Lisa K. (1990). Accelerating the coping process. *Journal of Personality and Social Psychology, 58,* 528–527.

• **Pennebaker, James W., & Harber, Kent D.** (1993). A social stage model of collective coping: The Loma Prieta earthquake and the Persian Gulf War. *Journal of Social Issues, 49*(4), 125–145.

Pennebaker, James W.; Hughes, Cheryl F.; & O'Heeron, Robin C. (1987). The psychophysiology of confession: Linking inhibitory and psychosomatic processes. *Journal of Personality and Social Psychology, 52,* 781–793.

Pennebaker, James W.; Kiecolt-Glaser, Janice; & Glaser, Ronald (1988). Disclosure of traumas and immune function: Health implications for psychotherapy. *Journal of Consulting and Clinical Psychology, 56,* 239–245.

• **Peplau, Letitia A.** (1991). Lesbian and gay relationships. In J. C. Gonsiorek & J. D. Weinrich (eds.), *Homosexuality: Research findings for social policy.* Newbury Park, CA: Sage.

• **Peplau, Letitia A., & Conrad, Eva** (1989). Beyond nonsexist research: The perils of feminist methods in psychology. *Psychology of Women Quarterly, 13,* 379–400.

Peplau, Letitia A., & Gordon, Steven L. (1985). Women and men in love: Gender differences in close heterosexual relationships. In V. O'Leary, R. Unger, & B. Wallston (eds.), *Women, gender, and social psychology.* Hillsdale, NJ: Erlbaum.

Pepperberg, Irene M. (1988). Comprehension of "absence" by an African gray parrot: Learning with respect to questions of same/different. *Journal of the Experimental Analysis of Behavior, 50,* 553–564.

Pepperberg, Irene M. (1990). Cognition in an African gray parrot *(Psittacus erithacus):* Further evidence for comprehension of categories and labels. *Journal of Comparative Psychology, 104,* 41–52.

• **Pepperberg, Irene M.** (1994). Numerical competence in an African gray parrot *(Psittacus erithacus). Journal of Comparative Psychology, 108,* 36–44.

Perdue, Charles W.; Dovidio, John F.; Gurtman, Michael B.; & Tyler, Richard B. (1990). Us and them: Social categorization and the process of intergroup bias. *Journal of Personality and Social Psychology, 59,* 475–486.

Perlman, Daniel (1990). Age differences in loneliness: A meta-analysis. Paper presented at the annual meeting of the American Psychological Association, Boston.

• **Perloff, Robert** (1992, Summer). "Where ignorance is bliss, 'tis folly to be wise." *The General Psychologist Newsletter, 28,* 34.

• **Perry, Samuel W., & Heidrich, George** (1982). Management of pain during debridement: A survey of U.S. burn units. *Pain, 13,* 267–280.

• **Persons, Ethel S.** (1986). Manipulativeness in entrepreneurs and psychopaths. In W. H. Reid, D. Dorr, J. I. Walker, & J. W. Bonner (eds.), *Unmasking the psychopath.* New York: Norton.

Persons, Jacqueline B. (1991). Psychotherapy outcome studies do not accurately represent current models of psychotherapy: A proposed remedy. *American Psychologist, 46,* 99–106.

Pert, Candace B., & Snyder, Solomon H. (1973). Opiate receptor: Demonstration in nervous tissue. *Science, 179,* 1011–1014.

• **Pervin, Lawrence A.** (1992). The rational mind and the problem of volition [feature review]. *Psychological Science, 3,* 162–164.

Petersen, Anne C. (1989). Developmental transitions and their role in influencing life trajectories. Paper presented at the annual meeting of the American Psychological Association, New Orleans.

• **Peterson, Bill E., & Stewart, Abigail J.** (1993). Generativity and social motives in young adults. *Journal of Personality and Social Psychology, 65,* 186–198.

Peterson, Lloyd R., & Peterson, Margaret J. (1959). Short-term retention of individual verbal items. *Journal of Experimental Psychology, 58,* 193–198.

• **Peterson, Marilyn R.** (1992). *At personal risk: Boundary violations in professional-client relationships.* New York: Norton.

• **Pfungst, Oskar** (1911/1965). *Clever Hans (The horse of Mr. von Osten): A contribution to experimental animal and human psychology.* New York: Holt, Rinehart and Winston.

• **Phillips, D. P.; Ruth, T. E.; & Wagner, L. M.** (1993, November 6). Psychology and survival. *Lancet, 342*(8880), 1142–1145.

Phinney, Jean S. (1990). Ethnic identity in adolescents and adults: Review of research. *Psychological Bulletin, 108,* 499–514.

Piaget, Jean (1929/1960). *The child's conception of the world.* Paterson, NJ: Littlefield, Adams.

Piaget, Jean (1932). *The moral judgment of the child.* New York: Macmillan.

• **Piaget, Jean** (1951). *Plays, dreams, and imitation in childhood.* New York: Norton.

Piaget, Jean (1952). *The origins of intelligence in children.* New York: International Universities Press.

Piaget, Jean (1984). Piaget's theory. In P. Mussen (ed.), *Handbook of child psychology* (4th ed.), W. Kessen (ed.), *Vol. 1: History, theory, and methods.* New York: Wiley.

• **Pickens, Jeffrey** (1994). Perception of auditory-visual distance relations by 5-month-old infants. *Developmental Psychology, 30,* 537–544.

Pines, Ayala M. (1986). Marriage. In C. Tavris (ed.), *Everywoman's emotional well-being.* New York: Prentice-Hall.

Pines, Maya (1983, September). The human difference. *Psychology Today,* 62–68.

• **Pinker, Steven** (1994a, April 5). The game of the name. *New York Times,* opinion page.

• **Pinker, Steven** (1994b). *The language instinct: How the mind creates language.* New York: Morrow.

• **Pittenger, David J.** (1993). The utility of the Myers-Briggs Type Indicator. *Review of Educational Research, 63,* 467–488.

Plante, Thomas G., & Rodin, Judith (1990). Physical fitness and enhanced psychological health. *Current Psychology: Research and Reviews, 9,* 3–24.

Plomin, Robert (1988). The nature and nurture of cognitive abilities. In R. J. Sternberg (ed.), *Advances in the psychology of human intelligence,* Vol. 4. Hillsdale, NJ: Erlbaum.

Plomin, Robert (1989). Environment and genes: Determinants of behavior. *American Psychologist, 44,* 105–111.

• **Plomin, Robert; Corley, Robin; DeFries, J. C.; & Fulker, D. W.** (1990). Individual differences in television viewing in early childhood: Nature as well as nurture. *Psychological Science, 1,* 371–377.

• **Plomin, Robert, & Daniels, D.** (1987). Why are children in the same family so different from one another? *Behavioral and Brain Sciences, 10,* 1–16.

• **Plomin, Robert, & DeFries, John C.** (1985). *Origins of individual differences in infancy: The Colorado Adoption Project.* New York: Academic Press.

Plous, Scott L. (1991). An attitude survey of animal rights activists. *Psychological Science, 2,* 194–196.

• **Plutchik, Robert** (1988). The nature of emotions: Clinical implications. In M. Clynes & J. Panksepp (eds.), *Emotions and psychopathology.* New York: Plenum.

• **Plutchik, Robert; Conte, Hope R.; Karasu, Toksoz; & Buckley, Peter** (1988, Fall/Winter). The measurement of psychodynamic variables. *Hillside Journal of Clinical Psychology, 10,* 132–147.

Polefrone, Joanna M., & Manuck, Stephen B. (1987). Gender differences in cardiovascular and neuroendocrine response to stressors. In R. C. Barnett, L. Biener, & G. K. Baruch (eds.), *Gender and stress.* New York: Free Press.

Poley, Wayne; Lea, Gary; & Vibe, Gail (1979). Alcoholism: *A treatment manual.* New York: Gardner.

• **Polich, John; Pollock, Vicki E.; & Bloom, Floyd E.** (1994). Meta-analysis of P300 amplitude from males at risk for alcoholism. *Psychological Bulletin, 115,* 55–73.

Pollitt, Katha (1991, December). Reading books, great or otherwise. *Harper's, 34,* 36. [Excerpt from "Why we read," paper delivered at Columbia University Center for American Culture Studies, 1991.]

• **Pomeranz, B. H.** (1989). Transcutaneous electrical nerve stimulation (TENS). In G. Adelman (ed.), *Neuroscience year.* Boston: Birkhauser.

• **Pomerleau, Andree; Bolduc, Daniel; Malcuit, Gerard; & Cossette, Louise** (1990). Pink or blue: Environmental gender stereotypes in the first two years of life. *Sex Roles, 22,* 359–367.

• **Poole, D. A., & White, L. T.** (1991). Effects of question repetition on the eyewitness testimony of children and adults. *Developmental Psychology, 27,* 975–986.

• **Poole, Debra A.; Lindsay, D. Stephen; Memon, Amina; Bull, Ray** (1995). Psychotherapy and the recovery of memories of childhood sexual abuse: U.S. and British practitioners' opinions, practices, and experiences. *Journal of Consulting and Clinical Psychology. 63,* 426–437.

• **Pope, Harrison G., & Hudson, James I.** (1992). Is childhood sexual abuse a risk factor for bulimia nervosa? *American Journal of Psychiatry, 149,* 455–463.

• **Pope, Harrison G., & Katz, David L.** (1992). Psychiatric effects of anabolic steriods. *Psychiatric Annals, 22,* 24–29.

Pope, Harrison G., Jr.; Keck, P. E.; & McElroy, S. L. (1986). Frequency and presentation of neuroleptic malignant syndrome in a large psychiatric hospital. *American Journal of Psychiatry, 143,* 1227–1233.

Pope, Kenneth, & Bouhoutsos, Jacqueline (1986). *Sexual intimacy between therapists and patients.* New York: Praeger.

• **Portenoy, Russell K.** (1994). Opioid therapy for chronic nonmalignant pain: Current status. In H. L. Fields & J. C. Liebeskind

(eds.), *Progress in pain research and management.* Vol. 1 of *Pharmacological approaches to the treatment of chronic pain: New concepts and critical issues.* Seattle: International Association for the Study of Pain.

Postman, Neil (1985). *Amusing ourselves to death.* New York: Viking Penguin.

• **Poulin-Dubois, Diane; Serbin, Lisa A.; Kenyon, Brenda; & Derbyshire, Alison** (1994). Infants' intermodal knowledge about gender. *Developmental Psychology, 30,* 436–442.

Poulos, Constantine X., & Cappell, Howard (1991). Homeostatic theory of drug tolerance: A general model of physiological adaptation. *Psychological Review, 98,* 390–408.

• **Powell, Russell A., & Boer, Douglas P.** (1994). Did Freud mislead patients to confabulate memories of abuse? *Psychological Reports, 74,* 1283–1298.

Pratkanis, Anthony, & Aronson, Elliot (1992). *Age of propaganda: The everyday use and abuse of persuasion.* New York: Freeman.

Premack, David, & Premack, Ann James (1983). *The mind of an ape.* New York: Norton.

• **Prentky, Robert A., & Knight, Raymond A.** (1991). Identifying critical dimensions for discriminating among rapists. Special Section: Theories of sexual aggression. *Journal of Consulting and Clinical Psychology, 59,* 643–661.

Press, Gary A.; Amaral, David G.; & Squire, Larry R. (1989, September 7). Hippocampal abnormalities in amnesic patients revealed by high-resolution magnetic resonance imaging. *Nature, 341,* 54–57.

Pribram, Karl H. (1971). *Languages of the brain: Experimental paradoxes and principles.* Englewood Cliffs, NJ: Prentice-Hall.

Pribram, Karl H. (1982). Localization and distribution of function in the brain. In J. Orbach (ed.), *Neuropsychology after Lashley.* Hillsdale, NJ: Erlbaum.

Prioleau, Leslie; Murdock, Martha; & Brody, Nathan (1983). An analysis of psychotherapy versus placebo studies. *Behavioral and Brain Sciences, 6,* 275–285.

Pryor, Karen (1984). *Don't shoot the dog!* New York: Simon & Schuster.

• **Ptito, Alain; Lepore, Franco; Ptito, Maurice; & Lassonde, Maryse** (1991). Target detection and movement discrimination in the blind field of hemispherectomized patients. *Brain, 114,* 497.

• **Pulver, Ann; Carpenter, William; Adler, Lawrence; & McGrath, John** (1988). Accuracy of diagnoses of affective disorders and schizophrenia in public hospitals. *American Journal of Psychiatry, 145,* 218–220.

• **Pynoos, R. S., & Nader, K.** (1989). Children's memory and proximity to violence. *Journal of the American Academy of Child and Adolescent Psychiatry, 28,* 236–241.

Rabkin, Judith G.; Williams, Janet B.; Remien, Robert H.; Goetz, Raymond; et al. (1991). Depression, distress, lymphocyte subsets, and human immunodeficiency virus symptoms on two occasions in HIV-positive homosexual men. *Archives of General Psychiatry, 48,* 111–119.

Rachman, S. J., & Wilson, G. Terence (1980). *The effects of psychological therapy* (2nd ed.). Oxford, England: Pergamon.

Radetsky, Peter (1991, April). The brainiest cells alive. *Discover, 12,* 82–85, 88, 90.

• **Raine, Adrian; Brennan, Patricia; & Mednick, Sarnoff A.** (1994). Birth complications combined with early maternal rejection at age one year predispose to violent crime at age 18 years. *Archives of General Psychiatry, 51,* 984–988.

• **Raine, Adrian; Buchsbaum, Monte S.; Stanley, Jill; et al.** (1994). Selective reductions in prefrontal glucose metabolism in murderers. Paper presented at the annual meeting of the American Psychological Association, Los Angeles.

• **Ram, Ranganathan; Bromet, Evelyn J.; Eaton, William W.; Pato, Carlos; et al.** (1992). The natural course of schizophrenia: A review of first-admission studies. *Schizophrenia Bulletin, 18,* 185–207.

• **Randi, James** (March, 1982). The 1980 divining tests. *The Skeptic,* 2–6.

• **Rareshide, Margaret, & Kern, Roy** (1991). Social interest: The haves and have nots. *Individual Psychology: Journal of Adlerian Theory, Research & Practice, 47,* 464–476.

• **Ratcliff, Roger** (1990). Connectionist models of recognition memory: Constraints imposed by learning and forgetting functions. *Psychological Review, 97,* 285–308.

Rathbun, Constance; DiVirgilio, Letitia; & Waldfogel, Samuel (1958). A restitutive process in children following radical separation from family and culture. *American Journal of Orthopsychiatry, 28,* 408–415.

Ravussin, Eric; Lillioja, Stephen; Knowler, William; Christin, Laurent; et al. (1988). Reduced rate of energy expenditure as a risk factor for body-weight gain. *New England Journal of Medicine, 318,* 467–472.

Raz, Sarah, & Raz, Naftali (1990). Structural brain abnormalities in the major psychoses: A quantitative review of the evidence from computerized imaging. *Psychological Bulletin, 108,* 93–108.

Rechtschaffen, Allan; Gilliland, Marcia A.; Bergmann, Bernard M.; & Winter, Jacqueline B. (1983). Physiological correlates of prolonged sleep deprivation in rats. *Science, 221,* 182–184.

Reed, Geoffrey M. (1990). Stress, coping, and psychological adaptation in a sample of gay and bisexual men with AIDS. Unpublished doctoral dissertation, University of California, Los Angeles.

• **Reedy, F. E.; Bartoshuk, L. M.; Miller, I. J.; Duffy, V. B.; Lucchina, L.; & Yanagisawa, K.** (1993). Relationships among papillae, taste pores, and 6-n-propylthiouracil (PROP) suprathreshold taste sensitivity. *Chemical Senses, 18,* 618–619.

• **Regier, Darrel A.; Narrow, William E.; Rae, Donald S.; Manderscheid, Ronald W.; et al.** (1993). The de facto US mental and addictive disorders service system: Epidemiologic Catchment Area prospective 1-year prevalence rates of disorders and services. *Archives of General Psychiatry, 50,* 85–94.

• **Reisenzein, Rainer** (1994). Pleasure-arousal theory and the intensity of emotions. *Journal of Personality and Social Psychology, 67,* 525–539.

• **Reppert, Steven M.; Weaver, David R.; Rivkees, Scoff A., & Stopa, Edward G.** (1988). Putative melatonin receptors in a human biological clock. *Science, 242,* 78–81.

Rescorla, Robert A. (1968). Probability of shock in the presence and absence of CS in fear conditioning. *Journal of Comparative and Physiological Psychology, 66,* 1–5.

Rescorla, Robert A. (1988). Pavlovian conditioning: It's not what you think it is. *American Psychologist, 43,* 151–160.

Rescorla, Robert A., & Wagner, Allan R. (1972). A theory of Pavlovian conditioning: Variations in the effectiveness of reinforcement and nonreinforcement. In A. H. Black & W. F. Prokasy (eds.), *Classical conditioning II: Current research and theory.* New York: Appleton-Century-Crofts.

Restak, Richard (1983, October). Is free will a fraud? *Science Digest, 91*(10), 52–55.

• **Restak, Richard M.** (1994). *The modular brain.* New York: Macmillan.

Revenson, Tracey; Wollman, Carol; & Felton, Barbara (1983). Social supports as stress buffers for adult cancer patients. *Psychosomatic Medicine, 45,* 321–331.

Reynolds, Brent A., & Weiss, Samuel (1992). Generation of neurons and astrocytes from isolated cells of the adult mammalian central nervous system. *Science, 255,* 1707–1710.

Reynolds, David K. (1987). *Water bears no scars: Japanese lifeways for personal growth.* New York: Morrow.

• **Rhoades, David F.** (1985). Pheromonal communication between plants. In G. A. Cooper-Driver, T. Swain, & E. E. Conn (eds.), *Research advances in phytochemistry,* Vol. 19. New York: Plenum.

• **Rhode, Deborah L. (ed.)** (1990). *Theoretical perspectives on sexual difference.* New Haven, CT: Yale University Press.

Ricaurte, George A.; Forno, Lysia; Wilson, Mary; deLanney, Louis; Irwin, Ean; Mulliver, Mark; & Langston, J. William (1988). (+ or −) 3, 4-Methylenedioxy-methamphetamine selectively damages central serotonergic neurons in nonhuman primates. *Journal of the American Medical Association, 260,* 51–55.

• **Ricciardi, Joseph N.** (1993). "Increasing frequency of the diagnosis of obsessive-compulsive disorder": Comment. *American Journal of Psychiatry, 150,* 682.

Rice, Mabel L. (1989). Children's language acquisition. *American Psychologist, 44,* 149–156.

Richards, Ruth L. (1991). Everyday creativity and the arts. Paper presented at the annual meeting of the American Psychological Association, San Francisco.

Richardson-Klavehn, Alan, & Bjork, Robert A. (1988). Measures of memory. *Annual Review of Psychology, 39,* 475–543.

• **Richmond, Barry J., & Optican, Lance M.** (1990). Temporal encoding of two-dimensional patterns by single units in primate primary visual cortex. II. Information transmission. *Journal of Neurophysiology, 64,* 370–380.

Ridley, Charles R. (1984). Clinical treatment of the nondisclosing black client. *American Psychologist, 39,* 1234–1244.

Riessman, Catherine K. (1990). *Divorce talk: Women and men make sense of personal relationships.* New Brunswick, NJ: Rutgers University Press.

• **Rimland, Bernard** (1994). New warning about drug danger. *Autism Research Review International, 8,* 1.

• **Ristau, Carolyn A. (ed.)** (1991). *Cognitive ethology: The minds of other animals.* Hillsdale, NJ: Erlbaum.

Roberts, Susan B.; Savage, J.; Coward, W. A.; Chew, B.; & Lucas, A. (1988). Energy expenditure and intake in infants born to lean and overweight mothers. *New England Journal of Medicine, 318,* 461–466.

Robertson, John, & Fitzgerald, Louise F. (1990). The (mis)treatment of men: Effects of client gender role and life-style on diagnosis and attribution of pathology. *Journal of Counseling Psychology, 37,* 3–9.

Robins, Lee N.; Davis, Darlene H.; & Goodwin, Donald W. (1974). Drug use by U.S. Army enlisted men in Vietnam: A follow-up on their return home. *American Journal of Epidemiology, 99,* 235–249.

• **Robins, Lee N.; Tipp, Jayson; & Przybeck, Thomas R.** (1991). Antisocial personality. In L. N. Robins & D. A. Regier (eds.), *Psychiatric disorders in America.* New York: Free Press.

Robinson, Leslie A.; Berman, Jeffrey S.; & Neimeyer, Robert A. (1990). Psychotherapy for the treatment of depression: A comprehensive review of controlled outcome research. *Psychological Bulletin, 108,* 30–49.

Robitscher, Jonas (1980). *The powers of psychiatry.* Boston: Houghton Mifflin.

Rodgers, Joann (1988, April). Pains of complaint. *Psychology Today,* 26–27.

Rodin, Judith; Silberstein, Lisa R.; & Striegel-Moore, Ruth H. (1990). Vulnerability and resilience in the age of eating disorders: Risk and protective factors for bulimia. In J. E. Rolf et al. (eds.), *Risk and protective factors in the development of psychopathology.* Cambridge, England: Cambridge University Press.

Roediger, Henry L., III (1990). Implicit memory: Retention without remembering. *American Psychologist, 45,* 1043–1056.

Roehrs, Timothy; Timms, Victoria; Zsyghuizen-Doorenbos, Ardith; Buzenski, Raymond; et al. (1990). Polysomnographic, performance, and personality differences of sleepy and alert normals. *Sleep, 13,* 395–402.

Roehrs, Timothy; Timms, Victoria; Zsyghuizen-Doorenbos, Ardith; & Roth, Thomas (1989). Sleep extension in sleepy and alert normals. *Sleep, 12,* 449–457.

Rogers, Carl (1951). *Client-centered therapy: Its current practice, implications, and theory.* Boston: Houghton Mifflin.

Rogers, Carl (1961). *On becoming a person.* Boston: Houghton Mifflin.

Rogers, Ronald W., & Prentice-Dunn, Steven (1981). Deindividuation and anger-mediated interracial aggression: Unmasking regressive racism. *Journal of Personality and Social Psychology, 41,* 63–73.

• **Rogers, Stuart** (1992–1993, Winter). How a publicity blitz created the myth of subliminal advertising. *Public Relations Quarterly,* 12–17.

• **Rogoff, Barbara, & Mistry, Jayanthi** (1985). Memory development in cultural context. In M. Pressley & C. Brainerd (eds.), *The cognitive side of memory development.* New York: Springer-Verlag.

Rokeach, Milton, & Ball-Rokeach, Sandra (1989). Stability and change in American value priorities, 1968–1981. *American Psychologist, 44,* 775–784.

Rollin, Henry (ed.) (1980). *Coping with schizophrenia.* London: Burnett.

Rook, Karen S. (1987). Social support versus companionship: Effects on life stress, loneliness, and evaluations by others. *Journal of Personality and Social Psychology, 52,* 1132–1147.

• **Rosaldo, Renato** (1989). *Culture and truth: The remaking of social analysis.* Boston: Beacon Press.

Rosch, Eleanor H. (1973). Natural categories. *Cognitive Psychology, 4,* 328–350.

• **Rose, Suzanna; Zand, Debra; & Cini, Marie A.** (1993). Lesbian courtship scripts. In E. D. Rothblum & K. A. Brehony (eds.), *Boston marriages.* Amherst: University of Massachusetts Press.

• **Roseman, Ira J.; Wiest, Cynthia; & Swartz, Tamara S.** (1994). Phenomenology, behaviors, and goals differentiate discrete emotions. *Journal of Personality and Social Psychology, 67,* 206–221.

• **Rosen, B. R.; Aronen, H. J.; Kwong, K. K.; et al.** (1993). Advances in clinical neuroimaging: Functional MR imaging techniques. *Radiographics, 13,* 889–896.

• **Rosen, Gerald M.** (1981). Guidelines for the review of do-it-yourself treatment books. *Contemporary Psychology, 26,* 189–191.

• **Rosen, Gerald M.** (1993). Self-help or hype? Comments on psychology's failure to advance self-care. *Professional Psychology: Research and Practice, 24,* 340–345.

Rosen, R. D. (1977). *Psychobabble.* New York: Atheneum.

• **Rosenberg, Harold** (1993). Prediction of controlled drinking by alcoholics and problem drinkers. *Psychological Bulletin, 113,* 129–139.

Rosenhan, David L. [D. L.] (1973). On being sane in insane places. *Science, 179,* 250–258.

Rosenthal, Norman E.; Sack, David A.; et al. (1985). Antidepressant effects of light in seasonal affective disorder. *American Journal of Psychiatry, 142,* 163–169.

Rosenthal, Robert (1966). *Experimenter effects in behavioral research.* New York: Appleton-Century-Crofts.

• **Rosenthal, Robert** (1994). Interpersonal expectancy effects: A 30-year perspective. *Current Directions in Psychological Science, 3,* 176–179.

Rosenthal, Robert; Hall, Judith A.; Archer, Dane; DiMatteo, M. Robin; & Rogers, Peter L. (1979). The PONS test: Measuring sensitivity to nonverbal cues. In S. Weitz (ed.), *Nonverbal communication* (2nd ed.). New York: Oxford University Press.

Rosenthal, Robert, & Jacobson, Lenore (1992). *Pygmalion in the classroom: Teacher expectation and pupils' intellectual development.* New York: Irvington.

Rosenzweig, Mark R. (1984). Experience, memory, and the brain. *American Psychologist, 39,* 365–376.

• **Rosnow, Ralph L., & Rosenthal, Robert** (1989). Statistical procedures and the justification of knowledge in psychological science. *American Psychologist, 44,* 1276–1284.

• **Ross, Catherine E.** (1994). Overweight and depression. *Journal of Health and Social Behavior, 35,* 63–79.

Ross, Lee (1977). The intuitive psychologist and his shortcomings: Distortions in the attribution process. In L. Berkowitz (ed.), *Advances in experimental social psychology,* Vol. 10. New York: Academic Press.

Ross, Michael (1989). Relation of implicit theories to the construction of personal histories. *Psychological Review, 96,* 341–357.

Ross, Michael, & Fletcher, Garth J. O. (1985). Attribution and social perception. In G. Lindzey & E. Aronson (eds.), *Handbook of social psychology,* Vol. II (3rd ed.). New York: Random House.

Rothbaum, Fred M.; Weisz, John R.; & Snyder, Samuel S. (1982). Changing the world and changing the self: A two-process model of perceived control. *Journal of Personality and Social Psychology, 42,* 5–37.

Rothman, Barbara (1989). *Recreating motherhood.* New York: Norton.

Rotter, Julian B. (1966). Generalized expectancies for internal versus external control of reinforcement. *Psychological Monographs, 80* (Whole no. 609, 1–28).

• **Rotter, Julian B.** (1982). *The development and applications of social learning theory: Selected papers.* New York: Praeger.

• **Rotter, Julian B.** (1990). Internal versus external control of reinforcement: A case history of a variable. *American Psychologist, 45,* 489–493.

Roueché, Berton (1984, June 4). Annals of medicine: The hoofbeats of a zebra. *The New Yorker, LX,* 71–86.

• **Rovee-Collier, Carolyn** (1993). The capacity for long-term memory in infancy. *Current Directions in Psychological Science, 2,* 130–135.

• **Rozin, Paul; Lowery, Laura; & Ebert, Rhonda** (1994). Varieties of disgust faces and the structure of disgust. *Journal of Personality and Social Psychology, 66,* 870–881.

Ruda, M. A. (1982). Opiates and pain pathways: Demonstration of enkephalin synapses on dorsal horn projection neurons. *Science, 215,* 1523–1525.

Ruggiero, Vincent R. (1988). *Teaching thinking across the curriculum.* New York: Harper & Row.

Rumbaugh, Duane M. (1977). *Language learning by a chimpanzee: The Lana project.* New York: Academic Press.

• **Rumbaugh, Duane M.; Savage-Rumbaugh, E. Sue; & Pate, James L.**

(1988). Addendum to "Summation in the chimpanzee (*Pan troglodytes*)." *Journal of Experimental Psychology: Animal Behavior Processes, 14,* 118–120.

• **Rumelhart, David E., & McClelland, James L.** (1987). Learning the past tenses of English verbs: Implicit rules or parallel distributed processing. In B. MacWhinney (ed.), *Mechanisms of language acquisition.* Hillsdale, NJ: Erlbaum.

Rumelhart, David E.; McClelland, James L.; & The PDP Research Group (1986). *Parallel distributed processing: Explorations in the microstructure of cognition,* Vols. 1 and 2. Cambridge, MA: MIT Press.

Rush, Florence (1980). *The best kept secret: Sexual abuse of children.* Englewood Cliffs, NJ: Prentice-Hall.

Rushton, J. Philippe (1988). Race differences in behavior: A review and evolutionary analysis. *Personality and Individual Differences, 9,* 1009–1024.

• **Rushton, J. Philippe** (1993). Cyril Burt: Victim of the scientific hoax of the century. Paper presented at the annual meeting of the American Psychological Association, Toronto.

Russell, Diana E. H. (1990). *Rape in marriage* (rev. ed.). Bloomington: Indiana University Press.

Russell, James A. (1991a). Culture and the categorization of emotion. *Psychological Bulletin, 110,* 426–450.

Russell, James A. (1991b). In defense of a prototype approach to emotion concepts. *Journal of Personality and Social Psychology, 60,* 37–47.

• **Russell, James A.** (1994). Is there universal recognition of emotion from facial expression? A review of the cross-cultural studies. *Psychological Bulletin, 115,* 102–141.

• **Russell, James A., & Fehr, Beverley** (1994). Fuzzy concepts in a fuzzy hierarchy: Varieties of anger. *Journal of Personality and Social Psychology, 67,* 186–205.

Russell, Michael; Peeke, Harmon V. S.; et al. (1984). Learned histamine release. *Science, 225,* 733–734.

• **Ryan, Alan** (1994, November 17). Apocalypse now? *New York Review,* 7–11.

• **Ryle, Gilbert** (1949). *The concept of mind.* London: Hutchinson.

• **Rymer, Russ** (1993). *Genie: An abused child's flight from silence.* New York: HarperCollins.

Saarni, Carolyn (1989). Children's understanding of strategic control of emotional expression in social transactions. In C. Saarni & P. L. Harris (eds.), *Children's understanding of emotion.* Cambridge, England: Cambridge University Press.

Sabini, John, & Silver, Maury (1985, Winter). Critical thinking and obedience to authority. *National Forum (Phi Beta Kappa Journal),* 13–17.

• **Sackett, Paul R.** (1994). Integrity testing for personnel selection. *Current Directions in Psychological Science, 3,* 73–76.

Sacks, Oliver (1985). *The man who mistook his wife for a hat and other clinical tales.* New York: Simon & Schuster.

Safran, Jeremy D., & Segal, Zindel V. (1990). *Interpersonal process in cognitive therapy.* New York: Basic Books.

• **Sagan, Eli** (1988). *Freud, women, and morality: The psychology of good and evil.* New York: Basic Books.

Sahley, Christie L.; Rudy, Jerry W.; & Gelperin, Alan (1981). An analysis of associative learning in a terrestrial mollusk. 1: Higher-order conditioning, blocking, and a transient US preexposure effect. *Journal of Comparative Physiology, 144,* 1–8.

Saltz, Bruce L.; Woerner, M. G.; Kane, J. M.; Lieberman, J. A.; et al. (1991, November 6). Prospective study of tardive dyskinesia incidence in the elderly. *Journal of the American Medical Association, 266*(17), 2402–2406.

Salzinger, Kurt (1990). A behavioral analysis of human error. Paper presented at the annual meeting of the American Psychological Association, Boston.

• **Samel, Alexander; Wegmann, Hans-Martin; Vejvoda, Martin; Maass, Hartmut; et al.** (1991). Influence of melatonin treatment on human circadian rhythmicity before and after a simulated 9-hr time shift. *Journal of Biological Rhythms, 6,* 235–248.

Samelson, Franz (1979). Putting psychology on the map: Ideology and intelligence testing. In A. R. Buss (ed.), *Psychology in social context.* New York: Irvington.

Sameroff, Arnold J., & Seifer, Ronald (1989). Social regulation of developmental continuities. Paper presented at the annual meeting of the American Association for the Advancement of Science, San Francisco.

Sameroff, Arnold J.; Seifer, Ronald; Barocas, Ralph; Zax, Melvin; & Greenspan, Stanley (1987). Intelligence quotient scores of 4-year-old children: Social-environmental risk factors. *Pediatrics, 79*, 343–350.

• **Sanberg, Paul R.; Koutouzis, Ted K.; Freeman, Thomas B.; et al.** (1992). Cell transplantation for Huntington's disease. *Transplantation Proceedings, 24*, 3015–3016.

• **Sanberg, Paul R.; Koutouzis, Ted K.; Freeman, Thomas B.; et al.** (1993). Behavioral effects of fetal neural transplants: Relevance to Huntington's disease. *Brain Research Bulletin, 32*, 493–496.

Sanders, Diana; Warner, Pamela; Bäckström, Torbjörn; & Bancroft, John (1983). Mood, sexuality, hormones and the menstrual cycle. I. Changes in mood and physical state: Description of subjects and method. *Psychosomatic Medicine, 45*, 487–501.

• **Sanua, Victor D.** (1994). "Prescription privileges" versus psychologists' authority: Psychologists do better without drugs. Paper presented at the annual meeting of the American Psychological Association, Los Angeles.

Sapolsky, Robert M. (1987, July). The case of the falling nightwatchmen. *Discover, 8*, 42–45.

• **Sarbin, Theodore R.** (1986). The narrative as a root metaphor for psychology. In T. R. Sarbin (ed.), *Narrative psychology: The storied nature of human conduct.* New York: Praeger.

Sarbin, Theodore R. (1991). Hypnosis: A fifty year perspective. *Contemporary Hypnosis, 8*, 1–15.

Sarbin, Theodore R. (1992). The social construction of schizophrenia. In W. Flack, D. R. Miller, & M. Wiener (eds.), *What is schizophrenia?* New York: Springer-Verlag.

• **Sáry, Gyula; Vogels, Rufin; & Orban, Guy A.** (1993). Cue-invariant shape selectivity of macaque inferior temporal neurons. *Science, 260*, 995–997.

Satir, Virginia (1983). *Conjoint family therapy* (3rd ed.). Palo Alto, CA: Science and Behavior Books.

• **Saucier, Gerard** (1994). Separating description and evaluation in the structure of personality attributes. *Journal of Personality and Social Psychology, 66*, 141–154.

Savage-Rumbaugh, E. Sue (1986). *Ape language: From conditioned response to symbol.* New York: Columbia University Press.

• **Savage-Rumbaugh, Sue, & Lewin, Roger** (1994). *Kanzi: The ape at the brink of the human mind.* New York: Wiley.

Savage-Rumbaugh, Sue; Sevcik, Rose A.; Brakke, Karen E.; Rumbaugh, Duane M.; & Greenfield, Patricia M. (1990). Symbols: Their communicative use, comprehension, and combination by Bonobos (*Pan paniscus*). In C. Rovee-Collier & L. P. Lipsitt (eds.), *Advances in infancy research*, Vol. 6. Norwood, NJ: Ablex.

• **Saxe, Leonard** (1994). Detection of deception: Polygraph and integrity tests. *Current Directions in Psychological Science, 3*, 69–73.

Scarborough, Elizabeth, & Furumoto, Laurel (1987). *Untold lives: The first generation of American women psychologists.* New York: Columbia University Press.

• **Scarnati, James T.; Kent, William; & MacKenzie, William** (1993). Peer coaching and cooperative learning: One room school concept. *Journal of Instructional Psychology, 20*, 65–71.

Scarr, Sandra (1984). Intelligence: What an introductory psychology student might want to know. In A. M. Rogers and C. J. Scheirer (eds.), *The G. Stanley Hall Lecture Series*, Vol. 4. Washington, DC: American Psychological Association.

• **Scarr, Sandra, & McCartney, Kathleen** (1983). How people make their own environments: A theory of genotype→environment effects. *Child Development, 54*, 424–435.

Scarr, Sandra; Pakstis, Andrew J.; Katz, Soloman H.; & Barker, William B. (1977). Absence of a relationship between degree of white ancestry and intellectual skill in a black population. *Human Genetics, 39*, 69–86.

Scarr, Sandra, & Weinberg, Richard A. (1976). IQ test performance of black children adopted by white families. *American Psychologist, 31*, 726–739.

Scarr, Sandra, & Weinberg, Richard A. (1977). Intellectual similarities within families of both adopted and biological children. *Intelligence, 1*, 170–191.

Schachter, Stanley (1971). *Emotion, obesity, and crime.* New York: Academic Press.

Schachter, Stanley, & Singer, Jerome E. (1962). Cognitive, social, and physiological determinants of emotional state. *Psychological Review, 69*, 379–399.

Schacter, Daniel L. (1986). Amnesia and crime: How much do we really know? *American Psychologist, 41*, 286–295.

Schacter, Daniel L. (1987). Implicit memory: History and current status. *Journal of Experimental Psychology: Learning, Memory, and Cognition, 13*, 501–518.

• **Schacter, Daniel L.** (1990). Memory. In M. I. Posner (ed.), *Foundations of cognitive science.* Cambridge, MA: MIT Press.

Schacter, Daniel L., & Moscovitch, Morris (1984). Infants, amnesics, and dissociable memory systems. In M. Moscovitch (ed.), *Infant memory.* New York: Plenum.

• **Schafer, Roy** (1992). *Retelling a life: Narration and dialogue in psychoanalysis.* New York: Basic Books.

• **Schaie, K. Warner** (1993). The Seattle Longitudinal Studies of adult intelligence. *Current Directions in Psychological Science, 2*, 171–175.

Schank, Roger (with Peter Childers) (1988). *The creative attitude.* New York: Macmillan.

Schatzman, M.; Worsley, A.; & Fenwick, P. (1988). Correspondence during lucid dreams between dreamed and actual events. In J. Gackenbach & S. LaBerge (eds.), *Conscious mind, sleeping brain.* New York: Plenum.

Schein, Edgar; Schneier, Inge; & Barker, Curtis H. (1961). *Coercive persuasion.* New York: Norton.

• **Scherer, Klaus R., & Wallbott, Harald G.** (1994). Evidence for universality and cultural variation of differential emotion response patterning. *Journal of Personality and Social Psychology, 66*, 310–328.

Schlossberg, Nancy K. (1984). Exploring the adult years. In A. M. Rogers & C. J. Scheirer (eds.), *The G. Stanley Hall lecture series*, Vol. 4. Washington, DC: American Psychological Association.

Schmidt, Peter J.; Nieman, Lynnette K.; Grover, Gay N.; Muller, Kari L.; et al. (1991). Lack of effect of induced menses on symptoms in women with premenstrual syndrome. *New England Journal of Medicine, 324*, 1174–1179.

Schneider, Allen M., & Tarshis, Barry (1986). *An introduction to physiological psychology* (3rd ed.). New York: Random House.

• **Schneider, Kirk J., & May, Rollo** (1995). *The psychology of existence: An integrative, clinical perspective.* New York: McGraw-Hill.

Schnell, Lisa, & Schwab, Martin E. (1990, January 18). Axonal regeneration in the rat spinal cord produced by an antibody against myelin-associated neurite growth inhibitors. *Nature, 343*, 269–272.

• **Schooler, Jonathan W.** (1994). Seeking the core: The issues and evidence surrounding recovered accounts of sexual trauma. In W. P. Banks & K. Pezdek (eds.), *Consciousness and Cognition* (Special issue: The recovered memory/false memory debate), *3*, 452–469.

• **Schulkin, Jay** (1994). Melancholic depression and the hormones of adversity: A role for the amygdala. *Current Directions in Psychological Science, 3*, 41–44.

• **Schulman, Michael, & Mekler, Eva** (1994). *Bringing up a caring child* (rev. ed.). New York: Doubleday.

Schulz, Richard, & Decker, Susan (1985). Long-term adjustment to physical disability: The role of social support, perceived control, and self-blame. *Journal of Personality and Social Psychology, 48*, 1162–1172.

Schuman, Howard, & Scott, Jacqueline (1989). Generations and collective memories. *American Journal of Sociology, 54*, 359–381.

Schwartz, Barry, & Reilly, Martha (1985). Long-term retention of a complex operant in pigeons. *Journal of Experimental Psychology: Animal Behavior Processes, 11*, 337–355.

Schwartz, Gary E. (1990). The data are always friendly: A new look at repression and health? Paper presented at the annual meeting of the Western Psychological Association, Los Angeles.

• **Scofield, Michael** (1993, June 6). About men: Off the ladder. *New York Times Magazine*, 22.

Scogin, Forrest; Bynum, Jerry; Stephens, Gretchen; & Calhoon, Sharon (1990). Efficacy of self-administered treatment programs: Meta-analytic review. *Professional Psychology: Research and Practice, 21*, 42–47.

Scribner, Sylvia (1977). Modes of thinking and ways of speaking: Culture and logic reconsidered. In P. N. Johnson-Laird & P. C. Wason (eds.), *Thinking: Readings in cognitive science.* Cambridge, England: Cambridge University Press.

• **Seabrook, John** (1994, March). Building a better human. [Book review of "The Gene Wars" by Robert Cook-Deegan.] *The New Yorker*, 109–114.

Sears, Pauline, & Barbee, Ann H. (1977). Career and life satisfactions among Terman's gifted women. In J. C. Stanley, W. C. George, & C. H. Solano (eds.), *The gifted and the creative: A fifty-year perspective.* Baltimore, MD: Johns Hopkins University Press.

• Sebel, Peter, S.; Bonke, Benno; & Winograd, Eugene (1993). *Memory and awareness in anesthesia.* Englewood Cliffs, NJ: Prentice-Hall.

Segal, Julius (1986). *Winning life's toughest battles.* New York: McGraw-Hill.

• Segall, Marshall H. (1994). A cross-cultural research contribution to unraveling the nativist/empiricist controversy. In W. J. Lonner & R. Malpass (eds.), *Psychology and culture.* Needham Heights, MA: Allyn & Bacon.

Segall, Marshall H.; Campbell, Donald T.; & Herskovits, Melville J. (1966). *The influence of culture on visual perception.* Indianapolis: Bobbs-Merrill.

Segall, Marshall H.; Dasen, Pierre R.; Berry, John W.; & Poortinga, Ype H. (1990). *Human behavior in global perspective: An introduction to cross-cultural psychology.* New York: Pergamon.

Seiden, Richard (1978). Where are they now? A follow-up study of suicide attempters from the Golden Gate Bridge. *Suicide and Life-Threatening Behavior, 8,* 203–216.

Seidenberg, Mark S., & Petitto, Laura A. (1979). Signing behavior in apes: A critical review. *Cognition, 7,* 177–215.

Sekuler, Robert, & Blake, Randolph (1985). *Perception.* New York: Knopf.

Seligman, Martin E. P. (1975). *Helplessness: On depression, development, and death.* San Francisco: Freeman.

Seligman, Martin E. P. (1991). *Learned optimism.* New York: Knopf.

Seligman, Martin E. P., & Hager, Joanne L. (1972, August). Biological boundaries of learning: The sauce-Béarnaise syndrome. *Psychology Today,* 59–61, 84–87.

Sem-Jacobsen, C. W. (1959). Effects of electrical stimulation on the human brain. *Electroencephalography and Clinical Neurophysiology, 11,* 379.

• Serbin, Lisa A.; Powlishta, Kimberly K.; & Gulko, Judith (1993). The development of sex typing in middle childhood. *Monographs of the Society for Research in Child Development, 58*(2, Serial No. 232), v–74.

• Serdula, Mary K.; Collins, M. E.; Williamson, David F.; et al. (1993). Weight control practices of U.S. adolescents and adults. *Annals of Internal Medicine, 119,* 667–671.

• Serpell, Robert (1994). The cultural construction of intelligence. In W. J. Lonner & R. S. Malpass (eds.), *Psychology and culture.* Needham Heights, MA: Allyn & Bacon.

Shadish, William R., Jr.; Lurigio, Arthur J.; & Lewis, Dan A. (1989). After deinstitutionalization: The present and future of mental health long-term care policy. *Journal of Social Issues, 45*(3), 1–16.

• Shapiro, A. Eugene, & Wiggins, Jack G. (1994). A PsyD degree for every practitioner. *American Psychologist, 49,* 207–210.

• Shapiro, David A., & Shapiro, Diana (1982). Meta-analysis of comparative therapy outcome studies: A replication and refinement. *Psychological Bulletin, 92,* 581–604.

Shatz, Marilyn, & Gelman, Rochel (1973). The development of communication skills: Modifications in the speech of young children as a function of the listener. *Monographs of the Society for Research in Child Development, 38.*

• Shaver, Phillip R. (1994). Attachment and care giving in adult romantic relationships. Paper presented at the annual meeting of the American Psychological Association, Los Angeles.

Shaver, Phillip, & Buhrmester, Duane (1983). Loneliness, sex-role orientation, and group life: A social needs perspective. In P. B. Paulus (ed.), *Basic group processes.* New York: Springer-Verlag.

Shaver, Phillip, & Hazan, Cindy (1987). Romantic love conceptualized as an attachment process. *Journal of Personality and Social Psychology, 52,* 511–524.

Shaver, Phillip; Schwartz, Judith; Krison, Donald; & O'Connor, Cary (1987). Emotion knowledge: Further exploration of a prototype approach. *Journal of Personality and Social Psychology, 52,* 1061–1086.

Shaver, Phillip R.; Wu, Shelley; & Schwartz, Judith C. (1992). Cross-cultural similarities and differences in emotion and its representation: A prototype approach. In M. S. Clark (ed.), *Review of Personality and Social Psychology,* Vol. 13. Newbury Park, CA: Sage.

• Shaw, Daniel S.; Keenan, Kate; & Vondra, Joan I. (1994). Developmental precursors of externalizing behavior: Ages 1 to 3. *Developmental Psychology, 30,* 355–364.

• Shaywitz, Bennett A.; Shaywitz, Sally E.; Pugh, Kenneth R.; et al. (1995). Sex differences in the functional organization of the brain for language. *Nature, 373,* 607–609.

Shedler, Jonathan, & Block, Jack (1990). Adolescent drug use and psychological health. *American Psychologist, 45,* 612–630.

• Shedler, Jonathan; Mayman, Martin; & Manis, Melvin (1993). The illusion of mental health. *American Psychologist, 48,* 1117–1131.

Shepard, Roger N. (1967). Recognition memory for words, sentences and pictures. *Journal of Verbal Learning and Verbal Behavior, 6,* 156–163.

Shepard, Roger N., & Metzler, Jacqueline (1971). Mental rotation of three-dimensional objects. *Science, 171,* 701–703.

Sherif, Carolyn Wood (1979). Bias in psychology. In J. Sherman & E. T. Beck (eds.), *The prism of sex.* Madison: University of Wisconsin Press.

Sherif, Muzafer (1958). Superordinate goals in the reduction of intergroup conflicts. *American Journal of Sociology, 63,* 349–356.

Sherif, Muzafer; Harvey, O. J.; White, B. J.; Hood, William; & Sherif, Carolyn (1961). *Intergroup conflict and cooperation: The Robbers Cave experiment.* Norman: University of Oklahoma Institute of Intergroup Relations.

Sherman, Bonnie R., & Kunda, Ziva (1989). Motivated evaluation of scientific evidence. Paper presented at the annual meeting of the American Psychological Society, Arlington, VA.

Sherman, Lawrence W. (1992). *Policing domestic violence.* New York: Free Press.

Sherman, Lawrence W., & Berk, Richard A. (1984). The specific deterrent effects of arrest for domestic assault. *American Sociological Review, 49,* 261–271.

Sherman, Lawrence W.; Schmidt, Janell D.; Rogan, Dennis P.; et al. (1991). From initial deterrence to long-term escalation: Short-custody arrest for poverty ghetto domestic violence. *Criminology, 29,* 821–849.

Sherrington, Robin; Brynjolfsson, Jon; Petursson, Hannes; Potter, Mark; et al. (1988, November 10). Location of a susceptibility locus for schizophrenia on chromosome 5. *Nature, 336,* 164–167.

Sherry, David F., & Schacter, Daniel L. (1987). The evolution of multiple memory systems. *Psychological Review, 94,* 439–454.

• Sherwin, Barbara B. (1988). A comparative analysis of the role of androgen in human male and female sexual behavior: Behavioral specificity, critical thresholds, and sensitivity. *Psychobiology, 16,* 416–425.

Shields, Stephanie A. (1975). Functionalism, Darwinism, and the psychology of women: A study in social myth. *American Psychologist, 30,* 739–754.

Shields, Stephanie A. (1991). Gender in the psychology of emotion: A selective research review. In K. T. Strongman (ed.), *International Review of Studies on Emotion,* Vol. 1. New York: Wiley.

Shiller, R. (1987). The volatility of stock market prices. *Science, 235,* 33–37.

• Shogren, Elizabeth (1994, August 18). Treatment against their will. *Los Angeles Times,* A1, A14–16.

Shotland, R. Lance, & Straw, Margaret (1976). Bystander response to an assault: When a man attacks a woman. *Journal of Personality and Social Psychology, 34,* 990–999.

Shuchman, Miriam, & Wilkes, Michael S. (1990, October 7). Dramatic progress against depression. *New York Times Magazine,* Pt. 2, *The Good Health Magazine,* 12, 30ff.

Shumaker, Sally A., & Hill, D. Robin (1991). Gender differences in social support and physical health. *Health Psychology, 10,* 102–111.

Shweder, Richard A. (1990). Cultural psychology—What is it? In J. W. Stigler, R. A. Shweder, & G. Herdt (eds.), *Cultural psychology: The Chicago symposia on human development.* Cambridge, England: Cambridge University Press.

Shweder, Richard A.; Mahapatra, Manamohan; & Miller, Joan G. (1990). Culture and moral development. In J. W. Stigler, R. A. Shweder, & G. Herdt (eds.), *Cultural psychology: Essays on comparative human development.* Cambridge: Cambridge University Press.

Sibatani, Atuhiro (1980, December). The Japanese brain. *Science, 80,* 22–26.

Siegel, Alan B. (1991). *Dreams that can change your life.* Los Angeles: Jeremy Tarcher.

Siegel, Ronald K. (1989). *Intoxication: Life in pursuit of artificial paradise.* New York: Dutton.

• Siegel, Shepard (1990). Classical conditioning and opiate tolerance and withdrawal. In D. J. K. Balfour (ed.), *Psychotropic drugs of abuse.* New York: Pergamon.

Siegel, Shepard; Hinson, Riley E.; Krank, Marvin D.; & McCully, Jane (1982). Heroin "overdose" death: Contribution of drug-associated environmental cues. *Science, 216,* 436–437.

Siegel, Shepard, & Sdao-Jarvie, Katherine (1986). Attenuation of ethanol tolerance by a novel stimulus. *Psychopharmacology, 88,* 258–261.

• **Silver, Eric; Cirincione, Carmen; & Steadman, Henry J.** (1994). Demythologizing inaccurate perceptions of the insanity defense. *Law and Human Behavior, 18,* 63–70.

• **Silverman, Loyd, & Weinberger, Joel** (1985). Mommy and I are one: Implications for psychotherapy. *American Psychologist, 40,* 1296–1308.

Silverstein, Brett; Peterson, Barbara; & Perdue, Lauren (1986). Some correlates of the thin standard of bodily attractiveness in women. *International Journal of Eating Disorders, 5,* 145–155.

Simon, Herbert A. (1973). The structure of ill-structured problems. *Artificial Intelligence, 4,* 181–202.

• **Simon, Herbert A.** (1992). What is an "explanation" of behavior? *Psychological Science, 3,* 150–161.

Sims, Ethan A. (1974). Studies in human hyperphagia. In G. Bray & J. Bethune (eds.), *Treatment and management of obesity.* New York: Harper & Row.

• **Sinclair, Robert C.; Hoffman, Curt; Mark, Melvin M.; Martin, Leonard L.; & Pickering, Tracie L.** (1994). Construct accessibility and the misattribution of arousal: Schachter and Singer revisited. *Psychological Science, 5,* 15–19.

Singer, Jerome L. (1984). The private personality. *Personality and Social Psychology Bulletin, 10,* 7–30.

Singer, Jerome L., & Singer, Dorothy G. (1988). Some hazards of growing up in a television environment: Children's aggression and restlessness. In S. Oskamp (ed.), *Television as a social issue (Applied Social Psychology Annual,* Vol. 8). Newbury Park, CA: Sage.

• **Singer, Margaret T.; Temerlin, Maurice K.; & Langone, Michael D.** (1990). Psychotherapy cults. *Cultic Studies Journal, 7,* 101–125.

Skeptic (1994). Roper Poll highly exaggerated says Gallup. Skeptical News column, *Skeptic, 2*(4), 24.

Skinner, B. F. (1938). *The behavior of organisms: An experimental analysis.* New York: Appleton-Century-Crofts.

Skinner, B. F. (1948). Superstition in the pigeon. *Journal of Experimental Psychology, 38,* 168–172.

Skinner, B. F. (1948/1976). *Walden Two.* New York: Macmillan.

Skinner, B. F. (1950). Are theories of learning necessary? *Psychological Review, 57,* 193–216.

Skinner, B. F. (1956). A case history in the scientific method. *American Psychologist, 11,* 221–233.

• **Skinner, B. F.** (1968). The technology of teaching. New York: Appleton-Century-Crofts.

Skinner, B. F. (1972). The operational analysis of psychological terms. In B. F. Skinner, *Cumulative record* (3rd ed.). New York: Appleton-Century-Crofts.

Skinner, B. F. (1974). *About behaviorism.* New York: Knopf.

Skinner, B. F. (1983). *A matter of consequences.* New York: Knopf.

Skinner, B. F. (1990). Can psychology be a science of mind? *American Psychologist, 45,* 1206–1210.

• **Skinner, J. B.; Erskine, A.; Pearace, S. A.; Rubenstein, I.; et al.** (1990). The evaluation of a cognitive behavioural treatment programme in outpatients with chronic pain. *Journal of Psychosomatic Research, 34,* 13–19.

Skreslet, Paula (1987, November 30). The prizes of first grade. *Newsweek,* 8.

Slade, Pauline (1984). Premenstrual emotional changes in normal women: Fact or fiction. *Journal of Psychosomatic Research, 28,* 1–7.

• **Slobin, Daniel I.** (1970). Universals of grammatical development in children. In G. B. Flores d'Arcais & W. J. M. Levelt (eds.), *Advances in psycholinguistics.* Amsterdam, Netherlands: North-Holland.

Slobin, Daniel I. (1979). *Psycholinguistics* (2nd ed.). Glenview, IL: Scott, Foresman.

Slobin, Daniel I. (1985). *The cross-linguistic study of language acquisition,* Vols. 1 & 2. Hillsdale, NJ: Erlbaum.

• **Slobin, Daniel I. (ed.)** (1991). *The cross-linguistic study of language acquisition,* Vol. 3. Hillsdale, NJ: Erlbaum.

• **Smelser, Neil J.; Vasconcellos, John; & Mecca, Andrew (eds.)** (1989). *The social importance of self-esteem.* Berkeley: University of California Press.

Smith, Barbara A.; Fillion, Thomas J.; & Blass, Elliott M. (1990). Orally mediated sources of calming in 1- to 3-day-old human infants. *Developmental Psychology, 26,* 731–737.

• **Smith, Carlyle, & MacNeill, Christine** (1993). A paradoxical sleep-dependent window for memory 53–56 h after the end of avoidance training. *Psychobiology, 21,* 109–112.

Smith, Craig A., & Ellsworth, Phoebe C. (1987). Patterns of appraisal and emotion related to taking an exam. *Journal of Personality and Social Psychology, 52,* 475–488.

• **Smith, Craig A.; Haynes, Kelly N.; Lazarus, Richard S.; & Pope, Lois K.** (1993). In search of the "hot" cognitions: Attributions, appraisals, and their relation to emotion. *Journal of Personality and Social Psychology, 65,* 916–929.

Smith, James F., & Kida, Thomas (1991). Heuristics and biases: Expertise and task realism in auditing. *Psychological Bulletin, 109,* 472–489.

• **Smith, M. Brewster** (1994). Selfhood at risk: Postmodern perils and the perils of postmodernism. *American Psychologist, 49,* 405–411.

Smith, Mary Lee; Glass, Gene; & Miller, Thomas I. (1980). *The benefits of psychotherapy.* Baltimore, MD: Johns Hopkins University Press.

Smith Timothy W.; Sanders, Jill D.; & Alexander, James F. (1990). What does the Cook and Medley Hostility Scale Measure? Affect, behavior, and attributions in the marital context. *Journal of Personality and Social Psychology, 58,* 699–708.

Smith, Tom W. (1991). *What do Americans think about Jews?* New York: American Jewish Committee.

Smither, Robert D. (1988). *The psychology of work and human performance.* New York: Harper & Row.

• **Snarey, John R.** (1985). Cross-cultural universality of social-moral development: A critical review of Kohlbergian research. *Psychological Bulletin, 97,* 202–232.

Snodgrass, Mary Ann (1987). The relationships of differential loneliness, intimacy, and characterological attributional style to duration of loneliness. In M. Hojat & R. Crandall (eds.), *Loneliness: Theory, research, and applications* (Special Issue of the *Journal of Social Behavior and Personality), 2,* 173–186.

Snodgrass, Sara E. (1985). Women's intuition: The effect of subordinate role on interpersonal sensitivity. *Journal of Personality and Social Psychology, 49,* 146–155.

Snodgrass, Sara E. (1992). Further effects of role versus gender on interpersonal sensitivity. *Journal of Personality and Social Psychology, 62,* 154–158.

Snow, Barry R; Pinter, Isaac; Gusmorino, Paul; Jimenez, Arthur; Rosenblum, Andrew; & Adelglass, Howard (1986). Sex differences in chronic pain: Incidence and causal mechanisms. Paper presented at the annual meeting of the American Psychological Association, Washington, DC.

• **Snow, Margaret E.; Jacklin, Carol N.; & Maccoby, Eleanor** (1983). Sex-of-child differences in father-child interaction at one year of age. *Child Development, 54,* 227–232.

Snyder, C. R. (1989). Reality negotiation: From excuses to hope and beyond. Special Issue: Self-illusions: When are they adaptive? *Journal of Social and Clinical Psychology, 8,* 130–157.

Snyder, C. R. (1990). Self-handicapping processes and sequelae: On the taking of a psychological dive. In R. L. Higgins, C. R. Snyder, & S. C. Berglas (eds.), *Self-handicapping: The paradox that isn't.* New York: Plenum.

Snyder, C. R., & Shenkel, Randee J. (1975, March). The P. T. Barnam effect. *Psychology Today,* 52–54.

Snyder, C. R.; Higgins, Raymond L.; & Stucky, Rita J. (1983). *Excuses: Masquerades in search of grace.* New York: Wiley-Interscience.

• **Snyder, Robert A.** (1993, Spring). The glass ceiling for women: Things that don't cause it and things that won't break it. *Human Resource Development Quarterly,* 97–106.

Solomon, Anita O. (1991). Psychotherapeutic techniques for victims of destructive cults. Paper presented at the annual meeting of the American Psychological Association, San Francisco.

Solomon, Paul R. (1979). Science and television commercials: Adding relevance to the research methodology course. *Teaching of Psychology, 6,* 26–30.

Solomon, Robert C. (1994). *About love.* Lanham, MD: Littlefield Adams.

Sommer, Robert (1969). *Personal space: The behavioral basis of design.* Englewood Cliffs, NJ: Prentice-Hall.

Sommer, Robert (1977, January). Toward a psychology of natural behavior. *APA Monitor.* (Reprinted in *Readings in psychology 78/79.* Guilford, CT: Dushkin, 1978.)

Sontag, Susan (1978). *Illness as metaphor.* New York: Farrar, Straus & Giroux.

Sorce, James F.; Emde, Robert N.; Campos, Joseph; & Klinnert, Mary D. (1985). Maternal emotional signaling; its effect on the visual cliff behavior of 1-year-olds. *Developmental Psychology, 21,* 195–200.

Spangler, William D., & House, Robert J. (1991). Presidential effectiveness and the leadership motive profile. *Journal of Personality and Social Psychology, 60,* 439–455.

Spanos, Nicholas P. (1986). Hypnotic behavior: A social-psychological interpretation of amnesia, analgesia, and "trance logic." *Behavorial and Brain Sciences, 9,* 449–467.

Spanos, Nicholas P. (1994). Multiple identity enactments and multiple personality disorder: A sociocognitive perspective. *Psychological Bulletin, 116,* 143–165.

Spanos, Nicholas P.; Burgess, Cheryl A.; Roncon, Vera; Wallace-Capretta, Suzanne; & Cross, Patricia (1993). Surreptitiously observed hypnotic responding in simulators and in skill-trained and untrained high hypnotizables. *Journal of Personality and Social Psychology, 65,* 391–398.

Spanos, Nicholas P.; DuBreuil, Susan C.; & Gabora, Natalie J. (1991). Four month follow-up of skill training induced enhancements in hypnotizability. *Contemporary Hypnosis, 8,* 25–32.

Spanos, Nicholas P.; Stenstrom, Robert J.; & Johnson, Joseph C. (1988). Hypnosis, placebo, and suggestion in the treatment of warts. *Psychosomatic Medicine, 50,* 245–260.

Spearman, Charles (1927). *The abilities of man.* London: Macmillan.

Spelke, Elizabeth S.; Breinlinger, Karen; Macomber, Janet; & Jacobson, Kristen (1992). Origins of knowledge. *Psychological Review, 99,* 605–632.

Speltz, Matthew L.; Greenberg, Mark T.; & Deklyen, Michelle (1990). Attachment in preschoolers with disruptive behavior: A comparison of clinic-referred and nonproblem children. *Development and Psychopathology, 2,* 31–46.

Spence, Janet T. (1985a). Achievement American style. *American Psychologist, 40,* 1285–1295.

Spence, Janet T. (1985b). Gender identity and its implications for concepts of masculinity and femininity. In T. Sonderegger (ed.), *Nebraska Symposium on Motivation.* Lincoln: University of Nebraska Press.

Spencer, M. B., & Dornbusch, Sanford M. (1990). Ethnicity. In S. S. Feldman & G. R. Elliott (eds.), *At the threshold: The developing adolescent.* Cambridge: Harvard University Press.

Sperling, George (1960). The information available in brief visual presentations. *Psychological Monographs, 74*(498).

Sperry, Roger W. (1964). The great cerebral commissure. *Scientific American, 210*(1), 42–52.

Sperry, Roger W. (1982). Some effects of disconnecting the cerebral hemispheres. *Science, 217,* 1223–1226.

Spiegel, D.; Bloom, J. R.; Kraemer, H. C.; Gottheil, E. (1989, October 14). Effect of psychosocial treatment on survival of patients with metastatic breast cancer. *Lancet, 2*(8668), 888–91.

Spilich, George J.; June, Lorraine; & Renner, Judith (1992). Cigarette smoking and cognitive performance. *British Journal of Addiction, 87,* 113–126.

Spitzer, Robert L., & Williams, Janet B. (1988). Having a dream: A research strategy for DSM-IV. *Archives of General Psychiatry, 45,* 871–874.

Sprecher, Susan; Sullivan, Quintin; & Hatfield, Elaine (1994). Male selection preferences: Gender differences examined in a national sample. *Journal of Personality and Social Psychology, 66,* 1074–1080.

Spring, Bonnie; Chiodo, June; & Bowen, Deborah J. (1987). Carbohydrates, tryptophan, and behavior: A methodological review. *Psychological Bulletin, 102,* 234–256.

Squire, Larry R. (1986). Mechanisms of memory. *Science, 232,* 1612–1619.

Squire, Larry R. (1987). *Memory and the brain.* New York: Oxford University Press.

Squire, Larry R.; Ojemann, Jeffrey G.; Miezin, Francis M.; et al. (1992). Activation of the hippocampus in normal humans: A functional anatomical study of memory. *Proceedings of the National Academy of Science, 89,* 1837–1841.

Squire, Larry R., & Zola-Morgan, Stuart (1991). The medial temporal lobe memory system. *Science, 253,* 1380–1386.

Staats, Carolyn K., & Staats, Arthur W. (1957). Meaning established by classical conditioning. *Journal of Experimental Psychology, 54,* 74–80.

Stam, Henderikus J. (1989). From symptom relief to cure: Hypnotic interventions in cancer. In N. P. Spanos & J. F. Chaves (eds.), *Hypnosis: The cognitive-behavioral perspective.* Buffalo, NY: Prometheus Books.

Stanovich, Keith E. (1992). *How to think straight about psychology* (3rd ed.). New York: HarperCollins.

Stanton, Annette L., & Snider, Pamela R. (1993). Coping with a breast cancer diagnosis: A prospective study. *Health Psychology, 12,* 16–23.

Staples, Brent (1994). *Parallel time.* New York: Pantheon.

Stapley, Janice C., & Haviland, Jeannette M. (1989). Beyond depression: Gender differences in normal adolescents' emotional experiences. *Sex Roles, 20,* 295–308.

Stattin, Haken, & Magnusson, David (1990). *Pubertal maturation in female development.* Hillsdale, NJ: Erlbaum.

Staub, Ervin (1989). *The roots of evil: The origins of genocide and other group violence.* New York: Cambridge University Press.

Steele, Claude M. (1994, October 31). "Bizarre black IQ claims abetted by media." *San Francisco Chronicle,* op-ed page.

Stein, Marvin; Miller, Andrew; & Trestman, Robert L. (1991). Depression, the immune system, and health and illness: Findings in search of meaning. *Archives of General Psychiatry, 48,* 171–177.

Steinberg, Laurence D. (1990). Interdependence in the family: Autonomy, conflict and harmony in the parent-adolescent relationship. In S. S. Feldman & G. R. Elliott (eds.), *At the threshold: The developing adolescent.* Cambridge: Harvard University Press.

Stempel, Jennifer J.; Beckwith, Bill E.; & Petros, Thomas V. (1986). The effects of alcohol on the speed of memory retrieval. Paper presented at the annual meeting of the American Psychological Association, Washington, DC.

Stenberg, Craig R., & Campos, Joseph (1990). The development of anger expressions in infancy. In N. Stein, B. Leventhal, & T. Trabasso (eds.), *Psychological and biological approaches to emotion.* Hillsdale, NJ: Erlbaum.

Stephan, K. M.; Fink, G. R.; Passingham, R. E.; et al. (1995). Functional anatomy of the mental representation of upper movements in healthy subjects. *Journal of Neurophysiology, 73,* 373–386.

Stephan, Walter (1985). Intergroup relations. In G. Lindzey & E. Aronson (eds.), *Handbook of social psychology,* Vol. 2. New York: Random House.

Stephan, Walter, & Brigham, John C. (1985). Intergroup contact: Introduction. *Journal of Social Issues, 41*(3), 1–8.

Stephan, Walter G.; Ageyev, Vladimir; Coates-Shrider, Lisa; Stephan, Cookie W.; & Abalakina, Marina (1994). On the relationship between stereotypes and prejudice: An international study. *Personality and Social Psychology Bulletin, 20,* 277–284.

Stephan, Walter G., & Stephan, Cookie (1992). Reducing intercultural anxiety through intercultural contact. *International Journal of Intercultural Relations, 16,* 96–106.

Stephens, Beth (1993, June 24). Hypocrisy on rights. *New York Times,* A13.

Stephens, Mitchell (1991, September 20). The death of reading. *Los Angeles Times Magazine,* 10, 12, 16, 42, 44.

Stern, Daniel (1985). *The interpersonal world of the infant.* New York: Basic Books.

Sternberg, Robert J. (1986). *Intelligence applied: Understanding and increasing your intellectual skills.* San Diego: Harcourt Brace Jovanovich.

Sternberg, Robert J. (1988). *The triarchic mind: A new theory of human intelligence.* New York: Viking.

Sternberg, Robert J. (1994, Spring). Love is a story. *The General Psychologist, 30,* 1–11.

Sternberg, Robert J., & Kolligian, John, Jr. (eds.) (1990). *Competence considered.* New Haven, CT: Yale University Press.

Sternberg, Robert J., & Wagner, Richard K. (1989). Individual differences in practical knowledge and its acquisition. In P. Ackerman, R. J. Sternberg, & R. Glaser (eds.), *Individual differences.* New York: Freeman.

Sternberg, Robert J.; Wagner, Richard K.; & Okagaki, Lynn (1993). Practical intelligence: The nature and role of tacit knowledge in work and at school. In H. Reese & J. Puckett (eds.), *Advances in liftspan development.* Hillsdale, NJ: Erlbaum.

• Stevenson, Harold W.; Chen, Chuansheng; & Lee, Shin-Ying (1993, January 1). Mathematics achievement of Chinese, Japanese, and American children: Ten years later. *Science, 259,* 53–58.

Stevenson, Harold W.; Lee, Shin-ying; Chen, Chuansheng; Lummis, Max; et al. (1990a). Mathematics achievement in children in China and the United States. *Child Development, 61,* 1053–1066.

Stevenson, Harold W.; Lee, Shin-ying; Chen, Chuansheng; Stigler, James W.; et al. (1990b). Contexts of achievement: A study of American, Chinese, and Japanese children. *Monographs of the Society for Research in Child Development, 55*(1–2)

Stewart, Abigail; Sokol, Michael; Healy, Joseph M., Jr.; Chester, Nia L.; & Weinstock-Savoy, Deborah (1982). Adaptation to life changes in children and adults: Cross-sectional studies. *Journal of Personality and Social Psychology, 43,* 1270–1282.

• Stewart, Douglas; Cudworth, Christopher J.; & Lishman, J. R. (1993). Misperception of time-to-collision by drivers in pedestrian accidents. *Perception, 22,* 1227–1244.

Stickler, Gunnar B.; Salter, Margery; Broughton, Daniel D.; & Alario, Anthony (1991). Parents' worries about children compared to actual risks. *Clinical Pediatrics, 30,* 522–528.

Stoch, M. B., & Smythe, P. M. (1963). Does undernutrition during infancy inhibit brain growth and subsequent intellectual development? *Archives of Diseases in Childhood, 38,* 546–552.

• Stoerig, Petra (1993). Sources of blindsight. *Science, 261,* 493.

• Stoll, Andrew L.; Tohen, Mauricio; & Baldessarini, Ross J. (1993). Increasing frequency of the diagnosis of obsessive-compulsive disorder: A reply. *American Journal of Psychiatry, 150,* 682–683.

• Stone, Jeff; Aronson, Elliot; Crain, A. Lauren; Winslow, Matthew; & Fried, Carrie B. (1994). Inducing hypocrisy as a means of encouraging young adults to use condoms. *Personality and Social Psychology Bulletin, 20,* 116–128.

Stoner, James (1961). A comparison of individual and group decisions involving risk. Unpublished master's thesis, MIT, Cambridge, MA.

Storm, Christine, & Storm, Tom (1987). A taxonomic study of the vocabulary of emotions. *Journal of Personality and Social Psychology, 53,* 805–816.

Strack, Fritz; Martin, Leonard L.; & Stepper, Sabine (1988). Inhibiting and facilitating conditions of the human smile: A nonobtrusive test of the facial-feedback hypothesis. *Journal of Social and Personality Psychology, 54,* 768–777.

Strasser, Susan (1982). *Never done: A history of American housework.* New York: Pantheon.

• Straus, Murray A. (1991). Discipline and deviance: Physical punishment of children and violence and other crime in adulthood. *Social Problems, 38*(2), 133–154.

• Streissguth, A. P.; Aase, J. M.; Clarren, S. K.; Randels, S. P.; LaDue, R. A.; & Smith, D. F. (1991). Fetal alcohol syndrome in adolescents and adults. *Journal of the American Medical Association, 265,* 1961–1967.

• Streissguth, A. P.; Barr, H. M.; & Sampson, P. D. (1990). Moderate prenatal alcohol exposure: Effects on child IQ and learning problems at age 7½ years. *Alcoholism: Clinical and Experimental Research, 14,* 662–669.

• Strickland, Bonnie R. (1989). Internal-external control expectancies: From contingency to creativity. *American Psychologist, 44,* 1–12.

• Strickland, Bonnie R. (1995). Research on sexual orientation and human development: A commentary. *Developmental Psychology, 31,* 137–140.

Stroebe, Wolfgang; Stroebe, Margaret S.; & Domittner, Günther (1988). Individual and situational differences in recovery from bereavement: A risk group identified. *Journal of Social Issues, 44*(3), 143–158.

Strupp, Hans H. (1982). The outcome problem in psychotherapy: Contemporary perspectives. In J. H. Harvey & M. M. Parks (eds.), *Psychotherapy research and behavior change: The APA Master Lecture Series,* Vol. 1. Washington, DC: American Psychological Association.

Strupp, Hans H., & Binder, Jeffrey (1984). *Psychotherapy in a new key.* New York: Basic Books.

• Stunkard, Albert J. (ed.) (1980). *Obesity.* Philadelphia: Saunders.

Stunkard, Albert J.; Harris, J. R.; Pedersen, N. L.; & McClearn, G. E. (1990, May 24). The body-mass index of twins who have been reared apart. *New England Journal of Medicine, 322,* 1483–1487.

Sue, Stanley (1991). Ethnicity and culture in psychological research and practice. In J. Goodchilds (ed.), *Psychological perspectives on human diversity in America.* Washington, DC: American Psychological Association.

Sue, Stanley, & Zane, Nolan (1987). The role of culture and cultural techniques in psychotherapy: A critique and reformulation. *American Psychologist, 42,* 37–45.

Suedfeld, Peter (1975). The benefits of boredom: Sensory deprivation reconsidered. *American Scientist, 63*(1), 60–69.

Suedfeld, Peter; Little, B. R.; Rank, A. D.; Rank, D. S.; & Ballard, E. (1986). Television and adults: Thinking, personality and attitudes. In T. M. Williams (ed.), *The impact of television: A natural experiment in three communities.* San Diego: Academic Press.

Sundstrom, Eric; De Meuse, Kenneth P.; & Futrell, David (1990). Work teams: Applications and effectiveness. *American Psychologist, 45,* 120–133.

Suomi, Stephen J. (1987). Genetic and maternal contributions to individual differences in rhesus monkey biobehavioral development. In N. Krasnegor, E. Blass, M. Hofer, & W. Smotherman (eds.), *Perinatal development: A psychobiological perspective.* New York: Academic Press.

Suomi, Stephen J. (1989). Primate separation models of affective disorders. In J. Madden (ed.), *Adaptation, learning, and affect.* New York: Raven Press.

• Suomi, Stephen J. (1991). Uptight and laid-back monkeys: Individual differences in the response to social challenges. In S. Branch, W. Hall, & J. E. Dooling (eds.), *Plasticity of development.* Cambridge, MA: MIT Press.

• Super, Charles A., & Harkness, Sara (1994). The developmental niche. In W. J. Lonner & R. Malpass (eds.), *Psychology and culture.* Needham Heights, MA: Allyn & Bacon.

Susman, Elizabeth J.; Inoff-Germain, Gale; Nottelmann, Editha D.; et al. (1987). Hormones, emotional dispositions, and aggressive attributes in young adolescents. *Child Development, 58,* 1114–1134.

• Swain, Scott (1989). Covert intimacy: Closeness in men's friendships. In B. J. Risman & P. Schwartz (eds.), *Gender in intimate relationships.* Belmont, CA: Wadsworth.

Swedo, Susan E., & Rapoport, Judith L. (1991). Trichotillomania [hair-pulling]. *Journal of Child Psychology and Psychiatry and Allied Disciplines, 32,* 401–409.

Syme, S. Leonard (1982, July/August). People need people. *American Health, 1.*

Symons, Donald (1979). *The evolution of human sexuality.* New York: Oxford University Press.

Szasz, Thomas (1961/1967). *The myth of mental illness.* New York: Dell Delta.

Szasz, Thomas (1970). *The manufacture of madness.* New York: Harper Torchbooks.

• Szempruch, Joseph, & Jacobson, John W. (1993). Evaluating facilitated communications of people with developmental disabilities. *Research in Developmental Disabilities, 14,* 253–264.

• Taffel, Ronald (1990, September/October). The politics of mood. *The Family Therapy Networker,* 49–53, 72.

• Tajfel, Henri; Billig, M. G.; Bundy, R. P.; & Flament, C. (1971). Social categorization and intergroup behavior. *European Journal of Social Psychology, 1,* 149–178.

Tajfel, Henri, & Turner, John C. (1986). The social identity theory of intergroup behavior. In S. Worchel & W. G. Austin (eds.), *Psychology of intergroup relations.* Chicago: Nelson-Hall.

• Talley, P. Forrest; Strupp, Hans H.; & Butler, Stephen F. (1994). *Psychotherapy research and practice: Bridging the gap.* New York: Basic Books.

• Tanaka, Keiji; Saito, Hide-aki; Fukada, Yoshiro; & Moriya, Madoka (1991). Coding visual images of objects in the inferotemporal cortex of the macaque monkey. *Journal of Neurophysiology, 66,* 170–189.

• Tangney, June P. (1992). Constructive vs. destructive responses to anger: The moderating roles of shame and guilt across the lifespan. Paper presented at the annual meeting of the International Congress of Psychology, Brussels, Belgium.

• Tangney, June P., & Fischer, Kurt W. (eds.) (1995). *Shame, guilt, embarrassment, and pride: Empirical studies of self-conscious emotions.* New York: Guilford Press.

• Tanur, Judith M. (ed.). (1992). *Questions about questions: Inquiries into the cognitive basis of surveys.* New York: Russell Sage Foundation.

• Tartter, Vivien C. (1986). *Language processes.* New York: Holt, Rinehart and Winston.

Taub, David M. (1984). *Primate paternalism.* New York: Van Nostrand Reinhold.

• **Tavris, Carol** (1987, January). How to succeed in business abroad. *Signature,* 86–87, 110–113.

Tavris, Carol (1989). *Anger: The misunderstood emotion* (2nd ed.). New York: Simon & Schuster/Touchstone.

Tavris, Carol (1992). *The mismeasure of woman.* New York: Simon & Schuster/Touchstone.

• **Taylor, Donald M., & Porter, Lana E.** (1994). A multicultural view of stereotyping. In W. J. Lonner & R. Malpass (eds.), *Psychology and culture.* Needham Heights, MA: Allyn & Bacon.

Taylor, Shelley E. (1989). *Positive illusions: Creative self-deception and the healthy mind.* New York: Basic Books.

Taylor, Shelley E. (1991). *Health psychology* (2nd ed.). New York: McGraw-Hill.

Taylor, Shelley E., & Brown, Jonathon D. (1988). Illusion and well-being: A social psychological perspective on mental health. *Psychological Bulletin, 103,* 193–210.

• **Taylor, Shelley E., & Brown, Jonathon D.** (1994). Positive illusions and well-being revisited: Separating fact from fiction. *Psychological Bulletin, 116,* 21–27.

Taylor, Shelley E.; Lichtman, Rosemary R.; & Wood, Joanne V. (1984). Attributions, beliefs about control, and adjustment to breast cancer. *Journal of Personality and Social Psychology, 46,* 489–502.

Taylor, Shelley E., & Lobel, Marci (1989). Social comparison activity under threat: Downward evaluation and upward contacts. *Psychological Review, 96,* 569–575.

• **Taylor, Shelley E.; Peplau, Letitia A.; & Sears, David O.** (1994). *Social psychology* (8th ed.). Englewood Cliffs, NJ: Prentice-Hall.

Tellegen, Auke; Lykken, David T.; Bouchard, Thomas J., Jr.; et al. (1988). Personality similarity in twins reared apart and together. *Journal of Personality and Social Psychology, 54,* 1031–1039.

Temerlin, Jane W., & Temerlin, Maurice K. (1986). Some hazards of the therapeutic relationship. *Cultic Studies Journal, 3,* 234–242.

Terman, Lewis M., & Oden, Melita H. (1959). *Genetic studies of genius. V. The gifted group at mid-life.* Stanford, CA: Stanford University Press.

• **Terr, Lenore** (1994). *Unchained memories: True stories of traumatic memories, lost and found.* New York: Basic Books.

Terrace, H. S. (1985). In the beginning was the "name." *American Psychologist, 40,* 1011–1028.

• **Terry, Deborah J.** (1994). Determinants of coping: The role of stable and situational factors. *Journal of Personality and Social Psychology, 66,* 895–910.

Teyler, T. J., & DiScenna, P. (1987). Long-term potentiation. *Annual Review of Neuroscience, 10,* 131–161.

Thiriart, Philippe (1991, Winter). Acceptance of personality test results. *Skeptical Inquirer, 15,* 161–165.

Thoits, Peggy A. (1986). Social support as coping assistance. *Journal of Consulting and Clinical Psychology, 54,* 416–423.

Thoma, Stephen J. (1986). Estimating gender differences in the comprehension and preference of moral issues. *Developmental Review, 6,* 165–180.

Thomas, Alexander, & Chess, Stella (1980). *The dynamics of psychological development.* New York: Brunner/Mazel.

Thomas, Alexander, & Chess, Stella (1982). Temperament and follow-up to adulthood. In R. Porter & G. M. Collins (eds.), *Temperamental differences in infants and young children.* London: Pitman.

Thomas, Alexander, & Chess, Stella (1984). Genesis and evolution of behavioral disorders: From infancy to early adult life. *American Journal of Psychiatry, 141,* 1–9.

Thomas, Lewis (1983). *The youngest science: Notes of a medicine-watcher.* Toronto: Bantam.

• **Thomas, Sandra P.** (1993). Introduction. In S. P. Thomas (ed.), *Women and anger.* New York: Springer.

• **Thompson, Paul D.; Zmuda, Joseph M.; & Catlin, Don H.** (1993). Use of anabolic steriods among adolescents. *New England Journal of Medicine, 329,* 888–889.

Thompson, Richard F. (1983). Neuronal substrates of simple associative learning: Classical conditioning. *Trends in Neurosciences, 6,* 270–275.

Thompson, Richard F. (1986). The neurobiology of learning and memory. *Science, 233,* 941–947.

• **Thompson, Suzanne C.; Nanni, Christopher; & Levine, Alexandra** (1994). Primary versus secondary and central versus consequence-related control in HIV-positive men. *Journal of Personality and Social Psychology, 67,* 540–547.

Thorndike, Edward L. (1898). Animal intelligence. An experimental study of the associative processes in animals. *Psychological Review Monograph Supplement, 2* (Whole No. 8).

Thorndike, Edward L. (1903). *Educational psychology.* New York: Columbia University Teachers College.

• **Thornhill, Randy** (1980). Rape in Panorpa scorpion-flies and a general rape hypothesis. *Animal Behavior, 28,* 52–59.

Thornton, E. M. (1984). *The Freudian fallacy: An alternative view of Freudian theory.* Garden City, NY: Dial Press (Doubleday).

Tiefer, Leonore (1978/1995). The kiss. Reprinted in L. Tiefer (1995), *Sex is not a natural act and other essays.* Boulder, CO: Westview Press.

Tiefer, Leonore (1992). Critique of DSM-III-R nomenclature for sexual dysfunctions. *Psychiatric Medicine, 10,* 227–245.

• **Tiefer, Leonore** (1995). *Sex is not a natural act and other essays.* Boulder, CO: Westview Press.

Tolman, Edward C. (1938). The determiners of behavior at a choice point. *Psychological Review, 45,* 1–35.

Tolman, Edward C. (1948). Cognitive maps in rats and men. *Psychological Review, 55,* 189–208.

Tolman, E. C., & Honzik, C. H. (1930). Introduction and removal of reward and maze performance in rats. *University of California Publications in Psychology, 4,* 257–275.

Tomkins, Silvan S. (1962). *Affect, imagery, consciousness: I. The positive affects.* New York: Springer-Verlag.

Tomkins, Silvan S. (1981). The role of facial response in the experience of emotion: A reply to Tourangeau and Ellsworth. *Journal of Personality and Social Psychology, 40,* 355–357.

Torrey, E. Fuller (1988). *Surviving schizophrenia* (rev. ed.). New York: Harper & Row.

• **Torrey, E. Fuller; Bowler, Ann E.; Taylor, Edward H.; & Gottesman, Irving I.** (1994). *Schizophrenia and manic-depressive disorder.* New York: Basic Books.

Trafimow, David; Triandis, Harry C.; & Goto, Sharon G. (1991). Some tests of the distinction between the private self and the collective self. *Journal of Personality and Social Psychology, 60,* 649–655.

Tranel, Daniel, & Damasio, Antonio (1985). Knowledge without awareness: An autonomic index of facial recognition by prosopagnosics. *Science, 228,* 1453–1454.

Tranel, Daniel; Damasio, Antonio; & Damasio, Hanna (1988). Intact recognition of facial expression, gender, and age in patients with impaired recognition of face identity. *Neurology, 38,* 690–696.

• **Traub, James** (1993, June 7). The hearts and minds of City College. *The New Yorker,* 42–53.

Triandis, Harry C. (1990). Cross-cultural studies of individualism and collectivism. In J. J. Berman (ed.), *Cross-cultural perspectives: Nebraska Symposium on Motivation, 1989.* Lincoln: University of Nebraska Press.

• **Triandis, Harry C.** (1994). Culture and social behavior. In W. J. Lonner & R. S. Malpass (eds.), *Psychology and culture.* Needham Heights, MA: Allyn & Bacon.

• **Trimble, Joseph E., & Medicine, Beatrice** (1993). Diversification of American Indians: Forming an indigenous perspective. In U. Kim & J. W. Berry (eds.), *Indigenous psychologies: Research and experience in cultural context.* Newbury Park, CA: Sage.

Trivers, Robert (1972). Parental investment and sexual selection. In B. Campbell (ed.), *Sexual selection and the descent of man.* New York: Aldine de Gruyter.

• **Tronick, Edward Z.; Morelli, Gilda A.; & Ivey, Paula K.** (1992). The Efe forager infant and toddler's pattern of social relationships: Multiple and simultaneous. Special Section: Cross-cultural studies of development. *Developmental Psychology, 28,* 568–577.

• **Trumbach, R.** (1989). Gender and the homosexual role in modern western culture: The 18th and 19th centuries compared. In D. Altman, C. Vance, M. Vicinus, & J. Weeks (eds.), *Which homosexuality?* London, England: GMP Publishers.

Tsunoda, Tadanobu (1985). *The Japanese brain: Uniqueness and universality.* (Yoshinori Oiwa, trans.) Tokyo: Taishukan.

Tucker, Don M. (1989). Asymmetries of neural architecture and the structure of emotional experience. In R. Johnson & W. Roth (eds.), *Eighth event-related potentials international conference.* New York: Oxford University Press.

Tucker, Don M., & Williamson, Peter A. (1984). Asymmetric neural control systems in human self-regulation. *Psychological Review, 91,* 185–215.

Tulving, Endel (1985). How many memory systems are there? *American Psychologist, 40,* 385–398.

Tulving, Endel, & Schacter, Daniel L. (1990). Priming and human memory systems. *Science, 247,* 301–305.

Tversky, Amos, & Kahneman, Daniel (1973). Availability: A heuristic for judging frequency and probability. *Cognitive Psychology, 5,* 207–232.

Tversky, Amos, & Kahneman, Daniel (1981). The framing of decisions and the psychology of choice. *Science, 211,* 453–458.

Tversky, Amos, & Kahneman, Daniel (1986). Rational choice and the framing of decisions. *Journal of Business, 59,* S25l–S278.

• **Tzischinsky, Orna; Pal, I.; Epstein, Rachel; Dagan, Y.; & Lavie, Peretz** (1992). The importance of timing in melatonin administration in a blind man. *Journal of Pineal Research, 12,* 105–108.

• **Unger, Rhoda** (1990). Imperfect reflections of reality: Psychology constructs gender. In R. T. Hare-Mustin & J. Marecek (eds.), *Making a difference: Psychology and the construction of gender.* New Haven, CT: Yale University Press.

• **Usher, JoNell A., & Neisser, Ulric** (1993). Childhood amnesia and the beginnings of memory for four early life events. *Journal of Experimental Psychology: General, 122,* 155–165.

Vaillant, George E. (1983). *The natural history of alcoholism: Causes, patterns, and paths to recovery.* Cambridge: Harvard University Press.

• **Vaillant, George E. (ed.)** (1992a). *Ego mechanisms of defense.* Washington, DC: American Psychiatric Press.

• **Vaillant, George E.** (1992b, Spring). The historical origins and future potential of Sigmund Freud's concept of the mechanisms of defence. *International Review of Psycho-Analysis, 19,* 35–50.

• **Vaillant, George E.** (1993). Paper presented at the annual meeting of the American Psychiatric Association, Washington, DC.

Vaillant, George E., & Milofsky, Eva S. (1982). The etiology of alcoholism. *American Psychologist, 37,* 494–503.

• **Valatx, Jean-Louis** (1989). Rêve et memoire. Approche neurobiologique. [Dream and memory: Neurobiological approach.] *Etudes Psychotherapiques, 20,* 103–107.

Valenstein, Elliot (1986). *Great and desperate cures: The rise and decline of psychosurgery and other radical treatments for mental illness.* New York: Basic Books.

• **Valentiner, David P.; Holahan, Charles J.; & Moos, Rudolf H.** (1994). Social support, appraisals of event controllability, and coping: An integrative model. *Journal of Personality and Social Psychology, 66,* 1094–1102.

• **Valkenburg, Patti M., & van der Voort, Tom H. A.** (1994). Influence of TV on daydreaming and creative imagination: A review of research. *Psychological Bulletin, 116,* 316–339.

Van Cantfort, Thomas E., & Rimpau, James B. (1982). Sign language studies with children and chimpanzees. *Sign Language Studies, 34,* 15–72.

Vandenberg, Brian (1985). Beyond the ethology of play. In A. Gottfried & C. C. Brown (eds.), *Play interactions.* Lexington, MA: Lexington Books.

• **Vandenberg, Brian** (1993). Existentialism and development. *American Psychologist, 48,* 296–297.

Van Lancker, Diana R., & Kempler, Daniel (1987). Comprehension of familiar phrases by left- but not by right-hemisphere damaged patients. *Brain and Language, 32,* 265–277.

Vasquez, Melba J. T., & Barón, Augustine, Jr. (1988). The psychology of the Chicano experience: A sample course structure. In P. Bronstein & K. Quina (eds.), *Teaching a psychology of people.* Washington, DC: American Psychological Association.

• **Viken, Richard J.; Rose, Richard J.; Kaprio, Jaakko; & Koskenvuo, Markku** (1994). A developmental genetic analysis of adult personality: Extraversion and neuroticism from 18 to 59 years of age. *Journal of Personality and Social Psychology, 66,* 722–730.

Vila, J., & Beech, H. R. (1980). Premenstrual symptomatology: An interaction hypothesis. *British Journal of Social and Clinical Psychology, 19,* 73–80.

• **Vinokur, Amiram D., & van Ryn, Michelle** (1993). Social support and undermining in close relationships: Their independent effects on the mental health of unemployed persons. *Journal of Personality and Social Psychology, 65,* 350–359.

Vokey, John R., & Read, J. Don (1985). Subliminal messages: Between the devil and the media. *American Psychologist, 40,* 1231–1239.

Von Lang, Jochen, & Sibyll, Claus (eds.) (1984). *Eichmann interrogated: Transcripts from the archives of the Israeli police.* New York: Random House.

• **Vormbrock, Julia K.** (1993). Attachment theory as applied to wartime and job-related marital separation. *Psychological Bulletin, 114,* 122–144.

• **Voyer, Daniel; Voyer, Susan; & Bryden, M. P.** (1995). Magnitude of sex differences in spatial abilities: A meta-analysis and consideration of critical variables. *Psychological Bulletin, 117,* 250–270.

Wadden, Thomas A.; Foster, G. D.; Letizia, K. A.; & Mullen, J. L. (1990, August 8). Long-term effects of dieting on resting metabolic rate in obese outpatients. *Journal of the American Medical Association, 264,* 707–711.

Wade, Carole, & Cirese, Sarah (1991). *Human sexuality* (2nd ed.). San Diego: Harcourt Brace Jovanovich.

Wagemaker, Herbert, Jr., & Cade, Robert (1978). Hemodialysis in chronic schizophrenic patients. *Southern Medical Journal, 71,* 1463–1465.

Wagenaar, Willem A. (1986). My memory: A study of autobiographical memory over six years. *Cognitive Psychology, 18,* 225–252.

• **Wakefield, Jerome C.** (1992). The concept of mental disorder: On the boundary between biological facts and social values. *American Psychologist, 47,* 373–388.

• **Walker, Anne** (1994). Mood and well-being in consecutive menstrual cycles: Methodological and theoretical implications. *Psychology of Women Quarterly, 18,* 271–290.

Walker, Edward L. (1970). Relevant psychology is a snark. *American Psychologist, 25,* 1081–1086.

• **Walker, Lawrence J.** (1989). A longitudinal study of moral reasoning. *Child Development, 60,* 157–166.

• **Walker, Lawrence J.; de Vries, Brian; & Trevethan, Shelley D.** (1987). Moral stages and moral orientations in real-life and hypothetical dilemmas. *Child Development, 58,* 842–858.

Wallbott, Harald G.; Ricci-Bitti, Pio; & Bänninger-Huber, Eva (1986). Non-verbal reactions to emotional experiences. In K. R. Scherer, H. G. Wallbott, & A. B. Summerfield (eds.), *Experiencing emotion: A cross-cultural study.* Cambridge, England: Cambridge University Press.

Waller, Niels G.; Kojetin, Brian A.; Bouchard, Thomas J., Jr.; Lykken, David T.; & Tellegen, Auke (1990). Genetic and environmental influences on religious interests, attitudes, and values: A study of twins reared apart and together. *Psychological Science, 1,* 138–142.

• **Waller, Niels G., & Shaver, Phillip** (1994). The importance of nongenetic influences on romantic love styles: A twin-family study. *Psychological Science, 5,* 268–274.

Waller, Willard (1938). *The family: A dynamic interpretation.* New York: Dryden.

Wallerstein, Judith, & Blakeslee, Sandra (1989). *Second chances: Men, women and children a decade after divorce.* New York: Ticknor & Fields.

• **Walter, John L., & Peller, Jane E.** (1993). *Becoming solution-focused in brief therapy.* New York: Brunner/Mazel.

Wang, Alvin Y., & Thomas, Margaret H. (1992). The effect of imagery-based mnemonics on the long-term retention of Chinese characters. *Language Learning, 42,* 359–376.

Wang, Alvin Y.; Thomas, Margaret H.; & Ouellette, Judith A. (1992). The keyword mnemonic and retention of second-language vocabulary words. *Journal of Educational Psychology, 84,* 520–528.

• **Ward, L. Monique** (1994). Preschoolers' awareness of associations between gender and societal status. Paper presented at the annual meeting of the American Psychological Association, Los Angeles.

• **Washburn, David A., & Rumbaugh, Duane M.** (1991). Ordinal judgments of numerical symbols by macaques *(Macaca mulatta). Psychological Science, 2,* 190–193.

• **Waterman, Alan S.** (1993). Two conceptions of happiness: Contrasts of personal expressiveness (eudaimonia) and hedonic enjoyment. *Journal of Personality and Social Psychology, 64,* 678–691.

Watson, David, & Clark, Lee Anna (1984). Negative affectivity: The disposition to experience aversive emotional states. *Psychological Bulletin, 96,* 465–490.

Watson, David, & Pennebaker, James W. (1989). Health complaints, stress, and distress: Exploring the central role of negative affectivity. *Psychological Review, 96,* 234–254.

Watson, John B. (1913). Psychology as the behaviorist views it. *Psychological Review, 20,* 158–177.

Watson, John B. (1925). *Behaviorism.* New York: Norton.

Watson, John B., & Rayner, Rosalie (1920). Conditioned emotional reactions. *Journal of Experimental Psychology, 3,* 1–14.

Webb, Wilse B., & Agnew, H. W., Jr. (1974). Sleep and waking in a time-free environment. *Aerospace Medicine, 45,* 617–622.

Webb, Wilse B., & Cartwright, Rosalind D. (1978). Sleep and dreams. In M. Rosenzweig & L. Porter (eds.), *Annual Review of Psychology, 29,* 223–252.

Wechsler, David (1955). *Manual for the Wechsler Adult Intelligence Scale.* New York: Psychological Corporation.

• Weder, Alan B., & Schork, Nicholas J. (1994). Adaptation, allometry, and hypertension. *Hypertension, 24,* 145–156.

• Wegner, Daniel M. (1994). Ironic processes of mental control. *Psychological Review, 101,* 34–52.

• Wegner, Daniel M., & Gold, Daniel B. (1995). Fanning old flames: Emotional and cognitive effects of suppressing thoughts of a past relationship. *Journal of Personality and Social Psychology, 68,* 782–792.

Wegner, Daniel M.; Schneider, David J.; Carter, Samuel R., III; & White, Teri L. (1987). Paradoxical effects of thought suppression. *Journal of Personality and Social Psychology, 53,* 5–13.

Wehr, Thomas A.; Sack, David A.; & Rosenthal, Norman E. (1987). Seasonal affective disorder with summer depression and winter hypomania. *American Journal of Psychiatry, 144,* 1602–1603.

Weil, Andrew T. (1972/1986). *The natural mind: A new way of looking at drugs and the higher consciousness.* Boston: Houghton Mifflin.

Weil, Andrew T. (1974a, June). Parapsychology: Andrew Weil's search for the true Geller. *Psychology Today,* 45–50.

Weil, Andrew T. (1974b, July). Parapsychology: Andrew Weil's search for the true Geller—Part II. The letdown. *Psychology Today,* 74–78, 82.

Weinberg, Richard A.; Scarr, Sandra; & Waldman, Irwin D. (1992). The Minnesota transracial adoption study: A follow-up of IQ test performance at adolescence. *Intelligence, 16,* 117–135.

Weiner, Bernard (1986). *An attributional theory of motivation and emotion.* New York: Springer-Verlag.

Weiner, Bernard; Figueroa-Muñoz, Alice; & Kakihara, Craig (1991). The goals of excuses and communication strategies related to causal perceptions. *Personality and Social Psychology Bulletin, 17,* 4–13.

• Weiskrantz, L. (1992). Unconscious vision: The strange phenomenon of blindsight. *Sciences, 32,* 22.

• Weiss, Bahr; Dodge, Kenneth A.; Bates, John E.; & Petitt, Gregory S. (1992). Some consequences of early harsh discipline: Child aggression and a maladaptive social information processing style. *Child Development, 63,* 1321–1335.

• Weisse, Carol S. (1992). Depression and immunocompetence: A review of the literature. *Psychological Bulletin, 111,* 475–489.

Weisz, John R.; Rothbaum, Fred M.; & Blackburn, Thomas C. (1984). Standing out and standing in: The psychology of control in America and Japan. *American Psychologist, 39,* 955–969.

• Weisz, John R.; Weiss, Bahr; Alicke, Mark D.; & Klotz, M. L. (1987). Effectiveness of psychotherapy with children and adolescents: A meta-analysis for clinicians. *Journal of Consulting and Clinical Psychology, 55,* 542–549.

• Weisz, John R.; Weiss, Bahr; Han, Susan S.; Granger, Douglas A.; & Morton, Todd (1995). Effects of psychotherapy with children and adolescents revisited: A meta-analysis of treatment outcome studies. *Psychological Bulletin, 117,* 450–468.

• Wells, Gary L. (1993). What do we know about eyewitness identification? *American Psychologist, 48,* 553–571.

Welwood, John (ed.) (1983). *Awakening the heart: East-west approaches to psychotherapy and the healing relationship.* Boulder, CO: Shambhala.

Wender, Paul H., & Klein, Donald F. (1981). *Mind, mood, and medicine: A guide to the new biopsychiatry.* New York: Farrar, Straus & Giroux.

Werner, Emmy E. (1989). High-risk children in young adulthood: A longitudinal study from birth to 32 years. *American Journal of Orthopsychiatry, 59,* 72–81.

Werner, Emmy E., & Smith, Ruth S. (1982). *Vulnerable but invincible: A longitudinal study of resilient children and youth.* New York: McGraw-Hill.

• West, Candace, & Zimmerman, Don H. (1991). Doing gender. In J. Lorber & S. A. Farrell (eds.), *The social construction of gender.* Newbury Park, CA: Sage.

West, Melissa O., & Prinz, Ronald J. (1987). Parental alcoholism and childhood psychopathology. *Psychological Bulletin, 102,* 204–218.

Wheeler, Anthony (1990, Fall). Biological cycles and rhythms vs. biorhythms. *Skeptical Inquirer,* 75–82.

• Wheeler, Douglas L.; Jacobson, John W.; Paglieri, Raymond A.; & Schwartz, Allen A. (1993). An experimental assessment of facilitated communication. *Mental Retardation, 31,* 49–59.

• Whisman, Mark A. (1993). Mediators and moderators of change in cognitive therapy of depression. *Psychological Bulletin, 114,* 248–265.

• White, Michael, & Epston, David (1990). *Narrative means to therapeutic ends.* New York: Norton.

White, Robert W. (1959). Motivation reconsidered: The concept of competence. *Psychological Review, 66,* 297–333.

White, Sheldon H., & Pillemer, David B. (1979). Childhood amnesia and the development of a socially accessible memory system. In J. F. Kihlstrom & F. J. Evans (eds.), *Functional disorders of memory.* Hillsdale, NJ: Erlbaum.

• Whitehead, Barbara D. (1993, April). Dan Quayle was right. *The Atlantic Monthly, 271,* 47–84

Whitehouse, Wayne G.; Dinges, David F.; Orne, Emily C.; & Orne, Martin T. (1988). Hypnotic hypermnesia: Enhanced memory accessibility or report bias? *Journal of Abnormal Psychology, 97,* 289–295.

• Whitehurst, Grover J.; Arnold, David S.; Epstein, Jeffery N.; Angell, Andrea L.; Smith, Meagan; & Fischel, Janet E. (1994). A picture book reading intervention in day care and home for children from low-income families. *Developmental Psychology, 30,* 679–689.

Whitehurst, Grover J.; Falco, F. L.; Lonigan, C. J.; Fischel, J. E.; et al. (1988). Accelerating language development through picture book reading. *Developmental Psychology, 24,* 552–559.

Whiting, Beatrice B., & Edwards, Carolyn E. (1988). *Children of different worlds: The formation of social behavior.* Cambridge: Harvard University Press.

Whiting, Beatrice, & Whiting, John (1975). *Children of six cultures.* Cambridge: Harvard University Press.

• Whitney, Kristina; Sagrestano, Lynda M.; & Maslach, Christina (1994). Establishing the social impact of individuation. *Journal of Personality and Social Psychology, 66,* 1140–1153.

Widom, Cathy S. (1989). Does violence beget violence? A critical examination of the literature. *Psychological Bulletin, 106,* 3–28.

Wiggins, Jack G. (1991). Anxiety: A cooperative approach. Paper presented at the annual meeting of the American Psychological Association, San Francisco.

Wiley, James, & Camacho, Terry (1980). Life-style and future health: Evidence from the Alameda County Study. *Preventive Medicine, 9,* 1–21.

Williams, Kipling D., & Karau, Steven J. (1991). Social loafing and social compensation: The effects of expectations of co-worker performance. *Journal of Personality and Social Psychology, 61,* 570–581.

• Williams, Redford B., Jr. (1989). *The trusting heart.* New York: Random House.

Williams, Redford B., Jr.; Barefoot, John C.; & Shekelle, Richard B. (1985). The health consequences of hostility. In M. A. Chesney & R. H. Rosenman (eds.), *Anger and hostility in cardiovascular and behavioral disorders.* New York: Hemisphere.

• Williams, Walter (1986). *The spirit and the flesh: Sexual diversity in American Indian culture.* Boston: Beacon Press.

Wilner, Daniel; Walkley, Rosabelle; & Cook, Stuart (1955). *Human relations in interracial housing.* Minneapolis: University of Minnesota Press.

Wilson, Edward O. (1975). *Sociobiology: The new synthesis.* Cambridge: Belknap/Harvard University Press.

Wilson, Edward O. (1978). *On human nature.* Cambridge: Harvard University Press.

• Wilson, Edward O. (1994). *Naturalist.* Washington, DC: Island Press.

• Wilson, G. Terence, & Fairburn, Christopher G. (1993). Cognitive treatments for eating disorders. Special section: Recent developments in cognitive and constructivist psychotherapies. *Journal of Consulting and Clinical Psychology, 61,* 261–269.

Wilson, Melvin N. (1989). Child development in the context of the black extended family. *American Psychologist, 44,* 380–385.

Windholz, George, & Lamal, P. A. (1985). Köhler's insight revisited. *Teaching of Psychology, 12,* 165–167.

Winick, Myron; Meyer, Knarig Katchadurian; & Harris, Ruth C. (1975). Malnutrition and environmental enrichment by early adoption. *Science, 190,* 1173–1175.

• Winnicott, D. W. (1957/1990). *Home is where we start from.* New York: Norton.

• Winter, David G. (1993). Power, affiliation, and war: Three tests of a motivational model. *Journal of Personality and Social Psychology, 65,* 532–545.

Wispé, Lauren G., & Drambarean, Nicholas C. (1953). Physiological need, word frequency, and visual duration thresholds. *Journal of Experimental Psychology, 46,* 25–31.

• Witelson, Sandra F.; Glazer, I. I., & Kigar, D. L. (1994). Sex differences in numerical density of neurons in human auditory association cortex. *Society for Neuroscience Abstracts, 30,* Abstr. No. 582.12.

• Woo, Elaine (1995, January 21). Teaching that goes beyond IQ. *Los Angeles Times,* A1, A22, A23.

• Wood, James M.; Nezworski, M. Teresa; & Stejskal, William J. (in press). The comprehensive system for the Rorschach: A critical examination. *Psychological Science.*

• Wood, Wendy; Lundgren, Sharon; Ouellette, Judith A.; Busceme, Shelly; & Blackstone, Tamela (1994). Minority influence: A meta-analytic review of social influence processes. *Psychological Bulletin, 115,* 323–345.

• Woodward, Amanda L.; Markman, Ellen M.; & Fitzsimmons, Colleen M. (1994). Rapid word learning in 13- and 18-month-olds. *Developmental Psychology, 30,* 553–566.

Wooley, Susan; Wooley, O. Wayne; & Dyrenforth, Susan (1979). Theoretical, practical, and social issues in behavioral treatments of obesity. *Journal of Applied Behavior Analysis, 12,* 3–25.

Woolfolk, Robert L., & Richardson, Frank C. (1984). Behavior therapy and the ideology of modernity. *American Psychologist, 39,* 777–786.

Wright, R. L. D. (1976). *Understanding statistics: An informal introduction for the behavioral sciences.* New York: Harcourt Brace Jovanovich.

Wu, Tzu-chin; Tashkin, Donald P.; Djahed, Behnam; & Rose, Jed E. (1988). Pulmonary hazards of smoking marijuana as compared with tobacco. *New England Journal of Medicine, 318,* 347–351.

Wurtman, Richard J. (1982). Nutrients that modify brain function. *Scientific American, 264*(4), 50–59.

Wurtman, Richard J., & Lieberman, Harris R. (eds.) (1982–1983). Research strategies for assessing the behavioral effects of foods and nutrients. *Journal of Psychiatric Research, 17*(2) [whole issue].

Wyatt, Gail E., & Mickey, M. Ray (1987). Ameliorating the effects of child sexual abuse: An exploratory study of support by parents and others. *Journal of Interpersonal Violence, 2,* 403–414.

• Wylie, Mary S. (1993, September/October). The shadow of a doubt. *The Family Therapy Networker, 17,* 18–29, 70, 73.

Yalom, Irvin D. (1989). *Love's executioner and other tales of psychotherapy.* New York: Basic Books.

• Yalom, Irvin D. (1995). *The theory and practice of group psychotherapy* (4th ed.). New York: Basic Books.

• Yapko, Michael (1993, September/October). The seductions of memory. *The Family Therapy Networker, 17,* 30–37.

• Yapko, Michael (1994). *Suggestions of abuse: True and false memories of childhood sexual trauma.* New York: Simon & Schuster.

• Yates, William R.; Perry, Paul; & Murray, Scott (1992). Aggression and hostility in anabolic steriod users. *Biological Psychiatry, 31,* 1232–1234.

Yazigi, R. A.; Odent, R. R.; & Polakoski, K. L. (1991, October 9). Demonstration of specific binding of cocaine to human spermatozoa. *Journal of the American Medical Association, 266*(14), 1956–1959.

• Yee, Albert H.; Fairchild, Halford H.; Weizmann, Fredric; & Wyatt, Gail E. (1993). Addressing psychology's problems with race. *American Psychologist, 48,* 1132–1140.

• Yoder, Janice D., & Kahn, Arnold S. (1993). Working toward an inclusive psychology of women. *American Psychologist, 48,* 846–850.

Yoken, Carol, & Berman, Jeffrey S. (1984). Does paying a fee for psychotherapy alter the effectiveness of treatment? *Journal of Consulting and Clinical Psychology, 52,* 254–260.

• Young, Malcolm P., & Yamane, Shigeru (1992). Sparse population coding of faces in the inferotemporal cortex. *Science, 256,* 1327–1331.

• Young-Eisendrath, Polly (1993). *You're not what I expected: Learning to love the opposite sex.* New York: Morrow.

Zahn-Waxler, Carolyn; Radke-Yarrow, Marian; & King, Robert (1979). Child-rearing and children's pro-social initiations toward victims of distress. *Child Development, 50,* 319–330.

Zahn-Waxler, Carolyn; Kochanska, Grazyna; Krupnick, Janice; & McKnew, Donald (1990). Patterns of guilt in children of depressed and well mothers. *Developmental Psychology, 26,* 51–59.

Zajonc, Robert B. (1968). Attitudinal effects of mere exposure. *Journal of Personality and Social Psychology, 9, Monograph Supplement 2,* 1–27.

Zajonc, Robert B., & Markus, Gregory B. (1975). Birth order and intellectual development. *Psychological Review, 82,* 74–88.

Zajonc, R. B.; Murphy, Sheila T.; & Inglehart, Marita (1989). Feeling and facial efference: Implications of the vascular theory of emotion. *Psychological Review, 96,* 395–416.

Zellman, Gail, & Goodchilds, Jacqueline (1983). Becoming sexual in adolescence. In E. R. Allgeier & N. B. McCormick (eds.), *Changing boundaries: Gender roles and sexual behavior.* Palo Alto, CA: Mayfield.

• Zhang, Y.; Proenca, R.; Maffei, M.; et al. (1994). Positional cloning of the mouse obese gene and its human homologue. *Nature, 372*(6505), 425–432.

Zilbergeld, Bernie (1983). *The shrinking of America: Myths of psychological change.* Boston: Little, Brown.

Zillmann, Dolf (1983). Transfer of excitation in emotional behavior. In J. T. Cacioppo & R. E. Petty (eds.), *Social psychophysiology: A sourcebook.* New York: Guilford Press.

Zimbardo, Philip G. (1970). The human choice: Individuation, reason, and order versus deindividuation, impulse, and chaos. In W. J. Arnold & D. Levine (eds.), *Nebraska Symposium on Motivation, 1969.* Lincoln: University of Nebraska Press.

• Zimbardo, Philip G., & Leippe, M. R. (1991). *The psychology of attitude change and social influence.* New York: McGraw-Hill.

Zinberg, Norman (1974). The search for rational approaches to heroin use. In P. G. Bourne (ed.), *Addiction.* New York: Academic Press.

Zonderman, Alan B.; Costa, Paul T., Jr.; & McCrae, Robert R. (1989, September 1). Depression as a risk for cancer morbidity and mortality in a nationally representative sample. *Journal of the American Medical Association, 262,* 1191–1195.

Zuckerman, Marvin (1990). Some dubious premises in research and theory on racial differences: Scientific, social, and ethical issues. *American Psychologist, 45,* 1297–1303.

Zuckerman, Marvin; Kuhlman, D. Michael; & Camac, Curt (1988). What lies beyond E and N? Factor analyses of scales believed to measure basic dimensions of personality. *Journal of Personality and Social Psychology, 54,* 96–107.

• Zuckerman, Marvin; Kuhlman, D. Michael; Joireman, Jeffrey; Teta, Paul; & Kraft, Michael (1993). A comparison of three structural models for personality: The Big Three, the Big Five, and the Alternative Five. *Journal of Personality and Social Psychology, 65,* 757–768.

CREDITS

TEXT, TABLE, AND FIGURE CREDITS

CHAPTER 3   Page 49 from Susan Curtiss, GENIE: A Modern Day Wild Child, Academic Press; used by permission / Figure 2.4, from R. L. Wright, Understanding Statistics—An Informal Introduction for the Behavioral Sciences.© 1976, Harcourt Brace & Company; reprinted by permission of the publisher / Figure 2.5, from Sapolsky, "Opinion" illustration, 1987; courtesy of Discover magazine, © 1987.

CHAPTER 3   Table 3.1, from Steven Pinker, The Language Instinct. © 1994 by Steven Pinker. Reprinted by permission of William Morrow and Company, Inc. / p. 90, from Steven Pinker, The Language Instinct. © 1994 by Steven Pinker. Reprinted by permission of William Morrow and Company, Inc. / p. 90, from Helen Bee, The Developing Child. © 1989 Harper & Row, Publishers, Inc.; reprinted by permission / Figure 3.2, from Arnold J. Sameroff, "Intelligent quotient scores of 4-year-old children: Social-environmental risk factors," in Pediatrics, 79, pp. 343–350; reprinted with permission of the author; from Arnold J. Sameroff and Ronald Seifer, "Social Regulation of Developmental Continuities"; reprinted with permission of the authors.

CHAPTER 4   Figure 4.6, Orietta Agostoni / p. 144, from Richard Restack, "Is Free Will a Fraud?" Science Digest, 91,(10), October 1983; reprinted by permission of Science Digest.

CHAPTER 5   Figure 5.1, from Wilse B. Webb and H. W. Agnew, Jr., "Sleep and waking in a time-free environment," Aerospace Medicine, 45 (1974); reprinted with the permission of the authors / Figure 5.2, from Jessica McFarlane, Carol Lynn Martin, and Tannis M. Williams, "Mood changes in men and women," Psychology of Women Quarterly, 12, (1988), pp. 201–223; reprinted by permission of Cambridge University Press / Figure 5.4, from Dennis Kelly, "Physiology of sleep and dreaming," in E. Kandel and J. Schwartz (eds.), Principles of Neural Science. © 1981 by Elsevier Science Publishing Co.; reprinted by permission of the publisher / p. 191, from Edith Fiore, Encounters: A Psychologist Reveals Case Studies of Abductions by Extraterrestrials, 1989; reprinted by permission of Bantam Doubleday Dell.

CHAPTER 6   Page 197, from R. L. Gregory and J.C. Wallace, "Recovery from early blindness," Experimental Psychological Monograph No. 2 (Cambridge, 1963) / Figure 6.2, from Tom N. Cornsweet, "Information processing in human visual systems." Reprinted by permission from Issue 5, The SRI Journal. © January 1969, SRI International / Table 6.1, from "Sound intensity levels in the environment," reprinted with permission from the American Academy of Otolaryngology—Head and Neck Surgery, Washington, DC / Figure 6.14, from "Genetic and pathological taste variation: What can we learn from animal models and human disease?" by Linda M. Bartoshuk, The Molecular Basis of Smell and Taste Transduction, Ciba Foundation Symposium 179. © Ciba Foundation 1993, published 1993 by John Wiley & Sons Ltd. / Figure 6.15, from Maxwell M. Mozell et al., "Taste Test," Archives of Otolaryngology, 90, 1969, pp. 367–373. © 1969 American Medical Association; reprinted with permission / Figure 6.19, adapted from Jan B. Deregowski, "Pictorial Perception and Culture." © 1972 by Scientific American, Inc.; all rights reserved.

CHAPTER 7   Figure 7.2, from Ivan P. Pavlov, "Acquisition and extinction of a salivary response," Conditioned Reflexes, trans. G. V. Anrep, 1927, Oxford University Press, Oxford, England / Figure 7.5, from B. F. Skinner, "Teaching Machines." © 1961 by Scientific American, Inc.; all rights reserved / Figure 7.6, from Carl Cheney, "A rat's route," from Learning and Behavior, by Paul Chance, p. 125. © 1979 by Wadsworth Publishing Co., Inc.; reprinted by permission of the publisher / p.266 from Paul Chance, "Knock Wood," Psychology Today, October 1988, pp. 68–69. © P. T. Partners, L.P.; reprinted with permission from Psychology Today magazine / Figure 7.7, from D. Green and M. Lepper, "Intrinsic motivation: How to turn play into work," reprinted with permission from Psychology Today magazine. © 1974 (Sussex Publishers, Inc.) / Figure 7.7, by E. C. Tolman and C. H. Honzik, "Introduction and removal of reward and maze performance in rats," University of California Publications in Psychology, 4, (1930); reprinted by permission.

CHAPTER 8   Page 292, from Sylvia Scribner, "Modes of Thinking and Ways of Speaking: Culture and Logic Reconsidered," in P. N. Johnson-Laird and P. C. Wason (eds.), Thinking: Readings in Cognitive Science, 1977, Cambridge University Press, New York; reprinted by permission / Table 8.1, from Kathleen Galotti, "Two kinds of reasoning," Psychological Bulletin, 105,© 1989 by the American Psychological Association; reprinted with per-

mission / p. 297, from Patricia M. King and Karen Strohm Kitchener, *Developing* Reflective Judgment: Understanding and Promoting Intellectual Growth and Critical Thinking in Adolescents and Adults."© 1994 Jossey-Bass, Inc., publishers; reprinted by permission / Figure 8.2, from Lee J. Cronbach, "Performance tasks on the Weschler tests," adapted from Essentials of Psychological Testing, 4th edition, p. 208.© 1984 by Harper & Row, Publishers, Inc.; reprinted by permission / Table 8.2, from Lewis M. Terman and Maud A. Merrill, "Sample items from the Stanford-Binet Intelligence Scale," 1973 by Houghton Mifflin Co.; reprinted by permission of Riverside Publishing Co / Table 8.3, from Lee J. Cronbach, "Verbal items similar to those on the WISC-R and WAIS-R," adapted from Essentials of Psychological Testing, 4th edition, p. 208.© 1984 by Harper & Row, Publishers, Inc.; reprinted by permission.

CHAPTER 9   Figure 9.5, from Elizabeth Loftus, "Serial position effect," Memory, p. 25.© 1980, Addison-Wesley Publishing Co., Inc., Reading, MA; reprinted by permission / Figure 9.6, from Michael G. Wessell, "Retention in short term memory," adapted from Cognitive Psychology, p. 98.© 1982 by Harper & Row, Publishers, Inc.; reprinted by permission / Figure 9.10, from Hermann Ebbinghaus, Memory: A Contribution to Experimental Psychology, 1885/1964, Dover Publications, Inc.; reprinted by permission / Figure 9.11, from Marigold Linton, "I remember it well" reprinted with permission from Psychology Today magazine.© 1979 (Sussex Publishers, Inc.).

CHAPTER 10   Page 385, from Debi Howell, "Detecting the Dirty Lie" (interview with Paul Ekman), This World, 7, August 8, 1993; reprinted by permission of the author.

CHAPTER 11   Page 413, from Robert Sternberg, "Love Is a Story," *The General Psychologist*, 30,© 1994; reprinted by permission of the author.

CHAPTER 12   Page 453, from Sigmund Freud, The Ego and the Id, trans. by James Strachey.© 1960 by James Strachey; used by permission of W. W. Norton and Co., Inc. / Figure 12.2, O. W. Wooley, Body Dissatisfaction: Studies Using the Color-A-Person Body Image Test (unpublished manuscript) / p. 472, from C. R. Snyder, "The P. T. Barnum Effect" reprinted with permission from Psychology Today magazine.© 1989 (Sussex Publishers, Inc.)

CHAPTER 13   Table 13.1, from Helen Bee, The Developing Child,© 1989 Harper & Row, Publishers, Inc.; reprinted by permission / Table 13.2, from Paul H. Mussen et al., Child Development and Personality, 1984, Harper & Row, Publishers, Inc.; reprinted by permission / Figure 13.3, from Ren[Unknown character: Courier New 142]e Baillargeon, "How Do Infants Learn About the Physical World?" Current Directions in Psychological Science, Vol. 5 (1994); reprinted with the permission of Cambridge University Press and the author / p. 491, from Daniel Slobin, Psycholinguistics.© 1979; reprinted by permission of HarperCollins College Publishers / Figure 13.4, from George A. Miller, "How children use words," *Scientific American*, September 1987, p. 98; reprinted by permission of Scientific American / Figure 13.5, from Kay Bussey and Albert Bandura, "Gender-linked activities," Child Development, Vol. 63.© The Society for Research in Child Development, Inc.; reprinted by permission / Figure 13.6, "U.S. child poverty is far above the European level," from San Francisco Chronicle, September 23, 1993.© San Francisco Chronicle. Reprinted by permission.

CHAPTER 14   Figure 14.1, from David Holmes, "Fitness and health," Abnormal Psychology.© 1991 by HarperCollins Publishers. Reprinted by permission of HarperCollins Publishers / Figure 14.2, from David Holmes, "Fitness and health," Abnormal Psychology,© 1991 by HarperCollins Publishers. Reprinted by permission of HarperCollins Publishers.

CHAPTER 15   Page 563, from Pamela King, "The Chemistry of Doubt" reprinted with permission from Psychology Today magazine. 1975 (Sussex Publishers, Inc.) / Figure 15.2, by Robert Hare, "Antisocial personality disorder," Journal of Psychology, 1965, p. 369; reprinted with permission of the Helen Dwight Reid Educational Foundation. Published by Heldref Publications, 1319 Eighteenth Street NW, Washington DC 20036–1802; 1965 / Table 15.2, by Stanton Peele, Archie Brodsky, and Mary Arnold, The Truth about Addiction and Recovery.© 1991 by Stanton Peele and Archie Brodsky with Mary Arnold; reprinted by permission of Simon & Schuster, Inc. / Figure 15.3, from Lee N. Robins, Darlene N. Davis, and Donald W. Goodwin, "Drugs and Vietnam veterans," American Journal of Epidemiology, 99, 1974, pp. 235–239; reprinted by permission of the American Journal of Epidemiology and the authors / p. 583, from Eugen Bleuler, Dementia Praecox or the Group of Schizophrenias, 1950, International Universities Press, Madison, CT; reprinted by permission.

CHAPTER 16   Figure 16.1, from Monica McGoldrick and Randy Gerson, "O'Neill family—repetitive functioning patterns," reprinted from Genograms in Family Assessment, with the permission of W. W. Norton & Company, Inc. © 1985 by Monica McGoldrick and Randy Gerson / Figure 16.2, from Robert Hobson, "Psychotherapy in action" in Forms of Feeling, pp.11–13, 1985. Reprinted by permission of Tavistock Publications (Hampshire, England) / Table 16.1, from Michael J. Lambert and Allen E. Bergin, Handbook of Psychotherapy and Behavior Change, 4th edition. © 1994 John Wiley & Sons, Inc.; reprinted by permission of John Wiley & Sons, Inc. / Figure 16.3, from Kenneth I. Howard, "The dose–effect relationship in psychotherapy," American Psychologist, 41, February 1986, p. 160. © 1986 by the American Psychological Association; reprinted by permission of the publisher and author.

CHAPTER 17   Page 633, from Stanley Milgram, Obedience to Authority. © 1974 by Stanley Milgram; reprinted by permission of HarperCollins Publishers / p. 656, from Eva Fogelman, Conscience & Courage: Rescuers of Jews During the Holocaust, 1994; reprinted by permission of Doubleday, a division of Bantam Doubleday Dell Publishing Group, Inc.

CHAPTER 18   Table 18.1, from Edward T. Hall and Mildred Hall, Understanding Cultural Differences. © 1990, reprinted by permission of Intercultural Press, Yarmouth, ME / Figure 18.2, from Hazel Markus and Shinobu Kitayama, "Culture and the self: Implications for cognition, emotion, and motivation." © 1991 by the American Psychological Association; reprinted with permission / p. 678, from Nancy Mairs, "On Being a Cripple," Plaintext: Deciphering a Woman's Life. © 1986 University of Arizona Press; reprinted by permission of University of Arizona Press / p. 679, from Steven Pinker, "The Game of the Name." © 1994, The New York Times Company; reprinted by permission / p. 692, from Gordon W. Allport, The Nature of Prejudice, pp. 13–14. © 1979 by Addison-Wesley Publishing Company Inc.; reprinted by permission of the publisher / p. 697, from Sheldon Harnick, "Merry Little Minuet," © 1958 Alley Music Corp. and Trio Music Co., Inc.; reprinted by permission.

PHOTOGRAPHS AND CARTOONS

Unless otherwise acknowledged, all photographs are the property of Scott, Foresman and Company. Page abbreviations are as follows: (T) top, (C) center, (B) bottom, (R) right.

CONTENTS   Page iv Photograph courtesy of Michael B. Smith, Ph.D., Shizhe Li, Ph.D., and Christopher Collins, Center for NMR Research, Department of Radiology, The Milton S. Hershey Medical Center of The Pennsylvania State University College of Medicine, Hershey, PA 17033 / p. v Howard Sochurek / p. vii Reprinted from Games Magazine (19 West 21st St., New York, NY 10010). Copyright © 1981 B. & P. Publishing Co., Inc. / p. ix National Portrait Gallery, London / p. x Terry McCrea/Warshaw Collection, Archives Center Smithsonian Institution 91–11799 / p. xi Library of Congress. Hand Colored by Cheryl Kucharzak / p. xii Robert Fludd, Utriusque Cosmi, 1619–1621. Hand Colored by Cheryl Kucharzak.

CHAPTER 1   Page 2 Photograph courtesy of Michael B. Smith, Ph.D., Shizhe Li, Ph.D. and Christopher Collins, Center for NMR Research, Department of Radiology, The Milton S. Hershey Medical Center of The Pennsylvania State University College of Medicine, Hershey, PA 17033 / p. 3 Anne Frank Foundation / p. 4 Randa Bishop/Uniphoto / p. 5(L) Mark E. Gibson/The Stock Market / p. 5(C) William Thompson/The Picture Cube / p. 5(R) Kevin Vessel/Adventure Photo / p. 8 Bettmann Archive / p. 9 Archives of the History of American Psychology / p. 10 Harvard University Archives / p. 11 Archives of the History of American Psychology / p. 12, 13, 15, 16, 17, 18 Gem[Scaron]ldegalerie, Berlin/Staatliche Museen Preussischer Kulturbesitz, Berlin / p. 14 Mary Evans/Sigmund Freud Copyrights of W. E. Freud / p. 25(L) Roe Di Bona / p. 25(R) Vladimir Lange/The Image Bank / p. 26 Alan Levenson/Tony Stone Images / p. 27(L) Steve Skloot/Photo Researchers / p. 27(R) Ed Kashi / p. 31 The Bizarro cartoon by Dan Piraro is reprinted by permission of Chronicle Features, San Francisco / p. 32 Dick Ruhl / p. 34(T) Dick Ruhl / p. 34(B) Bent Offerings by Don Addis. By permission of Don Addis and Creators Syndicate / p. 38(TL) Stuart Franklin/Magnum Photos / p. 38(TR) A. Crickmay/International Stock Photography Ltd. / p. 38(B) Lauren Wilder / p. 39(TL) Tannenbaum/Sygma / p. 39(TR) Dennis Brack/Black Star / p. 39(LC) Courtesy of Natural Nectar Corp. / p. 39(BL) Jim Anderson/Woodfin Camp & Associates / p. 39(BR) Daniel Lain[Unknown character: Courier New 142].

CHAPTER 2   Page 40 Jean-Loup Charmet / p. 41 Alan Carey/The Image Works / p. 42(L) Charles Moore/Black Star / p. 42(R) Dan McCoy/Black Star / p. 46 Gale Zucker/Stock Boston / p. 50 Copyright © 1990/Los Angeles Times Photo / p. 51(L) J.Guichard/Sygma / p. 51(R) Brian Smith/Stock Boston / p. 52 Will and Deni McIntyre/Photo Researchers / p. 54 Bob Daemmrich/Stock Boston / p. 55 Copyright © 1994, Los Angeles Times Syndicate. Reprinted with permission / p. 59 Joseph Schuyler/Stock Boston / p. 62 Tom McCarthy/The Picture Cube / p. 64 Miss Peach by Mell Lazarus. By permission of Mell Lazarus and Creators Syndicate / p. 70 Nydia Velasquez/Monkmeyer Press Photo Service / p. 71 Hank Morgan/Rainbow.

CHAPTER 3   Page 78 Richard G. Rawlins/Custom Medical Stock Photo / p. 79 Richard Hutchings/Photo Researchers / p. 80 Biophoto Associates/SS/Photo Researchers / p. 83(BOTH) Suzanne Szasz / p. 84 Copyright the British Museum / p. 85(BOTH) Breck P. Kent. / p. 86(L) Harlow Primate Laboratory, University of Wisconsin / p. 86(C) Laura Dwight / p. 86(R) Chuck Fishman/Woodfin Camp & Associates / p. 88 Marc Asnin/SABA / p. 89 American Health: Fitness of Body and Health, © 1986 American Health Partners / p. 93 Alex Webb/Magnum Photos / p. 94 Art Wolfe/Tony Stone Images / p. 98 Kathryn Abbe/Frances McLaughlin-Gill ©1979 / p. 100 Bob Kramer/The Picture Cube / p. 101(TL) Dennis Stock/Magnum / p. 101(TR) Victor Englebert/Photo Researchers / p. 101(B) Yoav Levy/Phototake / p. 102 Michael Jensen/Frozen Images / p. 105 Dan Bosler/Tony Stone Images / p. 106(L) Shelly Katz/Black Star / p. 106(R) Lawrence Migdale/Photo Researchers / p. 108 Brown Brothers

CHAPTER 4   Page 116 Howard Sochurek / p. 117 Howard Sochurek/The Stock Market / p. 120 Roe Di Bona / p. 124 Biophoto Associates/Photo Researchers / p. 130 Dan McCoy/Rainbow / p. 131 Fritz Goro/Life Magazine/Time Warner Inc. / p. 132 Figure 4.8a Courtesy of Dr. Michael E. Phelps and Dr. John C. Mazziotta, UCLA School of Medicine p. 132 Figure 4.8b Richard Haier, Department of Psychiatry, Univeristy of California, Irvine / p. 132(B) Figure 4.9 Howard Sochurek / p. 133 Figure 4.10 Alan Gevins, EEG Systems Laboratory, San Francisco / p. 138(BL) Figure 4.14 Warren Anatomical Museum, Harvard Medical School / p. 138(BR) Figure 4.14 from "The Return of Phineas Gage: Clues About the Brain from the Skull of a Famous Patient" By Hanna Damasio, Thomas Grabowski, Randall Frank, Albert M. Galaburda, Antonio R. Damasio. Science, May 20, 1994. Courtesy Hanna Damasio, M.D. / p. 145 Courtesy of Natural Nectar Corp. / p. 147(BOTH) Howard Sochurek / p. 149 Copyright © 1992, The Time Inc. Magazine Company. Reprinted by permission / p. 150 Figure 4.17 B. A. Shaywitz et al., 1995 NMR/Yale Medical School.

CHAPTER 5   Page 156 The Dickens House / p. 157 The Granger Collection, New York / p. 159(L) Earl Scott/Photo Researchers / p. 159(R) Tom Evans/Photo Researchers / p. 161 Chris Steele Perkins/Magnum Photos / p. 168(T) AP/Wide World / p. 168(BL) Melissa Hayes English/Photo Researchers / p. 168(BR) Earl Roberge/Photo Researchers / p. 170(BOTH) Walter Chandoha / p. 171 Peter Ward/Bruce Coleman Inc. / p. 173(L,C) Allan Hobson/SS/Photo Researchers / p. 173(R) J. A. Hobson/Harvard Medical School/Photo Researchers / p. 177(L) Mehmet Biber/Photo Researchers / p. 177(C) Tibor Hirsch/Photo Researchers / p. 177(R) Collection of Ronald K. Siegel / p. 180(BOTH) Omikron/Photo Researchers / p. 182(L) Paula Lerner/The Picture Cube / p. 182(R) Tom McCarthy/Unicorn Stock Photos / p. 185 National Library of Medicine / p. 187 Ernest Hilgard, Stanford University / p. 188 Bettmann Archive. Hand Colored by Cheryl Kucharzak.

CHAPTER 6   Page 196 Ren[Unknown character: Courier New 142] Magritte, La condition humaine, gift of the Collectors Committee. © Board of Trustees, National Gallery of Art, Washington / p. 202(BOTH) Gary Retherford / p. 204(L) Tony O'Brien / p. 204(R) B. Nation/Sygma / p. 205 Michael Beasley/Tony Stone Images / p. 212 Figure 6.8 Ron James / p. 212 Figure 6.9a Kaiser Porcelain Ltd. (Artist: Judy Cousins) / p. 215 Figure 6.10a Erik Svensson/The Stock Market / p. 215 Figure 6.10b J. Williamson/Photo Researchers / p. 215 Figure 6.10c Roy Schneider/The Stock Market / p. 215 Figure 6.10d Nicholas De Sciose/Photo Researchers / p. 215 Figure 6.10e Milt and Joan Mann/Cameramann International, Ltd. / p. 215 Figure 6.10f Larry Fleming/The Image Works / p. 215 Figure 6.10g Barrie Rokeach / p. 221 Molly Webster © 1982/Discover Syndication / p. 226 Arthur Tress/Photo Researchers / p. 228(L) Figure 6.17 Enrico Ferorelli Enterprises, Inc. / p. 232 Arnaud Borrel/Gamma-Liaison / p. 232 Figure 6.18 Tony Schwartz / p. 239(BOTH) Magic, Dover Publications. Hand Colored by Cheryl Kucharzak.

CHAPTER 7   Page 244 Library of Congress / p. 245 Don and Pat Valenti / p. 246(T) The Granger Collection, New York / p. 251 Cameramann/The Image Works / p. 256 Joe McNally / p. 258 Adam Woolfitt/Woodfin Camp & Associates / p. 260 Jester, Columbia / p. 265 Randy Taylor/Sygma / p. 266(T) Grant Heilman/Grant Heilman Photography / p. 268 David Young-Wolff/PhotoEdit / p. 269 Marion E. Hilton / p. 270 Ira Wyman/Sygma / p. 276 Adam Woolfitt / p. 281(ALL)Figure 7.9 R. Epstein, "Insight in the Pigeon," Epstein et al., 1984.

CHAPTER 8   Page 286 Reprinted from Games Magazine (19 West 21st St., New York, NY 10010). Copyright © 1981 B. & P. Publishing Co., Inc. / p. 287 The Metropolitan Museum of Art, Gift of Thomas F. Ryan, 1910 (11.173.9) p. 288 Cary Wolinsky/Stock Boston / p. 289(L) Peter Marlow/Sygma / p. 289(C) Benaroch/Lazic/Facelly/SIPA / p. 289(R) Naguet/SIPA / p. 290 Grapes-Michaud/Photo Researchers / p. 291(B) Kindra Clineff/The Picture Cube / p. 295 Jim Pickerell/Black Star / p. 296 Malcolm Hancock / p. 303 Prouser/SIPA / p. 304 Art Seitz/Sygma / p. 306 Bob Daemmrich/Stock Boston / p. 309(T) The National Archives / p.

309(B) Sidney Harris / p. 311 Richard Hutchings/Photo Researchers / p. 313(T) Charles Feil/Stock Boston / p. 313(BL) Tom Queally/Shooting Star / p. 313(BC) Bruce Roberts/Photo Researchers / p. 313(BR) Peter Vadnai/The Stock Market / p. 314 Harvey Lloyd/The Stock Market / p. 317 Jeff Foott / p. 319 Elizabeth Rubert / p. 320 Michael Goldman/Sisyphus / p. 325 Reprinted from *Games* Magazine (19 West 21st St., New York, NY 10010). Copyright © 1981 B. & P. Publishing Co., Inc.

CHAPTER 9 Page 326 Romberch, *Congestorium Artificiose Memorie*, 1533. Hand Colored by Cheryl Kucharzak / p. 327 PhotoFest / p. 328 Rick Maiman/Sygma / p. 329 Bonnie J. Olsen / p. 331 NASA / p. 332(T) Paul Shambroom/Photo Researchers / p. 332(B) Pool/Gamma-Liaison / p. 333(BOTH) Elizabeth F. Loftus / p. 337 Figure 9.1 Copyright ©1985, 1958 by Robert L. May Co. Reprinted by permission of Modern Curriculum Press, Inc. / p. 337 Tony Freeman/PhotoEdit / p. 339 Library of Congress / p. 340 Karen Preuss/The Image Works / p. 342 Bill Pierce/Time Magazine / p. 343 Ed Carlin/The Picture Cube / p. 344 Richard Hutchings/Photo Researchers / p. 345 Hank DeLespinasse/The Image Bank / p. 347 Jerry Jacka Photography / p. 348(L) Figure 9.4 David Frazier/Photo Researchers / p. 348(C) Figure 9.4 Don and Pat Valenti / p. 348(R) Figure 9.4 Raoul Hackel/Stock Boston / p. 352 John McGrail/©1981 *Discover* Syndication / p. 353 Sidney Harris / p. 356 (BOTH) Figure 9.9 Larry R. Squire, Veterans Affairs Medical Center, San Diego, CA / p. 358 Wasyl Szrodzinski/Photo Researchers / p. 359 Sidney Harris / p. 362 Camera Press / p. 363 The Museum of Modern Art/Film Stills Archive / p. 366 Catherine Ursillo/Photo Researchers / p. 367 Carolyn Rovee-Collier / p. 368 Robert S. Oakes/National Geographic Image Collection.

CHAPTER 10 Page 374 Mansell Collection / p. 375 Universit[Scaron]tsbibliothek, Heidelberg / p. 376(L) William Karel/Sygma / p. 376(R) Tannenbaum/Sygma / p. 378(TL) Barry Lewis/Network/Matrix / p. 378(TC) Erika Stone / p. 378(TR) Ted Kerasote/Photo Researchers / p. 378(BL) Francie Manning/The Picture Cube / p. 378(BC) John Giordano/SABA / p. 378(BR) Bridgeman/Art Resource, New York / p. 379(L) A. Knudsen/Sygma / p. 379(R) G. Schachmes/Sygma / p. 381 David Young-Wolff/PhotoEdit / p. 386 Wasyl Szrodzinski/Photo Researchers / p. 387 Nancy Bates/The Picture Cube / p. 388 David Madison/Duomo Photography Inc. / p. 390 Laura Dwight / p. 392 Philip J. Griffiths/Magnum Photos / p. 393 David Austen/Stock Boston / p. 395 Tom McCarthy/The Picture Cube / p. 397(T) Ellis Herwig/The Picture Cube / p. 397(BL) Michael O'Brien / p. 397(BR) Joel Gordon Photography / p. 399 © 1985 Jim Goldberg. Reprinted by permission of Random House.

CHAPTER 11 Page 404 North Wind Picture Archives / p. 405 Focus On Sports / p. 407(TL) Ann Goolkasian/The Picture Cube / p. 407(TR) Linda Bartlett/Folio / p. 407(B) Figure 11.1 Harlow Primate Laboratory, University of Wisconsin / p. 409 Elizabeth Crews / p. 410 Harry Groom/Photo Researchers / p. 415 Bruce Ayres/Tony Stone Images / p. 417(L) PhotoFest / p. 417(R) The Poster "The Rape of the Sabine Women" was created by the Pi Kappa Phi fraternity in 1987 to raise sexual abuse awareness among its undergraduate members / p. 418(L) Catherine Noren/Photo Researchers / p. 418(C) Day Williams/Photo Researchers / p. 418(R) Jim Anderson/Woodfin Camp & Associates / p. 419 Eric Kroll / p. 421(L) Deborah Davis/PhotoEdit / p. 421(R) Zigy Kaluzny/Tony Stone Images / p. 425 David Young-Wolff/PhotoEdit / p. 426(L) Rick Friedman/Black Star / p. 426(CL) Dennis Brack/Black Star / p. 426(CR) Flip Shulke/Black Star / p. 426(R) Dennis Brack/Black Star / p. 427(L) Owen Franken/Sygma / p. 427(CL) Marvin Koner/Black Star / p. 427(CR) Duran/Giansanti/Sygma / p. 427(R) Daniel Simon/Gamma-Liaison.

CHAPTER 12 Page 428 Spencer Grant/The Picture Cube / p. 437(T) Fred Prousser/SIPA / p. 437(B) PhotoFest / p. 439 Ed Kashi / p. 441 Rob Nelson/Black Star / p. 444(T) Frank Siteman / p. 444(B,ALL) Evan Byrne, Laboratory of Comparative Ethology, National Institute of Child Health and Human Development / p. 446(TL) Herman Kokojan/Black Star / p. 446(TR) Glassman/The Image Works / p. 446(BL) Ed Kashi / p. 446(BR) M. Siluk/The Image Works / p. 448 Lisa Quinones/Black Star / p. 451(TL) Jeffrey E. Blackman/The Stock Market / p. 451(TR) S. Franklin/Sygma / p. 451(BL) S. Franklin/Sygma / p. 451(BR) John Kelly/The Image Bank / p. 454(B) Innervisions / p. 457 John Kelly/The Image Bank / p. 458 The Granger Collection, New York / p. 460 Tom McCarthy/The Picture Cube / p. 463(BL) Mimi Forsyth/Monkmeyer Press Photo Service / p. 463(BR) Innervisions / p. 464 Sidney Harris / p. 467(TL) M. P. Kahl/Photo Researchers / p. 467(TR) Innervisions / p. 467(CL) Cosimo Scianna/The Image Bank / p. 467(BL) Amy C. Etra/PhotoEdit / p. 467(BR) Tony Freeman/PhotoEdit / p. 468 AP/Wide World / p. 469 Catherine Ursillo/Photo Researchers / p. 471(TL) Wally McNamee/Woodfin Camp & Associates / p. 471(TR) Mark A. Mittelman / p. 471(BL) Timothy Egan/Woodfin Camp & Associates / p. 471(BR) Peter Menzel/Stock Boston / p. 472 © *Punch*/Rothco.

CHAPTER 13 Page 476 National Portrait Gallery, London / p. 477 Peter Beck/The Stock Market / p. 481 Sally and Richard Greenhill p. 482 J. Guichard/Sygma / p. 483(ALL) Marina Raith/Gruner & Jahr / p. 484 Doris Pinney Brenner / p. 487(L) Marcia Weinstein / p. 487(R) Mimi

Forsyth/Monkmeyer Press Photo Service / p. 489(BOTH) Jackie Curtis / p. 490(T) Mandal Ranjiz/Photo Researchers / p. 490(B) Erika Stone / p. 493(B) Margo Granitsas/Photo Researchers / p. 494 Lawrence Migdale/Stock Boston / p. 498 Sandra Lousada Collections / p. 501(L) Erika Stone / p. 501(R) Laura Dwight / p. 502 Robert Brenner/PhotoEdit / p. 503 Robert Brenner/PhotoEdit / p. 506(L) Diane M. Lowe/Stock Boston / p. 506(R) Betsy Lee / p. 509 Richard Hutchings/Photo Researchers / p. 510(L) Phil McCarten/PhotoEdit / p. 510(C) Bob Daemmrich/Stock Boston / p. 510(R) Jeff Greenberg/Unicorn Stock Photos / p. 512 Jean-Claude LeJeune/Stock Boston.

CHAPTER 14 Page 518 Terry McCrea/Warshaw Collection, Archives Center/Smithsonian Institution Center 91–11799 / p. 519 Jeffry Myers/Stock Boston / p. 521(L) Enrico Ferorelli Enterprises, Inc. / p. 521(R) Greenlar/The Image Works / p. 522 Manfred Kage/Peter Arnold, Inc. / p. 524 Paul Fusco/Magnum Photos / p. 525 Stanley Rice/Monkmeyer Press Photo Service / p. 527 Tom Sobolik/Black Star / p. 530 National Baseball Library & Archive, Cooperstown, NY / p. 531 National Baseball Library & Archive, Cooperstown, NY / p. 532 P. Jones Griffiths/Magnum Photos / p. 533 Roy Roper/Zuma Images / p. 536 Camilla Smith/Rainbow / p. 537 Malcolm Hancock / p. 539 The Kobal Collection / p. 541 Paolo Koch/Photo Researchers / p. 544 The Museum of Modern Art/Film Stills Archive / p. 545 Culver Pictures / p. 548 John Griffin/The Image Works.

CHAPTER 15 Page 553 Culver Pictures / p. 554(L) Fujifotos/The Image Works / p. 554(C) Art Wolfe/Tony Stone Images / p. 554(R) Les Stone/Sygma / p. 561 Bourseiller/Gamma-Liaison / p. 562 Bourseiller/Gamma-Liaison / p. 565 Jonathan Becker / p. 566 Courtesy of Dr. Michael E. Phelps and Dr. John C. Mazziotta, UCLA School of Medicine / p. 569 Bettmann Archive. Hand Colored by Cheryl Kucharzak / p. 570 AP/Wide World / p. 574 AP/Wide World / p. 575 David Young-Wolff/Tony Stone Images / p. 580 Carol Lee/The Picture Cube / p. 584(ALL) Al Vercoutere, Malibu, CA / p. 585(T) Alfred Gescheidt/The Image Bank / p. 585(B) Dick Bell/*Insight* Magazine / p. 586(BOTH) Howard Sochurek.

CHAPTER 16 Page 592 National Library of Medicine, Bethesda, MD / p. 593 Spencer Eth, M.D. / p. 594 Bettmann Archive. Hand Colored by Cheryl Kucharzak / p. 595 Alvin H. Perlmutter Inc. / p. 598 Bettmann Archive / p. 600 Erich Lessing/Art Resource, New York / p. 602 James Wilson/Woodfin Camp & Associates / p. 603 E. Wendell/H. Armstrong Roberts / p. 604(L) Alan D. Entin, Ph.D. / p. 604(R) Alan D. Entin, Ph.D. / p. 608 Sidney Harris / p. 609(BOTH) Christopher Morris/Black Star / p. 617(L) Courtesy of Dr. Giuseppe Costantino / p. 617(R) Photo by Xan Lopez / p. 622 Paul Fusco/Magnum Photos.

CHAPTER 17 Page 626 Library of Congress. Hand Colored by Cheryl Kucharzak / p. 627 Courtesy of Friends of Le Chambon / p. 628 Ulrike Welsch/Photo Researchers / p. 630 Michael Greenlar/Black Star / p. 632 (BOTH) Copyright 1965 by Stanley Milgram. From the film *Obedience*, distributed by Pennsylvania State University, PCR / p. 633 Copyright 1965 by Stanley Milgram. From the film *Obedience*, distributed by Pennsylvania State University, PCR / p. 635 Bob Krist/Tony Stone Images / p. 640 Philip Jon Bailey/The Picture Cube / p. 644 James Pozarik/Gamma-Liaison / p. 646 Alex Webb/Magnum Photos / p. 647(T) Guy Anderson/*Life* Magazine / p. 647(B) Dr. Philip G. Zimbardo / p. 649(L) Evan Agostini/Gamma-Liaison / p. 653(ALL) from *Intergroup Conflict and Cooperation: The Robbers Cave Experiment*, by Sherif, Harvey, White, Hood, and Sherif. Institute of Group Relations, University of Oklahoma, Norman, 1961. Courtesy Muzafer Sherif / p. 654 AP/Wide World / p. 655 Shelly Katz/Black Star / p. 657(L) AP/Wide World / p. 658 Sygma.

CHAPTER 18 Page 662 Biblioth[Unknown character: Courier New 143]que Nationale, Paris. Hand Colored by Cheryl Kucharzak / p. 663 James W. Terry/SIPA-Press / p. 665 Lionel Delevigne/Stock Boston / p. 669(L) M. Dalmasso/Gamma-Liaison / p. 669(R) Shahn Kermani/Gamma-Liaison / p. 670(L) Robert Azzi/Woodfin Camp & Associates / p. 670(C) AP/Wide World / p. 670(R) Bob Daemmrich/The Image Works / p. 671(BOTH) Adapted from Bernieri, Davis, Rosenthal, and Knee (1991) / p. 673 Eastcott/Momatiuk/The Image Works / p. 676(L) Robert Frerck/Odyssey Productions, Chicago / p. 676(C) James Mays/Unicorn Stock Photos / p. 676(R) David Young-Wolff/PhotoEdit / p. 681(L) National Anthropological Archives/Smithsonian Institution / p. 683 Denver Public Library, Western History Department / p. 685 Stephen Ferry/Gamma-Liaison / p. 687 Penny Tweedie/Woodfin Camp & Associates / p. 688(ALL) from S. Keen, *Faces of the Enemy: Reflections of the Hostile Imagination*. Copyright © 1986 by Sam Keen. All rights reserved. Reprinted by permission of HarperCollins Publishers Inc. / p. 692(TL) The New-York Historical Society, New York City / p. 692(TR) Julie Marcotte/Stock Boston / p. 692(LC) Dana Stone, Richmond, VA / p. 692(CR) Steve Kagan/Photo Researchers / p. 692(BL) B'nai B'rith / p. 693(TL) UPI/Bettmann / p. 693 Library of Congress / p. 693(CL) N. Calante/Gamma-Liaison / p. 693(CR) Bettmann Archive / p. 693(BL) Bob Daemmrich/Sygma / p. 693(BR) Michael Schwarz/Gamma-Liaison / p. 695 The Palm Beach Post/Don Wright / p. 699 Gerd Ludwig/Woodfin Camp & Associates / p. 703 Robert Fludd, *Utriusque Cosmi*, 1619–1621. Hand Colored by Cheryl Kucharzak.